D1252624

Television Characters

Television Characters

1,485 Profiles, 1947–2004

VINCENT TERRACE

McFarland & Company, Inc., Publishers
Jefferson, North Carolina, and London

LIBRARY OF CONGRESS CATALOGUING-IN-PUBLICATION DATA

Terrace, Vincent, 1948–
Television characters : 1,485 profiles, 1947–2004 / Vincent Terrace.
p.   cm.
Includes bibliographical references and index.

ISBN 0-7864-2191-6 (illustrated case binding : 50# alkaline paper) ∞

1. Television programs — United States.
2. Characters and characteristics in television programs.
I. Title.
PN1992.3.U5T465   2006   791.45'75 — dc22   2005026331

British Library cataloguing data are available

Cover image ©2005 Brand X Pictures

Manufactured in the United States of America

*McFarland & Company, Inc., Publishers
Box 611, Jefferson, North Carolina 28640
www.mcfarlandpub.com*

Contents

Preface

From a puppet named Howdy Doody to a mobster named Tony Soprano. From a girl who was brought to life from clay (Diana Prince) to a girl who was created from an ancient power source called the Key (Dawn Summers). From a man who enjoys being an idiot (Chris Peterson) to a man who is totally neurotic (Adrian Monk). And from a pickle king (Jonas Paine) to a stripper who battles evil (Erotica Jones). And let's not forget Archie Bunker, Gomez Addams, Herman Munster, Al Bundy or Rob Petrie and many, many others — in this comprehensive reference work presenting detailed profiles on characters that have graced the television screen from December of 1947 through January of 2005.

There are 1,485 characters in 1,173 numbered entries. Each is alphabetized by first name (an appendix lists all of them by last name). The date range shown following the series on which the character appeared represents the time of that character's run — *not* necessarily the complete series run: for example, Pernell Roberts played Adam Cartwright on *Bonanza* from 1959 to 1965, but the series ended in 1973; Shelley Long played Diane Chambers on *Cheers* only from 1982 to 1987 — not through the end of the series in 1993. Also, this is *not* a book of series storyline information. It is a book of character information compiled from dialogue. Storyline information was only used when it was necessary to help define a character.

Given the many thousands of television characters who have appeared over the years, it is impossible for anyone to compile a profile on each and every one. The compiler is aware that it is probably also impossible to select characters for such a book as this that will please everyone. The broad range of characters presented here are primarily from prime time network, cable and syndicated series. They were chosen from well known series and also obscure and cult series. An appendix of characters listed by the series on which they appeared, an appendix of characters listed by last names, and an index of performers are included. Some entries have cross references to associated characters. In many of the profiles the character's own words are quoted to describe aspects of their being.

In addition to biographical information, each character is profiled with their series information (that is, jobs, schools, favorite foods, clothing sizes, nicknames, etc.); there are over 200,000 such facts.

CHARACTERS

1. Abby O'Neill, *Dharma and Greg*, ABC, 1997–2002. Played by Mimi Kennedy.

Abigail O'Neill, called Abby is married to Larry Finkelstein and the mother of their flower child, Dharma. Abby and Larry were hippies who lived together for 30 years before marrying in 1999. They live at 1421 Bank Lane in Mill Valley, California, and have a pet goat named Goat.

Abby was born in Wisconsin and is a graduate of Berkeley College. She also has a degree in feminine issues from the Goddess Institute. Abby runs a charity thrift shop and when she moved in with Larry, Abby's mother put a curse on him.

Abby's hobby is painting (which she enjoys doing in the nude). She depends on the zodiac to guide her life and believes that for the first time in 600 years she has been reincarnated as a woman. Abby is a licensed Aroma Healer and prescribes eucalyptus butter tea to cure the common cold. Tofu cannoli is her favorite dessert and Harold Christian Finkelstein is the baby brother Dharma is presented with when Abby gives birth in 2001.

See also: Edward and Kitty Montgomery, Dharma Montgomery, Greg Montgomery, Larry Finkelstein.

2. Adam Cartwright, *Bonanza*, NBC, 1959–1965. Played by Pernell Roberts.

Adam Milton Cartwright was born in Boston, Massachusetts, in 1842. He is the eldest son of Ben Cartwright and his first wife, Elizabeth Stoddard. He has two brothers, Hoss and Little Joe, and is the most sensitive of the Cartwrights (the owners of the Ponderosa Ranch near Virginia City, Nevada). Adam is well educated and loves to read (his middle name reflects Ben's favorite writer, John Milton). He is fast on the draw, tough when angered and enjoys singing, dancing and playing the guitar. Adam has a good business sense and "was best at judging horse sense; better than anyone in the whole territory."

As Adam grew older he became disillusioned with the West. He left the Ponderosa to further his education (in New York and Abroad). It was in England, while studying architecture that he married and had a son (Adam Cartwright, Jr.).

See also: Ben Cartwright, Hoss Cartwright, Little Joe Cartwright.

3. Adam Kane, *Mutant X*, Syn., 2001–2004. Played by John Shea.

Adam Kane was a chief biochemist with Genomex, a secret branch of U.S. Intelligence that was established to remake the world by creating perfect men and women through genetic manipula-tion. Adam felt enormous guilt for going against the laws of nature and creating what he called "genetic mistakes." When he was unable to convince his superiors that what they were doing was wrong, he broke lose from Genomex and retreated to a secret mountain hideaway that he called Sanctuary. Here he established an elaborate base of operations and created Mutant X, a group of rogue, genetically enhanced agents, who battle evil wherever they find it.

Adam possesses no special powers and appears to have abilities far beyond those of a bio-chemist. He is considered by some to be the smartest man in the world and is a brilliant strategist and tactician as well. His interest in science began in early childhood and Adam has devoted his whole life to improving mankind through technical advances. In addition to constructing Mutant X, he has created a series of sophisticated computer complexes and developed the Helix, an amazing space craft for use by his agents.

See also: Brennan Mulray, Emma DeLauro, Lexa Pierce, Shalimar Fox.

4. Adam Troy, *Adventures in Paradise*, ABC, 1959–1962. Played by Gardner McKay.

Adam Troy is the captain of the *Tiki*, a 60-foot, two-mast, five sail schooner that hauls cargo and passengers throughout the South Pacific. Adam was born in Connecticut and is a graduate of Yale University. He is a veteran of the Korean War and his dream is to one day settle down and own a ranch. He is, however, a victim of the wanderlust and purchased the schooner as a means of saving for his dream and fulfilling his thirst for adventure. Adam is said to live by a code ("There are certain things Adam will do and there are certain things he won't do") and follows a constellation called The Southern Cross ("Find those stars and you'll never lose your way in the South Pacific"). Adam has type A-B negative blood and was the skipper of a barge in Pusong before earning the money to buy the *Tiki*. Adam now calls Papeete Harbor in Tahiti home (his address is the Schooner *Tiki*).

5. Addie Loggins, *Paper Moon*, ABC, 1974–1975. Played by Jodie Foster.

Adelaide Loggins, called Addie, was born in Oak View, Kansas, on November 19, 1922 (she weighed 6 pounds, 2 ounces). Her mother was Essie Mae Loggins but her father is unknown (Essie Mae met a man in a bar, had an affair and he left when Addie was born). Addie was raised by Essie Mae and lived at 47 Bridge Corner in Ophelia, Kansas. She became an orphan in 1933 when her mother was killed in a car accident. Addie believes her father is Moses Pray (Christopher Connelly), a con artist who resembles her — "I look like you," she tells him, but Moses, called Moze, insists "I don't look like you. I'm not your father." Despite the objections, Addie attaches herself to Moze and becomes part of his con — salesman for the Dixie Bible Company. They travel throughout the Midwest in a 1931 Roadster (plate 68132) and Addie takes care of the finances ("If it wasn't for me, we'd be broke all the time"). Addie also calls herself Addie Pray and keeps her treasures in an old cigar box.

6. Adrian Monk, *Monk*, USA/ABC, 2002 (current). Played by Tony Shalhoub.

Adrian Monk is a man with an encyclopedic knowledge of strange and obscure facts. He has a photographic memory and the deductive skills of Sherlock Holmes. He can spot things at a crime scene that even the most highly trained specialists can overlook. He can study a crime scene and deduct, quite accurately, whether the killer was male or female, white or black and even height and weight. Adrian can rearrange shredded documents and everything must make perfect sense in order for him to perform properly. That was Adrian Monk as a member of the 14th Division of the San Francisco Police Department. He was married to Trudy Ellison, an investigative reporter for the *Examiner*, and lived on Cole Street. In 1988 Trudy was killed in a car bombing. The tragedy triggered a rare anxiety disorder in Adrian that now makes him germ phobic and afraid of virtually everything. The condition interfered with his job and he was given a 315 temporary suspension (a psychological discharge). To help him cope with life Adrian hired nurse Sharona Fleming (Bitty Schram), and together they established Monk as a private consultant to help people in trouble (at $500 a day plus expenses).

Monk was born in the small town of Tewkesbury and lived on Pine Street. He has a brother named Ambrose and as a child was excessively neat. He went to the store for the first time alone when he was 15; he first drove a car when he was 23; and his first date with a woman occurred at the age of 26. Although his parents are rarely mentioned, Monk acknowledged that his father abandoned the family when he was eight years old. He lost his mother in 1994.

Adrian is now scared all the time. Heights, germs, crowds, the dark and even milk are a small fraction of the fears Adrian must overcome. He is a compulsive cleaner and does not like to be touched. He is superstitious and afraid of cars.

He worries about everything and has great difficulty thinking because he is always worrying. Adrian must have a five-watt night-light to sleep and takes three showers a day. He carries his good luck charm (a key chain given to him by Trudy) with him at all times and is determined to solve Trudy's death (was she working on a story? Did she get too close to something? These are the questions that drive Adrian to constantly review the facts in the hope that he will find her killer).

A person who is neat and tidy impresses Monk and when he assists the police it is on an observer basis only. Adrian plays the clarinet and Willie Nelson is his favorite singer.

Aeryn Sun *see* **John Crichton**

Agent 86 *see* **Maxwell Smart**

Agent 99 *see* **99**

7. Al Borland, *Home Improvement*, ABC, 1991–1999. Played by Richard Karn.

Al Borland, known for wearing flannel shirts, is the co-host of *Tool Time*, a local Detroit cable home improvement series hosted by Tim Taylor. Al was born in Michigan and now lives in an apartment (505) with his never seen, supposedly overweight mother. Al served a hitch in the Navy and worked for a year as a heavy crane operator (Local 324) before assisting Tim. He has a superior knowledge of tools and construction and invented a board game called "Tool Time." He made a home video ("How to Assemble Your Tool Box") and takes a correspondence course ("Getting in Touch with the Square Dancer in You"). Al is part owner of Harry's Hardware Store at 3rd and Maine in Royal Oak and Big Mike's is his favorite eatery. As a kid Al had a business called "Little Al's Lemonade Stand" (his slogan was "When It Comes to Lemons I'm Your Main Squeeze"). Al is a graduate of Gilmore High School and he named his first sawhorse Lily. Al was also the host of *Cooking with Irma*, the show that follows *Tool Time*, and plays miniature golf at Put Put Panorama.

See also: Jill Taylor, Tim Taylor, Wilson Wilson, Jr.

8. Al Bundy, *Married ... With Children*, Fox, 1987–1997. Played by Ed O'Neill.

Al Bundy is a shoe salesman. He makes $12,000 a year and is married to Peggy, an adverse to any kind of work wife. He has two children, Kelly and Bud, and a pathetic life. The greatest moment of his life occurred in high school when, as a member of the football team, he scored four touchdowns in one game and was voted the Most Valuable Player of 1966. He was offered a college scholarship but turned it down to marry his high school sweetheart, Peggy Wanker. He has regretted it ever since.

Al was born in Chicago and now lives at 9674 Jeopardy Lane (also seen as 9764). He attended James K. Polk High School and works for Garry's Shoes and Accessories for the Beautiful Woman in the New Market Mall. His pride and joy is his collection of *Playboy* magazines and he drives (when not pushing) a run down 1974 Dodge (plate F3B 359). Al frequents the Jiggly Room of the Nudie Bar and reads a girlie magazine called *Big 'Ums*. He watches such "hooter classics" as *Planet of the D Cups* and *Breast Monsters from Venus* and his favorite TV shows are *Psycho Dad*, *Tube Top Wrestling* and *Friends* ("because if you mute the sound and watch through binoculars you can see that Jennifer Aniston [Rachel] isn't wearing a bra").

Al's favorite drink is Girlie Girl Beer. He wore jersey 38DD on a baseball team called Chicago Cleavage and his favorite motto is "Hooters, hooters, yum, yum, yum. Hooters, hooters on a girl who's dumb." Al made a TV commercial for Zeus Athletic Shoes and attempted to start a TV telephone service called "Dr. Shoe." He was also the founder and president of MA'AM (the National Organization of Men Against Amazonian Masterhood) and had another bright spot in his dull life. On November 26, 1995, the Kyoto National Bank named him the greatest football player ever at Polk High. The scoreboard was dedicated to him and the field named The Al Bundy Field.

See also: Bud Bundy, Kelly Bundy, Marcy Rhoades, Peggy Bundy.

9. Al Calavicci, *Quantum Leap*, NBC, 1989–1993. Played by Dean Stockwell.

Al Calavicci is a project observer on Quantum Leap, a secret government project concerned with time travel (it is concealed in the desert 30 miles outside the town of Destiny County, New Mexico). Al appears as a hologram to Sam Beckett, the man who travels through time to help people overcome a mistake they made in the past (Sam accomplished this through a sophisticated computer he has named Ziggy. Al communicates with Sam via a slightly defective hand-held version of Ziggy and supplies Sam with the information he needs to know about the person whose life he assumes).

Al was born on June 15, 1945, and grew up in an orphanage (where he had a pet roach named

Kevin). He ran away from the orphanage to join a circus and later enlisted in the Navy (he was an ensign in 1957 and called "Bingo" by his buddies). In 1969, Al married Beth, the only girl he says he ever loved. Two years later, while serving in Vietnam, Al was reported as missing in action and assumed dead. He was found in 1973. He learned that Beth had remarried and he never returned to her. Al relaxes by smoking a good cigar (a habit he picked up in Vietnam).

See also: Sam Beckett.

10. Alan Brady, *The Dick Van Dyke Show*, CBS, 1961–1966. Played by Carl Reiner.

Alan Brady is the over bearing, always exasperated, always yelling star and executive producer of *The Alan Brady Show*, a variety show that airs at 8:30 p.m. on an unnamed network opposite *Yancy Derringer* (which was on CBS). Alan is married to Margaret and lives in the Temple Towers on East 61st Street in Manhattan. Mel Cooley is his producer and "yes man." Rob Petrie, Sally Rogers and Buddy Sorrell are his comedy writers. Alan believes he should be held in admiration when he is in public places and considers his viewers (his adoring public) "the little people." Alan is perceived as outwardly crude but believes he has a soft heart.

Alan's business ventures pay the bills. The Ishomoto Company, which produces motorcycles, pays Rob's salary. Buddy and Sally were originally paid by Tam-O-Shatner, Ltd., which made Dean Martin and Jerry Lewis coloring books. When it folded, Alan's mother-in-law's company, Barracuda, Ltd., paid them. The show's band is paid by Brady Lady, Alan's wife's company. Alan is also sensitive to the fact that he is bald and has a series of hair pieces he calls "Fellas" (it became nationally known that Alan was bald when Rob's wife, Laura, exposed the secret on *The Ray Murdock X-Ray Show*). According to the CBS special, *The Dick Van Dyke Show Revisited* (May 11, 2004), *The Alan Brady Show* was cancelled after *The Dick Van Dyke Show* ended its run because Rob hadn't worked for Alan for over 40 years. Alan was also said to have several ex-wives and when he is cheerful, he was the most dangerous (he wants something).

See also: Buddy Sorrell, Laura Petrie, Ritchie Petrie, Rob Petrie, Sally Rogers.

11. Alan Carter, *Space: 1999*, Syn., 1975. Played by Nick Tate.

Alan Carter is a captain and pilot (of ships called Eagles) who is one of 300 people marooned on the moon after a radioactive chain reaction blasted it out of its orbit. The moon, part of a project called Moonbase Alpha, now wanders seeking a new planet to which to affix itself (the moon was colonized to build an early warning system to repel alien invaders).

Alan was born on a cattle ranch in Australia in 1966. He became an excellent horseman and had a dream to fly one day; when he was a teenager his dream came true when he piloted the family's private plane. After graduating from college Alan joined the Australian Air Force and eventually became an astronaut in the combined U.S./Australian Space Program. In 1997 he explored Mars and next embarked on an exploration of Venus. He then became Chief of Reconnaissance on the Moonbase Alpha project. Alan was also a test pilot (flew the Eagle Transport and the Mark IX Hawk).

See also: Helena Russell, John Koenig, Maya, Victor Bergman.

12. Alecia Alcott, *All About Us*, NBC, 2001–2002. Played by Alecia Elliott.

Alecia Alcott and her closest friends, Christina, Nikki and Sierra, attend Belmont High School in Chicago. Alecia was born in Alabama and relocated to Chicago when her father received a job transfer.

Alecia is a very pretty 16-year-old girl who is also a talented singer and songwriter (of rock ballads). She hopes to become a professional singer. Alecia is a friendly person who will go out of her way to help people in trouble. She hates confrontation and always excuses herself when she has to face one. Alecia had a steady boyfriend in Alabama and at her high school's Winter Festival they were voted "Cutest Couple" (she has not yet found a boyfriend in Chicago). Alecia has a difficult time figuring out boys and says, "He's a guy — who knows what he thinks." Alecia is a planner and thinks before acting — something her girlfriends do not do and she is the peacemaker of the group when they get into a scramble. Alecia has a gorgeous figure and eats what she wishes without ever gaining weight. Alecia's favorite song is "Rainy Day" (recorded in 1965 by The Celestials) and "Revolver" by The Beatles is her favorite album. Playing the guitar cheers Alecia up when she is sad. She has such a unique way with words that she can make anything sound romantic. She hangs out at a teen club called The Loft and sang with a band called Cool with Me.

See also: Christina Castelli, Nikki Merrick, Sierra Jennings.

13. Alex Burton, *Going Places*, ABC, 1990–1991. Played by Heather Locklear.

Alexandra Burton is a writer on the mythical television series *Here's Looking at You* (a *Candid Camera* type of show). Dawn St. Claire (Holland Taylor) produces the program at National Studios in Hollywood.

Alex, as Alexandra likes to be called, chose the nickname to confuse people — people expect to see a man, not a gorgeous blonde. Alex was born in Denver, Colorado, on August 31, 1965. She is the daughter of Mark and Cassandra Burton. She was an innocently mischievous child (liked playing practical jokes) and is a graduate of Colorado State University (where she acquired a degree in communications). Alex immediately acquired a job producing a local morning show called *Wake Up, Denver*. Two years later she applied for a writing position (devising practical jokes) on *Here's Looking at You* and was hired.

Alex lives at 1800 Beach Road and has a plush rabbit named Mr. Fluffy. She is a sexy blonde bombshell and loves to cook. She claims to have once gained weight — "I blew up to 103 pounds when I stopped smoking." Alex has a healthy outlook on life and has an impressive answer for everything. Alex later works as a writer on *The Dick Roberts Show* (a daily talk show) when *Here's Looking at You* is cancelled and replaced by a show called *America's Funniest Most Wanted*.

14. Alex Mack, *The Secret World of Alex Mack*, NIK, 1994. Played by Larisa Oleynik.

Alexandra Louise Mack, called Alex, is a 13-year-old girl who lives at 2344 Clemson Lane in Paradise Valley, California, with her parents, Barbara and George, and he older sister, Annie. Alex attends Atron Junior High School and is an average student. She is very sweet and very pretty but believes "I'm boring, plain and simple." She reads *13* magazine, has a collection of troll dolls and carries a troll lunchbox to school. Alex is somewhat of a tomboy and has an interest in sports. She is learning to play the piano and enjoys a game of miniature golf. Alex is also a very special girl. She possesses a series of super powers as a result of coming in contact with chemicals from the Paradise Valley Chemical Plant called GC 161 (a truck carrying the chemical swerved to miss hitting Alex. A container fell off the truck, burst open and doused Alex). She can now levitate through thought, dispense electrical charges through her fingers and turn herself into a silvery liquid by concentrating. Her worst enemy is the common cold (if she sneezes, her powers are set free and she has no control over them). Despite her enhancement, Alex uses her powers to help people overcome obstacles ("I don't want to use them to turn the world on its head").

See also: Annie Mack.

15. Alex Moreau, *Poltergeist: The Legacy*, Showtime, 1996–1998; Sci Fi, 1999; Syn., 1999–2001. Played by Robbie Chong.

Alexandra Moreau, called Alex, is a member of the Legacy, a group of people who protect the innocent "from the creatures that inhabit the shadows of the night." Alex works as a researcher at the San Francisco Legacy House. She is a brilliant student of anthropology and possesses an innate curiosity and psychic abilities. Alex has a natural gift for the paranormal, which she acquired from her grandmother, a Creole woman deeply involved in the occult. Alex has a university education in science and a highly developed social conscience as well as an outstanding talent for difficult research

See also: Derek Rayne, Kristen Adams, Nick Boyle, Rachel Corrigan.

16. Alex Murphy, *RoboCop*, Syn., 1999. Played by Richard Eden.

Alexander Murphy, nicknamed Alex, is a Delta City police officer in 21st century Detroit. He is married to Nancy and is the father of a son (Tommy). He and his family live at 548 Principal Drive. Alex is an Irish Catholic and attended Mother Theresa Elementary School, St. John Paul High School and Holy Trinity College. He attends Sunday mass at St. John Paul Cathedral and wears badge number 2120. That was Alex's past. He is now RoboCop, a part human, part machine law enforcer attached to the Crime Prevention Program of the Metro South Precinct of Old Chicago. His wife and son believe that Alex is dead. Alex was shot several times during a robbery investigation. With only one hope of saving his life, he was given to Security Concepts, a cybernetic institute that rebuilt him as RoboCop (total body prosthesis, titanium skin, on-board computer assisted brain, instant reflexes). Because he cannot be the husband and father he once was, Alex has chosen to distance himself from his family.

Alex is now programmed with three prime directives: Serve the Public Interest, Uphold the Law and Protect the Innocent. He carries a specially encoded Omni Consumer Products gun that can only be fired by him and he never stays in one place long enough "because somewhere there is a crime happening."

17. Alex P. Keaton, *Family Ties*, NBC, 1982–1989. Played by Michael J. Fox.

Alexander P. Keaton, called Alex, is the brilliant son of Elyse and Steven Keaton, a happily married couple who live in the Leland Heights section of Columbus, Ohio. He has a younger brother, Andrew, and two sisters, Mallory and Jennifer.

Alex was born in a commune in California where his then hippie parents had contemplated naming him Moon Muffin. Alex first attended Harding High School then Leland College (where he was an economics major). He worships money, is a staunch Republican and prides himself on being different. He was president of Leland's Young Businessman's Association and the Young Entrepreneurs Club. Alex won the Matthews, Wilson, Harris and Burke Scholarship, reads the *Wall Street Journal* and was host of his own show on WLEL (Leland College radio) called "Syncopated Money" (blues music and business news).

Alex carries his resume with him at all times and held jobs at the Harding Trust Company and the American Mercantile Bank. The first day of school is Alex's favorite day of the year and he has a collection of report cards from nursery school through college. In the last episode, Alex accepts a job offer from the Wall Street firm of O'Brien, Mathers and Clark.

See also: Jennifer Keaton, Mallory Keaton, Steven and Elyse Keaton.

18. Alex Reiger, *Taxi*, ABC, 1978–1982; NBC, 1982–1983. Played by Judd Hirsch.

Alex Reiger is a driver for the Sunshine Cab Company in New York City. He says 'I'm a cab driver and I don't mind," which is his way of taking pride in accepting things the way they are (it is also his excuse for having no ambition). Alex is divorced (from Phyllis) and is the father of an adult daughter (Cathy). Alex's father, Joe, considered himself a ladies' man and walked out on the family when Alex was a child. Alex now lives in Apartment 2A. He is the oldest of the cabbies and the authority figure in the company garage (the hangout). He listens to the other cabbies and offers them advice.

See also: Elaine Nardo, Jim Ignatowski, Latka Gravas, Louie DePalma.

19. Alex Young, *I'm with Her*, ABC, 2003–2004. Played by Teri Polo.

Alexis Young, better known as Alex, is America's Sweetheart, a beloved movie actress who receives $10 million a film. She lives in Beverly Hills in a house that was previously owned by Liberace and Madonna is her current neighbor. Alex is 31 years old and has been in show business for 12 years. She made her debut in a movie called *Cause for Alarm* playing Hooker Number 3 (her only line was "Keep driving Buddy, you can't afford me"). She next made a horrible slasher film called *All About Evil*, which she considers to be the most embarrassing thing she has ever done. This did not discourage Alex as twenty additional films came her way, including *And Baxter Makes Three*, *Carnival Man*, *The Prosecution Rests*, *All Blondes Are Dangerous*, *Swing Baby*, the Oscar nominated *September Song* and a little known cult film called *My Name Is I Don't Know*.

Alex has a star on the Hollywood Walk of Fame and performs at charity functions "so I can sing. Nobody else lets me sing." Alex was the subject of the E-Network's *E True Story* and when Alex does TV interviews she gets so nervous that she misuses words. Alex is allergic to almonds, enjoys double stuffed Oreo cookies and had her first teen crush on singer Duran Duran. Orchids are Alex's favorite flower and she reads *US* magazine.

Alex rescues stray dogs and names them after the places she finds them (for example, Found by the Freeway, Found by the Airport). She believes Halloween is the most wonderful time of the year.

Alex's real name is Alexis Baldzikowski. She was born in Tennessee and raised by her mother, Suzanne (Cybill Shepherd), an actress who gave up her career to have her and her sister, Cherie (Rhea Seehorn). Suzanne drank, smoked and was a bit wacky (she lived in a tree for three years; cooked food in pickle juice and always embarrassed Alex. At her high school graduation, Suzanne's blouse just happened to pop open and reveal her breasts; at Alex's first movie premiere, Suzanne's blouse again just happened to pop open). Suzanne had her only success as the female lead in *The Music Man* at the Lamplight Theater. Feeling that she would never regain her glory, Suzanne pushed Alex toward a life in show business. Alex took acting and dancing classes and by the age of seven began dreaming of Oscar night, wearing a gorgeous dress, looking beautiful and walking down the red carpet — "It was like a wedding to me." Although Alex was able to show her stunning figure as a contestant in the Miss Tennessee Pageant, she and Cherie were overweight growing up (they spent a summer at a fat camp). Alex is now with the William Morris Agency and Cherie works by her side as her hairdresser, makeup woman, publicist and wardrobe girl. Cheri is 29 years old and is hoping to become a fashion designer. She has a fascination with fire, mimics Joan Rivers and loves to roller blade in hot pants. She paid 22,000 pesos for breast implants in Mexico and she appears naked shooting a machine gun on the Internet (at *www.gunsandbuns. net*). She and Alex have a pet goldfish named Garbo (after actress Greta Garbo).

See also: Patrick Owen (the school teacher Alex is dating).

20. Alexander Scott, *I Spy*, NBC, 1965–1968. Played by Bill Cosby.

Alexander Scott, called Scotty, is a U.S. government agent whose cover is that of a trainer/masseur for Kelly Robinson, an agent who poses as a tennis pro.

Scotty is a Rhodes scholar and can speak eight languages. He was born in Philadelphia and mentioned he would have become a basketball coach at Allentown High School had he not become a spy. Scotty possesses a black belt in the martial arts and has the instincts of an alley cat. He had training as a chemist and is an expert on explosives (he can make a bomb out of almost anything). He will shoot to kill (or shoot first and ask questions later).

See also: Kelly Robinson.

21. Alexandra Cahill, *Walker, Texas Ranger*, CBS, 1993–2001. Played by Sheree J. Wilson.

Alexandra Cahill is the Assistant District Attorney of Fort Worth, Texas. She was born in Texas and is dating Cordell Walker, the Texas Ranger who calls her Alex (they married in May of 2000 and became the parents of a girl, Angela, in the series last episode). Alex teaches law enforcement classes at the Irving Campus of Mid-Texas University and conducts a Victims of Crime women's support group at the south shore of Stuart Lake that she calls Camp Cahill. Alex is also the founder of a help center called H.O.P.E. (Help Our People).

Alex is stubborn and will fight for what she believes in. She cares about people and will put her job on the line to see that justice is done. She loves horses (she has one named Amber) and *Sparticus* is her favorite movie (May is her favorite month of the year).

See also: Cordell Walker, Jimmy Trevette.

22. Alexandra DeMonaco, *Just Cause*, PAX, 2002. Played by Elizabeth Lackey.

Alexandra Sandra DeMonaco is an ex-con who is seeking to begin a new life. She was born in East Los Angeles and attended Roosevelt High School. Her father was a military man and she was considered an "army brat." Alex, as she is sometimes called, married a lawyer after graduation. After raising their daughter, Mia, Alex began working as her husband's office manager. Unknown to Alex, her husband was working with unethical doctors to defraud insurance companies. When an investigation into her husband's affairs showed that Alexandra manipulated the books, she was arrested and convicted of insurance fraud. Her husband disappeared, taking their daughter with him.

Alexandra was sentenced to five years at the Mendincino's Women's Prison. Angered at the wrong done to her, Alexandra studied law under Bay City College's internet program. She acquired her degree but is a felon and unable to practice law. Alexandra was a model prisoner and is now out on parole. She is a bright and determined woman with the mind of a detective. Her enthusiasm and sleuthing skills impress Hamilton Whitney, III, a senior partner in the San Francisco law firm of Burdick, Whitney and Morgan, who hires her as a paralegal. Alexandra is now determined to prove she was framed so she can practice law.

Alexandra lives at 1196-B Hayes Avenue in San Francisco. Her case is numbered B0-96301 and in prison she was assigned to kitchen detail (where she claims "I developed a talent for reading people"). Alexandra is allergic to dust and wears expensive ($15 a pair) sheer pantyhose. She is persistent once she is on a case, but sometimes becomes too emotionally involved and puts her life in jeopardy.

See also: Hamilton Whitney, III.

23. Alexx Woods, *C.S.I.: Miami,* CBS, 2002 (current). Played by Khandi Alexander.

Alexx Woods is a medical examiner with the Crime Scene Investigation Unit of the Miami Dade County Police Department. She was born in Queens, New York, on August 13, 1960, and stands five feet, four inches tall (she weighs 115 pounds). Alexx has a Bachelor of Science degree in chemistry from New York University and an M.D. from Rutgers University. She is married and the oldest of five brothers and sisters. When her parents worked long hours to keep the family out of poverty, Alexx became a substitute mother and cared for her siblings. As a result she became compulsively neat. By the age of 12, Alexx wanted to become a doctor. Her parents encouraged this and Alexx's determination earned her college scholarships. At Rutgers she kept to herself and became a top student. She began work in the New York City Coroner's Office but left that position for a job with the state-of-the-art crime lab in Dade County. Alexx has an unusual affinity with the victims of violent crimes and promises them closure.

See also: Calleigh Duquesne, Erik Delko, Horatio Caine, Tim Speedle.

24. ALF, *ALF,* NBC, 1986–1990. Voiced by Paul Fusco.

Gordon Schumway, called ALF (Alien Life Form), is an extraterrestrial who lives with an Earth family (the Tanners) at 167 Hemdale Street in Los Angeles. ALF became a part of their lives when his space ship crashed into their garage and he became stranded.

ALF is short and furry (burnt sienna color) with off black eyes, a large snout, four teeth and an enormous appetite. ALF's home world was a planet called Melmac, which has since been destroyed by an explosion. It had a purple moon and its good luck charms were a mouse and a Tupperware lid. ALF is 229 years old. He first said he was born on the twenty-eighth of Nathanganger, then to parents Bob, Biff and Flo on August 12th and October 2nd of 1757. ALF's body temperature is 425 degrees; he has eight stomachs and a craving for cats (his favorite breakfast was Cats Benedict).

ALF attended Melmac High School for 122 years and Melmac State College for two years. He holds degrees in software and pedestrian crossing. He was known as Mr. Science and held the following jobs: bearded lady in a circus, TV show host, car salesman and Orbit Guard. He became a male model at the age of 150 and later co-captioned the Codsters, a bouillaiseball team, for three years (played like Earth baseball, but on ice with shellfish).

On Earth ALF believes TV cartoons reflect real life. *Gilligan's Island* and the mythical *Polka Time* are his favorite TV shows. *Shana, Mistress of the Universe* is his favorite comic book and he orders pizza as "Alf Tanner" via the house account at the Pizza Barge. Too much food causes Melmacians to explode if they are not careful. Dieting is also a problem. It causes an enzyme imbalance and ALF could revert to Wolf, a primitive Melmacian hunting machine.

Willie Tanner (Max Wright) is the head of the Earth family that includes his wife, Kate (Anne Schedeen) and their children, Lynn (Andrea Elson) and Brian (Benji Gregory). Willie works for the Los Angeles Department of Social Services and considers ALF "my own personal hell" for all the trouble he causes. The family pet is Lucky, a cat ALF calls Flipper.

25. Alice Holliday, *This Is Alice,* Syn., 1958–1959. Played by Patty Ann Gerrity.

Alice Holliday is the pretty but mischievous

daughter of Chet and Clarissa Holliday. She was born on May 14, 1948 and lives at 857 Elm Street in the small town of River Glen, New Jersey. Chet is a reporter for the local newspaper, the *Star Herald*; Clarissa was born in Georgia, where her family owns a peanut plantation.

Alice, a fourth grader at the River Glen Elementary School, is president of the All for One Club ("Friends to the end" is their slogan). She has a pet frog (Rudolph), a pony (Pegasus) and two flies (Henry and Madeline). Alice is very smart but doesn't always apply herself at school. She has a kind heart and feels obligated to help people she feels are in trouble — even if they don't ask for it.

26. Alice Hyatt, *Alice*, CBS, 1976–1985. Played by Linda Lavin.

Alice Spevak Hyatt is a widow and the mother of a young son, Tommy. She was born in New Jersey and is a graduate of Passaic High School (where she was voted "Girl with the Best Knees"). Alice formed her own singing group, Alice and the Acorns, and was called "Pudge Spevak" when she was overweight as a child. Alice first worked at Vito's Bar and Grill in Newark. It was here that she met her future husband, Donald Hyatt, a big rig trucker. When Donald was killed in a job related accident, Alice decided to head west and pursue her dream of becoming a singer. Car trouble and a lack of money stranded her in Phoenix, Arizona, where she found work as a waitress at Mel's Diner. She and Tommy first lived at the Sun Apartments (Room 103) then at the Phoenix Arms (Apartment 108).

Alice was a Brownie as a child and became interested in singing at an early age. She becomes depressed when she feels her big break will never come. While the waitress job was only supposed to be a temporary stop off until she got herself back on her feet, Alice remained in Phoenix for nine years. She performed at the local clubs (Herman's Hitching Post, the Saddle Sore and Vinnie's House of Veal) and in the series last episode got her big break when she moved to Nashville to sing with a country/western singer named Travis Nash.

See also: Flo Castleberry, Jolene Hunnicutt, Mel Sharples, Vera Gorman.

27. Alice Kramden, *The Honeymooners*, CBS, 1955–1956. Played by Audrey Meadows.

Alice Kramden is the patient, understanding wife of Ralph Kramden, a driver for the Gotham Bus Company. She lives at 728 Chauncey Street in Bensonhurst, Brooklyn, New York, in an apart-

ment that she hates ("Living in a tent would be an improvement," she says). Alice was born in Brooklyn and married Ralph in 1941 (see Ralph Kramden for information on their meeting). They first lived with her mother, Mrs. Gibson, on Canarsie Street before moving into their one and only apartment.

Alice did not have a TV, radio or any modern appliance. She apparently cleaned all day and Ralph refused to let her get a job (as he was "The king of my castle" and felt the need to support her). Alice did, however, revolt against the king and held two temporary jobs: donut jelly stuffer at Krausmeyer's Bakery (later promoted to donut taster) and secretary to a man named Tony Amico. Prior to meeting Ralph, Alice worked in a laundromat then as a typist. Her birth sign is Aquarius (born February 8) and she was chosen "Cleaning Lady of the Year" by Glow Worm cleanser.

When they were first married, Ralph called Alice "Bunny" (she called him "Old Buttercup"). Now it's constant arguing with Ralph waving his fist and telling Alice "You're going to the moon" or "Pow! Right in the kisser." Despite his temper, Ralph deeply loves Alice and shows his affection by hugging her and telling her "Baby, you're the greatest."

See also: Ed Norton, Ralph Kramden.

28. Alice Nelson, *The Brady Bunch*, ABC, 1969–1974. Played by Ann B. Davis.

Alice Nelson is the all-giving housekeeper to Mike and Carol Brady and their children, Marcia, Greg, Jan, Peter, Cindy and Bobby. She resides with the family in the spacious Brady home at 4222 Clinton Avenue in Los Angeles. Mike, an architect, designed the home and Alice has a room to the right side of the kitchen. She also cares for the children's pets: Tiger (dog) and Fluffy (cat).

Alice was born in California and is a graduate of Westdale High School. She cooks, cleans, offers advice but never eats dinner at the same table with the Bradys. She began working for Mike and his family in 1962 (his wife had died shortly after Bobby was born). Alice likes to bowl, enter jingle writing contests and watches *Perry Mason* reruns on TV. Alice has had few relationships and is dating Sam Franklin (Allan Melvin), the owner of Sam's Butcher Shop; they married in 1981.

See also: Carol and Mike Brady, Greg Brady (also for information on Peter and Bobby), Marcia Brady (also for information on Jan and Cindy).

29. Alicia Lambert, *Step by Step*, ABC, 1991–1997; CBS, 1997–1998. Played by Christine Lakin.

Alicia Lambert, called Al by those who know her, is the daughter of Frank Lambert, a divorced contractor who lives with his second wife, Carol Foster, at 201 Winslow Street in Port Washington, Wisconsin. Alicia has two brothers, J.T. and Brendon, and shares the house with Carol's children, Dana, Karen and Mark.

Alicia is a very pretty tomboy. She first attended Miss Daisy's Ducky Room Preschool then Port Washington Junior High and Port Washington High School. She always fears the worst in a situation and has a rattlesnake's head preserved in a jar; she also has a pet pig named Bullet. Alicia is a catcher for the Beavers Little League baseball team and is a smart aleck (Dana thinks she needs an attitude adjustment and calls her "You little criminal").

Alicia is the "son" Frank wishes he had (although she shows great potential for construction, "Lambert and Daughter Construction" is a dream that Frank feels will never come true). Alicia rents movies (from Dave's Video Store) to do school book reports and played drums in an all-girl band called Chicks with Attitudes (their first gig was at Greco's Bowl-a-Rama). Her first job was as a waitress at Mr. Chips, the cookie store in the mall. Alicia next worked as the waitress Peggy Sue at the 50s Café.

Alicia has set her goal to become an actress. She starred as Lola Fonatine in the Community Playhouse production of *Death of a Salesman* and she also did a print ad for Stop Jeans.

See also: Carol and Frank Lambert, Dana Foster, J.T. Lambert, Karen Foster.

30. Alicia Smith, *Flying Blind*, Fox, 1992–1993. Played by Tea Leoni.

Alicia Smith is a freelance artist and fashion model who lives at 386 Bleecker Street in New York's Greenwich Village. She is beautiful, wild and unpredictable and her friends say "I should be committed." Alicia was born in a New York suburb and first realized she had sex appeal when she was 14 years old (on hot summer days Alicia would run through the sprinklers in a see-through sundress and drive her neighbor, an elderly doctor, crazy. He begged for just 15 minutes of her time. Alicia's constant refusals led him to develop the artificial aorta). Alicia attended the Zurich Academy for Girls in Switzerland and has an uneasy relationship with the somewhat psychotic father (Peter Boyle), a man of mystery who claims that "If I tell you what I do for a living I'll have

to kill you." He has no name and works for some ultra-secret government agency. When Alicia wants to visit him, she has to be blindfolded and stuffed in the trunk of a car (a Fiat).

Alicia loves to wear clothes that reveal her breasts in sexy bras and claims that her most embarrassing moment occurred when she was dating a U.N. dignitary "who stole a pair of my panties and sold them to a third world country as their flag." When she first began modeling, Alicia called herself "Kero"; when she tired of that, she became "Chloe" for several months. When jobs were scarce, Alicia went to Mexico to star in the movie *Bride of the Marsh Monster*. It became such a hit in the Philippines that the government issued an air mail stamp with Alicia's picture on it.

See also: Neil Barash (the man Alicia is dating).

31. Allie Lowell, *Kate and Allie*, CBS, 1984–1989. Played by Jane Curtin.

Allison Julie Charlotte Adams Lowell, called Allie, is the divorced mother of two children, Jennie and Chip. She is best-friends with Kate McArdle and they live together in New York's Greenwich Village.

Allie was born in New York City and was married to Charles Lowell, a doctor who now resides in Connecticut with his second wife, Claire. Allie and Kate are longtime friends who met as kids as an orthodontist's office. She and Kate moved in together to save on expenses.

Allie cooks, cleans and cares for the children, including Kate's daughter, Emma, while Kate works. Allie attends night classes at Washington Square College and held several part time jobs: bookstore salesgirl, box office cashier (at the 9th Street Cinema) and volunteer at Channel G, a Manhattan cable TV station. Allie later used her talent at cooking to form a company with Kate called Kate and Allie Caterers, which they operated from their home. Allie also found a new life when she married Bob Barsky, a sportscaster for WNTD-TV, Channel 10, in Washington, D.C. Bob commutes from New York to Washington and they moved into their own apartment (21C) on West 55th Street (Kate remained in their original apartment).

See also: Kate McArdle.

32. Allison and Kate Foster, *Double Trouble*, NBC, 1984–1985. Played by Jean and Liz Sagal.

Allison and Kate Foster are identical 18-year-old twins. They have brown hair and brown eyes and are each five feet, three inches tall (they each weigh 95 pounds and their driver's licenses expire on October 9, 1987).

Allison and Kate live at 1555 North Ridge Drive in Des Moines, Iowa, with their widowed father, Art Foster, the owner of Art's Gym. Allison is quiet and serious; Kate is a bit wild and mischievous. The girls, recent graduates of Des Moines High School, work as aerobic instructors at their father's gym. Halfway through the series, the format changed to focus on Allison and Kate's career goals. They moved to New York City and into the home of their aunt, Margo Foster at 49 West 74th Street (later given as 51 West 74th Street). Allison began her career of becoming a fashion designer by enrolling in the Manhattan Fashion Institute; Kate, who hopes to become an actress, takes whatever jobs become available (she works most often as a dancer at the Wacko Weiner Works Company, promoting their line of frankfurters).

33. Ally Barone, *Everybody Loves Raymond*, CBS, 1996–2005. Played by Madylin Sweeten.

Ally Barone, the daughter of Raymond and Debra Barone, was born in 1991. She lives at 320 Fowler Street (although 135 can be seen on the front door) in Lynbrook, New York, and has two siblings, twins Jeffrey and Michael. Ally attends Our Lady of Faith Elementary School (where she played a yam in the school's Thanksgiving play). Ally has a doll named Savannah and eats Flutie Flakes cereal for breakfast (later Post Alpha Bits). She is a member of the Frontier Scouts and *Beauty and the Beast* is her favorite movie. Ally is also a member of the Lynbrook T-Ball team (sponsored by Nemo's Pizza Parlor, it teaches children the spirit of baseball without the competition).

See also: Debra Barone, Frank and Marie Barone, Raymond Barone, Robert Barone.

34. Ally McBeal, *Ally McBeal*, Fox, 1997–2002. Played by Calista Flockhart.

Ally McBeal is a professional woman who lives in her own universe. She is beautiful and intelligent and hoping to become a partner in the Boston-based law firm of Cage and Fish. Ally was born in Boston and is a graduate of Harvard Law School. She lives at 1412 Dalton Lane. When Ally was ten years old she wanted to become an artist "and paint the world with beautiful pictures." In high school Ally was a cheerleader and voted "Most Likely to Become Julie Andrews" (Ally was considered perky like actress Julie Andrews).

Ally becomes nervous on first dates and wears what she calls "My lucky white bra" to give her confidence. She also has a problem with lesbians. Ally believes other women are attracted to her and she has mixed feelings about kissing another woman ("Some women gross me out but others I find attractive and don't gross me out"). Ally had been troubled by erotic gay dreams and found one such dream becoming a reality when she kissed a client (Ling Woo, played by Lucy Liu). Ally didn't say she didn't like it — "I kissed a woman — and can she kiss!" In a later episode Ally mentions her first date good luck charms as being "a pair of old shoes and my lucky lingerie."

Ally is blonde, always fashionably dressed and addicted to wearing micro miniskirts "because I like to." When she becomes upset or depressed, she raises her skirt hemlines to make her feel better (but comments "If things don't change I'm bound to get arrested for indecent exposure").

Ally claims to have a strange allergy: "I'm allergic to criminals" and also says "I get the sniffles if I'm put in jail for contempt to court." Ally is (or appears to be) dangerously thin (so much so that she wishes she were heavier just to have cleavage). Despite her slim figure, Ally (as Calista) is content with her slim figure and not suffering from an eating disorder (as had been assumed by the press and Calista's fans).

If Ally has a tough decision to make she stares into a mirror until she decides what to do. Ally also has fantasies and illusions. She is most famous for seeing a computer generated "Dancing Baby" (assumed to be an indication that Ally's biological clock is ticking). Ally mentioned that she also had visions as a child and at the age of eight saw a unicorn.

Ally feels that when she is happy she needs mental help ("I'm not use to it"). She likes Ben and Jerry's ice cream and in the end achieves success when the law firm becomes Cage, Fish and McBeal.

See also: John Cage, Elaine Vassal, Ling Woo.

35. Amanda, *Highlander: The Raven*, Syn., 1998–1999. Played by Elizabeth Gracen.

Amanda (no last name) is an Immortal, a mysterious person who cannot die except by beheading. Amanda is said to be 1200 years old in dialogue, but 1000 years old in the opening theme narration. She has lived for centuries as a rougish beauty who is attracted to the good things in life. She is never malicious and not without scruples. Her history is a mystery and no explanation is given as to who she really is or where she actually came from. Amanda says only that she belongs to a privileged class called the Immortals. She has lived and died many times and recalled her first birth as a young girl in Normandy in A.D. 850. This life was cut short when she was killed for stealing a loaf of bread. She was reborn that same day, but was unaware of her destiny. She was found and taken in by a mysterious woman named Rebecca Horne. It was Rebecca who cared for Amanda until she became a young woman. At this time Amanda was taught the martial arts and the art of swordplay. She was also told that she was an Immortal and that to survive, she must defeat the evil Immortals who seek to plunge the world into darkness. Amanda recalled her other lives as being a duchess, slave and woman of nobility.

36. Amanda King, *Scarecrow and Mrs. King*, CBS, 1983–1987. Played by Kate Jackson.

Amanda King is a suburban housewife who works as an operative for the Agency, a secret branch of the U.S. government that handles matters of national security. Amanda is divorced and the mother of two children, Philip and Jamie. She lives with her mother, Dotty West, at 4247 Maplewood Drive in Arlington, Virginia. Amanda attended the University of Virginia and has a degree in American Literature with a minor in photo-journalism. She was a cheerleader in high school and in college was a member of the drama club (she played the Tigress in a play called *Wailing Walrus*). Amanda does housework to exercise tapes, is a Bedside Bluebell (volunteer) at Galilee Hospital and works on behalf of United Charities (usually as the Refreshment Director). Amanda is also head of Mothers for a Safe Environment and manager of the Bombers, her sons' Little League baseball team. Pot roast with succotash is Amanda's favorite dinner. She is allergic to horses and took driving lessons at Barney's Driving Instructor School (she drives a station wagon with the plate JRY 502). Amanda earns extra money as an occasional reporter for the *Washington Blaze*.

Amanda is first a seasonal employee at the Agency (clearance level GS-7) and while assisting agent Lee Stetson (Bruce Boxleitner) on assignments, also transcribed tapes. After training at the Agency's Spy School, Station One, Amanda acquired a Grade 10 security clearance (her office is in the building's Film Library). Amanda and Lee grew close and married on February 13, 1987, shortly before the series ended.

See also: Lee Stetson.

37. Amanda Wickham, *Sabrina, the Teenage Witch*, ABC, 1999–2002. Played by Emily Hart.

Amanda Wickham is a pre-teen witch and the adorable but very mischievous cousin of Sabrina Spellman. Amanda was a full-fledged witch by the age of nine and enjoys popping in on Sabrina

at the most inconvenient times. Amanda is from the Fourth Galaxy in the Other Realm. She doesn't mean to be evil, but things just happen when she casts a spell. She currently attends the Witchwright School for Witches but was previously expelled from 14 different schools. Amanda sent 12 teachers into early retirement and one into a straight jacket. Amanda takes her toy box with her wherever she goes and, according to Sabrina, 'is a special rotten brat." Amanda is the daughter of Marigold and Harold and may appear as "bubbly and sweet" but she is one to fear if someone angers her (she will cast a spell on them). She also throws a tantrum if she doesn't get her way and teaching her a lesson is the only way to control her and make her listen.

See also: Hilda Spellman, Roxie King, Sabrina Spellman, Salem Saberhagen.

38. Amber Mariens, *Clueless*, ABC, 1996–1997; UPN, 1997–1999. Played by Elisa Donovan.

Amber Princess Mariens is a student at the posh Bronson Alcott High School in Beverly Hills, California. She is best friends with Cher Horowitz and Dee Davenport. Amber is the daughter of a wealthy doctor and lives at 111 Jeannie Court. She is beautiful and fashion conscious, but believes "people see me as a self-centered wacko." Amber has red hair ("Smoldering cherry, please, not red") and is sometimes called "Big Red" (her father calls her "Rose Petal," "Candy Cane" and "Buttercup"). Amber hopes to attend Stanhope College with Cher and Dee and previously attended Rodeo Drive Pre-School and the Rodeo Drive Elementary School. Amber flirts with male teachers to get better grades and flaunts 20-dollar bills to female teachers for that passing grade (she is normally an average student). Amber adores herself and Cher claims "she has super model delusions and is in love with herself." Amber seeks to marry rich ("If you date me," she says, "never buy me a gift from a store with barn in its name"). Amber has a pet dog (Tippy) and is very proud of the fact that her father donated a large sum of money to the local zoo and that officials named an animal after her (she is unaware that it is an orangutan). Amber does give of her time by volunteering at the Retired Actors Home.

See also: Cher Horowitz, Dee Davenport.

39. Amos McCoy, *The Real McCoys*, ABC, 1957–1962; CBS, 1962–1963. Played by Walter Brennan.

Amos McCoy, fondly called Grandpa, owns a 20-acre farm in California's San Fernando Valley. He resides on the farm (located on the Back Road) with his grandson, Luke, Luke's wife, Kate, and Luke's sister and brother, Hassie and Little Luke. Amos, a widower, was born in Smokey Corners, West Virginia, in 1894. His late wife was named Julie. Amos is an expert at birdcalls and uses the "McCoy Tonic" to cure his ailments (an alcoholic beverage recipe that has been in the family for over 100 years). When it comes to planting crops, Amos knows what goes where by tasting the dirt ("I got a taste for dirt"). He claims the family history includes two moonshiners, a horse thief and a riverboat gambler. Amos enjoys pitching horseshoes, fishing, playing checkers and relaxing in his rocking chair on the front porch. He is a member of the Royal Order of the Mystic Nile Lodge (where he is Grand Imperial Mummy) and president of the West Valley Grange Association. Amos is musically inclined (he plays the jug that usually holds moonshine) and in his youth, was the only spooner with a record player in his canoe. He calls his tractor Iron Mule (it is stubborn and rarely starts) and also has a 1920s Model A Ford Touring car (plate LBU 179) he calls Gertrude (later Emily). Amos is most embarrassed by the fact that he cannot read or write.

See also: Hassie and Little Luke McCoy, Kate and Luke McCoy.

Amy Barone *see* **Robert Barone**

40. Amy Tompkins, *It's a Living,* Syn., 1985–1989. Played by Crystal Bernard.

Amy Tompkins is a waitress at Above the Top, a 13th floor Los Angeles restaurant that features Sky High Dining (it is owned by Pacific Continental Properties). Amy was born in Snyder, Texas, and attended Middleton Elementary School. She is a graduate of Snyder High School and is an expert shot. She owns a chrome-plated .357 Magnum with a six-inch barrel and is a member of the American Gun Owners Association. Amy keeps her gun "in my pink jammy bunny with a zipper in its tummy."

Amy is undecided about her future and came to Los Angeles to better her life (she left home with these words from her father: "Keep your chin up and your skirt down"). Amy now lives at the Carrie Nation Hotel for Women in Los Angeles and has a plush rabbit she calls Snuggle Bunny.

See also: Cassie Cranston, Dot Higgins, Ginger St. James, Jan Hoffmeyer, Lois Adams, Sonny Mann.

41. The Ancient One, *BeastMaster,* Syn., 1999–2001. Played by Grahame Bond.

In an era before time began; in a world of magic and the supernatural sciences, there existed a being known only as the Ancient One. As animal life began to evolve on Earth, the Ancient One appeared in human form to control destiny and create an army of beautiful Sorceresses to maintain the balance of life. A Sorceress who proved weak would be imprisoned in a crystal rock for all eternity.

The powers of the Ancient One are unsurpassed. He can control the elements of earth, sea and sky. He can erase memories, create or destroy desires, and manipulate time. He is the link to a more powerful, unknown source; a source that could easily destroy the universe if it so pleased.

See also: Arina, Curupira, Dar, Iara, The Sorceress, Tao.

42. Andrea Thomas, *Isis,* CBS, 1975–1978. Played by JoAnna Cameron.

Andrea Thomas is a very special young woman. She possesses the ability to transform herself into Isis, the Egyptian goddess of fertility, to protect good from evil.

Andrea was born in Larkspur, a small town in California. She attended Mermount Grammar School, Larkspur High School and is a graduate of U.C.L.A. (where she acquired a degree in science). As long as Andrea can remember, she was interested in science, especially in the myths that surrounded the gods and goddesses of ancient Rome and Egypt. In 1975, an opportunity allowed Andrea to become part of an expedition to Egypt. While exploring on her own, Andrea found a magic amulet that was once worn by Isis (the amulet was given to Isis by the Royal Sorcerer. It had been buried for centuries and legend states that it will grant its owner special powers). Andrea conceals her find from the other members of the expedition. Upon her return to Larkspur, Andrea places the amulet around her neck. She utters the words "O Mighty Isis" and became the goddess (the skies darkened around her, the symbol of Isis was seen and Andrea was magically transformed into the goddess. She was able to soar and had the power over animals and the ability to control the elements of earth, sea and sky).

Andrea teaches science at Larkspur High School. She lives at 21306 Baker Place (apartment 4A) and has a pet crow named Tut. Her car license plate reads 69 CBE and 555-3638 is her phone number. As Isis, Andrea wears a white tunic with a short skirt and a tiara that allows her to see beyond her normal vision. Her hair also increases in length — from Andrea's mid-back length to hip length for Isis. Conservative dress, glasses, and a ponytail are the "disguises" Andrea uses to conceal her secret identity. To perform any feat, Isis must recite a special rhyme to the task at hand; the rhyme she most often uses is "O zephyr winds which blow on high, lift me now so I may fly."

43. Andromeda, *Andromeda*, Syn., 2000–2005. Played by Lexa Doig.

Andromeda is a three dimensional hologram that runs the *Andromeda Ascendant*, a futuristic Commonwealth battleship captioned by Dylan Hunt. The Shining Path to Truth and Knowledge Institute designed Andromeda, called Rommie by Dylan. She was originally the voice of the ship's computer and appeared only as an image on a screen. Her body was "humanized" and she now appears as a beautiful woman who is also the ship's aviator ("I am a warship and I don't like walking away from a fight"). Her official title is "Artificial Intelligence GRA 112; Serial Number XMC-10-182." Rommie thinks of herself as a real person and is only supposed to know what she is programmed to do but has adapted and can go beyond that and make decisions on her own. Rommie can pick up signals from all frequencies and all crafts in outer space. Very high frequencies usually stump Rommie because they indicate an object on which nothing is known. Rommie uses logic to make conclusions and for a hologram is an expert shot and fighter (the martial arts). Although Rommie has feelings for Dylan, she is forbidden to be anymore than just a servant (Commonwealth rules prohibit relationships between artificial intelligence and humans).

See also: Beka Valentine, Dylan Hunt, Trance Gemini.

44. Andy Campbell, *Strong Medicine*, Lifetime, 2003–2005. Played by Patricia Richardson.

Andrea Campbell, called Dr. Andy, is the head of the Rittenhouse Women's Health Clinic in Philadelphia. Andrea is from a military family and spent much of her youth in the Army Medical Corps (she retired as a colonel). She is a skilled general surgeon and woman's health specialist. Andrea is single, loves Oreo cookies (the new chocolate crème kind) and feels that her greatest achievement was graduating from airborne school. She fears failure and has to be perfect in everything she does. Andrea may have been influenced by her favorite TV show, *Combat*, to join the army.

See also: Dana Stowe, Kayla Thornton, Lana Hawkins, Luisa Delgado, Nick Biancavilla, Peter Riggs.

45. Andy Taylor, *The Andy Griffith Show*, CBS, 1960–1968. Played by Andy Griffith.

Andrew Jackson Taylor, called Andy, is the sheriff of Mayberry, a small, mythical town in North Carolina. He is a widower and the mother of a young son (Opie). Andy was born in Mayberry and is a graduate of Mayfield Union High School (class of 1945). He lives at 322 Maple Street (also given as 14 Maple Street) and is cared for by his Aunt Bee.

Andy does not carry a gun and is a bit old fashioned. He'd rather talk a criminal into giving up rather than use force to accomplish the same goal. He carries his emergency equipment, a rake and a shovel, in the trunk of his car and his duties in the virtually crime free town include patrolling, helping children across the street, handing out parking tickets and replacing lids on garbage cans.

Andy enjoys singing and playing the guitar and a good home cooked meal (although he eats lunch at the Junction Café, also called the Diner). Andy's greatest fear is that one day "Mayberry is going to turn into a sin town."

Andy first dated Ellie Walker (Elinor Donahue), a pharmacist at the Walker Drug Store (he called her "Miss Ellie"). He later dated and married Helen Crump (Aneta Corsaut), the local grammar school teacher.

See also: Barney Fife, Bee Taylor, Gomer Pyle, Goober Pyle, Opie Taylor.

46. Angel, *Angel*, WB, 1999–2004. Played by David Boreanaz.

The character of Angel first appeared as a recurring character (1997–1999) on *Buffy the Vampire Slayer*. Angel is actually Angelus, a once evil vampire who uses his skills of the undead to help people as the owner of Angel Investigations in Los Angeles.

Angel was born as Liam in Ireland. He was seduced by a beautiful vampire (Darla) and turned into a creature of the night. Exactly when this happened varies by episodes. Angel was first said to have been born in 1746, making him 251 years old in 1997. Shortly after he was 241 years old (born in 1756) and then 18 years old in 1775 (making his birth year 1757). A last mention of a birth year occurs in 2000 when Angel says he was born in 1723, making him 277 years old. Darla was first said to have bitten Angel in 1757, when he was 18; she later claims it happened in 1753. The exact date of Angel's restoration (turning good) is also a mystery. In the late 1850s Angel killed a young Gypsy girl. Her clan cursed him by restoring his soul and with it his conscience. Overcome with guilt for the misery he caused,

Angel fled to America and vowed never to feed on humans again. Angel rejected the life of a vampire and chose to remain above ground to atone for the sins of his past. The restoration is later mentioned as occurring in the 1920s and finally in 1898.

As Angelus, Angel terrorized Europe as "The vampire with the angelic face." After killing his victims, Angel would carve a cross on their left cheek to let people know he was there. Although Angel has a soul, he still possesses vampire traits. He cannot function in sunlight ("He uses the rat-infested sewers to get around in the daytime") and survives on pig's blood. He wears a long black trench coat and can be killed by a stake through the heart.

When a fire destroyed the small downtown office of Angel Investigations, Angel set up operations at the Hyperian Hotel. Wolfram and Hart, located at 1127 Spring Street in Los Angeles, is a law firm dedicated to evil (unleashing and protecting demons). A change in series focus occurred in 2003 when Angel and his assistants become part of the law firm they battled for years. Angel accepted an offer to run the L.A. branch to fight evil before it gets out of hand. Angel acquires a plush office, a vampire secretary (Harmony) and anything he needs to battle the awesome forces of evil.

See also: Buffy Summers, Cordelia Chase, Dawn Summers, Fred Berkel, Rupert Giles, Spike, Willow Rosenberg, Xander Harris

47. Angela Bower, *Who's the Boss?*, ABC, 1984–1992. Played by Judith Light.

Angela Bower is an attractive divorcee and the mother of a young son (Jonathan). She lives at 3344 Oak Hills Drive in Fairfield, Connecticut, and is president of the Wallace and McQuade Advertising Agency in New York City. She is later the owner of her own company, the Angela Bower Agency, at 323 East 57th Street in Manhattan. Her ex-husband is named Michael.

Angela is the daughter of Mona and Robert Robinson and was born on October 16 (year not mentioned) in Connecticut. She attended the Montague Academy for Girls and considered herself a loner. She had a small bust line and felt larger breasts would make her one of "the cool kids." She tried padding her bra with tissues but was still rejected. She used food to suppress her sorrows and became overweight. She cleaned up her act when she learned to accept herself. Angela is a graduate of Harvard Business School and is now in the 39 percent tax bracket. She manages a softball team called John's Giants and men-

tioned that her first job was rowboat manager at the Fairfield Boat Club. Angela attempted to play the cello but was so bad that the only way her mother could get her to stop was to hide the instrument in the attic. Angela was a member of a singing group called The Curletts in college and at a summer camp called Cataba, she used the name Ingrid when she shared her first kiss with a boy named Tony Micelli (the man who would later become her housekeeper).

See also: Samantha Micelli, Tony Micelli.

48. Angela Doolan, *Phenom*, ABC, 1993–1994. Played by Angela Goethals.

Angela Doolan is a natural at tennis, "a child blessed by the hand of God; something that comes along once in a lifetime." Angela was born in 1978 and is the daughter of Diane and Jack Doolan. She lives at 1728 Avalon Drive in Agora, California, and has an older brother (Brian) and a younger sister (Mary Margaret). Angela is Catholic and attends the Miraculous Medal Elementary School then its high school. She is a teacher's dream student; she is left in charge of the class when the teacher steps out and has been voted "most likely to join the order" by the nuns of her school.

Angela practices tennis 35 hours a week and is struggling with the demands of potential stardom while at the same time be a normal 15-year-old girl. She is coached by Lou Della Rose, owner of the Lou Della Rose Tennis Academy in La Hoya. Angela won the Sixteen and Under championship of Southern California and her most embarrassing moment occurred during a tournament match when her halter top slipped and exposed her left breast. Her dream is to win Wimbeldon.

49. Angelique, *Dark Shadows*, ABC, 1966–1971. Played by Lara Parker.

Angelique is a very beautiful and powerful witch whose hauntingly blue eyes and blonde hair can mesmerize any man she encounters. Angelique was born sometime in the 1780s (possibly 1780 or '81) and raised on the shores of Martinique in France. When her mother was discovered to be a witch, she was hanged and Angelique was sent to live with her alcoholic and abusive father. As she grew she practiced her craft and by the time she was a young woman she had perfected her skill as a powerful witch. It was also at this time that Angelique became the handmaiden to the wealthy Josette DuPres. It was when Angelique accompanied her mistress to America (Collinsport, Maine) that she fell in love with Barnabas Collins, the eldest son of the wealthy

Collins family. Josette and Barnabas were lovers and Angelique could not come between them. When Barnabas rejected Angelique she cursed him for all time by turning him into a vampire. Angelique, however, was later discovered to be a witch and hanged. Her body was placed in an unmarked grave on a desolate hillside. Her spirit, however, was not destroyed. A supernatural bolt of lightning struck her grave and restored her life. She has now manifested herself as a strikingly beautiful woman who is the exact image of the original Angelique. She is now more powerful than ever and has come back to carry out her vow of revenge. Angelique never thinks before she acts and rarely learns from her mistakes.

Angelique still loves Barnabas but Barnabas still loves Josette. She is often driven to the point of madness by her unfulfilled desires with Barnabas. Angelique destroys everything Barnabas loves and has remained single, determined to one day reclaim her lost love. Angelique dresses in modern-day clothes but relaxes at home in bosom-revealing and flowing negligees. She wears her blonde hair as a girl would have worn it in the 18th century and appears to be financially secure, as she has no job. The occult appears to be Angelique's best friend as she summons all the powers of darkness to do her bidding.

See also: Barnabas Collins, Roger Collins, Victoria Winters, Willie Loomis.

50. Ann McNeal, *Ann Jillian*, NBC, 1989–1990. Played by Ann Jillian.

Ann McNeal is the manager of Aunt Betty's Coffee and Bean Shop, a quaint eatery in the small town of Marvel, California. Ann is a recent widow and the mother of Lucy (Lisa Rieffel), a 15-year-old girl who attends Marvel High School.

Ann was born in Queens, New York, and lived at 1027-64 South Ferry Street. She is a graduate of Saint Michael's High School and a talented dancer who worked as a Radio City Music Hall Rockette. Ann's husband, Eddie, was a fireman for the City of New York who was killed in the line of duty (they were high school sweethearts). Ann needed to get away from it all and chose to begin a new life in Marvel (which was founded by Jacob Sweeney in 1921. While driving to San Francisco, his Model T Ford experienced a flat tire. Rather than fix the flat, he decided to stay where he was and start a town).

Ann and Lucy now live at 805 Etchfield Street. Ann has an account at the Fidelity Mutual Bank and is afraid of thunderstorms (she snuggles up in bed with Lucy when she hears thunder). As a teenager Ann would hang upside down to get color in her cheeks and later worked as the Activities Director of the Marvel Mall (her job was to make the mall a happy place).

51. Ann Marie, *That Girl*, ABC, 1966–1971. Played by Marlo Thomas.

Ann Marie is a young woman who has moved to New York City to follow her dream of becoming an actress. She was born in Fenwick, New York, in 1945 and is the daughter of Lou and Helen Marie. Ann later lived in Brewster, New York, when her family relocated to be closer to their business, the La Parisienne Restaurant. As a child Ann was called "Punky Puss" and would arrange her dolls by name. She won a medal for best actress at Camp Winnepoo and was voted "Best snowball thrower in Putnam County" (wherein Brewster lies). When she was five years old, Ann managed to get her elbow stuck in a peanut butter jar (in adult life Ann tried toe bowling and got her big toe stuck in a bowling ball). Ann is a graduate of Brewster College and was a member of the Brewster Community Playhouse actors group. She worked as a meter maid in Fenwick and was called "Twinkle Fingers Marie, the Speedy Steno" for her rapid shorthand skills. Before leaving Brewster Ann taught elementary school.

In Manhattan, Ann first lived at the East End Hotel on East 70th Street then at 344 West 78th Street (Apartment 4D). Her final address was 627 East 54th Street, Apartment 2C. Ann is a very pretty brunette who stands five feet, five and one half inches tall and weighs 100 pounds (later 108 pounds). She wears a size six dress and a 6A shoe. Ann was represented by the Gilliam and Norris Theatrical Agency and enrolled in classes at the Benedict Workshop of the Dramatic Arts. Her rent was $88.43 a month and Plaza 3-0598 was her phone number.

Ann made her television debut as a mop on the children's series *The Merry Mop-a-Teers*. She appeared as a contestant on the game shows *Get Rick Quick* and *The Mating Game*. She appeared on two unnamed soap operas playing first the character of Sheila then Doris, the ding-a-ling, a woman with multiple personalities. Her most embarrassing moment occurred on a live broadcast of the series *The Lady Killer* (she played a dead bank teller who opened her eyes on camera). Ann's television commercials were for the following products: Jungle Madness Perfume, No Freeze Anti-Freeze, Action Soda, POP Soft Drink and Creamy Soap.

Ann appeared in the following Broadway plays: *Gypsy* (a two-week Lincoln Center revival with

Ethel Merman), *The Knights of Queen Mary* (at the Empire Theater) and *The Revolutionary Heart* (starring Barry Sullivan). Her off–Broadway credits were: *And Everything Nice* (tried and closed in Philadelphia), *The Queen of Diamonds* (in St. Louis), *Funny Man* (Las Vegas) and *A Preponderance of Artichokes, Honor's Stain* and *North of Larchmont* (all in Manhattan). Ann was also the understudy to Sandy Stafford, a famous Broadway star.

As a model Ann held the following jobs: Miss Everything for the New York Has Everything at the Coliseum; pajama model at Unifit; Girl Friday Productions model; Miss Chicken Big (spokesgirl for the Chicken Big, Inc., fast food chain — "We Fry Harder"); fashion model to British photographer Noel Prince; roving clothes model at Sardi's Restaurant (she performed scenes from movies while modeling); and spokes girl for the Women in Space Air Force Program. Ann also appeared nude in *Playpen* magazine (her face on another girl's body).

Ann's very first job when arriving in Manhattan was as a waitress. Her other non–show business jobs were cosmetics salesgirl at Best and Company; perfume sales girl at Macy's; door-to-door sales girl for Smart and Stunning Shoes; waitress at the Cave (a nightclub); department store Christmas elf; and department store sales announcer.

Ann can play the violin and is a talented tap dancer. Her dream is to purchase the rights to the book *A Woman's Story* by Joseph Nelson and star in the movie version of it. Ann is single but is dating Donald Hollinger, a reporter for *Newsview* magazine.

See also: Donald Hollinger.

52. Ann Romano, *One Day at a Time*, CBS, 1975–1984. Played by Bonnie Franklin.

Ann Romano is a very independent woman who works as an account executive for the Connors and Davenport Advertising Agency in Indianapolis, Indiana. Ann is divorced from Ed Cooper but retains her maiden name "because I want to be a liberated woman and the master of my own fate." Her daughters, Julie and Barbara, carry their father's last name. Ann, Julie and Barbara live in Apartment 402 at 1344 Hartford Drive; 555-4142 is their phone number.

Ann was born in Logansport, Indiana, and is a graduate of Logansport High School. She next attended the University of Indiana and acquired a degree in advertising. She is the daughter of Kathryn and Michael Romano and was even independent as a child, putting up a fuss until she got what she wanted.

Ann first dated David Kane, her divorce lawyer (with the firm of McInerney, Wollman, Kollman and Schwartz) but later met and married Sam Royer, an architect, on May 16, 1983 (they moved into Apartment 422 at 322 Bedford Street). Before marrying Sam, Ann dated Nick Handris and quit Connors and Davenport to open her own agency, Romano and Handris (later called Handris and Associates). When this failed, Ann teamed with her friend, Francine Webster, to open the Romano and Webster Ad Agency. Ann wears a size 34A bra (although she is braless in many episodes) and loves almond mocha ice cream.

See also: Barbara Cooper, Dwayne Schneider, Julie Cooper.

53. Annabelle Hurst, *Department S*, Syn., 1971–1972. Played by Rosemary Nicols.

Annabelle Hurst is an agent for Department S, a Paris, France–based unit of Interpol (the International Police Force). Annabelle is young and beautiful and is at her best when she is behind a desk and at her computer. She is an expert at deciphering the most complex codes and can detect counterfeit money simply by touching it ("Who needs micro chemical analysis when we have Annabelle," says fellow agent Stewart Sullivan). Annabelle worked previously as a computer analyst for the Metro Police Force.

Annabelle also assists her partners, Jason King and Stewart Sullivan, in the field. She can pick locks and open safes but she is opposed to using a gun. The smallest details of a case intrigue Annabelle — it is from these insignificant clues that she comes up with the evidence Stewart and Jason need to solve a complex crime. Annabelle wears a 34B bra and lives at 86 Le Parses Drive; her white sedan license plate reads 874 Y3L (later LBY 143).

See also: Jason King, Stewart Sullivan.

54. Anne Shirley, *Anne of Green Gables*, PBS, 1986. Played by Megan Follows.

"Green Gables is a beautiful dream that will always haunt me," said Anne Shirley of the farm she called home whenever she had to leave it. Green Gables, called "the prettiest acreage" on the North Shore of Prince Edward Island in Canada (early 1900s), is owned by Marilla and Matthew Cuthbert, an elderly sister and brother who are the adoptive parents of Anne Shirley, a very pretty, fiercely independent orphan girl.

Anne was born in Fairfax, Canada, and orphaned at the age of three months when her parents, Walter and Bertha, "died of the fever." Anne was sent to and raised at the Fairview Orphanage in Nova Scotia. "My life is a graveyard of buried hopes," Anne would say of her days at Fairview; her only friend was Katie Moore, her "imaginary window friend" (Anne's reflection in a window). When Marilla and Matthew put in a request to adopt an orphan boy to help with the farm work, they were sent Anne—"It was Providence that brought her to us. It was He who knew that we needed her," said Marilla when Anne changed her bitter outlook on life.

In describing herself, Anne remarks "I'm skinny, a little freckled and have green eyes. I'm blessed with a wonderful imagination and want to be beautiful when I grow up." Anne has the ambition to be a writer and insists that her first name be spelled "Anne with an *e*" ("It's more distinguished and vibrant than plain old Ann without an *e*"). Anne feels that her downfall is her temper, which she attributes "to the curse of my red hair" (she gets highly charged when someone remarks negatively about her hair). When Anne promises to keep a secret "Wild horse couldn't drag it from me" and her philosophy is "Tomorrow is always fresh with no mistakes in it."

Anne's greatest wish "is to have a bosom friend, a really kindred spirit." She acquires a life long friend when she meets Diana Barry, the teenage girl living nearby on Orchid Slope. Anne first attends the Avonlea Public School then Queens College to obtain her teaching license. She became a teacher at the Avonlea School then an English teacher at the Kingspoint Ladies College in Charlotts Town, New Brunswick. It is at this time that Anne has her first book published, *Avonlea Vignettes*. Anne had a mischievous cow named Dolly and was gentle and kind to her students. She yearned for a home and love as an orphan and thanks to the kindness of Marilla and Matthew, became a person greater than she could ever imagine.

Annie Camden *see* **Eric and Annie Camden**

55. Annette McCleod, *Annette* (segment of *The Mickey Mouse Club*), ABC, 1958. Played by Annette Funicello.

Annette McCleod is a student at Old South High School in the small town of Ashford, Nebraska. Annette was born in the farming community of Beaver Junction, Nebraska, on May 29, 1943. She was a student at Beaver Junction High School when her parents, Brice and Blanche McCleod, were killed in an automobile accident. With only one living relative, her father's brother Archie McCleod (Richard Deacon), Annette

moved to Ashford to live with Archie and his wife Lila (Sylvia Field).

Annette lives at 149 Elm Street. She sleeps in the room next to her Aunt Lila (which was Lila's grandmother's room). She likes eggs, toast and milk for breakfast, is fond of chicken soup and just adores ("my ultra favorite") a burger with pickle relish, mustard and chips. Annette is program chairman of the Activities Committee at school and when she becomes a friend, she is true and loyal and a friend for life. She is a best friend with Jet Maypen (Judy Nugent), the farm girl who lives on Spring Branch Road. Annette will do what she can to help someone else. She is a bit more developed than the other girls in her class but she never accentuates her assets to become more popular. If someone does not accept her as she is without putting on airs, she prefers not to associate with them. Annette has a lovely singing voice but other than performing at school functions or at parties, she never mentions pursuing a professional singing career (in real life, Annette Funicello did release several albums).

56. Annie, Bess and Nora Bernstein, *Three Sisters*, NBC, 2001–2002. Played by A.J. Langer, Katherine LaNasa, Vicki Lewis.

Annie, Bess and Nora are three close sisters who live in Los Angeles. They are the children of Honey and George (Dyan Cannon, Peter Bonerz) and as different as night and day.

Annie. Annie is the youngest (25) of the sisters. She likes French fries with mayonnaise, clown paintings ("But not so much the clowns") and fresh strawberries. She was also the only sister who never got a first birthday. Before acquiring a steady job as a bartender at the Canteen on Sunset ("Although I don't know anything about pushing beer or mixing drinks"), Annie held a number of jobs: Annie's Doggie Day Care, a pot belly pig farm, receptionist, and glazer for a vase maker. She also auditioned for (but lost) a job as host of a TV show called *The Real World*, attended blackjack training school, psychic school (to become a medium) and ship captain's school. Annie is so sweet and so disarming that people fall in love with her and like to do things for her—how she got the bartending job (although she won't admit it, showing cleavage also helps her).

Bess. Bess, the middle sister, is sweet and charming and not as prone to showing cleavage as Annie. She is married to Steve Eubanks (David Alan Basche), who says, "I'm married to my wife and her sisters" as their problems become his problems. Steve is a sports complex architect at Keats and Riley; Bess is a marketing executive for

McClaren and Clark Foods (where she is called "Bossy Miss Snooty Pants" for all her work and no play attitude). Bess has a Barbie doll collection and was a cheerleader in high school. Although very pretty and sexy, Bess is not as busty as her sisters; to compensate, she wears the Satin Air Support Bra.

Nora. Nora is the most unstable of the sisters. She has a fear of rejection but she rejects people before they reject her. Nora is a graduate of Stanford University and works as a documentary film-maker for the Discovery Channel. She also held a temporary job as a producer on a multi-million dollar Imax film. She later works as professor of film production at the University of Southern California. When at Stanford Nora wrote a term paper on the Elizabeth Taylor movie *Who's Afraid of Virginia Woolf*; it led her teacher to believe she was a lesbian. Nora's office is in Room 104. Nora smokes and drinks and is divorced from Elliott (who left her when he realized he was gay). For fun as a child Nora would cut the heads off Bess's Barbie dolls. When *I Dream of Jeannie* became Bess's favorite TV show she got even by making Nora dress as Jeannie and become her master.

Honey and George. Honey and George are a very liberal couple and have been married 35 years. George, a graduate of Oxford University, is a university professor. Honey is a former Playboy Bunny who still relishes in the fact that she has the body of a 20 year old. She teaches yoga classes (Beyond Yoga) out of her home and is a graduate of UCLA. She is an L.A. Lakers fan and on Mother's Day, she observes a strange tradition: she goes to the beach at five in the morning, strips down and runs naked into the ocean. Honey is also a legend: when she was a Bunny, Hugh Hefner asked her to pose nude for his magazine and she refused.

57. Annie Mack, *The Secret World of Alex Mack*, NIK, 1994. Played by Meredith Bishop.

Annie Mack is a brilliant 16-year-old girl who attends Paradise Valley High School in Paradise Valley, California. She lives at 2344 Clemson Lane with her sister, Alex, and parents Barbara and George.

Annie believes "genius is lonely" and has few friends. She has maintained a 4.0 grade average since pre-school and takes advanced classes, hoping to one day win the Nobel Peace Prize in science. Annie involves herself in her schoolwork because she feels she has to accomplish something big. She understands atom splitting and gravity waves but is hesitant to go bowling because she fears rolling a gutter ball. Annie is working on a millennium DNA structure model (to create a fabrication of how life will evolve in the 21st century) and won the Ninth Annual Paradise Valley Chemical Plant Fair Award for her project on Ion Beam Acceleration.

See also: Alex Mack.

58. Annie O'Donnell, *Can't Hurry Love*, CBS, 1995–1996. Played by Nancy McKeon.

Anne O'Donnell, called Annie, is a single girl looking for Mr. Right. She was born in Manhattan and attended the Holy Cross Grammar School and St. Catherine's High School. She lives at 423 West 28th Street (Apartment 302) and works for the People Pleasers Employment Agency in New York City.

Annie has a $400 limit on her Visa card and "The Mystery Puddle in my living room" ("I clean it up but it keeps coming back from under the floor boards"). Annie calls her breasts "Thelma and Louise" and dreams of a charming guy who will bring her roses and sweep her off her feet ("I know he's out there but I haven't found him"). Men say Annie "has teeth like sparkling porcelain stars"; "It's a curse," says Annie. Annie frequents a bar called Wrecks and has named the two pigeons who call her windowsill home, Bill and Henry.

59. Annie Spadaro, *Caroline in the City*, NBC, 1995–1999. Played by Amy Pietz.

Annie Viola Spadaro is a professional dancer. She was born in Paissac, New Jersey, and attended Paramus High School. Her family owns the Spadaro Funeral Parlor and as a child, Annie idolized Carol Brady (Florence Henderson on *The Brady Bunch*). Annie now lives in an apartment in Manhattan and was a regular cast member of the Broadway play *Cats* (at the Winter Garden Theater). She did a TV commercial for Dr. Furman's Foot Powder and appeared in an unsold (and unnamed) TV pilot. When she left Broadway, she became Princess Neptuna, the model for a cartoon character. Annie was also the understudy for Julie Andrews in *Victor/Victoria* and was the inspiration for "The slutty next door neighbor" in her neighbor, Caroline Duffy's comic strip, *Caroline in the City* (although Annie insists "My breasts are bigger than Caroline draws them").

See also: Caroline Duffy, Richard Karinsky.

60. Anthony Anderson, *All About the Andersons*, WB, 2003. Played by Anthony Anderson.

Anthony Anderson is a single father who lives with his parents (Joe and Flo) and son (Tuga) at 266 Crestview Drive in Englewood, California.

Anthony, who does not like to be called Tony, is a hopeful actor. He had been living in New York City and was married to Cherie. She "just took off" when Tuga was six years old. Anthony returned to his hometown to raise Tuga and pursue his acting career.

In elementary school Anthony had a crush on the office secretary. He wears a size 13EEE shoe (the same size as his mother) and is called "Pop Pop" by Tuga (who attends the same school as his father did—Dwight Elementary). In high school, when the somewhat overweight Anthony joined the cheerleading squad, Joe called him "Sara Lee" for years.

When in New York Anthony performed in some off–Broadway plays—in Baltimore. In Los Angeles his auditions are so few that he had to resort to working two days a week for his father in the family business, Joe and Flo's Barber and Beauty Salon. He later joins with a friend to make extra money by throwing lingerie parties for San Pierre Lingerie.

Anthony is a free spirit and likes to express his ideas. He takes Tuga to the mall as bait to meet women. Anthony also instituted a house rule. If anyone uses a swear word in front of Tuga they must give Tuga a dollar. When Anthony's father was a kid his family was so poor that he had a tin can as a pet he called Rusty. He fought to work his way out of poverty and made a success of his life. That is the image Anthony hopes to implant in Tuga (Anthony's mother was a singer with a group called A Lady Among Giants). Anthony calls his father "Pops."

61. Anthony Bouvier, *Designing Women*, CBS, 1986–1993. Played by Meshach Taylor.

Anthony Bouvier works first as a deliveryman than as a partner in the Sugarbakers Design Firm (later Sugarbaker and Associates) in Atlanta, Georgia. He was born in Atlanta and is an ex-con. He was arrested for participating in a convenience store robbery (he later says it was a liquor store) and served time in Cell Block D of Atlanta State Prison. Anthony attended law school and does volunteer work at the Home for Wayward Boys. He is also director of the Atlanta Community Theater and married Etienne Toussant (Sheryl Lee Ralph), a former Las Vegas showgirl (at the Tropicana Resort and Casino). Etienne likes to be called "E.T." and calls Anthony "Tony" ("because he's my tiger"). E.T. believes she is one of the most beautiful women in the world and calls herself "The Ebony Princess." E.T.'s mother was one of 14 children; E.T. is one of nine and wants four children with Anthony ("After four

you can't get your figure back"). Anthony's contracting license is L-3303.

See also: Charlene Frazier, Julia Sugarbaker, Mary Jo Shively, Suzanne Sugarbaker.

62. Anthony Nelson, *I Dream of Jeannie*, NBC, 1965–1970. Played by Larry Hagman.

Anthony Nelson, called Tony, is a Captain (later Major) with the NASA Space Center at Cape Kennedy in Cocoa Beach, Florida. He lives at 1030 Palm Drive and is the owner of a genie, "not your average everyday Jeannie, but a beautiful genie who can grant any wish."

Tony was born on July 15 (year not mentioned) in Fowlers Corners, Ohio, and attended Fowlers Corners High School (where he was called "Bunky Nelson"). He now lives in Florida and his address was also given as 811 Pine Street and 1137 Oak Grove Street. Tony weighs 181½ pounds and 555-7231 is his phone number. Tony has piloted *Apollo 14*, *Apollo 15*, *Stardust 1*, the *X-14*, *Trail Blazer* and the *T-38* (the first fully automated plane). It was while testing the *Stardust 1* that a malfunction occurred and he crash-landed on a deserted island in the South Pacific. While seeking debris to make an S.O.S. signal, he found a strange-looking green bottle and opened it. A pink smoke emerged and materialized into a gorgeous genie dressed as a harem dancer. Tony called the genie Jeannie and wished for a rescue helicopter. Jeannie crossed her arms across her chest, nodded her head and blinked her eyes. The copter appeared and Tony set Jeannie free—although Jeannie didn't want to be set free—"she wanted to have fun and she wanted to have it with Captain Nelson." Jeannie concealed herself in Tony's survival kit and became a part of his life when he was rescued.

Tony, now unable to get rid of Jeannie, struggles to keep her presence a secret (he fears repercussions if the Air Force discovers he has his own personal genie). Jeannie calls Tony "Master" and, although she thinks she is being helpful, complicates Tony's life with her unpredictable magic.

See also: Jeannie.

63. Anthony Russo, *Blossom*, NBC, 1991–1995. Played by Michael Stoyanov.

Anthony Russo is the eldest child of Nick and Madelyn Russo. He lives at 465 Hampton Drive in Southern California with his father (now divorced), his sister, Blossom, and his younger brother, Joey.

Anthony is a graduate of Grant High School but had been a serious drug user for four years (he is now clean). He attributes his addiction to when he was 12 years old and attended Camp Mountain High (where he smoked his first joint). He has written a play called *Naked Chick Academy* that he hopes will make him $3 million. He first worked as a delivery boy for Fatty's Pizza then as a counter waiter at Dante's Donut Shop before finding a career as an E.M.T. (Emergency Medical Technician). In 1993, Anthony met and married Shelley Lewis (Samaria Graham); a year later they became the parents of a boy they named Nash Metropolitan.

See also: Blossom Russo, Joey Russo, Nick Russo, Six LeMeure.

64. April Dancer, *The Girl from U.N.C.L.E.*, NBC, 1966–1967. Played by Stefanie Powers.

April Dancer is an agent for U.N.C.L.E. (the United Network Command for Law and Enforcement), an international organization that is housed in New York City (behind the guise of Del Flories Taylor Shop) that battles the evils of THRUSH, an organization bent on world domain.

April is petite (five feet, five inches tall), very beautiful and capable of speaking several languages (Italian, French, Spanish, Japanese and Polish). She was born in Maine but received an international education (her father was a constantly uprooted serviceman). She settled long enough in Maine to graduate from a New England university. She joined U.N.C.L.E. Academy shortly after (1966) and was teamed with agent Mark Slate upon graduation.

Although April is a spy she is also a very typical girl. She becomes easily frightened and is not above making mistakes. She dresses rather conservatively (not one for showing too much skin) and is very frugal. She carries a gun but is reluctant to use it (only if absolutely necessary). April is trained in unarmed combat and her fashion accessories are also weapons. Her coat buttons double as explosives; her makeup case conceals gas capsules and her lipstick can be used as a tranquilizer dart gun and communicator (April also contacts headquarters with the standard issue communicator pen).

See also: Mark Slate.

April Giminski *see* **The Girls of Baywatch**

65. Archie, *Duffy's Tavern*, NBC, 1954. Played by Ed Gardner.

Archie (no last name given) is the manager of Duffy's Tavern, a rundown bar in a friendly neighborhood in a shabby section of New York City on Third Avenue. Archie claims the bar is "where the elite meet to eat" and where, with a beer, the free lunch costs 15cents. Archie also claims that Duffy's Tavern is not hard to find, especially if you are on Fifth Avenue: "Go into the street. You'll see a lot of these dames with the new look — long dresses. Well just keep going east until you see knees."

Archie is a grammar school educated con artist who runs the bar for the never seen Mr. Duffy. He uses the bar as his base of operations to conduct his harebrained moneymaking schemes. Archie is a graduate of P.S. 4. He claims to be an expert in medicine ("For years I watched *Dr. Kildare* movies") and a crack lawyer ("For ten years I worked for Muelbacker, Bushwacker, Millstone and Briggs painting the ipos on the factos"). Even without that extensive experience Archie is also an expert on anything else — from women to mixing drinks.

Archie claims the bar loses money on rainy nights ("Who wants to go out and lay in the gutter?") He says the bar has a caring attitude about its customers: "At Duffy's we have ethics. We don't roll customers until they're drunk." The safe is a hole in the wall and according to Archie, "The books are a little unbalanced."

Archie dates Peaches LaTour (Veda Ann Borg), a gorgeous stripper at the Burlesque Palace (later called the Bijou Burlesque) and fears only one person — Miss Duffy (Patte Chapman), Duffy's nosey daughter. She works as the cashier and Archie fears she will catch him in one of his not-so-legal schemes (he calls her "Mother Nature's revenge on peeping toms").

Archie admires people who are married. He claims he is single because "I wanted my wife to have everything — money, a mansion, a big car, a yacht. But I ain't found the right dame yet."

66. Archie Bunker, *All in the Family*, CBS, 1971–1979. Played by Carroll O'Connor.

The character of Archie Bunker also appeared on the series *Archie Bunker's Place* (CBS, 1979–1983). Archibald Bunker, called Archie, and his wife, Edith, are a quarrelsome married couple who live at 704 Hauser Street in Queens, New York ("The only house on the block with a paid-up mortgage," says Archie). They are also the parents of Gloria, a liberated young woman who is married to Mike Stivic, the liberal college student who also lives with them.

Archie works as a dock foreman for the Prendergast Tool and Dye Company and drives a cab at night to make extra money. Archie grew up during the Great Depression. As a child he was called "Shoe Bootie" by the other kids (he wore one shoe and one bootie when his destitute parents couldn't afford to buy him a pair of shoes). He is, today, a bigoted, uncouth, loud-mouthed conservative. Many of these traits came from his upbringing where he was erroneously taught to believe in the superiority of his own race and to distrust foreign-born people of all kinds. Archie is of normal intelligence and this, coupled with his environment, prevents him from learning much of anything new (he feels very threatened by all things he was never taught to fear). During World War II ("The Big One" as he calls it), Archie was first stationed at Fort Riley in Kansas. He later served 22 months in Italy with the Air Corps (where he was second in command of the motor pool). His hitch in the service earned him the Purple Heart, a good conduct medal and "a butt full of shrapnel — which is why I ain't danced with my wife for 30 years."

Archie is a strict conservative and pro law and order at any cost. He drinks Schlitz beer, reads the New York *Daily News*, and is a member of the Royal Brotherhood of the Kings of Queens Lodge. His blood pressure varies between 168/95 and 178/90. Cigars are his only vice.

Archie met Edith, whom he calls "Dingbat," in 1941. He later becomes the owner of his own bar, Archie Bunker's Place. He is a big fan of John Wayne movies and believes that "if it appears in *The Enquirer*, it's true."

See also: Billie Bunker, Edith Bunker, Gloria Stivic, Mike Stivic, Stephanie Mills.

67. Arina, *BeastMaster*, Syn., 1999–2002. Played by Marjean Holden.

Many demons exist in the age of darkness and nature. In addition to Curupira and Iara (see entries), there was Arina, "The demon who lives in the forest." Arina is actually a good demon befriended by Dar, the BeastMaster. Arina was born in a village called Narmead in the Great Desert. When Arina was a young girl, evil Terron warriors attacked her village. To protect her daughter, Arina's mother hid her in a field of wild flowers. It saved her life, but she also became the lone survivor of her people. Arina grew up alone and now, as an adult, Arina trusts only Dar and his companion, Tao, and will lie, steal, cheat and even kill to defeat an enemy. She later teams with Dar to battle the evil Terrons.

See also: The Ancient One, Curupira, Dar, Iara, The Sorceress, Tao.

68. Arnold Horshack, *Welcome Back, Kotter*, ABC, 1975–1979. Played by Ron Palillo.

Arnold Horshack is a teenager who says that his last name "is an old and respected name. It means

the cattle are dying." He also says he is the last of the Horshacks "because after they made me they broke the mold." Arnold is a Sweathog (a special education student) at James Buchanan High School in Bensonhurst, Brooklyn, New York.

Arnold was born in Brooklyn and as a kid had a wooden rocking horse named Pepper. His father drove a cab and Arnold grew up on the streets, not so much becoming a problem child but finding it difficult to do school work. He is now part of "the menagerie" (as the principal calls the Sweathogs) and usually only speaks when the head Sweathog, Vinnie Barbarino, gives him permission. Arnold's catchphrase is "ooh ooh ooh" and he often raises his hand to ask a question then forgets why he did so when he is called upon. Arnold worked part time at Orshack's of Fifth Avenue, his uncle's costume shop (his uncle dropped the *H*). Arnold's greeting is "Hello, how are you?"

See also: Freddie Washington, Gabe and Julie Kotter, Juan Epstein, Vinnie Barbarino.

69. Arnold Jackson, *Diff'rent Strokes*, NBC, 1978–1985; ABC, 1985–1986. Played by Gary Coleman.

Arnold Jackson is the young, adoptive son of Phillip Drummond, the wealthy owner of Drummond Industries. Arnold and his older brother, Willis, are the sons of Lucy Jackson, Phillip's housekeeper. When Lucy died, Phillip kept a promise to care for her sons if anything happened to her.

The Jacksons lived at 259 East 135th Street (Apartment 12) in Harlem. Arnold and Willis now reside at 679 Park Avenue (Penthouse A) in Manhattan. Arnold loves model railroading and has a pet goldfish (Abraham) and cricket (Lucky). As a baby he had a plush cow (Fuzzy Wuzzy Moo Moo) and a ratty old doll (Homer). Arnold was born in Harlem and attended the following schools: P.S. 89, P.S. 406, Roosevelt Jr. High, Edison Jr. High and Garfield High. He was a reporter for the P.S. 89 newspaper, *The Weekly Woodpecker* and was editor of *The Beacon* at Edison. Hamburger Heaven (later called the Hamburger Hanger) is his favorite hangout and he was champ at a video arcade game called "Space Sucker" (where he scored one million points).

Arnold was a member of the Super Dudes Gang and formed a band called Frozen Heads. He considers himself a magician and calls himself "Arnoldo." His first job was handing out fliers for Guido's Pizza Parlor on 63rd Street. His catch phrase is "What you talkin' about..."

See also: Edna Garrett, Kimberly Drummond, Willis Jackson.

70. Artemus Gordon, *The Wild Wild West*, CBS, 1965–1969. Played by Ross Martin.

Artemus Gordon is a brilliant actor turned undercover intelligence agent (Secret Service) for President Ulysses S. Grant during the 1870s. He works with Agent James T. West. Artemus is often called Artie and uses the wizardry of his craft (disguises) to help apprehend criminals who pose a threat to the safety of the country.

Artemus and Jim's mobile base of operations is the Nimrod, a railroad passenger coach that is pulled by an 1860 2-4-0 steam engine. In addition to his living quarters aboard the train, Artemus has several homing pigeons (Henry, Henrietta, Annabelle and Arabella). His favorite color is red and he gets the less glamorous assignments — nondescript characters that help Jim. Artie can read and write in English, Latin, Greek, German, Chinese and Braille; he can't read Russian but can speak it. Artemus's everyday wardrobe accommodates smoke bombs, putty explosives and knockout powders.

Artemus is always careful during assignments. He always calculates a move before acting upon it; however, because Jim is impulsive, he sometimes finds himself blowing his cover and acting on the spur of the moment to save Jim. After retiring from the Secret Service in 1890, Artemus returned to acting and began his own road company — the Deadwood Strolling Players Traveling Tent Show (they performed the play "The Society Lady's Revenge").

See also: James T. West.

Arnold Ziffel *see* **Fred and Doris Ziffel**

71. Arthur Carlson, *WKRP in Cincinnati*, CBS, 1978–1982. Played by Gordon Jump.

Arthur Carlson is the station manager of WKRP, a 5,000-watt radio station (1590 AM) in Cincinnati, Ohio. The station was founded on December 7, 1941, by his father, Hank, and has been managed by Arthur since 1955 (when his father died and his stern mother, "Mama" Lillian Carlson, took over). Arthur fears his mother and does whatever she asks of him.

Arthur is married to Carmen and the father of Arthur Carlson, Jr. He rarely listens to the station (he dislikes the rock format) and enjoys playing with toys or practicing golf and fishing in his office to pass the time. He enjoys reading *Ohio Fisherman* magazine and in his youth was a ball player called "Moose." He is called "Big Guy" by employee Herb Tarlek.

See also: Bailey Quarters, Dr. Johnny Fever, Herb Tarlek, Jennifer Marlowe, Les Nessman, Venus Flytrap.

Arthur Fonzarelli *see* **Fonzie**

72. Arthur Spooner, *The King of Queens*, CBS 1998 (current). Played by Jerry Stiller.

Arthur Eugene Spooner is a senior citizen who lives at 3121 Aberdine in Rego Park, Queens, New York, with his daughter, Carrie and son-in-law, Douglas Heffernan.

Arthur was born in New York and lived on a farm for three years (ages seven through ten). He loves to scream and yell at people and as a child had a fear that he would lose his voice and no one would hear him. He recalled that the happiest day of his life occurred when he was a child and received a pair of 3-D glasses. Arthur is a veteran of World War II (served with the 71st Infantry) and held the following jobs: riveter on the Empire State Building, owner of a trout farm, decorative ribbon salesman, assembly line worker at the Corbin Bowling Ball Company, crab cannery worker in Maryland, typist for former New York Mayor Abe Beame. After his retirement he worked as a counter clerk at the Big Hot Pretzel then at Aneglo's Pizza Parlor. Arthur next tried to invent an alternate screw and driver called Arthur's Head. He also attempted to start two businesses: Arthur Spooner, Music Teacher and Arthur Spooner, Candle Maker. Arthur plays the harmonica and failed in an attempt to start a blues band. He was first married to Lily (divorced) then Tessie (deceased). He was also said to have a wife named Sophia.

Arthur has a collection of 78 RPM records and exercises to the song "Hello Mudder, Hello Fadder." "Tijuana Taxi" is his favorite song. He hangs out at OTB (Off Track Betting) and the Nudie Nude Bar. Arthur steals fruit from the neighbor's lemon tree and claims someone stole the idea for moist toweletts from him. He has a problem with long plane flights ("I tend to panic and scream like a woman") and had a parrot named Douglas. Arthur also has his own walker, Holly (Nicole Sullivan), whom Carrie hired to walk him so he could get some exercise. Arthur loses his temper quite often and threatens people with his catch phrase "You want a piece of me?"

See also: Carrie Heffernan, Douglas Heffernan.

73. Arvid Engen, *Head of the Class*, ABC, 1986–1991. Played by Dan Frischman.

Arvid Engen is a student in the I.H.P. (Individual Honors Program) at Fillmore High School in New York City. Arvid is a math major and has perfect attendance. He has not missed one day of school since he first started. Arvid is a member of the glee club, the school orchestra (he plays triangle) and runs the school radio station, WFHS (410 on the AM dial). He also plays the accordian and Carl Sagan is his favorite writer. He wears a size nine shoe, usually brown, and had the nickname "Badges" (he has a 4.0 grade average and won many awards). Arvid was born in Manhattan and was a Boy Scout (Troop 645). He was also the lunchroom monitor and when he gets upset he speaks to a picture of Albert Einstein that he carries in his wallet. In the last episode, Arvid chose to attend Cal Tech.

See also: Charlie Moore, Darlene Merriman, Dennis Blunden, Simone Foster.

74. Ashley Banks, *The Fresh Prince of Bel Air*, NBC, 1990–1996. Played by Tatyana M. Ali.

Ashley Banks was born in 1979 and is the youngest child of Philip and Vivian Banks, a wealthy lawyer and his wife who live in fashionable Bel Air, California. Ashley reads *17* magazine and first attended the Hollywood Preparatory Institute. She next attended the Bel Air Academy then transferred to the less strict Morris High School. Her older sister, Hilary, is proud of the fact that she is dating right and becoming as beautiful as she is. Ashley plays the violin and her favorite video game is Tetris. Ashley is also a talented singer and dancer. She danced on *The Soul Train 25th Anniversary Show* and made a recording of a song she wrote called "Make Up Your Mind." Ashley is a brilliant student and her most embarrassing moment occurred at an honor awards ceremony. She was sitting with her legs crossed. When she was called on to receive an English citation, she got up, but her leg had fallen asleep and she fell on her face.

See also: Carlton Banks, Hilary Banks, Philip Banks, Will Smith.

75. Atlanta Shore, *Stingray*, Syn., 1965. Voiced by Lois Maxwell.

Atlanta Shore is a controller at the Marineville Base, headquarters for the World Aquanaut Security Patrol, a futuristic organization that patrols and protects the ocean floor. Atlanta is the daughter of Sam and Elaine Shore (her father is the commander of the Marineville Base). Atlanta was born in 2042 and grew up around the activities of the marine base; naturally, she developed a keen interest and followed in her father's footsteps. Atlanta enrolled in the Marineville School and upon graduation trained for the Submarine Service at the World Naval Academy. She became

a part of the Security Patrol in 2062 and a year later was promoted to lieutenant. Atlanta has eyes for Troy Tempest, the captain of the submarine *Stingray*, and a keen interest in the world beneath the sea. *Stingray* is a Gerry Anderson puppet series filmed in Supermarionation.

See also: Marina, Troy Tempest.

76. Audra Barkley, *The Big Valley*, ABC, 1965–1969. Played by Linda Evans.

Audra Barkley is the beautiful 19-year-old daughter of Victoria and Thomas Barkley, the owners of the 30,000-acre Barkley Ranch in the San Joaquin Valley in Stockton, California (1870s). She has four brothers, Jarrod, Nick, Heath and Eugene, and is proud of her birthright, the name of Barkley, a name that stands for right against wrong and a name that others can look up to for wisdom and leadership in troubled times. Although she is the only daughter, Audra fiercely protects the land her father died for (see Victoria Barkley for information). Audra often says "This is Barkley land — and I'm Audra Barkley" when she encounters trespassers.

As a child Audra had a canary (Bo Peep) a cat (Sasafrass) and an undying love for horses (when she was eight, she began showing horses at county fairs). Audra buys her dresses at Ida Nell's Seamstress Shop and does volunteer work at the Children's Orphanage (located next to the Old Mill). Audra also teaches Saturday Bible Class at the community church and has a tendency to fall for men with shady backgrounds.

See also: Heath Barkley, Jarrod Barkley, Nick Barkley, Victoria Barkley.

Automan *see* **Walter Nebecher**

77. Ava Newton, *Evening Shade*, CBS, 1990–1994. Played by Marilu Henner.

Ava Newton is 33 years old and married to Wood Newton, a former football player who now teaches P.E. at Evening Shade High School. Ava is also the mother of Molly, Will, Taylor, and Emily, and lives at 2102 Willow Lane in the small Arkansas town of Evening Shade.

Ava has been married to Wood for 15 years and is the town's first female prosecuting attorney. She was born in Evening Shade and is the daughter of Evan Evans, the publisher of the town's newspaper, *The Argus*. Ava is a graduate of Evening Shade grammar and high schools and has a law degree from the University of Arkansas. Although slim and attractive, Ava's pre-teen years were difficult; she was overweight and called "Chubby Evans" (Evans is her maiden name). Ava's most prized possession is her antique bathroom window and she and Wood honeymooned at Harrison Point (where they stayed in the Peach Blossom Suite of the hotel).

See also: Wood Newton.

78. B.A. Baracus, *The A-Team*, NBC, 1983–1987. Played by Mr. T.

Elliott Baracus, called B.A. (Bad Attitude) is a member of the A-Team, military fugitives who help people in trouble (see Hannibal Smith for further information).

B.A. was a sergeant in Vietnam and served with Hannibal Smith, Templeton Peck and H.M. Murdock. B.A. was the toughest and meanest member of the team and grew up in Chicago (he lived at 700 Foster Avenue and his mother called him "Scooter."). His Social Security number is 554-04-3106 and 61-5683-3 is his FBI file number.

B.A. loves children (he runs a day care center in his spare time) and gold jewelry (which he wears in chain-like necklaces). B.A. lives in an apartment at the Regina Hotel in Los Angeles and drives the team's main means of transportation, a black with red trim GMC van (license plates seen as 2E 14859, 218 3000, S96 7238, and 2A 22029). B.A is afraid of heights, loves milk and is also called Bosco Baracus. His catch phrase is "I pity the fool."

See also: Hannibal Smith, H.M. Murdock, Templeton Peck.

Baby Sinclair *see* **Charlene Sinclair**

79. Bailey Quarters, *WKRP in Cincinnati*, CBS, 1978–1982. Played by Jan Smithers.

Bailey Quarters is a young woman who works at WKRP, a 5,000-watt radio station (1590 on the AM dial) in Cincinnati, Ohio. She was born in Cincinnati and is a graduate of the University of Ohio (where she acquired a degree in journalism). Bailey originally worked as the traffic manager (scheduled commercials) then as an on-the-air personality doing two of the ten daily "WKRP News Roundups" (Golden Bean Coffee sponsor's her broadcasts).

Bailey stands up for what she believes in, especially the issue of equal rights for women. She often finds herself standing alone when she protests something at the station (others fear losing their jobs) and was originally depicted as a "Plain Jane" (glasses, non-flattering clothes, pulled back hair). As the series progressed, Bailey became more glamorous but did not lose her independent flair and liberal outlook.

See also: Arthur Carlson, Dr. Johnny Fever,

Herb Tarlek, Jennifer Marlowe, Les Nessman, Venus Flytrap.

80. Bailey Salinger, *Party of Five*, Fox, 1994–2000. Played by Scott Wolf.

Bailey Salinger is the 16-year-old son of Nicholas and Diana Salinger, the owners of Salinger's Restaurant in San Francisco. He lives at 3324 Broadway with his brothers (Charlie and Owen) and sisters (Julia and Claudia). He also helps care his younger siblings (Claudia and Owen) since the tragic death of their parents in a car accident.

Bailey is first a junior at Grant High School and a member of the football team (the Possums) and wrestling team. He scored a 900 on his SAT test and his dimples pulse when he lies. He later attended San Francisco State College and began a downward spiral when he met a girl (Sarah Reeves) and became addicted to alcohol (which he later overcame). When Bailey began college, Claudia and Julia gave him a lunch box based on the movie *Jumanji*. Bailey's first day at kindergarten holds an embarrassing memory for him: he became ill when he forgot the alphabet.

See also: Charlie Salinger, Claudia Salinger, Julia Salinger.

81. Balki Bartokomous, *Perfect Strangers*, ABC, 1986–1993. Played by Bronson Pinchot.

Balki Bartokomous is a sheepherder who has come to the big city (Chicago) to begin a new life. Balki was born in the small Mediterranean island of Mypos. When Balki discovered he had an American cousin (Larry Appleton) who was one-sixty-fourth Myposian, he found him and moved in with him at 711 Caldwell Avenue, Apartment 209 (they originally lived at the Caldwell Hotel, Apartment 203, at 627 Linden Boulevard).

Balki originally worked as a salesclerk at the Ritz Discount Store, then as a mail clerk at the Chicago *Chronicle* (where he also drew the kids' comic "Dimitri's World," about a cuddly little sheep).

Balki takes night classes at Chicago Community College to improve his knowledge of America. His favorite meal is eel wrapped in grape leaves and Sheepherder's bread with a side dish of Ding Ding Mac Mood (pig snout). For breakfast he eats yak links. Balki is famous for his bibibobacas, a cream puff–like pastry that has to be baked slowly or "the bib in the baca goes boom" (explodes). Wayne Newton is his favorite singer and *Uncle Shaggy's Dog House* his favorite TV show. He has a parrot (Yorgi), two pigeons (Steve and Edie), and as a kid had a horse (Trodsky) and a dog (Koos Koos). Balki uses Mr. Ducky Bubble Bath and had a plant named Margie (he also names his shoes — Phil and Andy).

When someone lies, Balki fears revenge from the Myposian Fib Furies (Eva, Magda and Zsa Zsa). Balki does volunteer work at Chicago General Hospital (he won "Bed Changer of the Month" award). He ran for student body president of his college under the slogan "Pro Sheep, Anti Wolf" and became a short-lived rap music star called Fresh Young Balki (he recorded the song "Balki B" for Knight Records).

Balki found romance with Mary Ann Spencer (Rebecca Arthur), an airline stewardess and married her on April 18, 1992. They became the parents of a boy they named Robespierre Bonkie on August 6, 1993.

See also: Larry Appleton.

Banacek *see* **Thomas Banacek**

82. Barbara Cooper, *One Day at a Time*, CBS, 1975–1984. Played by Valerie Bertinelli.

Barbara Cooper is the youngest daughter of Ann Romano, a divorcee who lives at 1344 Hartford Drive, Apartment 402, in Indianapolis, Indiana. She has an older sister, Julie, and carries her father, Ed's, last name (Ann uses her maiden name).

Barbara was a tomboy who evolved into a beautiful young woman. She first attended Jefferson High School and was a member of the girls basketball team (she wore jersey 4). After graduating with a B average, she attempted college life but dropped out of City University when she found she couldn't handle the workload. Barbara first worked as a counter girl at Quickie Burger then as a salesclerk at Olympic Sporting Goods. She found dissatisfaction with these jobs and settled into a cozy position as a booking agent at Gonigan Travel. She later met Mark Royer (Boyd Gaines), a dentist, and married him.

Barbara's biggest disappointment in life came when she learned a medical condition prevented her from having children. Rocky road is Barbara's favorite flavor of ice cream and a banana split is her favorite snack. As a kid Barbara ate a caterpillar when Julie told her it was a fuzzy Tootsie Roll. While attractive in high school, Barbara felt she needed to be more so and pretended to be on the pill — and paid dearly when she attracted a boy who thought he could have his way with her.

See also: Ann Romano, Dwayne Schneider, Julie Cooper.

83. Barbara Gordon, *Batman*, ABC, 1968. Played by Yvonne Craig.

Barbara Gordon is a young woman who is secretly Batgirl, a mysterious crime fighter in Gotham City. Barbara was born in Gotham City and is the daughter of Police Commissioner Gordon. She attended Woodrow Roosevelt High School and grew up admiring Batman, the city's mysterious crime fighter. His exploits so influenced Barbara that she too decided to become a crime fighter. After graduating from Gotham State University, Barbara began her dual life by becoming a librarian at the Gotham City library. She then rented an apartment (8A) and built a secret closet behind her bedroom wall to conceal her Batgirl costume (she conceals her mode of transportation, the Batgirl Cycle, in a secret freight elevator in the back of her building). When the need arises, she becomes Batgirl.

Barbara has a pet bird (Charlie) and is chairperson of the Gotham City Anti-Littering Committee. As Batgirl she received the first Gotham City Female Crime Fighting and Fashion Award, the Battie, for her crusade against crime and her sexy dark purple costume. Barbara's favorite opera is *The Marriage of Figaro*. She is a martial arts expert and was called "The Dazzling Dare Doll" in the pilot (she forms the Terrific Trio when joining Batman and his sidekick, Robin, the Boy Wonder).

See also: Barbara Gordon (next title), Bruce Wayne, Dick Grayson.

84. Barbara Gordon, *Birds of Prey*, WB, 2002–2003. Played by Dina Meyer.

Barbara Gordon, a resident of New Gotham City, is a crime fighter who battles evil as the mysterious Batgirl. She was trained by Batman and like her hero, waged a war against the evil Joker. One night while showering, the Joker broke into Barbara's apartment and shot her. The Joker's bullet, however, failed to kill Barbara. It crippled her and set her in motion to crusade against evil as Oracle.

Barbara, a graduate of New Gotham High School and College, is a master of the cyber realms "and a mentor and trainer to heroes." While confined to a wheelchair, Barbara is working on a way to make her legs mobile again (she has developed a device to activate her motor-driven wheelchair by thought processes; she is hoping to adopt this technology to her spine. She has developed an experimental neural response device that allows her to walk; however, in its primitive stages, it could further damage her spinal column).

Barbara works as a teacher at New Gotham High School. She lives in her crime-fighting lab-apartment in the Clock Tower of a skyscraper (where she monitors criminal activity throughout the city). It is from here that she directs her protégé, Helena Kyle, to bring criminals to justice (if Barbara leaves the complex, the computer alerts her to pending trouble on her beeper with the message "Delphi Alert").

See also: Barbara Gordon (above title), Dinah Lance, Helena Kyle.

Barbara Jean Hart *see* **Reba Hart**

85. Barbara Weston, *Empty Nest*, NBC, 1988–1992. Played by Kristy McNichol.

Barbara Weston is the middle daughter of Harry and Libby Weston and lives with her father (now a widower) and older sister, Carol, at 1755 Fairview Road in Miami Beach, Florida. Her younger sister, Emily, is away at college (but joins the family in 1993 when manic depression forces Kristy to leave the series in 1992).

Barbara is first an officer then sergeant with the Miami Police Department (she has been with the force since 1983). She is perky, upbeat and carefree but terrible with money. Barbara plunges into the unknown without thinking first and co-wrote (with her father) the children's book *Jumpy Goes to the Hospital.* "Beetle Bailey" is Barbara's favorite comic strip. She collects backscratchers and uses Zippy "The official antiperspirant of the Miss Junior Teen U.S.A. Pageant." Barbara attended Camp Weemawalk as a child and was called "Swim Like a Fish"; Carol calls her "Barbie Barb." Barbara's absence from the series is explained as her being on vacation or on assignment.

See also: Carol Weston, Emily Weston, Harry Weston.

Baretta *see* **Tony Baretta**

86. Barnabas Collins, *Dark Shadows*, ABC, 1967–1971. Played by Jonathan Frid.

The mysterious Barnabas Collins is the oldest living member of the wealthy Collins family of Collinsport, Maine. Barnabas was born in Maine in 1781. He is the son of Joshua and Naomi and has a younger sister named Sarah. Barnabas lost Sarah to a high fever in 1795 and was deeply affected by her death. Shortly after, as he began to take a vested interest in his family's ship building business, he fell in love with a woman named Josette DuPres. His love for her, however, angered Angelique Bouchard, Josette's maid, who also loved him. Angelique is a powerful witch. When Barnabas rejects Angelique's love she vows to destroy him and curses him to become a vampire. Barnabas is now a creature of the undead and must kill to survive (drink human blood).

The Collins family history states that Barnabas traveled to England and remained there after completing a business deal. This was to cover up the actual disappearance of Barnabas. Barnabas had approached his father and told him what he had become. Joshua could not fulfill his son's request to end his suffering by driving a stake through his heart; instead he placed Barnabas in a coffin and sealed it with heavy chains. It is 175 years later when Willie Loomis, the Collins family caretaker, becomes intrigued by the legend of the Collins jewels, especially those worn by an ancestor named Barnabas Collins. Willie breaks into the Collins crypt at Eagle Hill cemetery and removes the chains from the coffin of Barnabas Collins. He opens it and restores life to Barnabas. Willie becomes his slave and Barnabas, dressed as he was in the 19th century, is now alive in a new era. He quickly adjusts and when he sees the Old House (from his time) is still standing, he pretends to be a descendant of the original Barnabas Collins and is given permission to live in the Old House on the pretense that he will be restoring it. In actuality, he is seeking a way to end his curse and live a normal life (he has also made it clear that he has come to Maine to start a new life where his family originated (he is wealthy and would like to invest in a ship building business just like the "original" Barnabas Collins).

Barnabas displays old world courtesy and charm. He is extremely polite (especially to women) and displays antiquated manners. He is strongly opposed to killing but his curse prevents him from being moral. He still loves Josette and is still seeking her — whether in a ghostly form or in the reincarnation of a modern-day girl. Barnabas's picture hangs in the hall of the new house on the Collins grounds and Barnabas wears a distinctive ruby ring on his right hand. He also wears a cape and carries a large silver walking cane with him at all times.

See also: Angelique, Roger Collins, Victoria Winters, Willie Loomis.

87. Barnaby Jones, *Barnaby Jones*, CBS, 1973–1980. Played by Buddy Ebsen.

Barnaby Jones is a senior citizen who doesn't believe in old age. He feels he is as vibrant as he was when he was a young man and has the needed wisdom to continue in his capacity as a private detective. He operates Barnaby Jones Investigations at 3782 Clinton Avenue in Los Angeles. His daughter-in-law, Betty Jones (Lee Meriwether), and cousin Jedediah Romano "J.R." Jones (Mark

Shera), assist him. Barnaby can be reached by phone at 467-7935 (then at 555-7650); he rents office 615. Barnaby also solves cases for the California Meridian Insurance Company. Mark is a law student who tackles cases between classes; Betty was married to Barnaby's late son, Hal, and now works as the office secretary and receptionist.

Barnaby is a skilled investigator who likes to analyze the clues he finds. He claims to be "a long looker and a slow thinker." He has knowledge of forensic medicine and chemistry and is well versed in clinical psychology. He owns a ranch in Sun Valley (where he raises horses) and enjoys fishing in his spare time. His favorite drink is milk. Barnaby's appearance, relaxed manner and positive attitude combine to make him a criminal's worst nightmare.

88. Barney and Betty Rubble, *The Flintstones*, ABC, 1960–1966. Voiced by Mel Blanc (Barney), Bea Benaderet and Gerry Johnson (Betty).

Barney and Betty Rubble are a prehistoric couple who live next door to Fred and Wilma Flintstone in the town of Bedrock. Barney was born in Granite Town and lived at 142 Boulder Avenue. He was a Boy Scout and a member of the Saber-Toothed Tiger Troop. Barney attended Bedrock High School and was a member of the Beta Slatta Gamma Fraternity. In the year 1,000,056 B.C. (16 years before the series is set), Barney worked as a bellboy for the Honeyrock Hotel. It was here that he met Betty Jean McBricker, a waitress and fell in love. They married shortly after and set up housekeeping on Stone Cave Road.

Barney first worked for the Pebble Rock and Gravel Company then for the Slaterock Gravel Company (but also called the Rockhead Quarry Construction Company, the Bedrock Quarry Gravel Company, the Bedrock Gravel Company and the Rockhead and Quarry Cove Construction Company). Barney coaches the Giants Little League baseball team and eats Rock Toasties cereal for breakfast. He is a member of the Bedrock Quarry baseball team and bowls at the Bedrock Bowling Alley.

Betty is a content housewife but is apparently unable to have children. One night she and Barney wish upon a falling star for a baby. The following morning they find an orphan on their doorstep with a note attached asking them to care for their little Bamm Bamm, who has incredible strength. They also have a pet Hoparoo named Hoppy.

See also: Fred and Wilma Flintstone.

89. Barney Fife, *The Andy Griffith Show*, CBS, 1960–1965. Played by Don Knotts.

Bernard Fife, called Barney, is a deputy sheriff in the mythical town of Mayberry, North Carolina. He is the cousin of the town's sheriff, Andy Taylor, and was given three different middle names: Milton, Milton P. and Oliver.

Barney is a graduate of Mayfield Union High School, class of 1945. He has been a deputy for five of the 12 years Andy has been sheriff. He is a bachelor and lives at 411 Elm Street. He wears a size 7½ B shoe.

Barney wears a gun but is not allowed to keep it loaded (he carries the one bullet Andy allows him to have in his shirt pocket). Barney weighs 132 pounds, is easily excited and not taken seriously by lawbreakers (he waves his arms, makes speeches and rants). Barney pretends to be brave to impress people but deep down he is a coward (Andy realizes this and always helps Barney save face). When Barney is permitted to use his gun, he does so to start the potato race at the Mason's Picnic. In addition to patrolling the streets, Barney's duties include fly swatting and changing the jail's bed sheets.

Barney enjoys relaxing with Andy on his front porch and playing the harmonica. He enjoys meals at the Junction Café and is dating Thelma Lou (Betty Lynn), his longtime girlfriend. Barney left Mayberry in 1965 for a job in nearby Raleigh in traffic with the Raleigh Police Department (he is later promoted to the position of staff detective). In the 1986 NBC TV movie, *Return to Mayberry*, Barney returns to Mayberry and again becomes Andy's deputy.

See also: Andy Taylor, Bee Taylor, Gomer Pyle, Goober Pyle, Opie Taylor.

90. Barry Allen, *The Flash*, CBS, 1990–1991. Played by John Wesley Shipp.

Barry Allen is a man who leads a double life: chemist for the Central City Police Department in Central City and the Flash, a superhero who uses the power of speed to battle crime.

Barry was born in Central City ("The place where the corn dog was invented") and attended Central City High School (where he was a member of the Latin and science clubs). He lives in an area called North Park (Apartment 34) and drives a car with the license plate DLW 647. He has a pet dog (Earl) and enjoys eating at Burger World and Lucky Dogs. His life changed one day while working in his lab. A bolt of lightning from an approaching storm struck a shelf of chemicals and doused Barry with a variety of volatile chemicals. The chemicals altered Barry's DNA and enhanced his bone and muscle tissues. He is now capable of fantastic speeds (up to 620 mph) but he must consume enormous amounts of food to replenish the energy he uses to sustain himself. Barry wears a modified red friction Soviet-made deep-sea suit and a red mask as a costume to conceal his true identity. A lightning bolt adorns the front of the costume (so villains will fear him).

91. Barry Tarberry, *The 100 Lives of Black Jack Savage*, NBC, 1991. Played by Daniel Hugh-Kelly.

Barry Danforth Tarberry is a multi-billionaire and number 18 on the FBI's 20 most wanted list. He is the owner of Tarberry Industries and was arrested for insider trading (violating Federal Statute 1678). He escaped while out on bail and now lives in Blackbird Castle on the Caribbean island of San Pietro.

Barry was born in New York City and quickly took the world by storm with his brilliant business sense, turning a small investment company into a mega empire. Barry has written a book (*Dealing, Not Stealing*), and has appeared on the cover of *Forbes* magazine. He became a celebrity of sorts and appeared on TV (on such shows as *Jeopardy, The Mike Douglas Show, Circus of the Stars, Hollywood Squares* and *The $100,000 Pyramid*). He was also grand marshal of the 1990 Macy's Thanksgiving Day Parade.

See also: Black Jack Savage (for information on the ghost Barry helps save lives. Barry learns through Black Jack that he is a candidate for Hell but can redeem himself by helping Black Jack save 100 lives).

92. Bart Simpson, *The Simpsons*, Fox, 1990 (current). Voiced by Nancy Cartwright.

Bartholomew J. Simpson, called Bart, is the eldest child of Homer and Marge Simpson, a happily married couple who live at 742 Evergreen Terrace in the town of Springfield. He has two younger sisters, Lisa and Maggie. Bart is a 10-year-old wisecracking brat. He is in the fourth grade at Springfield Elementary School and spends more time in detention than he does in the classroom. He has a pet frog (Froggie) and a dog (Santa's Little Helper) and enjoys "Radio Active Man" comic books. His favorite TV shows are *Itchy and Scratchy* (a violent cat and mouse cartoon) and *Krusty the Clown* (about a very nasty clown on whom Bart has based his whole life. Bart has badge number 16302 in the Krusty the Clown Fan Club).

Bart has Double O-Negative blood, is allergic to butterscotch and is a champ at the video game "Slugfest." As kids, he and Lisa played the board

games "Hippo in the House," "The Game of Lent" and "Citizenship." Bart delights in playing practical jokes and his catch phrases are "Don't have a cow, man" and "My name is Bart Simpson, who the hell are you?" Bart is a member of the Hole in the Underwear Club ("No Girls Allowed") and sits in the back of the classroom "because the front is for geeks."

See also: Homer Simpson, Lisa Simpson, Marge Simpson.

Batgirl *see* **Barbara Gordon (two entries)**

Batman *see* **Bruce Wayne**

93. Beaver Cleaver, *Leave It to Beaver*, CBS, 1957–1958; ABC, 1958–1963. Played by Jerry Mathers.

Theodore Cleaver, nicknamed Beaver, is the youngest son of Ward and June Cleaver. He lives with them and his brother, Wally, at 211 Pine Street then 211 Lakewood Avenue in Mayfield (the original house address was also given as 211 Maple Drive and 211 Pine Avenue).

Theodore is named after June's Aunt Martha's brother. He acquired the name "Beaver" from Wally (who couldn't pronounce Theodore and said "Tweder." Ward and June thought "Beaver" sounded better). Beaver attends the Grant Avenue Grammar School then Mayfield High School. He wears a green baseball cap, hates "mushy stuff," and "likes to mess around with junk and would rather smell a skunk than see a girl." He likes to fish at Miller's Pond and walks in the gutter on his way home from school. His poorest subject in school is math.

Beaver played a tree in his kindergarten play, a mushroom in "Flowers and Feathers" in grammar school and Hans in his fifth grade play, *The Little Dutch Boy*. He took up the clarinet for the school orchestra and had a teddy bear named Billy. As a baby, Beaver would fall asleep in his bowl of cereal and when he gets upset, he locks himself in the bathroom. When he does something wrong, he hides in a tree, in the cave near Miller's Pond or near the railroad tracks. He had a pet monkey (Stanley), a rat (Peter Gunn; named after the detective show of the time), racing pigeons (Miss Canfield and Miss Landers; after "The two best teachers I ever had"), and a frog (Herbie). Beaver held a job as a caddy and is sometimes called "Beave." He also appeared on the TV show *Teenage Forum*.

In the TV movie update, *Still the Beaver* (CBS, March 19, 1983), Beaver is married to Kimberly (Joanna Gleason) and the father of Corey and Oliver (Corey Feldman, John Snee). In the updated series, *The New Leave It to Beaver* (TBS, 1986–1989), Beaver is now divorced and lives with his mother and sons at 211 Pine Street. He is also partners with Lumpy Rutherford (Frank Bank from the original series) in the Cleaver and Rutherford Company (exactly what they do is not revealed). The role of Kip is now played by Kipp Marcus.

See also: Eddie Haskell, June Cleaver, Lumpy Rutherford, Wally Cleaver, Ward Cleaver.

94. Becca Thatcher, *Life Goes On,* ABC, 1989–1993. Played by Kellie Martin.

Rebecca Thatcher, nicknamed Becca, is the 15-year-old daughter of Libby and Drew Thatcher and lives at 305 Woodridge Road in Glen Brook, Illinois, with her half sister, Paige, and brother Corky.

Becca weighs 85 pounds and attends Marshall High School. She is a bright student and a member of both the debating club and gymnastics team. Becca is also a talented ballerina and hopeful writer (she is on the staff of *The Underground Marshall,* the school's forbidden tabloid). While attractive, Becca fears her figure will never develop (in the opening theme she looks sideways into a mirror, and referring to her breasts, remarks, "Come on, where are you guys already?"). When Becca turned 16 (October 20, 1991), she developed and was called "a major babe" by her sister. The compliment helped Becca shed "the ugly duckling" image she held of herself. After graduating from high school, Becca enrolled in Brown University (she hopes to become a doctor and attend Harvard Medical School).

See also: Corky Thatcher, Libby and Drew Thatcher, Paige Thatcher.

Becker *see* **John Becker**

95. Becky Conner, *Roseanne,* ABC, 1988–1997. Played by Lecy Goranson, Sarah Chalke.

Rebecca Conner, called Becky, is the oldest daughter of Dan and Roseanne Conner, a middle class couple who live at 714 Delaware Street in Lanford, Illinois. Becky was born on March 15, 1975 and has a younger sister (Darlene) and brother (D.J.).

Becky attended the James Madison Elementary School then Lanford High School. She is sweet and feminine and much closer to her mother than she is to her father. As the series progressed, Becky became aggressive, independent and constantly defied parental authority. She received an allowance of $10 a week and had her first job at the Buy 'n' Bag Supermarket. Red is her favorite color and she feels eating Dannon yogurt will help keep her slim figure.

Becky left the family when she married Mark Healy (Glenn Quinn), a mechanic at the Lanford Custom Cycle Shop. They moved to Minneapolis (where Becky worked as a waitress at the Bunz Restaurant) but eventually returned to Illinois and moved into the Lanford Trailer Park. Becky then enrolled in the University of Illinois to pursue her dream of becoming a nurse.

See also: Dan and Roseanne Conner, Darlene Conner, Jackie Harris.

96. Bee Taylor, *The Andy Griffith Show,* CBS, 1960–1968. Played by Frances Bavier.

Beatrice Taylor, called Aunt Bee, is the woman who knows all that goes on in Mayberry, a small, mythical town in North Carolina. Bee is the aunt of Andy Taylor, the town's sheriff. She cares for him and his young son, Opie (Andy is a widower). Aunt Bee attended the Sweetbriar School and was a member of its basketball team. She is noted for her cooking and her ability to maintain a vegetable garden. Bee is famous for her homemade pickles and pies (apple and butterscotch pecan are Andy's favorites). Aunt Bee won assorted prizes for her cooking knowledge on the TV show *Win or Lose* and was awarded a trip to Mexico for winning the Tampico Tamale Contest.

Aunt Bee is a member of the Mayberry Church Choir, the Greater Mayberry Historical Society and the Mayberry Garden Club. She wrote the town's sentimental song, "Mayberry, My Home Town" and her catch phrase is "Oh, fiddle faddle."

See also: Andy Taylor, Barney Fife, Gomer Pyle, Goober Pyle, Opie Taylor.

97. Beka Valentine, *Andromeda,* Syn., 2000–2005. Played by Lisa Ryder.

Rebeka Valentine, called Beka, is a crew member on the *Andromeda Ascendant,* a futuristic battleship piloted by Captain Dylan Hunt. Prior to this, Beka was captain of the salvage ship *Eureka Maru,* and worked for ten years as the skipper of a freighter. As a child Beka was called "Rocket" by her father; she also learned the art of deception from him as he pulled elaborate scams to survive. Beka inherited her father's ship six years ago and will do what it takes to get what she wants. She will put herself in the line of fire to save her crewmates and is "one hell of a pilot" according to Dylan. While Beka enjoys the adventures she encounters, her main objective is to gather what treasures she can salvage in the various worlds she explores.

See also: Andromeda, Dylan Hunt, Trance Gemini.

98. B'Elanna Torres, *Star Trek: Voyager*, UPN, 1995–2001. Played by Roxann Dawson.

B'Elanna Torres is chief engineer on the star ship U.S.S. *Voyager NCC-7465*. She was born in the 24th century (possibly in the 2350s) and is half human and half Klingon. Her human father was named John Torres and her Klingon mother, Miral. B'Elanna grew up on the planet Kessik IV with her mother. Her father abandoned them when B'Elanna was a child and B'Elanna believes it was her Klingon heritage that drove him away.

B'Elanna is tough, knowledgeable and independent. She attended Starfleet Academy seeking and engineer's degree but quit when her Klingon and human sides began to clash. Before being assigned by Kathryn Janeway as chief engineer of *Voyager*, B'Elanna fought to save the Maquis by joining its rebellion against the Cardassians in the early 2370s. On *Voyager*, B'Elanna fell in love with crewmate Tom Paris. They were married by Captain Janeway and became the parents of a girl (Klingon in appearance) they named Miral in 2378.

See also: Chakotay, The Doctor, Harry Kim, Kathryn Janeway, Neelix, Seven of Nine, Tuvok.

99. Ben Cartwright, *Bonanza*, NBC, 1959–1973. Played by Lorne Greene.

Benjamin Cartwright, called Ben, is the owner of the 1,000-square mile timberland ranch, the Ponderosa, in the Comstock Lode Country of Virginia City, Nevada. Ben was born in 1825 to a shop owner in Jonns Common, Massachusetts. He became interested in the sea at an early age and at 20 worked as a third officer on the *Wanderer*, a ship captained by Morgan Stoddard, the father of the woman he loved (Elizabeth Eloise Stoddard). After several years at sea, Ben quit to open a ship chandler's shop in Boston. Ben and Elizabeth married shortly after and moved into a small home on Baldwin Lane. In 1842, shortly after giving birth to their son, Adam, Elizabeth died. Ben possessed a dream of settling in California. Motivated by Elizabeth's strong desire for him to pursue that dream, Ben sold his business and headed west.

Ben and Adam, now five years old, settled temporarily in St. Joseph, Missouri. It was here that Ben met Inger Borgstrom, a Swedish girl who ran the local grocery store. They eventually fell in love and married. Inger persuaded Ben to continue his journey west. They joined a wagon train and Ben took on the responsibility of guiding settlers to California. During the hazardous trek through the rugged Nevada territory, Inger gave birth to a son they named Eric Hoss (in 1848). Shortly after,

during an Indian attack, Inger was struck by an arrow and killed. Ben abandoned his dream. After seeing the beautiful Nevada territory, Ben made Virginia City his home. After years of hard work and sacrifice, Ben established his Ponderosa Ranch (named after the Ponderosa Pine Trees that are native to the land). By 1856 Ben had a prosperous ranch. A short time later, Ben's foreman, Pierre DeMarne, was killed attempting to save Ben's life. Ben chose to personally tell his widow, Marie, what happened and traveled to New Orleans. A romance developed and Ben and Marie married in 1856. A year later, Ben's third son, Joseph, was born. The ranch house seen by viewers was built under Marie's guidance. In 1859 tragedy struck again when Marie was thrown from her horse and killed. It is the 1880s when the series begins.

At one point in his life Ben was a Major with the 116th Militia but it is difficult to place because there are no flashback sequences regarding it. Ben is well respected and has a strong sense of justice. He is the largest depositor at the Virginia City Bank and collects firearms as a hobby. Ben was also the owner of a riverboat (the *Dixie*, which he operated on Lake Tahoe) and invested in a railroad (the High Sierra Shortline) Ben was also on the board of the Golden State Marine Bank and Trust Company and was head of the Virginia City School Board. Ben also raised cattle and paid his ranch hands quite well—$30 a month, a bunk and meals. Ben rode a horse named Buck.

The 1988 TV movie, *Bonanza, the Next Generation*, reveals that Ben died in 1903.

See also: Adam Cartwright, Hoss Cartwright, Little Joe Cartwright.

100. Ben Matlock, *Matlock*, NBC, 1986–1992; ABC, 1992–1995. Played by Andy Griffith.

Benjamin Layton Matlock, called Ben, is a wealthy lawyer based in Atlanta, Georgia. Ben is a Gemini and was born in the small town of Mount Harlan, Georgia (where his father owned a gas station). He is a graduate of Harvard Law School and worked as a public prosecutor before beginning his own law practice. Ben attends law seminars "because you're never too old to learn" and teaches law at Eaton University. He has a doctorate degree in law from Baxter University where they have named a chair after him. Ben drives a car with the license plate RAF 285 and is known for two things: eating hot dogs, usually with grape soda, and wearing white suits (he has a closet full of them). This tradition began in 1969 when a case brought Ben to Los Angeles. He became ill after eating several pieces of bad fish and was taken to Community General Hospital. He was treated by a young resident intern named Dr. Mark Sloan (Dick Van Dyke from the series *Diagnosis Murder*). Ben was just starting his law practice and Mark convinced him to invest his life savings of $5,000 in the hottest new item, 8-track tapes. The system proved to be a failure and Ben lost everything. Cheap white suits off the store rack and hot dogs were all he could afford.

Ben charges $100,000 a case and is known for his high rate of success in defending clients. He rises each morning at 5:00 A.M. ("It's the best time for thinking") and constantly complains about paying taxes. He lives in a house on Mill Pond Road, collects old coins and usually defends clients at the Fulton County Courthouse.

Ben sang in a church choir in his youth and occasionally plays the guitar. He despises a paper called the *Informer* because it reports on his cases and hampers his chances of freeing his clients. He also has little faith in police labs; "They're not working to help my clients." He prefers to do his own investigating. Ben doesn't make unsubstantiated charges and will occasionally takes a case for free. Ben was voted Man of the Year by the Atlanta Chamber of Commerce in 1991 and will not allow anyone to smoke in his office, "not even my best-paying clients." Ben is known as a great storyteller and knows how to appeal to a jury. Ben is also the father of two daughters, Charlene (Linda Purl) and Lee Ann (Brynn Thayer), both of whom worked with him (Charlene, 1986–87; Lee Ann, 1987–1994).

101. Ben Miller, *My Life and Times*, ABC, 1991. Played by Tom Irwin.

From an unidentified retirement home in the year 2035, 85-year-old Benjamin Miller speaks to the audience: "I wouldn't say I've seen it all, but I've seen a lot. I've seen the world change. I've seen myself change. I've watched footsteps on the moon; I've seen myself stumble. I've made a fortune. I've lost a fortune. I've loved and lost and lived to love again. The one thing I know, life is an adventure. You've got to hold on and let it carry you away. It carried me all the way to the year 2035. And I'm here to tell the tale. I'm Ben Miller and this is my life and times."

Ben was born in 1950 and is first seen as a journalism student at Northwestern University in 1968. After graduating he moved to New York City to pursue a writing career. In 1978 it was learned that Ben had written a story about an enchanting girl (Jesse) he met for the Illinois *Review*. At age 35, Ben worked as a reporter for the New York *Globe*. At some point between 1989 and 1998, Ben wrote two books, *A Break in the Clouds* and *Come the Redeemer*.

Ben left the *Globe* (possibly in 1986) for a job driving a Checker Cab in Manhattan. He also bought 900 shares of stock in a company called Lightbridge Systems and lost everything ($2,300) when the stock market fell 500 points on Black Monday. In 1988 Ben moved to Seattle, Washington, and found work as a bookkeeper with Colby-Stern, a government contracting company. Eleven years later, Ben moved to St. Louis to take a factory job. Ben remained at this job until his retirement in 2035. His favorite candy was Milk Duds.

Ben had married twice. His first wife was Rebecca Miller (Helen Hunt) who presented him with two children, Melanie and David. Rebecca died of cancer on Labor Day of 1999. A year later he married Lily Matheson (Lisa Zane); her fate was not revealed.

102. Ben Richards, *The Immortal*, ABC, 1970–1971. Played by Christopher George.

Ben Richards is 43 years old and stands six feet tall. He works in the automotive testing division of Braddock Industries in California and possesses type O-Negative blood. Ben has never been sick and has never had any childhood diseases. He was abandoned by his parents as an infant and adopted. He is unaware of who his parents are but has learned that he has a brother but has never seen him.

Everybody has immunity factors in their blood; factors that make them immune to certain diseases. Ben's blood contains every factor there is, making him immune to every disease. This mixing of genes also makes him immune to old age and a transfusion of his blood could give others a second or third lifetime. Did his parents (or at least one) possess the same blood factors? Was it a trick of nature? Does his brother possess the same immunity? These are the questions Ben seeks when he finds himself on the run from his employer, Jordan Braddock (Barry Sullivan), a dying billionaire who requires Ben's blood to live again. Ben remained on the run and seeking answers when the series ended.

103. Benjamin Franklin Pierce, *M*A*S*H*, CBS, 1972–1983. Played by Alan Alda.

Benjamin Franklin Pierce, nicknamed Hawkeye, is a Captain with the 4077th M*A*S*H (Mobile Army Surgical Hospital) unit in Korea during the war. Hawkeye, as he is most often called, was named by his father after the main character in *The Last of the Mohicans*. "My father was crazy about that book. He was crazy about Indians." Hawkeye was born in Crabapple Cove, Maine. When he was seven years old, Hawkeye almost drowned while fishing. He fell out of the boat and was rescued by a friend. When he was older, Hawkeye worked at Balinger's Drug Store, delivering prescriptions on his bicycle.

Hawkeye has the dog tag number 19095607 and had a practice in Boston when he was drafted into the Army. He chases nurses, will not carry a gun and calls the 4077 "a cesspool" and his tent "the swamp." He is considered the best "cutter" (surgeon) in the unit and is certified in chest and general surgery. He is a Captain and his official position is Chief Surgeon (for which he earns $413.50 a month). Hawkeye loves to wear his Hawaiian shirt and is on a quest "to find the driest martini in these parts" (he has a still for making martinis in his tent that he calls "The wellspring of life").

Hawkeye misses "a mattress thicker than a matzoh, my own bathroom and any woman out of uniform and the entire state of Maine." He thinks of himself as "The social director of the heart" for all the temporary relationships he has with nurses. He also says "We eat fish and liver day after day. It's against the Geneva Convention. I've eaten a river of liver and an ocean of fish." Hawkeye reads *The Joys of Nudity* magazine and starred in the Army documentary *Yankee Doodle Doctor* (as a wacky, Groucho Marx–like surgeon). Hawkeye tries to turn his mind off to the war in the hope that it will go away "But it doesn't work. You go back to your job and try to forget there is a war going on." To relax, Hawkeye collapses after a day of surgery and drinks. He also says "that at night I dream I'm awake." As a kid, Hawkeye had an imaginary friend named Tuttle that he blamed for doing things that got him into trouble. Hawkeye loves the theater, especially Broadway musicals.

See also: B.J. Hunnicutt, Charles Winchester III, Frank Burns, Henry Blake, Margaret Houlihan, Radar O'Reilly, Sherman Potter, Trapper John McIntire.

104. Benjamin Sisko, *Star Trek: Deep Space Nine,* Syn., 1993–1999. Played by Avery Brooks.

Benjamin Lafayette Sisko is a Captain and commanding officer of the Starfleet ship U.S.S. *Defiant NX-74205.* Benjamin was born in New Orleans, Louisiana, in the year 2332. His father, Joseph, was a gourmet cook and ran a family restaurant called Sisko's. As a child, Ben harvested vegetables from the family garden and later worked at the restaurant. Joseph's wife, Sarah, de-

serted the family shortly after Ben was born. Ben has a love for baseball and during his years at Starfleet Academy (2350–54), he was captain of the wrestling team. Ben was first married to Jennifer, a woman he met in 2354. They were blessed with a child, Jake (born in 2355) but in 2367 Jennifer was killed in a battle with the evil Borg at Wolf 359. A shattered Ben exiled himself on Mars at Utopia Planetia and had seriously considered resigning from Starfleet. Eight years later he found a new love, Kasidy Yates, and married for a second time.

Ben's first assignment was aboard the U.S.S. *Livingston.* Shortly after, when he was promoted to Lieutenant Commander, he served aboard the U.S.S. *Saratoga* and finally in 2371, he captained the U.S.S. *Defiant.* He also served a term as commander of *Deep Space Nine,* Starfleet's space station.

See also: Ezri Dax, Jadzia Dax, Kira Nerys.

105. Bentley Gregg, *Bachelor Father,* CBS, 1957–1958; NBC, 1958–1961; ABC, 1961–1962. Played by John Forsythe.

This entry also contains information on Kelly Gregg (Noreen Corcoran), Bentley's niece.

Bentley Gregg is a suave and sophisticated bachelor who lives at 1163 Rexford Drive in Beverly Hills with his orphaned 13-year-old niece, Kelly. Bentley was born in Beverly Hills and when he learned that girls weren't soft boys he became fascinated by them. He was the Romeo of his grade school, the ladies' man of his high school and by the time he had reached college he had become an expert on women. He knows how to sweet talk, dine and treat the fairer sex without ever having to make a commitment to a steady relationship or even the more frightening (to him) marriage.

Bentley is a graduate of Harvard Law School and sometimes wonders why he didn't become a doctor when his clients give him a hard time ("One of my professors said, 'Why Bentley, with hands like that you'd make a brilliant surgeon'"). Bentley rents office 106 in the Crescent Building on Crescent Drive in downtown Los Angeles.

Bentley is not only sophisticated in his dress, but his conversations are smooth and romantic. Girls swoon as he always manages to say the right thing. His houseboy Peter Tong (Sammee Tong) calls him "The greatest general in the romancing department"; Kelly says, "Gosh Uncle Bentley, you look beautiful" when she sees him in his "dating clothes" (a tuxedo or suit).

Bentley enjoys playing golf and tennis and treats his dates to dinner at the Coconut Grove and dancing at the Ambassador Room. While Bentley dates the most gorgeous women on TV, he says, "The toughest thing about being a bachelor is remaining one."

Kelly Gregg is the daughter of Bentley's brother and wife. When they were killed in an automobile accident, Bentley took on the responsibility of raising Kelly (hence the series title). Kelly is a student at Beverly Hills High School (where her best subject is math); Bill's Malt Shop is the after school hangout. Kelly has an 11 P.M. curfew (at age 15) and ever so often Bentley gives her "a cost of living increase in her allowance." Kelly is a loyal friend and puts herself out to help others. She is very polite and always stylishly dressed. Kelly is always a lady. She is charming, elegant for one so young and well versed on the opposite sex. Watching her Uncle Bentley "operate" has made her choosy about boys and she is looking to date one that has been cast in the shadow of her uncle. Before she found her dream man in last season episodes (lawyer Warren Dawson; played by Aaron Kincaid), Kelly dated the unpolished Howard Meechim (Jimmy Boyd), a boy she tried to mold into the image of her uncle but never could.

106. Bernie Mac, *The Bernie Mac Show*, Fox, 2001 (current). Played by Bernie Mac.

Bernie Mac is a standup comedian and star of the feature film *The Kings of Comedy*. He was born in 1958 and raised by a family who couldn't tolerate disobedience (he feared "Big Mama's black belt" because "I was wuped when I was bad"). Bernie grew up in a tough Chicago neighborhood and in his youth was a boxer. He liked to make people laugh and turned his talents to becoming an actor and comedian. He now lives in a swanky house in Encino, California, with his wife, Wanda (Kellita Smith), a vice president with AT&T.

Bernie enjoys a weekly game of poker with his friends and smoking a good cigar (mostly illegal Cubans, which he gets "through the Cuban connection" for $20 a piece). He does charity work for the Children's Council and plays golf with his personalized clubs.

Bernie has three favorite movies: *Cooley High* (his favorite Chicago film), *Car Wash* (Los Angeles), and *Cotton Comes to Harlem* (New York). He has another New York favorite, *Claudine*, which he uses as the password to the house alarm. Bernie lost the lead role in *Training Day* to Denzell Washington; the lead in *Beggar Vance* to Will Smith; and had to give up the lead in *Conrad's Prerogative* when he found he couldn't play an

athlete's attempts to overcome a heart attack dramatically ("I want only to make people laugh"). Bernie's license plate reads 410R 1019; Wanda's is first VP ATT then 4JRY 932.

Bernie and Wanda are the guardians of Vanessa, Jordan and Bryanna Tompkins (Camille Winbush, Jeremy Suarez, Dee Dee Davis), his sister's children. They became part of the family when Bernie sent his drug-addicted sister to rehab (their father is serving a 10 year prison sentence for tax evasion). Vanessa was born in 1988 and attends the Baha Vista Jr. High School. Jordan, born in 1993, attends Damian Elementary School; and Bryanna, born in 1998, is enrolled in the Wellington School. Vanessa is called "Nessa" by Bernie and is on the school's gymnastics team. In Chicago she practically raised Jordan and Bryanna. Jordan is a pre-asthmatic, a troublemaker, and he cries over everything. Bryanna, called "Baby Girl" by Bernie, has a doll named Precious and won a good citizenship award (which Bernie proudly displays in "The Mac Hall of Fame," a trophy cabinet in the den; it also contains his football trophy from high school).

Bernie was born in Chicago and worked as a deliveryman for Atlas Parcel Service when he met Wanda Thomas, the daughter of a customer. Bernie was performing as a comic on the L-Train and at Tickles, a comedy club. It was 1987 and it was Wanda who encouraged him to go further and seek fame. Wanda completed the executive program at Chicago Telecom when she and Bernie married and moved to California (where she found work with West Coast Wireless and Bernie became a hit on the standup comedy circuit).

Bernie is the only one who is aware of a viewing audience and he talks directly to them, calling them "America" (for example, "Listen, America..." or "Now I ask you, America...").

107. Beth Barry, *Dave's World*, CBS, 1993–1997. Played by DeLane Matthews.

Elizabeth Barry, called Beth, is the wife of humorist Dave Barry and the mother of their children, Tommy and Willie. She was born in Texas and now works as a teacher at the Collins Elementary School in Miami Beach, Florida. As a child Beth had a pet guinea pig named Boris. She was independent and sentimental and both qualities followed her into adulthood. She has a piece of her wedding cake (18 years old) preserved in her freezer and hides her "secret stash" ($300) in the lining of her wedding dress.

Beth is naturally beautiful and uses little makeup; when she gets angry she over-moisturizes and when she loses her temper she flies off the handle and takes her frustrations out on who ever ticked her off. Beth enjoys romantic movies (at the Multi-Plex Cinema) and although she is an excellent cook, she enjoys a night out at Columbo's Restaurant. Beth looks forward to a break from the kids by spending a romantic weekend with Dave at the Spanish Moss Inn.

See also: Dave Barry, Kenny Beckett, Tommy and Willie Barry.

108. Bette, *Bette*, CBS, 2001–2002. Played by Bette Midler.

The title character is assumed to be actress/singer Bette Midler although this is not specifically stated. Bette (no last name given) is a wife and mother, singer, dancer and actress. She is married to Roy (Kevin Dunn, Robert Hays), a professor at UCLA, and the mother of Rose (Lindsay Lohan, Marina Malota), a 12½ year-old girl who attends Fairfax Jr. High School.

Bette was born in Honolulu, Hawaii, on December 1, 1945. She has brown eyes and naturally blonde hair. As a kid she had a pet goldfish (Dinah Shore) and is a graduate of Radford High School, class of 1963. Bette majored in drama at the University of Hawaii and worked for a short time at the Dole pineapple processing plant in Hawaii. She found work as a singer with the Harletts and released her first album, "The Divine Miss M," shortly after. She has since won four Grammy Awards and ends each concert with the song "Ya Gotta Have Friends."

Before her marriage to Roy, whom she met on a flight from New York to L.A., Bette would frequent Benny's Boom Boom Room looking for dates. Although she is attractive, Bette feels she needs plastic surgery and constantly knocks her looks. She is a compulsive eater and feels she is a bit too busty ("I have to hold my breasts when I walk fast"). Bette claims to have no ego ("Just ask the millions of my adoring fans") and is a nervous wreck before she appears on a TV show. On television, Bette has guest starred on *Family Law*, *The Dolly Parton Special* and *The View*. On the big screen, Bette has starred in such movies as *The First Wives Club, Jinxed, Drowning Mona, Beaches*, and *The Rose*. Bette, called "The Divine Miss M," records on the Warner Bros. Label and is with the Endeavor Talent Agency (she was originally with the William Morris Agency but quit when they suggested she do a comedy series for TV).

Bette is good friends with Dolly Parton (whom she calls "Apple Fritter; Dolly calls Bette "Pudding Head"). Bette hates Sally Field (who won an Oscar for *Norma Rae*, beating Bette who was nominated for best actress for her role in *The Rose*).

Bette made a PSA (Public Service Announcement) for the Red Cross (on water safety) and was voted Woman of the Year for her in-flight entertainment movie, *For the Boys*, by the AFI (Airline Film Invatational). Bette enjoys Almond Joy and M&M candies and is famous for her "homemade waffles" (which she takes out of a box from the freezer). When Bette attends a movie, she brings extra coats with her to place on the seat in front of her "so heads don't get in the way." Bette looks forward to trick or treating with Rose each Halloween and admitted to making love to another woman ("But that was in college"). While Rose attempts to earn money by selling Bette's bras as "Bette Memorabilia," Bette sought extra money by selling hideous green and orange jump suits for $59.95 (item number 8690) on the mythical TV Club Shopping Network. She failed to sell any of the 4,000 units she had.

109. Beverly Crusher, *Star Trek: The Next Generation*, Syn., 1987–1994. Played by Gates McFadden.

Beverly Cheryl Crusher is the Chief Medical Officer aboard the Starship *Enterprise NCC 1701-D*. She was born on October 13, 2324, in Copernicus City, Luna. Her parents are Paul and Isabel Howard and she is currently a widow (she married Jack Crusher in 2348. He died in 2355; their son, Wesley Robert, was born on July 29, 2349).

Beverly is a graduate of Starfleet Academy (2342–46) and Starfleet Medical School (2346–50). She did her medical internship on the planet Delos IV and eleven years later, in 2363, passed the Starfleet Bridge Officers Examination (which permitted her to work on a starship). The year 2364 saw her first assignment: Chief Medical Officer under Jean-Luc Picard, Captain of the U.S.S. *Enterprise NCC 1701-D*. Beverly was withdrawn from Picard's crew in 2365 to head Starfleet Medical School for one year; she was then reinstated the following year. When the *Enterprise NCC 1701-D* was lost in battle, Beverly was assigned to Picard's senior staff aboard the newly developed Sovereign Class Starship U.S.S. *Enterprise NCC 1701-E*.

Beverly has a keen interest in stage arts. She is an excellent dancer (called "The Dancing Doctor" in medical school) and formed her own theater group aboard the *Enterprise* (she performed such plays as *The Pirates of Penzance, Cyrano de Bergerac* and *Frame of Mind*). Beverly is also an expert at poker and is fond of fine woven metallic fabrics.

See also: Data, Deanna Troi, Geordi La Forge, Jean-Luc Picard, Natasha Yar, William Riker.

110. Bill Davis, *Family Affair*, WB, 2002–2003. Played by Gary Cole.

William Lloyd Davis, better known as Bill Davis, is a wealthy, playboy bachelor who lives in a luxurious apartment (18A) at 85 Park Avenue in New York City. He was born in Terre Haute, Indiana, and at an early age showed an interest in building things. His parents encouraged his fascination and Bill pursued those goals throughout his school life. He became an engineer after graduating from Indiana State University and wealthy through his innovative designs. He eventually formed his own company (Davis-Hartwell-Newberg Industries) and set up operations in Manhattan (the company was first called Hartwell-Davis Engineering). Bill enjoys a good cigar, his lifestyle and traveling (via Executive Air Service) to his many meetings around the world. In September of 2003, however, Bill's life changed. He became the guardian of his late brother (Ken) and his wife's (Laura) three children when they were killed in a car accident. Cissy Davis and twins Buffy and Jody Davis now reside with him and his butler/valet/housekeeper/best friend, Giles French (Tim Curry).

In the original version of the series, CBS, 1966–1971, Brian Keith played Bill Davis as a swinging bachelor and president of the Davis and Gaynor Construction Company in New York City. Bill, the children and Bill's gentleman's gentleman, Giles French (Sebastian Cabot), reside in Apartment 27A at 600 East 62nd Street in Manhattan.

See also: Buffy and Jody Davis, Cissy Davis.

111. Bill Miller, *Still Standing*, CBS, 2002 (current). Played by Mark Addy.

William Miller, called Bill, is the son of Al and Louise Miller. He was born in Chicago and is a graduate of Thomas Jefferson High School, class of 1981. Bill was all city line back on the football team (jersey 24) and the hot dog eating champion (ate 32 franks in one sitting). Bill met his future wife, Judy Michaels, at school and they married shortly after graduation. Bill became a bathroom fixtures salesman at the Oak Street Mall and Judy a dental assistant. They also became the parents of Lauren, Brian and Tina.

Bill claims he has had a pain in his neck for 13 years. To avoid doing chores, Bill has ingenious solutions (for example, it was easier to cut down the tree in the backyard than to constantly rake up leaves). When he has to discipline the children he becomes "The Big Angry Guy." Bill drinks Miller High Life beer and enjoys eating at the Churchill Room (not so much for the food, but the full-breasted waitresses). As a child Bill's mother called him "Silly Billy"; and Bill has no problem with lying because he lies all the time.

See also: Brian Miller, Judy Miller, Lauren Miller.

112. Billie Bunker, *Archie Bunker's Place*, CBS, 1979–1982. Played by Denise Miller.

Barbara Lee Bunker, called Billie, is a waitress at Archie Bunker's Place, a bar-restaurant in Astoria, Queens, New York, that is owned by her uncle, Archie Bunker. Billie is the daughter of Fred Bunker (Archie's brother) and came to live with Archie (at 704 Hauser Street) when Fred fell on hard times and was unable to care for her.

Billie cares for Archie (a widower) and Stephanie, the daughter of Archie's late wife's "no good cousin" Fred. Billie is 18 years old and was born on Long Island. She attended P.S. 43 grammar school and had her first crush when she was 12 years old on her orthodontist ("I wanted to see him so badly I would go to see him every Saturday just to have my braces tightened"). Billie grew up poor and treasures the little things in life. She was an excellent student at Gramercy High School but due to her family situation was unable to attend college. Her father did what he thought was right and sent her to live with Archie. Archie originally refused to have another mouth to feed but felt, without his wife Edith, she could help him raise 13-year-old Stephanie and help her deal with all those "womanly situations" he fears facing.

Billie is a very private girl and enjoys a quiet evening at home (Archie doesn't have to worry about her staying out all night "and doing who knows what with who knows who"). She enjoys Nestle's Quick chocolate mix for a quick burst of energy.

See also: Archie Bunker, Stephanie Mills.

113. Billie Chambers, *Fastlane*, Fox, 2002–2003. Played by Tiffani-Amber Thiessen.

Wilhelmina Chambers, called Billie, is a Los Angeles Police Department lieutenant who heads the Candy Store, a warehouse that stores seized cars and weapons. The contents are used by her team (Deaquon Hayes, Van Ray) to help bring criminals to justice.

Billie was born in Los Angeles and grew up in a rough neighborhood. It was her exposure to drugs, hoods, hookers and corruption that instilled her with a determination to fight crime when she grew up. After graduating from UCLA, Billie enrolled in the L.A. Police Academy. She first worked undercover as a narcotics cop. Her work for the unit earned her a gold shield, but it almost cost her her life. During one case she posed as a crooked cop. It worked, but in order to prove herself and break up a heroine ring, she shot heroine and became addicted. Her superior pulled her off the case and saved her life, but it cost Billie an important collar. Billie was then assigned to the Candy Store to apprehend criminals who appear too dangerous for ordinary law enforcers to handle.

Billie is beautiful and sensuous and strictly business — you play by her rules or face dismissal. She often finds herself breaking her own commandments to bring a criminal to justice. Billie's favorite actor is Steve McQueen ("I identify with him") and his movie, *Bullet*, was another inspiration for her to become a cop. Billie's red Corvette license plate reads 2QCE 265 and "Billie Club" is her beeper code.

See also: Deaquon Hayes, Van Ray.

114. Billy Grant, *Dr. Vegas*, CBS, 2004. Played by Rob Lowe.

William Grant is a highly skilled physician with an office in the Metro Hotel and Casino in Las Vegas. Billy, as he is called, takes only "plastic or cash" for his services. He calls himself "The House Doctor" and tends to the needs of the high stakes rollers and patrons of the casino. People often tell him, "That's kinda weird." He always responds with, "That's Vegas." But Vegas was not always a part of Billy's life. Billy worked as a doctor in the emergency room of Las Vegas General Hospital. When he saved the life of a gunshot victim (casino owner Tommy Banko) Billy became fascinated by Tommy's glamorous life style. Billy felt unfulfilled working in the ER and longed to start his own practice — to help people on a more personal basis. Billy's life changed when Tommy (Joe Pantoliano) offered him the opportunity to start his own practice from a suite in the Metro. (Tommy was born in Hackensack, New Jersey, and grew up on the wrong side of the tracks — "I had potential of becoming a second story man." He came to Vegas to change his life and started at the bottom, from carhop to bellman until he worked his way to the top.)

Billy is an expert poker player, survives on very little sleep and loves to gamble. He relaxes by playing the guitar and singing and dreams of one day becoming a high roller by participating in a no-bet limit game. Billy treats all patients as equals and often claims to have a God complex — "When people hurt I put myself on the line." However, while Billy is sympathetic to his patients needs, he says, "I'm not good when it comes to worrying."

115. B.J. Hunnicutt, *M*A*S*H*, CBS, 1975–1983. Played by Mike Farrell.

Captain B.J. Hunnicutt, called B.J., is a surgeon attached to the 4077 M*A*S*H (Mobile Army Surgical Hospital) unit in Korea during the war. He was born in Mill Valley, California, and graduated top 10 in his class at Stanford Medical School (his father and grandfather were also doctors). He was drafted just as he hoped to start a practice. He did his army residency in Salsalido and had five weeks of training at Fort Sam Houston. B.J. is a clean-cut, even-tempered family man who most misses his wife, Peggy, and daughter Erin. He is best friends with Hawkeye Pierce and shares his tent. B.J., like Hawkeye, relaxes by "horseplay — taking your frustrations out on other people." Although tempted by some of the beautiful nurses that surround him, B.J. remains faithful to Peggy ("I'm hopelessly and passionately in love with my wife"). B.J. would never reveal what his initials stood for; it was rumored they stood for the first names of his parents — Beatrice and Joseph.

See also: Benjamin Franklin Pierce, Charles Winchester III, Frank Burns, Henry Blake, Margaret Houlihan, Radar O'Reilly, Sherman Potter, Trapper John McIntire.

116. B.J. McKay, *B.J. and the Bear*, NBC, 1979–1981. Played by Greg Evigan.

Billie Jo McKay, called B.J. for short, began his TV career as an independent trucker who would haul anything legal anywhere for $1.50 a mile plus expenses. He rode with his simian companion, Bear, and battled injustice wherever he found it.

B.J. drives a red with white trim Kenworth 18-wheeler. He was born in Milwaukee and found Bear while serving as a chopper pilot during the Vietnam War (B.J. was captured and imprisoned by the enemy. A stray chimpanzee brought him food to help him survive. When he was rescued, B.J. brought Bear with him. B.J. named him Bear after Paul "Bear" Bryant, a football coach for the University of Alabama). B.J. is tough when he has to be and tries to avoid confrontation but the unethical characters who are part of the trucking industry often give him no alternative but to fight violence with violence. B.J. hopes to one day settle down, but right now he appears to enjoy the lure of the open road. He plays piano and sang with a band called Ghettaway City. B.J. calls Bear "Kid" or "The Kid." His favorite hangout is the Country Comfort Trucker's Stop in Bowlin County; The Milwaukee Kid is his C.B. handle and UT 3665 is his truck license plate number (also seen as 806 356, 635 608 and RT 3665).

A change in format in 1980 took B.J. away from the road (for the most part) and placed him in an office as the owner of Bear Enterprises, a trucking company based at 800 Palmer Street over Phil's Disco in Hollywood, California. He employs seven beautiful female truckers and they act more like detectives (solving crimes) than big rig truckers. B.J.'s seven lady truckers are:

Jeannie Campbell (Judy Landers). Jeannie is a gorgeous blonde whose shapely measurements (37C-24-36) have earned her the nickname "Stacks" (and Jeannie lives up to her name by revealing considerable cleavage). While somewhat of a dumb blonde, Stacks is very sweet and very feminine. Perilous situations do not phase her until she thinks about what is happening to her. Then her senses kick in and she becomes logical and intelligent. While not totally vain, Stacks knows she is a very beautiful girl and loves to have cheesecake pictures taken of herself, especially if she is wearing a bikini or low cut blouse. Stacks dreams of getting married but falls for characters who always shatter those dreams. Her truck license plate reads 4JJ 0167.

Callie Everett (Linda McCullough). Callie is very pretty but dresses in jeans and shirts that somewhat hide her attractive figure. She is the toughest and most physically violent of the girls. She can handle herself in a fight (although B.J. prefers she not fight) and, as B.J. says, "Callie has a smart mouth" (which often gets her and B.J. into more trouble than they are already in). Callie has a secret crush on B.J. and believes "B.J. sees me only as a girl who can drive a rig and fix a tire." Her truck license plate reads 1XT 403.

Geri and Teri Garrison (Candi and Randi Brough). Geri and Teri are identical twins who also work as waitresses at Phil's Disco. Geri is impatient and likes to take matters in her own hands. Teri calls her a hot head. Teri is patient and prefers to take things slow and easy. They are very feminine and not as actively involved in the rough stuff like Stacks and Callie. Their truck license plate reads UJJ 4004.

Angie Cartwright (Sheila DeWindt). Angie is the only African-American member of the team. She is gorgeous, very feminine and not as actively involved on cases as the other girls. She spends most of her time moonlighting as a radio disk jockey called "The Nightingale." Her truck license plate reads 040 3777.

Samantha Smith (Barbra Horan) and **Cindy Grant** (Sherilyn Wolter) share an 18-wheel truck with the license plate XTR 7162. Samantha is sweet and very feminine and not prone to violent confrontations. While she does accompany B.J.

on assignments, she usually looks after Bear while B.J. investigates. Cindy is the daughter of Rutherford T. Grant, a corrupt police officer who heads S.C.A.T. (Special Crime Action Team), Southern Division of the L.A.P.D. Cindy despises her father's corrupt ways and is placed in a very difficult situation: she works for B.J. and B.J. is seeking a way to end Rutherford's reign of crime and corruption. Cindy is easily upset and a bit irrational. She has knowledge of criminal law and often warns B.J. that what he is about to do to crack a case could be considered as breaking the law (as B.J. often has to break the rules to get the job done). Cindy always sides with B.J. over her father because she knows that what he is doing is totally against the law.

117. Black Jack Savage, *The 100 Lives of Black Jack Savage*, NBC, 1991. Played by Stoney Jackson (pilot), Steven Williams.

Black Jack Savage is a ghost who must save 100 lives to redeem himself to find eternal peace. Black Jack was born in the 17th century as Niamu in the Monokanga Kingdom of Africa. When he was a young man, Portuguese slave traders abducted him. One night, an intoxicated sailor forgot to lock Niamu's chains. Niamu freed himself, began a revolt and killed 25 sailors. He set the slaves free and retreated to the Caribbean island of San Pietro, where he built a home he called Blackbird Castle. The British press dubbed him "Black Jack Savage" for killing the sailors. Niamu became a pirate and sailed the seas on his ship the *Blackbird*, pillaging and killing 100 people in the years that followed. Black Jack was eventually captured and hanged. His ghost is now cursed to remain in Blackbird Castle until he can save an equal number of lives to make up for those he took.

Black Jack is incapable of affecting physical matter. He can possess lower life forms and fears Snarks—"Little Dirt Bags" that will send him to Hell if he leaves the castle (Snarks are actually ghostly creatures in a different dimension. If they catch Black Jack they can transport him to Hell by bringing him to the roots of the tree where he was hanged; the roots lead to Hell).

See also: Barry Tarberry (a wanted fugitive who now owns Blackbird Castle and to save himself from Hell, must help Black Jack save 100 lives).

118. Blair Warner, *The Facts of Life*, NBC, 1979–1988. Played by Lisa Whelchel.

Blair Warner is a student at the Eastland School for Girls in Peekskill, New York. She is the daughter of Steve and Monica Warner and was named after her grandfather, Judge Carlton Blair. Blair is heir to Warner Textile Industries and says "I'm best at spending money."

Blair is the most beautiful girl at Eastland ("I'm cashmere and caviar"). She was voted Eastland Harvest Queen and received a blue ribbon for being Most Naturally Blonde. She sold cosmetics (as a Junior Beauty Ambassador) for Countess Calvet Cosmetics and won the Small Business-woman's Association Award for inventing contour top sheets. Blair reads *Vogue* magazine and is a member of the Fur of the Month Club. She has a horse named Chestnut and is hoping to become a lawyer.

Blair worked at Edna's Edibles, a gourmet food shop at 320 Main Street, and at Over Our Heads, a novelty shop (both of which were run by Edna Garrett, the school's former dietician). Blair next attended nearby Langley College and was a member of the Gamma Gamma Sorority. The last episode found Blair becoming head mistress of the Eastland Academy when she purchases the school to save it from bankruptcy.

The ABC TV movie, *The Facts of Life Reunion* (November 18, 2001) reveals that Blair is now the owner of the Warner Park Hotel in New York City. She is also married to a real estate tycoon named Tab Warner (making her Blair Warner-Warner).

See also: Edna Garrett, Jo Polniaszek, Natalie Greene, Tootie Ramsey.

119. Blanche Devereaux, *The Golden Girls,* NBC, 1985–1992. Played by Rue McClanahan.

Blanche Elizabeth Devereaux proudly boasts that her initials spell *BED.* She is totally liberated and flaunts her sexuality to get what she wants from men. Blanche lives at 1651 Richmond Street in Miami Beach, Florida, with three women over the age of fifty: Rose Nylund, Dorothy Zbornak and Dorothy's mother, Sophia Petrillo. Blanche, over 50 herself, insists she is 42 "because living with women who look older than me makes it look possible." Blanche is eager to show cleavage and is known to have had many affairs. She was born in Atlanta, Georgia, and is a Baptist. She works as a museum curator and is divorced from George Devereaux (Blanche's maiden name is Hollingsworth). She has a sister (Virginia), a brother (Clayton), two children (Charmayne and Rebecca), and a grandchild, Melissa (by Rebecca). Her mother is deceased; her father is Curtis "Big Daddy" Hollingsworth.

Blanche's favorite dessert is chocolate cheese-cake. In 1989 she was chosen as the Citrus Festival Queen and a year later became a model; her picture appeared on the cover of the Greater Miami Penny Saver for Ponce de Leon Itching Cream. Each year on her wedding anniversary, Blanche tries on her wedding gown. If it doesn't fit she drastically diets to regain her figure. Blanche was a member of the Alpha Gams Sorority House in college and her favorite hangout is the Rusty Anchor Bar.

See also: Dorothy Zbornak, Rose Nylund, Sophia Petrillo.

120. Blossom Russo, *Blossom,* NBC, 1991–1995. Played by Mayim Bialik.

Blossom Russo "is the perfect combination of a little sugar and a little spice." She is 13 years old and lives with her father, Nick Russo, at 465 Hampton Drive in Southern California. She has two brothers, Anthony and Joey; her mother, Madelyn, was married to Nick for 20 years. She left the family to pursue her dream of becoming a singer in Europe.

Blossom first attended the Crestridge School for Girls, then Tyler High School when she discovered they had a better band (she plays trumpet—"a little bit classical, a little bit jazz"; she hopes to become a musician like her father). Blossom sleeps with her ALF doll, drinks Bailey's Diet Cola and "became a woman" in the first episode (as her friend, Six, said "Blossom blossomed"). Blossom is called "a borderline babe" by her brother, Joey ("You're in the Honor Society, you play the trumpet, but you haven't been visited by the hooter fairy yet").

Blossom is very smart and hates people who show a lack of intelligence. She has a scar on her chin (as the result of falling off the monkey bars) and as a kid had a pet cat (Scruffy) and a teddy bear (Dwight). Blossom won the National Spelling Bee and loves green peppers and artichoke hearts as a pizza topping. When she gets upset she eats ice cream and pound cake. The last episode finds Blossom being accepted by the following colleges: UCLA, Berkeley, Harvard and Northwestern. She chooses to attend UCLA.

See also: Anthony Russo, Joey Russo, Nick Russo, Six LeMeure.

Bo Duke *see* **Daisy Duke**

121. Bob and Carol Chase, *Quintuplets,* Fox, 2004–2005. Played by Andy Richter, Rebecca Creskoff.

This entry also contains information on their quintuplet children: Paige (Sarah Wright), Penny (April Matson), Parker (Jake McDorman), Pearce (Johnny Lewis) and Patton (Ryan Pinkston).

Bob and Carol Chase are a happily married couple who live at 3 Barrington Drive in Nutley, New Jersey. Bob sells office cubicles for a living and he and Carol met and fell in love in high school (North Nutley High, where Bob was in a band called the Black Sparrows and never achieved a grade higher than a C). Carol had high hopes of studying dolphins after college but her pregnancy stopped her (in another episode she says she had been working as an editor in a publishing house). She had taken fertility drugs and as a result became the mother of quintuplets in 1989 (as Bob says, "I know five seems like a lot but we'll get through this horrible, horrible nightmare"). While Bob and Carol received much attention, it was Carol who became the neighborhood celebrity: "People waved at me and called me 'The Mom of the Quints'"). Bob is a sports fanatic and would rather watch a Knicks basketball game than have a romantic encounter with Carol upstairs. To find serenity from the family, Bob has constructed a secret room in the backyard that he calls "Camp Bob." At Christmas time Bob and Carol are always short of cash and give their children drawings of what they will get for presents. On the day after Christmas, Bob and Carol shop for the items on sale and the family celebrate Quintmas.

Paige. Paige is a very beautiful blonde who is also a bit dense (Penny calls her "Bimbo the Clown"). She is 15 years old and attends North Nutley High School (as do all the quints). If Paige knew what a sexpot was she would be one. She dresses to be alluring but doesn't realize how much "damage" she does when boys see her. Paige is not too work oriented. When it comes to school projects she chooses to work with a nerd (for Paige, filing her nails is work).

Carol shudders when Paige wears white pants and will be around pizza sauce. She also doesn't like Paige to wear cleavage-revealing blouses when she goes to the movies because the air conditioning tends to give her a chest cold. Paige carries a knife in her purse and while you would never expect it from seeing her, Paige confessed, "That I had my nipples pierced." She also said, "I let strange men pay for my haircuts" and has constructed a scale model of the Nutley Mall so she can study it to know exactly where to go when there is a sale. Her expertise seems to be applying makeup and claims "I have great hair and personality." Paige is happiest at Christmas time because she enjoys caroling.

Penny. Penny (and Paige) use the line "We're cool teen detectives out to solve a crime" when they do not want their mother to know where they are going. Penny is very smart and says "I accomplish things by science — it can't be explained." Penny is rather self-centered and Carol has to pay for her affection and for her help cooking and cleaning. When Penny (as well as the other kids) lie and manipulate Carol, Carol seems to enjoy it "because we are doing things together." Penny loves to read (Paige loves to gossip and talk on the phone). Penny is shrewd, cunning and rather proud of herself when she manipulates someone to accomplish something. She claims to be real and intellectual. However, what she does sexually is a mystery as she said, "I have a video out there that I'm not too proud of" (and she's only 15). Her goal is to become a Broadway show director and is the only quint that wears glasses. Penny has anger issues and curses when she gets mad.

Pierce. Pierce is the weird child. He has a higher pitched voice than his brothers and seems to live in a world of his own (he functions in the real world but everything must make sense to him). He is opposed to any kind of violence; is an advocate of animal rights and is incapable of lying. He watches TV with the set turned off (views his reflection in the picture tube, which he finds fascinating) and talking to Pierce, "is like trying to nail Jell-O to a tree stump." Pierce will listen but forms opinions that apparently come from a source other than his own mind. He is a good student at school and is the basketball team mascot, Cugie the Cougar. Pierce needs to be prepared for every contingency and goes to extremes to make sure he is. At school he raises a pirate flag instead of his hand to answer a question. He is happiest when he does nice things for other people.

Parker. Parker considers himself the handsome brother of the family. He also considers himself a hunk and is considered a ladies' man at school. Parker took ballet lessons for three years and fears it will become his downfall if it leaks out. He is on the school's basketball team, the Cougars, and can't stand rejection.

Patton. Patton is the shortest of the Chase children. He is constantly teased for this but tries not to let it bother him. He has the hots for any girl he sees and honestly thinks he is a "cool dude" and a strikingly handsome ladies' man. Patton endlessly pursues girls but never succeeds. He worked as a shoe salesman in the mall (but only as a means by which to hit on girls). If Patton thinks something will impress a girl he will do it no matter how foolish it makes him look.

122. Bob and Emily Hartley, *The Bob Newhart Show*, CBS, 1972–1978. Played by Bob Newhart, Suzanne Pleshette.

Robert Hartley is a psychologist with an office in the Rampo Medical Arts Building in Chicago (his office phone number is 726-7098 and his office door number varies by episodes; it's both 715 and 751). Robert, called Bob, is a Virgo and 352-22-7439 is his Social Security number. He is married to Emily and lives in Apartment 523 in a building owned by the Skyline Management Corporation.

Bob is the son of Herb and Martha Hartley and served with the 193rd Combat Support Orchestra during the Korean War. Bob, who played drums in high school, was noted as having "the best wrists South of the 38th Parallel." Hoping to become a professional drummer, Bob went to New York after his army hitch and auditioned for the Buddy Rich Orchestra. While Bob thought he did great, Buddy had only three words for him: "You stink, man." Though depressed, Bob decided to enter college and study psychology.

Emily is the daughter of Cornelius and Aggie Harrison and was born in Seattle, Washington. She and Bob married on April 15, 1970, and Emily turned her love for children into her career of teaching. She first taught third grade at Gorman Elementary School; she is later principal of Tracy Grammar School.

123. Bob Collins, *The Bob Cummings Show*, NBC, 1955; 1957–1959; CBS, 1955–1957. Played by Bob Cummings.

Robert Collins, called Bob, is a swinging young bachelor who works as a fashion photographer. He was born in Joplin, Missouri, and is descended from Scottish ancestors. He lived in a house built by his grandfather in the early 1900s (the house was so drafty that Grandfather Collins died of pneumonia). Bob is a graduate of Joplin High School and Missouri State College (UCLA is also mentioned) and served a hitch in the Air Force during World War II. He developed an interest in flying and photography at an early age and made his love of photography his life's occupation (he also discovered a fascination for girls at the age of four, when he first began playing post office).

Bob lives at 804 Grummond Road in Los Angeles with his widowed sister, Margaret MacDonald (Rosemary DeCamp) and her teenage son, Chuck (Dwayne Hickman). Bob has a studio in Hollywood and runs Bob Collins Photography with the help of Charmaine Schultz (Ann B. Davis), called simply Schultzy.

Bob owns his own airplane (a rarely seen twin engine Beechcraft) and uses cologne called Moustache "that drives girls crazy." Bob considers the women he photographs "lumps of clay. I mold them into bright, shimmering butterflies. I give them grace, style and charm." Bob, called " The Casanova of the Camera," by Margaret, cannot resist an beautiful woman and insists he is a confirmed bachelor — "I'm married to my camera and marriage is a serious commitment. I need my time before settling down. I need to find the right person no matter how many girls I have to date to find her."

124. Bob McKay, *Bob*, CBS, 1992–1993. Played by Bob Newhart.

This entry also contains information on Bob's wife, Kaye (Carlene Watkins) and their daughter, Trisha (Cynthia Stevenson). *Mad Dog*, "Mankind's Best Friend," is a comic book drawn by Bob McKay, a cartoonist who lives at 134 Oak Street in Chicago with his wife, Kaye, and their daughter, Trisha.

Mad Dog is the story of Dr. Jeffrey Austin, a veterinarian who acquires the glands of his Doberman pinscher, Blackie, and gains the powers of a dog when a scientific experiment backfires. He adopts the alias of Mad Dog to battle evil. Bob created the concept in 1964 when he was dating Kaye. He sketched the idea on a napkin and sold it to a publisher. It never caught on and was discontinued. Bob then went into the greeting card business. In 1992 Ace Comics hired Bob to revise the comic and *Mad Dog* was born again.

Bob was born in Chicago and as a kid had a dog named Freckles (he now has a cat named Otto, who hides when company comes). Issue number one of *Mad Dog* is Bob's most prized possession and he still has one of his baby teeth ("It's a medical oddity"). Bob won the Buster Award (comic book achievement) for Best New Comic Creator and Artist (*Mad Dog* won for Best New Comic). He previously won the Doily Award for Best Creativity in the greeting card business. In 1993, when Ace Comics stops publishing *Mad Dog* ("The company didn't stand behind it," says Bob), Bob finds work at the Schmitt Greeting Card Company. Bob hates substitute foods (for example, egg substitute "because it's too chewy") and dislikes fresh-squeezed orange juice (he prefers Tang "because the astronauts drink it").

Kaye works at the Museum Shop and she and Bob attend Mass at the Our Lady of Constant Sorrow Church. Bob and Kaye were married in a hospital in Wisconsin (when they stopped at the side of the road to pick wild flowers, Bob was stung by 100 bees. He had an allergic reaction and married Kaye while recuperating in the hospital). Bob based Penny, the girl who assists Mad Dog, after Kaye.

Trisha works as Bob's colorist. She previously worked as a "wench waitress" at a pub (the Keg and Cleaver) and as a waitress at the World of Pies and Cowboy Tom's Fast Food. Every December Trisha jumps rope for a charity called "The Children's Medical Benefit — Jump for Joy for Girls and Boys." As a baby, Trisha slept through the night; she never experienced "the terrible twos." Trisha was always perky and followed the rules. "The one thing I did that was bad was to let my mind wander one Sunday while attending mass."

125. Bob Patterson, *Bob Patterson*, ABC, 2001. Played by Jason Alexander.

I Know More Than You Think and *I Still Know More Than You Think* are the two best-selling books of Robert "Bob" Patterson, a professional speaker who uses psychology to make people believe what they need to believe — "If you can envision it, you can get it." Bob was born in Los Angeles and is a graduate of UCLA. He is divorced from Janet, who walked out on him and "hates him more than life itself." Bob first worked in an appliance store selling big screen TV sets. Here he found a gift for talking people into buying something they really didn't need and decided to make it his life's career.

Bob is not everything people think Bob Patterson is. Bob works tirelessly to make people think he is the man he writes about — but it doesn't always work (some people would prefer it if Bob nodded instead of talked). Bob is insecure in his personal life (feels he is unappealing to women) and runs a company called Patterson Seminar Training (his website is *www.bobpatterson-online.com*). Bob strolls to work at 10:00 A.M. and is often mistaken for actor Danny DeVito. He becomes easily upset if anyone uses his private bathroom (it is his only place of refuge from work). Bob posed nude for a book called *Naked Power* and was nominated for (and lost) seven book award prizes. He made an infomercial with actress Connie Sellecca and hangs out at the Tip Top Bar and Grill. His company's slogan is "To the Top."

Bobby Brady *see* **Greg Brady**

126. Bobby Ewing, *Dallas*, CBS, 1978–1991. Played by Patrick Duffy.

Robert Ewing was born in 1952 and grew up in the oil fields of the Southfork Ranch in Braddock, Texas. He is the son of Jock and Ellie Ewing and is the younger brother of J.R., "The man everybody loves to hate."

Bobby, as he is called, first worked as a roadman for Ewing Oil (the company run by J.R.). He later becomes an executive (1978) then C.E.O. (1980). He also headed Ewing Oil Construction and in 1981 became a Texas State Senator. After a falling out with J.R. Bobby became the C.E.O. of a rival oil company (Petro) and finally the owner of Southfork in 1991.

Bobby was originally in love with Jenna Wade, his childhood sweetheart (she left him when she ran off to Europe). Bobby next dated then married Pamela Barnes, the daughter of the family's archrivals, the Barnes family. Bobby and Pamela's escapades made them the Romeo and Juliet of Braddock. They married in 1978, divorced in 1983 and married again in 1986. They are the parents of two children: Lucas (with Pamela) and Christopher (adopted).

See also: J.R. Ewing, Pamela Barnes, Sue Ellen Ewing.

127. Bobby Tannen, *Good Sports*, CBS, 1991. Played by Ryan O'Neal.

Robert Tannen, called Bobby and "Downtown" Bobby Tannen, is co-host of *Sports Central*, an information program on the Rappaport Broadcasting Systems ASCN (All Sports Cable Network). He also hosts *Sports Chat* (interviews) and *Sports Briefs* (updates) with Gayle Roberts.

Bobby is 42 years old. He was born in Miami and was the number one draft pick from the University of Miami (jersey 12) but quit football after two years to manage the career of his wife, singer-stripper Yvonne Pomplona. Three weeks later, following his divorce, Bobby made a comeback with the L.A. Rams (jersey 13). He next became an Oakland Raider and wrote the tell-all book *Panty Raiders*. When team member Lyle Alazado read the book "he broke Bobby's body and tore his face off." Bobby appeared in bandages on the cover of *Look* magazine with the headline "Bye Bye Bobby." He then attempted a recording career and became "Downtown" Bobby Tannen (his only album was "Downtown Sings 'Downtown' and Other Chart Busters — Including the Hit Single 'Wichita Lineman'"). He next worked as a pizza delivery boy for the Friends of Pizza when he was discovered by station owner R.J. Rappaport (who teamed him with Gayle). Bobby lives in an apartment at the Landmark Building in Los Angeles. He collects beer cans (he has 47 unopened brands from 98 countries). When Bobby scored a touchdown at Shea Stadium the organist would play the song "Downtown."

See also: Gayle Roberts.

128. Boss Hogg, *The Dukes of Hazzard*, CBS, 1979–1985. Played by Sorrell Booke.

Jefferson Davis Hogg, also called Boss Hogg and J.D. Hogg, is the totally corrupt commissioner, bank president and justice of the peace of Hazzard County, Georgia, a town he seeks to own but finds his schemes foiled by the honesty of the Duke family (Bo, Daisy, Luke and Uncle Jesse).

Boss was born in Georgia and was originally a moonshine runner. He saved, deceived and conned his way to the top. He now owns most of the town (his top priority is to acquire the Duke farm and sell it to the Crystal Mountain Brewery).

Boss's business enterprises include Road Hogg Towing, Hogg Used Cars, the Boar's Nest Bar and the town radio station, WHOGG. Boss sells Hogg Alarm Systems, Hoggoco Motor Oil, J.D. Shocks, the Hoggo Car Charger Kit, Hoggo Mufflers and Hogg's Happy Burgers ("The only burger that makes you straighten up and fly right").

Boss has a plaque on his office wall that reads "Do Unto Others Before They Do Unto You" and the "J.D. Hogg War Memorial — Dedicated to J.D. Hogg and Less Important War Heroes." He rides in a car called the "Gray Ghost" and has established the Hogg Celebrity Speed Trap (which catches famous country and western singers and forces them to perform at the Boar's Nest). In Hazzard County, Boss has declared that hunting season is "Three weeks for deer, two weeks for quail and open season on Dukes and moonshiners."

See also: Daisy Duke (for information on Bo, Daisy, Luke and Uncle Jesse Duke).

129. Brad Steele, *Once a Hero*, ABC, 1987. Played by Jeff Lester.

Brad Steele is a schoolteacher at Pleasantville High School in the town of Pleasantville. Brad uses this identity as a cover for his true being — Captain Justice, a daring crime fighter. Pleasantville is located in Comic Book World, a world beyond the third dimension. Brad, his girlfriend Rachel Burke (Dianne Kay) and her sister, Tippy (Dana Short) live the lives created for them by Abner Bevis, a real world artist who created a comic book called *Captain Justice*.

Captain Justice wears a red costume with blue gloves and a blue triangle on his chest (a gold *C.J.* is in the center). He doesn't wear a cape but has these powers: ability to fly, immunity to harm, incredible strength and infrared and X-ray vision. His sole purpose is to protect the citizens, especially Rachel and Tippy, from evil villains (like Max Mayhem) who plague Pleasantville.

Captain Justice eats only peanut butter and jelly sandwiches with milk "except when I see a ballgame at Pleasantville Stadium. Then I have two hot dogs and lemonade." The Captain always tells the truth and his moral code prevents him from killing anyone. He received the key to the city 103 times and "has a bad habit" (as criminals say) of showing up in the nick of time to save Rachel and Tippy. When Captain Justice comes to their rescue Rachel sighs "Captain Justice"; Tippy exclaims "The Crimson Crusader" (the other name by which he is known).

Brandon Walsh *see* **Brenda and Brandon Walsh**

130. Breanna Barnes, *One on One*, UPN, 2001 (current). Played by Kyla Pratt.

Breanna Barnes is the 14-year-old daughter of Flex Washington, a sportscaster at Baltimore TV station WYNX. Breanna was born on November 18, 1987, to an 18-year-old mother (Nicole) who was the poster girl for "Babies Having Babies — Don't Let This Happen to You." Although Flex and Nicole married, they later divorced. Breanna had been living with her mother until Nicole applied for a grant to study aquatic wild life. When Nicole was sent to Nova Scotia, Flex agreed to care for Breanna (whom he called "My newly found tax exemption").

Breanna attends McKinley High School, where she is a cheerleader and member of the drama club, the McKinley Players. She was crowned Harvest Queen of her sophomore class and can't understand why "with this Victoria's Secret type body and all this cuteness" she can only manage a C in home economics (she is smart, as she scored a 220 out of a possible 240 on her PSAT pre college tests).

Breanna uses Neutrogena and Dark and Lovely beauty products. When first introduced, Breanna was sensitive about her figure, especially her breasts (she was told "You have small boobies" by a girl at school). This was at age 14. By the age of 16 (2203), Breanna had developed and yearned to buy her bras at Victoria's Secret — but her father refused to let her, feeling they were too sexy for a young girl. When Breanna needed $400 for her school ring she stuffed her bra and found a job at Dinner with a Movie (where large breasted girls recite lines from movies as they serve). When Breanna found that her breasts were getting more notice than her acting ability she quit.

Breanna has ambitions to become an actress. Flex would like her to attend Maryland State University while her mother hopes she will attend Harvard. Breanna first worked as her father's intern at the TV station (he hoped to show her responsibility) then as the mascot for the Chicken Shack fast food store. She attempted to start her own business, Bu Bu (Buy Us Buy Us) with a $6.95 cell phone hat. Breanna's favorite president is Gerald Ford ("He was so clumsy and misunderstood") and *Save the Last Dance* is her favorite movie. Breanna had a dog named Petey and doesn't mind sharing the cheerleading spotlight with eight other girls "because I'm the cutest." Breanna likes living with her father "because he treats me like an adult" (her mother treated her like a child).

See also: Duane Odell Knox, Flex Washington.

131. Bree Van DeKamp, *Desperate Housewives,* ABC, 2004 (current). Played by Marcia Cross.

Bree Van DeKamp is a very beautiful and sexy woman who lives at 4354 Wisteria Lane in the perfect house in the perfect suburb of a city called Fairview. Bree is married to Rex and is the mother of Danielle and Andrew.

Bree is always impeccably dressed and appears all too perfect in everything she does. She despises loose ends and she always displays confidence in her sensual eyes. In addition to being considered the perfect wife and mother, Bree loves gardening (she is famous for having the best lawn in the neighborhood), makes her own clothes and even makes muffins from scratch (even prepares exotic meals for her family). Bree is a member of the Monthly Wisteria Lane Book Club and strange as it may seem, this delicate, extremely feminine woman is also a member of the NRA (National Rifle Association). Bree is a sentimental woman who enjoys each and every holiday the year has to offer. She most enjoys Christmas for the peace and joy the season offers.

Although Bree seems content all the time, she suffers from feelings of guilt. As a child she felt guilty for not getting straight A's; as a teenager, she felt guilty for letting her boyfriend sexually take advantage of her; as an adult she first felt guilty when it took her three weeks to send out thank you notes for her wedding gifts. Bree overcame these feelings of guilt by reading the *Bible.* Bree loves her children but can't forgive them for growing up so quickly. Her car license plate reads EPW 755.

See also: Edie Britt, Gabrielle Solis, Lynette Scavo, Susan Mayer.

132. Brenda and Brandon Walsh, *Beverly Hills, 90210,* Fox, 1990–1998. Played by Shannen Doherty, Jason Priestley.

This entry also contains information on Kelly Taylor (Jennie Garth), Donna Martin (Tori Spel-

ling) and Andrea Zuckerman (Gabrielle Carteris), friends of Brenda and Brandon.

Brenda and Brandon are the fraternal twin children of Jim and Cindy Walsh. They were born in Minneapolis, Minnesota, in 1984 and lived at 1408 Walnut Avenue. When they turned 16, Jim, an accountant for the firm of Powell, Gaines and Yellin, received a transfer to the West Coast. The family now lives at 933 Hillcrest Drive, Beverly Hills, California 90210.

Brenda. Brenda is four minutes older than Brandon. She now attends West Beverly Hills High School and is a straight A student (at her prior school she was a member of the drama club and the student council). She has a keen interest in acting and hopes to become an actress one day.

Brenda is beautiful but feels "I'm not California beautiful" and desperately wants to change her image and become as popular as her girlfriends. As the series progressed, Brenda learned to accept herself for who she is. As for clothes, Brenda is not rich and "I make for free what the trendy stores sell for $150."

Brenda has a porcelain doll collection and uses Colgate brand toothpaste. She is deathly afraid of heights and is totally honest. As a kid she rode a horse named Sylvester. When she was thrown and too frightened to ride again, her father bought her a plush horse she named Mr. Pony (she also has a plush lion called Mr. Lion). Brenda had four dogs in Minnesota: Ruby (who was uncontrollable), Bruno (who bit the mailman), Mr. Pepper (who froze to death. Brenda was nine years old "and how was I suppose to know about wind chill factors?"), and Wally (a stray she adopted). Brenda played Juliet in her seventh grade production of *Romeo and Juliet. Keep It Together* is Brenda's favorite TV show and she acquired a temporary job at the local diner hangout, the Peach Pit (where she used the name Laverne); her father calls her "Beautiful."

Brandon. Brandon is also a straight A student. In Minnesota he enjoyed hiking near Gull Lake and was called "Mr. Popularity" at school. He was also a member of the swim team and wrote for the school newspaper. He has a Godzilla alarm clock and is the sports editor for the West Beverly High School newspaper, the *Blaze.* He has a 1965 yellow Mustang (plate 2BR1 645) and works as a waiter at the local diner, the Peach Pit. He also worked as a cabana boy at the Beverly Hills Beach Club during the summer of 1991 (in Minnesota he was a lifeguard at the community swimming pool). Jim calls him "Big Guy."

Kelly Taylor. Kelly is beautiful, fashion conscious and worships the sun. She is a rich, spoiled girl who has been called "The Rich Bitch" by some of the boys who have dated her at West Beverly High School. At the 1991 Junior Prom Spring Dance, Kelly was voted Spring Queen. She has a dog named Max and is forced to play parent to her divorced, man-hungry mother Jackie, whose questionable moral practices she sometimes finds herself copying. Kelly longs for a decent relationship but her slutty reputation often prevents her from finding happiness. She and Brenda take exercise classes at Bob Silvers World.

Donna Marie Martin. Donna is tall, very pretty and very bright but suffers from a learning disability that makes it extremely difficult for her to score well on written tests under pressure (some teachers realize this and allow her to take oral exams). Donna lacks confidence and does not always make a good first impression when she tries to impress a boy. Donna fantasizes about what it would be like to be beautiful and popular. Her favorite movie is *Pretty Woman* and she fantasizes about "running away, becoming a hooker and meeting Richard Gere on Hollywood Boulevard." She was born on December 25, 1974, and has an account at the National Bank of the West. The Peach Pit (a diner) and the nightclub After Dark are her Kelly and Brenda's hangouts.

Andrea Zuckerman. Andrea is the editor of the West Beverly High newspaper, the *Blaze*. She is also Brandon's on and off girlfriend. She (and Brenda) are volunteers at the Rap Line (to help troubled students) of the local social services center. Andrea is a very sweet girl who will give of herself to help others. She is also attending West Beverly Hills High illegally. She lives outside the school district and lies about where she lives so she can attend to take advantage of its programs. Andrea is the classic overachiever. The Peach Pit (a diner) and After Dark (a nightclub) are her hangouts.

133. Brennan Mulray, *Mutant X*, Syn., 2001–2004. Played by Victor Webster.

Brennan Mulray is a product of genetic manipulation. He is one of the "children" of Adam Kane, a bio-chemist who sought to create a world of perfect men and women. Brennan, like mutants Shalimar Fox and Emma DeLauro, was enhanced as an infant (his genetic profile was BK 401 5678 Q61789). Brennan realized at an early age that he was different. He grew up on the streets and used his emerging powers to commit petty crimes. As he grew older, the crimes became more serious (he was arrested for breaking and entering and grand theft auto). When Adam became aware of his actions, he stopped his life of crime and recruited him as an agent for Mutant X, a group of genetically enhanced people who battle evil.

Brennan has the power to control electricity. He can discharge such bolts from his fingers and create a ball of energy by placing his hands in a circle. The electricity also gives Brennan incredible strength and a split second burst of invisibility to pass through solid objects. Brennan now hopes to use his powers for good and put his past behind him.

See also: Adam Kane, Emma DeLauro, Lexa Pierce, Shalimar Fox.

134. Bret and Bart Maverick, *Maverick*, ABC, 1957–1962. Played by James Garner, Jack Kelly.

Bret and Bart Maverick are brothers. They are gentlemen gamblers who roam the Old West in search of rich prey. They are also cowards, but more often than not, help people in trouble. Bret and Bart are unconventional, self-centered and untrustworthy but they possess a genius for outwitting con men.

Although Bret and Bart served in the Confederacy during the Civil War, they became Union soldiers when they were captured (they figured it would be better to help the enemy than spend time in a Union prison camp). As "Galvanized Yankees" (as Bart put it), they were assigned to keep the Indians under control out west. At this same time, it was mentioned that another Maverick, Cousin Beau, became a disgrace when he was honored as a hero. The head of the family, Beauregard "Pappy" Maverick, instilled in his sons cowardice and con artist genius. When Pappy, as he was called, learned that his nephew Beau did something to bring honor to the Maverick name, he branded him "the white sheep of the family" and banished him to England. (Actually, Beau had been captured. While playing poker with a Union general, the Confederates attacked the camp. When the general lost the game and said "Son, I give up," Confederate troops entered the tent and Beau was credited with the capture.) To make up for this family disgrace, Beau (Roger Moore) spent five years tarnishing his "good name" and was actually brought on in 1960 (to 61) to replace James Garner, who left the series.

It is against a Maverick's principles to drink alone and they have one serious vice — curiosity. The Mavericks are from Little Bent, Texas, and a sheriff is not their best friend. A Maverick is not fast on the draw (if there is a way to get out of a gunfight, they will find it). Bret promised Pappy that on his thirty-eighth birthday he would find a wife and raise 12 Mavericks. Bart, who enjoys a good cigar, often says "Sometimes it frightens me what I'll do for money." Bret calls Bart "Brother Bart."

In addition to many proverbs (for example, "As my Pappy would say, no use crying over spilled milk, it could have been whiskey"), Pappy left each of his sons a $1,000 bill (which they each pin to their shirt pocket) and these profound words of wisdom: "Never hold a kicker and never draw to an inside straight."

In the series update, *Bret Maverick* (NBC, 1981–82), James Garner returned to the role of Bret Maverick. He was said to be "Twenty years older and forty years wiser." He ended his life of roaming and settled in the town of Sweetwater, Arizona, where he runs the Red Ox Saloon and the Lazy Ace Ranch — both of which he won in a poker game.

135. Brett Sinclair, *The Persuaders*, ABC, 1971–1972. Played by Roger Moore.

Brett Sinclair is a titled English Lord "who was born with a silver spoon in his mouth and all he does is lick the jam from it." Sinclair was a once proud and noble name that stood for justice and defended freedom — but that was before immense wealth changed it.

Brett was born in England and attended the finest universities. He is a first class athlete, a connoisseur of the arts and a gourmet with a lusty taste in wine and women. Money means nothing to him. He has it so he spends it. He can speak seven languages but all he uses them for is to order drinks in the various high-class bars he frequents (his favorite drink is a Creole Scream — "next to women and dogs, a man's best friend is a Creole Scream").

A Creole Scream consists of a jigger of white rum, a dash of bitters, chilled vermouth and a measure of grenadine. It is then mixed, crushed ice is added and the contents are strained and poured. But is it topped off with one or two olives? Brett insists one; his friend, Danny Wilde claims it is two. Brett and Danny couldn't agree, fought, were arrested, and saved from doing time by Judge Fulton (Laurence Naismith) who offers them a choice: work for him and bring criminals to justice or serve time in jail. Naturally they choose to work for the judge (being a playboy and the thought of spending his nights in jail convinces Brett to work with Danny and help the judge).

See also: Danny Wilde.

136. Brian Miller, *Still Standing*, CBS, 2002 (current). Played by Taylor Ball.

Fourteen-year-old Brian Miller lives at 209 Evergreen in Chicago with his parents, Bill and Judy, and his siblings, Lauren and Tina. Brian first attended the Radford Academy Grammar School then Thomas Jefferson High School (also the alma mater of his parents). Brian is excessively neat and quite intelligent. He is a member of the school's debate team and engineering, chess and math clubs. He is called "Bry Bry" by his mother and built a working robot her called Mr. Nuts and Bolts. Brian is also a member of the Cougars, the school's football team (first as a player, then cheerleader, mascot and finally team statistician). Brian's first job was that as salesman in a bookstore.

See also: Bill Miller, Judy Miller, Lauren Miller.

137. Bridget Hennessey, *Eight Simple Rules for Dating My Teenage Daughter*, ABC, 2002–2005. Played by Kaley Cuoco.

Bridget Erin Hennessey is the 16-year-old daughter of Paul and Cate Hennessey. She lives on Oakdale Street in Michigan with her sister, Kerry, and brother, Rory.

Bridget is a sophomore at Liberty High School. She is a C student and studies for final exams by reading the first and last lines of a paragraph. When she was in the second grade, Bridget drew a picture of a six-legged dog that her parents placed on the refrigerator door. Her second posting occurred 10 years later when she scored a 92 on her high school aptitude test and beat ultra smart Kerry (who scored an 88). Bridget is a member of the school's drama club (she starred in *The Diary of Anne Frank*), the pep squad, the tennis team ("The tennis shorts make me look sexy") and the chorus.

Bridget is a material girl and believes she can do no wrong ("I'm a winner at everything"). She can't resist new clothes ("I look good in anything") and is obsessed with her looks ("I'm a goddess"). She believes she can get through life by her looks alone. She loves Valentine's Day ("It's a day set aside for beautiful girls") and wears what she calls "Boob dresses, leg dresses and butt dresses" (Paul, however, never lets her leave the house "dressed like that"). Bridget also wears sexy, cleavage revealing bras and thong panties but will not wear such clothes to church. She has her nice bras but "I can never find my respectable panties" (Paul doesn't object to Bridget's lingerie and allows her to wear it as long as she doesn't make it obvious).

Bridget's favorite dinner is macaroni and cheese. She has an interest in music and took up the drums (because it was the only instruments that came in a color she liked — purple). She has a dream of performing in an all-girl band. Bridget is a fanatic about her makeup and has trouble with eye shadow "because of my combination skin." Bridget has an 11:30 P.M. curfew and is addicted to speaking on the phone. She has set her goal to become a beautician and had a first job as a salesgirl at a clothing store called Strip Rags; she later worked at the local YM/YWCA. Paul called Bridget "Bridge," "Beej" and "Cup Cake."

See also: Cate Hennessey, Kerry Hennessey, Paul Hennessey, Rory Hennessey.

138. Brisco County, Jr., *The Adventures of Brisco County, Jr.,* Fox, 1993–1994. Played by Bruce Campbell.

The time is 1893. Brisco County, Jr., is a latter day West bounty hunter. He was born in Boston and is the son of Brisco and Ruth County. As a child Brisco was fascinated by his father's occupation as a bounty hunter. His parents, however, did not want him to take that path; they groomed him to become a lawyer. Brisco obliged them and attended Harvard University. He majored in English and law but claims "I mostly learned drinking songs and how to unbutton women's unmentionables." After graduating, Brisco opened a law practice but soon felt it wasn't what he wanted. He craved excitement and the only way he knew to get it was to become a bounty hunter.

Brisco is looking for "the coming thing. It's 1893 and we're only seven years away from the new century. If I knew what the coming thing was I wouldn't be looking for it." Brisco is rather flamboyant and works for the Tycoons, a society of wealthy San Francisco businessmen who have hired him to capture John Bly, an outlaw who is plaguing their railroad operations. Brisco also has foresight. He talks about the future and predicts there will be trolley cars, electricity "and rockets charting the stars."

Brisco claims "I can out shoot and out ride anyone." He rides a horse named Comet (who likes green apples but "he don't know he's 'a horse. He thinks he's human and has to go where I go").

Brock Hart *see* **Reba Hart**

139. Bronco Layne, *Bronco,* ABC, 1958–1960. Played by Ty Hardin.

Bronco Layne is an ex–Confederate Army Captain who wanders from town-to-town fighting injustice in the post–Civil War West.

Bronco was born in Texas ("Down around the Old Panhandle") and "There ain't a horse that he can't handle, that's how he got his name." His grandfather was a "Yankee" and Bronco continued the proud family tradition by serving with the Texas Confederacy. When the war ended, Bronco returned home to become partners with his friend, Enrique Cortez, in the Layne and Cortez General Store. But Bronco, who longed to travel, disliked staying in one place and left town "to go where the grass may be greener."

Bronco carries a Colt .45 with the inscription "Courage is the Freedom of Honor." He had a gold pocket watch that plays the song "Deep in the Heart of Dixie" and a cat he called Elmira (a reminder of his involvement in the Battle of Elmira). Inside the watch there is a picture of Redemption McNally, Bronco's one and only true love (they grew up together in Texas). Although he preferred to avoid trouble, Bronco refused to stand by and see others abused ("You've never seen a twister, mister, 'til someone gets him riled").

140. Brooke McQueen, *Popular,* WB, 1999–2001. Played by Leslie Bibb.

Brooke McQueen is one of the more popular girls at John F. Kennedy High School in Los Angeles. She is a member of the cheerleading team, the Glamazons, and is a reporter for the school newspaper, the *Zapruder Reporter.* With her blonde hair and slim figure, Brooke appears to be perfect. She is not. "I wish I had breasts that bounce and have a bad habit of starring at myself in the mirror" (thinking that she is fat).

Brooke was born in Los Angeles. When she was eight years old her mother abandoned her and her father. Brooke thought that because she was overweight, her mother left. Hoping to bring her mother back, Brooke went on a diet. She got herself down to 85 pounds — but she was too thin; she broke a rib when she sneezed. Her mother never returned. Brooke is now very weight conscious and constantly watches what she eats.

Brooke talks in her sleep. She is also a member of the Honors Society at school and was a Homecoming Queen. She enjoys hanging out with her friends at the Coffee Shop and at a diner called Roscoe's. Although she is as smart as she is beautiful, an aptitude test revealed that Brooke should prepare herself to be a rodeo clown.

See also: Mary Cherry, Samantha McPherson.

141. Bruce Wayne, *Batman,* ABC, 1966–1968. Played by Adam West.

Bruce Wayne is the alias of Batman, a mysterious caped crusader who battles evil in Gotham City. Bruce was born in Gotham City and is the son of millionaire industrialist Thomas Wayne and his wife, Martha. They live in Stately Wayne

Manor and are cared for by Alfred Pennyworth, the Wayne family butler.

One summer night when Bruce was 10 years old, his parents were the victims of a jewel robbery and killed. Bruce, suddenly orphaned, vows to get even — "I swear by the spirits of my parents to avenge their deaths by spending the rest of my life fighting criminals. I will make war on crime!"

Backed by his family's enormous wealth and cared for by Alfred, Bruce works in almost total isolation to become a master scientist and perfects his mental and physical skills. With Alfred's help, Bruce creates the world's greatest crime lab (later to be called the Batcave) beneath Wayne Manor.

Ten years later, on the anniversary of that tragic night, Bruce feels it is time for him to fulfill the promise he made. "I must have a disguise," he tells Alfred, "Criminals are a superstitious, cowardly lot. So my disguise must be able to strike terror in their hearts. I must be a creature of the night. Black, mysterious." Just then, Bruce and Alfred hear a noise at the window. They see a bat that has been attracted by the light. "That's it," says Bruce, "It's an omen; the perfect disguise. I shall become a bat!" Bruce then develops his Bat costume, his special utility belt and the Batmobile. Bruce soon becomes a legend ("The Caped Crusader") and the police are quick to use his help in apprehending criminals.

Bruce next establishes the Wayne Foundation (to support worthwhile projects) and becomes known as Millionaire Bruce Wayne, the mild-mannered, generous head of Wayne Industries. Bruce has a glass of milk and a sandwich after every Batman mission and never mixes fighting with eating.

See also: Barbara Gordon (two entries), Dick Grayson.

142. Buck Russell, *Uncle Buck*, CBS, 1990–1991. Played by Kevin Meaney.

Buck Russell is an insensitive, uncouth and ill-mannered man who cares for Tia, Maizy and Miles Russell, the children of his late brother (Bobby) and his wife (Margaret).

Buck is totally unprepared for the responsibility and solves family problems by accident. He drives a beat-up, muffler-smoking sedan with the license plate 521 214. His hangout is Rafe's Place ("Pool, Food, Friendship"). He is a Chicago Cubs fan and was the guest announcer at Wrigley Field on the TV show *Call an Inning with Harry*. As a kid Buck barely managed to graduate from grammar school. He would cut classes to learn the art of the con by the master con artist of his neigh-

borhood, Pete O'Halahan. Pete's hangout was the local drugstore and he taught Buck how to work scams, from three-card Monte to handicapping. Buck was expelled from high school for planting cherry bombs in the bathrooms. His only pleasure appears to be his yearly fishing trip to Wisconsin (where he stays in Room 13 of the Stark Weather Lodge).

See also: Maizy Russell, Tia Russell.

143. Bud Bundy, *Married ... With Children*, Fox, 1987–1997. Played by David Faustino.

Budrick Bundy, called Bud, is the son of Al and Peggy Bundy, "the shoe salesman and his wife" who live at 9674 Jeopardy Lane in Chicago (the address is also seen as 9764). He has one sibling, a sister named Kelly (who calls him "Rat Boy" and "Toad Boy" and claims he watches *Star Trek* reruns "to get a glimpse of Klingon cleavage").

Bud first attended Polk High School, where he was a member of the soccer team, the Rippers (he wore jersey 5). He next attended Trumaine College, where he was a member of the Gamma Gamma Sigma Pi Fraternity. Bud wants a girl but can never seem to attract any. He pretended to be the street rapper, Grand Master B to impress girls and uses Open Sesame after-shave lotion. He watches *Dateless Dude Late Night Theater* when he can't get a date and calls his cowboy pajamas, his love clothes. Bud reads the girlie magazine *Boudoir* and "became a man" at 18 when Al took him to the Nudie Bar.

Bud worked at the Department of Motor Vehicles but was fired for being a go-getter (tried to help people). He next became a chimney sweeper then a volunteer at the Community Service Center's Virgin Hotline (1-800-ZIPP UP). Bud also worked for a short time as King Roach in the Verminator TV commercial exhibit at the Chicago TV World Theme Park.

See also: Al Bundy, Kelly Bundy, Marcy Rhoades, Peggy Bundy.

144. Buddy Lembeck, *Charles in Charge*, CBS, 1984–1985; Syn., 1987–1990. Played by Willie Aames.

Buddence Lembeck, nicknamed Buddy, is simple-minded person who is best friends with Charles (no last name), a college student who babysits to earn money. Buddy was born in California but now lives in the dorm on the campus of Copeland College in New Jersey (he is banned from performing chemistry experiments and bringing live stock into the room). As a child, Buddy had a hand puppet he called Handie and in high school was voted Class Flake. He has an autographed Mickey Mantle baseball that he signed on behalf of Mickey (who wasn't around at the time). He is afraid of clowns (one scared him as a child) and tried to break a Guinness world record for smashing beer cans against his forehead but passed out after smashing 57 cans ("I could have done more if the cans were empty").

Buddy is a Leo and only takes courses with five or fewer books to read (any more and it will cause him to cheat). His major is political science; aptitude tests rated him as a Jack of no trades and best suited for jury duty. At Copeland, Buddy has his own radio program (*The Buddy Lembeck Show* on WFNZ) and is a member of the scuba club. In California Buddy had a dog named Kitty; he now has two pets: Lloyd (a lizard) and Arlo (an ant who lives in a plastic ant farm). Buddy believes singer Barbara Mandrell is in love with him (she sent him an autographed photo signed "Love, Barbara") and he claims he receives mind transmissions from the planet Zargon. The first thing Buddy does after getting up in the morning is take a nap. His favorite hangouts were first the Lamplight (a hamburger joint) then Sid's Pizza Parlor and finally the Yesterday Café.

See also: Charles, Jamie Powell, Lila Pembroke, Sarah Powell.

145. Buddy Sorrell, *The Dick Van Dyke Show,* CBS, 1961–1966. Played by Morey Amsterdam.

Maurice Sorrell, called Buddy, is Rob Petrie's co-worker, a comedy writer on *The Alan Brady Show.* Buddy has the ability to make a joke out of any word in the English language. He previously worked on *The Billy Barrows Show* and had his own TV series called *Buddy's Bag.* He is married to Fiona (called Pickles) and has a German shepherd named Larry. Buddy plays the cello at every opportunity and his favorite drink is tomato juice. He performs on occasion with co-writer Sally Rogers in a variety act called Gilbert and Solomon at Herbie's Hiawatha Lodge.

See also: Alan Brady, Laura Petrie, Ritchie Petrie, Rob Petrie, Sally Rogers.

Buffalo Bob Smith *see* **Howdy Doody**

146. Buffy and Jody Davis, *Family Affair,* WB, 2002–2003. Played by Sasha Pieterse, Jimmy Pinchak.

Called "The Runts" by their older sister, Cissy, six-year-old twins Buffy and Jody Davis reside with their uncle, Bill Davis, in Apartment 18A at 85 Park Avenue in New York City. The twins came to live with Bill after their parents were killed in a car accident in their hometown of Terre Haute, Indiana. Bill first enrolled Buffy and Jody in the Bairwood-Calder Academy on the Upper East Side. When Bill found the school's curriculum unsuitable, he enrolled them in the Dove Tail School (which caters to the individual child).

The guest room serves as Buffy and Jody's bedroom. Jody is the more mischievous twin and both appeared in their school play, "Winter Wow" (Buffy was a snowflake; Jody played the blizzard). Buffy is very sensitive and treasures her best friend, her doll, Mrs. Beasley, which was her mother's doll as a child (the doll was made in 1964 by Ziggy Toys and is actually a Curly Boots doll). Buffy doesn't like people to call Mrs. Beasley a doll—"she's my friend."

In the original CBS series (1966–1971) Anissa Jones and Johnnie Whitaker played Buffy and Jody Davis. Johnnie appeared in an episode of the new series on December 12, 2002 ("A Family Affair Christmas") as an actor (Kevin) Bill hired to play Santa Claus for Jody, who is sick with the flu.

See also: Bill Davis, Cissy Davis.

147. Buffy Summers, *Buffy the Vampire Slayer,* WB, 1997–2001; UPN, 2001-2203. Played by Sarah Michelle Gellar.

Buffy Anne Summers is a very special 16-year-old girl. She is "The Chosen One," the one girl in the world with the power to slay vampires and other evil creatures. Buffy has remarkable strength and agility and was born of a legend that is countless centuries old. It was at a time when evil ruled the world that the Shadow Men, mysterious and powerful forces for good, gathered to endow one girl with the necessary power to battle evil that surrounded them. From that moment on and for each generation that passed, one girl was chosen to become the Slayer.

Buffy is a sophomore at Sunnydale High School. She is the daughter of Joyce and Hank Summers and was born in Los Angeles, California, on May 6, 1979 (later said to be October 24, 1980). Buffy now lives at 1630 Rivello Drive in Sunnydale. As a child Buffy imagined herself as a super crime fighter she called Power Woman. She had a plush pig (Mr. Gordo) and a security blanket (Mr. Pointy). Buffy was fascinated with Dorothy Hamill and dreamed of becoming an ice skater.

Buffy likes cheese, Sunshine Crisp cereal and has a 2.8 grade average. When she turned 16, she discovered she was the Slayer and the one fate had chosen to protect her generation from evil.

Buffy is guided by her Watcher, Rupert Giles, a man with special abilities who has been chosen to help Buffy defeat whatever evil a Hellmouth dispenses (Sunnydale High is the center of a Hellmouth, a mysterious portal that attracts evil).

Buffy wished she were a normal teenage girl. Her strange behavior kept her out of the "in crowd" and instead bonded her with Willow Rosenberg and Xander Harris, outsiders who helped her and Giles battle evil. Buffy and her friends hang out at the Bronze, a nightclub for teenagers. Buffy's weakness is her inability to leave anyone behind — even if it means risking her own life. Buffy calls a new grouping of vampires "a fang club." After graduating from high school and before becoming a freshman at the University of Sunnydale, Buffy worked as a waitress at a diner called Helen's Kitchen.

At college Buffy resides in Room 214 of Stevenson Hall. She was first romantically involved with Angel, the vampire who helped her defeat evil. When Angel left Sunnydale to battle evil in Los Angeles, Buffy found romance with Riley Finn, a member of the Initiative, a secret government organization that hunts demons. She lost Riley when he was recalled by the military. Buffy next had an on-and-off relationship with Spike, a vampire who first wanted to kill her rather than love her.

Buffy's parents were divorced. When Joyce dies from a complication after an operation to remove a brain tumor, Buffy is forced to leave college to support herself and her sister, Dawn. Buffy held a number of odd jobs, including "slinging hash" at the Double Meat Palace before she found a permanent position as the guidance counselor at Sunnydale High School (helping students overcome their problems while still fighting demons; she says "I'm the thing monsters have nightmares about").

The January 27, 2004, episode of *Angel* informs viewers that Buffy had quit her job at Sunnydale High to live in Europe and become part of a team that trains new Slayers.

See also: Angel, Cordelia Chase, Dawn Summers, Rupert Giles, Spike, Willow Rosenberg, Xander Harris.

148. Bull Shannon, *Night Court*, NBC, 1984–1992. Played by Richard Moll.

Nostradamus Shannon, called Bull, is the tall, bald bailiff who serves in the courtroom of Harry T. Stone, a night court judge in New York City. Bull acquired his nickname from his mother who said "Bull" when she found out she was pregnant.

Bull's friends think "I'm dumber than dirt" despite the fact that he scored 181 on a judicial system I.Q. test. Bull was born in New York City and

as a young man worked as an usher at the Majestic Theater. He attempted to write a children's book called *Bully the Dragon* (but it scared kids). He then wrote *The Azzari Sisters: An Adventure in Fun, The Snake Pit of Chuckie's Mind* and *Bull on Bull*. When *Bull on Bull* was rejected by 426 publishers, he had it printed by the vanity press Random Author and bought enough copies (at $11 each) to make it a best seller.

Bull's favorite TV show is *The Smurfs* and he has a pet python named Bertha (he later has one named Harvey). Bull eats Frosted Neon Nuggets cereal for breakfast. His address is given as only Apartment 7 (there is a giant B on his front door). He has a concrete sofa ("durable, practical and easy to patch") that he made himself. The apartment is next to the subway line and shakes when a train passes.

Bull weighs 250 pounds and earns $320 a week. He uses lacquer thinner to remove the shine from his bald head and is a member of the Volunteer Father's Organization. When Bull gets depressed, he retreats to the Museum of Natural History to talk to the early man exhibit. The last episode finds Bull being taken to the planet Jupiter to become somebody — "The man who can reach items on their top shelves."

See also: Christine Sullivan, Dan Fielding, Harry T. Stone, Mac Robinson.

Buster Bluth *see* **Michael Bluth**

149. Byron Sully, *Dr. Quinn, Medicine Woman*, CBS, 1993–1998. Played by Joe Lando.

Rugged mountain man Byron Sully was born in Colorado in 1829; he now resides in the town of Colorado Springs. Sully worked as a miner and is compassionate to the Cheyenne Indians (he is good friends with the tribal chief and is learned in both the way of the Indian and white man). Sully (as he is most often called) married a woman named Abigail. It was at this time that Sully built a log cabin for her on the outskirts of town. Several years later, Abigail lost her life during childbirth — a tragedy that also took the life of their unborn child. (It is difficult to pinpoint dates for Sully's marriage. Abigail was said to have been born in 1839. She married Sully when she was 18 in 1857; Sully was then 28. A camera shot of Abigail's tombstone reveals that she died in 1865, which would make him a recent widower when he first meets Dr. Michaela Quinn, his future wife. Based on dialogue, Sully was a widower for several years when Dr. Quinn arrived.)

Despite the year, Sully abandoned his cabin when he lost Abigail and retreated to the life of a mountain man, earning a living selling skins and doing odd jobs. He also has a true friend, a wolf he calls Boy. Sully uses a tomahawk as a weapon and was afraid of horses (he finally rode when Dr. Quinn talked him out of his fear).

Sully was the first person to trust Dr. Quinn. They became close friends and married two years later in 1867 (they take up residence in the cabin Sully originally built for Abigail, which also doubles as Michaela's clinic; they later become parents of a daughter they name Katie). Sully later becomes the Personal Indian Agent in Colorado to President Grant. He last worked for the Bureau of Land Management (which sets aside land for national parks). His first assignment was to survey Yellowstone National Park.

See also: Michaela Quinn.

150. Caitlin Cross, *Nash Bridges,* CBS, 1998–2000. Played by Yasmine Bleeth.

Caitlin Cross is an inspector with the Internal Affairs Division of the San Francisco Police Department. She was born in San Francisco and is a graduate of Union High School and State University. Caitlin grew up in the posh Sea Cliff section and became interested in law enforcement at an early age as the result of her exposure to police dramas on television. After college Caitlin joined the San Francisco Police Academy and graduated with top honors. She first worked for the FBI but quit "when I couldn't tell lies from truths." Caitlin next worked an as analyst for the CIA, Russian Intelligence Division ("I analyzed documents all day long"; as a result, she can speak and read Russian). She resigned after five years when the Mayor of San Francisco hired her for her current assignment: oversee the procedures of the S.I.U. (Special Investigative Unit) of the S.F.P.D. It is here that she develops a romantic relationship with Captain Nash Bridges, the head of the unit.

Caitlin lives in an apartment at 440 California Avenue. Her eyes are listed as "Sultry Blue" on her driver's license and she is totally self-sufficient. Caitlin is beautiful and knows it, but she does not use that asset to accomplish things. She has a difficult time asking for help and hates it when Nash calls her "Sister" (for example, "I've got a hot lead for you, Sister, trust me"). Caitlin drives a Xebra Roadster electric car with the license plate XEBRA. She is also the coach of a Police Athletic League soccer team called the Cougars.

See also: Nash Bridges.

151. Caitlin Moore, *Spin City,* ABC, 1999–2002. Played by Heather Locklear.

Caitlin Moore is a stunning blonde who works as the campaign manager for Randall Winston, the Mayor of New York City. Caitlin was born in Vermont and majored in political science in college (she was President of the Young Democratic Society; another episode claims Caitlin was born in Massachusetts, attended Harvard and majored in psychology). She is divorced from Trevor Wolfe and uses her maiden name. Caitlin was also a contestant on the TV show *Star Search* but lost (an awful singer). She is a founding shareholder in Microsoft, likes jazz music, bike riding and going to the theater. Every two months Caitlin's mother, Jane, puts a personal ad in the paper (the *New York Post*) to find her a man (Caitlin is the last single girl in the family).

Caitlin lives in an apartment (5C) in Manhattan and first had a romantic relationship with Mike Flaherty, the Deputy Mayor, then Charlie Crawford, Mike's replacement. Caitlin's father deserted the family when she was six; her mother worked two jobs to support the family. Caitlin is a terrible liar and when she becomes nervous she compulsively cleans her hands. See Charlie Crawford for additional information on Caitlin.

See also: Charlie Crawford, Michael Flaherty, Paul Lassiter, Randall Winston, Stuart Bondek.

Caitlin Ryan *see* **The Girls of Degrassi**

152. Calleigh Duquesne, *C.S.I.: Miami,* CBS, 2002 (current). Played by Emily Procter.

Calleigh Duquesne is a ballistics expert for the Crime Scene Investigation Unit of the Miami Dade Police Department. Calleigh was born in Darnell, Louisiana, on February 28, 1974, and is five feet, three inches tall (she claims to weigh 105 pounds). She has a degree in physics from Tulane University and is also an expert on firearms and tool marks. Calleigh is single and speaks fluent Spanish.

Darnell is a rural town where Calleigh's once wealthy mother and father, a public defender, set up housekeeping. It was a mismatched marriage and Calleigh grew up amid their bickering and drinking. Her father did, however, teach Calleigh the ins and outs of a gun. She learned she was capable of doing everything a man could do and that upholding justice was the highest call of all. After graduating from college, Calleigh began her career as a street cop for the New Orleans P.D. Her knowledge of firearms earned her the nickname "The Bullet Girl" and was reassigned to the crime lab. Calleigh soon became a member of the Miami C.S.I. when its head, Horatio Caine, recruited her.

See also: Alexx Woods, Erik Delko, Horatio Caine, Tim Speedle.

Callie Everett *see* **B.J. McKay**

153. Callisto, *Xena: Warrior Princess*, Syn., 1999–2001. Played by Hudson Leick.

Callisto is a beautiful but extremely vengeful warrior of ancient Greece (she, like Xena, did not actually exist in either Greek or Roman mythology). Callisto was born in the village of Cirra and had a normal childhood. She enjoyed her family and the simple pleasures of her life in Cirra. She was a bright girl and learned much from her mother — how to keep house, how to cook, how to fend for herself and most importantly, she was being groomed to become the perfect wife (Callisto had contemplated marriage when she became of age). Her life changed drastically when she was a teenager. Xena's army invaded her village. Despite her reputation, Xena would not harm women or children. However, during the raid, a fire was accidentally started. Callisto managed to escape a fire that killed her family and destroyed her home. At that moment Callisto became filled with rage and vowed to destroy Xena for what she caused to happen.

While not explained, Callisto somehow managed to survive on her own. She honed her fighting skills and hatred as she grew to become as ruthless as the woman she hated. Callisto dresses in a rather provocative, bosom-revealing outfit and is an expert with a sword, as well as her fists. She is blonde, coy and has pity for no one. She has set her goal on killing Xena and that desire is her driving force. She destroys whatever stands in her way and feels she is non stoppable. She has killed many people (some just for fun) and has her followers — men who will go into battle and die for her. Callisto's attempts to kill Xena are the focal point of episodes that feature her (a recurring character who, through her devious deeds, became an immortal, then a god and finally an angel. She never achieved her goal).

See also: Gabrielle, Xena.

154. Candace DeLorenzo, *The Division*, Lifetime, 2001–2004. Played by Tracy Needham.

Candace DeLorenzo, called C.D., is a detective with the Homicide Division of the San Francisco Police Department. She was born in San Francisco and is 32 years old. She has been on the force since 1991 and is the chronic overachiever. Candace is totally devoted to her job, very professional and full of ambition (she wants to quickly move up the departmental ladder).

Candace expresses confidence in everything she does. She likes the idea of the power she has as a woman in blue and once she has her mind set on

something she is inflexible — she has to see it through. Candace is tough when she has to be — and feminine when the situation calls for elegance. Her ambitions often alienate her and she has few friends; but to those who are her friends, she is loyal and trustworthy.

See also: Jinny Exstead, Kate McCafferty, Magda Ramirez, Raina Washington, Stacy Newland.

Captain Justice *see* **Brad Steele**

155. Captain Liberty, *The Tick*, Fox, 2001. Played by Liz Vassey.

Janet (no last name given) is beautiful, single and lonely. She was born in a U.S. locale called The City and grew up admiring superheroes like Batman, Superman and Wonder Woman. After graduating from City College, Janet enrolled in Superhero School. She stood for justice and took the name Captain Liberty. When the U.S. government realized they needed to do something about crime, they hired Janet to be their symbol of everything that is good. Janet wears a gold costume with a cutout star on her chest to reveal cleavage. She wears a Statue of Liberty Crown and carries a plastic torch as a symbol of freedom. But Janet is not all sugar and spice. She keeps an array of weapons in her apartment and will not hesitate to use them to foil evil.

Janet is 29 years old and feels that her superhero status leaves her no time for romance (she constantly complains about being lonely). She drowns her sorrows at the Lonely Panda Bar and mentioned that she should learn to curtail her drinking as she was just out of rehab. To make extra money, Captain Liberty posed "buck naked on a Harley motorcycle wearing only boots" for a strange magazine called *Peek and Boom*.

See also: The Tick.

156. Captain Magenta, *Captain Scarlet and the Mysterons*, Syn., 1967. Voiced by Gary Files.

Captain Magenta (no other name given) is an agent for Spectrum, an organization that safeguards the Earth from alien invaders (all agents are named after the colors of the spectrum). Captain Magenta was born in Ireland in 2034. His family emigrated to America shortly after. Magenta was brought up in a poor New York suburb in an environment of poverty and crime. He worked hard at school, earned a scholarship to Yale and graduated with degrees in physics, electrical engineering and technology. Magenta was still not satisfied. He yearned for a life of adventure and big money and turned to crime. He soon became a big time operator and ruthless mastermind who controlled two-thirds of New York's crime organization. Spectrum's selection committee needed such a man, trusted and respected in the underworld, in their security division (someone to work on the inside and get into the heart of criminal activity). He was offered the job and accepted. The program is a puppet series filmed in Supermarionation.

See also: Captain Ochre, Captain Scarlet, Destiny Angel, Harmony Angel, Melody Angel, Rhapsody Angel, Symphony Angel.

157. Captain Ochre, *Captain Scarlet and the Mysterons,* Syn., 1967. Voiced by Jeremy Wilkins.

Captain Ochre (no other name given) is an agent for Spectrum, a 21st century organization that protects the world from alien invaders. All agents are named after the colors of the spectrum.

Captain Ochre was born in the U.S. and grew up as a normal child. He was an average student and did not excel in anything. He became fascinated by only one thing — aviation. He studied everything he could about flying and earned his pilot's license when he was 16 (in the year 2050). After graduating from high school, he went to work for the World Government Police Corps and was decorated for breaking up one of the most ruthless crime syndicates in America. When he turned down a promotion because he preferred action to paperwork, he was hired by Spectrum to become an agent. He is quick-witted and a brilliant conversationalist but has a bad habit of playing practical jokes. The program is a puppet series filmed in Supermarionation.

See also: Captain Magenta, Captain Scarlet, Destiny Angel, Harmony Angel, Melody Angel, Rhapsody Angel, Symphony Angel.

158. Captain Scarlet, *Captain Scarlet and the Mysterons,* Syn., 1967. Voiced by Francis Matthews.

Captain Scarlet (no other name given) is a man who cannot be killed. He is the top agent for Spectrum, a 21st century international organization that protects the security of the world. Its headquarters are on Cloudbase and all its male agents are named after the colors of the spectrum; women assist as glamorous pilots called Angels.

Captain Scarlet was born in England in the year 2036 and is from a family of distinguished soldiers. He was an exceptional student in school and possesses degrees in math, history and technology. He joined the military after college and received training as a field combat soldier. His skills as a soldier and his brilliant academic career

led the newly formed Spectrum to recruit him as one of their agents. It was during the initial development of Spectrum that Captain Scarlet would become extraordinary. It began when Spectrum was exploring the planet Mars and its inhabitants, the Mysterons, mistook their efforts as an unprovoked attack. They declared a war of revenge on Earth and felt they needed an agent on Earth to keep them informed of Spectrum's activities. They killed Captain Scarlet then restored his life. The captain absorbed Mysteron characteristics (invincibility) but failed to become one of them; he instead became their indestructible enemy.

Captain Scarlet is a professional agent and carries out orders immediately and efficiently. He is popular with all the Spectrum agents, especially the Angels. The program is a puppet series filmed in Supermarionation.

See also: Captain Magenta, Captain Ochre, Destiny Angel, Harmony Angel, Melody Angel, Rhapsody Angel, Symphony Angel.

159. Carl Kolchak, *Kolchak: The Night Stalker,* ABC, 1974–1975. Played by Darren McGavin.

Carl Kolchak is a newspaper reporter who believes in only one thing: finding stories and reporting them to the public. Unfortunately Carl writes about supernatural-based stories that are never seen by the public; they are lost, destroyed or suppressed by his editor Tony Vincenzo (who believes nobody would believe the vampires, werewolves, mummies and other unearthly creatures Carl claims are real).

At first sight Carl appears to be wearing clothes that are wrinkled and out of style (he wears off white tennis shoes, battered seersucker suits and a straw boater hat). He first worked for the Las Vegas *Daily News* (in the 1972 TV movie *The Night Stalker*) then for the Seattle, Washington *Daily Chronicle* (in the 1973 TV movie *The Night Strangler*). He found his way to Chicago for the TV series and became a reporter for the Independent News Service (I.N.S.), a low budget wire service (supplies stories to newspapers).

Carl risked his life to write the stories nobody would ever read. He is a fast-talking, wise cracking crusader whose stories would normally start off with a tip or by stumbling upon a crime. His further investigation would involve him with the bizarre creatures that he would inevitably have to destroy to survive. Carl is, if nothing else, relentless. If he felt there was a story to tell he would go to all lengths to tell it. Dumb luck was Carl's friend and combined with his persistence and wits, he was able to overcome the most bizarre of circumstances.

160. Carl Winslow, *Family Matters*, ABC, 1989–1997; CBS, 1997–1998. Played by Reginald Vel-Johnson.

Carl Otis Winslow and his wife, Harriette, live at 263 Pinehurst Street in Chicago, Illinois. Carl is a sergeant (later lieutenant) with the Chicago Police Department; Harriette worked originally as the elevator operator for the Chicago *Chronicle*; later as the paper's security director. They are the parents of three children (Eddie, Laura and Judy) and are the next-door neighbors of Steve Urkel, the nerd with a crush on Laura.

Carl and Harriette met as students at Vanderbilt High School. Carl is with the Metro Division of the 8th Precinct (his car code is 2-Adam-12) and he held a temporary job as the WNTW, Channel 13, traffic reporter. In high school (mentioned also as being Kennedy High), Carl was in a singing group called The Darnells and was called "Rack and Roll Winslow" at the Corner Pocket Pool Hall. Carl has an account at the Investor's Bank and his car license plate reads L95-541. When Carl was a street cop he had a dog named Rex as a partner.

Carl believes he is a handyman, but is not as Harriette constantly tells him "Hire a professional." Carl and Harriette enjoy meals at Chez Josephine and Carl constantly finds his life plagued by Steve's antics (just when he doesn't think anything could get worse, Steve shows up). Jo Marie Payton played Harriette in all but the last episode, when it was played by Judyann Elder.

See also: Laura Winslow, Steve Urkel.

161. Carla LeBec, *Cheers*, NBC, 1982–1993. Played by Rhea Perlman.

Carla is the rather nasty waitress who works at Cheers, a Boston bar. She has been married three times and her full name is Carla Maria Victoria Angelina Theresa Appollonia Lozupone Tortelli Ludlow LeBec.

Carla was born in Boston and was a mischievous child; it was so bad that her parents enrolled her in Saint Clete's School for Wayward Girls. At the age of 16 Carla danced on the TV show *The Boston Boppers* and in 1991 she entered the Miss Boston Barmaid Contest. She "became nice for the duration" and won the Miss Congeniality Award. Carla was named after her grandmother's stubborn mule and as a kid was called "Muffin" by her brothers (who stuffed her ears with yeast and tried to bake her face). Carla first worked at a bar called the Broken Spoke before acquiring the job at Cheers.

Carla has eight children, all of whom are known to roll drunks. Five (Anthony, Sarafina, Lucinda, Gino, Anne Marie) are by her first husband, Nick Tortelli; Ludlow, by her second husband, Dr. Bennett Ludlow; and twins Elvis and Danny by her third husband, Eddie LeBec.

Carla's humor is always at someone else's expense ("It makes me laugh"). She used the "Le Mans" method of childbirth ("I screamed like a Ferrari") and refused to follow a family tradition by giving her first-born son (Anthony) her father's name and her mother's maiden name (which would have made him Benito Mussolini). Carla can be reached by phone at 555-7834.

See also: Cliff Claven, Diane Chambers, Ernie Pantusso, Norm Peterson, Rebecca Howe, Sam Malone, Woody Boyd.

162. Carlton Banks, *The Fresh Prince of Bel Air*, NBC, 1990–1996. Played by Alfonso Riberio.

Carlton Banks, the son of Philip and Vivian Banks, lives in fashionable Bel Air, California. He was born on August 4, 1974, and as a child had a dog named Scruffy. He first attended the Bel Air Academy and has a 3.9½ grade point average. He is a member of the poetry and glee clubs at school and has a dream of becoming a lawyer like his father. Carlton next attends the University of Los Angeles and hopes to get his law degree at Princeton University (his dream college; he feels he has a big advantage over every other applicant because he has been faxing Santa Claus for years requesting a Princeton entrance gift certificate. In another episode, Carlton mentions Harvard as being his dream law school).

Carlton works as the manager of The Peacock Stop, the college bookstore and believes he is a great singer and dancer (he hopes to break into show business as Carlton Banks, Soul Brother Number One. He embarrassed himself with his weird dancing techniques on *The Soul Train 25th Anniversary Show* on television). Carlton eats Fruity Pebbles cereal for breakfast and had his first crush on Tootie from *The Facts of Life*; he still hopes to meet her one day. Carlton firmly believes the world has gone crazy "since M&M's introduced the blue ones."

See also: Ashley Banks, Hilary Banks, Philip Banks, Will Smith.

163. Carmela Soprano, *The Sopranos*, HBO, 1999 (current). Played by Edie Falco.

Carmela Soprano is the wife of Anthony "Tony" Soprano, a ruthless wise guy for the DeMeo family. Carmela was born in New Jersey and is no stranger to mobster activity: her cousin, a wise guy, was gunned down in front of his own house. While Tony grew up in a violent atmosphere (his father was a mobster), Carmela had a relatively normal upbringing. But it was in high school, when she met Tony, that her life would change forever. Although popular and studious, Carmela set her sights on the uninspired Tony and gave up her dream of majoring in business administration at Montclair State University to marry him. They set up housekeeping in a fashionable and expensive home and became the parents of Anthony Jr. and Meadow.

Carmela is considered the First Lady of the New Jersey Mob. Although she appears to hate it, she also seems to enjoy the financial benefits of such a title. She is determined to raise her children on the straight and narrow but has become increasingly impatient with Tony's extra marital affairs. Despite the infidelity, Carmela feels she has a good life with Tony, better than she would have had without him.

See also: Janice Soprano, Meadow Soprano, Tony Soprano.

164. Carmen Lopez, *The George Lopez Show*, ABC, 2002 (current). Played by Masiela Lusha.

Carmen Lopez is the teenage daughter of George and Angie Lopez, a happily married couple who live at 3128 Rose Avenue in Los Angeles. Carmen is proud of her Cuban-Mexican heritage and tries to be the perfect daughter. She earns money first by baby-sitting then as a waitress on weekends at Carrello's, a local fast food burrito store.

Carmen has always been her father's little girl. In the seventh grade Carmen played Anna in the school play *The King and I*. George was there to "support her" (third seat from the rear and asleep). George was looking forward to Carmen becoming a teenager. He thought she would lock herself in her room and never speak to him. As it turned out, the bud blossomed into a very pretty young woman and everything in her life becomes a crisis—"and trying to solve them is wiping me out," says George.

Carmen would like to wear sexy lingerie like her girlfriends, but George (and Angie) refuse to let her buy any (he feels the day Carmen buys a thong will be the day he loses his little girl). Carmen would also like a cell phone—but that will not happen either (George doesn't fear her getting kidnapped "because my taxes pay for the Amber Alert"). Although she is allowed to have boys over to do homework, she is not permitted to date until she is 16. Carmen attends the Allendale School, where she is a member of the poetry club. She is also a talented dancer and attends dance classes. Carmen later attends St. Theresa's High

School when she is expelled from Allendale for behavior unbecoming of a student: 32 violations for showing public affection; six uniform violations (skirt too short); and eight tardiness violations.

See also: George and Angie Lopez.

165. Carol and Frank Lambert, *Step by Step*, ABC, 1991–1997; CBS, 1997–1998. Played by Suzanne Somers, Patrick Duffy.

Carol and Frank Lambert are a newlywed couple with children from previous marriages. Carol Foster was a widow with three children (Dana, Karen and Mark) and Frank Lambert was the divorced father of three children (Alicia, J.T. and Brendon). Frank and Carol were married at the Wedding Shack in Jamaica and set up housekeeping in their hometown of Port Washington, Wisconsin (at 201 Winslow Street).

Carol, whose maiden name was first mentioned as Baker, then Williams, operates Carol's Beauty Boutique from her home. She is neat (for example, she alphabetizes soup cans; irons Karen and Dana's lingerie) and tries to run the house on a schedule. Breakfast is ready at 7:30 A.M. and dinner at 6:30 P.M. Carol was born in Port Washington and is a graduate of Port Washington High School. She sang in a band and in 1971 was first runner-up in the Miss Small Curd Cottage Cheese Beauty Pageant ("I lost to a girl with bigger curds"). Carol was a cheerleader in high school (for the Wildcats) and hates to be called a nag by Frank.

Frank's first wife left him to become a lounge singer in Las Vegas. He and the kids are, according to Carol, "slobs." Frank is an independent contractor and owns Lambert Construction. He is a member of the Mallard Lodge and drives a GMC pickup (plate 129 815; later 527 P9) that he polishes with Royal Carnuba Wax (at $15 a can at Auto World). Frank attended Port Washington High School and was a member of the Sheboygan Super Bears bowling team and president of the Milwaukee Tile and Grout Association. Frank coaches the Cubs, a Little League baseball team. He hates to be called a liar by Carol. Frank uses a construction site story to relate aspects of life to the children; Carol uses a beauty parlor story.

See also: Alicia Lambert, Dana Foster, J.T. Lambert, Karen Foster.

166. Carol and Mike Brady, *The Brady Bunch*, ABC, 1969–1974. Played by Florence Henderson, Robert Reed.

Carol Ann Tyler Martin is a widow with three

daughters (Marcia, Jan and Cindy). Michael Paul Brady, called Mike, is a widower with three sons (Greg, Peter and Bobby). Carol and Mike are now married and they and their children live together in a four bedroom, three-bathroom home at 4222 Clinton Avenue in Los Angeles.

Carol (maiden name Tyler) was born in Los Angeles and attended West Side High School. She grew up as an ordinary child and was called "Twinkles" by her friends. She is content as a housewife and enjoys singing, needlepoint and cooking. She helps the children with their school projects, shops, cleans and with Mike's help, tries to give the children the right advice as they approach adulthood. Carol wrote an untitled article about her family for *Tomorrow's World* magazine.

Mike works as an architect (for an unnamed company) and designed the house in which the family lives. As a kid he was the checkers champion of Chestnut Street and in 1969 received the Father of the Year Award. Mike relaxes by playing golf and drives a sedan with the license plate TEL 635. Mike is the wise and understanding father who always thinks things out before teaching the children a valuable lesson about life. Mike also helped the children with their school projects and always put his family above everything else.

In the first series update, *The Brady Girls Get Married* (NBC, 1981; later called *The Brady Brides*), Carol is seen as an agent for Willowbrook Realty; Mike is still an architect. Carol held the same position in the 1990 CBS series update, *The Bradys*, but Mike is now retired and a Fourth District Councilman (his middle name was also changed to Thomas).

See also: Alice Nelson, Greg Brady (for information on Greg, Peter and Bobby Brady), Marcia Brady (for information on Marcia, Jan and Cindy Brady).

167. Carol Post, *Mister Ed*, Syn., 1960–1961; CBS, 1961–1966. Played by Connie Hines.

Carol Post is the wife of Wilbur Post, an architect and owner of Mister Ed, a talking horse. Fortunately, for Carol, she is unaware that the horse talks and is thus considered the normal one in the family (Mister Ed's antics cause Wilbur to be looked upon as a fool).

Carol is a gorgeous former dancer who measures 36-22-36. She was born in California and now lives at 17230 Valley Spring Lane in Los Angeles. Carol studied dance as a child and is a graduate of Hollywood High School. She worked as an instructor at Miss Irene's Dance Studio in Hollywood before marrying Wilbur and enjoys playing tennis. She takes pride and joy in her vegetable garden and is a member of the neighborhood Women's Club. Carol is self-conscious about her weight and tells people she weights 102 pounds when asked (she actually weighs eight pounds more).

Carol claims that "you really don't know a man until you marry him. I did and I still don't" (she is referring to all the nutty things Wilbur does because of Mister Ed). But no matter how much trouble Wilbur gets into, Carol assures him that she'll stand by him (Mister Ed assures Wilbur that if Carol should ever leave him, he'll clean and keep house for him).

See also: Mister Ed, Wilbur Post.

168. Carol Seaver, *Growing Pains*, ABC, 1985–1992. Played by Tracey Gold.

Carol Ann Seaver is the eldest daughter of Jason and Maggie Seaver, a psychologist and his wife, who live at 15 Robin Hood Lane in Huntington on Long Island in New York. She has two brothers (Mike and Ben) and a younger sister (Chrissy).

Carol is sensitive, smart and very pretty but wishes she could shed her brainy image and be thought of as "dangerous, provocative and sexy; not the kind of girl who is voted recording secretary, left in charge of the class when the teacher leaves and immaculate." Carol attended Wendell Wilkie Elementary School, Dewey High School and Columbia University. She dropped out of Columbia in 1990 to take a job as a computer page breaker at GSM Publishing. The following year she returned to Columbia to study law.

At the age of seven, Carol was a member of the Happy Campers. She was voted the 1988 Dewey Homecoming Queen and was president of the Future Nuclear Physicians Club in high school. Carol also worked with her father at the Health Clinic.

Carol's bedroom walls are decorated with posters of comics W.C. Fields, the Marx Brothers and Laurel and Hardy. When Tracey Gold developed an eating disorder (late 1991–early '92) her character does not appear; Carol is said to be in London attending school. The ABC TV reunion special, *The Growing Pains Movie* (November 5, 2000) finds that Carol had graduated third in her class at Columbia and is now helping people start new businesses on Wall Street in New York City.

See also: Jason and Maggie Seaver, Mike Seaver.

169. Carol Weston, *Empty Nest*, NBC, 1988–1995. Played by Dinah Manoff.

Carol Olivia Weston is the eldest child of Harry and Libby Weston. She lives with her father (a widower) and younger sister, Barbara, at 1755 Fairview Road in Miami Beach, Florida.

Carol is in her mid-thirties and has been divorced (from Gary) for five years when the series begins (the marriage was so bad that Carol had a nervous breakdown and required therapy to overcome it). Carol laughs too loud, can't sew and has a dream of opening a self-help bookstore. Carol is good with money but had ten jobs before the series began (she quit the last one because the air conditioning was too cold). Her first regular series job was that of Assistant Director of the University of Miami Rare Books Library (which she quit after three years to start her own catering business, Elegant Epicure).

Carol has fat attacks each spring and is a member of a support group called Adult Children of Perfectly Fine Parents. She has a difficult time finding boyfriends and tends to drop them abruptly. As a child Carol attended Camp Weemawalk and was called "Stay in Tent." After an affair with a destitute sculptor (Patrick Arcola), Carol gives birth to a baby she names F. Scott Weston (after her favorite author, F. Scott Fitzgerald).

See also: Barbara Weston, Harry Weston.

170. Carole Stanwyck, *Partners in Crime*, NBC, 1984. Played by Lynda Carter.

Carole Stanwyck is a gorgeous brunette who is partners with Sydney Kovack, an equally gorgeous blonde, in the Caulfield Detective Agency (which they inherited from their late husband, Raymond. Carole was Ray's first wife; Sydney, his second).

Carole was born in New York City and is heir to the Stanwyck Tea Bag Company. She acquired a great deal of money when she turned 21, but has squandered it and lost most of it through bad investments. Carole is a former debutante. She measures 38-25-37 and earns a living as a freelance photographer. Carole wears a size medium dress and is always elegantly attired. Her biggest worry is that she may be inappropriately dressed for an undercover assignment. Carole admits to one bad habit ("I'm always losing keys") and despises wearing an electronic bug during an assignment (which she places in her bra).

Carole is very concerned about her figure and will not eat junk food ("too many fats, calories and carbohydrates"). She has a strict dating rule and will never call a man for a night out ("I never did and I never will"). Carole lives at 654 Verona Drive and has a car with the license plate IFL 896. "We're not exactly Sherlock Holmes and Dr. Watson," says Carole, "but we get the job done."

See also: Sydney Kovack.

171. Caroline Duffy, *Caroline in the City*, NBC, 1995–1999. Played by Lea Thompson.

"Caroline in the City" is a daily newspaper comic strip written and drawn by Caroline Duffy and based on her experiences as a single girl living in New York City. Caroline was born in Wisconsin and attended the Webster Memorial Grammar School. When she was ten years old she had a dog named Sparky and developed a sudden interest in art. She wanted breasts "and I drew boobs on everything." Caroline got the figure she wanted in high school (Matheson High) but put her interest in art on the back burner. After dropping out of Wisconsin State College during her sophomore year, Caroline took a job as a copywriter but was fired shortly after for doodling; those doodles became the inspiration for her comic strip, which is now syndicated in 565 newspapers.

Caroline now lives in Manhattan (Apartment 2A) and has a pet cat named Salty. Caroline hates to miss a deadline because papers run two "Cathy" strips (and "I hate that girl," says Caroline). Caroline also designed cards for the Cassidy Greeting Card Company, which later became Eagle Greeting Cards. Caroline's favorite drink is ginger ale and Remo's Restaurante is her favorite eatery. The Dartland Food Company marketed a puffed wheat cereal based on the character called "Sweet Carolines." Caroline cooks chicken to impress a date but when she breaks up with a man, she goes to the museum to talk to the exhibits.

See also: Annie Spadaro, Richard Karinsky.

Caroline Holden *see* **The Girls of Baywatch**

172. Caroline Weldon, *Living Dolls*, ABC, 1989. Played by Deborah Tucker.

Caroline Weldon is a teen model for Trish Carlin (Michael Learned), a former super model who now runs the Carlin Modeling Agency from her home at 68th Street and Madison Avenue in New York City.

Caroline enjoys shopping for clothes at Bloomingdale's and the biggest challenge she faces all day comes in the morning — "What should I wear today?" Caroline attends Lexington High School and has little confidence in anything she does that is not related to modeling. She hopes for at least a C grade at school ("You don't know how hard I try") and tries to compliment people on everything — even if they are not deserving of a compliment.

Caroline has limited academic knowledge and tries to impress people with her knowledge of experience. She hates to read books for school and is a member of the Book on Tape Club. She relates aspects of life based on her favorite TV show (*Star Trek*) and believes in what she calls "Model Unity" ("we have to stick together when things get tough for one of us"). Caroline is a bit dense and tries to be bright but her efforts always fail (especially since she has to write notes on the palms of her hands to remember what she has to say to appear smart). She finds inspiration in music and the Care Bears.

See also: Charlie Briscoe, Emily Franklin, Martha Lambert.

173. Carolyn Muir, *The Ghost and Mrs. Muir*, NBC, 1968–1969; ABC, 1969–1970. Played by Hope Lange.

Carolyn Muir is the daughter of Emily and Brad Williams. She was born in Philadelphia in 1931 and earns a living as a free-lance writer. She was married (now a widower) and is the mother of Candy and Jonathan. Hoping to escape the memories of her life in Philadelphia, Carolyn uses her life savings to move to Schooner Bay, Maine, and into Gull Cottage, a quaint home that is haunted by the ghost of its builder, Captain Daniel Gregg (see entry for more information).

Carolyn is a devoted mother to her children. She tries to handle the problems they encounter with wisdom and understanding and never becomes harsh or hands out a stiff punishment. She encourages them to be themselves, respect other people and do the best they can even if they think their best will not please her.

Carolyn finds Gull Cottage to be the house of her dreams ("a dear, gentle, lovely little cottage") and Schooner Bay to be the perfect town in which to raise her children. She has adjusted to the fact that she lives with a ghost and is determined to remain despite the Captain's ramblings. Carolyn has made the Captain's former bedroom ("The Captain's Cabin") her bedroom. While Carolyn is a good cook, she and the family sometimes enjoy a meal at The Lobster House, the local restaurant. She assists the local community theater and attempted to write a book dictated by Captain Gregg called *Maiden Voyage* (when the Captain added spice to the book by making Carolyn look promiscuous, she objected and the book was never published).

See also: Daniel Gregg.

174. Carrie Bradshaw, *Sex and the City*, HBO, 1998–2004. Played by Sarah Jessica Parker.

Carrie Bradshaw is a beautiful sex columnist (for the *New York Star*) who writes about living (and loving) in New York City. Carrie lives in Manhattan and is best friends with Samantha Jones, Charlotte York and Miranda Hobbes. They share stories about men and sex and Carrie has been known to write the juiciest columns in town (her bus billboards read "Carrie Bradshaw Knows Good Sex").

Carrie is single and very fashion conscious. She likes high heels (wears a size 7½ shoe), tight (and often bright) dresses and miniskirts. At one point in her life she became addicted to floral patterns and her wardrobe reflected flowers. Carrie does not need to dress to the hilt to attract a man. She is so attractive that no mater what she wears she turns heads. And this is where Carrie is most vulnerable: she just has no luck when it comes to men. The charismatic Mr. Big (as he is only called) first broke her heart when he left her. Next her relationship with Aidan Shaw ended when Carrie found she couldn't get over (the now married) Mr. Big and began having an affair with him. She also lost him for a second time. Despite all the advice she gives to readers, Carrie doesn't listen to what she writes. Following these heartbreaks, Carrie quit her job for a position as a fashion reporter for *Vogue* magazine. Carrie also became an author when Clearwater Press turned her best sex columns into a book (even with this added fame Carrie was unable to find the man of her dreams). Carrie's favorite drink is a Cosmopolitan. Carrie is the only four of the female regulars that does not appear nude at anytime on the series. She wears the laciest and sexiest lingerie but never does anymore than show off her sexy figure in them. Her computer screen name is "Shoegal" and she enjoys eating Whoppers candy when she goes to the movies.

See also: Charlotte York, Miranda Hobbes, Samantha Jones.

175. Carrie Heffernan, *The King of Queens*, CBS, 1998 (current). Played by Leah Remini.

Carrie Heffernan is the wife of Doug Heffernan, a driver for IPS (International Parcel Service). Carrie was born in New York's Greenwich Village in 1968. She is the daughter of Arthur and his first wife, now deceased, Sophia (another episode claims Carrie's mother is Lily and divorced from Arthur). The family moved to Queens, New York, shortly after when Arthur acquired a job as a decorative ribbon salesman.

As a child, Carrie learned to knit from her mother and to pick fights with everyone from her father. She was a Brownie and at the age of one developed a severe case of croup. Carrie is Catholic and attended St. Claire's Elementary School. As a pre-teen during the summer of 1977, she attended Camp Unity where she picked fights and mooned truckers off Route 9. Carrie is also a graduate of Monsignor Scanlon High School and Queens College and first worked as a checker at Foodtown on Northern Boulevard. She met her future husband, Douglas Heffernan, at a nightclub called Wall Street in Queens (Doug was the bouncer; another episode claims they met over Jell-O shots on Foxy Boxing Night). They dated and married three years later in 1995. They first lived in their own apartment then moved in with Arthur to save money for the house in which they currently live (3121 Aberdine Avenue in Rego Park, Queens).

Carrie next found work as a legal secretary at a mid–Manhattan firm called Haskell and Associates (later known as Kaplan, Hornstein and Steckle). Carrie arranges for the muffins at the morning meetings and a good day for her is getting positive feedback from the tight skirts and cleavage revealing blouses she wears. In November of 2003, Carrie loses her job due to downsizing and first attempted to sell rather awful looking home made designer cell phone cases. She next acquired a job as a secretary at the Dugan Group, a real estate development firm in Manhattan.

Carrie is naturally grouchy and bitchy. She is not a happy person by nature and enjoys seeing other people miserable. She cheats at board games and stuffs her bra with cotton to bring more attention to herself. When Carrie has a martini or similar drink, she becomes mellow and nice. Doug likes it when Carrie attends his softball games because she uses the best foul language when yelling at the opposing team.

Carrie shops at Greenbaum's Supermarket and will buy any greeting card she sees that she likes even if she has no need for it. Carrie's mother was a good cook. "I buy frozen foods and defrost them. That's what I do," says Carrie. Carrie's station wagon license plate reads FEM 291, then FBC 291.

See also: Arthur Spooner, Douglas Heffernan.

176. Carter Nash, *Captain Nice,* NBC, 1967. Played by William Daniels.

Carter Nash is the alias for Captain Nice, an heroic crime fighter who protects the citizens of Big Town, U.S.A., a metropolis of 112,000 people, from evil.

Carter was born in Big Town and is the son of Esther and Harvey Nash. He is mother dominated and his father, who cannot remember his name, calls him "Spot." Carter grew up with a fascination for science and is a graduate of Big Town

University, where he acquired a degree in physics. Carter is shy, timid and helpless. He believes he is ordinary and doesn't stand out. He is afraid of the dark (in the daytime) and thinks of girls as round men. Feeling a need to serve his country, Carter tried to join the army but "they burned my draft card." When he enrolled in a self-defense class "they said I should carry an axe." Through a connection with his mother, the sister of the city's mayor, Carter found work at the Big Town Police Department as a crime lab chemist. Here, while experimenting, Carter created Super Juice, a liquid that transforms him into the heroic Captain Nice (named after the C.N. initials on his belt buckle). It was his mother, however, who convinced Carter to use his abilities for justice: "This place we live in is a typical American town full of crooks, hoodlums and gangsters. It's up to you to do something about it." Esther made him his red, white and blue costume, mask and cape and had suggested the names "Wonder Man" and "Muscle Head."

As Captain Nice, Carter has incredible speed and strength, the ability to fly and an immunity to harm. He is described as "The man who flies like an eagle," "The man with muscles of lead" and "The masked enemy of evil." "From now on," Carter says, "The forces of evil will have to watch out for Captain Nice!"

177. Casey McAfee, *Nurses,* NBC, 1993–1994. Played by Loni Anderson.

Cassandra McAfee is a beautiful blonde who measures 36-24-36. She is the corporate representative for the Healthweb Corporation, owners of the Community Medical Center in Miami Beach, Florida. Cassandra feels the job is beneath her and took it because "It is only a pit stop on my way to the top."

Casey, as she is called, was born in Florida and is the daughter of Ed and Melanie McAfee. Ed was a puppeteer and Casey had a very unsteady childhood (the family moved from place to place; "we had to go where the work was"). Casey attended several different grammar schools but got her degree in business administration from Miami University.

Casey was a beautiful child and she learned at an early age how to use her looks to manipulate people. She first worked as a waitress at Little Stephanie International (which seemed only to employ busty blonde girls) and quit "because all the girls looked like me." After college she acquired a job with Healthweb and found her looks could not influence the corporate heads. She is now angry that she has to work like everybody else. The pressures of work have made Casey see life in a different light and it has become too much for her. She has instituted "Me Time" and sets aside about 12 minutes a day to relax and argue with herself for what she is doing. Casey lives in a posh corporate-paid apartment at the Health-web Towers and collects snowball domes as a hobby ("the ones you shake").

178. Cassidy Bridges, *Nash Bridges*, CBS, 1996–2001. Played by Jodi Lynn O'Keefe.

Cassidy Bridges is the only child of Nash Bridges and his first wife, Lisa (now divorced). Nash is a police captain; Lisa runs a catering company. Cassidy lives with her father at 855 Sacramento Street in San Francisco, California.

Cassidy was born in San Francisco and first attended Bay High School. She is a graduate of Berkeley College and originally had aspirations to become an actress but later found an interest in law enforcement and joined the S.F.P.D. after graduating from its police academy.

As an actress, Cassidy appeared topless in an avant-garde play (*Tears of the Monkey*). When she became a police officer she was first assigned to patrol the Sea Cliff section of San Francisco. She was later transferred to her father's unit at the S.I.U. (Special Investigative Unit) as a uniformed officer. Nash was uneasy with Cassidy becoming a cop as he was with her doing nude scenes in plays.

Cassidy is rarely defiant and loyal to her father. If she does get angry, she takes her frustrations out on the police gym punching bag. Chocolate is her favorite flavor of ice cream.

See also: Caitlin Cross, Joe Dominiquez, Nash Bridges.

179. Cassie Cranston, *It's a Living*, ABC, 1980–1982; Syn., 1985–1989. Played by Ann Jillian.

Katie Lou Cranston, called Cassie, is a beautiful waitress at Above the Top, a 13th floor Los Angeles restaurant that features "Sky High Dining." Cassie was born in Kansas and dropped the Katie Lou so people wouldn't think of her as a hick. She was an exceptionally pretty girl and had all the boys at Beth Grammar School and Kansas City High wrapped around her little finger. After graduating from high school, Cassie sought to make her mark on the world and headed to Los Angeles. She took the waitress job as a means of finding a rich man to marry.

Cassie is very sexy and loves to flaunt her breasts in low cut uniforms. Although she cannot cook, Cassie tells men "I'm a terrific cook" (her one cooking talent is making toast). Cassie lives

in Los Angeles at the Sun Palace Condominium Complex and on her only night off, reads to senior citizens at the Willow Glen Rest Home. Cassie appears to be self-centered but is really quite giving and will help a friend in need.

See also: Amy Tompkins, Dot Higgins, Ginger St. James, Jan Hoffmeyer, Lois Adams, Sonny Mann.

180. Cassie McBain, *She Spies*, Syn., 2002–2004. Played by Natasha Henstridge.

Cassandra Ann McBain, called Cassie, is a member of the She Spies, a government organization designed to battle crime and corruption.

Cassie was born in Los Angeles on May 4, 1976 (another episode claims she was born in Morris Town, New Jersey). Her hospital I.D. bracelet (as an infant) was B 379-4789. At the age of six, Cassie would steal her mother's lipstick and pretend to be just like her. Cassie's mother, Catherine, called herself "the stars"; Cassie was her "sun" (Cassie's bedroom reflected this as she had stars on her ceiling). Cassie's father, however, was a con artist and taught her how to lie, steal, cheat and scam. She became a part of his schemes and it eventually cost Cassie her freedom when one of her cons backfired and she was arrested on the day she was to be married. Cassie was booked on November 9, 2000, and her L.A.P.D. file is 7833509, case number 354. Cassie was sentenced to Terminal Island Prison in San Pedro, California, but freed by the government when they required a girl with extraordinary skills.

Cassie is a Phi Delta Gamma who earned her way into college by conning bankers and CEO's. She is a brilliant career criminal and the self-proclaimed leader of the She Spies (who include D.D. Cummings and Shane Phillips. They live together in a house provided by the government). Cassie is an expert at bugging and loves pretending to be someone else to get information from suspects. She also enjoys walking on the beach and relaxes by playing pool. Her least favorite thing "is being chained to a bomb." As a child, Cassie had dreams of becoming an astronaut.

See also: D.D. Cummings, Shane Phillips.

181. Cate Hennessy, *Eight Simple Rules for Dating My Teenage Daughter*, ABC, 2002–2005. Played by Katey Sagal.

Cate, a nurse, is the wife of sportswriter Paul Hennessey and the mother of Bridget, Kerry and Rory. She lives on Oakdale Street in Michigan and became a widow in the fall of 2003 when Paul died of a heart attack. Prior to meeting Paul at a "geek party for writers" (which she crashed with a friend), Cate would only date musicians and "bad boys." Cate doesn't talk about her former boyfriends around Paul because he always asks "Is he cuter than me?"

Cate is the daughter of Jim and Laura Egan and was born in Florida. She attended Garfield High School (where she was on the drill team and recalls herself as being "hot and smart'). She suffered an embarrassing moment in Garfield Junior High: while performing in a Christmas pageant she lost her pace and fell into the orchestra pit. As a child, Cate had a fantasy about singing in a smoke-filled bar and wearing a sexy dress. She never pursued it because her father thought it was frivolous. In later life she took the plunge and sang "My Old Man" on Open Mike Night at the Green Bottle Bar. Cate hides her old love letters in a box labeled "Taxes."

Cate is addicted to coffee and doesn't mind any family vacation as long as she doesn't have to cook. Cate had more control over the kids than Paul and returned to nursing while Paul worked at home "because Bridget is two years away from college and with her grades she will never get a scholarship." Cate is the recording secretary of the PTA and later gets help in raising the children when her father, Jim (James Garner), a retired engineer, moves in with her. In the fall of 2004, Cate quits her job at the hospital for a position as the nurse at Liberty High School (the school attended by Bridget and Kerry).

See also: Bridget Hennessey, Kerry Hennessey, Paul Hennessey, Rory Hennessey.

182. Catherine Chandler, *Beauty and the Beast,* CBS, 1987–1990. Played by Linda Hamilton.

Catherine Chandler is the "beauty" of the title, an investigator for the Manhattan District Attorney, who receives help in solving crimes from the mysterious Vincent (the "beast" of the title), a deformed man who lives beneath the streets and helps her whenever she is in trouble.

Catherine was born in New York City and is the daughter of a wealthy corporate attorney. She is a graduate of Columbia University and first works for her father as a corporate attorney. She is 30 years old and lives in an apartment (21E) off Central Park West; her car license plate reads CLO 426.

Catherine's life changed dramatically one night when she was mistaken for someone else and abducted off the street after leaving a social gathering. She was severely beaten and slashed across the face. Her lifeless body was dumped near Central Park. She was found by Vincent and taken to his world beneath the streets and healed by Father,

the leader of Vincent's world. After recovering, Catherine vowed to keep Vincent and his world a secret.

Catherine felt that after her near-fatal experience, she needed to do more than just work in a law office. Becoming an investigator and helping gather the evidence needed to bring criminals to justice is now her way of fighting back at the wrong done to her. At first Catherine was cautious, always reminded of what happened to her by the large scar on the right side of her chin and neck that resulted from the slashing. When the scar became less visible and mysteriously disappeared, Catherine took on more dangerous assignments and sought the more deadly criminals. Vincent was able to help her but in the end her enthusiasm was too great and it cost Catherine her life when a master criminal she sought ended his nightmare by killing her. The criminal, Gabriel, was even smart enough to outwit Vincent.

See also: Vincent.

183. Catherine Gale, *The Avengers,* British TV, 1962–1965; American TV (A&E), 1991. Played by Honor Blackman.

Catherine Gale, called Cathy, is an Avenger, a Ministry agent who battles the enemies of the British government. Cathy, an amateur, is partners with the Ministry's top agent, John Steed.

Cathy was born in England. She is a graduate of Oxford University and possesses a Ph.D. in anthropology. She is a widow and works for the British Museum (she was recruited by the Ministry after her husband, an anthropologist, was killed in a Mau Mau raid in Kenya, Africa).

Cathy is a skilled mechanic, expert photographer and highly knowledgeable in the use of firearms. She possesses scientific knowledge, martial arts abilities and, unlike her partner, finds it necessary to carry a gun. Cathy lives at 14 Primrose Hall and rides a Triumph motorcycle with the license plate 987 CAA.

Cathy is impetuous and plunges head first into situations without really thinking first. She became more of a professional as she worked and learned from Steed and loved to dress in sexy black outfits while on assignments.

See also: Emma Peel, John Steed, Tara King.

184. Catherine Willows, *C.S.I.: Crime Scene Investigation,* CBS, 2000 (current). Played by Marg Helgenberger.

Catherine Willows is a senior investigator for the Crime Scene Investigation Unit of the Metropolitan Las Vegas Police Department. She was born in Bozeman, Montana, on March 26, 1963.

She grew up on a farm but Catherine craved excitement and a rural life was not for her. She left home at an early age and headed for Seattle where she found work as a waitress. When this failed, she returned to Montana to find that her parents had divorced and sold the farm. With no place to call home, Catherine settled in Las Vegas where she first worked as a waitress, then as an exotic dancer. With the money she made from dancing, Catherine enrolled in West Las Vegas University (she later graduated with a Bachelor of Science degree in medical technology). It was also at this time that she met a low-life music producer named Eddie. They eventually married and had a daughter, Lindsay. It was not a marriage made in heaven. Constant bickering led to a breakup. Eddie left Catherine with ten dollars, a cocaine habit and Lindsay to raise. Catherine then woke up and turned her life around. She became an officer with the Las Vegas P.D. and was spotted by Gil Grissom, a field service officer, who recruited her to work at his C.S.I. lab. Over a ten-year period Catherine worked her way up from assistant technician to her current status as a C.S.I. Level Three.

Catherine loves her job ("we're like a bunch of kids getting paid to work on puzzles"). She scrutinizes every crime scene to collect evidence and can recreate what happened by piecing together the evidence she has found. Her specialty is blood splatter analysis.

See also: Gil Grissom, Nick Stokes, Sara Sidle, Warrick Brown.

185. C.C. Babcock, *The Nanny,* CBS, 1993–1999. Played by Lauren Lane.

Chastity Claire Babcock, called C.C., is the business associate of Maxwell Sheffield, a widow with three children. He lives on New York's Park Avenue and runs Maxwell Sheffield Productions (produces Broadway shows); C.C. later becomes his partner (Sheffield-Babcock Productions).

C.C. was born in New York City to a wealthy family and is second in line to inherit a fortune (her mother, B.B., is first; her sister, D.D., is third). C.C. has a pampered dog (Chester) and believes people think of her as "a self-centered, cold-hearted witch." C.C. tries to be nice, sincere and sensitive "but my nasty attitude can't make it happen."

While C.C. makes the Sheffield home her second home, she lives at 407 East 86th Street in Manhattan. Her computer password is Good and Plenty and she has a terrible memory for names (she calls Maxwell's children, Macy, Bob and Nancy; their real names are Maggie, Bryton and

Gracie); she calls the children's nanny, Fran Fine, "Nanny Fine." C.C. constantly tries to impress Maxwell with her knowledge of business, celebrities and the Broadway stage in the hope that he will one day marry her (but she failed when Maxwell married Fran).

See also: Fran Fine, Gracie Sheffield, Maggie Sheffield, Maxwell Sheffield.

186. Cedric Robinson, *The Steve Harvey Show,* WB, 1996–2002. Played by Cedric the Entertainer.

Cedric Jackie Robinson is the coach (of the Cheetas basketball team) and the health teacher at Booker T. Washington High School in Chicago. He is engaged to (and later marries) Lovita Jenkins, the school's administrative assistant. Cedric is called "Ceddie" and "Ceddie Bear" by Lovita and drives what Lovita calls "The Ceddie Mobile." Cedric has been nominated for "Teacher of the Year" eight times and has lost each time. He runs an inner city company for youths called The Cookie Man. He is sentimental (has a "little black box" that contains his childhood memories) and shares an apartment with his best friend, Steve Hightower, the school's music teacher. When Cedric and Lovita marry, they first live with Steve; they later move to the vacant apartment across the hall. Cedric calls Steve "Dawg" (Steve calls him "Ced").

Cedric performs with Steve at Charity functions as The Soul Teachers and once had an idea of opening a culturally friendly hardware store called "Homey Depot" (he also fizzled out with "Bro Black — black golf balls for black golfers"). Since Lovita can't cook, Cedric claims "Nobody dials take out like my baby." Cedric's Grandma Puddin' is the eldest and most respected member of the Robinson family (Cedric often mentions his mother, who is apparently grossly overweight and constantly calls on him to get her out of the bathtub when she gets stuck).

See also: Lovita Jenkins, Regina Grier, Steve Hightower.

187. Chakotay, *Star Trek: Voyager,* UPN, 1995–2001. Played by Robert Beltran.

Chakotay, a Native American descendant, is First Officer on the Starship U.S.S. *Voyager.* Chakotay, the son of Kolopak, was born in 2329 and has a Mayan background (his ancestry can be traced back to the Rubber Tree People of Central America). When Chakotay was 15, his father traced his people's ancestral home to the Central American jungles. It was at this time in 2344 that Chakotay began allying himself with the Starfleet crews patrolling the border. Shortly after, Chakotay decided to attend Starfleet Academy. He graduated in 2348 and became an instructor in Starfleet's Advanced Tactical Training Program. He resigned in 2370 and left the Alpha Quadrant to join the Maquis rebellion and fight the invading Cardassians on the tribe's home world along the Demilitarized Zone when they threatened their way of life. He returned to the Alpha Quadrant in 2387 as First Officer of *Voyager*.

Chakotay is a gentle man. He cherishes his Mayan background and uses a spirit summoned from his medicine bag for guidance. He also wears a tattoo over his left eye as a symbol of his heritage.

See also: B'Elanna Torres, The Doctor, Harry Kim, Kathryn Janeway, Neelix, Seven of Nine, Tuvok.

188. Chance Harper, *Strange Luck*, Fox, 1995. Played by D.B. Sweeney.

"If I see a situation where someone needs help I get involved." These are the words of Chance Harper, "the guy they call when nobody else wants the job." Here, the "they" are unknown forces that compel Chance to be in a specific place at a specific time to see the person he must save from bad luck (or an unfortunate accident).

Chance himself is not always lucky — he has 23 murder charges on police file (he just happened to be in the wrong place at the wrong time) but none of the cases were ever brought to trial. Chance believes that "This all happened when I was a child." Thirty years ago, when Chance was a young boy, he was on a plane with his parents when the engine caught fire and the plane crashed. All 106 aboard were killed — except Chance. He believes Lady Luck saved him and now, as an adult, he uses his mysterious relationship with Lady Luck to help others.

Chance has little memory of his childhood; he is not even sure of his exact birth date. He was orphaned by the plane crash and raised by the fireman who rescued him. Chance never knows what is going to happen, "But I'm always there when it does." Chance's real first name is Alex, but he goes by Chance — the name the fireman called him (as it was one chance in a billion that he survived the plane crash)

189. Chandler Bing, *Friends*, NBC, 1994–2004. Played by Matthew Perry.

Chandler Bing grew up on Long Island (New York) and is the son of world famous novelist Nora Bing (and a transvestite father, Charles). Chandler attended Lincoln High School and is best friends with Monica, Rachel, Phoebe, Joey and Ross. He hangs out with them at a coffee shop called Central Perk. Chandler lives in an apartment building at Grove and Bedford Streets in Manhattan and works at an unnamed company in data analysis and statistical information. He quit the job on December 12, 2002, when he found he had to work on Christmas Eve and could not be with his wife, Monica (whom he married on May 17, 2001). Chandler later works as a copywriter in an unnamed advertising agency.

Chandler hides the fact that "I have a third nipple" and has *TV Guide* delivered to him under the name "Chandler Bong." His favorite TV shows are *Baywatch*, *Wonder Woman* and *Xena: Warrior Princess*. Before marrying Monica, Chandler suffered through three stages when he broke up with a girl: the sweat pants phase; the strip club phase; and the envisioning himself with other girls phase. In high school Chandler was afraid of bras ("I can't work them") and was called "Sir Limpsalot" after schoolmate Monica Geller accidentally dropped a knife that cut off the tip of his pinky toe. *The Velveteen Rabbit* was Chandler's favorite book as a child and in college (N.Y.U.), he was in a band called Way No Way.

On Thanksgiving Day of 2003, Chandler and Monica learn they will become adoptive parents (they are unable to have children naturally) and on January 15, 2004, they announce they are moving to Westchester. In the final episode, May 6, 2004, Chandler and Monica become the parents of twins (Erica and Jack) when their substitute mother, Erica, gives birth.

See also: Joey Tribbiani, Monica Geller, Phoebe Buffay, Rachel Greene, Ross Geller.

190. Charlene Frazier, *Designing Women*, CBS, 1986–1990. Played by Jean Smart.

Charlene Frazier works as the office manager for the Sugarbaker Design Firm at 1521 Sycamore Street in Atlanta, Georgia. Charlene is the daughter of Ben and Ione Frazier and was born in Little Rock, Arkansas. Her family moved shortly after her birth and Charlene grew up in the small town of Poplar Bluffs, Arkansas. She attended Three Rivers Secretarial School in Missouri and Claraton University in Atlanta (where she studied psychology).

Charlene is a Baptist and also held a part time job as a salesgirl for Kemper Cosmetics. Charlene wears a size eight shoe and "I'll Be Seeing You" is her favorite song; Dolly Parton is her favorite singer. She co-wrote the children's book, *Billy Bunny*, with her friend Mary Jo Shively and fell in love with and married Bill Stillfield (Douglas

Barr), a U.S. Air Force Colonel (the ceremony was held on the rooftop garden of the Dinwoodie Hotel in 1989; "Ave Maria" was their wedding song). Charlene next purchased the Grand Ghostly Mansion of Atlanta as a home for herself, Bill and their newborn baby, Olivia. When Bill received a transfer to England, Charlene quit her job to join him (at which time she left the series). Charlene's pride and joy is her autographed picture of Elvis Presley.

See also: Anthony Bouvier, Julia Sugarbaker, Mary Jo Shively, Suzanne Sugarbaker.

191. Charlene Sinclair, *Dinosaurs*, ABC, 1991–1994. Voiced by Sally Struthers.

This entry also contains information on Charlene's older brother, Robbie (Jason Willinger) and her infant brother, Baby Sinclair (Kevin Clark). Charlene, Robbie and Baby are prehistoric dinosaurs who speak and live as the people of today. They are the children of Earl and Fran Sinclair and live in the city of Pangaea in the year 60,000,003 B.C.

Twelve-year-old Charlene and 14-year-old Robbie attend Bob LaBrea high School. Robbie is a precocious visionary (he believes, for example, the caveman might have a bright future); Charlene is a material girl and cares little about what the future might hold. Robbie is a B student while Charlene is an average student (C grades) and strives to remain so — "So I can be average." Charlene is fashion conscious and buys her cosmetics at Fifth Avenue Scales. She is a bit vain and must have perfect hair, dress and makeup before she leaves the house. Robbie, always dressed in his high school jacket (Rampaging Trilobites is printed on the back), is a herbivore who studies "prehistory" in school. He was a member of the Scavengers Gang and has a poster of the movie *Teenage Mutant Ninja Cavemen* on his bedroom wall.

Baby Sinclair was hatched in the first episode. Baby (his official name) seems to know who everyone is except his father, Earl. When Earl cares for him, Baby says "Not the Mama" and hits him on the head with a Myman Frying Pan. When Fran complained to the company that their pan breaks when Baby hits Earl, the company created the unbreakable P-2000 and featured Baby and Earl (as Sir Pan) in TV commercials. Baby's first word was the gutter word "Smoo." Baby Sinclair is a TV addict and his favorite shows are *Mr. Ugh* (about a talking caveman), *Raptile* (a talk show), and *Ask Mr. Lizard* (a science program). Whenever he does something wrong, Baby remarks "I'm the Baby, gotta love me."

See also: Earl and Fran Sinclair.

192. Charles, *Charles in Charge*, CBS, 1984–1985; Syn., 1987–1990. Played by Scott Baio.

Charles (no last name) is a student at Copeland College in New Jersey (pursuing a degree in education). He works as a live-in housekeeper (baby sitter) to earn the money for tuition. Charles was born in Scranton, Pennsylvania; his mother, Lillian, is the owner of the Yesterday Café in New Jersey (information about his father is not given). Lillian called Charles "Doodlebug" as a child and claims he was a very neat and tidy boy. Charles attended Middletown Grammar School (where he won a spelling bee) and Scranton High School (where he was in a band called the Charles Tones). He also had a ventriloquist act with a dummy named Muggsy when he was in the fifth grade.

Charles first worked for Jill and Stan Pembroke and lived with them and their children, Lila, Douglas, and Jason, at 10 Barrington Court in New Brunswick. When the series switched to syndication, the Pembrokes had moved and sublet their home to the Powell family (Ellen, her husband, Robert; their children, Jamie, Sarah, and Adam; and Robert's father, Walter). Because Robert was a naval commander stationed overseas, Charles found employment as their live-in housekeeper.

Jill worked as a writer for the New Jersey *Register*; Stan was one of 49 vice presidents in an unnamed company. Ellen worked as a real estate broker. Charles tries to solve the problems he encounters with wisdom and understanding and uses logic to explain what is right and wrong to the children. He finds "help" from his friend, Buddy Lembeck, a not-too-bright student at Copeland College, whose antics impress the children and hinder Charles's efforts to discipline them. Charles also held a job as a teacher's aide at Central High School and in the last episode, Charles left the Powells to pursue his teaching degree at Princeton University. The Lamplight Café, Sid's Pizza Parlor and the Yesterday Café were Charles and Buddy's hangouts.

See also: Buddy Lembeck, Jamie Powell, Lila Pembroke, Sarah Powell.

193. Charles Tucker, *Star Trek: Enterprise*, UPN, 2001–2005. Played by Connor Trinneer.

Charles Tucker, III, is Chief Engineer aboard the U.S.S. *Enterprise*. He was born in Florida on the planet Earth in an unspecified year (possibly the 2120s or the early 2130s). He has the nickname "Trip" (short for "Triple" as both his father and grandfather were also named Charles).

Trip (as he is often called) has been with Starfleet for 12 years and was involved in its NX-test program (the testing ground for what would eventually launch the U.S.S. Star Ships and their designations, such as *Enterprise NX-01*). Trip is an experienced orbital engineer with an offbeat sense of humor. He has the ability to repair a Starship in orbit and became the only human male to experience a pregnancy (although briefly, when he encountered Ahilein, a Xyrilliam female). Trip has only one known sibling, Elizabeth, who was killed in 2153 when a race called the Xindi attacked Earth and killed over seven million people. As kids, he and Elizabeth had a dog named Bedford.

See also: Hoshi Sato, Jonathan Archer, Phlox, T'Pol, Travis Mayweather.

194. Charles Winchester, III, *M*A*S*H*, CBS, 1977–1983. Played by David Ogden Stiers.

Major Charles Emerson Winchester, III, is a doctor with the 4077th Mobile Army Surgical Hospital (M*A*S*H) unit in Korea during the war. He became the new tent mate to Hawkeye Pierce and B.J. Hunnicutt when Major Frank Burns was transferred stateside. Charles is a pompous Bostonian. He is a Harvard Medical School graduate and had been working at Tokyo General Hospital before his transfer to Korea. He reads the *Boston Globe* (sent to him by his sister, Honoria) and is called "Major Windbag" by chief nurse Margaret Houlihan when he talks about himself. Charles, a gourmet, feels that "breakfast at the 4077 makes you look forward to lunch." He is an expert at chess and loves fine wine. Charles sends a tape-recorded message home to his parents and claims "Classical music reminds me that there is still some grace and culture in the world" (Gustav Mahler is his favorite composer).

Charles claims that "three generations of Winchesters have never lost an argument" and that he is a good doctor "because I do one thing at a time. I do it very well, then I move on." However, he says, "The meatball surgery that is performed in the OR (operating room) is causing my skills to deteriorate; they're wasting away."

See also: Benjamin Franklin Pierce, B.J. Hunnicutt, Frank Burns, Henry Blake, Margaret Houlihan, Radar O'Reilly, Sherman Potter, Trapper John McIntire.

195. Charlie Briscoe, *Living Dolls*, ABC, 1989. Played by Leah Remini.

You would never know by her name, but Charlie Briscoe is actually Charlene Briscoe, a very pretty street-wise teenage girl who has "The Look" — the face and figure to become a fashion model.

Charlie (as she likes to be called) was born in Brooklyn, New York, on May 16, 1973. She attends Lexington High School and is under contract with the Carlin Modeling Agency in Manhattan (the agency is located at 68th Street and Madison Avenue and is run by Trish Carlin [Michael Learned], a former high fashion model). Charlie has a tough exterior but is a softie on the inside. She does not believe she is as beautiful as people tell her she is and likes to be herself ("What you see is what you get"). Charlie is rarely impressed by anything — even when she is told she is special ("A good burger is special, not me"). Charlie's specialty is insulting people. When she doesn't respond to a perfect opportunity her friends know something is troubling her. Charlie will stand up for the little guy — she is a product of the streets and had her fair share of trouble. She learned the hard way (fighting) to stand up for herself and feels this is how she became independent. Charlie will tell people off when they annoy her and may appear pushy, but when she faces the cameras she becomes a soft, sweet and feminine young woman (but don't let that fool you. Once the photo shoot ends, its back to jeans, a T-shirt and a nasty attitude).

See also: Caroline Weldon, Emily Franklin, Martha Lambert.

196. Charlie Crawford, *Spin City*, ABC, 2000–2002. Played by Charlie Sheen.

Charlie Crawford is the Deputy Mayor to Randall Winston, the Mayor of New York City (Charlie replaced Michael Flaherty, the former Deputy Mayor). Charlie is a ladies' man and had been raised by a father (Roy) with few morals (he took Charlie to pool halls beginning at age seven and a year later Charlie had his first taste of beer at Callahan's Tavern).

Charlie's work philosophy is "I do all the work of the Mayor without the glory, pay or prestige." Charlie has been voted number eleven of the sexiest men in New York even though he has a string of embarrassing exploits in Washington, D.C., prior to coming to New York. Even though Charlie doesn't smoke, he carries a pack of cigarettes "in case a girl asks me for a smoke." He claims "I've been dating 23-year-old girls for 20 years" and fears any type of commitment (he is especially afraid of dating a woman with children "because I'm not good with kids"). Even though Charlie began a romantic relationship with co-worker Caitlin Moore (the Mayor's campaign manager), he still makes passes at women. Caitlin doesn't like to dine with Charlie because he hits on waitresses, makes rude noises, and is a bad conversationalist. Caitlin also calls the Italian silk shirts Charlie wears "blouses." Charlie's one good trait seems to be cooking, where he is famous for his stuffed salmon. Charlie lives in Apartment 7D and before dating Caitlin, he and Caitlin worked out a scam to get him out of a date: when Charlie phones Caitlin with a code red, Caitlin comes to where he is (usually a restaurant), pretends she is pregnant and discourages the date so she will leave (for Charlie, a month is a long term commitment). Charlie attended and was expelled from Michigan State College, Arizona State, Alabama State, Syracuse University and Northeastern State College.

See also: Caitlin Moore, Michael Flaherty, Paul Lassiter, Randall Winston, Stewart Bondek.

197. Charlie Moore, *Head of the Class*, ABC, 1986–1990. Played by Howard Hesseman.

Charles Moore, called Charlie, is an I.H.P. (Individual Honors Program) teacher at Fillmore High School in New York City. He was born in Idaho and attended Wesssur High School then Idaho State College. Charlie found an interest in the theater and acting and wrote and directed his high school musical, *Goodbye Weesur, Hello Broadway*. With a dream to make it on the Great White Way, Charlie made Manhattan his home. He staged the off–Broadway play *Hamlet* at the Playhouse Theater in Newark, New Jersey (where he started a small group of players). He began his acting career in 1969, and his most embarrassing moment occurred when he appeared in the play *Hair* and did the nude scene in the wrong act. Charlie also appeared in plays by Chekhov and Ibsen and directed an off–Broadway production of *The Little Shop of Horrors*. When he found himself without work he turned to teaching. He became a substitute teacher at Fillmore and a faculty member when the previous I.H.P. teacher left.

Charlie lives next to the Plant Store and appeared in TV commercials as "The King of Discount Appliances" for Veemer Appliances. Charlie left Fillmore High in 1990 when he accepted the lead in the road company production of *Death of a Salesman*. Charlie held his classes in Room 19. He disliked the taste of anchovies and his favorite eatery was Casa Falafel. Before leaving Fillmore, he directed his class in a production of *Grease*.

See also: Arvid Engen, Darlene Merriman, Dennis Blunden, Simone Foster.

198. Charlie Salinger, *Party of Five*, Fox, 1994–2000. Played by Matthew Fox.

Charles Salinger, called Charlie, is the oldest son of Nicholas and Diane Salinger. He has four siblings (Julia, Bailey, Claudia and infant Owen) and through a tragic accident (the death of their parents in a car accident) has taken on the responsibility of caring for his brothers and sisters.

The Salingers live at 3324 Broadway in San Francisco. Income is provided by the family-owned restaurant, Salinger's. Charlie, a womanizer and somewhat irresponsible, is 24 years old. He attended Grant High School and later Berkeley College. He dropped out of Berkeley and at Grant High he was responsible for setting the boys bathroom on fire and drilling a peephole in the girls locker room. Charlie first worked as a bartender at the family restaurant. He later turned his wood working skills into a furniture making business. He would attempt to impress girls by pretending to be the suave Lloyd W. Loomis.

See also: Bailey Salinger, Claudia Salinger, Julia Salinger.

199. Charlie Townsend, *Charlie's Angels*, ABC, 1976–1981. Played by John Forsythe.

Charles Townsend, called Charlie by those close to him, is the owner of the Los Angeles-based Townsend Investigations (the detective agency is also called the Townsend Detective Agency, Charles Townsend, Private Investigations, and Townsend and Associates). Charlie, who is never seen (only heard over a speaker phone) has three beautiful private detectives he calls Angels: Sabrina Duncan, Jill Monroe and Kelly Garrett (Kris Monroe, Tiffany Welles and Julie Rogers became later Angels). Charlie also owns the all-girl Venus Trucking Company.

Charlie is basically a man of mystery. With the exception of John Bosley, his right-hand man, none of the Angels have seen him. It is assumed Charlie remains invisible to them so he can protect them (Charlie has sent many people to prison; people who will be getting out sooner or later and may seek revenge. Not revealing himself to the Angels is his way of protecting them in the long run). It was revealed only that Charlie was in the military during World War II and has many important connections throughout the world. He is apparently very wealthy and a man of leisure. He relaxes by pools, lives in plush surroundings and is always with a beautiful woman by his side. Charlie is not all play; he does help the Angels with computer checks and uses his many contacts to help them solve crimes. Mildred is Charlie's favorite fish in scenes that show his aquarium.

See also: Jill Monroe, Julie Rogers, Kelly Garrett, Kris Monroe, Sabrina Duncan, Tiffany Welles.

200. Charlotte York, *Sex and the City*, HBO, 1998–2004. Played by Kristin Davis.

Charlotte York is a hopeless romantic who prides herself on being poised and polished. She is extremely feminine and always fashionably and provocatively dressed. Charlotte dreams of a marriage and a family; however she tends to panic when she tries on a wedding dress. She collects decorating magazines and fabric samples for her dream home — a country cottage.

Charlotte lives in New York City and works as an art gallery dealer. She will only date wealthy men and sometimes goes to extremes to land one. She claims, "you only get two great loves in your life." She would also like it to always be known that she is 35 years old. Charlotte, who was born in Connecticut, faced her first trauma when she was 36 years old: she learned she was unable to conceive naturally; in order to have children she must endure hormone therapy. This cost her a first marriage to Dr. Trey McDougal (she later converted to Judaism to marry Harry Goldenblatt, her Jewish divorce lawyer).

Charlotte enjoys spending time with her girlfriends, Carrie, Samantha and Miranda, and her favorite drink is a Cosmopolitan. Charlotte is also obsessed with shoes. Her footwear must be as elegant as her outerwear. Her wardrobe is basically pastel with accessories that highlight her feminine side. She feels sexiest in her black evening gown (which she wears to charity benefits and the ballet).

See also: Carrie Bradshaw, Miranda Hobbes, Samantha Jones.

201. Chatsworth Osborne, Jr. *Dobie Gillis*, CBS, 1959–1963. Played by Steve Franken.

Chatsworth Osborne, Jr., is the spoiled son of the fabulously wealthy Clarissa Osborne and the late Chatsworth Osborne, Sr., the owners of the Osborne National Bank. Chatsworth was born in Central City in 1943. He is heir to the family fortune and lives in the 47-room Louis XIV home "on top of the hill with the broken glass embedded in the wall that surrounds it."

Chatsworth is the richest kid in town and is friends with the dirt poor Dobie Gillis and his equally impoverished friend, Maynard G. Krebs. He attends Central High School then S. Peter Pryor Junior College. Chatsworth is a member of the Downshifters Club, is president of the Silver Spoon Club (for snobs) and he claims to have type "R" (for royal) blood. Chatsworth has a misguided approach to life and believes money can get him anything. He is an average student and his dream is to attend Yale University. He calls

Dobie "Dobie Do" and his mother, "Mumsey." His mother has little patience with Chatsworth and is constantly belittling him (she calls him "You Nasty Boy"). When something doesn't go his way, Chatsworth exclaims "Mice and Rats."

See also: Dobie Gillis (also for information on Thalia Menninger and Zelda Gilroy), Maynard G. Krebs.

202. Cher Horowitz, *Clueless*, ABC, 1996–1997; UPN, 1997–1998. Played by Rachel Blanchard.

Cher Horowitz is a beautiful teenage girl who knows she is beautiful. She is a student at the posh Bronson Alcottt High School in fashionable Beverly Hills. Cher is Jewish and the daughter of a wealthy family (her father, Mel, is a lawyer; her mother is deceased). Cher lives at 2232 Karma Vista Drive and plans to attend Stanhope College after graduation. She previously attended Rodeo Drive Pre-School and the Rodeo Drive Elementary School. Cher was also a member of the Girl Scouts and played Glenda, the Good Witch, in a school production of *The Wizard of Oz*.

Cher has a passion for fashion and is always elegantly dressed. She is a bit self-conscious over the fact that she has a small bust line and wears her "Bust Builder '98," a bra, made especially for her, that gives her a fuller look. Cher has a 10:00 P.M. weeknight and a midnight Saturday curfew. Cher gets depressed "when I'm boyfriend challenged" and believes in "The Three C's" when approaching a boy — "casual, cool and collective."

Cher writes the advice column, "Buzzline," for the school's newspaper, *The Alcott Buzz* and had the lead in the senior high production of *Grease*. Cher is best friends with Dee Davenport and Amber Mariens and the swank Koffee House is their favorite hangout.

See also: Amber Mariens, Dee Davenport.

Cherry White *see* **Laurette Barber**

203. Cheryl, *According to Jim*, ABC, 2001 (current). Played by Courtney Thorne-Smith.

Cheryl (no last name given) is the wife of Jim, an architect who owns a construction company called Ground Up Designs. She is the mother of Gracie, Ruby and Kyle and lives at 412 Maple Street in Chicago.

Cheryl is a beautiful woman who likes to be liked. When driving she stops at stop signals and pulls over for ambulances (Jim says she does so to be liked). Cheryl speaks fluent French but is totally tone deaf. She likes her steak rare; hamburgers medium well done. Cheryl has a scar on her forehead from when she was six years old and ran into the refrigerator. She was a straight A student in high school and was in the National Honors Society for four straight years. She was also a cheerleader and majored in business administration in college. Cheryl held a job as a claims adjuster in an insurance company but quit when she became pregnant. She has been a housewife and mother ever since.

Cheryl's middle name is Mabel. She wears size 34C bra and periwinkle blue is her favorite color. She had a cat named Mr. Finney and worries that after her friends meet Jim (who is a bit uncouth) will her friends still like her. The Beatles are Cheryl's favorite singing group and she can't get rid of her old clothes ("Everything looks good on me"). Cheryl believes "Jim pretends to be a moron to cover up being a jackass." She prepares spaghetti and meatballs when she becomes depressed and deals with problems in a civilized manner, taking things one step at a time (Jim panics and seeks the fastest way to resolve a problem, especially when he doesn't want Cheryl to know he was responsible for causing a problem).

See also: Jim.

204. Chester and Peg Riley, *The Life of Riley*, NBC, 1953–1958. Played by William Bendix, Marjorie Reynolds.

Chester A. Riley and his wife, Margaret (called Peg and Peggy), are a happily married couple who live at 1313 Blue View Terrace in Los Angeles, California. They are the parents of Babs (Barbara) and Junior (Chester Riley, Jr.). Chester, most always called Riley, is a riveter for Cunningham Aircraft and Associates.

Chester was born in Brooklyn, New York. He met his future wife, Peggy Barker (also born in Brooklyn) at Bensonhurst High School. They were in love and married shortly after graduating. It could be seen as a mistake as they were broke and had to move in with Peggy's parents. Shortly after, when Peggy became pregnant, she quit her secretarial job and Chester, previously unemployed (it was the era of the Great Depression), found work as a milkman for the Sunbeam Dairy. He made four dollars a day and had a route with "mostly the beer-drinking crowd." With their newfound prosperity, Chester and Peggy moved into their own $15 a month basement apartment located under a bowling alley near the East River and next to the subway. It was after the birth of their first child (Babs) that they moved to Los Angeles. It is not explained how Chester went from milkman to riveter, but he was now making $59 a week.

Chester is an honest, hard-working man who finds trouble in whatever he does. Peggy is a loving housewife and mother who finds herself embroiled in her husband's mishaps (and is usually the one who solves them). When Chester finds he has bumbled something yet again, he exclaims "What a revoltin' development this is." Their later addresses are 5412 Grove Street and 3412 Del Mar Vista. An earlier version of the series appeared on the DuMont network with Jackie Gleason (Chester Riley) and Rosemary DeCamp (Peg Riley).

205. Cheyenne Bodie, *Cheyenne*, ABC, 1955–1963. Played by Clint Walker.

Cheyenne Bodie is a drifter who wanders across the American Frontier of the 1860s. He is a strong, quiet man who fights for the rights of others.

Cheyenne is unaware of who his birth parents are. On the third day of the ninth moon of the Indian calendar (September 12th; this calendar has 13 moons each year with 28 days in each month), a wagon train traveling through Wyoming territory is attacked by Cheyenne Indians. Chief White Cloud spares the life of a baby boy and raises him as his son. The boy, whom White Cloud said "was so quiet and solemn that he must have the brain of a wise grey fox," was given the name Grey Fox. At the age of 12, Grey Fox chose to live the life of the white man and took the name Cheyenne Bodie. He left his home "south where the river winds at the foot of the hills" and set out on his own (it is not mentioned how one so young managed to survive alone).

Cheyenne worked as a ranch hand, cavalry scout, army undercover agent, deputy, trail boss, wagon train guide and whatever he could do to earn his keep. He is proud of his heritage and is dedicated to helping the army build up the land and establish a peace treaty with his blood brothers (Cheyenne can read smoke signals and is trusted by Indian Chiefs). Cheyenne carries a hunting knife on the left side of his holster (his gun is on the right side) and is looking for a place to settle down and call home (he hopes to one day buy a ranch and raise horses).

Cheyenne Montgomery *see* **Reba Hart**

Chiana (*Farscape*) *see* **John Crichton**

206. The Chief, *Get Smart*, NBC, 1965–1969; CBS, 1969–1970. Played by Edward Platt.

A man known only as Thaddeus, but called Chief by his agents, is the head of C.O.N.T.R.O.L, a supposedly top secret government organization that battles the evils of KAOS, an organization bent on dominating the world.

"Sorry about that Chief," the words constantly spoken by fumbling agent Maxwell Smart, often try the Chief's patients. Thaddeus is a kind and gentle man but often loses his temper (and sanity) when Max bungles a case. When he is needed in the field, Thaddeus goes undercover as Harold Clark, the head of the Pontiac Greeting Card Company (for which Max is also a salesman on such assignments; the Chief's cover is also known to be Howard Clark).

The Chief is apparently married (he mentions a wife in some episodes) and he lives in a comfortably furnished apartment where he enjoys smoking his pipe. He frequents the Regency Club and is fond of playing chess. He was a member of the glee club in college and the only family member ever seen is his niece Phoebe.

Thaddeus possibly began his career as a spy in the 1930s at which time he joined C.O.N.T.T.O.L and became Agent Q. His mentor was its then chief, Admiral Harold Harmon Hargrade. Thaddeus replaced Hargrade when he retired and became the new Chief (possibly in the late 1950s). Thaddeus is a skilled marksman and is knowledgeable in many languages.

See also: Maxwell Smart, 99.

207. Chris Cagney, *Cagney and Lacey*, CBS, 1982–1988. Played by Meg Foster, Sharon Gless.

Christine Cagney, called Chris, is a sergeant with the Homicide Division of the Manhattan 14th Precinct and is partners with Mary Beth Lacey. Chris originally worked as an undercover detective with the John Squad of the 23rd Precinct (posing as a prostitute to nab men who pay for sex).

Chris was born in Manhattan and is the daughter of a father (Charlie) who is an alcoholic. She attended Holy Cross Grammar School and Mount St. Michael High School. She now lives in an apartment at 11 West 49th Street and drives a car with the license plate 562 BLA (later 801 FEM). Chris wears badge number 763 and is a member of the precinct's Community Board (where she oversees minor cases). Chris has a drinking problem and is trying to break the habit (she attends A.A. meetings but still frequents a bar with Mary Beth called Flannery's; later O'Malley's Bar).

Chris is single "because I understand about commitment and responsibilities" something she can't handle since a psychic told her she was going to marry, live on a farm and have four children. Chris's car code is first 312, then 27 and finally 394. Chris hates to lose at anything and when she becomes angry, she has to kick or punch something.

See also: Mary Beth Lacey.

208. Chris Lorenzo, *Silk Stalkings*, CBS, 1991–1993; USA, 1993–1995. Played by Rob Estes.

Christopher Lorenzo, called Chris, is a sergeant with the Crimes of Passion Unit of the Palm Springs, Florida, Police Department. He and his partner, Rita Lee Lance, investigate Silk Stalkings, murders related to members of high society.

Chris was born in Philadelphia on April 12, 1963. His parents, Ben, a lawyer, and Anna Alexis, a former actress, divorced when he was ten years old. Chris was sent to live with his grandmother, Rose, in Palm Beach when he objected to his constant shifting from parent to parent

Chris is a graduate of Palm Beach High School and Florida State College (where he earned a criminology degree in 1985). He began work as a patrol cop and in 1988 was assigned to the robbery unit; he was next made a sergeant and teamed with Rita.

Chris enjoys playing the saxophone and is a former Boys' League basketball coach. He lives at 4613 Fairway and drives a car with the plate 284 736 (his dream car is a 1965 Thunderbird). Chris's car code is 1-X-Ray 13, then 1-X-Ray 9.

See also: Rita Lee Lance.

209. Chris Peterson, *Get a Life*, Fox, 1990–1992. Played by Chris Elliott.

Chris Peterson is a 30-year-old man who never forgot what it is like to be a kid. He is the son of Fred and Gladys Peterson and lives with his parents at 1341 Meadow Brook Lane in the small town of Greenville, Minnesota. Fred and Gladys believe Chris "is like a diamond in the rough that needs polishing" (in other words, Fred says, "an idiot"). His friends and neighbors all agree "Chris is a gas-headed idiot who gets on everyone's nerves." Chris believes "I have a happy-go-lucky outlook on life. I'm happy being an idiot."

Chris works as a newspaper delivery boy for the *Pioneer Press*, a job he has held since 1971. Chris is a failure at everything but he is the last one to realize it. He watches *Fraggle Rock* on TV every morning, believes Darryl Hannah is the greatest actress since Lillian Gish and worries that the local video store will be discontinuing the X-rated section ("I can't tell you how many nights I lost sleep over that").

Chris has a ventriloquist doll he calls Mr. Poppy and has been psychotically obsessed with a girl named Stacey since he first met her in the sixth grade at Greenville Grammar School. Chris's male ancestors dressed as women to get off the *Titanic*; he likes turkey — "but only the dark meat"; and his proudest moment occurred when he had his picture taken with Adam West (TV's *Batman*).

Chris believes he was meant to be many things but was dealt a cruel hand by fate. He attempted to become a male model ("Sparkles" Peterson) and enrolled in the Handsome Boy Modeling School. When he thought he should be an actor, he landed the role of a wildebeest in "Zoo Animals on Parade" at the Greenville Musical Theater. Last season episodes find Chris moving to 1804 York Avenue and into the garage of Gus Borden, an embittered ex-cop with a drinking problem.

210. Chrissy Snow, *Three's Company*, ABC, 1977–1980. Played by Suzanne Somers.

Christmas Snow, called Chrissy, was born in Fresno, California, on December 25 (hence her name). She is one of three roommates who share Apartment 201 of the Ropers' Apartment House in Santa Monica, California. The locale was also said to be Los Angeles and her roommates are Jack Tripper and Janet Wood.

Chrissy is the daughter of a minister and grew up feeling she had to be the best in bible class, the best in school, the best at everything. This affected her in later life as she has a habit of sleepwalking (in a short nightgown) when she goes to bed worried. Chrissy works as a secretary for an unnamed company (possibly J.C. Braddock & Company as her employer is a woman named J.C. Braddock). She also sold Easy Time Cosmetics to make extra money.

Chrissy is blonde, beautiful and a bit naïve at times (she can turn men on without realizing she is doing it). Chrissy wears a 36C bra, but often goes braless as she was part of the era of "Jiggle TV." She is sweet and trusting and cries when she gets upset. Chrissy is a member of Harvey's Health Spa and can come up with a plan on the spot but isn't sure what it is until after she realizes what the situation is. Chrissy always tries to answer the telephone with her left ear "because if I don't, I'll be listening with the wrong ear." Despite the dumb things she does, Chrissy claims "I always make sense. Other people are just not smart enough to understand me."

Chrissy leaves lip-gloss on half-eaten donuts, the cap off the toothpaste tube and says "If I have to listen to a dumb idea, I hope I'm not around to hear it." Chrissy snorts when she laughs and when she loses something she claims "Before it got lost was the last time I saw it." She enjoys a drink at the Regal Beagle Bar.

A contract dispute forced Suzanne Somers to leave the series. She was first seen in cameos (a quick phone call to her roommates telling them she is in Fresno caring for her sick mother); she was then written out when her equally gorgeous cousin, Cindy Snow, arrived to become Jack and Janet's new roommate.

See also: Cindy Snow, Ralph Furley, Stanley and Helen Roper, Jack Tripper, Janet Wood, Terri Alden.

211. Christie Love, *Get Christie Love*, ABC, 1974–1975. Played by Teresa Graves.

Christine Love, better known as Christie, is not only a beautiful and sexy woman when not working, but she is just as gorgeous on the job — as an undercover police woman with the Homicide Division, Metro Bureau, of the L.A.P.D.

Christie is the daughter of Mel and Rose Love. She was born on April 19, 1953, and was brought up to respect the law. Mel was a police detective and while not groomed to be a cop, Christie chose the life of a police officer. Christie wears badge number 7332 and lives at 3600 La Paloma Drive; 462-4699 is her phone number and her car license plate reads 343 MCI (later 089 LIR).

Christie is television's first African-American police woman and the first such female action star. She is an expert shot and keeps her skills sharp by practicing at a shooting range called Hogan's Alley. She never shoots to kill — "Just enough to stop 'em." Christie does, however, use her stunning good looks to help her in her undercover work. She measures 36-24-34 and will show cleavage and wear short skirts to accomplish a goal. Christie tries to go by the book, but sometimes the book doesn't agree with what Christie has in mind when investigating a case. Christie's car code is 5-Baker-5. She is also not as "mean" as she appears to be. She panics and tends to scream when she finds herself in a tight situation. While Christie claims to be a good cook, she prefers to dine out at her favorite eatery, Papa Caruso's Restaurant. She is fond of using the word "Sugah" and when she finally gets her man, she says, "You're under arrest, Sugah."

212. Christine and Jimmy Hughes, *Yes, Dear*, CBS, 1999–(current). Played by Liza Snyder, Mike O'Malley.

Christine and Jimmy Hughes are transplanted New Yorkers who now live in Los Angeles in the home of Kim and Greg Warner — Christine's sister and brother-in-law. Christine and Jimmy are the parents of Dominick and Logan and very laid back when it comes to disciplining their children. Christine and Jimmy met in high school and their first date involved watching a football game and drinking beer in his parents' basement. They lived together before marrying. They first lived in his parent's basement then in a cheap apartment (F) at 611 Sutton Street. Jimmy worked as a pizza deliveryman; Christine was a waitress at Howard Johnson's.

Greg looks upon Jimmy as a 20-year-old single guy without any responsibilities for the carefree lifestyle he lives. Jimmy was originally unemployed when the series began but through Greg acquired a job as a security gate guard at CBS-TV (Gate C, Building 3); his prior job was the giant sponge at a car wash.

Jimmy is the son of "Big" Jimmy and Kitty Hughes and as a child had a dream of becoming a baseball umpire (his dream is now to collect permanent disability). He was also in the emergency room eight times for hurting himself by doing stupid things (for example, trying to run through a wall like characters in cartoons; seeing if he could parachute off a roof with a bed sheet). Jimmy is cheap (makes his own books on tape "because the real ones are too expensive" and when at a strip club he folds dollar bills to make them look like tens). Jimmy can spot a strip club from a mile away "but put a check in front of him in a restaurant and he turns into Mr. Magoo."

Christine and Jimmy are never hard on their children (they rarely scold them; let them stay up as late as they want; and use TV as a babysitter). Christine is also not overly concerned if the kids eat food that falls on the floor (she couldn't care less about germs) and often relies on McDonald's take-out for their "nourishment" (she does complain that doing so deprives her kids of their vegetables). Christine doesn't seem to mind what Jimmy does (for example, she never complains about his strip club visits). In high school Christine was "the loose sister" (Kim was the prudish one) and called herself "a big high school slut." Christine was a constant worry to her mother for her habit of not wearing a bra or panties under her school uniform. Christine is basically responsible for raising Dominick and Logan. Jimmy doesn't help, doesn't clean and does what he wants to do. As a kid, Christine had a Crying Cathy Doll.

See also: Kim and Greg Warner.

213. Christine Armstrong, *Coach,* ABC, 1989–1996. Played by Shelley Fabares.

Christine Armstrong is the girlfriend, then wife, of Hayden Fox, coach of the Minnesota State University Screaming Eagles football team. Christine was born in Kentucky and is a graduate of St. Mary's High School and the University of Kentucky (where she acquired a degree in communications). Christine first worked as a sportscaster on KCCY-TV, Channel 6 in Minneapolis. Her segments on the local news were so popular that she was given her own weekly series, *Christine's Sports Round Up.* When the show was cancelled due to low ratings, she hosted the pilot episode for an unsold series called *Magazine America.* Christine next became the host of *Wake Up, Minneapolis,* but left the job when she and Hayden moved to Florida. Hayden now coached the Orlando Breakers (an NFL expansion team) and Christine became the host of *Coach's Corner,* a Breakers post-game show on Channel 5.

Christine is a logical, sensible woman who takes things in stride. She tries not to let the little things upset her but when they do she has "to be by myself" to work things out. She and Hayden met in 1986 at the United Charity Ball; they married on November 25, 1992.

See also: Hayden Fox.

214. Christina Castelli, *All About Us,* NBC, 2001–2002. Played by Alicia Lagano.

Christina Castelli is a very pretty 16-year-old girl who, because of her love of sports, is called Castelli by her friends. Christina is a sophomore at Belmont High School in Chicago. She lives at 934 Highland Avenue and often works after school as a waitress at the family business, Castelli's Pizza (she hates to work on Wednesday as the kids hate "Fat Free Wednesday"). Christina's trademark is her writing smiley faces on the customers' checks.

Although Christina likes sports, especially basketball (she is a member of the school's basketball team, the Bulldogs), she is still very feminine. She appears to be very sweet but if she feels she has been betrayed, "she can hold a serious grudge." Christina becomes a bit nervous around boys and twirls her hair with her finger to ease her nerves (she says, "I always have crushes but I'm never the crushee"). Christina and her girlfriends (Sierra, Nikki and Alecia) are members of the Martha Stewart Cooking Club (they get together every Sunday to test new recipes) and calls E.C.S. (Emergency Chat Sessions) to help the group resolve a problem. Her favorite hangout is the Loft, a teen club.

See also: Alecia Alcott, Nikki Merrick, Sierra Jennings.

215. Christine Sullivan, *Night Court,* NBC, 1984–1992. Played by Markie Post.

Christine Sullivan is the very beautiful and always fashionably dressed legal-aid attorney who defends clients in the courtroom of Harry T. Stone, a rather unorthodox night court judge in New York City.

Christine was born in the small town of North

Tonawanda (near Buffalo, New York). As a young girl she had a dog named Puddles and dreamed of becoming an Olympic gold medal ice skater. The ice stopped her ("It's slippery on that stuff"). Christine is a graduate of Tonawanda High School and Buffalo State College (where she majored in psychology and is now an expert on depression). Christine measures 37-23-35 and with her stunning looks and figure entered the 1978 Miss Greater Buffalo Pageant; she lost for taking a stand on women's rights.

Christine lost her first case (she cried hysterically, hyperventilated and had to be dragged out of the courtroom. The case involved a man who tried to dismantle a record store with his bare hands). Christine likes to wear sexy bras that reveal cleavage; however, she becomes easily upset and paces and has a tendency to "jiggle" (she often remarks "I should have worn my underwire bra").

Christine is a member of "Ha Ha" (Happy Alone, Happy Adults; their slogan is "Happy to Be Happy"). She was the inspiration for street artist Ian McKee who painted a large, nude mural of her on a warehouse door called "The Naked Body of Justice." Christine has a collection of Princess Diana porcelain thimbles and likes her job "because I serve justice and help the down trodden" (she also says "that the most artistic people I get as clients are hookers with makeup skills").

In 1990, Christine had an affair with undercover cop Tony Juliano and became pregnant. Nine months later (May 2, 1990), Christine gave birth to a son she named Charles Otis Juliano. She later wrote a children's book based on her experiences called *Mommy's World* under the pen name Mother Sullivan (she also divorced Tony one year after marrying him). Christine next ran for and was elected Congresswoman of the 13th District. The last episode (May 13, 1992) finds Christine moving to Washington, D.C., to pursue that goal. As a child, Christine's father, Jake, called her "Peaches."

See also: Bull Shannon, Dan Fielding, Harry T. Stone, Mac Robinson.

216. Christopher Titus, *Titus*, Fox, 2000–2002. Played by Christopher Titus.

This entry also contains information on Christopher's father, Ken Titus (Stacy Keach), Christopher's brother, Dave (Zack Ward), their mother, Juanita (Connie Stevens) and Christopher's girlfriend, Erin (Cynthia Watros).

Titus High Performance ("We Build Hot Rods") is a company owned by Christopher Titus, the son of a dysfunctional family. Christopher talks directly to the audience and says he pictured life as a television series he called "Life Is Swell." What he got, however, was life "with a mean spirited and evil father" and "a psychotic mother who believed in hurting people."

Christopher lives in California and is engaged to his high school sweetheart, Erin Fitzpatrick, the girl who is drawn to Christopher but frightened to death of Ken, whom she calls "Papa Titus." Juanita is also disturbed. She has multiple personalities and has apparently killed several people (she is currently in the psychiatric ward of a hospital but does manage to escape to visit her family). Ken calls her "The Crazy Bitch." Ken has been married five times but still chases women; he also smokes, drinks and curses. Christopher and Dave were brought up in a home of constant fighting by a bullying father who called them "wussies." Normal people now terrify Christopher and Dave (because when something happens they can't handle it). Ken's favorite watering hole is Mullany's Bar; Dave moonlights as a valet at the Rusty Cannon, a gay bar.

Christopher and Erin attended Seacliff High School (Erin was a cheerleader; Christopher, dressed as a pirate, was the football team mascot). After graduating, Erin enrolled in State College (hoping to become a psychiatrist); Christopher became a used car salesman before starting his own business. Ken is not all bad, says Christopher, "He never missed a smoke or drink or house payment in his life." Christopher also has a dark side: when he was a teenager he robbed a liquor store and was scolded and punished by Ken — not for the deed, but for not taking his brand of beer. When growing up, Christopher and Dave were also terrified by Apples, Juanita's insane German shepherd.

217. Christy Huddleston, *Christy*, CBS, 1994; PAX (2000). Played by Kellie Martin (CBS), Lauren Lee Smith (PAX).

Christine Huddleston, called Christy, is a young woman who cares about helping other people. She was born in Nashville, Tennessee, in 1893. She is the only child of a wealthy family (her baby sister, Amelia, died of scarlet fever two days before her second birthday. Christy was eight and says "It is the saddest day of my life"). One day in 1912, when Christy was 19 years old, she attended a sermon by Miss Alice Henderson, a Quaker missionary. The sermon so impressed Christy that she abandoned her life of luxury for a life of squalor in Cutter's Gap, Tennessee, in the heart of the Smokey Mountains.

Christy wants her life to count for something —

more than being married and having children. She is a graduate the Nashville Teaching College and believes she was meant to be in Cutter's Gap, an impoverished backwoods community. She also believes "I can change this place" and with what little money she has, she begins a quest to educate the children "with no notebooks, little paper, if any, and five tattered textbooks." Although Christy is surrounded by squalor, she says "I'm also surrounded by beauty."

Christy feels that living in Cutter's Gap "is like stepping back 100 years in time" (few people work and rely on growing their own food for survival). To help her get around, Christy has a horse (Jerome) and a donkey (Theo). Christy is called "Teacher" by her students.

218. Chuck Hookstratten, *Hey Landlord!*, NBC, 1966–1967. Played by Sandy Baron.

Charles Hookstratten, called Chuck, is best friends with Woody Banner, a recent college graduate who runs a ten room apartment house in Manhattan.

Chuck was born and raised in New York City. He was, as he says, "a rotten kid." He is the son of Leon and Fanny Hookstratten, and wanted to do what he wanted when he wanted. His parents had little control over him. He grew up on the streets and became a wise acre. He wrote on the school walls, stuck chewing gum under the seats and once tried to burn down the school. While not explained, he somehow managed to escape juvenile hall and graduate from both grammar and high schools. He next attended Ohio State University, where he met and befriended Woody. Chuck has ambitions to be a comedian and after graduation moved to New York with Woody (a potential writer) to pursue that goal. Chuck shares Woody's messy ground-floor apartment and assists Woody in running the building (he is called "Chuckula" by some tenants). Chuck and Woody take whatever jobs they can find but pursuing girls is uppermost on their agenda. Chuck worked as a model for Sedgewick Socks and takes shredded coconut in his hot tamales.
See also: Woody Banner.

219. Cindy and Allen Campbell, *Married People*, ABC, 1990–1991. Played by Megan Gallivan, Chris Young.

Cynthia and Allen Campbell are a newly married couple seeking careers in New York City. They live in Apartment 3 of a three family home at 862 Central Park North (at 73rd Street) in what is actually Harlem; however, the tenants call it "Central Park North" after the street sign on the corner.

Cindy, as Cynthia likes to be called, and Allen were born in Mineral Wells, Indiana. They chose to move to the big city after their high school graduation so Allen could attend Columbia University (while not made exactly clear, apparently to become some sort of scientist). Cindy, like Allen, is 18 years old. She was a cheerleader in high school and hopes to become a professional dancer. She works as a waitress at the East Side Diner and attends as many show auditions as she can. She acquired her first professional job with the Exotic Porthole Dancers and in the last episode acquired the role of Girl Number 2 in the Broadway play *The Phantom of the Opera* at the Majestic Theater.

In Mineral Wells Cindy had a pet cat named Simone and was famous for her "Sticky Treats" (a gooey Rice Krispies cereal and marshmallow snack). Cindy and Allen were childhood sweethearts. Cindy is very pretty but very protective of Allen because she fears another girl will try and steal him. Allen does associate with beautiful girls at school, but he is totally devoted to Cindy (something he has a hard time convincing her of). Allen works after classes in the school's lab. In New York he is allergic to hazelnuts; in Indiana he was allergic to walnuts. Cindy's favorite meal to prepare is three-bean and marshmallow casserole.
See also: Elizabeth and Russell Meyers.

Cindy Brady *see* **Marcia Brady**

Cindy Grant *see* **B.J. McKay**

220. Cindy Lubbock, *Just the Ten of Us*, ABC, 1988–1990. Played by Jamie Luner.

Cynthia Anne Lubbock, called Cindy, is a sophomore at Saint Augustine's Catholic High School in Eureka, California. She is 16 years old and the daughter of Graham and Elizabeth Lubbock, the parents of eight children. Cindy was born on Long Island in New York on July 3, 1972.

Cindy is the third oldest child. She is beautiful and knows it but has no common sense and is not too bright. She never used her middle name because for years she wasn't sure if it was Anne or Diane. Cindy wears as 36C bra and size eight dress. Cheese is her favorite food and she has a slight weight problem (she is a member of the Diet Control Clinic). She is boy crazy but doesn't realize she is a tease. She has a tendency to lead boys on but quits when she realizes "What am I doing? I can't lead myself." Her sisters believe Cindy's body is like a flashing neon sign — "Open All Night, No Waiting."

Cindy admits she can't sew and make sweaters,

"but I sure know how to wear one." She first worked as a receptionist at the Eureka Fitness Center (at $8 an hour) and she was the host of her own radio program, *What's Happening, Saint Augie's*, over the school's radio station, KHPO. She says "Hi-eee" and "By-eee" for hello and goodbye. Cindy formed the singing group, The Lubbock Babes, with her sisters, Marie, Wendy and Connie.

See also: Connie Lubbock, Graham and Elizabeth Lubbock, Marie Lubbock, Wendy Lubbock.

221. Cindy Snow, *Three's Company*, ABC, 1980–1982. Played by Jenilee Harrison.

Cynthia Snow, called Cindy, is the gorgeous, blonde cousin of Chrissy Snow, the girl who shares an apartment with Janet Wood and Jack Tripper. Cindy is actually the replacement for Chrissy when Suzanne Somers left the show (explained as leaving to care for her sick mother).

Cindy was born in a small town in California and felt she needed to change her dull life by moving to the big city to find excitement. Chrissy arranged for her to stay with Jack and Janet (although she forgot to tell them) and set her up with a job as a secretary at her company (with a Mr. Hadley). Cindy shares the same bedroom Chrissy shared with Janet.

Cindy is clumsy and, according to Jack, a walking disaster area (he calls her "a perfect ten on the Richter Scale").

Cindy's father is a traveling salesman. She has a basset hound named Wilbur, that she has had since she was 10 years old. Cindy cannot lie and is a bit naïve (she tends to believe what people tell her). She believes that Jack, who often stretches the truth, is the best liar she has ever met. Cindy later attends UCLA and hires herself out as a maid to make extra money. She left the show when she moved into the dormitory on campus. Jack had always been on the receiving end of Cindy's mishaps; he most missed her "Oops" when she did something wrong. She was replaced by Terri Alden.

See also: Chrissy Snow, Ralph Furley, Stanley and Helen Roper, Jack Tripper, Janet Wood, Terri Alden.

222. Cissy Davis, *Family Affair*, WB, 2002–2003. Played by Caitlin Wachs.

Sigournay Elizabeth Davis, better known as Cissy, was born in Terre Haute, Indiana, in 1988. She is the daughter of Ken and Laura Davis and has a younger sister and brother, twins Buffy and Jody. Tragedy struck the family when Cissy turned 15: her parents were killed in an automobile accident. Cissy was sent to her Aunt Jenny and Uncle Doug in Ohio; the twins were relocated to New York to live with their uncle, Bill Davis. Cissy's life would again change shortly after. When Jenny and Doug sell their house and buy a mobile home, Cissy felt she would be a burden and traveled to New York (via bus) with a hope that she would find a new home with her Uncle Bill. Although Cissy's unexpected arrival shocked Bill, he saw how much she, Buffy and Jody needed each other and made his study her bedroom.

Cissy, a talented young girl, can write poetry, sing, dance, and act, and dreams of becoming an actress. Bill sets that dream in motion by enrolling her at the High School for the Lively Arts at 79th Street and Broadway (the school is also called the Performing Arts High School). Cissy played Eliza Dolittle in the school's production of *Pygmalion* and was a member of the Antionettes, a social club for young ladies.

In the original CBS version of the series (1966–1971), Kathy Garver played the role as Catherine "Cissy" Davis, a typical teenage girl who attended Lexington High School in Manhattan. Kathy appeared in the new version of the series on December 5, 2002 ("A Family Affair Christmas"), in the role of a passenger at the airport.

See also: Bill Davis, Buffy and Jody Davis.

C.J. Parker *see* **The Girls of Baywatch**

Clair Huxtable *see* **Cliff and Clair Huxtable**

223. Claire McCarron, *Leg Work*, CBS, 1987. Played by Margaret Colin.

Claire McCarron is a beautiful young woman with a job that requires a considerable amount of walking. She is a private detective who owns McCarron Investigations at 307 Avenue of the Americas in Manhattan.

Claire is the daughter of Michael and Linda McCarron. She was born in New York City and grew up in a family of law enforcers: her father was a police captain; her brother, Fred, is a lieutenant with the Office of Public Relations.

Claire is a graduate of New York University and first worked as an assistant district attorney at Foley Square. The job bored Claire as she yearned for excitement. She quit to become her own boss. Claire charges $500 a day plus expenses and lives at 365 East 65th Street with her dog Clyde. She drives a silver Porsche (plate DEX 627) and 555-4365 is her mobile phone number. When a case bothers Claire she makes oatmeal raisin cookies — one of two foods she can prepare (the other is coq au vin — chicken in wine sauce).

Claire's pride and joy is her collection of very rare Lionel "O" gauge pre–World War II electric trains that she inherited from her father.

Claire is not one for wearing pants or slacks. She loves wearing dresses or miniskirts that show off her shapely legs and keeps in shape by doing a lot of walking because her car is always in need of repair. Claire is cautious when it comes to cases. She likes to have all the facts before she begins her investigations (an old habit she picked up while working for the D.A.). Claire does have a gun but she prefers not to use it (she is almost totally opposed to violence but feels there has to be some violence in the world or she would be out of a job).

224. Clarissa Darling, *Clarissa Explains It All*, NIK, 1991–1994. Played Melissa Joan Hart.

Clarissa Marie Darling is a very pretty 13-year-old girl who speaks directly to the TV audience "to explain all the things that go on around here." Clarissa is the daughter of Marshall and Janet Darling and lives at 464 Shadow Lane in Baxter Beach, Florida, with her obnoxious brother, Ferguson.

Clarissa attends Thomas Tupper Junior High School and receives an allowance of three dollars a week; she shops at the Willow Mall. She has a "security alligator" (Elvis) who lives in "The Heartbreak Hotel" (a small plastic pool in her bedroom). Clarissa's dream is to own a 1976 apple red Gremlin ("the car, not the creature"). She has a collection of hubcaps on her wall and a 28-foot gum chain made from "recycled gum." Clarissa wears fish earrings, likes junk food (especially Twizzlers licorice and jawbreakers) and says she hates "the kind of pixie haircuts your mom gives you at home and I hate germs everywhere." Clarissa earns money by walking Sarge, the neighbor's collie. At one point, when she appeared to have a bad case of E.P.S. ("Empty Pockets Syndrome"), Clarissa went looking for a job and found five: clerk at Bert's Bait Bucket; waitress at Weenie Drive-Thru Hot Dog Shack; assistant at the Precious Poodle Playpen; salesgirl at Planet Fantastic 2000 Comic Books; and research assistant at the public library. Her first real job was Kiddie Attendant (as Little Bo Peep) at the Baxter Beach Carnival. Her favorite cult movie is *Revenge of the Nerds* and sour cream and onion is her favorite flavor of potato chips. Her favorite TV show is *21 Jump Street*.

Clarissa's most embarrassing moment occurred when her brother brought her bra to school for "show and tell." Her most frightening experience occurred on her seventh birthday when she stuck her head in the sour cream dip and almost drowned. As a kid, Clarissa had a rocking horse named Trigger and "starred" in several school plays: the tail of a T-Rex in "The Prehistoric Pageant"; a Wiseman in "The Christmas Pageant"; and a pillar in "The Greek Day Pageant." Peanut butter swirl is Clarissa's favorite flavor of ice cream. *The Little Mermaid* is her favorite Disney movie. Clarissa wrote for the school newspaper, *The Thomas Tupper Times*. The final episode was the unsold pilot for a CBS series in which Clarissa moved to New York to become an intern at a newspaper called *The Daily Post*.

See also: Ferguson Darling.

225. Clark Kent, *The Adventures of Superman*, Syn., 1953–1957. Played by George Reeves.

Clark Kent is a man with three separate identities. His real name is Kal-El and he was born on the now extinct planet Krypton (1926 Earth time). He is the son of Jor-El, a leading scientist, and his wife, Lara.

Jor-El was a member of the Scientific Council when he discovered that Krypton was being drawn closer to its sun and destruction. When the council marked him as a fool for his theories, Jor-El began preparations to save his family from the impending disaster. Jor-El, however, miscalculated and had only time to build a small, experimental rocket. Jor-El and Lara placed the infant in the rocket and Jor-El programmed it to land on Earth, a planet he knew to be inhabited. Just as the rocket cleared Krypton space, the planet exploded and scattered billions of particles of Kryptonite, the only substance that can harm Kal-El, into the universe. The rocket and its infant passenger crash-landed near the Jones farm in Smallville, U.S.A. on April 10, 1926.

Eben and Sarah Kent, a childless farm couple, witnessed the landing. Eben risked his life to save the baby. Kal-El, wrapped in red and blue blankets, was miraculously unharmed. Seconds later, the rocket exploded, destroying all evidence of its ever having been there.

Realizing that no one would ever believe their fantastic story, Eben and Sarah decided to raise the baby as their own and named him Clark. As Clark grew, each year brought to life evidence of Clark's amazing powers: X-ray vision, incredible strength, exceptional hearing, the ability to fly, immunity to disease and incapable of being hurt. Twenty-five years later, after the death of Eben, Sarah urges Clark to use his great abilities to help mankind. She makes him a costume from the blankets that were originally wrapped around him. To keep his true identity a secret, Clark maintains the alias of mild-mannered Clark Kent and moves to Metropolis, where he becomes a reporter for the *Daily Planet*, a crusading newspaper. Clark takes up residence at the Standish Arms Hotel (Apartment 5H); West 3-0963 is his phone number. To further conceal his true identity as Superman, Clark pretends to be somewhat of a coward when threatening situations arise. He always manages to sneak away, which gives him the opportunity to reappear as Superman. He works for Perry White, editor of the *Planet*, and with reporter Lois Lane and photographer Jimmy Olsen.

The above information was compiled from episodes of the original series. Other versions (movies, TV and comic books) name Clark's parents as Martha and Jonathan or Sarah and Jonathan. Smallville is said to be located in Kansas and Kal-El was a small child, not an infant when he was found by the Kents.

See also: Lois Lane.

226. Claudia and Sean Finnerty, *Grounded for Life*, Fox, 2001–2002; WB, 2003–2005. Played by Megyn Price, Donal Logue.

Claudia and Sean Finnerty are a busy married couple who live at 856 Winslow Place on Staten Island in New York. They are the parents of Claudia, Henry and Jimmy, and have a dog named Murphy.

Claudia Bustamonte and Sean Finnerty met in high school (St. Finian's). They fell in love and married shortly after graduating. Claudia found work as a waitress while Sean "worked in a dump" as a sanitation landfill supervisor. He is later an electrician, then construction supervisor for the New York Subway System. Sean found the subway job dirty and noisy (working in tunnels all day) and quit to open a bar called the Red Boot Pub. After raising their children, Claudia also found work — "hostess at a very popular SoHo restaurant" (a later episode claims Claudia became pregnant at 17 and married Sean after the birth of Claudia).

At 32, Sean considers himself "a cool, young thinking father"; Claudia, very immature in high school, was also child-like through most of her marriage. She matured when the series switched networks. Sean wears a size 10½ D shoe; hates cell phones ("they annoy me'); and when he makes homemade pizza, he does so with ketchup on pita bread. Claudia is a very sexy woman who relishes in the fact that after three children she can still turn men's heads. Her flamboyant style and dress have earned her the nickname "The Neighborhood Hot Mom." Claudia is taking classes at Wadsworth College "to improve my mind" and uses "embarrassing Raggedy Ann checks" ("the bank sent them so I use them").

Claudia and Sean were heavy smokers in their youth. Although they are a two-income family, they can't afford to take the family on a decent vacation and always wind up at the Jersey Shore. Sean drives a car with the license plate CQP 293 (later STY 293) and believes his New York Knicks basketball jersey is lucky (the team always wins when he wears it).

See also: Claudia Finnerty.

227. Claudia Salinger, *Party of Five*, Fox, 1994–2000. Played by Lacey Chabert.

Claudia Salinger is 11 years old and in the fifth grade. She is the youngest daughter of Nicholas and Diana Salinger, the owners of Salinger's Restaurant in San Francisco (her parents were killed in a tragic car accident by a drunk driver). She lives at 3324 Broadway with her brothers (Charlie, Bailey and Owen) and sister, Julia.

Claudia is very sweet but also a very private person She loves the TV show *Sesame Street* and hopes to become a concert violinist (like her mother). Claudia feels it is her duty to keep the family together. She also believes she has all the solutions to the problems that arise but nobody will listen to her. Following her parents' death, Claudia felt she needed her own space and moved out of the bedroom she shared with Julia. She first set up a tent in the dining room then slept in the shower stall when an earthquake frightened her. She finally returned to her old bedroom when Julia moved into the attic.

When Claudia turned 12 she began classes at Walt Whitman Jr. High School and immediately felt inadequate, especially about her figure. Hoping to develop a bustline, Claudia increased her breast size by purchasing the Incredi-Bra. Claudia got the attention she sought but found it too much to handle and discarded the bra. She turned "evil" when she met a girl named Jody and began to smoke, drink and use foul language. She overcame this when she realized her new attitude was offending people, not impressing them.

Although Claudia was considered one of the Bay areas most gifted young musicians, she gave up the violin after she broke her arm while ice-skating. Claudia wrote the column, "I Claudia," for the school newspaper and tried out for but lost a role in the school play *The Crucible*.

See also: Bailey Salinger, Charlie Salinger, Julia Salinger.

228. Cleopatra, *Cleopatra 2525*, Syn., 2000–2001. Played by Jennifer Sky.

This entry also contains information on Sarge (Victoria Pratt) and Hel (Gina Torres), the women who assist Cleopatra in the battle against evil in the year 2525.

Cleopatra (no other name given, but also called Cleo) was born in Phoenix, Arizona, but raised in California when the family relocated shortly after her birth. Cleo had a dog named Pants and at the age of eight received 12 stitches in her arm when she fell off her roller blades (she now has a scar on her elbow). She attended Glendale High School and with a desire to become an actress, enrolled in Glendale Community College (she drove a red Mustang she called Maggie at the time). After graduating, she took the stage name Cleopatra when the only job she could find was that of a stripper in nightclubs. Cleopatra found the job rewarding but felt larger breasts would benefit her act. She made arrangements for the necessary operation. During the enhancement process "something went wrong" (all that we are told) and Cleo was cryogenically frozen "until a cure can be found." The year was 2001, when Cleo turned 21.

Cleo's body "remained on ice" until she was "thawed out" in the year 2525 to save the life of a girl named Sarge, a resistance fighter who had been seriously injured and needed a replacement kidney (Cleo's genetic makeup was found to be a perfect match for Sarge). Whatever the reason for Cleo being preserved apparently healed itself as no mention is made of it. Cleo awakens following the operation, looks down at her breasts and says "good work." Seconds later, the lab is attacked by the enemies of the resistance and Cleo quickly learns of her fate. She is now part of Sarge and joins with her and Sarge's partner, Hel, to battle the enemies of the Earth — alien machines called Bailies.

Cleo is an excellent mimic and tends to scream, cry and whimper. She is always seen wearing a pink miniskirt and low-cut pink blouse. Sarge, real name Rose, was originally a soldier with the Black Watch Resistance Fighters. She is impulsive and plunges into violent confrontations without thinking first. She has been "wounded and repaired" many times and owes her life to Cleo.

Hel, short for Helen, is the leader of the group. She receives information on Bailey activities from the unseen, mysterious Voice, through an implant behind her ear. Hel is rational and her approach to each situation is logically planned. Her most treasured possession is a wood tube that holds a picture of her father (wood is now extremely rare).

229. Cliff and Clair Huxtable, *The Cosby Show*, NBC, 1984–1992. Played by Bill Cosby, Phylicia Rashad.

Dr. Cliff Huxtable, his wife, Clair, a lawyer, and their children (Sondra, Denise, Theo, Vanessa and Rudy) live at 10 Stigwood Avenue in Brooklyn, New York. Cliff is a gynecologist-obstetrician with offices at home and at both the Children's Hospital and Corinthian Hospital. Clair is with the firm of Greentree, Bradley and Dexter.

Cliff is the son of Russell and Anna Huxtable; Clair is the daughter of Al and Carrie Hanks. They met and fell in love at Hillman College in Georgia (Clair called Cliff "Baby Cakes"; Cliff called Clair "Lum Lum"). They married after graduation on February 14, 1964, and honeymooned at the Caralu Hotel in the Caribbean.

Cliff, whose real name is Heathcliff, loves jazz music and calls himself "Mr. Jazz." He enjoys watching rodeo events on TV and is also a fan of western movies (his favorite is *Six Guns for Glory* starring Colt Kirby). Jake's Appliance Store is his favorite hangout (where Clair says he has no sales resistance). As a kid, Cliff had a pet bird (Charlie) and a bike he called Bob. His ambition at the time was to become a drummer. He and Clair read a daily paper called the *City Sun*. Cliff likes to eavesdrop on Clair and the kids as it is sometimes the only way he knows what is going on in his own house.

Cliff has a tendency to gain weight and is often restricted by Clair to eating only healthy foods (although Cliff tries to sneak a piece of junk food whenever he can). Clair is very careful about what she eats and becomes very upset if she gains any weight (at which time she goes to drastic measures to lose it). Her weakness is Mexican food (which she and Cliff enjoy at the El Grande del Restaurante). Clair wears a size eight dress and was a panelist on *Retrospective*, a Channel 37 TV show that explored history. Clair is calm and restrained; Cliff is more of an alarmist and feels that if anything will go wrong it will go wrong in his presence. Clair is the one who usually yells at the kids when they do something wrong while Cliff sits by and listens. When Clair is done Cliff always agrees —"And that goes for me too."

See also: Denise Huxtable, Sondra Huxtable, Theo Huxtable, Vanessa and Rudy Huxtable.

230. Cliff Claven, *Cheers*, NBC, 1982–1993. Played by John Ratzenberger.

Clifford Claven, called Cliff, is a regular at Cheers, the Boston bar owned by Sam Malone. He was born in Boston and as a child was fascinated by anything and everything. He continued this by acquiring knowledge and today has an opinion on everything and believes he knows everything there is to know about anything.

Cliff works as a letter carrier for the U.S. Post Office. He was originally assigned to the Meadow View Acres route near the airport then a route for the South Central Branch. He was later promoted to District Supervisor, Subdivision A, Grid L. Cliff feared the day the now extinct Sears catalogue came out as it put an extra strain on him (he also fears the Flannigan's dog, which is on his route). Cliff is a member of a lodge called the Knights of the Semitar and he watches the Weather Channel for only one reason — the Weather Bunnies ("You sort of develop a fatherly feeling after a while").

Cliff believes he is "the wing nut that holds Western Civilization together." His car trunk contains an inflatable raft and several cans of tuna fish (he is prepared for the East Coast flooding that will occur if the Polar Ice Caps melt due to global warming). He is also an amateur inventor and enjoys Twinkies as a snack.

See also: Carla LeBec, Diana Chambers, Ernie Pantusso, Norm Peterson, Rebecca Howe, Sam Malone, Woody Boyd.

231. Clint Cassidy, *Doc,* PAX, 2001–2005. Played by Billy Ray Cyrus.

Clint Cassidy was born in a rural section of Montana where he enjoyed fishing, sleeping under the stars and helping his father with chores around the family farm. Tragedy struck when Clint was 10 years old. His father died of cancer. Clint felt helpless during the ordeal and vowed to become a doctor and help people. He graduated from medical school in North Dakota and returned to his hometown to work at the Johanson Medical Center, where he doubled as a physician as well as a much-needed veterinarian. Clint, however, had dreams of beginning a practice in New York City. He had always been hesitant to follow that dream until he woke up one morning and thought "What if I never tried it?" Through a connection with a friend, a writer for *Ultra Elite* magazine, Clint applies for and receives a position at the Westbury Clinic on the Upper West Side of Manhattan (the clinic works in conjunction with Manhattan General Hospital). Clint now resides in an apartment (7) and pays $1900 a month rent.

Clint treasures the last thing his father gave him, his gold money clip. Clint wears jeans and boots and, as people say, "looks like he's ready to ride a horse." Clint has an unusual "talent"— he can pick pockets like an expert. Female patients find him handsome and irresistible. Clint listens to patients and cares about them. His country ways are unusual, not dramatic and unconven-tional. He even makes house calls and will not compromise his patients. Clint is a Cincinnati Reds baseball fan and Johnny Bench is his favorite sports figure. Luigi's Restaurant is his favorite eatery. (In later episodes, the clinic is seen as the Woodbury Clinic and the hospital as Manhattan Memorial.)

232. Cole, *Tracker,* Syn., 2001. Played by Adrian Paul.

Cole is the Earth name taken by Daggon, an alien from the planet Cirron. Daggon has come to Earth to recapture 218 dangerous criminals who have escaped from the prison planet Sartop, before they wreck havoc on the planet.

Daggon was born on Cirron, one of six planets in the Migar Solar System. He was an educator and studied many different fields in college; one of his specialties was the planet Earth (he believes human physiology is very primitive). Daggon was married and had a daughter. They were apparently killed by a female criminal named Ree. To avenge their deaths, Daggon became a Tracker (bounty hunter) and captured Ree. He was assigned to guard her, but she managed to escape through a wormhole that led to the Earth (218 additional prisoners followed her). Daggon discovered the wormhole and he too found his way to Earth (this information was compiled from bits and pieces of dialogue from various episodes; nothing is really explained and it has been placed in logical order to continue Daggon's life with what follows).

The wormhole deposits Daggon near Highway 88 in Illinois. A bit dazed, Daggon begins to wander and stops near a highway billboard for Cole (men's briefs). He assumes the image of the model depicted in the ad. Daggon then approaches a stranded motorist (Mel Porter) and helps her (he places his hand on the car and the engine starts). As Mel speaks to thank him, Daggon begins to understand English. When Mel suggests "You look like the Cole guy," Daggon assumes Cole as his name.

Mel (Amy Price-Francis) owns a bar called the Watchfire in Chicago's Criminal Courts District. It is not made quite clear why a very trusting Mel allows Cole to live in a room above the bar, but she fears for him and does become involved in his crusade when he reveals his true nature to her.

Cole wears clothes that were left by one of Mel's former boyfriends and enjoys all types of Earth foods, especially corn on the cob. He can mentally stop time and alter it for a split second. Cole can manipulate electronic equipment with powers he emits from his fingers. He can also change his appearance by studying a picture of someone and assuming that image. Cole has incredible strength and can leap to fantastic heights. Extraordinary feats weaken Cole ("It takes one solar day for me to regenerate") and he becomes numb when exposed to cold weather. He works at the bar to protect his true identity.

233. Colleen McMurphy, *China Beach*, ABC, 1988–1991. Played by Dana Delany.

Colleen McMurphy is a triage nurse stationed at China Beach, the U.S. Armed Forces R&R facility in DaNang, Republic of Vietnam. She is attached to the 510th Evac Hospital, 63rd Division.

Colleen, an Irish Catholic, was born in Lawrence, Kansas, in 1948. She began her career as a nurse in 1966 at the age of 18 (she was inspired by John F. Kennedy that she can make a difference). She joined the army, trained in Houston and volunteered for service in Vietnam (she is representative of the 50,000 women who actually served in Nam). Colleen wears a size 34C bra and her serial number is N91574. She was called "F.N.G." (Fairly New Guy) when she first arrived on China Beach. Colleen is desperately trying to do her job while at the same time struggling to overcome her feelings of frustration and make sense out of an unjustified war and senseless killing.

Colleen served as a lieutenant in Vietnam for two years (1967–69) and feels she made a difference — "I couldn't save them all, but I saved some. I mattered. We all did." In 1967, Colleen had one wish — "a day without choppers" (helicopters brought the wounded). It never came true. Three years later, Colleen returned home to Kansas and took a job as a nurse at the local hospital. By 1972, she was "a wild at heart free spirit who took to the open road via a motorcycle."

The year 1975 saw Colleen taking to the road again, this time in a car (plate CN3 679) to escape the memories of her past. She drifted for a few years and finally settled in Portland, Oregon, where she acquired a job as a hospital administrator. In 1985, she married architect Joseph Arenberry. By 1988 (the last we know of her character), Colleen is the mother of a three-year-old girl named Maggie.

See also: K.C., Laurette Barber (for information on Laurette, Cherry White, Waylou Marie Holmes and Lila Garreau, the nurses on China Beach).

234. Colt Seavers, *The Fall Guy*, ABC, 1981–1986. Played by Lee Majors.

Colt Seavers is a man who makes money by getting killed, blownup, shot, punched, pushed off cliffs or whatever peril is required. He is a stuntman for the Fall Guy Stunt Association in Hollywood. He also works as a bounty hunter for the Los Angeles Criminal Courts System.

Colt was born in California and grew up in a rural area. He became fascinated by stunts he saw performed in movies and was taught to hunt and track by his father. While attending UCLA, Colt met and befriended "Wild" Dan Wilde, a famous stuntman who taught him the ropes.

Colt is now somewhat of a loner. He considers himself the best tracker in the business and charges $500 a day plus expenses to find bail jumpers. He lives in what people call "a shed in the woods." Despite the fact that it is off the beaten path and always in need of repair Colt calls it home (his favorite pastime is soaking in his outdoor tub). Colt uses a movie stunt gun with three-quarter load blanks — "To impress people." His favorite watering hole is the Palomino Club and his car license plate reads FALL GUY.

Colt works with Jody Banks (Heather Thomas) and his cousin, Howie Munson (Douglas Barr). Jody is a shapely stuntwoman (36-24-36) who also assists Colt on cases. She lives at 146 Del Mar Vista (in the Marina) and drives a car with the license plate 1GS 1267. Howie is Colt's business manager and apprentice stuntman. He has spent seven years in college. At Iowa State he specialized in Latin America Culture; he was boxing champion at Yale University; took accounting at Oklahoma State; majored in business at Harvard but also attended Cornell, Cal State and Fresno State College. Colt calls him "Kid."

235. Columbo, *Columbo*, NBC, 1971–1978; ABC, 1989–1991. Played by Peter Falk.

Columbo (no first name) is a lieutenant with the Homicide Division of the Los Angeles Police Department. He is first said to be with the Hollenbeck Division then Central Division. He was born in New York City and attributes his becoming a police officer to the Edward G. Robinson, Humphrey Bogart and James Cagney gangster pictures of the 1930s that he watched as a child. They instilled him with a passion for justice. Columbo joined the army after high school. After serving in Korea, he became an officer with the N.Y.P.D. In 1958, he moved to Los Angeles and joined the L.A.P.D.

Columbo rarely uses his gun and often neglects his yearly firing range tests. He is rarely in his office due to his field investigations. When it comes to dancing he claims "I have two left feet." Columbo drives a rundown 1952 Peugeot (plate

448 DBZ) that people say is in bad shape (even though the car needs a painting, Columbo parks it in the shade "because the sun wrecks havoc with the paint").

Columbo is a master of deductive reasoning but claims to have a bad memory. His badge number is 436 (also seen as 416) and he wears a rumpled raincoat virtually every place he goes. He tends to slouch, is always early for appointments and studies peoples' faces for their reactions to his questions. He is persistent and fascinated by the evidence he finds. Little insignificant details bother him and he will not rest until he can tie up every loose end. He believes there is something wrong with him because "I seem to bother people and make them nervous," especially when he approaches a suspect and says "Oh, just one more thing."

Columbo always appears to be working on a case. He would like Saturday nights off but "I can't take it off if duty calls." He enjoys comedy and variety shows on television and gave up listening to the radio — "Perry Como and Louis Armstrong I understand, but those rock groups give me an earache." He also likes to play pool and he considers himself an excellent cook. He dislikes flying and boating as they tend to make him sick.

Columbo taught a criminology course at Freemont College and enjoys a hot cup of tea ("I don't like luke warm tea") and hot, strong black coffee ("no decaf for me"). He does have a bad habit of smoking cigars — "I know it's a filthy habit and that I should have given it up years ago. Even my wife complains and sends me out to the porch." His wife, Kate, would like him to smoke a pipe "but that's too much for me to carry around." (Columbo's wife is never seen. She is only referred to by Columbo as "The Wife" or "Mrs. Columbo.") Columbo has a basset hound called both Fang and Dog ("He's a dog so we call him Dog"). Peter Falk first played the role in the NBC TV Movie *Prescription Murder* on February 20, 1968.

See also: Kate Columbo.

236. Connie Brooks, *Our Miss Brooks*, CBS, 1952–1956. Played by Eve Arden.

Constance Brooks is young, pretty and single and looking for a man in her life. She works as an English teacher at Madison High School and lives at Mrs. Davis's Boarding House on Carroll Street in the small town of Madison.

Connie, as she is called, was born and raised in Madison and is herself a graduate of Madison High. She is very dedicated to her job and always gives of herself to help students who are falling be-

hind. She is also soft hearted and can't turn down anyone with a hard luck story. Connie puts in long days and is genuinely tired when she gets home; it is then that she enjoys what she calls "School Teacher's B&B" ("Bath and Bed").

Connie enjoys pancakes and tomato juice for breakfast and likes jellybeans ("but only the purple ones"). She often complains about how small her paycheck is and how hard it is for her to make ends meet. She sometimes resorts to hocking items at Fisher's Pawn Shop. Connie enjoys the holidays (especially Christmas) and when she first became a teacher she looked forward to the first day of school. Her years of experience has taught her to now fear it for it means the beginning of another hard working year. Connie is a bit absentminded at times and often forgets her own birthday. Last season episodes find Connie teaching at Mrs. Nestor's Elementary School in California's San Fernando Valley when Madison High is torn down to make way for a highway.

Connie's fantasies revolve around Philip Boynton (Robert Rockwell), the extremely shy biology teacher on whom she has a crush. "Philip is bashful when it comes to women. I don't mind that. It's just this one particular English teacher who I mind him being bashful with." Connie wishes Philip would take "brave shots" as women appear to frighten him off. He is not romantic and treats Connie with respect (too much Connie believes). When Connie lucks out and Philip becomes romantic, something always happens to interrupt him and he loses his confidence. Connie also has frequent dreams about Philip "and as usual, nothing happens." Despite the lack of affection and kisses, Connie loves Philip and hopes to make a man out of him.

Philip was born in Seattle and is a graduate of Cavendish High School. He met Connie in 1948 when he came to Madison (he has a pet lab frog named McDougal). He is the school's track coach and a member of the Elk's Club. Philip plays the ukulele and carries jellybeans with him at all times ("The dextrose contained in them is one of the best sources of quick energy known to science").

237. Connie Lubbock, *Just the Ten of Us*, ABC, 1988–1990. Played by JoAnn Willette.

Constance Lubbock, called Connie, is the 15-year-old daughter of Graham and Elizabeth Lubbock. She is a freshman at Saint Augustine's High School in Eureka, California and is the most sensitive of her seven siblings. She was born on Long Island, New York, on May 16, 1973.

Connie hopes to become a journalist and writes for the school newspaper, the *Herald-Gazette*. She wears a size five dress, a 34A bra and is jealous of girls with larger breasts (she believes girls with ample cleavage get all the attention. She wore falsies and found she was right; she went back to being herself when she felt uncomfortable being someone else). Connie (jersey 8) loves to play basketball with her father (who is determined to beat her) and considers herself and her older sister, Marie, "the two Lubbock sisters who are not man crazy." She also feels Marie is the only person she can talk to about guys. Connie's first job was sweeping animal entrails at the MacGregor Slaughter House for $4 an hour. Connie became the fourth "babe" when Wendy, Cindy and Marie formed the singing Lubbock Babes (who performed regularly at Danny's Pizza Parlor).

See also: Cindy Lubbock, Graham and Elizabeth Lubbock, Marie Lubbock, Wendy Lubbock.

238. Cookie Brody, *Aliens in the Family*, ABC, 1996. Played by Margaret Trigg.

This entry also contains information on Cookie's husband, Doug (John Bedford Lloyd), and their children Heather (Paige Tiffany), Adam (Chris Marquette), Spit (Michelan Sisti), Snizzie (Alice Dinnear) and Bobut (voice of John Kennedy).

Cookie is a strikingly beautiful alien from the Neutron Galaxy. She is divorced and the mother of Snizzie, Spit and Bobut. Cookie worked as a DNA scientist and is extremely intelligent (she has an I.Q. of 5,000 by Earth standards). Her ability to use her entire brain has earned her a high ranking in her galaxy and has the coveted job of experimenting on lower life forms from other galaxies. Cookie is heartless. Her job involves extracting brains for research and she shows no remorse for destroying a life form. On a medical voyage to the backward planet Earth, Cookie spots Doug Brody barbequing in his backyard. Cookie kidnaps him and brings him aboard her ship. Cookie is about to extract his brain when she falls in love and spares his life. He also falls in love with her and she gives up her life on Neutron to live with his family in Sherwood Hills. Cookie is now delegated to the role of housewife and mother (she is human in appearance but with blue ears) but her children are all bug-eyed and fish-faced like their biological alien father. Doug is the father of Heather and Adam and works at a company called Trans Global International. He is content being the husband of an alien (they married at an unspecified time after leaving Neutron). Heather, Spit and Snizzie attend Sherwood Hills Memorial High School; Adam is enrolled at the Sherwood Hills Elementary School; Bobut is another story.

Bobut is a super intelligent alien baby (a puppet) who believes he is the center of the universe (he is being groomed by Cookie to become the Emperor of the Neutron Galaxy). Bobut wears size three diapers "with little ducks on the sticky tapes." His favorite food is pudding and he has a plush dog name Sugar Pie. Bobut believes mothers are the most intelligent life forms on Earth. He expects his family to bow down to him but he gets little respect from them in that aspect. Bobut likes to rule the house (and practice his future dictatorship) from his high chair in the kitchen.

239. Cordelia Chase, *Angel*, WB, 1999–2004. Played by Charisma Carpenter.

The character of Cordelia Chase first appeared as a regular on *Buffy the Vampire Slayer* on the WB from 1997 to 1999. Cordelia Chase, called Cordy, assisted Buffy Summers, then Angel, in their fight against evil. She was born in Sunnydale, California, in 1980 and is the daughter of a wealthy family. She was a member of the Cordettes, the clique of rich girls at Sunnydale High School, and looked down upon those she thought were weird (like Buffy). It was Buffy, however, who changed Cordelia's life when she saved her from an invisible female demon who despised Cordelia's beauty and sought to disfigure her. Cordelia then became a part of Buffy's circle of demon fighters.

In high school Cordelia would only wear dresses made especially for her ("off-the-rack clothes give me hives") and drove a car with the license plate QUEEN C. Life again changed for Cordelia when she graduated from Sunnydale High and learned her parents lost their wealth. Rather than attend college, Cordelia chose to become an actress and moved to Los Angeles. With no job or money, she found employment as secretary to Angel, the vampire with a soul who helps people. Angel did not appear to need money, but it was Cordelia who suggested he charge for his services and open Angel Investigations (Cordelia also designed the business cards with a drawing of an angel and the slogan "We Specialize in Strange"). Shortly after, Cordelia becomes Angel's contact with the Other World when "The Powers That Be" select her to become their eyes, or as Cordelia says "Vision Girl." When Cordelia receives a vision of what is about to happen, she says "It gives me mind-bending, bone-cracking vision headaches." To make the visions bearable for Cordelia, the Powers That Be changed her being to incorporate the essence of a demon; without the change, she would not survive. While Cordelia could see who would die, she could also cause more harm than good. When her demon implant fought to control her human destiny, Cordelia fell into a mystic coma. She remained hospitalized for several months until she awoke for the series 100th episode (February 4, 2004) to tell Angel of a vision she had in which he was threatened by a man with strange tattoos. Cordelia helped Angel defeat the demon but could not remain with him. As Cordelia seemed to vanish Angel received a phone call from the hospital informing him that Cordelia had died and never awoke from her coma. It can be assumed that the Powers That Be removed the demon and allowed Cordelia one last vision to save Angel.

Cordelia first lived above Angel's loft, then in a small dingy apartment. Before moving into a room at their new headquarters at the Hyperian Hotel, Cordelia lived in Apartment 212 at 118 Silver Lake Road with a ghost named Dennis. As long as Dennis did his haunting quietly and didn't invade her privacy, Cordelia put up with him (Dennis was bricked up behind a wall by his mother when she found this the only way to stop him from marrying a prostitute).

See also: Angel, Buffy Summers, Dawn Summers, Fred Berkel, Rupert Giles, Spike, Willow Rosenberg, Xander Harris.

240. Cordell Walker, *Walker, Texas Ranger*, CBS, 1993–2001. Played by Chuck Norris.

Cordell Walker is a Texas Ranger with the Department of Public Safety who exceeds authority to get the job done. He is skilled in the martial arts and uses his upbringing as a Cherokee Indian to help him outwit and capture criminals.

Cordell is the son of John Firewalker, a full-blooded Cherokee, and Elizabeth, a white woman John met at a rodeo. Cordell was ten years old when his parents were killed by three intoxicated thugs at a Texas county fair (a fight ensued when Elizabeth was insulted "for marrying a red skin"). Cordell was then raised on the Cherokee Reservation by his Uncle Ray. He was given the Indian name Warshaw (Lone Eagle) and raised in both the ways of the Indian and white man. When the series begins, Cordell is living with his Uncle Ray on his parents' ranch on South Road 8 in Springfield, Texas (555-4928 is his phone number). Dialogue from other episodes changes Cordell's upbringing. It is next said his parents were killed in a car crash and he was sent to the Cherokee Reservation in Oklahoma to be raised. Next, after the death of his parents, Cordell was sent to the Santa Rosa Orphanage in Texas to be raised.

Cordell was a captain in the Vietnam War and was called "The Nighthawk" for his deadly maneuvers against the enemy in the dark. He joined the Texas Rangers shortly after the war ended. He was a kickboxing champion in 1978 and began a drug free program for children called Kick Drugs Out of America (where he also teaches karate). Turkey meatloaf is Cordell's favorite meal and he rode three horses throughout the series run: Cookie, Amigo and Ranger. Cordell also drove a Dodge 4X4 with three different license plates: DV4 708, 495 3XA, AUQ 075. Walker's car code is 8157 and he bears a remarkable resemblance to Hayes Cooper, a former Old West Texas Ranger (played by Chuck Norris in flashback sequences). Cordell is partners with Jimmy Trevette and is romantically involved with Alexandra Cahill, the assistant D.A. Their favorite hangout is C.D.'s Bar and Grill.

See also: Alexandra Cahill, Jimmy Trevette.

241. Corky Sherwood, *Murphy Brown*, CBS, 1988–1997. Played by Faith Ford.

Corky Lynn Sherwood is a reporter for *F.Y.I.* ("For Your Information"), a CBS-TV, Washington, D.C.–based newsmagazine series. Corky was born on a farm in Louisiana and is a graduate of Eastern Louisiana University (where she acquired a degree in journalism). She is the daughter of Edward and Bootsie Sherwood and has two sisters, Cookie and Kiki Sherwood.

Corky can recite all the books of the Bible by heart. At the age of 19 she was crowned Miss America and worked previously as a model (she was "The Check Girl" for the First Bank of New Orleans). Corky has a First Lady doll collection, a pet cat named Mr. Puffy, and is the cheerleader for the Bulletins, the show's football team. Her first special on the network was an interview show called *Corky's Place* and she won the 1989 Humboldt Award for her story, "A Woman's Touch at West Point." Corky appeared on *Circus of the Stars* (did a trapeze act with Robert Urich) and lives in Apartment 304. She wears a size 34B bra and 555-7261 is her phone number. In 1989 Corky married Will Forrest (Scott Bryce), a struggling writer she met at the Air and Space Museum (he penned a book called *The Little Dutch Boy*; she became Corky Sherwood-Forrest). They divorced three years later due to incompatibility (he wanted her to quit her job and devote all her time to him). Corky is a very sweet and trusting girl who will give of her time to help others. She has a difficult time saying no and she sometimes finds people taking advantage of that asset.

See also: Frank Fontana, Jim Dial, Miles Silverberg, Murphy Brown.

242. Corky Thatcher, *Life Goes On*, ABC, 1989–1993. Played by Christopher Burke.

Charles Thatcher, nicknamed "Corky" and "The Cork," is the son of Libby and Drew Thatcher and lives at 305 Woodridge Road in Glen Brook, Illinois, with his sisters, Paige and Becca. Corky was born in 1971 and has Down syndrome (making him the first real life handicapped person to be a regular on a prime time series).

Corky first attended the Fowler Institution, then Marshall High School. He first worked as a newspaper delivery boy, then at the family diner, the Glen Brook Grill. His only series job was as an usher at the Glen Brook Theater (where he earned $165 every two weeks). Corky is older than the other students in his class (he became a senior at the age of 21 and was not permitted to graduate with his fellow class mates. Corky chose to enter a mainstream school rather than a special school. As a result, his grades suffered, especially math. The school board refused to grant special privileges to a disabled person; "not consistent with our policy." Corky's family held a special ceremony and presented him with his own diploma).

Throughout the series Corky proved that despite a handicap he could become a part of society and do what other kids do — from playing the drums to running for class president to competing in the Glen Brook 50K Bike Race (he was number 277 and although he came in last, it was a victory for Corky because he was able to accomplish something). His favorite sandwiches are sliced turkey on raisin bread and ham and cheese on whole wheat.

Like most people, Corky made mistakes. He impulsively married Amanda Swanson (Andrea Friedman), a girl with Down syndrome. She attended college and they lived off the money Corky made as an usher. The series ended with them struggling to make the marriage work.

See also: Becca Thatcher, Libby and Drew Thatcher, Paige Thatcher.

243. Corliss Archer, *Meet Corliss Archer*, CBS, 1951–1952; Syn., 1954–1955. Played by Lugene Sanders (1951), Ann Baker (1954).

Corliss Archer is a vibrant teenage girl. She was born on March 3, 1935, and is the daughter of Harry and Janet Archer. Corliss lives at 32 Oak Street and is a sophomore at Midland Heights High School.

Corliss is very pretty and eager to grow up. She has a penchant for getting herself into trouble and has a weekly allowance of one dollar ("Gee, I wish I could get my father to increase my allowance; a

dollar doesn't go far these days"). Corliss is a big movie fan, especially of Gregory Peck films ("He's so dreamy. I just love going to his movies"—which cost 25 cents). Corliss has a nice figure for a 16-year-old girl but is jealous of the more developed and popular Betty Campbell ("I just know that scatterbrain puts on acts just to woo the boys").

Corliss enjoys two eggs, toast and orange juice for breakfast and lasagna is her favorite dinner. She has a tendency to drop the toothpaste tube cap down the drain and isn't the tidiest when it comes to keeping her bedroom clutter free. Corliss would like to be more active at school but she just doesn't have what it takes. She is not athletic enough for the sports teams, she tried out for the Pep Squad ("They said I had no cheer in my cheers") and the glee club ("If I sang with the glee club they said there would be no glee in the glee club").

Dexter Franklin (Bobby Ellis) is the boy Corliss dates and hopes to one day marry. He also receives an allowance of one dollar a week and is a steak and potatoes man. Corliss is trying to shape him into the man of her dreams but has little success. Dexter is a big fan of Marilyn Monroe movies (which makes Corliss jealous — "What does Marilyn Monroe have that I don't?") and he puts up with all of her nonsense because he loves her.

244. Cory Matthews, *Boy Meets World*, ABC, 1993–2000. Played by Ben Savage.

Cory Matthews is the 11-year-old son of Amy and Allan Matthews. He was born at St. Vincent's Hospital and lives at 311 Pinehurst in Philadelphia. Cory first attended Jefferson Elementary School, then John Adams Jr. High School, John Adams High School and finally Pennbrook University. He joined a band called the Exits to attract girls and first hung out at an eatery called Chubbys (later called Peg Leg Pete's Diner, then Captain Randy's).

At John Adams High, Cory was a reporter for the school's TV station program, *The News Now*. Cory grew up with a very pretty girl named Topanga Lawrence and although he dated other girls, always returned to Topanga when he was dumped. It took time, but when Cory finally realized Topanga was the girl for him, he proposed and the two married (see Topanga Lawrence for further information). Cory was a good kid, presented few problems for his parents and always realized that when he did something wrong he needed to be punished. His father was the manager "of the largest grocery store in the area"; his mother was a real estate agent. He also has a younger sister (Morgan) and older, mischievous brother (Eric).

245. Cosmo Kramer, *Seinfeld,* NBC, 1990–1998. Played by Michael Richards.

Cosmo Kramer, most always called Kramer, is an eccentric who lives in Apartment 5B at 129 West 81st Street in Manhattan. He is the neighbor of Jerry Seinfeld and is friends with Elaine Benes and George Costanza. Kramer has also made Jerry's apartment (5A) his apartment (he enters when he wishes and helps himself to whatever he wants).

Kramer appears to be a self-styled entrepreneur (although he did admit to once having a regular job as a bagel technician at H&H Bagels in Manhattan. He has been on strike for 12 years). Kramer also conceived a company called Kramerica and hopes to start a chain of make your own pizza parlors. He also "worked" as a broker for Bryant-Leland when he was mistaken for an employee and decided to become part of the team (he was fired for not knowing what he was doing). Other jobs held by Kramer: Santa Claus at Coleman's Department Store; stand-in for the father of an eight-year-old child on *All My Children;* medical actor (performs illnesses for interns to identify); ball boy at the U.S. Open Tennis Tournament; author of *The Coffee Table Book of Coffee Tables* (published by Pendant Publishing).

Kramer acted on the series *Murphy Brown* (as Steve Snell, one of Murphy's wacky secretaries) and had one line in an unnamed Woody Allen movie ("Boy, these pretzels are making me thirsty"). Kramer invented a cologne called The Beach and was an underwear model for Calvin Klein. Kramer also took advantage of the Adopt-a-Highway program and was responsible for keeping one mile of Highway 114 of the Arthur Burkhardt Highway clean.

Kramer eats Kellogg's Double Dip Crunch for breakfast and likes hot dogs from Papaya King, a local fast food store. Kramer enjoys fresh fruit and when he wanted eggs from uncaged chickens he mistakenly bought a rooster he named "Little Jerry Seinfeld."

Golf is Kramer's favorite sport. He has a habit of snooping into other people's medicine cabinets and enjoys shopping at the airport's duty-free shop. He is banned from the local fruit store (for returning a bad peach), likes extra MSG in his Chinese food and is a member of the Polar Bears Club. Kramer's dream is to drive the rear end of a hook and ladder fire truck (he feels he knows the shortcuts firemen don't). His car license plate

reads ERB 224, but was mistakenly issued ones that read ASSMAN. He also posed for a portrait that has become known as "The Kramer." Kramer's phone number is 555-3455, then 555-8643; early episodes show his apartment as being 3B. His favorite hangout is Monk's Café.

See also: Elaine Benes, George Costanza, Jerry Seinfeld.

246. Courtney Martin, *Molloy,* Fox, 1990. Played by Jennifer Aniston.

Courtney Martin is the daughter of Paul and Lynn Martin. She was born in 1974 and lives at 6113 Fullerton Drive in Beverly Hills, California, with her half-sister, Molloy, and brother, Jason.

Courtney attends the Beverly Hills Private School. She is considered the most beautiful girl at the school and Molloy says she is deserving of the title "but beneath all that beauty she is just an airhead." Courtney is totally devoted to herself and her number one priority is looking gorgeous. She is easily distracted from whatever she is doing and becomes very upset over the simplest of things (like a strand of hair out of place or a chip in her fingernail polish). Courtney feels she possesses an aura that attracts only the good things in life. However, should something go wrong or should Courtney not get her way, she becomes a "cry baby" (as Molloy calls her) and puts up a fuss until she gets what she wants. Courtney believes her stunning good looks, perfect figure and natural fashion sense, make her a role model to other girls, especially Molly (Molly agrees and would like to look like Courtney—"but without the dullard interior).

See also: Molloy Martin.

247. Courtney Rae, *Whoopi,* NBC, 2003–2004. Played by Wren T. Brown.

Courtney Rae is the son of Lawrence and Viveca Rae and the conservative brother of Mavis Rae, a liberal who owns the LaMont Hotel in New York City. While Mavis set her sights on becoming a professional singer, Courtney set his goal on becoming a lawyer. He is a graduate of the Columbia School of Law and worked at Enron for five years before he lost his job to the corporate scandal that destroyed the company. He lives in Room 37 of his sister's hotel and is dating Rita Nash, a woman Mavis dislikes. She also dislikes Courtney for his political views—he is a Republican and Mavis believes Republicans are responsible for all that is wrong with the U.S. Before acquiring a job with the President George W. Bush Re-Election Campaign in 2004, Courtney worked as a limo driver for Rita's father's company, a researcher for the law firm of McMillan and Lohman, and a men's fine suit salesman at Suit King.

Courtney doesn't dance in public ("I'm not comfortable with public movement"). He likes lemon yogurt and is afraid of surprises (when he was a child, his parents had to take away his Jack in the Box fearing something might happen when the Jack popped out). Rita calls Courtney "Boo."

See also: Mavis Rae, Rita Nash.

248. Courtney Scott, *Grosse Pointe,* WB, 2000–2001. Played by Bonnie Sommerville.

Courtney Scott is one of the three female leads on the mythical television series *Grosse Pointe.* She plays Laura, a student at Grosse Point High School and was given the role to add sex to the series (she wears a 36C bra and a big breasted cheerleader was needed to boost the ratings).

Courtney was born in Arizona and attended Lanfield Elementary School. She was the first girl in her class to physically develop and teased by the boys for wearing a bra. While it bothered Courtney at first, she overcame the teasing and took an interest in performing in school plays. She found she liked acting and made it her life's goal. After graduating from Emerson High School, Courtney enrolled in the University of Arizona Theater Arts Program. She performed in the school's production of *A Doll's House* and landed the role of Laura on *Grosse Pointe* when she auditioned in a very low cut blouse.

Courtney's ample bosom has made the show a hit in Japan (where she is known as "Miss Big Breasts") and when nude pictures of Courtney, taken by her ex-boyfriend, appeared in *Playboy* magazine (in a layout called "Courtney's Grand Tetons"), the show's ratings jumped 22 percent. Courtney enjoys the publicity her figure gives her. She has been offered movie roles, but refuses to appear in any film that requires a nude scene.

See also: Hunter Fallow, Marcie Sternfeld.

249. Craig Stirling, *The Champions,* NBC/Syn., 1968. Played by Stuart Damon.

Craig Stirling is an agent for Nemesis, an international organization that battles evil. Craig is the American member of the British team that includes Sharron Macready and Richard Barrett. Craig was born in New York City on December 1, 1939 and joined Nemesis in 1965 after serving in the U.S. Air Force. Craig, like Sharron and Richard, possesses extraordinary powers that he uses to safeguard freedom and democracy (see Richard Barrett for information on their powers).

Craig is intelligent and well versed in the mar-

tial arts. He is also the strongest of the three and often the one who receives the worst of it in a confrontation with the enemy. When Richard fails to come up with a plan he likes, Craig usually devises an on-the-spot plan that often works. Craig lives at 487 Hampton Drive and prefers to take his time when a plan is set in motion rather than rush in and take his chances (as Richard likes to do).

See also: Richard Barrett, Sharron Macready.

250. Curupira, *BeastMaster,* Syn., 1999–2002. Played by Emilie de Ravin.

Curupira is a beautiful but deadly demon that rules the forests and animals in a time when nature and magic ruled the world. Curupira cares only about her animals and some humans (like Dar, the BeastMaster). If a man kills her animals, she kills him. Tao, Dar's friend, calls her "The Little Demon." Curupira is incredibly strong. She has blonde hair, a normal flesh face but she is green from the neck down. Her feet are backwards and to kiss her means death (she drains the life force from those who kiss her). She can burn with her breath and control the weather to protect her forests. Curupira's appearance is that of an adolescent — charming and innocent and she is most fond of her white tiger, Mohan. Her enemy is Iara, a demon who calls her "an immature, unpleasant little girl," and who seeks to take over her forests.

See also: The Ancient One, Arina, Dar, Iara, The Sorceress, Tao.

251. Cybill Sheridan, *Cybill,* CBS, 1995–1998. Played by Cybill Shepherd.

Although sexy and beautiful, Cybill Sheridan says "I'm an aging actress who loses jobs to younger girls." Cybill lives at 11291 Moss Canyon Drive in Los Angeles and has two daughters, Rachel (by her first husband, Jeff Robbins) and Zoe (by second husband Ira Woodbine).

Cybill was born in Memphis, Tennessee, and got her first taste of show business as a child when she entered a beauty contest and was crowned "Miss Pickled Pigs Feet." From that moment on Cybill set her sights on becoming a star. As a young actress, Cybill starred in the all-nude off-Broadway version of *Death of a Salesman.* She made her network TV debut on a sitcom called *Family House* ("I played the husband's secretary") and next played the Lizard Woman in an episode of *Star Trek.* When she finally got her big break, the leading role on a series called *Island Cop,* the six filmed episodes were so bad that they never aired in the U.S.; however, they did run in Russia and *Island Cop* became the number one show for seven years.

Cybill's other TV roles include: Booty the Clown (a clown with a big butt) on the children's show, *Major Milo*; co-host of the morning talk show, *Julie and Cybill*; Sara McCullum on *Life Forms*, a science fiction series about a woman who battles aliens (Cybill says "The actual stars of the show are my breasts and legs, which receive more air time than the rest of me"). She also played Galaxy Girl on the series *Invincible Girl* and appeared on the reality series *Stories of the Highway Patrol* ("I was hit by a bus").

Cybill's television commercials include: spokesperson for the Psychic Pals Network; Femgel (a female product); Fraunmeiser Beer; Granny's Snack Cakes; and Can-Do Supermarkets. Cybill also appeared in several movies, including *Punchout*, *Oliver Twisted* ("The worst horror film ever made"), and *What She Did for Love* (which Cybill says contains her first filmed nude scene).

Cybill drives a 1964 Dodge Dart (plate UPU 838) and has her own chalked-in star on the Hollywood Walk of Fame (which she placed next to actress Jean Harlow).

252. Daisy Duke, *The Dukes of Hazzard*, CBS, 1979–1985. Played by Catherine Bach.

This entry also contains information on Bo Duke (John Schneider), Luke Duke (Tom Wopat) and Uncle Jesse Duke (Denver Pyle).

Daisy Duke was born in Hazzard County, Georgia. She lives with her uncle Jesse and cousins Bo and Luke on the Duke family farm on Mill Pond Road (18 miles outside of town). The family is noted for running moonshine. Daisy is a graduate of Hazzard High School (where she was considered "The Wildest Girl"). She works as a waitress at the Boar's Nest, the local bar. Daisy also held a position as part-time reporter for the Hazzard County *Gazette*. She entered "The Miss Tri Counties Beauty Pageant" and won the title "Best All Around Gal in Three Counties" (for her "beauty, mechanical abilities and driving skills").

Daisy originally drove a yellow Dodge Charger (destroyed by Bo and Luke when they lost control and the car went off a cliff), then a white Jeep Eagle she called "Dixie." Daisy shops at the Capitol City Department Store and is den mother to the Junior Patrol, a Girl Scout troop. The red bikini Daisy is seen wearing in the opening theme and the short shorts she wears during the show (the Daisy Dukes) were created by Catherine Bach.

Bo and Luke Duke were also born in Hazzard County and are graduates of Hazzard High

School. Luke is the older of the cousins and saw much of the world during his hitch with the Marines after high school. Bo was a linebacker on the school football team and boasts that he can talk any girl into a date for Saturday night. They enjoy fishing at Sunset Lake and share the "General Lee," a souped-up 1969 orange Dodge Charger (with a Confederate flag on the roof, the racing number 01 on the door, and the license plate CNH 320). Luke is famous for the "hood slide" (sliding across the roof from the driver's side to the passenger side). They race it in the Cherokee County Dirt Road Classic and the Smokey Hollow Race.

Uncle Jesse is the Duke family patriarch. He now stands for law and order but once ran moonshine in the Range Runner Association (in a car he first called "Sweet Tillie" then "Black Tillie"). He has a pet goat named Bonnie and believes that "The law is the law and us Dukes gotta obey it no matter what."

The Dukes have teamed to keep Hazzard County honest by fighting its corrupt Justice of the Peace, Boss Hogg. Bo and Duke do not use any guns (they use dynamite-tipped arrows as weapons) and have C.B. codes while on the road: Shepherd (Jesse), Lost Sheep (Bo and Luke), and Bo Peep (Daisy).

See also: Boss Hogg.

253. Dan and Roseanne Conner, *Roseanne*, ABC, 1988–1997. Played by John Goodman, Roseanne.

Dan and Roseanne Conner are a middle class married couple who live at 714 Delaware Street in Lanford, Illinois. They are the parents of Becky, Darlene and D.J. and first met at Lanford High School. Dan was an athlete (nicknamed "Yor") and Roseanne Harris had aspirations to become a writer.

Dan is the son of Ed and Audrey Conner; Roseanne is the daughter of Al and Beverly Harris. Roseanne mentioned that her and Dan's first date was on his Harley Davidson Motorcycle at the A&W Drive-In. It was on their second date, at the Blue Swan Café off Highway 72, that Dan proposed to her. They married after graduation but neither became what they wanted. Dan went into construction and eventually formed his own company, 4 Aces Construction. When this failed years later, Dan turned his love of motorcycles into a repair and sales shop called Lanford Custom Cycles. Overdue mortgage payments closed the business. He next free-lanced in construction, became "the guy who fixes trucks" at the Lanford Garage, and finally partners with Roseanne and her sister, Jackie Harris, in the Lanford Lunch Box, a diner off Route 9.

Roseanne first worked as an assembly line worker at Wellman Plastics. She eventually formed a partnership with her sister to open the Lanford Lunch Box, but prior to doing so, she held the following jobs: telephone solicitor for Discount House magazines; order taker at Divine Chicken; bartender at the Lobo Lounge; clean-up lady at Art's Beauty Parlor; waitress at Rodbell's Luncheonette; commentator ("Roseanne Reports from the Heartland") on WERG-TV, Channel 4.

Dan reads the girlie magazine *Girls, Girls, Girls*; beer is his favorite drink; cake his favorite desert and Oscar Meyer franks his favorite food. He is famous for his chocolate chip shakes and gets upset when the kids leave toast crumbs in the butter (Roseanne gets upset when the kids leave jelly in the peanut butter jar). Roseanne gave birth to a fourth child (Jerry) in 1996 and had all their problems solved when she and Dan won $108 million in the Illinois State Lottery. Dan is often gentle in dealing with the kids and their problems; Roseanne takes a more dramatic stance and feels being tough is the only way to make them understand right from wrong.

See also: Becky Conner, Darlene Conner.

254. Dan Fielding, *Night Court*, NBC, 1984–1992. Played by John Larroquette.

Dan Fielding is the prosecuting attorney assigned to the courtroom of Harry T. Stone, an unorthodox New York City night court judge.

Dan's real name is Reinhold Fielding Elmore (he changed his name when he started school). He is the son of "Daddy" Bob and Musette Elmore and was born on a farm in Paris, Louisiana. His parents were rural and he lived with pigs in his room. He was six before he realized he wasn't related to them. As an infant Dan thought he had a pet turtle named Scruffy (he was two years old when he found out his father had painted a potato to look like a turtle). During the summer of 1967, when Dan was a teenager, he worked as a lifeguard at the Lone Star Beach Club in Galveston, Texas.

Dan now lives in an apartment on Hauser Street on Third Avenue in Manhattan. He drives a Mercedes with the license plate HOT TO TROT (he is a ladies' man and calls his car "The Dan Mobile"). Dan is an army reservist and has stock in a company called the Fletko Corporation (which is famous for tearing down landmarks).

Dan hosted an insult TV show called *In Your Face* and picks up girls at the Sticky Wickey Club. He first mentions his dream job is to become a

judge ("to wear satin and send people to jail"); he later says it is to be a lawyer with the firm of Taylor, Woods and Johnson.

See also: Bull Shannon, Christine Sullivan, Harry T. Stone, Mac Robinson.

255. Dan Tanna, *Vegas*, ABC, 1978–1981. Played by Robert Urich.

Dan Tanna is a tough private detective with a penchant for finding and helping beautiful women in trouble. He is based in Las Vegas and has a spacious office on the ground floor of the Desert Inn Casino and Hotel. His office also doubles as his garage (where he parks his prized red 1957 Thunderbird). Although Dan resides at the Desert Inn and is friends with its owner (Philip Roth) he is not bound to cases involving the hotel and its guests; he is free to help wherever and whoever he wants (Dan will take all types of cases except divorces, which he feels are too disturbing). He also refuses to take cases that involve body guarding.

Dan was born in Nevada and appears to know many people, especially the celebrities who frequent the Desert Inn. He carries a .44 Magnum and milk is his favorite drink. Dan is handsome, cool and a smooth talker when it comes to the fairer sex. He surrounds himself with beauty — whether on a case or just relaxing in his office. Filling the bill are two Desert Inn showgirls: Bea Travis (Phyllis Elizabeth Davis) and Angie Turner (Judy Landers). Bea is a sensible brunette with her feet planted firmly on the ground. She first held a job as Dan's secretary but later became more of an assistant than a note taker. Angie was a beautiful, busty "dumb blonde" who was not only a knockout on the Las Vegas stage but a drop dead gorgeous secretary. Dan was never distracted by her attributes. Angie was an expert when it came to dancing on stage but appeared to be a bit naïve when it came to working for Dan. Angie is so disarming that her looks make up for all her mistakes.

256. Dan Troop, *Lawman*, ABC, 1958–1962. Played by John Russell.

Dan Troop is a legendary lawman who is known as "The Famous Gun from Texas," a daring U.S. Marshal who upholds the law at any cost.

Dan was born in Texas and worked in a hash house as a kid. Becoming a lawman was the furthest thing on Dan's mind. Fate, however, changed his path. When a girl Dan considered special is killed in a senseless gunfight by a stray bullet, he vowed to avenge her death by upholding the law. Dan was first Marshal of Abilene,

Texas, then Laramie, Wyoming (1879), "a town that is tough on lawmen and horse thieves."

Dan believes that a man has to wear a gun because of the way things are; he also believes that there will be a time when it will not be necessary. He is fast with his guns as well as his fists. He is very high-priced and likes his pay once a month — waiting for him in the bank. Dan is always dressed in white and will not use his guns unless circumstances offer him no other choice. He does shoot to kill and wants Laramie to be a town where its citizens can walk the streets without being afraid.

Dan is assisted by his deputy, Johnny McKay (Peter Brown) and has a close relationship with Lily Merrill (Peggie Castle), the owner of the Birdcage Saloon. Dan and Johnny enjoy meals at the Blue Bonnett Café.

257. Dana Foster, *Step by Step*, ABC, 1991–1997; CBS, 1997–1998. Played by Staci Keanan.

Dana Foster is a beautiful 16-year-old girl who attends Port Washington High School in Wisconsin. She was born in Port Washington on January 15, 1976 at 10:47 P.M. and lives at 201 Winslow Street with her mother, Carol, and siblings, Karen and Mark. Also living with them is Carol's second husband, Frank Lambert, and his children, Alicia, J.T. and Brendon.

Dana is a straight A student and first attended Lincoln Elementary School. At Port Washington High, where she is an Honors Student, Dana also writes for the school's newspaper, *The Wildcatter*. She later attends East Wisconsin University (nicknamed Cheese Whiz U.), where she is studying to become a lawyer. It was at college that Dana received her first and only D on a paper for "using big words with no meaning."

Dana is always impeccably dressed and sensitive to the fact that she has small breasts (as Alicia puts it "You're smart and it's a good thing because you have no boobs"). Dana shares her bedroom with Karen and Alicia and Carol keeps a "Dana Book," a photographic record of Dana's life — from her first tooth, first step, and even first kiss (Carol just happened to be in a tree with an infrared camera and zoom lens). As a child Carol called Dana "Princess Bubble Bath" when it was time for her bath. Dana worked as the assistant manager of the 50's Café and does volunteer work at the Tri County Mission.

See also: Alicia Lambert, Carol and Frank Lambert, J.T. Lambert, Karen Foster.

258. Dana Palladino, *Love and War*, CBS, 1994–1995. Played by Annie Potts.

Dana Palladino is a professional chef at a New York restaurant called Chez Wally on 72nd Street. Dana was born in New York but raised in Europe. She became fascinated with cooking at an early age and by the age of ten could cook the most complicated meals to perfection (she so impressed the owner of Harry's Bar in Paris that she was given her own table). Before returning to the U.S., Dana worked at the Le Petite Bateau in France but was fired for standing up for her rights (she was passed over for an executive position by a man). She is the daughter of a famous artist (Dante) and worked as the personal chef to singer Mick Jagger during his Steel Wheels Tour. Dana has to be perfect at anything she cooks and do what it takes to ensure that perfection (she spent a year, for example, on the Alaska Pipeline just to learn how to cook salmon).

Dana now lives in a Manhattan loft with the name "Schaefer Sewing Machine Company" on the building. She has a cat named James and uses Morton brand salt in her salt shakers. Her favorite movie is *Casablanca*.

See also: Jack Stein, Wally Porter.

259. Dana Plant, *Snoops*, ABC, 1999. Played by Paula Marshall.

Dana Plant was a detective with the Santa Monica Police Department who quit her job to work as a private detective for Glenn Hall, Inc., a high tech agency in California.

Dana was born in Santa Monica and was a straight A student at Santa Monica High School. She next attended State College, then the Santa Monica Police Academy where she graduated with top honors. She was assigned to the homicide division but found the job unrewarding; she felt she could find more freedom in the private sector and went to work for Glenn Hall (a gorgeous female detective). The detective in Dana never rests, an ability she acquired from watching police oriented shows on television. Dana has been trained to do certain things certain ways (like taking notes during an investigation). This upsets Glenn, who says, for example, "Good detective don't take notes. If you have to take notes, do it when we get back to the office." Glenn also considers Dana to be a bit too eager to use a gun and is reluctant to let her carry one (even the tranquilizer gun they use to collar suspects).

As a child and even as an adult, Dana never broke a rule. She was the perfect child and made her parents proud. She became a good cop but found shortly after joining the agency that Glenn breaks the rules all the time. "The cop in me won't let me break the law" and her inability to abide by Glenn's rules forced her to return to the force

("I enjoyed my job as a private detective but it's not my world"). She became Glenn's link with the police department.

See also: Glenn Hall, Roberta Young.

Danny Partridge *see* **Shirley Partridge**

260. Dana Scully, *The X-Files,* Fox, 1993–2002. Played by Gillian Anderson.

Dana Katherine Scully is an agent for the X-Files, a government organization that investigates paranormal activity. Dana is the daughter of William and Margaret Scully. She was born on February 23, 1964, and has two brothers (William Jr. and Charles) and an older sister (Melissa). Dana has red hair and blue eyes and stands five feet, three inches tall. She is a graduate of Maryland University (medical diploma) and the University of California (physics degree). She was recruited by the FBI after graduation and began her career teaching at the FBI Academy in Quantico, Virginia. Two years later she was teamed with Fox Mulder to investigate unnatural happenings as part of the X-Files.

Dana does not believe everything she sees and feels there is a logical explanation for the supernatural events she investigates (everything has to be logical and make sense to her). Dana is extremely scientific and tries to debunk the unexplained phenomena she encounters (much to Fox's objections, as he believes what he sees).

Dana had a dog named Queequeg and was called "Starbuck" by her father. She is a Catholic (wears a necklace with a cross) and has a tattoo on her back (a snake biting its tail). She likes coffee with cream and no sugar and enjoys an occasional glass of wine. Pizza, fried chicken and lobster are her favorite foods. She also enjoys plain yogurt with honey. Dana watches the Discovery Channel and enjoys horror films (such as *The Exorcist and Poltergeist*). Classical music relaxes her; JTT0331613 is her badge number. She resides in an apartment (35) in Georgetown. Her e-mail address is *Scully@FBI.gov/queequeq0925@hotmail. com*; 555-3564 is her cell phone number.

See also: Fox Mulder.

261. Dana Stowe, *Strong Medicine,* Lifetime, 2000–2003. Played by Janine Turner.

Dana Stowe is a doctor so dedicated to her work (she wants to become the U.S. Surgeon General) that she has no time to watch television. She is the daughter of a Nobel Prize nominee (her mother) and a doctor (father) and has devoted her life to medical research (particularly in women's health issues). Dana comes from a prestigious

family and is struggling to achieve fame by finding a cure for breast cancer. She works at the Rittenhouse Women's Health Clinic in Philadelphia and is regarded as one of the top women's health experts.

Dana is a stickler for rules and constantly comes in conflict with her co-workers. If Dana makes it through a day without bucking heads with anyone she is happy. She is not a fancy girl. Clothes do not impress her and the simpler the jewelry she wears the better she likes it. Despite the fact that she is a doctor (and should know better) she has a passion for junk food. Dana feared ending up alone and it was that fear that caused her to leave the series when she adopted two young girls and moved back to her home in Virginia to begin a new life.

See also: Andy Campbell, Kayla Thornton, Lana Hawkins, Luisa Delgado, Peter Riggs, Nick Biancavilla.

262. Daniel Gregg, *The Ghost and Mrs. Muir,* NBC, 1968–1969; ABC, 1969–1970. Played by Edward Mulhare.

Daniel Gregg is a ghost. He now haunts the home he built, Gull Cottage in the New England town of Schooner Bay. He shares the home with the very alive, attractive widow, Carolyn Muir, her children (Candy and Jonathan), their housekeeper (Martha Grant) and their do (Scruffy).

Life for Daniel began in Schooner Bay in 1828. Daniel grew up amid the fishing industry that supported the town and eventually became a fisherman himself. He learned all he could about the sea and ships and soon became the captain of his own ship. He was, as he calls himself, "a scoundrel," a notorious ladies' man with a girl in every port. He claims he was never engaged and lived a free life style. In 1868 the Captain planted a Monkey Puzzle Tree in the front of Gull Cottage, which he built for himself but eventually planned to turn into a home for retired sailors. One night in 1868 a southwest gale approached the town. Daniel closed his bedroom windows. While sleeping "I kicked the blasted gas heater with my blasted foot" and was killed by escaping fumes. The coroner's jury brought in a verdict of suicide because "my confounded cleaning woman testified that I slept with my windows open." In order to save Gull Cottage, the Captain's present-day, wimpy descendant, Claymore Gregg (Charles Nelson Reilly) leased it to Carolyn Muir to avoid a state takeover for unpaid back taxes.

Daniel balks at having to share his home but he and Carolyn have come to terms and they accept each other (Daniel sees that Carolyn loves the house and he allows her to stay). Daniel has never once allowed a woman aboard his ship (or house) and he watches over Carolyn each night by standing watch on the porch above Carolyn's bedroom (his "Bridge," as he calls it); his beloved telescope remains in the bedroom. The Captain now considers the Wheel House (the attic) his only retreat from Carolyn and her family. "Blast" and "Blasted" are the Captain's favorite expressions. He calls Carolyn "Madame" and Carolyn can predict when Daniel becomes angry by the barometer on the living room wall (it reads "Stormy Weather"). Martha and the children can also see the Captain. Martha calls him "The Old Barnacle" and he sometimes enjoys watching the children — although he will never admit it.

See also: Carolyn Muir.

263. Daniel Jackson, *Stargate SG-1*, Sci Fi, 1997 (current). Played by Michael Shanks.

Daniel Jackson is a member of Stargate SG-1, a U.S. Air Fore project that enables travel to various planets (see Jack O'Neill for details).

Daniel is a student of ancient culture whose archaeological expertise allowed him to crack the code that activated the Stargate (the alien time portal). Daniel was born in New York City on July 8 (possibly in 1964 or 1965). His parents, Melburn and Claire were killed while working on a Museum of Modern Art exhibit (a stone pillar fell and crushed them). Eight-year-old Daniel was raised by a foster family. Daniel had a keen interest in the mysteries of the past and made archaeology his life's career. After graduating from college he went to work for the government and was assigned to the Creek Mountain Complex (which originally housed the Stargate). He deciphered the mysterious symbols that he concluded were star constellations (the seventh constellation symbol is the key to activating the Stargate).

Daniel sees the world in scientific circles. He is totally devoted to his work and is sometimes unaware of what is happening around him. He also has a somewhat negative view of life (which could account for his stubborn streak and drive to dig deeper for the truth).

See also: Jack O'Neill, Samantha Carter, Teal'c.

264. Danny Tanner, *Full House*, ABC, 1987–1995. Played by Bob Saget.

Daniel Tanner, called Danny, is a widower with three daughters (D.J., Stephanie, and Michelle), who lives at 1882 Gerard Street in San Francisco, California. His late wife, Pamela, was killed in a car accident shortly after the birth of Michelle.

Danny was born in San Francisco. He is a neat freak and attributes his condition to his fifth birthday when his mother gave him, her "special helper," a set of vacuum cleaner attachments. He also had a "friend" named Terry, the talking washcloth. Danny is a graduate of Golden Bay Union High School (where he was called "Dan Dan") and State College (where he hosted a campus TV show called *College Pop*).

Danny was originally a sportscaster on KTMB-TV, Channel 8's *Newsbeat*; he is later co-host (with Rebecca Donaldson) of *Wake Up, San Francisco*. Danny is also a health food fanatic and buys his special low-salt gherkins at Pickle Town. Danny drives a car he calls Bullet (plate 4E11 449) and has a dog named Comet. When dealing with the children and their problems, Danny is warm and gentle and feels the subtle approach is the best way to help them learn about the adult life.

See also: D.J. Tanner, Jesse Cochran, Joey Gladstone, Michelle Tanner, Stephanie Tanner.

265. Danny Taylor, *The Reporter*, CBS, 1964. Played by Harry Guardino.

Danny Taylor is a man who is angry at the world's injustices. He works as a crime reporter for the *New York Globe* and fights crime and corruption through the power of the press.

Danny was born in Manhattan and raised in a crime ridden, poor section of Third Avenue. His schooling was both teacher taught in a building and hoodlum taught on the streets. Danny witnessed many acts of violence and when he grew up he knew he had to do something about it. He felt becoming a police officer would bound him to strict rules, but becoming a crime reporter would allow him to spread his cause beyond a single police station.

Lou Sheldon (Gary Merrill) is the man who believes in Danny's plight and took a chance on him. He is the editor of the *Globe* and he pushes Danny "to the last heart breaking expenditure of effort that only a champion in the making can give." He treats Danny like family (and acts as his trainer, task master and conscience).

Danny has been called "A man who cares about people, not a man who stands about with a notebook jotting down facts. He is a man standing up to his armpits in facts." Danny is aggressive and tough with his fists when he has to be. When Danny takes on assignments he becomes personally involved with that story and will not rest until he has the facts that will bring justice. He resides at 63 East 46th Street in Manhattan.

266. Danny Wilde, *The Persuaders*, ABC, 1971–1972. Played by Tony Curtis.

Daniel Wilde, called Danny, is a nobody who became somebody — a multi-millionaire. He was born in the Bronx, New York, and lived in one of its poorest sections. He grew up on the streets but never went above the law to accomplish a goal. He had a natural flair for business and his optimism, courage, and sense of humor pushed him to the top of the financial ladder. He made millions, lost millions, and made millions again. Making money has become so easy for him that he bothers only when he needs it.

Danny is a playboy and just drifts from country to country, gambling, drinking and womanizing. At a bar in the Hotel du Somme in France, Danny overhears Lord Brett Sinclair order his favorite drink, a Creole Scream. It is a mixture of white rum, bitters, chilled vermouth and grenadine. It also has to be topped off with an olive. But how many? Brett tells the bartender one olive. Danny interrupts and says "Two olives. That way you can see them gently bounce up against each other." Brett and Danny can't agree. A fight ensues and they are arrested but saved from a lockup by a retired judge (Fulton) who offers them a choice: work for him and help bring criminals to justice or spend time in jail. Danny and Brett are like nitro and glycerin. Apart they are harmless; together they are deadly — and the judge requires their help (which they agree to when Danny realizes his nights in jail will keep him away from the ladies).

See also: Brett Sinclair.

267. Dar, *BeastMaster*, Syn., 1999–2002. Played by Daniel Goddard.

Dar is a BeastMaster, a warrior who can communicate with animals in a time when magic and nature ruled the world. He is also called the last of his tribe, the Soulas (destroyed by the evil King Zad and his Terron Warriors). Two versions were given regarding Dar's creation.

In the first version, Dar was said to have been born in a village in the Midlands. When the Terrons attacked, a beautiful demon named Curupira saved him. Curupira rules the forests. She was keeping a promise she made to Dar's father, Eldar, many years ago: in return for helping her protect her domain, she would always watch over Dar. Now that Eldar was dead, Curupira required a new champion for her cause; someone to protect her forests and animals if anything should happen to her. She bestows upon Dar the power of a BeastMaster (control and communicate with animals).

The second version takes place two years later when Dar was said to be a member of the Soulas

tribe in a land called Ericon. Here Dar's father was the true king of the land. When the evil King Zad invaded the village, the infant Dar — the future true king of Ericon — was brought to the village of Dimor to be raised by its chief until he became of age to assume his destiny. It is now established that Curupira did not transform Dar into a Beast-Master. How he became such a being is not explained.

Dar is now a man without a home. His village has been destroyed and he is the last of his tribe. He now battles evil with a human companion (Tao), his pet tiger (Ruh), ferrets (Kato and Poto) and Sharak, an eagle through whose eyes Dar can see what he sees. Dar can command animals, think as they do and he learned how to fight by observing them. Dar first used a white staff as a weapon; later, his father's magic sword. He will not kill unless a predator — human or animal — gives him no other choice.

See also: The Ancient One, Arina, Curupira, Iara, The Sorceress, Tao.

268. Darcy Fields, *Darcy's Wild Life*, Discovery Kids on NBC, 2004 (Current). Played by Sara Paxton.

Darcy Fields is the beautiful 14-year-old daughter of Victoria Fields, a famous, highly sought after movie actress (Darcy's father is a rock drummer whose constant road tours caused her and Victoria to split up. Darcy has few memories of her father as she rarely saw him). Darcy knows a lot about fashion ("I think I was born with it") and relishes in the glamorous life her mother's career affords her. Though not an actress, Darcy gained a reputation for her parties — "A Darcy Fields party was the kind of party that got written up in newspapers." She even appeared with her mother on the Celebrity Mother-Daughter Fashion Channel. After completing such movies as *Death Knocks at Midnight*, Victoria realized that Darcy not only lacks direction and responsibility but also has an uncanny knack for finding fun. To give Darcy a normal life, Victoria moves from Malibu, California, to a farm in a rural town called Bailey. Suddenly Darcy's life changes and she must now adjust to a new life, new friends and responsibility (she has a job at a veterinary clinic called Creature Comforts).

Darcy is a Sagittarius and abides by her mother's wishes (she believes her mother wanted to leave "that crazy show business behind for simple values and simple pleasures"). Darcy now has to live by new rules — "If I want something I have to earn the money for it." Darcy's new life style has prompted her to start a computer journal she calls "Darcy's Dish," wherein she records her daily activities. When something upsets Darcy she buys something. However, when something makes Darcy happy she buys something. Darcy also claims she doesn't always know what she is talking about — "It makes life interesting, doesn't it?" When Darcy gets a cut she likes to use the "pink sparkly bandages." A bright spot in Darcy's life occurred shortly after her arrival in Bailey when she appeared in a TV commercial for Giraldi's Car Corral.

269. Darcy Walker, *Black Scorpion*, Sci Fi, 2001. Played by Michelle Lintel.

Darcy Walker is a beautiful woman who is secretly Black Scorpion, a daring crime fighter who protects the people of Angel City. Darcy is a second-generation police officer. Her father, Lieutenant Stan Walker, was a maverick cop who took the law into his own hands and was eventually suspended from the force.

Darcy was born in Angel City and as a child her father allowed her to monitor the police radio band. He also told her a strange bedtime story about a scorpion that wanted to cross a river. The scorpion, unable to swim, asked a frog for a ride on his back. The frog was hesitant, fearing to get stung. The scorpion assured the frog she would not sting him. Halfway across the river, the scorpion stung the frog. "Now we're both going to drown. Why did you sting me?" asked the frog. "Because I'm a scorpion," she said. Darcy told her father she didn't understand the story. He told her not to worry — "one day you will."

Darcy's interest in police work led her to graduate from the Angel City Police Academy and become a detective with the 21st Precinct. A short time later, her father, now a security guard, is killed. Darcy takes the law into her own hands to solve the case, but is suspended for doing so (later reinstated). Bitter and disillusioned, Darcy retreats to her apartment. While trying to make sense about what happened, Darcy spots a birthday gift left to her by her father. She opens it and finds a black ring with a silver scorpion as its stone (representing her birth sigh). Darcy needs everything to make sense to her. She feels the ring is an omen and as she recalls her father's story she begins to understand the meaning — a scorpion strikes when least expected. She feels her father meant for her to be more than just a police officer and devises a way to bring to justice the criminals the cops can't. She becomes Black Scorpion.

With only her skills in the martial arts as her initial weapon, Darcy creates a sexy and revealing black leather costume and mask. Her exploits first

earned her the name Masked Vigilante, then Masked Marauder. She became known as Black Scorpion when a girl rescued by Darcy described her as "dressed in black with her hair in a braid like a scorpion's tail."

Darcy monitors the police band to learn of crimes. She also modifies her father's stun gun to create an immobilizer (laser-like rays that emanate from the scorpion ring). Darcy's apartment becomes her headquarters (where she has a pet black scorpion and an array of guns and knives). Her costume is secured behind a secret wall in her living room and she hides her car, the Scorpion Mobile, in the garage of an adjacent building. While Darcy stands for good, her enthusiasm places her in an awkward position. She is a criminal's worst nightmare, but she is also a criminal herself — she is wanted by the police for breaking a number of laws (from speeding to leaving the scene of a crime).

270. Darien Lambert, *Time Traxx*, Syn., 1993. Played by Dale Midkiff.

Darien Lambert is a cop of the future who travels back in time to apprehend criminals. He was born at Longham Hospital in Middle City at 8:05 A.M. on August 17, 2160. He was unclaimed by his parents and was raised in an orphanage in Unclave 1–6, an area previously known as Chicagoland. Darien was allowed to choose his own name. He chose Darien for the hero of the Just War of 2129; and Lambert, the surname of the woman who bore him, as his last name even though all he has of her is a photograph.

Darien was a normal child. He has an I.Q. of 204; speed memorization rate of one point two pages per second and an amazing athletic ability. He can run 100 meters in 8.6 seconds; the mile in 3 minutes, 38 seconds. His heartbeat is a normal 35 beats per minute and his life expectancy is 120 years. His lungs are also average, capable of storing up to six minutes of air. Beta Wave Training has given his generation mind control abilities; one of these is the ability to slow down the speed of visual images reaching the brain (called Time Stalling, it takes rigorous training to accomplish). Darien was a solitary child and lived among his memories. He loved his native land, once called America, and knew every detail of her history. He admired the early Fugitive Retrieval Specialists (U.S. Marshals) and this led him to enter the International Police Academy at West Point.

Darien excelled at school. He learned Masti, a mental improvement on the martial arts. He became an expert with the PPT (Pellet Projection Tube), the police weapon of the day. He graduated first in his class and was commissioned to Detective Junior Grade (a Marshal). In the summer of 2192, Darien was promoted to Captain of the Fugitive Retrieval Section (based at Metro Headquarters; SM-3 is his code). He was also given SELMA (Specified Encapsulated Limitless Memory Archive), a micro miniature computer that contains all information ever printed since Guttenberg's Bible.

Darien next became a member of TRAXX (Trans-Time Research and Experimentation), a time machine project located in the sub-basement of the Smithsonian Institution in Washington, D.C. Here, through the use of a pill (TXP), Darien is able to travel through time (the TXP pill aligns a person's molecules to the delta wave transmissions of TRAXX, thus enabling the transfer of molecules). When Darien travels in time he is supplied with clothes, money, and identification pertinent to the era in which he is sent. He uses his knowledge of the future to apprehend criminals who have escaped into the past seeking freedom from punishment.

271. Darlene Conner, *Roseanne*, ABC, 1988–1997. Played by Sara Gilbert.

Darlene Conner is the daughter of Dan and Roseanne Conner. She has a sister (Becky) and brother (D.J.) and lives with them at 714 Delaware Street in Lanford, Illinois. Darlene has a beautiful first name, but she is mean and nasty. She went from tomboy to moody teenage girl. She lost an interest in sports, found an interest in boys and constantly defied parental authority. She lived, to some extent, in her own little dream world.

Darlene attended South Elementary School, Lanford Jr. High, Lanford High and the Chicago School of the Arts. Her allowance was $5 a week and she loved Fruit Rings and Frank 'n' Berries cereal for breakfast. She also loved helping her father put up drywall and hanging out with him (she was closer to him than her mother). Her life changed, for the worst part, when she met David Healy (Johnny Galecki), the lazy brother of her sister's boyfriend. David, a busboy at Pizza World, whom Darlene eventually married. They had a child they named Harris Conner Healy.

See also: Becky Conner, Dan and Roseanne Conner.

272. Darlene Merriman, *Head of the Class*, ABC, 1986–1991. Played by Robin Givens.

Darlene Merriman is a student in the I.H.P. (Individual Honors Program) at Fillmore High School in New York City. She is the daughter of a wealthy family and lives on Park Avenue (she was born in Manhattan). Darlene is a descendant of Sally Hemmings, the black woman by whom Thomas Jefferson had children. Her specialty is speech and debate and she believes she is very attractive to men ("I represent the physical and intellectual ideals men want"). Darlene believes very few girls can match her beauty and places herself on a pedestal. She is also the editor of the school newspaper, *The Spartan*. In the last episode, Darlene accepts a scholarship to Stanford University.

See also: Arvid Engen, Charlie Moore, Dennis Blunden, Simone Foster.

Darrin Stevens *see* **Samantha Stevens**

273. Darryl Hughley, *The Hughleys*, ABC, 1998–1999; UPN, 1999–2002. Played by D.L. Hughley.

Darryl L. Hughley is a high school dropout who became a success. He is the owner of the Hughley Vending Machine Company in West Hills, California, and is married to Yvonne, a beautiful, well-educated college graduate. He and Yvonne live at 317 Crestview and are the parents of Sydney and Michael.

Darryl grew up in a lower class Los Angeles neighborhood at 135th and Avalon Street. Although his father, Henry, worked as an airport janitor, Darryl claims his family was so poor that they couldn't afford a television set that worked properly ("We had two sets — one for sound and one for picture"). Darryl was the shortest child in his kindergarten class and was called "Scooter" by his mother, Hattie Mae. By the age of ten Darryl had a newspaper route and a lemonade stand but became increasingly uneasy about school. At the age of 16, Darryl worked for three months at his Aunt Jesse's beauty parlor, the Kurl 'n' Knaps Salon. A year later, during his junior year at South Central High School, Darryl felt he wasn't smart enough to continue and dropped out. He claims to have gotten "my master's degree in life" (years later he returned to school to get his G.E.D. at Ulysses S. Grant High School). Rather than wasting time hanging out at the Jay Bones Pool Hall, Darryl found a job with the Perrymore Vending Machine Company, first delivering then repairing them (the Vendamatic 86 was the first machine he serviced). Darryl saved his money and learned all he could about vending machines. When he felt the time was right, he started his own business and became a success.

Darryl believes computers will be the downfall of mankind. He likes to insult people (make jokes) but hates to admit he is wrong. He is afraid of no one — except Yvonne, whom he fears. He always sits furthest from the front door "because you never know who is going to break into this place." He watches TV waiting for unscrambled moments on the Playboy Channel, reads *Ebony* magazine, and has his hair cut at Magic Shears. Otis Redding is his favorite singer and he drives a Lexus. Darryl hates low fat milk but unknowingly drinks it because Yvonne tells him it is whole milk.

See also: Sydney and Michael Hughley, Yvonne Hughley.

274. Data, *Star Trek: The Next Generation*, Syn., 1987–1994. Played by Brent Spiner.

Data, an android, is the Science Officer under Jean-Luc Picard, Captain of the Star Ship U.S.S. *Enterprise NCC 1701-E*. Data was found by members of the U.S.S. *Tripoli* after a crystalline entity drained the life force from his 411-member colony. He was brought to the Omicron Theta Science Colony and reactivated on February 2, 2338, by Dr. Noonien Soong and his fiancé, Dr. Juliana O'Donnell. Data was sent to Star Fleet Academy in 2341 to learn how to become human. He graduated with honors and is an expert in probable mechanics and exobiology. Data was first an ensign then a lieutenant and was first assigned to the U.S.S. *Trieste*. He next served with Picard as the Operations Officer on the U.S.S. *Enterprise NCC 1701-D* and finally on the Sovereign class *Enterprise NCC 1701-E*.

See also: Beverly Crusher, Geordi La Forge, Jean-Luc Picard, Natasha Yar, William Riker.

275. Dave and Linda Lewis, *Good Morning, World*, CBS, 1967–1968. Played by Joby Baker, Julie Parrish.

Dave Lewis is the co-host (with Larry Clark) of *The Lewis and Clark Show*, a 6:00 to 10:00 A.M. radio program of comedy, music and news in Los Angeles (no call letters or AM or FM designation is given). Dave is married to Linda and they live at 63 Court Place.

Dave was born in Los Angeles and began his show business career as a nightclub comedian. He met fellow comic Larry Clark (Ronnie Schell) at a club and they became a team. When the nightclub circuit began to falter for them, they were hired by Hawaiian radio station (KOUA) to host a morning show. Linda, born in San Francisco, was working as the station's receptionist and switchboard operator when she and Dave met. It was a love at first sight and the two married shortly after (at the Prince Kali Hiki Tiki Lodge). Los Angeles radio station owner Roland B. Hut-

ton Jr. heard Dave and Larry's show while vacationing in Hawaii and hired them for his station.

Dave and Linda have been married one year when the series begins. Dave is a happy-go-lucky guy who takes what life dishes out. Linda, on the other hand, tries to overcome obstacles and not let misfortune depress her.

Dave's hobby is building model airplanes (although Linda says "The wings always fall off"). His dream was to fly a plane but after taking lessons at the Speed Gonzales Flying School, he learned he had an inner ear "malfunction" and could never fly. Dave calls Linda "Pumpkin" and clams oreganta with garlic bread is his favorite lunch. Linda, a beautiful woman, receives compliments regarding her stunning looks (from both men and women). "She may be beautiful," Dave says, "but I hate it when she wears a flannel nightgown." Linda is also very neat and tidy and says that Dave suffers from frequent attacks of clumsiness.

See also: Rolland B. Hutton, Jr.

276. Dave Barry, *Dave's World*, CBS, 1993–1997. Played by Harry Anderson.

David Barry, called Dave, is a humorist and author of the books *Helluva Time* and *Barry Picking* (a collection of articles from his Miami *Record Dispatch* newspaper column, "Dave's World"). Dave is married to Beth and is the father of Tommy and Willie. They live "West of Maple Street" in Dade County and have a dog named Ernest. Their phone number is 555-7433 and 6PU 16R is Dave's car license plate number.

Dave was born in the small town of Pewuckatucket and as a kid had a cat (Mr. Stubbs) and a dog (Sparky). He practiced kissing on a pillow he called Phyllis. He is a graduate of Miami State University (where he acquired a degree in journalism; he also did "a little experimenting with drugs" which caused him to see things — "My hair brush became a tribe of Pygmies who worshiped me").

Dave began his career as a reporter for the *Record Dispatch*; he then wrote a series of romance novels for Pinafore Publishing under the pen name Letitia DeVore (his heroine was Lady Millicent).

Dave "writes about funny things in an odd way" and claims to be mechanically inclined ("It took me only three days to master the Clapper"). Dave is always late with his articles and enjoys snacking on peanut butter ice cream and beer. When it comes to giving advice to the kids, Dave does what he does best — nothing.

See also: Beth Barry, Kenny Beckett, Tommy and Willie Barry.

277. Dave Blassingame, *The Westerner*, NBC, 1960. Played by Brian Keith.

Dave Blassingame is a cowboy who roams the West of the 1890s looking for work and eventually a place to settle down. He rides a spotted horse; has a dog named Brown and carries a 405 Winchester repeating rifle with a telescopic sight. Dave can't read or write, tends to get drunk and is often defeated in fights. His past is a mystery. He was raised in a town called Coleman by an uncle. He first rode a horse when he was eight years old and had ambitions to be a rancher. Dave calls Brown, a stray dog he found, Brown "'cause he's a brown dog." Dave works most often as a ranch hand or as a wrangler on a cattle drive. People call Dave "a cheap tin horn with a two bit reputation who doesn't have enough guts to carry a gun." He can, "break broncs with the best of 'em," rides "'cause it's a big country" and has the utmost respect for women ("Women must be God's favorites," Dave says," "'cause he made 'em finer than anything in creation").

278. Dave Starsky, *Starsky and Hutch*, ABC, 1975–1979. Played by Paul Michael Glaser.

David Michael Starsky, called Dave, is a detective with the Metropolitan Division of the L.A.P.D. (also given as the Bay City Police Department). He is partners with Ken Hutchinson and their car code is Zebra 3.

Dave was born in New York City and has a brother named Nick (their father was a cop; their mother a homemaker). While a birth date was not given, episode dialogue places his birth between 1943 and 1945. Dave is Jewish. His father died when he was a young boy and Dave moved to California in late 1958. He served a hitch in the army and after his discharge enrolled in the L.A. Police Academy. It was here that he met his future partner, Ken Hutchinson. Dave became a uniformed police officer in early 1970 and was assigned to the Metro Division 18 months later. In 1974 he became an undercover cop.

Dave lived in three apartments throughout the series run. Only the second one was given an address (2000 Ridgeway Drive). He drives a candy apple red car with a white stripe (plate 537 ONW) and carries a 39–9 Smith and Wesson gun. Dave likes junk food, expensive watches, Laurel and Hardy movies, and rock music. He is a bit afraid of heights and dogs and enjoys the holidays, especially Christmas. When he was a child, he imagined his backyard as a magical play land called Doodletown.

Dave is a neat freak, ladies' man, and looks for the good in people — no matter how bad they may appear. He is also impetuous and would rather take action than sit back and watch things happen. Dave is still close to his mother and calls her every Friday.

See also: Ken Hutchinson.

279. David Addison, *Moonlighting*, ABC, 1985–1989. Played by Bruce Willis.

David Addison, Jr., is a private detective employed by Maddie Hayes, a former model who runs the Blue Moon Detective Agency in Los Angeles. He is the son of David Sr. and Irma, and was born on March 23, 1956 (later mentioned as November 27). He lived on Bainbridge Street in Philadelphia as a child and his father remarried after Irma's death (his stepmother is named Stephanie); his only sibling is his brother, Richard.

David was undecided about his life and first worked as a bartender before choosing to become an investigator (where he thought he could make more money). He is immature, deceitful and totally distrustful of people. He is optimistic about everything but constantly jokes, makes lewd sexual remarks and sings whenever the opportunity permits, even when it doesn't. Money is his number one priority and he will take whatever cases come along to make it (even by going behind Maddie's back; he calls her "Blondie Blonde"). "Do bears bare?" and "Do bees be" are his catch phrases. He drives a car with the license plate 2900 LB, likes R&B music and bowling; he hates foreign films and seafood.

See also: Maddie Hayes.

280. David Bradford, *Eight Is Enough*, ABC, 1977–1981. Played by Grant Goodeve.

This entry also contains information of David's younger brothers, Tommy (Willie Aames) and Nicholas (Adam Rich).

David. David is the oldest of the eight Bradford children (which also includes Mary, Nancy, Susan, Joanie and Elizabeth). They live at 1436 Oak Street in Sacramento, California, and are the children of Tom and Joan Bradford. David is a contractor and worked for the Mann Construction Company, then Joseph Jenkins and Associates before forming the Bradford Construction Company. David is a graduate of Sacramento High School (class of 1977) and was the first of the children to move to his own apartment (207) and marry (Janet McCarther, played by Joan Prather. Janet is a lawyer with the firm of Goodman, Saxon and Tweedy; later the firm of Ted O'Hara and Associates. Marital tensions led to their separation and eventual divorce in 1981).

Tommy. Tommy is the most troublesome of the children. He constantly rebels against parental authority and longs to become a rock musician (he plays guitar). He attended Sacramento High School and formed a band called Tommy and the Actions. His hangouts are Bernie's Burger Bin and the Cluck 'n' Chuck (fast food chicken).

Nicholas. Nicholas is the youngest of the Bradfords. He attended the Goodwin-Knight Elementary School and had a neighborhood courier service (N&M Delivery Service). Nicholas loves basketball, has two hamsters (Ron and Marsha) and had a job selling a wrinkle remover called Guaca Dew door-to-door. He was also the ring bearer at his father's wedding when he married his second wife, Abby (Joan, his first wife, had died of cancer).

In the first update *Eight Is Enough: A Family Reunion* (NBC, October 18, 1987), David is now an architect and marries Marilyn Fulbright (Nancy Everhard) in the second update, *An Eight Is Enough Wedding* (NBC, October 15, 1989). Tommy is a struggling lounge singer and Nicholas is attending college.

See also: Mary Bradford (for information on Mary, Joanie, Susan, Nancy and Elizabeth Bradford), Tom Bradford (for information on Tom, Joan and Abby Bradford).

281. David Palmer, *24*, Fox, 2001–2004. Played by Dennis Haysbert.

David Palmer is the mythical, first black president of the United States and personally in charge of the CTU (Counter Terrorism Unit; it is headed by agent Jack Bauer). David is divorced and the father of Nicole and Keith. He was a senator (representing Maryland) and a member of the Senate Commerce Sub Committee, the Senate Appropriations Committee, the House Ways and Means Committee, and the House National Security Sub Committee.

David has a degree from the Maryland School of Law and a Bachelor of Arts degree in political economy from Georgetown University. He also served with the law firm of Fidley, Barrow and Bain. David played basketball in college and was called College Player of the Year by *Sporting News* and won the Wooden Award (Player of the Year) and Defensive Player of the Year (Big East Conference). He was also NCAA All-American in men's basketball. David is a powerful force for justice. While he doesn't rule with an iron hand he expects only the best from the agents he commands as head of the CTU.

See also: Jack Bauer, Tony Almeida.

282. Dawn Summers, *Buffy the Vampire Slayer*, WB, 2000–2001; UPN, 2001–2003. Played by Michelle Trachtenberg.

Dawn Summers is a very pretty 14-year-old girl who did not exist in human form prior to the year 2000. She is the sister of Buffy Summers, the only child of Joyce and Hank Summers, and lives at 1630 Revello Drive in Sunnydale, California. Dawn attends Sunnydale High School and her memories were drawn from Buffy and Joyce. Buffy and Joyce's memories were altered to accept the fact that Dawn was always a part of their lives (Joyce is divorced and Hank is no longer a part of her life).

Dawn is actually the Key, an unknown power source that operates beyond a normal reality. The Key is centuries old and its origins are unknown. The monks of the Byzantine Order discovered the Key and sought to control its power. When Glory, an evil goddess learned of the Key, she set her goal on encompassing its powers. To prevent Glory from acquiring the Key, the monks transformed its power into human form as a sister for Buffy, a powerful slayer of demons, to protect.

Dawn enjoys salami and peanut butter sandwiches and eats Sugar Bombs cereal for breakfast. She invented a not-so-tasty peanut butter and banana waffle and is sometimes called Dawnie by Buffy. At first Dawn was unaware of exactly who she was. She appears as a girl but deep inside she feels she is something else. She often wonders "Who or what am I" and believes Buffy thinks of her as "a dumb little sister" and "Little Miss Nobody." Buffy, however, cares for Dawn — "It doesn't matter where you came from or how you got here. You're my sister and I love you." Dawn has memories of growing up with Buffy and her mother (who called her "Pumpkin Belly" as a kid). Dawn keeps a diary of her activities and becomes a valuable aid to Buffy as she battles demons. Dawn learns to accept herself when she discovers she is the Key but that aspect is played down when the series switched to UPN. Dawn is portrayed as a typical high school girl with an uncanny interest in demons (she wants to learn all she can so she can help Buffy battle evil).

See also: Angel, Buffy Summers, Rupert Giles, Spike, Willow Rosenberg, Xander Harris.

283. D.D. Cummings, *She Spies*, Syn., 2002–2004. Played by Kristen Miller.

Deedra Cummings, called D.D., is a member of She Spies, a government organization that battles crime and corruption. D.D. was born in Washington, D.C. Her father was a CIA agent who was framed for spying. D.D. knew he was innocent and the only way she could prove it was to hack into the government's database. She managed to prove her father was innocent but was arrested for stealing state secrets. Her police booking number is 83-7648-8; she served time in Terminal Island Prison in San Pedro, California but was freed by the government who required her extraordinary skills.

D.D. attended St. Mary's Middle School where she learned to speak French. In high school she was voted most likely to coordinate talent. She also played Shell Number One in the school production of *The Little Mermaid*. D.D. is a graduate of Harvard University (she hacked her way into the school's computer system to arrange for a diploma). She is an expert on computers, foreign languages and explosives. Her favorite drink is a banana cream (banana liqueur, vodka, orange juice, nonfat milk). She has a plush teddy bear (Uncle Blue Bear) and a talent for what she calls "wall walking" (balancing herself between two walls in a horizontal manner). A Kit Kat bar is her favorite candy and her least favorite thing to do is jump through a window to escape. D.D. was an Indian Princess Scout as a child and was called "Ray of Sunshine." Her dream as a young girl was to grow up and become a princess.

D.D. is very careful when she is on a case. She likes to think about what she is going to do before she does it. Sometimes, however, there is no time to think and she just does it; she often says, "That's what I would have done if I had time to think about it." D.D. carries a gun but is reluctant to use it (she'll only use it if she has no other choice). While very attractive, D.D. sometimes shows more skin than usual to help her and her teammates, Cassie and Shane, get through an assignment.

See also: Cassie McBain, Shane Phillips.

284. Deanna Troi, *Star Trek: The Next Generation*, Syn., 1987–1994. Played by Marina Sirtis.

Deanna Troi is the daughter of a human father (Starfleet Lieutenant Ian Troi) and a Betazoid mother (Ambassador Lwaxana). She was born on March 29, 2336, near Lake El-Nar on the planet Betazed. Deanna serves as the counselor under Jean-Luc Picard, captain of the U.S.S. *Enterprise*.

Deanna lost her father when she was seven. She treasures the Earth-based stories and songs he would relate to her each night at bedtime. She learned in later life that she had a six-year-old sister, Kestra, who drowned when Deanna was an infant (but never told about the incident).

Deanna has telepathic powers and can emotionally bond with other species. She is knowl-

edgeable in language and linguistics and loves desserts, especially anything chocolate ("I never met a chocolate I didn't like"). Deanna attended Starfleet Academy (2355-59). After graduation, she attended the University of Betazed for advanced studies in psychology. In 2364 she became a lieutenant commander and was assigned to *Enterprise NCC 1701-D*. Six years later she became a commander and in 2372 was transferred with Captain Picard to the Sovereign class *Enterprise NCC 1701-E*.

See also: Beverly Crusher, Data, Geordi La Forge, Jean-Luc Picard, Natasha Yar, William Riker.

285. Deaquon Hayes, *Fastlane*, Fox, 2002–2003. Played by Bill Bellamy.

Deaquon Lavelle Hayes is a detective attached to the Candy Store, a division of the L.A.P.D. that uses seized cars and weapons to help bring criminals to justice. Deaquon was born in Torrence, California. He drifted to New York and ran with a gang before he turned his life around. He joined the police academy and first worked as an undercover narcotics cop for the N.Y.P.D. Deaquon uses his street smarts to deal with crime. He is partners with Van Ray and lives at 200 Country Club Road in Santa Monica, California. He eats Post Cocoa Puffs cereal for breakfast and his beeper code is "Purple Hayes."

See also: Billie Chambers, Van Ray.

286. Debra Barone, *Everybody Loves Raymond*, CBS, 1996–2005. Played by Patricia Heaton.

Debra Barone is the wife of sportswriter Raymond Barone and the mother of Ally, Jeffrey and Michael. She lives in Lynbrook, New York, at 320 Fowler Street (although 135 can be seen on the front door) and is the daughter of Warren and Lois Whalen. As a teenager, Debra enjoyed making trips to Manhattan with her mother for a mother and daughter day of tea and shopping. She is a graduate of St. John's University (where she studied behavioral psychology and wrote her thesis on the book *To Kill a Mockingbird*). Dialogue from various episodes tells us that Debra met her future husband, Raymond, while in college (she ordered a bed from Claude's Futons and Raymond was sent to install it). They married after graduation and set up housekeeping in a small apartment in Lynbrook. Raymond found work as a sportswriter at *Newsday* while Debra acquired a job in Manhattan in a public relations firm. It was at this time that she became pregnant and quit her job when her daughter, Ally, was born (1991). When the house next to Raymond's parents, Frank and Marie, became available, she and Raymond purchased it.

Debra has a tendency to be moody and critical. She has a knack for being late for anything she and Raymond have to attend (which makes Raymond uneasy, as he hates to be late for anything). Debra spent her summers as a kid at Lake Sagatuck in Connecticut. She likes craftsman furniture, is famous for her lemon chicken and lillies of the valley are her favorite flower. Debra does volunteer work at St. Theresa's Hospital and held a temporary job as a copywriter at the Charlotte Sterling PR Agency in Manhattan. Raymond proposed to Debra on Valentine's Day and she believes "I inherited a freak show next door" (referring to the constant intrusion of her in-laws, especially Marie, who is super critical of her cooking, cleaning, and care of the children).

See also: Ally Barone, Frank and Marie Barone, Raymond Barone, Robert Barone.

287. Dee Davenport, *Clueless,* ABC, 1996–1997; UPN, 1997–1999. Played by Stacey Dash.

Dionne Davenport, called Dee, is a beautiful teenage girl who is also exceptionally bright. She is a member of the National Honors Society and the daughter of a wealthy family. She lives at 607 Chantilly Lane in Beverly Hills, California, and attends the posh Bronson Alcott High School. She previously attended Rodeo Drive Pre-School and the Rodeo Drive Elementary School. Dee hopes to attend Stanhope College with her best friends, Cher Horowitz and Amber Mariens. Their hangout is the Koffee House.

Dee believes she is not only gorgeous but also physically perfect. She dresses in the latest clothes, loves to show cleavage and is looking to marry into wealth. While Dee finds a day at school trying, she relaxes by "shopping the retail experience." When Dee breaks up with a boy she "shrinks into a bottomless pit of bumming." Dee does have one problem, although she won't admit it — she often talks on and on about something that bothers her; Cher calls it "Bimbo Babble."

See also: Amber Mariens, Cher Horowitz.

288. Dee Dee McCall, *Hunter,* NBC, 1984–1990; 2003. Played by Stepfanie Kramer.

Dee Dee McCall is a beautiful detective sergeant with Division 122 of the Los Angeles Police Department. She is partners with Rick Hunter and is tough and honest; these attributes have earned her the nickname "The Brass Cupcake." Dee Dee resides at 8534 Mezdon Drive in Los Angeles, then at 808 McKenzie Street when she transfers to the Robbery-Homicide Division of the San Diego Police Department (2003). Her car codes (Los Angeles) were 1-Adam 43, Charles Albert 420, and L-59. In San Diego, her car code was 930-Sam; 794 her badge number. Dee Dee loves children and teaches music at the San Diego Juvenile Center in her spare time.

Dee Dee is a perfectionist; she likes to take her time on a case and everything must make sense to her. She will try to avoid violent confrontations if she can, but often finds herself as impatient as her partner (who likes to rush in and get the job over with). Dee Dee is a widow; her late husband, Steve McCall, was a sergeant killed in the line of duty. She is again teamed with Rick when he also transfers to San Diego in 2003 (in a new version of the series called *Hunter*).

See also: Rick Hunter.

289. Dee Dee Star, *Heart's Afire,* CBS, 1992–1993. Played by Beth Broderick.

Dee Dee Star is a woman who is motivated by patriotism and a love of country (or as some people put it, "She feels that any time a man plays an important role in world events, Dee Dee finds it her patriotic duty to throw her skirt over her head"). Dee Dee works as the office receptionist to Strobe Smithers, a somewhat senile, conservative Southern Senator, in Washington, D.C.

Dee Dee was born in Amarillo, Texas, and as early as she can remember she has been concerned about her looks. She was the class beauty at Amarillo High School and became a beautician after graduation. She worked at the Beauty Pit Salon in Texas but felt the need to try bigger and better things. She moved to Washington, D.C., where she found work at the local Foto Mat. Exactly how she became Strobe's receptionist is not mentioned (it can be assumed that Strobe, a married ladies' man, spotted her and hired her).

Dee Dee's wild sexual activities have earned her the nickname "The last bimbo on the Hill." She thinks women are threatened by her looks and to prove she is not all beauty and no brains she started her own business: Mail Order Bras and Panties. Dee Dee does not care what people think about her and relishes in the fact that she is thought of as easy and a tease ("It makes me happy").

See also: Georgie Ann Lahti.

290. Dee Dee Thorne, *Half and Half,* UPN, 2003 (current). Played by Essence Atkins.

Dee Dee Thorne was born in San Francisco and grew up in the swank Sea Cliff section. She is the daughter of "Big" Dee Dee and Charles Thorne and has a half sister named Mona Thorne.

Dee Dee grew up in luxury. She was given anything she wanted and attended private grammar and high schools (in high school, Dee Dee was one of only two black girls. The other girl, Aurora, was overweight, so Dee Dee became "The Hot Black Chick").

Dee Dee has lived up to her high school reputation and dresses in only designer clothes. She graduated top in her law class at Berkeley and is now taking graduate courses in law. She lives in a $2,000 a month apartment (3A) in the same building as Mona (at 36 Briarcliff). The building is owned by her father and Dee Dee's wealthy mother pays her rent. At Berkeley, Dee Dee was voted "Best Dressed" by her sorority. She is afraid of spiders, cleans when she becomes upset and to prove her independence, she took a job as a waitress at the local eatery, the Lunch Lounge. Dee Dee is very particular about her appearance. If she is not in full makeup it is an indication that something is bothering her. Though rich, she is not a snob and will give of herself to help others, especially Mona, whom she feels needs all the help she can get.

See also: Mona Thorne.

291. Delenn, *Babylon 5*, TNT, 1993–1999. Played by Mira Furlan.

Delenn, an Ambassador of the planet Minbari (a race of spiritual people), is the second wife of John Sheridan, captain then president of *Babylon 5*, a five-mile long space station built in the 23rd century and located in neutral space. Its purpose is to maintain the peace between the various alien races that inhabit the galaxy.

Delenn was a member of her planet's ruling body (the Grey Counsel) who underwent an operation to make her appear human (to blend in with humans. The Minbari not only distrust humans, they are appalled by their appearance). Delenn is a strong, levelheaded woman with sacred political beliefs (she was chastised for her affair with John because mating with a human could contaminate the Minbari bloodline).

Delenn is later head of the Minbari Religious Chaste and is always by John's side. She is totally dedicated to him and even served with him as his co-commander in the Army of Light. She is a firm believer that if something was meant to happen it will happen and no force can change fate. Prior to her marrying John, Delenn was the leader of the Conspiracy of Light, a group of rangers who battled the evils that threatened their planet.

See also: Elizabeth Lochley, John Sheridan, Lyta Alexander, Susan Ivanova.

Della Street *see* **Perry Mason**

292. Delta Bishop, *Delta*, CBS, 1992–1993. Played by Delta Burke.

Delta Bishop is a woman with a powerful dream: to become a country and western singer. Delta was born in the town of Goose Neck, which is on the Mississippi Delta ("I was named Delta because Mississippi was not the right name for me"). Ever since she was a young girl, Delta wanted to write and sing country music but never had the opportunity to pursue that goal. She is a graduate of Goose Neck High School and attended beauty school after graduation. It was here that she met Charlie Bishop, a lumberyard worker she fell in love with and married. Charlie was reckless with money and would spend foolishly, thus denying Delta her chance to go to Nashville. As the years passed, Delta became restless and was eager to follow in the footsteps of her idol, singer Patsy Cline, and become a country music star. After eight years of waiting, Delta quit her job as a hairstylist at Mona's House of Hair and moved to Nashville (she later divorced Charlie). She found an apartment (over the garage of her cousin, Lvonne Overton), an agent (The Tune Mogul of the Universal Artists and Others, Inc.), and a job — waitress at the Green Lantern (at 211 East Grange), where Patsy Cline once sang. Delta then dyes her blonde hair black and begins her quest to fulfill a dream.

293. Denise Huxtable, *The Cosby Show*, NBC, 1984–1992. Played by Lisa Bonet.

The character of Denise Huxtable also appeared on *The Cosby Show* spinoff, *A Different World* (NBC, 1987–1988). Denise is the daughter of Cliff and Clair Huxtable and lives at 10 Stigwood Avenue in Brooklyn, New York. She has three sisters (Sondra, Vanessa and Rudy) and a brother (Theo).

Denise is the most mischievous of the children. She is beautiful but very insecure. She is careless, irresponsible and terrible when it comes to money matters. Denise is a graduate of Central High School but dropped out of Hillman College (in Georgia) after three semesters (unable to handle the work load; she received five Ds, one C, and seven incompletes. She had an undecided major and lived in Room 20Y of the Gilbert Hall Dorm).

Denise returned home after quitting college and held jobs at the Wilderness Store, then Blue Wave Records (where she earned $25 a week as the assistant to the executive assistant). She next worked as a photographer's assistant. While on assignment in Africa, she married Martin Kendall (Joseph C. Phillips), a Navy Lieutenant with a young daughter named Olivia (Raven-Symone). While caring for Olivia, Denise recalled that she once had a dream of teaching children. She decided to pursue that goal by taking education classes at the Medgar Evers College of the City University of New York. This too may not come to pass as in the last episode Denise announced he was pregnant.

See also: Cliff and Clair Huxtable, Sondra Huxtable, Theo Huxtable, Vanessa and Rudy Huxtable.

294. Dennis Blunden, *Head of the Class*, ABC, 1986–1991. Played by Dan Schneider.

Dennis Clarence Blunden is a student in the I.H.P. (Individual Honors Program) at Fillmore High School in New York City. He is the class clown (loves to play practical jokes) and is skilled in chemistry and physics. Dennis holds the record for being sent to the principal's office more times than any other student (in the office he stares at the picture of George Washington that is on the wall).

Dennis was born in Manhattan and lives at 63 West 45th Street (the school is downtown at 16th Street and Irving Place). Dennis showed potential for greatness at an early age but felt he was out of place and covered his brilliance by joking all the time. He carried a John Travolta lunch box in grammar school but now prefers to eat out at Izzy's, a fast food store (Dennis loves to eat but says he can't stand the school's cafeteria food). Dennis's locker combination is 27-14-5 and he held a part time job as a waiter at an eatery called Casa Falafel.

See also: Arvid Engen, Charlie Moore, Darlene Merriman, Simone Foster.

295. Dennis Finch, *Just Shoot Me*, NBC, 1997–2003. Played by David Spade.

Dennis Finch is a schemer who works as the assistant to Jack Gallo, the publisher of *Blush*, a Manhattan-based fashion magazine. Jack sees his magazine as his castle and Dennis as his gargoyle.

Dennis was born in Albany, New York, and worked as a gift wrapper at Bloomingdale's, then a movie theater usher before his job at the magazine (which he sees as an opportunity to meet beautiful girls). Dennis is a yuppie. His favorite song is "Time in a Bottle" and he writes an advice column called "Dear Miss Pretty." He collects old TV action figures (for the money he can get for them) and ceramic kittens (which he loves and saves). He has a pet cat (Spartacus), uses

"Finch Fry" as his computer password and reads *Teen Scream* magazine. He spends his time "thinking of women's breasts and bottoms" and has "a gift for hearing words like 'nude' and 'sex' from great distances." Dennis believes he works hard, gets little pay and is given no respect.

See also: Jack Gallo, Maya Gallo, Nina Van Horn.

296. Derek Rayne, *Poltergeist: The Legacy*, SHO, 1996–1998; Sci Fi, 1999; Syn., 1999–2001. Played by Derek DeLint.

Derek Rayne is a man who says "I was born into the fight against evil." He is the house leader of the San Francisco–based Legacy, people with special gifts who protect the innocent from supernatural forces.

Derek possesses doctorates in theology and biological anthropology. He has psychic abilities and an extensive knowledge of science, mythology and the Legacy itself. Derek is the son of Winston Rayne, a former head of the San Francisco House. When Derek was 15 years old he accompanied his father to Peru to search for the mysterious Chests of the Five Angels (the chests contain the spirits of evil angels who were banished from Heaven. They wrecked havoc on the world until they were stopped by a group of Druids who imprisoned them). Winston's search led him to one of the chests. His curiosity got the best of him and he opened the forbidden chest. An angel's spirit emerged and killed him. Derek felt he had to take over his father's quest and destroy the remaining chests. He spent many years searching and has found three others; he still needs to find the fifth one to complete his mission (destroying the chest also destroys the evil).

Derek studies ancient scrolls and seeks the truth even if it is not what he wants it to be. He is embittered and sometimes torn between his own desires and his destiny with the Legacy. He stays because he knows "all it takes for evil to triumph is for good people to do nothing."

See also: Alex Moreau, Kristen Adams, Nick Boyle, Rachel Corrigan.

297. Destiny Angel, *Captain Scarlet and the Mysterons*, Syn., 1967. Voiced by Liz Morgan.

Destiny Angel is one of five beautiful girls who work as pilots for Spectrum, a futuristic organization that safeguards the Earth from alien invaders.

Destiny was born in Paris and attended the finest universities in Europe. After college Destiny joined the World Army Air Force. Her extraordinary skills and feats of daring earned her a transfer to the Women's Flight Squadron. Three years later, she started her own firm of flying contractors. This led her to being hired by Spectrum. Her intelligence, leadership abilities and talent in flying earned her the position as leader of the Angels. The program is a puppet series filmed in Supermarionation.

See also: Captain Magenta, Captain Ochre, Captain Scarlet, Harmony Angel, Melody Angel, Rhapsody Angel, Symphony Angel.

298. Dharma Montgomery, *Dharma and Greg*, ABC, 1997–2002. Played by Jenna Elfman.

Dharma Freedom Montgomery Finkelstein is the daughter of Abby O'Neill and Larry Finkelstein, an offbeat couple who lived together for 30 years before marrying in 1999. Dharma is a very beautiful woman and is now married to Greg Montgomery, a wealthy attorney she met and married on their first date.

Dharma was born at home in an old standalone bathtub and is referred to by her hippie parents as "Our Flower Child" (Dharma's mother-in-law, Kitty, refers to her as "A big blonde lump of clay that needs molding"). Dharma's childhood was quite bizarre, which could account for her strange behavior as an adult. Her baby bed was a rope-tied hammock with a banana leaf as a blanket (Abby felt "cribs were little jails for babies"). As a toddler, Dharma would crawl under the house to play with Fluffy (Dharma wasn't sure what kind of animal it was — "but it sure was fluffy").

As a kid, Dharma did not have a Jack in the Box ("I had a mouse under a Dixie cup") and she was not allowed to play with dolls (Abby felt it fostered unnecessary motherly instincts). Dharma was given substitutes: she had a dump truck that she would dress up and call Barbie; her Ken doll was an ant farm. Dharma also played with a "shoeboat" (an old sneaker) and her baby stroller was a homemade blanket tied to the back of her father's bike. When Dharma was 12 years old she learned that people eat meat. Curious to try it, she bought a hamburger at Tasty Freeze. She was caught by her mother and scolded. The next day she had her first period and now associates meat with periods. At age 13 Dharma began to develop and wanted a bra like her girlfriends. When Abby refused to buy her one ("too constricting"), Dharma stole one from the Sears lingerie department. A year later, Dharma shaved her head, hoping her straight hair would grow in curly. It didn't; she had to wear a wig, "but I did learn how to wiggle my ears." Dharma took ballet classes as a child and was called "The Graceful Little Bas-

tard" by other students (her parents were not married at the time).

Dharma is a graduate of Berkeley College (where she had a number of lesbian friends) and later took classes at the University of Central California. She worked as a blackjack dealer, a NASCAR pit crew girl, mermaid in a Florida theme park, and waitress at Jerry's Rice Bowl. She currently trains dogs and teaches yoga classes at night. She and Greg live in a renovated battery factory building in San Francisco. Dharma has a beaded Mona Lisa curtain that acts as a room divider and a pop-up toaster she calls Willie. Every spring Dharma dances nude on her building's roof in a ritual to celebrate the annual rebirth of the Earth.

When something goes wrong, Dharma believes the universe is trying to tell her something. She speaks four languages (English, French, Spanish and can swear in Mandarin) and believes UFO's exist. Although she wanted a bra as a teenager, she now rarely wears one (a 38C) and calls her breasts Lyle and Eric.

Dharma has a hand painted watercolor birth certificate (made by her father). She can play drums and was in two bands: the Jamaican Steel Band (which played on Fisherman's Wharf) and Snot's Army (a garage band). As a child, Dharma had a dog named Doobie; she now has one named Stinky and Stinky has his own dog, Nunzio (whom Dharma gave to Stinky on his Bar Mitzvah); she bathes them at the You Wash Doogie Place.

An image of Dharma appeared in a comic book as the Blonde Tornado, a super hero who battled evil by turning herself into a tornado (Dharma also posed as her at a comic book convention).

Tofu barley soup is Dharma's favorite meal. She loves organ music and has her clothes cleaned at the Fluff and Fold Laundry. She operated an illegal two-watt radio station called Radio Dharma and ran for a seat on the San Francisco Board of Supervisors (but lost; her slogan was "Improve Your Karma, Vote for Dharma"). Dharma wears jersey 13 as a member of the Sheeps, an all-girl softball team and she appeared on TV in commercials for Anaconda Beer.

See also: Abby O'Neill, Edward and Kitty Montgomery, Greg Montgomery, Larry Finkelstein.

299. Diana Prince, *Wonder Woman*, ABC, 1976–1977; CBS, 1977–1979. Played by Lynda Carter.

Diana Prince is a beautiful young woman who appears to be in her mid-twenties. In actuality, she is very old (mentioned as being 27 million years old in an unaired pilot). Diana is a woman of great strength and courage and protects all that is good as Wonder Woman, a mysterious, indestructible figure for justice.

Diana's creation can be traced back to the year 200 B.C. when the rival gods Mars and Aphrodite fought for control of the Earth. It was at this time that Aphrodite created a race of super women called Amazons and established a home for them on a still uncharted and unknown landmass in the Bermuda Triangle. Here, the goddess Hippolyta became their queen and named their home Paradise Island ("There are no men here. It is free of their wars and barbaric ways. We live in peace and sisterhood"). Mars, however, could not abide by such a ruling and used Hippolyta's own weapon of love to seduce and defeat her. Mars won the battle but Paradise Island remained untouched (it is concealed by the refraction of light). To receive forgiveness, Hippolyta fashioned a small statute out of clay and offered it to Aphrodite. Aphrodite forgave Hippolyta and brought the statue to life as the baby Diana, a baby Hippolyta was to raise and groom to become a future ruler. As the centuries passed, Diana grew into a stunningly beautiful woman with the necessary abilities to rule Paradise Island.

Diana is immortal. As Wonder Woman, a name given to her by Hippolyta ("In the words of ordinary men, you are a Wonder Woman"), Diana wears a red, white and blue costume (a sexy one piece bathing suit). She also wears a gold belt to retain her cunning, strength and immortality away from Paradise Island, and a gold tiara with a red ruby in the middle. Diana also carries her magic lariat (which compels people to tell the truth when placed around them) and wears a pair of gold bracelets, made from Feminum, to deflect bullets ("The Amazon mind is conditioned for athletic ability and academic learning. Only we have the speed and coordination to attempt bullets and bracelets").

When Diana is away from Paradise Island she lives at 2890 West 20th Street in Washington, D.C. (ABC episodes; set during World War II). Capitol 7-362 is her phone number. She poses as a Navy yeoman and works as secretary to Steve Trevor of Air Corps Intelligence. CBS episodes are set in modern times with Diana as the assistant to Steve Trevor, Jr., at the I.A.D.C. (Inter-Agency Defense Command) in Washington, D.C.

Diana becomes Wonder Woman by doing a twirling striptease. She travels from Paradise Island to Washington, D.C. via her invisible plane.

300. Diane Chambers, *Cheers*, NBC, 1982–1987. Played by Shelley Long.

Diane Chambers is prim and proper and works as a barmaid at Cheers, a Boston bar owned by Sam Malone. She was born in Boston and is the daughter of Spencer and Helen Chambers. Diane was called "Muffin" by her father and had a pet cat named Elizabeth Barrett Browning (after her favorite poet). She also had a plush toad (Freddy Frogbottom), giraffe (Mr. Jammers), bee (Mr. Buzzer) and Brian the Lion and Gary Gorilla. Diane is a graduate of Boston University (where she worked as a substitute teacher). She is also an art student and held jobs at the Third Eye Bookstore and as a checkout clerk at Hurley's Supermarket.

Diane is interested in rare first-edition books and had an on-and-off love affair with ballet since she was seven years old (she abandoned that dream to become a novelist). She first dated bar patron Dr. Frasier Crane but left him at the altar when she felt the marriage wouldn't work (she then went on a sexual spree in Europe but saved herself by checking into the Abbey of St. Anshelins in Boston. Here, the Sisters of the Divine Serenity returned Diane to her old self). She next had a rocky romance with Sam Malone and used the pen name Jessica Simpson Bordais to help him write a book (that never materialized) about his days as a relief pitcher for the Red Sox baseball team. She then left Sam in 1987 to pursue a writing career. This too failed. However, when her publisher, Houghton Mifflin Publishing, suggested she trim several thousand pages and turn it into a screenplay, Diane found success. Six years later her book became a TV movie (*The Heart Held Hostage*) and won the cable TV Ace Award for Best Telefilm.

Diane was a dreamer "and I have a habit of making those dreams come true," she said. She entered the 45th Annual Miss Boston Barmaid Contest and won based on her beauty, perkiness and congeniality. In high school, Diane was voted "Most Likely to Marry into Old Money" and in college was a member of the Phi Epsilon Delta Sorority.

See also: Carla LeBec, Cliff Claven, Ernie Pantusso, Norm Peterson, Rebecca Howe, Sam Malone, Woody Boyd.

301. Dick and Joanna Loudon, *Newhart*, CBS, 1982–1990. Played by Bob Newhart, Mary Frann.

Dick and Joanna Loudon are the owners of the 200-year-old Stratford Inn at 28 Westbrook Road in River City, Vermont. Dick Loudon and Joanna McKenna met in New York City at an ad agency where they both worked (their first date was at a Memorial Day picnic). They married shortly after and quit their jobs to pursue different goals: Dick, a "How To" book author, and Joanna, a real estate broker. Years later they pooled their resources to settle down as the owners of a country inn.

Dick was born in Chicago and attended Cunningham Elementary School. At State College, where he majored in journalism, Dick was a drummer in a band called the Jazz Tones (he had the nickname "Slats Loudon"). As a kid Dick had a goldfish he named after actress Ethel Merman. He attended Camp Cowapoka and for some strange reason, his favorite sport is diving. Dick's books include *How to Make Your Dream Bathroom*, *Pillow Talk* (making pillows), and *Installation and Care of Your Low Maintenance Lawn Sprinkler*. His first novel was *Murder at the Strately* (a mystery based on the Stratford Inn).

Dick wears a size 8½ DDD shoe and hosts the local TV show *Vermont Today* on WPIV, Channel 8. Dick's most devastating act was accidentally burning down the French restaurant Maison Hubert (he carelessly tossed a lit cigarette in the men's room waste basket).

Joanna was born in Gainsville, Ohio. She loves to wear sexy sweaters but on their anniversary, Dick always gives her a yellow scarf. Joanna first hosted the Channel 8 TV show *Your House Is My House*, then to capitalize on Joanna's sexy look, the show became *Hot Houses*. Joanna also holds the town's record for renting the video *60 Days to a Tighter Tummy*.

See also: George Utley, Larry, Darryl and Darryl, Stephanie Vanderkellin.

302. Dick Grayson, *Batman*, ABC, 1966–1968. Played by Burt Ward.

Richard Grayson, called Dick, is actually Robin, the Boy Wonder, the teenage crime fighter who helps Bruce Wayne, alias Batman, battle evil. Dick was born to a family of circus performers called the Flying Graysons. He grew up in traveling tent shows and was educated by his mother. One day, while performing their high wire act in Gotham City, tragedy strikes: the rope snaps and young Dick's parents are killed in the ensuing fall. Bruce Wayne, who had been attending the performance, quickly changes into his Batman costume and investigates. He discovers racketeers had cut the rope to force the circus owner to pay protection money. Batman approaches the young orphan and tells him what he has discovered. He also tells him about the tragic circumstances that led to his becoming Batman (see Bruce Wayne for information). "If only I could do something

like that," Dick says, "It will help avenge their deaths. Let me join you, please." "With your acrobatic skills plus what I could teach you, maybe you can make the grade," says Batman.

Bruce takes on the responsibility of raising Dick and eventually becomes his legal guardian. Dick perfects his mental and physical skills and adapts the alias of Robin, the Boy Wonder (when working together they are called the Dynamic Duo). Dick attends Woodrow Roosevelt High School and his cover is that of Bruce Wayne's young ward. As Robin, Dick's catch phrase is the word "Holy" followed by a term (for example, "Holy Crucial Moments" or "Holy Strawberries Batman, We're in a Jam"—the one term Burt Ward wanted to say but was never permitted to).

See also: Barbara Gordon, Bruce Wayne.

303. Dick Solomon, *Third Rock from the Sun*, NBC, 1996–2001. Played by John Lithgow.

On the Home Planet, a world 30 trillion miles away, four aliens are assigned by their leader, the Big Giant Head, to study life on Earth. The aliens travel across three billion galaxies and take up residence at 417 Pensdale Drive in Rutherford, Ohio. Here, the leader becomes Dick Solomon. The Security Officer, Sally, is appointed as his sister; the Transmitter becomes Harry, Dick's brother; and the Information Officer becomes Tommy, who is Dick's son in some episodes, his brother in others.

Dick's cover is that of a quantum physics professor at Pendleton University. His classes are held in room 239 and his office is in room 109 in the Hunt Hall Building. Dick is pompous, judgmental, self-absorbed and extremely naïve when it comes to life on Earth (he takes everything literally and makes a fool of himself). Dick enjoys Lucky Charms and Cheerios cereal for breakfast and carries a U.S. Post Office logo lunch box to work. When he gets lonely or depressed, Dick goes to the planetarium to find comfort. In some episodes, Dick is single and was never married; in others, he claims to be a widower ("My wife burned up on re-entry"). Dick enjoys a drink at Balaska's Bar and drives a red Rambler with the license plate DLW 4S7. He enjoys ice cream from the Mr. Frostie Smooth truck.

Dick prepares the daily status reports in limerick form for the Big Giant Head. When he needed extra money, Dick became a counter clerk at the Rusty Burger. After several years on Earth, Dick felt heat, electricity and cooked meats had made him weak.

Dick dated Dr. Mary Albright (Jane Curtin), a professor of anthropology at Pendleton. Mary first shared office 109 with Dick but was given her own office (108) when she was promoted to the Dean of the Arts and Sciences Department. Mary believes she teaches "half-baked morons at a second rate university." As a kid Mary had a dream of becoming a torch singer named Marlena Albright and in her youth posed nude for black and white photos in an art class. She has a dog named Pepper and wrote a book based on Dick's weird life called *Where's Mommy: Dissecting the Typical American Family.*

In the last episode, Dick and the family are transported back to the Home Planet.

See also: Harry Solomon, Sally Solomon, Tommy Solomon.

304. Dinah Lance, *Birds of Prey,* WB, 2002–2003. Played by Rachel Skarsten.

Dinah is the daughter of Carolyn Lance, a great espionage agent with amazing abilities who was known as the Black Canary. Carolyn feared for her daughter's safety and abandoned Dinah when she was six years old. Carolyn left Dinah with the Redmond family in Opal, Missouri. Dinah, however, did not grow up as a normal child. She was blessed with the abilities of her mother and of her unknown father to become a Medahuman (a person with abilities no one else has). Dinah has telekinetic powers and at the age of seven began having visions that would dictate her future destiny.

Dinah's earliest visions were of a woman being shot, but surviving as a cripple; and of her joining a team of crime fighters. When Dinah turned 16, she ran away from home (her foster parents were going to send her "someplace to make my powers stronger"). Her visions took her to New Gotham City where she was rescued by Helena Kyle, alias Huntress, the protégé of Barbara Gordon, a trainer of super heroes (Barbara is the woman Dinah envisioned as a child. Barbara was crippled by a bullet meant to kill her. Barbara and Helena are the team she envisioned joining).

It is Barbara's philosophy "to take people like Dinah in and mentor them." Though Dinah would like to join Barbara and Helena, Barbara tells her "We don't need a junior super girl." However, with Dinah's ability to see the future, she becomes a part of the team — "As long as you go to school and develop your physical and mental skills."

Dinah has the power to open the hidden doors of the mind simply by touching someone. She can see what they have seen or what their future holds. She can also move objects by thought. Dinah attends New Gotham High School and lives with Barbara in her headquarters, the Clock Tower that overlooks New Gotham City.

See also: Barbara Gordon, Helena Kyle.

305. D.J. Tanner, *Full House,* ABC, 1987–1995. Played by Candace Cameron.

Donna Jo Tanner, called D.J., is the oldest daughter of Danny and Pamela Tanner. She has two sisters, Stephanie and Michelle; her mother was killed in a car accident shortly after the birth of Michelle. D.J. was born in San Francisco and lives at 1882 Gerard Street.

D.J first attended the Frasier Street Elementary School. She was then said to attend Beaumont Junior High, Van Allen Junior High and finally Van Allen High School. She is the editor of her unnamed school newspaper and has her own phone (555-8722 is her number). As a kid, D.J. was much like her father — a neat freak and father's little helper (cleaning the house). She also had a pillow she called "Pillow Person." She lost an interest in cleaning when she discovered boys.

D.J. loves to shop at the mall "and spend hours in the bathroom" preparing herself to be as pretty as she can be. D.J. has a flair for fashion and wears Passion Plumb eye shadow. D.J. held a job as "The Happy Helper" at Tot Shots (a mall photographer) and has a dream to own her own horse (she briefly had one named Rocket when she was in the sixth grade). She has a dog named Comet and now dislikes Friday's (it's "mop till you drop day").

See also: Danny Tanner, Jesse Cochran, Joey Gladstone, Michelle Tanner, Stephanie Tanner.

306. Dobie Gillis, *Dobie Gillis,* CBS, 1959–1963. Played by Dwayne Hickman.

This entry also contains information on Dobie's friends, Thalia Menninger (Tuesday Weld) and Zelda Gilroy (Sheila James).

Dobie Gillis is the son of Herbert T. Gillis and his wife, Winnie, and lives at 285 Norwood Street in the mythical community of Central City. Dobie is a teenage ladies' man but is always in need of money to impress them. He is the son of "a cheap father" ("I'm not only penniless, but dimeless, quarterless and dollarless") and works in the family business, the Gillis Grocery Store, to earn his allowance.

Dobie first attends Central High School, then after a hitch in the army, he becomes a student at S. Peter Pryor Junior College (Dobie's army platoon was referred to as Company A, Company C and finally Company Q). In college, Dobie was the second assistant editor of the school's newspaper, the *Pryor Crier.*

Dobie is an average student; if he applied himself to his schoolwork he could be brilliant. But he is a thinker not a doer and spends a great deal of time seeking ways to impress girls. He is most famous for his infatuation with Thalia Menninger, a beautiful blonde who liked Dobie but needed to marry money to support her family — "a 60-year-old father with a kidney condition, a mother who isn't getting any younger, a sister who married a loafer, and a brother who is becoming a public charge."

Thalia had hopes that Dobie could one day make "oodles and oodles of money" but deep down she knew he couldn't and always left him for a boy with money. Thalia's rich tastes included fine food, luxurious clothes and "MMMMM," a perfume that cost $18 an ounce.

Zelda Gilroy is pretty, very smart, full of ambition and desperately in love with Dobie. They grew up together and she even taught him how to play the guitar. Zelda wants Dobie "with all my heart and soul"; Dobie, however, sees Zelda as only a pain and constantly tells her "Zelda, get off my back." Dobie doesn't see her inner beauty and Zelda feels she isn't attractive to Dobie because she is too smart (although when Dobie breaks up with a girl, Zelda is always there for him, knowing one day he'll see she is the girl for him). Zelda lovingly calls Dobie "Poopsie." She is the daughter of Walter and Edna Gilroy and has six sisters.

Dobie hangs out with his good friend, Maynard G. Krebs, at Charlie Wong's Ice Cream Parlor. Dobie talks directly to the audience while sitting or standing near a statute of the Thinker in the park. He expresses his feelings about school, work and especially about a girl he is trying to impress.

On May 10, 1977, CBS presented the unsold pilot for an update of the series called *Whatever Happened to Dobie Gillis?* In it, Zelda had gotten her wish and she and Dobie were now married and the parents of Georgie. They were also partners with Dobie's father in the expanded Gillis Grocery Store. The TV movie update, *Bring Me the Head of Dobie Gillis* (CBS, February 21, 1988), finds Dobie and Zelda as the owners of the Gillis Market and Pharmacy.

See also: Chatsworth Osborne, Jr., Maynard G. Krebs.

Doc Adams *see* **Matt Dillon**

The Doctor (*Doctor Who*) *see* **Doctor Who**

307. The Doctor, *Star Trek: Voyager,* UPN, 1995–2001. Played by Robert Picardo.

"Please state the nature of the medical emergency" are the words spoken by The Doctor, Chief Medical Officer aboard the Starship U.S.S. *Voyager NCC-7465,* when he is summoned. The Doctor, as he is called, is actually a hologram, an EMH (Emergency Medical Hologram, designation AK-1) that has been programmed to perform all types of medical procedures. He is a combination of light force fields powered by an atomic computer. The Doctor was activated at the Jupiter Holo-Programming Center in the year 2371. He was programmed by Dr. Lewis Zimmerman of Starfleet and has the knowledge of 3,000 cultures and over 5,000 medical surgeries. His office is located in Sick Bay on Deck Five. He is able to move about the ship by use of his mobile emitter and his first oath as a doctor is "Do No Harm." He enjoys music, especially opera, and has taken on qualities far beyond those for which he was programmed (due to his interaction with the various races he treats).

See also: Chakotay, Harry Kim, Kathryn Janeway, Neelix, Seven of Nine, Tuvok.

308. Dr. Johnny Fever, *WKRP in Cincinnati,* CBS, 1978–1982. Played by Howard Hesseman.

Dr. Johnny Fever is the broadcast name for Johnny Caravella, a spaced-out disc jockey who earns $17,500 a year at WKRP, a 5,000-watt AM radio station (1590 on the dial), in Cincinnati, Ohio.

Johnny is addicted to gambling. He lives at the Gone with the Wind Estates and is always late paying bills. He was born in Los Angeles and worked previously under the names Johnny Cool, Johnny Midnight and Johnny Sunshine. Johnny was fired from his prior job at an L.A. station for using the word "booger" on the air. He drifted around the country and wound up in Ohio, where he found a job at the newly formatted WKRP (changed from beautiful music to rock music; Johnny calls the station "The Mighty KRP").

Johnny has a bad habit of listening to conversations behind closed doors (his way of knowing whether or not to join in). He is also addicted to alcohol and although it is against station rules, keeps a bottle of some unknown brew in the broadcast booth (fellow employee Jennifer Marlowe tasted it an remarked "I think Johnny gets it in a hardware store").

Johnny resurfaced during the second season of the series update, *The New WKRP in Cincinnati* (1992–93 episodes), as his old self, this time as the host of the midnight to 6:00 A.M. slot. He left WKRP in 1982 and moved to New York (where he lived in a loft in Greenwich Village). He worked at various D.J. jobs while attempting to write a book about rock and roll music. When this failed, he went back to WKRP, the only station he really called home.

See also: Arthur Carlson, Bailey Quarters, Jennifer Marlowe, Les Nessman, Venus Flytrap.

309. Doctor Who, *Doctor Who*, Syn., 1973. Played by: William Hartnell (Doctor 1), Patrick Troughton (Doctor 2), Jon Pertwee (Doctor 3), Tom Baker (Doctor 4), Peter Davidson (Doctor 5), Colin Baker (Doctor 6), Sylvester McCoy (Doctor 7).

Doctor Who is a traveler in time who battles evil. He is rarely called Doctor Who and is known as "The Doctor" or "Doctor." The Doctor is really a Time Lord from the planet Gallifrey. He travels through time in his TARDIS (Relative Dimensions in Time and Space), a machine that resembles a 1960s British Police Call Box (telephone booth).

Gallifrey is a planet in the constellation Casterborus and appears to be covered by vast wastelands as citizens live in domed cities that are governed by the Cardinals; the High Command is concerned with the aspect of time. Scientists who work for the High Command are called Time Lords. Each Time Lord has the ability to regenerate himself 12 times (the cast list above represents seven of the rejuvenations the Doctor has undergone). The Doctor possesses two hearts, two pulses, a body temperature of 60 degrees, and a bypass respiratory system. The Doctor we see is said to be over 700 years old; however, nothing is revealed about his family or his youth.

The Doctor has built-in resistance to any form of violence—except self-defense. At college ("The University"), he had the nickname "Feta Sigma"; his specialty was thermodynamics. The doctor thrives on challenge and his favorite drink is carrot juice. "Street Blowing Jazz" is his favorite type of music. Doctor 4 was fond of a candy called Jelly Babies and was lost without his sonic screwdriver. The Doctor claims to have the directional instincts of a homing pigeon. Doctor 2 thinks he is at his best when he plays his flute (which he calls his "recorder").

The Time Lords of Gallifrey have a goal of possessing all knowledge and achieving eternal life. Their source of power is the Eye of Harmony, a large black stone through which awesome forces make time travel possible. The Time Lords originally designed TARDIS to resemble a study lab (our Doctor stole a TARDIS to pursue his desire for knowledge). Its original form is that of a metal cabinet with a sliding door. The TARDIS is supposed to disguise itself wherever it goes; because of a malfunction, the Doctor's TARDIS is stuck in the guise of a telephone booth. The TARDIS appears to be small in its outward appearance. It is actually quite large and represents the Doctor's lab. The Doctor's enemies are anything that threatens to destroy life (he was most famous for

his battles against the Master, the Daleks and the Cybermen). The series began in England in 1963 and was first syndicated to the U.S. in 1973.

310. Dr. Zachary Smith, *Lost in Space*, CBS, 1965–1968. Played by Jonathan Harris.

This entry also contains information on the Robot (played by Bob May; voiced by Dick Tufeld), the environmental control unit for the *Jupiter II*, the Earth ship that became lost in space when it was sabotaged by Dr. Smith to prevent it from reaching a planet orbiting the star Alpha Centauri (Smith, an enemy agent, was hired by unknown superiors to stop the ship from reaching the planet first).

Dr. Smith was born in England and is a graduate of Oxford University (where he was champion of the chess club for three years). He operated under the code Aeolus-14 Umbre for an enemy of the U.S. (how he was recruited was not revealed). Dr. Smith is called an intergalactic doctor of environmental psychology. He was trapped aboard the *Jupiter II* while attempting to sabotage it and is now stranded with the Robinsons (the family chosen to colonize the new planet). Smith's only goal is to find a way to get back to Earth.

Dr. Smith is an evil person. He looks out only for himself and if necessary to save himself, will put someone else in harm's way. He is a coward and greedy (if an opportunity arises to make money, he will take advantage of it; as an example, he turned the *Jupiter II* into a hotel called Smith's Happy Acres Hotel to fleece visiting aliens). Dr. Smith likes peanut butter and salmon sandwiches before bed and his over eagerness to return home is often responsible for a setback. He sees the Robot as a slave and calls it such names as "Bucket of Bolts," "Potbellied Pumpkin," "Tin Plated Tattletale" and "Disreputable Thunderhead." His favorite name for it is "Booby" ("Move it Booby," "Silence Booby"). The Robot most often obeys Dr. Smith, but does object at times to his constant demands: "A robot does not live by programming alone. Some culture is required to keep my tapes in balance. My computer tapes are not programmed for day and night work. I need eight hours of rest like other robots." The Robot defends itself with electrical discharges.

See also: John Robinson (for information on John and his family: Maureen, Penny, Judy and Will Robinson).

311. Don Diego de la Vega, *Zorro*, ABC, 1957–1959. Played by Guy Williams.

Don Diego de la Vega was born in Monterey, California, in 1799. He is the son of Don Alejandro and has been cared for by Bernardo (Gene Sheldon), his mute servant, since the death of his mother as a child.

The de la Vegas are the most important family in Southern California. They are rich, well educated and powerful. When Don Diego reaches the age of 17, he is sent to the University of Spain to further his education. During his absence, a tyrant named Enrique Monasterio (Britt Lemond) imposes harsh taxes in his quest to become the richest man in Old California. In 1820, Don Diego receives a letter from his father asking for help in defeating Monasterio. Aboard ship, on his way home to Monterey, Don Diego and Bernardo come up with a plan to defeat Monasterio. Don Diego assumes the guise of Zorro, a masked swordsman who fights for right. To convince everyone that he is perfectly harmless, Don Diego poses as "a man of letters, an innocent scholar interested only in the arts and sciences." As Don Diego adopts his secret alias, Bernardo becomes "the eyes behind my back. You cannot only not speak, you hear nothing."

As Zorro, Don Diego dresses in black. He carries a sword and a whip and carves the sign of the Z when he completes his mission. Zorro rides a horse named Tornado (Don Diego's horse is Phantom). Don Diego's base of operations is a secret cave below his hacienda in Monterey (the entrance is through the fireplace. Don Diego discovered it when he was a child and believes it was built by his grandfather as a means of escaping Indian raids). While Zorro is an excellent swordsman, Don Diego pretends to be inexperienced at fencing (at the University, he was the fencing champion). Although Zorro helps people, he is considered criminal by the authorities (1000 pesos has been offered for his capture — dead or alive). Zorro is called by the citizens "a friend of the people," "defender of the oppressed" and "the champion of justice."

312. Dona Alvarado, *The Queen of Swords*, Syn., 2000–2001. Played by Tessie Santiago.

Dona Maria Teresa Alvarado, called Tessa, was born in Santa Helena, a small town in Old California, in 1797. She is the daughter of Don Alvarado, a wealthy and prominent citizen. Dona enjoyed her life, growing up in a small town. When she turned 18, her father thought it best she receive a university education and sent her to Madrid, Spain. During Dona's absence, the evil military leader, Luise Montoya (Valentine Pelka) came into power and began a quest to rule the land. Don Alvarado resisted and was killed for doing so. Word is sent to Tessa that her father

died in a horse-related accident. It is 1817 when Tessa returns to Santa Helena. She sees the townspeople living in fear and the once glorious Alvarado mansion in shambles and about to be repossessed by Montoya for unpaid back taxes. Tessa is unable to pay the taxes and believes her father, an expert horseman, did not die as she was told. Tessa vows to remain in Santa Helena and avenge her father's death.

That night, Don Alvarado's ghostly image appears to Tessa. It tells her his "Avenging Angel" will make things right. The spirit directs Tessa to the wine cellar and to a rare bottle of Santa Rita wine. When Tessa pulls the bottle from the rack, a secret door opens to reveal a picture painted of Tessa when she was seven years old. It has the caption "My Little Angel." As Tessa looks at the picture she decides to become that Avenging Angel the spirit mentioned. Tessa dons a lacy black mask, tight black blouse and pants (with a red scarf around her waist) and a calling card — the Queen of Swords (taken from the tarot deck of cards). Although Tessa battles the evils of Montoya, she is branded a villain and a reward of 1000 Reales is offered for her capture — dead or alive.

Tessa appears as an aristocrat who has returned to her homeland to take over the family estate (which she does when she pays the back taxes with money hidden by her father in the wine cellar). She reveals her secret identity only to her faithful servant, Marta (Paulina Galvez). Tessa rides a brown horse she calls Chico. Tessa is skilled in the art of swordplay and was called El Caita by her father as a child (her mother passed away when Tessa was an infant). Tessa carries a small spare sword in her boot and the Queen is called "a miracle of God for all the good she does" by the padre. Montoya believes the Queen is no ordinary woman, but "an evil spirit who threatens the very destiny of the public."

313. Donald Hollinger, *That Girl*, ABC, 1966–1971. Played by Ted Bessell.

Donald Hollinger, called Don at times, is a reporter for *Newsview* magazine and the boyfriend of Ann Marie, the upstate New York girl who has come to the Big City to seek fame and fortune as an actress. Don is the son of Bert (also called Ed and Harold) and Mildred (also called Lillian) Hollinger and was born in 1934 in Toledo, Ohio (later said to be Shelton, Ohio, then St. Louis, Missouri). He is a rather sloppy housekeeper and now lives in an apartment (1) on West 54th Street in Manhattan; Bryant 9-9978 is his phone number.

Don wrote an unpublished novel (*City of*

Strangers) and drinks milk with corned beef sandwiches. He won the Humanitarian Award for his writing and drives a red Mustang with the license plate 4G82 H9. Don is 13 years older than Ann. They became engaged at the start of the last season but a wedding never occurred. He and Ann enjoy dinner at Nino's Restaurant; Don's office is located at 1330 Sixth Avenue and he always wears a suit or sports jacket to work (as well as on a date with Ann). In the unaired pilot version of the series, Ted Bessell played Don Blue Sky, Ann's Native American agent and boyfriend.

See also: Ann Marie.

314. Donna Garland, *Out of This World*, Syn., 1987–1991. Played by Donna Pescow.

Donna Garland is a woman with a most unusual husband — an alien from the planet Anterias. She is also the mother of their half Earthling, half Anterian daughter, Evie.

Donna Froelich (her maiden name) was born in Marlowe, California, in 1954. She is the daughter of Michael and Barbara Froelich and is a graduate of Marlowe High School. In 1972, when Donna held a job as a waitress at Natural Norman's Organic Ice Cream Parlor, Troy Ethel Garland, a being from the planet Anterias, was sent on a mission to get help from the other planets in his galaxy to battle the warring Frigians (from the planet Frigid). During his mission, Troy's mortal enemy, Krangel the Skull Basher, shot at Troy and disabled his ship. Troy crash-landed on Earth. Sometime after (not specified), Troy, who had taken human form, wandered into Natural Norman's and ordered a Raspberry Radish Rocket Ship. A love at first sight developed when Troy and Donna saw each other. They dated and married on July 22, 1974 (at Our Lady of the Wedding Chapel in Las Vegas), and blended life forms. Shortly after, Donna gave birth to a girl they named Eve Ethel Garland (called Evie). Troy repaired his ship, completed his long overdue mission and returned to Anterias. Donna raised Evie and they now live at 17 Medvale Road in Marlowe. They communicate with Troy (voice of Burt Reynolds) through Evie's genetic-link crystal cube that allows voice transmission.

Donna first ran the Marlowe School for Gifted Children, then became owner of the Donna Delights Planning and Catering service. She gave up the business to become the mayor of Marlowe. She hosts the public access show, *Meet the Mayor* (on Channel 108) and has a fear of Jell-O ("It's not right the way it wiggles"). As a kid, Donna rode Mr. Trotter, the ten-cent a ride horse at Sherman's Market.

Troy (who is never seen) is also called Troy of Anterias. "Doo-whop" was his favorite type of Earth music. He was in the Interplanetary Air Force for 14 years and Loni Anderson (Burt Reynolds's wife) is his favorite TV star; *Evening Shade* (Burt's CBS series) is his favorite TV show (which is running on Anterias).

See also: Evie Garland, Kyle Applegate.

Donna Marco *see* **The Girls of Baywatch**

315. Doogie Howser, *Doogie Howser, M.D.*, ABC, 1989–1993. Played by Neil Patrick Harris.

Douglas Howser, called Doogie, is the son of David and Katherine Howser. He was born on September 21, 1973, and lives in Brentwood, California. Doogie is a fan of Humphrey Bogart movies and summarizes the day's activities in his computer diary, "The Personal Journal of Doogie Howser, M.D." Doogie's father is a doctor and his mother, 15 years younger than David, was a member of the rock group Mother Earth and the Penguins. Neither of them have I.Q.s that are extraordinary, yet Doogie possesses such a high I.Q. that at the age of 16 he is a second year resident physician at the Eastman Medical Center (he is later a third year resident and the supervisor of interns). Doogie can prescribe drugs but can't buy beer. At the age of six, Doogie attained a perfect SAT score. He completed high school in nine weeks and graduated from Princeton at the age of 14.

Doogie's home phone number is 555-9980 and appeared on the quiz show *High I.Q.* He also did public service announcements called "Ask Dr. Doogie" and despite all the attention, tries to live the life of a normal teenager. Doogie feels that after a battle with leukemia when he was six years old something happened and turned him into a genius; he believes becoming a doctor and helping people is a way of putting his gift to the best use he knows.

Dora Calderon *see* **Peter Farrell**

316. Dorothy Jane Torkelson, *The Torkelsons*, NBC, 1991–1992. Played by Olivia Burnette.

Dorothy Jane Torkelson is the 14-year-old daughter of Millicent and Randall Torkelson. Dorothy Jane lives off Farm Route Two in the small town of Pyramid Corners, Oklahoma, with her mother (now divorced) and four siblings (Ruth Ann, Mary Sue, Steven Floyd and Chuckie Lee).

Dorothy Jane is a very pretty and sensitive girl who longs "for a life of poetry, romance and beauty." She believes her family is weird and is convinced she was switched at birth and her real family lives in Palm Springs. The only sanctuary she has is her bedroom (the tower room with a wrap-a-round balcony that overlooks the street); she calls it "my sanctuary from the storm." Here, at night, she confides her dreams, joys, sorrows and ambitions to "The Man in the Moon."

Dorothy Jane was born in Pyramid Corners. She attended Will Rogers Jr. High School, then Pyramid Corners High School. She is the only kid in her class who wears clothes that were once something else (for example, her mother turned curtains into a dress for her). Dorothy Jane played Juliet in her high school production of *Romeo and Juliet*. At school Dorothy Jane was fascinated by Callie Kimbrough, "a highly sculptured ice princess" who had the attention of all the boys. Hoping to attract boys herself, Dorothy Jane changed her wholesome image for that of a sexy dumb blonde. She dyed her hair Playful Minx blonde and became Dottie—"I'm not a young lady anymore. I'm a teenage bombshell" (she achieved her goal and went back to being her old self "because it felt goofy being someone else").

In the revised version of the series (*Almost Home*, NBC, 1993), Dorothy Jane is living in Seattle, Washington, in the home of a lawyer (Brian Morgan) where her mother (Millicent) works as a live-in nanny for Brian's children, Molly and Gregory. Dorothy Jane feels she has now shed her "Oklahoma Milk Maid image" and loves her new environment. She attends Lincoln High School and works as a countergirl at the Chicken in the Hat fast food restaurant.

See also: Millicent Torkelson.

317. Dorothy Zbornak, *The Golden Girls*, NBC, 1985–1992. Played by Bea Arthur.

Dorothy Zbornak is one of four women, over 50, who lives at 6151 Richmond Street in Miami Beach, Florida. Her housemates are Blanche Devereaux, Rose Nylund and Sophia Petrillo (Dorothy's mother).

Dorothy is the most outrageous of the women. She is the daughter of Sophia and Sal Petrillo and was born in Brooklyn, New York (where she lived on Carnarsie Street). Dorothy now works as a substitute English teacher in the Florida public school system. She was married to Stan Zbornak, a novelty salesman, for 38 years; they are the parents of Michael and Kate Zbornak. Dorothy's favorite TV show is *Jeopardy* and she was the first one in her family to graduate from college (where she majored in U.S. history). In the series' last episode, Dorothy marries Blanche's uncle, Lucas Hollingsworth, and moves to Atlanta, Georgia, to begin a new life.

See also: Blanche Devereaux, Rose Nylund, Sophia Petrillo.

318. Douglas Heffernan, *The King of Queens*, CBS, 1998 (current). Played by Kevin James.

Douglas Heffernan, called Doug at times, is the son of Janet and Joe Heffernan. He was born in Queens, New York, and attended St. Gregory's High School (also said to be St. Griffin High School). Doug has always been overweight and on the school's football team he was nicknamed "Heifer Legs." Food is an important factor in Doug's life (as a kid he would shoplift candy from local stores). He had a dog named Rocky, dreamed of owning a monkey and has an uncanny knack for making delicious sandwiches (he also has a dream to one day open his own sandwich shop).

Doug's father had hoped his son would follow in his footsteps and take over the family hardware business. One day, while helping his father, an I.P.S. (International Parcel Service) man brought in a package and Doug was hooked—he knew he had to become an I.P.S. deliveryman.

When the series begins, Doug has been working for I.P.S. for eight years. He was originally assigned to Zone 12 ("the boonies") but was transferred to the prestigious Zone 8 in Queens. In 1995, Doug worked nights as a bouncer at a nightclub called Wall Street in Queens. It was here that he met his future wife, Carrie Spooner (another episode claims Doug and Carrie met at the bar over Jell-O shots and Foxy Boxing Night). They dated, married shortly after and set up housekeeping at 3121 Aberdine Avenue in Rego Park, Queens. Prior to marrying Carrie, Doug lived in Apartment 5 at 63rd Street; his car license plate reads 428 DIP.

Doug bowls at Bowl-A-Rama on a team sponsored by Cooper's House of Ale. He is also on a softball team (Brother's Pizzeria) and has the nickname "Moose." Doug wears a size 11 shoe, enjoys beer at Murray's Bar and snacks on Pringle's Potato Chips.

Doug and Carrie see movies at the Loyola Theater (also seen as Cinema Village). Doug has a collection of porn tapes he hides from Carrie by labeling the boxes "The Bad News Bears Go to Japan." Doug has anger but doesn't like confrontations; he takes his frustrations out on himself. At I.P.S, Doug's I.D. number is 62287. He appeared in the "Men of I.P.S." calendar as Mr. April and was voted Driver of the Month for fewest lost packages, most deliveries and a perfect time record. Doug sold Sparkle Top Water Filters to make extra money and hates it when Carrie wears her hair in a bun (makes her look old and unattractive).

See also: Arthur Spooner, Carrie Heffernan.

319. Drew Carey, *The Drew Carey Show*, ABC, 1995–2004. Played by Drew Carey.

Drew Aliceson Carey is a bachelor who lives in a private house (with a pool table in the backyard) at 720 Sedgwick Road in Cleveland, Ohio. He is the son of George (deceased) and Beulah Carey and was born in Ohio. Drew makes $26,000 a year as the Personnel Director at the Winford-Louder Department Store and is best friends with Oswald Harvey, Lewis Kiniski and Kate O'Brien.

Drew has cubicle 17 at the store ("The Drew-bicle") and hosts "The House of Easy Living" show on the store's web site, *www.winloud.com*. Drew's dream job is to be the director of 6 Flags Amusement Park. He attended Rhodes High School and has a dog named Speedy. His favorite TV show is *Xena: Warrior Princess* (he writes to star Lucy Lawless under the name "Junior Warrior Drew Carey") and believes Cher is the most beautiful woman in the world. As a kid he had a crush on Oswald's beautiful, busty mother, Kim (Adrienne Barbeau). At this time he had a dog named Nibbles and his first kiss occurred on a golf course with a 14-year-old girl who preferred kissing girls.

Drew is Protestant and his car license plate reads DLW GA3. He hangs out at the Warsaw Tavern and he, Lewis and Oswald invented a beer-coffee mix called Buzz Beer ("The Working Man's Beer"). In high school the three were in a band called The Horndogs. Drew first had a romance with Kate, then with a former high school classmate, Kellie Newkirk (Cynthia Watros), who became a bartender at the Warsaw Tavern in 2002. Kellie was born in Bay Village, Ohio, and is the daughter of Don and Annette Newkirk.

Prior to his job at Winford-Louder, Drew worked as a waiter at Antonio's Restaurant. His Winford-Louder work history is as follows: Assisatnt Personnel Director (1987–95); Personnel Director (1995–2000); Head of Personnel then Store Manager (2001–02); the Internet Expediency Analyst (when Winford-Louder went bankrupt and became the internet company *www.neverendingstore.com*; 2002–04). Drew's on-line name is Beer Stud 2 and he also held the following jobs when he was laid off from the store: Hash slinger in his former high school cafeteria; security guard at the Rock and Roll Hall of Fame.

See also: Kate O'Brien, Lewis Kiniski, Mimi Bobeck, Oswald Harvey.

320. Duane Odell Knox, *One on One*, UPN, 2001 (current). Played by Kelly Perine.

Women and alcohol are the two things Duane Odell Knox thinks about most. He is best friends with Flex Washington and the godfather of Flex's daughter, Breanna Barnes. Duane and Flex grew up together in Baltimore and attended McKinley High School. Duane now works as a salesman for Big Sal's Used Cars. In high school, he and Flex were members of a band called Midnight Gold and while he is reluctant to admit it, Duane danced on a highway off ramp for change.

Duane has the ability to dance and as a kid dreamed of joining the Dance Theater of Harlem. Before moving into Apartment 7 opposite Flex (Apartment 8), Duane lived in the basement of his mother's house. He has nightmares about the Hamburger Helper Hand (from TV commercials).

See also: Breanna Barnes, Flex Washington.

321. Duke DePalma, *Team Knight Rider*, Syn., 1997–1998. Played by Duane Davis.

Duke DePalma is the toughest member of Team Knight Rider, a branch of the Foundation for Law and Enforcement, that battles crime. Duke was born in Chicago and fought his way out of the slums to become a small time boxer. His background of crime and corruption also made him feel the need to help others. He became a police officer and tried to do what was right, but he took the law into his own hands and broke too many rules. He was suspended but his activities brought him to the attention of TKR (Team Knight Rider) and he was hired as an agent (they required an agent who was in touch with the common man; Duke's cop-on-the-beat experience makes him the only team member who possesses these qualities). While he appears tough, Duke's actions are slow and thought out; he never rushes head first into anything.

Duke drives a Ford F-150 truck called Beast (also Attack Beast). The car is able to talk (via a computer) and has a gruff, hostile voice. Beast and Duke are sent in to do the hard work (like crashing through walls). BSF-1 is Best's license plate.

See also: Erica West, Jenny Andrews, Kyle Stewart, Trek Sanders.

322. Duncan MacLeod, *Highlander*, Syn., 1992–1998. Played by Adrian Paul.

Duncan MacLeod appears to be an ordinary man. He lives in a typical American city (unspecified) and has his own business, The Antique Shop. Duncan is, in reality, an Immortal. Although he looks to be 35, Duncan was born in the Scottish Highlands 400 years ago. He knows only that he was brought to his father as an infant by a midwife when the baby that was born to his mother died at birth. It was not until Duncan was a young man that he learned he was an Immortal. During a battle with a rival clan, Duncan was mortally wounded. Duncan's father praised him as a brave warrior; but when Duncan's wounds healed and he returned to life, his father condemned him, saying he was in league with the devil. Although cast out by his parents, Duncan kept the only name he knew.

Duncan is now represetative of the Clan MacLeod. He is seeking to become the last Immortal and acquire all the powers of all Immortals to rule the world for good. Legend states that all knowledge is controlled by the Immortals. When one Immortal encounters another, the Gathering is held. This is followed by the Quickening (combat by sword) to acquire additional strength. An Immortal can only be killed by beheading. When this happens, the surviving Immortal acquires the other's strength. As Duncan seeks to fulfill his destiny, he helps people who have become the victims of crime and dispenses justice with his ornamental Japanese sword.

See also: Amanda.

323. Dwayne and Denny Mullet, *The Mullets*, UPN, 2003. Played by Michael Weaver, David Hornsby.

When most people think of Dwayne and Denny Mullet they associate them with idiots. Dwayne and Denny are spaced-out brothers who run a roofing company called Mullet Brothers Roofing (they claim to have the largest ladder in the San Francisco area).

Dwayne and Denny are the sons of Mandy (Loni Anderson) and a father called "Mad Dog" who deserted Mandy to follow the rock group REO Speedwagon 20 years ago (he is still following them according to Mandy). Mandy is now married to Roger Hydecker (John O'Hurley), the host of a TV game show called *Quizzadry*. Mandy is an exceptionally beautiful woman who absolutely delights in showing ample cleavage. Mandy met Roger when she became a contestant on his show. She picked the category "Famous Quotations" and said, "I've got a dream." He said "Yabba Dabba Do" and it was a love at first sight. Mandy works as a lypo suction technician and raised her sons to live life to the fullest. They do. They live together in a cheap apartment on Bayside Way in Roseta, California, and drink beer (Pabst Blue Ribbon) at every opportunity. They

hang out at a convenience store called Honk 'n' Go and quite frequently drink on the job and injure themselves falling off roofs. Dwayne is the more idiotic of the brothers (supposedly older and wiser) and calls himself "The Dwayniac." He also says he uses built up Dwayne energy to accomplish things. The more sedate (but just as idiotic) Denny does whatever Dwayne tells him and is forever getting into trouble for doing so. The brothers hate to upset their mother with their antics. She gets mad and does "The Mandy Mullet Silent Treatment" and pretends they do not exist (Roger is always in awe as to how such a sweet and sensible woman could have raised two moronic sons).

324. Dwayne Schneider, *One Day At a Time*, CBS, 1975–1984. Played by Pat Harrington, Jr.

Dwayne F. Schneider is the superintendent for an apartment building at 1344 Hartford Drive in Indianapolis, Indiana. He lives in the basement (Apartment 1) and is a member of I.B.M. (Indianapolis Building Maintenance). Dwayne was born in Secaucus, New Jersey, and is a graduate of Irvington High School. He married in 1957, but the marriage lasted only one week (his wife got up one morning, hot-wired his truck and just took off. However, in the first episode, Dwayne is married; in a later episode, Dwayne says he was married for five days and got a divorce). Dwayne's first job was at the age of two months when he was a model in a diaper ad.

Dwayne is a ladies' man and he uses the C.B. handle "Super Stud." He is a member of the Secret Order of the Beaver's Lodge, North Central Chapter (where he is the activities chairman and entertainment producer for the lodge). Dwayne frequents the Boom Boom Room of the Purple Pig Club and the Alibi Room Bar (not just for the drinks — but as a hot spot to pick up girls). He is good-friends with tenants Ann Romano and her daughters, Julie and Barbara.

See also: Ann Romano, Barbara Cooper, Julie Cooper.

325. Dwayne Wayne, *A Different World*, NBC, 1987–1993. Played by Kadeem Hardison.

Dwayne Creofus Wayne is a student at Hillman College in Georgia. He was born in Michigan and is majoring in math at a college that is not just tough, "it's a butt breaker." Dwayne is up to the challenge and has been blessed with a gift for numbers. He "wears those funny-looking flip-down sunglasses that drive you crazy" and hits on almost every girl he sees ("over 12 billion bothered").

Dwayne has a music and talk show on the school's radio station (WHZU) where he works as Darryl Walker. Dwayne graduated in 1990 and remained at Hillman to pursue his Ph.D. in math. He became a professor in 1992 and was teaching math at Hillman when the series ended. He also became engaged to fellow student Whitley Gilbert in the fall of 1991 and married her in May of 1992. Whitley called Dwayne "Pookie Bear."

See also: Whitley Gilbert.

326. Dwight Davis, *Davis Rules,* ABC, 1991; CBS, 1991–1992. Played by Randy Quaid.

Dwight Ulysses Davis is a widower who lives at 631 Evergreen in the town of Pomahac (an island across from Seattle). He is the father of three children (Robbie, Charlie and Ben) and works as the principal of Pomahac Elementary School.

Dwight is a big fan of western movies. At the age of 15 he broke his nose playing football; in high school (Pomahac High) he drove a red Corvette; before his current job, he was a minor league pitcher in Lodi, California (his career ended when he fell in the dugout and injured himself). Dwight then became a teacher before taking over the job as principal. He loves golf but only plays three times a year (he hangs out at a store called Par for the Course, where he is known as "a browse-a-holic"). Dwight is also called "a penny-pinching, coupon-snipping miser." He uses a cologne called Sweaty Lad and enjoys fishing at Bee's Lake.

327. Dwight White, *Nikki,* WB, 2000–2002. Played by Nick von Esmarch.

Dwight White was born on Long Island, New York, in 1976. He was raised by strict parents and groomed by his mother to become a corporate tax lawyer. Dwight, however, loved sports, especially wrestling, and dreamed of becoming a professional wrestler. He put those dreams aside to please his mother.

Dwight wrestled in high school and was all-state champion. His mother, however, made him quit the team when he broke his nose. Dwight turned his attention to studying and was accepted into Pepperdine University. On the night Dwight was attending a going away party thrown by his friends, a girl named Nikki Carmichael began a motor trip to Las Vegas to fulfill her dream of becoming a show dancer. En route, her car broke down and somehow (not explained) crashed Dwight's party, looking for a ride to Vegas. It was a love at first sight for Nikki and Dwight. It was also Nikki who convinced Dwight to give up Pep-

perdine and follow his dream. En route to Las Vegas, Nikki and Dwight married.

Nikki and Dwight now live at 262 Linden Drive, Apartment C (also seen as Apartment 25) in Las Vegas. Nikki works as a dancer while Dwight has become a member of the CWF Wrestling Federation. He performs at the Las Vegas Pavilion under the name "The Cry Baby" (Dwight's boss calls Nikki "Mrs. Cry Baby"). When the CWF folded, Dwight became a wrestler with the WXL League owned by Creative Development. Dwight, however, is more of an oiler (puts oil on other wrestlers) than a wrestler. When this was not to his liking, he quit and joined the VWF (Very Violent Wrestling) League (which was just established when the series ended). Dwight was scheduled to perform in the league's Ring of Death.

See also: Nikki White.

328. Dylan Del'Amico, *Undercover,* ABC, 1991. Played by Anthony John Denison.

Dylan Del'Amico is an agent for the Company, a branch of the N.I.A. (National Intelligence Agency) that concerns itself with the why of a case (the reason behind an agent's decision to take a case).

Dylan is married to Kate and is the father of Megan, Emily and Marlon. They live in suburban Maryland and Dylan and Kate lie to their children about their jobs (Dylan's cover is that of a security consultant for a company called Langley; Kate, a Company agent also, has the cover of a State Department employee).

Dylan was born in the Bronx, New York, and is a graduate of Fordham University. He is the son of a father who was a police officer and first worked as an insurance agent. When he saw the inscription on the Lincoln Memorial, he believed the words and wanted to make a difference. He was 20 years old and joined the N.I.A. (in 1975). He has strayed from the church and calls himself "a fallen Catholic." Dylan drives a red vintage Corvette and is a New York Yankees baseball fan. Dylan speaks Russian and Italian and loves action and fun (he especially likes setting people up for practical jokes). He values loyalty and does things his own way. Brandy is his favorite drink.

See also: Kate Del'Amico.

329. Dylan Hunt, *Andromeda,* Syn., 2000–2005. Played by Kevin Sorbo.

Dylan Hunt is the captain of the *Andromeda Ascendant,* a battleship of the High Command in the Systems Commonwealth, a highly developed futuristic society. Dylan is a man who never walks into a situation without a plan for getting out. He could be considered a futuristic ladies' man as women either want to love him or kill him. "I hate that effect," he says. Dylan served for twenty years as a High Guard officer to the Systems Commonwealth. He began his career as an enlisted soldier. He was first assigned to the local Home Guard. He next attended the High Guard Academy, where his academic abilities placed him above other students. He did post graduate work at the Antares Command Lyceum and at the Imperial Strategy College. He first commanded the *Crimson Eclipse* (a Low Observation Warfare Craft), then *Andromeda*.

The Commonwealth spanned three galaxies, had over one million member worlds, orbital habitats and asteroid colonies. In an instant it was all gone when the evil Nietzchen Empire attacked the Commonwealth and its 10,000 war ships destroyed what was once the greatest civilization in history. The *Andromeda*, however, managed to escape but was sabotaged and drawn into a black-hole where it remained suspended in time for 300 years. The *Andromeda* was found by a salvage crew (Beka, Trance and Seamus), and dragged out of the black hole. The only survivor of the craft, Dylan Hunt, was found and revitalized. He was told of his fate and that the Commonwealth no longer exists. He disbelieves it and has set out to restore the Commonwealth and "rekindle the light of civilization" (he also says "on the starship *Andromeda* hope lives again"). Dylan embraces darkness—"That's how I fight. Victory comes from accepting the unexpectable." His security code is H.E. 5095C2.

See also: Andromeda, Beka Valentine, Trance Gemini.

330. Earl and Fran Sinclair, *Dinosaurs*, ABC, 1991–1994. Voiced by Stuart Pankin, Jessica Walter.

Earl, age 43, is a Megalasaurus; Fran, 38, is an Allosaurus. They are husband and wife and live in the city of Pangaea in the year 60,000,003 B.C., at a time when dinosaurs came out of the forests to marry and raise a family. Earl and Fran are also the parents of Charlene, Robbie and Baby Sinclair.

Earl works as a tree pusher (knocks down trees) for the Wesayso Development Company. He earns $4 an hour, has a caveman alarm clock and eats Sugar Frosted Boo Boo cereal for breakfast. Earl is a member the YMCA (Young Man's Carnivore Association) and his favorite hangout is the Meteor Tiki Bar. He reads a daily paper called the *Tribune*; 555-3000 is his phone number and 000-00-0018 is his Social Security number.

Fran has been married to Earl for 19 years (Earl keeps their marriage license under the TV set to balance it). Fran watches the Dinosaur Shopping Network on TV, shops at the Swamp Basket (later called the Food Chain) and worked part time as a TV advice host on *Just Advice with Fran*. Fran, a Pisces, frequents the Kave Mart Department Store and serves waffle meat pancakes for breakfast (her specialty is refrigerator mold pies). Fran (maiden name Hinkleman) later worked for the Turf and Surf Center for Amphibians (a halfway house for amphibians seeking to make it on land).

See also: Charlene Sinclair (for information on Charlene, Robbie and Baby Sinclair).

331. Ed Norton, *The Honeymooners*, CBS, 1955–1956. Played by Art Carney.

Edward L. Norton, called Norton by most everyone, is married to Trixie and lives at 728 Chauncey Street in Bensonhurst, Brooklyn, New York. Ed works as an "Engineer in Subterranean Sanitation" (a sewer worker for the Department of Sanitation). He says the L in his name stands for Lilywhite (his mother's maiden name) and that he majored in arithmetic at vocational school (in another episode he mentions attending P.S. 31 in Oyster Bay, Brooklyn). As a kid Ed had a dog named Lulu (although in another episode he is allergic to dogs) and did a hitch in the Navy (he later took up typing on the G.I. Bill). Ed found that he couldn't stand being couped up in an office, so he took the job in the sewer (which he started in 1938). Ed's astrological sign was given as both Capricorn and Pisces. *Captain Video* is his favorite TV show (he is Ranger Third Class in the Captain Video Fan Club) and his hero is Pierre Francois de la Brioski (whom Ed thought designed the sewers of France; in reality, he condemned them). Ed can play the piano but needs to warm up with the song "Swanee River." He coaches the Cougars stickball team and calls his best friend, Ralph Kramden, "Ralphie Boy."

Ed and Trixie had been living in the apartment house prior to Ralph and his wife Alice renting the downstairs apartment. When Ed came down to invite Ralph and Alice to dinner they became instant friends. Ed is a member of the Raccoon Lodge and enjoys bowling and playing pool with Ralph. He loves to eat and enjoys Alice's cooking as much as Trixie's (no background information is given on Trixie).

See also: Alice Kramden, Ralph Kramden.

332. Eddie and Honey Smith, *Big Eddie*, CBS, 1975. Played by Sheldon Leonard, Sheree North.

Edward Smith, called Big Eddie, is a former

gambler turned owner of the Big E, an East Side Manhattan sports, entertainment and civic center. Eddie is married to Honey and they are the guardians of Ginger Smith (Quinn Cummings), Eddie's eight-year-old granddaughter.

Eddie was born on the Lower East Side of New York and grew up during the Great Depression. His family was poor and to earn money, Eddie would take whatever jobs he could find. Eddie, however, had no drive or ambition for school; he'd rather cut classes to make money. Being in an environment of mobster-controlled rackets, Eddie soon found a fascination with the underworld and was soon a hood himself, stealing, conning and cheating his way to the top.

With the outbreak of World War II in 1941, Eddie felt it his patriotic duty to serve and was assigned to the European Theater of War. It was in Hungary that he fell in love with and married Countess Margaret. They had a son but the marriage ended long before the war. When Eddie was discharged he returned to New York to become a big time gambler and head racketeer.

In 1973, Eddie's son and wife were killed in a car accident. To gain custody of his granddaughter, Ginger, Eddie was ordered to clean up his act. He married his longtime girlfriend, Honey, and established the Big E. He then moved his family into a glamorous apartment at 450 East 56th Street in Manhattan. Honey was a former Las Vegas showgirl whom Eddie met on one of his many trips to Vegas. She danced in the Follies Bergere, did some exotic dancing and eventually moved to New York to be with Eddie (she now performs at the various clubs where Eddie has considerable power, although she has cleaned up her act, now that she is a substitute mother to Ginger). Eddie too has changed his ways and seeks to keep low life associates from becoming a part of Ginger's life.

333. Eddie Capra, *The Eddie Capra Mysteries*, NBC, 1978–1979. Played by Vincent Baggetta.

Edward Capra, called Eddie, is an attorney with the firm of Devlin, Linkman and O'Brien in Los Angeles. He was born in Brooklyn, New York, and is a graduate of Brooklyn Polytech High School and the New York University School of Law.

Eddie lives at 64 Holland Avenue and drives a car with the license plate 836 PCE; 656-1656 is his phone number. Eddie is not a conventional lawyer. He does not wear a three-piece suit and prefers to dress casually. He takes a real interest in his clients' problems and will do what it takes to prove their innocence — even if it means break-

ing all the rules and causing friction with his employers. He is not tough by nature, although when he becomes frustrated, he will use his fists (he prefers to stray from the use of firearms).

334. Eddie Haskell, *Leave It to Beaver*, CBS, 1957–1958; ABC, 1958–1963. Played by Ken Osmond.

Edward W. Haskell, called Eddie, is the son of George and Agnes Haskell and lives at 175 Grant Avenue (also said to be 531 Grant Avenue) in the small town of Mayfield. He is best friends with Wally Cleaver (they met in second grade) and is extremely polite to adults (he fears their authority) but mean to everybody else, especially Wally's younger brother, Beaver (whom he calls "Squirt"; he calls Wally "Sam," "Gertrude" and Ellwood"). Eddie tries to hide the fact that he can be nice to people.

Eddie attended the Grant Avenue Elementary School, Mayfield High School and State College (although he had aspirations to first attend Annapolis then MIT). Although he has the middle initial of W and his father's name is George, Eddie claims his full name is Edward Clark Haskell, Jr. He also has "a genuine police dog" named Wolf.

Eddie's father owns a garage and Eddie worked there as well as at the Mayfield Dairy (where he was assigned to the loading dock); he also drove a truck for the Mayfield Diaper Service. Eddie will go out of his way to stay after school to watch cheerleading practice. He is poor at sports but manages the Mayfield High track team. He is allergic to mayonnaise; chocolate pudding is his favorite desert; and *Woody Woodpecker* is his favorite TV show. He was the first one of his friends to get a credit card (number 06212312) from the Universal Gas and Oil Company.

In the TV movie update, *Still the Beaver* (CBS, March 19, 1983), Eddie is married to the never seen Gert and the father of Eddie Haskell, Jr. The updated series, *The New Leave It to Beaver* (TBS, 1986–1989), finds Eddie as the owner of the somewhat shady Eddie Haskell Construction Company. He is still married to Gert and is the father of two boys, the wisecracking Freddie and the mischievous Bomber.

See also: Beaver Cleaver, June Cleaver, Lumpy Rutherford, Wally Cleaver, Ward Cleaver.

335. Eddie Munster, *The Munsters*, CBS, 1964–1966. Played by Butch Patrick.

Edward Wolfgang Munster, called Eddie, is the eight-year-old werewolf son of a Frankenstein-like father (Herman) and a vampire mother (Lily).

He lives at 1313 Mockingbird Lane in the town of Mockingbird Heights and has a werewolf doll (Woof Woof). He also has a pet snake (Elmer) who lives under the garbage pail in the backyard, and Spot, a fire-breahting dragon (who lives under the front staircase in the living room).

Eddie attends Mockingbird Heights Elementary School and is more accepting of the fact that he is different from others (he is green and has pointy ears). He also has fangs and always wears his Little Lord Fauntleroy suit. Eddie won an award at school for writing a composition called "My Parents: An Average American Family" (in the reddest ink his teacher had ever seen — blood). Eddie is on the track team at school and plays, rather badly, the trumpet. He also has a bad habit of biting his nails — not on his fingers, but those found in hardware stores.

In the updated series, *The Munsters Today* (Syn., 1988–91), Jason Marsden plays Eddie as a teenager and attending Mockingbird Heights High School. He has a pet Tasmanian devil named Irving and has set his sights on becoming a rock video producer when he grows up. He buys his clothes at Kiddie Casuals and is a member of the Dukes Little League baseball team.

See also: Grandpa, Herman Munster, Lily Munster, Marilyn Munster.

Eddie Winslow *see* **Laura Winslow**

336. Edie Britt, *Desperate Housewives,* ABC, 2004 (current). Played by Nicollette Sheridan.

Edie Britt lives on Wisteria Lane in a tranquil, fantasy-like suburb of a city called Fairview. Wisteria Lane appears to be immaculate and its residents perfect. Edie is a flirtatious divorcee and could be considered the black sheep of the neighborhood — "a slut" according to some residents as she is always boasting of her romantic conquests.

Edie works for the Fairview Realty Company at 125 North Main Street. People who know only of Edie's reputation consider her trash; her friends (Bree, Lynette, Susan and Gabrielle) know she is easy "but she's still a human being" and welcome her into their circle (although Susan finds her a threat to her finding happiness as Edie uses her sexy style to steal Susan's men). Edie doesn't like to worry because she feels it will give her wrinkles. She feels a need to show other people her fabulous body in sexy clothes and explains her numerous sexual escapades as "a healthy sex life." Her license plate reads UMH 380.

See also: Bree Van DeKamp, Gabrielle Solis, Lynette Scavo, Susan Mayer.

337. Edith Bunker, *All in the Family,* CBS, 1971–1979. Played by Jean Stapleton.

Edith Bunker is a simple housewife who is married to Archie Bunker, an uncouth dock foreman. They are the parents of Gloria and live at 704 Hauser Street in Queens, New York.

Edith Baines was born in Queens in 1922. She grew up in a loving family and is a graduate of Fillmore High School, class of 1940. She met and fell in love with Archie in 1941 when they first saw each other at the Puritan Maid Ice Cream Parlor. They dated and married shortly after. They became the parents of Gloria in 1944. Edith worked for a short time for the Hercules Plumbing Company but spent most of her married life caring for Archie, Gloria and the house. They purchased their first TV set in 1950.

Edith is lovingly called "Dingbat" by Archie, who also tells her to "stifle it" for talking too much. Edith tries to see only the good in people. She is totally honest and intuitive. Archie is a loud mouth and her best defense for survival with him is her ability to know when to turnoff, when to make a comment or when to say nothing.

Edith buys her meat at Klemer's Butcher Shop and earns $2.65 an hour as a Sunshine Lady at the Sunshine Home for the Elderly. She considers stealing a five cent O'Henry bar from the candy counter of F.W. Woolworth to be her most despicable act (she was only six years old at the time and went back at a later time to make restitution but had to pay a dime as the price had gone up).

As the World Turns is Edith's favorite TV show and she has an account at the First Friendly Bank of Queens. Edith was the first sitcom character to openly face menopause — a situation that caused the doctor to prescribe pills for Archie (who can't deal with "female problems"). When Jean Stapleton wanted to leave the series in 1979, her character was written out when Edith suffered a fatal heart attack in her sleep.

See also: Archie Bunker, Gloria Stivic, Mike Stivic.

338. Edna Garrett, *Diff'rent Strokes* (NBC, 1978–1979), *The Facts of Life* (NBC, 1979–1987). Played by Charlotte Rae.

Edna Garrett began her TV career as a housekeeper working for Philip Drummond, a New York millionaire (on *Diff'rent Strokes*). She cared for his daughter Kimberly and his adopted sons Arnold and Willis Jackson. Edna was divorced from Robert Garrett and was the mother of Raymond and Alexander. She was born in Appleton, Wisconsin, and is a caring woman who is totally devoted to her job. Edna is an excellent cook and housekeeper and looks out for the welfare of the Drummonds (Philip lived at 697 Park Avenue and owned Drummond Industries, which was also called Trans-Allied, Inc.).

Kimberly was a student at the Eastland School for Girls in Peekskill, New York. Edna became the school's dietician (*The Facts of Life*) when the prior housemother quit. Kimberly transferred to a Manhattan school (Garfield High) and Edna became close to four students: Blair, Jo, Tootie and Natalie.

Edna quit Eastland when her pension disappeared and she was refused a raise. Her son Raymond, an accountant, set her up in a business called Edna's Edibles, a gourmet shop at 320 Main Street in Peekskill (in the location of a former deli called Aera's). Jo, Blair, Tootie and Natalie work for her as they attend school — Jo and Blair at Langley College; Tootie and Natalie at Eastland. The store catches fire in 1985 and is destroyed. Edna uses the insurance money to reopen the store as Over Our heads, a novelty shop. Her four girls again work for her. Edna left the series a year before it ended when she married Dr. Bruce Gaines and moved to Africa to work with him in the Peace Corps. Edna's sister, Beverly Ann Stickle (Cloris Leachman), took over the store and ran it until the series ended in 1988.

See also: Arnold Jackson, Blair Warner, Kimberly Drummond, Jo Polniaszek, Natalie Greene, Tootie Ramsey, Willis Jackson.

339. Edward and Kitty Montgomery, *Dharma and Greg*, ABC, 1997–2002. Played by Mitchell Ryan, Susan Sullivan.

Edward and Kitty Montgomery are the parents of Greg Montgomery, the lawyer who married Dharma Finkelstein, the slightly off center girl Kitty feels is ruining her son's life.

Edward is the owner of Montgomery Enterprises, which is based in San Francisco. Kitty's parents own the Standard Oil Company. After serving as a Green Beret in Korea, Edward found work as a barber then as a fry cook. He later joined his father's company and eventually became its CEO (he also worked as a shoe salesman in the company owned Coach's Corner store). The Tijuana Brass is Edward's favorite group while "Tijuana Taxi" is his favorite song. He collects Calypso music records, likes the color sky blue and enjoys the movie *The Piano*.

Edward has a gift for hair styling while Kitty is an expert at pool. Kitty grew up in a world where looks and courtesy meant everything. She had the looks but was not a people person. Kitty is a graduate of Vassar and had a dream to win a beauty contest (as a young woman, she entered many contests, like "Young Miss Newport Beach," "Miss Congeniality of Santa Barbara" but always came in second. Kitty mentioned she wears a size 36C bra). Kitty stopped having children after Greg "because it hurt too bad. Smart women never forget that pain." Kitty is a member of the Women's Charity Committee (where she won the Evelyn Hofsteder Humanitarian Award). She feels Dharma is "a nutty diamond in the rough" and is determined to make a Montgomery out of her.

See also: Abby O'Neill, Dharma Montgomery, Greg Montgomery, Larry Finkelstein.

340. Edward Stratton, *Silver Spoons*, NBC, 1982–1986; Syn., 1986–1988. Played by Joel Higgins.

Edward Stratton, III, is a 32-year-old divorced millionaire who loves to play with toys. He was born on Long Island, New York, and is the son of Edward Stratton II, the stern, penny-pinching head of Stratton Industries. Edward lives with his 12-year-old son, Ricky, at 123 Mockingbird Lane in Shallow Springs on Long Island; 516-555-9898 is their phone number.

Edward runs the Eddie Toys Division of Stratton Industries. He attended the Shallow Springs grammar and high schools and is a graduate of Aspen Junior College in Colorado. As a child, Edward had an invisible friend he called Clarence. Edward wears a size 10½ shoe and held a summer job as a counselor at Camp Al Bernstein.

Edward is the kid who never grew up. He is not a responsible businessman but is fascinated by the toys his company produces. Edward was married to Evelyn Bradford, a woman of social class and status. Their marriage broke up after six days due to their social incapability.

Edward tends to take after his grandfather, Edward Stratton, a novice inventor who became rich by accident and founded Stratton Industries (Grandfather Stratton invented an inner tube one year before the car was invented so he would not sink when he went to the beach. When Henry Ford invented the car a year later, he used Stratton's invention and Edward became rich). That is the philosophy Edward III has — invent the perfect toy, sit back, collect the money and enjoy life (although he has not yet hit upon that idea. His first board game was called Endangered Species. The game sold only six of the 50,000 units produced — and two were returned). Edward is famous for riding a large-scale model train from room to room.

See also: Kate Summers, Ricky Stratton.

341. Elaine Benes, *Seinfeld*, NBC, 1990–1998. Played by Julia Louis-Dreyfus.

Elaine Marie Benes is close friends with Jerry Seinfeld, Cosmo Kramer and George Costanza, and hangs out with them at Monk's Cafe in Manhattan. Elaine was born in Baltimore and now lives at 16 West 75th Street (Apartment 2G) and uses the Tri-State Wakeup Service. She is the daughter of Alton Benes, a famous writer, and attended five Eastern universities (where she was a debate and equestrian champion). She is an Orioles baseball fan and is allergic to cats.

Elaine first worked as a proofreader for Pendant Publishing. She next worked as the personal assistant to author Justin Pitt (who hired her because she reminded him of his idol, Jacqueline Kennedy). She last worked as a description writer for the J. Peterman Mail Order Catalogue (specializing mostly in clothes).

Elaine has to have things her way. She is nasty when something goes wrong and takes her anger out on other people. When Elaine is nice, it is an indication that she wants something.

A life size mannequin of Elaine appears at a clothing store called Renitzi's. She wears a size 7½ shoe and she created a sensation when the antique button on her blouse popped off and revealed her breasts in a low-cut, cleavage-revealing bra. She also created a stir when she distributed a Christmas card picture of herself (taken by Kramer) that showed her nipple. She wasn't wearing a bra and explained that she simply missed buttoning a button. For this she was nicknamed "Nip."

Elaine orders take out fish from the China Panda Restaurant, brushes her teeth with Close-Up toothpaste and has a weakness for Jujyfruit candy. She has a fear of dogs and was "best man" at a lesbian wedding. Her catch phrase is "Get Out" (which she says when she becomes excited; she also pushes someone when she says it).

See also: Cosmo Kramer, George Costanza, Jerry Seinfeld.

342. Elaine Nardo, *Taxi*, ABC, 1978–1982; NBC, 1982–1983. Played by Marilu Henner.

Elaine Nardo is a woman with two jobs: driver for the Sunshine Cab Company in New York City and art appraiser for the Hazelton Galleries. Elaine was born in New York City on February 4, 1952 and is the divorced mother of two children, Jennifer and Jason. She attended Eastside High School (where she was voted "Most Likely to Succeed") and previously worked as a secretary for an unnamed company. Elaine is the only female cabbie with a speaking part; she is thus a natural target for the advances of her lecherous boss, Louie DePalma (who calls her breasts "Headlights" and has made a peephole in the ladies' room so he can watch Elaine undress). Elaine is sympathetic and although she has her share of problems, will lend a hand to help a fellow cabbie in trouble.

See also: Alex Reiger, Jim Ignatowski, Latka Gravas, Louie DePalma.

343. Elaine Vassal, *Ally McBeal*, Fox, 1997–2002. Played by Jane Krakowski.

Elaine Vassal is a lawyer with the Boston-based law firm of Cage and Fish. She is beautiful, ambitious and shrewd. She measures 36-24-36 and presents herself as a sexual person even though she believes most people "see me as a slut." Elaine is the inventive one in the law firm and not only devises clever defenses but has invented some not-so-practical devices (for example, the Pregnant Dress — "to give women the pregnant look so they will get special attention even though they are not pregnant"; and the Face Bra — "to strengthen facial muscles"). Elaine enjoys being a snoop and eavesdrops on her fellow employees (via wire tapping) "to find out all the secret stuff that goes on." She and fellow employee, Ally McBeal, enjoy meals and a drink at Jasper's Restaurant.

See also: Ally McBeal, John Cage, Ling Woo.

344. Electra Woman and Dyna Girl, *Electra Woman and Dyna Girl*, ABC (segment of *The Krofft Super Show*), 1976–1977. Played by Deidre Hall, Judy Strangis.

Electra Woman and Dyna Girl are a crime fighting team who help electronics expert Frank Heflin (Norman Alden) battle evil.

Electra Woman is actually Laurie (no last name), a reporter for *Newsmaker* magazine. Dyna Girl is Judy Bennett, a journalism student rescued from a villain by Laurie when Judy was a child. Laurie and Judy are modern-day superheroes. Laurie wears a reddish-orange costume with a yellow cape, boots and tights (to match her blonde hair). The letters *EW* appear on the front of the costume. Judy dons a red costume, cape and boots with pink tights (*DG* appears on the front of her costume).

Electra Woman is fearless and resourceful in the face of danger. She thinks before acting. Dyna Girl is a teenager who is a bit impetuous and lunges into situations without thinking. She uses terms such as "Electra Wow" and "What and Electra Mess" when in a jam. Laurie and Judy possess no abnormal powers. They are activated with abilities by the gadgets they wear (all controlled by Electra Base, the headquarters for

Crime Scope, a computer that pinpoints criminal activity). The Electra Charge allows Laurie and Judy to go from their street clothes to their crime fighting outfits. They travel in either the Electra Car or the Electra Plane and use the power of electricity to its fullest potential. The Electra Comp is the wrist-worn portable link to Electra Base. The Electra Strobe allows them to perform anything at 10,000 times normal speed. Electra G adds gravity to their bodies when activated and Electra Power gives them a sudden burst of energy to help them in difficult situations.

In 2001 an unsold pilot called *Electra Woman and Dyna Girl* was produced for the WB. The story reunited Laurie and Judy as the crime fighting team after they had parted company. Judy (Anne Stedman) left Crime Scope to become a super model. Although Laurie (Markie Post) had a good job, she became "a disillusioned, foulmouthed trailer park alcoholic." When evil again threatens the city, Judy finds Laurie, straightens her out and the two resume their former lives as super heroes.

345. Elizabeth and Jessica Wakefield, *Sweet Valley High,* Syn., 1994–1997. Played by Cynthia Daniel (Elizabeth), Brittany Daniel (Jessica).

Elizabeth and Jessica Wakefield are identical 16-year-old twins who live in the small town of Sweet Valley. Both girls are blonde and beautiful but not equally intelligent. Elizabeth is the intellectual; Jessica, the flighty more down to earth sister. According to Jessica, she and Elizabeth "share the same D.O.A." (she means, of course, D.N.A.).

Jessica is obsessed with her figure, fashion and makeup. She is a flirt "and a tease" and loves her Wonder Bra ("It gives me just the right amount of cleavage to show"). She reads the *National Tabloid* ("You're nothing until you appear in it") and claims to have read a book, a romance novel called *The Silos of Billings, Montana.* Jessica's dream is to become an actress. She (and Elizabeth) appeared in a TV commercial for Nirvana Cosmetics and Jessica was co-host of a local television talk show called *Frankly Speaking.*

Elizabeth keeps a diary of her activities. She is sensitive and treasures her childhood memories (she keeps, for example, her money in her Holly Hobby Music Box). Elizabeth and Jessica are sophomores at Sweet Valley High School. Jessica is head cheerleader for the school's basketball team, the Gladiators; Elizabeth writes "The Eyes and Ears" column for the school newspaper, the *Oracle;* she later becomes its editor. Elizabeth yearns to become a journalist and later acquired a job with the Sweet Valley *Tribune.* She had her first story, "Platinum Blonde," published in *Teen Lit* magazine (the story of a spy named Platinum Blonde). "Elizabeth will never tell a secret or hurt anyone," says Jessica, "she's like Mother Theresa in a mini skirt." The community minded Elizabeth also worked as a candy stripper at Sweet Valley Hospital.

Elizabeth Bradford *see* **Mary Bradford**

346. Elizabeth and Russell Meyers, *Married People,* ABC, 1990–1991. Played by Bess Armstrong, Jay Thomas.

Elizabeth and Russell Meyers are a happily married professional couple who live in Apartment 2 of a three family home at 862 Central Park North (at 73rd Street) in New York City. Their rent is $500 a month.

Elizabeth is 36 years old "but looks 32." She is a graduate of Yale Law School and works as an attorney for the Wall Street law firm of Michaelson and Michaelson; she is later a partner and adds her name to the firm title. Elizabeth claims to have "lived on coffee and cheese doodles" while attending Yale and did her internship for a judge who called her "Toots."

Russell is 37 years old "but looks 42." He is a freelance writer who has penned articles for such magazines as *TV Guide* and *The New Yorker.* He also writes a monthly column for *Manhattan Life* magazine called "The Worst of New York" (wherein he reviews the worst things each month — from diners to landlords). He is a graduate of the Columbia School of Journalism and hates to be called "Russie" (his mother, Evelyn, was in labor for 52 hours with him).

Elizabeth is sweet, always happy and a perfectionist when it comes to her appearance and the apartment. While not a slob, Russell is a bit untidy and not the best dresser in the world. He likes "man food" not "the girlie foods" (healthy, no fat meals) Elizabeth prepares. Elizabeth shops for groceries at the 85th Street Market. She and Russell became parents in the episode of November 14, 1990, when Elizabeth gave birth to an eight pound, five ounce boy they named Max (Elizabeth shops for baby clothes at Bob's World of Babies). The Meyers can be reached by phone at 212-555-8247. Russell attended Woodstock in 1969 and claims the gray spot on the album cover that was released in his tent.

See also: Cindy and Allen Campbell.

347. Elizabeth Cooper, *Major Dad,* CBS, 1989–1993. Played by Marisa Ryan.

This entry also contains information on Elizabeth's sisters, Robin (Nicole Dubuc) and Casey Cooper (Chelsea Herford). Elizabeth, Robin and Casey are the daughters of Polly and Sandy Cooper. They live with their mother (a widow) in Oceanside, California (later with their stepfather, Major John MacGillis, when Polly remarries; they also relocate to Camp Hollister in Virginia).

Elizabeth first attended Keefer High School (Oceanside) then the Hollister Base High School. R.E.M. is her favorite music group and purple is her favorite color. While beautiful and sexy, Elizabeth feels she is slightly deformed ("My little toes are double jointed"). Elizabeth is fashion conscious, concerned about her makeup but worries about how her hair looked when she browses through the family album.

Robin, the middle child, attended Martin Elementary School (Oceanside, where she was a member of the Condors basketball team) then the Hollister Base School (where she is on the girls softball team, the Hollister Hornets). Robin, a tomboy, loves sports and enjoys drinking Minute Maid orange juice and Welch's grape juice.

Casey is the youngest of the girls and attends the same schools as Robin. She has two dolls (Henrietta and Ruby), a teddy bear (Mr. Smithers), and a plush toy (Mr. Whoobie). Casey played "the only squash with a solo" in the school's Harvest play and likes Ocean Spray cranberry juice.

See also: John and Polly MacGillis.

Elizabeth Walton *see* **Mary-Ellen Walton**

348. Elizabeth Lochley, *Babylon 5*, TNT, 1998–1999. Played by Tracy Scoggins.

Elizabeth Lochley is the ex-wife of John Sheridan, the captain of *Babylon 5*, a five-mile long floating city that was built in the 23rd century as a meeting ground to keep peace between the various races that inhabit the galaxy.

Elizabeth is the replacement for Susan Ivanova and became a captain when Susan left to take command of the Army of Light. Elizabeth and John had a rocky relationship. They were married for only a few weeks before they separated and later divorced. They remained friends over the years and were reunited again when Elizabeth was assigned to work with John.

Although Elizabeth shows intelligence and resourcefulness in everything she does, her life as a young adult was anything but responsible. She could be called a 23rd century "pot head" as she would use drugs and party. Her life changed after her roommate, a girl named Zoe, died from an apparent drug overdose (although Elizabeth believes Zoe may have committed suicide). Elizabeth has carried her memories of Zoe throughout her life and even uses the Code "Zoe's Dead" to gain access to *Babylon 5*'s computer files (in a flashback sequence, Zoe appeared to Elizabeth to confirm her suspicions that she did kill herself because she felt her life was meaningless).

Elizabeth appears to be all work and no play. She is rather stern looking when on the job, but she is extremely sexy in her off hours; she can bedazzle the viewer with her skimpy, bosom-revealing outfits.

See also: Delenn, John Sheridan, Lyta Alexander, Susan Ivanova.

349. Ellen Morgan, *Ellen*, ABC, 1994–1998. Played by Ellen DeGeneres.

Ellen Inez Morgan is the owner of a bookstore and coffee shop called Buy the Book in Los Angeles. Ellen was born in Louisiana in 1961. As a child Ellen took ballet lessons, had a pet goldfish (Goldie) and was an average student at Amsterdam Grammar School. Ellen's family relocated to Los Angeles when Ellen turned 14. Ellen attended Edgemont High School (class of 1978) and became fascinated with girls. She was not sure what was happening but soon after felt she was different. Ellen first worked as a waitress at Burger World before acquiring the bookstore. She lives in an apartment (7) on North Sweeter in Los Angeles and when we first see Ellen, she has come to terms with her sexuality and is comfortable with the fact that she is a lesbian. The first girl Ellen kissed was her straight friend, Paige Clark (Joely Fisher), an executive at Tri-Global Pictures.

Ellen has two goldfish (Lyle and Eric); she shops at the Buy and Bag Supermarket and has an account at the Interstate Bank. Ellen later sells the bookstore to the Tom and Larry Corporation but remains as its assistant manager. As a follow-up to her earlier ballet training, Ellen performed the lead in "Giselle" at the Edward Dru Hollywood Dance Studio. Ellen is a very attractive woman who doesn't hide the fact that she is different. She enjoys the company of men, but will not date them. She is not attracted to all women and is seeking just the right one; one who will compliment her fun outlook on life.

350. Ellen Richmond, *The Ellen Show*, CBS, 2001–2002. Played by Ellen DeGeneres.

Ellen Richmond was born in the small town of Clark, New Jersey. She attended Clark grammar and high schools and made her mark on the world — she won "The Spreading Your Wings

Award" for becoming the most successful person ever to achieve success from Clark.

Ellen started four internet companies and made over $16 million. However, one by one, the companies failed; when the last one (*www.homelearn. web*) lost its funding, Ellen found she was broke and returned home to live with her widowed mother, Dot, and her sister, Cathy.

As a child Ellen was fascinated by girls. She had posters of the TV series *Charlie's Angels* and *Wonder Woman* on her bedroom wall; when she was older, she replaced those posters with ones of singer K.D. Lang and tennis star Billie Jean King. Her hangout was a candy store called McIntire's. Ellen is now an openly admitted lesbian. She also admits to being a coffee freak ("but I can't seem to find a good cup of coffee") and enjoys the music of the band U-2. Ellen was interviewed for an article in *Vanity Fair* magazine ("Dot comers — Where Are They Now?"); she now has a net worth of only $800. Ellen, a graduate of Union State College, was a teacher before venturing into the business world. With that experience, she became the guidance counselor at Grant High School, which was founded in 1895.

351. Ellie Riggs, *Watching Ellie,* NBC, 2002–2003. Played by Julia Louis-Dreyfus.

Eleanor Riggs, better known as Ellie, is a woman whose life unfolds in 22 minutes each week (a ticking clock is seen on the left side of the screen). Ellie is trying to live her dream of becoming a famous singer. As a child, Ellie would dream of touring with a band, sing at Carnegie Hall, make records and become famous. Ellie is a singer in her adult life. However, it is not her dream; she seems to work long hours, perform at the worst clubs and is famous only as a bar-restaurant and wedding singer.

Ellie is vivacious and that quality landed her a series of singing television commercials: Cheese Doodles Snack Foods (to the song "You Made Me Love You") and Muni Electronics; and radio commercials for Fruit Shots (a brick pack liquid aimed at teenagers) and a butter substitute product called Butter Switch. Ellie lives in Apartment 3E at an unspecified address. She takes three sugars in her coffee and drives a car with the license plate 124 AVO. Ellen is not an easy person to get along with and one can expect trouble if she is not approached in the right manner. She is easily angered, always out to get even if someone does something to her, and becomes extremely frustrated when things do not go her way.

352. Ellie Walker, *High Society,* CBS, 1995–1996. Played by Jean Smart.

Ellie Walker is a wealthy New York socialite and novelist. She was born in Pittsburgh and is the daughter of Mel and Hazel Worshorsky (Ellie's real name is Eleanor Antoinette Worshorsky). As a child Ellie had a dog named Goochi and set her goal on having only the best things in life. She was an avid reader and also eager to learn about life. She developed a bit early and began wearing a bra in the fourth grade. This made her very popular with the boys but girls became jealous of her developing figure. Though she was rather young she claims she was voted "Best French Kisser of the Fourth Grade" (at Center Grammar School). While Ellie does not mention any additional shameful behavior, she no doubt was promiscuous in high school and college. She is now the successful author of trashy love stories and most of her readers believe she has lived the hot romances she writes about. Ellie mentioned writing the following books: *Pool Boys Plunge, Hermaphrodite, Swedish Meat Boys, Hung Jury, Street Walker, Stiletto Summer, Submissive Samurai, The Naked and the Deadline* and *Cops and Throbbers.*

Ellie changed her name when she began writing. She lives at 511 Sutton Place in Manhattan and 555-3000 is her phone number. She is always elegantly dressed (even when lounging around the apartment) and is sassy, loud and totally dedicated to the pursuit of the opposite sex (she is known for her numerous affairs). Ellie also drinks a bit too much and always eats out but does not like corner tables in restaurants "because no one can see me." Ellie likes being in the spotlight and makes sure she stays there by making her next book even trashier than the prior one. Emerson Publishing, a company that is number one in travel and leisure books, is Ellie's publisher.

353. Elly Mae Clampett, *The Beverly Hillbillies,* CBS, 1962–1971. Played by Donna Douglas.

Elly Mae Clampett is the daughter of Jed Clampett, a poor mountaineer who struck oil and became rich. She lives with him and her cousin, Jethro Bodine, and grandmother, Granny, in a mansion at 518 Crestview Drive in Beverly Hills, California.

Elly Mae was born in a log cabin near Blueberry Ridge in the Ozark Mountains in 1944. Jed raised Elly Mae as best he could after his wife, Rose Ellen, died. He brought her up like a boy and taught her everything from fishing to fighting to hunting. Elly Mae is now a beautiful young woman who dresses like a boy (when she got her first bra she thought it was "a store-bought lace-trimmed double-barreled sling shot"). Elly Mae knew she was different "when the buttons started to pop off her blouse." She was fearful of dressing like a girl because the boys called her "sissy." Jed wanted her to become refined like her mother, but ever since she could walk, "she's been climbin' trees and cuddlin' creatures." When Elly is mistaken for a boy by the clothes she sometimes wears, she says "Why thank you." "Boys came a courtin'" when Elly Mae was 12 and she fought them off (she had to prove she was better than any man by "wrestlin'" them to the ground"). Jed tried to teach Elly Mae about the birds and the bees but hasn't had much success as Elly sees them in a literal light (she says "Gee Paw, I'm fond of those little creatures").

Living in Beverly Hills has refined Elly a bit. She still has a special place in her heart for animals (which she calls "critters"). She has a rooster (Earl, who can play dead), two chimpanzees (Skipper and Beth; Beth is also called Bessie), a jaguar (Jasper), squirrel (Nicki), cat (Rusty), a duck (Charley) and a bear (Fairchild, who loves liquor).

While Elly Mae had some "schoolin'" in the Ozarks, she also attended the all-girl Willows Academy for Select Young Ladies in Beverly Hills. She was also a member of the Biddle Bird Watchers Club. "The big tree out front" is Elly Mae's favorite hiding place on the Clampett property. In the 1981 CBS TV movie update, *The Return of the Beverly Hillbillies*, Elly Mae is seen as the owner of Elly's Zoo in Beverly Hills.

See also: Granny, Jed Clampett, Jethro Bodine.

354. Emilia Rothschild, *Jack of All Trades,* Syn., 2000–2001. Played by Angela Dotchin.

Emilia Smythe Rothschild is a secret agent who has been assigned to stop the French expansion and save Pulau Pulau, a small East Indies island, from French rule. The time is 1801.

Emilia works on behalf of the British government. She is a brilliant scientist and has a secret lab in the basement of her home. Her cover is that of an exporter. Emilia was born in England and is the daughter of an aristocratic family. She is a graduate of Oxford University and became a spy to help free the oppressed. Emilia measures 36-24-36 and uses her sexuality to achieve her goals. She believes God is a woman and follows a long-standing tradition of daily breaks for tea. Emilia is very inventive and has created such military weapons as ginger spray, knockout gas, bulletproof clothing and a submarine.

The secret entrance to Emilia's lab is through the fireplace in the living room (it has an illusionary fire made from candles and mirrors). Emilia is courteous and carefully plans each action before she proceeds, a trait she learned from her father, a British agent who calls her "Fu Fu."

See also: Jack Stiles (the American agent who assists Emilia).

355. Emily Franklin, *Living Dolls,* ABC, 1989. Played by Halle Berry.

Emily Franklin is a teenage model that hates to be called a "Human Hanger," the term for a girl who is so pretty that she can't be smart. Emily is not only pretty she is beautiful and very smart. She is a straight A student at Lexington High School in Manhattan and hopes to become a doctor.

Emily was born on July 3, 1973 and is under contract with Trish Carlin, a former super model who runs the Carlin Modeling Agency from her home at 68th Street and Madison Avenue in New York City. Emily is very studious and gets extremely upset if she scores badly on a test. She fears that if her grades slip "the closest I will ever come to being a doctor is modeling lab coats." Emily is called "M" by her friends and goes out of her way to impress people. She is very fashion conscious and is always stylishly dressed. Emily tries to help her friends by dispensing advice that only she seems to understand (for example, "Follow your heart no matter what your heart says"). Emily is eager to achieve success. She hates rejection and believes if she does something good she should be complimented for it. She relaxes by playing racquet ball.

See also: Caroline Weldon, Charlie Briscoe, Martha Lambert.

Emily Gilmore *see* **Richard and Emily Gilmore**

Emily Hartley *see* **Bob and Emily Hartley**

356. Emily Stewart, *Raising Dad,* WB, 2001–2002. Played by Brie Larson.

Eleven-year-old Emily Stewart is an excellent cook, sports fanatic and a B student at Octavius Elementary School. She lives at 803 Linden Avenue in Massachusetts with her father, Matt, and sister, Sarah. Emily is called "Emmy" by her friends and "M" by Sarah. She likes popping plastic packing bubbles and is a bit mischievous. She listens in on Sarah's phone calls; reads her e-mails and preys into her "private stuff."

Emily's favorite dessert is apple pie and she holds the school record for getting her bra snapped 15 times in one day by "the cool guys" (something that was not objected to by the school or Matt, who is very protective of her and Sarah). Sarah's enjoys doing homework, housework (her mother is deceased), cooking and reading — things Matt fears she will grow out of when she gets older and becomes interested in boys.

See also: Matt Stewart, Sarah Stewart.

357. Emily Weston, *Empty Nest,* NBC, 1993–1995. Played by Lisa Rieffel.

Emily Weston is the youngest daughter of Harry and Libby Weston. Harry, now a widower, lives with Emily's sisters, Barbara and Carol, at 1755 Fairview Road in Miami Beach, Florida. Emily is 23 years old and was mentioned many times but not seen until Kristy McNichol (Barbara) left the series. Emily was born in Miami and was first said to be living in New York, then "attending college up north." Emily appeared for the first time on January 2, 1993. She had been in Italy and was pursued by an unwanted admirer. She returned home to work out her boyfriend problems (Harry believed Emily was attending college, the Hollyoak Girls' School, and was unaware that she had been globe trotting). At school Emily had heard about a program offering work in a Vietnam clinic and put school on hold to pursue it. When she lost interest, she took a moped over the Himalayan Mountains. She next went to Japan (where she worked as a karaoke waitress) and finally to Italy where she became a hand model.

Emily is independent, bad with money and unable to remain in one place for long periods of time. She calls her father "Harry" (Carol and Barbara call him "Daddy").

See also: Barbara Weston, Carol Weston, Harry Weston.

358. Emma DeLauro, *Mutant X,* Syn., 2001–2003. Played by Lauren Lee Smith.

Emma DeLauro is a genetically enhanced woman. Her genes were manipulated prior to her birth at Genomex, a secret genetics lab (see Adam Kane for information on Genomex). At the age of five, Emma realized she was different (she was attending a rock concert with her parents and became separated from them. She closed her eyes and was able to visualize their whereabouts and found them). Five years later, Emma's parents "ran off" and she was raised in an orphanage. When Adam learned of Emma's whereabouts, he recruited her as a member of Mutant X, a group of genetically manipulated agents who battle evil.

Emma's telepathic powers are only the beginning. She has "enormous untapped powers" that have yet to surface. As the series progressed, Emma obtained the ability to sense the feelings of others and the power to kill by thought (for example, choking someone simply by thinking it). Emma worked as a salesgirl when Adam found her. Here, she used her gifts to manipulate her customers into buying her products. Adam calls Emma one of his "children," as he helped create her. He also says "she is cautious and can be read like a book." An explosion took the life of Emma while investigating a case at the end of the second season.

See also: Adam Kane, Brennan Mulray, Lexa Pierce, Shalimar Fox.

359. Emma Peel, *The Avengers,* ABC, 1966–1968. Played by Diana Rigg.

Emma Peel is a totally emancipated and beautiful woman who works with John Steed, a suave Ministry agent, to avenge crimes committed against the British government. While Steed was a professional, Emma was an amateur and never officially a Ministry agent (she was loyal to the government and helped Steed for the sheer love of adventure).

Emma was born in England and was first said to be the daughter of a rich ship owner; later she is said to be the daughter of Sir John Knight, the owner of Knight Industries (located in the Knight Building in London). Emma, maiden name Knight, became the head of Knight Industries when she turned 21 (at which time her father died; no mention is made of her mother or if Emma still has a vested interest in the company). Emma appears to be wealthy and is either living off a trust fund or from money her company generates. At one point in her life (not stated) she married Peter Peel, a test pilot who was lost in the Amazonian Jungle and is presumed dead. Through dialogue it is learned that Emma and Steed (as he is called) met over a minor car accident. She became fascinated by him and attached herself to him.

Emma is a skilled karate expert and is interested in science and anthropology (she has a mini lab in her rooftop penthouse in Hampstead). She enjoys rock sculpting (which she does in her living room) playing bridge (she had an article, "Better Bridge Through Applied Mathematics" published in *The Bridge Players International Guide*).

Emma's "fighting clothes" are sexy two-piece outfits called "Emmapeelers." She carries a small handgun for protection and drives a 1966 Lotus Elan with the license plate SJH 4990 (then HNK 9996 and HN 9996). Emma is the replacement for Steed's prior partner, Catherine Gale; Tara

King replaced Emma when Peter Peel was found alive and Emma returned to him.

See also: Catherine Gale, John Steed, Tara King.

360. Endora, *Bewitched*, ABC, 1964–1972. Played by Agnes Moorehead.

Endora is a powerful witch and the mother of Samantha, the witch who married a mortal (Darrin Stevens). She is several thousand years old and chairwoman of the Witches' Council (also called the Witches' Committee), the governing body that rules witches. Endora speaks many languages and is also a lecturer on the Witches' Council Convention Circuit. She enjoys many hobbies, including shopping, lunching in Paris, and mountain climbing. Endora has a fiery temper and demands respect from everyone. Anyone who disrespects her feels her wrath (in the form of a spell). Endora's favorite breakfast is fried raven's eggs and she can temporarily lose her powers if she mixes eye of newt with oysters or is exposed to black Bavarian roses. She enjoys art (she frequents avant garde galleries) and purple is her favorite color. Endora claims mortals cannot pronounce her last name and she is divorced from Maurice, a very powerful and respected warlock who loves to quote from Shakespeare.

See also: Samantha Stevens.

361. Eric and Annie Camden, *7th Heaven*, WB, 1996 (current). Played by Stephen Collins, Catherine Hicks.

Eric and Annie Camden are a happily married couple who live in Glen Oak, a small community in California. They are the parents of seven children (Matt, Mary, Lucy, Simon, Ruthie and twins Sam and David) and live in a rather large home with the street number 527 (555-0517 is their phone number). Happy is the family dog.

Eric is a minister (Protestant) at the Glen Oak Community Church. Eric was a teenager when he found his true calling in life. He was a summer camp counselor and enjoyed helping people. This led to other such jobs and eventually the ministry. Eric attended Binghamton Elementary School. In high school he was a member of a band called the Flower and Vegetable Show. He is the author of an unpublished novel (*Lover, Can You Hear Me?*). He was also host of a call-in talk show on the Crawford College radio station, KRHC, 106.9 FM.

Roasted chicken and potatoes was the first meal Annie prepared for Eric. Annie's maiden name is Jackson and she was a psychology major at Crawford College (where she and Eric first met and soon after married). Annie later dropped out of college when she became pregnant with their first child (Matt). She became a full time mother and housewife over the next 20 years. Despite her limited free time, Annie has managed to return to college to get her degree in child psychology and hold a job as a morals teacher in a private school. Annie is a Jill of all trades (can cook, clean, repair broken pipes) and never leaves the house without lipstick ("No lipstick, that's bad," says Ruthie). When Annie was pregnant with Mary she took up plumbing; when pregnant with Lucy, she took up electricity; with the twins it was gardening. Eric calls these phases "Pregnancy Projects."

Eric and Annie do not believe in video games and will not allow their children to have any. Mary and Lucy feel that when it comes to their dating life, their father has nothing but time and no one can embarrass them like their mother. All the children were born at Glen Oak Hospital. As a child, Matt sang the theme to *The Mary Tyler Moore Show* ("Love Is All Around") to his mother when Mary was born. The show and song were Annie's favorites and the singing of that song has become a tradition with the births of Simon, Lucy, Ruthie and the twins.

See also: Lucy Camden, Mary Camden, Matt Camden, Ruthie Camden, Simon Camden.

362. Erica West, *Team Knight Rider*, Syn., 1997–1998. Played by Kathy Tragester.

Erica West is a beautiful blonde with a mysterious and mostly unknown past. She is a member of TKR (Team Knight Rider), a branch of the Foundation for Law and Government that tackles highly sensitive and dangerous matters. Erica West is the name this girl has chosen. She is a smooth talking con artist who can manipulate people into giving her exactly what she wants. Since she was old enough to fend for herself, Erica has thrived on scams. Her schemes always paid off and Erica thought she was invincible. However, during one scam, she made a mistake and was apprehended. She was tried, convicted and spent three years in prison before she was released to the Foundation, who required such a person in their organization. She was accepted as Erica West and agreed to use her talents to help TKR.

Erica rides a highly sophisticated (talking and thinking) motorcycle named Kat. Kat is a by-the-books vehicle and will not allow Erica to misuse her on the road (Kat is aware of road rules and will not jeopardize her or Erica's safety to accomplish a goal. Kat has been programmed with a safety conscious computer chip that no one can override).

See also: Duke DePalma, Jenny Andrews, Kyle Stewart, Trek Sanders.

363. Erik Delko, *C.S.I.: Miami*, CBS, 2002 (current). Played by Adam Rodriquez.

Erik Delko is a detective with the Crime Scene Investigation Unit of the Miami Dade Police Department. He was born in Miami on December 19, 1976 and stands six feet, one inch tall; he weighs 180 pounds. Erik has a B.S. degree in chemistry from the University of Miami and his special skills are finger print analysis and drug identification. He is also single and fluent in Spanish.

Erik was conceived in Cuba but born in the U.S. His father, Pavel Deletorsky, was a Russian engineer working in Cuba (early 1970s). Here, he met Clorinda, a young Cuban woman he later married. They had three daughters. When Pavel learned that their fourth child was to be a boy (Erik), he smuggled his family out of Cuba across the Straits of Florida. It was the only way for Pavel knew to give his unborn son a future. Pavel found work in his chosen field; Clorinda worked with the various Cuban charities in Miami. Erik learned to help others from this. Although Erik excelled in science in grammar and high school, it was in high school that he discovered his true love — swimming. He graduated with a swimming degree and enrolled in college. After graduation, he used his skills as a swimmer for the Miami Police Department's Underwater Recovery Unit. During a bomb scare investigation, Erik met Horatio Caine, the head of the C.S.I. unit. Horatio became impressed with Erik and recruited him as the first member of his C.S.I. unit. Erik calls Horatio "Boss" and often doubles as the unit's photographer.

See also: Alexx Woods, Calleigh Duquesne, Horatio Caine, Tim Speedle.

Erin Walton *see* **Mary-Ellen Walton**

364. Ernest Frye, *Amen*, NBC, 1986–1991. Played by Sherman Hemsley.

Ernest Frye is deacon of the First Community Church of Philadelphia. He is stubborn, opinionated, tight with money but devoted to God, his church and concerned about the welfare of his parishioners. Ernest's father founded the church and Ernest continues in a tradition that is decades old and somewhat behind the times.

Ernest was born and raised in Philadelphia. Being the son of a minister, Ernest was groomed to follow in the ways of the Lord and one day become his disciple on Earth. Ernest, however, felt it was not his true calling; at least not yet. He hoped to become a lawyer. It was while he was in law school that Ernest met his future wife, Laraine Tillman (Ernest worked for Al's Delivery Service. While delivering flowers to a patient at County General Hospital, Ernest saw Laraine, a nurse, and it was a love at first sight). Ernest and Laraine married and had a daughter (Thelma). They enjoyed five happy years together before Laraine's passing. Ernest had become a lawyer by this time but now felt he needed to thank the Lord for the prosperity and happiness he enjoyed with Laraine and took over the reigns of the church from his father.

Ernest has a law office (Room 203) on 56th Street (his shingle reads "Attorney-at-Law, Ernest Frye — Where Winning Is Everything"). Ernest has A-positive blood, reads *Popular Gospel* magazine and drives a sedan with the license plate KNC 481. Ernest is deathly afraid of spiders and loves meatball-topped pizza. Later episodes find Ernest becoming a judge and cutting back somewhat on his duties as a deacon.

See also: Reuben Gregory.

365. Ernie Paine, *Thicker Than Water*, ABC, 1973. Played by Richard Long.

Ernest Paine, called Ernie, is the son of Jonas Paine, a man who loved pickles so much that he turned his love into an empire (Paine's Pure Pickles). Ernie was born in 1937 and was groomed to take over the family business. In 1955, Ernie's mother Frances passed away. Eight years later, Jonas became chronically ill. In 1965, Ernie had it with pickles and left home. His older sister, Nellie, remained behind to care for Jonas and run the pickle factory.

In school Ernie was teased by other kids and called "Ernie Gherkin." For eight years it appeared that Jonas missed Ernie. Every day, when someone would enter his room, Jonas would call out "Ernie, is that you?" Although it was never Ernie, Jonas knew that one day Ernie would return "because blood's thicker than water." It also appeared that Jonas would never live to hear the answer he yearned for. In 1973, when Ernie learns that Pop (as he calls Jonas) has taken a turn for the worse, he returns home, hoping to collect his share of the family fortune. Ernie enters Pop's room. We hear Jonas say "Ernie, is that you?" "Hey Pop," responds Ernie, "It's me." "Well who the hell is me?" replies Pop. "It's me, Ernie, don't you recognize me?" "How do I know it's Ernie? Maybe you're just out to steal the secret of my Gherkins." "Gherkins!," responds Ernie, "who wants your Gherkins you silly old codger." Jonas then realizes it is Ernie and they hug; but Ernie is in for a shock. To inherit $75,000, he must live in the family residence for five years and run the pickle plant.

Ernie is a ladies' man and studiously avoids work. He drinks, chases women and has a talent for getting the prize out of a Crackerjack box without opening it. Ernie hangs out at Vito's Atomic Bar, the Purple Cow and the Golden Slipper bars (if he gets lucky, it's off to the Hideaway Hotel). As a child, Ernie had a doll that looked so much like him that it was called "The Ernie Doll."

See also: Jonas Paine, Nellie Paine.

366. Ernie Pantusso, *Cheers*, NBC, 1982–1985. Played by Nicholas Colasanto.

Ernie Pantusso, affectionately called "Coach," works as a bartender at Cheers, the Boston bar owned by Sam Malone. Ernie was the Boston Red Sox pitching coach at the same time Sam was a relief pitcher. Sam gave Ernie the job when he became somewhat senile and was let go by the Sox. Ernie holds the record for being hit by more pitched balls than any other coach in minor league history.

Ernie also had the nickname "Red" (not because he had red hair, but because he once read a book). He considers the blackouts he has to be a nice break in the day and has chosen 1:37 in the morning as his favorite time of the day ("I don't know why, I just like it"). His favorite movie is *Thunder Road* starring Robert Mitchum and Ernie has a habit of banging his head on the bar's serving area next to the beer dispensers.

Ernie was married (his late wife was named Angela) and he was the coach of a Little League baseball team called the Titans. Ernie was kind and gentle and always gave of himself to help someone in need. In a fond tribute to Nicholas Colasanto after his death in 1985, the picture of Geronimo that he kept in his dressing room was placed on the *Cheers* set (upper left stage wall) to remind the cast and crew of Ernie.

See also: Carla LeBec, Cliff Claven, Diane Chambers, Norm Peterson, Rebecca Howe, Sam Malone, Woody Boyd.

367. Erotica Jones, *Stripperella*, Spike TV, 2003–2004. Voiced by Pamela Anderson.

Erotica Jones is a beautiful stripper who works at a club called the Tender Loins. She is extremely intelligent but she hides that attribute by wearing revealing tops and miniskirts. Erotica also has another life: she is Stripperella, a daring crime fighter for T.H.U.G.G., a secret agency that battles evil wherever it exists.

Erotica, as Stripperella, is sexier than any Playboy Playmate. She calls herself a "Double D Cup Superhero" but her official code is Agent Double 069 (she is sometimes called 0069 and Agent 69). Erotica has a heart of gold and a passion for animals (all profits from her line of Stripperella merchandise, like lunch boxes, go to her favorite charity, All Animals Need Universal Support). Erotica wears pink when she is herself; black or dark blue when she becomes Stripperella.

Erotica's life as a crime fighter leaves her little time for a social life. She is impervious to all temperatures and weather conditions. She rides a motorcycle and can cut glass with her fingernails. The naval jewelry Erotica wears is actually a control device her superior, Chief Stroganoff, uses to contact her for an assignment. Erotica's enhanced hair enables her to float safely from tall buildings. She conceals a lie detector in her bra and a digital scanner, placed under her tongue, allows her to download information into a computer. The animated series contains no information regarding Erotica's past or how she acquired her abilities.

Ethel Mertz *see* **Fred and Ethel Mertz**

368. Eve Madison, *Mann and Machine*, NBC, 1992. Played by Yancy Butler.

Eve Madison is young, beautiful and extremely feminine. She is also a highly sophisticated and perfectly formed female robot. Eve was created by Anna Kepler, a doctor with the Artificial Intelligence Program, an agency that is experimenting with robots as police officers.

Eve functions as a normal woman. She is a sergeant with the L.A.P.D. and is learning to become human. Her body is a combination of plastic compounds and metal alloys. Her brain functions like the human brain and is capable of assimilating artificial material. Eve is the prototype for a project called "The Protector" ("The future partner of every police officer"). Eve is highly advanced in technical terms, but emotionally she is very young (the age of a seven-year-old girl). She has the deductive reasoning of Sherlock Holmes and a genuine sense of humor (she will laugh if she feels something is funny). Eve eats, sleeps and daydreams. Her eyes are capable of emitting laser beams; her tears are a lubricant and she can speak 40 languages.

Eve watches television to learn about life (*The Mod Squad* and *The Three Stooges* are her favorite shows). But the only way Eve can really grow is to experience life — "the good, the bad and the ugly of it." Eve's brain downloads directly into the advanced A.I. Workstation Computer in her apartment (1407 at the Metropolitan Hotel). She can access any computer through a special earplug adapter.

Eve believes she was built for only one purpose — to enforce the law. She is a retrieval expert ("I'm an information specialist. There isn't a mainframe in the country I can't access"). Eve was built in Danville in the Silicone Valley and was first assigned to the San Francisco Police Department. She has a worm collection and her lucky number is the algebraic term *pi*.

369. Evie Garland, *Out of This World*, Syn., 1987–1991. Played by Maureen Flannigan.

Eve Ethel Garland, called Evie, is not your average, everyday teenage girl. She is half alien. Her father is Troy Ethel Garland, a being from the planet Anterias; Donna Froelich, an Earth girl, is her mother (see Donna Garland for further information).

Evie is 13 years old and is a student at the Marlowe School for Gifted Children, then Marlowe High School. She lives with her mother at 17 Medvale Road in Marlowe, California; 406-555-4669 is their phone number (Evie's father has since returned to Anterias. Evie is able to speak with him via a genetic-link crystal cube. Troy calls her his "Earth Angel").

Evie can freeze and unfreeze time, gleep (rearrange molecules by concentrating) and teletransport (move from one place to another). She has a plush cat (Twinky) and she frequents a soda shop called the Goodie Goodie. Evie is third string on the school's basketball team, the Fighting Hamsters, and a member of the Marlowe Teenage Bowling Team. Evie's favorite breakfast is orange juice, hot cakes and bacon. She loves to wear earrings ("I'm an earring-holic") and rents movies at Vic's Video Rentals (Kevin Costner is her favorite film star). The mythical soap opera, *All My Yesterday's Tomorrow*, is her favorite TV show. She has a midnight curfew on non-school nights.

See also: Donna Garland, Kyle Applegate.

370. Ezri Dax, *Star Trek: Deep Space Nine*, Syn., 1993–1999. Played by Nicole de Boer.

Ezri Dax is a station counselor on *Deep Space Nine*, a former Cardassian mining station that was revitalized as a critical space station by Starfleet and the Bajoran government. Ezri was born as Ezri Tigan on the planet Trill but grew up in the Suppora System. Like Jadzia Dax (see entry), Ezri was chosen by the Symbiosis Institute to become host for a Dax life force (at which time she became known as Ezri Dax).

Ezri graduated from Starfleet Academy's medical program with a degree in psychology. In 2372, two years after graduating, Ezri was assigned to the U.S.S. *Destiny* for field training. One year later she acquired the counselor's position at *Deep Space Nine*.

See also: Benjamin Sisko, Jadzia Dax, Kira Nerys.

371. Faith Fairfield, *Hope and Faith*, ABC, 2003 (current). Played by Kelly Ripa.

April Storm and her twin sister, Ashley, were the two characters actress Faith Fairfield played on the mythical ABC soap opera, *The Sacred and the Sinful*. After a ten year run, Faith was written out of the story when April shot Ashley then killed herself. With no money, no house and no place to live, Faith left Hollywood and returned to her home town of Glen Falls, Ohio, to live with her older sister, Hope, her husband, Charlie, and their children, Sydney, Hayley and Justin, at 22 Cherry Lane.

Faith has every episode of her ten year run on the soap opera on tape. She cherishes her one Daytime Emmy Award and claims "For the first time in my life I have no role. I just don't know who to be." She is now 33 years old and relates incidents about life she thinks are real but are actually scenes from her series. Faith calls her breasts "The Girls" and believes her greatest talent is her ability to cry on cue (Hope calls her "a famous star with a Daytime Emmy and fake boobs").

Faith grew up in Glen Falls. She was irresponsible from the beginning. When she was 13, she used her father's stamp collection to mail invitations to her upcoming birthday party (she also used her father's coin collection to pay for the invitations). Faith attended U.S. Grant High School and had a dog named Pickles. She first showed a talent for acting when she was in the third grade (she played a pirate in *The Pirates of Penzance*). Her mother encouraged her and her first professional job was in a TV commercial for a cold medicine. She next appeared on *Star Search* (but lost) and with the great body she feels she has, wound up as the star of a sexy and steamy cable movie called *Weapons of Mass Seduction* (wherein she had her first nude scene — she had to remove her bra and use it to stop the bleeding when her partner was shot). Locally, Faith appeared in a series of TV commercials for Handsome Hal's Used Cars. She next got an agent (Animal and Artists Talent Agency) and had her first job in a red bikini modeling jackhammers at a local trade show. Faith also held a job as a columnist for the Glen Falls *Gazette* writing "Life in the Star Pool Lane." Her father calls her "My Little TV Star."

See also: Hope Shanoski.

372. Father Dowling, *Father Dowling Mysteries*, NBC, 1989; ABC, 1990–1991. Played by Tom Bosley.

Father Frank Dowling is a Catholic parish priest with the mind of a detective. He is pastor of Saint Michael's Roman Catholic Church in Chicago and says "I'm in the business of helping people."

Frank was born in Chicago and attended Saint Michael's elementary and high schools. Although Frank was an altar boy and would always try to attend mass on Sunday, he never showed an interest in becoming a priest. It was when Frank worked as a counselor for a parish youth group that he had thoughts about entering the priesthood. However, he was in love with a girl named Mary Ellen Connell and also wanted to raise a family. Frank proposed to Mary Ellen and she accepted. After a brief romance Mary Ellen realized Frank was destined to become a priest and convinced him to enter the seminary. Frank did and recalls "I knew she was right."

Frank is a priest first and a detective second. He is an avid mystery fan and fancies himself as an amateur sleuth (he works with Sister Steve to solve crimes).

Frank has been a priest since 1958 and the pastor of Saint Michael's for nine years (he replaced the former pastor, Father Hunnicker). Frank is a Cubs baseball fan and the fictional character, Sherlock Holmes, is his mentor. Frank reads *Amateur Sleuth* magazine and his exploits became the basis of an unsold TV series called "Father Flannigan Investigates."

See also: Sister Steve.

373. Felix Unger, *The Odd Couple*, ABC, 1970–1975. Played by Tony Randall.

Felix Unger is an excessively neat perfectionist who owns a photography business called Portraits a Specialty. He shares Apartment 1102 at 1049 Park Avenue (at 74th Street and Central Park West) in New York City with Oscar Madison, an irresponsible slob.

Felix first mentions he was born in Chicago. As a youngster he moved to Oklahoma, then to Glenview, New York, where he grew up on a farm (in another episode, Felix mentions Toledo, Ohio, as his home town). He was a neat child, perfect student in school and became a radio actor as a teenager (he is a member of the Radio Actor's Guild and appeared on the series *Let's Pretend*); in college he hosted is own radio show, *Felix*. Following his college graduation, Felix enrolled in the army and was stationed in England during World War II (with the 22nd Training Film Platoon,

Educational Division of the Special Services). He starred in the army training film, *How to Take a Shower* and originated the line, "Men don't let this happen to you." He also won the Silver Canteen Award for his song about Hitler called "To a Sour Kraut." Felix, a lieutenant at the time, was next transferred to Greenland and two years later retired as a captain. He now serves two weeks a year in the Army Reserves.

Felix's first job was as a photographer for *Playboy* magazine (he worked under the name Spencer Benedict because "You don't think I'm going to use my real name to shoot nudes"). He was also engaged to his now ex-wife Gloria at the time (Gloria worked as a bunny in the Manhattan Playboy Club). Felix and Gloria were married for seven years before Gloria asked him for a divorce (he would buy Gloria's clothes, do the cooking, clean after she cleaned; he simply drove her to a point of not being able to stand him any longer. They became the parents of two children, Edna and Leonard).

Felix and Oscar first met as jurors at the trial of Leo Garvey, a man accused of driving his roommate crazy. When Gloria got rid of Felix, Oscar acquired him when he agreed to let Felix move in with him. Felix has an annoying and loud sinus problem. He is allergic to animals (even plush ones); when he was a kid "I curled up with a sponge." He had a pet parrot (Albert) and says "That ever since I played Hamlet in junior high school, I have been fascinated by ghosts." Felix loves the opera and ballet and is a member of the Edward Vilella Ballet Appreciation Club, the Lexington Avenue Opera Club, and a band called the Sophisticates. He subscribes to the *Opera News* magazine and becomes embarrassed in public because he cries at operas. Felix won the Dink Advertising Award for directing a TV commercial for Fataway Diet Pills and prides himself on knowing the best French restaurants in Manhattan.

Felix's boyhood friend was Orville Kruger ("the boy with the odd-shaped head"); his first girlfriend was "Big Bertha." When they were kids, Felix and his brother, Floyd, were called "Spic and Span" (Floyd now makes Unger Bubble Gum). Felix called Floyd "Little F;" Floyd called Felix "Big F."

See also: Oscar Madison.

374. Ferguson Darling, *Clarissa Explains It All*, NIK, 1991–1994. Played by Jason Zimbler.

Ferguson Darling, called "Ferg Face" by his sister, Clarissa, is the son of Marshall and Janet Darling, and lives at 464 Shadow Lane in Baxter Beach, Florida.

Clarissa best describes Ferguson: "That dork boy has been a burn on my butt since he was born. He was a normal, ugly baby. Sometimes I think he was just envious of my natural grace and good looks. Sometimes I think he's related to Freddy" (Freddy Kruger from the *Nightmare on Elm Street* movies).

Ferguson attends Thomas Tupper Junior High School and, as Clarissa says, "Living with my brother is like having your hair set on fire, then putting it out with a sledge hammer." Ferguson is annoying and has to get his way. *Bugs Bunny and Friends* is his favorite TV show and he sneaks down to the living room late at night to watch *Spine Tingly Theater*. Ferguson is a Republican and vice president of the Dan Quayle Fan Club (there is no president — "you can't have an office higher than your idol"). As a kid, Ferguson attended Camp Can Do and appeared with Clarissa on the TV show *Brain* (they lost when Ferguson went about explaining what a pie was when the host meant the algebraic term *pi*). Ferguson was born on February 13th and had a public access TV show called *Boy Thoughts* (wherein he gave his opinions).

See also: Clarissa Darling.

Festus Haggen *see* **Matt Dillon**

375. Finn, *The Lost World*, Syn., 2002. Played by Lara Cox.

Finn (no other name given) joined the cast of *The Lost World* in 2002. It is 1924 when Finn, a young woman from the future, is propelled back in time through a time warp to become allies with George, Marguerite, Veronica, John, and Ned, explorers stranded on a lost plateau of prehistoric creatures in the Amazon.

Finn is from the year 2033. She was born in 2010 in New Amazonia, the future name for the plateau on which the Challenger Expedition is stranded. In this futuristic world, there are cities but all traces of prehistoric creatures have vanished. It is also a world that has been devastated by a great holocaust and is being ravaged by scavengers. Finn had become a warrior to survive.

Finn, like the Challenger Expedition, is seeking the secret of the way off the plateau. She calls Veronica, the one she is closest to, "Vee" and George, "The Big Guy." Finn is proficient with her crossbow and like her comrades, remained lost forever on the plateau when the series ended before allowing their escape.

See also: George Challenger, John Roxton, Marguerite Krux, Ned Malone, Veronica Layton.

376. Fitz Fitzgerald, *The Fighting Fitzgeralds*, NBC, 2001. Played by Brian Dennehy.

Fitz Fitzgerald, otherwise known as Pop Fitzgerald, is a cantankerous senior citizen who lives at 5780 Valley Road on Long Island in New York. Other than "Pop" or "Fitz," he has no other name. Pop grew up in New York and is proud of his Irish heritage. He was a fireman with the New York City Fire Department (Fire Station 17) for 37 years and is now retired. As a kid, his older sister, Rose, called him "Little Boo Boo" and there is a strong indication that he hated that nickname as it made him the bitter, always ready for an argument man he is today.

Pop enjoys reading the New York *Post*, recalling his days with the Marines and painting — "It gets me through retirement." Dusty Springfield and Bobby Darin are Pop's favorite singers and he enjoys a beer (and an argument) at the local pub, Gibson's Tavern. Pop is a widower (he was married to his late wife, Maggie, for 40 years) and is part owner of an Irish restaurant called Mickey O'Shea's. Pop claims the family history includes a burlesque dancer ("We don't talk about her") and a sweatshop worker ("who learned the value of a dollar"). Pop drives a Lincoln and changes the oil every 10,000 miles because "fat cat oil companies want you to believe it has to be changed every 3,000 miles." Besides his knack for arguing, Pop can't keep a secret (at the firehouse, for example, Pop was never let in on anything).

377. Flex Washington, *One on One*, UPN, 2001 (current). Played by Flex Alexander.

Flex Washington is the professional name for Flex Barnes, the son of a middle class Baltimore family whose mother, Eunice, was a teacher, and whose father, Richard, ran a barber shop business called Barnes and Son (now called Phathead's and managed by Flex following his father's retirement; the shop has been in the family for 50 years).

Flex was born in 1968 and showed an interest in sports at an early age. He excelled at basketball and played on the McKinley High School basketball team. He won a basketball scholarship to college and majored in communication arts as a backup to his professional sports career. After graduating from Maryland State University, he joined the NBA. During his second season, he threw his knee out and was unable to play. He fell back on his college degree and acquired a job as Flex Washington at WYNX-TV, Channel 3, as the station's sports commentator on *The Flex Files*.

Flex is a single father and is caring for his 14-year-old daughter, Breanna Barnes, while her mother, Nicole, is in Nova Scotia studying marine life (Breanna eventually lives with Flex on a permanent basis. Flex and Nicole were high school sweethearts. Nicole became pregnant at the age of 18 and had Breanna shortly after. Flex and Nicole married but soon divorced. Breanna had been living with her mother. When Nicole acquired a grant, Flex agrees to care for their daughter). Nicole now works as the research director for Save the Oceans United League.

Flex's first car was a 1979 Pontiac he called Thriller. He was in a high school band called Midnight Gold and tried to revive his career in 2003 as "The NBA's Oldest Rookie" with the L.A. Clippers but failed to make the grade (he wore jersey 35). Flex did a TV commercial for Mattress King and the TV show *MTV Crib* did a profile of Flex. In the 1980s, Flex had a crush on the singer Vanity and he has a collection of NBA hats (he also won a trophy in a hot dog eating contest). His hangout is a bar called Peanuts.

See also: Breanna Barnes, Duane Odell Knox.

378. Florence Jean Castleberry, *Alice,* CBS, 1976-l980. Played by Polly Holliday.

Florence Jean Castleberry, nicknamed Flo, is the wisecracking, sassy waitress who works for Mel Sharples, the stingy owner of Mel's Diner in Phoenix, Arizona.

Flo was born in Cowtown, Texas. She has a sister named Fran and her mother is a feisty little woman named Velma. Flo attended Cowtown grammar and high schools and after graduation, she decided to make her mark on the world. She bought a mobile home and drifted from state to state, working at whatever jobs she could find. She settled, temporarily, in Phoenix, when she found the job at Mel's Diner.

Flo is a very sexy woman who dresses to make that fact known. Her non-working attire is tight pants, tight blouses and "a peek-a-boo nightgown" at bedtime. Flo will not take anything from anyone and has a difficult time holding her temper when someone aggravates her. She used the comeback line "Kiss My Grits" as a way of verbally getting back at someone.

Flo lives at the Desert Trailer Park and frequents a bar called Shake Chug-a-Lug. She is known for her many affairs and Lookout Mountain is her favorite make out spot (she keeps a memento of every date she has). Her most prized possessions are an imitation leopard bedspread, a blue velvet painting of singer Johnny Cash, and a plush rabbit she won at the Corpus Christi County Fair. She left Mel's Diner in 1980 to open her own diner in her hometown.

See also: Alice Hyatt, Jolene Hunnicutt, Mel Sharples, Vera Gorman.

379. Fonzie, *Happy Days,* ABC, 1974–1984. Played by Henry Winkler.

The time is the 1950s. His "offices" can be found in the "Guys Room" of Arnold's Drive-In, a hamburger hangout for teenagers in Milwaukee, Wisconsin. He is a high school dropout who receives great respect because he is "cool." He rides a motorcycle, wears a leather jacket and asks to be called "Fonzie" or "The Fonz," but never by his real name, Arthur Herbert Fonzarelli.

Fonzie was born in Milwaukee and had an uneasy childhood. He was raised by his grandmother after his parents "split" (Fonzie first says his father deserted the family when he was three years old; later it was when Arthur was two; his mother, according to dialogue, "split two years later"). Although Fonzie's grandmother fondly called him "Skippy," she was not able to properly raise him. The streets did. Fonzie fell in with the wrong crowd (gang motorcyclists) and found school a bore. He dropped out of Jefferson High to ride with a gang called the Falcons. When he realized his life was heading nowhere, he left the Falcons for a job as a mechanic at Otto's Auto Orphanage (then Herb's Auto Repairs and finally Bronco's Auto Repairs). Fonzie soon became the idol of students at Jefferson High. He also became close to the Cunningham family (Richie, his sister, Joanie, and their parents, Howard and Marion).

Fonzie later returned to Jefferson High to get his diploma and become a shop teacher at the school. He later became the Dean of Boys at the rowdy George S. Patton High School. He first lived in an apartment (154) at an unspecified address then in a room above the Cunningham's garage at 618 Bridge Street.

Fonzie commands attention by snapping his fingers. He is a ladies' man and "Aaagh" and "Whooa" are his catch phrases. The Lone Ranger is Fonzie's hero (he has a Lone Ranger toothbrush); he uses Mr. Musk after-shave lotion and he has a dog named Spunky. He also has a bathrobe and a toolbox that say "Sweetums" ("hey, it's a gift from a girl") and an autographed picture of then famous *Mickey Mouse Club* "Mouseketeer" Annette Funicello ("She gave me hers, I gave her mine"). Fonzie later becomes partners with Al Delvecchio in Arnold's Drive-In when it burns down and they rename it "Arnold's — Fonzie and Big Al, Proprietors."

Fonzie was best known for his relationship with Pinky Tuscadero, a biker who dressed in pink;

and Ashley Pfister, a widow with a young daughter named Heather.

See also: Howard and Marion Cunningham, Joanie Cunningham, Richie Cunningham.

380. Fox Mulder, *The X-Files*, Fox, 1993–2002. Played by David Duchovny.

Fox William Mulder is an agent for the X-Files, a government organization that investigates supernatural occurrences. He is the son of Bill and Tina Mulder and was born in Maryland on October 13, 1961. He has brown hair, green eyes and stands six feet tall. He lived at 2790 Vine Street and had a younger sister named Samantha. When Samantha was eight years old (Fox was 12) she mysteriously disappeared (Fox claimed she was kidnapped by aliens. He was paralyzed by a bright light and unable to help her. He recalls hearing the aliens say Samantha would be cared for). This incident led Fox to believe the supernatural exists and he became obsessed with such phenomena (UFO sightings, witchcraft, alien abduction — anything that can't be explained in normal terms).

Fox attended Oxford University and joined the FBI after graduation. He has a degree in psychology and has a photographic memory. Fox worked for the FBI's Violent Crimes Unit and earned a reputation for defying authority to do things his way. Shortly after joining the bureau (1986) he stumbled upon the X-Files while working in the bureau's behavioral sciences department (as an analyst). He was eventually teamed with agent Dana Scully and became the backbone of the X-Files Bureau.

Fox has the nickname of "Spooky" for his beliefs and ability to process information and come to a logical conclusion. He is a fan of the TV series *Star Trek*. He also likes nuts, especially pistachio, and sunflower seeds. Fox is color blind and a fan of both the New York Knicks (basketball) and the Washington Red Skins (football). He has a habit of bouncing a ball when he becomes bored and swims and runs to keep fit. Fox enjoys ice tea, classic rock music and is a collector of adult videos (porn). He watches the Playboy Channel and enjoys the centerfolds in girlie magazines.

Fox is agent number 22791 (JJT 047101111 is his badge number). He lives at 2360 Hegal Place, Apartment 42 in Alexandria, Virginia; 555-9355 is his phone number.

See also: Dana Scully.

381. Fran Fine, *The Nanny*, CBS, 1993–1999. Played by Fran Drescher.

Francine Fine, called Fran and Franny, is a gorgeous 29-year-old woman who works as the live-in nanny for Maggie, Gracie and Bryton, the children of Maxwell Sheffield, a wealthy widower who runs a Broadway show producing company called Maxwell Sheffield Productions. They live in a fashionable 19-room house on New York's Park Avenue.

Fran is the daughter of Sylvia and Morty Fine and was born in Flushing (Queens, New York) in 1964 (another episode makes her younger, giving her birth date as November 26, 1970). Fran was first said to have attended P.S. 19 grammar school, then P.S. 165. As for high schools, it was first said to be Flushing High, then Hillcrest High. Her Sweet 16 Party was held at Benny's Clam Bar (in the Half Shell Room). She attended Camp Kindervelt during the summer of 1974 and had a pet goldfish (Goldie).

Fran was in the cosmetology club at Flushing High and later attended the Ultissima Beauty Institute (she became a licensed cosmetologist; she later says she attended the Barbizon School of Modeling and was a foot model for two years). No matter what was said, it was Fran's fascination with beauty at an early age that led her to become an expert on hair, makeup and clothing (although she claims "some women believe I'm a hooker by the clothes I wear"; the clothes include size two miniskirts, cleavage-revealing blouses and very bright colors).

Fran first worked at the Bridal Shoppe in Flushing. She was fired for rejecting the advances of her boss. She began selling Shades of the Orient Cosmetics door-to-door. At the Sheffield home she was mistaken for an agency nanny and hired when she impressed Maxwell's children.

Fran has her hair done at the Chatterbox Salon. She is an expert on 1960s television shows and appeared on *Jeopardy* (where she won $200). Her favorite soap opera is *The Young and the Restless* (as a child it was the fictional *Edge of Life*). Although Fran is Jewish, she played the Catholic Reverend Mother in her high school play, *The Sound of Music* (her prior starring role was in her third grade production of *Fiddler on the Roof*). Barbra Streisand is Fran's favorite singer (she believes *Yentl* is the best movie ever made) and she paid $200 for a framed wad of bubblegum that came from the bottom of one of Barbra's shoes. Fran is a member of Shopper's Anonymous (when she gets depressed she shops) and played Juliet in an off-Broadway retelling of *Romeo and Juliet*.

Fran tries to solve all problems with flair and style. She does not have a voice that is powerful enough to demand respect (it's more nasal) and tries street psychology to solve the problems she encounters as a nanny. Last season episodes find

Fran marrying Maxwell and giving birth to twins they name Eve Kathryn and James Samuel.

See also: C.C. Babcock, Gracie Sheffield, Maggie Sheffield, Maxwell Sheffield.

Fran Sinclair *see* **Earl and Fran Sinclair**

382. Francis Muldoon, *Car 54, Where Are You?,* NBC, 1961–1963. Played by Fred Gwynne.

Francis Muldoon is an officer with the 53rd Police Precinct on Tremont Avenue in the Bronx, New York. He is assigned to Car 54 and is partners with Gunther Toody.

Francis is from a long line of police officers (his father was a captain; his grandfather, a deputy police commissioner). Francis is single and lives with his mother and sisters (Cathy and Peggy) at 807 East 157th Street in the Bronx (address also given as 17th Street). Francis was born in the Bronx and is a graduate of Holy Cross High School (where he was a member of the basketball team); he was also said to have attended Bryant High and Newtown High School.

Francis is tall ("I'm six feet, five inches tall and five feet, six inches is all face") and was called "Horse Face" as a kid in grammar school. He is afraid of girls and rarely dates. He weighs 183¾ pounds and was named after his mother's idol, film star Francis X. Busman (his mother also calls Francis "My Big Baby Boy"). Francis is famous for his homemade salad dressing and has a mind like a computer (he can recall any police regulation). He collects stamps (is a member of the Bronx Stamp Club) and wrote the play *Tempest in the Tropics* for a policeman's benefit show.

Francis enjoys life and the simple pleasures it offers. He is easily upset and prefers to listen to people rather than talk to them. He is a member of the precinct's Singing Whippoorwills and the Brotherhood Club. He also coaches (with Gunther), the Wildcats, a PAL (Police Athletic League) basketball team. Francis wears badge 723 (originally 787).

See also: Gunther Toody, Leo Schnauser

383. Frank and Marie Barone, *Everybody Loves Raymond,* CBS, 1996–2005. Played by Peter Boyle, Doris Roberts.

Frank and Marie Barone are the parents of Raymond and Robert Barone. They live in Lynbrook, New York, and met in 1955. Frank immediately fell in love with Marie for her cooking. She prepared braciole (an Italian meat dish) and has been in love with her cooking ever since. Frank lives to eat since he has retired (first said to be an accountant with Polk Accounting, then a real estate bro-

ker). His favorite part of the turkey—"The part that goes over the fence last—the caboose." He believes the only way to do things is to do it his way. Frank is an Italian Catholic and is an usher at Our Lady of Faith Church. He drives a 1972 Valiant (plate W7F 540) and had a story published in *Reader's Digest* magazine based on his Korean War stories (in the "Humor in Uniform" section). His catch phrase is Holy Crap (which he says when something doesn't go his way).

Marie loved Valentine's Day until she met the unromantic Frank. She takes pride in her cooking and claims she doesn't cook from recipes but from the heart. Marie loves to look at other people's mail and lives to intrude into other people's lives (especially her son, Raymond, and his wife, Debra). Marie panics if anyone asks for one of her recipes. She taught piano lessons and takes folk dancing lessons on Thursday evenings.

See also: Ally Barone, Debra Barone, Raymond Barone, Robert Barone.

384. Frank Burns, *M*A*S*H,* CBS, 1972–1977. Played by Larry Linville.

Major Frank Burns is a doctor with the 4077 M*A*S*H (Mobile Army Surgical Hospital) unit in Korea during the war. He shares a tent with Hawkeye Pierce and had the nickname "Ferret Face." Frank had a lucrative practice in Indiana before being drafted. Hawkeye claims that Frank became a doctor for the money ("He married money and is crazy about money"). Frank claims he toyed with the idea of becoming a doctor in high school then decided to do so when his mother asked him ("She's the guiding light in my life"; he keeps a picture of her in a silver frame by his bed).

Frank brags about his $35,000 home and two cars. He keeps in touch with his patients with his "What's Up Front Doc" letters so they will not forget him. Frank most misses his country club and 30-foot yacht. He doesn't miss his wife because of an affair he is having with Major Margaret Houlihan, the head nurse (although he fears his wife finding out). In high school Frank was president of the stamp club; in college he played the lead in a production of *Romeo and Juliet.* He likes his pork chops with extra fat and keeps abreast of the stock market with the brokerage house of Sanders, Landers and Flynn in New York City. Although Frank is a major he gets little respect from his subordinates, especially Hawkeye and his tent-mate, Trapper John McIntire (later B.J. Hunnicutt). Frank set his goal to expose Hawkeye for constantly defying military rules (Hawkeye would like to see Frank transferred to another base—"preferably an enemy base").

When Margaret dumped Frank for Major Donald Penobscott, Frank had a nervous breakdown and was transferred to a stateside hospital in Indiana. He also received a promotion to lieutenant colonel and returned to his wife Louise.

See also: Benjamin Franklin Pierce, B.J. Hunnicutt, Charles Winchester, III, Henry Blake, Margaret Houlihan, Radar O'Reilly, Sherman Potter, Trapper John McIntire.

385. Frank Fontana, *Murphy Brown*, CBS, 1988–1997. Played by Joe Regalbuto.

Frank Fontana is an investigative reporter for *F.Y.I.* ("For Your Information"), a CBS-TV, Washington, D.C.-based series. Frank was born in New York City. He is the son of Frank and Rose Fontana and was babied as a child. He had a dog named Cocoa and is a graduate of the Bishop Fallon High School for Boys. He attended the Columbia School of Journalism and first worked for the *New York Times*. He quit his job as a newspaper reporter and joined *F.Y.I.* in 1977. Frank won the 1991 Humboldt Award for his story, "A Death in Dade County" and wrote a 4¼ hour play called *Life Changed*. Frank has issue problems and has been in therapy "for 13 or 14 years" (he has lost track). Frank's favorite movie is *The Maltese Falcon* and he regrets seeing the film *Poltergeist*, as he now has to sleep with his closet door open. Frank follows the rules of broadcasting and will not compromise his integrity for the benefit of a story. He will work with what he has and make the best of it. Frank hosted the premiere of the network's *Overnight News* and no matter how many times he complains to them, *TV Guide* still lists his name as "Fred Fontana" in program listings.

See also: Corky Sherwood, Jim Dial, Miles Silverberg, Murphy Brown.

Frank Lambert *see* **Carol and Frank Lambert**

386. Frank Poncherello, *ChiPs*, NBC, 1977–1983. Played by Erik Estrada.

Francis Llewellyn Poncherello, called both Frank and Ponch, is a motorcycle officer with the California Highway Patrol (ChiPs). He was born in the barrio on March 16, 1949, and has two brothers (Martin and Robert) and a sister (Patricia). He wears badge number B600 (also given as 2140) and has the mobile codes 7-Mary-3, LA 15-Mary-2, and LA 15-Mary-6. His motorcycle license plate reads 16A95.

While Ponch is known for flashing his pearly white teeth, he is also fond of junk food, especially snack cakes. He drives a Pontiac Trans Am (plate 8003 IF) and lives in a mobile home (where he is not the tidiest housekeeper), before acquiring an actual apartment. Ponch is a sports enthusiast and has a black belt in karate.

See also: Jon Baker (his partner).

387. Frankie Colletti, *The Great Defender*, Fox, 1995. Played by Kelly Rutherford.

Francesca Colletti is a gorgeous Christian woman who prefers to be called by her nickname — "I'm a Frankie not a Francesca." She works as an investigator for Lou Frischetti, a Boston lawyer who is called "The Great Defender" (not so much for his work but by his TV ads).

Frankie, the daughter of a middle-class Italian-American family, was born in Boston. She grew up as a tomboy and joined all the sports teams at school. She was better than most boys but as she began to develop her figure she quickly became a young lady with other pursuits and her tomboyish ways quickly came to end. She is a graduate of Boston University with a degree in business management. Frankie worked for a year in her chosen field but quickly became disenchanted. It was dull and boring. She felt unfulfilled until she saw an ad on TV for "The Great Defender" and approached then budding lawyer Lou Frischetti for a job. Lou required an investigator — someone who would work cheap and hired Frankie.

Frankie knows she is an alluring woman and uses her assets to help Lou bring a case to a successful conclusion. Frankie is single and lives at 01342 Arlington Drive, Apartment 703.

See also: Lou Frischetti.

388. Franny Byrd, *The Byrds of Paradise*, ABC, 1994. Played by Jennifer Love Hewitt.

Frances Byrd, better known as Franny, is a 15-year-old girl who attends the Palmer School in Honomolu, Hawaii. She is the daughter of Sam Byrd, a college professor who now teaches at the school. Franny previously lived in New Haven, Connecticut, where she was happy and well adjusted. She became rebellious when her mother, Holly, was killed in an ATM cash machine robbery. Hoping to provide a better life for his family, Sam gave up his job as a university professor and moved to Hawaii.

Franny has a dog named Heidi and a tattoo of a falcon on her hip ("I paid $50 for it and I love my tattoo"). Although Franny is very pretty, she believes she is not as beautiful as other people see her. She has a negative attitude about everything and is having a difficult time overcoming the loss of her mother. Franny also believes that if weird things can happen, they will happen to her. She was plagued by a lingerie thief and busted for possession of drugs (after a loss of two bras and five pairs of panties, Franny was arrested for drug possession. It seems a police narcotics dog wandered onto the Byrd property and while in the house found drugs in Franny's lingerie laundry basket. "I just wanted to try it," she said, and promised her father she would never use it again). On the brighter side, Franny is a cheerleader for the Palmer School pep squad, where she used her talent as a dancer to add excitement to the cheers.

389. Frasier Crane, *Cheers* (NBC, 1984–1993); *Frasier* (NBC, 1993–2004). Played by Kelsey Grammer.

Profile from *Cheers*: Frasier Crane is a private practice psychiatrist who finds relief from the pressures of work by frequenting a bar called Cheers in Boston. He was born in Seattle, Washington, and claims to have degrees from Harvard and Oxford. He moved to Boston after graduating to begin his practice. He is married to Lilith Sternin (Bebe Neuwirth), a somber-looking woman who, according to Frasier "rules the roost in her bra and panties." They are the parents of a son (Frederick), who was born in the back of a cab.

Frasier collects first edition books and considers himself "the solver of all problems personal." He conducts traveling self-help seminars called "The Crane Train to Mental Well-Being" and charges $350 for the sessions. Charles Dickens is his favorite author; he has a dog named Pavlov and a spider collection.

Lilith is a psychiatrist and on call at Boston Memorial Hospital. She wrote a book called *Good Girls/Bad Boys* and has two favorite lab rats, Whitey and Whiskers.

Profile from *Frasier*: Following the closure of his favorite bar hangout, Cheers, in Boston (and his pending divorce from Lilith Sternin), Frasier returns to his home town of Seattle, Washington, to open a new practice and host *The Frasier Crane Show*, a daily (2:00 P.M. to 5:00 P.M.) call in advice program on KACL, 780 on the AM dial. He lives at the Elliott Bay Towers (Apartment 1901) with his father, Martin (a retired police detective; in *Cheers*, Frasier had mentioned his father as being deceased). He has a brother, Niles, and as children, they wrote a series of detective yarns called "The Crane Boys Mystery Stories"; they lived on Wallace Lane at the time.

Frasier attended the Brice Academy and in high school he accidentally joined the girl's soccer team when he signed up in the "F-list" (the "F"

stood for female, not freshman as he thought). He next attended Harvard University and majored in psychology (minored in music) and was a member of the crew team. Frasier attributes his becoming a psychiatrist to his mother, Hester. When he was eight years old, a school bully threw his book, *The Fountainhead*, under a bus. When he came home from school crying, his mother explained to him why children are mean. It was then, he says, that he became a student of humanity. He has an I.Q. of 129.

Frasier is the recipient of the Seattle Broadcaster's Lifetime Achievement Award and the Stephen R. Schaefer Lifetime Achievement Award (for his work at the station). He first ended his program with "Good Day and Good Mental Health"; it was later "Good Day Seattle and Good Mental Health." Frasier was also the host of *A.M. Seattle*, on TV when his radio program was bumped for a weekday series called *Car Chat*. A caricature of Frasier (which he calls "The Frasier Cranium") appears on the wall of his favorite eatery, Stefano's Restaurant; the Café Nervosa is his favorite coffee house and he drives a car with the license plate 330 WPT. He uses Bartok's classic "Concerto in C" as his radio series theme song. Frasier was also the spokesperson for Redwood Hot Tubs. He enjoys a low high fiber breakfast "so I can start the day off right."

Frasier's first love was his baby sitter, Ronnie Lawrence (who is now his father's romantic interest). He was first married to Nanette Goodsmith, a woman who works as a children's entertainer called "Nanny Gee." He was next married to the stern Lilith, who is the mother of his son, Frederick. He next met Charlotte, a matchmaker (owner of Charlotte's Web) and fell in love with her. The final episode ("Goodbye, Seattle"; May 13, 2004), finds Frasier supposedly heading to San Francisco for a new job in radio, but in actuality, going to Chicago to be with Charlotte.

See also: Martin Crane, Niles Crane.

390. Fred and Doris Ziffel, *Green Acres*, CBS, 1965–1971. Played by Hank Patterson (Fred); Fran Ryan, Barbara Pepper (Doris).

This entry also contains information on Arnold Ziffel, the pig Fred and Doris raised like their own son. Fred and Doris are farmers in the small town of Hooterville. While Fred is dressed as a typical farmer in overalls, it is his wife, Doris, who really wears the pants (she plants, cooks, feeds the animals, keeps house). Fred appears more like a supervisor and offers what he considers sound advice to anyone who asks him for an opinion. Fred and Doris were born in Hooterville and were not able to have children. They raised a pig as if it were their own son and named him Arnold.

Fred takes great pride in Arnold and is proud that he turned out so well (he is hoping he will become a veterinarian when he grows up). Arnold is quite intelligent and is respected by the citizens as Fred and Doris's son. Arnold is in third grade at Hooterville Elementary School. He can speak several languages (English, French and Japanese; heard in pig grunts, but placed in captions for viewers). He can write his name, plays practical jokes, can predict the weather with his tail and enjoys playing a game of cricket (he even has his own cricket bat). Arnold likes lime soda and enjoys tea and crumpets with his neighbor, Lisa Douglas.

Arnold has a job (delivering newspapers), plays the piano, and picks up his "parents" mail. Arnold is friends with everyone but becomes shy in front of beautiful women. His favorite TV show is *The CBS Evening News with Walter Cronkite*. He was also the star (as Columbo the dog) in the Hooterville Theater play "Who Killed Jacques Robin."

See also: Oliver and Lisa Douglas.

391. Fred and Ethel Mertz, *I Love Lucy*, CBS, 1951–1957. Played by William Frawley, Vivian Vance.

Fred Mertz and his wife, Ethel, are the owners of an apartment house at 623 East 68th Street in Manhattan; it is also the residence of their good friends, bandleader Ricky Ricardo and his wife, Lucy.

Fred Mertz and Ethel Potter were singers and dancers who worked in vaudeville. Fred worked in an act called Mertz and Kertz before he met Ethel (it is difficult to pinpoint when they married. They gave up performing in 1925 and it is assumed Fred and Ethel married. In another episode it is mentioned they have been married for 18 years in 1951, making their marriage in 1933; still another episode claims they have been married for 15 years in 1952, making 1927 their marriage year). Fred was born in Steubenville, Ohio; Ethel was born in Albuquerque, New Mexico, and was called "Little Ethel" by her Aunt Martha and Uncle Elmo. Ethel was also given three middle names: Louise, Mae and Roberta.

Fred is a cheapskate and loves money (parting with any is a traumatic experience for him; Ethel has become frugal over the years because of this). Ethel is easily upset (Fred just slips her a tranquilizer to calm her down) and has failed numerous times to get him to change his cheap ways. Fred is seeking a way to make money by investing in something (he had an idea "but is mad at Edison for coming up with the idea of the light bulb before him"). Ethel likes to eavesdrop and Fred feels the only way she can keep a secret is not to hear it. Fred sometimes works as Ricky's band manager when he goes on the road. Fred and Ethel have a dog (Butch) in one episode (but not again) and their phone number is Plaza 5-6098 (later Circle 2-7099). Fred and Ethel also attempted to run a diner called A Big Hunk of America.

See also: Lucy and Ricky Ricardo

392. Fred and Wilma Flintstone, *The Flintstones*, ABC, 1960–1966. Voiced by Alan Reed (Fred), Jean VanderPyl (Wilma).

Fred and Wilma Flintstone are a prehistoric modern family who live at 345 Stone Cave Road in the town of Bedrock in the year 1,000,040 B.C. (their address is also given as Cobblestone Lane). Fred and Wilma have been married for 16 years and are the parents of a daughter named Pebbles.

Fred works as a dino operator for the Slaterock Gravel Company (also seen as the Rockhead Quarry Construction Company, the Bedrock Quarry Gravel Company, the Bedrock Gravel Company, and the Rockhead and Quarry Cove Construction Company). Fred is also a member of the Royal Order of the Water Buffalo Lodge (originally the Loyal Order of Dinosaurs). He is also a member of the Bedrock Quarry baseball team and enjoys bowling at the Bedrock Bowling Alley.

Fred was a Boy Scout (Saber-Toothed Tiger Troop) and attended Rockville Center High School (he was a member of the football team and the baseball team, where he was called "Fireball Freddy"). Fred was born in Bedrock and his catch phrase is "Yabba Dabba Doo."

Wilma is a Capricorn (born in November) and "fixes the best roast dodo bird in Bedrock." Her maiden is Slaghoople and she worked as a waitress at the Honeyrock Hotel when she first met Fred, a bellboy at the same hotel. It was a love at first sight and they married shortly after. Wilma is a patient housewife and puts up with Fred and his endless antics because she truly loves him. Wilma held a job as a singer on *The Rockinspiel Happy Housewives Show* (for the Bedrock Radio and TV Company). She also became animated TV's first pregnant woman. She and Fred have a pet Snarkasaurus named Dino (who is purple with black spots on his back).

See also: Barney and Betty Rubble.

393. Fred Berkel, *Angel*, WB, 2001–2004. Played by Amy Acker.

Winifred Berkel, called Fred, is a beautiful woman who helps Angel, the vampire with a soul, battle demons. Fred is the daughter of Roger and Trish Berkel and was born on a small farm in the Midwest. She had a plush rabbit named Figenbaum and while she worked on the farm, she was extremely bright and showed an uncanny interest in science. Fred excelled in school and sought to better her education by attending the University of California in Los Angeles (where she majored in physics). One day, while doing research for a school project, Fred removed an old book from the library shelf and was pulled through a time portal and propelled to a world called Pylea. Here, humans were treated as slaves and to survive, Fred became a fugitive. She stole food and lived in a cave (she was rescued five years later when Angel was transported to Pylea. Fred found excitement with Angel and became part of his team. Her experiences in Pylea have given her the power to see and battle demons).

Life again changes for Fred when she finds a sarcophagus and opens it. A mysterious gas is released and Fred is overcome by Illyria, the spirit of an ancient demon from a place called the Deep Well. Illyria has re-emerged to reclaim her army and rule the world. But her world has since been destroyed and she is now without a purpose and must learn to accept a new life. Illyria retains Fred's appearance and memories, but in actuality, she is pure evil.

See also: Angel, Spike.

394. Fred Sanford, *Sanford and Son,* NBC, 1972–1977. Played by Redd Foxx.

Sanford and Son Salvage is considered to be a junkyard empire by its owner, Fred G. Sanford, a 65-year-old widower who refuses to retire. He is the father of Lamont and believes he is living in the lap of luxury (the junkyard is located at 9114 South Central in Los Angeles).

Fred was born in Georgia in 1917 and is the son of a very poor family (they slept five to a room). Fred attended the Dickinson Elementary School but had to drop out in eighth grade to help support his family. Fred showed great promise as a singer and dancer while growing up. He turned that talent into a career and performed in vaudeville; he later teamed with a woman named Juanita. Fred eventually quit show business when he met the woman of his dreams, Elizabeth, and established his junkyard. Fred lost Elizabeth in 1959 and raised Lamont (born in 1938) as best he could on his own.

Fred is an ornery and cantankerous and set in his ways. He is distrustful of people and when he doesn't get his way, he feigns a heart attack (he puts his hand on his heart, looks up to Heaven and says: "I'm coming Elizabeth; this is it, the big one"; he had his 15th major heart attack in the first episode). Fred always develops a sudden case of "arth-i-ritis" when there is work to be done. When someone irritates him, Fred makes a fist and responds with "How would you like one across your lips?"

Fred is comfortable where he is and enjoys relaxing with a glass of his homemade "Ripple" (an alcoholic beverage). Fred needs to wear glasses but refuses to see an eye doctor. He has a desk drawer filled with pairs of discarded eyeglasses that he rummages through when he needs to read something.

Fred's romantic interest is Donna Harris, a woman who is much younger than Fred. In the 1980–81 series update, *Sanford,* Fred is seen dating Evelyn Lewis, a wealthy woman who didn't mind dating beneath her social scale (Fred's address was changed to 4707 South Central in Watts).

See also: Lamont Sanford.

395. Freddie Washington, *Welcome Back, Kotter,* ABC, 1975–1979. Played by Lawrence-Hilton Jacobs.

Frederick Washington, called Freddie, is a Sweathog, a special education student at James Buchanan High School in Bensonhurst, Brooklyn, New York. Freddie likes to play the bass guitar but says his nickname of "Boom Boom" doesn't come from the instrument's deep sounds, "but because I like Boom Boom."

Freddie is a below average student (as are all the Sweathogs) and would like to improve himself and become an architect (he dreams of designing the world's largest building, "Boom Boom Towers"). Freddie was born in Brooklyn and was an obedient child but from the beginning he had a difficult time in school. He had an invisible duck named Ralph (who would sit on his shoulder) and considers himself a ladies' man. Freddie is a member of the school's varsity basketball team (jersey 1) and his catch phrase is "Hi There." He was also the host of *Hi There,* a radio talk show on station WBAD.

See also: Arnold Horshack, Juan Epstein, Gabe and Julie Kotter, Vinnie Barbarino.

396. Freddie Wilson, *My Little Margie,* CBS, 1952–1953; NBC, 1953–1955. Played by Don Hayden.

Frederick Wilson, called Freddie, is both fortunate and unfortunate. He has a gorgeous girlfriend (Margie Albright) but is unmotivated and disliked by Margie's father, Vern (who wishes Margie would show more taste in boy friends).

Margie insists "There is nothing wrong with Freddie." "Goof ball" and "Droop" are two terms used to describe Freddie. He seems permanently suited for unemployment. He works at various jobs and is the only person Vern knows "who got fired from five different jobs in one week." It is also said "that Freddie is too lazy to work. One night he only dreamed he was working and he was pooped for the next two days." Margie believes Freddie is smart ("He's won several contests working crossword puzzles") and ambitious (he did hold two jobs for longer than a day: night watch man, of which he says "Not one night was stolen when I was watching them"; and as a store window mattress demonstrator doing what Freddie does best — sleep — at Farley's Furniture Store).

Freddie tries, but he just can't seem to find his place in life. He tried enlisting in the army, but was rejected by his draft board (he was sent home with a note pinned to his shirt saying "If this is dead we don't want it. If this is alive, we don't believe it").

Freddie and Margie have been sweethearts since they were three years old. It was at this time that Margie first learned about men — "Freddie pointed one out to me." When Freddie does manage to find a job, Margie misses him (as they would spend the afternoon together). Freddie enjoys the leftovers he finds in Margie's refrigerator and believes he can one day find a job, get rich and make Margie (and Vern) happy. He wrote a play called *Girl Against the World* ("The heartwarming story of Gwendolyn Lovequist , a typical American girl with the odds stacked up against her") and enjoys watching *Captain Stratosphere* on TV.

See also: Margie Albright, Vern Albright.

397. Gabe and Julie Kotter, *Welcome Back, Kotter,* ABC, 1975–1979. Played by Gabe Kaplan, Marcia Strassman.

Gabriel Kotter, called Gabe, is a special education teacher at James Buchanan High School in Bensonhurst, Brooklyn, New York. He is married to Julie Hanson and they live in a small apartment (3C) at 711 East Ocean Parkway; later, after the birth of their twin daughters (Rachel and Robin), they move into a spacious apartment (409) at 1962 Linden Boulevard.

Gabe was born in Brooklyn in a neighborhood "that was so tough that gangs didn't carry guns, they inserted the bullets manually." While not as dangerous as some of those gang members, Gabe

was influenced by their actions and became a radical student at James Buchanan High School. He was assigned to a special education class and coined the term "Sweathogs" to describe such students. Gabe was on the school's basketball team and was blamed for the cafeteria riots. After graduating, Gabe found a whole new outlook on life. He wanted to help students who were much like he was and set out to get his teaching degree. Ten years later he returned to his alma mater and became a special remedial academics teacher to a new breed of incorrigible Sweathogs: Vinnie, Juan, Freddie and Arnold. Gabe is looking for a meaningful relationship between himself and his students. His classes are held in Room 11 and he is also the Sweathogs homeroom teacher. Gabe believes the antics of Vinnie, Juan, Freddie and Arnold are like those of old time movie comics, the Marx Brothers (Groucho, Harpo, Chico and Gummo); "Only I have four of my own — Wacko, Stupo, Jerko and Dumbo."

Julie was born in Nebraska and is famous for her tuna casserole (which Gabe hates and says, "it will deter dinner guests from returning." Her secret ingredient is either prunes or coffee beans. While Gabe constantly makes fun of Julie's casserole, Julie constantly pokes fun as his endless array of relatives). Julie works as a volunteer at the Free Clinic and makes $5 an hour for every 1,000 envelopes she stuffs with polyester fabric samples; she later works as the school secretary to the principal, Michael Woodman. When Julie doesn't have enough money to buy Gabe a birthday present, she gives him a card that reads, "I owe you one giant favor."

Gabe is the faculty advisor for the school newspaper, the *Buchanan Bugle*. He has a pressed flower in his high school yearbook that he bought for his prom date "but she never showed up." About Julie he says "If it wasn't for you, I would have married somebody else." Julie and Gabe appear at the opening and closing of each episode so Gabe can relate an often humorous tale about one of his many relatives ("Julie, did I tell you about...").

See also: Arnold Horshack, Freddie Washington, Juan Epstein, Vinnie Barbarino.

398. Gabriel Bird, *Gabriel's Fire,* ABC, 1990–1991. Played by James Earl Jones.

Gabriel Bird is a private investigator who works as a legman for Victoria Heller (Laila Robins), a lawyer for the firm of Heller and Klein. Gabe, as he is called, was born in Chicago in 1939. He is the son of Albert and Lillie Bird and grew up in a poor section around Emerald Street. Gabe's early life was tainted by the crime and corruption that surrounded him. But instead of becoming a victim Gabe had a plan to become a cop and take back the streets. He was side tracked, however, when he was drafted for service in the Korean War (he served with the 24th Infantry). He showed unusual bravery on the battlefield and was decorated four times. He was discharged with honors and returned to Chicago and enrolled in junior college. In 1959 he enrolled in the Chicago Police Academy and was one of the few African-Americans to graduate top in his class. He was assigned to patrol a beat in his old neighborhood and he was determined to advance the cause of the black man within the system. His neighborhood felt safe and people looked up to him. He married a girl named Ellie and they had a daughter (Celene). In 1969 Gabe became the only black man on the state's new Attorney Prosecuting Team.

Things were looking up for Gabe. However, on December 21, 1969, Gabe's unit raided an apartment on Hampton Street, an address believed to be the armed headquarters of the Black Liberation Army. It was a witch-hunt but Gabe didn't know it. Inside the apartment was the family of John C. Elner. Elner and his two brothers were killed. Just as Gabe's partner was about to kill a woman and her child, Gabe killed him. Gabe was considered a Black Liberation supporter and disowned by the department. He was falsely convicted of murder one; but because of his outstanding war record he was not sentenced to death (he was given life imprisonment instead). Two years into his sentence Ellie divorced him. Gabe's case number is 2266 and D-72721 is his prison number. After serving 7,271 days Gabe is released when Victoria Heller becomes interested in his case and clears him. He accepts Victoria's offer to become her investigator. Two hot dogs with everything on them is the first thing Gabe has when he is released.

Josephine Austin (Madge Sinclair) owns a restaurant called Empress Josephine's Soul Food Kitchen on Emerald Street. Gabe was the cop on the beat when Josephine's husband died. He came by with candy for the kids and groceries when they needed them. He took the kids to the park and became a substitute father to them. Gabe returns to Emerald Street. When Josephine sees "a ghost from her past," she repays a favor she never forgot by offering Gabe free room and board in the attic above the restaurant.

Gabe goes to extremes to catch a criminal and keeps a diary of everything he does. He says, "It's a big world out there and I'm having a great time getting to know it again." Victoria is a tough,

dedicated attorney who will fight for any cause she believes in. Her offices are located at 14301 North LaSalle Street; 555-4748 is her phone number and her license plate reads K87 463.

In the spinoff series, *Pros and Cons* (ABC, 1991–1992), Gabe moves to Los Angeles and opens his own agency, Gabriel Bird Investigations, when Victoria leaves her practice to become a judge. He later teams with Mitch O'Hannon (Richard Crenna), a reckless private eye in a firm they call Bird and O'Hannon, Private Investigators (at 1122 North Plaza; 555-6464 is their phone number). Gabe and Josephine also marry and set up housekeeping at 808 Magnolia Drive. She becomes the manager of a restaurant called the Angel City Grill. Mitch lives in an apartment (705) at 455 Lane Street. He served in Korea with the 40th Sunburst Unit.

399. Gabrielle, *Xena: Warrior Princess*, Syn., 1995–2001. Played by Renee O'Connor.

Gabrielle, called "that irritating little blonde who travels with Xena," is an adventurous but peace-loving young woman who attaches herself to Xena, the Warrior Princess, to become her friend and traveling companion. Like Xena, Gabrielle did not exist in ancient Greek or Roman mythology. Gabrielle was born in the Greek village of Potidaea. It was when Xena saved Potidaea from the warlord Draco that Gabrielle became fascinated by her. Gabrielle yearned for excitement and adventure and with her gift of gab, talked Xena into letting her tag along.

Gabrielle is sweet and innocent. She solved conflicts with words and stories. It is with her stories that Gabrielle found her true calling as a bard. She kept records called "The Xena Scrolls" that detailed her and her mentor's adventures. She had one produced in the style of a Broadway called "Gabrielle and Xena: A Message of Peace." Gabrielle later attended the Academy for Performing Bards in Athens. She later wrote a play called "Fallen Angel" and was called "The Visionary Voice of Athens." Gabrielle also became one of the Followers of Eli (a religious profit who professed love). Daisies are Gabrielle's favorite flower and she loves to cook (she treasures her frying pan). Gabrielle's life changed somewhat when she saved the life of Ephiny, the Amazon queen. An Amazon is a warrior of Ares, the God of War. To repay Gabrielle for saving her life, Ephiny bestows the title of Amazon Princess and teaches her how to fight (something she was previously reluctant to learn from Xena, but now found it necessary for her and Xena's survival).

See also: Xena.

400. Gabrielle Solis, *Desperate Housewives*, ABC, 2004. Played by Eva Longoria.

Gabrielle Solis is a beautiful, world-famous ex-model who gave up her life of glamour for a rich husband (Carlos) and a big house. What she didn't count on was a life on Wisteria Lane, a perfect neighborhood in a seemingly perfect city (Fairview).

Gabrielle lives at 4349 Wisteria Lane and finds life boring. As a model Gabrielle had a taste for rich food and rich men. She was, as she admits, "a slut" and thought her old ways would vanish when she married Carlos. They didn't. Being unfaithful excites Gabrielle and makes life on Wisteria Lane bearable. Though living in an elegant house and being showered with expensive gifts by Carlos, she risks it all to have what she calls "fun" (she won't divorce Carlos and enjoys the thrill of having affairs behind his back. She is prepared to pack it up and leave should he discover her secret life). "To sleep like a baby" Gabrielle needs to do something good. She constantly worries that Carlos will discover her extramarital affairs and has difficulty sleeping. She discovered that by involving herself with charity work she could find peace of mind for a good night's sleep.

See also: Bree Van DeKamp, Edie Britt, Lynette Scavo, Susan Mayer.

401. Gaby Stepjak, *Someone Like Me*, NBC, 1994. Played by Gaby Hoffman.

Twelve-year-old Gabrielle Stepjak, called Gaby, is the daughter of Jean and Steven Stepjak. She was born in Parkwood, St. Louis, and lives at 1402 Manton Drive with her sister (Samantha) and brother (Evan).

Gaby is a pretty bundle of energy and attends the Walter Mondale Middle School. She is a good student and anxious to grow up, date boys, but most of all "to get breasts as great" as Samantha. Gaby practices kissing on her hand and is a member of the swim team at the local hangout, the Park Recreation Center.

Gaby feels the worst punishment she can get is no phone privileges ("it's barbaric"). When she was younger, Gaby cut the hair off her Barbie dolls (thinking it would grow back). When she does something wrong, her mother gives her "the anybody can become President speech." Gaby is allowed to wear minimal makeup, but she "over doses" on bubblegum-flavored lip-gloss. Gaby hasn't made a decision about her future yet ("I'm only in the sixth grade") but has set her future goal "to become beautiful."

See also: Samantha Stepjak.

402. Garrett Macy, *Crossing Jordan*, NBC, 2001 (current). Played by Miguel Ferrer.

Dr. Garrett Macy is the Chief Medical Examiner for the Commonwealth of Massachusetts, Office of the Medical Examiner. Garrett runs the center on a shrinking shoestring budget and says "This place is going to hell and it's about to get crazier due to budget cuts."

Garrett was born in Massachusetts. He became interested in crime solving at an early age and felt forensics was the way to go. He is divorced (from Maggie) and the father of a rebellious teenage girl (Abby). Garrett's job guarantees him several things: worries, ulcers, high blood pressure and insomnia (he keeps a bottle of Pepto Bismol in his desk drawer for the indigestion that also goes along with the job when it comes to dealing with office matters).

Garrett has a problem dealing with people (he tends to suppress his anger) and is seeing a psychiatrist in an attempt to become more forceful (he has a dog hand puppet "that my shrink gave to me to say things to that I can't say to other people"). Garrett collects old records (mostly jazz and blues from the 1920s and '30s) and says "I'm more than a medical examiner, I'm an interesting guy." He relaxes by writing poetry and playing jazz drums. As a kid he was a big comic book collector, something he wishes he kept up because he once found it enjoyable (and joy is something Garrett rarely experiences any more).

See also: Jordan Cavanaugh.

403. Gary Hobson, *Early Edition*, CBS, 1996–2000. Played by Kyle Chandler.

Gary Hobson is a man who reads tomorrow's newspaper today. He is not sure why it happens or why he was chosen. He only knows that he was selected by higher powers to prevent tragedies by acting on them today and changing the lives of people who would otherwise face a horrible fate and become tomorrow's headline.

Gary was born in Hickory, Indiana, in 1965 and is the son of Lois and Barney Hobson. In Chicago at this same time, a mysterious man named Lucius Snow was a linotype setter at a paper called the *Sun Times*. Lucius was not an ordinary typesetter. He set type for tomorrow's stories today. In 1976 Gary was a finalist in the *Sun Times* Bicentennial Essay Contest. Gary and his family were flown to Chicago and Gary was supposed to die that day when he was hit by a truck. But just as the events predicted in the newspaper were about to unfold, Lucius pulled Gary from the approaching truck and saved his life. The newspaper headline disappeared — as did Lucius.

Fate had determined that Gary possessed the qualities to become the paper's future champion.

Gary eventually married and became a stockbroker. Life was not all roses. His marriage was breaking up and he lost his job. He used what savings he had to move into a hotel. One day at 6:30 in the morning he heard a cat meowing at his front door. He opened the door to find the cat and tomorrow's edition of the *Sun Times* (it took him a half a day to figure out what he had and what he had to do. Gary knows he is successful when the newspaper headline automatically changes).

Gary has to constantly lie to people to explain his actions (suddenly leaving to be someplace). Although Gary has advanced knowledge of the stock market reports, lottery results and horse racing results, he does not use them for profit. Gary later becomes the owner of McGinty's Bar (where he also lives) on Illinois and Franklin streets. Through research Gary discovered that the cat who appears with the paper appears to be the same cat that is pictured with Lucius in archival photographs. Gary believes the cat possesses Lucius's spirit but is still not sure why Lucius chose him.

404. Gayle Roberts, *Good Sports*, CBS, 1991. Played by Farrah Fawcett.

Gayle Roberts is the co-host (with Bobby Tannen) of *Sports Central*, an information program on the Rappaport Broadcasting System ASCN (All Sports Cable Network). She also hosts *Sports Chat* (interviews) and *Sports Brief* (updates).

Gayle is 40 years old and lives in an apartment at the Landmark Building in Los Angeles. She was born in California and is called "The Doris Day of the Sports World" for her wholesome image and perky outlook on life. Her birth name, however, is Gayle Gordon (she changed her last name to Roberts to avoid confusion with Gale Gordon, Lucille Ball's longtime sidekick, Mr. Mooney; for example, on *Here's Lucy*).

Gayle was a very beautiful baby who grew up to be a very beautiful woman. She was also a sports fanatic and wanted to become a sportscaster but it was basically a male only field at the time. With the advantage of her stunning good looks, Gayle turned her attention to modeling. She appeared on the covers of many fashion magazines but her biggest thrill came when she appeared on the cover of *Sports Illustrated*. The cover so impressed station owner R.J. Rappaport that he hired Gayle as the network's first female sportscaster. She was an instant hit with the viewing audience.

Gayle does charity work for the Los Angeles Mission and has a pet goldfish named Frankie. "Fog" by Carl Sandburg is her favorite poem by her favorite poet. Gayle is allergic to goat cheese, can't eat baby back ribs and "I hate the word bitch."

See also: Bobby Tannen.

405. Geordi La Forge, *Star Trek: The Next Generation*, Syn., 1987–1994. Played by LeVar Burton.

Geordi La Forge is the chief engineer under Jean-Luc Picard, captain of the Starfleet space ship *Enterprise NCC-1701E*. Geordi was born in the African Confederation on Earth on February 16, 2335. He is the son of Commander Edward M. La Forge and Captain Silva La Forge. Geordi is unique among Starfleet officers as he is blind (from birth) but able to "see" by a device called a *Visor* (attached at the temple through implants that are connected directly to the brain. By concentrating, Geordi is able to see images). As cybernetic technology progressed, Geordi was outfitted with ocular implants that employ complex sensors and filters that simulate a real eye.

Geordi attended Starfleet Academy (2353–57) and was first assigned as an ensign aboard the U.S.S. *Victory*. A year later (2364), he was promoted to lieutenant junior grade and assigned to *Enterprise* under Captain Picard. While totally dedicated and capable of performing his job, Geordi is insecure in his private life, especially about dating and female relationships. He enjoys playing poker with his fellow officers and his hobbies include building scale models of old sailing ships, swimming, chess, and skin diving. He also speaks a number of languages and enjoys iced coffee and pasta dishes.

See also: Beverly Crusher, Data, Deanna Troi, Jean-Luc Picard, Natasha Yar, William Riker.

406. George and Angie Lopez, *The George Lopez Show*, ABC, 2002 (current). Played by George Lopez, Constance Marie.

George Lopez is a Mexican-American who was the first one in his family to graduate from high school. His upbringing was difficult. His mother, Benita, was reckless. She smoked, drank, cursed, and is not sure who is the father of George (George is the result of an affair she had. She believes George's father is a man named Manny). During his high school years, George worked as often as he could as a waiter at Carrello's, a local fast food burrito store. After graduating, George found employment as an assembly line worker for Powers and Sons Aviation in Los Angeles. Although he was good at his job, he was treated a bit unfairly (for the first five years he was called "Senor Pumpkin Head" by his boss). Twelve years later, George would become the company's manager (the company, which can't make parts as good as Boeing, is known for making the best knockoffs. It is also called Power Brothers Aviation).

Two years after acquiring the assembly line job, George married Angela "Angie" Palmero and purchased a home at 3128 Rose Street near Alan Avenue. There, they became the parents of Carmen and Max. They also have a dog named Mr. Needles (diabetic; needs insulin shots).

Angie, a Cuban-American, is the daughter of Vic and Melina Palmero. She is a sales representative for LaMarie Cosmetics and loves gardening, charity work and helping out with any cause she can find. Angie blames George's mother for everything that is wrong with George. Angie wears a size 34B bra and does volunteer work at the Allendale High School Library. She is more patient in dealing with the kids than George (who flies off the handle when they do something wrong). When LaMarie Cosmetics folds and Angie loses her job she uses her ability for detail and organization to become a wedding planner.

George enjoys a beer at Thirsty's Bar and drives a 4X4 with the license plate 4QS W102. His favorite dinner is lasagna and he practices his golf swing to relax when something bothers him. George was also honored with the Rising Star Award from the Minority Businessman's Association.

See also: Carmen Lopez.

407. George and Dorothy Baxter, *Hazel*, NBC, 1961–1965. Played by Don DeFore, Whitney Blake.

George Baxter is an attorney with the firm of Butterworth, Hatch, Noll and Baxter in an unspecified Eastern city. He is married to Dorothy and they are the parents of Harold. Caring for them is their live-in maid, Hazel Burke. They reside in a comfortable home at 123 Marshall Road; Klondike 5-8372 (later 555-8372) is their phone number.

George is a graduate of Dartmouth and began practicing law in 1949. He is a member of the board of regents of the City University Law School and each year delivers the Oliver Wendell Holmes Memorial Lectures. He is also the private council for the city's Symphony Association. George enjoys a good cup of coffee, Hazel's "peachy keen pecan brownies" and reading the *Daily Chronicle*, the city's newspaper.

Dorothy has been married to George since 1950. She is a freelance interior decorator (no business name given) and is a member of the I.D.S. (Interior Decorator's Society). She is also a member of the local neighborhood Women's Club. Dorothy is an attractive woman who dresses rather conservatively (keeping in style with her husband's line of work and the clients he has to impress). She buys her dresses at Montique's Boutique and her lingerie (she wears a size eight negligee) at Blackstone's Department Store.

George has a tendency to gain a little weight and is constantly nagged by Hazel to stay on his diet. George also finds it a mistake to tell Hazel anything about his job as Hazel will butt in and try to help George ("It's remarkable," George says, "Two years of pre-law training, four years of law school and 12 years of successful practice and I still haven't learned to keep my mouth shut around Hazel").

See also: Hazel Burke.

408. George and Katherine Papadopolis, *Webster*, ABC, 1983–1987; Syn., 1987–1988. Played by Alex Karras, Susan Clark.

George and Katherine Papadopolis are a married couple who live in Apartment 14B at 534 Steiner Boulevard in Chicago; 555-8775 is their phone number. George and Katherine are also the guardians of Webster Long, the son of George's late friend and wife (see Webster Long for information).

George is a 41-year-old former pro football player who works as a sportscaster for WBJX-TV, Channel 6 (he hosts *Papadopolis on Sports*). George wore jersey 71 and tried to make a comeback via the Warriors football team but was found to be too old to play again.

George was born in Chicago and as a kid attended the Tumbleweed Ranch in Arizona (he stayed in bunkhouse 7). George loves to wear white socks with black shoes and enjoys chili cheese dogs at Sloppy Eddie's and a pizza at Angelo's Pizzeria. George calls Webster "Web" and Katherine "Jelly Bean" (she calls George "Cuddle Bunny"). When George gets upset he sings songs from *Carmen*.

Katherine Calder-Young met and fell in love with George during an ocean voyage. She is 37 years old and the daughter of a wealthy family (as a child she had a butler named Chives). She also had two dogs (Derek and Farnsworth) and a horse she called Binky ("His real name was Mortimer, but we called him Binky"). Katherine first worked as a consumer advocate for the mayor of Chicago. She quit the job to enter the University of Chicago and pursue her dream of becoming a child psychologist.

See also: Webster Long.

409. George and Louise Jefferson, *The Jeffersons*, CBS, 1975–1985. Played by Sherman Hemsley, Isabel Sanford.

George and Louise Jefferson are an argumentative married couple who live in a luxurious high rise apartment (12D) in Manhattan. They are the parents of a son (Lionel) and previously lived on Hauser Street in Queens, New York (the neighbors of Archie and Edith Bunker from *All in the Family*, from which *The Jeffersons* is a spinoff).

George is not only wealthy, but he is a snob as well. He is the owner of the successful Jefferson Cleaners (stores in Manhattan, the Bronx, Brooklyn, Harlem and Queens) and feels it is his right to be who he is after the difficult life he has lived. George was born in Georgia and Christmas was the worst time for him. His family was very poor and his parents sacrificed to make one day of the year special for him. The family moved to Harlem when George was a child and he lived in Apartment 5C at 984 West 125th Street. George was a good student in school and did manage to graduate. He served a hitch in the Navy on an aircraft carrier (where he was assigned to the galley as a cook). He has type O blood and is always ready for an argument. He is also thought of as cheap. George mentioned that he was 12 years old when he developed his first crush on a girl named Paula Vincent.

George has been married to Louise Mills for 25 years and, according to George, the reason why the marriage lasts is "because I put up with all her faults." Louise is actually the one who puts up with all of George's nonsense. She is practical and understanding and learning to avoid arguments with George is why the marriage has lasted so long. When first married (and before George started his business) they lived on 13th Street and Amsterdam Avenue in Manhattan. Louise, called "Weezie" and Weez" by George, is den mother to the Robbins, a Girl Scout troop. She also works as a staff member at the Neighborhood Help Center.

410. George and Marsha Owens, *Mr. Belvedere*, ABC, 1985–1990. Played by Bob Uecker, Ilene Graff.

George and Marsha Owens are a happily married couple who reside at 200 Spring Valley Road in Beaver Falls, Pittsburgh. They are the parents of Heather, Kevin and Wesley, and are cared for by Mr. Belvedere, a British butler.

George was born in Cleveland and is a graduate of Cleveland High School. He was not exactly the best kid in the world and would skip school to play pinball at the arcade on First Avenue, stay out until midnight, then sneak into his room. George was a big sports fan and turned his love of the game into his career. He was originally the host of *Sports Page* (later *Sports Rap*), a radio program on WBK-AM. He is later the sports anchor of WBN-TV, Channel 8's *Metro News* and writer of the "Sports Beat" column for the Pittsburgh *Bulletin*. George's favorite dinner is meatloaf, potato logs and creamed corn; pork rinds and Spam dip are his favorite snacks. Shopping at Lumber Rama is his favorite pastime. George has a fear of flying and to overcome it he closes his eyes and pretends he is on a bus.

Marsha was born in Pittsburgh and has a law degree from the University of Pittsburgh (she spent $30,000 on tuition and ranked 76 out of 278 students). She joined the firm of Dawson, Metcalfe and Bach in 1987 but quit after one year to become an attorney for the Legal Hut. Marsha had dreamed of helping the underdog. When she couldn't find it at the Legal Hut, she quit and became Babs, a waitress at the Beaver Falls Diner.

Marsha's maiden name was given as both Cameron and McClellan. Her favorite dinner is lobster thermadore and she has a never-seen Porsche she calls Wolfgang. George and Marsha's favorite restaurant is McSwarley's. Their wedding date is mentioned as both September 2, 1967, and September 17, 1967 (later in 1968). They honeymooned at the Altoona Motor Lodge and stayed in room14.

See also: Heather Owens (for information on Heather, Kevin and Wesley Owens), Lynn Belvedere.

411. George and Nancy Henderson, *Harry and the Hendersons*, Syn., 1991–1993. Played by Bruce Davison, Molly Cheek.

George Henderson is a marketing executive for the People's Sporting Goods Store in Seattle, Washington. He is married to Nancy and is the father of two children, Sarah and Ernie. They live at 410 Forest Drive and have a permanent houseguest — a legendary Big Foot (called Harry) who became a part of their family after he was struck by George's van on Interstate 5.

George and Nancy were born in Seattle. As a child George had a dream to travel to Hollywood and meet his idol, Annette Funicello, and sing with her on TV's *The Mickey Mouse Club*. George is a graduate of Seattle State University and later becomes the publisher of a magazine he calls *A Better Life*. When George gave Nancy her engagement ring (June 26, 1972), he wrapped it in a piece of paper with a note saying "Dear Nancy, will you murry me" (*murry* was a typo).

Nancy Gwen Douglas has been married to George for 19 years. She works for the Student Council Exchange of Seattle and has more control over the children and Harry (George tends to be a bit laid back trying to deal with and solve their problems). As a kid, Nancy had a pet frog (Slimey) and played the triangle in her high school marching band. She claims that the most risqué thing she ever did "was not to wear a bra between 1972 and 1975." She was later arrested (civil disobedience) for protesting without clothes on a nude beach. When Nancy gets upset, she eats a half-gallon of Breyer's Rocky Road ice cream.

See also: Sarah and Ernie Henderson.

412. George Challenger, *The Lost World*, Syn., 1998–2002. Played by Peter McCauley.

The time is 1920. George Edward Challenger is a respected British professor of anthropology who possesses a journal and believes a lost world of unknown civilizations and prehistoric animals exists within our own world. George stumbled upon a dying explorer who claimed to have seen prehistoric creatures and presented him with his journal. Through an arrangement with the Royal Zoological Society, an expedition was arranged and George, along with fellow explorers John Roxton, Marguerite Krux and Ned Malone, become marooned on a plateau after they use a hot air balloon to escape hostile natives. It is here that they befriend Veronica Layton, a young woman stranded on the plateau, who allows them to live in her tree house.

George is determined to find a dinosaur egg and bring it back to England with him. Unfortunately, the secret of the way off the plateau is unknown to him and his fellow explorers. George has a habit of talking to himself while working or exploring and collects insects for his research (he has what he believes is a beetle and calls it Arthur). George's knowledge of science enables him to make life comfortable and safe. He has built a windmill to provide power; an electric fence for protection; gunpowder for their bullets; and rubber for various uses. The series ended before the secret of the way off the plateau was found.

See also: Finn, John Roxton, Ned Malone, Marguerite Krux, Veronica Layton.

413. George Costanza, *Seinfeld*, NBC, 1990–1998. Played by Jason Alexander.

George Costanza considers himself "a short, fat, bald man who lives with his parents" (although he later has his own apartment, 609, on 86th Street in Manhattan). George is the son of Frank and Estelle Costanza and was born in Queens, New York (where he lived at 1344 Queens Boulevard). George's dream job is to be an architect. Although he uses the alias Art Van Delay, architect, to impress people, his dream never happened. He first worked as a real estate broker for Rick Bar Properties (he quit when the boss refused to let him use his private bathroom. George has an obsession with quality bathrooms). He next became a proofreader for Pendant Publishing (fired for having sex on his desk with the cleaning lady). George's third job was assistant to the traveling secretary for the New York Yankees (fired when he pretended to be a hen supervisor for Tyler Chicken to impress a girl). Pretending to be handicapped ("bum leg") cost George his fourth job, executive at Play Now, a playground supply company. His final series job was for Krueger Industrial Sanding, a company that sands and smoothes anything.

George is best friends with Jerry Seinfeld, Elaine Benes and Cosmo Kramer. George and Jerry were childhood friends and attended Camp Hotchapee together; they are also graduates of Edward R. Murrow Jr. High School, J.F.K. High School and Queens College. They attempted to write a TV series based on Jerry's life as a comedian called "Jerry" ("a show about nothing"); a pilot was produced by NBC. It was at this time that George met and fell in love with NBC executive Susan Ross (Heidi Swedelberg). They planned to be married but miserly George bought cheap wedding invitations from Melody Stationary that contained poison envelope glue that killed Susan. To remember Susan, her parents set up the Susan Ross Foundation with George as a senior board member assigned to distribute money to worthy causes.

George is an expert on chocolate candy bars, especially his favorite, the Twix Bar. His ATM code is Bosco (after his favorite chocolate drink) and he is a member of the Champagne Video Store. George frequents Monk's Café and in high school he did accomplish something — he scored 860,000 points on the video game Frogger at Mario's Pizza Parlor. George drives a 1976 Chevy Impala with the license plate QAG 826 and if he were an adult film star, he would choose the name Buck Naked.

See also: Cosmo Kramer, Elaine Benes, Jerry Seinfeld.

414. George Utley, *Newhart*, CBS, 1982–1990. Played by Tom Poston.

George Utley is a man of few words. He works as the handyman for Dick and Joanna Loudon, the owners of the Stratford Inn in River City, Vermont. George was born in Vermont and feels he is capable of repairing anything (his most prized possession is "Old Blue," a hammer handed down to him by his father). He is an avid birdwatcher and finds Johnny Kaye Lake to be a prime bird spotting location.

George is a member of the Beaver Lodge and looks forward to the annual Memorial Day Beaver Bash (where the featured meal is a spaghetti and tomato sauce sit-down dinner). George's father passed on to him his knack for fixing things. George put all that knowledge into a board game he created called "Handyman: The Feel Good Game." As a child George's favorite radio show was *The Goldbergs*; on TV he enjoys *Barnaby Jones* and the mythical *It's Always Moisha* (a comedy starring Don Rickles). For good luck, George keeps a penny in his shoe or sock.

See also: Dick and Joanna Loudon, Larry, Darryl and Darryl, Stephanie Vanderkellen.

415. Georgie Lahti, *Hearts Afire*, CBS, 1992–1993. Played by Markie Post.

Georgia Anne Lahti, called Georgie, is a liberal feminist who works as the speechwriter for Strobe Smithers, a somewhat senile, conservative Southern Senator.

Georgie was born in Chicago. Her mother died shortly after her birth; her father, George, was a lawyer; their housekeeper, Miss Lula, actually raised Georgie as George's work kept him absent from most of his daughter's life. As a kid Georgie had a snow cone stand, won a Davy Crockett Bravery Award, and wanted to wear her Halloween costume (a devil) to school every day. When she took her SAT test, she was singled out for writing the longest answers ever given on a multiple choice test ("I wasn't satisfied with E — none of the above").

Georgie has a degree in journalism and began her career as a question writer on the TV game show *Jeopardy* (she created the category "Potent Potables"). She then wrote an episode of the series *Rhoda* before returning to Chicago to work on the *Chicago Tribune*, then the *Chicago Post*. She was with the *Tribune* for eight years and left the *Post* to write a book based on her life with Fidel Castro called *My Year with Fidel*. Although Georgie thought the story should be told, the book didn't sell. She next went to France, where she became "a cultural liaison in Paris" ("I worked at Euro Disney helping people on and off the teacup ride"). Before returning to the U.S., Georgie stopped off in Rome, Italy, where "I ran around the Trevi Fountain in my bra and panties." When she learned of an opening for a speechwriter, she applied for and got the job in Washington, D.C.

Georgie is broke ("My credit line is not enough to buy a Vivien Leigh commemorative plate") and smokes but can't quit ("I smoke when I get upset and I get upset a lot"). Georgie also says that because of her gorgeous figure and good looks "I have a problem being taken seriously."

Georgie also wrote several romance novels under the pen name Dusty Silver: *Flamingo Summer*, *Lust Beyond Tomorrow* and *Naked Spring*. Georgie plays the trumpet and eats Kix cereal for breakfast. She began a romance with John Hartman (John Ritter), Strobe's senatorial aide. John lived at 1184 Arlington Drive and his wife, Diandra, left him for another woman. Georgie and John eventually married and became the parents of a girl they named Amelia Rose.

See also: Dee Dee Star.

416. Georgie Reed, *Sisters*, NBC, 1991–1996. Played by Patricia Kalember.

This entry also contains information on Georgie's sisters, Alex Reed (Swoosie Kurtz), Teddy Reed (Sela Ward) and Frankie Reed (Julianne Phillips).

Georgiana (called Georgie), Alexandra (Alex), Theodora (Teddy) and Francesca (Frankie) are four close knit sisters who are more than sisters "we're best friends," says Teddy. The girls live in Winnetka, a small town near Chicago. They are the daughters of Tom and Bea Reed and each have a male nickname because Tom had hoped for boys. They attended West High School. A mythical TV movie was made based on the sisters' lives called *A Sister's Love — Four Sisters for Each Other Forever*.

Georgie. Georgie is 35 years old. She is married to John Whitsig and is the mother of Trevor and Evan. She works as a real estate broker for Maple Leaf Realties and has become the main support of her family since John quit his job as a C.P.A. to become a singer (his dream is to release a record album called "The Sound of Whitsig").

Georgie is a graduate of Chicago University and has a Ph.D. in anthropology (she had to give up her dream of becoming anthropologist when she became pregnant). She enjoys blueberry pancakes for breakfast and is a member of the Maple Leaf Rags bowling team (where her skills have earned her the name "Striker Whitsig"). Georgie is a caring woman who loves John and her children very much (the reason why she lets him follow his dream). She is an excellent cook and housekeeper and truly enjoys the holidays, especially Christmas (she complains that the only holiday video tape she has is the Christmas episode from the TV series *Eight Is* Enough). Georgie lives in house number 844; 555-7842 is her phone number and PC2 726 is her car license plate. Georgie also has a dog named Watson. She enrolled in college in last season episodes seeking to become a therapist.

Alex. Alex is 39 years old and considered the miser of the family. She will drive 20 miles out of her way to save ten cents on an item without realizing the cost of wear and tear on the car. She is married to Wade Halsey, a plastic surgeon, and is the mother of Reed. In 1992 Alex and Wade divorced when Wade left Alex for a younger woman.

Alex has a small lightning bolt tattoo on her right breast. She is organized and loves yard sales (she is a shopaholic). Alex has a shotgun under her bed for protection. She had a TV interview program on Channel 3 called *Alex Live*. She also cares for Reed as a single mother and is having a somewhat difficult time. Reed (Kathy Wagner, Ashley Judd, Noelle Parker) is quite rebellious. She first attended a Catholic high school then a private school in Paris. She was expelled for immoral conduct. Alex then enrolled her in the Plumdale Private School in Chicago. Alex was in labor with Reed for 24 hours. Reed later joined a cult (The Nature of Science) and changed her name to Ineka. She next married a filmmaker (Kirby Philby) and moved to Los Angeles when his film, *Pigs to the Slaughter*, won acceptance at the American Academy of Film. Alex also dated (and later married) Big Al Barker (Robert Klein), "The Prince of Price Town." He called her "Little Al." Alex drives a car with the license plate 89F 890. Alex's bout with breast cancer became a recurring storyline beginning with the 1993 episodes.

Teddy. Teddy is 32 years old and divorced from Mitch Margolis. She is a recovering alcoholic and is regarded as the unstable sister. Teddy has a carefree attitude about life and will go anywhere the wind blows when the mood strikes her. She takes whatever jobs she can find and is a budding architect. Teddy first worked as a waitress at a soda shop called Sweet 16 (when she was 16 years old). She next tried her hand at telephone sales at 555-MOAN, a line for lonely men (she used the name Ramona; the cost was $5 for three minutes). A job as a salesgirl at Wonderful You Cosmetics followed as did fashion consultant at the Chandler-Klein Department Store. She next attempted to design a line of affordable clothes called Teddy Ware. When this failed she became the Chief Financial Officer for the IDH Corporation in New York City. In her youth Teddy posed nude for

pictures that later found their way to the Douglas Gallery in Chicago.

Teddy is also struggling to raise her beautiful 15-year-old daughter Catherine (Heather McAdam). Catherine, called Cat, and Teddy, live with Georgie. Cat is very close to her mother and longs for a stable home. Cat likes clothes that are "stylin'" but around the house she likes to parade around in her bra and panties (a habit Georgie is desperately trying to break). Teddy's sisters each claim she has "the perfect breasts."

Frankie. Frankie is the youngest of the sisters. She is single and originally worked as a marketing analyst for the firm of Frye, Birnbaum and Coates (Teddy also worked there for a short time). Frankie later opens a restaurant called Sweet 16 (where Cat works as a waitress). Teddy calls Frankie "Stinkerbell." Frankie appears to have her feet planted firmly on the ground. She knows what she wants and how to get it. Ever since she was 12 years old she has had a crush on Teddy's husband, Mitch (Ed Marinaro), the owner of a fresh fish store called Mitch's Catch of the Day (she went into the store to buy some sea bass, saw Mitch and fell in love with him). When Teddy divorced Mitch in 1988, Frankie began dating him and married him in 1993. Mitch has a pet lobster named Louie.

417. Georgy De La Rue, *Princesses*, CBS, 1991. Played by Twiggy Lawson.

Princess Georgina, better known as Georgy De La Rue, lives at 4107 5th Avenue in New York City. She is the Princess of Scilly, a group of islands off the South Coast of England. Georgy was born in England but not to a wealthy or royal family. She grew up in a middle class working family and for as long as she can remember wanted to be a dancer. After graduating from the Royal Academy of the Arts, Georgy became a tap dancer then a chorus girl. She was performing in a play called *No No Prime Minister* when Frederick, the elderly Prince of Scilly, spotted her. Despite the age difference, they fell in love and married. A short time later Frederick died, leaving Georgy with money and these words: "Don't be sad. I've had a good, long life."

Though wealthy, Georgy is actually penniless. Frederick's children never considered their stepmother worthy of the title and have protested a will that leaves her all of their father's money. With only the clothes on her back (and those in a trunk), Georgy headed for the U.S. to begin a new life ("I'm just a single princess looking for work"). Georgy sings in the key of A and now performs at the Blue Cord Club. She auditioned (but lost) the role of Hooker Number 2 in the play *Street Tango* and was the TV spokes-girl for Buckingham Airlines.

418. Gidget Lawrence, *Gidget*, ABC, 1965–1966. Played by Sally Field.

Frances Lawrence, better known as Gidget, is a 15½-year-old girl who loves the beach and surfing. She was born in Santa Monica, California, and is the daughter of Russell Lawrence, an English Professor at U.C.L.A. (her late mother's name is not mentioned).

Gidget lives with her father at 803 North Dutton Drive and says "I was the typical American girl until June 23, 1965, the day I fell in love with surfing." It was her new friends who gave her the name Gidget ("A girl who is neither tall nor a midget — a Gidget").

Gidget is a student at Westside High School (where she is president of the Civics Club and author of the "Helpful Hannah" advice column for its newspaper, the *Westside Jester*). Gidget is aware of a viewing audience and speaks directly to the camera to relate her feelings as stories progress. She is very philosophical for one so young; she wonders "why we can't be born with maturity and lose it as we grow older and don't need it." Gidget cherishes her privacy and has a pink Princess phone in her bedroom (Granite 5-5099; later 477-0599 is her phone number). Gidget applies Perpetual Emotion pink polish to her toe nails and has an understanding with her father: "If either of them has a problem, they can turn to the other for help." When Gidget hears "Frances" from her father, she knows she has done something wrong.

Gidget hangs out at soda shops called the Shaggy Dog, the Shake Shop, and Pop's. She was in a band called The Young People (later changed to Gidget and the Goories) and sees movies at the Spring Street Theater. She often uses the term "Tootles" to bid the audience a goodbye.

In the syndicated (1986–88) series update, *The New Gidget*, Caryn Richman plays Gidget. She is now 27 years old and married to Jeff Griffin. She is the owner of the Gidget Travel Agency in Los Angeles and lives at 656 Glendale. It is mentioned here that when Gidget first learned to surf she was teased about needing training wheels on her surfboard. As a kid she appeared on the TV show *Romper Room* (where she was called a "Perky Doo-Bee") and is a fan of musician Lawrence Welk. She also turned her love of surfing into a home video called *Gidget's Guide to Surfing*.

419. Gil Grissom, *C.S.I.: Crime Scene Investigation*, CBS, 2000 (current). Played by William Petersen.

Gil Grissom is head of a level three C.S.I. team for the Metropolitan Las Vegas Police Department. He was born in Santa Monica, California, on August 17, 1956. His father was head of an import/export business and his mother ran an art gallery (his mother also suffered from a hearing disability — something that would also affect Gil in his later life). Gil's childhood was anything but normal. At the age of eight he would go to the beach at Marina Del Rey in the early morning to collect dead birds (or anything else he could find) to perform autopsies. As he grew older, he would find dead cats and dogs and do the same thing, teaching himself the ins and outs of death. By the time Gil was a teenager, he had a reputation and found work helping the local authorities determine the cause of death in animals. By the time he was 16, he was an unofficial intern for the L.A. County Morgue. By this time his parents had divorced. With the money he earned, Gil put himself through college (U.C.L.A.) and graduated with a Bachelor of Science Degree in biology. By the age of 22 he became the youngest coroner in the history of Los Angeles County. Eight years later, he was recruited by the Las Vegas P.D. to run their field office. He was promoted to head of the crime lab when his superior, Captain Jim Brass, was transferred to the department's homicide division.

Gil's expertise is entomology (the study of insects). He gets a migraine headache about once a year and gets frustrated if he can't solve a case. He enjoys chocolate covered grasshoppers for a quick burst of energy. He experiments with the why and how of a killing. He can speak sign language (due to his mother's affliction). He also likes to think he is smarter than the criminal and find the evidence he may have left behind and overlooked ("I hate it when the criminal is smarter").

See also: Catherine Willows, Nick Stokes, Sara Sidle, Warrick Brown.

420. Gilligan, *Gilligan's Island*, CBS, 1964–1967. Played by Bob Denver.

Gilligan, proposed to have the first name of Willie (but never used) was the first mate aboard the S.S. *Minnow*, a small charter ship owned by Jonas Grumby (the Skipper) and based in Hawaii. Gilligan, the Skipper and five castaways (Ginger, Mary Ann, the Professor, and Thurston and Lovey Howell) are now stranded on a deserted island after the *Minnow* was caught in a tropical storm at sea and beached.

Gilligan is a well-meaning young man who will go out of his way to help someone in trouble. Unfortunately, he is accident-prone and all his good intentions prove fruitless in the end. Gilligan was born in Pennsylvania (where he had a pet turtle named Herman and his best friend was Skinny Mulligan). He was president of his grammar school camera club and worked in a gas station before joining the Navy (where he met Jonas). The two remained friends through their service careers and Gilligan became Jonas's first mate when he bought the *Minnow*.

On the uncharted island on which they are marooned, Gilligan has a pet duck (Gretchen) and his bumbling antics always foil the castaways efforts to get off the island. He enjoys coconut, papaya and tuna fish pie and is called "Little Buddy" by Jonas. Gilligan carries a not-so-lucky rabbit's foot and his image is carved in wood on the top of a totem pole (he resembles the former native inhabitants king). Gilligan is responsible for most of the work on the island and shares a hut with Jonas. He also does the fishing and enjoys listening to kid shows on the radio (the only means of communication they have with the outside world). The Mosquitoes is his favorite rock group and he misses TV, hot dogs and licorice.

See also: Ginger Grant, Mary Ann Summers, The Professor, The Skipper, Thurston and Lovey Howell.

421. Gina Tribbiani, *Joey,* NBC, 2004 (current). Played by Drea de Matteo.

Gina Tribbiani is a woman who is proud of her breasts. She not only shows ample cleavage but also brags about her breast enlargement operation — "I went up three cup sizes." She is also outspoken and not afraid to say what is on her mind. She is the sister of Joey Tribbiani (from the series *Friends*) and the mother of a 20-year-old son (Michael).

Gina lives in Los Angeles and close to Joey (who relocated from New York to further his acting career). Gina takes it as a compliment when people say she looks like a Hooters waitress and doesn't realize she dresses like a tramp until she sees herself in a mirror (and then smiles and shows an expression of "Wow, am I hot!"). Gina now works as a hairdresser at Salon Viktor but originally held a job with a dentist — "I was called the Southland's most dangerous dental technician by Channel 5." Gina is also banned from two K-Mart stores — "I didn't respect their return policy."

Gina believes that if you think young you are young. She lies about her age to everyone and honestly believes she has the body of a 22-year-old girl (while not stated, Gina is 34 based on the fact that she was said to have had Michael when she was 14). Gina makes homemade soup like her mother did ("A box of Lipton Chicken Noodle Soup and cut up hot dogs") giving the impression she can't cook. In another episode, Gina is said to be a great cook and if you want to stay on her good side, never insult her cooking or say you've tasted better). Telling Michael what to do is her favorite thing to do. Her favorite TV show is *JAG*.

See also: Joey Tribbiani.

422. Ginger Grant, *Gilligan's Island,* CBS, 1964–1967. Played by Tina Louise.

Ginger Grant is a beautiful Hollywood movie star who has starred in such films as *Belly Dancers from Bali Bali, Mohawk Over the Moon, The Rain Dancers of Rango Rango, San Quentin Blues* and *Sing a Song of Sing Sing.*

Ginger was born in California and lived in Hollywood before she became ship wrecked on an uncharted island in the South Pacific (as the result of a cruise that turned tragic when the ship, the S.S. *Minnow,* was beached after being caught in a tropical storm). Ginger now calls the deserted island home with the Skipper, Gilligan, the first mate, and fellow passengers, Mary Ann, the Professor and Thurston and Lovey Howell.

Ginger is first said to measure 38-27-35 then 36-25-36. She was called "Miss Hour Glass" ("They said I had all the sand in the right places") and broke into show business in a mind reading act with Merlin the Mind Reader. With her gorgeous features, Ginger changed her style to emulate those of her idol, Marilyn Monroe. Ginger became a popular star of romantic comedies but felt she could have been a major star with her role of Cleopatra in the Broadway production of *Pyramid for Two* (the role she was offered before the ship wreck).

Ginger has virtually no wardrobe (she originally had only the gown she wore for the cruise; she later makes a skin-tight dress from the ship's sail). Despite the deplorable conditions on the island, Ginger always remains alluring and sexy and uses the salvaged radio to keep informed of Hollywood gossip. Ginger shares her hut with Mary Ann and has learned to fend for herself, cooking, gathering firewood and food, and doing the laundry.

See also: Gilligan, Mary Ann Summers, The Professor, The Skipper, Thurston and Lovey Howell.

423. Ginger St. James, *It's a Living,* Syn., 1985–1989. Played by Sheryl Lee Ralph.

Virginia St. James, nicknamed Ginger, is the only African-American waitress at Above the Top, a posh 13th floor Los Angeles restaurant that offers "Sky High Dining." Ginger, like her fellow waitresses, Jan, Cassie, Dot and Amy, adds an air of sophistication to a restaurant that seems to cater to the rich and famous.

Ginger was born in Buffalo, New York, and is a graduate of Buffalo High School. While comfortable with her figure now, Ginger's high school years were all but satisfying. She was slow to develop and became jealous of girls with fuller figures. Hoping to fit in and attract boys, Ginger stuffed her bra with socks. She was found out and called "Booby Soxer" for her efforts. Ginger excelled in school and was a B-plus student. She has a flair for fashion and hopes to turn that skill into a career. She moved to California after graduating from Buffalo State University, but for reasons that are not explained, became a waitress at Above the Top. Ginger dreams of attracting the opposite sex have come true. She has many admirers (sometimes too many, she claims); one even named his boat after her—*Ginger Snaps*. It appears at times Ginger is looking to marry (she flirts with rich patrons and has visions of wealth). For the time being, however, Ginger is surviving on the tips she makes and shares a small apartment with fellow waitress Amy Tompkins.

See also: Amy Tompkins, Cassie Cranston, Dot Higgins, Jan Hoffmeyer, Lois Adams, Sonny Mann.

424. The Girls of Baywatch, *Baywatch*, NBC, 1989–1990; Syn., 1991–2001.

This entry contains information on the glamorous Los Angeles County Lifeguards who worked with senior lifeguard Mitch Buchannon at Baywatch in Malibu Beach.

April Giminski (Kelly Packard, 1997–1999). April is a young woman who gives of herself to help others. She was born in Wisconsin and had her first experience as a lifeguard at Lake Watanabe. April is very sweet and adorable and is seen by others as the wholesome girl next door. April will not deny this fact. She loves being thought of as an old fashioned girl because that is the way she really is. She sees no need to change her squeaky-clean image. If a man cannot accept her for whom she really is than she feels he is not worth her time. April does not go out of her way to impress people. She is not one for fancy clothes and does not put on airs. April is not as busty as her counterparts and she never lets this bother her. She accepts herself for who she is and is very careful when it comes to sea rescues; she never rushes in without thinking first.

Caroline Holden (Yasmine Bleeth, 1994–1998). Caroline is the strikingly beautiful sister of Stephanie Holden, a senior lifeguard at Baywatch. Caroline was married and initially came to Los Angeles to be with Stephanie when she caught her husband (Frank) cheating on her (they later divorced). Caroline shared an apartment with Stephanie and lifeguard C.J. Parker and eventually became a lifeguard herself although she showed an interest in acting.

Caroline is a beautiful brunette who, in the tradition of most Baywatch girls, wears tight, cleavage-revealing swimsuits (she relaxes in bikinis in her off duty hours). As a kid Caroline's favorite TV show was *Charlie's Angels*. Caroline is very sweet and sensitive and easily hurt. She became more of an adult when she rebelled against Stephanie's treatment of her like a child. Caroline was able to take considerable amounts of time off from work to attend auditions and left Baywatch when she acquired a role in a TV soap opera called *Shannon's Hope*. She worked out of Tower 1.

C.J. Parker (Pamela Anderson, 1992–1997). Casey Jean, who likes to be called C.J., is the bustiest of the lifeguards (she wears a 38D bra) "and where ever C.J. goes, men are not far behind." She works out of Tower 25 (later 163). C.J. was born in Nevada; her mother, Shelley Sands (Connie Stevens) works as an exotic dancer in Las Vegas. C.J. uses her stunning figure to get what she wants and believes in fortune telling and karma. She has a talent for working with animals and drives a sports car with the license plate 3DT 368 (also seen as 3JMJ 193). C.J. is also seen as the pilot of the rescue boat *Lifeguard One* (Rescue One is its code). C.J. originally left Baywatch to marry a rock star but is later seen in Hawaii and married to a hotel waiter named Lorenzo (who worked out of the Turtle Bay Resort and Marina).

Donna Marco (Donna D'Errico, 1996–1998). Donna uses the name D.J. Marco "because it makes business easier." She is a glamorous and wealthy businesswoman who owned a nightclub called Nights in Malibu on the series *Baywatch Nights* (1995–1997). When this spinoff from *Baywatch* ended, Donna's character was given less money and became a lifeguard. Donna finished second in her class at lifeguard school and seemed too perfect to be a lifeguard—a blonde bombshell that should be admired not working. Donna, however, was very athletic (especially skilled in rock climbing) and proved her abilities to be a responsible lifeguard. Donna knows she has a great body and almost lost her job because of it. She posed nude for *Playboy* magazine but used her Baywatch swimsuit as part of the layout. She was reprimanded for presenting the wrong image about female lifeguards (who are role models).

Jesse Owens (Brooke Burns, 1998–2000). Jessica, who likes to be called Jesse, is the liveliest of the *Baywatch* girls although her past is not squeaky clean. She was arrested and convicted of riding in a stolen car with her boyfriend. Jesse was underage (16) and was not criminally prosecuted and the incident was not placed on her permanent record. Jesse was not the best kid in school and was often troublesome to her parents. She left home at 19 and drifted from town to town and job to job. She found her way to the Baywatch lifeguard headquarters and began working in its maintenance department to pay for her lessons in stunt work for movies and TV. Jesse is very athletic and an excellent swimmer. One day while walking on a deserted beach she performed a rescue at sea and disappeared after doing so. She did this several times more and gained a reputation as a mysterious girl who rescues people then just vanishes. When senior lifeguard Mitch Buchannon discovered Jesse's secret he convinced her to become a lifeguard. Jesse is always eager, always full of life and gives of herself to help others.

Jill Riley (Shawn Weatherly, 1989–1990). Jill was one of the first Baywatch girls. She is tall and eager to do her job. She was born in Wisconsin and is the daughter of a middle-class family. Jill was somewhat of a tomboy and enjoyed sports. At the age of 15 she found a love for fishing. Every weekend she would take a rowboat out on Lake Motawanakeg and read while she fished. Halfway through the book *Wuthering Heights* she got a nibble, then a bit and reeled in a large stripped bass — which she gutted and had for supper that night.

Jill is a lifeguard when the series begins (she is assigned to Outpost Tower 27 with Mitch Buchannon). Jill always gives of herself to help others. She was never careless; she always figured out what to do before entering the water to save someone. Such was the case when she entered the water to save children during a shark sighting. Though as careful as anyone could be, Jill was attacked by a shark and lost a great deal of blood. She suffered massive internal injuries and required over 200 stitches. She seemed to be recovering at Webster Memorial Hospital but complications set in when and Jill died from a blood embolism. Jill never had the opportunity to finish reading *Wuthering Heights*.

Lani McKenzie (Carmen Electra, 1997–1998). Lailani, nicknamed Lani, was a lifeguard who was more of a dancer than a lifeguard. She yearned to be a dancer and spent every free moment practic-ing to achieve her goal. Lani was born in Hawaii (her father is a naval officer of Scottish descent). Lani is proud of her Hawaiian heritage and is not a person one wants to get angry — she has the fiery temper of her father (her mother is calm and mellow). Lani felt her rookie school training and work as a lifeguard was vital to her becoming a dancer. Her mind was changed when she injured her ankle during a rescue. She missed auditions and resented Baywatch. Although Lani earned money as a dancer (under the name Kyla) at the Club Rio, she moved to New York to further her career.

Neely Capshaw (Gena Lee Nolin, 1995–1998). While Caroline is the girl you can't help but love, Neely is the girl you love to hate. Neely was a girl who had to have what she wanted. If she couldn't have it she schemed to get it. She was cold and calculating and didn't care whom she hurt to get results. Neely believes that being a good swimmer is the most important part of being a lifeguard — "If you're not a good enough swimmer to reach the victim than nothing else matters."

Neely is gorgeous and knows her looks could get her out of trouble. She defied rules (like drinking on the job, flirting with beach goers) and always managed to come out on top. Neely worked previously at Huntington Beach and was transferred to Baywatch in 1995. She did a sexy layout for *Inside Sports* magazine and left Baywatch to become a businesswoman. Though Neely was deceitful and took advantage of everyone, she found the error of her ways when she injured her back skiing and became dependant upon pain killers. It was her fellow lifeguards who literally saved her life by getting her over her addiction. The "stiff punishments" she received for her evil ways amounted to switchboard duty. Mitch Buchannon, her superior, knew Caroline and C.J. hated Neely but he knew "Neely is a dam good lifeguard" (C.J. claimed she would rather be stationed in Cleveland than work with Neely). Neely always has to be the star attraction wherever she goes. But when there is a crisis, Neely will risk her life to save a drowning victim.

Shauni McClain (Erika Eleniak, 1989–1992). Shauni was the first of the new lifeguards when the series switched from NBC to syndication. She is the daughter of wealthy parents and is a graduate of South Central High School. She now lives at 3360 North Canyon Drive. She commands Outpost Tower 17 and is also the pilot of Rescue Boat One. Shauni is later said to have attended Valley High School (where her parents gave her $50 for every A on her report card). Shauni began a relationship with fellow lifeguard Eddie Kramer

(Billy Warlock) and married him in 1992. She left the series when she learned she was pregnant and she and Eddie moved Australia to raise a family.

Stephanie Holden (Alexandra Paul, 1992–1997). Stephanie is the older, domineering sister of lifeguard Caroline Holden. Stephanie is tall, not as busty as Caroline, and almost all work and no play. She shares a room with C.J. Parker (and later Caroline) and beside Mitch Buchannon, was the only lifeguard to move up the ranks (to become a lieutenant). Stephanie was assigned to Outpost Tower 18 and originally left the series in 1994 when she set sail on a round-the-world tour. She returned five months later when she found she missed Baywatch.

Stephanie was well versed in all operations at Baywatch — from rescuing people at sea to commanding a boat. She was also the head of the Junior Lifeguards (teenage girls who want to become lifeguards). In 1997, a sudden storm engulfs a boat called *Chance of a Lifetime*. Stephanie, a passenger on the boat, is killed when a mast, broken by the wind, strikes her. Her car license plate read 2HEX 864.

Summer Quinn (Nicole Eggert, 1992–1994). Roberta Quinn is a beautiful teenage rookie lifeguard who likes to be called by her nickname of Summer. She was born in Pittsburgh and drifted to California with her mother, Jackie Quinn (Susan Anton). Summer is 17 years old and lives with her mother in a trailer park. She trained to become a lifeguard at Baywatch while attending Malibu Beach High School. She is assigned to Tower 26 and her greatest fear during training was diving off the 100-foot pier. Summer was the youngest of the lifeguards and quite heroic for one so young. She left the series when she returned to Pittsburgh to attend Penn State College.

See also: Mitch Buchannon.

425. The Girls of Degrassi, *Degrassi Junior High*, Syn., 1987–1989.

This entry contains information on the popular students at Degrassi, a junior high school in the mythical town of Degrassi, Canada. The after-school hangout is 13 Busy Street (fast food).

Caitlin Ryan (Stacie Mistysyn). Caitlin is considered the seventh grade class beauty. She writes for the school newspaper, the Degrassi *Digest* and considers herself to be the school's lone crusader (she will back any cause she believes in — from protecting animal rights to fighting pollution). Caitlin is a promising journalist but suffers from epilepsy (she has it under control with medication). She is also a member of the Degrassi swim team and played Elizabeth in the school's pro-

duction of "Love's Fresh Face." She was also a contestant on the TV quiz show *Quest for the Best*.

Erica and Heather Farrell (Angela Deiseach, Maureen Deiseach). Erica and Heather are identical twins (birth sign Gemini). They are in the eighth grade and identical in almost every way. As they matured they also changed. Heather remained the sweet, conservative one while Erica chose "to live on the wild side." While Heather preferred to enjoy her evenings at home with a good book or doing homework, Erica chose to date. She soon acquired a loose reputation and became pregnant at age 16. Erica's pregnancy tore the family apart. While she had the support of her parents, she thought she lost the close relationship she one shared with Heather. The situation began to eat away at Erica and when she decided to have an abortion, she found an unexpected helping hand from Heather, who helped her through the ordeal. They became close again and together won first place honors with a report on eating disorders at the school science fair.

Kathleen Mead (Rebecca Haines). Seventh grader Kathleen Mead is one of the smartest and prettiest girls at Degrassi. Kathleen feels the only way she can make her mother proud is to do beyond her best. If she acquires anything less than an A she feels her mother will be disappointed in her (her mother is an alcoholic and takes little interest in what she does). Kathleen cooks her own meals, cleans the house and does whatever else she can to make her mother proud of her. Kathleen is not beyond crying when she sees her efforts fall on eyes blinded by alcohol. Kathleen wants to be an actress and won the drama award at Degrassi. She is the founder of the school's Environmental Action Committee and fears gaining weight and becoming unattractive.

Larraine Delacorte (Amanda Cook). Lorraine is called "L.D." by her friends. She is a seventh grader and captain of the girls' swim team. L.D. is a staunch supporter of girls' sports and lives with her widowed father, the owner of a gas station. At the age of 15 L.D. developed leukemia and missed most of her freshman year at Degrassi High. During chemotherapy L.D. allowed only her dearest friend, Lucy Fernandez, to see her (for her sixteenth birthday, Lucy made L.D. a video of her friends wishing her a happy birthday).

Lucy Fernandez (Anais Granofsky). Lucy is a very pretty African Canadian who seems to take care of herself (her parents are never seen and are seldom at home). She is in the eighth grade and has been in trouble with the law for minor infractions (shoplifting). Lucy has aspirations to become both a dancer and a filmmaker (in the episode "It Creeps," Lucy filmed a female slasher movie called *It Creeps* in which her friend, Caitlin played the slasher). She also made a music video for a band called The Zit Remedy and is famous for giving wild parties.

Melanie Brody (Sarah Ballingall). Melanie is a boy shy 12-year-old seventh grader. She has opinions on everything and is anxious to grow up. Melanie was the first girl in her class to develop her figure and apparently, by the episode "The Great Race," was the first in her class to wear a bra (which she bought with her friend L.D. when L.D. got fed up with Melanie's complaining that she needs one but her mother will not get her one. Her mother feels that Melanie is too young to accentuate her developing figure). Melanie is a member of the swim team. She hates reptiles and played a witch in the school play, "Love's Fresh Face." She won honorable mention with a project on air pollution in the school's science fair.

Stephanie Kaye (Nicole Stoffman). Stephanie is a stunning 14-year-old girl who is considered not only the most beautiful girl at school but also the sexiest (at 14 she is already well developed and shows cleavage). She is the eighth grade class president (she won the election by trading kisses for votes). Stephanie displays her figure in low cut, tight blouses and mini skirts. Steph, as she is called, leaves home dressed in typical conservative school clothes; at Degrassi she changes into her sexy attire ("My mother would kill me if she knew"). Stephanie craves attention and feels this is the only way she can get it. Although she means no harm by her appearance, she earned a reputation as the school sleaze.

Gladys Porter *see* **Peter Porter**

426. Glenn Hall, *Snoops*, ABC, 1999. Played by Gina Gershon.

You wouldn't expect it from the name, but Glenn Hall is an extremely beautiful and sexy woman who operates Glenn Hall, Inc., a high tech private detective agency in Santa Monica, California. Glenn charges $500 a day plus expenses plus a $5,000 retainer.

Glenn was born in Santa Monica in 1965 and has little memory of her mother and the name of her father. Glenn was the result of an affair her mother had with her high school sweetheart. The girl was left to raise her baby alone after the father deserted them. Glenn was three years old when her mother placed her on a carousel horse at the pier and abandoned her. Glenn was raised in four different foster homes and became bitter

as she grew older. She resented what had been done to her but was helpless to do anything about it. Becoming a detective was her way of helping people who face situations in which they are helpless to act. Her uneasy upbringing has made Glenn tough and she becomes extremely angry when clients take advantage of her (she usually takes her frustrations out on her staff).

Glenn is an expert at computers and hacking. She also says, "We have to be bad and break laws because we are after bad guys and it's the only way to catch them." She also claims she can go undercover better than any cop and despises skip tracing cases (apprehending escaped convicts for a reward; "It's not cost effective. There's no billing and it's dangerous"). Glenn is a certified pilot and uses a tranquilizer gun as a weapon. She has devised what she calls "a digital nipple cam" (worn on her breast, it takes stills through her bra and blouse); her one bad habit is falling for handsome clients.

See also: Dana Platt, Roberta Young.

427. Gloria and Mike Stivic, *All in the Family*, CBS, 1971–1977. Played by Sally Struthers, Rob Reiner.

Gloria Stivic is the married daughter of Archie and Edith Bunker. She lives with her husband, Mike Stivic, in her parent's home at 704 Hauser Street in Queens, New York.

Gloria was born at Bayside Hospital in Queens in 1944 (the hospital bill was $131.50). Gloria grew up as a normal girl but has been babied all her life, ever since Edith learned she was anemic. Edith has protected Gloria and consequently, Gloria has done little housework. She is accustomed to being pampered and likes it (she doesn't move out because if she does she will have to grow up and she is not ready for that).

Archie calls Gloria "Little Girl." She dropped out of Queens High School at 16 to take a secretarial course. She next acquired a job in Manhattan and met Michael Stivic, a liberal she became fascinated with (she believes he is the most intelligent person she has even known); a later episode claims Gloria met Mike, a hippie, when a girlfriend set her up on a blind date. Gloria later quits her secretarial job for that of a salesgirl at Kresler's Department Store (at $80 a week).

Gloria has lived a sheltered life but is beginning to learn about the world from Mike. She is also realizing that her parents are wrong about a lot of things.

Mike lives in a vacuum. He has no job, is married to Gloria but doesn't support her (Archie supports both of them and calls Mike "Meathead" and "You dumb Polack"). He believes Archie's conservative ways are harmful to the world and he believes Edith is ignorant to the ways of the world. Mike is hoping to make Gloria more liberal (which he succeeded in doing when he gave her permission to pose nude for an artist. He then saw the world in a different light and became as uptight as Archie when she did it).

Mike is attending college and hoping to become a teacher. Before doing so and moving to California when a good teaching job becomes available, he and Gloria become the parents of a son they name Joey.

In the spinoff series, *Gloria* (CBS, 1982–83), Gloria returns to Queens when Mike is unable to deal with society and abandons Gloria and Joey. Gloria becomes a single mother and finds a job as a veterinary assistant in upstate New York in a town called Fox County.

See also: Archie Bunker, Billie Bunker, Edith Bunker, Stephanie Mills.

Gob Bluth *see* **Michael Bluth**

428. Gomer Pyle, *Gomer Pyle, U.S.M.C*, CBS, 1964–1969. Played by Jim Nabors.

Gomer Pyle is a private with the U.S. Marine Corps. He is stationed at Camp Henderson in Los Angeles and is with the Second Platoon, B Company. Gomer was born in Mayberry, North Carolina, and worked as an attendant at Wally's Filling Station before he joined the Marines.

Gomer is a single man. He asks little from life and is satisfied with everything he does. He asks no favors but will give of himself to help others. He is a graduate of Mayberry Union High School and lives in a room in back of the gas station. He appears to be naïve and was saving his money to go to college and become a doctor. However, when he learned he was expected to serve a term of military duty, he enlisted with the Marines and put his medical career on hold. Gomer is proud of the fact that he knows all the words to the *Marine Hymn* ("From the Halls of Montezuma to the Shores of Tripoli..."), which he learned from the back of a calendar put out by Nelson's Funeral Parlor. Gomer had a dog named Spot as a kid and likes Limburger cheese and onion sandwiches. He says "Shazam" when something goes wrong. When he leaves he says "Lots of luck to you and yours"; when something fascinates Gomer he says "Golll-lllly." His greeting is "Hey" (for example, "Tell the captain Gomer says hey") and "Surprise, surprise, surprise" is another of Gomer's catch phrases. Gomer was promoted to Private First Class in 1968 and was champion of

the platoon's foot race (he was called "Crazy Legs Gomer").

Gomer's girlfriend is Lou Ann Poovie (Elizabeth McRae), a singer at the Blue Bird Café. His superior is Vince Carter (Frank Sutton), a tough sergeant who always finds himself in trouble due to Gomer's antics. The character of Gomer Pyle first appeared on *The Andy Griffith Show*.

See also: Andy Taylor, Barney Fife, Bee Taylor, Goober Pyle, Opie Taylor.

429. Gomez Addams, *The Addams Family*, ABC, 1964–1966. Played by John Astin.

Gomez Addams is a man of considerable wealth who resides in the town of Cemetery Ridge. He is married to Morticia and is the father of Wednesday and Pugsley. Although his mother, called Grandmamma Addams, lives with them, his father is not mentioned. Gomez has a mixed ancestry, including American, Spanish and Egyptian. The earliest known Addams was Maumud Kali Pashu Addams who, in the year A.D. 270 set the Egyptian Library at Alexandria on fire. Gomez enjoys a good cigar and is an expert swordsman. He claims the second *d* in their names distinguishes them from "the embarrassingly famous and historic John Adams and family."

While Gomez does not seem to work (he dabbles in the stock market), he was at one time a defense attorney and responsible for putting more men behind bars than any other lawyer in the United States. He has an elephant herd in Africa, a nut plantation in Brazil, a salt mine and an animal preserve in Nairobi (for vacations in its subterranean bat caves). Gomez is a member of the Zen Yoga Society and Ivan the Terrible is his favorite person in history. Halloween is his favorite holiday.

Gomez's favorite stock, Consolidated Fuzz, has made him rich. He has little trust in banks and hides money in the house, most notably in desk drawers. For relaxation, Gomez enjoys running his Lionel O-gauge electric trains (for the thrill of collisions and explosions). He enjoys gloomy weather, exploring caves and moon bathing. He has a polka dot wooden polo pony he calls Kelso and he calls Morticia "Tish," "Cara Mia" and "Caita." As a child Gomez's constant companion was Thing, a human right hand; Thing now works as a family servant.

See also: Morticia Addams, Uncle Fester, Wednesday and Pugsley Addams.

430. Goober Pyle, *The Andy Griffith Show*, CBS 1965–1968. Played By George Lindsey.

Goober Pyle is the cousin of Gomer Pyle and

a car mechanic who works at and later owns Wally's Filling Station in the town of Mayberry, North Carolina. Goober was born in Mayberry, attended Mayberry Union High School and earns $1.25 an hour. He played on the school's football team and learned his trade in nearby Raleigh. He also served a hitch in the National Guard.

Goober reads comic books and loves playing checkers. He also considers himself a great impersonator but does a rather poor imitation of Cary Grant's then famous "Judy, Judy, Judy" movie line. His pickup truck license plate reads M37 9054.

Goober is a bit dense but a kind and generous man. He has a teddy bear (Buster), a canary (Louise) and a spotless dog named Spot. Corn on the cob is his favorite food and when it comes to women, Goober is all thumbs. He is extremely shy and awkward and has no serious relationships.

Goober loves to hang out at the Courthouse and barbershop and is a member of the Royal Order of the Golden Door Good Fellowship. He is also a member of the town choir and manager of the Giants, a Little League baseball team.

The character of Goober continued on the spinoff series *Mayberry, R.F.D.* (CBS, 1968–1971). Here Goober aligned himself to Sam Jones (Ken Berry), the Mayberry town councilman. George Lindsey revived his Goober Pyle character for CBS in an unsold 1978 pilot called *Goober and the Truckers' Paradise*. Here Goober moved to a small town outside of Atlanta to open a truck stop (Truckers' Paradise) with his older sister Pearl Pyle (Leigh French) and younger sister Toni Pyle (Lindsay Bloom). He is also seen with his gorgeous niece, Becky Pyle (Audrey Landers).

See also: Andy Taylor, Barney Fife, Bee Taylor, Gomer Pyle, Opie Taylor.

431. Grace Adler, *Will and Grace*, NBC, 1998 (current). Played by Debra Messing.

Grace Elizabeth Adler is an interior designer who runs her own company (Grace Adler Designs) out of the Buck Building in Manhattan. Grace was born in Schenectady, New York. She is Jewish and attended Sunday school for 10 years. She had a dog named Toki and had her biggest childhood disappointment when she discovered that hamsters can't fly. Grace has A-B negative blood and a scar on her thigh "from a cousin who was sleep walking and thought I was a salami." She has an older sister (Janet) and her mother, Bobbie, is a singer.

Grace attended Hawthorne High School then New York University (where she met her best friend, Will Truman). They were in an improv

group called the Zanies). Grace next attended the Fashion Institute then started her own business (due to a typo, the Yellow Pages lists her as "The Breast Designer" instead of "The Best Designer").

The lily is Grace's favorite flower. She likes Twizzler's licorice (strawberry flavor) and Hershey's Chocolate Dove Bar. Grace can appreciate a bargain. She shops for clothes at Designer Mark Downs at the Paramus Mall in New Jersey. She fears getting old "really old," and tends to cry when she thinks about it. She claims the worst day of her life occurred at Bloomingdale's "I cried a river of tears when a young girl bumped into me and said 'Excuse me, ma'am.'" The neighborhood cleaner calls Grace "Nice lady" and Grace enjoys coffee at Kitty's Coffee Shop. When she gets mad she eats cheesecake; when Grace is upset, she has a slice of white bread. She believes *The Pet Psychic* is the best TV series ever and usually watches whatever is on when she switches on the TV "because I'm here [on the couch] and the remote is over there [on top of the TV]." Lifetime is her favorite network. Grace hates flavored coffee and clowns ("because they think they're so funny").

Grace knows she is very pretty but feels her shortcoming is her boyish figure, especially her small breasts (she shudders when people refer to her breasts as "boobies"). Grace's well-endowed assistant, Karen Walker, constantly reminds Grace that she "has no breasts" (Grace's mother was so desperate for Grace to have breasts that she padded her high school gym uniform. Grace even tried to acquire some fullness by wearing a water bra "for extra perkiness." The bra worked for a short time until it sprung a leak and totally embarrassed her).

Grace loves to attend concerts but gets carried away and tends to sing along. At Joni Mitchell's concert, Joni asked Grace to leave. At one for Melissa Manchester, Melissa called security.

Grave first lived at 155 Riverside Drive with Will in Apartment 9C. Will is gay; Grace is straight. They found the living arrangement perfect (Grace admits to making love to another woman "but it wasn't my thing"). Grace later moved across the hall into her own apartment (9A), then back with Will. She also had a brief marriage to a doctor (Leo Marcus) that ended when he abandoned her (at this time she lived in Brooklyn in Apartment 2K). Grace believes people mistake her actress Julia Roberts.

See also: Jack McFarland, Karen Walker, Will Truman.

432. Grace Kelly, *Grace Under Fire*, ABC, 1993–1998. Played by Brett Butler.

Grace Kelly is 36 years old, divorced, and the

mother of three children (Libby, Quentin and Patrick). She lives at 455 Washington Avenue in Victory, Missouri, and works as the office manager at the Reliance Construction Company.

Grace was born in Huntsville, Alabama; her maiden name is Burdette. She is a graduate of Huntsville High School and married Jimmy Kelly shortly after graduating. Grace had a severe drinking problem. Jimmy was a womanizer. They were unable to live with each other and divorced. After cleaning up her act, Grace moved to Victory and found work as a waitress at Stevie Rays's Bar. She next became a field worker in Section 7 of the CBD Oil Refinery. She quit this job for the one at Reliance and was later promoted to crew chief. Grace was also a volunteer for the Crisis Center (where she used the name Chris); she later returned to school (Missouri State College) to pursue a degree in English. The Equator Coffee House was her favorite off campus hangout.

Grace claims she stopped drinking "when I saw a big red dog jump out of my lingerie drawer." She buys her lingerie at Bras, Bras, Bras and drives a car with the license plate FXB 352 (later AEH 497). She later moved to the house across the street (446) when the landlord sold the home she was renting; 555-0159 is her phone number. Grace enjoys strawberry ice cream, Little Debbie Swiss Cake Rolls, and for breakfast, she treats herself to Canadian bacon.

433. Grace Musso, *Parker Lewis Can't Lose*, Fox, 1990–1992. Played by Melanie Chartoff.

Grace Musso is the principal of Santo Domingo High School in California. She is stern and demanding and asks for only one thing—"a cup of coffee and a little peace and quiet in the morning." Grace rarely gets what she asks for. She feels her students are little monsters and keeping them in line is a never-ending job.

Grace was born in Santo Domingo and was herself a student at the school she now rules. It was perhaps an incident in 1970, when Grace was a junior that turned her happy outlook on life to one of bitterness. Grace was the obedience helper to the school's principal and disliked by the other students. On prom night she was dowsed with 60 gallons of lime Jell-O. She now feels it is her duty to keep the school "crime free" and the only way she knows how is by being strict.

Grace is a very attractive woman. She wears tight skirts and blouses and causes havoc when she attends basketball games as the boys leer at her and often lose the game (she says she dresses to please herself and no one else).

Grace earns $38,000 a year but lives in a $600,000 home and owns a cabin on Sky Lake. She is singer Donny Osmond's biggest fan (she has written him thousands of letters) and revealed that the Bee Gees rock group and men with beards turn her on. Grace has had 1,357 blind dates since becoming principal and not one was a match for her (her parents feel that a hunting lodge or a rifle range is a good place for her to meet a man).

Grace "is more than a principal, she is a psychopath with tenure" as she is feared by everyone and demands respect. When students are sent to her office, Grace delights in sending them to detention (where the punishment is showing them home videos of Grace's life—from infancy).

See also: Parker Lewis, Shelly Lewis.

434. Gracie Sheffield, *The Nanny*, CBS, 1993–1999. Played by Madeline Zima.

Grace Sheffield, lovingly called Gracie, is the adorable six-year-old daughter of Broadway producer Maxwell Sheffield, a widower who lives on New York's Park Avenue. Gracie has an older sister (Maggie) and brother (Bryton) and is cared for by her nanny, Fran Fine (who calls her "Angel").

Gracie is far wiser than her age. She is "a complicated girl with multiple personalities" and attends therapy sessions to treat her introversion and insecurities (she worries, for example, about the Polar Ice Caps melting and thus cannot have fun at school). Gracie first attends the Holy Cross School, then Lexington Academy (she played the Itty Bitty Spider in the school's play, *Mother Goose on Broadway*).

Gracie is a member of the Red Robbins (a Girl Scout troop) and believes the showgirls that audition for her father's Broadway shows are "giant Barbie dolls." She has a teddy bear (Mr. Fuzzy; later called Teddy), two hamsters (Miss Fine and Mr. Sheffield), and an invisible friend she calls Imogene. Gracie is a very obedient girl and is very close to Fran, whom she considers a substitute mother.

See also: C.C. Babcock, Fran Fine, Maggie Sheffield, Maxwell Sheffield.

435. Graham and Elizabeth Lubbock, *Just the Ten of Us*, ABC, 1988–1990. Played by Bill Kirchenbauer, Deborah Harmon.

Graham and his wife Elizabeth are the parents of eight children (Marie, Wendy, Cindy, Connie, Sherry, J.R. and infant twins, Michelle and Harvey). They live in Eureka, California, with a dog named Hooter and a milk cow called Diane; 555-3273 is their phone number. Graham works as the athletic director at Saint Augustine's, a Catholic High School (where he is also coach of the football, team, the Hippos); Elizabeth is a content homemaker.

Elizabeth and Graham were born on Long Island in New York. They met at a C.Y.O. (Catholic Youth Organization) mixer and fell in love at first sight. They married in 1970. Shortly after, Graham became the athletic director at Dewey High School on Long Island. They moved to California in 1988 when Graham was offered a free house and a better paying job at Saint Augustine's.

Elizabeth is deeply religious and is delighted by the fact that eldest daughter, Marie, is contemplating becoming a nun. Elizabeth wanted to become a nun also but her mother, who ruled with an iron fist, talked her out of it—"You should find a husband while you still have your looks." Elizabeth treats each of her children equally and deals punishments accordingly (she usually deprives the child in trouble of what they like to do the most for a week). Graham, on the other hand, is a man surrounded by six females and tends to favor J.R. (Graham Lubbock, Jr.) over the girls as he feels he is the only child he can really bond with. Graham is a bit overweight and tries to remain on the diets Elizabeth creates for him. But when his favorite foods, Ovaltine and Ho Ho's call, he has little resistance. Elizabeth does volunteer work at the Food Bank; Graham was forced to take a second job as a counter boy at the Burger Barn (where he worked as Mitch) to make ends meet.

See also: Cindy Lubbock, Connie Lubbock, Marie Lubbock, Wendy Lubbock.

436. Grandpa, *The Munsters,* CBS, 1964–1966. Played by Al Lewis.

Count Vladimir Dracula is a prince among vampires. He is the father of Lily Dracula, the beautiful vampire who married a Frankenstein look-a-like named Herman Munster. For reasons that are not explained, Vladimir is also called Grandpa Munster. Grandpa is not only a creature of the undead, but he is a mad scientist as well. He lives with Herman, Lily, their son Eddie, and niece, Marilyn, at 1313 Mockingbird Lane in the town of Mockingbird Heights; he has his lab in the dungeon.

Grandpa was born in Transylvania in 1586. He has been married 167 times (his wife, Katja, gave birth to Lily in 1664; Katja left Grandpa when she became tired of ironing capes and moping dungeons). Grandpa is a graduate of the University of Transylvania (where he majored in philosophy). He is a member of the A.V.A. (American Vampire Association) and operated a blood bank in his hometown. Grandpa also worked as a guillotine janitor and as the owner of a fang-sharpening business.

Grandpa enjoys experimenting in his lab (especially with electricity) and has a pet bat named Igor ("a mouse with wings who joined the Transylvanian Air Force"). He was once a professional magician (his magic has soured over time) and has a book that contains a variety of centuries-old recipes from curing headaches to curing the bubonic plaque. Grandpa is proud of his newly transistorized diving rod (which picks up reruns of *My Little Margie*) and sometimes wishes he were back in the old country where, when the full moon rose, he could roam free as a wolf. Grandpa mentioned that *My Three Sons* was his favorite TV show.

See also: Eddie Munster, Herman Munster, Lily Munster, Marilyn Munster.

437. Granny, *The Beverly Hillbillies,* CBS, 1962–1971. Played by Irene Ryan.

Daisy Mae Moses, called Granny, is the mother-in-law of Jed Clampett, the Ozark mountaineer who became rich when he struck oil. He moved his family (his daughter, Elly Mae, and nephew, Jethro Bodine) to a mansion in Beverly Hills (at 518 Crestview Drive) and Granny now must endure the pleasures of "living high off the hog."

Granny was born in Tennessee sometime in the 1850s. She grew up poor and loves the real simple life because it is the only life she has ever known. At some point (possibly the 1890s), Daisy's family moved to the Ozark Community of Sibley (Daisy mentioned that she was not sure of her age and that when she was a child her mother fell in a swamp and drowned).

Daisy entered the Bug Tussle Bathing Beauty Contest at the Expo of 1897 and won "The Miss Good Sport Award." She was a teenager at the time and nearly became a spinster, as she had not yet been married. She did marry shortly after and had a daughter named Rose Ellen (who would one day marry Jed Clampett).

Daisy, now called Granny, is a widow. She lives with Jed but longs for the good life she lived in the backwoods. She believes Jefferson Davis is the President of the U.S. and her life savings of $5,000 is in Confederate money. She has a double-barreled 12-gauge shotgun she uses "to get rid of revenuers" and plays a 200-year-old lap organ. Granny has an all-around cure for ailments called Granny's Spring Tonic. Her perfume is "pure vanilly extract" and she is famous for her homemade lye soap (with fumes so toxic "it can peel the bark off a tree and bring a full grown mule to its knees"). Granny has a still in the backyard for making her "Rheumatiz medicine" and claims she is the only family member who can hold a grudge. She can also predict when it is going to rain by "twinges" ("aches in my bones"). Granny is also the family cook and possum stew and boiled buzzard eggs are a favorite of everyone. Granny was also a backwoods doctor and likes to practice her innocent "doctorin' ways" on the sick people she encounters (she, has for example, a sure-fire cure for the common cold — a spoonful of tonic, plenty of fluids and rest and within seven to ten days it's gone). Granny watches the TV soap opera *Journey to Misery* and had a race horse named Ladybelle.

See also: Elly Mae Clampett, Jed Clampett, Jethro Bodine.

438. Greg Brady, *The Brady Bunch*, ABC, 1969–1974. Played by Barry Williams.

This entry also contains information on Greg's brothers, Peter (Christopher Knight) and Bobby (Michael Lookinland). They live with their parents, Mike and Carol, and sisters, Marcia, Jan and Cindy, at 4222 Clinton Avenue in Los Angeles.

Greg. Greg is the oldest of the Brady brothers. He attends Westside High School (where he is a member of the basketball team). Greg enjoys singing and playing the guitar. He attempted to break into show business as a singer named Johnny Bravo. He had a band called the Banana Convention, then formed The Brady Six with his siblings (later changed to The Brady Kids; "Time to Change" was the first song they sang). Greg also attempted to become a filmmaker (he used his family as Pilgrims in a production of the first Thanksgiving). While he appeared to be an all-American boy, Greg did get into the normal childhood mischief and possibly getting caught smoking a cigarette by his parents was the worst. As a child Greg was a Frontier Scout and had a hamster named Myron.

Greg became a doctor in the 1981 NBC TV movie, *The Brady Girls Get Married*. He is seen married to Nora (Caryn Richman) in the 1988 CBS TV movie *A Very Brady Christmas* and in the series update, *The Bradys* (CBS, 1990), Greg is working in the same hospital as Nora, a nurse. They are the parents of Kevin.

Peter. Peter, the middle son, is the most insecure of the male Bradys. He feels he has no personality and is dull and unattractive to girls. He likes science fiction movies and George Washington is his hero. Peter first attended Clinton Elementary School then Fillmore Junior High School. He was also a member of the neighborhood Treehouse Club.

Peter joined the Air Force in the 1981 TV movie *The Brady Girls Get Married*. He is engaged to Valerie Thomas (Carol Huston) in the TV movie, *A Very Brady Christmas* (1988). In the 1990 series update, *The* Bradys, Peter is now married and assists his father who is the Fourth District City Councilman.

Bobby. Bobby, the youngest male Brady, attends Clinton Elementary School (where he is a safety monitor). He had a parakeet named Bird and claims that his hero is outlaw Jesse James. Bobby often gets into innocent mischief and found getting rich quick schemes often don't work (he sold Neat and Tidy Nature Hair Tonic for $2 a bottle; it turned hair orange).

Bobby is a college student (in the 1981 TV movie, *The Brady Girls Get Married*) and became a racecar driver in the series update, *The Bradys* (CBS, 1990). He is also married to Tracy (Martha Quinn) and suffered a terrible accident during a race that has left him paralyzed from the waist down.

See also: Alice Nelson, Carol and Mike Brady, Marcia Brady (for information on Marcia, Jan and Cindy Brady).

439. Greg Montgomery, *Dharma and Greg*, ABC, 1997–2002. Played by Thomas Gibson.

Gregory Clifford Montgomery, called Greg, is a conservative U.S. Attorney for the Justice Department in San Francisco. He is married to Dharma, a somewhat kookie girl he met, fell in love with and married on their first date. Greg is the son of Edward and Kitty Montgomery, the wealthy owners of Montgomery Industries. He was born in San Francisco and attended Brookside Academy as a kid. He is a graduate of Harvard University and has a law degree from Stanford. He organizes his credit cards by expiration date ("If the top card isn't expired, you're in good shape with the rest of them"). Greg loves to cook and he spends two weeks a year as a captain in the Army Reserves (Dharma uses his captain's bars the rest of the year as thumb tacks on their bulletin board).

Greg and Dharma live in a renovated battery factory in San Francisco. When Greg felt his government job was not fulfilling, he quit to become a private practice attorney. Shortly before the series ended, he relinquished this career and embarked on a journey of self-discovery. He worked in a cannery (as a squid skinner) then diner cook before becoming a member of the Montgomery Industries legal team.

Greg is captain of Dharma's softball team, the Sheeps. At the age of 18, Greg was the youngest delegate ever to attend the Republican National Convention. When Dharma ran for political office (a seat on the San Francisco Broad of Supervisors) Greg was "stamp licker" (a position he pulled from "the job hat"). Greg is Episcopalian (Dharma is Jewish) and is allergic to macadamia nuts. He likes vanilla ice cream and collects stamps.

See also: Abby O'Neill, Dharma Montgomery, Edward and Kitty Montgomery, Larry Finkelstein.

440. Gregory House, *House*, Fox, 2004 (current). Played by Hugh Laurie.

Gregory House is a doctor of diagnostic medicine who is on staff at the Princeton-Plainsboro Teaching Hospital in New Jersey. He also works in the hospital's clinic and he prefers to treat the illness, not the patient (he has made it a policy to avoid patients if possible — "Treating illness is why I became a doctor. Treating patients is what makes doctors miserable").

Gregory has a team of three highly over qualified specialists who assist him (Allison Cameron, Eric Foreman and Robert Chase) but he still calls himself "a lonely infectious disease guy." Gregory does not dress like a doctor (he refuses to wear hospital whites or greens) and walks with a cane; he doesn't want people to see a doctor who is sick (a heart attack left him with a partially crippled right leg). He also takes pain-killers (vicodin) as a result.

Gregory's philosophy is "We treat. If the patient gets better we're right. If not, we learn something else." He does not believe in pretense; he says what he thinks. If a case intrigues Gregory he will break his rule and talk to a patient. He has a degree in infectious diseases and balks at having to work the common cases in the hospital's clinic (He is six years behind on his obligation to the clinic and says, "I'm here from nine to five").

Gregory enjoys watching *General Hospital* on TV and plays video games for inspiration. He has an encyclopedic knowledge of medicine and is best when he is faced with a baffling medical condition. It is then that he puts his team to work to help him solve the mystery. Gregory claims he hired Allison (Jennifer Morrison) because she is pretty; "It's like having a nice piece of art in the lobby." Allison was not at the top of her class and did her internship at the Mayo Clinic. Taylor (Omar Epps) is a graduate of Johns Hopkins and has a juvenile arrest record for breaking and entering.

Gregory is smug ("smugness is easy to maintain"), rude and has no bedside manner. Dr. Lisa Cuddy (Lisa Edelstein), the hospital administrator won't fire him because "The son of a bitch is the best doctor we have." Gregory will lie, steal and cheat to get what he needs if it means helping a patient. Gregory's insane diagnosis and treatment procedures are usually right. He thinks outside the box to find solutions. He has been a doctor for 20 years. The series is also seen on screen as *House, M.D.*

441. Greta Hanson, *How to Marry a Millionaire*, Syn., 1958–1959. Played by Lori Nelson.

Greta Hanson is young, beautiful and desirable. She is also broke and seeking to marry a millionaire. She shares Penthouse G at the Tower Apartment House on Park Avenue in New York City with Loco Jones and Mike McCall, two other women seeking to marry a rich man.

Greta was born in Manhattan and works as the hostess of a TV game show called *Go for Broke*. She has the ability to wear anything and look great. Because of her lack of funds, she is the borrower of the group (she especially enjoys Mike's wardrobe) and is a bit untidy (she rarely makes her bed and hates housework). To ensure she finds the right man, Greta uses the book *Who's Who in America* as her research material. Greta hopes there is a millionaire out there for her and finds him "before he has to whisper sweet nothings into my ear trumpet." A year before the series ended, Greta found true love; not the oil man she dreamed of marrying, but "a man who owned a gas station." She and her new love moved to California (Greta was replaced by Gwen Kirby, another girl seeking a rich husband).

See also: Gwen Kirby, Loco Jones, Mike McCall.

442. Gunther Toody, *Car 54, Where Are You?*, NBC, 1961–1963. Played by Joe E. Ross.

Gunther Toody is a police officer with the 53rd Precinct of the N.Y.P.D. on Tremont Avenue in the Bronx. He rides in patrol car 54 with Francis Muldoon and is married to the always-nagging Lucille.

Gunther was born in the Bronx on August 15th and stands five feet, eight inches tall. He is a graduate of Fairview High School (where he was called "Bull" on the football team) and Hunter College. He next joined the army and was stationed at Fort Dix in New Jersey (where at base dances he was called "Lover Lips"). After the service, Gunther worked for the Department of Sanitation before joining the Police Academy (he showed no potential for law enforcement and the rookie school lieutenant said, "If Toody ever graduates I'll shot myself." Toody graduated and the lieutenant is fine). Gunther hopes to become a detective and "studies" by watching *Dragnet, Checkmate* and *Perry Mason* ("I've gotten so good that I can solve the crime by the third commercial").

Gunther married his high school sweetheart, Lucille Hasselwhite, in 1948. They live in a five room, rent controlled $45 a month apartment. Gunther wears badge 432 (although camera angels and lighting make it look like 1432 and 453). The gravel-voiced Gunther claims to be related to the famous Singing Toodys, but he has not inherited a singing voice. Gunther enjoys bowling (if he misses a game, his teammates say, "He must not only be sick, he must be on the critical list") and reads a daily paper called the *News Journal*. Gunther has an account at the Bronx Home Savings Bank and is a coach (with Francis) of the Wildcats, a PAL (Police Athletic League) basketball team.

See also: Francis Muldoon, Leo Schnauser.

443. Gus Witherspoon, *Our House*, NBC, 1986–1988. Played by Wilford Brimley.

Gus Witherspoon is a widower who lives at 14 Ashton Street in Los Angeles with his daughter-in-law, Jessie and her children Kris, David and Molly. Jessie was married to Gus's late son, John.

Gus is 65 years old and righteous. He has strong beliefs and is set in his ways (his neighbors feel he is stubborn and hard to get along with). He was a corporal with the Marines during World War II (dog tag reads 212 4027). Judging by his hobby of H-O scale model railroading, Gus (who dresses as a train engineer when running them) was an engineer for the Santa Fe Railroad. He now does part time work as a blacksmith (shoeing horses).

Gus's late wife was named Mary. He also has a younger daughter, Sarah, and an estranged son, Ben (when Sarah was three years old and very sick, Gus wrote her a series of stories called "Stories by Angus Shea" to cheer her up; the stories were never published).

Gus has breakfast at 7:15 A.M. and walks two miles a day for exercise. He is a member of the Monona Service Club (helps the community) and is on a bowling team (with Kris) called Cliff's Clippers. He calls Kris "Sweetheart," Molly "Buttons" and David "Champ." Gus's best friend is his neighbor Joe Kaplan (Gerald S. O'Loughlin); they have their hair cut at the Mid-Town Barber Shop. Arthur, the family dog, will eat everything but Gus's chili. Joe ran a bookstore ("I just sold 'em,

I didn't read 'em") and is also a veteran of World War II (two bronze stars, a purple heart "and shrapnel in the butt"). Gus can be reached by phone at 555-4847 (later 555-1680).

See also: Jessie Witherspoon (also for information on Kris, David and Molly Witherspoon).

444. Gwen Cross, *Moon Over Miami*, NBC, 1993. Played by Ally Walker.

Gwenevere Cross, called Gwen, is a secretary employed by the Walter Tatum Detective Agency (also called Walter Tatum, Inc.) at 668 Strand in South Beach, Miami, Florida.

Gwen was born in Florida and is the daughter of a wealthy family. Her father, Arthur, was a powerful attorney and babied Gwen all her life. It made Gwen feel different, but she enjoyed the attention she received as a child. As she grew, she came into contact with children of lesser wealth and began to resent the pampering. After graduating from the University of Miami, Gwen felt "My life has no meaning" and left home. She drifted for a while and found employment at the agency (where she helps its owner, Walter Tatum, solve crimes).

Gwen lives in an apartment on Lomax Drive. She is weight conscious and very careful about what she eats ("I don't eat desserts because they are unnecessary indulgences"). Gwen is very meticulous and often comes up with a plan of action for her and Walter to follow. She cherishes her privacy and is adjusting to her new life as an average wage earner quite well.

See also: Walter Tatum.

445. Gwen Kirby, *How to Marry a Millionaire*, Syn., 1959–1960. Played by Lisa Gaye.

Gwen Kirby is a woman who lives beyond her means. She dresses in elegant clothes, lives in a luxurious Park Avenue Penthouse (in the Tower Apartment House) and has a Marilyn Monroe-like figure and aura that attracts men all the time — although the type of men Gwen wishes to attract are the millionaires — not the working class man.

Gwen was born in Illinois, was a Girl Scout, and enjoyed the simple life. She began to develop at an early age and became spoiled by all the attention given to her by boys. She grew up wanting more, but her job with a local magazine was not getting her what she wanted. With what little money she had, Gwen moved to New York and with luck on her side found a job as editor for *Manhattan Magazine*. She next spotted an ad in the *Journal News* for a roommate and joined forces with Loco Jones and Mike McCall, two other strikingly beautiful women with the same credo: "Have Money, Will Marry."

Gwen is almost a clone of Greta Hanson, Mike and Loco's former roommate. She prefers not to do housework, loves to take long bubble baths and enjoys borrowing Mike and Loco's clothes. Gwen is a bit more particular than Loco or Mike but hopes to find her million-dollar dream man before her thirtieth birthday.

See also: Greta Hanson, Loco Jones, Mike McCall.

446. Hamilton Whitney, III, *Just Cause*, PAX, 2002. Played by Richard Thomas.

Hamilton Whitney, III, is a man who loves San Francisco, the home of his birth. Hamilton is the senior law partner in the firm of Burdick, Whitney and Morgan at 2325 Battery Street. He appears to be rich, stuck up and all work and no play. Whitney is a graduate of Harvard Law School and has an undergraduate degree in Asiatic languages (he later says he went to Princeton). Whitney came from a family of professionals: his father was a surgeon; his uncle, a criminal lawyer, wrote the book, *Just Cause*.

Whitney is called "Whit" by his friends and will not violate a court order to achieve a goal. He is strictly professional and will not compromise that professionalism at any cost (one of the reasons why he commands high fees and is a much sought after criminal lawyer; he compares this to fishing: "I like fishing, but I throw the little ones back. I like to wade out deep and catch the big ones"). Whitney has been married three times; he maintains a working relationship with his third wife, Rebecca, an FBI agent he met when she interrogated him during a case.

See also: Alexandra DeMonaco.

447. Hannibal Smith, *The A-Team*, NBC, 1983–1987. Played by George Peppard.

John Smith, nicknamed Hannibal, is the head of the A-Team, military fugitives who help people who are unable to help themselves. Hannibal was a colonel in Vietnam and served in the 5th Special Forces Group with B.A. Baracus, H.M. Murdock and Templeton Peck. On January 27, 1971, the team was ordered to rob the Bank of Hanoi by a Colonel Morrison. After completing the assignment, Morrison, a Vietnam supporter, framed the team for the robbery and escaped with the money by staging his own death. Unable to prove their innocence, the team was arrested; but before they could be court-martialed, they escaped and set themselves up as the A-Team in Los Angeles.

Hannibal lives in Los Angeles. His Social Security number is 844-31-3142 and 61-56831 is his FBI file number (wanted as a fugitive). Hannibal is also a part-time actor and takes roles in horror movies (playing either the Slime Monster or the Aquamaniac). He is famous for his expression "I love it when a plan comes together" and has a gun, an M-60, he calls "Baby." Hannibal also claims he gets "on the jazz" (a feeling of excitement during each assignment). He also plays Mr. Lee, the elderly Chinese owner of Mr. Lee's Laundry Shop in Los Angeles (each client must meet with Mr. Lee before the team will take an assignment. Hannibal believes this deception is necessary as they are wanted by the military and it could be a trap).

See also: B.A. Baracus, H.M. Murdock, Templeton Peck.

448. Harley Random, *LAX*, NBC, 2004. Played by Heather Locklear.

Harley Random is a young woman with a high pressure, highly responsible job: runway manager (also called co-director) at Los Angeles International Airport (LAX for short). Harley was born in California but never surfed — "I was a Valley Girl; tanning was our sport." She was also brought up, with her sister Julie, in a house that her father ran like a military unit. When she rebelled she was kicked out of the house and began a new life wherein she estranged herself from her family. Harley is single and has never been married — "I haven't gotten around to that."

Harley brings her personal life to work — "and it makes her a real bitch" say her co-workers. She believes firmly in helping people in trouble and hates to owe people anything. She likes to do things her way — "the hell with procedure when my way is better." People say Harley has a bad temper — "It's not temper," she says, "It's passion. My job has no passion and if that makes me a touch cranky sometimes, too bad."

Harley lives in Venice, California, with her dog Finnegan. She is an expert on birds ("I dated a bird freak once") and suffers from an attention disorder problem. Two martinis is her limit; "three makes me stupid." When Harley needs to impress people she shows a bit more cleavage than normal. Despite the numerous problems — and headaches she gets from dealing with countless crises, Harley claims, "This is the best job I ever had."

449. Harmony Angel, *Captain Scarlet and the Mysterons*, Syn., 1967. Voiced by Shin-Lian.

Harmony Angel is a pilot for Spectrum, a futuristic organization that battles evil from outer space. Harmony was born in Tokyo, Japan, and is the daughter of a wealthy flying taxi service owner. Harmony grew up in the world of high speeds and became a member of the Tokyo Flying Club. Hoping to become the first woman to break a record, Harmony flew around the world nonstop. Her determination, courage and experience brought her to the attention of Spectrum, who immediately hired her as a pilot. Harmony loves sports and spends her spare time teaching judo and karate to the other angels. The program is a puppet series filmed in Supermarionation.

See also: Captain Magenta, Captain Ochre, Captain Scarlet, Destiny Angel, Melody Angel, Rhapsody Angel, Symphony Angel.

450. Harriman Nelson, *Voyage to the Bottom of the Sea*, ABC, 1964–1968. Played by Richard Basehart.

Harriman Nelson is an admiral in the U.S. Navy and the creator of the *Seaview*, an awesome, atomic-powered submarine. Harriman, the son of William and Elizabeth Nelson, was born in Boston, Massachusetts. His father was a wealthy banker and Harriman was being groomed to follow in his father's footsteps. Harriman, however, had a dream to join the Navy. He entered the Naval Academy against his father's wishes to study marine biology and nuclear engineering. Harriman became interested in submarines at this time and set out to learn all he could about them. With his superior knowledge of submarines, Harriman was appointed commander of the *Nautilus*, the Navy's first nuclear sub. The assignment was short lived (as the *Nautilus* was being decommissioned) but the experience gave Harriman the idea for a similar submarine that could be used for undersea research.

Harriman was next assigned to the Office of Naval Intelligence. He then taught at Annapolis and retired shortly after. With time and resources at his disposal, Harriman established the N.I.M.R. (Nelson Institute for Marine Research) off the Southern Coast of California. Here he built his dream, the *Seaview*.

Harriman is an expert in military history and tactics. He enjoys music and a good Scotch. He won the Nobel Prize for his work in biology. Although Harriman built the *Seaview* for research, it more often than not encounters evil beneath the sea and the sub becomes a means by which to protect mankind. "The *Seaview* is never finished," says Harriman, "as long as there are evil forces active in the world."

See also: Lee Crane.

451. Harrison Destry, *Destry*, ABC, 1964–1965. Played by John Gavin.

Harrison Destry is a rugged and handsome Old West cowboy. He stands six feet, four inches tall and possesses a great sense of humor. He is the son of Tom Destry, a rugged gunfighter and respected lawman; but Harrison has not followed in his footsteps. Harrison is not fast on the draw, but he's tough when he has to be. He prefers to avoid confrontations and his philosophy is peace ("I'm the most peaceful man there is"). Money interests him ("I'll do most anything for it") and women find him irresistible ("Nothing can stop me from coming to the aid of a beautiful damsel in distress"). If there is a way to avoid trouble, Harrison will find a way. His easy-going ways have also made him a patsy. He was framed for a robbery, arrested, tried and found guilty. He served time in the Texas State Penitentiary and was released early for good behavior. He now roams the West seeking the man who framed him.

452. Harry Kim, *Star Trek: Voyager*, UPN, 1995–2001. Played by Garrett Wang.

Harry Kim, Operations Officer on Starfleet's U.S.S. *Voyager*, was born in the year 2349. He attended Starfleet Academy (2367–71) and graduated with a degree in engineering and analytical operations. He was engaged at the time of his assignment on *Voyager* (2371) and previously played clarinet in the Julliard Youth Symphony. He was also editor of the Starfleet Academy Newsletter for one year. Harry is brilliant in certain applications, but he appears to lack knowledge of his own Earth history as he never heard of Amelia Earhart and was vague on events dealing with aviation.

See also: B'Elanna Torres, Chakotay, The Doctor, Kathryn Janeway, Neelix, Seven of Nine, Tuvok.

453. Harry McGraw, *The Law and Harry McGraw*, CBS, 1987–1988. Played by Jerry Orbach.

Harlan H. McGraw, III, better known as Harry McGraw, is a tough detective who owns Harry McGraw Private Investigations in Boston. Harry was born in Massachusetts and became fascinated with crime solving by watching movies of the great detective of his youth (Charlie Chan, Philip Marlowe and The Thin Man). He was untidy as a child and he is untidy as an adult (he lives in a cluttered apartment on Melrose). He developed an interest in gambling at an early age and this too has been carried into his adult life (he loves to bet on the horses but he has virtually no luck and is always in need of money; he claims "I never forget a nag I lose on").

Harry is totally disorganized and easily irritated. He is reluctant to tell the whole truth (or "The Straight Skinny," as he calls it) and believes he attracts the worst clients (he considers such people missions of mercy clients). Harry rarely gives out his business card ("I'd give you a card but I'm fresh out. I'm in the book"). He rarely uses a gun and relies on his fists ("Okay, I get busted up a bit, but at least I get a case solved"). He claims that murder cases have a way of bringing out the worst in people and that if you need protection he's the guy who can give it to you. However, once on a case, Harry's seedy and abrasive side appears. He becomes relentless and a determined fact finder despite the dangerous obstacles he might encounter. He is also a master of disguises and uses such deception to trick suspects into revealing information.

Harry is not all that innocent himself. He has a police record (arrested by the Boston police for suspicion of murder and robbery) and has had his private investigator's license suspended four times in three years. When he gets the chance, he enjoys a drink at Gilhooley's Bar. The character first appeared on several episodes of *Murder, She Wrote*.

454. Harry Orwell, *Harry O*, ABC, 1974–1976. Played by David Janssen.

Harry Orwell is a bitter private detective working out of San Diego. He lives in a beach house and is repairing a boat he calls *The Answer* ("which I'll have as soon as I put it back together. I'm going on the ocean where they have no telephones; telephones bug me").

Harry was disabled in 1969 when on active duty (he was shot in the back while investigating a burglary-in-progress at a drugstore). He never discusses politics or the shooting that disabled him. Harry has been living on his disability pension and supplementing his income by moonlighting as a detective. The bullet has lodged near his spine and vigorous activity like running after a suspect causes pain.

Harry has a gun but rarely uses it. He also has a car but does a lot of walking. The car, an ancient Austin-Healey MG, needs numerous repairs—all of which he can't afford. He will ride the bus or spring for a cab when he needs transportation ("It's tax deductible"). Harry isn't particularly friendly but a good friend to those who know him. He is grouchy, more stubborn than he was before, and he is now just realizing that his chances for a true romance are becoming increasingly slimmer as he grows older. "I wish I was 17 again because when I was 17 I once said 'A woman

is like a bus. They'll be another one along in a few minutes.' Now that was a long time ago."

Second season episodes place Harry in Santa Monica, California, where he lives at 1101 Coast Road; 555-4617 is his phone number. Harry found romance with Sue Ingram (Farrah Fawcett), an airline stewardess with a Great Dane named Grover (who just doesn't seem to like Harry).

455. Harry Solomon, *Third Rock from the Sun*, NBC, 1996–2001. Played by French Stewart.

Four aliens from the Home Planet, a world 30 trillion miles away, are dispatched by the Big Giant Head, to study life on Earth. The aliens travel across 3 billion galaxies and establish themselves at 417 Pensdale Drive in Rutherford, Ohio. Harry Solomon is the name taken by the group's transmitter (relates messages to the Big Giant Head). His leader becomes his older brother, Dick; the information man becomes Tommy, his younger brother; and the Security Officer takes the form of Sally, Dick's sister.

Harry loves watching television. He gets severe headaches if he can't watch *Good Morning, Rutherford* and *Good Afternoon, Rutherford*, his two favorite talk shows (in that order). Harry is dim witted and naïve and easily fooled. He is hoping to get into the Guinness Book of World Records with the world's largest soda can collection. He held jobs as a bartender (at McSorley's Bar), radio talk show host (at WBDL), and as Hargo the Alien at the LePine County Fair. On the Home Planet, Harry had a lower life form pet named Pickles.

See also: Dick Solomon, Sally Solomon, Tommy Solomon.

456. Harry T. Stone, *Night Court*, NBC, 1984–1992. Played by Harry Anderson.

Harry T. Stone is an unorthodox Manhattan night court judge (he is famous for his $55 fines and time served sentences). He presides in Room 808 (sometimes 1808) of the Criminal Courts Building and processes 12 percent fewer cases than any other judge in his position (due to the long lectures he gives defendants).

Harry was born in Chesapeake, Ohio. As a child he had a teddy bear (Jamboree) and two dogs (Oliver and Otto). As a teenager he stole a 1964 Cadillac for a joy ride and received two nights in jail and two weeks in a reformatory for crashing into a liquor store. It was at this time, when Harry saw the error of his ways that he began to develop an interest in the law. He is a graduate of East Chesapeake State College and acquired a law degree from Princeton University.

Harry lives in a small apartment in Manhattan with his pet rabbit (Cecil) and his stuffed armadillo (Clarence). He is a big fan of singer Mel Torme and claims to own every record Mel has made (he has also vowed to marry the first girl who is impressed by that). He is also a fan of 1930s actress Jean Harlow (a large picture of her is on the wall behind his office desk; a picture a Mel is on his desk).

Harry carries a Mercury-head dime as a good luck charm and he teaches law at the Ed Koch Community College (named after the former New York mayor); he is also faculty advisor for the school's newspaper, the *Harpoon*. Harry has been voted "Man of the Month" by the Society of Goodfellows and "Most Fascinating Judge in New York" by the Empire Magician's Society (Harry's first true love is magic. Harry Houdini was his hero and *Magic Time* was his favorite TV show as a kid).

Harry eats Zipp Bitts cereal for breakfast and likes cherry Kool-Aid and Fresca soda. He bowls at Bowl-a-Lane Alleys and always appears to be restrained; he never loses his temper and calmly deals with all defendants, no matter how obnoxious they may be.

See also: Bull Shannon, Christine Sullivan, Dan Fielding, Mac Robinson.

457. Harry Weston, *Empty Nest*, NBC, 1988–1995. Played by Richard Mulligan.

Harold Weston, called Harry, is a widowed pediatrician who lives at 1775 Fairview Road in Miami Beach, Florida (555–3630 is his phone number). Harry is the father of Carol, Barbara and Emily; his late wife was named Libby.

Harry was born in Florida and is a graduate of the Bedford Medical School, class of 1959. His mentor was Leo Brewster, a doctor who took Harry under his wing and inspired him to enter the medical field.

Harry originally had the tenth floor office at the Community Medical Center in Miami Beach; he later moves to the second floor when the Greykirk Corporation purchases the building. Harry is also the host of *Ask Dr. Weston*, a call-in radio program on station WWEN (990 on the AM dial). Harry later sells his practice to become a doctor at the Canal Street Clinic (a poor people's center next to Ernie's Garage). Although the focus changed from children to adults, Harry treated the adults as he did children — with kindness and respect. Harry tries to remain calm in all situations. He is easily exasperated and talks to himself when he becomes upset (especially over the antics of his adult daughters). He is also proud of his family crest, "The Sword of Weston." Harry has a dog named Dreyfuss (whom he also talks to when he becomes upset) and frequents Gerard's and Bernadette's Restaurant.

See also: Barbara Weston, Carol Weston, Emily Weston.

458. Hassie McCoy, *The Real McCoys*, ABC, 1957–1962. Played by Lydia Reed.

This entry also contains information on Little Luke McCoy (Michael Winkelman), Hassie's brother. Tallahassee McCoy, called Hassie, is the sister of Luke McCoy, a farmer in California's San Fernando Valley.

Hassie. Hassie was born in Smokey Corners, West Virginia, in 1944. Little Luke, the only McCoy to be born in a hospital, is actually the younger brother of Luke McCoy (Luke's parents were so excited when the baby was born that they named him Luke, forgetting they already had a son named Luke. He was called Little Luke to distinguish them). Luke's parents are deceased. Luke and his wife, Kate, now care for Hassie and Little Luke. The family relocated to California when Luke's grandfather, Amos McCoy, inherited his late brother's farm.

Hassie attends Valley High School and is a member of the Alpha Beta Sigma sorority; she later joined "The Bunch," the "in crowd" of girls at the school. Red and silver are Hassie's favorite colors and she has her hair done at Armond's Beauty Parlor (she was the first one in her school to wear the latest craze from France, the buffet beehive, which cost her $3.50). Hassie's after school hangout is the Malt Shop (later called the Soda Fountain). She earns money by babysitting.

Little Luke. Little Luke attends Valley Elementary School and is a member of the Valley Town Tigers Little League baseball team (he wears jersey 4). Little Luke's school is also referred to as "that school Little Luke attends" (Grandpa believes "It's a prison with all those rooms"). Little Luke enjoys fishing (sometimes cutting school to do so) and had his first job delivering newspapers. When Little Luke has noting to say it means something is bothering him. In one episode Little Luke had a dog named Mike (that appeared to be part of the family; it never turned up again). Hassie is said to be attending college and Little Luke is "at camp" in their last appearances on the show in 1962 (the series ended in 1963).

See also: Amos McCoy, Luke and Kate McCoy.

459. Hayden Fox, *Coach*, ABC, 1989–1996. Played by Craig T. Nelson.

Hayden Fox is coach of the Screaming Eagles, the football team of Minnesota State University. Hayden was born in Spokane, Washington, and is a graduate of Spokane High School and Georgetown University (another episode mentions Minnesota State University). Hayden has appeared on the covers of *Sports Illustrated* and *Collegiate Sports Digest* magazines and has been coaching the Eagles for 21 years. He is a patient man and hopes to one day win enough games to enter a bowl competition (such as the Pineapple Bowl in Hawaii). Hayden is also the host of *The Hayden Fox Show*, a weekly sports interview and update program on KCCY-TV, Channel 6.

Hayden cherishes his privacy. He lives away from people in a cabin in an unspecified forest-like area. There is a wooden Indian on his front porch, a basketball hoop, rubber tire on a rope (for football tossing), and a tree house in the backyard. Hayden drives a truck (which he has cleaned at Helen's Car Wash) and holds a weekly poker game (with a two dollar limit). Hayden is famous for his "five alarm chili." His favorite hangout is the Touchdown Club, a bar.

Hayden is divorced (from Beth) and the father of Kelly, a student at the university. Hayden is dating Christine Armstrong, a sportscaster for Channel 6. In 1995 Hayden left Minnesota State for a job in Orlando, Florida, coaching the Orlando Breakers, an NFL Expansion Team. Hayden's years of dedication won him the Curley O'Brien Award for Excellence in Coaching.

See also: Christine Armstrong, Luther Van Dam.

460. Hazel Burke, *Hazel*, NBC, 1961–1965; CBS, 1965–1966. Played by Shirley Booth.

Hazel Burke is the kind of woman you can pal around with. She is friendly and kind, a good sport, and a woman who will give of herself to help others. She is a bit overweight and she hasn't many male admirers. Hazel feels she will never find true romance again. Her only true love was Gus Jenkins, a merchant marine she met in the Observation Tower of the Empire State Building. He was throwing paper airplanes and called her "Brown Eyes." It was a love at first sight and Hazel would have married him if he asked her. He was strictly military and she knew things would never work out.

Hazel works as a maid and considers her employers, George and Dorothy Baxter (and their son Harold) to be her family. She has been working for the Baxters since 1950 and lives with them

at 123 Marshall Road in an unspecified Eastern city. Hazel calls George "Mr. B," Dorothy "Missy," and Harold "Sport."

Hazel is an especially good cook and housekeeper. She attempted to write her recipes for a book called *Hazel's Handy Recipes* and is President of the Ladies' Society of Domestic Engineers. She is famous for her fudge brownies and she was the TV spokeswoman for Aunt Nora's Instant Cake Mix. Hazel is also a member of the Sunshine Girls, a society of local neighborhood maids. Hazel was voted "Maid of the Month" by *American Elegance* magazine and, according to George she is the only person who knows the true meaning of Christmas ("she makes her own presents").

Hazel has 11 shares of stock in the Davidson Vacuum Cleaner Company and has an insurance policy to cover her back when she bowls. She keeps her government bonds in her footlocker.

Thursday is Hazel's day off and she takes time on Sunday to attend mass. She serves breakfast at 7:00 A.M.; lunch at 12:15 P.M.; dinner at 6:00 P.M. She has an account at the Commerce Trust Bank and never tells a lie (George says, "She has George Washington heroics"). Hazel loves her job and loves meddling in (and trying to solve) George's problems (she says, "Just dustin' these cobwebs off Mr. B's law books makes me feel smart"). CBS episodes find Hazel becoming the maid to George's brother, Steve Baxter, his wife, Barbara, and their daughter, Suzie, when George is transferred to the Middle East. Steve is the owner of the Baxter Realty Company and lives at 325 Sycamore Road.

See also: George and Dorothy Baxter.

461. Heath Barkley, *The Big Valley*, ABC, 1965–1969. Played by Lee Majors.

Heath was a man who described himself as "a tumbleweed in the wind, going from town to town and job to job" before he learned of his birthright — the name of Barkley. Heath is the illegitimate son of Tom Barkley, a man of vision who established the Barkley Ranch in the San Joaquin Valley in Stockton, California, in the 1830s.

Tom and his wife, Victoria, became the parents of Jarrod and Nick after establishing their ranch. A few years later a business venture brought Tom to the town of Strawberry to invest in some mines. Two thugs attacked Tom one night. He was beaten and left for dead behind a saloon. A girl named Leah Simmons found Tom and nursed him back to health. Tom had a brief affair with Leah but left her before he knew she was pregnant. Tom loved Victoria. He was on his way to becoming rich and famous and couldn't afford a scandal if he stayed with Leah. Tom returned to Victoria and never told her about Leah. They eventually had two additional children, Audra and Eugene. Leah too had a child — Tom's son, whom she named Heath (Leah never contacted Tom to tell him about Heath). Nine years later Tom was killed defending his land from those who wanted to take it (railroad officials).

Leah and two friends, Hannah and Rachel, raised Heath. It is six years after the death of Tom Barkley (1876) that Leah dies. Heath learns from Hannah that Tom Barkley was his father. Heath leaves Strawberry to seek his birthright. He hires on as a ranch hand at the Barkley ranch. A confrontation with Nick, the foreman (who believes Heath is a railroad spy) reveals the truth about Heath. Victoria eventually accepts Heath as her son (Victoria later rode to Strawberry and discovered through a letter written by Tom to Leah that Heath was Tom's son, but that he never knew about him).

Heath is bitter, full of painful memories and angry at the world. He helps Nick run the ranch and his famous for his bullfrog stew on the trail. He carries a rattlesnake's rattler for good luck and rides a horse named Charger. His favorite dinner is wild duck.

See also: Audra Barkley, Jarrod Barkley, Nick Barkley, Victoria Barkley.

462. Heather Owens, *Mr. Belvedere*, ABC, 1985–1990. Played by Tracy Wells.

Heather Owens is the middle child of George and Marsha Owens and lives at 200 Spring Valley Road in Beaver Falls, Pittsburgh, Pennsylvania, with her brothers, Kevin and Wesley.

Heather is very pretty but feels her brown hair makes her less attractive to boys (she wishes she were a blonde and became one for a time when she dyed her hair blonde. Heather was suddenly getting whistled at, had doors opened for her, and even "got free food from the guy in the cafeteria." She went to being her old self when her new look was more than she could handle. A year later, she felt she needed a more sophisticated name and called herself Bianca).

Heather is an average student at Van Buren High School. She is happy with her B and C grades and feels she does not have the ability to become an A student. Heather is a cheerleader for the school's football team, the Beavers, and is a member of the Iron Maidens, a community group that reads to the elderly. Heather entered the Miss Beaver Falls Beauty Pageant, performed a patriotic tap dance and came is second. She held an after school job at Traeger's Record Store and has her hair done at Snyder's Beauty Salon. When Heather gets depressed over losing a boyfriend, she eats Rocky Road ice cream then shops at the mall. She is called "Kitten" by George and eats Kellogg's Corn Flakes for breakfast.

See also: George Owens, Kevin Owens, Lynn Belvedere, Marsha Owens, Wesley Owens.

463. Helen and William Girardi, *Joan of Arcadia*, CBS, 2003–2005. Played by Mary Steenburgen, Joe Mantegna.

Helen and William Girardi, a happily married couple, live at 2320 Euclid Avenue in Arcadia, Maryland, with their children, Joan, Kevin and Luke. Sixteen-year-old Joan performs missions for God (see Joan Girardi).

Helen's maiden name is Brody. She is an artist (paints landscapes) and first worked in the administrative office at Arcadia High School, then as its art teacher (she is also the yearbook advisor). Helen is a caring mother who loves her very different children with equal devotion but with different approaches. Joan is pretty, a bit insecure and not easily motivated. Kevin is handicapped (injured his spine in a car accident) and self-pitying; Luke is the youngest, a brilliant student who stays mostly to himself.

Helen's early artwork reflects a dark side in her life: a man broke into her college dorm and raped her; to this day he remains at large. Red wine makes Helen tipsy and she insists that she do the family laundry.

William was originally the Chief of Police of Arcadia (a scandal within the department demoted him to head of the detective unit). He was born on September 5, 1955, and attended Mother Cabrini High School. He is a graduate of Morton Jr. College and immediately went into police work. Shortly after, he was brought in to help the overworked Arcadia Police Department to get the kinks out of the system. He succeeded and was a good cop until he relied on a false tip to bust a drug dealer. The tip didn't hold up under scrutiny and William was demoted to fieldwork. He eventually proved himself to be a good cop and was promoted to police chief. He served for several years before another scandal hit the department. William's car license plate reads PRZ 3S5 and L-100 is his car code. William was never in the delivery room with Helen "because I can't see my wife in pain."

See also: Joan Girardi.

464. Helena Kyle, *Birds of Prey*, WB, 2002–2003. Played by Ashley Scott.

Helena Kyle is a resident of New Gotham City. Her father is millionaire Bruce Wayne, alias the caped crusader, Batman; her mother was the villainous Cat Woman. Helena, however, is unaware that Bruce Wayne is Batman. When Helena was a young girl, her mother and father were engaged in a desperate effort to capture the evil Joker. The Joker's plan to defeat Batman was to drive him insane. He succeeded by killing Cat Woman. This so depressed Batman that Bruce Wayne left Gotham City without ever knowing that he had a daughter (Cat Woman kept her secret from Batman to protect her from the forces of evil). The orphaned Helena was adopted by Barbara Gordon, a close friend of Cat Woman, and raised to fight crime as Huntress (Helena's only wish is "to find the man who killed my mother and I want that man dead").

Bruce Wayne's genes and Cat Woman's unique villainous chemistry have made Helena a Medahuman (a person who possesses abilities that no one else does). Helena's eyes turn cat-like when she is angered and says, I'm the Huntress — you're the prey" when approaching a villain. She has the instincts of a cat and can leap. Helena is very strong and well versed in the martial arts. Although Helena lives at Stately Wayne Manor, she works as a bartender at the Dark Horse Bar. Helena attended New Gotham High School and was voted "Most Likely to Inspire Energy" (she was captain of the pep squad).

Helena, as Huntress, dresses in black and doesn't wear a mask ("It's itchy and ruins my mascara"). She doesn't carry a weapon "because I'm a weapon." Sometimes she says, "I just want to be like an ordinary girl."

See also: Barbara Gordon, Dinah Lance.

465. Helena Russell, *Space: 1999*, Syn., 1975–1977. Played by Barbara Bain.

Helena Susan Russell is a doctor with Space Services who is now attached to the Moonbase Alpha Medical Center (in 1999 the moon was conquered and an early warning system was established to repel alien invaders. A radioactive chain reaction blasted the moon out of its orbit and Dr. Russell and 300 personnel are now marooned on the moon as it wanders, seeking a new planet on which to affix itself).

Helena was born on August 5, 1960. She is the daughter of a physician and chose to follow in her father's footsteps. She majored in space medicine and was immediately drafted by the Space Commission to work in its medical unit. It was at this time that Helena met and married Lee Russell, an astronaut who later disappeared dur-ing an Astro 7 mission. She joined the Space Service in 1992 and won the Donnelmeyer Award for her academic excellence (the award is a replica of a microscope once used by Louis Pasteur). She is noted for her work transforming duty periods from dull recreation rooms to exotic gardens of relaxation. Helena strives for perfection; not only in her work but in the work of others. She is hard on herself when she fails at something. She is also not one to sit around and wait for something to happen. She will risk her life on missions outside of Moonbase to help others. Her hobby is sculpting (she even created a self portrait of herself in clay).

See also: Alan Carter, John Koenig, Maya, Victor Bergman.

466. Henry and Muriel Rush, *Too Close for Comfort*, ABC, 1980–1983; Syn., 1984–1986. Played by Ted Knight, Nancy Dussault.

Henry Rush and his wife Muriel are a happily married couple that live in a red Victorian two-family house on Buena Vista Street in San Francisco. They are also the parents of Jackie and Sarah, two very beautiful girls who live in the downstairs apartment.

Henry is the creator and artist of the comic strip "Cosmic Cow" (a space crime fighter; his biggest challenge "is to draw an udder so it is not offensive"). Henry was born in San Francisco and is a graduate of State College (where he studied art). He first worked as an artist by painting turtles. While working with animals he had an idea of an animal that fights crime and sold the idea to Random Comics, a division of Wainwright Publishing.

Henry met Muriel, a singer with Al Crowler and His Orchestra, one night while dining at a nightclub. Henry found an instant attraction to Muriel and asked her for a date. Several months later they were married (they honeymooned at the Golden Pines Hotel). Muriel gave up her career to raise Jackie and Sarah while Henry's income from the comic strip increased as "Cosmic Cow" merchandise became popular.

Henry draws his comic in a section of the bedroom that he has set aside as a mini office (he draws the comic with a "Cosmic Cow" hand puppet by his side). Henry is a very protective father and constantly worries about Jackie and Sarah, more so than ever, since they moved into their own apartment and has less contact with them. Muriel is more relaxed and trusts her girls to do the right thing (something she cannot convince Henry of doing). Henry is constantly thinking the worst and it is Muriel who brings peace and serenity to the household. While Muriel had some regrets about giving up her singing career, she put that part of her life behind her. When the girls were old enough to care for themselves, she found work as a freelance photographer (a job she still holds). Henry gives Muriel $150 a week to run the house.

In the syndicated version of the series, Henry and Muriel move to Marin County, California, after Jackie and Sarah move away. Henry becomes co-owner of a weekly paper called the Marin Bugler; Muriel becomes a mother again when she gives birth to a son she and Henry name Andrew.

See also: Jackie Rush, Sarah Rush.

467. Henry Blake, *M*A*S*H*, CBS, 1972–1975. Played by McLean Stevenson.

Colonel Henry Blake was a doctor in charge of the 4077 M*A*S*H (Mobile Army Surgical Hospital) unit in Korea during the war. Henry was born in Bloomington, Illinois, and is married to Lorraine. He claims, "I left a growing practice and a wife with a fistful of credit cards at home." Henry loves fishing and is often seen wearing his green fishing cap. He tries to impress nurses with fishing stories and gets little respect from his officers, especially Hawkeye Pierce and Trapper John McIntire. Henry was more like "one of the boys" as opposed to being a leader and put up with Hawkeye and Trapper's antics as he knew it was their way of letting off steam. Although in charge, Henry was actually lost without the help of the company clerk, Radar O'Reilly. Henry ordered adult films from the Tabasco Film Company in Havana, Cuba, and had to resort to sending notices to the various tents to make announcements (as nobody listened to him when he spoke). He believed Major Frank Burns "is the biggest horse's patootie on this post" and "the only thing G.I. about him is athlete's foot." Henry's joyous transfer turns to sadness when the 4077 hear that his transport plane was shot down over the Sea of Japan and there were no survivors. Henry was often seen wearing a black sweater with a red *I* (for Illinois State College); he drinks from a mug with the same colors. Colonel Sherman Potter replaced him.

See also: Benjamin Franklin Pierce, B.J. Hunnicutt, Charles Winchester, III, Frank Burns, Margaret Houlihan, Radar O'Reilly, Sherman Potter, Trapper John McIntire.

468. Herb Tarlek, *WKRP in Cincinnati*, CBS, 1978–1982. Played by Frank Bonner.

Herbert R. Tarlek, II, called Herb, is the obnoxious sales manager for WKRP, a 5,000-watt AM radio station (1530 on the dial) in Cincinnati, Ohio. Herb is married to Lucille and is the father of Bunny and Herbert III.

Herb was born in Cincinnati and majored in business at State College. He wears rather loud clothes and constantly fears getting fired for the difficult time he has selling time to advertisers. WKRP is not a top ten station (it is number 16 in an 18 station market). Advertisers are reluctant to spend money and Herb feels his ingenious ways of acquiring sponsors is the only thing that keeps his paycheck coming.

When a meeting is called, Herb wonders "Am I in trouble?" He also has a rule: "When it comes to petitions, Herbert R. Tarlek doesn't sign anything."

Herb appears to have a comfortable relationship with Lucille (although Lucille believes that sex is a reward and will only give it when Herb does something to earn it; for example, "Mow the lawn Herb or no num num tonight"). While Herb is faithful to Lucille, he does hit on (annoy) every girl he sees. He especially has an innocent crush on Jennifer Marlowe, the station's ultra sexy secretary (who constantly rejects his advances). He calls the station's boss, Arthur Carlson, "Big Guy."

See also: Arthur Carlson, Bailey Quarters, Dr. Johnny Fever, Jennifer Marlowe, Les Nessman, Venus Flytrap.

469. Hercules, *Hercules: The Legendary Journeys*, Syn., 1994–2000. Played by Kevin Sorbo.

This entry also contains information on Iolaus (Michael Hurst), Hercules's traveling companion.

Hercules. Hercules is a hero of Ancient Greece who uses his mighty strength to help those who are threatened by evil. Hercules is half mortal and half god. His father is Zeus, the King of the Gods, and his mother is Alcmene, a mortal woman with whom Zeus had an affair. Hera, Zeus's wife, the all-powerful Queen of the Gods, frowns upon infidelity and has sworn to kill Hercules because he is a constant reminder of her husband's infidelity.

Hercules has chosen to live among mortals and help them. He travels with Iolaus to help wherever they are needed. Hercules is kind and gentle and never seeks to kill. He believes the Earth is round and that the sun revolves around it ("It is the reason why there are seasons." Iolaus believes, like others, that the Earth is flat). Hercules can sew and make clothes ("My mother taught me") and devised the first Olympic games (as a means to avoid a bloody conflict between the Spartans and Elans). Hercules has a certain knack for arriving just as a crisis erupts and, being of kind heart, feels honor bound to resolve the conflict (peacefully if possible).

Iolaus. Iolaus is a mortal who believes he is a great comedian (he tells jokes and is often the only one who laughs at them). He is two years older than Hercules and was a thief (as a child he stole donuts from villagers). It was Hercules who turned his life around. Iolaus is the son of Skouros, a professional soldier who spent little time at home and was later killed in battle. Although Iolaus does not possess the strength of Hercules, he often becomes offended when Hercules thinks he cannot defend himself and steps into help. He believes he and Hercules find trouble without looking for it and is always on the lookout for some fiendish plot Hera has devised to kill Hercules.

470. Herman Brooks, *Herman's Head*, Fox, 1991–1993. Played by William Ragsdale.

Herman Brooks is a magazine fact checker and researcher for the Warterton Publishing Company in New York City. Herman was born in Millbury, Ohio, and is the son of a tire salesman and his wife. He is a graduate of Millbury High School and Ohio State College. As a kid Herman had a parakeet named Pookie. Herman now lives at 564 West 58th Street, Apartment 3C in Manhattan. He earns $22,500 a year and hopes to become a writer. Herman is of average intelligence and the audience is permitted to see "inside" his head as characters representing his anxiety, intellect, lust, and sensitivity battle over his actions.

A woman named Angel represents Herman's sensitivity. Without her, Herman would lack tenderness, honesty and love. Just the opposite is Lust, represented by Animal ("Without me he'd miss out on all the good stuff; you know, fun, food, babes"). Keeping Herman out of trouble is Wimp, who represents Herman's anxiety. And without Genius, representing Herman's intellect, Herman would not be capable of accomplishing any feat. Herman is fearful of confrontation and Angel appears to be the emotion that most often wins. Herman's favorite watering hole is McNally's Pub and Restaurant.

471. Herman Munster, *The Munsters*, CBS, 1964–1966. Played by Fred Gwynne.

Herman Munster is the successful creation of Dr. Frankenstein. He was assembled from body parts at the Heidelberg School of Medicine in Germany ("I was in several jars for six years"). Herman was brought to life by electricity in 1814. Count Dracula, Herman's father-in-law (better known as Grandpa), owns the only known set of blueprints for his creation.

Herman resembles the 1930s movie screen monster, Frankenstein. He stands seven feet, three inches tall and weighs "three spins on the bathroom scale." Herman has a body temperature of 62.8 degrees; a blood pressure reading of minus three; a pulse of 15 and no heartbeat. He has been married to Lily Dracula since 1865 and they have an eight-year-old werewolf son named Edward Wolfgang. They live at 1313 Mockingbird Lane in the town of Mockingbird Heights.

Herman works as a gravedigger for the Gateman, Goodbury and Graves Funeral Parlor. Doris Day is his favorite actress and "Goldilocks and the Three Bears" is his favorite fairy tale (he can't wait for it to be made into a movie). Herman is a poet of sorts and he contributes his morbid verses to a magazine called *Mortician's Monthly* (where his first poem, "Going Out to Pasture," was published). He has a ham radio with the call letters W6XRL4 and drives a hot rod with the license plate HAJ 302. To earn extra money, Herman held the following jobs: bronco buster at a rodeo; Chinese laundry presser; welder at a shipyard; and private detective (Agent 702 for the Kempner Detective Agency). When Herman gets mad he stomps his feet (and shakes the house) and says, "Darn, darn, darn" when something goes wrong.

John Schuck plays Herman in the 1988–91 syndicated series update, *The Munsters Today*. The following new information is given: Herman was born in Dr. Frankenstein's lab in Transylvania over 300 years ago. His teeth squeak when he gets thirsty; his eyes are brown, blue and undetermined; and his neck bolts (for the electricity that supplied life) itch when he gets an idea. For a bedtime snack, Herman enjoys refried armadillo bladders (which also give him nightmares) and weasel burgers; his favorite breakfast is "legs benedict"; rack of lamb is his favorite dinner. Herman was the first person in Mockingbird Heights to eat sushi and he possesses the Golden Shovel Award for being the best gravedigger. His favorite TV show is *Married ... With Children* (he is a member of the Christina Applegate [Kelly on the show] fan club) and Judge Wopner (from *The People's Court*) is his hero.

See also: Eddie Munster, Grandpa, Lily Munster, Marilyn Munster.

472. Hikaru Sulu, *Star Trek*, NBC, 1966–1969. Played by George Takei.

Hikaru Sulu was born in San Francisco, California, in the year 2237. He is of Asian descent and attended Starfleet Academy (2255–59). He began his career as a physicist before becoming a lieutenant under James T. Kirk, captain of the

Starship, U.S.S. *Enterprise NCC-170l*. A year later (2266) he became a helm officer and worked on the bridge alongside Captain Kirk.

See also: James T. Kirk, Leonard McCoy, Mr. Spock, Montgomery Scott, Pavel Chekov, Uhura.

473. Hilary Banks, *The Fresh Prince of Bel Air*, NBC, 1990–1996. Played by Karyn Parsons.

Hilary Banks is the daughter of Philip and Vivian Banks and lives in fashionable Bel Air, California. She was born in 1969 and is beautiful, extremely feminine and conceited. Hilary grew up in the lap of luxury and was given anything she wanted. At the age of nine Hilary attempted to play the violin but had to give it up ("It irritated my chin"). She next tried ballet but had to stop "because I thought I would get feet like Fred Flintstone." In high school Hilary was a cheerleader but quit "because they expected me to cheer at away games and travel by bus."

Hilary dreams of a glamorous job so when people ask what she does she can see them turn green with envy. She enrolled in UCLA but quit when she found it too difficult. She first worked at the Bel Air Mall then as the personal assistant to a has-been movie star (Marissa Redmond). When her father took her credit cards away ("You spend more money on clothes than some small nations spend on grain") Hilary found a job with Delectable Eats Catering. When this didn't suit her she became the TV weather girl on KFPB, Channel 8's *News in Action* (a paper called "The I Hate Hilary Newsletter" was published criticizing her skimpy wardrobe and lack of weather knowledge). This led to her hosting her own talk show, *Hilary*.

Hilary has her hair done at a salon called Black Beauty and posed nude for a *Playboy* magazine layout on weather girls called "Warm Fronts" (Hilary's breasts were covered by clouds). Hilary reads *17* and *She* magazines and will never wear the same clothes twice. She has a knack for losing her house keys (she has 30 copies made each month and hopes someone will return the ones she lost; her address is on each key).

See also: Ashley Banks, Carlton Banks, Philip Banks, Will Smith.

474. Hilton Lucas, *Cosby*, CBS, 1996–2000. Played by Bill Cosby.

Hilton Lucas and his wife Ruthie (Phylicia Rashad) live at 1539 Blake Street in Astoria, Queens, New York, with their daughter Erica (T'keyah Crystal Keymah). Hilton was born in Queens in 1936 and attended P.S. 168 (grammar school) and Queens Point High School. He next served a four-year hitch in the Navy before ac-

quiring a job as a baggage handler for National West Airlines. He is now retired (forced out of work after 30 years when the airline claimed they were losing money and laid off 10,000 employees).

Hilton is a man who has to be involved with something to occupy his time. He held several additional jobs, ranging from magazine telemarketer, salesman at Winchester Antiques, video store sales clerk, and security guard for Hollinger Security. Hilton enjoys performing a magic act for the Children's Charity Fund and appeared on TV as Cowboy Bob on the kiddie series *Mr. Jay's Crib*.

Hilton enjoys a beer at the Steinway Pub and is intrigued by reruns of the TV series *I Spy* (the character of Alexander Scott, played by Bill Cosby, bears a striking resemblance to Hilton Lucas). Hilton banks at Trust Savings and Loan (later called the Astoria Savings Bank) and has a specific rule for guests about smoking in the house: they must join him in the smoking room — the city block outside his home. Hilton is a fan of jazz music (he calls his stereo record player "Old Betsy") and enjoys barbequing in the backyard on a grill he calls "Bob."

Hilton likes veggie burgers "if they're wrapped in meat," says Ruthie, who has been married to Hilton since 1966. Ruthie works with her friend Pauline Fox in a café/flower shop (later café/book shop) they call The Flower Café. In their spare time Hilton and Ruthie coach basketball teams at the Community Center: Hilton is captain of the Warriors; Ruthie captains the Fireflies. Their favorite restaurant is Marino's.

Hilton's daughter, Erica, is first a law student then lawyer with the firm of Muldrew and Renwick. She quit the firm to become a chef; gave up on that to become a flight attendant (for National West Airlines); and finally decided on becoming a schoolteacher.

475. H.M. Murdock, *The A-Team*, NBC, 1983–1987. Played by Dwight Schultz.

H.M. Murdock is a member of the A-Team, military fugitives who help people in trouble (see Hannibal Smith for further information). H.M., who claims his initials stand for "Howling Mad," is not wanted by the military (he was on another assignment in Vietnam when his teammates, Hannibal Smith, B.A. Baracus and Templeton Peck, were captured and tried for robbing a bank). H.M. was a pilot for the Thunderbirds before the Vietnam War (where he performed heroic missions). He was discharged as a captain and now pretends to be insane (as a result of the war) for free food and shelter (at Building 16 of the V.A.

Hospital in Los Angeles). The military suspects that H.M. is a member of the A-Team, but can't prove it (Hannibal devises unique plans to get Murdock out of the hospital for brief periods so he can join the team on assignments). H.M. has type A-B negative blood, an invisible dog (Billy) an alligator (Wally Gator) and a plant ("The Little Guy"). "The Range Rider" (from the 1950s TV show) and Captain Bellybuster of the Burger Heaven Food Chain are his heroes. H.M. has been diagnosed with paranoid delusions and ammonia is the key word that triggers his aggression. Although H.M. is pretending to be crazy, B.A. believes "he ain't pretending, he's crazy" (for all the nutty things Murdock does, like talking to Billy on assignments).

See also: B.A. Baracus, Hannibal Smith, Templeton Peck.

476. Holly Aldridge, *Café Americain*, NBC, 1993–1994. Played by Valerie Bertinelli.

Holly Aldridge is a 30-year-old woman struggling to rebuild her life after an unpleasant divorce. Holly was born in Minneapolis in 1963. She is the daughter of George and Marilyn and was pampered as a child. She attended the Middleton Elementary School, U.S. Grant High School and State College (where she majored in languages). Details about Holly's marriage and divorce are sketchy, but after the breakup, she headed to Paris to begin a new life. She found work as "a translator of English to English" (taking the dry language and translating it into everyday American talk at an undisclosed company). When her boss tried to seduce her, she quit. Holly is walking along the street, hoping to find inspiration about what to do next, when she wanders into the Café Americain, a famous French eatery. She befriends its owner, Margaret Hunt, and acquires the job of assistant manager when she helps Margaret acquire a contract with the JuVal Soft Drink Company. While Holly has the title of manager, she says, "I have no actual title. It's whatever Margaret tells me to do."

Holly is a Scorpio and has a unique way of dealing with people. She lives in a very small apartment with a view of the Eiffel Tower ("if you hold a mirror out the window and angle it just right you can see the Tower"). Holly is a very trusting woman. She is still heartbroken about her husband cheating on her and is afraid to take another chance; she has quit dating for the time being. She is afraid of heights ("It's not so much height as it is the uncontrollable urge to jump off") and loves to snack on Hostess Sno-Ball cakes.

477. Holly Tyler, *What I Like About You*, WB, 2002 (current). Played by Amanda Bynes.

Holly Ann Tyler is a very pretty 16-year-old girl who lives with her sister, Valerie Tyler on Bleeker Street (Apartment 34C) in Manhattan. She and Valerie later live in a loft on Spring Street. Holly is a sophomore at Styvesant High School and came to live with her older sister when their father, a salesman, was transferred to Japan (their mother is deceased).

Holly is trouble prone, inquisitive and very nosey. She is also very bright and very independent for one so young. Holly likes to do things her way and frowns when a situation doesn't always turn out exactly as she expected. She dreams of attending Columbia University and claims to be a loose cannon—"I do whatever comes to my mind." She hangs out at the Liberty Diner, likes ketchup on her hot dog and her cooking specialty is omelets. Holly first worked at an unnamed restaurant as a busgirl (responsible for "bread, water and clearing tables"). She next worked as Valerie's assistant (then mail room girl) at the P.R. firm of Harper and Diggs; and assistant salesgirl at a duplicating company called Copy That. Holly enjoys various Post cereals for breakfast (Fruity Pebbles, Honey Bunches of Oats and Blueberry Morning). Her father sends her $60 a week as an allowance (Valerie takes out $20 and adds $30 of her own for Holly's college education). After graduating from high school Holly spent the summer of 2004 on a scholastic internship in Paris. She enrolled in N.Y.U. in the fall of 2004 (Valerie had attended Columbia and Holly felt she would be living in Valerie's shadow if she also attended).

See also: Lauren, Valerie Tyler.

478. Homer Simpson, *The Simpsons*, Fox, 1990 (current). Voiced by Dan Castellaneta.

Homer J. Simpson is a 34-year-old, 239-pound buffoon who works as a safety inspector in Sector 7G of the Springfield Nuclear Power Plant. He is married to Marge and is the father of Bart, Lisa and Maggie.

Homer was born in Springfield in 1956 but was abandoned by his mother when he was seven years old. He attended Springfield Elementary School and is a graduate of Springfield High School (where one flashback episode shows Homer and Marge meeting here for the first time in 1974. A later flashback shows Homer and Marge meeting in 1980 when he worked at the Springfield Fun Center and Marge was a waitress at Burgers Burgers).

Homer and his family now live at 742 Evergreen Terrace in the town of Springfield. Homer enjoys eating, drinking Duff's Beer and sleeping. He can't fix things and he can't build things. He enjoys calling the local radio station with fake traffic jam tips and is boastful of the fact that he knows the words to the Oscar Meyer Weiner TV commercial jingle ("I wish I were an Oscar Meyer Weiner..."). He is afraid of spiders and vowed never to read a book after he read *To Kill a Mockingbird* and never learned how to kill one.

Homer has A-positive blood and pork chops are his favorite food. He hangs out at Moe's Tavern and was "Dancin' Homer," the mascot for the Isotopes baseball team. Homer also created his own drink—"Flaming Homer" (liquor mixed with cough syrup). He held a second job as a driver for Classy Joe's Limo Service and wrote (with Lisa's help) a food critique column for the Springfield Shopper. Homer is called "Homey" by Marge and was responsible for launching the career of Lerlena, a country and western singer he discovered but sold her contract for $50.

See also: Bart Simpson, Lisa Simpson, Marge Simpson.

479. Honey West, *Honey West*, ABC, 1965–1966. Played by Anne Francis.

Honey West is a shapely blonde who measures 36-24-34. She dresses in the latest fashions, has a swanky apartment and appears to be a lady of leisure, sophisticated and wealthy (having a pet ocelot named Bruce sort of establishes her as being linked to high society). However, she is not what most people would suspect—a private detective and owner of H. West and Company in Los Angeles.

Honey was born in California and brought up in an atmosphere of murder and mayhem (her father was a private detective. When he passed away, Honey inherited the business—and all the danger that accompanies it).

Honey's base of operations is her apartment at 6033 Del Mar Vista in Los Angeles. She is shrewd, uncanny, and capable of defending herself. Although she does possess a black belt in karate, Honey does take an occasional beating. She incorporates the latest in scientific equipment (for example, her lipstick, earrings and makeup compact double as a transmitter). She has a mobile base of operations disguised as a TV repair truck (H. West TV Repairing); license plate 1406 122 (later IET 974). Honey carries a gun—and uses it. Her earrings also double as miniature gas bombs when thrown and broken. When Honey becomes upset, she takes her anger out on target practice figures (and always hits the bulls-

eye. "I come here for practice, not therapy," she says).

Honey is not always successful and does let clients down. She often risks her life by going undercover to solve a case (she especially likes a society woman or wealthy playgirl). Honey tries to cooperate with the police but she can't always promise she will go by the book.

Honey is a born cynic and believes every case is connected to a murder. She is also not as effective as her father when he ran the company. She lets cases pile up and becomes too focused on a case when it gets the best of her. The innocent looking ballpoint pen Honey gives to certain clients is actually a miniature transmitter she uses for tracking purposes. Honey works alongside Sam Bolt (John Ericson), her father's partner, whom she also inherited.

480. Hope Shanoski, *Hope and Faith*, ABC, 2003 (current). Played by Faith Ford.

Hope Marie Shanoski is a 35-year-old housewife and mother who lives at 22 Cherry Lane in Glen Falls, Ohio, with her husband, Charlie (an orthodontist), and their children, Sydney, Hayley and Justin. Hope is the sister of Faith Fairfield, a once famous soap opera star who is down on her luck and now resides with Hope. While Hope and Faith grew up together and attended the same schools, they took different life paths: Faith became an actress; Hope chose to raise a family.

Hope is not as sexy or flamboyant as Faith (at U.S. Grant High School, for example, Hope was self conscious about her developing figure and would shower in a two piece bathing suit after gym class). Hope claims that the only reason Faith's breasts are bigger "is because she had a boob job" (Faith holds it over Hope that she wears a bra to bed. "I need the support," says Hope).

Hope is a simple girl who likes life to be uncomplicated. She is a bit of a control freak and loves to go shopping. She always buckles her seat belt; always reports for jury duty ("It's a civic responsibility") and loves celebrating special occasions (like birthdays and anniversaries). Hope is president of the Grant High School P.T.A., chairman of the Glen Falls Hospital and Volunteer Committee, and hostess for her weekly book club meetings. Hope admits to doing daring things ("I found a broken egg in a carton and replaced it with another egg from another carton before buying it"). She stands by the fact that the strongest drug she has ever taken was Ibuprofen ("aspirin upsets my stomach"). Hope had a dog named Pickles as a kid and her father called her "Sunshine." Hope mentioned she turned down a job with the *Chicago Tribune* to marry Charlie. However, she put her journalistic abilities to the test when she took a job with the Glen Falls *Gazette* as a columnist (for "Life in the Carpool Lane").

See also: Faith Fairfield

481. Horatio Caine, *C.S.I.: Miami*, CBS, 2002 (current). Played by David Caruso.

Horatio Caine is a lieutenant with the Crime Scene Investigation Unit of the Miami Dade Police Department in Florida. His expertise is arson and explosives. Horatio was born in Miami on April 17, 1960. He is six feet tall, weighs 180 pounds, and has a Bachelor of Science degree in chemistry from Florida State University. As a child Horatio grew up in an era of drugs, race riots and Cuban freedom fights. Horatio was 17 years old when his mother stood up to a drug dealer and was killed. Horatio knew he had to do something and helped the police find her killer. He also knew that he found his true calling—protecting the city he loves. Horatio entered the Miami Police Academy after graduating from high school. However, when he was assigned to walk a beat he found it boring. Soon afterward, when he discovered it was the C.S.I. Unit that actually solved major crimes, he enrolled in a four-year criminology program at Miami University. Horatio graduated as a Level 1 criminologist and eventually became the head of the Miami Dade C.S.I. unit.

Horatio is a three dimensional thinker and has the ability to place pieces of a puzzle together. He knows science provides the solutions to a crime and he incorporates all the field has to offer. When he catches a killer he is satisfied. The motive doesn't appear to matter to him.

See also: Alexx Woods, Calleigh Duquesne, Erik Delko, Tim Speedle.

482. Hoshi Sato, *Star Trek: Enterprise*, UPN, 2001–2005. Played by Linda Park.

Hoshi Sato is an ensign and the communications officer under Jonathan Archer, captain of the Starship U.S.S. *Enterprise NX-01*. Hoshi was a teacher of exo-linguistics at Amazon University in Brazil when she was asked by Jonathan to become a part of his crew and initiate man's thrust to explore other worlds. She studies languages to make unique connections with people. Hoshi was born in the 22nd century (possibly the early 2120s) and is an expert at translating alien languages.

See also: Charles Tucker, Jonathan Archer, Phlox, T'Pol, Travis Mayweather.

483. Hoss Cartwright, *Bonanza*, NBC, 1959–1972. Played by Dan Blocker.

Eric Hoss Cartwright was born in 1848 and is the middle child of Ben Cartwright and his second wife, Inger, a Swedish girl Ben married that same year. Hoss, as Eric is called, has two brothers, Adam and Little Joe. Hoss is the Swedish mountain name for a big friendly man—something Inger knew the boy would become even though she only lived long enough to see him as an infant (she was killed during an Indian attack; see Ben Cartwright for further information).

Hoss was a big man (six feet, four inches tall, 270 pounds) with a powerful punch and a big friendly smile. He was feared for his strength but had a heart of gold and often gave of himself to help others. He wore a white 10-gallon hat and loved to eat (he felt he would perish without meals prepared by the ranch cook, Hop Sing). Hoss had a habit of bringing home hopeless cases and trying to reform them. Every spring Hoss would come down with a severe case of Spring Fever Clumsiness, which Ben controlled with a mixture of sulfur and molasses. Hoss was sensitive and shy around women. When he called a girl "filly" it meant, according to Adam, a high compliment. In addition to performing all the heavy chores around the family's timberland ranch, the Ponderosa, Hoss held the position of temporary sheriff in both Virginia City (the town near the Ponderosa in Nevada) and of a town called Trouble, California. He rode a horse named Chub. Hoss lost his life in 1881 while attempting to save a woman from drowning.

See also: Adam Cartwright, Ben Cartwright, Little Joe Cartwright.

Hot Lips Houlihan *see* **Margaret Houlihan**

484. Howard and Marion Cunningham, *Happy Days*, ABC, 1974–1984. Played by Tom Bosley, Marion Ross.

Howard and Marion Cunningham are a happily married couple who live at 618 Bridge Street in Milwaukee, Wisconsin, during the 1950s. They have been married since 1936 and are the parents of Chuck, Richie and Joanie.

Howard and Marion were both born in Wisconsin. Howard currently owns the Cunningham Hardware Store on 8th and Maine; Marion is content as a housewife and mother. When Howard was a teenager, he went to the hardware store to buy a plunger. He became fascinated by the various items lining the shelves and became hooked—hardware was in his blood. He began working at that store as a stock boy and by 1946 he owned the store. Howard's work history in dialogue from other episodes contradicts this story. At one point in his life (not specified) Howard worked as a hot dog vendor at Yankee Stadium in the Bronx, New York. He also served a hitch in the army during World War II (where he had the nickname "Cookie").

Howard is a republican and a member of the Leopard Lodge (Local 462). He likes the color blue and drives a black DeSoto (plate F-3680). Omelets are his favorite breakfast. Howard's back goes out if he has an irritating day at work and he gets a headache if he doesn't have dinner by 7:00 P.M.

Marion worked as a secretary before marrying Howard (they honeymooned at the Holiday Shore Lodge in Lake Geneva and stayed in Suite 325. They danced to the song "Moonlight in Vermont" on their wedding night). As newlyweds Howard called Marion "Baby Cakes"; she called him "Snookums." Marion is a member of the Milwaukee Women's Club and bowls with Howard on a team called The Ten Pins. *The Edge of Night*, *As the World Turns* and *The Secret Storm* (actual soaps at the time) are Marion's favorite TV serials. Marion (maiden name Kelp) is allergic to cayenne pepper and has a drinking glass with a picture of movie star Rudolph Valentino on it. When it comes to disciplining the children, Marion and Howard always agree that a firm hand is the proper way to earn their respect.

See also: Fonzie, Joanie Cunningham, Richie Cunningham.

485. Howdy Doody, *Howdy Doody*, NBC, 1947–1960. Voiced by Bob Smith.

The marionette Howdy Doody and his twin brother, Double Doody, were born in Texas on December 27, 1941. Their parents were ranch hands and earned a living by performing chores for the owner. Howdy and Double enjoyed life on the ranch but their lives would change forever when they turned six. It was at this time that their rich uncle, Doody, died and bequeathed them a small parcel of land in New York City. Uncle Doody struck oil in Texas and created a town its future citizens called Doodyville. Uncle Doody traveled east before the twins were born and had always regretted that business kept him from returning to see them.

Each of the boys had a dream: Howdy wanted to run a circus while Double wanted to become a ranch owner. When NBC television needed land to build a studio they approached Mr. Doody and offered to buy the land his son had inherited. Mr. Doody arranged a deal to include Howdy's dream. The land eventually became the home of NBC's New York headquarters, 30 Rockefeller Plaza. NBC built circus grounds and appointed one of their radio performers, Buffalo Bob Smith, as a guardian for the six-year-old boy.

Howdy traveled alone by bus from Texas to New York. He met Buffalo Bob at the bus terminal and the two became instant and life-long friends. Howdy's dream became a reality on his birthday in 1947 when NBC premiered a circus show they called *Howdy Doody*.

Howdy is a red-haired, freckle-faced (72 freckles), blue-eyed boy with an enormous grin who dresses in dungarees, a plaid work shirt and large bandana. He is honest, good-natured and always eager to help people in trouble. While he has a lot of friends, Howdy is saddened that Phineas T. Bluster, a mean 70-year-old man, opposes his circus and seeks to shut it down.

Bob Smith, called "Buffalo Bob" for his adventurous past, dresses in a pioneer costume and oversees the circus for Howdy. He is supposedly descended from Buffalo Bill. Clarabell Hornblow, a skilled clown hired by Howdy when no other circus would stand for his habit of playing practical jokes, assists Buffalo Bob. Clarabell remains silent and "speaks" by honking a "yes" or "no" horn.

486. Hunter Fallow, *Grosse Pointe*, WB, 2000–2001. Played by Irene Molloy.

Hunter Fallow plays the part of Becky, a student at Grosse Point High School on the mythical television series *Grosse Pointe*. Hunter grew up in Los Angeles and was pushed by her mother into becoming an actress. She appeared in diaper commercials when she was an infant and in cereal ads when she was six. Hunter is a graduate of the UCLA Theater Department and has guest starred on such real shows as *Blossom* and *Remington Steele*. She auditioned for a role in an Oliver Stone movie called *The Monica Lewinski Story* but lost the role to Reese Witherspoon.

Hunter made an appearance on *Buffy the Vampire Slayer* before acquiring the role of Hunter on *Grosse Pointe*. She and *Buffy* star, Sarah Michelle Gellar, didn't get along and Hunter has started her own Internet web page (*www.ihatesarahmichelle.com*) where fans can send messages about Sarah on the WB network (where *Buffy* aired at the time).

While Hunter is very attractive, she feels her small breasts are her downfall. She feels the lack of ample cleavage prevents her from getting juicy parts and is responsible for her not having a boyfriend. Hunter is a health food nut and likes beet juice with a carrot chaser. She drinks ginseng tea and has a serious problem — she shoplifts.

See also: Courtney Scott, Marcie Sternfeld.

487. Iara, *BeastMaster*, Syn., 1999–2001. Played by Samantha Healy.

Iara is an enchanting demon who is as deadly as she is beautiful. She rules in an era of magic and nature and has the power of the mist (a white, cloud-like vapor that traps her victims). Iara derives strength from water and uses it to project false images of herself (for example, transform herself from seductress to venomous snake).

Iara seeks to become all-powerful. One of the demons that stands in her way is Curupira (see entry), who rules the forests and its animals. After several confrontations, Iara defeated Curupira and imprisoned her beneath her waters (although it was later said Curupira "was imprisoned neck deep in snakes"). At this point Iara assumed Curupira's powers and was called "The demon who rules the animal kingdom."

See also: The Ancient One, Arina, Curupira, Dar, The Sorceress, Tao.

488. Illya Kuryakin, *The Man from U.N.C.L.E.*, NBC, 1964–1968. Played by David McCallum.

Illya Kuryakin is an agent for U.N.C.L.E. (The United Network Command for Law and Enforcement), a secret New York–based agency that battles the evils of THRUSH. The Del Floria Taylor Shop on 2nd Avenue and 40th Street fronts for U.N.C.L.E. Illya works with Napoleon Solo and wears badge number 2. He communicates with headquarters via his pen, which is set on Channel D. He uses a Magnum 35, a refined version of the Magnum 44.

Illya was born in Russia but speaks with what appears to be a British accent. He first attended the University of Georgia in the Ukraine (where he learned gymnastics), then the Sorbonne in France (post graduate work) and finally England's Cambridge University (where he acquired a degree in mechanics). Illya next served a hitch in the Russian Navy and graduated from the U.N.C.L.E. Survival School in 1956.

Illya is knowledgeable in many areas and is well versed in the martial arts. He is also an expert shot and archer. While not much of a drinker (prefers only beer or wine), he is a gourmet eater, not cook. Illya takes his coffee black and prefers cats to dogs. He is a Scorpio and is prone to catching colds (due to his allergies). In the TV movie update, *The Man from U.N.C.L.E.: The 15 Years Later Affair*, it is learned that Illya quit U.N.C.L.E. to open his own fashion line of clothes called Vanya.

See also: Napoleon Solo.

489. Inara Serra, *Firefly*, Fox, 2002. Played by Morena Baccarin.

Inara Serra is a renegade and a member of the *Serenity*, a Firefly class transport vessel that transverses a futuristic galaxy seeking to avoid capture by the Alliance and find jobs on planets that are outside of its grasp (Inara, as well as the ship's captain, Malcolm Reynolds, opposed the Union of Planets that was formed after a deadly civil war. They are now renegades and sought by the governing council of the Alliance of Planets).

Inara is a very beautiful woman who is actually a high priced prostitute. She is from a society called Companion Guild. Malcolm does not avail himself of Inara's services but has chosen to call her the ship's Ambassador as a Companion is necessary to open the door of communication on the many planets they encounter. Prior to her joining the *Serenity*, Inara had her own space shuttle. She dresses in very revealing outfits and her whole life is devoted to sex. She services only rich clients and uses her living quarters in the *Serenity*'s shuttle bay as her business office. Inara doesn't like to be referred to by the old Earth term "whore" and enjoys the title bestowed upon her by Malcolm as she finds it the perfect way to expand her clientele.

See also: Malcolm Reynolds, River Tam.

Iolaus *see* **Hercules**

490. Irma Peterson, *My Friend Irma*, CBS, 1952–1954. Played by Marie Wilson.

This entry also contains information on Jane Stacey (Cathy Lewis) and Kay Foster (Mary Shipp), Irma's roommates.

Irma Peterson is a gorgeous, shapely blonde, who would be referred to (at the time) as "a dumb blonde," or "a dizzy dame." She believes, for example, "that a meatball is a dance where lonely butchers go looking for romance." She claims to have gotten a bird dog as a puppy, but when it grew up "it never did learn how to fly." Irma finds life exciting, especially life in the big city. She was born in Minnesota (also said to be Montana) and was raised on a farm. But Irma wanted more than just chickens, cows and crops; she wanted to make her mark on the world. After graduating from high school, where she learned secretarial skills, Irma ventured onto New York City where she found a job with Milton J. Clyde, the owner of the Clyde Real Estate Company at 631 East 41st Street. She also found an apartment (3B; later 2C) at Mrs. O'Reilly's Boarding House at 185 West 73rd Street in Manhattan. She first shared the apartment with Jane Stacey (1952–53) then Kay Foster (1953–54).

Irma is sweet and sensitive and realizes she is not as smart as other people (as Jane says, "If she thinks it could be dangerous"). Irma talks to walls "so I can clear the cobwebs out of my mind" and reads "Flash Gordon" comics to learn about the future. When "I don't want people to know I know something, I pretend I'm dumb," says Irma.

Irma is always fashionably dressed (if she is not good at anything else, she is an expert on looking beautiful). She is also a good housekeeper and an ample cook (although she has a hard time figuring out some fruits. When Irma eats a banana, for example, she peels it, tosses the fruit aside and munches on the inside of the skin).

Irma is so sweet and so innocent that you can't help but love her. She has a tendency to cry when she doesn't get her way and she rarely ever realizes she said or did something dumb. Jane best describes Irma's predicament: "Mother Nature gave some girls brains, intelligence and cleverness. But with Irma, Mother Nature slipped her a Mickey."

Jane was born in Connecticut and lived with her parents at 1362 Post Valley Road. She moved to New York City to fulfill a dream: marry a rich man. Jane works as a secretary for Richard Rhinelander, the wealthy owner of the Richard Rhinelander Investment Company at 113 Park Avenue. She believes only money can buy happiness. When Jane was transferred to Panama in 1953, Irma acquired a new roommate, Kay Foster, a bright and beautiful reporter for the New York *Globe*. Kay was born in Ohio and majored in journalism at State College. Kay, like Jane, speaks directly to the audience to comment on the situations that arise and develop due to Irma's scatterbrained antics.

Isis *see* **Andrea Thomas**

491. Jacey Wyatt, *Movie Stars*, WB, 1999–2000. Played by Jennifer Grant.

Jacey Wyatt is a gorgeous movie star who has earned the reputation as "America's Favorite Leading Lady." She lives in Malibu, California, with her husband, Reese Hardin ("America's Leading Action Star") and their children, Lori, Apache and Moonglow.

Jacey is a three time Oscar nominee and "gets the movies that receive praise." She has made such films as *Heartland*, *Joan of Arc* and *A Perfect Fool*. Jacey is sometimes called "The biggest chick star around" by the tabloids.

Jacey was born and raised in Bakersfield by her beautiful mother Audrey (Loni Anderson), after her father deserted the family. Audrey was a stripper at the Extreme Turbulence Room, who posed nude for *Playboy* magazine in a layout called "Moms of the Stars." Jacey is a graduate of Bakersfield High School and although she was raised in a nightclub atmosphere, she has not followed in her mother's footsteps. She has earned respect and will not due a nude scene. Jacey's most embarrassing moment occurred during a live interview with Barbara Walters. She had an allergic reaction to Barbara's perfume and swelled up. The tabloids dubbed it "The Blow Fish Incident." Jacey is represented by the William Morris Agency.

See also: Lori Hardin, Reese Hardin, Todd Hardin.

492. Jack and Norma Arnold, *The Wonder Years*, ABC, 1988–1993. Played by Dan Lauria, Alley Mills.

Jack and Norma Arnold are a working class married couple. They are the parents of Kevin, Karen and Wayne, and live in a large home in an unspecified American suburb during the latter 1960s.

Jack was born on November 6, 1927. He served in the Army during the Korean War and now works in a job he hates — manager of distribution and product support services for a government company called Norcom Enterprises. Jack gets up at five in the morning, fights traffic, "busts his hump all day," comes home and pays taxes. He later quits ("the job is killing me") and opens a furniture store.

Norma, like Jack, was born in the same city. She and Jack married in 1949 (they honeymooned in Ocean City) and moved into their current home (street number 516) a year later. Norma worked as a secretary before giving up her job to raise a family. When the children were old enough to fend for themselves, Norma went back to work and found a job as a secretary in the attendance room at Kennedy Junior High School. However, her years away from the work force dulled her skills and she was let go for poor typing and dictation. She enrolled in River Community College to improve her skills and acquired a job as comptroller at Micro Electronics, a computer software company, at $225 a week.

As a child, Norma had a dream of becoming a singer after high school. She and Jack were average students in high school, although Norma was a bit more daring than Jack — she was caught smoking on campus and suspended for two weeks. Jack often feels the whole world is against him. He is very strict in disciplining the children and rarely takes any nonsense from them. Norma is a more gentle, trusting person and tries to be subtle when dealing with family issues; her wisdom and understanding is actually the glue that holds the family together.

See also: Kevin Arnold, Winnie Cooper.

493. Jack Bauer, *24*, Fox, 2001 (current). Played by Kiefer Sutherland.

This entry also contains information on Kimberly Bauer (Elisha Cuthbert), Jack's daughter. Jack Bauer is a top notch CIA agent who heads the President's Counter Terrorism Unit (CTU). He is a widower (his late wife was named Teri) and is the father of Kimberly (a CTU employee).

Jack is a graduate of the University of California (Los Angeles, where he acquired a Bachelor of Arts degree in English literature) and Berkeley (where he has a Master of Science degree in criminology and law). Jack then joined the L.A.P.D. and enrolled in its S.W.A.T. (Special Weapons and Tactics) school. After graduating he took a Special Forces Operations training course. Jack also served a hitch in the army where he was assigned first to the Combat Alliance Group then the Delta Force Counter Terrorist Unit. He became a section captain for the L.A.P.D. and later (2000) team leader of Operation Proteus. His prior experiences include the S.W.A.T. team and two CTU assignments: Special agent in charge of the Los Angeles Domestic Unit and Director of Field Operations for the L.A. Domestic Unit. Experience has taught Jack to be careful, very careful as the slightest mistake could have serious repercussions. He handles each assignment with kid gloves and executes each carefully planned maneuver with precise accuracy.

Kimberly is single and works with her father in the Domestic Unit of the L.A. Counter Terrorism Unit (where she is a Level One Analyst). She dropped out of Santa Monica High School but later acquired her GED and attended Santa Monica College (where she acquired an Associate of Arts degree in computer programming).

See also: David Palmer, Tony Almeida.

494. Jack Gallo, *Just Shoot Me*, NBC, 1997–2003. Played by George Segal.

Jack Gallo is the wealthy owner of *Blush*, a Manhattan-based fashion magazine. Jack founded the magazine in 1967 to encourage women to express their sexuality and encourage them "to drop their mops and pick up a briefcase." *Blush* is the first magazine to give a voice to female politicians; however, most women see it as just another magazine that treats females like trophies.

Jack is the father of Maya, his articles editor, with his first wife, Eve. His second daughter, Allison, is by his second wife, Allie, who is 30 years his junior (Jack is in his 60s). Jack runs his magazine like his blood type — B-positive. He loves electronic gadgets and watching old Marx Brothers movies cheers him up when he is depressed. Jack must have his coffee with Sweet and Low; he gets very upset if there is none in the office. He enjoys eating soft shell crabs "because it makes me feel powerful like a shark" and eats lunch at the Carnegie Deli. Jack has a racehorse named Tax Dodge and uses an after-shave lotion called Meadow After a Rainstorm. Jack is supposed to write the "From the Publisher" page but has grown tired of doing it and lets someone else do it (he never bothers to read it anyway). He is also the author of a book called *Don't Back Down* and while he may have worked hard to establish his magazine at first he is now more relaxed and relies on others to do the hard work for him.

See also: Dennis Finch, Maya Gallo, Nina Van Horn.

495. Jack Harper, *Tru Calling*, Fox, 2004–2005. Played by Jason Priestley.

Jack Harper was an accomplished E.M.T. (Emergency Medical Technician) who felt that after five years he needed to do something else. He now works at the New York City Morgue (330 West 7th Street) and has a mysterious link with the dead, as he himself was once dead.

Jack worked at Sinclair Hospital, the Lexington Medical Center, Pearson Health Services and St. Vale's Children's Hospital prior to his job at the morgue. During an emergency call to help a child who was the victim of a shooting, Jack took several bullets that were meant for the child. Jack's heart stopped for three minutes and 28 seconds before he was brought back from the dead (for an unknown purpose at first. As time passed it appeared Jack was to help co-worker Tru Davies save the lives of people who die before their time; Tru has the ability to relive the past 24 hours and change events to save lives. The 2004 season finale revealed Jack to be a being capable of reliving days — but to see that people who die are not saved by Tru).

Jack lives at 109-567 Charleston Road (address on his I.D. card); 555-0183 is his phone number. His web address is *JHARPER@EXGENT.WEB.*

See also: Tru Davies.

496. Jack McFarland, *Will and Grace*, NBC, 1998 (current). Played by Sean Hayes.

Jack McFarland is an admitted gay who calls himself a West Village singer, actor, dancer and choreographer. Jack was born in 1968 but does not know his biological father. His mother, Judith, had sex at a pool party with a man wearing a Richard Nixon mask and never saw him again. She had Jack as a single mother and later married Daniel McFarland, Jack's stepfather. Jack now lives in New York City.

Jack reads *Guy's World* magazine and had a parrot (Guapo) and a dog (Klaus Von Puppy; later called Gus). He gets nervous when he thinks about making love to a woman but claims he knows all about them because he had a "Growing-Up Skipper Doll" as a kid. Jack has a one-man show at the Duplex Theater called *Just Jack*, wherein he sings, dances and acts (he updated the show to *Just Jack 2000* and *Jack 2001: A Space Odyssey*). His web site is *www.justjack.com*.

Jack wrote a Caribbean fantasy called *Love Among the Coconuts* (which he changed to *Untitled Jack in Three Parts* when he was told it stinks) and dreams of starring in a gay Hollywood movie and having a line of gay action figures. He starred in a TV commercial for Senor Mattresses and made a training film about sexual harassment for the Canterville Plate Glass Company. Jack conducts acting classes in the rectory of St. Mary's Church in Manhattan and wrote an unpublished novel called *To Weep and to Willow*.

Jack held several jobs: caterer for Starlight Enterprises; salesman in the men's clothing department at both the Banana Republic and Barney's; usher for two performances of the Broadway show *Les Miserables*; man's hand bar soap distributor at Le Spa; and failed student at the Acrylic Nail School. He worked as a backup dancer to singers Jennifer Lopez and Janet Jackson and attempted to become a male nurse (Jack graduated from nursing school and was voted "Most Popular Student." While giving his farewell speech he realized he had dreams to become an actor and gave up nursing to pursue that dream). Jack tried to make money by marketing his invention, The Subway Tush (a train seating cushion he promoted with a hand puppet called Buttford, the Pantyhose Butt Puppet). In 2004 he became an employee of Out TV, a gay-run and oriented television station in Manhattan. Jack mentioned that in grammar school he was an altar boy at St. Margaret's Church.

Smart men scare Jack off. He is best friends with Grace Adler, an interior decorator; Will Truman, a gay lawyer; and Karen Walker, a fabulously wealthy woman who calls Jack "Poodle." Cher is Jack's idol and his dream house is Jeannie's bottle (from the series *I Dream of Jeannie*). Although there are several gay oriented series on TV, Jack mentions *Buffy the Vampire Slayer* as being his favorite (he finds the lesbian character, Willow, intriguing). Jack believes God is a woman and also believes that every TV and movie robot is gay. He has watched *Star Wars* many times in an effort to prove CP-30 is gay.

See also: Grace Adler, Karen Walker, Will Truman.

497. Jack Malloy, *Unhappily Ever After*, WB, 1995–1999. Played by Geoff Pierson.

Jack Malloy is a man who lives a miserable life. He has been married for 16 years (to Jennie) and is the father of three children, Tiffany, Ryan and Ross. He is not very fond of the children, except for Tiffany, and calls them "the accident," "the girl" and "the mistake."

Jack makes $40,000 a year as a salesman at Joe's Used Cars. He lives in the basement of his home at 30220 Oak Avenue in Van Nuys, California (he and Jennie are separated but Jennie has allowed Jack to still live in the house). Jack has a companion, his son Ross's plush rabbit, Mr. Floppy. Mr. Floppy (voice of Bobcat Goldthwait) comes to life (only for Jack and the audience) to help him cope with his pathetic life.

Jack loves basketball, and young busty babes but also fears the fact that he is getting older. He likes to watch Spanish TV "for the girls in bikinis and high heels" and talks constantly (to Mr. Floppy) about women's breasts and super models. Jack is actually a terrible father. He is overly protective of Tiffany and couldn't care less about Ryan or Ross (for example, if a boy breaks Tiffany's heart, Jack goes for the rifle in the den. If Ryan is not needed, Jack sends him to other WB shows to cause trouble for someone else. As for Ross, well, Jack tells him at the beginning of an episode whether or not he will be needed. This does not happen to Tiffany because, as Jack says, "We're not crazy; if it weren't for Tiffany [gorgeous Nikki Cox] the WB would have cancelled us long ago").

Mr. Floppy has his share of problems also. He is the son of Yogi Bear, but Yogi was a big star at the time and couldn't be saddled with a kid "so he tossed me into the toy bin." Mr. Floppy is a ladies' puppet and has had many affairs (especially with a Barbie doll take off called Berbie "in the toy box"). Mr. Floppy longs for (but can't get) Luscious Locks Loni, the doll of his dreams. Mr. Floppy has a crush on actress Drew Barrymore and constantly urges her to come on the show ("Drew, if you're watching..."). She never did.

See also: Jennie Malloy, Ryan Malloy, Tiffany Malloy.

498. Jack Mannion, *The District*, CBS, 2000–2004. Played by Craig T. Nelson.

Jack Mannion is the Police Chief of Washington, D.C. He was hired to do what no one else could: clean up the District, which has the worst crime rate in the nation.

The *New York Times* called Jack "the most innovative crime fighter." He was born in Manhattan and worked as a New York City Transit Cop (Badge 203) after serving in the Vietnam War. Jack was next Police Commissioner of Newark, New Jersey, then the Police Chief of Boston.

Jack is, as he calls himself, "a numbers guy." He believes in gathering crime statistics on a daily basis and crunching them relentlessly to see what is happening in D.C. and to know who is responsible for what. At times Jack can be considered caring and compassionate; but he is also arrogant, pushy, tasteless and smug. The word "no" is not in his vocabulary. When he declares a war on crime he uses military lingo. Jack is a movie fan and says, "I'm a cross between *Forrest Gump* and *Rain Man*."

Jack has a dog (Cujo) and enjoys relaxing on his boat, the *Betty-O*, which is docked at Slip 38 at the Washington Channel and Marina. He enjoys a drink at a bar called Teddy R's and keeps a bag of jellybeans in his desk drawer for a quick burst of energy. Jack also likes opera, cheese, white asparagus and a milk chocolate covered candy called Jiffy Bar. Jack plays the accordion and has been married and divorced twice. As a kid he had a pet cat (Cleopatra) and basis his tactics on the theory that "to win the war on crime first you believe you can."

499. Jack Moran, *Queens Supreme*, CBS, 2003. Played by Oliver Platt.

Jack Moran is a judge of the Queens Supreme Court in Queens, New York (8281 is his telephone extension). He is also not a typical run-of-the-mill judge. He is described as "smart, clever, a problem solver and he acts like a 12 year old." Jack is Irish and carries a gun in a shoulder holster. He keeps his favorite snack, jellybeans, on the Scales of Justice in his office. He is the author of the book *Moran on Justice* and he does outrageous things in his court to prove his point.

Jack is an outspoken Democrat who sometimes eavesdrops on jury deliberations (via the bathroom vents). He was born in New York, is a graduate of Queens College and enjoys meals at Brooks Diner.

500. Jack O'Neill, *Stargate SG-1*, Sci Fi, 1997 (current). Played by Richard Dean Anderson.

Jack O'Neill is first a colonel then a general with the U.S. Air Force's Stargate Command at the Cheyenne Mountain Operations Center in Colorado. Jack heads SG-1, a team of explorers who travel from planet to planet via a mysterious alien gate that allows for intergalactic travel. The Stargate, as it is called, was created eons ago by a civilization called the Ancients and scattered throughout the universe. Its circular center contains an energy field that emits a wormhole that allows almost instantaneous travel to any planet that also contains a Stargate (it is activated by pushing symbols similar to those of a telephone number).

Very little is known about Jack. He was born in Chicago but raised in Minnesota. He was married to Sarah and had a son (Charlie). He joined the Air Force and worked his way up to colonel but was forced into retirement when his son was accidentally killed (he found Jack's handgun and fatally shot himself). Jack went into a deep depression and was no longer capable of working. Sometime later he was asked to return to active service to head the Stargate missions. His intense work with Stargate also cost him his marriage and he and Sarah divorced.

Jack loved a family life. Prior to the Stargate Command he found pure pleasure with his wife and son. He is now a loner and has a difficult time making close relationships. Jack has a sharp mind and a deep concern for the inhabitants he encounters on distant planets (he is a by-the-books commander and not prone to violence unless circumstances force his hand. If he can resolve a situation without gunfire he feels he has accomplished something important) Jack has a keen sense of humor and strong convictions. He often disagrees with the suggestions of his team (most notably Dr. Daniel Jackson, a scientist whose theories sometimes seem implausible to Jack) and has to show authority to get things done the way he wants (following his plans).

See also: Daniel Jackson, Samantha Carter, Teal'c.

501. Jack Stein, *Love and War*, CBS, 1992–1995. Played by Jay Thomas.

Jack Stein is a 42-year-old newspaper columnist for the *New York Register* (he writes the column "The Stein Way"). He is a regular at the Blue Shamrock Bar and dates its female owner, Wally Porter. Jack was born in Brooklyn, New York. He attended Camp Olympus as a child and is a graduate of Brooklyn Poly Tech High School and the Columbia School of Journalism (where he was a member of the Sigma Chi Fraternity). He lives on

West 61st Street (Apartment 4C) and has a dust ball under his bed he named Milt. Jack loves jazz music and eats breakfast at Maurice's House of Steaks and Waffles. He won the Algonquin Award for a story on illiteracy and wears Old Spice cologne. He buys his shoes at Sears and *Betty and Helen* was the first movie he and Wally saw together at the Clairmont Theater in Manhattan. On their two-month anniversary, they gave each other the same gift: red satin boxer shorts. For a charity event, Jack and fellow columnist Jimmy Breslin ran naked across the Brooklyn Bridge. Jack writes about his observations on life, more often than not, basing those observations on his life at the Blue Shamrock.

See also: Dana Palladino, Wally Porter.

502. Jack Stiles, *Jack of All Trades*, Syn., 2000–2001. Played by Bruce Campbell.

Jack Stiles is an American agent working on orders from President Thomas Jefferson to protect the East Indian island of Pulau Pulau from Napoleon's plan to conquer it (the time is 1801). Jack works with his British counterpart, Emilia Rothschild and only she knows his secret: he is the Daring Dragoon, a local folk hero who helps good defeat evil.

Jack, as the Daring Dragoon, wears a black mask and hat with a red cape. He rides a horse named Nutcracker and fights for the people—"I am an enemy of all crime." Jack hangs out at a pub called The Drunken Pig and has a scar on his chin (as a young boy in a Catholic grammar school, he cut himself while trying to carve a hole in the stained glass window in the nun's convent). Jack jokes endlessly about everything and has an eye for the ladies (although he often gets his face slapped when approaching them). He plays the harmonica and is a graduate of West Point Military Academy. Although called "The Masked Weasel" by those he has sworn to fight, Jack continues his crusade, always disappearing after completing a mission. Jack's cover is that of Emilia's attaché (Emilia poses as an exporter).

See also: Emilia Rothschild.

503. Jack Tripper, *Three's Company*, ABC, 1977–1984. Played by John Ritter.

Jack Tripper is a male cooking student who shares Apartment 201 of the Ropers Apartment Building in Santa Monica, California, with two beautiful girls (Chrissy Snow and Janet Wood) but must pretend to be gay to remain with them (as the landlord, Stanley Roper, refuses to let a straight man live with two girls).

Jack attends the L.A. Technical School and is

specializing in French cuisine (poached salmon aspic is his specialty). Jack was born in San Diego and as a kid was a fan of the TV series *Davy Crockett* (in another episode, Jack says he was born in Arizona and had a dog named Coco. His mother and father met at a church picnic). He is a graduate of San Diego High School (where he won a trophy as a member of the track team). He then served a hitch in the Navy (where he got a tattoo on his behind that says "The Love Butt"). Because of his asthma he was put to work in the galley.

When Stanley and his wife, Helen, sell their apartment house to Bart Furley in 1979, his brother, Ralph Furley (Don Knotts) becomes the landlord. Jack must still pretend to be gay because "Bart would never allow a guy living with two girls." When Chrissy leaves to care for her sick mother in 1981, Jack and Janet acquire first acquire Cindy Snow (Chrissy's cousin) then nurse Terri Alden as their new roommate.

When Jack buys six pounds of prime rib, it is an indication to Janet and Chrissy that he has a special date with a girl. He and the girls enjoy a drink at the Regal Beagle Pub. When Jack graduates from school in 1980 he first acquires a job as a chef at Marconi's Diner, then at Angelino's Italian Restaurant. He next opens his own French eatery (Jack's Bistro) at 834 Ocean Vista in Los Angeles. The last episode of the series introduces Vicky Bradford (Mary Cadorette), a stewardess Jack met on a return flight from a chef's convention in San Francisco. The spinoff series, *Three's a Crowd* (ABC, 1984–1985), picks up the story line with Jack and Vicky moving into Apartment 203 over the bistro (now located at 834 Ocean Vista in Ocean Vista, California). Vicky is a flight attendant for Trans-Allied Airlines and "the crowd" is Vicky's father, James (Robert Mandan), their landlord, who constantly intrudes in their lives.

See also: Cindy Snow, Chrissy Snow, Janet Wood, Ralph Furley, Stanley and Helen Roper, Terri Alden.

504. Jackie Harris, *Roseanne*, ABC, 1988–1997. Played by Laurie Metcalf.

Jackie Harris is the sister of Roseanne Conner, a housewife and mother who lives in Lanford, Illinois. Jackie's real name is Marjorie, but as a baby, Roseanne could not pronounce it and called her "My Jackie." Jackie stuck and replaced Marjorie.

Jackie was born in Lanford and is the daughter of Al and Beverly Harris. She attended the Wild Oaks Summer Camp as a kid and is a graduate of James Madison Elementary School and

Lanford High School. Jackie first worked as an assembly line worker at Wellman Plastics. She next became an officer with the Lanford Police Department when a printing company took over Wellman. Jackie trained in nearby Springfield but quit the force when she fell down a flight of stairs and injured herself while tackling a pervert. After recovering she turned to acting and joined the Lanford Theater Company (she starred in a production of *Cyrano de Bergerac*). When this failed, Jackie became "a perfume bottle squitter" at the makeup counter in the Lanford Mall. This soon bored her and she quit to become a big rig trucker. Jackie soon tired of this and became partners with Roseanne in the Lanford Lunch Box (a diner).

As a kid Jackie had a doll (Mrs. Tuttle). She first lived in an apartment (A) then a house (number 465). She was married for a short time to a loser (Fred) and became the mother of their son (Andy). Jackie is a worrier and becomes upset over the simplest of things. She finds it hard to relax because of all the stress in her life; if she finds a moment of peace each day she is content — until the next crisis arises and she is back to worrying, complaining and seeking a way to cope with life.

See also: Becky Conner, Dan and Roseanne Conner, Darlene Conner.

505. Jackie Rush, *Too Close for Comfort*, ABC, 1980–1983. Played by Deborah Van Valkenburgh.

Jacqueline Rush, called Jackie, is the daughter of Henry and Muriel Rush and lives with her sister, Sarah, in a red Victorian home on Buena Vista Street in San Francisco.

Jackie was born in San Francisco on July 3, 1968. She is a graduate of Union Bay High School and San Francisco State College (where she majored in business). Jackie is very pretty, neat and tidy. She dislikes people who are sloppy and disorganized. Everything around her must be in order for her to perform properly. Jackie has a great sense for fashion but is very jealous of girls with large breasts. Jackie wears a size 32A bra and honestly believes her small bust line prevents her from advancing her position in life.

Jackie has a dream to become a fashion designer but for reasons that are not really made clear, she doesn't pursue that goal until she left the series in 1983. She first worked as a teller at the Bay City Bank. She next became a salesgirl at Balaban's Department Store. This led her to designing her own clothes. When she felt the time was right, she started her own freelance business, Designs by Jackie.

See also: Henry and Muriel Rush, Sarah Rush.

506. Jackie Thomas, *The Jackie Thomas Show*, ABC, 1992–1993. Played by Tom Arnold.

Jackie Thomas is a famous television star who can't act and think at the same time. He is conceited, demanding and obnoxious and his mere presence strikes fear into the hearts of his co-stars, writing staff and network executives. Jackie is allowed to do what he does because his program, *The Jackie Thomas Show*, is a big hit for the network and to lose him would mean huge advertising loses (Jackie plays a wacky father with a wife and two kids on the show).

Jackie was born in Ottumwa, Iowa (in Wapello County). It is not said how Jackie became a star, but he worked previously in a slaughterhouse (his TV character is a butcher). His favorite TV show and theme song is *Green Acres* and he has started his own charity, Jackie Thomas Save Our Universe. He treasures his privacy and lives in a beach house, but nobody knows where ("and I'd like to keep it that way," he says). Jackie has to be in the spotlight all the time. He becomes angry when a co-star becomes too popular, gets too much fan mail, or gets too much airtime. Jackie has two goals in life: to get Arnold Ziffel (the pig from *Green Acres*), a star on the Hollywood Walk of Fame ("He's a pig among pigs," says Jackie); and win an Oscar for his show (not realizing that TV shows win Emmys). Jackie's favorite sport is owl hunting ("in Iowa, where it's legal").

507. Jade O'Keefe, *2000 Malibu Road*, CBS, 1992. Played by Lisa Hartman.

Jade O'Keefe is a beautiful high-priced call girl who lives in a luxurious beachfront house at 2000 Malibu Road in Malibu Beach, California. She shares the house with actress Lindsay Wallace; Lindsay's sister and agent, Joy Wallace; and Perry Quinn, a criminal attorney.

Jade O'Keefe is the name taken by Victoria Page Tremont to distance herself from her controlling family, the influential Tremonts of Virginia (who have a net worth of $500 million). Victoria was brought up under the strictest of circumstances; everything she did was for a purpose: to carry on the family tradition. She was told what to eat, who to date, who to marry and even how many children to have. When Victoria turned 17 she couldn't stand it any longer and ran away from home. Becoming a prostitute was the only way she found she could support herself (she can now command as much as $4,000 a night). That is the true story. Jade tells a different one: "I was dirt poor and hungry and became a prostitute to survive. I thought I could sell my body without selling my soul, but it didn't work that way. There is still enough of me left for something better." Jade is hoping to do just that — but without help from her family.

See also: Lindsay Wallace.

508. Jadzia Dax, *Star Trek: Deep Space Nine*, Syn., 1993–1999. Played by Terry Farrell.

Jadzia Dax, a member of Starfleet, performs double duties: helm officer of the Starship U.S.S. *Defiant NX-74205* and science officer aboard *Deep Space Nine*, a former Cardassian mining station that was built in 2351 and abandoned 18 years later. It was then occupied by the Bajoran and finally by Starfleet who, at the request of the Bajoran Provisional Government, turned it into a strategic space station.

Jadzia is actually a combination of two life forms — a Trill and a symbion Dax (which lives through its host). Jadzia is a beautiful female and the eighth Dax host. Unlike previous hosts, Jadzia retains memories of her previous male host, Curzon Dax.

Jadzia was born on the planet Trill and joined with the Dax Symbion in 2341. She attended Starfleet Academy (2359–63) and was responsible for discovering the critical Bajoran wormhole to the Gamma Quadrant.

Jadzia is a fan of Galeo-Manada style wrestling. She enjoys the night and has an uncanny interest in forgotten composers, Klingon operas and Yirdian symphonies. In addition to her male-female conflicts, Jadzia has also inherited from her former hosts a liking for steamed azna and two favorite drinks: a Black Hole and iced raktajino with extra cream.

See also: Benjamin Sisko, Ezri Dax, Kira Nerys.

509. Jaime Sommers, *The Bionic Woman*, ABC, 1976–1977; NBC, 1977–1978. Played by Lindsay Wagner.

Jamie Sommers is a young woman who lives in Ojai, California. She is a schoolteacher (grade levels seven, eight and nine) at the Ventura Air Force Base and appears to be just that — a schoolteacher. Jaime, however, is very special. She is part bionic and an agent for the O.S.I. (Office of Scientific Intelligence), a branch of the government that tackles seemingly impossible assignments.

Jaime was born in Ojai and is a graduate of Ojai High School. She dated Steve Austin (the astronaut who would become "The Six Million Dollar Man") and was on her way to becoming a great tennis star when she suffered a terrible tragedy: while sky diving her parachute failed to open and Jaime plunged to the ground — "Her legs have so many breaks that we can't count them; her right ear is hemorrhaging and her right arm and shoulder are crushed beyond repair." Seeing that a bionic operation is the only way to save Jaime, Steve convinces Oscar Goldman, head of the O.S.I., to arrange for one. In a cost-classified operation, Jaime's legs (Bionic neuro link bi-pedal assembly), arm (Bionic neuro link forearm, upper right arm assembly), and ear (Bionic audio sensor) are substituted for Jaime's damaged limbs.

The operation saves Jaime's life and makes her the world's first female cyborg (a cybernetic organism). She has incredible strength and speed (she can run the mile in 58 seconds) and super fine hearing. Jaime feels she owes Oscar and the government a debt and relinquishes her tennis career to become an agent for the O.S.I. NBC episodes find Jaime working with a bionic dog she calls Max (Oscar named him Maximillion after the cost of the operation needed to replace his legs and jaw when he was injured in a fire). Jaime is very careful on assignments. She realizes her powers can kill but always restrains herself from letting them get the best of her.

See also: Steve Austin.

510. James and Florida Evans, *Good Times*, CBS, 1974–1979. Played by John Amos, Esther Rolle.

James and Florida Evans are a very hard working lower-income family who live on the South Side of Chicago at 963 North Gilbert (Apartment 17C of the Cabrini Housing Project; address also given as 763). They are the parents of three children (J.J., Thelma and Michael) and pay $104.50 a month in rent; 555-8264 is their phone number.

James is totally devoted to Florida. The times are bad and James struggles to provide a decent life for his family by taking whatever work he can find. He is a loving but stern father. He is easily upset by the antics of his children, especially J.J., and is very protective of Thelma. While Florida takes a subtle approach to disciplining the children, James believes in tough love; he was brought up by a strict father and he feels that a gentle touch is no way to deal with today's kids — even his own (some yelling and threatening works best for James).

Florida originally worked as a maid but quit the job when James objected and he moved the family from Tuckahoe, New York, to Chicago in an attempt to find a better life (in these early episodes of the series *Maude*, John Amos played Florida's husband as Henry). In 1976, after graduating from trade school, an opportunity arose for James in rural Mississippi to work in a garage. The family had been preparing to move when they received word that James had been killed in a car accident (John Amos's way of leaving the series). Florida suddenly became the head of the house and took a job as a school bus driver for the Roadway Bus Company. A year later, Florida met and fell in love with Carl Dixon (Moses Gunn), the owner of a small appliance shop. They were married in an off-camera wedding during the summer of 1977. As a child, Florida was called "Pookie Poo."

See also: J.J. Evans, Thelma Evans.

511. James T. Kirk, *Star Trek*, NBC, 1966–1969. Played by William Shatner.

James Tiberius Kirk, called Jim, was born in Riverside, Iowa, on March 22, 2233. He is captain of the Starfleet ship U.S.S. *Enterprise NCC-1701* and, at age 34, holds the record for being the youngest captain in Starfleet history. He also holds the record for being involved in 17 different temporal violations. On the plus side, he holds the record for bringing *Enterprise* back after its five-year mission in one piece.

Jim has an interest in American history (his ancestors were pioneers on the frontier of the 1800s). At the age of 13, Jim witnessed the massacre of 4000 people during a famine by Kodos the Executioner, the nickname for the governor of Tarsus IV. Through the efforts of a friend, Jim entered Starfleet Academy in the year 2250. It was at this time that he earned the rank of ensign and was assigned to the U.S.S. *Republic*. Four years later, Jim graduated and was promoted to lieutenant (assigned to the U.S.S. *Farragut*). In 2264, Jim became a captain and assigned to the U.S.S. *Enterprise* for its historic five-year mission "and go where no man has gone before." He was promoted to Admiral at the end of that mission.

Jim received Awards of Valor, the Medal of Honor, the Prantares Ribbon of Commendation and the Palm Leaf of the Axanar Peace Mission. Jim was involved in the very beginnings of the Klingon peace mission and for television history, shared the first interracial kiss with Uhura, his communications officer.

See also: Hikaru Sulu, Leonard McCoy, Mr. Spock, Montgomery Scott, Pavel Chekov, Uhura.

512. James T. West, *The Wild Wild West*, CBS, 1965–1969. Played by Robert Conrad.

James T. West is a major in the Secret Service of the 1870s. He is officially an underground intelligence officer and works for President Ulysses S. Grant. His partner is Artemus Gordon.

Jim, as he is most often called, had been in the cavalry for ten years before he was selected by the President to apprehend criminals who pose a threat to the safety of the country. Jim's mobile base of operations is a government loan: a train (an 1860 2-4-0 steam locomotive [engine number 3], a coal car and the Nimrod, a luxurious passenger coach). As far as the outside world is concerned, the train is the sole property of Jim West, a big spender from the East who is known as "The dandiest dude who ever crossed the Mississippi in his own train."

Jim has an assortment of weapons on the Nimrod (rifles, guns, knives and explosives). He also has a secret wardrobe for his undercover assignments and a pool table for relaxation. Jim always gets the more glamorous assignments. He has pop-out guns up his coat sleeves, a tiny derringer is concealed in two parts in the heels of his boots, a skeleton key is hidden behind his coat lapel, a sword is kept in his pool cue and smoke bombs are located under his holster. Jim is impulsive and quick to use his fists. He likes things to happen now, not later and this usually complicates the assignment, as Artemus has to expose his cover and come to the rescue. Jim is a ladies' man and this too becomes a problem when the villain is a beautiful woman Jim has unknowingly become fond of. Jim retired from the service in 1890 and moved to Mexico to begin a new life.

See also: Artemus Gordon.

513. Jamie and Paul Buchman, *Mad About You*, NBC, 1992–1999. Played by Helen Hunt, Paul Reiser.

Jamie Buchman is the regional vice president of the Ferrah-Ganz Public Relations Firm on Madison Avenue in Manhattan. She is married to Paul Buchman, a filmmaker, and they live at 142 West 81st Street (Apartment 11D).

Jamie is the daughter of Gus and Theresa Stemple. She was born in New Haven, Connecticut, in 1962 and has a sister named Lila (Jamie was called "Peanut" by her father). Jamie is a graduate of Yale University and likes to be liked by other people. She gets extremely upset if people don't like her and goes out of her way to impress them so they will like her (in high school, Jamie was known as "the Stemple sister who showed a boy her boobs to be liked").

Jamie is very pretty, has a sexy voice and has a knack for telling pathetic stories about herself and having people believe her. Jamie was a counselor at Camp Winneway and her image appears in the comic book *Mega Void*, as the evil Queen Talin. When Jamie is laid off from the PR firm, she first works as a press agent for the Mayor of New York. She then joins her friend, Fran Devanow (Leila Kenzle) to open her own public relations firm (Buchman-Devanow).

As a child growing up in New York City, Paul Buchman's favorite TV show was *Spy Lady*. However, it was not until he saw his first movie, *Attack of the 50-Foot Woman*, that he became fascinated by filmmaking and decided to become a filmmaker himself. After graduating from the NYU School of Film, Paul established his own documentary company, Buchman Films. When this failed years later, he found a job as a producer and director for a cable network called the Explorer Channel. *A Day in the Life of a Button* was the first film he made and he is famous for directing the "classic" film, *Hooter Vacation*.

Paul and Jamie have a dog named Murray. Paul previously lived at 129 West 81st Street (Apartment 5B) before moving into Jamie's apartment. In 1997 Jamie gave birth to a girl she and Paul name Mabel. Their favorite eatery is Riff's and they rent movies from Video Village.

514. Jamie Powell, *Charles in Charge*, Syn., 1987–1990. Played by Nicole Eggert.

Jamie Powell is the 16-year-old daughter of Ellen and Robert Powell. She was born in New Jersey and lives at 10 Barrington Court in New Brunswick with her sister Sarah and brother Adam.

Jamie attends Central High School and yearns to be a model. She has the beauty, the look and the style, although she sometimes worries that her small breasts will keep her out of the limelight. Jamie is a fanatic about makeup and clothes (everything has to be just right before she leaves the house). She is a cheerleader at school and hangs out at an eatery called the Yesterday Café. Jamie held a job as a waitress at Sid's Pizza Parlor and was a contestant in the Miss New Brunswick Beauty Pageant. Although she lost this contest, she was crowned Queen of The Yesterday Café Beauty Pageant. Jamie is also a student at the Better Image School of Modeling and through it, acquired a TV commercial for Banana Cream Shampoo and Hair Lotion. Jamie wears a size five shoe and is called "Little Scooter" by her father.

See also: Charles, Lila Pembroke, Sarah Powell.

Jan Brady *see* **Marcia Brady**

515. Jan Hoffmeyer, *It's a Living*, ABC, 1980–1982; Syn., 1985–1989. Played by Barrie Youngfellow.

Janice Hoffmeyer, called Jan, is a waitress at Above the Top, a posh Los Angeles restaurant that features "Sky High Dining." Jan was born in Philadelphia in 1948. She is the daughter of Will and Phyllis Frankel and is the mother of a young daughter named Ellen. Jan is divorced from Lloyd Hoffmeyer and becomes Jan Grey when she marries Richard Grey in 1985.

Jan is a graduate of Templar High School (class of 1966) and Berkeley College (where, during a protest, she was arrested for mooning a cop). Jan is an intelligent woman who sees her current job as only a stepping-stone for her dream of becoming a lawyer. She is attending the North Los Angeles School of Law and says, "I plan to do more with my life than hand out menus." Jan has a second job, hand writing invitations, to help pay for Ellen's ballet lessons.

See also: Amy Tompkins, Cassie Cranston, Dot Higgins, Ginger St. James, Sonny Mann.

516. Jane Cooper, *Zoe, Duncan, Jack and Jane*, WB, 1999–2000. Played by Azura Skye.

Jane Cooper is a very pretty but slightly off-center teenage girl. She is best friends with Zoe Bean and has a fraternal twin brother (Jack).

Jane lives in Manhattan (Chelsea District) and first attends Fielding High School, then Mid Manhattan College. Jane is a bit insecure and masks that insecurity with a deadpan sense of humor and cool attitude. She also believes her shoulders are out of alignment ("I lean a bit to the left"). Jane is very sexy but studies other girls to see what makes them sexy and copies what she feels will work for her. Jane has small breasts but doesn't complain about that fact. She makes the best of the situation and before each date wears a push-up bra "for cleavage purposes only." Although Jane is not a lesbian, she becomes extremely jealous if Zoe attaches herself to another girl (Jane changes her personality to match those of the girl Zoe has befriended). Jane is cynical and sour "and that's what I like about you," says Zoe.

At college Jane is studying to become a photographer. She works first as a photographer's personal assistant then as his camera assistant. She also shares an apartment (9H) with fellow college student Zoe.

See also: Zoe Bean.

Jane Stacey *see* **Irma Peterson**

517. Janet and Marshall Darling, *Clarissa Explains It All*, NIK, 1991–1994. Played by Elizabeth Hess, Joe O'Connor.

Janet and Marshall Darling are a happily married couple who live at 464 Shadow Lane in Baxter Beach, Florida. They are the parents of Clarissa and Ferguson and have been married for 15 years.

Marshall is an architect with the firm of Waterson, Baker and Kleinfield; Janet is head of the Children's Museum and won the Phineas Fiddlecarp Award for outstanding curator. Janet is a vitamin fanatic and health food nut who prepares such "tempting" meals as zucchini lentil surprise and carob pudding cake with whipped tofu topping. *Casablanca* is Janet's favorite movie and in college, she was in the Modern Ballet Dance Troupe (she starred in a ballet called "The Red Rabbits of Dawn"). When Janet becomes upset or depressed, she watches tapes of the movies *The Red Shoes* and *The Turning Point*.

Marshall watches *This Old House* on TV (he feels he has the ability to do the work he sees being done but never has the time to put his theories to the test) and reads *Architect World* magazine. He also reads a daily paper called *The Dispatch*. When it comes to disciplining the children, Marshall and Janet are lucky as both Clarissa and Ferguson are relatively good kids. What mischief they cause is easily remedied by talking things over.

See also: Clarissa Darling, Ferguson Darling.

518. Janet Wood, *Three's Company*, ABC, 1977–1984. Played by Joyce DeWitt.

Janet Wood is a pretty salesgirl who shares Apartment 201 of the Ropers Apartment House in Santa Monica, California, with Jack Tripper and Chrissy Snow (later with Cindy Snow and Terri Alden).

Janet is practical, sensitive, smart and witty. She works at the Arcade Flower Shop (later its manager) and after a hard day working "I could just sit down and take root." Janet has black hair and measures 34-22-34. She feels her breasts are small and thus not as attractive to men as she could be (she contemplated but rejected breast implants); she later felt it was her hair and bought a blonde wig (which she discarded when she found it was changing her personality from nice to mean).

Janet was born in Massachusetts. She talks and nags and usually gets her way by doing so ("People just give in to shut me up"). Janet is a member of Harvey's Health Spa and enjoys a drink at the Regal Beagle Pub. She likes to find "love, adventure and romance at the library" and tends to panic when she gets upset. At the age of seven Janet took ballet lessons (she dreamed she would grow up and become a dancer just like her teacher). In adult life, Janet took dance lessons

and starred in the play *Annie Get Your Gun* in Laguna Beach. Janet stated from day one that she was looking to marry and settle down. This occurred in the last episode when she married her boyfriend, Philip Dawson, an art dealer.

See also: Chrissy Snow, Cindy Snow, Jack Tripper, Ralph Furley, Stanley and Helen Roper, Terri Alden

519. Janice Soprano, *The Sopranos*, HBO, 1999 (current). Played by Alda Turturro.

Janice Soprano, alias Parvati Wasatch, is the daughter of mobster Johnny Boy Soprano and his wife, Livia. She is also the older sister of wise guy Tony Soprano. Tony followed in his father's footsteps; Janice found it difficult to live with her parents, especially her mother, who taunted her about her weight. She left her home in New Jersey when she turned 18. Janice first lived in California, where she worked for a moving company. It was at this time that Janice changed her name to Parvati (after a Hindu goddess) Wasatch (after a Utah mountain range). She next traveled to Europe where she found romance (she married a man named Eugene and they had a son they named Harpo). When Janice became disgusted with her marriage, she returned to the U.S. She found work in Seattle as a counter girl in an espresso bar. When she claimed operating the espresso machine gave her carpal tunnel syndrome and convinced a Workman's Compensation Board of it, she was granted disability payments.

Janice's father died before she left home. When Janice learned her mother had a stroke, she decided to forgive her for past discretions. Janice dropped her alias and returned to New Jersey to care for Livia. When Livia died shortly after, Janice's urge to travel subsided and she chose to live in her childhood home (where she wrecks havoc in her search for love, taking what she wants whenever she wants).

See also: Carmela Soprano, Meadow Soprano, Tony Soprano.

520. Jarrod Barkley, *The Big Valley*, ABC, 1965–1969. Played by Richard Long.

Jarrod Thomas Barkley is the eldest child of Tom (deceased) and Victoria Barkley, a married couple from Ohio who risked their lives to establish the Barkley Ranch in the San Joaquin Valley in Stockton, California, in the 1830s. The series is set in the 1860s; his siblings are Nick, Heath, Audra and Eugene.

Jarrod is now 32 years old and a lawyer. He has a strong sense of justice and will not compromise the name of Barkley for any reason. Tom and Victoria established themselves as a name for right against wrong; a name the people of the valley could look up to for wisdom and leadership in troubled times. Jarrod strongly believes in that principle and like his father, who was killed for standing up for his rights (by railroad officials who wanted to take his land), Jarrod will put his life on the line for justice.

Jarrod has offices in Stockton (the town nearest to the ranch) and in San Francisco. He oversees the massive Barkley holdings, which include the 30,000-acre ranch, its crops (peaches, olives, apples, oranges and grapes), the Barkley-Sierra Gold Mine and the Barkley Lumber Company. While Jarrod would love to do things by the book to defend clients (even members of his own family when they get into trouble), he sometimes finds himself becoming as tough as his brother Nick (the ranch foreman) when fists or guns sometimes becomes the only way to deal with certain situations.

See also: Audra Barkley, Heath Barkley, Nick Barkley, Victoria Barkley.

521. Jason and Maggie Seaver, *Growing Pains*, ABC, 1985–1992. Played by Alan Thicke, Joanna Kearns.

Jason Roland Seaver and his wife Maggie live at 15 Robin Hood Lane in Huntington on Long Island in New York. They are the parents of Mike, Carol, Ben and Chrissy and they met while they were students at Boston College. Jason is 13 months older than Maggie and was a psychology major. He was also a member of a rock group called The Wild Hots and as a kid his imaginary friend was 1950s TV game show host Bud Collyer ("who would come over to my house and play games"). Jason originally worked at Long Island General Hospital before establishing a private practice in his home. He also does volunteer work for the Free Clinic to help the people of his community.

Maggie first majored in child psychology then switched her major to journalism. She married Jason after graduating from college and worked as a researcher for *Newsweek* magazine before quitting to raise a family. She later returned to work using her maiden name, Margaret Malone. She was first a reporter for the Long Island *Daily Herald*, then a TV reporter for *Action News* on Channel 19. Maggie also worked as a columnist ("Maggie Malone, Consumer Watchdog") for *The Sentinel*. The last episode finds Jason moving his practice to Washington, D.C., when Maggie becomes the Executive Director of Media Relations for an unseen senator. Their youngest children,

Ben and Chrissy, relocate with them. The ABC TV movie update, *The Growing Pains Movie* (November 5, 2000) finds Jason is still a psychologist and has written a series of mystery books called *Dr. Dick Hollister*. Maggie was now the press secretary for district congressman, Mac Robinson. When she is fired, she and Jason return to Long Island and Maggie runs for a seat in Congress against Mac (whom she feels is unfit for the job). Jason re-establishes his practice and Maggie's campaign ("Maggie Malone — I'm on Your Side") wins her a seat in Congress as the Long Island representative.

See also: Carol Seaver, Mike Seaver.

522. Jason King, *Department S*, Syn., 1971–1972. Played by Peter Wyngarde.

Jason King is a mystery writer and published author who also works for Department S, a special branch of Interpol (the International Police Force). Jason was born in Darjeeling, India, and worked as a freelance journalist and forensic advisor for the Hong Kong Police before joining Department S.

Jason writes Mark Caine mystery novels and attempts to solve each case for Department S as if it were a plot for one of his books (he often says, "What would Mark Caine do?"). Jason mentioned writing the following books: *High Fashion Murder* and *Two Plus One Equals Murder*. Jason has a vivid imagination and is an incurable romantic ("I thrive on excitement"). He enjoys relaxing in the sun on Jamaica "to unravel my thoughts," skiing, romancing the ladies and an occasional drink (he carries a flask with him at all times for the times he can't frequent a bar or supper club).

Jason lives at 43 Pilchard Street in Paris, France (the headquarters of Department S) and drives a car with the license plate BE2083E. He has an excellent memory for details and can sketch the likeness of a suspect he has seen. Jason is also somewhat accident prone and likely to take a beating while investigating a case.

See also: Annabelle Hurst, Stewart Sullivan.

523. Jason McCord, *Branded*, NBC, 1965–1966. Played by Chuck Connors.

"What do you do when you're branded and you know you're a man?" That is the dilemma facing Jason McCord, a U.S. Army Captain who survived the Battle of Bitter Creek (1869) but was court-martialed and branded a coward for doing so (military brass believed Jason deserted his troops. Jason has no recollection of what happened. "I was knocked unconscious [by attacking Comanche Indians] and when I awoke three days later, I was being treated by a farmer miles from the battle ... maybe I did run").

Jason was dishonorably discharged — stripped of his rank, left with only a broken sword and branded "The Coward of Bitter Creek." Horace Greeley wrote about Jason's trial and through his newspaper columns, the name Jason McCord has become a household name to associate with cowardice. Jason now wanders across the country, using the experience he gained as a geologist in the army to survive.

Jason was born in Washington, D.C., and attended West Point (where he graduated at the top of his class. He even coached George Armstrong Custer, a cadet one year behind him, on his entrance exams). Jason fought in the Battle of Shiloh and was a soldier in the Army of the Ohio (stationed at Ford Ohio). He met General Ulysses S. Grant at the Battle of Vicksburg (May 1863) and was a lieutenant with the Union Army during the Civil War. He was later stationed at Fort Lincoln.

In 1871, two years after wandering, President Grant summoned Jason to Washington, D.C. Grant believed the court-martial was the right decision; however, "whatever the facts, Bitter Creek doesn't nullify all your years as a good soldier... You've already been marked as a coward; how would you like to be branded a traitor as well?" Grant needs an undercover agent and he finds Jason is the perfect man for the job. Jason accepts and his assignments for President Grant are another aspect of Jason's life that is depicted.

The last we know of Jason occurs in the last two episodes. Jason is surveying a path for the railroad near the town of Panament when he meets an old flame, Ann Williams (Lola Albright), the editor of the town newspaper, *The Banner*. They eventually fall is love and plan to marry. Jason next decides to settle in Panament and establishes (with his grandfather, General Joshua McCord), a business called McCord and McCord, Survey Engineers.

Jason Walton *see* **John-Boy Walton**

524. Jay Sherman, *The Critic*, ABC, 1994; Fox, 1995. Voiced by Jon Lovitz.

Jay Sherman is the adopted son of the wealthy but senile Franklin Sherman (the former governor of New York) and his socialite wife, Eleanor. Jay was born in 1968 but abandoned by his parents. He was raised at Orphan City (where his first words as a baby were "Feed me"). Franklin and Eleanor adopted him shortly after.

Jay is now overweight, bald and divorced; he is also a much-disliked TV film critic. He lives in an unspecified address in Apartment 1202 and is the host of *Coming Attractions* on Channel 67 (owned by the Phillips Broadcasting Company). Jay does his own off-stage announcing as Skip Fisher and is proud of the fact that he can sink a $50 million movie just by saying the word "crap." Jay's show is dubbed into 11 languages; in Mexico, Jay scares people and the station runs a disclaimer stating that Jay is insane. Jay had a small part in the film *Dances with Wolves* and panned his own screenplay *Ghost Chasers 3* as the worst movie ever made.

Jay attended the New York School for the Performing Arts and wrote a Pulitzer Prize winning book called *What I Do in the Dark*. He also won a pie-eating contest when he was a kid at summer camp. Jay was also the host of a cable access show called *English for Cab Drivers*.

525. Jaye Tyler, *Wonderfalls*, Fox, 2004. Played by Caroline Dhavernas.

Jaye Tyler is a very pretty 24-year-old girl who works as a salesgirl at the Wonderfalls Gift Emporium in Niagara Falls, New York. Jaye was born on January 22, 1980, and is the daughter of Dr. Alec Tyler and his wife, Karen, the successful author of travel books. She has an older sister, Sharon, who is an immigration lawyer and a partner in the firm of Merifield, Harrison and Eldridge; and a younger brother, Eric, who is the youngest non–Asian to win the Fulton Scholarship for Religious Studies and is now pursuing a doctorate in comparative religion.

Jaye attended Niagara Falls High School and is a graduate of Brown University (where she acquired a degree in philosophy). Jaye attended high school because she had to; she did nothing extra (the caption next to her 1998 yearbook photo states "Clubs, sports, honors: none"). Jaye is not easily motivated. She has a slight slouch and a subtle sense of humor that seems to repel others. Jaye feels the whole universe is conspiring against her. She refuses to make eye contact with the elderly and children and tries to avoid everything that surrounds her in everyday life. Jaye likes billiards, hangs out at the Barrel (a bar) and doesn't perform acts of kindness. She lives in a mobile home at the High and Dry Trailer Park and feels her life is a reaction to the choices her family has made. Jaye also thinks she may be "clinically insane" because inanimate objects ask her to help people. Jaye is not sure why it is happening but believes it has something to do with the legend of the Maid of the Mist. The Maid of the Mist is a statue that serves as a wishing well opposite her store. Before Niagara Falls became known as one of the Seven Wonders of the World, there was a god who lived in the waterfall. The local Native Americans feared the god because they believed he killed people by eating them. To appease the god, the Indians chose to offer a sacrifice. The chief's daughter, a beautiful princess, was selected. The princess was placed in a canoe and sent down the river. As the canoe plunged over the falls, the god swallowed the princess. The god was appeased by her beauty and spared her life. The princess agreed to live with the god in his cave and in turn he would protect her people and enchant her land for all time. A legend was born as the princess became the Maid of the Mist, making Niagara Falls an enchanted wonderland.

Jaye is seated on the fountain ledge eating her lunch when she tosses a quarter into the fountain. The quarter hits the statute and bounces back, striking Jaye in the head. She passes it off as nothing until she returns to work and a small wax lion talks to her, asking her not to give a customer a cash refund. Jaye disregards it and gives the customer a refund. Outside the store the customer is robbed. "The lion with the smushed face" (as Jaye calls it) tells Jaye she should have listened to him and from that moment Jaye becomes an errand girl for inanimate objects (if Jaye doesn't do what they ask, they constantly sing to make her succumb to their requests).

Jaye is Presbyterian; her sister is a lesbian and her parents are happy if she is happy. Disappointing her family is an extreme sport for Jaye — "They all work very hard each day and they are extremely dissatisfied. I can be dissatisfied by hardly working at all." In addition to the lion, Jaye also has a monkey statute that commands her to perform good deeds.

526. Jean-Luc Picard, *Star Trek: The Next Generation*, Syn., 1987–1994. Played by Patrick Stewart.

Jean-Luc Picard was born on Earth (France) on July 13, 2305. He is the son of Maurice and Yvette Picard and is single. He is captain, then commander of Starfleet's U.S.S. *Enterprise NCC-1701E.*

As early as he can remember, Jean-Luc had dreamed of joining Starfleet. He took piano lessons to please his mother but quit when performing in public bothered him. As his interest in space grew, he built airships in bottles and wrote reports on starships. He was able to read the ancient Bajoren language in the fifth grade, was school president, a star athlete and valedictorian of his graduating class.

Jean-Luc later attended Starfleet Academy

(2323–27). He became the only first-year student to win the Academy's marathon and graduated at the top of his class. His first assignment occurred in the year 2332 when he was commissioned as a first officer, then captain of the U.S.S. *Stargazer.* Twenty years later he was made commander of *Enterprise NCC-1701-D*, the first of the newly designed Galaxy-class Star Ships. In 2371, when *Enterprise NCC-1701-D* was lost opposing the El Aurians, Jean-Luc was chosen to captain *Enterprise NCC-1701-E*, a new Sovereign-class Star Ship.

Jean-Luc has an inquisitive mind and a keen interest in archaeology. He is also a tactician and an accomplished diplomat. Jean-Luc is a career officer and has no desire to marry and raise a family. He is troubled by deep personal issues and has a difficult time controlling them. Although he defends Starfleet's Prime Directive (which prohibits interference in alien cultures) he does break it if it is necessary to accomplish a goal.

See also: Beverly Crusher, Data, Deanna Troi, Geordi La Forge, Natasha Yar, William Riker.

527. Jeannie, *I Dream of Jeannie*, NBC, 1965–1970. Played by Barbara Eden.

Jeannie is a beautiful genie who can grant her master any wish. Her current master is Anthony Nelson, an astronaut who found her on a deserted island in the South Pacific. She lives with him in a modest home at 1030 Palm Drive in Cocoa Beach, Florida.

Jeannie (the name given to her by Anthony) was born in Baghdad on April 1, 64 B.C., at a time when the planet Neptune was in Scorpio. When she became of age, the Blue Djin, the most powerful and most feared of all genies, asked for her hand in marriage. When the girl refused, the Blue Djin turned her into a genie, placed her in a bottle, and sentenced her to a life of loneliness on a deserted island. She remained there for 2000 years. She was released when Major Nelson found her bottle and opened it.

Jeannie lives in her green bottle. When opened, a pink smoke emerges and materializes into Jeannie (who wears a two piece, cleavage-revealing pink harem costume). Jeannie first weighs 109 pounds (although she insists, "I have never weighed over 107 pounds"), then 127 pounds. To activate her powers, Jeannie crosses her hands over her chest and blinks her eyes. When she becomes unhappy, Jeannie's powers weaken; if she becomes very sad, she begins to vanish. Jeannie has green blood and Pip Chicks is her favorite homemade candy (it has a strange effect on non-genies: it brings out their hidden fantasies).

Jeannie becomes excited if Anthony asks her

for a favor (as he has forbidden her to use her magic for all the trouble it gets him into). Jeannie first mentions, "that if a mortal marries a genie only then will she lose her powers." She later says, "Only the power of Hadji [a powerful genie leader] can take them away." It was also said that a genie could not be photographed (yet Jeannie's picture appeared in a newspaper when she was crowned a rodeo queen).

Jeannie is all giving and only wants to please her master by using her powers to please him. Her magic is often misguided and causes unexpected problems for Anthony. Love eventually develops between Jeannie and Anthony and they married in 1969 (she then became Jeannie Nelson). Jeannie also has a mischievous genie dog named Gin Gin.

See also: Anthony Nelson.

528. Jeannie Bueller, *Ferris Bueller*, NBC, 1990. Played by Jennifer Aniston.

Jeannie Bueller is a student at Ocean Park High School in Santa Monica, California. She is the daughter of Bill and Barbara Bueller and was born on May 16, 1972. She lives at 164 North Dutton Place and has a brother named Ferris, a 17 year old who finds high school as only a place to keep track of friends.

Jeannie is beautiful and vivacious, but also vicious and nasty—and proud of it. She knows "I have a body other women would kill for" and loves to wear bikinis to the beach—but her mother refuses to let her; she tries but always gets caught ("What is the point of having a great body if I can't show it off," she sobs). While her mother is concerned about what Jeannie wears to the beach, she doesn't seem to mind the tight, short skirts and low cut blouses Jeannie wears to school (Jeannie calls these "my dress to kill clothes"). Jeannie also has what she calls "my innocent look" (she dresses as Pippi Longstocking—long dress and pigtails—to attract boys).

While Jeannie is absolutely gorgeous and appears to be perfect, she is not and her greatest fear is that her friends will find out she had her nose fixed. When a boy breaks up with Jeannie (usually because she is too demanding), she goes on an ice cream and chocolate sauce-eating binge ("Boys bad, ice cream good," she says). Jeannie is called "Princess" by her father and refuses to associate with or let it be known that she is related to Ferris—"He is a scrawny, immature pile of dog do. My life was perfect until he was born. At least I had one good year." Jeannie drives a car with the license plate 2PEK 635 (later 2RNJ 672).

529. Jed Clampett, *The Beverly Hillbillies*, CBS, 1962–1971. Played by Buddy Ebsen.

Jedidiah Clampett, called Jed, is a hillbilly who lives in a mansion at 518 Crestview Drive in Beverly Hills, California. Living with him are his daughter, Elly Mae Clampett; his mother-in-law, Granny; and his nephew, Jethro Bodine.

Jed was born in the Ozarks in Arkansas and lived in a small, run-down cabin near Blueberry Ridge. The cabin sits on a half-acre of land that "is mostly stumps and rocks." Jed is eight miles from his nearest neighbor and they are overrun with bobcats, possums, skunks and coyotes. They drink homemade moonshine, use kerosene lamps for light, cook on a wood-burning stove and wash with Granny's homemade lye soap. The outhouse is 50 feet from the cabin and to Jed, Elly and Granny (the cabin residents), they are living in the lap of luxury.

All this changes one day when Jed goes hunting for food. He spots a rabbit and fires his rifle. The bullet misses its target and strikes the ground near Jed's swamp. Oil emerges from the ground and suddenly Jed becomes a millionaire when the O.K. Oil Company purchases the oil rights for $25 million. Jed's money is deposited in the Commerce Bank of Beverly Hills and Jed's cousin, Pearl Bodine, convinces him to enjoy life and move to Beverly Hills (Jed likes the sound of "hills"). Pearl's son, Jethro, also moves with Jed, Elly Mae and Granny to experience life in the big city.

Jed found Beverly Hills to be exciting at first but longed to return to the life he loved in the Ozarks. He continues to dress in his shabby clothes (he is always mistaken for a person of unfortunate means) and hangs out with his hunting dog Duke. Mustard greens and possum innards are Jed's favorite meals ("There's just as good the second day"). When something pleases Jed he says, "Wheeee Doggies."

Jed is a widower; his late wife was named Rose Ellen and he raised Elly Mae as best he could. Jed's education was limited to the Oxford Grammar School in Arkansas (which is the only indication that the Clampetts are from the Arkansas Ozarks; other episodes do not state an exact backwoods locale). He is a simple man and asks very little from life. He cares only for providing for his family. While he appears simple, he is shrewd and his common sense guides him through the many situations he encounters.

Jed's money grew over the years (by 1971 it had reached $80 million). Through investments Jed became the owner of the Mammoth Film Studios in Hollywood. He also purchased a dress shop for

Granny (The House of Granny) and took a job as a garbage man ("for the nifty uniform"). He later became an executive at the O.K. Oil Company.

See also: Elly Mae Clampett, Granny, Jethro Bodine.

530. Jennie Malloy, *Unhappily Ever After*, WB, 1995–1998. Played by Stephanie Hodge.

Jennifer Malloy, called Jennie, lives at 30220 Oak Avenue in Van Nuys, California. She is separated from her husband, Jack (who lives in the basement) and is the mother of Tiffany, Ross and Ryan. Jennie has three dogs (Jasper, Emily and Annie), an unseen cat (Kitty) and a beloved glass-top living room table (Sheila). The dogs, the cat and the table are shown more love than the husband and the children.

Jack is a terrible father and Jennie is an irresponsible mother. As a child, Jennie had a dog (Buttons) and a cat (Snuffles). She played with dolls, helped her mother around the house and was good in school. But after 16 years of marriage and three kids, Jennie simply lost it and separated from Jack (although she allowed him to remain the basement of their home). Three years later (1998) Jennie left Jack for her lesbian lover (although Jack insists she was abducted by aliens). Prior to this Jennie was written out via a terrible accident: while tanning herself at Guy Macaroni's House of Tanning, Jennie drank, fell asleep on the table and was "turned into beef jerky remnants." She returned as a ghost to help guide her family but the storyline simply did not work and the salon incident was simply dropped (Jack called it "The writer's mistake" as he is aware of a viewing audience and often expresses his opinions to them).

Jennie has the internet name Vickie Vixen; at dinner she separates her food into three separate dishes "so I can have three distinct flavors." Slattery is Jennie's maiden name and her one regret is that she never played Juliet in her high school production of *Romeo and Juliet* (she lost it "to fellow classmate Charlene Tilton").

See also: Jack Malloy, Ryan Malloy, Tiffany Malloy.

531. Jennifer Farrell, *Jennifer Slept Here*, NBC, 1983. Played by Ann Jillian.

Jennifer Farrell was a very popular and beloved actress who died too young and way before her time (the cause was never revealed). She is now a ghost and she haunts her former residence, a mansion at 32 Rexford Drive in Beverly Hills (where she becomes a guiding light to the only person who can see her—Joey Elliott, the 14-year-old

son of the mansion's new owners, George and Susan Elliott).

Jennifer is the daughter of Alice and Mark Farrell and was born in Lanford, Illinois, in 1948. Jennifer became a fan of movies growing up and would spend the entire day on Saturday at the local movie theater idolizing the stars on the screen. She dreamed of becoming an actress and would practice scenes from movies in front of her mirror. Her mother, however, tried to discourage Jennifer and lead her on the path to becoming a beautician.

When Jennifer was six years old she was a tomboy and made a neighborhood kid eat dirt—literally. She attended the Pinehurst Elementary School and three years of Lanford High School (she dropped out in her senior year to pursue her dream). Her first job in Hollywood was as a waitress at Danny's Diner. She made her TV debut as a banana in the audience of the game show *Let's Make a Deal*. In 1966, 18-year-old Jennifer was hungry and flat broke. She posed nude for a calendar, but the calendar was never actually released (she acquired a job shortly after and bought up all the copies). Jennifer next landed a small role in the movie *Desire*, but it was her outstanding singing and dancing performance in her next film, *Stairway to Paradise*, that brought her overnight stardom. Jennifer soon became one of America's most glamorous and beloved stars. She was lost to the world in 1978.

Jennifer Hart *see* **Jonathan and Jennifer Hart**

532. Jennifer Keaton, *Family Ties*, NBC, 1982–1989. Played by Tina Yothers.

Jennifer Keaton is the youngest daughter of Steven and Elyse Keaton and lives in Leland Heights in Columbus, Ohio. She has an older sister (Mallory) and two brothers (Alex and Andrew).

Jennifer blossomed from adolescent to young woman. She was a member of the Sunshine Girls (Troop 247; patch 27) and first attended Thomas Dewey Junior High School, then Harding High School and Leland College. She is smart and finds school enjoyable. Jennifer is very respectful of her parents and causes little, if any, worries for them. She is not boy crazy and does what she is told (most of the time). Jennifer is pretty but not as fashion conscious or make-up crazy like her sister Mallory (Mallory is bad at school, a bit naïve and has a hard time grasping life. Mallory, however, has two things that Jennifer wishes she had: her beauty and taste in clothes). Jennifer is sweet, kind and enjoys helping other people. She held her first job as an order taker at Chicken Heaven, a fast food restaurant.

See also: Alex P. Keaton, Mallory Keaton, Steven and Elyse Keaton.

533. Jennifer Marlowe, *WKRP in Cincinnati,* CBS, 1978–1982. Played by Loni Anderson.

Jennifer Elizabeth Marlowe is the ultra-sexy receptionist at WKRP, a 5,000-watt AM radio station (1530 on the dial) in Cincinnati, Ohio.

Jennifer is the highest paid employee at the station and earns $24,000 a year. She will answer the phone and take messages, but will not take dictation or make coffee. Jennifer wears tight skirts and blouses and knows "I am a very sexy and desirable woman" (other women describe Jennifer as "the best-looking woman I have ever seen"). Jennifer also says, "Other women see me as a threat to their husbands."

Jennifer dates only wealthy, older men because she feels safer and more secure with them. She will never loan money to men or do any favors for them yet they buy her things — "Cars, acoustical ceilings, microwaves and appliances."

Jennifer was born in Rock Throw, West Virginia. She first lives in a gorgeous apartment (330) that is filled with appliances (gifts). Her doorbell plays the song "Fly Me to the Moon" and she has box seats at Cincinnati Reds games. Jennifer later moves to a Victorian house in the town of Landersville (location given as "across the lake") for which she paid $125,000.

Jennifer is a member of the International Sisterhood of Blonde Receptionists. She becomes upset if something doesn't go her way and her work philosophy is "Do your job but don't do too much of it." Jennifer also hosted, for a brief time, the call-in advice show, *Ask Arlene* (she quit when her flip answers caused a woman to become a victim of a beating).

In the syndicated (1991–1993) series update, *The New WKRP in Cincinnati,* Jennifer was a wealthy widow and engaged to Reynaldo Roberto Ricky Ricardo Goulegant, III, the European prince of a country called Rosario Roberto.

See also: Arthur Carlson, Bailey Quarters, Dr. Johnny Fever, Herb Tarlek, Les Nessman, Venus Flytrap.

534. Jenny Andrews, *Team Knight Rider,* Syn., 1997–1998. Played by Christine Steel.

Jennifer Andrews, called Jenny, is a member of TKR (Team Knight Rider), a branch of the Foundation for Law and Government that battles crime.

Jenny is a beautiful, tough ex–Marine sergeant.

She is an excellent gymnast and martial arts expert. She was raised in a military family. Her father was a general and her five brothers are all pursuing various military careers. Jenny fought in the 1991 Gulf War and received many accommodations. She is obsessed with guns. Her mother wished her only daughter would have pursued a more feminine career but knew at the age of ten Jenny was destined for a military career (at that time the tomboyish Jenny led a tactical assault on a rival neighborhood kids' clubhouse).

Jenny is very cautious when it comes to her personal life and rarely shows her soft, feminine side (her teammates call her "Xena: Warrior Princess"). Jenny is focused, driven and efficient and the one her superior, Kyle Stewart, worries about the most (fearing her enthusiasm could get her killed). Jenny mentioned that as a kid, *Josie and the Pussycats* was her favorite TV show.

Jenny drives Domino, a sophisticated (thinking and talking) Ford Mustang GT convertible. Domino is somewhat vocal and flirts with any cute guy she sees (causing the man to assume it is Jenny). Domino "just wants to be one of the girls" and feels she has "a hot body and smooth curves." She helps Jenny with an array of weapons (including energy blasts).

See also: Duke DePalma, Erica West, Kyle Stewart, Trek Sanders.

535. Jenny Garrison, *California Dreams,* NBC, 1992–1993. Played by Heidi Noelle Lenhart.

Jennifer Garrison is a talented singer who performs with the soft rock band California Dreams. Jenny, as she is called, is the daughter of Darryl and Melody Garrison. She was born on July 3, 1976, in California and lives at 128 Ocean Drive.

Jenny also plays keyboard and has aspirations to become a professional musician. She is a student at Pacific Coast High School and hangs out at Sharkey's, an eatery by the beach. Jenny is very pretty but never goes overboard to impress people with clothes or makeup. She likes being herself and being a down-to-earth girl makes her happy. Jenny has a collection of stuffed animals she calls "Stuffies" and a poster from the movie *Giant* graces her bedroom wall. Jenny is very particular about the boys she dates. When she breaks up with a guy she locks herself in her bedroom and watches reruns of *Thirty Something.* Jenny left the group in 1993 to further her dream by attending the Music Conservatory in Rome, Italy.

See also: Tiffany Smith.

536. Jenny McMillan, *Jenny,* NBC, 1997–1998. Played by Jenny McCarthy.

Jennifer McMillan, called Jenny, works at Inky Pete's High Speed Copying and Offset Printing in California. Jenny was born in Utica, New York, and was, as she says, "an obnoxious little brat." She cut classes, broke curfews and snuck into "R" rated movies. Jenny is the daughter of Guy Hathaway and Jennifer McMillan. Guy was a famous movie star and met Jennifer while filming *It Happened in Paris* in Utica. They had an affair and he left after the wrap party. A year later Jenny was born but Guy distanced himself. Jennifer raised her daughter alone.

Jenny attended Utica High School (where she wore jersey 22 as a member of the girls basketball team). She worked after school at Chubby Boy Burger and moved to California to begin a new life when Guy, who never forgot Jenny, willed her his Hollywood mansion, the Playpen.

Jenny's favorite sport is volleyball. She gets the hiccups when nervous and becomes edgy and hyper if she has too much coffee. Her idea of culture is to shop at the mall and when she watches the movie *Ghost* it becomes "a two hour weep-a-palooza" because Jenny cries and cries. When Jenny plays sports she becomes caught up in the competition "and becomes a monster." Jenny sells Skin So Nice cream on the side and 555-6127 is her phone number.

537. Jerome Daggett, *DAG*, NBC, 2000–2001. Played by David Alan Grier.

Jerome Daggett, nicknamed Dag (also the initials for the show's star) was born in Michigan. Jerome attended Littleton Grammar School and was a typical kid until he and his mother were driving home from school and the President's motor cade passed them. While everybody struggled to see the President, Jerome starred in awe at the Secret Servicemen who walk with the car. "I thought to myself," Jerome later said, "Those are the coolest guys I have ever seen." From that point on, Jerome knew what he wanted to do in life — protect the President of the United States.

After graduating from Michigan State College, Jerome applied for a job with the Secret Service. He began as a field agent but after 10,000 hours of such experience, he became the best in his field and was assigned to the White House's B-Team to protect the First Lady, Judith Whitman.

Jerome is a master at Code 12 (decoy missions) and is called "The Duke of Decoys" and "The Master of Confusion." The last episode finds Jerome's dream becoming a reality: he saves the life of President Whitman by preventing him from eating a slice of coconut cake. The President is allergic to coconut and Jerome is reassigned to the A-Team, the specially selected people who guard the President with their lives.

538. Jerry and Pamela North, *Mr. and Mrs. North*, CBS, 1952–1953; NBC, 1954. Played by Richard Denning, Barbara Britton.

Jerry and Pamela North are a happily married couple who live at 24 Sainte Ann's Place (Apartment 6A) in New York's Greenwich Village. They also help the police solve crimes.

Jerry was born in Manhattan and served as a lieutenant with the Navy during World War II. He became a private detective after his discharge but soon became bored with murder, mayhem and annoying clients and turned to the world of publishing (in some episodes Jerry appears to be a mystery book editor; in others the impression is given that Jerry is head of the unnamed company). Jerry enjoys his new life style: peace, tranquility and no real crimes — only those that are the figment of a writer's imagination.

Pamela is a very beautiful woman who worked as a secretary and married Jerry in 1948 (they wed on a Friday afternoon and honeymooned in Paris). Pamela has a suspicious mind and her curiosity often gets her into trouble. She has an uncanny knack for stumbling upon crimes (usually murders) and finds solving them a unique way to relieve the boredom of being a housewife. Pamela is not one for relaxation like Jerry. She is always full of energy — "I use to go to parties and dance and stay up all night and work the next day and go to another party that evening. I'm just as young as I ever was." Pamela's activities also disrupt Jerry's tranquil life, as he must now call on his former experiences as a detective to help Pamela solve crimes. He gladly does so because he fears for her safety ("Since I married Pam, disrupted plans are the one thing in life that I can positively depend on"). With or sometimes without Jerry's help, Pamela does manage to solve crimes. She is so unassuming that criminals are unaware of her brilliance and are caught by surprise (sometimes it is sheer dumb luck that allows Pamela to collar a culprit).

Pamela is always elegantly dressed and is always very feminine — even when she doesn't have to be (like being stalked by a killer or rummaging through garbage to find clues). Pamela and Jerry's address was also given as Apartment 408 at 23 Sainte Ann's Place (even though Apartment 6A is seen in the opening theme). Gramercy 3-4098; Gramercy 3-8099; and Gramercy 3-4370 were given as their phone numbers. Jerry's car license plate reads NN 1139.

539. Jerry Seinfeld, *Seinfeld*, NBC, 1990–1998. Played by Jerry Seinfeld.

Jerome Seinfeld, called Jerry, is a standup comedian who lives at 129 West 81st Street (Apartment 5A) in Manhattan (early episodes show the apartment as 3A and the building is located opposite Almo's Bar and Grill; KL5-2392, later 555-8383 are Jerry's phone numbers).

Jerry was born in Queens and is the son of Morty and Helen Seinfeld. He is a graduate of Edward R. Murrow Junior High School, J.F.K. High School and Queens College. At one point in his life, Jerry sold umbrellas on the street. He is a member of the New York Health Club and hangs out with his friends, Elaine, Kramer and George at Monk's Café. Jerry wears a size 40 suit gets his hair cut at Three Brothers Barbers. Jerry's refrigerator has magnets of the Statue of Liberty, the Comedy Central TV logo, the New York Mets and Superman (Jerry's ATM card pin number is Jor-El, Superman's father).

Jerry teamed with George to write a TV pilot about his life called *Jerry* ("a story about nothing"). They were paid $8,000 and a pilot was produced but it failed to generate a series. Jerry has a favorite T-shirt he calls Golden Boy (when it didn't make it through its last washing, Jerry replaced it with Golden Boy's son, Baby Blue).

Jerry performs at the Improv Club in Manhattan and appears often on *The Tonight Show*. He receives checks for eleven cents as royalty payments for his comedy segments on *The Super Terrific Happy Hour in Japan*.

Jerry is very generous with his money and appears to be successful although he will never admit to the fact. He drives a 1992 Saab (plate JUN 728) and often says, "That's a Shame" when something goes wrong.

See also: Cosmo Kramer, Elaine Benes, George Costanza.

Jesse Duke *see* **Daisy Duke**

540. Jesse Katsopolis, *Full House*, ABC, 1987–1995. Played by John Stamos.

Jesse Katsopolis is the brother-in-law of Danny Tanner, a widower with three daughters (D.J., Stephanie and Michelle). He now lives with Danny and helps him care for the children (Pamela, his sister, was married to Danny; she lost her life in a tragic car accident shortly after Michelle was born). They live at 1882 Gerard Street in San Francisco.

Jesse is Greek and has the real first name of Hermes (his last name was originally given as Cochran and was changed for unexplained rea-

sons). He is the son of Nick and Irene Katsopolis and was born in San Francisco. Jesse was named after his great grandfather. Because Jesse was teased at school and called "Zorba the Geek," his mother changed it from Hermes to Jesse. On his first day in pre-school, Jesse was goldfish monitor and killed the fish when he took it home without the bowl.

Jesse is a graduate of Golden Bay Union High School and originally worked with his father as a bug exterminator. He and his friend, Joey Gladstone, own J.J. Creative Services (also called Double J. Creative Services), a commercial jingle writing company. They also work together as D.J.'s ("The Rush Hour Renegades") on KFLH radio.

Jesse is a musician and his idol is Elvis Presley. In high school Jesse was in a band called both Disciplinary Action and Disciplinary Problem. He was next in a band called Feedback; he then formed two additional bands: Jesse and the Rippers and Hot Daddy and the Monkey Puppets.

Jesse has a contract with Fat Fish Records and plays at the Smash Club. He later inherits the Smash Club and rebuilds it as the family-oriented New Smash Club. In his youth Jesse rode a motorcycle and was known as Dr. Dare (he would take any dare). He has a Mustang (plate RDV 913) he calls Sally; "Have Mercy" is his favorite expression and he buys Elvis Peanut Butter.

Jesse fell in love with and married Rebecca Donaldson (Lori Loughlin), Danny's co-host on the TV show *Wake-Up, San Francisco*, on February 15, 1991; they honeymooned in Bora Bora. They first lived in Rebecca's apartment, then in the converted attic in Danny's home. Rebecca was born on a farm in Valentine, Nebraska (where she had a pet cow named Janice) and gave birth to twins she and Jesse named Nicholas and Alexander.

See also: Danny Tanner, D.J. Tanner, Joey Gladstone, Michelle Tanner, Stephanie Tanner.

Jesse Owens *see* **The Girls of Baywatch**

541. Jesse Spano, *Saved by the Bell*, NBC, 1989–1993. Played by Elizabeth Berkley.

Jessica Myrtle Spano, called Jesse, is a student at Bayside High School in Palisades, California. She is smart, very pretty and sensitive to the fact that she is tall. Jesse is a talented dancer and a member of the Honors Society. She won the French Award and hopes to attend Stanford University (although in her last appearance, she was accepted into Columbia University). She scored 1205 on her SAT test and reported the news on the school's radio station, Tiger Radio.

Jesse can turn any boy's head but dresses only to please herself (she is not one for tight skirts or cleavage-revealing blouses). She hates being called "chick" or "babe" as she feels it is demeaning to women. She appeared with fellow students Zack, Kelly and Lisa in a band called Hot Sundae (they sang the song "I'm Excited"). Jesse was the activist of her group. She had principles, believed in them and stood up for what she believed was right (although in one episode, Jesse went against everything she believed in when she posed in a bikini for "The Girls of Bayside High Swimsuit Calendar"; Jesse was Miss July). The photo led to a feature in *Teen Fashion* magazine where Jesse was "The Studious but Fashionable Girl." During the summer of 1991, Jesse worked as the receptionist at the Malibu Beach Sands Club. She and her friends hang out at an eatery called the Max.

See also: Kelly Kapowski, Lisa Turtle, Screech Powers, Zack Morris.

542. Jesse Warner, *Jesse*, NBC, 1998–2000. Played by Christina Applegate.

Jessica Warner is always the boot when she plays Monopoly. She drinks Chuck Full O'Nuts coffee (later Folgers) and when she has a ham and cheese sandwich, it has to be cheese, ham, cheese "because if the cheese is on the top it means it will touch the mustard — and two yellows can't touch."

Jesse, as she is called, lives at 346 McCord Avenue in Buffalo, New York. She is also divorced and the mother of a young son (John). Jesse was born in Buffalo and attended Fledgemore High School (where she was called "Bed Bug" when she was caught having sex in the back of her Volkswagen Bug. Jesse was 16 at the time and had to drop out of school when she became pregnant. She married the boy, Roy, but divorced him when she caught him in bed "with that chick from the video store"). Jesse works as a waitress in her father's German pub, Der Biergarten, and is hoping to become a nurse (she attends classes at the Rochester Nursing School). She later works part time as a nurse at the Student Health Center.

Jesse eats Kix cereal for breakfast and enjoys meals at the Lunch Hole. She likes the nickname "Skeeter" but no one ever calls her by it. When she has a bad dream, Jesse sees Kevin, the cigar smoking fish. Jesse originally drove an orange Volkswagen (plate AQN 249), for which she paid $300; when it was stolen, she replaced it with a 1984 beige Volvo she calls Petunia.

543. Jessica Fletcher, *Murder, She Wrote*, CBS, 1984–1996. Played by Angela Lansbury.

Jessica Beatrice Fletcher is a former high school English teacher turned best selling mystery writer. She lives at 698 Candlewood Road in Cabot Cove, Maine, and was married to the late Frank Fletcher, a real estate broker. Jessica McGill met Frank one summer at the Applewood Playhouse. They had a faithful marriage but were never blessed with children. After Frank's death from natural causes in the early 1980s, Jessica quit her teaching job of 19 years (at Cabot Cove High School) to devote time to her one indulgence — writing. The publication of her first book, *The Corpse Danced at Midnight*, became a best seller and began a new career for her as a mystery novelist and amateur sleuth. To always have Frank near her, Jessica wears a pendant near her heart that contains a picture of Frank. Jessica is sometimes called J.B. Fletcher.

Jessica was born in New England. Her mother had come from Ireland. As a child Jessica would skinny dip at the lake in back of the family house. Jessica's fascination for writing could be attributed to a college break when she worked as a reporter for a newspaper wire service. Covington House was her original publisher; later it was Sutton Place Publishing, Harper Publishing and finally Consolidated Publishers, all in New York City.

Jessica enjoys gardening, jogging, cooking and helping with local charities. She rarely drinks but when she does it is a glass of wine. She dislikes driving and refuses to get a license. She is friendly, talkative and uses her bicycle to get around town. In later episodes, Jessica acquires a job in New York City as a criminology teacher at Manhattan University. She resides in Apartment 4B at the Penfield Apartments (941 West 16th Street; 212-124-7199 is her phone number). She also teaches creative writing at the Inner City High School and does volunteer work on behalf of the Museum of Cultural History and the Library Foundation. Jessica is also a world traveler and is willing to help people wherever she goes. She is also eager to help the police solve crimes. Jessica is an expert on poisons due to her research and often says, "I think I know who the killer is. Now to prove it." Two of Jessica's fictional lead characters are Inspector Dison and Inspector Gelico. Damian Sinclair is the debonair jewel thief she created. An alphabetical listing of Jessica's books are as follows: *Ashes, Ashes, Fall Down*; *The Belgrade Murders*; *Calvin Cantebury's Revenge*; *A Case and a Half of Murder*; *The Corpse at Vespers*; *The Corpse Danced at Midnight*; *The Corpse Wasn't There*; *The Crypt of Death*; *The Dead Must Sing*; *Dirge for a Dead Dachshund*; *The Killer Called*

Collect; *A Killing at Hastings Rock*; *The Launch Pad Murders*; *Love's Revenge*; *Messenger at Midnight*; *Murder at Midnight* (Jessica's favorite book "because I didn't know who the killer was until the last 12 pages"); *Murder at the Asylum*; *Murder at the Digs*; *Murder at the Ridge Top*; *Murder Comes to Maine*; *Murder in a Minor Key*; *Murder on the Amazon*; *Murder Will Out*; *Runaway to Murder*; *Sanitarium of Death*; *The Stain on the Stairs*; *Stone Cold Dead*; *The Triple Crown Murders*; *The Umbrella Murders*; *The Uncaught*; *The Venomous Valentine*; and *Yours Truly, Damain Sinclair*.

Jessica Wakefield *see* **Elizabeth and Jessica Wakefield**

544. Jessie Hayden, *Jessie*, ABC, 1984. Played by Lindsay Wagner.

Dr. Jessica Hayden is a beautiful police psychiatrist. She was born in San Francisco on April 3, 1948, and is the daughter of Molly and James Hayden. Jessie, as she likes to be called, was an excellent student at school and showed a deep interest in other people's problems. She attended South Bay High School and received a degree in psychiatry from the University of San Francisco. She immediately joined the San Francisco Police Department and was assigned to the Metro Department's Behavioral Sciences Division.

Jessie grew up on the prestigious Winterhaven Street but now "lives in a little shack in the hills" (as she says). Jessie rejected a job "with big bucks" at Memorial Hospital and even nixed the idea of starting her own private practice to do what she wants to do: be a part of the action to help the police solve crimes through her psychological profiles and work with suspects. Jessie refuses to carry a gun ("I wouldn't know what to do with it. A doctor's duty is to preserve life not destroy it"). When Jessie sets her mind on something "trying to talk her out of it is a waste of time." Jessie does not drink coffee, likes Mexican food and rarely complains except when she is in her office: "People are always walking off with my pens."

545. Jessie Witherspoon, *Our House*, NBC, 1986–1988. Played by Deidre Hall.

This entry also contains information on her children, Kris (Shannen Doherty), David (Chad Allen) and Molly (Keri Houlihan).

Jessica. Jessica Witherspoon is a widow who now lives with her father-in-law Gus Witherspoon at 14 Ashton Drive in Los Angeles (555-4680; later 555-4847 and 555-1680 is her phone number). Jessie, as she is often called, and her late husband, John, lived in Fort Wayne, Indiana, where Jessie worked as a freelance photographer. When expenses became overwhelming, Gus, John's 65-year-old father, extended an invitation for her and her children (including their dog Arthur) to come and live with him. Jessie is a very caring mother and very strict with her children (sometimes Gus admires her for this; in turn the children are very respectful of her and their grandfather). Jessie first uses her skills as a photographer to work as a models photographer for Cathcart Architects. She is later employed as a photographer for the local newspaper, the *Post-Gazette*.

Kris. Kris is the oldest of the children and is determined to become an astronaut. She has set her sights on this goal since she was in the sixth grade and is eager to attend the Air Force Academy. Kris is an Honors Student at Highland Park High School (also said to be James K. Polk High School). Her pride and joy is her model of a Boeing ATF, a plane that took her three months to build (in some episodes Kris mentions she is interested in aviation and wants to become a test pilot). Kris earns extra money by babysitting and is called "Kleenex Chest" by her younger sister Molly (for the one time she stuffed her bra with tissues to bring attention to herself at school). Kris is a member of the Rockin' Robins, a softball team managed by Gus. To further her dream of becoming a pilot, Kris took Junior R.O.T.C. in her sophomore year at school.

David. David is the middle child. He is very smart and first attended the Chester A. Arthur Elementary School, then Naismith Junior High School. He is a member of the computer club and he and Kris take piano lessons (Kris appears to enjoy it while David seems to despise it—"Kris even likes going to the dentist to have her teeth cleaned and her gums bleed," he says). David's first job (at age 12) was painting numbers on curbs for homeowners.

Molly. Molly is the young entrepreneur of the family (she is also the only one who is left handed). She attends the Chester A. Arthur Elementary School and has a pet caterpillar named Charlie (whom she found on a squash plant in the backyard). Molly's first business venture was walking dogs; she then ventured onto a ten cent a glass lemonade stand. She is also proud of the fact that her mother allows her to stay up until 10:00 P.M. on non-school nights (otherwise it's bed at 8 P.M.).

See also: Gus Witherspoon.

546. Jethro Bodine, *The Beverly Hillbillies*, CBS, 1962–1971. Played by Max Baer, Jr.

Jethro Bodine is a hillbilly who is living high

off the hog. His uncle, Jed Clampett, struck oil on his property in the Ozarks and now he, Uncle Jed, Cousin Elly Mae and Granny (Jed's mother-in-law) live in a mansion at 518 Crestview Drive in Beverly Hills, California.

Jethro delights in the excitement of the big city. Unfortunately, he is not too bright. He was born on December 4 (no year given) in the Arkansas Ozarks (as he is a graduate of the sixth grade of the Oxford Grammar School in Arkansas). Jethro is the son of Pearl Bodine and has a sister named Jethrene. He spent two years in the first grade, three years in the fourth grade and brags that he "was educated and graduated from the sixth grade." He is considered the educated one in the family. In Beverly Hills he furthered his education at the Millicent Schyler Potts School.

Jethro's main goal in life is to attract the opposite sex "and find me a sweetheart." He had ambitions to be an astronaut ("to find moon maidens"), a streetcar conductor, "double naught spy," a pig farmer, "do brain surgerin,'" become a folk singer and a movie star (he did hold a job as a stunt double for film star Dash Riprock).

Jethro loves Granny's cooking, which he calls vittles, but is not permitted to indulge in Granny's moonshine until he gets married. At Oxford Jethro was the crawdad-eating champion. When something pleases Jethro, he yells "Yee Haw." Jethro also ran a diner (The Happy Gizzard) and appeared in a TV commercial for Foggy Mountain Soap. He receives an allowance of 50 cents a week.

In the CBS TV movie, *The Return of the Beverly Hillbillies* (October 6, 1981), Jethro is seen running one of his Uncle Jed's investments, Mammoth Film Studios in Hollywood.

See also: Elly Mae Clampett, Granny, Jed Clampett.

547. Jill Monroe, *Charlie's Angels*, ABC, 1976–1977. Played by Farrah Fawcett.

Jill Monroe is an Angel. Not quite a heavenly angel, but an operative for Charlie Townsend, the never-seen owner of Townsend Investigations in California (the agency is also called The Townsend Detective Agency and Charlie's female operatives are called Angels).

Jill was born in San Francisco in 1952. She is a graduate of Union Bay High School and San Francisco State College. Jill admits to being a fan of *The Roy Rogers Show* on TV when she was a child, but she also enjoyed the early police dramas (like *Dragnet)* and they whet her appetite to become a police officer. She attended the San Francisco Police Academy but being assigned to office work after graduation was not quite what she had in mind. She wanted excitement and quit the force to join the Townsend Agency.

Jill is blonde and gorgeous and has the ability to distract others so her partners (Sabrina and Kelly) can do their jobs. Jill is aggressive and always ready to help someone in trouble. She is also caring and impulsive. She loves skateboarding and drives a white Cobra II with the license plate 861 BMG. Jill lives in a house on the beach and meditates to relax. Jill is also sensitive and carries an old-fashioned pocket watch (given to her by her father) in her purse. Jill left the agency to pursue her car-racing career (she hopes to be the first woman to win Le Mans).

See also: Charlie Townsend, Julie Rogers, Kelly Garrett, Kris Monroe, Sabrina Duncan, Tiffany Welles.

Jill Riley *see* **The Girls of Baywatch**

548. Jill Taylor, *Home Improvement*, ABC, 1991–1999. Played by Patricia Richardson.

Jill Taylor is the wife of Tim "The Tool Man" Taylor, the host of *Tool Time*, a home repair program on local Michigan TV. Jill is also the mother of three sons (Randy, Mark and Brad)) and lives at 508 Glenview Road.

Jill Patterson was born in Michigan and was considered an army brat (her father, who called her "Jilly Dilly," was in the military). Jill first says she attended Adams High School; later it is the Huntley School for Girls and then the Hockaday School for Girls (where she played Juliet in the school's production of *Romeo and Juliet*). She met Tim at Michigan State College.

As a teenager Jill had a dog named Puddles and wore Tinker Bell Perfume. Jill considers herself a song expert and calls herself "The High Priestess of Pop Songs." Jill originally worked as a researcher for *Inside Detroit* magazine; when she was laid off, she returned to college to get her master's degree in psychology. Jill is rather strict with the children as she feels a firm upper hand is needed when disciplining them (Tim believes a lighter touch is more effective and is not as harsh with punishments as Jill).

See also: Al Borland, Tim Taylor, Wilson Wilson, Jr.

549. Jim, *According to Jim*, ABC, 2001 (current). Played by Jim Belushi.

Jim (no last name given) is the owner of an architectural company called Ground Up Designs. He lives at 412 Maple Street in Chicago and is married to Cheryl. They are the parents of Gracie, Ruby and Kyle (an infant).

Jim is a fast talker who basis much of what he says on articles he reads in *Playboy* magazine. He was born on April 5 and his favorite holiday is Halloween. He is allergic to MSG and is afraid of spiders. He has a "naked pen lady pen" he calls Bridget and his most prized possession is his eight glass collectables from Chevron gas stations. His favorite movies are *Ice Station Zebra* and *A Fistful of Dollars*. Jim calls his bowling ball "Rolling Thunder" and bowls on a team called the Ball Masters.

Jim has a "secret" jelly donut before dinner and hides "the good ice cream" in the back of the freezer behind the brussels sprouts (so the kids can't find it). He orders pizza from Speedy Tony's Pizza and the Lunch Wagon, the eatery near his business, has named a sandwich after him (the Big Jim — fried bologna and sauerkraut). Jim takes his shirt off to scare away Jehovah's Witnesses and he attempted to make money by inventing self-folding pants, liquor-filled donuts and a doll called Gassy Gus.

Jim enjoys a beer whenever he can and when he has to mind the kids he calls it "My watch." He also plays games with Ruby and Gracie — Frozen Man and Hammock Guy.

For Frozen Man, the girls play outside while Jim rests on the couch inside; for Hammock Guy, Jim rests outside while the girls play inside. Jim believes that if a woman sees you are good at something she will make it your job forever. In an attempt to get out of doing boring things with Cheryl, Jim has an imaginary friend named Gus Demas. Gus always manages to come to town when Cheryl has something boring planned. Jim uses the term "Hold the phone" when something does not go his way.

See also: Cheryl.

550. Jim and Joan Holliday, *Please Don't Eat the Daisies*, NBC, 1965–1967. Played by Mark Miller, Patricia Crowley.

Jim and Joan Nash are a happily married couple and the parents of four boys (Kyle, Joel and twins Trevor and Tracy). They live at 228 Circle Avenue in Ridgemont City and have a dog named Lad.

Jim Nash and Joan Holliday were born in Ridgemont City. They met at Ridgemont College in 1952 (Jim was a teaching assistant; Joan a journalism student). They married shortly after and set up housekeeping in a small apartment on Second Street ("one flight up, first door on the left"). It was a struggle to make ends meet and Jim had contemplated giving up teaching for a better paying job until Joan told him: "You love to teach and you've invested six years of your life into becoming a teacher. You love me and you want to do what is best for me. The best thing that ever happened to me was becoming Mrs. James Nash. And I love being married to a schoolteacher. If there are a few hardships along the way, that's fine and dandy because someday I'm going to be able to say, 'I want you to meet my husband, Professor James Nash.'"

It was on their tenth anniversary that Jim gave Joan a puppy (Lad). It was also at this time that Jim had been promoted to the position of instructor and that Joan announced she was having a baby (Kyle). The years passed and Jim became an English professor at Ridgemont City College and Joan, a housewife and mother, works out of her home as a freelance magazine writer (under the name Joan Holliday). Jim and Joan have been blessed with relatively good kids. They cause little trouble, but when they do misbehave, they do not receive harsh punishments from their parents. Jim and Joan believe in talking things over (usually together) to discipline their children. Joan's father was a world traveler; her grandfather, Albert Tennyson Kerns, was a Civil War hero and the first man in Ridgemont City to own a bathtub. Ridgemont City is said to have an urban legend called "The Big Train" (a mysterious storm that occurs every ten years and during which someone disappears).

551. Jim Dial, *Murphy Brown*, CBS, 1988–1997. Played by Charles Kimbrough.

Jim Dial is "America's Most Trusted Newsman," the senior anchor (with Murphy Brown) on *F.Y.I.* (For Your Information), a CBS-TV, Washington, D.C.–based newsmagazine series. Jim is married to Doris, has a dog named Victor (later called Trixie and Trixter), and lives at 3134 South Bedford Drive.

It is first mentioned that Jim has been with CBS news for 25 years. In 1956, he was the only correspondent to interview John F. Kennedy when he lost the presidential nomination. It is later said Jim started his career as a struggling reporter for Channel 9 in Chicago (where he doubled as the host of *Poop Deck Pete and Cartoons Ahoy*). In 1996, after a dispute with CBS (for refusing to run one of his stories), Jim walked off the set and found a job with the ICN Network in New York. Several months later CBS ran Jim's story and he returned to *F.Y.I.*

Jim wears expensive Italian suits, has a pink and blue fish-shaped coffee mug and before each broadcast, he orders fried rice from Wo Pong's. He also taps his knee three times for good luck.

Jim is Presbyterian and a member of the Dunfriars, a club for distinguished news people. Jim is part owner of a gay bar called The Anchorman and lamb chops, mashed potatoes and mint jelly is his favorite dinner.

See also: Corky Sherwood, Frank Fontana, Miles Silverberg, Murphy Brown.

552. Jim Ellison, *The Sentinel*, Syn., 1996. Played by Richard Burgi.

James Ellison is a police officer with highly developed hyperactive senses. He is a detective with the Major Crime Division of the Cascade, Washington Police Department who uses his powers to uphold the law.

Jim, as he is called, was born in Cascade and believes he acquired his powers when he was in service with the Army Rangers in Peru. Jim was a captain and in charge of a seven-man covert action team assigned to train local jungle tribes to protect trade routes against the guerilla army. During a battle, the team was killed and Jim was reported missing in action. Jim was actually rescued by natives from an isolated local tribe called the Chopec. He was chosen by the tribal chief to become a Sentinel, a protector of people. It was Jim's acts of courage in defending the tribes that showed he possessed virtue — the qualities of a Sentinel. Jim's powers had not yet developed and it was at this time that he was taught how to use his gifts. He was found 18 months later by a rescue unit when they stumbled upon him.

Jim has super sensitive hearing, exceptional vision (including the ability to see in the dark) and the ability to identify any substance by touch, taste or smell. His powers have been given to him to protect the people of his village (Cascade), which he does by joining the police force.

While Jim has powers he must also learn not to abuse them. If he becomes too focused on one sense he will become oblivious to his other senses and become vulnerable to danger. Jim is not immune to harm and his powers will not protect him if he becomes over confident. His powers will alert him to danger but he must be cautious as he investigates cases. Jim wears badge number 733 and lives in Apartment 307 at 852 Prospect; 555-7036 is his phone number and 409 GDT is his Ford license plate number.

553. Jim Ignatowski, *Taxi*, ABC, 1979–1982; NBC, 1982–1983. Played by Christopher Lloyd.

James Ignatowski, called Jim and nicknamed Iggie, is a driver for the Sunshine Cab Company in New York City. Jim was born in Boston and was a very studious child. His downfall occurred at Harvard University. It was here that he ate some brownies laced with drugs ("funny brownies") and ruined his life. He dropped out of Harvard, changed his name from James Caldwell to James Ignatowski because he thought *Ignatowski* was "Star Child" spelled backwards. He is now totally spaced out on drugs and believes he still lives in the 1960s. His drug habit has made him an expert on marijuana — he can tell you the day, week and year a particular weed was grown.

Although Jim's father was disappointed with Jim for what he had done with his life, he remembered him in his will and left him a great deal of money. Jim now fears opening mail because of the checks he gets from his father's estate ("If you cash them, what do you do with the money? Money can be lost, wasted or squandered and you'll feel terrible. Not me, I got checks"). Despite his appearance and apparent inability to do anything, Jim can play concert piano (although he has to do impressions, like a water cooler, before he starts. He claims, "I must a had lessons"). Jim doesn't realize he is the one doing something (like humming) when someone says, "Where's that coming from?" When Jim walks into a bank, the security guard unbuttons the flap on his holster.

Jim's heroes are actor Alan Alda, St. Thomas Aquinas, and his boss, Louie DePalma. *Star Trek* is Jim's favorite TV show; *Star Wars* and *E.T.* are his favorite movies. In 1968 Jim was arrested at the Democratic Convention for stealing decorations. Jim owned a racehorse (Gary) and lives in a condemned building in Manhattan. He also bought his favorite hangout, Mario's Bar and changed the name to Jim's Mario's. Jim always forgets to put the toothpaste cap back on the tube and screams for several hours in his sleep. Jim was also ordained as a minister in the Church of the Peaceful in 1968 and is sometimes called Reverend Jim. Jim's favorite color is blue and when the cab company temporarily went bankrupt Jim took a job selling Magic Carpet Wizard Vacuum Cleaners (although he thought he was selling encyclopedias door-to-door).

See also: Alex Reiger, Elaine Nardo, Latka Gravas, Louie DePalma.

554. Jim Rockford, *The Rockford Files*, NBC, 1974–1980. Played by James Garner.

James Scott Rockford, called Jim, is a tough private detective who takes the law into his own hands "because I don't like the alternatives." He is bitter because he was falsely convicted of armed robbery and sentenced to 20 years at San Quentin. He was given a full pardon after five years when new evidence cleared him. It is also the one thing Jim refuses to talk about with anyone.

Jim is a veteran of the Korean War (an army corporal with the Fifth Combat Regime) and now operates the Rockford Private Detective Agency (also called the Rockford Agency) from his mobile home at the Paradise Cove Trailer Colony in Malibu Beach, California (addresses given as 29 Palm Road, 29 Cove Road and 2354 Pacific Coast). He can be reached by phone at 555-2368 (later 555-9000) and his fee is $200 a day plus expenses. Jim dives a gold Firebird with the license plate 853 CNG (later OK 6853 and 853 OKG).

Jim stands six feet, two inches tall and weighs 200 pounds. He began his agency in 1968 and Scotch is his favorite drink. He relaxes by fishing and enjoys a meal at Casa Tacos (he always gives a ten percent tip "because it seems like ten percent is enough").

Jim owns a gun but rarely uses it (he keeps it in a coffee can in his home). Jim also does investigative work for the Boston Insurance Company and uses the alias Jerry Vanders, reporter for the L.A. *Sun*, to get into places his P.I. license won't allow.

555. Jimmy Trevette, *Walker, Texas Ranger*, CBS, 1993–2001. Played by Clarence Gilyard, Jr.

James Trevette was originally a Texas police officer. He was assigned to stop a riot and attacked by several hoods. From out of the shadows a Texas Ranger appeared and saved him. Jimmy, as he is called, saw the Ranger's badge and knew what he had to become — a Texas Ranger (it was not until Jimmy became a Ranger did he learn that his partner, Cordell Walker, was the mysterious Ranger who saved his life).

Jimmy was born in Baltimore on the wrong side of the tracks. He grew up on the streets but didn't turn to a life of crime; he saw first hand how crime can affect a community and wanted to become a law enforcer to stop it. He attended Penn Sate College and was first said to be a member of the wrestling team. This changed to a member of the football team where he showed potential for becoming a pro. A shoulder injury ended his chances. Somehow he found his way to Texas and joined the highway patrol. Shortly after he was assigned to the narcotics division of the Texas P.D. Another episode finds Jimmy as a pro football player for the Dallas Cowboys when he suffered a serious shoulder injury that ended his career. It was at this time that he met C.D., a former Texas Ranger, who helped him get his life back together and paved the way for him becoming a Texas Ranger (not Cordell as stated above).

The Lone Ranger is Jimmy's favorite TV show; he drives a car with the license plate 595 NYD (also seen as FY4 161, 278 566 and 853 4FP). Jimmy is also a member of the Brown's basketball team. Jimmy works side by side with Walker and is not as impulsive or as violent as Walker when it comes to facing the enemy.

See also: Alexandra Cahill, Cordell Walker.

556. J.J. Evans, *Good Times*, CBS, 1974–1979. Played by Jimmie Walker.

James Evans, Jr., called J.J., is the son of James and Florida Evans, a very hard working lower class family who live in the Cabrini Housing Projects (Apartment 17C) at 963 North Gilbert on the South Side of Chicago (address also given as 763). He has a sister (Thelma) and a younger brother (Michael).

J.J. was born in Tuckahoe, New York, in 1956. He is a talented artist and first developed an interest in drawing at the age of 12 when he painted a naked lady eating grits on an elevator wall ("I didn't know how to draw clothes then"). J.J. considers himself a teenage ladies' man and calls himself "The Ebony Prince" (his sister, Thelma, calls him "Beanpole" because he is so thin).

J.J. first worked as a delivery boy for the Chicken Shack. He later acquires confidence in his work and becomes the art director for the Dynomite Greeting Card Company (by coincidence, "Dyn-o-mite" is J.J.'s favorite expression). J.J. hides his money "in that sock in his dresser drawer." When first introduced, the character of J.J. was terribly stereotyped (he couldn't write, read or speak well). This was changed when Esther Rolle (Florida) insisted they make J.J. literate.

See also: James and Florida Evans, Thelma Evans.

557. Jinny Exstead, *The Division*, Lifetime, 2001–2003. Played by Nancy McKeon.

Jinny Exstead is an inspector with the San Francisco Police Department. She is 32 years old and grew up in a family of law enforcers (her father and three brothers are on the force). Jinny's constant exposure to police work has led her to chose the same career — but not only to protect the innocent but to prove that a woman can be as good or even better than a male cop.

Jinny is a graduate of South Bay High School and is an expert in the martial arts (she has a black belt in karate). She was, as she calls herself, "a wild kid," and often rebelled against parental authority (she wanted to do what she wanted to do). Jinny is now impulsive and self-assured but also somewhat reckless as she is not careful when it comes to sex; she enjoys one-night stands and sleeping around with strangers.

Jinny enjoys the challenges of her profession but becomes extremely angry if a bust goes wrong. She also likes to drink (a bit too much) but is a loyal friend if she chooses to make someone a friend. Her philosophy is "What is the point of planning for the future? I want the most out of today."

See also: Candace DeLorenzo, Kate McCafferty, Magda Ramirez, Raina Washington, Stacy Newland.

558. Jo Bhaer, *Little Men,* PAX, 1999. Played by Michelle Rene Thomas.

This entry also contains information on Bess Lawrence (Rachel Skarsten) and Nan Harding (Brittany Irvin), the female students at the Plumfield School for Boys in Concord, Massachusetts during the 1860s.

Jo. Josephine Bhaer, called Jo, is one of the four March sisters from the Louisa Mae Alcott book *Little Women.* When that story ended Jo and her husband Theodore opened the Plumfield School for Boys as an institution for children from all walks of life. Now, years later, Theodore's passing has left a void in Jo's life — "but in the children I see the promise of a new day and find the strength to keep our dream alive, no matter how hard the struggle."

Jo is fondly called "Mrs. Jo" by her students. She puts the needs of her children before her own and never favors one student over another. Each is treated with the same respect. The fall is Jo's favorite time of the year and on her birthday she makes "My birthday resolution — what I expect from the coming year." Jo has a dog (Mack) and a horse named Penny (whom she and her sisters rescued from a bog when she was 12 years old). She truly enjoys running the school, teaching and being a substitute mother to the children. "I treat my kids like people — not like other schools that give orders and you obey." Jo enjoys writing and keeps a daily record of her activities.

Nan. Anthea, called Nan, was the first girl admitted to Plumfield to increase revenue. Nan reminds Jo of herself when she was a girl — mischievous and a whirlwind of energy. She enjoys fishing and doing what the male students like to do. Nan is not all tomboy. She likes to "dress like a girl" and her cooking specialty is porridge (but eating it is another story). Her prized possessions are a frog skeleton and a music box given to her by her mother. Nan started a grape juice business with the grapes grown at the school (Plumfield

Grape Juice). She also has a keen interest in medicine and helps tend to the children when they are sick or get hurt. Nan also enjoys pulling harmless pranks.

Bess. Bess is the daughter of Jo's sister, Amy. Bess, like her mother, is sensitive, enjoys the finer things in life — reading, painting landscapes and elegant clothes. "I don't enjoy horseshoes, feeding pigs or breaking nuts on my head" (a tradition among the boy students). It was Bess's father who donated the books to the school and started its library. Bess is very genteel and very sensitive. She was raised to always be feminine and to be a standout in society. She sometimes wishes she could break that mold and be a kid like her best friend, Nan.

559. Jo Polniaszek, *The Facts of Life,* NBC, 1979–1988. Played by Nancy McKeon.

Jo Ann Polniaszek, called Jo, is a student at the Eastland School for Girls in Peekskill, New York. Jo was born in the Bronx, New York, and is the daughter of Charlie and Rose Polniaszek; she is attending Eastland on a scholarship (her mother works as a waitress; her father is in jail). Jo is very pretty but tough and burdened with an attitude problem. She rides a motorcycle and cares little about fashion and makeup. She gets along with almost everyone except fellow schoolmate Blair Warner, whom she considers snob (although they become friends as the series progresses).

Jo worked at Edna's Edibles, a gourmet food shop, and Over Our heads, a novelty store; she attempted to start her own business, Mama Rosa's Original Bronx Pizza, Inc., but failed when it became too much work. Jo later attends nearby Langley College, where she becomes a member of the Board of Regents. Jo was also a disc jockey for the Langley radio station, WLG, 90.8 FM, and worked as a counselor at the Hudson Valley Community Center. The last episode finds Jo marrying her boyfriend, Rick Bonner.

Nancy McKeon does not appear in the ABC TV movie *The Facts of Life Reunion* (November 18, 2001). Her character, Jo, is mentioned as being a Los Angeles police officer. She is married, has a daughter (Jamie) and was unable to attend the reunion because of duty (transporting a suspect to another city).

See also: Blair Warner, Edna Garrett, Natalie Greene, Tootie Ramsey.

560. Joan Clayton, *Girlfriends,* UPN, 2000 (current). Played by Tracee Ellis Ross.

Joan Carol Clayton is 29 years old, claims she is 26 but realizes she is nearing 30 and has no man in her life. She is a junior partner with the law firm of Goldstein, Sweedleston, Donald and Lee. She later quit the firm to open her own restaurant (The J Spot; originally called Joan's Place) when she found her chances for advancement very slim.

Joan was born in Fresno, California. She attended the Fresno Dance Academy for Girls and has a law degree from U.C.L.A. She lives on the North 700 block at Wilton Place in the historic Wilton District of Los Angeles. Joan is caring, sweet and always ready to help a friend in trouble (she sometimes wishes she could be "a bitch" like her girlfriend Toni Childs but realizes she can't "because I'm too kind").

Joan's father called her "Baby Girl" as a child. She was a Girl Scout and hustled cookies from K-Mart. At her high school prom Joan flashed her breasts to motorists as she rode in the limo. She loves to wear see-through blouses that reveal her sexy bras (and go braless under silky dresses). For her 30th birthday Joan decided to change her dull, boring life by doing something outrageous — she spent the day at a nude beach.

Joan's office is on the 27th floor. She has an encyclopedic knowledge of contract law and is hoping to become a full partner in the law firm. She has been a bridesmaid 14 times but never a bride. A vodka martini is Joan's favorite drink and she will not have sex with anyone unless she has been in a relationship with a man for at least three months.

Before becoming a lawyer Joan worked at the Gap (she invented a method of folding clothes that shaved three seconds off the official Gap folding time). She lunches at Skia's with her girlfriends (Toni, Maya and Lynn).

See also: Lynn Searcy, Maya Wilkes, Toni Childs.

561. Joan Gallagher, *What About Joan*, ABC, 2001. Played by Joan Cusack.

Joan Gallagher is a very pretty girl who says, "I'm not the type of girl who sweeps men off their feet. I'm the low maintenance, dependable girl who gets called by the men who get dumped by the girls who sweep them off their feet." Joan is single and lives at 300 Newberg Avenue, Apartment 31D in Chicago. She teaches English at Chicago High School and is also the head of the speech club.

Joan was born in Illinois and raised as a Catholic. She attended Holy Cross Grammar and High School. She graduated from Chicago State University with a degree in education. Joan takes notes on everything. When she has to face something she has to refer to her notes. Joan was called "Joanie Baloney" as a kid and her most embarrassing moment occurred at Sunset Beach when her breasts popped out of her bathing suit. Joan is a Chicago Cubs baseball fan and when guests come to visit, she entertains them with "a two ton photo album."

562. Joan Girardi, *Joan of Arcadia*, CBS, 2003–2005. Played by Amber Tamblyn.

Joan Agnes Girardi was born in Arcadia, Maryland, on November 24, 1987. She lives at 2320 Euclid Avenue with her parents, William and Helen, and her brothers, Kevin and Luke. Joan's social security number is 507-07-1113 and her driver's license, which expires on December 6, 2006, reads G-726 1871 73 136. Joan's favorite color is green and she likes her cantaloupe melon with a dash of salt.

Joan grew up as a typical girl, enjoying life and getting into all kinds of mischief. She broke her arm roller blading; she chipped a tooth when the training wheels were taken off her bike and she fell; she pulled a groin muscle while attempting to snow board.

Joan is prettier than she believes and has few friends. Those that she has she cherishes very much. At Arcadia High School, where Joan is a student, she is slightly above average with C-plus grades. When Joan turned 16 and became a sophomore, her life changed forever. It was at this time that God chose to appear to her to ask for help in resolving small problems for Him. God has chosen to appear in human form as a schoolgirl to a bus driver to a janitor so He can be seen and understood. Joan's first mission for God was to help a shop owner by acquiring a job at the Starlight Book Store. Joan has joined the school's debate team, chess club, band (playing drums) and the cheerleading team (the Eagelettes) on missions for God. Joan was skeptical at first, but believed she was talking to God and did what He asked (she explained her strange behavior as "I'm an adolescent girl searching for my position in life"). When God asks Joan to do something, it is not always obvious why He needs her help (for example, building a boat in her basement to bring her father and brother closer together when they took over the project). Joan always learns she is capable of doing something she didn't know she could do (like cutting wood for the boat and making the pieces fit together). After several assignments for God, a history class lesson on Joan of Arc made Joan realize that she is unique. Joan of Arc was known to have talked to God and He talked to her. Joan of Arc was a girl warrior and wore chain mail and led men into battle. Also uncanny is Joan's resemblance to Joan of Arc.

See also: Helen and William Girardi.

Joanie Bradford *see* **Mary Bradford**

563. Joanie Cunningham, *Happy Days*, ABC, 1974–1984. Played by Erin Moran.

Joanie Cunningham, the youngest child of Howard and Marion Cunningham, lives with her brother, Richie, at 618 Bridge Street in Milwaukee, Wisconsin (1950s).

Joanie was born in Milwaukee. Her father owns a hardware store and as a baby, Joanie constantly heard her father talking about the business. Her first word was *hardware*. Joanie was a member of the Junior Chipmunks and attends Jefferson High School (where she is a cheerleader). Joanie is called "Shortcake" and "Pumpkin" and has a pet hamster named Gertrude. Baked macaroni is her favorite meal. Joanie was a member the singing group, the Suedes (backup vocalist for singer Leather Tuscadero).

Joanie and her sexy friend, Jenny Piccolo (Cathy Silvers) hang out at Arnold's Drive-In, the local hamburger joint. Joanie is pretty and sensible; Jenny is wild and unpredictable and considers herself "the object of mad desire." Joanie was an obedient girl and rarely got into trouble; it was only when she befriended Jenny that she became a concern for her parents (as Jenny could easily talk Joanie into loosening up and having some fun).

Joanie also found romance with Charles Arcola (Scott Baio), a schoolmate with a band called the Velvet Clouds. Charles, called Chachi, could sing and play drums; Joanie could sing. Together they ventured off to Chicago to break into the world of music. Their attempts were seen in the spinoff series *Joanie Loves Chachi* (ABC, 1982–83); when they failed to make their mark (the series was cancelled), they returned to Milwaukee and married shortly after.

See also: Fonzie, Howard and Marion Cunningham, Richie Cunningham.

Joanna Louden *see* **Bob and Joanna Loudon**

564. Joe Dominiquez, *Nash Bridges*, CBS, 1996–2001. Played by Cheech Marin.

Joe Dominiquez is a member of the San Francisco Police Department's S.I.U. (Special Investigative Unit). He is partners with Nash Bridges (whom he calls "The Nashman") and is married to Inger (Caroline Langerfelt); they live at 4665 Laguna and in later episodes become the parents of a girl they name Lucia.

Joe was originally introduced as Nash's ex-partner. He had quit the force to become a private detective. Soon after, he was back on the force (first as an inspector then a lieutenant; he is also said to be semi-retired). Joe is part owner of a gay bar called The Tender Loin and is partners with Nash in a moonlighting business called Bridges and Dominiquez—Private Investigators (they have offices at 427 Grey Street in a building occupied by psychiatrists). They often become involved in private capers while on departmental matters. Joe is also part owner (with his family) of a company called Loco Joe's Salsa (he marketed his family's recipe and receives one percent of the profits).

Joe is a bit more laid back than Nash when it comes to investigating crimes (Nash has a shoot first ask questions later attitude). Joe often rides with Nash in his 1971 Plymouth Barracuda convertible (which doubles as Nash's squad car). Joe often uses department time to run errands (for Inger) and tend to business matters. No matter, he and Nash are the perfect team as they understand and respect each other.

See also: Caitlin Cross, Cassidy Bridges, Nash Bridges.

565. Joe Friday, *Dragnet*, NBC, 1951–1959; 1967–1970. Played by Jack Webb.

Joseph Friday, called Joe, is a sergeant with the Homicide Division of the Los Angeles Police Department. Joe wears badge 714 and solves crimes associated with robbery, car theft, homicide, and missing persons. He resides at 4646 Cooper Street (Apartment 12) and has been working on the force since 1940 (when he was a rookie and a graduate of the L.A. Police Academy).

Joe is a no nonsense plainclothes detective with virtually no sense of humor. He works strictly by the books and devotes all his energies to solving crimes. Joe prefers to take his time at crime scenes and study the evidence. He often goes on hunches and "I sometimes get a notebook full of notes and a crime lab full of evidence but nothing to tie them together. I've got the pieces; I've just got to put them together." And that is where Joe's brilliance comes into to play — he is an expert at solving crime puzzles. Joe drives a car with the license plate 58 0216 and his car code is Eighty-K (it also sounds like A-D-K). In addition to Joe's narration and stone cold approach to investigating, he became associated with the phrases "My name is Friday, I'm a cop" and, when questioning a woman, "Just the facts, ma'am."

566. Joe Mannix, *Mannix*, CBS, 1967–1975. Played by Mike Connors.

Joseph Mannix, the son of an Armenian vineyard owner in California, is a private detective—first with Intertect, a computerized investigative firm run by Lew Wickersham, then in 1968, his own boss (the owner of an agency at 17 Paseo Verdes in Los Angeles. Joe also lives here, but previously resided at 2742 Canyon Road when working for Lew).

Joe, as he is called, was a lieutenant in the air force during the Korean War. He is a graduate of Western California University (class of 1955) and acquired his private investigator's license a year later. Joe possesses a black belt in karate. He jogs and plays golf to stay in fit and his hobbies include sailing and swimming. Scotch is his favorite drink.

Joe is rather tough on suspects and suspects are rather tough on him (he does take serious beatings). He is not afraid to use his gun, although he will try to avoid killing if possible. Joe drove several cars throughout the series run: a Dodge, an Oldsmobile, and a Barracuda.

567. Joel Fleischman, *Northern Exposure*, CBS, 1990–1995. Played by Rob Morrow.

This entry also contains information on Maggie O'Connell (Janine Turner), Joel's girlfriend.

Joel Fleischman is a doctor in Cicely, a remote town of 214 people in Alaska (in the borough of Arrowhead in Anchorage). Joel was born in Flushing, New York. He is a graduate of Richfield High School and the Columbia University Medical School. He did his internship at Beth Sinai Hospital in New York City.

Joel has an office in the abandoned Northwestern Mining building. He reads *Golf Digest* and *The New Yorker* magazines and the town's only newspaper, *The World Telegram*. Joel enjoys a drink at the Brick Bar and eats at Rosalyn's Café. His truck license plate reads 5792 H2.

Although Joel is Jewish he celebrates Christmas (he believes in the spirit of the holiday and enjoys decorating a tree). He is a compassionate man and always giving of himself to help others—even though he sometimes has a hard time understanding the customs of the people he helps.

Joel was rejected for a medical school scholarship 74 times. He was forced to take out student loans and owed $125,000. His burden was dropped when he learned the state of Alaska would pay off his debt if he would spend four years in service to the state. Joel agreed. He began a relationship with Maggie O'Connell, a pretty bush pilot who was also his landlady. Three years later their relationship ended and Joel became depressed. He retreated to the remote fishing village of the Manonash Tribe to get over his lost love (the village is located up river from Dead Man's Gorge). Joel returned several months later and was let out of his contract. He returned to New York to begin his own practice. As a kid he attended Camp Indian Head.

Maggie's full name is Margaret Mary O'Connell. She was born in Gross Pointe, Michigan, and owns the one plane (I.D. number N8326; later N41492) O'Connell Air Taxi Service. She lives on the South Corner of Katunick and Washington and her pickup truck license plate reads 8346MA. People say Maggie is cursed when it comes to boyfriends; five have died under tragic circumstances: Harry (choked at a picnic on potato salad), Bruce (fishing accident), Glen (took a wrong turn in his Volvo onto a missile firing range), Dave (fell asleep on a glacier and froze), and Rick (killed by a falling satellite). It appears that Joel got off easy—only a broken heart. Shortly after Joel's departure, Maggie was elected the Mayor of Cicely.

568. Joey Gladstone, *Full House*, ABC, 1987–1995. Played by David Coulier.

Joseph Gladstone is friends with Jesse Katsopolis, the brother-in-law of Danny Tanner, a widower with three daughters (D.J., Stephanie and Michelle). He lives with them at 1882 Gerard Street in San Francisco and helps Danny and Jesse care for the children.

Joey, as he is called, was born in San Francisco and is the son of Colonel Gladstone and his wife Mindy. Joey is a graduate of Golden Bay Union High School and is partners with Jesse in J.J. Creative Services (later called Double J. Creative Services), a commercial jingle writing company.

Joey is also a standup comedian and cartoon voice impersonator. He appeared on *Star Search* and did a TV pilot called *Surf's Up* (he played Flip, the surfer-dude mailman. When the live action format didn't work, it was turned into a cartoon with Joey as Flip, the surfing kangaroo). Joey next became the host of KTMB-TV, Channel 8's *The Ranger Joe Show* (where he entertained kids from the Enchanted Forest with his hand puppet Mr. Woodchuck; Jesse was a regular as Lumberjack Jesse). Joey drives a 1963 Rambler (plate JJE 805) he calls Rosie and his favorite expression is "Cut it out."

See also: Danny Tanner, D.J. Tanner, Jesse Katsopolis, Michelle Tanner, Stephanie Tanner.

569. Joey Tribbiani, *Friends* (NBC, 1994–2004), *Joey* (NBC, 2004; current). Played by Matt Le Blanc.

Joseph Francis Tribbiani, Jr., called Joey, is a struggling actor. He was born in New York City and is the son of Joseph and Gloria Tribbiani. As a child Joey had an imaginary friend (Maurice, a space cowboy), and a cabbage patch doll (Elisha Mae Emory). He also had a plush bedtime toy called Hugsy the Penguin.

Joey hangs out at a coffee shop called Central Perk and is the dim-witted member of a group of friends that includes Monica, Rachel, Ross, Phoebe, and Chandler. Joey is represented by the Estelle Leonard Talent Agency and claims that his idol, Al Pacino, was his inspiration to become an actor (in later years Joey appeared in an Al Pacino film as his "butt double in a shower scene"). Joey also mentioned these roles: an unnamed porn movie; regular on the TV soap opera *Days of Our Lives* (as Dr. Drake Ramore); guest role on *Law and Order*; infomercial spokesman for the Milk Carton Spout; the role of Victor in an unnamed Broadway play at the Lucille Cortel Theater; the part of Mac in a TV series called *Mac and Cheese* (Mac was the human assistant to Cheese, a futuristic robotic crime fighter); soldier in an unnamed World War I film shot at Pier 59 Studios in Manhattan.

Joey lives in an apartment building at Grove and Bedford streets in Manhattan. He has posters of director Alfred Hitchcock and the films *Hurricane* and *Scarface* on his wall. He calls his recliner Rosita and his TV set Stevie. He is most fond of "the big white dog" (a plastic Greyhound). Joey can drink a gallon of milk in ten seconds and eat an entire turkey at one sitting. He also doesn't share food (if, for example, he takes a girl out to dinner and she takes food from his plate, it's over). Joey wears a size 7 shoe ("I have surprisingly small feet") and 5639 is his ATM pin number. To remember things, Joey writes messages on his arms. He had a pet chicken (called Chicken) and a duck (called Duck). Chandler called the chicken "Our Chicken" and "Little Yasmine" (after a real "chick"—Yasmine Bleeth of the series *Baywatch*).

Joey cries every time he sees the movie *Titanic*. He made a commercial for Ichabon (a lipstick for men) for Japanese TV. The Foosball is Joey's favorite game (he has a game table in the middle of his living room) and "How 'ya doin'" is his favorite expression.

Joey, the series spinoff, picks up from where the last episode of *Friends* left off. Joey has given up his role on *Days of Our Lives* (taped in New York) and has moved to Los Angeles in hopes of furthering his career. He acquires an agent and moves into an apartment (7) close to his older sister, Gina (Gina's 20-year-old son, Michael, lives with

him). Joey is still a fanatic about food and considers his savings his "face account" (he feels his face is his best feature and the money is for when he loses his looks). Joey has several scars "and each taught me a lesson—not to touch a hot stove; not to lick peanut butter off a steak knife; not to run with scissors in your mouth; and not to stand up in a roller coaster." Joey keeps a diary of his daily activities and is struggling to find decent roles. Before acquiring a role on a series called *Deep Powder* ("*Baywatch* on snow"), Joey performed in industrial industry videos "and silly commercials."

See also: Chandler Bing, Gina Tribbiani, Monica Geller, Phoebe Buffay, Rachel Greene, Ross Geller.

570. John and Blanche Bickerson, *The Bickersons*, Syn., 1951. Played by Lew Parker, Virginia Grey.

John and Blanche Bickerson are a happily married but quarrelsome couple who tied the knot in 1943. They live in Apartment 22 at 123 Englewood Drive and have a pet cat (Nature Boy) and an unnamed goldfish and canary. The only thing they have in common is their love of bickering about everything.

John is a vacuum cleaner salesman for Household Appliances. Blanche is the typical American housewife who is struggling to make ends meet on what little money John makes. Blanche seems to be okay with that, but it is John who has to struggle—"I have to pick fights with Indians because I can't afford a haircut. I sew sleeves on Blanche's old drawers and wear them for sweaters. And I cut down Blanche's old girdles to make suspenders." John's pride and joy is the one bedroom slipper he has. Blanche and a friend bought a raffle ticket and won a pair of slippers. They split the prize and John wound up with the right slipper—"It's the only slipper I have and I have to protect it with my life."

According to Blanche John "doesn't act human until he has his morning coffee." She also says, "He's the only man in town who eats duck eggs and drinks reindeer milk." John fancies himself as an expert repairman but Blanche says no. They have, for example, an electric orange juicer that John hooked up to a vacuum cleaner—"It now sucks up the orange juice and spits the pits in your face."

John is also a chronic snorer (he is so loud that the neighbors often call to complain). Blanche says, "Now I know what it is like to sleep at Cape Canaveral." A doctor prescribed two aspirin and a jigger of bourbon each night to cure John's snoring. John is six months behind on the aspirin and two years ahead on the bourbon.

Blanche is not as easy to live with either. She gets "dizzy spells every fifteen minutes that last a half hour." Blanche is a good cook and John doesn't hate her cooking—he just doesn't understand it (for example, powdered frog legs, frog omelets, deviled pancakes and two-foot long rhubarb pies). Because Blanche has so little money to spend she sometimes borrows from the money John saves for his life insurance payments (she tells the company to pay the premium "by deducting the money they will pay me when John drops dead"). John and Blanche keep their money in the sugar bowl; the ironing board doubles as the kitchen table and they have a huge ice box in the kitchen. John's favorite hangout is Murphy's Bar and Grill.

571. John and Olivia Walton, *The Waltons*, CBS, 1972–1981. Played by Ralph Waite (John), Michael Learned (Olivia).

The year was 1789. A pioneer named Rome Walton settled in the Blue Ridge Mountains of Virginia. He had only an axe, a plow and a mule to his name. He fought wars there (cold, disease, fire and flood) and raised a family there. The area came to be known as Waltons' Mountain (the family doesn't own it but "sort of hold it in trust"). The mountain has been passed down from generation to generation. In 1931 (the series setting when it begins) it is "owned" by John Walton and his wife Olivia. They live in Jefferson County (the area now surrounding Waltons' Mountain) with John's parents, Zeb and Esther, and their children John-Boy, Mary-Ellen, Erin, Elizabeth, Jason, Ben and Jim-Bob. Reckless is the family dog.

John and Olivia married in 1916 and established a timber mill in 1931. Olivia is a Baptist and very religious. Her parents objected to her marrying John because they considered him a "heathen" (he is not a church-going man and prefers to worship in his own way).

John is a dedicated, hard-working family man. He is stern with his children and offers them kindly advice and support. John's dream is to build a home on Waltons' Mountain itself. Olivia is a dedicated mother to her children. She finds comfort in reading the Bible and is also very stern when it comes to disciplining her children. She expects them all to help with the chores and help each other. Olivia tends to lose her temper when she has a bad day (John also has his bad days but often suppress his emotions). Olivia left the family to work as a nurse in an army hospital during World War II (John was a member of the Draft

Board at this time). Olivia later contracted tuberculosis and learned she could no longer have children as a result. Olivia is famous for her applesauce cake and in later years became a schoolteacher (third grade).

See also: John-Boy Walton (for information on John-Boy, Jason, Ben and Jim-Bob Walton), Mary-Ellen Walton (for information on Mary-Ellen, Erin and Elizabeth Walton), Zeb and Esther Walton.

572. John and Polly MacGillis, *Major Dad*, CBS, 1989–1993. Played by Gerald McRaney, Shanna Reed.

John D. MacGillis, called Mac, and Polly Cooper are lovers who marry and set up housekeeping in Oceanside, California. John is a major with the U.S. Marines (stationed at Camp Singleton); Polly was a widow with three daughters (Elizabeth, Robin and Casey) and works as a reporter for the Oceanside *Chronicle*. Later episodes are set in Farlough, Virginia, when John is transferred to Camp Hollister (which Polly calls "a military hell hole"). The family now resides at the base house (485) and John becomes "a staff weenie" (staff secretary to the general).

John was born in Snake River, Mississippi (where his parents owned a farm on Decater Road). His grandfather taught him how to whittle at the age of 11. When he was seven years old, John stole a $7.95 Zorro watch from Peavey's Five and Dime. John wound it up; but instead of it going "tick, tick, tick," it went "thief, thief, thief." Thirty-three years later, John called Mr. Peavey and confessed.

John majored in history at Vanderbilt College. He joined the Marines in 1967 (another episode claims 1969) and did his basic training on Parris Island. He then served three tours of duty as a corporal in Vietnam. When a typo on his retirement papers forced him to retire, John held a job as vice president of product relations for Teleteck Defense. He reenlisted in the Marines when the mistake was corrected. John enjoys sitting on the front porch and listening to the crickets chirp. He has three objections to living with four females: "a bedroom with pink walls; a Strawberry Shortcake shower curtain; and hair clogging the drains."

Polly and John met on September 11; they married on October 11 and honeymooned in Hawaii. Every month on the eleventh John gives Polly flowers. At Camp Hollister Polly becomes the managing editor of the camp newsletter, *The Bulldog*. She also writes the column "The Suggestion Box" and is in charge of the "At Ease" section of the newspaper. Polly is a Democrat and a member of the Officers' Wives Club. In her youth Polly worked for a radical magazine called *What's Left*. Her late husband was named Sandy.

See also: Elizabeth Cooper (for information on Elizabeth, Robin and Casey Cooper).

573. John Becker, *Becker*, CBS, 1998–2004. Played by Ted Danson.

John Becker is a neighborhood doctor with an office in the Bronx, New York. He is rude, gruff, loud and a chronic complainer. He is 50 years old and smokes, drinks and eats mostly only fast foods. He has an opinion (usually negative) about everything and hates to be wrong. His patients often barter for his services.

John lives in Apartment 3B on Katon Avenue; 555-0199 is his phone number and he pays $450 a month in rent (the reason: someone was murdered in his apartment "and nothing a chalk eraser, some bleach and an open window couldn't cure"). John has been married twice, divorced twice and says, "my next wife gets half of nothing" (he also says his first wife, Sandra, was "the castrating bitch from hell"). John attended Harding High School and is a graduate of Harvard Medical School, class of 1972 (he still wears the jacket he wore in college because "if you keep it long enough everything comes back in style"); he interned at Boston General Hospital. In his youth John was an expert juggler with bowling pins. He has no children "because kids annoy me."

John has a muffin and a cup of coffee every morning at his favorite eatery, Reggie's Diner (owned by Reggie Costas, then Christine Conner). While John and Reggie had a love-hate relationship, John and Christine had a more romantic one and would have married if the series had progressed.

John reads the *New York Post*, is afraid of spiders and walks around like he is better than everyone else (as Reggie says, "We're dirtying up his world"). John has been banned from Thrifty Mart stores for hitting a handicapped person (who tried to get ahead of him in the cash register line); and when he tries to stop smoking, John becomes irritable and edgy. John hates holidays, sentimentality and people who squander money.

574. John Beresford Tipton, *The Millionaire*, CBS, 1955–1960. Played by Paul Frees.

Silverstone is a fabulous 60-acre estate in an undisclosed location. It is the home of John Beresford Tipton, a mysterious multi-billionaire who lived a life of seclusion. He conducted his business empire from Silverstone and in 1955 was worth more than $500 million.

Mr. Tipton devoted his entire life to running his business empire. However, he was not born into wealth. He was from a modest family and born with a natural sense for business. He turned that gift into a fortune ("He was one of the very few men who ever earned, by the use of his phenomenal brain, a fortune that ran into the billions of dollars"). His ivory chess set was the first luxury he ever allowed himself. As the years passed and Mr. Tipton grew older, his health began to suffer. Mr. Tipton was advised by a doctor to sit back, relax and enjoy life; take up a hobby if he so desired. Mr. Tipton chose a most unusual hobby: giving complete strangers a tax-free cashier's check for one million dollars.

The recipients of each check (drawn on the Gotham City Trust and Savings Bank) were selected by a means known only to Mr. Tipton. Mr. Tipton remained anonymous. None of the selected individuals (188 in all) ever learned who their mysterious benefactor was (if they did learn, any remaining monies would be forfeited). Mr. Tipton chose his executive secretary, Michael Anthony (Marvin Miller), to hand out the checks. Each person was required to sign a document agreeing never to reveal the exact nature of the gift or its amount (only spouses were permitted to be told). Mike was told to keep an account of every transaction.

Mr. Tipton enjoyed his intrusion on fate (seeing how the money helped or hindered lives). Mr. Tipton was a student of human nature. "Every subject in his vast store of knowledge was close analysis and was always related to the behavior and destiny of man."

It was only after the death of Mr. Tipton that the will instructed Michael Anthony to reveal the files of people selected by Mr. Tipton to receive one million dollars. They are seen in flashback sequences. Two catch phrases became associated with the series: Mike (approaching Mr. Tipton): "You sent for me, Sir?; and Mr. Tipton, handing Mike the check: "Mike, our next millionaire."

575. John-Boy Walton, *The Waltons*, CBS, 1972–1981. Played by Richard Thomas, Robert Wightman.

This entry also contains information on John-Boy's brothers, Ben (Eric Scott), Jason (John Walmsley) and Jim-Bob (David W. Harper).

John-Boy. John Walton, Jr., called John-Boy, is the eldest child of John and Olivia Walton. He lives near the Blue Ridge Mountains in Jefferson County, Virginia, and longs to be a writer (he keeps a journal of his family's activities). He attended Boatwright University and established his own newspaper, *The Blue Ridge Chronicle*. During World War II, John-Boy became a reporter for *Stars and Stripes* (a military magazine) and traveled the world as a war correspondent. After the war he moved to New York to pursue his writing career. He acquired a publisher (Hastings House) and had several books published (he also worked as a wire service reporter). He also fell in love and married a girl named Janet (a magazine editor).

John-Boy was very family-oriented and cared very much for his siblings, especially Elizabeth, the youngest, with whom he felt he had a special connection. He is also stubborn and stands up for what he believes is right, even if it means going against his parent's wishes.

Jason. Jason, the second eldest son, is seeking musical fame (he wrote the song "Will You Be Mine"). He studied at the Clynburg Conservatory and played with Bobby Bigelow and His Hayseed Band. He was also a part of the Rhythm Kings and sang with the WQSR Radio Gospelites. Jason held a job at the Jarvis Used Car Lot and played guitar at the Dew Drop Inn (he eventually came to own the inn). He was also the church organist. Jason enlisted in the Army during World War II (stationed at Camp Rockfish) and fell in love with and later married a girl named Toni.

Ben. Ben, the third oldest son, enjoys helping his father run the family timber mill (he eventually takes over the business and turns it into the Walton Lumber Mill). Ben was the schemer of the family and the one who always seemed out to make money (and usually wound up in trouble for doing so). Ben worked as a civil defense worker during World War II. He fell in love with (and eloped to marry) Cindy Brunson. They had two children, Virginia and Charlie.

Jim-Bob. James Robert, called Jim-Bob, is the youngest son. He had a twin, but his brother, Joseph Zebulon, died (possibly at birth). He is a loner and constantly lost in his dreams. Jim-Bob wanted to be a pilot but was unable because of astigmatism (needed to wear eye glasses). His fascination with airplanes led him to become a motor mechanic and later opened his own business in Jefferson County. Jim-Bob has a ham radio in the barn and enjoys talking to people all over the world. During World War II Jim-Bob experimented with building his own airplane. It took several years but in late 1945 he flew for the first time when it lifted him into the air (his hobby was building model airplanes out of wood).

See also: John and Olivia Walton, Mary-Ellen Walton (for information on Mary-Ellen, Erin and Elizabeth Walton), Zeb and Esther Walton.

576. John Byers, *The Lone Gunmen*, Fox, 2001. Played by Bruce Harwood.

John Fitzgerald Byers and his partners Melvin Frohike and Richard Langley are the Lone Gunmen, publishers of *The Lone Gunman*, a Tacoma Park, Maryland–based computer oriented newsletter that attempts to expose conspiracies, injustices and criminal activities at all levels of society (the paper is singular in name because it is the only one in America).

John and his partners could be considered geeks. John was born in Idaho and named after President John F. Kennedy (his parents had originally intended to name him Bertram, after his father). John previously worked for the FCC (Federal Communications Commission) helping the government expose computer hackers. He quit when he discovered the government was conducting controlled experiments on civilians and concealing the truth about their activities from the public.

John is always neatly dressed (suit and tie) and often uses the government's Freedom of Information Office for research. He is a topnotch hacker and has proclaimed himself as the group's leader. He would prefer to resolve situations in a peaceful manner but often finds himself running for his life when Melvin and Richard become involved in a case. John mentioned that *Gentle Ben* was his favorite TV show as a kid.

See also: Melvin Frohike, Richard Langley.

577. John Cage, *Ally McBeal*, Fox, 1997–2002. Played by Peter MacNichol.

John Cage is the senior partner in the law firm of Cage and Fish (located at 415 8th Street in Boston). He is the more relaxed partner and tends to involve himself in his clients personal and professional lives.

John has a stuttering problem and his shoes tend to squeak when he walks. He often disrupts courtroom proceedings with nasal noises (which flare up when he becomes nervous) and has a remote control "bowl flusher" (which he uses for the series most unusual hangout, the unisex bathroom).

John likes to play the bagpipes to relax and has a pet frog named Stefan (who competes in frog jumping contests). When John was a child he heard the song "Something Stupid" (by Frank and Nancy Sinatra) and imagined Nancy was performing it just for him.

See also: Ally McBeal, Elaine Vassal, Ling Woo.

578. John Crichton, *Farscape*, Sci Fi, 1999–2004. Played by Ben Browder.

This entry also contains information on Chiana (Gigi Edgely), Zotoh Zhaan (Virginia Robyn Hey), Ka D'Argo (Anthony Simcoe) and Aeryn Sun (Claudia Black), other members of the space ship *Moya*.

John. John Crichton is a NASA astronaut who theorized that it is possible to use the Earth's gravity to propel a ship past the Earth's orbit and into deep outer space to explore distant planets. What works in theory doesn't always hold true in practice. John piloted a ship called *Farscape* out of the Earth's orbit but encountered a wormhole that propelled him to a distant galaxy and into the midst of a war between the Peace Keepers and the Leviathans. He was rescued by the crew of the *Moya*, a ship of freedom fighters battling the evil Peace Keepers, and helped them avoid capture by the enemy. John, now a member of the Moya, is seeking a way to return home while trying to survive the hostile aliens he encounters.

John is the son of an astronaut. He was raised mostly by his mother and rarely saw his father (space missions kept the family apart). John set his sights on space and graduated from college with a degree in theoretical science. He immediately went to work for NASA as a mission specialist (overseeing shuttle launches). John is idealistic and fiercely independent. He respects his crewmates and is not one to jump into a dangerous situation without thinking first.

Chiana. Chiana is a very beautiful and sexy alien. She was born on a planet called Nebari and is a skilled thief. She is quite intelligent and appears to be in her early twenties. However, when things do not go exactly as she wants, she tends to yell and appears more like a spoiled teenage girl than a young adult. Chiana has gray-toned skin and loves to show cleavage. She also likes to flirt to get what she wants. She can read situations and is a good listener and has a knack for placing the blame on somebody else when something goes wrong

Aeryn Sun. Aeryn Sun is a former Peacemaker (member of the Peace Keeper Commando). She is a very cold and calculating person and shows little compassion (possibly attributed to her upbringing). She was an orphan and shown little or no love). Aeryn Sun was brought up to be a soldier and she has not lost that aspect. She is aggressive yet attractive and possesses a proven ability to take care of herself in a fight.

Zotoh Zhaan. Zotoh Zhaan is a female priestess (called a Pa'u) from the planet Delvia. She evolved from a plant and is skilled in the medical sciences. Zotoh's people are peace loving and look to religion for comfort; they oppose war and confrontation. Zotoh has entered the tenth plateau in the Delvion Seek and is searching for the elusive answers that mean perfect understanding in everything. She has mystic and telepathic abilities and her main duties on the *Moya* include tending the sick and wounded.

Ka D'Argo. Ka D'Argo could be described as a two-legged animal (he possesses the characteristics of a lizard, dog and elephant). He is from a planet called Luxor and is an aggressive warrior (he has been decorated several times for his daring battle tactics). Ka is very loyal to his race and will kill anyone who threatens him or his people. His weapon of choice is his Qualta Blade (a large sword with blunt edges) that doubles as a rifle. At one point in his life, Ka was a slave of the Peace Keepers and worked the deadly mines of a maximum-security planet. In addition to his frightening looks, Ka has clear blood.

579. John Drake, *Danger Man* (CBS, 1961), *Secret Agent* (CBS, 1965). Played by Patrick McGoohan.

John Drake is a suave and sophisticated British Intelligence Agent who first performed assignments on behalf of NATO (The North Atlantic Treaty Organization) on the series *Danger Man*. He became a secret agent in the spinoff series and investigated situations that endangered world security.

John is a man with a strong moral sense and convictions. He was born in England and is dedicated to defending Her Majesty against all her enemies. John is totally dedicated to righting wrongs but he does not use unnecessary force (or gadgets) to achieve his goal. He carries a gun but will only shoot if he has to. His fists and his sharp wit are his most valuable weapon against crime (John uses quick thinking to get him out of tight situations, not gun battles).

John is handsome and could have his choice of any woman but his relationships with women are minimal (the most John ever experiences is a slight peck on the cheek). John does like women, especially intelligent ones and treats them with a great deal of respect. It can be assumed John's strict moral code prevents him from mixing business with pleasure (however, if a woman is in danger John will take risky steps to save her — and not even accept a kiss in gratitude). John tries to work by the code he has sworn to uphold. He most often does things according to the book but occasionally deviates, doing things his way to bring down the enemy.

580. John Koenig, *Space: 1999*, Syn., 1975–1977. Played by Martin Landau.

John Robert Koenig is a noted astronaut and is responsible for the success of the U.S. space missions, one of which was colonizing the moon for purposes of establishing an early warning system to repel alien invaders. John was appointed the commander of Moonbase Alpha (the project name) when a radioactive chain reaction blasted the moon out of orbit. He and 300 other astronauts are now marooned in space as the moon seeks a new planet on which to affix itself.

John was born in Brooklyn, New York, on March 17, 1957. He developed an early interest in space when he saw Neil Armstrong walk on the moon in 1969. He is a graduate of MIT and was married to a gifted artist named Diana Morris (who died in 1987). John first mission was to the Venus space station and was later a part of the Ultra Probe Mission of 1996 (the program that paved the way for the colonization of the moon). He was assigned the command of Moonbase Alpha in 1999 — the year it was blown out of orbit. John has a computer-like mind and is deeply concerned for the welfare of the people he commands. He insures the safety of others by putting his life on the line in dangerous situations. John paces back and forth to think, likes to play chess and has an interest in physics. He works closely with Dr. Helena Russell. He is also capable of piloting an Eagle, the ship used for missions away from Moonbase.

581. John Lacey, *Dear John*, NBC, 1988–1992. Played by Judd Hirsch.

John Lacey is an English teacher at the Drake Prep School in New York City (he has office 215). He is divorced (from Wendy) and lives in Apartment 4R on Woodlawn Boulevard. He is also a member of the 1-2-1 Club, a Manhattan based organization for divorced, widowed, lonely and separated people who need help in adjusting to the single life.

Club meetings are held on Friday evenings at 9:00 P.M. at the Rego Park Community Center. One hour before each meeting John teaches a literary class. John was born in Binghamton, New York, and was called "Moochie" as a kid. Pineapple strudel is his favorite dessert and he has an antique watch that has been handed down from generation to generation. John also cares for Snuffy, Fluffy and Snowball, the cats of his never-seen 93-year-old neighbor. John writes poetry in his spare time and hopes to one day be published. John's childhood dream was to play clarinet. At the age of 45 he fulfilled that dream by taking lessons at the Charlie Moreloft Music School.

See also: Kate McCarron, Kirk Morris, Louise Mercer, Mary Beth Sutton.

582. John McCallister, *The Master*, NBC, 1984. Played by Lee Van Cleef.

John Peter McCallister is the only occidental American ever to become a Ninja. He is a master and disciplined in the Japanese art of combat. John says he is now "a cantankerous old man who's lived a lot of years alone."

John was with the Army Air Corps during World War II "and found myself in Japan. The tranquility and the people kept me there" (in another episode, John mentions he found his way to Japan after the Korean War — where he was a prisoner of war and managed to escape via a motorcycle). John carries a black suitcase with him that contains all his worldly possessions. He helps people in trouble as he travels about the country and battles evil with his ornamental Japanese sword. John can scale buildings, catch an arrow in his hand, knock people out with a pinch to the temple, and can remain still for long periods of time ("Slow the heart beat and listen to the senses"). When engaging in a fight with the enemy, John uses "smokescreen and illusion. Give them what they expect and they will believe it. Do what they don't expect." John also says "I have a knack for getting into places people don't want me." John wears a medallion around his neck ("the symbol of my household") and wears his black Ninja outfit when battling his enemies.

583. John Reid, *The Lone Ranger*, ABC, 1949–1957. Played by Clayton Moore, John Hart.

John Reid is secretly the Lone Ranger, an early West lawman who helped people threatened by outlaws. John was born in Texas and was the son of a Texas Ranger. He and his brother Dan were groomed to be lawmen and joined the Rangers when they became of age. Dan, the older brother, had risen to the rank of Captain when John joined the force. It was also at this time that John would become the mysterious Lone Ranger.

John was one of six Rangers (led by Dan) who were tracking the Butch Cavendish Hole in the Wall Gang. At Bryant's Gap in Texas, the Rangers were ambushed by the gang and left for dead. Tonto (Jay Silverheels), a Potawatomi Indian hunting for food, found a lone survivor of the attack — John Reid. Tonto nursed John back to health.

As John recovered from his wounds, he chose to begin a crusade and bring outlaws to justice.

He made a black mask from his brother's vest, dressed in white and soon became known as the Lone Ranger—the one ranger who lived to avenge the others. With Tonto's help, John apprehends the Cavendish gang. Their reputation soon spreads and they become known as a force for good ("Where ever you find a wrong to be righted, that's where you'll find the Lone Ranger." John also says, "Keeping my identity a secret makes the pursuit of outlaws easier").

John is apparently from a wealthy family as he inherited a silver mine (while not stated, John had to let certain people know he is still alive—like Jim Blaine, the old miner who works the mine; and George Wilson, John's secret banker in Border City, who exchanges the silver for money). John's trademark is a silver bullet (to remind him to shoot sparingly and to remember the high cost of human life).

To help in a capacity other than the Lone Ranger, John uses various disguises to assist without arousing suspicion (for example, Don Pedro O'Sullivan, the Swede; Juan Ringo, the Mexican bandit; the Old Timer; and Professor Horatio Tucker, the medicine man). John has a distinctive voice and it is sometimes a threat to his secret identity when he goes undercover ("There's something about that voice," an outlaw would say, "but I can't place my finger on it").

The Lone Ranger rides a horse named Silver (whom he also calls "Big Fella"); Scout is Tonto's horse. The Lone Ranger wears a double holster; Tonto carries a single holstered gun (left side) and a knife (right side) Tonto also goes undercover as Red Dog, an outlaw Indian. Tonto calls John "Kemo Sabe" (translated as both "Faithful Friend" and "Trusted Scout").

584. John Robinson, *Lost in Space,* CBS, 1965–1968. Played by Guy Williams.

This entry also contains information on John's family: his wife Maureen (June Lockhart), and their children Judy (Marta Kristen), Penny (Angela Cartwright) and Will (Billy Mumy).

John Robinson is the head of a unique family. He is a professor of astrophysics; Maureen is a distinguished biochemist; Penny has an I.Q. of 147 and is interested in zoology; Will is an electronics wizard; and Judy is an heroic girl who will sacrifice what she loves to serve her country.

John was a professor at the University of Stellar Dynamics. Maureen, working with the New Mexico College of State Medicine, was the first woman in history to pass the International Space Administrations grueling physical and emotional screenings for intergalactic flight. Will graduated

from the Campbell Canyon School of Science at the age of nine and held the highest average in the school's history.

It is the future (1997) when the Robinson's are chosen to colonize an unnamed planet orbiting the star Alpha Centauri in an effort to relieve Earth of over crowding. Major Donald West is chosen to pilot the ship that will take them into outer space, the *Jupiter II.* An enemy agent (Dr. Zachary Smith) sabotages the *Jupiter II* (to prevent American from reaching the star first) and the Robinsons become lost in space.

John is an expert in applied geology. He quickly adapts to the conditions of the hostile worlds he encounters and becomes the leader of the stranded family (which also includes Donald West and Dr. Smith). John is an expert shot with a laser pistol. Maureen is a devoted wife and mother. Although trained in biochemistry, she rarely has an opportunity to use her skills. She is regulated to such wifely duties as cooking, cleaning and even gardening.

Judy is the oldest of the Robinson children. It was said that she "heroically postponed all hopes for a career in the musical comedy field" to join the family. Judy has no special skills (her beauty makes up for it) and helps her mother with the chores. Penny is the middle child. She has a vivid imagination and natural curiosity to explore (often getting into perilous situations). She also had an invisible friend she called "Mr. Nobody." Will, the youngest child, has an uncontrollable urge to investigate the new surroundings he encounters (and almost always becomes involved in dangerous situations that require the help of his family to save him).

See also: Dr. Zachary Smith.

585. John Roxton, *The Lost World,* Syn., 1998–2002. Played by Will Snow.

The time is 1920. Lord John Roxton is a famous hunter who joined the Challenger Expedition to stalk the greatest game of all time: prehistoric creatures on a mysterious plateau in the Amazon.

John was born on January 12, 1882, in Avery, England. He is the youngest son of a lord and inherited the title through a tragic accident (John and his brother, William, were on a safari when William was attacked by an ape. John shot the ape, but the bullet passed through it and killed William. John inherited what should have been William's title).

John is also a notorious ladies' man and the toast of society. He was voted "Most Elegant Speaker in the House of Lords" and is suspicious of everyone and everything. He likes his tea double blended with a splash of milk in a China cup. He lives by a creed that adventure is the only thing that makes life worth living.

See also: George Challenger, Finn, Marguerite Krux, Veronica Layton, Ned Malone.

586. John Sheridan, *Babylon 5*, TNT, 1994–1998. Played by Bruce Boxleitner.

John Sheridan is captain of *Babylon 5*, a five-mile long space station that was built in the 23rd century. It is located in neutral space and serves as a negotiating base to maintain the peace among the various alien races.

John came aboard during the second season. He has the respect of his crew and is especially close to his second in command, Susan Ivanova. John is clever and witty and has an impressive battle record. He fought in the Mimbari-Earth War and used his cunning to down strategic enemy ships. He was also responsible for (and almost killed) when he destroyed a large city on the home planet of the evil Shadows, an enemy of *Babylon 5*. John's daring is always apparent but he seeks to diplomatically resolve the problems he encounters — not only for the residents of *Babylon 5* but for the travelers, trades people, business personnel and criminals who visit the floating city.

John is married to Ann, a scientist who is believed to be dead (lost on an exploration on the planet Z'ha'dun). During the fourth season John was captured on Mars, interrogated by the Psi Corps (the evil militant group) and escaped to lead the Army of Light in a victorious battle to liberate the Earth from the tyranny of the Shadows. He then became the President of the Alliance (the agreement between planets) and remained on *Babylon 5* as an overseer.

See also: Delenn, Elizabeth Lochley, Lyta Alexander, Susan Ivanova.

587. John Steed, *The Avengers*, ABC, 1966–1969. Played by Patrick Macnee.

John Steed is an Avenger, a Ministry agent who battles the enemies of the British government. He works with Catherine Gale, Emma Peel and Tara King. Steed (as he is most often called) is debonair and he displays old world charm and courtesy.

Steed was born in England and is the scion of a wealthy family. He attended school at Eaton but spent much of his time in amateur stage productions. He left school in 1939 and joined the Royal Navy (where he was a lieutenant in command of a torpedo boat). After the war he captained an ex-naval launch in the Mediterranean that dealt with illegal cigarette trafficking. He gave this up

to become a civil servant in London. This led to him becoming an economic advisor to a sheik in the Middle East. When Steed settled a dispute between two neighboring states that made the sheik rich through oil deals, Steed was given life royalties from two of the oil wells by the sheik.

Steed first lived at 5 West Minster Mews, then at 3 Stable Mews in London. He is trained to withstand brainwashing and torture and is an expert on explosives, poison and codes. When it comes to fighting he uses every dirty trick in the book to get the best of his enemies. Steed carries no gun, but as part of his Edwardian-style wardrobe, he carries an umbrella with him at all times (the handle conceals a sword) and wears a bowler hat lined with metal. Steed is a connoisseur of fine wine plays piano and croquet and reads the Royal Edition of the *London Times*.

Steed's first car was a yellow 1926 Vintage Rolls Royce Silver Ghost, then a dark green 1929 Vintage 4.5 Liter Bentley (plate YT 3942; later RX 6180 and VT 3942). He also has a white Rolls Royce "that I usually keep in mothballs" as it doesn't always start and is used only for special occasions (like treating Mrs. Peel to lunch). Steed takes three sugars in his coffee and has a weakness for the opposite sex. He originally had a Great Dane named Juno, then a Dalmatian he called Freckles.

The character of John Steed originally appeared in 1961 on British television (at which time he worked with Dr. David Keel). The following year (to 1965) he was teamed with Catherine Gale. These episodes were first seen in the U.S. in 1991 on A&E.

See also: Catherine Gale, Emma Peel, Mike Gambit, Purdy, Tara King.

588. Johnny Marucci, *Thieves*, ABC, 2001. Played by John Stamos.

Johnny Marucci is an expert pickpocket and locksmith who works as a thief for the U.S. government (the Justice Department) to retrieve items that the government believes were stolen from them.

Johnny was a master debater in high school and considers himself a master thief—"I don't find things I take things. There are thieves and there are thieves. Don't lump them in one category." He lives in Apartment 1210 in Washington, D.C., and doesn't like shooting or being around shooting ("I break into people's homes when they're sleeping. If they wake up I leave"). Johnny also dislikes flying in helicopters ("It doesn't have any wings"). He likes to take things slow and easy (like opening a safe by listening for the tumblers in a combination lock — not by explosives). Johnny learned most of his skills on the streets (at the age of 18, for example, he learned how to hot wire cars). He is also superstitious and rambles on and on when he talks to someone.

See also: Rita (no last name), his partner in crime.

589. Johnny Midnight, *Johnny Midnight,* Syn., 1960. Played by Edmond O'Brien.

Johnny Midnight is a private detective who uses the craft of his former occupation as an actor to apprehend criminals. Johnny lives in a penthouse on West 41st Street and Broadway — "My favorite Street in my favorite town — New York City." Although Johnny gave up his career as an actor to help people in trouble, he found that "the curtain never comes down on the real things that happen on the Street of Dreams."

Johnny is the son of a show business couple and followed in their footsteps. He has his own Broadway theater, the Midnight Theater, and still frequents the actors' hangout, Lindy's Bar (where he likes to eat and keep in touch with his show business friends). Cost doesn't matter to Johnny when it comes to a client. If he sees that a person is in real trouble, the money becomes secondary. Johnny also works on behalf of the Mutual Insurance Company. Johnny is swift to use violence. He is calculating and careful but he feels the longer it takes to solve a crime, the easier it is for the criminal to escape the bounds of the law.

590. Johnny Ringo, *Johnny Ringo,* CBS, 1959–1960. Played by Don Durant.

Johnny Ringo is a gunfighter of the 1870s who is not quite sure how he became a legend — "I don't know, it just grew... All of a sudden you're a big man and you find yourself like a turkey in a shoot. Everybody wants to try their luck. You can't stop it. You wanna but you can't. You run but they catch you. You hide but they find you."

Johnny's reputation, "The fastest gun in the West," was also his saving grace. He became the town sheriff of Velardi, Arizona, and now helps people "the badge will make up for some of the things I did."

Johnny receives $200 a month and says, "Velardi didn't hire me. They hired my guns. I know that and got to live with it. Maybe someday it will be different." Johnny doesn't know much about the law and puts things on a personal basis. He philosophizes and people say he sounds more like a preacher than a gunfighter. Johnny sometimes poses as a wanted man and calls on his reputation as a gunfighter to apprehend outlaws.

Johnny never killed a man for money. His gun is a variation on the French firearm, the LeMet Special. It has been called a "seven shooter" and looks like a regular Colt .45 but it has a separate barrel for an extra shell — a .410 shotgun shell — "to even up the odds." Johnny's reputation was known from the Gulf of Mexico to the Pacific Ocean.

591. Johnny Staccato, *Johnny Staccato,* NBC, 1959–1960. Played by John Cassavetes.

Johnny Staccato is a private detective who works out of New York City. Waldo's, a jazz nightclub on MacDougal Street, is his base of operations. Johnny is a former jazz musician (head of the Staccato Combo) who gave up his career for a more lucrative job as a private investigator. Johnny was born in Manhattan and lives at 860 West 40th Street — "I'm a native, but I still ask questions, especially of pretty girls to get around." Johnny also knows a lot — "It's all from odd bits of information I picked up here and there."

Johnny relaxes by playing piano at Waldo's. He is tough with his fists and quick to use a gun. His clients are not the best society has to offer and he frequently takes the cases of people with little money and desperately in need of help. Johnny's world is that of the beatniks, strippers, hookers and low life's who come to life when the city turns on its lights at night. Johnny needed to do what he had to bring a case to a successful conclusion. If it meant drinking cheap liquor in a two-bit joint to get info or frequenting clip joints and dance halls, Johnny would do it. Johnny had his ethics but he was not beyond bending the rules to get what he needed.

592. Johnny Yuma, *The Rebel,* ABC, 1959–1961. Played by Nick Adams.

Johnny Yuma is an embittered, leather-tough, young ex–Confederate soldier who journeys West after the Civil War to seek his own identity. Johnny was born in the town of Mason, Georgia. He wanted to be a writer and work for the town newspaper, the Mason *Bulletin,* but he could not stay put. He ran away from home several times when he was 15 and joined the Confederate Army as a means of running away. Johnny's mother died when he was very young; his father, Ned Yuma, raised him.

Johnny now rides his late father's horse and carries his scattergun (Ned, the town sheriff, was killed in the line of duty). Johnny wears his Rebel uniform proudly wherever he goes. His saddle is his pillow; he never stays in any one place long enough to call home — "The things I gotta learn about aren't here, just another stop in an off place." Johnny keeps a record of his travels in a "book" as he calls it, and helps people in trouble (his strong sense of justice forces him into violent confrontations with those who oppose his beliefs). The war may be over, but hatred still exists — "Maybe I'll find my place one day."

593. Jolene Hunnicutt, *Alice,* CBS, 1982–1984. Played by Celia Weston.

Jolene Hunnicutt is a waitress at Mel's Diner, a less-than-fashionable roadside eatery in Phoenix, Arizona. Jolene was born in South Carolina and worked as a big rig trucker before quitting and trying her luck at a new profession. She previously worked in a "stuffing factory" ("stuff, staple, stuff, staple," she says). Mel, the boss, calls her "Blondie" (when he yells at her he says, "Bag it Blondie").

Jolene works with Alice Hyatt and Vera Gorman. She lives at the Pine Valley Apartments and dreams of one day opening her own beauty shop. Jolene hates to wear a hair net ("It makes your hair look like sofa stuffing"), reads mystery novels and the magazines *True Romance* and *Modern Crime.* She believes a coffee break "is a teensy weensy vacation with pay" and at the Laundromat she uses washers six and nine ("because number eight wobbles") and dryers 16 and 31. She sleeps on Snoopy sheets. As a kid, Jolene pretended that her tree house was a plane and she was a stewardess. To live that childhood dream, Jolene attended flight school and became a stewardess for Desert Airlines. After her first assignment (on flight 12) she quit when she realized she was afraid to fly. The last episode finds Jolene opening her own beauty parlor with the money she inherits from her grandmother.

See also: Alice Hyatt, Flo Castleberry, Mel Sharples, Vera Gorman.

594. Jon Baker, *CHiPs,* NBC, 1977–1983. Played by Larry Wilcox.

Jonathan A. Baker, called Jon, is a motorcycle police officer with the California Highway Patrol (CHiPs). He was born on August 8, 1948, in San Diego, California (another episode mentions Wyoming). He is single and has a brother and a sister. He wears badge 5712 (also seen as 8712) and drives a motorcycle with the plate 16A60. His mobile codes were given as 7-Mary-4 and LA-15-Mary-3.

Jon is a certified flight instructor and enjoys all types of sports (tennis, handball and skiing are his favorites). He teaches children how to bowl and enjoys riding his horse, Old Grey. When he gets a bit nervous, Jon adjusts his gun belt and

pulls on his gloves. Jon likes the outdoors, is neat and has a clean police record.

See also: Frank Poncherello (his partner).

595. Jonas Paine, *Thicker Than Water,* ABC, 1973. Played Malcolm Atterbury.

Jonas Paine is an American legend, a man who loved pickles so much that he turned his love for the Gherkin into an empire called Paine's Pure Pickles.

Jonas was born in 1881 and raised on a farm where he became fascinated by cucumbers and their pickling. He created a recipe that not only brought out the taste of a Gherkin but also kept it fresh and pure. He invested what little money he had and established a small business in 1910. His Gherkins caught on and an empire was born. A year later he won the gold medal for his Gherkins at the American Grain Association.

Jonas married a girl named Frances in 1932. They became the parents of Nellie (1933) and Ernie (1935). Jonas lost Frances in 1955 and eight years later became chronically ill. He has been cared for by Nellie ever since (Ernie left home when he was no longer able to stand the smell of pickles).

Jonas gets his medication from Pike's Pharmacy and almost every home in town (unnamed) has a jar of Paine's Pure Pickles. While Jonas did build the pickle factory up from nothing, he also invested in such losing propositions as a dude ranch in Chicago and electric fishing poles.

Jonas lived by two pickle rules that he insists his employees follow: "Never let your cucumber crumble" and "remember the Gherkin rule — no cucumber bigger than your finger."

See also: Ernie Paine, Nellie Paine.

596. Jonathan and Jennifer Hart, *Hart to Hart,* ABC, 1979–1984. Played by Robert Wagner, Stefanie Powers.

Jonathan and Jennifer Hart are a happily married and wealthy couple who are fascinated by crime. While not officially private detectives, they use their expertise as amateur sleuths to help people in trouble. They live at 3100 Willow Pond Road in Bel Air, California; 555-1654 (later 555-3223) is their phone number. Max (Lionel Stander), Jonathan's dearest friend, cares for them; and they have a dog named Freeway.

Jonathan is the owner of Hart Industries at 112 North Las Palmas in Los Angeles. It is a multi-billion dollar conglomerate that Jonathan began in 1965 with $1500 he borrowed from Max. By 1969, when the first issues of stock were offered to the public, Jonathan had become a millionaire.

Jonathan's past is a bit sketchy. He was born in

California and orphaned at an early age. He grew up on the streets and was headed for a life of crime when a stranger named Max stepped in and rescued him. Max made sure Jonathan graduated from high school and sent him to college. Jonathan studied business and with Max's help after graduation, began Hart Industries.

Jennifer (maiden name Edwards) was born in Hillhaven, Maryland (her father, Steven Edwards, is a former CIA agent). Jennifer grew up on a ranch and had a horse named Sweet Sue. She attended Gresham Prep School and an unnamed college (where she majored in journalism). After graduating, Jennifer moved to New York and became a free-lance journalist. It was while on an assignment in London for the *Herald*, that Jennifer met and fell in love with Jonathan (they met at a bar in the Hotel Ritz). They married after a brief courtship and honeymooned at the O'Berge Inn, Room 7, in San Francisco's Napa Valley.

Jennifer gets a bit tipsy from champagne and lunches at La Scala's. She has her hair done at Salvatore's on Wilshire Boulevard. Jennifer likes to cook (although Max does most of the cooking) and appeared in a bit part (party hostess) on her favorite TV soap opera, *Doctors' Hospital*.

597. Jonathan Archer, *Star Trek: Enterprise*, UPN, 2001–2005. Played by Scott Bakula.

Jonathan Archer, Captain of the U.S.S. *Enterprise NX-01*, was born in upstate New York in an unspecified year (possibly the early 2120s) but spent most of his adult life in San Francisco. He has type B-negative blood. Jonathan is the only member of *Enterprise* to have his own pet, his dog, Porthos. Jonathan is the son of Henry Archer, a scientist who developed the warp five-engine, an improvement on a warp drive created by Zefram Cochrane, (the new drive would allow the flight of U.S.S. Star Ships, the first of which was *Enterprise*). Jonathan dreamed of space travel and exploring new worlds. As a child he had memorized Dr. Cochrane's "Warp Five Complex" dedication speech. When he was eight years old, Jonathan received his first astronomy book, *The Cosmos: A to Z* by Laura Danly (this became the first book in his collection that he called "The Library of Admiral Jonathan Archer"). A year later, Jonathan was building models of low warp space ships that existed at the time. Shortly after, he made a ship that actually flew and got his first taste as a ship's commander. He would later find himself a part of the NX-Test Program. It was here that he improved on his father's design. With fellow officer Charles Tucker, they initiated the NX fleet of vessels.

Jonathan's quarters are on A Deck (in the Ready Room next to the Bridge). He is a born explorer and has an insatiable sense of adventure. He relies on his intuition and will go against protocol when he feels his instincts are right. Jonathan was Starfleet's choice to captain *Enterprise*, the first Star Ship to explore the vast, unknown regions of space.

See also: Charles Tucker, Hoshi Sato, Phlox, T'Pol, Travis Mayweather,

598. Jonathan Higgins, *Magnum, P.I.*, CBS, 1980–1988. Played by John Hillerman.

Jonathan Quayle Higgins is the major domo for Robin's Nest, the estate of pulp fiction writer Robin Masters (Robin is never seen; the estate is on Concord Road, later Kalohoa Drive, on the North Shore of Hawaii). It is also the estate on which private detective Thomas Magnum resides (he provides security in return for his living quarters in the main house).

Jonathan was born in England and served Her Majesty in five conflicts over 35 years, most notably as a member of England's MI (Military Intelligence)-5 and MI-6 during World War II. His greatest embarrassment was his expulsion from the prestigious Sandhurst Academy, something he does not talk about. In 1957, Jonathan ran a hotel called the Arlington Arms, which catered to the rich and famous. He enjoys talking to friends around the world (via his ham radio; call letters NR6 DBZ) and his hobbies are building model bridges and painting.

While Jonathan is well educated and very proficient at his job, he has an annoying habit — he tells long, boring stories about his life experiences. Jonathan is the chairman (also called managing director) of the King Kamehamela Club and is chairman of the Honolulu branch of the Britons Seaman's Fund Charity. He enjoys doing the Sunday *London Times* crossword puzzle and is writing his memories in a diary called *Crisis at Suez*. Jonathan is also a member of the Committee on Historical Preservation and he has created his own blend of tea he calls Lady Ashley Tea. Jonathan has two Great Danes, Apollo and Zeus, who patrol the grounds (he calls the dogs "Lads") and his mobile car code is N6DB2.

See also: Thomas Magnum.

599. Jonathan Smith, *Highway to Heaven*, NBC, 1984–1989. Played by Michael Landon.

This entry also contains information on Mark Gordon (Victor French), the mortal who assists Jonathan. Jonathan Smith is an angel who performs missions of good for God (whom Jonathan calls "The Boss").

Jonathan Smith is actually the heavenly name given to Arthur Morton, a man who worked as an honest lawyer all his life. Arthur was born in 1917 and died in 1948. He was married (to Jane) and was the father of a daughter (Mandy). Arthur was a kind and gentle man and devoted all his energies to helping people in trouble. He was a loving husband and father and was never unfaithful to his wife. At an unspecified time after his death, Arthur became an apprentice angel and given an assignment in order to earn his wings: help people on earth. Jonathan worked alone until he met Mark, a cynical ex-cop. When Jonathan restored Mark's faith in his fellow man and revealed himself to be an angel, Mark asked to let him help and Jonathan, with the approval of "The Boss," accepted ("It is not my decision to make. Higher authority deems we should be a team").

Mark was born and raised in California. He is a graduate of Lathrop High School (where he was called "Stick") and served with the Oakland Police Department for 15 years. Mark wears a California A's baseball cap and drives a Ford sedan (plate IDT 0458).

600. Jordan Cavanaugh, *Crossing Jordan*, NBC, 2001 (current). Played by Jill Hennessy.

Dr. Jordan Cavanaugh is a medical examiner for the Commonwealth of Massachusetts, Office of the Chief Medical Examiner ("I cut up dead people for a living," she says).

Jordan was born in Massachusetts and is the daughter of Max Cavanaugh, a Boston police officer (Jordan's mother died as the result of a shooting that is still unsolved). When Jordan was a child she would sneak out of her room at night to spy on her father as he sat at the kitchen table with a glass of Scotch and all the evidence in a case he was investigating laid out on the table. Max would stare at the evidence and envision himself as both the killer and the victim in an attempt to solve the crime. Max always knew Jordan was watching him and one night asked her "Would you like to be the victim or the killer?" "And that's how it started," says Jordan. "It was like our very own game of Clue; only I wasn't Colonel Mustard in the drawing room with a knife." Jordan later says the book *Catcher in the Rye*, which she read at the age of 15, changed her life and prompted her to become a medical examiner.

Jordan's favorite color is purple. She has a chipped tooth from an accident she suffered in the second grade. She received a rosary on her confirmation from her father (an old Irish Catholic tradition). Jordan is a graduate of St. Inez High School and Boston University (graduated top five in her class). Max believes Jordan is pigheaded and stubborn (she does have one serious problem — insubordination. She constantly clashes with her superiors and has an obsessive desire to solve crimes).

Jordan is opposed to injustice ("that pisses me off") and has a commendation from the Chicago Police Department for solving five murders. She has extraordinary skills, is compassionate about her work and is an excellent diagnostician. Jordan doesn't like to be challenged in her work and gets extremely emotional when a murder baffles her (she assures the victim "I'm going to find out who did this to you"). Jordan lives at 43 Victor Drive, Apartment 311 and thinks like a cop; she takes the simplest assignment and turns it into a murder investigation.

See also: Garrett Macy (Jordan's superior).

601. Josh Randall, *Wanted: Dead or Alive*, CBS, 1958–1961. Played by Steve McQueen.

"The law wants 'em and I want 'em too — dead or alive," says Josh Randall, a bounty hunter of the Old West (1870s). Josh is a man with a conscience — he will not kill his bounty unless he is given no other choice.

Josh is not a lawman but has made a lot of friends during his travels across the West (including many sheriffs and marshals who respect him). Josh doesn't wear a badge and can take the shortest distance between two people; he does not require the legalities to bring in a wanted man or woman.

Josh claims, "Being a bounty hunter wasn't a bad way to live. You got to see a lot of the country and meet a lot of people. It was a living and now and then a good one." Josh liked his life "and it seemed to like him." Though the world may be big and men can easily hide from the law, Josh finds that not to be a problem — "He's a man. There's no where he can lay down his feet that I can't walk — I'll find him." Josh has a motto: "If he's got a price on his head. I've got an empty pocket."

People say Josh asks a lot of questions for a bounty hunter. He feels he has to and make sure the person he is trailing is really guilty. Josh has compassion and sometimes finds himself in the position of protector, struggling to protect his prisoners from the less scrupulous bounty hunters.

Josh carries a .30-40 caliber sawed-off carbine he calls his "Mare's Leg." "It's kinda like a hog's leg but not quite as mean. If I have to use it, I want to get the message across."

Joy Wallace *see* **Lindsay Wallace**

602. J.R. Ewing, *Dallas,* CBS, 1978–1991. Played by Larry Hagman.

John Ross Ewing, called J.R., is the son of Jock and Ellie Ewing. He was born in Braddock, Texas (on the Southfork Ranch), in 1939. From an early age J.R. learned the ropes of the oil business (he would accompany his father to the office and observe). As J.R. grew he learned how to be a businessman — not the ranch owner his father had hoped he would become.

J.R. attended Braddock High School and the University of Texas. It was here that his love for women, fine food and drink would manifest itself into an uncontrollable urge in later life (bourbon is his favorite drink). J.R. next joined the army (1960). He was originally sent to Vietnam but that didn't please him. He used his knowledge of wheeling and dealing to manipulate the army brass and spent the rest of his service in Japan. After his discharge he became Vice President of Ewing Oil.

In 1967 J.R. became a judge for the Miss Texas Beauty Pageant and fell in love with its winner, Sue Ellen Shepherd. They married in 1971. Sue Ellen and J.R. simply did not get along and she left him 10 years later (but remarried him again in 1982 and divorced him for a second time in 1988). J.R. became "The man everybody loves to hate." He is a brilliant schemer and conniver with a glint of evil in his eye. He cares only about money and power and is a totally unfaithful husband (although Sue Ellen was no angel either). J.R. claims the name of the game is huge profits. In his tenure at Ewing Oil, his wheeling and dealing cost the company $2 billion in bad deals.

See also: Bobby Ewing, Lucy Ewing, Pamela Barnes, Sue Ellen Ewing.

603. J.T. Lambert, *Step by Step,* ABC, 1991–1997; CBS, 1997–1998. Played by Brandon Call.

John Thomas Lambert, called J.T., is the son of Frank Lambert, a divorced construction company owner, who is now married to Carol Foster, a widow with three children (Karen, Dana and Mark). J.T. has two siblings, Alicia and Brendon, and lives at 211 Winslow Street in Port Washington, Wisconsin.

J.T. is not the brightest student at Port Washington High School. He is a member of the track team and a walking disaster. He has no flair for the construction business but feels at home working as Carol's shampoo boy in her beauty salon (which she operates from the house). While Dana sees J.T. as "a pea-brained idiot," J.T. fancies himself as a teenage ladies' man. J.T.'s favorite meal is burritos and the Burger Palace is his after school hangout. He later worked as a waiter named Cubby at the 50s Café. J.T. and his cousin, Cody Lambert, hosted a cable access program called *J.T. and Cody's World,* wherein they gave their opinions on life, its problems and how to cope with them.

See also: Alicia Lambert, Carol and Frank Lambert, Dana Foster, Karen Foster.

604. Juan Epstein, *Welcome Back, Kotter,* ABC, 1975–1979. Played by Robert Hegyes.

Juan Epstein is a Sweathog, a special education student at James Buchanan High School in Bensonhurst, Brooklyn, New York. Juan has a Puerto Rican and Jewish background (he calls himself "a Puerto Rican Jew") and nine brothers and sisters. He is the toughest kid in school and has been called "Most likely to take a life."

Juan was born in Brooklyn and he is not easily motivated, especially when it comes to schoolwork. He cheats (writes answers on his arms when it is time for a test), uses *TV Guide* movie descriptions for his book reports and when he has to get out of a test (or an excuse for being late) he hands his teacher (Gabe Kotter) "a note from my mother" (composed by Juan and singed "Epstein's mother"). Juan's antics get him sent to the principal's office on a regular basis. On the plus side, Principal Lazarus has taken a liking to Juan and considers him to be like a son.

Juan has a dream to become "a typhoon" and open a string of Puerto Rican–Jewish restaurants. He is an animal lover and has an array of pets: Wally, Eddie Haskell, Lumpy and Jerry Mathers as the Beaver (lizards); Jimmy, Darlene, Cubby and Annette (white mice; his "Mouseketeers"); Florence, Harpo and John-Boy (hamsters); Truman Capote (turtle); and an unnamed chicken "who escaped from a butcher shop and crossed Bay Parkway" (which is near Juan's home). Juan has a bad habit of smoking, which he has been doing on and off since he was 12 years old.

See also: Arnold Horshack, Freddie Washington, Gabe and Julie Kotter, Vinnie Barbarino.

605. Judge Roy Bean, *Judge Roy Bean,* Syn., 1955–1956. Played by Edgar Buchanan.

Roy Bean is one of television's least likely western heroes. He is a bit on the heavy side, near sighted without his glasses and older than most lawmen. He is not quick on the draw and he does not carry a fancy gun. He does, however, possess a genius for figuring out the criminal mind and capturing outlaws.

Roy was born in Texas and grew up in an era of lawlessness. He is a self-appointed judge and owns Roy Bean's General Store in the town he founded — Langtry, Texas (Roy named the town after Lily Langtry, a showgirl who was once his lady love). Roy is also the sheriff and mayor and established the town 18 years ago (1870) when the railroads began laying tracks in the West. However, with the railroads also came the most vicious characters in the country. Soon, the desolate region West of the Pecos River became known as "The wildest spot in the United States. It took the courage of one man, a lone storekeeper who was sick of the lawlessness to change all this. His name was Judge Roy Bean."

Judge Bean enforces the spirit of the law, not so much the letter of the law (he has, for example, an unsigned search warrant that he constantly uses for his investigative work). Roy is fond of apple pie, has a horse named Maggie and feels that of all the items he bought for the store, the dress dummy was his worst purchase (he can't seem to sell it). Roy is assisted at the store by his beautiful niece Letty Bean (Jackie Loughery) and in his law enforcing by his deputy Jeff Taggard (Jack Beutel).

Letty is 19 years old (born June 9, 1869) and came to live with her uncle after the death of her parents. Letty is very feminine and dynamite with a gun (her dress conceals a gun strapped to her ankle). Jeff also runs a ranch (has 800 head of cattle) and is dating Letty. He sees Letty as "a big tomboy" and admires her ability to handle a gun — "You shoot just like a man." Letty is forever getting angry when Jeff sees her that way — "Can't you see me as a woman just once?" He tries, at least for the remainder of that particular episode.

606. Judson Cross, *Adventure, Inc.*, Syn., 2002–2003. Played by Michael Biehn.

Judson Cross is a marine archeologist and explorer who captains the boat *Vast Explorer* and runs a company called Adventure, Inc. He will recover any missing object for a price.

Judson likes to think of himself as a professional explorer. He is a diving expert and honest — he will not take a bribe to do research and will not withhold valuable objects for himself. If he did such a things "It would give the profession a worse reputation than it already has." Judson can live on water and knows exactly where to dive for something (he also mixes water with Coffee Mate non dairy creamer to produce milk for his breakfast cereal of corn flakes). For relaxation Judson enjoys fishing at Jackson's Cove in Florida

(his home base). He also uses a mini-sub called *Rover* to explore the ocean floor.

See also: McKenzie Previn (his assistant).

607. Judy Foster, *A Date with Judy*, ABC, 1951–1953. Played by Patricia Crowley, Mary Linn Beller.

Judy Foster is a very pretty 16-year-old girl with a knack for finding trouble. She is the daughter of Melvyn and Dora Foster and lives at 123 State Street in a locale referred to as the City. Judy was born on May 16, 1935 and is a sophomore at City High School. She receives an allowance of two dollars a week and says things like "Oh, caterpillars" and "Oh, butterflies" when something goes wrong. Judy is vibrant, eager to enjoy life and eager to express her endless opinions about everything. However, she believes nobody appreciates what she has to say, especially her family — "I think people who are related to me are unsympathetic and full of a lack of understanding. Every time I offer something constructive and valuable in the way of something constructive, I get stepped on before the germ of my idea ever gets a chance to bud into blossom."

Judy is not one for school athletics (just getting through a day of classes is an effort) and keeping her bedroom neat and tidy is another chore she often neglects. Judy has a nice figure and appears not to be jealous of the more developed girls in her class. The Coke Parlor (later Pop Scully's Soda Fountain) is the after-school hangout.

Oogie Pringle (Jimmy Sommers) is the object of Judy's affections. She fell in love with him on the day she ran over him with her tricycle and has made it her goal to make him the man of her dreams. Judy's father owns the Foster Canning Company and she has a younger brother named Randolph.

608. Judy Miller, *Still Standing*, CBS, 2002 (current). Played by Jami Gertz.

Judith Miller, called Judy, is the daughter of Helen and Gene Michaels. She was born in Illinois and attended the Pixey Pre-School, Hamilton Grammar School and Jefferson High School (class of 1981). As a child, Judy was a Blue Bell Girl Scout. In high school, where she met her future husband, Bill Miller, Judy was an activist and stood up for what she believed was right. Before marrying, Judy worked as a dental office receptionist (later becoming a dental assistant); Bill acquired a job as a bathroom fixtures salesman (a job he still holds). Judy and Bill eventually had three children (Lauren, Brian and Tina) and set up housekeeping at 209 Evergreen in Chicago.

Judy overcooks the chicken, sings all the time (even though she can't carry a tune), constantly talks while Bill is watching TV and always puts words in Bill's mouth. When the children get out of hand, Judy disciplines them by becoming "Tight-lipped, scary voice Mom." Judy feels she is the better parent — "Bill isn't a bad parent, he's just a stupid man doing the best he can." Judy's favorite movie is *Terms of Endearment* and has her hair done at a salon called Hair by Gary. To get a discount when shopping for appliances, Judy wears a sexy halter-top. Judy tried to make extra money by selling hand-painted outdoor chairs at swap meets.

See also: Bill Miller, Brian Miller, Lauren Miller.

609. Julia Salinger, *Party of Five*, Fox, 1994–2000. Played by Neve Campbell.

Julia Salinger is the 15-year-old daughter of Nicholas and Diana Salinger, the owners of Salinger's Restaurant in San Francisco. She lives at 3324 Broadway with her brothers (Charlie, Bailey and Owen) and sister (Claudia). Julia also helps care for her siblings after the tragic death of her parents in a car accident.

Julia is a sophomore at Grant High School. She is a straight A student and wrote a story about her family called "The Children's Room" (published by *San Francisco Magazine*; she was paid $1,000). Julia is so smart that graffiti on the boys' bathroom wall claims she is "The Girl Most Boys Want to Cheat Off Of."

Julia's middle name is Gordon (her mother's maiden name) and worked briefly at Parker Patterson Press. She is allergic to shrimp and was a cheerleader for less than a half-hour (she gave it up because she found it difficult to smile all the time). Julia enjoys writing poetry but feels she is not as pretty as other girls at Grant High. She dressed older and lied about her age (18) to work as a waitress at Stage 18, an after hours coffee house.

See also: Bailey Salinger, Charlie Salinger, Claudia Salinger.

610. Julia Sugarbaker, *Designing Women*, CBS, 1986–1993. Played by Dixie Carter.

Julia Sugarbaker and her sister, Suzanne, are the owners of the Sugarbaker's Design Firm (later called Sugarbaker and Associates — Interior Design) at 1521 Sycamore Street in Atlanta, Georgia (404-555-8600; later 555-6787 is their phone number).

People describe Julia and Suzanne simply as "Julia got the brains and Suzanne got the boobs."

Julia is well educated, fashion conscious, outspoken, and totally dedicated to women's equality. She was born in Georgia and is a graduate of Chapel High School and Southern State University. She also studied art in Paris (the Gallery Pouzette exhibited a series of her fruit bowl paintings). Julia is easily stressed out and "to get a vacation from myself" (to find her spiritual self), she became Giselle and sang at the Blue Note Night Club.

Julia lives above the firm and wears a size seven shoe. She began the company (something she always wanted to do) after her husband, Hayden, died. She is the sponsor of a Little League baseball team called the Sugarbaker Giants and has a birth certificate with no year on it (a gift from her mother).

See also: Anthony Bouvier, Charlene Frazier, Mary Jo Shively, Suzanne Sugarbaker.

611. Julia Wallace, *Maybe This Time*, ABC, 1995–1996. Played by Marie Osmond.

This entry also contains information on Gracie Wallace (Ashley Johnson), Julia's daughter.

Julia Wallace is a beautiful young woman who looks like she just stepped out of the pages of a fashion magazine. She is 35 years old, divorced (from Frank) and the mother of a 12-year-old daughter. Julia now lives at 136 Old Oak Lane in a small Pennsylvania college town and earns a living by helping her mother Shirley Sullivan (Betty White) run the family diner, The Coffee Dog Café.

Julia loved to roller skate, was obedient, a good student and an overall good child. She is now a modern girl with modern ideas about how to run the café. She believes she has initiative when it comes to the café and hopes to build up the clientele by appealing to the college crowd.

Julia has a strong sense of honesty and ethics. She approaches each situation with a calm, understanding attitude and strives to resolve problems without raising her voice or losing her temper. Everything in life appears to be in black and white to Julia; she never sees the gray and is optimistic that everything will work out for the best. She believes a person can never be wrong if one does the right thing. She stands her ground and always tells the truth.

Julia keeps herself so busy with the café and school activities for Gracie that she has no social life. She does things for others but never for herself — "Doing things for others is like doing it for myself."

When it comes to Gracie, her advice is "Gracie, you're a good girl and always do what your conscience tells you is right" (Julia's way of keeping Gracie on the right track). Gracie would like to change her looks but Julia says, "You're too adorable for a makeover." Gracie is in the sixth grade at P.S. 117 and receives an allowance of $5 a week. She reads *Tiger Beat* and *Sassy* magazines and loves actor Keanu Reeves (she hopes to become his wife one day). She is very obedient and loves to roller skate just like her mother did when she was a child.

612. Julie Cooper, *One Day at a Time*, CBS, 1975–1984. Played by Mackenzie Phillips.

Julie Cooper is the older sister of Barbara Cooper and the daughter of Ann Romano. She lives at 1344 Hartford Drive, Apartment 402, in Indianapolis, Indiana, and carries her father's (Ed) last name (Ann is divorced and uses her maiden name).

Julie is a very independent girl and a constant source of aggravation for her mother. Trouble could be called Julie's middle name. Julie is a graduate of Jefferson High School and first worked as a receptionist for a veterinarian at the Curran Animal Center. When she became dissatisfied with this, she attempted to use her flair for fashion to become a designer. When this failed she found her true calling — counselor at the Free Clinic. She gave up her job to marry Max Horvath (Michael Lembeck), a flight attendant for PMA Airlines, on October 10, 1979. Julie attempted to further her education by attending classes at the Berkum Management Institute and later became the manager of a donut shop and the mother of a daughter she and Max name Annie.

As a child Julie had a plush bear named Tu Tu Bear. She wears a size 32B bra and likes snacking on celery stalks (sometimes dipping them in ice cream). Julie felt her small breasts were her downfall and to attract boys often stuffed her bra with tissues (she was most envious of the never seen, well-endowed Trish the Dish).

See also: Ann Romano, Barbara Cooper, Dwayne Schneider.

613. Julie Kanisky, *Gimme a Break*, NBC, 1981–1986. Played by Lauri Hendler.

Julie Kanisky is the daughter of Carl and Margaret Kanisky. Carl is a police chief; Margaret is deceased. Julie lives at 2938 Maple Lane in Glen Lawn, California, with her sisters, Katie and Samantha, and their live-in housekeeper, Nell Harper.

Julie was born in Glen Law and is the smartest of the sisters (she has an I.Q. of 160). She attends Lincoln High School and claims "I can hold my breath for two whole minutes under water." She collects coins and enjoys watching TV with Nell (whom she considers to be a substitute mother).

Julie is pretty but she is unsure of herself. She wears glasses and feels comfortable being plain and simple. Although she will not admit it, she is jealous of Katie and wishes she could be more like her (popular and beautiful). Katie feels Julie dresses like "an awning on a pizza shop" and has no taste in clothes (younger sister Samantha thinks Julie buys her clothes at garage sales).

Julie is sensitive and relaxes by reading. She was the only one of the sisters to marry (Jonathan Silverman) and have a baby (Little Nell). They moved to San Diego to begin new lives a year before the series ended.

See also: Katie Kanisky, Nell Harper, Samantha Kanisky.

614. Julie Rogers, *Charlie's Angels*, ABC, 1980–1981. Played by Tanya Roberts.

Julie Rogers is a girl with a troubled past who became an Angel — an operative for Charlie Townsend, owner of Townsend Investigations in Los Angeles.

Julie was born in New York City and raised street tough. Her father deserted the family when Julie was too young to remember him. Her mother died in 1978 in a charity hospital of acute alcoholism. Julie is gorgeous and through the efforts of a friend became a model. She appeared on the cover of *Elite* magazine and was the spokes girl for Joggerade Health Juice. But as fast as the jobs came, they also became difficult to find. Julie drifted to Los Angeles. She was broke and soon after arrested for shoplifting a dress she needed for a job interview.

After serving time in jail, Julie was released and found work with the Woodman Modeling Agency. It was here that she met Angels Kris Monroe and Kelly Garrett and helped them find a killer of young models. Her work so impressed Charlie that he hired her when Angel Tiffany Welles left to pursue a modeling career in New York.

Julie is rather impulsive and street smart. She uses her knowledge of the streets to help overcome most of the situations she encounters. While pretty, she rarely uses that asset to help achieve a goal.

See also: Charlie Townsend, Jill Monroe, Kelly Garrett, Kris Monroe, Sabrina Duncan, Tiffany Welles.

615. June Cleaver, *Leave It to Beaver*, CBS, 1957–1958; ABC, 1958–1963. Played by Barbara Billingsley.

June Cleaver is an excellent cook and house-wife. She is married to Ward Cleaver and is the mother of Wally and Beaver. She lives at 211 Pine Street (then 211 Lakewood Avenue) in Mayfield; KL5–763 is their phone number.

June's early background varies by dialogue in various episodes. She was born June Evelyn Bronson in 1920. She had an uncle who was a judge and her grandfather was nearly a genius. When she did something wrong as a child she would wish it were tomorrow. It is first mentioned that June and her family moved to Mayfield when she was a child. She attended the Grant Avenue Elementary School, then a boarding school and State College. In boarding school she told her classmates her mother was a famous actress (LaVerne Laverne) who gave up her career to marry her father. Here she was captain of the girls' basketball team and also a member of the swim team. She also worked at a department store selling books and was with the U.S.O. (United Serviceman's Organization). When she was 16 years old she met Ward (which would make them both high school students). However, in a later episode, June mentions she was a teenager when she moved to Mayfield (thus she never attended Grant Avenue Grammar School). She met Ward at State College and married him after graduating.

June loves to wear jewelry and is a member of the Ladies' Club of the Grant Avenue Elementary School. In the TV movie update, *Still the Beaver* (CBS, March 19, 1983), June is seen as a widow but still living in Mayfield with her children, Wally and Beaver. In the TBS series, *The New Leave It to Beaver* (1986–1989), June is living in the original series house at 211 Pine Street with her son Beaver (divorced from Kimberly) and his two sons, Kip and Oliver. June is also a member of the Mayfield City Council.

See also: Beaver Cleaver, Eddie Haskell, Lumpy Rutherford, Wally Cleaver, Ward Cleaver.

616. J.Z. Kane, *Dog and Cat*, ABC, 1977. Played by Kim Basinger.

J.Z. Kane is an officer with the 42nd Division of the Los Angeles Police Department. She is also called "Cat," a female officer who is partners with a male (the "Dog"); here with Sergeant Jack Ramsey (Lou Antonio).

J.Z. (full name not revealed) lives at 2317 Englewood Road. She was born and raised in Georgia and attributes her expertise as a police officer to "my uncle back in Georgia" (who apparently taught her how to take care of herself— from shooting a gun to defending herself with her fists). J.Z. is blonde and gorgeous and looks more like a model than an undercover police officer. She is street wise, despite her upbringing on a farm. She loves animals and country and western music. J.Z. is not a picky eater. She hates cooking and lives off frozen TV dinners. She is also an expert on cars (especially engines) and has installed a Porsche 912 engine in her Volkswagen (the car is now capable of high speeds). How J.Z. came to be a police officer is not really explained; she says only that she held a job as a cashier at the Greenwich Theater (which shows porno films) while "working my way through the police academy." Prior to being teamed with Jack, J.Z. worked as an undercover cop amid the hookers, sleazy producers and pornographic filmmakers of Venice (it was the department's idea to experiment with a male-female team and paired J.Z. with Jack). Jack is a hothead who is J.Z.'s direct opposite — "I'm from the pavement," he says, "and you (J.Z.) are from the streets." No matter what Jack and the department think, J.Z. always comes through "because I do things by female intuition."

Ka D'Argo *see* **John Crichton**

617. Kai, *Lexx*, Sci Fi, 2000–2002. Played by Michael McManus.

Kai is an undead assassin and the last member of the Brunnen-G, a once proud and noble race of romantic warriors who, overtime, became isolated and easily defeated when they went into battle (their battle song, "Va Va Ra, Brunnen-G," is the series theme song). Kai and his people lived on a planet in the Light Universe. Kai was a leader and philosopher and it was foretold that Kai would be the one to end the reign of His Divine Shadow, the leader of an invading race ruled by His Divine Order. In a devastating battle between His Divine Shadow and the Brunnen-G, Kai was killed. His Divine Shadow, however, would not let Kai remain dead. He restored Kai's essence by proto-blood and used his services as an assassin. Kai obeyed His Divine Shadow for 2,000 years. He was a heartless killing machine and to receive the proto-blood did what he was told. Without warning the memories of all those he killed became a powerful source of wisdom, strength and information for Kai. Although dead, Kai begins to think for himself and uses his newfound knowledge to end the reign of the Divine Order by killing His Divine Shadow.

Kai has no heart and doesn't breathe. He can move and is technically alive, but he lacks color. Kai is a being of deep thought and has little to say. He observes the situations he encounters and accepts the fact that he is dead. He dresses in black and is often called "The Man in Black" by those who see him. He travels with Zev Bellringer and Stanley H. Tweedle aboard an exploratory spacecraft called *Lexx*. He is able to transport himself from place to place by firing his brace (a bracelet-like device he wears on his wrist that emits a sharp hook and a long rope when fired). And, "for a dead guy, Kai has an interest in certain legends related to certain places" (the reason he is exploring the Dark Universe).

See also: Robot Head 790, Stanley H. Tweedle, Zev Bellringer.

618. Karen Foster, *Step by Step*, ABC, 1991–1997; CBS, 1997–1998. Played by Angela Watson.

Karen Foster knows that at 14 years of age she is beautiful ("I'm what the guys call a babe"). She was born in Port Washington, Wisconsin, in 1978 and is the daughter of Carol Foster, a widow who is now married to Frank Lambert. Karen has two siblings, Dana and Mark, and also lives with Frank and his children (Alicia, J.T. and Brendon) at 201 Winslow Street in Port Washington.

Karen first attended Lincoln Elementary School, then Port Washington High School. She is often mistaken for a model and says, "I just look like one but I'm not." Karen is very concerned about her appearance, especially her makeup ("A mirror is my best friend"). Her mother believes her obsession started the day she gave Karen a Brooke Shields fashion doll. Alicia believes Karen "is a wuss because everything frightens her." Karen reads *Chic* and *Cosmopolitan* magazines and worked as a teen model at Peterson's Department Store. Karen can't resist a sale at the mall; if she is five minutes late, she feels there are people buying things meant for her. Before each date Karen listens to the tape "Teenage Dating Tips." As a child, Karen had a washcloth with a mouse on it she called "Mouthy" (Carol called it "Mousy," but Karen pronounced it as "Mouthy"). In high school Karen is a cheerleader for the Wildcats football team. Cherry Cha Cha is her favorite shade of lipstick.

See also: Alicia Lambert, Carol and Frank Lambert, Dana Foster, J.T. Lambert.

619. Karen Sisco, *Karen Sisco*, ABC, 2003. Played by Carla Gugino.

Karen Sisco is a tough and seductive Miami Beach based U.S. Marshal. She is the daughter of Marshall and Julie Sisco and has been raised in an atmosphere of good always triumphs over evil. Her father is a rugged, respected private detective who helped the police collar many lawbreakers (he charges $5,000 a case plus ten percent up front for expenses).

Karen is a graduate of North Central High School and Miami State University. She is stubborn and insists on doing things her way. She is an expert at poker and steals evidence from crime scenes (and worries about the consequences — "It's 3 to 5 years if I'm caught." She feels she is better equipped to solve a case if she can study the evidence she gathers first hand). Karen is angry over the fact that she can only work on warrants and cannot legally do anything without one. At times circumstances prevent Karen from securing evidence. When she is faced with such situations, she does what she does best — bend the rules to bring a case to a successful conclusion (figuring what her boss doesn't know won't hurt him).

Karen lives in an apartment at 7841 North Alameda; 565-555-1095 is her cell phone number and Del Monaco's is her favorite eatery. While gorgeous without showing too much skin, Karen finds that revealing a bit more of her bosom gets her into places she would normally have trouble accessing. When a case becomes difficult Karen often seeks the help of her father and together they manage to bring a culprit to justice.

620. Karen Walker, *Will and Grace*, NBC, 1998 (current). Played by Megan Mullally.

Karen Walker is a rich, beautiful woman who works as the assistant to Grace Adler, an interior decorator in Manhattan. Karen is married to the grossly overweight, rich owner of Stanley Walker, Inc.; she works only to get away from Stan and her stepchildren.

Karen is the daughter of Lois Whitley. Her father died when she was seven years old and to support herself and Karen, Lois moved from town to town living off scams. Karen, called Kiki by Lois, had an unstable childhood and was often a part of a con. When she became a teenager, Karen and Lois had a falling out and Karen ran away when she was no longer able to live of scams (Lois now works as a waitress at Paddy's Pub in Yonkers, New York). While no jobs are mentioned, Karen managed to survive and even attended college. Karen apparently met Stan after graduating from college. Just prior to this she starred in an X-rated fetish film first called *Next to Godliness* (she later says it was called *Dirty Little Pig Boy*); she did it "because I was broke and needed the money." Karen appeared in the film under the name Karen Delaney. Karen also says that she appeared in an episode of the TV series *Mama's Family*, but her scene as a bank teller was cut out. On their first wedding anniversary, Stan gave Karen $1 million is cash — "because paper is the symbol of the first anniversary."

Karen believes she is fabulous. She calls her ample breasts "a killer rack" and considers herself a fantastic dresser. While Karen prides herself on her physical beauty, she revealed a shocking secret about her life in high school: "I was flat chested." Karen felt she had to do something and "I took horse pills." By the time she was 16, she prided herself on wearing a 36D bra. She immediately put her newfound assets to work by "lifting my blouse for votes in the student body election" (naturally, she won). She now fells that showing her breasts is an easy way to accomplish a goal (she is now a 38D). Karen also revealed that she is sometimes drawn to beautiful women and did experiment with making love to a woman almost as beautiful as she is (she will rarely admit that any woman is prettier than her). She never actually said she disliked it (she does look at other women and she has kissed other women including her friend, Grace Adler).

Karen is also neurotic. She takes a blue pill, labeled "Beautiful Feeling," every 15 minutes but also has a pill for anything that bothers her ("If they don't have a pill for my ailment, they will make it for me"). When Karen wants to "pig out" (as she says) she uses the name Anastasia Beaverhaven so people won't know who she really is (she uses the alias, for example, to eat at Taco Time). Karen loves Halloween for the sexy "boobs up and out" costumes she can wear and has weekly facials at Yolanda's Salon. Karen does not know how to work a computer, fax or phone, but she knows people and can get Grace what she needs; she also gets back from lunch in time for dinner.

Stanley Walker is Karen's second husband (she never talks about hubby number one). She has a racehorse (Lamar) and is most proud when people "admire my large bosom." She finds comfort in drinking and carries a flask with her at all times.

Karen has a home in the country and a luxurious penthouse suite in Manhattan. Her life changes when Stanley is arrested for tax evasion and dies shortly after from a heart attack (while having sex with his mistress, Lorraine). Karen becomes the head of what is now called Walker, Inc., and hires her friend Will Truman as the company lawyer (she sends her stepchildren off to live with Stan's first wife). Karen next fell in love with Lyle Finster (John Cleese) and married him in the season finale on April 29, 2004 (Lyle makes money by selling rat traps to breweries).

See also: Grace Adler, Jack McFarland, Will Truman.

621. Kate Benson, *Special Unit 2*, UPN, 2001–2002. Played by Alexondra Lee.

Kate Alice Benson believes that there is an evil presence in the world — something that is hard to see but something that exists. Kate works for Special Unit 2, a secret undercover unit of the Chicago Police Department that investigates bizarre cases involving Links — everything that is not man or beast.

Kate was born in a Chicago suburb and as a child saw a troll. Nobody believed her and she never mentioned the incident again (especially since she was teased at school for saying such a thing). Kate attended Pioneer High School and was being groomed by her parents to become a doctor (something she did not want to do. The creature she witnessed as a child had haunted her. She believed what she saw and no one could tell her otherwise). For reasons that are not explained, Kate chose to become a police officer. Perhaps it was fate because shortly after graduating from the Chicago Police Academy, Kate witnessed another bizarre incident. While patrolling the docks late one night a sea serpent destroyed a barge. Her report was disbelieved — until it crossed the desk of Captain Richard Paige (Richard Gant), the head of Special Unit 2. Paige believes something lurks in the dark and knows Kate believes it too. He hires her for his unit and teams her with Nicholas O'Malley, an agent with a grudge: a link killed his partner and he is now out to get them.

Kate doesn't chase men and likes to be by herself. She is totally honest ("I say what I think") and is very cautious. She knows her job could cost her her life at any time and likes to plan things before pursuing a Link. "Caution," as she says, "is our best weapon against the unknown."

See also: Nicholas O'Malley.

622. Kate Columbo, *Mrs. Columbo*, NBC, 1979. Played by Kate Mulgrew.

Kate Columbo is the wife of famed police lieutenant Columbo of the Los Angeles Police Department. Kate was never seen or mentioned by a first name on the *Columbo* series. It was also not revealed that Columbo had a daughter named Jenny (Lili Haydn). Columbo, however, never appeared here with Kate; he was always said to be on a case or away on business.

Kate and Jenny live at 728 Valley Lane in San Fernando, California. Kate first worked as a writer for *The Weekly Advertiser*, then *The Weekly Advocate*. Jenny attends the Valley Elementary School; Kate's phone number is 555-9861 (later 555-9867); 859 KTL is her sedan license plate number (later seen as 304 MGD).

According to Columbo, "The Mrs." (as Kate was called on *Columbo*) would always pick the wrong person as a killer when they watched a movie (in her own series Kate suddenly inherits her husband's sleuthing abilities as she enjoys solving crimes). Kate has a habit of writing her grocery list with her brown eyeliner pencil. She buys Maidenform lingerie and loves orange marmalade, flowers and painting. Kate is a great cook and housekeeper and her favorite musical piece is "Madame Butterfly." Kate also cares for the family dog, Fang (but also called Dog) and her husband's rundown Peugeot.

When *Mrs. Columbo* was replaced by the revised *Kate Loves a Mystery* (NBC, 1979), Kate was still a newspaper reporter but she had divorced the lieutenant and was now working under her maiden name of Callahan (the Peugeot was also gone, but the house, daughter [now Jenny Callahan] and the dog remained).

See also: Columbo.

623. Kate Del'Amico, *Undercover*, ABC, 1991. Played by Linda Purl.

Kate Del'Amico is an agent for the Company, a branch of the NIA (National Intelligence Agency) of the U.S. government. Kate is married to Dylan and is the mother of Emily and Marlon and stepmother to Megan, Dylan's 16-year-old daughter from a previous marriage.

Kate is the only child of Edmond and Margaret Singleton. She was born in Europe in 1955 but grew up in the United States. She attended the Concord Boarding School in Boston and became the first woman operative of the CIA. Kate's special skills are risk management, damage control, investigation, masquerading and master recruiting. She can also speak Chinese and Russian. Kate is voracious reader and has a knack for losing her keys. Scotch on the rocks is her favorite drink. Kate will only kill in self-defense and will not participate in a sexual liaison. Her Achilles' heel is Dylan (whom she married in 1980 and whom she fears for the most when they are on separate assignments). The most distressing part of the job for Kate is lying to her children about her work (to maintain her cover she tells them she works for the State Department).

See also: Dylan Del'Amico.

624. Kate Farrell, *I Married Dora*, ABC, 1987–1988. Played by Juliette Lewis.

Katherine Farrell, called Kate, is the 13-year-old daughter of divorced architect Peter Farrell, and lives at 46 La Paloma Drive in Los Angeles. She is a young girl who wants to become a woman. She has gorgeous features and could be mistaken for a teen model (she considers her luxurious hair to be her best asset). Kate knows she is attractive and likes to feel sexy (she wears a perfume called Sensual and often dresses in short skirts and tight blouses "to show people how hot I am"). Kate loves Beatles music and feels she possesses the three P's to be popular: "positive, pretty and perky." And because she is a teenager, Kate feels it is her job "to whine and complain and be moody."

Kate was born in Los Angeles on May 16, 1974. She attends Kennedy Jr. High School and is also a bit dense. She believes going around the world "is like going from her (her home) to the mall a lot of times." Kate straightens her hair by clamping it in a vice and plays the saxophone in the school band (she auditioned to be a cheerleader but was found to be stiff in her movements. She was offered the opportunity to wear the team mascot costume, the Badger, but turned it down and joined the band "because a guy would like to see a girl play the sax rather than a girl dressed as an animal"). Kate is always concerned about her makeup and plays golf with her father at Putter World.

Kate was a Brownie when younger and hates public speaking class "because you have to give a three minute speech and I hate giving speeches. There's so many words to choose from and you actually have to know what you are talking about. Is that pressure or what?" Kate is growing up fast. It was when Peter opened Kate's bedroom closet door and saw a poster of singer Bon Jovi that he knew "my little girl is growing up" (she previously had a poster of Strawberry Shortcake).

See also: Peter Farrell.

625. Kate McArdle, *Kate and Allie*, CBS, 1984–1989. Played by Susan Saint James.

Katherine Elizabeth Ann McArdle, called Kate, is divorced (from Max) and the mother of Emma. Kate shares a Greenwich Village, New York, apartment with her closest friend, Allie Lowell, and her children, Jennie and Chip. Kate was born in Manhattan. She and Allie met as kids at the orthodontist's office; they remained friends ever since and have moved in together to save on expenses. Kate works as a travel agent for the Sloane Travel Agency and was a radical during the latter 1960s (she attended Woodstock, burned her bra, protested the bomb, and participated in sit-ins and college demonstrations). In 1986 she teamed with Allie to begin Kate and Allie Catering, a business they ran from their apartment. Emma (Ari Meyers) is a relatively good girl and rarely causes problems for her mother. However, when Emma does do something wrong, Kate is quite lenient (she doesn't believe in being strict a feels talking things over can resolve any difficulties).

See also: Allie Lowell.

626. Kate McCafferty, *The Division*, Lifetime, 2001–2004. Played by Bonnie Bedelia.

Kate McCafferty is the no-nonsense captain of the Homicide Division of the San Francisco Police Department. She is 44 years old, divorced and the mother of a rebellious teenage daughter (Amanda). Kate has one goal on the force: to prove that a woman can do anything a man can do—"just as well if not better." She is determined to be the best captain the S.F.P.D. can have.

Kate entered the force twenty years ago—at a time when women were not a welcome part of the unit. She proved her abilities by working her way up the ranks and has the greatest respect for the women she commands. Kate is competent and feels she is a role model to the other girls in the squad. She is like a mother figure to them and inspires them to do their best.

Kate appears to be all work and no play. But despite the pressures of her job and her rocky relationship with Amanda, Kate enjoys being a woman—becoming "a fox" and dating (most often) younger men.

See also: Candace DeLorenzo, Jinny Exstead, Magda Ramirez, Raina Washington, Stacy Newland.

627. Kate McCarron, *Dear John*, NBC, 1988–1992. Played by Isabella Hoffman.

Kate McCarron is a member of the 1-2-1 Club, a Manhattan-based organization for divorced, widowed, lonely and separated people who need help in adjusting to the single life.

Kate was born in New York City and is the daughter of Harry and Elizabeth Foster. She is a graduate of Columbia University (where she acquired a degree in business administration) and is divorced from Blake McCarron. She assists Louise Mercer in running the club (at the Rego Park Community Center).

As a child Kate had a dog named Skipper. She was a neat and tidy child and loved to help her mother cook. She turned that love into a business and now owns a restaurant called Kate's Place. Kate is beautiful and always fashionably dressed. She is looking for Mr. Right—a man who will see her for her intellectual side, not for her looks alone. Kate enjoys helping people but tends to become too personally involved and finds someone else's problems becoming her problems (until she finds a way to resolve the problem, then she becomes her old cheery self).

See also: John Lacey, Kirk Morris, Louise Mercer, Mary Beth Sutton.

Kate McCoy *see* **Luke and Kate McCoy**

628. Kate McCrorey, *Down Home*, NBC, 1990–1991. Played by Judith Ivey.

Katherine McCrorey, called Kate, was born in the small coastal fishing town of Hadley Cove in New England. The town has its own phone book, "The Yellow Page," and Kate is the first person to leave and become a success on her own (she moved to New York and became an executive with a designing firm. She returned after 15 years to once again live the simple life).

Kate attended Hadley Cove Grammar and high schools and nearby Fullerton College (where she acquired a degree in business). She grew up working in the family business, McCrorey's Landing (a combination café, mooring dock, bait, fish, tackle and gas store) and now helps her widowed father, Walt, run the 40-year-old business.

In New York Kate was famous for engineering the takeover of a Fortune 500 company. In Hadley Cove, she won an award for playing Golda in her high school production of *Fiddler on the Roof.*

629. Kate O'Brien, *The Drew Carey Show*, ABC, 1995–2002. Played by Christa Miller.

Kathryn O'Brien is a young woman who lives in Cleveland, Ohio, in a home near "a naked guy with binoculars who lives in the house across the alley." Kate, as she is called, is a friend with Drew Carey, Lewis Kiniski and Oswald Harvey. She is a graduate of Rhodes High School and enjoys drinking beer.

Kate claims, "I save my sick days for hangovers and soap opera weddings." Kate however, didn't appear to work at one job long enough to acquire sick days. Her jobs: waitress at the Sizzler; receptionist at a car body shop; cosmetics salesgirl at the Winford-Louder Department Store; Soup on a Stick waitress; house sitter; Massage on the Job therapist; personal director to the owner of Winford-Louder; catering company employee; waitress at her favorite watering hole, the Warsaw Tavern; security guard at the Rock and Roll Hall of Fame.

Kate has a problem with men: she will date them but finds it difficult to make a commitment. Those she has dumped have formed a website devoted to her (www.coldheartedbitch.com). Kate's inability to commit was dropped when she met Kirk, a navy fighter pilot she later married (and relocated to be with him in Germany).

Kate helped Drew establish his homemade beer-coffee brew (Buzz Beer) and had an on-and-off romance with Drew before meeting Kirk. Kate is Catholic and calls her breasts "The Kids."

See also: Drew Carey, Lewis Kaniski, Mimi Bobeck, Oswald Harvey.

630. Kate Sommers, *Silver Spoons,* NBC, 1982–1986; Syn., 1986–1988. Played by Erin Gray.

Katherine Sommers is the wife of Edward Stratton, III, the head of the Eddie Toys Division of Stratton Industries. Kate, as she is called, is the stepmother to Edward's son, Ricky, and lives in a mansion at 123 Mockingbird Lane in Shallow Springs on Long Island in New York.

Kate was born in Columbus, Ohio, on June 9, 1950, and previously worked as Edward's secretary before marrying him; she now helps him run Eddie Toys. Kate has two cats (Fluffy and Snickle Fritz) and claims she is a shoe nut — she worries about matching everything with her shoes ("I've always been a shoe worrier. I almost checked myself into the Buster Brown Clinic").

Kate is a graduate of Columbus High School (where on her first day of classes, a naïve Kate was sold an elevator pass to an elevator that didn't exist) and State College (where she majored in business administration). Kate is always fashionably dressed and feels she has to look her best at all times — even when she gets out of bed in the morning. She is a loving mother to Ricky and kind of keeps the family together as Edward is a kid who never grew up (likes to play with toys). Edward's first wife, Evelyn, was a woman of social status who left him after six days due to their social incompatibility. Kate understands Edward and loves him — and puts up with his nonsense. The first toy Kate created for the company was the Berserk Warrior — a Viking doll with an attitude problem.

See also: Edward Stratton, Ricky Stratton.

631. Katherine Spencer, *18 Wheels of Justice,* TNN, 2000–2001. Played by Lisa Thornhill.

Katherine Spencer is an agent for the Justice Department who was instrumental in developing the Kenworth Project, the prototype for an 18-wheel truck that transports key witnesses in criminal prosecution cases.

Katherine was born in Louisville, Kentucky, in 1972. Her mother was a high school teacher; her father, a law professor. Katherine is one of five children. She was educated in a private school in Charlotte and is a graduate of Virginia Tech (where she specialized in micro technology). Katherine acquired a job with the Justice Depart-

ment working on surveillance technology. During one case she became an instrumental witness in a high profile murder case. An internal leak exposed Katherine as the key witness and a contract was put out on her life. To protect her, the department gave her a new identity (Cie Baxter), relocated her to California (from Washington) and put her to work on the Kenworth Project.

Katherine considers the truck "my baby" and rides with its driver, Chance Bowman, to insure its safety. Katherine has modified a blue aerodynamic Kenworth T-2000 Advanced Technology Truck to include weapons; a fingerprint identification system (to identify individual truckers); a navigation system that can talk and drive to a destination; and a safety monitoring system that even detects drowsiness in a driver.

Kathleen Mead *see* **The Girls of Degrassi**

632. Kathryn Janeway, *Star Trek: Voyager,* UPN, 1995–2001. Played by Kate Mulgrew.

Kathryn Janeway, Captain of the Starship U.S.S. *Voyager,* is the daughter of Edward and Gretchen Janeway. She was born in Indiana on May 20 (the year is unspecified, but in late 2330 or early 2340). As a child Kathryn studied ballet (performed in "The Dying Swan" at the age of six) and was playing tennis by the age of 12. Unlike others in her rural hometown, Kathryn wanted to be more than just a farmer. She had a yearning to explore new worlds and made that her goal in life. She enrolled in Starfleet Academy and graduated with top honors. Her first assignment was as Science Officer aboard the U.S.S. *Al-Batani.* Her knowledge of science combined with her ability to command enabled her to become a captain in 2371 and command the U.S.S. *Voyager NCC-7465,* a new class star ship that became lost in the Delta Quadrant while pursuing a Maquis ship. *Voyager* remained lost for seven years until Kathryn and her crew managed to incorporate a Borg Transwarp Conduit to return to Earth. She was then promoted to Admiral.

Kathryn is one of the best captains in Starfleet. She is tough and not afraid to take chances. She is well educated in math and science and has studied chromo-linguistics and American Sign Language. She loves music but regretted she never learned to play an instrument. She had an Irish setter named Molly that she rescued from a pound.

Kathryn is most often called Captain and dislikes "sir" or "ma'am." For relaxation, Kathryn enjoys the Holodeck room where she is able to experience role-playing in Gothic novels, skiing and sailing. She mentioned *Dante's Inferno* as being her favorite book. Amelia Earhart was her heroine and possibly gave her the motivation to achieve her dream.

See also: B'Elanna Torres, Chakotay, The Doctor, Harry Kim, Neelix, Seven of Nine, Tuvok.

633. Katie Fox, *Miss Match*, NBC, 2003. Played by Alicia Silverstone.

Katherine Fox, called Katie, is a divorce lawyer who works for her father, Jerrold (Ryan O'Neal), head of the Los Angeles firm of Jerrold Fox and Associates.

Katie is fresh from law school (Harvard) and works as a junior associate. She is blonde, beautiful and single. She is also good a matching people (she feels her natural instincts are more accurate than those of a computer). Her exposure to divorcing couples has led her to believe she can bring people together for everlasting relationships. She now mixes law with match making and once the match is made Katie takes a back seat to let nature take its course.

Katie was born in Los Angeles. She is a graduate of UCLA and now lives at 4860 Linden Street (555-8731 is her phone number). She says, "I spend my days tearing relationships apart and I try to create the occasional relationship. Helping depressed women bounce back from a devastating divorce is part of my job to me."

634. Katie Joplin, *Katie Joplin*, WB, 1999. Played by Park Overall.

Katherine Joplin, better known as Katie, was born in Knoxville, Tennessee, and is now the host of *The Katie Joplin Show*, a six-hour overnight radio program on station WLBP (87.5 FM) in Philadelphia.

Katie's home life in Knoxville was not easy. She came from a poor family and had to work 16-hour days at the local bottling plant. She was not able to complete her education at Knoxville High School, but is well learned in the life of hard knocks. When she felt the time was right she left home and headed for what she hoped would be a better life in Philadelphia. Here she first worked at the Crescent Corset Company then as a salesgirl at Car City. It was at Car City that Katie's flamboyant sales pitch impressed the station manager at WLBP and was offered the overnight hosting job. Katie speaks her mind and Jockey Shorts was the first sponsor to buy time on Katie's program.

635. Katie Kanisky, *Gimme a Break*, NBC, 1981–1986. Played by Kari Michaelsen.

Katie Kanisky was born in Glenlawn, California, and is the oldest daughter of Carl and Margaret Kanisky. Carl is the town's police chief; Margaret is deceased. She lives at 2938 Maple Lane with her sisters, Julie and Samantha, and live-in housekeeper, Nell Harper.

Katie is the prettiest of the sisters. She attends Lincoln High School and was a member of a club called the Silver Slippers (the members, including Katie, are not especially bright. Julie claims "The biggest thing those girls have going for them are their bra sizes"). Katie also formed a rock group called The Hot Muffins (they performed the song "I Can't Stop the Fire" at the Impromptu Club).

Katie despises sports (she once tried to bowl and, according to her father, "threw herself down the alley"). Katie is always fashionably dressed, has perfect hair and makeup and is a bit conceited. She turned her flair for fashion into her own business, Katie's Clothing Store in the Glenlawn Mall. A year before the series ended, Katie moved to San Francisco to become a clothing buyer for the Chadwick Department Store.

See also: Julie Kanisky, Nell Harper, Samantha Kanisky.

636. Katy Mahoney, *Lady Blue*, ABC, 1985–1986. Played by Jamie Rose.

Kathleen Mahoney, called Katy, is an Irish-American cop with a violent approach to fighting crime — shoot first, ask questions later. Katy was born in Chicago and is a detective with the Violent Crimes Division of the 39th Street Station of the Chicago Metro Police Department.

Katy grew up amid the crime and corruption of the city she has now sworn to protect. She is the daughter of a police officer and apparently followed in her father's footsteps so she could legally use a gun (she is called ABC's "Dirty Harriet" in press release information). Katy plays by her own rules. While she respects the law she bends it to accomplish her objectives and keep the city free of thugs. Katy "can read a crime scene in progress like most guys read the sports page." She has been reprimanded many times for the frequent use of her gun, but warnings seem to have no effect — she reverts immediately back to what she has been told not to do. Katy is single and lives at 1107 West Brandis Place. Her car license plate reads 4DJ 56 and her badge number is 28668 (688 in the pilot episode).

637. Kay Simmons, *V.I.P.*, Syn., 1998–2002. Played by Leah Lail.

Kay Simmons is a very sexy secretary who works for V.I.P. (Vallery Irons Protection), a high profile Los Angeles–based protection service that charges $25,000 a day plus expenses.

Kay Eugenia Simmons is not only beautiful but she is brilliant. She is a computer genius and is the only other girl (beside Vallery) who shows ample cleavage. Kay would like to become more active in the field (like co-workers Nikki and Tasha) but her unique skills make her the perfect office associate ("I can be mean and vicious as long as I don't hurt anyone"). Kay hates her middle name ("I rather it be Danger; anything is better than Eugenia").

Kay was born in California and was a brilliant child. At the age of seven her parents enrolled her in Neo Tech, "a school for brainy kids." She won the seventh grade science fair "with my Black Plaque in a shoebox diorama." Her brilliance also caused her some trauma. She was teased for being smart (this would make her cry and she acquired the nickname "Cry Baby Kay").

Kay was editor of her college yearbook for three years "including one year after I graduated." She is a *Star Trek* fanatic and is a member of the Champions of Freedom, a conservation group. Her favorite TV show is the daily talk show *Donny and Marie*.

Kay lives at 817 Oakdale (818-KL5-9415 is her phone number). When Kay is allowed to help the team on assignments she gets a nervous stomach "and I need to take my Mylanta." VIP KAY is Kay's minivan license plate. "Muffin Girl" is her computer password; curiosity is her Achilles' heel.

See also: Nikki Franco, Quick Williams, Tasha Dexter, Vallery Irons.

638. Kayla Thornton, *Strong Medicine*, Lifetime, 2004 (current). Played by Tamera Mowry.

Kayla Thornton is a first year resident in emergency medicine at the Rittenhouse Women's Health Clinic in Philadelphia. She is 26 years old and hopes to return to her rural hometown of Mount Union (Pennsylvania) when she finishes her residency to help the people of her community. Kayla was motivated to become a doctor when she was ten years old. Her younger brother was accidentally shot by a friend while playing with a rifle. Kayla desperately tried to save her brother but she was unable to stop the bleeding. The nearest doctor, being 25 miles away, arrived too late. Because of this incident, Kayla's greatest fear is not being able to help a patient in dire need.

Kayla put herself through medical school and hopes to one day write a book. She enjoys TV soap operas and dancing. She also loves to read (a trait she acquired from her mother, a school teacher) and the outdoors (which she learned to appreciate from her father).

See also: Andy Campbell, Dana Stowe, Lana Hawkins, Luisa Delgado, Peter Riggs, Nick Biancavilla.

639. K.C., *China Beach*, ABC, 1988–1991. Played by Marg Helgenberger.

Karen Charlene Colosky prefers to be called K.C. (after her home town of Kansas City). She is the only civilian on China Beach, the U.S. Armed Forces R&R facility in Da Nang in the Republic of Vietnam during the war (the facility houses the medical personnel of the 510th Evac Hospital of the 63rd Division).

K.C. is a beautiful prostitute who charges $100 an hour for her services. She is an expert at telling pathetic stories about herself and having people believe her. As a child Karen loved the rain (it made her feel safe when she snuggled under the bed covers). On China Beach the rains provide K.C. with the only sense of safety and security she can find amid the devastation that surrounds her.

K.C. became best friends with nurse Colleen McMurphy. They first met in 1967 in the women's shower (K.C. noticed Colleen starring at her navel and said, "Never seen an outie before?" They joked and became close friends). It is through Colleen that we learn of K.C.'s life.

In 1967, K.C. became pregnant by a general (A.M. "Mac" Miller). Later that year, while in Saigon for a rest, Colleen runs into K.C. and helps deliver her baby, a girl K.C. names Karen. K.C. is unable to care for Karen and hires a Vietnamese woman (Trieu Au) to care for the child "until I get my life together."

K.C. left China Beach in 1969 without Karen (now two years of age). She moved to Bangkok and began an import/export business. In 1975 she had a nightclub called K.C.'s. It is at this time that K.C. seeks Karen but it is also a time of great concern as it is the fall of Saigon. K.C. has only a precious short time to spend with Karen before she realizes she must get her to safety. At an American military base K.C. manages to get Karen (now eight) onto a helicopter. With only seconds remaining, K.C. tells Karen to look up Boonie Lanier (a soldier from China Beach who loved her) "who'll take care of you."

In Santa Cruz, California, in 1976, K.C. sees that Karen is safe, attending school and living with Boonie. She leaves without revealing herself to Karen.

A Christmas card sent to Colleen from K.C. revealed that in 1977 K.C. owned a diner called The Answer. By 1988 K.C. is a high-powered businesswoman and sees Karen for the first time in 12 years. Karen Lanier, as she is now called, is attending college. She is living with Boonie and she considers Boonie to be her father and uses his last name. Boonewell G. Lanier, called Boonie, was with the First Marine Division, Icor, on China Beach. He always called K.C. "K.C. from K.C."

See also: Colleen McMurphy, Laurette Barber (for information on Laurette, Cherry White, Chloe Webb and Waylou Marie Holmes).

Keith Partridge *see* **Shirley Partridge**

640. Kelly Bundy, *Married ... With Children*, Fox, 1987–1997. Played by Christina Applegate.

Kelly Bundy is the daughter of Al and Peggy Bundy and lives at 9674 (also seen as 9764) Jeopardy Lane in Chicago. Kelly is gorgeous. She has blonde hair, blue eyes and dresses in tight jeans, tight miniskirts and low-cut blouses (her mother calls her "a hussy. She became a hussy when she learned to cut her diapers up the side"). Kelly is also naïve, dense and the typical stereo typed dumb blonde.

Kelly first says she was born in February ("I'm an aquarium") then on November 27. She writes her name on her palm so she can look at it to remember who she is. She is a very poor student at James K. Polk High School (she only attends school because she considers it a place to keep in touch with friends and supply the family with pens and pencils).

Peggy got Kelly her first job at the age of five — selling kisses. Jobs Kelly later acquires are as follows: Weather Bunny Girl on Channel 8's *Action News* (her stunning good looks boosted ratings but the job was lost when she couldn't read the teleprompter); roller skating waitress at Bill's Hilltop Drive-In; a model for Weenie Tots (hot dogs wrapped in bread and fried in lard). Kelly's ability to jiggle her breasts in what she calls "The Bundy Bounce," got her a job as the Allanti Girl (showgirl for a foreign car called the Allanti).

Vital Social Issues and Stuff with Kelly was the cable access show on Channel 99 hosted by Kelly. With topics like "Slut of the Week," "Bad Perms" and "Hunks," it was picked up by the mythical NBS Network (but cancelled when it was cleaned up and the "vital stuff" became milk and books).

Kelly next enrolled in the Larry Storch School of Modeling and acquired such jobs as the Verminator Girl at the Chicago TV World Theme Park (Verminator is an insect killer made by Pest Boys. When Kelly refused to wear a skimpy bikini she was fired); model in a TV commercial for Easy

Off Jeans; Rock Slut in a Gutter Cats music video; the wife in Romantic Roast Instant Coffee commercials; a sexy dog for Hungry Puppy dog food; figure model for Waist-Away Diet Drink; spokes girl for Ice Hole Beer ("The micro brewed beer"); and dressed in a bikini, the window display for the Kyoto Bank (she held a sign reading "Check Out Our Assets").

In modeling school Kelly got tension headaches from smiling but was called a natural leg crosser ("I can do it at will"). Kelly is a member of the Northside Aerobics Studio, dresses with the window shades up each morning and has a lucky see-through blouse that she can never seem to find ("It's see-through," she explains). Veal is Kelly's favorite meal; Al calls her "Pumpkin." Kelly has a real talent for dating losers (from men one step away from jail to motor-cycle riding hoods) and honestly believes she is "an intelligent woman" (she doesn't realize she does and says dumb things). Al can recall doing only two things for Kelly: carrying her home form the hospital (although he left her on the car roof) and buying her ice cream when she was ten years old.

See also: Al Bundy, Bud Bundy, Peggy Bundy.

641. Kelly Callahan, *Lenny*, CBS, 1990–1991. Played by Jenna Von Oy.

Kelly Callahan is the 13-year-old daughter of Lenny and Shelly Callahan and lives at 11 Cherry Wood Lane in Boston with her younger sister, Tracy.

Kelly is a student at Saint Theodore's Catholic Grammar School. She receives an allowance of three dollars a week and complains about (and has a negative view of) everything. Although she is slim and very pretty, Kelly feels "I'm overweight, unattractive and going to be flat chested." Kelly has not yet developed and is extremely jealous because her girlfriends have ("I want cleavage like my other girlfriends"). Shelly refuses to let Kelly pad her bra as she feels Kelly's negative attitude and the attention boys will suddenly give her is something she can't handle (Kelly broods and complains, but she learned to accept "my shortcomings").

Kelly hides her money in a box under her bed and eats Nutri Grain cereal for breakfast. She is smart but could do better if she applied herself to her schoolwork (shopping, boys and fun appear to be all that is on her mind). While she can't wear a padded bra, Kelly was allowed have her ears pierced (which she did at Hadley's Jewelry Store).

See also: Lenny and Shelly Callahan, Tracy Callahan.

642. Kelly Garrett, *Charlie's Angels*, ABC, 1976–1981. Played by Jaclyn Smith.

Kelly Garrett is a private detective called Angel by her employer, Charlie Townsend, the never-seen owner of Townsend Investigations in Los Angeles. Kelly is the only Angel who believes she may have seen Charlie. In the last episode, "Let Our Angel Live," Kelly is shot in the head and near death. During the operation to save her life, Charlie was by Kelly's side (dressed in hospital greens) and Kelly believes it was Charlie, but she was in a dazed state and can't be sure.

Kelly was born in San Diego in August of 1955 but never knew her real mother or father. Kelly was an infant, riding with her mother in a car, when her mother was killed in a 23-car pileup on a Texas highway. In a rush to get victims to hospitals, Kelly was lost (misplaced). When no one claimed the infant girl she was sent to the St. Agnes Home for the Orphaned in Dallas (it was not mentioned what happened to Kelly's father. It is also not mentioned how the infant received the name of Kelly; her last name, Garrett, was the family name of one of the sisters of the orphanage who cared for her). Kelly was adopted in 1964 and raised by foster parents (she says she learned how "to shoot from my father"). Kelly later moved to Los Angeles and entered the police academy, hoping to fight crime and bring criminals to justice. What she got was school crossing guard. She quit when she became discouraged and joined the Townsend Agency when Charlie was just setting up business.

Kelly is concerned and caring and has the ability to sing and dance (she was lead alto in a glee club). She is brilliant at deciphering complex clues and is an expert shot. Kelly is also a master at bugging devices and picking locks. Tequila straight up with a lime chaser is her favorite drink. Guido's Italian Diner is her favorite eatery.

See also: Charlie Townsend, Jill Monroe, Julie Rogers, Kris Monroe, Sabrina Duncan, Tiffany Welles.

643. Kelly Kapowski, *Saved by the Bell*, NBC, 1989–1993. Played by Tiffani-Amber Thiessen.

Kelly Kapowski is 16 years old and considered the most beautiful girl at Bayside High School in Palisades, California. She was born in Palisades and lives at 3175 Fairfax Drive (555-4314 is her phone number).

Kelly is also the most popular student at school. She is head cheerleader (for the Bayside Tigers football team), captain of the girls' softball, volleyball and swim teams, and is the Bayside Homecoming Queen. Kelly hosts *Kelly Desire*, a pro-gram of romantic music on Tiger Radio (the school's radio station, KKTY, 98.6 FM). She was also a contestant in the Miss Bayside Beauty Pageant (she sang, off key, "Blue Moon"). Kelly was also "Miss November" in "The Girls of Bayside High Swimsuit Calendar" (which led to a photo layout in *Teen Fashion* magazine where Kelly was "The All-American Girl").

Kelly could suddenly sing (and quite well) when she became a part of Hot Sundae, an all-girl group formed by her on-and-off boyfriend, Zack Morris (the group was later called The Zack Attack). Kelly was a bright student and in her last appearance (graduation) had decided to attend Palisades Community College. She scored an 1100 on her SAT test and had a German shepherd named Freddie. Kelly and her friends hang out at the Max (a diner).

During the summer of 1991 Kelly worked as a lifeguard at the Malibu Sands Beach Club. She resurfaced in the spinoff series, *Saved by the Bell: The College Years* (NBC, 1993–1994) as a freshman at California State University (where she is studying to become a doctor; she works at the Student Health Center). The TV movie *Saved by the Bell: Wedding in Las Vegas* (NBC, October 7, 1994) picks up from the final episode of *The College Years* (when Zack proposed to Kelly) and relates the mishaps that occur as Kelly and Zack wed.

See also: Jesse Spano, Lisa Turtle, Screech Powers, Zack Morris.

644. Kelly Robinson, *I Spy*, NBC, 1965–1968. Played by Robert Culp.

Kelly Robinson and Alexander Scott are espionage agents for the U.S. government (their exact affiliation is not mentioned; they call their "boss" "Our People," "Our Superiors" or "Washington"). Kelly's cover is that of a tennis pro (Scott poses as his trainer/masseur).

Kelly, called Kel by Scott, was born in Ohio. He is a graduate of Princeton University (where he studied law and played on two Davis Cup [tennis] teams). He is skilled in karate but still manages to take a beating from the enemy. Kelly loves fishing, golfing and duck hunting and has a habit of repeating what the person he is talking to says. He also enjoys eating (especially steamed clams) and he is warned by Scott to curtail his culinary pursuits "or you'll look like a lox on the court." Kelly calls himself "a tennis bum" and has won Davis Cup trophies (when asked why he chose such a life he responds with "It's better than digging ditches"). Although he travels around the world to compete Kelly doesn't always win (for example, he lost in five sets at Forest Hills).

Kelly and Scott have a tendency to argue over everything especially over how a case should progress. Kelly likes to joke around but also has a bad habit — the smokes (too much) and drinks. He is also a ladies' man but finds romance lasting only as long as the assignment on which he met the girl lasts.

See also: Alexander Scott.

645. Ken Hutchinson, *Starsky and Hutch*, ABC, 1975–1979. Played by David Soul.

Kenneth Hutchinson nicknamed Ken but called Hutch, is a plainclothes detective with the Metro Division of the Los Angeles Police Department. His partner is Dave Starsky; their car code is Zebra 3 (they are also said to be with the Bay City Police Department).

Hutch was born in California and resides at the Venice Apartments at 1027½ Ocean in Sea Point. He drives a scratched, dented, gas-eating, muffler-smoking, gray car (plate 552 LQD) with a bumper sticker that reads "Cops Need Love Too." Hutch is a health food nut and vitamin fanatic (he overdoses on Vitamin E and puts wheat germ in the meals he cooks). He is also a ladies' man and takes his gun wherever he goes (on a date, to the store, to visit his mother). Hutch sings, plays the piano and guitar, and is not too fond of holidays. As a kid Hutch bought toys from Uncle Elmo's Toy Shop; it's now Uncle Elmo's Adult Toy Shop. At Xavier High School Hutch was called "The Pauper" (he was from a poor family and was friends with a rich kid). Hutch was also class valedictorian and voted "Most Likely to Succeed." Ken's dream is to quit the force and live life as the captain of a ship. He carries a .357 Magnum gun.

See also: Dave Starsky.

646. Kenny Beckett, *Dave's World*, CBS, 1993–1997. Played by Shadoe Stevens.

Kenneth Beckett is a close friend of Dave Barry, the humorist who writes the newspaper column "Dave's World" for the Miami *Record Dispatch.* Kenny, as he is called, was born in the small town of Pewuchatucket and is a graduate of its high school.

Kenny lives at 4703 El Camino Terrace in Florida. He first worked as Dave's editor at the newspaper. When he lost his job to downsizing, Kenny became a reader for Books on Tape (he is called "The Voice"; his first audio book was *The Three Musketeers*). He later became the weatherman for Channel 5.

Kenny is allergic to peanuts and wears a size 10½ shoe. As a kid he had a plush dog (Rusty) and

an imaginary friend (Too Too). His office and home phone have three buttons: business, personal message, screening dates.

See also: Beth Barry, Dave Barry.

647. Kerry Hennessey, *Eight Simple Rules for Dating My Teenage Daughter*, ABC, 2002–2005. Played by Amy Davidson.

Kerry Hennessey is the 15-year-old daughter of sportswriter Paul Hennessey and his wife Cate, a nurse. She lives on Oakdale Street in Michigan with her older sister (Bridget) and younger brother (Rory). Kerry is very pretty but feels she is not as glamorous or as sexy as Bridget (whom she calls "Little Miss Blonde Bobble Head: My name is Bridget. I can't believe how much my head shakes when I talk"). Kerry is a freshman at Liberty High School. She is very bright and an Honors Student. She is a member of the Owls cheerleading team and with the drama club (builds sets and paints scenery; "I hate the drama club," she says). Kerry is also on the debate team but is a wise acre and very negative about everything. She also cares too much about what other people think about her or what they may think about her.

Kerry is always hard on herself when she fails at something. She is a talented artist (the first picture she drew for her father was a giraffe — although Paul thinks it looks like a rabbit). Bridget calls Kerry "Psycho Sister" for all her concerns about everything. Kerry made a video for a school project about what life is like for Bridget called "How the Beautiful People Have It So Much Easier."

As a kid Kerry had a pet rabbit (Mr. Wiggles) and a plush dog (Muttsy). She played soccer in third grade and has always been fond of animals. Paul called her "Care Bear."

See also: Bridget Hennessey, Cate Hennessey, Paul Hennessey, Rory Hennessey.

648. Kevin Arnold, *The Wonder Years*, ABC, 1988–1993. Played by Fred Savage.

Kevin Arnold is the son of Jack and Norma Arnold and lives in a suburban home in Any Town, U.S.A. He has an older sister (Karen) and brother (Wayne). Stories are set in the latter 1960s and early '70s.

Kevin was born on March 18, 1956. He attended Hillcrest Grammar School, Robert F. Kennedy Junior High School and William McKinley High School. Kevin wears a New York Jets football jacket and keeps a picture of actress Raquel Welch on the inside of his locker door. He is undecided about his future and has aspirations to become a writer, astronaut, or center fielder for the San Francisco Giants baseball team. Kevin was a member of the Kennedy Junior High Glee Club and was also with a band called Electric Shoes. The Pizza Barn is his favorite hangout and he receives an allowance of 50 cents a week (1969), $2.50 (1970), and $3.00 (1971). He has a dog (Buster) and skates at the Moonlight Roller Rink.

Kevin worked as a caddy ($20 a game), stock clerk at Harris and Son Hardware, delivery boy (later waiter) at Chong's Chinese Restaurant, then clerk at the family furniture store. He had an on-and-off relationship with Winnie Cooper, the pretty girl next door. In the last episode it is learned that a number of years had passed and that Kevin and Winnie were still friends but Kevin had married and had a son.

See also: Jack and Norma Arnold, Winnie Cooper.

649. Kevin Owens, *Mr. Belvedere*, ABC, 1985–1990. Played by Rob Stone.

Kevin Owens is the eldest child of George and Marsha Owens. He has a sister (Heather) and brother (Wesley) and lives at 200 Spring Valley Road in Beaver Falls, Pittsburgh. Lynn Belvedere, a British housekeeper, cares for the family.

Kevin was born in 1967 in Beaver Falls. His parents contemplated calling him either Moon Shadow (if a girl) or Moon Doggie (if a boy). But when he was born he looked more like a Kevin. Kevin attends Van Buren High School and was a drummer in a band called The Young Savages. He later attends the University of Pittsburgh and moves into his own apartment (5) in a building next to a sewage treatment plant. Kevin is allergic to raisins and worked part time at Mr. Cluck's Fried Chicken and at Phil's Friendly Motors (a used car lot).

See also: George and Marsha Owens, Heather Owens, Wesley Owens.

650. Kim and Greg Warner, *Yes, Dear*, CBS, 1999 (current). Played by Jean Louisa Kelly, Anthony Clark.

Kim and Greg Warner are newlyweds who live in a comfortable home in a sedate section of Los Angeles. They are the parents of Emily and Sam and overly protective of them (at night Kim, for example, gets up every hour on the hour to make sure their children are still breathing). Greg is first said to work as an executive at Bradford Studios; later he is a business affairs executive for CBS-TV in Burbank. Greg is allergic to strawberries and does whatever Kim asks of him (she only has to ask once and Greg does it). He is the son of

Tom and Natalie Warner. In grammar school Greg was considered a nerd and constantly picked on. He took home economics in high school because his mother said he would make a good catch if he could cook. Greg relaxes by singing and playing the guitar. He is proud of his Mark Spitz American Flag bathing suit. He also likes jazz music, old movies and *Joan of Arcadia* is his favorite TV show. Greg enjoys playing pool and he and Kim dine at a pool hall–restaurant called Earl's.

Kim and Greg attended a pottery class on their first date (they met in college). Kim majored in art and now makes her own baby soap. She is the daughter of Don and Gina Lutkey. As a child Kim had a pet rabbit that she held and petted so much that she gave it a bald spot. She is famous in high school for not wearing anything under her graduation gown. The wind blew and a censored picture of her wound up in the yearbook. Kim likes to get flowers, especially roses and is saddened when she has to stop breast-feeding—"I like the boobs. I never had anything like them before and I hate giving them back."

Kim has a book for every problem she thinks her children will encounter—from not eating to not walking. Kim buys oven mitts every few months "because they get brown spots on them." Greg drives a car with the license plate 3ASB 506 and Kim devotes all her energies to ensuring Greg, Emily and Sam's happiness. Having a family is the most important thing in the world to Kim.

See also: Christine and Jimmy Hughes.

651. Kimberly Drummond, *Diff'rent Strokes*, NBC, 1978–1984. Played by Dana Plato.

Kimberly Drummond is the daughter of Phillip Drummond, a widower and owner of Drummond Industries in Manhattan. She lives at 679 Park Avenue (Penthouse B; also seen as Penthouse A) with her adopted brothers, Arnold and Willis Jackson.

Kimberly is a pretty, bubbly teenage girl. She first attended the Eastlake (later called the Eastland) School for Girls in Peekskill, New York, then Garfield High School in Manhattan. She is a prima ballerina and played the lead in Eastland's production of *Swan Lake* (Kimberly is a member of the swim team at Garfield).

Kimberly receives an allowance of $10 a week and held a job at the Hula Hut (fast food). When Kimberly had aspirations to become a world-class ice skater, her father arranged for to have lessons from Dorothy Hamill (Kimberly's Olympic dreams fell apart at the seams when she found practicing too demanding and quit). Kimberly next became the spokes girl for Mother Brady's Shampoo. She developed bulimia when she became a fashion model at Baum's Department Store (she felt she was gaining weight and stopped eating). Dana Plato left the series in 1984; Kimberly's absence is explained as her attending school in Paris.

See also: Arnold Jackson, Edna Garrett, Willis Jackson.

652. Kimiko Fannuchi, *Murphy's Law,* ABC, 1988–1989. Played by Maggie Han.

Kimiko Fannuchi, sometimes called Kim, lives with her boss, insurance investigator Patrick Murphy, at 3116 Hillside in San Francisco, California.

Kim is a beautiful Eurasian model whose claim to fame is being the calendar girl for Morgan Power Tools. Kim is the daughter of an Italian father and Japanese mother and has been blessed with stunning good looks and a gorgeous figure. Yet with these assets she cannot seem to achieve the status of models with lesser qualities. She believes her strong moral upbringing is responsible for her dilemma. Kim has been asked to pose nude for several high profile magazines but has refused to do so. She is also very picky about the kinds of layout she will do (she likes elegant fashion) and refuses to do any that feature her in a string bikini.

Kim is bright and very intuitive. She has the instincts of a detective and helps her boss solve crimes. She drives an old Saab and will dress in skimpy clothes while in the privacy of her own home.

See also: Patrick Murphy.

653. Kira Nerys, *Star Trek: Deep Space Nine,* Syn., 1993–1999. Played by Nana Visitor.

Kira Nerys is a Bjoran Militia Colonel assigned to Benjamin Sisko, captain of the Starfleet ship U.S.S. *Defiant NX-74205.* Kira was born on the Dakhur Providence of the planet Bajor in the year 2343. She possesses strategic and tactical skills and is a survivor of many tragic events that began in her early childhood. Her father was a farmer (killed in a resistance battle); her mother, an icon painter, died in a Singha refugee camp of malnutrition. Kira's early childhood was spent in this camp (she learned to play Bajoran springball and was taught crafts, such as finger painting). Her life changed shortly after when she was sent to work in the Bajoran mines. At the age of 12, Kira was cleaning weapons and running errands for the Shakaar resistance cell. Kira's thirteenth birthday saw her becoming a full member of the Bajor re-

sistance against the Cardassians. She fought bravely against her planet's oppressors, learned to pilot antique raider crafts but suffered dearly for the next ten years (2360–70) when she and her cell mates took to the Dahkur Hills caves to evade their enemies. Kira was a major force in the Bajor's liberation from the Cardassians and was responsible for many deaths in the process (something she regrets but couldn't avoid). It was at this time that Kira accepted a major's commission as the Bajoran Military Attaché to Benjamin Sisko of the space station *Deep Space Nine* (the Bajorans are part of Starfleet Academy).

See also: Benjamin Sisko, Ezri Dax, Jadzia Dax.

654. Kirk Morris, *Dear John,* NBC, 1988–1992. Played by Jere Burns.

Kirk Morris is a member of the 1-2-1 Club, a Manhattan based organization for lonely, divorced, separated or widowed people who need help in adjusting to the single life. Kirk is now single; his wife, Carol, left him for another woman.

Kirk was born in Scranton, Pennsylvania. He grew up on the streets and learned how to con and scam. He carried that tradition into his adult life. He is apparently without a regular job and survives by taking advantage of people. A catering service called Cuisine by Kirk; Kakemono Tours (a tourist service for Japanese visitors in New York); K-Burns (jeans with a *K* on the rear pocket) and Standby Airline Tickets (to Hawaii via Trans Universal Airlines) are some of the cons Kirk uses to make money.

Kirk lives at 36 Amsterdam Avenue (Apartment 306) and claims to be a published author (via letters to *Playboy* magazine). Other than finding ways to make money, women are uppermost on his mind and he has an arsenal of pickup lines and techniques to impress the ladies. However, when Kirk first sees a pretty girl, he thinks of only one thing — "does her bra unhook from the front or the back?" He joined the 1-2-1 Club for only one reason — to meet lonely women.

See also: John Lacey, Kate McCarron, Louise Mercer, Mary Beth Sutton.

655. KITT, *Knight Rider,* NBC, 1982–1986. Voiced by William Daniels.

KITT is a Knight Industries Two Thousand black Trans Am car (plate KNIGHT) that was created by Knight Industries for the Foundation for Law and Government to battle crime. It is made of a molecular bonded shell and has the series number Alpha Delta 277529. The car is able to talk via its ultra sophisticated and elaborate micro circuitry. Microprocessors make it the world's safest car and it has been programmed with a chip to protect human life. KITT has long-range tracking scopes, turbo boost, normal and auto driving and pursuit modes (that give KITT extra speed). KITT is also programmed to avoid collisions and is equipped with a mini-lab (in the dashboard) and a third stage aquatic synthesizer that allows it to ride on water. KITT also carries S.I.D. (Satellite Infiltration Drone), a bugging device that can go where KITT cannot.

KITT was updated for *Knight Rider 2000* (NBC, May 19,1991), an unsold pilot attempt to continue the series. KITT is now the Knight Industries 4000. It cost $10 million and has a three-liter, 300 horsepower engine that can go from zero to 300 mph in a matter of seconds. KITT now runs on nonpolluting hydrogen fuel refined from gasses emitted by algae fields. KITT also has an aroma detector and sonic booms to immobilize criminals. A collision factor analyzer tells its driver when it is safe to run a red light or speed through traffic. Virtual reality allows its driver to look through the windshield to see an enhanced simulation of the road's topography and vehicles in pursuit. Digital sampling allows KITT to analyze voice patterns and duplicate them exactly. The thermal expander heats the air in the tires of fleeing cars and explodes them.

See also: Michael Knight (KITT's driver).

Kitty Russell *see* **Matt Dillon**

Kojak *see* **Theo Kojak**

656. Kris Monroe, *Charlie's Angels*, ABC, 1977–1981. Played by Cheryl Ladd.

Kris Monroe is a private detective and the younger sister of Jill Monroe, the Angel she replaced when Jill left Townsend Investigations to pursue her racing career (she hopes to become the first woman to win Le Mans).

Kris was born in San Francisco and is a graduate of the San Francisco Police Academy. Kris (and Jill's) parents are not mentioned but it was Jill who had been paying for Kris's college education (at State University, where Jill thought Kris was studying to become a teacher; instead she had been taking criminology courses). Kris had hoped to put her knowledge of law enforcement into action but was assigned office work (like answering the switchboard). When Jill knew that her boss would require another Angel (investigator) to replace her, she asked Charlie to hire Kris.

Kris, like Jill, is gorgeous and also an expert at distraction. She cares about people, a little too much at times, and this is her biggest fault (as it could get her killed because of the business she is in). Kris is also very sensitive and carries two very special items with her when she travels: a Raggedy Ann doll she had as a child and the book *Hansel and Gretel* (given to her by her mother; she considers the book a good luck charm. In the book is a picture of Kris as a girl with her mother). Kris mentioned that at Union Bay High School she was the first in a class to learn pig latin. Scotch on the rocks is her favorite drink and she drives a white Cobra with the license plate 590 VGG. "Angel Eyes" is the C.B. handle Kris used when she went undercover a big rig trucker.

See also: Charlie Townsend, Jill Monroe, Julie Rogers, Kelly Garrett, Sabrina Duncan, Tiffany Welles.

657. Kristen Adams, *Poltergeist: The Legacy*, Sci Fi, 1999. Played by Kristin Lehman.

Kristen Adams is a member of the San Francisco Legacy House, an organization that battles the evils of the supernatural. Kristen was born in Boston, Massachusetts. She is the daughter of Justin Adams, a noted professor in New England who specialized in the study of the unnatural. Kristen grew up hearing about myths and legends and the possibilities of the supernatural and has geared her education toward that goal. She is very bright and graduated from Harvard University in three years with a degree in anthropology.

Justin had been a consultant to the Boston Legacy House for a number of years. Several years ago he mysteriously disappeared while working on a Legacy dig in Istanbul. Kristen immediately joined the Legacy to find her missing father and help defeat evil.

Kristen was originally a part of the Boston Legacy House but is currently on loan to the San Francisco House. She possesses brilliance and drive and has her own opinions about how to battle evil; she often puts her life on the line to follow them.

See also: Alex Moreau, Derek Rayne, Nick Boyle, Rachel Corrigan.

658. Kristen Yancey, *Kristen*, NBC, 2001. Played by Kristen Chenoweth.

Kristen Yancey was born in Tulsa, Oklahoma. As a child Kristen would watch movie musicals on television and became so influenced by the singing and dancing that she dreamed of becoming a Broadway star. After graduating from Broken Arrow High School, Kristen found a job as weight counselor at the Jenny Craig Fitness Center in Oklahoma.

Kristen has a good singing voice and can dance

well. With those assets she took the first step and moved to New York. She found work in two off-Broadway plays (*Peter Pan* and *A Kiss Before Midnight*). The plays, however, never made it past rehearsals and Kristen needed money. She found work as a receptionist at Ballantine Enterprises, a mid–Manhattan architectural firm. She still hopes for that Broadway dream and attends every audition she can find.

Kristen has a tendency to talk too much. When she gets nervous she sings the song "Put Your Best Foot Forward" to find confidence. Kristen knows it sounds old fashioned, but "I never tell a lie." She lives in a small apartment (E) and her favorite drink is Moo Hoo (a chocolate milk drink) "that gives me all my vitamins."

659. Kurt Franklin, *Run of the House*, WB, 2003–2004. Played by Joseph Lawrence.

This entry also contains information on Kurt's siblings: Sally (Sasha Baresse), Brooke (Margo Harshman) and Chris (Kyle Howard).

Kurt Franklin is the eldest child of the four Franklin children. They live at 4375 Ryerton Drive in Grand Rapids, Michigan, and are basically on their own (health concerns forced their parents to move to the warmer climate of Arizona for the winter. Another cold season in Michigan would have killed their father, who suffers from a weak heart).

Kurt. Kurt runs the family business, Franklin Office Supplies. He dropped out of college to pursue his dream of becoming a pro ball player (pitcher) for a minor league team called the Lansing Lugnuts (he was eventually cut from the team and returned home to help run the family business). He is actually the only responsible one and has a difficult time making the others obey him. He tries acting like a father but often gets little respect. Kurt fancies himself as a ladies' man but his obligations at home often give him little or no time to pursue romantic relationships.

Brooke. Brooke is the youngest member of the family (15 years old). She is first said to attend Kirkfield Academy then Henderson High School (which was also attended by Kurt, Sally and Chris). Brooke enjoys living without her parents because she feels she can now have a social life (Kurt sees to it that she doesn't as he feels she is too young to be dating). Brooke is proud of her developing figure (she calls her breasts "The Girls") and finds that boys are "finally beginning to notice me." She eats Honey Toasted Oats cereal for breakfast and is quite studious when it comes to school and homework.

Sally. Sally was the Homecoming Queen of Henderson High School and is conceited. She feels she is not capable of looking bad. She works as a buyer for an unnamed fashion company but doesn't borrow clothes or dress to impress people. She is a rather conservative dresser and feels she doesn't need to show skin to attract a man. She is the quietest of the children and usually avoids trouble by keeping silent during brother-sister confrontations with Kurt. Sally is a fussy eater (watches her weight) and more of a homebody than the rest of the family.

Chris. Chris is described as being "as dumb as a post." He attended Princeton University and majored in philosophy. He dropped out to attend law school and gave that up to become a waiter at the local pub (O'Rourke's) at 23rd Street. Chris is rather naïve and prone to misadventure. If he sets out to do something, it is inevitable that he will foul things up and rely on Kurt to resolve the situation for him. He is of little help to Kurt in caring for Brooke as Brooke is more mature and responsible and can easily manipulate him.

660. Kwai Chang Caine, *Kung Fu*, ABC, 1972–1975. Played by David Carradine.

Kwai Chang Caine, called most often Caine, is a Shaolin priest who battles evil on the American Frontier of the 1870s.

Kwai Chang was born in China in the 1850s. He is the son of an American father and a Chinese mother and was orphaned at the age of six (the cause of his parents death is not mentioned). With no apparent relatives, Kwai Chang appeared at the Temple of Whonon (a training ground for Shaolin priests). He was accepted by Master Teh to live and study to become a priest. He was also to learn the art of Kung Fu, the medieval Chinese science of disciplined combat developed by Buddhist and Taoist Monks. It is here that he befriends Master Po (Keye Luke), the blind Shaolin priest who would become his mentor.

Kwai Chang first learns the knowledge of the Inner Strength "to discover a harmony of body and mind in accord with the flow of the universe." A short time later, while in the garden with Master Po, Kwai Chang is asked, "What do you hear?" "I hear the water. I hear the birds," responds Kwai Chang. "Do you hear the grasshopper at your feet?" asks Master Po. "Old man, remarks Kwai Chang, "how is it that you hear these things?" "How is it that you do not," responds Master Po. From that moment on Kwai Chang would always be called "Grasshopper" by Master Po.

The years pass and Kwai Chang, now a young man, completes his training. He approaches a cauldron of burning coals and places his arms around the sides. The symbol of a tiger and a dragon are branded into Kwai Chang's arms — the final step in his becoming a Shaolin priest. Kwai Chang leaves the temple with the final words of Master Teh: "Remember, the wise man walks always with his head bowed, humble like the dust." Kwai Chang's strict training in China is seen in flashbacks as he encounters situations that parallel those of his past.

661. Kyle Applegate, *Out of This World*, Syn., 1987–1991. Played by Doug McClure.

Kyle X. Applegate is a former Hollywood film and television star who is now the mayor of Marlowe, California (1987–90). He is then the police chief (he calls his patrol car Betsy).

Kyle was born in California in 1948 and caught the acting bug at an early age. He dropped out of high school the night before his last test in senior year to play a cannibal in the movie *Please Don't Eat the Daileys* in 1962. He then appeared in the film *Gidget Goes to Gettysburg*. However, it was his role as Cowboy Kyle that brought him fame (Cowboy Kyle films include *The Good, the Bad and the Unattractive* and *Gunfight at the Pretty Good Corral*). The movies were so popular that they were turned into the TV series *Cowboy Kyle* (Kyle had a horse named Myron and was Marshal of Laramie Heights. Sheldon Moskowitz the frontier dentist assisted him. On the show Kyle wore fancy shirts with ruffles; off the set he was called "The Ruffleman").

Kyle was also the star of two other TV series: *The Floridian* and *Mosquito Man* (wherein he played a crime fighter dressed in a mosquito outfit). Kyle thought he was a fine actor and deserved an award. He crashed the 1976 Emmy Awards presentation and pretended to be John Travolta to pick up an Emmy. Kyle is also famous in Marlowe. During his tenure as sheriff he caught the biggest villain the town had ever seen — the cereal thief (he broke into 7-11 stores to steal cereal. Kyle caught him with 200 boxes of Rice Krispies).

See also: Donna Garland, Evie Garland.

662. Kyle Stewart, *Team Knight Rider*, Syn., 1997–1998. Played by Brixton Karnes.

Kyle Stewart is the head of TKR (Team Knight Rider), an agency of the Foundation for Law and Government that battles criminal elements. His team includes Jenny Andrews, Erica West, Duke DePalma and Trek Sanders.

Kyle and his team are based in *Sky One*, a large cargo plane that serves as their mobile headquarters (to be ready at a moment's notice to help any city or town that requires their assistance).

Kyle is a former CIA operative whose daring exploits and rate of success had earned him the nickname "America's James Bond." Kyle was a brilliant strategist whose assignments took him to the world's hot spots where he performed near-impossible missions successfully. His career came to an abrupt end when his cover was blown behind enemy lines. He was then hired by the Foundation to head TKR. Kyle once took daring risks. That has all changed. He looks at life in a different way and is cautious. He worries about the safety of his team, the moral issues of an assignment and the state of the world in which he lives.

See also: Duke DePalma, Erica West, Jenny Andrews, Trek Sanders.

Kyra Hart *see* **Reba Hart**

663. Lamont Sanford, *Sanford and Son*, NBC, 1972–1977. Played by Demond Wilson.

Lamont Sanford was born in Los Angeles in 1938. He is the son of Fred and Elizabeth Sanford and heir to Sanford and Son Salvage, a junk empire owned by his father, now a 65-year-old widower.

Lamont is 34 years old and called "Dummy" by Fred. Lamont can't stand being poor and doesn't see the business as an empire ("It's a junkyard"). He refuses to call himself a junk dealer ("I'm a collector") and is regulated to doing all the work while Fred supervises. Lamont is a graduate of South Central High School and was unable to attend college because Fred never saved for such an occasion. He lives with his father in the back of the "empire" at 9114 South Central in Los Angeles. Lamont attempted to break into show business as the manager of an all-girl singing group called Three Degrees.

Lamont is hoping to one day leave the junk business and build himself a better life but feels he can't because Fred is too dependent on him. Lamont puts up with all of Fred's gruff and abusive behavior; in 1977, however, he left the business for a job on the Alaska Pipeline.

See also: Fred Sanford.

664. Lana Hawkins, *Strong Medicine*, Lifetime, 2000 (current). Played by Jenifer Lewis.

Lana Hawkins enjoys watching *General Hospital* on TV and is the outspoken receptionist at the Rittenhouse Women's Health Clinic in Philadelphia. She first worked as a cashier at the now defunct F.W. Woolworth chain of stores. She then turned to a life of prostitution to survive the harsh streets of South Philly. She became pregnant during this time and had two sons (both of whom she raised on her own). She also managed to see the fault of her lifestyle and took it upon herself to change it. She befriended Dr. Luisa Delgado at Rittenhouse and was hired as the receptionist.

Lana's experiences on the streets have made her a wiser person. She knows the dangerous situations a woman can face and she calls upon her own hidden secrets to help those she feels are heading down the same destructive path she once traveled. Lana is not afraid to speak her mind and feels that it is not the fashion that makes the woman but the woman who makes the clothes (her philosophy is "If you've got it, flaunt it"). Her secret desire is to spend at least 45 minutes alone with the man of her dreams, actor Billy Dee Williams.

See also: Andy Campbell, Dana Stowe, Kayla Thornton, Luisa Delgado, Peter Riggs, Nick Biancavilla.

665. Larry Appleton, *Perfect Strangers*, ABC, 1986–1993. Played by Mark Linn-Baker.

Lawrence Appleton is the assistant to the city editor at the Chicago *Chronicle*. Larry, as he is called, was born in Madison, Wisconsin, on May 30. He had a dog named Spot as a kid and is a graduate of Madison High School. Larry asked 12 girls to the senior prom; 13 girls turned him down (one came up to him and said, "Don't even think of asking me"). Larry next attended Chicago University (where he acquired a degree in journalism). He first worked as a salesman at the Ritz Discount store before acquiring the newspaper job.

Larry shares an apartment with his cousin Balki Bartokomous. They live in Apartment 203 in the Caldwell Hotel at 627 Lincoln Boulevard. Larry gargles to the song "Moon River" and exclaims "Oh, My Lord" when something goes wrong (he is easily excitable and becomes upset over everything). Larry drives a car with the license plate KYP 758 (later 999 753) and wrote a play called *Wheat*. He married his longtime girlfriend Jennifer Lyons (Melanie Wilson) on September 27, 1991; they set up housekeeping on Elm Street with Balki and his wife, Mary Anne. Jennifer worked as an airline stewardess and gave birth in the last episode to a boy she and Larry named Tucker.

See also: Balki Bartokomous.

666. Larry, Darryl and Darryl, *Newhart*, CBS, 1982–1990. Played by William Sanderson (Larry), Tony Papenfuss (Darryl One), John Volstad (Darryl Two).

Larry and his two brothers, Darryl One and Darryl Two, are residents of the town of River City, Vermont. Larry is the only brother who speaks (when he enters a room he always says, "Hello. My name is Larry. This is my brother Darryl, and this is my other brother, Darryl"). The brothers are rather unkempt looking and appear to be backwoods trappers but in reality operate the Minuteman Café (located next to the Stratford Inn) on Westbrook Road.

Darryl and Darryl only nod *yes* or *no* when Larry speaks to them. The brothers will tackle any job (usually something disgusting, like cleaning drainage ditches, that no one else will handle). The brothers also look like hillbillies but are well educated. Larry is a graduate of the Mount Pilard Technical School; Darryl One was enrolled in Oxford University; and Darryl Two attended Cambridge University (where he majored in royalty under a rowing scholarship). According to Larry, the Darryls never speak because nothing upsets them. They all take what life has to offer and through Larry's speeches, never find fault with anything. The last episode, which is set five years in the future, finds Larry married to Rhonda; Darryl One has wed Sada; and Darryl Two is married to Zora. The occasion marks the first time the Darryls speak — to yell "Quiet" to their arguing wives.

See also: Bob and Joanna Loudon, George Utley, Stephanie Vanderkellen.

667. Larry Finkelstein, *Dharma and Greg*, ABC, 1997–2002. Played by Alan Rachins.

Myron Lawrence Finkelstein, called Larry, is married to Abby, the mother of their flower child Dharma. Larry and Abby were liberals who lived together for 30 years before marrying in 1999. Larry is a man without a Social Security number ("I don't want to be part of the grid and I don't want to be found") and on the run from the government. He is a revolutionary and in 1968 protested the Vietnam War. In an attempt to "cripple the Vietnam War machine," Larry broke into the draft board office and set the building on fire. Although the sprinkler system put out the fire, Larry escaped before knowing this. He believes the government is looking for him and has been in hiding ever since (Abby says, "Every day he is free is a gift").

Larry worked in Canada as a janitor before meeting Abby. He wrote a song called "One Thing About Angels" and had anticipated a music career but gave it up when no one would publish his song. He next tried starting his own church (the Church of Larry) but had to abandon it when the IRS began an investigation. He found his talent at handcrafting furniture "with handcrafted tools I handcrafted." He sells the furniture at the East Bay Swap Meet in San Francisco.

Larry has to finish what he starts no matter how long it takes "because if I don't I forget." He also worked as a rodeo clown and invented spray-on gravy but no one would market it. Larry hears a constant metal hum ("Like a factory making metal shoes") but can't figure out why. He wrote a five-hour Watergate rock opera and has a pet goat (Goat). He drives an old ice cream truck and is famous for his vegetable chili (the secret ingredient is chopped meat). His favorite song is "Hey Jude" and his favorite movies are *Fritz the Cat* (an X-rated cartoon) and *Lawrence of Arabia*. He and Abby became the parents of a baby they name Harold Christian Finkelstein in 2001.

See also: Abby O'Neill, Dharma Montgomery, Edward and Kitty Montgomery, Greg Montgomery.

668. Latka Gravas, *Taxi*, ABC, 1978–1982; NBC, 1982–1983. Played by Andy Kaufman.

Latka Gravas is a mechanic for the Sunshine Cab Company in New York City. He is an immigrant from an unidentified country and speaks with an understandable (at times) accent. He is Orthodox and says, "Mindless superstitions and pointless rituals are the only thing that separates people in my country from the animals."

Latka's childhood was very difficult. For the first eight years of his life he lived outdoors with a wood bucket and a chair. When his father got a raise at work they moved indoors. His mother (Greta) was mean, says Latka, because she forced him to spend summers with his Uncle Bobka, who tried to make a man of him. Latka feels that he is very lucky because he won first prize in his country's lottery — a fly swatter.

When it comes to women Latka is shy and insecure. To become attractive, he took time off from work to study *Playboy* magazine "and alter my life to fit the Fastlane." He returned as his alter ego, Vic Ferrari, "the secure ladies' man" (who also spoke perfect unaccented English). A side effect was a second alter ego — Arlo the Cowboy. Latka tried to make money by selling Grandma Gravas' Old Fashioned Oat Meal Cookies (which was based on an old family recipe but used drugs as the main ingredient). When the cab company suffered a financial setback, Latka took a job as a busboy at Mario's, the local hangout.

Simka Dahblitz (Carol Kane) is a girl from the same country as Latka but from a different tribe (Latka's tribe made cruel jokes about Simka's). She speaks the same strange language and eventually married Latka. Simka is romantic, moody and feared by men when she becomes angry (although Latka finds her temper romantic).

See also: Alex Reiger, Elaine Nardo, Jim Ignatowski, Louie DePalma.

669. Laura Holt, *Remington Steele*, NBC, 1982–1986. Played by Stephanie Zimbalist.

Laura Holt is young, beautiful and elegant. She appears to be a corporate executive but in reality operates Remington Steele Investigations. Laura had a fascination for crime since she was a child. She enjoyed watching crime dramas (although she mentions *Atomic Man* as being her favorite show). She was called "Binky" and is a graduate of Stanford University (where she was a member of the glee club. She shared a fourth floor dorm room with three girls and they were known as "The Four East"). After graduating, Laura became an apprentice detective with the Havenhurst Detective Agency. When Laura felt she had learned enough, she quit to open her own agency — Laura Holt Investigations. Most people believed that because of her sex, Laura was not right for the job ("It takes more brains than brawn to make a detective," she says). When Laura's business began to falter she finally believed that perhaps "a female detective is too feminine." She invented a mythical boss (Remington Steele) by combining the first name of a typewriter (Remington) with a singular version of her favorite football team (the Steelers). Suddenly business was booming (before a stranger came into her life to pose as Remington Steele, Laura would explain Mr. Steele's absence to a client as "he functions best in an advisory capacity").

Laura weighs 110 pounds and lives at 800 Tenth Avenue, Apartment 3A in Los Angeles in a building owned by The Commercial Management Corporation (her agency is located in Suite 1157 of an office building at 606 West Beverly Boulevard; 555-9450; 555-3535; and 555-9548 are its phone numbers). Laura has a pet cat (Nero) and 555-6235 is her home phone number. For relaxation Laura listens to radio station KROT. Her clock radio rings at 6:00 A.M.

Laura never carries a gun ("I never found the need for one"). She is practical but intuitive, logical and brilliant no matter how bleak the situation. Laura never loses her sense of humor. The reading glasses Laura wears date back to her college days when she bought them to impress her calculus professor ("to make me look brainy"). While seemingly perfect, Laura is plagued by "The Holt Curse," a craving for chocolate.

See also: Remington Steele.

670. Laura Petrie, *The Dick Van Dyke Show*, CBS, 1961–1966. Played by Mary Tyler Moore.

Laura Petrie is the wife of comedy writer Rob Petrie (of *The Alan Brady Show*) and the mother of their young son, Ritchie. She lives at 148 Bonnie Meadow Road in New Rochelle, New York, and her antics often provide Rob with sketches for the show.

Laura's background is a bit sketchy. Her maiden name is first mentioned as Meeker then Meehan. She is well educated and apparently a high school graduate (if not college also). However, she met Rob at the age of 17 (although she told him she was 19). At this time Rob was a sergeant stationed at the Camp Crowder Army Base in Joplin, Missouri. Laura was a dancer with the U.S.O. (United Serviceman's Organization) and performed in variety shows. It was Rob who fell in love with Laura; she wanted nothing to do with him until they danced together to the song "You Wonderful You" in a show (at which time Rob broke Laura's toes by stepping on her foot. He romanced her with flowers and recipes and her hatred turned to love. A marriage occurred shortly after). Laura won the title "Bivouac Baby" of Camp Crowder but no mention is made of Laura's education (being 17, she was either a dropout or smart enough to graduate early).

Laura weighs 112 pounds and moo goo gai pan is her favorite food. *Town of Passion* is her favorite TV show and she hides her old love letters (from her high school boyfriend Joe Coogan) behind some loose bricks behind the furnace in the basement. When first married, Laura posed for a clothed portrait of herself called "October Eve" that she planned to give to Rob. It became a nude painting when the artist envisioned — and painted — Laura without clothes. Laura attempted to write a children's book called *Be Yourself: The Seven Days of Danny* under the pen name Samantha Q. Wiggins. Laura believes her motherly instincts can tell her when a child is sick (especially when he refuses a cupcake) and her favorite, sobering expression is "Oh Rob" (which she says when something goes wrong). In the series update, *The Dick Van Dyke Show Revisited* (CBS, 2004), Laura and Rob have moved to Manhattan. Rob has retired and Laura works as a dance instructor.

See also: Alan Brady, Buddy Sorrell, Ritchie Petrie, Rob Petrie, Sally Rogers.

671. Laura Winslow, *Family Matters*, ABC, 1989–1997; CBS, 1997–1998. Played by Kellie Shanygne Williams.

This entry also contains information on Laura's older brother, Eddie Winslow (Darius McCrary).

Laura and Eddie Winslow are the children of Carl and Henrietta Winslow, a happily married couple who live at 263 Pinehurst Street in Chicago. Laura and Eddie attend Vanderbilt High School. Laura is pretty, fashion conscious, bright and frightened by the fact that her nerdy next-door neighbor, Steve Urkel, loves her. She and Steve first met in kindergarten. Laura made Steve eat Play-Doh and took an instant dislike to him; he felt it was love at first sight. Laura feels Steve is loud, obnoxious, clumsy, pushy and immature — and those are his good qualities (see Steve Urkel for more information).

Laura was voted the 1992 Vanderbilt High Homecoming Queen and was a cheerleader for the Muskrats basketball team. She wears Rainbow Cloud perfume and worked as a waitress at Rachel's Place, the after school hangout (she also attempted her own business — the Winslow Baby Sitting Service but failed due to a lack of employees).

Edward James Arthur Winslow was born on January 28, 1974, and believes that when it comes to good looks God smiled on the men in his family. He is not too bright and is known as "Fast Eddie Winslow" at the local pool hall. At school he is a member of the Muskrats basketball team (jersey 33) and will not sleep without his Scooby-Doo nightlight. He worked as a waiter at the Mighty Weiner and became a police officer (following in his father's footsteps) before the series ended.

See also: Carl Winslow, Steve Urkel.

672. Lauren, *What I Like About You*, WB, 2002 (current). Played by Leslie Grossman.

Lauren (no last name given) is a girl who knows she is beautiful and alluring. She uses her sex appeal, especially her breasts, to get what she wants from men (even women). She says, however, "I didn't always look like this. In high school I was considered big boned and undateable."

Lauren is an advertising agency executive and first worked at the Harper and Diggs Agency in Manhattan; she later works as a partner (with Valerie Tyler) in an agency called Valco.

Lauren has a criminal record for robbery. She was overweight in grammar school and had her nose fixed when she was 16 years old. She wears a size 36C bra and calls her breasts "The Maids of Honor" (a year later she calls them "The Girls"). Lauren says, "I am not just as hot piece of meat, I have a lot to offer." She hates sports and if she dates a man who likes sports she says, "I'll change him." She also says, "I don't take crap from anyone" and if she is with a man she doesn't like she gets out of the date by saying "I'm a lesbian."

It is unusual to see Lauren thinking about something that bothers her. She is impulsive and doesn't think before she acts. She claims to be a people person although she is pushy. "Sugar is my pimp," she says, as she is addicted to sweets (peanut brownies are her favorite snack). Lauren lives in Apartment 42 in New York's Greenwich Village and is looking to marry a rich man. She claims to be an overachiever. But when Val asks her to do something extra she says, "No way."

Lauren is forever giving meaningless advice; it shocks her when somebody actually takes it. Lauren worships money and would roll around in it if she had any. Even if she doesn't agree with what a man is saying, Lauren forces herself to agree to keep him interested in her.

See also: Holly Tyler, Valerie Tyler.

673. Lauren Miller, *Still Standing,* CBS, 2002 (current). Played by Renee Olstead.

Thirteen-year-old Lauren Miller is the daughter of Bill and Judy Miller, a happily married couple who live at 209 Evergreen in Chicago. Lauren attended the Radford Academy Grammar School and is currently a student at Thomas Jefferson High School (where she was a member of the choir until she found out it was for losers). She eats Alpha Bits cereal for breakfast and is attempting to play the cornet. Lauren finds that housework makes her look forward to school (something that does not excite her). Lauren sleeps with a pillow she calls Dawson (after the TV series *Dawson's Creek*) and loves to see her grandfather "because I can really use the money."

Lauren's first job was as a babysitter and she attempted to make money by selling goose clothes for plastic lawn ornament geese. She enjoys shopping for clothes with her mother because Judy knows how to manipulate people to get her what she wants. Lauren is not overly fashion conscious and is comfortable wearing what she likes. Bill calls her "Pumpkin."

See also: Bill Miller, Brian Miller, Judy Miller.

674. Laurette Barber, *China Beach,* ABC, 1988–1991. Played by Chloe Webb.

This entry also contains information on Cherry White (Nan Woods), Lila Garreau (Concetta Tomei) and Waylou Marie Holmes (Megan Gallagher), personnel stationed on China Beach during the Vietnam War (they are with the 510th Evac Hospital, 63rd Division).

Laurette. Laurette Barber was the sweet U.S.O. (United Serviceman's Organization) singer and dancer who involved herself with the soldiers she entertained. If an extra hand was needed, she was there to help the wounded. Laurette was orphaned at an early age and grew up at the Lady of Perpetual Hope Orphanage. She learned to care from the sisters who raised her and that experience has always made her give of herself to help others. Laurette faced horrific situations and never refused to help where she could. She was not a nurse and when her troupe was assigned to another base, Laurette was obligated to move along with it. Laurette loved to entertain and it is assumed she found a career in show business after the war.

Cherry. Cherry White was a nurse truly dedicated to helping the victims of a war she felt was unjust. She was an A.R.C. (American Red Cross) nurse whose greatest hope was to find her brother, Rick, who had been reported missing in action. Cherry was extremely kind and giving and was well liked by everyone on China Beach. She was close to Colleen McMurphy and tried to be the best nurse she could. Cherry received an unkind fate: she was killed during the Tet Offensive by an enemy bomb. She never learned of Rick's fate.

Lila. Lila Garreau was a major whose life was the army. She was the hospital administrator and was nicknamed "Scooter." She most often pushed herself (and her nurses) beyond the call of duty. She was well liked and although brought up by a strict military father, she sometimes regretted having to be so strict with her nurses; she realized they needed to have fun to relax but the times were difficult and fun was not a part of the game. Lila married a sergeant (Bartholomew Pepper) after the war and moved to Alabama to run a gas station.

Waylou. Waylou Marie Holmes was the U.S. Air Force television reporter who covered the misery of China Beach for the U.S. networks. While Marie became an active part of the war (helping as a nurse where needed), her only thought was to do a job good enough to acquire bigger and better things. Her efforts paid off when she became a reporter for ABC-TV in New York in 1968. It is later learned that Marie became the host of a series called *This Morning*.

See also: Colleen McMurphy, K.C.

Laurie Partridge *see* **Shirley Partridge**

675. Laverne DeFazio, *Laverne and Shirley,* ABC, 1976–1983. Played by Penny Marshall.

Laverne DeFazio is a single girl who shares Apartment A at 730 Knapp Street in Milwaukee, Wisconsin, with her best friend, Shirley Feeney. The time is the 1960s and the address is also given as 730 Hampton Street.

Laverne, an Italian Catholic, was born in Milwaukee. She works in the beer bottle capping division of the Shotz Brewery (at $1.35 an hour) and shops at Slotnik's Supermarket. Laverne is a graduate of Fillmore High School (where she was a member of a singing group called The Angora Debs). She served a hitch in the army as a private (stationed at Camp McClellan; she and Shirley played prostitutes in the army training film *This Can Happen to You*).

Laverne is cynical, street smart and outspoken. While comfortable with her current lifestyle she has the feeling that other people look down on her. Laverne wears a large capital *L* on all her clothes (including her lingerie). She has a fear of small places and she loves to mix Pepsi Cola with milk. Scooter Pies are her favorite snack and sauerkraut on raisin bread is her favorite sandwich. As a little girl Laverne had the nickname "Messy Pants."

After five years on the job Laverne moves to California to better her life. She finds an apartment at 113½ Laurel Vista Drive and first worked as a gift wrapper at Bardwell's Department Store. She later finds work with the Ajax Aerospace Company.

See also: Lenny and Squiggy, Shirley Feeney.

676. Lee Crane, *Voyage to the Bottom of the Sea*, ABC, 1964–1968. Played by David Hedison.

Lee Crane is Captain of the *Seaview*, an atomic research submarine developed by his mentor, Admiral Harriman Nelson. Lee was born in Providence, Rhode Island, and is the son of David and Helen Crane. Lee was seven years old when his father, a naval commander, died in an explosion that occurred on his ship. As Lee, now being raised alone by his mother, grew up, he became interested in the sea and ships. He excelled in high school and attended the U.S. Naval Academy at West Point. It was during a class in marine biology that he met Harriman Nelson, the man who became a father figure to him. Lee served with Harriman on the submarine *Nautilus* (its last voyage before decommission) and on the *Kingfisher* before permanent assignment on *Seaview* ("The most extraordinary submarine in all the Seven Seas." Its public image is that of an instrument of marine research; in actuality it is the mightiest weapon afloat and is secretly assigned the most dangerous missions against the enemies of mankind).

Lee is a by-the-books commander who earns the respect of his crew. He does not just give orders; he becomes an active part of each mission and risks his life to protect others. Lee is trusting, sometimes too much so, and feels that when

necessary, he must resort to violence to achieve a goal.

See also: Harriman Nelson.

677. Lee Stetson, *Scarecrow and Mrs. King*, CBS, 1982–1987. Played by Bruce Boxleitner.

Lee Stetson, codename "Scarecrow," is a top field operative for The Agency, a secret branch of the U.S. government that handles matters of national security (it operates under the cover of International Federal Film — which actually makes movies). Lee is partners with Amanda King, a real housewife whose cover is that of a housewife.

Lee was orphaned at the age of four and raised by a military uncle on a number of army bases. Lee's education in various military schools peaked his interest in serving his country. He joined the Agency in 1973 and became a member of the Oz Team (where he received his codename; other members of the team were "The Wizard," "The Tin Man" and "The Lion"). Lee's expertise in the field led him to becoming one of the Agency's top agents.

Lee lives in an apartment at 46 Hamblin in Washington, D.C. (he hides the spare key under the potted plant in the hallway). He combs his hair with a plastic comb that is missing two teeth ("It's the right comb for my hair") and practices karate, kickboxing and fencing at home. He drives a classic 1953 Porsche 350 (plate 3NG 105; later 9S1 407 and 7G4 928). Lee enjoys chilidogs at Milo's Daffy Dog and a drink at Ned's Washington Pub (the bar is later called Emilio's). Lee is a member of the University Athletic Club and works out when he gets upset. He also has two unnamed pet fish (Siamese fighting fish). Although Lee is a spy he doesn't care for that word and prefers to be called an Intelligence Operative. Love eventually developed between Lee and Amanda and they married in last season episodes.

See also: Amanda King.

678. Lenny and Shelly Callahan, *Lenny*, CBS, 1990–1991. Played by Lenny Clarke, Lee Garlington.

Leonard Joseph Callahan and Shelly Morrison met as teenagers. Leonard, called Lenny, had to borrow ten dollars for their first date. When he brought Shelly home to meet the family, his younger brother (Eddie) remarked, "What great torpedoes — and what a tush." Despite Lenny's lack of money and his brother's crude sexual references, Shelly stayed with Lenny and they married shortly after graduating from St. Theodore's Catholic High School in Boston. After living with Lenny's parents (Patrick and Mary) for a year,

Lenny and Shelly moved into their own home at 11 Cherry Wood Lane. There they became the parents of three daughters: Kelly, Tracy and Elizabeth.

Lenny was born in 1953; Shelly in 1954. Lenny works two jobs to support his family: gasman for Boston Utility, and doorman at an unnamed hotel at night. Shelly is kept busy caring for the house and children.

As a kid Lenny had a teddy bear named Buzzer. The Boston Celtics is his favorite baseball team and Fielding Insurance handles his life insurance. Lenny enjoys cold pizza in the morning and his one claim to fame is his ability to belch the song "White Christmas." His favorite robe is a terry cloth he stole from his honeymoon hotel.

Shelly is the glue that holds the family together. She is logical and her common sense resolves most of the family's problems. Lenny has trouble dealing with the children, especially 13-year-old Kelly, as she progresses into young adulthood (Lenny can't handle "female issues" and leaves all those problems for Shelly to solve). Shelly knows their daughters can manipulate Lenny and is wise to all their moves. Shelly is also very good with money and handles all the household finances. She fears giving Lenny any extra money because she feels he is an easy touch ("A friend in need is a friend of Lenny's"). Lenny calls Shelly "Shell" and "Love Muffin."

See also: Kelly Callahan, Tracy Callahan.

679. Lenny and Squiggy, *Laverne and Shirley*, ABC, 1976–1983. Played by Michael McKean (Lenny), David L. Lander (Squiggy).

Leonard Kosnoski and Andrew Squigman are best friends and roommates who like to be called by their nicknames — Lenny and Squiggy. They live at 730 Knapp Street (also given as 730 Hampton Street) in Milwaukee, Wisconsin (1960s) and are the upstairs-neighbors of Laverne DeFazio and Shirley Feeney.

Lenny and Squiggy work as beer truck delivery drivers for the Shotz Brewery. Lenny is a bit naïve but very sincere and caring. He claims that, "my home away from home is the gutter." He likes sports and horror movies and apparently from a poor family as the only toy he had as a kid was sauerkraut. Squiggy was apparently his only friend and even animals had a hard time accepting Lenny (his pet turtle killed itself trying to scratch Lenny's name off its back).

Squiggy is the son of Helmut and Gwen Squigman and has a rather manly looking sister named Squendelyn Squigman (also played by David L. Lander). Squiggy is a hothead and outspoken. He

will argue with anybody on anything and often learns that what he is saying is wrong. He has been "blessed" with the Squigman birthmark (a big red blotch shaped like Abraham Lincoln). A moth collection is his most prized possession. He collects toenail clippings and likes old sandwiches.

After five years at Shotz, Lenny and Squiggy move to California to begin new careers: the co-owners of the Squignoski Talent Agency of Burbank. As talent agents they wrote a movie called *Blood Orgy of the Amazon*. They also had a sideline — ice cream vendors with a truck called Squignoski's Ice Cream. Lenny and Squiggy's favorite food is Bosco — which they put on everything.

See also: Laverne DeFazio, Shirley Feeney.

680. Leo Schnauser, *Car 54, Where Are You?*, NBC, 1961–1963. Played by Al Lewis.

Leo Schnauser is a police officer with the 53rd Precinct on East Tremont Avenue in the Bronx, New York. He wears badge number 1062 and is married to the former Sylvia Schwartzcock (Charlotte Rae), a woman who keeps a tight reign on him.

Leo was born in the Bronx on Friday the 13th and has been on the force for 20 years (he has been married to Sylvia for 15 years and believes that when he was born a black cat crossed his path for all the bad luck he has). Leo his six sisters, yet he is considered the pretty one in the family. Leo was a mounted policeman (he rode a horse named Sally) for 16 years before becoming a patrolman with the 53rd. He coaches a basketball team called the Tigers in his spare time. He and Sylvia live in Apartment 6A. They are an argumentative couple. Sylvia believes that each time Leo goes out with the boys he is having a secret affair with Marilyn Monroe. Leo hates night duty "because I get home in time to see Sylvia getting out of bed."

Sylvia was an actress and ballet dancer and tried painting before marrying Leo. She is writing a book based on the 53rd called *Precinct Place*. She believes in psychics and what the tea leaves tell her. Leo calls her "Pussycat."

See also: Francis Muldoon, Gunther Toody.

681. Leo Wyatt, *Charmed*, WB, 1998 (current). Played by Brian Krause.

Leo Wyatt is a White Lighter, a guardian angel of witches. He was born in 1924 and from the beginning possessed the qualities sought by the Elders, a society of powerful beings who battle evil through the powers of good witches. Leo was chosen to become a White Lighter during World War

II. He was serving as a battlefield medic when he was killed. He was then rescued by the Elders to serve as a guardian angel.

When first seen, Leo is working as a handyman to his charges, the three Halliwell sisters (Prue, Phoebe and Piper), good witches who are also known as the Power of Three. Leo has the power to heal, but not himself or animals. His enemies are Dark Lighters, who seek to destroy witches and create evil.

As Leo worked with the Halliwell sisters he became close to Piper and eventually married her. They became the parents of a mystical baby (Matthew Wyatt Halliwell) and set up housekeeping in the Halliwell sister's home at 1329 Prescott in San Francisco. It is also at this time that Leo becomes an Elder and Piper becomes responsible for raising Wyatt (Leo's duties leave him little time to spend with Piper and Wyatt). Piper became pregnant for a second time a year later and gave birth to a son she and Leo named Chris. It was shortly after this that Leo became an Avatar, an all-powerful being capable of both good or evil.

See also: Paige Matthews, Phoebe Halliwell, Piper Halliwell, Prue Halliwell.

682. Leonard McCoy, *Star Trek*, NBC, 1966–1969. Played by DeForest Kelley.

Dr. Leonard McCoy, nicknamed "Bones" by his friend James T. Kirk, is a graduate of the University of Mississippi (2245–49) and its associated medical school (2249–53). He is divorced and the father of a daughter named Joanna (a nurse). Dr. McCoy enjoyed an active practice for 12 years before he joined Starfleet. At that time he developed a neural grafting procedure that is still used. His first Starfleet assignment was Chief Medical Officer under Captain Kirk aboard the U.S.S. *Enterprise NCC-1701*. During his Starfleet career Dr. McCoy won awards of Valor and was decorated by the Legion of Honor.

See also: Hikaru Sulu, James T. Kirk, Mr. Spock, Montgomery Scott, Pavel Chekov, Uhura.

683. Les Nessman, *WKRP in Cincinnati*, CBS, 1978–1982. Played by Richard Sanders.

Lester Nessman, called Les, is the self-proclaimed "News Beacon of the Ohio Valley." He is the news director of WKRP, a 5,000-watt radio station (1590 AM) in Cincinnati. Les signs on with the 8:00 A.M. news and ends the day with the 6:00 P.M. newscast. He also does the sports, a celebrity interview program (*Show Beat*) and *Eyewitness Weather* ("I look out the window for that eyewitness aspect"). Les works in an open office

atmosphere but has imaginary walls and a door (marked with tape on the floor) that his co-workers respect.

Les was born in Dayton, Ohio, and is a graduate of Xavier University. He took violin lessons as a kid and thought he would make a good handyman until he tried making a footstool and he blew out the back of the garage. He enjoys exploring dark basements and attics (hoping to find a ghost or some unearthly being) and is a member of the Ho Down Square Dancing Club. He has a nasty dog (Phil) and one record in his collection ("Chances Are" by Johnny Mathis). Les uses his motor scooter as the WKRP Mobile News Unit and has won the Silver Sow Award for his hog reports (which he believes are the most important part of his newscasts; he keeps informed by reading *Pig American* magazine). Les has also won the Buckeye News Hawk Award for his newscasts and ends his reports with "This is Les Nessman saying this is Les Nessman" or "This is Les Nessman saying good day and may the good news be yours."

See also: Arthur Carlson, Bailey Quarters, Dr. Johnny Fever, Herb Tarlek, Jennifer Marlowe, Venus Flytrap.

684. Lewis Kiniski, *The Drew Carey Show*, ABC, 1995–2004. Played by Ryan Stiles.

Lewis Kiniski, Drew Carey, Oswald Harvey, and Kate O'Brien are best friends. They are all graduates of Rhodes High School and ventured into business together (in a beer-coffee brew called Buzz Beer, which they make in Drew's garage and sell at their favorite watering hole, the Warsaw Tavern).

Lewis and Oswald are often mistaken for a gay couple (although they are not). They live over the Warsaw Tavern in Cleveland, Ohio, and spend much of their time together. Lewis was originally a maintenance man (then janitorial manager) at the DrugCo Chemical Company. DrugCo experiments with what appear to be strange and dangerous drugs. The drugs used often affect Lewis and his dream job "is to be stud monkey at DrugCo."

Lewis has a sock puppet (Professor Von Sock) to help him out of tight situations. He is allergic to strawberries and fish and on Wednesday nights conducts "Beer Robics" at the Warsaw. Although Lewis considers himself a ladies' man, he has a difficult time finding a date. When he is without a girl for a time, he sets up candle light dinners with a Pat Benatar album. To discourage telemarketers, Lewis screams Chinese into the phone when they call. He is a fan of the TV shows *Star*

Trek, *Babylon 5* and *Buffy the Vampire Slayer*. Lewis is an expert on serial killers. In high school he, Drew and Oswald were in a band called the Horndogs. Drinking beer is Lewis's favorite activity.

See also: Drew Carey, Kate O'Brien, Mimi Bobeck, Oswald Harvey.

685. Lexa Pierce, *Mutant X*, Syn., 2003–2004. Played by Karen Cliche.

Lexa Pierce is a stunning woman with a mysterious, shadowy past. She works for a secret organization called the Dominion (which controls the world's technology) and has been placed in charge of Mutant X (beginning in 2003), the organization of genetically enhanced agents who battle evil (its former leader, Adam Kane, has gone into hiding to avoid an unknown assassin). Lexa was genetically manipulated and has the power to bend light to appear invisible. She was Adam's first subject at Genomex, a secret U.S. Intelligence agency that sought to create perfect men and women through genetic enhancement (Lexa was classified as Mutant X-1.0). Lexa can change her molecules to pass through solid objects and discharge power from her hands. She has used her powers for good and has been involved in covert operations for several U.S. intelligence and security agencies.

See also: Adam Kane, Brennan Mulray, Emma DeLauro, Shalimar Fox.

686. Libby and Drew Thatcher, *Life Goes On*, ABC, 1989–1993. Played by Patti LuPone, Bill Smitrovich.

Elizabeth Giordano, called Libby, and Andrew Thatcher were adults when they first met. Libby was a singer and dancer. Andrew, called Drew, was a divorced construction worker with a young daughter (Paige). Libby and Drew were born in Ohio and on their first date (in Drew's old Plymouth) they saw the movie *Curse of the Swamp Creature*. They married shortly after meeting and set up housekeeping at 305 Woodridge Road in the town of Glen Brook, Ohio. They had three children together: Becca, Corky and Nicholas James. The family dog is named Arnold.

Drew first worked for the Quentico Construction Company but quit to open his own business, the Glen Brook Grill (a diner). Libby worked under the stage name Libby Dean and starred in a production of *West Side Story*. She gave up show business to raise a family; she later worked as an account executive at the Berkson and Berkson Ad Agency.

Libby's favorite TV soap opera is *Forever and a Day*. She is very frugal and buys mostly store brand (no frills) products at the supermarket. She is the daughter of Sid and Teresa Giordano and is very strict with the children. Drew, the son of Jack and Mary Thatcher, is a man who understands what it is like to be a kid in trouble and while strict, he is a bit more tolerant when disciplining their mostly obedient children. Drew's dream car is an Austin Healey 3000.

See also: Becca Thatcher, Corky Thatcher, Paige Thatcher.

687. Libby Kelly, *Grace Under Fire*, ABC, 1993–1998. Played by Kaitlin Cullum.

Elizabeth Louise Kelly, nicknamed Libby, is the adorable daughter of Grace Kelly, a single mother (divorced) who lives at 445 Washington Avenue in Victory, Missouri. She has two brothers, Quentin and Patrick.

Libby attends Glenview Elementary School (where she is a member of the girl's soccer team). Libby is in the fourth grade and won her class "Why I Like Our State" essay contest (she also entered the Little Miss Muppet Pageant. She sang the song "Tomorrow" and came in next to last). Libby feels that she can be a musician and has taken up the trumpet (Grace wonders for how long as she is so bad). Libby has a knack for really getting interested in something then dropping it on the spur of the moment. She is a *Star Trek* fanatic and has a pet squirrel (Spot) and a goldfish (Fishy Fisherman). Libby has a favorite doll named Helen and keeps her Barbie dolls in the refrigerator's butter dish "because Ken likes his Barbie cold." Libby is very respectful of her mother and looks up to her not only as an authority figure but also as a good friend. Despite the fact that she lives with a brother (Quentin) who constantly disobeys Grace, Libby has not been influenced by his behavior and has remained what Grace calls "a good girl."

See also: Grace Kelly.

Lila Garreau *see* **Laurette Barber**

688. Lila Pembroke, *Charles in Charge*, CBS, 1984–1985. Played by April Lerman.

Lila Beth Pembroke is a teenage girl who dots her i's with hearts. She is the daughter of Jill and Stan Pembroke and lives at 10 Barrington Court in New Brunswick, New Jersey. She has two brothers, Douglas and Jason, and is cared for by Charles, their live-in babysitter.

Lila first attended Lincoln Elementary School then Northside High School. She reads *Co-Ed* magazine and is a member of the Circle of Friends

Club. Lila is eager to grow up. She loves to wear makeup and high heels and can't wait to develop a bust line. She is very sweet and causes little trouble for Charles (her parents are rarely home; her mother is a theater critic for the New Jersey *Register*; her father is vice president of an unnamed company). When a problem does arise (even female ones) Charles does his best to resolve them by telling stories about his youth. Lila has a never-seen feline (Putty Cat) and enjoys Kellogg's Corn Flakes for breakfast.

See also: Buddy Lembeck, Charles, Jamie Powell, Sarah Powell.

Lilith Sternin *see* **Frasier Crane**

689. Lily Finnerty, *Grounded for Life*, Fox, 2001–2002; WB, 2003–2005. Played by Lynsey Bartilson.

Lillian Finnerty lives at 856 Winslow Place on Staten Island in New York. She is the 14-year-old daughter of Claudia and Sean Finnerty and attends St. Finian's High School. Lily, as she is called, wears her plaid school skirts much too short, shows cleavage and is a cheerleader. She is also a member of the Dance Squad and the science club, the Science Nauts.

Lily treasures her privacy; the sign on her bedroom door reads, "Stop. Keep Out. Trespassers Will Be Shot." Lily reads *Tres Chic* magazine and has a fake I.D. card under the name Lillian Winterhaven. She has a tattoo on her lower back of a golden sprite and uses the computer screen name Lily Fin.

Lily believes her father "lives to humiliate me." She is jealous of her mother flaunting her sexuality because she believes nobody notices her. As a little girl Lily put a cigarette in her mouth and pretended to smoke, copying what she saw her parents do (this caused Claudia and Sean to quit. Lilly also saw her mother flaunt her breasts. She copied this when she got older but Claudia has not stopped doing it). At the age of 13 Lily had the nickname "Freckle Monster." She loves the soundtrack to the movie *Grease* and her favorite hangout is Mocha Joe's. Fiddle Faddle and Fruit Rings cereal (which she eats dry from the box) are Lily's favorite snacks. Lily's sexuality became apparent in the tenth grade when she performed a very racy version of the song "Big Spender" in a school play. Lily's first job was sweeping up in a butcher shop.

See also: Claudia and Sean Finnerty.

690. Lily Munster, *The Munsters*, CBS, 1964–1966. Played by Yvonne DeCarlo.

Lily Munster is the daughter of Count Vladimir Dracula and the wife of Herman Munster, a gravedigger for the Gateman, Goodbury and Graves Funeral Parlor. They are the parents of a werewolf son (Edward Wolfgang) and live at 1313 Mockingbird Lane in the town of Mockingbird Heights.

Lily is a hauntingly beautiful vampire and was born in Transylvania in 1660 (she is 304 years old). She met Herman in the early 1860s and they married in 1865. They were forced to leave Transylvania when angry villagers drove them out of town with torches and threatened to burn them at the stake. Lily is a proficient housekeeper and assures that their home is always nice and gloomy (she untidies rooms and applies dirt and cobwebs). Lily is an excellent cook, caring mother and devoted to Herman no matter how many dumb things he does. She and Herman enjoy bat milk yogurt and Bundles for Transylvania is Lily's favorite charity. She calls Herman (who resembles Frankenstein's Monster) "Poopsie." Lily's cleavage revealing dress is made from coffin lining (which Herman gets for her at his job).

In the 1988–91 syndicated series update, *The Munsters Today*, Lee Meriwether played the role of Lily. Lily was now 324 years old (born in 1654) and married Herman 299 years ago (in 1689). Before marrying, Lily worked as a singer at Club Dead in Transylvania. She won the beauty pageant title "Miss Transylvania of 1655" and the Silver Shroud Award for fashion design. Her normal body temperature is 25.8 degrees and "Transylvania the Beautiful" is her favorite song. Lily is called "Lilikins" by Herman and gives birth within 24 hours of becoming pregnant (a tradition with vampires in her family).

See also: Eddie Munster, Grandpa, Herman Munster, Marilyn Munster.

691. Lily Rush, *Cold Case*, CBS, 2003 (current). Played by Kathryn Morris.

Lily Rush is a young woman fascinated by unusual crimes — crimes that are labeled "Cold Case" and have never been solved. Lily is detective with the Homicide Bureau of the Philadelphia Police Department who investigates long unsolved cases based on new evidence that emerges.

Lily was born in Philadelphia and grew up on Kensington Avenue. In her youth it was a respectable area where a child could grow up in tranquil surroundings. "Today," she says, "it is an area infested with hookers and drug dealers." Lily was fascinated by the crime shows on TV and it is that exposure that led her to becoming a police officer. She believes cold cases are more important "because they have been waiting longer." She also prefers these cases to current crimes "because I don't like bastards getting away with murder." Lily is an optimistic when it comes to solving cold cases. She feels the new evidence, coupled with the cold case file, holds the answers to a crime; it is that enthusiasm that drives her and eventually allows her to close the file on a previously unsolved crime.

When Lily feels there is a new direction it means there is hope in solving a cold case — "People shouldn't be forgotten; they mater. They should see justice too." Lily is a vegetarian and Scotch and soda is her favorite drink. She despises people who believe that because she is a woman she became a cop "because of a bad education and limited talent." Lily is highly educated, very talented and never gets praise, as a cold case appears to be a non-newsworthy event. Lily is a very beautiful woman but her private life is just that, private. She enjoys evenings at home, an occasional date, but reveals little else about herself.

Lindsay Funke *see* **Michael Bluth**

692. Lindsay Wallace, *2000 Malibu Road*, CBS, 1992. Played by Drew Barrymore.

This entry also contains information on Joy Wallace (Tuesday Knight), Lindsay's sister. Lindsay Wallace is a stunningly beautiful but relatively unknown actress who lives at 2000 Malibu Road in Malibu Beach, California. She shares the house with her sister (Joy), a high priced call girl (Jade O'Keefe) and a lawyer (Perry Quinn).

Lindsay is an aspiring actress who appears to have little confidence in her abilities. She is well endowed and accentuates her breasts in low cut blouses. She is managed by her sister and Joy believes the sexier Lindsay is the better her chances of getting work. While Lindsay is gorgeous she believes "there are thousands of girls who are a lot prettier and a lot bustier than I am."

Lindsay is very sweet and very trusting (she is called "Honey Bunny" by Joy). She works under the professional name of Lindsay Rule. Lindsay is also afraid to take a chance on love (her high school sweetheart stood her up at the altar). She now fears giving of herself only to be hurt again. Lindsay currently plays the younger daughter on the mythical DBS network series *The Jessica Rolley Show*.

Joy is Lindsay's direct opposite. She is deceitful and devious. She has a gift for telling pathetic stories about herself or Lindsay and having people believe her to get what she wants. Joy also believes in psychic powers, tarot cards and Ouija

boards. She is very nosey and pries into everyone's business (information she uses to blackmail people and help Lindsay). Her aim is to make Lindsay the biggest name in show business.

See also: Jade O'Keefe.

693. Ling Woo, *Ally McBeal*, Fox, 1997–2002. Played by Lucy Liu.

Ling Woo is a strikingly beautiful woman with many talents. She was first introduced as the manager of a steel factory who sought help on a legal matter from the Boston-based firm of Cage and Fish. Although Ling is a shrewd lawyer herself, she preferred to have her legal matters resolved by someone else "because practice causes wrinkles." Ling is noted for suing anyone who crosses her and found it more profitable to make money through her various businesses (in one business, for example, she was said to make between $80,000 and $90,000 a year by running an escort service that would supply beautiful girls as dates for high school boys). Ling doesn't mind being a defendant or plaintiff "but being a plaintiff gives me a martyr glow." Shortly after her introduction Ling became a lawyer with Cage and Fish for the excitement it offers (wrinkles don't seem to matter anymore). Ling designs clothes in her spare time. She is considered to be an ice princess by people who know her. Ling is also a very loving woman but her cold approach to business makes it very difficult for her to express her tender side.

Ling liked men, but she also liked women, especially co-worker Ally McBeal. It is after a dinner date that the two become curious about being tender with a woman and share two passionate kisses (they remain friends but not lovers). Ling's main talent at Cage and Fish is using her gift of "magnetism" (to bring people into court who would otherwise go unnoticed).

See also: Ally McBeal, Elaine Vassal, John Cage.

Lisa Douglas *see* **Oliver and Lisa Douglas**

694. Lisa Simpson, *The Simpsons*, Fox, 1990 (current). Voiced by Yeardley Smith.

Lisa Simpson is the eight-year-old daughter of Homer and Marge Simpson, a married couple who live at 742 Evergreen Terrace in the town of Springfield. She has an older brother (Bart) and a younger sister (Maggie).

Lisa has an I.Q. of 159 and is in the second grade at Springfield Elementary School. She is precociously intelligent and is a budding saxophone player (the street musician, Bleeding Gums Murphy, is her inspiration). *The Little Mermaid* is Lisa's favorite movie; *Casper the Friendly Ghost* is her favorite comic book; and *The Itchy and Scratchy Show* (a violent cartoon) is her favorite TV program. Lisa reads *Teen Screen*, *Teen Dream* and *Teen Steam* magazines. She had four pet cats (Snowball I, Snowball II, Snowball III and Coltrane) and wears a size 4B shoe. "The Broken Neck Blues" is her favorite song and she and Bart enjoy eating at Krusty Burger. Homer wanted to name Lisa "Bartzina" and her first word as a baby was Bart.

See also: Bart Simpson, Homer Simpson, Marge Simpson.

695. Lisa Turtle, *Saved by the Bell*, NBC, 1989–1993. Played by Lark Voorhies.

Lisa Marie Turtle is a student at Bayside High School in Palisades, California. She was born in Palisades and is the daughter of Henry and Judy Turtle, two wealthy and respected doctors.

Lisa is 14 years old and says, "I'm beautiful, charming and always in fashion." She prides herself on her ability to always be perfect and has an uncanny knack for being able to guess the contents of a gift before opening it. Her one true passion is shopping at the Palisades Mall ("Lisa is my name, shopping is my game. If it's sold, I can find it").

Lisa is friends with Kelly, Jesse, Slater and Screech and hangs out with them at the Max (a diner). Lisa loves to gossip and eavesdrops whenever she can. Her natural sense of snoop earned her a job as "The Galloping Gossip" on the school's radio station, Tiger Radio. Lisa's beauty also earned her a place in The Miss Bayside Beauty Pageant (where she played the violin) and as Miss October in The Girls of Bayside High Swimsuit Calendar (this led to her appearing in a photo layout in *Teen Fashion* magazine as "The It's Happening Now Girl"). Lisa was also a singer in a band first called Hot Sundae (then The Zack Attack and finally The Five Aces). Lisa scored 1140 on her SAT test and enrolled at the Fashion Institute after graduating.

See also: Jesse Spano, Kelly Kapowski, Screech Powers, Zack Morris.

696. Little Joe Cartwright, *Bonanza*, NBC, 1959–1973. Played by Michael Landon.

Joseph Francis Cartwright, called Little Joe, is the youngest son of Ben Cartwright, the owner of the Ponderosa Ranch in Virginia City, Nevada, and his third wife, Marie. Joe was born in 1857 and has two brothers, Adam and Hoss. Early in the series Joe claims he was called Little Joe "because Hoss is so big." He later says, "That's what

I get for being the youngest member of the family." The flashback episode, "Marie My Love," relates how Ben met Marie (Marie's husband, Jean Pierre, worked for Ben as a ranch hand. When Jean Pierre dies saving Ben's life, Ben travels to New Orleans to personally tell Marie. A relationship eventually develops and they marry. Marie, like Ben's previous wives [Elizabeth and Inger] dies shortly after Joe's birth when she is thrown from her horse). In the pilot episode Joe mentions his mother's name as Felicia and that Ben met her on a business trip.

Joe stood a quarter inch less than five feet, ten inches tall. He had jet-black hair and was as handsome as older brother Adam. He was also a ladies' man but quick-tempered and too fast to use his fists (which constantly got him into trouble). Joe was fond of animals, especially horses, and rode a Pinto named Cochise. Joe also liked to play practical jokes and sought to make money anyway he could, mostly through hair-brained schemes (for example, entering Hoss is a wrestling match, boxing match, pie eating-contest).

In the 1988 TV movie, *Bonanza: The Next Generation*, it is learned that Little Joe had married a woman named Annabelle and they had a son they named Benji (after Joe's father). During the Spanish American War Joe became a member of Teddy Roosevelt's Rough Riders. He was listed as missing in action in 1899 and was presumed killed.

See also: Adam Cartwright, Ben Cartwright, Hoss Cartwright.

697. Liu Tsong, *The Gallery of Madame Liu Tsong*, DuMont, 1951.

Liu Tsong is a beautiful Oriental woman whose name means "Frosted Willow." She is a good girl against bad men; "a combination of the daughter of Fu Manchu and the daughter of the Dragon" as she battles the enemies of the art world.

Liu was born in Los Angeles (Chinatown) and is the daughter of parents who operated a Chinese laundry. Liu worked after school and on weekends at the laundry ironing clothes and at an early age developed an appreciation for art. She learned all she could about art in school and carried that fascination with her into her adult life. She began her own business, The Gallery of Madame Liu Tsong in San Francisco and often has to become her own detective to solve the crimes associated with the art world (forgers and thieves who crave great works of art). Liu was not a superhero and she possessed no great powers (not even martial arts abilities). She appeared as a gentle, delicate flower, not someone who chases bad guys. Liu was very clever and shrewd and used her wits to bring criminals to justice. Liu spoke fluent Chinese but with an American accent and mentioned that Groucho Marx (of the Marx Brothers) was her favorite comedian. Anna May Wong became the first Oriental personality to star in an American TV series.

698. Liz and Bob Pitts, *The Pitts*, Fox, 2003. Played by Kellie Waymire, Dylan Baker.

Elizabeth and Robert Pitts, called Liz and Bob, believe "life is a bowl of cherries — but you can't have cherries without the pits." They are the parents of Faith (Lizzie Caplain) and Petey (David Henrie). The Pitts may look like a normal family but they are not because, as Faith believes, they are cursed with bad luck.

The Pitts live at 1313 Shadow Road in Nevada; 555-5555 is their phone number and their house is located across from a mountain with a giant boulder perched at the edge and about to fall. Liz is 34 years old and met Bob, also 34, at Statesville High School. Each was plagued by bouts of bad luck and they fell in love. They married after high school and combined their bad luck to live a life where what goes wrong is normal to them.

Bob and Liz are the owners of a store called Mail Boxes and Mail More. Their children have inherited their bad luck and have few friends because of the misfortune that hangs over their heads. They have a dog named Lucky.

Bob has been struck by lightning on several occasions and naturally fears thunderstorms. He is allergic to peanuts and shellfish. Liz, maiden name Wilson, claims to wear Jaclyn Smith original dresses. She is very pretty and has a nice figure; but when she attempts to look extra special, a sudden weight gain plagues her.

Faith, a student at Statesville High School, believes the family is cursed by demons, not bad luck. She believes boys are afraid of her because of all the crazy things that happen around her (books falling out of lockers, students tripping, water fountains over flowing, doors getting stuck). Faith has a car (plate 217 MJS) and a violin (which she believes is haunted) and no blood or ability to feel pain (when the hot water boiler in their home exploded it sent a pipe through Faith's head). She was embarrassed to attend school with a pipe as part of her head and joined Zeke's Freaky Show (where she became "Little Bo Pipe"). She was relieved of her burden when a stray concession dart hit the pipe and it popped out leaving Faith with a hole in her head but no brain damage and no visible blood. She earns money by babysitting.

Petey likes the thought of being cursed by bad luck. He is weird without the need for bad luck. He likes to taunt people (he goes to health clubs "to laugh at fat guys") and likes going to the kitchens of Korean restaurants "to look for cat parts."

699. Lizzie McGuire, *Lizzie McGuire*, Disney, 2001–2004. Played by Hilary Duff.

Elizabeth Brooke McGuire, better known as Lizzie, is the 13-year-old daughter of Sam and Jo McGuire, a happily married couple who live at 804 Linwood Drive in an unspecified city. Lizzie is very pretty and is considered "a good girl prototype" by her friends for all the good deeds she does. Lizzie always does what is right. She believes the only reason her parent's live with her is to make her life miserable. Lizzie oversleeps, trips over things, keeps her room a mess, snores, leaves hair on her brush, sleeps with the windows closed, the door open and requires ocean wave sounds to get a good night's sleep. She hates alarm clocks ("they wake me up") and oven roasted chicken is her favorite dinner. She is the only one in the house who can work the picture-in-picture feature of the TV set (she watches MTV and cartoons at the same time).

Lizzie first attended Eldridge Elementary School then Bayridge High School. She is a B-plus student and her favorite class is lunch. She never misses it. Lizzie wrote an entertainment column for the school newspaper at Eldridge and when she ran for class president (Bayridge) she did so with the slogan "Voice of the People — McGuire's on Fire." Lizzie is on the school dance committee and holds the record in the Presidential Fitness Challenge (hanging from an iron bar). Lizzie danced in a music video for teenage heartthrob Aaron Carter and made a music video with her friends Miranda and Gordo called "Detention." Lizzie's most embarrassing moment occurred in a math class. She dropped the chalk while at the blackboard, bent over to pick it up and ripped her pants. Her face turned red because she was wearing her Wednesday panties on a Tuesday.

Lizzie's home phone number is 555-0101. A smoothie is her afternoon pickup and she bowls on a team called Sunrise Fireballs. She would like a job babysitting "but I don't baby sit — I get baby sat." Lizzie worked briefly as a busgirl at the Digital Bean, her favorite hangout. Lizzie wears a size 32A Young Misses Bar (which she got at age 13) and has a plush rabbit named Mr. Snuggles.

See also: Matt McGuire.

700. L.K. McGuire, *Easy Street*, NBC, 1986–1987. Played by Loni Anderson.

Linda Kaye McGuire, better known as L.K., is a girl who lives on easy street. She is a gorgeous ex–Las Vegas blackjack dealer who inherited a mansion and the easy life following the accidental death of her husband, Ned, in a plane crash.

L.K. is a stunning blonde who measures 36-24-36. She was born in California and is the daughter of George and Alma Stevenson. George and Alma were not rich and L.K. enjoyed a comfortable life growing up. She knew at an early age that she was beautiful and used her looks to get what she wanted from people. This became so natural to her that as she grew she found that manipulating people was almost as much fun as earning money.

L.K. began her work career as a waitress but that was too much like work. She befriended a girl whose ambition was to become Las Vegas stage dancer and quit her job to follow her. L.K.'s stunning looks got her a spot as dancer on the Vegas stage but she apparently had a knack for cards. When casino owner Ned McGuire spotted L.K. in the chorus he felt her assets were being wasted and took a personal interest in her. He taught her how to deal cards and made her a blackjack dealer (the low-cut blouses she wore while dealing also added greatly to the popularity of her table). Ned also fell in love with her. They married and moved to a mansion at 4163 Hillcrest Drive in Beverly Hills.

L.K. aspires to the good life. She loves parties and wears stunning bosom-revealing dresses and blouses. L.K. may be rich but she never forgot her roots. She is a generous person and will help people genuinely in need of assistance. L.K. runs the McGuire Empire and knows what it means to be poor. It's a life she never wants to see again.

701. Loco Jones, *How to Marry a Millionaire*, Syn., 1958–1960. Played by Barbara Eden.

Rita Marlene Gloria Claudette Jones, nicknamed Loco, is a gorgeous fashion model seeking only one thing — a millionaire husband. She was born in North Platte, Nebraska, on February 25. She is a graduate of North Platte High School (where she was voted "The One Most Likely to Go Further with Less Than Anyone"). Loco is blonde, a bit naïve and very sweet and trusting. She is also nearsighted and needs to wear glasses but feels men will not find her attractive if she does. The resulting chaos costs her perspective husbands.

A modeling job brought Loco to New York. She was renting a small apartment on Amsterdam Avenue when she met Greta Hanson and Mike McCall, two girls with a scheme — pool their resources, rent a swanky penthouse and sell themselves as wealthy girls seeking rich husbands. Loco became a part of their plan and now lives on Park Avenue in Penthouse G of the Tower Apartment House. She is also broke all the time as pretending to be rich is more costly than she expected.

Loco works for the Travis Modeling Agency (later the Talbot Agency) and is called "a fabulous blonde with an hourglass figure." She has her photos taken at Marachi's Studio and reads *Fashion Preview* magazine. Although Loco wears tight dresses with low necklines and low cut backs, she worries about short skirts that show too much leg (Greta assures her it is okay "because a man can't appreciate the flower of womanhood unless he can see the stems"). Loco has an encyclopedic knowledge of comic strips and keeps abreast of all the comic happenings by reading *Super Comics* magazine. Loco was voted "Queen of the Madison Square Garden Rodeo" in 1958 and has a habit of falling for "strays" (men who are anything but rich). She enjoys feeding the pigeons in Central Park.

See also: Greta Hanson, Gwen Kirby, Mike McCall.

702. Lois and Hal Wilkerson, *Malcolm in the Middle*, Fox, 2000 (current). Played by Jane Kaczmarek, Bryan Cranston.

This entry also contains information on Francis, Malcolm, Reese and Dewey, their mischievous children.

Lois and Hal. Lois and Hal are a married couple who truly love each other but often wonder how their genes produced such troublesome children (their favorite song is "Tears of a Clown"). They have been voted "The Most Hated Family in the Neighborhood" and live in an unspecified town at 123341 Maple Road. Lois and Hal's approach to parenting is also their approach to marriage: "Love each other, love your kids and don't sweat the small stuff." They are not easily impressed and care very little about status. Hal originally worked as a systems supervisor at a company called G.N. Industries ("Making the World Safe with Our Products" and "We've Got the Solution if You've Got the Problem"). He is later laid off when the company CEO uses funds to buy his wife a recording studio. Hal later works at various jobs, including salesman at a store called U Buy It. He is rather lenient when it comes to punishing the kids and confessed that certain cartoon characters frighten him. Hal is also addicted to roller-skating and calls it "The

Brotherhood of the Wheel." When he was 15, Hal had such a crush on Farrah Fawcett that he bought her an engagement ring hoping she would marry him. In college Hal was "The Voice of the Little Man" on an illegal pirate radio station. A vodka martini is his favorite drink.

Lois was born in Manitoba, Canada, and is the daughter of Ida and Victor. She has asymmetrical shoulders that throw the third and fourth vertebrae of her back out of alignment when she gets upset. Lois is totally stressed out by the kids. She cares little about modesty (she walks around the house in her bra and sometimes without her bra) and is very strict when it comes to disciplining the children, especially Reese (the most troublesome). Sleep is the only escape Lois has from the responsibilities of motherhood.

Lois is also abrupt, short tempered and rude (in high school she was called "The Mouth" for taking her frustrations out on other people). She feels she always has to be right even if she is wrong. She is so overpowering that Hal is terrified of her (rather than cause an argument he always agrees with her).

Lois's dream family is having obedient girls (in a dream sequence, she is seen as the mother of three obedient daughters—Mallory, Renee and Daisy). She works as a salesgirl at a department store called Lucky Aide (where she has the nickname "Beans"). Lois once thought of becoming a blackjack dealer on an Indian reservation "but stubby thumbs stopped me." On her birthday Lois gives each of the children $10 to buy her a present. She enjoys milk shakes and hopes to one day give birth to a girl. This failed to happen when she gave birth to another boy (Jamie) in 2003.

Malcolm (Frankie Muniz). Malcolm is the genius of the family. He has an I.Q. of 165 and excels in math (he is part of the gifted program at school). He is the only one who is aware of a viewing audience and speaks directly to them. Malcolm's first job was as a babysitter and he later worked with his mother at Lucky Aide (store 167). Malcolm attends North High School and volunteers at Memorial Hospital three times a week.

Francis (Christopher Kennedy Masterson). Francis is the oldest of the children. His mischievous ways have forced his parents to send him to the Marlin Military Academy for rehabilitation. He is now married to Piami (Emy Coligado) and held several jobs after Marlin: waiter in an Alaskan diner (where he met Piami), logger at a logging camp (where he was a member of the Logs Ice Hockey Team) and foreman of the Grotto Ranch. As a kid Francis had a pet snake named

Otis and he is the only one of the kids to beat his mother at what he calls "Lois's Punchout Tactics" (her way of getting the kids to tell who did something bad by threatening them). Despite his bad reputation, Malcolm, Reese and Dewey look up to Francis as their hero, the one they can turn to for help in dealing with their parents.

Reese (Justin Berfield). Reese is following in Francis's footsteps and solves all his problems by fighting. He attends North High School and is a D student, but uses the right shade of ink his teacher uses to change grades on his report card. He is also quite naïve and is easily taken advantage of. Reese has a "shiny box" under his bed "for shiny things I find." He likes clouds for "the sky kittens" he sees and has what he calls "a wishing hole" (a tree on Jefferson Street with a hole in it that he makes wishes upon). Reese's only talent appears to be gourmet cooking. He believes he is a ladies' man (although he never seems to be able to find a date) and to impress girls he joined the Wildcats cheerleading team at school.

Dewey (Erik Per Sullivan). Dewey is the most conniving of the children (he uses what he calls "turning on the cute" to get things from people). He attends Grace Elementary School and has a plush teddy bear (Domingo). He also has a pet fly (Tony), an adopted dog he found (Marshmallow) and a grossly overweight rabbit (Gordo). Dewey cuts school to perform as Le Great El Foldo (squeezes himself into a box for money). He never had piano lessons but can play like an expert. He believes he can understand what dogs are saying and when he becomes upset he hides under the house.

703. Lois Adams, *It's a Living,* ABC, 1980–1981. Played by Susan Sullivan.

Lois Adams is a waitress at Above the Top, a 13th floor Los Angeles restaurant that features "Sky High Dining." Lois is the sophisticated, older waitress. She is in her mid-thirties, very attractive and the one the other waitresses look to for guidance when they have a problem. Lois lives at 8713 Mercer Street in Los Angeles and is married to the never seen Bill. She is also the mother of Amy and Joey and is struggling to make ends meet (Bill is a salesman).

Lois was born in Minnesota and worked as a secretary before marrying. She loves art and reading and rejoined the work force when a night position opened up at the restaurant. Lois is a loving and caring mother and all her energies are devoted to providing for her family. Lois's childhood was not easy as her parents had to sacrifice to give her things. She doesn't want it to be the same way for her children. Lois has her share of problems and tries to resolve them by herself. It is not obvious when something bothers Lois (she is good at hiding it) but when it is noticed she finds help from fellow waitress Cassie Cranston.

See also: Amy Tompkins, Cassie Cranston, Dot Higgins, Ginger St. James, Jan Hoffmeyer, Sonny Mann.

704. Lois Lane, *The Adventures of Superman,* Syn., 1953–1957. Played by Phyllis Coates, Noel Neill.

Lois Lane is a gutsy reporter for the *Daily Planet,* a crusading newspaper in Metropolis. Lois was born in the small town of Clifton-by-the-Sea. She is the daughter of Sam and Ellen Lane and now lives in Apartment 6A of an unidentified building; she drives a car with the license plate ZN 18683. Lois often works with cub reporter Jimmy Olsen and is very stubborn. Once she has her mind set on something, it is impossible to change. She loves to investigate stories associated with crime and takes uncalculated risks to follow a lead — leads that often become perilous and a risk to her life. Her guardian angel, Superman, always arrives in the nick of time to save her.

Lois has an attraction for danger and wants the headline-making stories. She has a love-hate relationship with Clark Kent, a reporter at the *Planet* who is also her rival for stories. Clark appears to be mild-mannered and Lois suspects he is really Superman but can't prove it. Her suspicions are aroused when she is with Clark and Clark suddenly makes an excuse to be someplace else when something happens. Superman suddenly appears and Lois is trying to let it all make sense. Clark appears to be a coward and has led Lois to believe it is the reason why he disappears when they encounter a troublesome situation.

See also: Clark Kent.

705. Lorelai Gilmore, *Gilmore Girls,* WB, 2000 (current). Played by Lauren Graham.

Lorelai Victoria Gilmore is a 32-year-old single mother who lives with her 16-year-old daughter, Rory, in Stars Hollow, Connecticut. Lorelai is the daughter of Richard and Emily Gilmore and was born in Hartford, Connecticut, in 1968. At the age of four she had a pet rabbit named Murray. She believes that wonderful things happen when it snows (her first kiss, Rory's birth). When it does snow she says, "Hey, that's my present" and recalls one night when she was five years old and bedridden for a week with a bad ear infection. One night she wished something wonderful would happen. When she awoke the next morn-

ing it had snowed and everything was better. She now claims she can predict when it is going to snow "by the smell in the air." Lorelai's summers were spent at camps. She was expelled from one camp for refusing to call a counselor Peaches (the counselors took names after summer fruits) and from another (Chatoquoy) for freeing the horses. While she liked it as a kid, Lorelai now dislikes her mother's concoction of mashed banana on toast (which she was given when she was sick). Lorelai also worked for one summer as a counselor at the Dean Forrester Hills Inn.

Life changed for Lorelai when she turned 16. She had an affair with her high school boyfriend (Chris Hayden) and became pregnant. Lorelai's parents disapproved but Lorelai stood her ground. She refused to marry Chris, feeling they were too young and the marriage would not work. Lorelai's inability to get along with her parents, especially her controlling mother, forced her to leave home about a year after Rory was born. Lorelai and Rory found refuge at the Independence Inn in Stars Hollow. Here, the inn's owner, a friend of Emily, hired Lorelai as a maid and gave her a place to live. Rory grew up in Stars Hollow and Lorelai worked her way up to managing the inn. She also made peace with her parents (who live in Hartford).

Watching someone else work makes Lorelai feel happy. She can take things that are unattractive and make them pretty (for example, dressing Rory's liquid paper bottle in a dress. "She's not crazy," says Rory, "she just sounds like it"). Daisies are Lorelai's favorite flower; "Shadow Dance" is her favorite song; and the all-girl singing group the Bangles, were her favorites in high school. Lorelai uses Dream Fresh laundry detergent and carries the following flavors of lip gloss with her at all times: chocolate, vanilla, strawberry and marshmallow. She wears a size nine shoe and drives a jeep with the license plate 937 G5R. Luke's Diner is her favorite eatery (Lorelai rarely cooks. When she does, she serves meals on her good china — a set of "Charlie's Angels" dinner plates). Lorelai orders Chinese take out food from Al's Pancake World and does grocery shopping at Doose's Market.

Lorelai is a member of the Stars Hollow Video Club (card number 6247; *Willy Wonka and the Chocolate Factory* is her favorite movie). She is a coffee junkie and is obsessed with sweaters and breast size (she claims "an evil, crazed spirit obsessed with bra size takes over my body and makes me go nuts"; she has had arguments with Rory over whose breasts are bigger). Lorelai is also obsessed with mail order catalogues — the more she gets the happier she is (she has made up the names Squeegee Buckingham and Tootie Clothespin to get even more). When Lorelai went fishing for the first time she caught a large carp. She placed it in her bathtub and called it Jayne Mansfield. In the 2003 Stars Hollow Festival of Living Pictures (people dress up as famous paintings) Lorelai was the Renoir Girl.

Lorelai's dream is have her own inn. When the Independence Inn closes after a fire, Lorelai and her friend, Sookie, begin the Independence Catering Company. Later they pool their resources and buy (and renovate) the abandoned Dragon Fly Inn (their first reservation was for May 8, 2004).

See also: Paris Geller, Richard and Emily Gilmore, Rory Gilmore.

706. Lori Harden, *Movie Stars*, WB, 1999–2000. Played by Marnette Patterson.

This entry also contains information on Apache (Zack Hopkins) and Moonglow (Rachel David), Lori's siblings. They are the children of movie stars Reese Harden and Jacey Wyatt and live in Malibu Beach, California.

Lori is Reese's daughter from a previous marriage. She came to live with her father "when things got too hot in Ohio. You burn down one Dairy Queen and they never forget." Lori first attended Buchanan Prep School ("Geek Prep," as she called it) then the "cool" Crosswinds High School. Lori is 17 and gorgeous. She has a love-hate relationship with Jacey (she also borrows much of Jacey's wardrobe—"which look great on Jacey but fabulous on me").

Lori has aspirations to become a star although her only acting credit since arriving in Los Angeles has been in a music video called "The Last Goodbye." For reasons that are not explained, Lori's last name became Lansford in 2000 (even though Reese Harden is her father).

Moonglow trades headshots of Jacey to her friends for Pokemon cards. She and her brother, Apache, attend Buchanan Prep. Apache hates his name and Reese explains: "that I was into the American Indian movement and my spiritual guide said for me to name you after a famous Indian." Moonglow seems to be content with her name. Apache walks the dogs of celebrities to earn extra money. Moonglow has a pet hamster (Popeye) and a turtle (Sammy). She played Gretel in her first grade production of "Hansel and Gretel." Apache and Moonglow eat Fruit Pebbles cereal for breakfast.

See also: Jacey Wyatt, Reese Harden, Todd Harden.

707. Lou Frischetti, *The Great Defender*, Fox, 1995. Played by Michael Rispoli.

Lou Frischetti is a Boston-based lawyer who will use every trick in the book to defend his clients whether they are accused of petty theft or murder.

Lou was born in Boston and is the son of Pearl and Louis, Sr. Lou is a Catholic and always showed an interest in helping people. He was a poor student at school and becoming a lawyer seemed impossible — until he enrolled in the East Podoc School of Law and acquired his degree. He figured television was the best way to acquire clients and began running a series of ads called "The Great Defender" ("Do you need a lawyer? Call me, Lou Frischetti. Divorce. Accident. Criminal. Call me at 1-800-55-Legal").

Lou is a fast talker and usually represents the clients nobody else wants — from hookers to bookies. Lou believes in justice for all, is a bit unethical and knows what is going on — in the courtroom, the police precincts and on the streets. He sometimes invents his own theories about the law and promises his clients "If there is trouble, I'll be there on the double." Lou later works at the Beacon Hill law firm of Osborne, Merritt and De-Witt when its senior partner, Jason DeWitt (Richard Kiley) feels Lou is the man he needs to get his firm out of a rut. Lou lives at 462 Marlon Road.

See also: Frankie Colletti (Lou's investigator).

708. Lou Grant, *The Mary Tyler Moore Show*, CBS, 1970–1977. Played by Edward Asner.

Louis Grant, called Lou, is first the producer then executive producer of *The Six O'clock News* on WJM-TV, Channel 6 in Minneapolis, Minnesota. Lou has been a distinguished newsman all his life but he knows that what he has now is the best he can hope to achieve at this point in his life. His program is always at the bottom of the ratings and he knows it will never crack the top ten.

Lou is grouchy, bossy and easily exasperated. He is divorced (from Edie) and finds solace in only one thing — a drink. He frequents the Happy Hour Bar but also has a bottle of liquor in the bottom drawer of his desk. There is a picture of Lou dressed in his college football uniform on his office wall. When situations become stressful he retreats to his office and closes the door behind him. John Wayne is his favorite actor. Edward Asner revised his character on *Lou Grant* (CBS, 1977–1982) as the city editor of the Los Angeles *Tribune*, the second largest paper in the city.

See also: Mary Richards, Rhoda Morganstern, Ted Baxter.

709. Louie DePalma, *Taxi*, ABC, 1978–1982; NBC, 1982–1983. Played by Danny DeVito.

"If God had a reason for creating snakes, lice and vermin he had a reason for creating Louie," say people about Louie DePalma, the nasty, dishonest dispatcher for the Sunshine Cab Company in New York City.

Louie's office in the cab company garage is called "The Cage" and he considers it "My window on the world" (as he spies on the cabbies from it). Louie considers all his drivers losers, people who will never amount to anything. Louie lives for his job and has been working there for 15 years—first as a driver then as the dispatcher (he began driving in 1963 and claims his first fare was actor Errol Flynn). When it comes to his cabbies only three things make him happy: "Keep bookings high, call 24 hours in advance if you can't work, and never but never say the word *accident*." Beside his worship of money, Louie is lecherous and mean. He considers himself a ladies' man and will pursue any woman he thinks is worthy of him. He had a brief romance with Zina Sherman (Rhea Perlman), the candy machine-vending lady.

The difference between Louie and other people is two million years of evolution. When he needs something from one of his drivers he announces "Who wants a good cab today?" He gives retiring cabbies a speech and a calendar featuring the highways of America. "When one sees repulsive things floating around in the water one should think of Louie. He'd like that."

See also: Alex Reiger, Elaine Nardo, Jim Ignatowski, Latka Gravas.

710. Louise Mercer, *Dear John*, NBC, 1988–1992. Played by Jane Carr.

Louise Mercer is a British woman who conducts the 1-2-1 Club, a New York City organization for divorced, widowed, lonely and separated people who need help in adjusting to the single life.

Louise was born in Cheshire, England, and had a strict upbringing by aristocratic parents. She attempts to implement that upbringing on the people she supervises as head of the club. Louise now lives in Manhattan in Apartment 5G.

Louise was married but became deeply depressed after her divorce and had to spend time at Meadowbrook, a mental hospital. She is the mother of the never seen but always talked about Nigel. She claims to be friends with the Queen of England. Before leaving England, Louise entered a beauty pageant and was crowned "Miss Cheshire" (she was actually the first runner up but when the winner's bathing suit strap broke and

exposed her breasts she ran off stage and disqualified herself). Louise struggles to take an interest in everybody's problems but often becomes depressed when she realizes she also has problems.

See also: John Lacey, Kate McCarron, Kirk Morris, Mary Beth Sutton.

711. Lovita Jenkins, *The Steve Harvey Show*, WB, 1996–2002. Played by Terri J. Vaughn.

Lovita Alizay Jenkins is the administrative assistant to Regina Grier, the principal of Booker T. Washington High School in Chicago. Lovita is a very sweet yet complex girl who dated (and later married) Cedric Robinson, the school's athletic coach. Lovita calls Regina "Boss Lady" and has a dream for her and Cedric to move to Florida to open a store called Ceddie and Lovita's House of Honda Parts and Hair (Lovita, who calls Cedric "Ceddie," is a talented hair stylist).

Lovita buys her cosmetics from Rite Aid and believes in séances, voodoo and her ability to contact spirits. Lovita is unable to cook "because my mother never taught me." Her mother used the kitchen for a beauty shop. When Lovita attempted to cook her first meal she fried catfish in Afro-Sheen and nearly killed her father. Believing that she could be a playwright, Lovita took a course at the Intercity Arts Center and wrote a play called "Madame Sister President" (about a girl from the ghetto who goes from fashion designer to President of the U.S.). Lovita learned her hair styling ability at Miss Claudine's School of Style and Hair Weaving in her hometown of Alabama.

See also: Cedric Robinson, Regina Grier, Steve Hightower.

712. Lucy and Ricky Ricardo, *I Love Lucy*, CBS, 1951–1957. Played by Lucille Ball, Desi Arnaz.

Lucille Esmerelda McGillicuddy and Ricky Ricardo Alberto Fernando Acha (also known as Alberto Ricardo, IV) met on a blind date in New York City in 1941 (the date was arranged by Lucy's friend Marian Strong; another episode claims Lucy met Ricky while on a vacation in Havana, Cuba). Ricky proposed to Lucy at the Byrum River Beagle Club in Connecticut on Christmas Eve (their song was Jingle Bells as it was the only song Ricky knew the words to in English). They married shortly after and set up housekeeping in Apartment 3B (later 3D) at 623 East 68th Street in Manhattan (they moved into the converted brownstone on August 6, 1948 and pay $125 a month in rent; Murray Hill 5-9975; later Murray Hill 5-9099 is their phone number; Fred and Ethel Mertz are their landlords). They later become the parents of a son (Ricky Ricardo, Jr., better known as Little Ricky).

Lucy, as Lucille is called, was born in Jamestown, New York, on August 6, 1921 (another episode claims she was born in West Jamestown in May of 1921 and Taurus is her astrological sign). Lucy has been juggling her age for so long "that I kinda lost track of how old I am." In grade school Lucy was called "Bird Legs" and played Juliet in her Jamestown High School production of *Romeo and Juliet* (a later episode claims she attended Celeron High School). Lucy also played the saxophone in the school band ("Glow Worm was the only song she ever learned to play). She also studied ballet for four years.

Lucy gets the hiccups when she cries ("It's happened since I was a little girl") and is famous for her "spider noise" ("Eeeuuuuu") when something doesn't go her way. She is a member of the Wednesday Afternoon Fine Arts League and appeared on the TV game show *Females Are Fabulous* ("Any woman is idiotic enough to win a prize"). Lucy loves to read murder-mystery novels and has a hard time managing the family budget. She did a TV commercial for Vitameatavegamin on *Your Saturday Night Variety Show* (the vitamin product contained meat, vegetables, minerals and 23 percent alcohol; Lucy became intoxicated during rehearsal). She also tried to market her Aunt Martha's recipe for salad dressing as Aunt Martha's Old-fashioned Salad Dressing.

Lucy yearns to be in show business but Ricky will not allow it (he feels her place is in the home). When Lucy's antics upset Ricky, he takes her over his knee and spanks her. Ricky was born in Cuba and is a graduate of Havana University. He is a drummer and works with his band at the Tropicana Club in Manhattan. In 1956 Ricky bought controlling interest in the club and renamed it The Babalu Club (after his favorite song. The club was also called The Ricky Ricardo Babalu Club). Ricky plays the conga drums and sings. He likes roast pig and Lucy claims she married Ricky in 1922 when she was 22 years old (1942) and weighed 110 pounds at the time (she now weighs 132 pounds).

Ricky and Lucy were interviewed on the TV program *Face to Face* and were hosts of a morning show called *Breakfast with Ricky and Lucy* (sponsored by Phipps Drug Store). They also did a TV benefit for the Heart Fund. Lucy wrote an article about Ricky for *Photoplay* magazine called "What It Is Really Like to Be Married to Ricky Ricardo."

Ricky made a TV pilot for an unrealized series called *Tropical Rhythms* and traveled to Hollywood to star in a movie called *Don Juan*. He is also a member of the Recreation Club and appeared with their friends Fred and Ethel Mertz, on the TV game show *Be a Good Neighbor*. Ricky and Lucy were also the owners of a diner called A Little Bit of Cuba.

Little Ricky was born in 1953 and is learning to play the drums. He has the following pets: Fred (dog), Alice and Phil (parakeets), Tommy and Jimmy (turtles), Hopalong (frog), and Mildred and Charles (fish). He is a very good child (except for endless crying as an infant) and causes very few problems for his parents.

See also: Fred and Ethel Mertz.

713. Lucy Camden, *7th Heaven*, WB, 1996 (current). Played by Beverley Mitchell.

Lucille Camden, called Lucy, owns a professional tool belt and does minor repairs around her parent's home. She is the third-born child of Eric and Annie Camden, a Protestant minister and his wife. She also has six siblings (Matt, Mary, Simon, Ruthie and twins Sam and David) and lives in Glen Oak, California.

Lucy is very bright, sassy, emotional and carefree. Rocky road is her favorite flavor of ice cream and she receives an allowance of $5 a week (first season). As a kid she attended what she called Camp All By Myself (she was the only camper assigned her own bunk). Lucy is also an expert at fixing cars and first attended Walter Reed Jr. High School. She then attended Kennedy High School and is currently enrolled at Crawford College (where she is studying theology; she hopes to become a minister like her father). At Kennedy High Lucy was voted Homecoming Queen and used her carpentry skills as a volunteer for Habitat for Humanity (builds homes for deserving people).

Lucy became engaged to Kevin Kinkirk (George Stults) and married him in April of 2003. Kevin is a police officer and he and Lucy set up housekeeping in a converted room over her parent's garage.

See also: Eric and Annie Camden, Mary Camden, Matt Camden, Ruthie Camden, Simon Camden.

Luke Duke *see* **Daisy Duke**

714. Lucy Ewing, *Dallas*, CBS, 1978–1991. Played by Charlene Tilton.

Lucy Ewing was born in Texas in 1961 and is the daughter of Gary and Velene Ewing (Gary is the younger brother of the notorious J.R. Ewing, head of the Ewing Oil Empire). Lucy grew up on the Southfork Ranch in Braddock, Texas. She was a student at Southern Methodist University but dropped out after two years (1981) to become a Young Miss Dallas fashion model for Ward Publications. She spent the next year as a freelance model for the Blair Sullivan Agency. When jobs became scarce, she became a waitress at the Hot Biscuit in Fort Worth, Texas. She next became partners in a construction business and finally a patron of the arts.

Lucy appeared to be sweet and innocent. She was anything but. She was very promiscuous and had many meaningless affairs. Lucy appeared to date, marry and divorce only losers. She had an abortion, was kidnapped, raped and had a bout with drug addiction. But through it all, Lucy always managed to bounce back. She felt that what happened once couldn't happen again.

See also: Bobby Ewing, J.R. Ewing, Pamela Barnes, Sue Ellen Ewing.

715. Luigi Basco, *Life with Luigi*, CBS, 1952–1953. Played by J. Carrol Naish, Thomas Gomez.

Luigi Basco is an Italian immigrant who runs a small antique shop in Chicago's Little Italy. Luigi was born in Italy in the town of Cant Loma in 1910. He ran a small business in his hometown but possessed a dream to travel to America and begin a new life. His inspiration was his hero, America's first President, George Washington. Luigi possessed a bust of George Washington that was made in 1833. He became fascinated by it and learned all he could about his hero. He soon pictured America as a land where dreams could come true. In 1947 Luigi decided to fulfill that dream.

When the series begins Luigi has settled in Chicago's Little Italy and owns a store called Luigi Basco's Antiques at 21 Halstead Street (he lives in the back of the store and his phone number is Circle 2-0742). Luigi is a kind and gentle man who will give of himself to help others. He loves America and is hoping to become one of its citizens. He has an account at the Chase National Bank and pays $40 a month in rent. He wears a size 38 suit and attends night classes at the Halstead Street School (taking English and history as he prepares for his citizenship test). Luigi enjoys meals at Pasquale's Spaghetti Palace, a restaurant owned by a dear friend of Luigi's Mama Basco in Italy. Pasquale came to America 26 years ago (1921) and had arranged for Luigi's transportation. In April of 1953 (when Thomas Gomez took over the role), Luigi found he needed to make more money and gave up his antique business to work as a waiter for Pasquale (Alan Reed), a jovial, overweight man with one goal in his life—find a

husband for his terribly plump daughter Rosa (Jody Gilbert, Muriel Landers). His choice: Luigi. Luigi, however, is not interested in marriage and wants only to enjoy the wonders of America. Pasquale calls Luigi "Cabbage Puss" and "Banana Nose."

716. Luisa Delgado, *Strong Medicine*, Lifetime, 2000 (current). Played by Rosa Blasi.

Dr. Luisa Delgado, called "Lu," is co-founder (with Dr. Andy Campbell) of the Rittenhouse Women's Clinic in Philadelphia. She is a single mother (of Marc) and put herself through medical school (she originally founded the South Philly Women's Clinic, which went bankrupt). Luisa was born in South Philly and is determined to give back everything she can to the neighborhood in which she was raised—first by her mother, then her grandmother (her mother died of breast cancer when Luisa was 10 years old). She is still haunted by the death of her mother and says that Marc is the most important thing in her life.

The Ricki Lake Show is Luisa's favorite TV program and her greatest fear is losing touch with the people who live and work in her poor neighborhood. Luisa first held a job as a cocktail waitress and goes beyond the call of duty to help people who really need help, not a fast diagnosis and non-caring help.

See also: Andy Campbell, Dana Stowe, Kayla Thornton, Lana Hawkins, Nick Biancavilla, Peter Riggs.

717. Luke and Kate McCoy, *The Real McCoys*, ABC, 1957–1963; CBS, 1962–1963. Played by Richard Crenna, Kathleen Nolan.

Luke McCoy and Kate Purvis are newlyweds. They were born in Smokey Corners, West Virginia, and married in 1957, shortly before moving to San Fernando, California, to run a farm inherited by Luke's grandfather, Amos McCoy. Luke's parents are deceased and he and Kate care for his sister, Hassie and brother, Little Luke.

The 20-acre McCoy farm is located "on the Back Road" about 4½ miles outside of town. Luke has the responsibility of running the farm while Amos oversees its operations (the growing of tomatoes, lettuce, potatoes, apples, peaches and alfalfa). Luke's real name is Lucius. He and Kate honeymooned at the Colonial Palms Motel and stayed in room 204. "Margie" was the song they danced to when they first met at the June Social (another episode claims they met in Sunday School). Luke calls Kate "Sugar Babe" ("Honey Babe" in the pilot).

Luke is a member of the Valley Co-op Poultry

Association, the Grange Association and the Mystic Knights of the Nile Lodge. Luke was the state arm wrestling champion of West Virginia and was a member of its Tri State Militia Marching Band. In his youth he wrote a song called "In the Name of Rotten Love" and entered an amateur radio contest (where he sang "In the Hills of West Virginny"). When the farm was between crops Luke took a job as a dogcatcher (badge 7014; car code AR-31).

Kate is a devoted wife and cares for the house and Hassie and Little Luke as if they were her own children. She is an excellent cook and won the Prize Foods of California Home Baking Preserves Contest with her piccalilli (she received a blue ribbon). She also received a $50 gift certificate as the winner of the Mrs. Homemaker Contest at the Carter Brothers General Store. Kate is a member of the Charity Clothing Drive and the Ladies' Auxiliary of the Mystic Nile Lodge. She earns extra money by taking in sewing and cares for the family's finances (she keeps the money in the sugar bowl in the kitchen). Kathleen left the series at the end of the 1962 season. When the series returned for its final season (CBS episodes) Luke has been a widower for a year-and-a-half (no mention is made of how Kate "died"). Luke was now ready to date other women as he felt enough time had passed and he should start looking for another wife.

See also: Amos McCoy, Hassie McCoy (for information on Hassie and Little Luke).

718. Lumpy Rutherford, *Leave It to Beaver,* ABC, 1958–1963. Played by Frank Bank.

Clarence Rutherford, nicknamed Lumpy, is the son of Fred and Geraldine Rutherford (Fred's wife is later said to be named Gwen. Lumpy originally had a sister [Violet] and two brothers who were offered football scholarships; later he has only his sister Violet). Being overweight has caused Clarence's friends to call him Lumpy. He lives in Mayfield and attends the Grant Elementary School, Mayfield High School and finally State College. He is a year older than his best friends, Wally Cleaver and Eddie Haskell, and the age difference was explained as his having to repeat sophomore year in high school (although when he was first introduced he was several years older [16] than Wally or Eddie and was the bully of the neighborhood). At Mayfield High Lumpy plays clarinet in the school band (later the tuba) and throws the discus (although when he spins around he gets dizzy and passes out). He drives "a sickly purple" 1941 Ford convertible (plate PZR 342) and 433–6733 is his phone number.

In the series update, *The New Leave It to Beaver* (TBS, 1986–1989), Lumpy is now married and the father of J.J. He is also partners with Wally's younger brother, Beaver, in the Cleaver and Rutherford Company (exactly what they do is not said).

See also: Beaver Cleaver, Eddie Haskell, June Cleaver, Wally Cleaver, Ward Cleaver.

719. Luther Van Dam, *Coach,* ABC, 1989–1996. Played by Jerry Van Dyke.

Luther Van Dam has been an assistant coach for 38 years. He was born in Danville, Illinois, and is a graduate of Danville High School. Luther became interested in sports at an early age but he was more interested by what happened behind the scenes as opposed to actually playing the game. He now earns $32,000 a year as the assistant coach to Hayden Fox, coach of the Minnesota State University Screaming Eagles football team.

Luther feels comfortable assisting people. He fears the day he has to coach. He lives in a small apartment with his dog (Quincy) and parrot (Sunshine); he received Sunshine from his father when he was ten years old. Luther eats Sweeties, the Full Sugar Cereal, for breakfast and enjoys whatever is available at the time for dinner. He hates school recesses because he gets what he calls "the summer blues" (eats, gains weight and spends all fall working it off). Luther later moves to Florida (1995) with Hayden to help him coach the Orlando Breakers, an NFL Expansion Team. He now lives in a condo at Leisure Town. He also held a one-week job coaching at Aberdeen College but was fired for breaking NCAA rules.

See also: Christine Armstrong, Hayden Fox.

720. Lydia DeLucca, *That's Life,* CBS, 2000–2001. Played by Heather Paige Kent.

Lydia Denise DeLucca is the daughter of Frank and Dolly DeLucca. She was born in Bellefield, New Jersey and works as a bartender. Her father is a toll taker for the New Jersey Turnpike and her mother would like her to get married and have children. Lydia does not want children but does want to make something of her life.

Lydia is attending Montville State University and taking classes in human behavior, human sexuality, pottery, post modernism and photography. Ever since she was five years old, Lydia dreamed about book reports, cramming, tests and a tree-covered campus. She is a graduate of Bellefield High School (where she went to her prom with a temperature of 104 degrees); she put college on hold to work. Before finding steady employment at the After Hours Bar, Lydia held 58 jobs. Those she mentioned were as follows: chauffeur, stripper, urologist, gynecology assistant, bus driver, lawyer's assistant, receptionist at the Department of Age Discrimination, caddy, postal worker, camp counselor, dog walker, cab driver, veterinary assistant, ice cream vendor, produce clerk at Grundel's Grocery, waitress at Rivetti's Pizza Parlor, secretary at Wolfstein Associates, and salesgirl at Sally's House of Flowers.

Lydia is Catholic and was considered a great athlete in high school (she broke all kinds of records). She was a bridesmaid 17 times and lives in Apartment E above the Runco Brothers Printing Company. Lydia won $10,000 playing a Crazy 8's scratch-off lottery game and has a stubborn car she calls Stanley (plate T 4210). When the car isn't running (which is often) Lydia takes the 086-bus to school. Lydia buys her lingerie from Victoria's Secret and frequents Micelli's Bar for its karaoke nights.

When Lydia was fired from the bar for refusing to serve alcohol to an intoxicated customer, she first acquired work at a beauty parlor called Jackie O's Beauty Salon, then at the family restaurant, Cucina DeLucca ("Great Food at Fair Prices." Her father started the business when he got fed up with the turnpike and quit).

721. Lynette Scavo, *Desperate Housewives*, ABC, 2004 (current). Played by Felicity Huffman.

Lynette Scavo was a high-powered businesswoman who ran an advertising company that employed 85 people. She was glamorous and had an acute business sense. She was known for her eye-catching presentations and ruthlessness for destroying the competition. Lynette gave it all up for a marriage, four mischievous children and a new life at 4356 Wisteria Lane, a spotless neighborhood in a perfect suburb of a city called Fairview.

Lynette often regrets her decision to marry because she is constantly depressed and harassed by her children. She constantly lies about her life as a mother but says, "It's the best job I ever had" (she tries to cover the fact that if she stayed at the agency she would have become a company president). Lynette has been worn out caring for her children. She is not as glamorous as her girlfriends, Bree, Gabrielle and Susan, and delights in the little pleasures in life — like the monthly meeting of the Wisteria Lane Book Club (which gives her a break from the kids). Lynette was once a woman who spoke her mind (she was thrown out of Disneyland for lewd behavior) and commanded respect. Her life consisted of client meetings, decision-making and creating. She is now mellow, neurotic and the only meetings she at-

tends are those to visit the school principal when the kids get into trouble. Lynette calls the kids "Little Monsters" and is a Boy Scout troop den mother. To relax, Lynette often takes the kids ADA medication.

See also: Bree Van DeKamp, Edie Britt, Gabrielle Solis, Susan Mayer.

722. Lynn Belvedere, *Mr. Belvedere*, ABC, 1985–1990. Played by Christopher Hewett.

Lynn Aloysius Belvedere is a respected British butler who worked for English royalty — from Winston Churchill to Queen Elizabeth II. He is now employed by George Owens, a TV sports anchor, and cares for him and his helpless family (his wife Martha and their children Kevin, Heather and Wesley). They live at 200 Spring Valley Road in Beaver Falls, Pittsburgh.

Lynn was born in Stonehedge, England. He lived on Highby Road and attended the Pennington School. He appeared on the cover of *World Focus* magazine ("Housekeeper of the Year") and possesses medals for climbing Mount Everest and winning the Pillsbury Bake-off. Lynn possesses a $750,000 Faberge egg (given to him by a sheik for saving his life) and he is most proud of the fact that he served as a housekeeper to Ghandi.

Lynn keeps a daily diary of his activities with the Owens family. He wrote a book based on his experiences called *An American Journal: The Suburban Years*. Lynn is affected by the Stonehedge Curse once every seven years (a force that strikes the people of his hometown. It makes him bounce back and forth between himself and someone else. The cure is to wait it out or return home and dance around the statue of Stonehedge, the founder of the town).

The last episode finds Lynn marrying Louise Gilbert, an animal behaviorist he met at a laundromat. Lynn leaves the Owens family to join Louise in Africa when she is asked to return to the University of Boutari to take a gorilla census. In the final moments of the episode, Lynn remarks that he left his weekly journals at the Owens home with a possibility that he may one day return for them. He never did.

See also: George and Marsha Owens, Heather Owens, Kevin Owens, Wesley Owens.

723. Lynn Searcy, *Girlfriends*, UPN, 2000 (current). Played by Persia White.

Lynn Ann Searcy is a beautiful young woman who first appears to be a permanent grad student at U.C.L.A. She is unstable, not easily motivated and not very responsible. She has five degrees and owes over $200,000 in student loans. Lynn has no money, no job and lives with her girlfriend Joan Clayton. Although she has a masters' degree in clinical psychology, she has not followed through on it with a job. She takes whatever odd jobs she can find (like waitress, secretary) and when she is desperate for money she sells her blood ("I like to do it before four p.m. before all the good cookies are gone").

Lynn finally completed her college education in 2001 but did not find her career until two years later when she became a documentary filmmaker (her films: *Lives in the Balance: The African-American Woman and the AIDS Crisis* and *Life in the Balance: Single Mothers*). The Thompson Foundation provides Lynn's funding. Prior to this, Lynn worked as a waitress at Amie's Diner. When she tried living on her own, she called a converted garage on Florence Street home. Lynn has a dog named Vosco and volunteers at the South Side Free Clinic, a telephone hotline service. She also earns money by writing trashy soft-porn stories for Climaxxx Publishing.

Lynn was born in Charlottesville, Virginia, on February 9, 1971 (later said to be in 1970). It was first said that Lynn was abandoned by her black parents and raised by a white family. Later, it is revealed that Lynn's mother, Sandy, was white and had an affair with a black man (Ken). Lynn was given up for adoption and raised by a black family (Ed and Beth). This second version appears more credible when Lynn is reunited with her white birth mother, Sandy (Karen Austin) in 2003. To further complicate matters, it was also said that Sandy's parents paid Lynn's father (Ken) money to disappear because they didn't want their daughter marrying a black man.

Lynn mentions she has degrees in "geology, anthropology, psychiatry, science and I can't remember the fifth one." She is allergic to cashew nuts and dines with her girlfriends at Skia's Restaurant. Lynn later gave up her job as a filmmaker to find herself. She became a tour guide, a street-performing robot (like a mime but dressed in silver), host of a public access TV show called *Ambush* (wherein she degrades guests), and a celebrity photographer (her jobs as of January 31, 2005).

See also: Joan Clayton, Maya Wilkes, Toni Childs.

724. Lyta Alexander, *Babylon 5,* TNT, 1993–1999. Played by Patricia Tallman.

Lyta Alexander is a stunning mind reader who resides on *Babylon 5,* a five-mile long floating city that was built in the 23rd century to maintain the peace among the various alien races.

Lyta was created by a race called the Vorlons as a weapon in their battle against the evil Shadows. In 2257, shortly after *Babylon 5* was built, Lyta became the city's first telepath. She can control dreams and manipulate people and is seeking one important goal (at least to her)—a home world for her and other telepaths. Lyta blends in with the other residents of *Babylon 5* and will not use her powers unless she feels threatened. She can destroy minds if she is not careful and is a bit uneasy about becoming close to people who are not of her race.

See also: Delenn, Elizabeth Lochley, John Sheridan, Susan Ivanova.

725. Mac Robinson, *Night Court,* NBC, 1984–1992. Played by Charles Robinson.

Mac Robinson is the clerk in the courtroom of Harry Stone, an unorthodox night court judge in New York City. Mac was born in Manhattan. He was a singer with a group called the Starlights but left before they became famous. He did a tour of duty in Vietnam during the war and risked his life to help a Vietnamese family overcome the ravages of a recent bombing. It was at this time that a 12-year-old girl named Quon Le Dac fell in love with him. Years later (1985) Quon Le (Denice Kumagai) left Vietnam when the new regime took over and traveled to New York to find Mac. Mac married her in an attempt to keep her in the U.S. They had planned to annul the marriage but decided against it when they discovered they loved each other. Mac and Quon Le set up housekeeping in a small apartment and Quon Le acquired work as a checker at the Vegetable Mart. She and Mac attempted to market a cookie they called "Mac Snacks."

Mac is a devoted husband to Quon Le. They realize they are in a difficult marriage (she is Vietnamese; he is African-American and much older) but they are determined to make it work. Mac had originally planned on becoming a lawyer and began taking classes in law at City College. He later switched his major to film when he became interested in making movies.

See also: Bull Shannon, Christine Sullivan, Dan Fielding, Harry T. Stone.

726. MacGyver, *MacGyver,* ABC, 1985–1991. Played by Richard Dean Anderson.

Angus MacGyver is a survival expert and scientific genius who tackles seemingly impossible missions for the Phoenix Foundation. MacGyver worked previously for the Department of External Services, U.S. Intelligence and The Company.

Mac, as MacGyver is called, was born in Mission City, Missouri, in March of 1951. He is the son of James and Ellen MacGyver but raised mostly by Ellen and Ellen's father, Harry Jackson, after his father and grandmother were killed in a car accident. Mac, called "Bud" by Harry, was taught the value of fair play. It was at this time that Mac developed a dislike for firearms: his best friend was accidentally shot to death. Mac attended Mission High School and is a graduate of Western Technical College. During his summer vacations he worked as an usher at Met baseball stadium.

Mac is now based in California as a troubleshooter for the Phoenix Foundation. He first lived on a houseboat then, in 1991, when a fire destroyed the boat, in a loft in Los Angeles. Mac is a vegetarian and his favorite sport is ice hockey. He first drove a Jeep (plate IRQ 104) then a sedan (plate 2ASB 795). Mac has the ability to use duct tape (his "best friend") to help him overcome virtually any obstacle he encounters. He is mechanically inclined and can make use out of seemingly useless items (to help free himself from precarious situations).

727. Madame, *Madame's Place*, Syn., 1982–1983. Voiced by Wayland Flowers.

Madame (a puppet controlled and voiced by Wayland Flowers) is the host of a late-night talk show called *Madame's Place*. The show is broadcast from Madame's mansion in Hollywood and the unnamed network on which the program airs has established the Madame Scholarship for Male Freshman at the University of Georgia (in honor of Madame's fascination for younger men. Madame is from Georgia and is, or appears to be, in her late 50s). Madame also has a line of designer jeans ("They're hard to get out of, but easy to get into").

Madame was born with show business in her blood. She began her career as a standup comedian and found herself working the dingy nightclub circuit. She made it "big" in the movies. She starred with Clint Eastwood in *A Woman Named Hey You* and was set to star with Tab Hunter in *Ride the Wild Surf* but lost the role to Barbara Eden (who looked stunning in a bathing suit). In an attempt to win back the role, Madame accused Barbara of "painting stretch marks" on her bikini. Madame's next picture, *Trampoline Honeymoon*, got rave reviews and made her a star.

Madame has been married six times (seven was mentioned in the pilot) and estimates she has had 200 boyfriends; her third husband was a fan who sent a picture of himself playing polo in the nude. And like many stars, Madame has had her harrowing moments: she was kidnapped by Egbert Tegley, a famous criminal known as "Sweet Tooth Tegley," who held her hostage at an Atlantic City salt water taffy stand. She was also the target of a crazed fan who believed she was the most beautiful woman in the world (despite her large nose and witch-like appearance; but he also believed that when the moon is full he turns into a parakeet).

Madame enjoys reading the *Enquiring Star* (for all the dirt she can find on herself) and is a member of the Fetish-of-the-Month Club. She uses Me Tarzan — You Jane Body Rub (which she orders from the House of Pleasure Catalogue). Madame is a notorious for her relationships with men and flirts with male guests on her show. She drives a Rolls Royce with the license plate MADAME. Her competition is *Naked All-Star Bowling*.

See also: Sara Joy Pitts (Madame's niece).

728. Maddie Hayes, *Moonlighting*, ABC, 1985–1989. Played by Cybill Shepherd.

Madeline Hayes is a beautiful and sophisticated model who owns Blue Moon Investigations, a detective agency in Los Angeles. Maddie, as she is called, is the daughter of Alexander and Virginia Hayes. She was born in Chicago on February 4, 1951, and lived at 88 East Oak Avenue (another episode mentions October 11 as the birth month and day). Maddie had a dog (Spot) and never wanted for anything growing up. She was a beautiful child and her looks got her into modeling. She appeared on the covers of such magazines as *Fashion*, *Vogue*, *Glamour* and *Vanity Fair* and was the television spokes-girl for Blue Moon Shampoo. Maddie had everything — until her business manager embezzled her funds and left her penniless. One of her business holdings was a detective agency called City of Angels Investigations. This became Blue Moon Investigations (also called The Blue Moon Detective Agency) when employee David Addison talked Maddie out of selling it (to recoup loses) and become his partner in the agency.

Maddie fears she made a big mistake listening to David as they are broke and have few clients ("We are standing on the decks of the *Titanic*. No one calls, no one comes in, and it is bankrupting me. Why am I living like this? I don't deserve this," says Maddie). Maddie is a constant worrier (not only about how she looks, but how to keep her sanity in a new life situation as a detective). Maddie has to be in control of a situation. If she is not, she begins to babble and act incoherently. She appears to place herself above everyone else, but as she begins to meet people from the lower classes (the sleazy clients the agency attracts) Maddie becomes soft hearted and vulnerable to their causes (she puts aside her feelings to help them). David calls Maddie "Blondie Blonde."

See also: David Addison.

729. Magda Ramirez, *The Division,* Lifetime, 2001–2004. Played by Lisa Vidal.

Magda Ramirez is a 32-year-old detective with the Homicide Division of the San Francisco Police Department. She is Puerto Rican and one of seven children. As the youngest child growing up in a poor section of the City by the Bay, Magda experienced crime and corruption first hand. She set her goal at a young age to make the world a better place. Magda was not the best student in school or in the police academy but she did her best and found fulfillment when she became a police officer.

Magda is a down-to-earth girl. She enjoys singing (which she does while getting dressed for work) and helping make people happy by solving their problems. Magda loves her job but she is a single mother and feels uncomfortable when she has to be away from her son (Ben). Working seems to put her mind at ease and she is able to function. Magda is sensitive and honest but has mistrust issues when it comes to men. She is afraid to make another commitment because Ben's father deserted her when she told him she was pregnant.

See also: Candace DeLorenzo, Jinny Exstead, Kate McCafferty, Raina Washington, Stacy Newland.

730. Maggie Briggs, *Suzanne Pleshette is Maggie Briggs,* CBS, 1984. Played by Suzanne Pleshette.

Margaret Briggs is a very beautiful and sexy woman who sometimes gives one the impression that she is anything but. She often wears a male cologne called Lug Nut, has not fainted, become ill or screamed over the sight of a murder victim, and is quite bossy and arrogant and has to get her own way.

Maggie, as she likes to be called, is a hard news reporter for the City Side section of the *New York Examiner,* a daily newspaper that is in financial difficulty. Maggie was born in Nebraska and is a graduate of St. Barnabas High School and the New York School of Journalism. She became interested in journalism when a reporter (Walter Holden) spoke at her high school on career day. Maggie was the editor of her high school and college newspapers and yearbooks and worked as a stringer covering fires, strikes, shootings and murders. She acquired the job with the *Examiner*

shortly after. After 15 years of hard news she was reassigned to the feature department's *Modern Living* magazine in an attempt to breathe some new life into the section (her new desk is two desks away from her old one). Maggie now covers items like fashion, cooking and movie and TV reviews. She does not particularly like it, but she is determined to make the magazine self-sufficient so she can do what she loves best — cover the hard news.

731. Maggie McBirney, *It's a Living,* ABC, 1982. Played by Louise Lasser.

Margaret McBirney is a waitress at Above the Top, a 13th floor Los Angeles restaurant that offers "Sky High Dining." Maggie, as she is called, is attractive, sweet, somewhat of a loner and very insecure. She lives by herself in a spacious house at 1417 Brook Avenue and is afraid to come out of her shell. Maggie was married to Joseph, a salesman for Kitchen Help Dishwashers. Joseph pampered Maggie all their married life. When Joseph died Maggie lost a husband and best friend "my guiding light, my reason for living." Maggie tries to hide her sadness when working but it is obvious she is having a difficult time doing so. Her efforts to help co-workers with their problems bring up memories of Joseph and send Maggie back into a state of depression. Maggie began to improve as the series progressed but the character was just not working and was dropped. Maggie was born in Ohio and her one regret is that she and Joseph were never blessed with children.

See also: Amy Tompkins, Cassie Cranston, Dot Higgins, Ginger St. James, Jan Hoffmeyer, Sonny Mann.

Maggie O'Connell *see* **Joel Fleischman**

Maggie Seaver *see* **Jason and Maggie Seaver**

732. Maggie Sheffield, *The Nanny,* CBS, 1993–1999. Played by Nicholle Tom.

Margaret Sheffield is the 14-year-old daughter of Maxwell Sheffield, a Broadway show producer. She lives in a 19-room dwelling on New York's Park Avenue with her sister Gracie and brother Bryton. Her mother is deceased. Fran Fine, the live-in nanny cares for her.

Maggie, as she is called, is tall, very pretty and looks as though she just stepped out of a page of a teen fashion magazine. Maggie, however, does not see herself in a positive light. She is tall but "I'm a worthless, pathetic unlovable nothing." She also believes that she has no personality and will never fall in love. Maggie quickly grew out of that phase when Fran taught her to use what she has to its best advantage. Makeup, sexier (but still conservative) clothes, and a more positive attitude gave Maggie the confidence she needed to change her negative outlook on life. Maggie and Fran became close as the series progressed and Maggie considers Fran to be her best friend, not a nanny.

Maggie first attends Holy Cross Grammar School then the Lexington Academy High School. She is a top student and not only enjoys school, but rarely complains about homework. Maggie's gorgeous looks came to the attention of the Chloe Simpson Modeling Agency. Maggie was tested for a potential series as a stylish teenager for a magazine layout. She was disappointed to learn her test shots revealed her to be "vacant and lifeless." Maggie's first job was as a volunteer candy stripper at Bellmont Hospital.

See also: C.C. Babcock, Fran Fine, Gracie Sheffield, Maxwell Sheffield.

733. Maggie Winters, *Maggie Winters*, CBS, 1998. Played by Faith Ford.

Margaret Elaine Winters, better known as Maggie, was born on July 3, 1968, in a small town called Shelbyville. When Maggie was three years old she would embarrass her mother by stripping when company arrived. Maggie attended Shelbyville Grammar School and is a graduate of Hull High School. At Hull High Maggie was called "Maggie the Lion Heart" for her ability to imitate a mother's voice and call in for supposedly sick kids who would then cut classes. Maggie next attended the Fashion Institute in New York City and graduated with a degree in design. She married and thought she would live happily ever after until she found her husband had cheated on her. Maggie left him and returned to Shelbyville to begin a new life. She now works as the assistant to the Woman's Apparel Buyer at Hendley's Department Store. Her favorite hangout is Sonny's Restaurant (a bar-diner). Maggie is very sweet, very trusting and will give of herself to help others. She never lies (she becomes nervous if she tries) and tries to always do what is right.

Magnum *see* **Thomas Magnum**

734. Maizy Russell, *Uncle Buck*, CBS, 1990–1991. Played by Sarah Martineck.

Maizy Russell is an adorable seven-year-old girl with a smart mouth. She has a sister (Tia) and brother (Miles) and is cared for by her uncle, Buck Russell (he became her legal guardian after her parents, Robert and Margaret, were killed in a car accident. Robert was Buck's brother).

Maizy attends the Livingston Avenue Grammar School in Chicago. She receives an allowance of 50 cents or 60 cents a week (Buck isn't sure) and is called "Freckle Butt" by her brother (for the birthmark she has on her behind). Maizy is first a Blue Bell then Tulip in the Girl Scouts. She is also on the girl's basketball team, the Pigtails at school (she wears jersey 11). Maizy claims, "I want to be a doctor when I grow up because I care about people." She has a *Jetsons: The Movie* poster on her bedroom wall and is very close to her older sister Tia. Maizy is the only person to whom Tia cannot lie (Tia calls her "Sprout"; Buck calls her "Maze"). Maizy eats Kellogg's Corn Flakes for breakfast, is good at school and a relatively good kid.

See also: Buck Russell, Tia Russell.

Major Nelson *see* **Anthony Nelson**

735. Malcolm Reynolds, *Firefly*, Fox, 2002. Played by Nathan Fillion.

Malcolm Reynolds, called Mal, is captain of the *Serenity*, a Firefly-class transport vessel that roams a futuristic universe seeking to escape the grasp of the Union of Planets (governed by the Alliance) that was established after a bloody civil war. Mal commands a crew of renegades who fought against the Alliance (refusing to live in a controlled regime). They now live aboard the ship and seek jobs on the border planets that are just out of the reach of the Alliance.

Mal was born on a ranch on the planet Shadow and raised by his mother. He served as a sergeant in the war but upped his rank to captain when he appropriated the *Serenity*. He is content in his new life style but not very trusting of other people. He is also quite bitter (perhaps due to the fact that his ranch was destroyed in the war) and rude to everyone. He appears to be happiest when he is by himself and his nasty behavior could be attributed to the fact that his side lost the war and he must now live the life of a renegade aboard a ship.

See also: Inara Serra, River Tam.

736. Mallory Keaton, *Family Ties*, NBC, 1982–1989. Played by Justine Bateman.

Mallory Keaton is the daughter of Steven and Elyse Keaton, a professional couple who live in the Leland Heights section of Columbus, Ohio. Mallory has a younger sister (Jennifer) and two brothers (Alex and Andrew).

Mallory is a very beautiful girl who dreams of becoming a fashion designer. She first attends Harding High School then Grant College (where she majored in fashion design and was a member of the Gamma Delta Gamma sorority). Mallory is not very bright (she is smart in her own ways) and finds schoolwork difficult (her teachers report that she does not apply herself. Alex mentioned that he once tried to teach Mallory long division but got a concussion from banging his head against the wall).

Mallory is always fashionably dressed and has a gift for being able to tell fabrics apart blindfolded (she hates polyester). She also wrote the advice column "Dear Mallory" for the *Columbus Shoppers Guide*. Mallory is very naïve and tends to believe what people tell her. She found romance with an unlikely boyfriend, an artist named Nick Moore (Scott Valentine). Nick finds Mallory's naivety intriguing and appears to be a tough biker; he is actually quite charming and cares deeply for Mallory.

See also: Alex P. Keaton, Jennifer Keaton, Steven and Elyse Keaton.

Mandy Mullet *see* **Dwayne and Denny Mullet**

Mannix *see* **Joseph Mannix**

737. Marcia Brady, *The Brady Bunch,* ABC, 1969–1974. Played by Maureen McCormick.

This entry also contains information on Marcia's sisters, Jan (Eve Plumb) and Cindy (Susan Olsen). They live with their mother (Carol) and stepfather (Mike) and their stepbrothers (Greg, Peter and Bobby) at 4222 Clinton Avenue in Los Angeles.

Marcia. Marcia is the oldest of the Brady girls. She first attends Fillmore Junior High School (where she was class president and editor of its paper, *The Fillmore Flier*) and Westside High School (where she was a cheerleader for the Bears football team). While good at schoolwork, Marcia found history to be her worst subject ("I get confused with dates"). She takes ballet lessons at the Valley School of Dancing and was a member of the Sun Flower Girl Scout Troop. Marcia worked after-school as a counter girl at Hanson's Ice Cream Parlor; the Pizza Parlor is her favorite hangout. As Marcia progressed into young womanhood and found an attraction to boys, she also found herself being spied upon by Jan and Cindy (whom she called the "Nosey Bradys").

Marcia marries the wacky Wally Logan (Jerry Houser) in the 1981 NBC TV movie *The Brady Girls Get Married.* Wally works as a designer for the Tyler Toy Company (later Prescott Toys); Marcia is now a fashion designer for Casual Clothes. They live in the same house as Jan and her husband Philip. In the 1990 CBS series update, *The Bradys,* Marcia (now played by Leah Ayres) and Wally are the owners of the Party Girls Catering Company. They are also the parents of Jessica and Mickey.

Jan. Jan is the middle daughter. She attends Fillmore Junior High School and later Westside High. Jan describes herself as "pretty, smart and kind." But because she wears glasses she feels "I'm not as beautiful as Marcia." While Jan delights in playing practical jokes, she is insecure, especially around boys (she invented a boyfriend named George Glass to show everyone that boys liked her). Jan also tried wearing a brunette wig to change her personality so "I'm not a blonde Brady." Jan worked at Hanson's Ice Cream Parlor and loves cinnamon spice cookies. The term "Marcia, Marcia, Marcia" became associated with Jan (which she says when she becomes jealous of Marcia).

The 1981 TV movie *The Brady Girls Get Married* finds Jan (an architect in her father's company) marrying Philip Covington, III (Ron Kuhlman), a college chemistry professor. To save on expenses they share a house with Marcia and her husband Wally. Jan has become head of her father's company in the 1990 CBS series update, *The Bradys.* She and Philip are also the parents of an adopted daughter (Patty).

Cindy. Cindy is cute and charming and the youngest Brady sister. She attends the Dixie Canyon Elementary School and has two pet rabbits (Romeo and Juliet). She has a favorite doll (Kitty Carry-All) and Joan of Arc is her hero. Cindy has a bad habit of eaves dropping and tattling on her brothers and sisters (and often getting into trouble for doing so).

In the 1990 CBS series update, *The Bradys* Cindy has graduated from college and is now the host of her own radio program, *Cindy at Sunrise* on station KBLA. Jennifer Runyon played Cindy in the 1988 CBS TV movie, *A Very Brady Christmas.*

See also: Alice Nelson, Carol and Mike Brady, Greg Brady (for information on Greg, Peter and Bobby Brady).

738. Marcie Sternfeld, *Grosse Pointe,* WB, 2000–2001. Played by Lindsay Sloane.

Marcie Sternfeld is a Jewish girl who plays the role of Kim Peterson, a Catholic girl on the mythical TV series *Grosse Pointe* (about students at Grosse Point High School).

Ever since Marcie was a child she has worried about everything. She feels her co-stars, Hunter Fallow and Courtney Scott, are sexier than her. She is also concerned about what the press says about her and what her fans think.

Marcie was born in Los Angeles and is a graduate of Berkeley University. Throughout her school life Marcie was a cheerleader; on the series she plays the head cheerleader and was even honored by the National Cheerleader Association for her work on the small screen.

Marcie also worries about being written out of the show. When she gets upset she goes to a deserted soundstage and screams. Marcie tries to be a role model for the show's teenage fans but often fails. She is not obsessed with her breasts (although she has been said "to thrust her breasts when she shows emotion") and is always criticized by the fashion magazines for her poor taste in clothes (she often makes the "What Was She Thinking" columns).

Marcie was the host of a WB-TV special (*The WB Beach Party*) and watches everything she eats ("I know the calorie count for everything. I keep a food log of everything I eat"). To avoid the calories on a pizza, for example, Marcie orders one made with brown rice bread, low fat cheese and tofu everything else. Marcie has a terrible time attracting guys and feels she makes a fool of herself when she tries to impress someone.

See also: Courtney Scott, Hunter Fallow.

739. Marcy Rhoades, *Married ... With Children*, Fox, 1987–1997. Played by Amanda Bearse.

This entry also contains information on Steve Rhoades (David Garrison), Marcy's first husband, and Jefferson D'Arcy (Ted McGinley), her second husband.

Marcy is a vegetarian and a feminist who works as a loan officer at Kyoto National Bank in Chicago. She lives on Jeopardy Lane and is a neighbor to the Bundy family (Al, Peggy, Kelly and Bud).

Marcy was raised by a three times married mother. She had three dogs (Bella, Chester and Winkems) a cat (Gringo) and a cuckoo clock (Petey). She cannot speak in public due to a traumatic childhood incident: she was giving a speech in school when a roach started climbing up her leg. She screamed, ran around the room, took her dress off and revealed "my 'Hey, Hey, We're the Monkees' panties." She was teased the rest of the term. At this time she had an invisible friend named Jennifer.

Marcy and neighbor Al do not get along and constantly insult each other (Al calls her "Chicken legs." Marcy also has small breasts and is constantly made aware of this fact by Al's insults). To battle Al's all male organization MA'AM (the National Organization of Men Against Amazonian Masterhood), Marcy formed FANG (Feminists Against Neanderthal Guys).

Steve Rhoades worked as a loan officer at the Leading Bank of Chicago. He calls Marcy "Angel Cups" (she called him "Sugar Tush"). They were married on Valentine's Day and in high school Steve was a member of a band called the Tuxedos. On the first sunny day in May Steve and Marcy "go to the beach and shake hands with Mr. Sunshine." Steve lost his job when he loaned Al, a shoe salesman, $50,000 to start a failed telephone service called Dr. Shoe (shoe advice over the phone). He found work as a cage cleaner at Slither's Pet Emporium then as a ranger at Yosemite National Park (at which time he left Marcy and the series). At a banking seminar we learn that Marcy was a party animal and woke up in bed with Jefferson D'Arcy, a man she married at Clyde's No Blood Test Needed Chapel. Jefferson is a con artist and out on parole (arrested for stealing money from investors). Jefferson also claimed to be a covert operations agent for the CIA (code name "Bullwinkle") who was let go because he would not kill a man he befriended — Fidel Castro. Jefferson rarely works and relies on Marcy for his spending money. He calls Marcy "Bon Bon Bottom" (she calls him "Cinnamon Buns"). He often sides with Al against Marcy (he appears to have married her for her money) and finds Al's insults about Marcy refreshing.

See also: Al Bundy, Bud Bundy, Kelly Bundy, Peggy Bundy.

740. Margaret Houlihan, *M*A*S*H*, CBS, 1972–1983. Played by Loretta Swit.

Major Margaret Houlihan, nicknamed "Hot Lips," is the head nurse with the 4077th M*A*S*H (Mobile Army Surgical Hospital) unit in Korea during the war. Margaret earns $400 a month. She has a spotless record and has been a chief nurse for ten years. She "is a woman of passion but a stickler for rules" ("which sometimes alienates me from my nurses who never make me a part of their activities").

Margaret was raised by a military father and is regular army; she would like all doctors and nurses to behave in a military manner but realizes they won't ("They're terribly unruly and undisciplined and I thank God for each and everyone of them when the casualties roll in"). Margaret is a beautiful and alluring woman who tries to be just that despite the deplorable conditions that surround her. She uses her sex appeal to get what she needs and acts tough. Deep down she is just as frightened as everyone else ("I don't like being afraid, it scares me").

Margaret misses "the beauty shop in Tokyo and a sense of order and discipline." She treasures the brushes her father gave her (which she uses to brush her hair 100 times a night). She writes the beauty column, "About Faces," for the camp newsletter, *M*A*S*H Notes*.

Margaret and Major Frank Burns became an item when she began an affair with the married man. Margaret was turned on when Frank "flared his nostrils" ("I get so excited") and knew "He thinks of me as a bag of desirable bones." When Margaret found Donald Penobscott, a major who respected her mind, she dumped Frank and married him.

See also: Benjamin Franklin Pierce, B.J. Hunnicutt, Charles Winchester, III, Frank Burns, Henry Blake, Radar O'Reilly, Sherman Potter, Trapper John McIntire.

741. Margaret Kim, *All-American Girl*, ABC, 1994–1995. Played by Margaret Cho.

Margaret Kim is young Korean woman who grew up in San Francisco. She is the daughter of Benjamin and Kathryn Kim and has two brothers, Stuart and Eric.

Margaret was born on August 7, 1975, and was brought up by parents who believe in their old world Korean customs. They would like their children to carry on that tradition.

Margaret, however, was influenced by television and has grown to love the American way of life.

Margaret is a graduate of Union Bay High School and is currently majoring in economics at the University of San Francisco. She lives at 7364 Hyde Place with her family and works part time in the perfume department at the mall in a store called Drummond's Cosmetics Counter. Margaret also worked for her father, the owner of Kim's Books, when she was in high school.

Margaret reads *Metal Head* music magazine and loves the TV series *Charlie's Angels* (she fantasizes that if she were one of the Angels she would be Farrah Fawcett's Jill Monroe character). Margaret is pretty and vibrant but she speaks first and thinks later — a habit that constantly gets her into trouble.

Margaret is very respectful of her parents. If she does something wrong and is punished, she will not rebel. She would like to preserve her family's traditions and date only Korean boys but she cries, "I wanna date American boys." This is a concession her parents allow her — provided they are upstanding and decent. Margaret is also forbidden to mention the name of Mary Lou Retton (the 1984 Olympic gymnastics champion) in the house. During the 1984 Olympic gymnastic competition Kathryn was rooting for the Korean girl to win

while Margaret was rooting for her hero, Mary Lou Retton, to win. She did and thus the rule.

The last episode (March 15, 1995) finds Kim living on her own (Apartment 23 at 861 Foster Way) and working as the Assistant to the Assistant to the Associate Vice President of Bleach Records. This was the pilot for an unsold attempt to revive the series as *The Young Americans*.

742. Marge Simpson, *The Simpsons*, Fox, 1990 (current). Voiced by Julie Kavner.

Marjorie Bouvier is an intelligent woman who fell in love with and married a literal moron named Homer Simpson. They are the parents of Bart, Lisa and Maggie and live at 742 Evergreen Terrace in the town of Springfield.

Marge, as she is called, was born in Springfield in 1956 and attended Springfield Elementary and high schools. In a flashback sequence it is revealed that Marge met Homer at Springfield High in 1974. In a later flashback they are seen meeting for the first time in 1980 when Marge was a waitress at Burgers Burgers and Homer worked at the Springfield Fun Center.

Marge has blue hair and wears a size 13AAA shoe. She believes her life is dull. She shops, does housework, cooks and cares for the kids; she even caters to Homer's whims. To become different (and possibly add some excitement in her dull life) Marge underwent breast implant surgery and increased her bust size to 48D. Before having them removed due to back problems, Marge's new assets allowed her to work as the Oven Mitt Convention Spokeswoman and for Global Shoe Horns.

Marge's favorite TV show is *Search for the Sun*. She wrote a novel called *The Harpooned Heart* (about a whaling father and his family). She also enrolled in art classes at Springfield Community College (in high school Marge had aspirations of becoming an artist but was discouraged by her teacher; she painted only one picture: her idol Ringo Starr). Marge makes her own Pepsi Cola ("It's a little tricky though"); has her hair done at Jake's Unisex Hair Salon; and worked as a police officer (assigned to patrol Junk Town) to earn extra money. As a kid Marge had a hamster named Cinnamon.

See also: Bart Simpson, Homer Simpson, Lisa Simpson.

743. Margie Albright, *My Little Margie*, CBS, 1952–1953; NBC, 1953–1955. Played by Gale Storm.

Marjorie Albright is a beautiful 21-year-old woman who lives with her father, investment counselor Vern Albright, in Apartment 10A of the Carlton Arms Hotel in New York City; Carlton 3-8966 is their phone number.

Margie, as she is called, is single. She was born in Manhattan in 1931 and was raised by Vern (her mother apparently died during childbirth according to Vern: "I've been both mother and father to her since she was born"). When Margie was young Vern had control over her. When she disobeyed "I took her roller skates away for a week." But as Margie grew she began to develop a stubborn, independent mind and now sort of listens to her father but mainly does what she wants.

Margie is described as "pretty, shapely and attractive." She attracts men like bees to honey and she uses her beauty to get men to do what she wants them to (especially her lazy, unemployed, not easily motivated boyfriend, Freddie Wilson). Margie has Irish blood (and temper) from her mother. She hates to be told she is wrong and will go out of her way to prove a point (no matter how much trouble she and Freddie get into). Margie is a talented dancer and dreams of attending the International Ball (but was never able "because it was for bluebloods").

Margie attended Gorman Elementary School, Lexington High School and Manhattan College. She does not have a regular job and appears to live off an allowance given to her by Vern. Margie mentioned her first job was "beauty consultant" (handing out samples of cosmetics at Stacey's Department Store). She also held such various part time jobs as waitress, dance instructor, and sales clerk. She was also the co-host (with Vern) on a TV show called *Captain Stratosphere*. This looked to be a regular job and was touched upon in the episode "Margie's Millionth Member" (but not seen or mentioned again).

Margie loves to meddle in her father's business affairs (and always winds up in hot water for doing so). Margie appears to be the ideal dream girl of any red-blooded American male. But she does have one bad habit: she smokes (she is seen reaching for, lighting up and smoking a cigarette — just a sign of the times on early TV).

See also: Freddie Wilson, Vern Albright.

744. Margie Clayton, *Margie*, ABC, 1961–1962. Played by Cynthia Pepper.

Marjorie Clayton is a pretty and vibrant 16-year-old girl. She is the daughter of Harvey and Nora Clayton and has a younger brother named Cornell. Margie, as she likes to be called, lives in the town of Madison during the 1920s. She was born on July 17, 1911, and lives at 34 Oak Tree Lane (Central 4734 is her phone number).

Margie is a sophomore at Madison High School and is fascinated with life. She lives in a small town but manages to find misadventure in everything she does. She is editor of her school newspaper, *The Madison Bugle* and also writes the gossip column, "Through the Keyhole." Crawford's Ice Cream Parlor is the after-school hang-out. Margie wears, as most teenage girls did at the time, a dress and professes no ambition of becoming a flapper (a girl who seeks only fun).

Margie is the daughter of a banker (at the Great Eastern Savings Bank) and has not yet learned the value of a dollar. She goes through her 50-cent weekly allowance rather quickly and is always looking for a temporary job to earn additional cash (those nickel ice cream sodas eat up her savings when she treats her friends). Margie is a loyal friend and has an unrelenting urge to help people she believes are in trouble (but often complicates matters). Margie feels she is an expert at match making but rarely succeeds in matching the right girl with the right boy. She is dating Heywood Botts (Tommy Ivo) and is a best friend with the school's most beautiful girl, Maybelle Jackson (Penny Parker)

745. Margaux Kramer, *Punky Brewster*, NBC, 1984–1986. Played by Ami Foster.

Margaux Kramer is a very pretty, very rich and very spoiled young girl. She lives in a mansion on Oak Lane (in suburban Chicago) with "so many rooms that you need a map to find your way around." There are metal detectors at each door; Margaux's room is in the east wing; 555-RICH is her phone number.

Margaux has been spoiled by her mother (who pampers her; she is currently learning how to fire servants). Margaux is only eight years old and already has her own masseuse, beautician and manicurist. She has to always be in style ("I even look gorgeous when I'm nervous") and had a harrowing experience one winter day: "I almost got a snowflake on my hair." When it comes time for marriage Margaux says, "I'll look through *Who's Who* to see who has what."

Margaux has a collection of dolls made by her personal doll maker (her most cherished one is a dancing ballerina that plays the song "Beautiful Dreamer." "She comforts me when I'm sad," says Margaux). Margaux had never known what (she considers) poverty was until she befriended Punky Brewster, the orphaned girl who lives with Henry Warnimont. Henry is not wealthy and lives in an apartment in the city (which Margaux considers "the poverty pit"). Despite Punky's lower social level, she and Margaux became close friends.

They attended Camp Kookalookie together and entered an old time radio contest and won a trip to Disneyland with their story "Gruesome Ghost Stories — The Mystery of Horror House."

See also: Punky Brewster.

746. Marguerite Krux, *The Lost World,* Syn., 1998–2002. Played by Rachel Blakely.

The time is 1920. Marguerite Krux is a beautiful, wealthy and mysterious woman with no scruples. Marguerite Krux is the name she uses but it is only one of several she supposedly has. Marguerite was born in Essex, England, but never knew her parents. She was raised in a series of boarding schools and was given the finest education but no love. She has an extensive knowledge of subjects and an incredible ability with languages. She has a strange birthmark on her right shoulder that resembles the symbol of the moon, the serpent and the sun. The symbol is that of a Druid Princess and Marguerite believes she is the reincarnation of one such ancient princess.

Marguerite, a graduate of Oxford University, has a keen interest in geology and astrology. She is also especially fond of diamonds and other precious stones. When she learns that George Challenger (see entry) is organizing an expedition to a supposedly lost world of prehistoric creatures, Marguerite appears and offers to fund the project. Soon after the expedition begins, Marguerite, George, and fellow explorers Ned Malone and John Roxton, become stranded on a seemingly inescapable plateau in the Amazon. Here they befriend Veronica Layton, a girl born on the plateau, who allows them to live in her tree house.

Marguerite believes the mysteries of the plateau are never ending. The most important thing to her is finding the rare gems that are abundant on the plateau. Marguerite is an expert with a gun, rifle and knife, and can take care of herself—"I always have and I always will."

See also: Finn, George Challenger, John Roxton, Ned Malone, Veronica Layton.

Marie Barone *see* **Frank and Marie Barone**

747. Marie Lubbock, *Just the Ten of Us,* ABC, 1988– 1990. Played by Heather Langenkamp.

Marie Lubbock is a senior at St. Augustine's, a Catholic high school in Eureka, California. She was born on June 9, 1970, on Long Island in New York and is the eldest daughter of Graham and Elizabeth Lubbock. She has seven siblings and is the most religious member of the family.

Marie is a very attractive girl who believes God has chosen her to become a nun ("I love God and deep down I know this is the best way to serve him"). Marie wears a size five dress, a 34C bra and hides her beauty behind glasses, pulled back hair and loose fitting clothes (she dropped her dull look when she and her sisters Wendy, Cindy and Connie formed a sexy singing group called the Lubbock Babes). Marie held a job serving food at the Eureka Mission and Saturday is Marie's day to buy the groceries and cook. She believes she is normal but when she becomes excited she feels people see her as a little insane "because I don't always phrase things properly." Marie lost her urge to become a nun after she backed down from a two-week seminar at St. Bartholomew's Convent. She began to dress and act more like a normal girl although she had some doubts about giving up her life as a nun. The series ended without resolving Marie's dilemma.

See also: Cindy Lubbock, Connie Lubbock, Graham and Elizabeth Lubbock, Wendy Lubbock.

748. Marilyn Munster, *The Munsters,* CBS, 1964–1966. Played by Beverley Owen, Pat Priest.

Marilyn Munster is young, blonde and beautiful. Her looks make her the black sheep of the Munsters, a family who resemble movie monsters of the 1930s. The Munsters believe they are normal and other people (like Marilyn) are weird.

Marilyn's history is somewhat sketchy. She lives at 1313 Mockingbird Lane in the town of Mockingbird Heights with her Uncle Herman (Frankenstein-like), her Aunt Lily (a vampire), Lily's father (Grandpa) and her nephew, Eddie (a werewolf). Herman and Lily are not sure whose side of the family produced such a hideous creature as Marilyn (she is said to be from Herman's side of the family, then Lily's side of the family. In the episode "All-Star Munster," Herman pinpoints Marilyn as "Lily's sister's kid"). Exactly how Marilyn came to live with the family or who her parents are (normal or monster) is not revealed.

Marilyn appears lovely to the viewer but is grotesque in her family's eyes. She attends Westbury University and is studying art. Her bedroom is bright and cheery in a house that is dark, dreary, dusty and covered with spider webs (Lily attributes this to her good housekeeping skills). Marilyn accepts her family but feels "I'm so ugly that I will never attract a man" (she fails to realize that when a new boyfriend sees Herman, it is he who scares them off, not Marilyn).

Hilary Van Dyke plays Marilyn in the syndicated (1988–91) series update, *The Munsters Today.* Marilyn is now younger (17 years old) and a student at Mockingbird Heights High School (she was 21 in the prior series). Marilyn is somewhat boy crazy and feels her small breasts, not Herman, is why she has a difficult time finding boyfriends (she claims, "I wanna be a 36D"). She reads *Teen Scene* magazine and mentioned she was studying art but also wanted to be an actress then a magazine writer-editor. Marilyn has a porcelain bunny collection and won the Bronx Cheer Pom Pom Award as a member of the school's cheerleading team. She also appeared in the school's production of *To Kill a Mockingbird*.

See also: Eddie Munster, Grandpa, Herman Munster, Lily Munster.

749. Marina, *Stingray*, Syn., 1961. Character is non-speaking.

Marina is the daughter of Aphony, ruler of the undersea kingdom of Pacifica. She was born in the year 2046 and is a princess. Troy Tempest, captain of the submarine *Stingray*, discovered her kingdom. Marina now works with Troy as a member of the World Aquanaut Security Patrol.

Marina is unable to speak (a characteristic of her people) and communicates by mental telepathy or by sign language. She has an extensive knowledge of the ocean floor and travels with her pet seal Oink. Marina is capable of breathing water as well as air and helps Troy to further her knowledge of what she calls the surface world. *Stingray* is a Gerry Anderson puppet series filmed in Supermarionation.

750. Mark Harris, *The Man from Atlantis*, NBC, 1977–1978. Played by Patrick Duffy.

Mark Harris is believed to be the sole survivor of the Lost Kingdom of Atlantis. He was found on a California beach after a storm deep within the Pacific Ocean injured him and washed him ashore. The Atlantian was brought to the Naval Underwater Center and labeled The Project Atlantis Affair. Elizabeth Merrill, the doctor who saved his life, named him Mark Harris.

Mark requires the sea for survival. His life expectancy out of water is estimated to be 16 hours. On land Mark's eyes are sensitive to light and he tires easily by physical activity. In his natural habitat, Mark is perfectly adapted to aquatic life. He has great strength and agility and his chest cavity has gill-like membranes in place of lung tissue. His eyes are catlike and he can see in almost total darkness. His diet consists of kelp and plankton. Mark can swim faster than a dolphin and can go to depths of 36,000 feet.

Mark is now part of the Navy's O.R.F. (Oceanic Research Foundation). He has chosen to work with mankind to further his knowledge of humans (and allow scientists to learn more about his race).

751. Mark Sloan, *Diagnosis Murder*, CBS, 1993–2001. Played by Dick Van Dyke.

Mark Sloan is a doctor at Community General Hospital in Los Angeles. He was born in Los Angeles and is the son of James Sloan, a homicide detective who abandoned his family when Mark was ten years old. Mark grew up loving magic and uses that talent to entertain children at the hospital. Mark treats patients as individuals and refers them to specialists if necessary. Her performs 17 percent more CAT scans and MRIs than other doctors at Community General.

Mark is a widower (his late wife was named Catherine). He is in his 60s and keeps in shape by walking five miles a day (although at times he just paces back and forth in his office to make up for walking when something bothers him). His office is cluttered but one can see posters of magicians Harry Blackstone and Thurston on the walls. Mark roller skates to work when his car breaks down, constantly forgets to activate his beeper and serves as a special medical consultant to the L.A.P.D. ("I'm a homicide consultant for the police department although I give them more problems than solutions." In one episode it was mentioned that Mark solved over 150 murders; in another, Mark was said to have the honorary title of Police Consultant). Once Mark gets involved in a case "and I get something in my head, I have to go with it until I solve the crime."

Mark takes his coffee with cream and three sugars. As an intern Mark worked part-time for the free clinic at the docks. He frequents a bar called Jax and drives a Jaguar with the license plate 55 JAB (also seen as YEB 257, 55 186, 200 PCQ, and OSRQ 590). Mark was an intern, then administrator and finally head of internal medicine at Community General. He assists his son, Detective Steve Sloan, on cases and won $150,000 on the TV game show *Through the Roof* (he donated the money to the Children's Aid Relief and to breast cancer research).

752. Mark Slate, *The Girl from U.N.C.L.E.*, NBC, 1966–1967. Played by Noel Harrison.

Mark Slate is an agent for U.N.C.L.E. (the United Network Command for Law and Enforcement), a New York-based organization that battles the evils of THRUSH, an organization bent on world domain.

Mark was born and raised in England. He joined the Royal Air Force after graduating from college and became a pilot. After resigning he joined the London branch of U.N.C.L.E. Shortly after, he applied for a transfer to the New York branch and was teamed with April Dancer, a recent graduate.

Mark has technical ability (from his days with the air force) and is an expert shot. He is trained in unarmed combat and can speak several languages. He is also a young, swinging bachelor and loves women and fast cars (but not so much a fast life). He enjoys playing the guitar and singing (but not at every opportunity) and while flirtatious, he never makes a pass at April (he looks upon her as his little sister; she sees him as a big brother). Mark stands five feet, eleven inches tall and is often seen wearing some sort of hat, usually a battered old woolen cap.

See also: April Dancer.

Marsha Owens *see* **George and Marsha Owens**

753. Martha Lambert, *Living Dolls,* ABC, 1989. Played by Alison Elliott.

Martha Lambert, nicknamed "Pooch," is a teen model with the Carlin Modeling Agency in Manhattan (at 68th Street and Madison Avenue). She was born in Idaho on June 9, 1973 and now attends Lexington High School.

Martha loves to talk about her home state and is an A student at school (although she claims she has to work very hard to achieve her grades). She loves the attention modeling gives her but she is not overly fashion conscious when it comes to clothes when she is not working. Martha enjoys relaxing at home after school or work by listening to music or reading a book. She treasures her simple, uncomplicated upbringing in Idaho and hopes to one day settle down and raise a family. She feels best when she helps one of her friends overcome a problem.

See also: Caroline Weldon, Charlie Briscoe, Emily Franklin.

754. Martin Crane, *Frasier,* NBC, 1993–2004. Played by John Mahoney.

Martin Crane is the father of Frasier and Niles Crane, psychiatrists who live in Seattle, Washington. Martin is a retired police detective and lives with Frasier at the Elliott Bay Towers (Apartment 1901). Martin is a veteran of the Korean War and in his youth was a mounted policeman (he rode a horse name Agadies). He is obsessed with solving a 20-year-old murder case called "The Weeping Lotus Murder" (someone killed a hooker and tried to stuff her body into a bowling ball bag. He feels he is overlooking a crucial clue but can't figure out what it is). Martin loves fishing and each year embarks on a fishing trip to Lake Noomeheegan. He also has a secret shoebox that contains 30-year-old songs he wrote for Frank Sinatra but never sent.

Martin is a widower; his late wife was named Hester (whom he met at a crime scene. She was a psychiatrist hired by the police department to work on the profile of a killer). Martin has an eyesore of a recliner that Frasier feels clashes with his décor and a dog named Eddie who constantly stares at Frasier. Eddie has a pigeon friend (Barney) who visits him on the patio and they stare at each other. Martin drinks Ballantine beer and has a drink with friends at McGinty's Bar. He later acquired a job as a security guard for Keckner Security and began a romantic relationship with Ronnie Lawrence (Wendie Malick), a girl who once babysat Frasier and Niles. Ronnie plays piano at the Wellington Hotel (in the Rendezvous Room). She also recorded a record album (that sold seven copies) called "Ronnie Lawrence — Mood Swings."

See also: Frasier Crane, Niles Crane.

755. Martin Payne, *Martin,* Fox, 1992–1996. Played by Martin Lawrence.

This entry also contains information on Gina Waters (Tisha Campbell), Martin's girlfriend then wife.

Martin Payne and Gina Waters are lovers. Martin was originally the host of a radio talk show called *The Insane Martin Payne* on Detroit radio station WZUP (he broadcasts from Studio B). He later hosted his own Channel 51 TV show *On the Street.* Gina is a marketing executive with the Whitaker Advertising Agency. She originally lived in her own apartment at 549 Springdale; she moved into Martin's apartment (42) on 23rd Street after their marriage.

Martin discusses the important issues of the day on his show. Unfortunately, Martin is opinionated and hates to be told he is wrong. He is also loud and makes sure he is heard when he speaks. It is only when he is with Gina that we see another side of him: his sensitivity — a side he will never show any one else. Martin has to be king of his household. It is something he insists upon and it is something Gina lets him enjoy doing. Martin attempted to make money by opening a restaurant called Marty Mart's Meat Loaf and Waffles. He also has a collection of *Playboy* magazines that offends Gina. Gina also believes that Martin has loaned his apartment out to many friends for all the female clothing she finds — "I could open a Victoria's Secret Catalogue with all the lingerie I find here."

Gina is the daughter of Dr. Cliff Warner and his wife Nadine (Gina was born in Philadelphia; Martin in Detroit). She is rather sweet and Martin's direct opposite (she usually contradicts what Martin has to say and knows how to silence herself to keep their relationship working). While she puts up with much of Martin's nonsense, Gina really loses her cool when she (while not mentioned by name) becomes a source of amusement for one of Martin's broadcasts. Martin's favorite expression is "Whazz Uuup!" The last episode finds Martin and Gina moving to Los Angeles to pursue new jobs: Gina as head of the L.A. branch of her company; Martin as the host to a network version of his local show.

756. Mary Ann Summers, *Gilligan's Island*, CBS, 1964–1967. Played by Dawn Wells.

Mary Ann Summers is one of seven castaways marooned on an island in the South Pacific. Her cruise ship, the S.S. *Minnow*, was beached after a tropical storm at sea. She, fellow passengers, Ginger, the Professor and Thurston and Lovey Howell, as well as the ship's captain (Jonas Grumby) and his first mate (Gilligan), have made the island their home.

Mary Ann is a very pretty farm girl from Horners Corners, Kansas, (she later says she was born in Winfield, Kansas). She worked as a clerk in the town's general store and helped her parents operate their farm. Her knowledge of plants and crops added greatly to their diet of fish and fruit.

Mary Ann is gentle and kind, very honest and down-to-earth. She shares a hut with Ginger and while as sexy as Ginger, Mary Ann downplays her sexuality (although her tight shorts and stomach-revealing blouses made her appear sexy). Mary Ann, Ginger and Lovey formed a singing group called The Honey Bees on the island and Mary Ann most misses her life on the farm.

See also: Gilligan, Ginger Grant, The Professor, The Skipper, Thurston and Lovey Howell.

757. Mary Beth Lacey, *Cagney and Lacey*, CBS, 1982–1988. Played by Tyne Daly.

Mary Beth Lacey is a plainclothes detective with the Homicide Division of the 14th Precinct in New York City. She is partners with Chris Cagney and was originally an undercover detective with the John Squad of the 23rd Precinct (Mary Beth hated the job, posing as a prostitute, "because cops' feet aren't made for hookers' shoes").

Mary Beth was born in Queens, New York, and is a graduate of St. Catherine Grammar School and St. Helena's High School. She is married to

Harvey and is the mother of Harvey Jr., Michael and Alice. She first lived in Manhattan (Apartment 9) then Jackson Heights, Queens, at 7132 West 46th Street; 555-1519 is her home phone number. Mary Beth's badge number is 340.

Mary Beth dislikes being assigned to missing person's cases as she gets moody and takes it personally (her father, Martin Biskey, is missing. He disappeared when she was a child and she is not sure if he is dead or alive). In the fifth grade Mary Beth was called Mary Beth Number Two to distinguish her from Mary Beth Number One — Mary Beth Lazonne. Mary Beth has a bad habit of smoking. Her favorite watering hole is Flannery's Bar (later called O'Malley's Bar). Mary Beth and Chris work well together. They have their disagreements, especially over how to proceed on a case, but always manage to agree with one another and successfully bring cases to a conclusion.

See also: Chris Cagney.

758. Mary Beth Sutton, *Dear John*, NBC, 1988–1992. Played by Susan Walters.

Mary Beth Sutton is a member of the 1-2-1 Club, a Manhattan-based organization for widowed, divorced, lonely and separated people who need help adjusting to the single life. Meetings are held at the Rego Park Community Center.

Mary Beth is a very attractive woman who believes that no one appreciates her. She always expects the bad to happen but is not sure how to act when something good happens. Mary Beth was born in New York City and works as a columnist for *Above the Clouds*, an airline industry magazine (she previously worked as a writer on the TV series *The Divorced Heart*). Mary Beth's father pampered her as a child. He called her "Sunshine Girl" and "Little Honey Bunny" and gave her anything her heart desired. When her father started a baby food company he named it after her (The Sunshine Baby Food Company) and used her baby picture on the jars.

Mary Beth lives in Apartment 3A of an unidentified building. She attended private schools, was a homecoming queen, and beauty pageant winner. Mary Beth feels she may be too perfect and finding a man who can measure up to her standards is one of the reasons why she joined the club. Mary Beth and fellow club members enjoy a drink at Clancy's Bar after each Friday evening meeting.

See also: John Lacey, Kate McCarron, Kirk Morris, Louise Mercer.

759. Mary Bradford, *Eight Is Enough*, ABC, 1977–1981. Played by Lani O'Grady.

This entry also contains information on Mary's younger sisters, Joanie (Laurie Walters), Nancy (Dianne Kay), Susan (Susan Richardson), and Elizabeth (Connie Needham). They also have three brothers (David, Tommy, and Nicholas) and live at 1436 Oak Street in Sacramento, California. They are the children of Tom and Joan Bradford.

Mary. Mary is the most studious of the children. She is attending medical school when the series begins and later interns at St. Mary's Hospital (she previously attended Sacramento Central High School and Berkeley College). Mary stands up for what she believes in (at college she was a radical and arrested for protesting the Vietnam War). She enjoys cold pizza for breakfast.

Joanie. Joanie is named after her late mother (died of cancer). She has her mother's eyes, smile and sensitivity. She also has something her mother didn't — frizzy hair (she uses Frizz Free Shampoo). Joanie is first a researcher then reporter for KTNS-TV, Channel 8, in Sacramento. She also entertains (as a clown) at the Charles Street Children's Home. Joanie originally had aspirations to become an actress (she appeared without clothes in a play called "Shakespeare in the Nude"). Joanie (dressed as an ice cream cone) and Susan (a banana split) worked as walking advertisements for the Sweet Tooth Dessert Shoppe (at $3.25 an hour).

Nancy. Nancy is the prettiest of the Bradford girls. She attended Sacramento Central High School (where she was a cheerleader) and Sacramento State College (but dropped out when she couldn't handle the work load). Nancy first worked for Hot Wires (singing telegrams over the telephone). She was next a model (she appeared on the cover of *Epitome* magazine and was "The Sunshine Soda Girl" in TV commercials). Nancy gave up possible stardom when she refused to show her breasts in an ad for Vernon Isley Jeans (Nancy believed she could break into modeling "with my outgoing personality and nice features"). Her nice features did land her a steady job as a receptionist at the Bates, Callahan and Chester Brokerage House (later called Fenwick, Hargrove and Elliott Brokerage). Nancy plays tennis, rides horses and uses extra body shampoo.

Susan. Susan is the most sensitive of the children. She is a graduate of Sacramento Central High School but traveled a different path to discover her goal. She attempted a number of jobs but her biggest disappointment came when she failed the physical endurance test to become a police officer. Susan has a true fondness for children and discovered her goal in life when she took over a day care center started by Nancy (who couldn't

make a go of it). Susan married Merle "The Pearl" Stockwell (Brian Patrick Clarke), a pitcher for the Cyclones, a minor league baseball team. He later became a pitcher for the New York Mets. His career ended a year later when he injured his arm while riding a bike. He then became the athletic coach at Central High School. Susan and Merle also became the parents of a daughter they name Sandra Sue.

Elizabeth. Elizabeth is the youngest of the Bradford girls. She attends Sacramento Central High School then Sacramento Junior College. She is studying dance and hopes to become a professional dancer. Elizabeth is very pretty but feels awkward around boys ("I'm like a cross between Marie Osmond and a kewpie doll"). If Elizabeth misses her 11:30 P.M. curfew she is grounded for two weeks "with no time off for good behavior."

In the fourth grade Elizabeth wore braces and was called "Metal Mouth" (this caused her to fight with the name callers and become a hero with the girls; she was also her class blackboard monitor). Elizabeth was not permitted to graduate with her high school class (she dropped a water balloon from the second floor as part of a prank and accidentially caused a teacher to fall and break her leg). When Elizabeth becomes upset she sulks and locks herself in the bathroom.

In the TV movie update, *Eight Is Enough: A Family Reunion* (NBC, October 18, 1987), Mary has become a doctor; Joanie became an actress and was married to a filmmaker named Jean Pierre; Nancy was also married (to a sheep rancher named Jeb); and Susan and Merle were still happily married.

See also: David Bradford (for information on David, Tommy and Nicholas Bradford), Tom Bradford.

760. Mary Camden, *7th Heaven,* WB, 1996 (current). Played by Jessica Beal.

Mary Camden is the eldest daughter of Eric and Annie Camden, a minister and his wife, and lives in Glen Oak, California. She has six siblings (Matt, Simon, Ruthie, Lucy and twins Sam and David) and is the most troublesome of the Camden children. Mary attended Kennedy High School and wore jersey 3 as captain of the Wildcats, the girls' varsity basketball team. Mary had a recurring dream that she would become a professional player for the L.A. Lakers. Her hopes were shattered when she injured her knee and was no longer able to play ball. It was during her time with the Wildcats that Mary and trouble became partners: she was arrested for trashing the school gym when the coach cancelled the basketball season due to the team's poor grades. It was also at this time that Mary became a victim of sexual abuse when her coach tried to seduce her.

In high school Mary wanted to take on the world. However, after graduation, she found she was undecided about her future. She drifted from job to job (waitress at Pete's Pizza and Eddie's' Pool Hall) and when she felt her parents didn't think of her as an adult, she attempted to become a fire fighter but failed to focus and flunked the endurance test. She then hit rock bottom and became a dead beat: spending what little money she had, maxing out credit cards, not paying bills, quitting jobs, driving while intoxicated, and falling in with the wrong crowd. Shortly after, Eric and Annie stepped in and sent Mary to live with his father, a disciplined, retired army colonel, in Buffalo, New York. Mary began work at the Community Center for the Homeless and enrolled in college (at which time Jessica Beal left the series). Several months later, a reformed Mary returned to Glen Oak to surprise her father on his birthday. Mary also surprised her family by announcing she had become a flight attendant for Jet Blue Airlines (she now lives in Fort Lauderdale, Florida). Mary's favorite dinner is pot roast and apple pie. Although not a regular, Mary appears on occasion.

See also: Eric and Annie Camden, Lucy Camden, Matt Camden, Ruthie Camden, Simon Camden.

761. Mary Cherry, *Popular*, WB, 1999–2001. Played by Leslie Grossman.

Mary Cherry is a very beautiful 16-year-old blonde. She is the daughter of Cheri Cherry, a fabulously wealthy businesswoman (owner of the Cheri Cherry Corporation) and is a very popular girl at John F. Kennedy High in Los Angeles. Mary lives at 4420 Red Cherry Lane with her mother. There is no background information on Mary. All that is known is that "she is a mysterious transfer from Dallas" and that she was born with webbed hands and feet (12 operations were needed to cure her hands; her toes, for unexplained reasons, remain webbed). It was also revealed that at the age of four, Mary was overweight. To help her slim down her mother allowed her to smoke cigarettes.

Mary is a member of the school's gorgeous cheerleading team, the Glamazons. She has what she calls "my teen autograph book" (which contains the autographs of teen stars she meets). Gwyneth Paltrow is her favorite movie star ("I've seen *Shakespeare in Love* 12 times") and enjoys dinner at Croutons (a lobster restaurant). Her

after school hangout is the Coffee Shop and Roscoe's, the local diner. Mary's locker combination is 34-8-34.

Mary's mother, Cheri (Delta Burke), was a Dallas Cowboys Cheerleader and has been married eight times. She has raised Mary in the lap of luxury and Mary is extremely spoiled. She got a taste of poverty when an accounting error showed that Cheri lost her money. Mary came to school in a Hefty trash bag dress, cardboard box shoes and a new outlook on life: "Poverty is challenging." She survived by collecting and redeeming empty soda cans and by working in the school's cafeteria.

Mary idolizes her mother and has to be the star of her life (her mother knows Mary is not very smart but claims, "She is as loyal as a Rockweiller"). The results of a school aptitude test showed that Mary should prepare herself to become a serial killer.

See also: Brooke McQueen, Samantha McPherson.

762. Mary-Ellen Walton, *The Waltons*, CBS, 1972–1981. Played by Judy Norton-Taylor.

This entry also contains information on Mary-Ellen's sisters, Erin (Mary Elizabeth McDonough) and Elizabeth (Kami Cotler). Mary-Ellen, Erin and Elizabeth are the daughters of John and Olivia Walton. They live with their brothers (John-Boy, Jason, Ben and Jim-Bob) near the Blue Ridge Mountains in Jefferson County, Virginia, during the 1930s.

Mary-Ellen. Mary-Ellen is the oldest daughter and grew up as a tomboy. She loved sports, fishing and hiking and also had a fondness for caring — both people and animals (when she became upset she would go to the barn and hug a cow to feel better). Mary-Ellen became a nursing student and eventually the county nurse. She contemplated becoming an army nurse during World War II but found she was needed more in Jefferson County than at the warfront. Mary-Ellen found her first true romance with Willard Curtis, a doctor who established a practice in the county. He and Mary-Ellen married and had a son (John Curtis Walton Willard). Curtis joined the Army Medical Corps and was sent overseas during the war. He was reported as missing in action and presumed dead. Mary-Ellen received help in raising her son from her family; she married Arlington "Jonesy" Westcott after the war.

Erin. Erin, the middle daughter, is a best friend with Mary-Ellen (although they fight and have their differences, they always make up and are very close). Erin worked as an operator at the

Jefferson County Phone Company and later works at the Pickett Metal Products Company. Erin is the prettiest of the sisters but not the most studious (she is an average student at school). Her first love was George "G.W." Haines (reported as killed in action during World War II). She later married Paul Northridge.

Elizabeth. Elizabeth, the youngest daughter, has a mind of her own. She shares John-Boy's love of reading and writing. She is also carefree and anxious to grow up (and she does grow from young child to young woman over the course of the series). Elizabeth was best friends with Aimee Godsey and worked as a clerk in her father's store, Godsey's General Merchandise. Elizabeth had a pet cat (Calico) and nursed a sick raccoon (Pete) back to health.

See also: John and Olivia Walton, John-Boy Walton (for information on John-Boy, Jason, Ben and Jim-Bob Walton), Zeb and Esther Walton.

763. Mary Hartman, *Mary Hartman, Mary Hartman*, Syn., 1976–1977. Played by Louise Lasser.

Mary Penelope Hartman is a very pretty housewife and mother who lives at 343 Bratner Avenue in the small town of Fernwood, Ohio. She is married to Tom (Greg Mullavey) and the mother of Heather (Claudia Lamb).

Mary is the daughter of George and Martha Schumway. She was born in Fernwood on April 8, 1945. She attended Woodland Heights Elementary School and is a graduate of Fernwood High School. Mary was a typical kid. She enjoyed playing with dolls and helping her mother around the house. She was good in school and had planned to work with her father at the Fernwood Auto Plant (the main industry in town). Her life changed when she entered high school. She discovered boys and immediately began a steady relationship with Tom who is four years her senior (Mary was a freshman and Tom a senior when they met). Tom acquired a job at the auto plant when he graduated and continued to date Mary. They married when Mary turned 17 and first lived with her parents.

Mary's so-called wild life ended when she became pregnant soon after. She quickly settled into the role of housewife and mother and 14 years later (when the series begins) has a dull and boring life. Mary has become totally dependant on Tom and lives for the time they can spend together at night. Mary enjoys a cup of coffee in the morning but worries "about the yellow waxy build-up on the kitchen floor" all the time. Her wardrobe is totally conservative and she rarely dresses to be alluring or sexy. She is not as attractive as she once was or could now be and has created a shell around herself, believing she is not capable of being anything more than a housewife.

Mary was once a romantic girl who craved all the affection she could get. She is now often depressed, not as romantic and not always in need of attention. She has sex with Tom only because she knows she will lose him if she doesn't (he has cheated on her and she suspects it but can't prove it). Mary is a constant worrier. She worries about everything — from getting a good night's sleep to whether Heather will live up to her expectations and develop large breasts (she doesn't seem to worry about Heather's school grades. Even though 12-year-old Heather has not physically developed yet, Mary bought her a training bra "to show her I have faith in her"). Mary is mesmerized by TV soap operas (she feels for the characters) and she smokes a cigarette when she gets nervous (often lighting the filter tip end and smoking the non filtered end). When she becomes upset she says, "I need a glass of water." She appears to get a lot of help from a magazine called *It's a Woman's World* and when she begins talking about something she constantly rambles. While sex doesn't always please Mary, getting rid of that waxy yellow build up keeps her going. She's determined to find a way to get rid of it.

764. Mary Jo Shively, *Designing Women*, CBS, 1986–1993. Played by Annie Potts.

Mary Jo Shively works as a decorator and buyer for Sugarbaker and Associates — Interior Design at 1521 Sycamore Street in Atlanta, Georgia. Mary Jo was born in Atlanta and raised as a Baptist. She is a graduate of Franklin High School and Atlanta State College. She is divorced (from Ted) and the mother of two children (Claudia Marie and Quentin). She says, "The best time of my life was raising my two children."

Mary Jo has a small bosom and is envious of women with larger breasts. She also has a fixation about breasts "because a big bust means power and respect — not only from men, but also from women." She contemplated implants (to become a 36C) but decided against it. Mary Jo wears a size six shoe and has a dog named Brownie. She wrote the children's book *Billy Bunny* and was voted Parent Volunteer of the Year by the PTA in 1991. Mary Jo is a very devoted mother and puts her children before her work.

See also: Anthony Bouvier, Charlene Frazier, Julia Sugarbaker, Suzanne Sugarbaker.

765. Mary Kate and Ashley Burke, *Two of a Kind*, ABC, 1998–1999. Played by Mary Kate and Ashley Olsen.

Mary Kate and Ashley Burke are 12-year-old identical twins who have been raised by their father (Kevin) since the death of their mother (Janice) six years earlier. Mary Kate and Ashley were born in Chicago and live at 238 Belmont Avenue.

Although they are identical they are as different as night and day. Mary Kate is a tomboy; Ashley is glamorous and fashion conscious. Ashley has aspirations to become a model. Standing in front of a mirror and acting like a super model is her favorite activity ("I've been doing it since I could stand"). The girls share a bedroom. When Mary Kate is trying to fall asleep at night, Ashley keeps her awake by talking about clothes. If Ashley needs to wear something grubby, she borrows one of Mary Kate's shirts. At school Ashley has mirrors and makeup in her locker and wishes she had an electrical outlet for her curling iron. She attends dance classes and "going to the mall to spend Dad's money" cheers her up when she is depressed.

"People think of me as a tomboy but I'm a girl too and like to do girl things too," says Mary Kate. Mary Kate is untidy, likes camping and sports, and is slowly becoming interested in boys. She is not as smart as Ashley in school but was chosen over Ashley for her natural look for a fashion layout in *Real Teen* magazine. As the series progressed Mary Kate found makeup to be her friend and dressing like a girl to give her attention she never had before. The girls have to be in bed by 9:00 P.M. They buy their C.D.s at Mega Records and enjoy pizza at Pepperoni Joe's. Mary Kate has a pet pigeon named Harriet; green is Ashley's favorite color; and double fudge crunch bars are Ashley's favorite snack.

766. Mary Richards, *The Mary Tyler Moore Show*, CBS, 1970–1977. Played by Mary Tyler Moore.

Mary Richards is the producer of *The Six O'clock News*, on WJM-TV, Channel 12, in Minneapolis, Minnesota. She is attractive, single and in her thirties. At the present time she is not interested in marriage. Mary is sweet, trusting and speaks her mind (although at such times she becomes nervous and stammers). Mary is the daughter of Walter and Dotty Richards and was born in Roseberg, Minnesota, in 1940. She attended Leif Erickson High School (class of 1959), where she was a cheerleader and voted "Most Popular Girl" in the school.

Mary is a Presbyterian and lives in Apartment D at 119 North Weatherly. Her rent is $125 a month. She has an I.Q. of 118 and keeps a complete record of everything she does. She enjoys a chef's salad for lunch and makes chocolate chip cookies to impress guests. Mary does charity work for the YWCA and helps support her grandmother by sending her $45 a month.

Mary can type 65 words a minute. She has a large *M* on her living room wall and a picture of herself with a poodle on the desk near the front door. Mary's favorite drink is a vodka tonic. If somebody's stomach growls, Mary believes people will think it is hers. She washes her hair before she goes to the hairdresser and cares what other people think of her. Her favorite movie is *Gone with the Wind*. Mary was the associate producer and was hired because the job was open and her boss, Lou Grant, saw that she has "a nice caboose." When Lou made himself the executive producer, Mary became the producer. Mary is famous for her dinner parties, which never turn out right and are best described by Lou: "I've had some of the worst times in my life at your dinner parties."

In 1977, Mary was fired and left WJM and Minneapolis forever. In the ABC TV movie update, *Mary and Rhoda* (February 7, 2000), it is learned that Mary is a recent widow and the mother of Rose, an English major at N.Y.U. Her late husband, Steve Corwin, was a congressman who died in a rock climbing accident. Mary was now living in New York City at 415 84th Street and Central Park West and employed as a segment producer for WNYT-TV, Channel 6. She worked previously as an in-studio producer for ABC news.

See also: Lou Grant, Rhoda Morganstern, Ted Baxter.

Matlock *see* **Ben Matlock**

767. Matt Camden, *7th Heaven*, WB, 1996 (current). Played by Barry Watson.

Matthew Camden, called Matt, is the oldest son of Eric and Annie Camden, a Protestant minister and his wife. Matt has six siblings (Mary, Simon, Lucy, Ruthie and twins Sam and David) and lives with them in Glen Oak, California. Matt is attending Kennedy High School when the series begins. He was valedictorian of his graduating class and took a pre-college job as an intern in Washington, D.C., in First Lady Hilary Clinton's Summer Work Program. Matt's interest, however, turned away from politics to the medical profession. He enrolled at Crawford College and held a job as an orderly at the Free Clinic. He later acquired a position in the food services department at Glen Oak Hospital (then as an orderly when he became a pre-med student). His first job during high school was at the Dairy Shack.

Life changed drastically for Matt when he met fellow medical student Sarah Glass (Sarah Danielle Madison) and fell in love. Sarah is Jewish and had been raised to marry within her religion. Despite the objections of his parents, Matt converted to Judaism and married Sarah. They moved to Manhattan where they began their internship at New York Hospital (at which time Barry Watson left the series; he returned as an occasional "guest star").

See also: Eric and Annie Camden, Lucy Camden, Mary Camden, Ruthie Camden, Simon Camden.

768. Matt Dillon, *Gunsmoke*, CBS, 1955–1975. Played by James Arness.

This entry also contains information on Kitty Russell (Amanda Blake), Doc Adams (Milburn Stone) and Festus Haggen (Ken Curtis), friends of Matt.

Matthew Dillon, called Matt, is a U.S. Marshal stationed in Dodge City, Kansas (1870s). He is a tough, honest and fair lawman who is fast with his guns, but not always quick to use them. Matt will only kill if circumstances force his hand. He would like outlaws to surrender rather than fight because he believes a fair trial is a just means of deciding fate.

Matt has an office on Front Street and earns $100 a month (the office wall has five rifles chained together in a rack and the famous coffee pot with the rust stain seen in the closing theme over the credits is next to his desk). He has a horse named Marshall (with two l's) and pays $35 for a saddle.

Matt is a bachelor (never been married) and enjoys a drink at the Long Branch, a saloon run by Kitty Russell, an auburn-haired beauty who shares a platonic relationship with Matt. Kitty appears at times to be all business. She has had a hard life and struggled to succeed in a world where women were not meant to be anything but dressmakers, wives or saloon girls. Kitty broke that mold and now fiercely defends her livelihood.

Kitty and Matt never kissed; they were more in admiration of each other as opposed to being lovers. Matt, however, did have a much more meaning relationship with a woman named "Mike" Yardner (Michael Learned). Mike was introduced in the episode "Matt's Love Story" on September 24, 1973. She was a widow who found Matt suffering from amnesia after being ambushed by a murder suspect. Mike nursed Matt back to health and he had his first screen kiss. It was not revealed until the TV movie *Gunsmoke: The Last Apache* (CBS, March 18, 1990) that Matt is the father of a girl named Beth (Amy Stock). It appears that during Matt's recuperation in1973 that he and Mike had made love. Matt had amnesia and Mike never told him about the affair. Mike was now the owner of the Yardner Cattle Ranch. In the follow up TV movie, *Gunsmoke: To the Last Man* (CBS, January 10, 1992), Matt has become Beth's guardian after Mike dies from a high fever.

Galen Adams, fondly called "Doc," is the town's lone physician (Matt is his best customer as Doc is seemingly always digging a bullet out of him). Doc is well educated and has opinions about everything. He can only be as helpful as 1870s medical knowledge will allow and his prognosis is often "We'll have to wait and see."

Doc is a bachelor and has his office on Front Street. He enjoys a drink at the Long Branch Saloon and when puzzled or talking, he has a tendency to grab his ear or nose.

Festus Haggen is the Deputy Marshal to Matt Dillon (he replaced Matt's former deputy, Chester Goode [Dennis Weaver], a kind man who walked with a limp, called Matt "Mister Dillon" and brewed "a mean pot of coffee"). Festus is from a backwoods family and uneducated (although he does have what today could be called street smarts). He is very loyal to Matt, whom he considers his best friend. Festus is a bachelor who also takes whatever odd jobs he can find to make money. He rides a mule named Ruth.

769. Matt Houston, *Matt Houston*, ABC, 1982–1985. Played by Lee Horsley.

Matlock Houston is a millionaire oil baron, cattle rancher and notorious playboy who relaxes by helping people who are in deep trouble and unable to turn to the police for help. C.J. Parsons (Pamela Hensley), Matlock's beautiful business associate and lover, assists him in his adventures.

Matt, as he likes to be called, was born into wealth but does not sit back and let others do the work. He is actively involved in the daily operations of all his holdings. He trusts only a very few people and one of those is C.J. Although Matt was born in Texas, he has set up his base of operations for Houston, Inc. in Los Angeles at 200 West Temple Street (address later given as 100 Century Plaza). He also owns Houston Investigations, the agency through which he enjoys doing what he likes doing best — solving crimes (he does have a private investigator's license). He also owns the Houston Cattle Ranch in Texas.

Matt's everyday business car is his Rolls Royce (plate COWBOY 1); he does his investigative work in a car he calls *Excalibur* (plate 21 VE 124). He calls his computer "Baby" and N10907 is the I.D. number of the Houston Industries helicopter. C.J. lives at 8766 West Beverly, Apartment 3C; 555-3141 is Matt's office telephone number and his and C.J.'s favorite eatery is Mama Novelli's Restaurant.

770. Matt McGuire, *Lizzie McGuire*, Disney, 2001–2004. Played by Jake Thomas.

Matthew McGuire is the younger brother of Lizzie McGuire. They live with their parents, Sam and Jo, at 804 Linwood Drive in an unspecified city. Lizzie is the good child; Matt, as he is called, is the mischievous one. Matt is rarely good; when he is, his parent's suspect he is up to something.

Matt sleeps with the windows open, the door closed and with a psychedelic night-light. When Matt felt he needed a place of his own, he dug a cave for himself in the woods that he called "The Matt Cave." When he becomes bored Matt dresses as a super hero he calls "Matt Man" (who does good deeds around the neighborhood). Matt is a member of the Wilderness Cadets and his curfew is 6:00 P.M. (or when the street lights turn on). He likes to impress girls by saying things about himself that are not true. He appeared in a TV commercial for Cardio Punch, a sports drink for teenagers, and became famous as "The Goofy Face Kid" when he appeared on *The Uncle Wendell Show* and made a funny face. Matt had an interactive internet site called "Matt After Dinner," was in a band called Spoink, and invented a vanilla drink he tried to sell from his backyard in a night club setting he called Club Flamingo.

Matt attends the Main Street Grammar School. He is on the soccer team, but the worst player. He sneaks out of class to take naps with the kindergarten children. Matt had an invisible alien friend named Jasper and eats a breakfast cereal called Computers.

See also: Lizzie McGuire.

771. Matt Stewart, *Raising Dad*, WB, 2001–2002. Played by Bob Saget.

Matt Stewart is a widower who lives at 803 Linden Avenue with his daughters Sarah and Emily. He is a graduate of Boston College and now teaches creative writing at Barrington High School. Matt married his college sweetheart, Abby, in 1985. They first lived in a small apartment on Beacon Street (where Sarah was born in 1986). When Matt acquired full teacher status they moved to a home on Linden Avenue. Shortly after the birth of Emily (1991), Abby died from complications of childbirth. At this time the family had a dog named Mildred.

Matt has an office in the basement where he enjoys writing in his spare time. He is the author of a book called *Monheign Island* and is an "expert" on golf—"Ask me anything you want about it, except how to play well." Matt has an autographed copy of Hemingway's *The Sun Also Rises* and enjoys playing Scrabble with Sarah and Emily on Sunday evenings.

See also: Emily Stewart, Sarah Stewart.

Maureen Robinson *see* **John Robinson**

Maverick *see* **Bret and Bart Maverick**

772. Mavis Rae, *Whoopi*, NBC, 2003–2004. Played by Whoopi Goldberg.

Mavis Rae is a famous singer who now owns the LaMont Hotel in New York City. She is the daughter of Lawrence and Viveca Rae and was raised in a very strict household. She was a mischievous child and spanked when she was bad and spanked again by her mother for what she thought Mavis would do. She has a younger brother named Courtney (the good kid).

In her adult life Mavis is a liberal. She is loud, vulgar, crass and opinionated (as she says, "I smoke, drink, and cuss like a sailor"). In her professional career, Mavis had one hit record in 1986—"Don't Hide Love" (which, in 2004, gays and lesbians proclaimed to be their theme song). She was previously in an all-black group called The Ebony Blackbirds and had one hit with them, "Chocolate Love." Mavis bared all at Woodstock, played Las Vegas, spent time in jail (charges not stated) and won two Grammy awards.

Mavis is afraid of small spaces, a hockey fan (the N.Y. Rangers) and the rumba is her favorite dance. If Mavis acts nicely something is wrong. Bad news calls for Mavis to take a drink; really bad news and it's straight to the bottle. Mavis bought the hotel with the money she earned as a singer to provide for her retirement. She enjoys her weekly poker game with her cigarette-smoking, liquor-drinking girlfriends.

See also: Courtney Rae, Rita Nash.

773. Max Guevara, *Dark Angel*, Fox, 2000–2002. Played by Jessica Alba.

Max (rarely called by any other name) is a young woman who was designed to be the perfect soldier. Technically, she is a chimera (a mythological creature). She has eleven "brothers and sisters" and was created at a secret genetics lab called Manticore in the mountains of Gillette, Wyoming. The scientists at Manticore sought to produce superior humans for the military. Women were used to produce the children whose DNA was altered. The mother and child were never permitted to meet. Max was such a creation.

As Max grew she was placed in Block 12 with a group called X-5. Max has a barcode on the back of her neck for I.D. purposes (332960073952) and her file is X5–452. She is very strong and, as a child, excelled in telecommunications. The pupils in Max's eyes work like a telescope lens and can pinpoint distant objects. She can dodge a bullet and has a photographic memory. Max also has a genetic flaw — seizures and must take medication (tryptophan) to control them. Max is also on the run. She has escaped from Manticore (who want to retrieve her) and now, at age 19, supports herself as a bike messenger for the Jam Pony-X-Press Messenger Service. The time is 2019 at a time when computers have been wiped out by "The Pulse" and the United States is a third world country in a deep depression.

Max rides a Kawasaki motorcycle (plate JG 154) and breaks the law to get what she wants. She steals, cheats and lies without remorse. When she gets set to ride her cycle she says, "Gotta bounce." Max wears cherry lip baum and when she has to be by herself she seeks the serenity of the top of the Seattle Space Needle building ("I look down at the people and think how everybody has problems ... and if I sit up here long enough I start to feel like I'm one of those people, a normal girl").

Max is considered by Manticore to be a rogue X-5. She is top of the line (other X-5s have been affected by the aging process. Max's DNA is now needed to create flawless soldiers). When she was a child imprisoned at Manticore, Max found faith in the Lady of the Sacred Heart (whom she called "The Blue Lady" [for the blue garments she wore]). Although Max was genetically engineered to kill, she is opposed to guns. Max can see in the dark, prowl like a cat, and doesn't need to sleep. She resides in a small apartment in Seattle, Washington, but "lives a life on the run, always looking over my shoulder." Max is not all bad; she helps cyber journalist Logan Cale bring criminals to justice.

774. Maxwell Beckett, *Over My Dead Body*, CBS, 1990–1991. Played by Edward Woodward.

Maxwell Beckett is a British mystery story novelist who pretends to be a former Scotland Yard Investigator to give credibility to his books. He has led his readers to believe he was called "Beck-

ett of the Yard" and "The Catcher of Uncatchable Thieves, the Solver of Unsolvable Crimes." Maxwell has written six books, but only three were a success: *All That Glitters, The Fire Confrontations, Hanging Crimes, Hooker by Crook, Over My Dead Body* and *Taking the Heart.* He has also written a series of children's books (*M. Mongoose*) under the pen name A.J. Edison.

Maxwell lives in San Francisco, California. He is divorced (from Diane), drives a Rolls Royce (plate 2915 AJ), and donates money to a charity called the Fog City Shelter. He enjoys a meal at Alotta's Restaurant and 555-4242 is his phone number. Max now investigates crimes for story material and constantly argues with his publisher (who feel Max's books need more grit). After such conversations, Max goes to the local park to argue with himself.

See also: Nikki Page (the girl who assists Max).

775. Maxwell Klinger, *M*A*S*H*, CBS, 1972–1983. Played by Jamie Farr.

Maxwell Q. Klinger is a corpsman assigned to the 4077th Mobile Army Surgical Hospital (M*A*S*H) unit in Korea during the war. He is considered the company's "resident loon" as he pretends to be insane to get a Section 8 psychiatric discharge. He is first a corporal then a sergeant and dresses in women's clothes hoping to convince his superiors "that I'm nuts." He patrols in a skirt and purchases his gowns from Mr. Syd of Toledo, Ohio (his home town). Klinger (as he is always called) became the company clerk when Radar O'Reilly was given a hardship discharge. He hates "the damned army but I love the people." He calls the trucks that bring in the wounded "the bad humor trucks" and published the camp newsletter *M*A*S*H Notes* (he also wrote the advice column "Dear Aunt Sadie").

Klinger doesn't relax ("If I do someone will think I like it here"). In the last episode, Klinger married Soon-Lee (Rosalind Chao), a migrant farm worker. In the series update, *After-M*A*S*H* (CBS, 1983-84), Klinger and Soon-Lee move to Riverbend, Missouri, where Klinger accepts the offer of his former commander, Sherman Potter, to work at the General Pershing V.A. Hospital.

See also: Benjamin Franklin Pierce, B.J. Hunnicutt, Frank Burns, Henry Blake, Margaret Houlihan, Radar O'Reilly, Sherman Potter, Trapper John McIntire.

776. Maxwell Sheffield, *The Nanny*, CBS, 1993–1999. Played by Charles Shaugnessy.

Maxwell Sheffield is a widower with three children (Maggie, Gracie and Bryton) who lives on

New York's fashionable Park Avenue. A nanny (Fran Fine) cares for the children and Maxwell, a successful Broadway producer, runs Sheffield-Babcock Productions with his partner, C.C. Babcock (Maxwell originally ran the company as Maxwell Sheffield Productions).

Maxwell was born in England and attended the Eton School (where he was captain of the water polo team). He has a sister (Jocelyn) who called him "Puddle Duck" (he called her "Mopsey"). A strict nanny (Clara Mueller) raised Maxwell; Maxwell, however, is not strict with his children (nor is Fran). Maggie, Gracie and Bryton are basically good kids and require little disciplining. They are obedient, but when they disobey, a firm talking to usually resolves the problem

Maxwell produced his first play, *The Sound of Music*, at the age of 17. He has also produced *Annie 2*, *Norma*, *Whodunit*, *The Widower*, *Moby*, *Regardless* and *Loves Me Not* (but he considers his children his three greatest productions). His shows have won him three Tony awards. Maxwell has been listed by *Esquire* magazine as one of the most eligible widowers (his late wife was named Sarah). A love interest developed between Maxwell and Fran and they married (and became the parents of twins they named Eve Kathryn and James Samuel).

See also: C.C. Babcock, Fran Fine, Gracie Sheffield, Maggie Sheffield.

777. Maxwell Smart, *Get Smart*, NBC, 1965–1969; CBS, 1969–1970. Played by Don Adams.

Maxwell Smart, salesman for the Pontiac Greeting Card Company, is the cover used by Maxwell Smart, an agent for CONTROL, a secret U.S. government agency that battles the evils of THRUSH. CONTROL is located at 123 Main Street in Washington, D.C., and Max, as he is called, operates as Agent 86. He works most often with Agent 99, the woman he would eventually marry.

Max is accident-prone and believes his main weapons are his constant vigilance and his razor-sharp instincts. He wears a size 40 regular jacket and has a standard issue shoe phone (the Chief's means of contacting Max in the field). He drives a red sports car (plate 6A7 379) and has to use the voice-activated password *Bismark* to enter his booby-trapped apartment.

Max has a mostly unknown past. He was born and raised in Washington, D.C. (1930 is mentioned but it could be a cover). His parents are never seen or mentioned (the only relatives ever seen are his Uncle Albert and Aunt Bertha). Max is a college graduate and served a hitch in Korea during the war (where he was a corporal). He joined CONTROL after his enlistment to fight the forces of evil "and serve on the side of goodness and niceness." He wasn't the best student in spy school but did manage to graduate and become an agent under the supervision of Thaddeus (the Chief), a man who has been driven batty by Max's constant fumbling (but it is also that fumbling that enables Max to get the best of the bad guys and successfully complete a case. He was honored with "The Spy of the Year" Award"). Max was also chosen "Best Dressed" by the industry magazine *Popular Espionage*.

Max enjoys a good game of chess and poker and has a midnight snack before bedtime. He is afraid of lightning and sleeps with a teddy bear. Max can speak several languages and is a trained karate expert. Max's catch phrases are "Sorry about that, Chief," "Would you believe...," and "I asked you not to tell me that."

In the 1989 TV movie update, *Get Smart Again*, Max had become a protocol officer for the State Department when CONTROL was deactivated in 1974. He is back as a spy when KAOS threatens the world with a weather machine and CONTROL is reactivated. In the series update, *Get Smart* (Fox, 1995), Max is now the Chief of CONTROL and the father of a son (Zack) who is following in his father's fumbling footsteps.

See also: The Chief, 99.

778. Maya, *Space: 1999*, Syn., 1975–1977. Played by Catherine Schell.

Maya is a beautiful inhabitant of a planet called Psychon. She was born in the Manos Project on the Third Day of the Tayad (she is 6752 years old in Psychon years). Psychon is a world of peace with only one race, government, culture and religion. She is the daughter of Mentor, a famous scientist, and possesses the ability to morph (change into anything organic by concentrating). Maya is sensuous, emotional and has a computer-like brain. She now serves as the science officer on Moonbase Alpha and can analyze raw data in an instant (faster than the base's computers).

Moonbase Alpha was an Earth project designed to repel alien invaders by establishing an early warning system on the moon. In 1999 a radioactive chain reaction blasted the moon out of its orbit and marooned 300 astronauts in space. John Koenig, the commander of Moonbase Alpha, rescued Maya when her planet was destroyed. She is now the only alien resident of Moonbase Alpha. Maya's features changed slightly with episodes. During the first season she had brown ears and well-defined side burns. Less noticeable side burns and pink ears can be seen during the second season.

See also: Alan Carter, Helena Russell, John Koenig, Victor Bergman.

779. Maya Gallo, *Just Shoot Me,* NBC, 1997–2003. Played by Laura San Giacomo.

Maya Gallo is a beautiful young woman who works as the articles editor for *Blush,* a Manhattan-based fashion magazine owned by her father, Jack Gallo (her mother is Eve Gallo). Maya was born in Manhattan on January 1st and as a child wore her hair in pig tails and was overweight ("I was called Crisco by my schoolmates because I was fat in the can"). Maya attended the Westbridge School, the Columbia School of Journalism and Stanford University (where she did her undergraduate work). In another episode Maya mentions that she majored in Shakespeare in college. She appeared in 10 productions and named the family cat Othello. Earlier, when Maya had an interest in flying, she named her pet turtle Amelia Earhart (she also had a dog named Rags). She has B-negative blood.

Maya previously worked in the Channel 8 news department (she was fired for making an anchorwoman cry). She now lives in Apartment 803 and believes people "see me as a straight-laced, uptight school teacher. But I'm not. I like to have fun." Maya takes pottery classes, tutors children in her spare time and finds video games exciting. Maya hoped to launch her own magazine, *Emily* (named after her favorite poet, Emily Dickinson). The magazine was to be like *The New Yorker* "but without the flash." She was unable to do it because the market couldn't support another magazine, especially an intellectual one. Maya heads the magazine's charity wing and was awarded the Our Guardian Angel Award for her work for the Avalon Foundation Charity.

See also: Dennis Finch, Jack Gallo, Nina Van Horn.

780. Maya Wilkes, *Girlfriends,* UPN, 2000 (current). Played by Golden Brooks.

Maya Wilkes is the legal secretary to Joan Clayton at the Los Angeles law firm of Goldberg, Sweedlestein and Donaldson (later called McDonald, Sweedleson and Goldstein, then Goldberg, Sweedlestein, Donaldson and Lee). She was born on a farm in Fresno and attended U.C.L.A. for two years. She later enrolled at the City of Industry School of Life Science at the Monrovian School of Psychology. Maya lives in Unit 8 at the Leimert Park Village and is married (her husband is in the air force) and the mother of a son (Jubara).

Maya reads *Black Detective* magazine (she is hoping to stumble across a crime and write an article); her claim to fame is that her cousin is BernNadette Stanis (played Thelma on the TV series *Good Times*). Maya is a Baptist and a Democrat and is afraid of gaining weight. She dislikes cats and believes she is not only gorgeous but also brilliant. She put her writing ability to use and became the author of *Oh Hell, Yes,* a book published by Inner Vision Press, that tells what Maya is all about. She lunches with her girlfriends (Joan, Lynn and Toni) at a restaurant called Skia's.

See also: Joan Clayton, Lynn Searcy, Toni Childs.

781. Maynard G. Krebs, *Dobie Gillis,* CBS, 1959–1963. Played by Bob Denver.

Maynard G. Krebs is a young man who enjoys the simple, uncomplicated things in life. He was also something that no longer exists — a beatnik, a person who lived a simple existence with few worries or cares.

Maynard lives at 1343 South Elm Street in Central City and is best friends with Dobie Gillis, a fellow student at Central High School. He calls Dobie "Good Buddy." Maynard has a stuffed armadillo (Herman) and says the *G* in his name stands for Walter. He receives an allowance of 35 cents a week and he claims to have the world's largest collection of tin foil (which he collects as a large ball). Maynard loves to play the bongo drums and hang out at Riff's Music Store (where he plays jazz records so much he wears out the grooves).

Maynard has been turned down 46 times in six years for his driver's license and claims the longest word he can pronounce is delicatessen. His favorite movie is *The Monster That Devoured Cleveland* (apparently the only movie that ever plays at the Bijou Theater). Maynard enjoys simple activities like watching workmen paint a new white line down Elm Street or being there when they knock down the old Endicott Building. Maynard panics when he hears the word *work* and responds with "You Rang" when his name is mentioned.

Maynard's favorite after school hangout is Charlie Wong's Ice Cream Parlor. He was also in the army and later attended S. Peter Pryor Junior College (both with Dobie). In the 1977 series update, *Whatever Happened to Dobie Gillis?*, Maynard is seen as a rich and successful businessman (the same position he held in the 1988 CBS TV movie, *Bring Me the Head of Dobie Gillis*).

See also: Chatsworth Osborne, Jr., Dobie Gillis.

782. McKenzie Previn, *Adventure, Inc.*, Syn., 2002–2003. Played by Karen Cliche.

McKenzie Previn is a beautiful diving and demolition specialist who works for Judson Cross, a world famous marine biologist who runs an ocean salvage business called Adventure, Inc., a business that is more dangerous than it sounds for all the unscrupulous characters McKenzie and Judson must battle.

McKenzie was born in France but was raised in the U.S. She previously worked for the CIA as an expert on weapons and explosives. She is also good in math and takes care of Judson's business finances. McKenzie loves raspberries, lilies and small hotel rooms that overlook the water. Her looks are also deceiving. While she uses her attributes for distraction purposes during assignments, she is well versed in the martial arts and can take care of herself in any situation (a skill she attributes to her CIA training). McKenzie needs to look her best in any situation; she is particularly fussy about her nail polish — she needs to use the right shade for the job at hand. She is also very careful and will not rush into any situation without thinking first — another trait she can trace back to the CIA (she was almost killed during an assignment for being impulsive and not doing what she was taught).

See also: Judson Cross.

783. Meadow Soprano, *The Sopranos*, HBO, 1999 (current). Played by Jamie-Lynn DiScala.

Meadow Mari Angela Soprano is the first-born child of wise guy Tony Soprano and his wife Carmela. Meadow is currently studying law at Columbia University and volunteers at a legal clinic called the South Brown Law Center. Meadow was born in New Jersey and grew up believing her father was in the waste disposal business. During one Easter egg hunt, when Meadow found a .45 automatic pistol and $50,000 in Krugerands, she also learned the truth about her father's mob-connected business. Surprisingly, Meadow was not shocked; instead, she confessed that her father is just as respectable as the lawyers who work for the tobacco companies. Meadow was an Honors Student in high school and the least of Tony's problems. Meadow is smart and can survive on her own.

See also: Carmela Soprano, Janice Soprano, Tony Soprano.

784. Mel Sharples, *Alice*, CBS, 1976–1985. Played by Vic Tayback.

Melvin Emory Sharples is the owner of Mel's Diner, a less-than-fashionable roadside eatery at 1030 Bush Highway in Phoenix, Arizona.

Mel, as he is called, was born in Arizona and lives in Apartment 107 at 634 Plainview Drive (a poster of Farrah Fawcett, later Loni Anderson, can be seen on his living room wall). As a child in school Mel was worried about his nose. He was called "Hose Nose." In the navy his mates called him "Banana Nose." When he was shipped overseas to Japan, the Japanese dubbed him "Hanason" ("Mr. Nose"). He now has the distinction of being called "Super Schnoz" by the guys on his bowling team (in another episode, Mel complained that is school he was called "Smelly Melly" and "Jelly Belly"). Mel is also the landlord of the neighboring Mother Goose Preschool.

Mel is proud of his cooking (although he has been told his brownies taste like asphalt). He produced his own Mel's Diner T-shirts (his picture on the front; the diner on the back). He attended pastry school (where he learned how to make roses as cupcake toppers); was "Be Boppin' Mel Sharples" for a 25th anniversary celebration at Vinnie's House of Veal; and he took a temporary job with the R.J. Catering Company when he thought he should try something different (he quit when he couldn't be his own boss).

Mel never married "because I'm married to this diner." He has an account at the Desert Bank and keeps the diner's month old bills in a Thom McAn shoebox; older bills are placed in a Buster Brown shoebox. The only way Mel knows how to be nice to people (especially his waitresses) is to yell at them. He also stands up for what he believes in "and it doesn't matter which waitress gets into trouble for it." Mel buys his polyester suits at Syd's Stylist Shop. His car license plate reads NA 087 and his third-place bowling trophy sits on his desk in the diner's storeroom.

See also: Alice Hyatt, Flo Castleberry, Jolene Hunnicutt, Vera Gorman.

Melanie Brody *see* **The Girls of Degrassi**

785. Melissa Santos, *Ann Jillian*, NBC, 1989–1990. Played by Chantal Rivera-Batisse.

Melissa Santos is a 15-year-old girl who lives in the small town of Marvel, California. She was born on June 9, 1974, and lives at 3162 Turtle Dove Drive with her parents George and Carmen. Melissa attends Marvel High School and is conceited ("She cares only about how she looks and what the guys think"). Melissa believes no girl can match her beauty and hopes to become a future Miss America. She holds the beauty pageant titles "Miss Teenage Tomato" and "Miss Teen Avocado" and believes she has untapped talent as a singer and dancer "and I want to set it free" (she wants to be the next Madonna, whom she feels "is over the hill"). Melissa takes dancing lessons from Ann McNeal, the mother of her best friend, Lucy. Melissa has never heard of Ann's dancing idols, Fred Astaire and Cyd Charisse and has to cope with something that she feels makes her unattractive — "I wish I could do something about this sweating. It's so icky."

See also: Ann McNeal.

786. Melody Angel, *Captain Scarlet and the Mysterons*, Syn., 1967. Voiced by Sylvia Anderson.

Melody Angel is a pilot for Spectrum, a futuristic defense organization that protects the Earth from alien invaders. Melody was born on a cotton farm in Atlanta, Georgia. She grew up as a tomboy and loved sports, especially racing cars. As she grew older her interests peaked and she took up professional motor racing. Melody took a break from the circuit to attend college. It was while she was studying at a Swiss finishing school that she developed an interest in flying. Melody was also an unruly student and expelled for behavior unbecoming of a student. With an interest in flying, Melody joined the World Army Air Force (where she displayed amazing courage and nerves of steel). Her abilities led Spectrum to hire her as a pilot. The program is a puppet series filmed in Supermarionation.

See also: Captain Magenta, Captain Ochre, Captain Scarlet, Destiny Angel, Harmony Angel, Rhapsody Angel, Symphony Angel.

787. Melvin Frohike, *The Lone Gunmen*, Fox, 2001. Played by Tom Braidwood.

Melvin Frohike and his partners, John Byers and Richard Langley, are the Lone Gunmen, publishers of *The Lone Gunman*, a computer newsletter that exposes injustice on all levels of society. The paper is based in Tacoma Park, Maryland, and is singular in name because it is the only such paper in America.

Melvin was born in Michigan and ran a company called Frohike Electronics (his sideline was selling illegal cable boxes). Melvin feels he is the one "who risks his butt doing all the outside work while Richard is behind the scenes" (at his computer in his run down green, white and rusty van; plate TSD 596). Melvin is short and unshaven. He loves women but is not a great talker. He is also sarcastic (but sensitive) and is the photographer and surveillance expert of the group. Melvin is also the inventor of a device called "The Frojack," a gizmo for tracking cars.

See also: John Byers, Richard Langley.

788. Marlene and Harlan Eldridge, *Evening Shade*, CBS, 1990–1994. Played by Ann Wedgeworth, Charles Durning.

Marlene Frazier and Harlan Eldridge were born in the small town of Evening Shade, Arkansas. They are graduates of Evening Shade High School and although Harlan is older than Marlene, they are happily married. Harlan is the town's only physician and also works at nearby City Hospital (also called Evening Shade Hospital). He and Marlene live on a plush estate they call Tara (both have been influenced by the movie *Gone with the Wind*). Harlan is a member of the Civil War Society and is most proud of his trophy room, where he displays the various fish he has caught over the years. He most enjoys fishing and does so from his boat *Tara of the Sea*.

Marlene is a very sexy woman and believes she is a magnet for perverts. She is a talented singer and as a child formed a singing group (with her sisters Jolene and Lerlene) called the Frazier Sisters. Marlene is proud of three pictures that hang on her walls: an American Indian, Billy Graham and Tom Selleck. She is also quite frugal for one with money. She likes to use inexpensive items to make things that are elegant (for example, taking Styrofoam and turning it into Christmas reindeer). Marlene enjoys reading *Southern Comfort* magazine and takes great pride in her heritage.

See also: Ava Newton, Molly and Taylor Newton, Wood Newton.

789. Michael and Jay Kyle, *My Wife and Kids*, ABC, 2001–2005. Played by Damon Wayans, Tisha Campbell.

This entry also contains information on the Kyle's children: Claire (Jazz Ray Cole, Jennifer Nicole Freeman), Junior (George O. Gore II), and Cady (Parker McKenna Posey).

Michael and Jay. Michael and Jay are a happily married couple who live in a 4500 square foot home with maroon shingles and green shutters in Connecticut. Michael is a former UPS driver who now runs Kyle's Trucking Company. Jay was first said to be a stockbroker, then an investment broker who gave up her career to raise their children. She has a dream to open her own restaurant and did so in the episode of November 16, 2004, when she started Jay's Soul Kitchen (originally called The Cobbler).

Michael is fond of Jay's peach cobbler and makes it his business to get the last piece at dinner "because I'm the king of the castle around here and it's the only perk I get." Jay has a tendency to give Michael strange anniversary gifts (for example, wooden shoes, an afro pick — when he is bald). Michael is also a bit strange at times — he eats pie while watching football games with a baby fork (makes the pie last longer). When Michael does something unexpected for Jay she says, "Did you take a good husband pill or something?" as it totally surprises her. If Michael tells Jay she looks great in an outfit, she sighs and says, "Now I gotta change" (many episodes focus on Jay's attempts to lose weight). Michael also has a bad habit of placing embarrassing pictures of the family on the refrigerator door (he calls it "The Wall of Shame"). Michael had a first car he called Trudy (an Audie 5000) and now drives a car with the license plate 258 N3R. When one of the kids needs to be disciplined, Michael and Jay flip a coin to determine who is to be "the bad guy." Grilled chicken is Michael's favorite food. Jay's license plate reads 490 FSW. Michael tries to relax by playing golf.

Claire. Michael worries about Claire growing up and no longer being his little girl. Claire is 12 years old when the series begins and is an A student at school (she sulks if she gets a lower grade). Michael calls her "My Black American Princess." Claire is beautiful but self-centered. She loves looking in mirrors, store windows, or any reflective surface to see herself. Claire, middle name Marie, is a cheerleader at school, takes dance lessons and has a 7 P.M. weekend curfew. Claire buys her lingerie at Vivica's Lingerie and stuffs her bra with socks because she believes "bigger breasts attract boys." She later increases her breast size by wearing "The Bosom Buddy Bra" to please boys. "If you want to be popular you have to have something going on up top," she says. Claire feels she can cook (although her cooking can kill a plant if placed next to the meal she is preparing) and is a bit clumsy (she has a tendency to trip and fall down a lot). She volunteers her time as a Big Sister and works after school as a salesgirl at Ann Tailor, a designer clothes shop. Jay would like to spend more time with Claire but Claire objects — "You're twice my age and not cool."

Junior. Pork rinds, naked women and video games inspire Michael Kyle, Jr. His father calls him "an expert in the dork department" as he is not too bright and is a rather poor student at school (he scored 200 on his SAT test. Normally students are given 300 points just for signing their name. Junior misspelled his name — using a "y" in Junior and 100 points was deducted from his score). Junior receives an allowance of $10 a week and does show some promise as an artist. But he is irresponsible when it comes to sex. His girlfriend Vanessa (Meagon Good, Brooklyn Sudano) became pregnant and gave birth to a son they named Michael Jr. (called "Junior Junior" by the family). Prior to marrying Vanessa (November 30, 2004), Junior kept his room a mess "because I feel comfortable in a mess" (he now lives with Vanessa in the converted Kyle garage and is rather neat and tidy). Junior originally attended Reddington University (2003) but quit when Vanessa became pregnant to work for his father (at $300 a week).

Cady. Cady, the youngest child (five when the series begins), attends Tumble Tots Pre-K School (later Crestview Elementary School). She is allergic to peanut oil and has a doll named Little Pippi. Cady loves licorice and eats Lucky Charms cereal for breakfast. She has a pet hamster (Buddy) and is close friends with Franklin Aloysius Mumford (Noah Gray-Cabey), a super intelligent little boy. He is seven years old, has degrees from Harvard and MIT and is a whiz at playing the piano. He has encyclopedic knowledge about everything and when he sees Cody he sighs, "You make the sun come up, you make the birds sing, you make my heart flutter." Cady attempted to make money by selling "Lemon Aids" for five cents a glass.

790. Michael Bluth, *Arrested Development*, Fox, 2003 (current). Played by Jason Bateman.

This entry also contains information on Lindsay Funke (Portia De Rossi), Michael's twin sister, and his brothers, Gob (George Oscar) and Buster (Tony Hale).

Michael. Michael is the son of George and Lucille Bluth. He is the only sane and responsible member of an eccentric family and runs Bluth Enterprises for his father. The Securities and Exchange Commission arrested George for cheating investors and treating the company like his own personal piggy bank (he is now serving time in the Orange County Penitentiary). Michael's grandfather began the Bluth Empire in 1953 when he opened the Bluth Frozen Banana Stand on Balboa Island in California (a frozen banana on a stick now sells for $1.00). George (Jeffrey Tambor) turned the one stand into a franchise and built the family fortune. As a kid Michael worked at the stand and is now struggling to keep the company from going bankrupt. He is a widower and lives with his son, George Michael (Michael Cera) in Sudden Valley (in Orange County) in the model home for the proposed Bluth Development Company (the company is in such financial straits that the only vehicle it owns is the Bluth Company Airplane Ladder Truck). Michael is calm and collected despite the constant annoyances his family causes. He tackles each crisis with cool thinking and it is only by cutting corners that he manages to keep the company afloat. Michael's mother Lucille (Jessica Walter) is a spoiled socialite who lives in luxury at the Balboa Towers (an apartment the company cannot really afford). Lucille has the distinction of being one of the world's worst drivers (subject of the TV program *The World's Worst Drivers*). Her car (plate 4JBG 794) has a rock in the back seat that Buster found on an expedition but now can't figure how to get it out.

Lindsay. Lindsay Funke is a beautiful woman who has no concept of money and is addicted to shopping. She is married to Tobias Funke (David Cross) and they are the parents of Maebe (Alia Shawkat). They rely on an allowance from Michael for their income. Tobias is a would-be actor but has never had an audition. Prior to this he was a psychiatrist but developed a number of phobias and is now very insecure (he lost his medical license while on a cruise. He administered CPR to a person he thought was having a heart attack. The Newsport newspaper headline read: "Sleeping Tourist has Sternum Broken"). Tobias then decided to become an actor. (Tobias was Chief Resident in Psychiatry at Massachusetts General Hospital for two years. He did his fellowship in psychoanalysis at MIT.)

Lindsay and Tobias lived previously in Boston (where they were famous for their cheese and wine fund-raisers. They were also in a band called Dr. Funke's 100% Natural Good Times Family Band Solution, wherein they sang about food and vitamins). Lindsay was famous in high school for winning the annual "Best Hairstyle Award." She is also proud of her lingerie pose as Miss December in the Ladies of Literacy Calendar. She is also an activist and not the best of mothers for Maebe (she rarely keeps tabs on her and allows her to get away with much nonsense).

Gob. George Oscar Bluth, II, called Gob (pronounced Jobe), is Michael's older brother. He is a would-be magician who prefers that his acts be called illusions not tricks ("A trick is something a whore does for money"). He started the Alliance of Magicians, which blacklists any magician who reveals the secrets of an illusion. His life revolves around magic and he is somewhat of a loner because of it.

Buster. Byron Bluth, called Buster, is the middle brother. He is a bit strange and doctors attribute his behavior to the 11 months he spent in the womb (his odd behavior alienates people). He is a graduate of the Milford School "where children should not be seen nor heard." He studied everything from Native American tribal ceremonies to the mapping of uncharted territories. He also suffers from crippling panic attacks.

791. Michael Flaherty, *Spin City*, ABC, 1996–2000. Played by Michael J. Fox.

Michael Patrick Flaherty is the Deputy Mayor of New York City (under Mayor Randall Winston). He is hyper, controlling and highly competitive. He is a graduate of Fordham University in the Bronx and in high school had the nickname "Newt" ("Like the small lizard"). Michael began his career as an intern to Congressman Owen Kingston. Mike, as he is most often called, has a fear of commitment (he feels being intimate with a girl will lead to marriage, something he doesn't want right now). Michael does date but everything must revolve around him (he is known as "The king of failed relationships").

Mike enjoys playing the guitar and lives in an apartment that overlooks Central Park. He is a Capricorn and believes his biggest job is making the Mayor look good as circumstances always seem to put Randall in a bad light (for example, when asked to throw out the first ball in a Little League game "and throwing like a girl"). To accomplish his goal Mike struggles to show the public that the Mayor has compassion (like taking him to a children's hospital — but here too things go wrong. Randall gave a child in the diabetic ward a Hershey Bar).

Mike is all work oriented and has no time for leisure activity. He is often so overworked that he has fantasies about people that only he and the viewing audience see. He manipulates people and the press in order to make himself (and the Mayor) look good. However, when things do not go his way he sometimes "rants like an idiot in search of a village."

In September of 2002 Mike manages to settle a taxi strike, get hookers out of Times Square and get a contract to renovate Grand Central Station. However, in doing so, he accepted favors for giving contracts. A scandal hits the Mayor's office and Mike resigns to protect Randall. Six weeks later he secures a job in Washington, D.C., as an environmental lobbyist. Charlie Crawford becomes the new Deputy Mayor (Mike worked with Randall for four years). Mike also lost his fear of commitment when he returned for a visit and was seen married to a girl named Allison (Olivia D'Abo).

See also: Caitlin Moore, Charlie Crawford, Paul Lassiter, Randall Winston, Stewart Bondek.

792. Michael Longstreet, *Longstreet*, ABC, 1971–1972. Played by James Franciscus.

Michael Longstreet is a blind insurance investigator for the Great Pacific Casualty Company in New Orleans, Louisiana. He lives at 835 Charles Street and is aided by Pax, a German shepherd seeing-eye dog. Mike, as he is called, is also a widower. His late wife, Ingrid, was killed in an explosion that was meant to kill him (Mike had been working on a case involving jewel thieves. They rigged a bottle of champagne to kill Mike and end his pursuit). Mike was blinded but not discouraged. His strong will and sense of justice enabled him to continue in his capacity as an investigator. Nikki Bell (Marlyn Mason) taught him to read Braille; L. Tsung (Bruce Lee), an Asian art dealer, taught him how to fight. Mike also uses an advanced cane that is fitted with electronic sensors (allowing him to go places without Pax). As time passed Mike's other senses were honed and his sense of hearing, touch, taste and smell became valuable aids to his investigative work.

Mike has adapted to his new world quite nicely. He appreciates things he once took for granted and has a fond respect for people facing similar circumstances. Mike is not quick to solve a case. He likes to study the information he and Pax uncover and analyze it (sometimes with Nikki's help). He feels that just because he is blind he is no less a man. Criminals may think so, but Mike is determined not to let anyone get the best of him — not even the circus performers who killed Ingrid (he captured them at the end of the pilot episode).

793. Michael Knight, *Knight Rider*, NBC, 1982–1986. Played by David Hasselhoff.

Michael Knight is the driver of KITT (Knight Industries Two Thousand), a specially built black Trans Am car designed to battle crime. The Foundation for Law and Government built the car and Michael Knight did not exist before 1982. He is actually Michael Long, a police officer with the 11th Precinct of the L.A.P.D.

Michael wore badge number 8043 and lived at 1834 Shore Road. While on an undercover assignment Michael was shot in the face during a bust that went wrong. Michael was given little hope to survive until Wilton Knight, a dying billionaire and owner of Knight Electronics, provided life saving surgery: a new face (patterned after his own when he was young), a new identity (Michael Knight), and a mission — to apprehend criminals who are above the law. Michael now works for Devon Miles, the head of the Foundation for which KITT was built. Michael calls KITT "Buddy."

Michael Arthur Long was born in Reno,

Nevada, in 1949. He came from a middle class working family and joined the Green Berets when he turned 20. Her served a three-year tour of duty in Vietnam (working counter intelligence) and joined the Nevada Police Department after his discharge. He later moved to Los Angeles and joined its police department in 1982. It was shortly after that Michael Long became Michael Knight.

See also: KITT.

794. Michael Shayne, *Michael Shayne*, NBC, 1960–1961. Played by Richard Denning.

Michael Shayne, sometimes called Mike, is a private detective "who is practical and realizes he will never get rich at what he is doing." Mike has an office (322) at 483 Adams Street in the City of Miami (he often complains that his mail occasionally gets rerouted to Miami Beach by mistake). Mike can be reached by phone at 236-6236 and he never sees a client before ten in the morning.

Mike claims he was born to be a private eye ("I like to snoop") and enjoys his job despite the beatings he sometimes takes. He is relaxed and easy-going and tries not to fly off the handle when things do not quite go his way. Mike will avoid violence if possible and offers a cigarette to clients and suspects to relax them. He has an eye for the ladies and manages to sneak in a kiss when the client is a gorgeous female.

Mike is a stickler for evidence. He gathers what he can, sorts through it and then uses every dirty trick in the book to get the truth from both clients and suspects. Mike uses Braser's Chemical Lab for analysis work. He is a member of the Private Investigators of America and is assisted at times by Lucy Hamilton (Patricia Donohue, Maggie Regan), his ever-faithful secretary and sometimes "legman." Lucy can type 90 words a minute and lives at 8 Gower Street; 976-6616 is her phone number.

795. Michaela Quinn, *Dr. Quinn, Medicine Woman*, CBS, 1993–1998. Played by Jane Seymour.

Michaela Quinn is the fifth daughter of Michael and Elizabeth Quinn, a wealthy Boston couple. Michaela was born on February 15, 1833 and was expected to be a boy (her father, a man of science, believed that the odds would favor the birth of a son who would be named Michael. When this didn't happen, he named her Michaela). Michaela grew up admiring her father's work as a doctor and set her goal to follow in his footsteps (something that greatly pleased him). Michaela found it difficult to find a medical school that would allow women until she found acceptance at the Women's Medical College in Pennsylvania. Following her graduation, Michaela became a partner in her father's medical practice. They worked side by side for seven years. "When he died I lost my mentor, my advocate, my best friend. He spoiled me but gave me the freedom to discover myself. With my father gone our practice virtually disappeared. I was afraid my life as a doctor was over. But I promised him to carry on." Michaela found work at the Holy Mission Orphanage.

It was in 1865, while reading the *Boston Globe* that Michaela found an ad for a doctor in the Colorado Territory. Michaela responded and acquired the position. However, Michaela is a woman and people in Colorado Springs are distrustful of people from the East and especially women doctors. Michaela finds lodgings at Mrs. Cooper's Rooms and Meals, then a permanent home when she rents a cabin from Byron Sully for one dollar a month. Byron is the man Michaela would marry in 1867 (and become the mother of their daughter, Katie).

Michaela's acceptance as a doctor is slow. She has made friends but people are still reluctant to see a woman doctor. One of the people who trusted her was Charlotte Cooper, a widow with three children (Colleen, Matthew and Brian). Charlotte and Michaela became close. Tragedy strikes when Michaela is too late to save Charlotte when she is bitten by a rattlesnake. Charlotte's last request is for Michaela to care for her children. Colleen and Brian call her "Dr. Mike"; Brian calls her "Maw."

The local Cheyenne Indians believe Michaela is "a crazy white woman" because "only white man make medicine." However, when the tribal chief is wounded and Michaela saves his life, he gives her the name "Medicine Woman" (her cabin shingle reflects her new title: "Dr Quinn — Medicine Woman"). Dr. Quinn's mode of transportation is a horse named Flash in the Sky (a present from a Cheyenne Indian woman when Dr. Quinn saved the life of her child).

See also: Byron Sully.

796. Michelle Tanner, *Full House*, ABC, 1987–1995. Played by Mary Kate and Ashley Olsen.

Michelle Elizabeth Tanner was an infant when their mother (Pam) was killed in a car accident. She has two sisters, D.J. and Stephanie, and is being raised by her father, Danny Tanner, a TV personality (co-host of *Wake Up, San Francisco*). The family lives at 1882 Gerard Street and they have a dog named Comet.

Viewers were able to see Michelle grow from toddler to eight years of age. Michelle attended the Meadowcrest Preschool, then the Frasier Street Elementary School. On her first day at Meadowcrest, Michelle let Dave, the class bird, out of his cage and he flew away. In the first grade at Frasier, Michelle played the Statue of Liberty in the school's production of "Yankee Doodle Dandy." When older, Michelle was Officer Michelle of the Polite Police at school.

Michelle had an invisible friend (Glen) and two goldfish (Martin and Frankie). She eats Honey Coated Fiber Bears breakfast cereal and *The Little Mermaid* is her favorite movie. In 1994, when Michelle joined her sisters at Camp Lakota, she was called "Trail Mix."

Michelle is a typical child and Danny has the typical problems of raising her. Michelle looks up to her sisters but is also very independent when she wants something (she can be told no, but when she has her mind set she does what she wants). Danny is quite strict when it comes to punishment as he feels it is the only way to gain respect). Michelle's favorite term is "You got it dude."

See also: Danny Tanner, D.J. Tanner, Jesse Katsopolis, Joey Gladstone, Stephanie Tanner.

797. Mickey McKenzie, *We Got It Made*, NBC, 1983–1984; Syn., 1987–1988. Played by Teri Copley.

Mickey McKenzie is a young woman who works as a housekeeper. She measures 36-24-34 and is what a lot of men would call a blonde bombshell. She has a Marilyn Monroe aura about her (her speech, facial expressions and walk are reminiscent of Marilyn's). "That," she says, "is how men see me. But they don't see *me*." Mickey is referring to the sweet, innocent and rather sensitive girl she really is.

Mickey is afraid to take a chance (she fears failing at anything she tries). "All my life I've been afraid to take a chance. I didn't go out for cheerleading. I didn't apply to college. I didn't even take the Pepsi Challenge. I never took a risk. I never did anything exciting."

Mickey was born in the Midwest (an exact locale is not mentioned). She worked as a dancer and movie usher after graduating from high school. She craved for a life in the big city but was afraid to move. She quit the usher job for a position as a secretary at a company called American Fryer. She also found a boyfriend and things were finally looking up for Mickey. Then "tragedy" struck — her boyfriend ran off with her mother. Mickey quit her job and took the first chance in her life — she moved to Manhattan to escape her past. Mickey is now happy. She works as a housekeeper ("even though I have no housekeeping experience"). She lives at 1103 North Brewster Street and has a dream to become a standup comedian. She took a chance on that too by performing her act (rather badly) at a strip club called Marcel's Club Marcel. "With each little thing I try I get stronger, a little braver and a little freer."

798. Mickey Mulligan, *Hey Mulligan*, NBC, 1954–1955. Played by Mickey Rooney.

Michael Mulligan, called Mickey, is a page at the fictitious IBS (International Broadcasting Company) in Los Angeles. He works at the West Coast branch of the New York-based network, and insists his official title is "Guest Relations Staff." Mickey earns $47.62 a week take home pay and believes he is meant for better things.

Mickey was born in Los Angeles and is the son of Joe and Nell Mulligan. Joe is a retired police officer; Nell is a former vaudeville actress. Mickey is not a tall man. He stands five feet high and believes his height is preventing him from going places at the network; he calls himself "The tallest short man you'll ever meet." Mickey was raised in a show business environment (more so than one of law enforcement) and has been influenced by his mother. He enrolled in the Academy of Dramatic Arts in the hope of finding a career as an actor.

Mickey has a blue suit that he calls his "sincere suit" (the one he wears when he needs to make an impression). He has a girlfriend (Pat Harding, the station receptionist) and enjoys eating lunch at the Hamburger Hut. Mickey is very kind and trusting and will give of himself to help others.

799. Mike Gambit, *The New Avengers*, CBS, 1978–1979. Played by Gareth Hunt.

Michael Gambit is an Avenger, an agent of the Ministry who avenges crimes committed against the British government. His superior is John Steed, the Ministry's top agent. Mike, as he is called, was born in England and comes from a long and distinguished military background. He was groomed to be a soldier and as soon as he was old enough, Mike joined the British Army (where he served in the Parachute Regiment). He was later with Special Air Services. Mike acquired knowledge of guerilla warfare when he worked as a mercenary in Africa and the Middle East. He worked as a crocodile wrestler in the Congo and a professional racecar driver before he joined the Ministry.

Mike drives a Jaguar XJS, is an expert in unarmed combat and a skilled shot, archer and pilot.

Every morning at the crack of dawn, a sparrow Mike named Charlie, flies onto his windowsill "to sing his heart out and wake me up."

See also: John Steed, Purdy.

800. Mike McCall, *How to Marry a Millionaire*, Syn., 1958–1960. Played by Merry Anders.

Michelle McCall, nicknamed Mike, is one of three beautiful girls seeking to marry a millionaire. She shares a swank penthouse apartment (at the Tower Apartment House) with Loco Jones and Greta Hanson and each took the following pledge devised by Mike: "On my honor I promise to do my best to help one of us marry a millionaire. So help me Fort Knox."

Mike works as an analyst for the Wall Street firm of Hammersmith, Cavanaugh and Hammersmith. She reads the financial section of the newspaper and *Dunn and Bradstreet* for her research material. Mike believes that "the only way for a girl to be smart is to be dumb." She feels "that one of these days we're gonna make it big" and knows that women have to put on airs — "Men go for either the sophisticated Tallulah [Bankhead] type or the slinky Marilyn Monroe type." When Mike spots a potential prospect she sees dollar signs (as does the viewer when a money bag is superimposed over the subject). After an exhausting date, Mike likes to have her feet massaged.

See also: Greta Hanson, Gwen Kirby, Loco Jones.

801. Mike Mercury, *Supercar*, Syn., 1960–1961. Voiced by Graydon Gould.

Michael Mercury, called Mike, is the pilot of Supercar, a futuristic automobile that is capable of traveling on the land, the sea or in the air. Supercar was built by Dr. Beaker and Professor Popkiss and is hidden in an isolated laboratory at Black Rock in the Nevada desert.

Mike was born in 1930 and is the son of a U.S. Air Force pilot. Mike acquired a love for flying at an early age but suffered two tragedies: his father was killed while serving overseas during World War II and his mother died shortly after in a car accident. Mike was raised by an aunt and uncle and enlisted in the Air Force when he became of age. When Mike learned of the fledging U.S. space program of the 1950s, he transferred to its division. It was here that he met Professor Popkiss and Dr. Beaker. In 1958 he joined them in the construction of Supercar, a car that would be used to battle evil (especially those of Master Spy, a villain who seeks the car for his own sinister purposes). *Supercar* is the first puppet series from producer Gerry Anderson.

802. Mike Nelson, *Sea Hunt*, Syn., 1957–1961. Played by Lloyd Bridges.

Mike Nelson is an underwater troubleshooter. He says, "Three-fifths of the world is covered by the sea and most of us know little about it." From as early as he can remember Mike was interested in sea life. He studied all he could about it and was captain of his high school and college swim teams. Mike has a degree in oceanography and served as a Navy frogman during World War II. It was here that he gained knowledge of explosives, especially those dealing with underwater demolition. Mike now works as a freelance ocean detective and accepts assignments from civilians, law enforcement agencies and the government (scientific expeditions, testing underwater inventions). Mike also teaches diving lessons and stresses safety and always diving in pairs.

Mike is extremely careful in what he does. He approaches underwater targets cautiously and observes before acting. He will take daring chances — "I've done this in the war; that's what I was trained to do." Mike almost always operates alone and the slightest error in calculation could cost him his life. He does not like to dive with civilians (even experienced divers) but will work with trained government or law enforcement divers to help solve a crime. Mike has a boat called the *Argonaut* and a hand held water scooter called a Porta Sub for swift movement under water.

A revised version of the series, also called *Sea Hunt*, appeared in syndication in 1986 (to 1987). Ron Ely played Mike Nelson (here as an ex–Navy frogman). He had a boat called *Sea Hunt* and worked with his daughter Jennifer Nelson (Kimber Sissons).

803. Mike Olshansky, *Hack*, CBS, 2002–2004. Played by David Morse.

Michael Olshansky is a fallen police officer. He was a fan of the old TV series *Naked City* (which ended with the classic line "There are eight million stories in the Naked City. This has been one of them"). Mike, as he is called, tells viewers "There must be eight million and one because you sure don't know mine."

Mike was born in Philadelphia and attended Saint Victor's Grammar and high schools. He was an altar boy at Saint Victor's Church and was good friends with its pastor, Father Tom (whom Mike called "Grizz"). Mike grew up on the straight and narrow. He obeyed all the rules; he did everything he was told. In adult life he became a police officer with the Philadelphia Police Department.

As a cop Mike followed all the rules. He had a

record of 159 drug busts and was shot once in the shoulder. One day Mike woke up. He believed that being shot and risking his life everyday entitled him to hazard pay. The department thought differently. During a drug bust, Mike decided to make his own hazard fund and helped himself to money found on a table. He was caught and discharged ("no modified duty, no pension. Goodbye"). The scandal cost Mike his marriage (to Heather) and estranged him from his son (Michael Jr.).

Mike is under a felony indictment and is not permitted to carry a gun. He now drives a cab for the Victory Cab Company (although South Side Taxi Exchange can be seen on the door of his hack). Although he is not a cop, Mike can't stop thinking about crime. His police upbringing (six uncles in law enforcement) can't let crime-fighting go unnoticed ("I'm just a cab driver, but deep down I'm still a cop"). Mike most often works the night shift and takes on the responsibilities of a private detective even though he is not one officially (he will help if someone is in trouble or stop a crime if he encounters one). Mike's cab number reads P-2626; 555-0100 is the cab company phone number; TX-2300 is Mike's cab license plate number and Bernie's Tap is his favorite bar.

804. Mike Seaver, *Growing Pains*, ABC, 1985–1992. Played by Kirk Cameron.

Michael Aaron Seaver, called Mike, is the oldest child of Jason and Maggie Seaver, a psychologist and his wife, who live at 15 Robin Hood Lane in Huntington, Long Island, New York. He has two sisters (Carol and Chrissy) and a brother (Ben).

Mike attended Wendell Wilkie Elementary School, Dewey High School, Alf Landon Junior College and finally Boynton State College. Mike dreamed of becoming an actor. He starred in the Dewey High production of *Our Town* and had his first professional acting job on the TV series *New York Heat* as officer Bukarski. Mike was also a member of the Alf Landon Drama Club (where he starred in the play *The Passion*). Mike next appeared on the TV soap opera *Big City Streets* before he found an interest in teaching and acquired a job instructing remedial students at the Learning Annex of the Community Health Center. Mike's previous jobs: paperboy for the Long Island *Herald*, waiter at World of Burgers, salesman at Stereo Village, car wash attendant, night man at the Stop and Shop Convenience Store; singing waiter at Sullivan's Tavern. The ABC TV movie update, *The Growing Pains Movie* (November 5, 2000), finds Mike as the vice president of the Genasee Advertising Agency.

See also: Carol Seaver, Jason and Maggie Seaver.

Mike Stivic *see* **Gloria and Mike Stivic**

805. Miles Hawkins, *M.A.N.T.I.S.*, Fox, 1993–1994. Played by Carl Lumbly.

Miles Hawkins is a mysterious crime fighter whose costume reminds people of a Praying Mantis and is called M.A.N.T.I.S. (Mechanically Augmented Neuro-Transmitter Interception System). Miles was born in Port Columbia and now heads Hawkins Industries (also called Hawkins Laboratories). He grew up in the Lincoln Heights section and was a gifted child. He had an uncanny ability for understanding all aspects of science and was far superior then others of his own age. He graduated from high school at the age of 12 and four years later graduated with a degree in biophysics from MIT. Miles always felt science could be used to improve the quality of life. He used that belief to start his own company and was soon the third richest man in Port Columbia (called Ocean City in the pilot).

Miles is an African-American. In 1991 during a business conference in Los Angeles Miles was shot in the back during a race riot. He claims he was shot by a cop but could never prove it. The shooting crippled Miles and he is now wheel chair bound. This gives him the perfect cover for his activities as M.A.N.T.I.S. He created his alter ego as a way of fighting back.

Miles encompassed his genius to enable him to create the Hornet (later called the Exo-Skeleton), a black suit (costume) that gives him the ability to walk and a bug-like appearance. He also invented the Seapod, a futuristic flying machine that enables him to get to places fast. He uses paralyzing darts that stop his enemies in their tracks. He has a calling card with the symbol of a Praying Mantis on it; and when asked who he is, he responds simply "Just one man trying to help." The Seapod is also his base of operations. It is an undersea lab Miles built just before he was shot for sea farming. It is located beneath the lab building and he has a ship called the *Chrysalis*.

806. Miles Silverberg, *Murphy Brown*, CBS, 1988–1996. Played by Grant Shaud.

Miles Silverberg is the easily exasperated, always upset executive producer of *F.Y.I.* ("For Your Information"), a Washington, D.C.–based news magazine series. Miles believes the antics of his host, hard-hitting news reporter Murphy Brown, has driven him to the point of hysteria (and made

him a good candidate for ulcers and a heart attack. "I'm 27 years old and living on Mylanta"). Miles hears Murphy's voice in his sleep and says, "They should pipe it into cornfields to scare away the crows."

Miles was born in Washington and was a student at the Little Bo Peep Preschool. He had a hamster named Whitey and was a very smart child. He excelled in school and in Harvard (class of 1984) he was called "Miles Silverbrain." Miles gets donuts for the staff and crew at Marino's Bakery and was also the producer of *The New Wave*, a CBS news program. Miles left *F.Y.I.* on May 20, 1996 to become the head of news operations for CBS in New York. He drove a car with the license plate 400 928 (later 452 689).

See also: Corky Sherwood, Frank Fontana, Jim Dial, Murphy Brown.

807. Millicent Torkelson, *The Torkelsons*, NBC, 1991–1992. Played by Connie Ray.

Millicent Torkelson is a rural housewife who lives off Farm Route Two in the small town of Pyramid Corners, Oklahoma. She is divorced from Randall and the mother of five children (Dorothy Jane, Ruth Ann, Mary Sue, Steven Floyd and Chuckie Lee).

Millicent is poor but proud and devotes all her energies to raising her family. She makes homemade jellies and jams and sells them for one dollar a jar at the Torkelson Treats roadside stand. She also runs a small business (Millicent Torkelson — Custom Upholstery and Design) from her home.

Millicent is very pretty but has not dated since her husband walked out on her. She was born in Pyramid Corners and attended Will Rogers Jr. High and Pyramid Corners High School. Millicent speaks her mind on everything. She was raised by a frugal mother and hates the term *store bought* (if she can make it she will; for example, clothes for the children). Millicent (maiden name Dowd) is famous for her pickled vegetables (from a recipe begun by her grandmother and handed down by her mother. Dorothy Jane is next in line to receive it). Millicent has a dog named Fred and she and the family attend Sunday mass at the Pyramid Corners Community Church.

Almost Home (NBC, 1993), the series revival, finds Millicent and the family moving to Seattle, Washington, when Millicent's business fails and she loses her home. Millicent now works as the live-in nanny to a lawyer (Brian Morgan) and cares for his children (Molly and Gregory).

See also: Dorothy Jane Torkelson.

808. Mimi Bobeck, *The Drew Carey Show*, ABC, 1995–2004. Played by Kathy Kinney.

Mimi Bobeck is the secretary to the director of the Winford-Louder Department Store in Cleveland, Ohio. She is, as her co-worker, Drew Carey says, "800 pounds of trouble" (the two simply do not like each other and constantly play practical jokes on each other).

Mimi was born in Ohio and attended Sacred Heart High School. Before acquiring her present job, Mimi was in phone sales, a photographer's dark room assistant, and an office manager. Mimi's desk, which is opposite Drew's, is cluttered with troll dolls. She wears outlandish makeup and is angry with Drew for getting the job she wanted (personnel director). She has now made it her personal goal to make his life miserable (after she pulls a prank she tells Drew "Bit me, dough boy." She also calls Drew "Pig"). Mimi sells Sally Mae Cosmetics on the side and has a yearly business service called Mimi's Door-to-Door Christmas Tree Service. Her father is the owner of a successful trucking company and Mimi is also the landlord for the Winford-Louder real estate holdings.

Mimi lives in Apartment 24 in a neighborhood where the kids think she is a circus clown ("Do you have numbers on your skin so you know what colors go where?"). Her home also reflects her outlandish makeup ("Now I know what you do with your makeup when you take it off— you throw it against the wall" say people who have seen her home).

Mimi's life changed when she met Steve Carey (John Carroll Lynch), Drew's brother, a cross-dresser (and prison guard). She wore less makeup and he let go of his feminine side to marry "the most beautiful girl I have ever seen." They later became the parents of a baby they named Gus. Mimi worked beside (and annoyed) Drew throughout the series run. Her computer name was Honeybee 28.

See also: Drew Carey, Kate O'Brien, Lewis Kiniski, Oswald Harvey.

809. Mindy McConnell, *Mork and Mindy*, ABC, 1978–1982. Played by Pam Dawber.

Mindy McConnell is the daughter of Fred and Beth McConnell. She was born in Colorado in 1966 and was the first girl in Boulder to play Little League baseball. Mindy's mother died when Mindy was very young and she was raised primarily by her father. Mindy attended Boulder High School and majored in journalism at the University of Colorado. She first worked at her father's store (McConnell's Music Store) then as a news-caster at KTNS, Channel 31. Her warm on-air personality led her to become the host of *Wake Up, Boulder*. Mindy lives at 1619 Pine Street and drives a Jeep with the license plate ML 29HJ.

Mindy is a friendly girl who will lend a helping hand to anyone in need. Such a person was Mork, an alien who had been dispatched from the planet Ork to study life on Earth. Mindy became his guide and the two eventually fell in love and married. Soon after, Mork became pregnant and laid an egg. The egg hatched and they became the parents of an elderly baby they named Mearth (Orkin children are born old and become young with time). Mindy's experiences living with an alien brought her into contact with his world. She was the first human to eat Fleck, an Orkin food that brings out strange behavioral qualities. On Ork she was known as "The Soft-Lapped One" and the Necotrons, the enemies of Orkins, considered her a pretty pet that should be kept in a cage.

See also: Mork.

810. Miranda Hobbes, *Sex and the City*, HBO, 1998–2004. Played by Cynthia Nixon.

Miranda Hobbes is an elegant, extremely feminine lawyer with a prestigious Manhattan firm. She is the classic overachiever and a 16-hour workday is something that is normal for her. Yet, despite the long hours and tedious work, Miranda can turn a man's head simply by passing him. Miranda is very outspoken and not afraid to say what she thinks (her wise acre remarks, however, do not always work out for the best). Whether it is the courtroom or in the office, Miranda knows how to dress for success. Her conservative tailored suits coupled with her stylish look make Miranda the perfect fashion statement — but that is at work. At home it's T-shirts, jeans and sweats.

Miranda's self-assurance and ability eventually led her to become a partner in her law firm. It also gave her the money to move into a stylish Upper West Side apartment. Miranda is tough and down to earth and feels that being aggressive is the only way to succeed in the business world. Miranda mentioned that in high school she wore a size 36A bra and when she gets into one of her baked goods addictions, she makes Devil's Food cake.

Miranda has high expectations when it comes to dating (or at least she did at first). She dated what she considered boring businessmen until she found Steve Brady, a simple bartender whom she found to be a breath of fresh air (she eventually became pregnant by Steve and they had a son they named Brady Hobbes). Miranda's favorite drink is a Cosmopolitan.

See also: Carrie Bradshaw, Charlotte York, Samantha Jones.

811. Mister Ed, *Mister Ed*, Syn., 1960–1961; CBS, 1961–1966. Voiced by Allan "Rocky" Lane.

The barn adjacent to the house at 17230 Valley Spring Lane in Los Angeles is the home of Mister Ed, a horse who will only talk to his owner, architect Wilbur Post (Ed explained that he never talked before because Wilbur became the first human he liked well enough to talk to. He calls Wilbur "Buddy Boy").

Mister Ed, a Palomino, was born in May of 1952 at the Happy Time Stables and purchased by the previous owner of the house in which Wilbur now lives. That person left the horse when he moved. Ed's father was sold to a retired sailor (who had an anchor tattooed on the horse's left flank. He then sold the horse to a traveling carnival, where he now works). Ed's mother is still a resident of the stables. Ed weighed 68 pounds at birth (in another episode he says 98 pounds) and inherited the family curse: a fear of heights (began when his grandfather was chasing a filly and fell off a cliff). Ed is superstitious ("Why do think I walk around here in horseshoes?") and wears a size 9½ horseshoe. As a young horse, Ed had dreams of growing up and joining a circus.

Ed considers himself "the playboy horse of Los Angeles." He has an eye for the fillies (he considers *filly* to be the prettiest word in the English language) and wrote a song called "Pretty Little Filly" (he also wrote a book called *Love and the Single Horse*). Ed would like to move out of the barn and into a swinging bachelor pad and sometimes wishes he were a dog for all the trouble his mouth gets him into.

Mister Ed is a L.A. Dodgers baseball fan and enjoys *Open End* and *The Huntley-Brinkley Report* (two real shows) on TV (he has a set in the barn; later his favorite show is *Walter Cronkite and the News*). Ed also likes Wilbur to read him a fairy tale before bedtime. Ed dances, cooks and sews. He can read (with the aid of glasses), dials the phone and works crossword puzzles. Ed sleeps in a nightcap but doesn't realize he is standing when he sleeps. When Ed gets a leg cramp he calls it a "Charlie People" ("Horses get Charlie People; people get Charlie Horses"). Ed is also an expert at chess and he has a bad habit of eating apples from the neighbor's tree. He loves carrots (although too much carrot juice gives him a hangover).

Mister Ed likes to hangout at the Sunnybrook Stables "because the horses really swing there" (Ed has a 9:00 P.M. curfew). Ed never married because he never met a filly worthy of sharing his feedbag. Ed has a Social Security number (054-22-5551) that he applied for under the name Edward Post to provide for his old age (he created a drink called Wilburini — a combination of apple and carrot juice strained through day old hay). Although he works as Wilbur's assistant (Wilbur has his office in the barn), Ed also held a job at the Tally Ho Stables (where people rode him for a fee).

Mister Ed is a crusader for animal rights (he started the Society for the Prevention of Horseback Riding. Ed was the only member). When Ed needs someone else to talk to he uses his short wave radio (call letters NAG). Ed has to keep his stall clean or he loses his TV privileges. Last season episodes find Ed and Wilbur solving cases for the Secret Intelligence Agency.

See also: Carol Post, Wilbur Post.

Mr. Floppy *see* **Unhappily Ever After**

812. Mr. Roarke, *Fantasy Island*, ABC, 1978–1984. Played by Ricardo Montalban.

Mr. Roarke is a man of mystery. He appears to be an immortal as well as a messenger of God who has been sent to Earth to help deserving individuals by allowing them to experience or relive a past event at a mysterious tropical resort called Fantasy Island.

Mr. Roarke is known by no other name. He is debonair, dresses in white and possesses a suave Spanish accent. He has a deadly enemy — the Devil, who is seeking his soul. Mr. Roarke has battled Satan many times and has always defeated him. After each defeat Satan remarks, "We'll play again. We have all eternity before us. Sooner or later I vow to win." It was revealed that over 300 years ago Mr. Roarke was in love with a woman named Elizabeth but never married her. He did marry Helena Marsh, a fashion designer in 1979. The marriage was short lived: Helena died of an inoperable brain tumor.

"My dear guests, I am Mr. Roarke, your host. Welcome to Fantasy Island" is the greeting guests hear when they arrive on the island. Mr. Roarke is assisted by Tattoo, his good friend, and it is only known that he has a goddaughter named Julie.

See also: Tattoo.

813. Mr. Spock, *Star Trek*, NBC, 1966–1969. Played by Leonard Nimoy.

Mr. Spock, Science Officer aboard the star ship U.S.S. *Enterprise NCC-1701*, was born on the planet Vulcan in the year 2230. He is the child of an Earth mother (Amanda Grayson, a science teacher) and Ambassador Sarek, a Vulcan diplomat. As a result of his human–Vulcan heritage, Spock's childhood was difficult. He was torn between human emotion and an emotionless and strict Vulcan philosophy. Spock grew up on Vulcan. He had a pet sehlat (a bear-like animal) and was telepathically bonded with T'Pring, a young Vulcan girl, at the age of seven (this was necessary. When a Vulcan child becomes of age, he or she must mate once every seven years or die). As Spock grew he became interested in science and space exploration. In the year 2249 Spock joined Starfleet Academy. Three years later he was assigned as a cadet under Christopher Pike, the first captain of *Enterprise*. A year later (2265) he became an ensign (at the same time James T. Kirk became captain of *Enterprise*) and was later promoted to Science Officer.

Mr. Spock's lineal Vulcan name is, as he says, unpronounceable. He has an interest in poetry, music, literature and art and is an expert at a game called tri-dimensional chess. "Live long and prosper" is his catch phrase and he can penetrate the minds of others with the Vulcan Mind Meld.

See also: Hikaru Sulu, James T. Kirk, Leonard McCoy, Montgomery Scott, Pavel Chekov, Uhura.

Mr. Terrific *see* **Stanley Beemish**

814. Mitch Buchannon, *Baywatch*, NBC, 1989–1990; Syn., 1991–2001. Played by David Hasselhoff.

Mitch Buchannon is a handsome and rugged lifeguard for the Los Angeles County Lifeguards at Malibu Beach (also called Sunset Beach; Baywatch is the headquarters). Mitch says it is the same beach his father took him to when he was a child (although this statement by Mitch doesn't coincide with prior episode history).

Mitch was born in Phoenix, Arizona, and became so hooked on TV detective shows that he wanted to become a private investigator when he grew up (which he did, in part, on the spinoff series *Baywatch Nights*, Syn., 1995–1997). Mitch is the son of Al and Irene Buchannon and was groomed to follow in his father's footsteps and become an architect. He graduated from Arizona State University and tried to please his parents but quit two months after joining his father's firm because he felt miserable. He married his longtime Palisades High School girlfriend, Gayle (Wendie Malick) and they became the parents of Hobie (Brandon Call, Jeremy Jackson). Mitch's history stops here. He is next seen as a single fa-

ther (divorced from Gayle) and working as a lifeguard at Baywatch (Gayle works as a restaurant consultant for Captain Cluck's Chicken and Fixin' franchises in Columbus, Ohio). In 1995 Mitch acquires a new family member named Joie Jennings (Ashley Gorrell). Joie is a nine-year-old girl Mitch befriended when he helped her con artist mother out of a jam. He becomes her guardian when Joie's mother is killed in a car accident.

Mitch was assigned to Outpost Tower 33 as a rookie. He was later assigned Tower 27 then Tower 12 before being promoted to captain (1997) and assigned to an office at Baywatch headquarters. Mitch could work with anyone and never pushed his lifeguards beyond the call of duty. He urged his lifeguards to act with reason and never put them or a drowning victim at risk by doing something stupid (like acting before thinking). While Mitch hates to admit it, he says that sometimes there is no time for thinking and acting quickly is the only way to achieve a successful rescue (he prefers his lifeguards not do this because it is extremely dangerous and could cost them their lives). Mitch's car code was KF 295 then 208 Lincoln. His beach patrol car license plates read 200T 456, 3E9 1063 and 4J06 197. When Mitch feels the blues he "swims the towers" (goes from one tower to another) to cure himself. Before the series ended Mitch established the International Training Center for lifeguards in Hawaii.

See also: The Girls of Baywatch (for information on April Giminski, Caroline Holden, C.J. Parker, Donna Marco, Jesse Owens, Jill Riley, Neely Capshaw, Shauni McClain, Stephanie Holden, Summer Quinn).

815. Moesha Mitchell, *Moesha*, UPN, 1996–2001. Played by Brandy Norwood.

Moesha Denise Mitchell is a 15-year-old girl who can't wait to grow up. She is the daughter of a car dealership owner (her mother is deceased) and lives at 6653 West Post Road in Los Angeles with her father (Frank), stepmother (Dee) and brother (Miles).

Moesha is a straight A student at Crenshaw High School. She hangs out with her friends at The Den and works after school as a salesgirl at Class Act (a clothing store). Moesha tries always to be in style but is stopped from wearing cleavage-revealing tops and midriff blouses by her father (Frank feels she is too young to show skin and believes his gray hairs are all a part of raising a beautiful teenage daughter). Moesha believes her only flaw is "that I have a big butt." As she grew older Moesha balked at parental authority and was always punished for doing so.

Moesha's favorite TV show as a kid was *Spunky's World*. She hates to hear the words "Moesha, we have to talk" from her parents (as she knows she is in trouble). Moesha is very friendly and she likes to help people she believes are in trouble (and always makes the situation worse).

Moesha graduated from high school in 1999. She had planned to attend Northwestern University in Chicago. She was also accepted to USC, Harvard, Duke and Spellman. She chose not to attend college and took a job as a receptionist at *Vibe* magazine (hoping to become a writer). She was fired after several months (for interviewing Maya Angelou without permission) and then chose to enroll in college (California University).

816. Molloy Martin, *Molloy*, Fox, 1990. Played by Mayim Bialik.

Molloy Martin is a pretty 13-year-old girl who says, "I major in stuff." She is very knowledgeable for one so young and works as a professional actress on the children's TV series *Wonderland* on KQET in Beverly Hills. Molloy is the daughter of Paul Martin, a radio program director; her mother is deceased. She lives at 6113 Fullerton Drive with her father, stepmother Lynn (an interior decorator), half sister Courtney, and half brother, Jason. Molloy's parents were divorced when she was three years old (her mother's name was not mentioned, nor was a reason for the divorce. Molloy had been living with her mother before moving to California to live with her father and stepfamily).

Molloy is a brilliant student at Beverly Hills Junior High School. She is bright, cheery, and full of pep and energy. She is generous and always willing to help a friend in need. Molloy is not fashion conscious and feels comfortable wearing clothes that make her feel happy. She has just begun to use makeup and she admires Courtney's style, elegance and especially her beauty. She hopes that when she gets older she becomes like her "but without the dullard interior" (Courtney is somewhat of an airhead). Molloy plays one of the children of the forest on *Wonderland*, a series hosted by Joey the Squirrel.

See also: Courtney Martin.

817. Molly and Taylor Newton, *Evening Shade*, CBS, 1990–1994. Played by Candace Huston, Jay R. Ferguson.

Molly and Taylor Newton are the children of Wood and Ava Newton and live at 2102 Willow Lane in Evening Shade, a small town in Arkansas. They have a dog named Brownie.

Molly is eleven years old and attends Evening Shade Grammar School. She (and Taylor) were born in Evening Shade (at City Hospital). Molly is growing up faster than Wood and Ava would like as they think of her as nine ("so she can always be our little girl"). Molly wishes "they would stop treating me like a baby." Molly has just started to develop and wears a Littlest Angel Bra (she wears a size 5½ shoe). She has developed an interest in makeup and is starting to gain a fashion sense, but so far her parents have been spared the traumas of boyfriends: she still likes to pal around with her girlfriends. Molly is very pretty and entered the Little Miss Evening Shade Beauty Pageant. She lost when she attempted to walk in high heels and fell. *The Wizard of Oz* is her favorite movie and her and Taylor's favorite hangout is Doug and Herman's Ice Cream Parlor.

Taylor is fifteen years old and a student at Evening Shade High School. He believes he is a ladies' man and feels his face is his best feature (he would like to join the school's football team, the Mules, but fears damaging his face and thus ruining his chances of becoming an actor). Taylor and Molly are relatively good kids and cause few problems for their parents.

See also: Ava Newton, Marlene and Harlan Eldridge, Wood Newton.

818. Molly Stage, *Maybe It's Me*, WB, 2001–2002. Played by Reagan Dale Neis.

Molly Stage is a 15-year-old girl who chronicles the daily activities of her life in her computer journal. She lives in the small Rhode Island community of Wickets Town and is the only normal person in a large family of offbeat characters. Her father, Jerry, is an optometrist and has an excessive passion for girls' soccer (he coaches a team called the Terminators). Mary, her mother, is well meaning but insanely frugal (she keeps the house at "a comfortable 52 degrees," works as the lunch lady at Molly's school, and rings a cowbell to summon the family for breakfast). Her older brother, Rick, is a petty thief; Grant, her other brother, aspires to be a Christian music rock star; and her twin sisters, Cindy and Mindy, "are sweet-faced little terrors" (Molly is the only one who can tell them apart).

Molly first attends Wickets Town High School. She was, as she says, "a nerd. I was brainy, wore glasses and was a bit chubby. But all that changed when I went to high school. I'm still brainy but I lost the weight and got contacts." As a little girl Molly liked to take baths ("My mother nicknamed me Tubby"). Molly enjoys watching Mary Kate and Ashley Olsen videos and is a member of the Terminator's soccer team. She is an expert at chess and also a member of the chess club at school. Molly's e-mail address is *Yotevoyamer4@ aol.com.* Molly is also a cheerleader for the school's wrestling team, the Wolverines. In addition to her embarrassing family dinners at the Lobster Barn (where the twins "like to watch the lobsters twitch and die"), Molly was forced to enter (and won the title of) Miss Quahog in the town's annual festival celebrating clams (Molly received a crown of clams).

819. Mona Mullins, *Vinnie and Bobby*, Fox, 1992. Played by Joey Adams.

Beverly Hills, 90210 is the favorite television program of Mona Mullins, a gorgeous 17-year-old girl who lives at 623 Cypress Avenue (Apartment 4B) in Chicago. She considers herself "sensuous, desirous and sexy" and Kelly Bundy (the dumb blonde on *Married ... With Children*) is her idol (Mona tries to emulate Kelly's sexy style, including her trashy wardrobe).

Mona is the upstairs neighbor of Vinnie Verducci (Matt LeBlanc) and his roommate Bobby Grazzo (Robert Torti). Mona was born in Chicago and is the daughter of a father who owns a gun shop. She is attending James K. Polk High School and while she can have the choice of any boy at school, she has set her sights on Vinnie ("my heartthrob"), an older man (a former boxer turned worker for the Rand Construction Company). Vinnie wants nothing to do with Mona (he considers her jailbait) and tries to avoid her advances. Mona has made it her goal to marry Vinnie on her 18th birthday (she has given him a "Mona Countdown to Heaven Calendar" [sexy pictures of Mona in a bikini]. "I circled my 18th birthday. It's our wedding day").

While Mona tries to look like her idol, one can see aspects of Ginger Grant (*Gilligan's Island*) and actress Marilyn Monroe in the way she speaks and in her walk. Mona's parents are never seen and it is not made clear as to weather her mother is aware of Mona's attempts to seduce Vinnie or of her sexy wardrobe. As one observes Mona it is clearly evident she is a tease. She seems to acquire great satisfaction in playing a sex goddess and turning men on. But despite all her charm and apparent cheery outlook on life, Mona does get upset — and when she does, she goes to her room and cuts the heads off her Ken dolls.

See also: Vinnie Verducci.

820. Mona Thorne, *Half and Half*, UPN, 2003 (current). Played by Rachel True.

Mona Thorne has an ear for music, loves her job and would do it for free, but prefers to get paid for it. She is the daughter of Phyllis and Charles Thorne and has a rich, spoiled half sister named Dee Dee Thorne. Mona is 25 years old and was born in San Francisco. Phyllis raised Mona following her divorce from Charles. Mona is a graduate of San Francisco Union Bay High School and State College. She first worked during high school as a waitress at the Dairy Princess; then, after graduating from college, at Delicious Records. She was first an artist's representative, then a vice president.

Mona lives at 36 Briarcliff Avenue (Apartment 4A) in a building owned by her father; her rent is $1200 a month and she has a pet cat named Smokey. Mona is a Scorpio and claims, "The world is made up of Dee Dee's and Mona's. I wound up a Mona." As a kid Mona had a recurring dream "that a big dinosaur bird would swoop down from out of the sky and take Dee Dee and her mother ["Big" Dee Dee] off and dump them into the sea so my mother would move in with my father and we could live happily ever after." Her stepmother calls her "Kit Kat" and "Snicker Doodle."

Mona likes Dee Dee but feels she was raised in the lap of luxury "and got all the good stuff. I was treated like a big old Raggedy Ann doll." At times Mona feels like she will never find a man or happiness. At her favorite eatery, the Lunch Lounge, Mona orders "The Lonely Girl's Special."

See also: Dee Dee Thorne.

821. Monica, *Touched by an Angel*, CBS, 1994–2003. Played by Roma Downey.

Monica is an Angel, a messenger of God who performs missions to help deserving individuals. While Monica can talk directly to God, she receives her assignments from Tess (Della Reese), an angel as old as God, who considers Monica "My baby."

"There is no pay but the benefits are great," says Monica about becoming an angel and answering prayers. Monica's age is unknown. She began her heavenly life in the Angelic Choir and was moved to Special Appearances and finally to Search and Rescue to save souls. When she saved a doomed airliner she was promoted to Case Worker and granted more powers and assigned to Tess.

Monica, called "Miss Wings" by Tess, sometimes breaks tradition "when my instincts kick in" and she has to do things her way despite what higher powers believe. "I'm an Angel sent by God" is what Monica says when she reveals herself to the person she is helping (she is seen in a golden glow she calls "The Power of God's Love"). "If it were not for destiny I would not have a job," says Monica. Monica likes coffee more than anything else but can't explain why. She also became intoxicated for the first time when she had an Irish cream coffee. Monica is fascinated by earth foods (especially olives) and had a fear of water until she conquered it.

Although Monica was said to be in the choir, she is later apparently unable to sing and her greatest wish "is to sing like an angel" (her favorite song is "Panas Angelicas"). As the story goes, hundreds of years ago, after completing an errand of mercy, Monica stumbled upon the Heavenly Choir and sort of joined in. When it was found she could not sing, "I was kicked out and I wasn't even a member. I'm the worst singer you ever heard."

Although Monica is not human she can catch viruses like anger when she encounters someone who annoys her. Monica has an evil twin — Monique (Roma Downey in a dual role), a demon who takes on her appearance to cause confusion and destruction.

The last episode finds Monica parting company with Tess when she is promoted to Supervisor and begins a journey of her own. Before they parted company Tess presented Monica with her pride and joy — the red Cadillac (plate 758 R2G) she and Tess rode in traveling from assignment to assignment.

822. Monica Geller, *Friends*, NBC, 1994–2004. Played by Courteney Cox.

Monica Geller was born on Long Island in New York and is a graduate of Lincoln High School (where she was overweight and had an imaginary boyfriend named Jarrod). Monica is now slim and gorgeous but she is still haunted by the memories of a difficult childhood. She loved to eat and gained considerable weight. Mona's love for food was also her saving grace as it gave her the ambition to become a chef. It actually began "when I got my first Easy Bake Oven and opened Easy Monica's Bakery" (her brother, Ross, called her "The unbaked batter eater" because she couldn't wait for the light bulb to cook her brownies and would eat the dough raw). Monica also confessed, "that I couldn't tell time until I was 13. It's hard for some people."

Monica now lives in an apartment house at the corner of Grove and Bedford Streets in Manhattan. She first worked as the head chef at Alesandro's Restaurant. She earned extra money as the food critic for the *Chelsea Reporter* (she received a penny a word for her reviews). She next worked as a roller skating waitress (with a blonde wig and padded bra) at the Moon Dance Diner, then with her friend Phoebe in a short-lived catering business. She next found steady employment as a chef at the Java Restaurant.

Monica makes her own tile cleaner ("ammonia, lemon juice and a secret ingredient") and is famous for her annual Thanksgiving Day feasts (Ross claims that Monica makes the best turkey sandwiches in the world; her secret is "the moist maker, a gravy-soaked slice of bread in the middle of two slices of turkey and the outer bread"). Monica reads *In Style* magazine and numbers the bottoms of coffee mugs "so I can keep track of them." Monica will not make chocolate pies (she ate too many at one time and got sick).

Monica, Ross and their friends, Rachel, Joey, Phoebe and Chandler hang out at a coffee shop called Central Perk. Monica began a relationship with Chandler and married him on May 17, 2001. They announced on January 15, 2004, that they found a house and were moving to Westchester to have a home in which to raise their adopted twins. Monica loves to show cleavage and believes her breasts get her attention. She also has a pet peeve: seeing animals dressed as humans. The last episode finds Monica and Chandler preparing to move to their new home in the suburbs.

See also: Chandler Bing, Joey Tribbiani, Phoebe Buffay, Rachel Greene, Ross Geller.

Monk *see* **Adrian Monk**

823. Montgomery Scott, *Star Trek*, NBC, 1966–1969. Played by James Doohan.

Montgomery Scott, nicknamed Scotty, is the chief engineer under James T. Kirk, captain of the star ship U.S.S. *Enterprise NCC-1701*. Scotty was born in the year 2222 and graduated from Starfleet Academy in the year 2244. During his time at the academy Scotty served on eleven ships. The *Enterprise* was his first assignment as a chief engineer (in 2264). Scotty is proud of his Scottish heritage and sometimes wears his ceremonial kilts with his dress uniform. He plays the bagpipes and is known for his beverage collection (which he acquired from all areas of the galaxy). His favorite drink is Scotch and he takes offense if anyone speaks negatively about his "baby" (*Enterprise*).

See also: Hikaru Sulu, James T. Kirk, Leonard McCoy, Mr. Spock, Pavel Chekov, Uhura.

824. Morgan O'Rourke, *F Troop*, ABC, 1965–1967. Played by Forrest Tucker.

Morgan Sylvester O'Rourke is a 25-year career

officer who is stationed at Fort Courage, the U.S. Army's cavalry outpost in the Kansas wilderness of 1866. Morgan is a sergeant and sees the army as a way to become rich. He is an expert schemer and con artist and manipulates people for his own benefit.

Morgan uses the post's barracks and supply hut as his base of operations for the illegal O'Rourke Enterprises. Morgan is the president and fellow soldier Corporal Randolph Agarn is his vice president. The company owns the Fort Courage Saloon and the International Trading Company (which deals in souvenirs and anything else that will make money). Morgan has organized the friendly Hekawi Indians into his factory and they supply the goods he sells.

The fort's captain, Wilton Parmenter, is unaware of O'Rourke's operations (Morgan is a convincing liar and manages to talk Wilton out of what he thinks he sees). Morgan is the only trooper who can read smoke signals and he and Agarn are members of the Hekawi Playbrave Club (an 1860s version of the Playboy Club). Morgan is also the post's best judge of horses and although raised in America, Morgan was born in County Galway, Ireland.

825. Mork, *Mork and Mindy*, ABC, 1978–1982. Played by Robin Williams.

Mork is a resident of the planet Ork (about 200 million miles from Earth). Ork has three moons and its inhabitants, who resemble humans, evolved from the chicken (their space ships are egg shaped). Mork has been assigned by Ork's leader (Orson) to study life on Earth and report back via his Scorpio Reports (which are accomplished through mind transference). On Earth Mork befriends Mindy McConnell, a girl who becomes his "guide." They live together at 1619 Pine Street in Boulder, Colorado, and to fit in, Mork acquires a job as a counselor at the Pine Tree Day Care Center. He later marries Mindy and they become the parents of an elderly baby named Mearth (Mork produced an egg that hatched. Orkin children are born old and become young with time).

Mork was born in a test tube on Ork (there are no parents) and comes with a guarantee that covers rusted skin and ankle blowouts. He is a graduate of Ork Prep School and can travel through time via his red sequined Time Traveling Shoes (size 8). Mork has a pet Nauger Camp named Beebo (a furry ball-like creature). Mork worked as a dinner diver in a lobster tank and later was an explorer who charted 16 galaxies. He was then chosen by Orson to become an Earth Observer.

Mork is very naïve and believes what people tell him. He enjoys working with children but misses his life on Ork. He keeps the spirit of his planet alive by celebrating the Orkin holiday National Backwards Day. Because of his strange behavior people believe Mork should be in a mental institution. Mork relaxes by standing on his head and his greeting for hello is "Na-nu, na-nu."
See also: Mindy McConnell.

826. Morticia Addams, *The Addams Family*, ABC, 1964–1966. Played by Carolyn Jones.

Morticia Addams is the wife of Gomez Addams and the mother of his children Wednesday and Pugsley. They live at 000 Cemetery Lane in the town of Cemetery Ridge. Morticia is the daughter of Esther Frump and has a flaky sister named Ophelia (also played by Carolyn Jones). The Frump family ancestry dates back to the early witch burning days of Colonial Salem, Massachusetts.

As a child Morticia loved thunderstorms, gloomy weather and lightning. She dressed in black and played with headless dolls (her favorite was Anne Boleyn, a wife of Henry VIII). In contrast, Ophelia dressed in white, loved sunny days and water (she would jump into fountains and brooks and cook all day so she could wash dishes).

Gomez and Ophelia were a part of a prearranged marriage. The marriage never occurred. On that fatal day Gomez saw Morticia for the first time and knew she was the woman for him (especially when she spoke French and cleared up a sinus condition he had for 22 years). Fate stepped in. Ophelia saw Gomez's Cousin Itt and it was a love at first sight. They eloped thus allowing Gomez and Morticia to marry.

Morticia is a beautiful woman who wears a long skin-tight black dress (on their wedding day Gomez was driven wild by it. "I'll never wear another," she told him). Black is Morticia's favorite color ("It's so soothing and mysterious"). She has a carnivorous plant (an African Strangler) named Cleopatra (who loves zebra burgers) and keeps the house "nice and bleak." Morticia is also an excellent cook and always prepares Gomez his favorite meals—fried eyes of newt, fried yak and barbecued turtle tips. She is also famous for her dwarf's hair pie. Morticia plays the bagpipes, loves to paint and smokes (literally). She is also an expert at animal imitations (especially the bullfrog, which, in addition to French, makes Gomez romantic). Her favorite holiday is Halloween.

Morticia relishes in the idea that their house may be haunted and takes pride in her garden of deadly nightshade, quicksand, poison sumac and assorted weeds. She calls Gomez "Bubala." When the local grammar school banned the book *Grimm's Fairy Tales* as being too violent for children, Morticia wrote her own children's book *A Treasury of Mean Witches, Evil Giants, Wicked Goblins and Other Bedtime Stories*. She also cares for Kit Kat, the family's pet lion; Zelda, the vulture; and Tristan, the piranha.

See also: Gomez Addams, Uncle Fester, Wednesday and Pugsley Addams.

827. Murphy Brown, *Murphy Brown*, CBS, 1988–1997. Played by Candice Bergen.

Murphy Brown is the beautiful, hard-hitting anchor of *F.Y.I.* ("For Your Information"), a CBS-TV Washington, D.C.-based news magazine series.

Murphy was born in Chicago in May of 1948 and is the daughter of Bill and Avery Brown (another episode mentions her birthday as November 26, 1948). Because of her practical joke playing as a kid Murphy received the nickname "Stinky" (her father calls her "Suzy Q"). She had a dog (Butterscotch) and was editor of her high school newspaper. She claims her journalism professor (Ken Hamilton) gave her the inspiration to become a reporter. Murphy is a graduate of Penn State. She submitted a videotape audition to her hero, newsman Howard K. Smith, and received this reply: "You stink but you've got a nice tush."

At some point after this (not pinpointed) Murphy became a foreign correspondent. She auditioned for *F.Y.I.* on August 16, 1977 and won the role over newscaster Linda Ellerbe. Since then she has won the Robert F. Kennedy Journalism Award, an Emmy and eight Humboldt News Story Awards. Murphy has appeared on the covers of *Time, TV Guide, Newsweek, Esquire* and *Harper's Bazaar* and has been lampooned in the comics as "Mouth Brown" (for her continual habit of talking).

Murphy has a reputation for getting even with anyone who crosses her. She is easily exasperated and has a tendency to yell a lot. Despite her abrasive behavior Murphy does having a caring side — "I once fed the cat next door." People say Murphy could never have a pet — "But I got a Chia Pet to grow." Murphy drives a white Porsche (plate 189 347; later MURPHY) and likes Sterling Roses. Her favorite singer is Aretha Franklin ("Respect" is her favorite song). Murphy is also barred from the White House (she ran over former President George Bush, Sr., with her bicycle in 1990. Now every time Bush hears Murphy's name he screams and runs for his life).

Murphy lives on Cambridge Place. She was offered a role in the film *Deadline* but was fired for rewriting the script. Murphy had a five-day marriage to Jake Lowenstein in 1968 (they met at the Democratic National Convention). When he reentered her life in 1990 they had an affair and Murphy became pregnant. She gave birth to a boy she eventually named Avery (after her mother). Murphy was in labor for 39 hours and first called the boy Baby Brown. Murphy was the first TV character to have a website (*www.murphybrown. com*) and fellow newsman, Jim Dial, calls her "Slugger." Murphy also started her own business, the Murphy Brown School of Broadcasting and was co-host for the premiere of a new CBS show called *Overnight News*.

See also: Corky Sherwood, Frank Fontana, Jim Dial, Miles Silverberg.

828. Murray Updike, *Malibu, Ca.*, Syn., 1998–2002. Played by Brandon Brooks.

Murray Updike is the son of a wealthy businessman who rejected the corporate world to live the life of a surfer. Murray was born in Malibu Beach, California, and received his inspiration to become a surfer from the Annette Funicello and Frankie Avalon *Beach Party* movies of the 1960s. He earns a living by working at the Surf Shack, a Malibu Beach eatery. Murray calls himself a "surfer dude" and lives by the code of the surfer's king, The Great Kahuna. Murray resides in a rather posh apartment at 3116 Malibu Beach Road and has a pet electric eel named Sheila. His hero is the Silver Surfer (a comic book character) and he was host of the advice program "The Dude of Love" on radio station KPOV. Murray believes in helping people less fortunate than he is and hangs out at an eatery called the Lighthouse. He struck out in an attempt to make money when he tried to market see through raincoats with painted designs (the paint ran when it rained and they got wet).

See also: Tracee Banks.

Nancy Bradford *see* **Mary Bradford**

829. Nancy Drew, *The Nancy Drew Mysteries*, ABC, 1977–1978. Played by Pamela Sue Martin, Janet Louise Johnson.

This entry also contains information on Tracy Ryan as Nancy Drew (*Nancy Drew*, Syn., 1995–1996) and Maggie Lawson as Nancy Drew (*Nancy Drew*, ABC, 2002).

Nancy Drew "is a girl with a very inquisitive mind who loves to solve a mystery." She is a recent graduate of River Heights High School and works as an investigator for her father, Carson

Drew (William Schallert), a prominent lawyer. Nancy lives with her father at 8606 Bainbridge Street in River Heights, a small New England town.

Nancy is very pretty, always elegantly dressed and always looking for the answers to a mystery. She dislikes being told she is wrong and says, "I don't consider what I do prying. I just observe." Nancy rarely takes chances. She carefully calculates a move before she makes it. She is also very thorough. She looks beyond the obvious for the small (sometimes very elusive) clues that others may overlook but holds the key to solving a crime.

Carson has raised Nancy since she was three years old (at which time her mother died of a heart attack). Nancy grew up admiring her father's work but she chose the more exciting end of the field — the legwork and investigating (she hopes to become a private detective). She calls herself an investigator and Carson tries to keep her out of trouble by assigning her to research legal files and check driving records (something Nancy is said to do but she is never seen doing this; her efforts to solve crimes are seen). Nancy enjoys charity work and donates toys to the Children's Hospital. While you wouldn't expect it from seeing one dressed so elegantly, Nancy can trick ride on a motorcycle.

In the 1995 series Nancy is removed from her traditional setting of River Heights and is seen living on her own in Apartment 603 of the Callisto Hotel at 306 Marsh Avenue in an unidentified city. Nancy is now 21 years old and is still hoping to become a detective. She works at various jobs as an employee of the Temp Agency and is studying criminology at the University (as it is called). Like with the prior Nancy Drew, where ever Nancy goes mystery follows. Nancy is just as attractive as her predecessor but she now possesses the ability to pick locks and defeat alarm systems. Nancy likes ketchup on her hot dog and drives a car with the license plate NDY 7M2. Here River Heights is mentioned as being in Illinois (in the Pamela Sue Martin version River Heights is in Boston).

On December 15, 2002, ABC aired an unsold pilot for an updated version of the Nancy Drew character. Nancy is now 18 years old and a graduate of River Heights High School. She has just enrolled in college (River Heights University in Boston) and is living on campus in the Kelly Hall Dorm. She is smart, pretty and adventurous and has an uncanny knack for stumbling upon mysteries. She is a journalism student and drives a car with the license plate AV655 22; 6589 is her campus permit parking number. Nancy has a picture of herself with her parents and a photo of her inspiration, Sherlock Holmes, on her desk. Nancy mentioned that when she was in high school she was a reporter for the school newspaper, the River Heights *Inkwell*. She also has a dog named Butch.

830. Naomi Harper, *Mama's Family*, NBC, 1983–1984; Syn., 1986. Played by Dorothy Lyman.

Naomi Oates was born and raised in Raytown, U.S.A. She is a graduate of Raytown High School and now lives with her fifth husband, Vinton Harper, at 1542 Ray Way (also called Ray Lane). Naomi has been called "The sexiest woman in Raytown" and Vinton's mother, Thelma, believes Naomi is the kind of girl mother's fear their sons will marry. Naomi's previous husbands were Tom, Bill, Leonard and George. Vinton calls her "Skeeter."

Naomi first worked as a checker at Food Circus; she later became its manager. She had a dog named Marlon (named after her favorite actor, Marlon Brando) and is a kind and loving woman. Her sexy attire has given her a flamboyant reputation. Red licorice whips are her favorite candy and Naomi tries to get along with her mother-in-law but Thelma refuses to accept her as a respectable member of the family. Naomi wrestled briefly as "Queen Bee" in the Women's Wrestling League (Vinton was her ringside attendant, the Bee Keeper).

See also: Thelma Harper, Vinton Harper.

831. Napoleon Solo, *The Man from U.N.C.L.E.*, NBC, 1964–1968. Played by Robert Vaughn.

Napoleon Solo is an agent for U.N.C.L.E. (The United Network Command for Law Enforcement), a secret New York-based agency that battles the evils of THRUSH. The Del Flora Taylor Shop on Second Avenue and 40th Street fronts for the agency. Napoleon works with Illya Kuryakin and wears badge number 11. He communicates with headquarters via his pen, which is set on Channel D. Napoleon uses a refined version of a Magnum .44 called a Magnum .35.

Napoleon is a suave and sophisticated ladies' man. He lives at the Alexandria Hotel at 221 Fifth Avenue in Manhattan. He is an expert at chess and prefers a well-chilled martini (although he also orders one with two onions). He carries a flask and takes his coffee with cream and no sugar. His favorite dinner appears to be steak although he also enjoys chicken soup and Danish food.

Napoleon is single but longs for a wife and family. He is not wealthy (apparently working as a spy is not a well-paying job). Napoleon was born in Kansas City, Kansas, and served a hitch in Korea during the war (another episode claims he was born in Montreal, Canada, where his father owned a hotel and his mother was an actress). Napoleon is a college graduate and often quotes from the Bible, poets and Shakespeare. He can fly a helicopter, ride a motorcycle and is knowledgeable in several languages (Italian, Russian and French).

Napoleon is not a man of action; he would rather use his considerable charm to talk his way out of a situation rather than use physical force (although he is well versed in the martial arts. He is also an expert shot and a champion fencer). He has been called "The Top U.N.C.L.E. Agent in America."

Although it appeared that the head of U.N.C.L.E. (Alexander Waverly) had been grooming Napoleon to take his place, the TV Movie Update (*The Man from U.N.C.L.E.: The 15 Years Later Affair*) shows that Napoleon had quit the organization in 1968 to begin his own computer business.

See also: Illya Kuryakin.

832. Nash Bridges, *Nash Bridges*, CBS, 1996–2001. Played by Don Johnson.

Nash Bridges is an inspector with the S.I.U. (Special Investigation Unit) of the San Francisco Police Department. He has been married and divorced twice and is the father of Cassidy. He lives at 85 Sacramento Street with Cassidy and his father, Nick; his mother is deceased. Lisa, Nash's first wife, is Cassidy's mother (Kelly was Nash's second wife).

Nash was born in San Francisco on December 7, 1955. He had a dog named Old Jimbo, was interested in magic, especially sleight of hand, and was a member of the football team (jersey 55) at Bay High School. Nash attended the San Francisco Police Academy after graduating from State College and was the youngest cop to ever receive the Gold Star. Nash wears badge 22 and 5-George 31 is his mobile car code. He drives a 1971 yellow Plymouth Barracuda convertible with the license plate GQD 685. Nash calls the car "The Cuda" and in some episodes he says the car was made in 1970. He also tends to call people "Bubba."

Nash was first an inspector, then captain of the S.I.U. (headquarters were first located in an old building in downtown San Francisco. When an earthquake partially destroyed the building, operations were moved to a docked ferryboat called the *Eureka* on Hyde Street. The ferry was replaced two years later by a 177-foot barge that once housed the Allied Cannery Company then a rave club).

Nash likes to do things his way when it comes to investigating cases and balks at sharing information with the FBI ("They're too damned sure about everything," he says). Nash and his partner, Joe Dominiquez, also moonlight as private investigators in a business called Bridges and Dominiquez — Private Investigations.

See also: Cassidy Bridges, Joe Dominiquez.

833. Natalie Greene, *The Facts of Life*, NBC, 1979–1988. Played by Mindy Cohn.

Natalie Greene is a student at the Eastland Academy for Girls in Peekskill, New York. Other students consider Natalie the most honest person they have ever known. Natalie hopes to become a journalist and wears her thinking cap when she writes (a blue baseball cap with orange lightning bolts over each ear). She first worked as a waitress at a taco stand called El Sombrero then at Edna's Edibles, a gourmet food shop, and Over Our Heads, a novelty store. She later worked as a part time reporter for the *Peekskill Press* (where he first article, "An Eighth Grader Gets Angry," was published).

Natalie is best friends with Tootie Ramsey and is the peacemaker between the always-feuding Blair Warner and Jo Polniaszek. Natalie washes her hair when she gets angry and the last episode found her moving to New York's SoHo District to pursue her writing career. In the ABC TV movie update, *The Facts of Life Reunion* (November 18, 2001), Natalie was revealed as being a full-fledged newspaper reporter.

See also: Blair Warner, Edna Garrett, Jo Polniaszek, Tootie Ramsey.

834. Natasha Yar, *Star Trek: The Next Generation*, Syn., 1987–1994. Played by Denise Crosby.

Natasha Yar, called Tasha, was the Chief of Security under Jean-Luc Picard, captain of the star ship U.S.S. *Enterprise NCC-1701-D*. Tasha was born on the planet Turkana IV in the year 2337. She and her younger sister, Ishara, had a difficult if not violent upbringing. When Ishara was four-and-a-half years old, their parents were killed in a civil war that erupted on the planet. Tasha and Ishara were sent to a foster home but were soon abandoned and took to living on the harsh streets, managing to avoid the gangs, the drugs and death. In 2352, when the United Federation of Planets intervened and stopped the war, Tasha and Ishara parted company. Tasha joined the Federation but Ishara chose to remain behind. They never saw each other again. Sometime later, after Tasha risked her life to save a colonist in a minefield, Captain Picard's request to have her transferred to his command was granted.

Tragedy struck the crew of the *Enterprise* in 2364. During a rescue mission on Vagrall, Tasha was hit with an invisible energy blast and died of severe head trauma. She was athletic and well trained in the martial arts.

See also: Beverly Crusher, Data, Deanna Troi, Geordi La Forge, Jean-Luc Picard, William Riker.

835. Ned Malone, *The Lost World,* Syn., 1998–2002. Played by David Orth.

The time is 1920. Edward Malone, called Ned, is a journalist seeking the story of a lifetime: recording the events of the Challenger Expedition as they explore a lost word of unknown civilizations and prehistoric creatures (see George Challenger for further information). As a child Ned delivered newspapers. He became a copyboy for the *International Herald-Tribune* after graduating from college. He then served time overseas during World War I as a foreign correspondent. Ned's war experience serves him well as he encounters hostile tribes and fierce animals as he and his fellow explores (Roxton, Marguerite, George and Veronica) struggle for survival in a land that time forgot. Ned calls his journals "The Lost World."

See also: George Challenger, Finn, John Roxton, Marguerite Krux, Veronica Layton.

836. Neelix, *Star Trek: Voyager,* UPN, 1995–2001. Played by Ethan Phillips.

Neelix is a Talaxian and Morale Officer under Kathryn Janeway, captain of the star ship U.S.S. *Voyager.* Neelix was born on Rinax, a moon of the planet Talax in the Delta Quadrant. In addition to his duties as morale officer, Neelix is a goodwill ambassador and calls the galley his home (he is an excellent cook). He is also one of the few remaining Talaxians and left *Voyager* in 2378 to live with a fellow Talaxian (Dexa) and her son (Brax) on a Delta Quadrant asteroid (Talax was destroyed many years ago by an invading army. Neelix served Captain Janeway for seven years, leaving right before the series ended).

See also: B'Elanna Torres, Chakotay, The Doctor, Harry Kim, Kathryn Janeway, Seven of Nine, Tuvok.

837. Neesee James, *All of Us,* UPN, 2003 (current). Played by LisaRaye McCoy.

This entry also contains information on Robert James (Duane Martin), Neesee's ex-husband, and Tia Jewell (Elise Neal), Robert's fiancé.

Neesee James is very beautiful and always elegantly dressed woman who runs her own catering company in Los Angeles. She is divorced from Robert and is the mother of Robert Jr.

Neesee Harrison (her maiden name) was born and raised in California. Her mother raised her to be the belle of the ball and to always surround herself with elegance. She attended the Lanford Academy (an exclusive and expensive private girls finishing school) and is a graduate of UCLA. She met Robert in college and they married after graduation. Neesee became pregnant soon after and put her career (a chef) on hold to raise their son. Robert works as an entertainment reporter for a program called *Mr. L.A.* on KJSB-TV. They divorced after five years when Robert put his career above their relationship. Neesee retains her married name for her son's sake. She called Robert "Snookie" when they were married.

Tia understands Robert and Neesee's need to remain friends for their son's sake. Tia works as kindergarten teacher. She was in the drama club in high school and studied dance in college.

Neesee lives in a very luxurious apartment (9) at the El Royale Apartments (street number 450). She likes old movies, Oriental food and needless to say, she is an exceptional cook. Prior to starting her company Neesee tried writing a children's book ("It's a work in progress) and selling jewelry ("I was my best customer"). Neesee also claims she has a gift for dance—"and the body for it."

838. Neil Barash, *Flying Blind,* Fox, 1992–1993. Played by Corey Parker.

Neil Barash is a young man who is dating a wild, beautiful and unpredictable girl named Alicia Smith (see entry for more information).

Neil is the son of Jeremy and Ellen Barash. He was born in Hartsdale, New York, and now lives in a small apartment in Manhattan (he met Alicia at the Madison Bistro). Neil first worked in the advertising department of his father's snack food company, Hockman Foods. He quit the job to become independent and found work as a gopher for Dennis Lake, the sleazy owner of a B-horror movie company called Scepter Films (they have produced such "classics" as *Beverly Hills 9021-Dead, Panic at Three Mile Island, Massacre at Cleavage Farm, Revenge of the Ozone Mutant Mermaid* and *Frosty the Maniac*).

Neil is Alicia's complete opposite. He is laid back and not eager to do wild and crazy things on the spur of the moment (as is Alicia). It was a mismatched romance and Neil's inability (or lack of enthusiasm for) flying blind would have led to their breakup had the series continued. Neil had a parakeet named Mickey as a child and won the Most Improved Camper Award at Camp Tomahawk. His mother called him "Mo Bo."

839. Nell Harper, *Gimme a Break*, NBC, 1981–1987. Played by Nell Carter.

Nell Ruth Harper is a caring woman who gave up a singing career to honor the last request of her dearest friend (Margaret Kanisky): care for her three daughters (Katie, Samantha, and Julie). Although the girls have a father (Carl) Margaret felt Carl could not manage alone and asked Nell to help him. As time passed Nell became like a real mother to the young girls.

Nell was born in Alabama on April 13, 1950. She grew up on Erickson Road and attended Etchfield High School. Nell was raised in a musically inclined family and learned to sing and dance at an early age. She fine-tuned that talent as she grew and appeared in her school's musical productions over the years. When she felt the time was right she left home to make her mark on the world. It was a rough road and Nell worked the small clubs for little pay and virtually no recognition. She had talent but the breaks just weren't there.

Nell found great satisfaction in raising Katie, Julie and Samantha. Although her career was put on hold, Nell still managed to sing at the local clubs in Glen Lawn, California (where they live at 2938 Maple Lane). Nell became much a part of each girl's life. Samantha, who was too young to really remember her mother, looked upon Nell as her real mother; Julie and Katie felt very close to Nell and treated her with the same respect they showed their birth mother. Nell was married (and divorced from Tony Tremaine) but was never blessed with children of her own. Like most kids, Katie, Julie and Samantha are a bit mischievous (Katie most of all) and Nell deals a strict hand to deal with them (something Carl likes about her). While stories do allow for Nell to do an occasional song and dance, the singing career aspect was played down as the series progressed. Nell enrolled in Glen Lawn Junior College (pursuing a career in child psychology) and in 1986, after Carl's passing, moved to Littlefield, New Jersey with Samantha (Julie had married and moved to San Diego; Katie took a job as a department store buyer in San Francisco). Samantha enrolled in Littlefield College while Nell acquired a job as an editor at the McDutton and Leod Publishing House.

See also: Julie Kanisky, Katie Kanisky, Samantha Kanisky.

840. Nellie Paine, *Thicker Than Water*, ABC, 1973. Played by Julie Harris.

Nellie Paine is the daughter of Jonas Paine, an enterprising businessman who turned his love of pickles into the Paine's Pure Pickles empire. Nellie was born in 1933 and her brother, Ernie, in 1935. Their mother, Frances, passed away in 1955 and in 1963 Jonas became chronically ill. Two years later Ernie left home (unable to stand the smell of pickles anymore) and Nellie became a spinster, living at home and caring for an elderly, sick father who just won't kick the bucket.

Nellie is attractive but she downplays her looks, wearing little makeup and matronly clothes. She runs the pickle company for Jonas and feels she will never have a life of her own. Her childhood revolved around pickles. She was teased in school by other kids and called "Nellie, Nellie, Pickle Belly." She was studious and rarely dated. She dreamed of attending the prom but was never asked. Her life after high school was pickles, pickles and more pickles; but most importantly, keeping the secret of the Paine's Gherkin — the special pickle that launched the company — secret.

Nellie has always been frugal. Her parents were not stingy but tried to instill in her the value of a dollar (Ernie, on the other hand, is a spendthrift). Nellie buys her clothes at Harrison's Discount Store (35–45 percent off) and tries to run the household (and pickle factory) on a tight budget.

See also: Ernie Paine, Jonas Paine.

841. Nero Wolfe, *Nero Wolfe*, NBC, 1981; A&E, 2001–2002. Played by William Conrad (NBC), Maury Chaykin (A&E).

Nero Wolfe is television's most unusual private detective. He is overweight, a gourmet cook, horticulturist and connoisseur of fine wine. But most of all, he is a master criminologist. Nero is a wealthy recluse who is abrupt, insulting and arrogant. He lives in a New York brownstone but seldom leaves the house to solve crimes. His legman, private detective Archie Goodwin (Lee Horsley, NBC; Timothy Hutton, A&E) gathers the evidence for him. Nero is a perfectionist. He examines each piece of evidence with a fine toothcomb. His sharp mind enables him to piece together the evidence and pinpoint a killer. He gathers the suspects in his home (with the police present) and recaps the crime at hand. He then questions the suspects and reveals the culprit.

Nero claims he rarely leaves home "because I hate traffic." When a circumstance leaves him no other choice but to leave his home, he immediately misses its comforts and avails himself to the comforts of the house he is visiting. It is also at these times that Nero hopes for one thing — a meal prepared by a gourmet cook. These opportunities also give Nero the opportunity to pick up minute details the police often overlook.

Nero solves cases by hard facts not by imagining who did it. He usually sets a trap to catch a killer — "We can't go to him so we have to make him come to us." Nero relaxes by raising orchids "and sitting in my nice big easy chair and enjoying a delectable glass of beer." On NBC, Nero's address was given as 918 West 35th Street; on A&E he resides as 454 West 35th Street in Manhattan.

Nicholas Bradford *see* **David Bradford**

842. Nicholas Flemming, *Sable*, ABC, 1987–1988. Played by Lewis Van Bergen.

Nicholas Flemming is the name currently being used by Jon Sable, a wanted murderer who helps people in trouble. Nicholas lives at 2435 Lincoln Park West in Chicago and enjoys great success as the author of *The Friends of B.B. Flemm*, a best-selling series of children's books. He is also the creator of "Jon Sable, Freelance," a daily comic strip about a hero of the underdog.

Jon's past is very sketchy. It is only revealed that he lived in South Africa and was married. He was also the father of two children and ran a safari business. For unknown reasons Jon's wife and children were killed by poachers. Jon killed the men responsible and fled to Chicago to begin a new life (he actually owes his life to Eden Kendall [Rene Russo] his literary agent. She created Nicholas Flemming and got him out of Africa. Eden is also the only other person who knows that Nicholas is actually Jon Sable). Jon's pen name is also known to be B.B. Flemm and the locale is also said to be New York.

Nicholas lives his comic strip. He is part vigilante and part detective. He takes on the cases of people desperately in need of help but does so in makeup (dressed in black with stripes across his face; Eden says, "He looks like the Easter Bunny"). Nicholas chooses his clients very carefully — "I have to. I have a price on my head." Nicholas is not a hired killer. If a case involves a child he gets "crazy and careless because he couldn't stand to see what happened to him happen to someone else."

843. Nicholas Knight, *Forever Knight*, CBS, 1992. Played by Geraint Wyn Davies.

Nicholas Knight is a detective with the 37th Precinct of the Toronto Police Department in Canada. He only works at night and he is incredibly strong. Nicholas is also the city's most unusual crime fighter — an 800-year-old vampire who uses his amazing abilities to help good defeat evil.

Nicholas was born in the year 1192 in Europe. He grew up on the legends of the supernatural and the undead (vampires). When he turned 26 (in 1218) he wished for immortality. A master vampire named Lucien LaCroix arranged for Nicholas to have his wish. A beautiful vampire (Janette) bit Nicholas and turned him into a creature of the night. Nicholas, however, was unable to kill and turned his back on vampirism.

Nicholas can become mortal by facing his fears (for example, looking at a cross, which weakens him; or facing the light of day, which could destroy him). The jade glass of the Mayan Indians can also cure him (European legend states that if blood from a sacrificed victim is consumed from this glass, it will lift the blanket of evil from cursed individuals).

Nicholas is single and resides at 7 Curtis Avenue. He drives a 1962 Cadillac (plate 358 VY5) and doesn't kill for blood (he has a supply of cow's blood in his refrigerator to sustain himself). He works the night shift to avoid sunlight (he told his captain he was allergic to bright light) and frequents The Raven, a nightclub run by Janette (the same vampire who bit him).

844. Nick and Nora Charles, *The Thin Man*, NBC, 1957–1959. Played by Peter Lawford, Phyllis Kirk.

Nicholas Charles is a private detective (owner of Nicholas Charles — Confidential Investigations) in New York City; Nora Claridon is the spoiled, rich daughter of a wealthy San Francisco family. They meet by chance but sparks do not fly. To impress Nora, Nick, as he is called, buys her a wirehaired terrier. The dog, named Asta by Nora, impresses Nora and she and Nick become close. They marry and set up housekeeping in an apartment in New York's Greenwich Village. Nick gives up his job as a detective to become the mystery editor for a publishing house. Now, on the twenty-eighth of each year (month not mentioned) Nick and Nora celebrate the day they met as "Asta Day" (they married in 1950 and honeymooned at the Ambassador Hotel).

Nick is handsome, always well dressed and always a gentleman — at times too much of a gentleman for Nora when beautiful women become attracted by Nick's sophisticated style. Nick enjoys his new career as an editor for the peace and quiet it affords him. However, he still has to call on his sleuthing abilities to help Nora solve the crimes she has an uncanny knack for stumbling upon.

Nora is beautiful, fashion conscious and a standout at society functions. She is extremely jealous when other women "make goo goo eyes" at Nick (it is at these times that she calls him "Nicholas!"); her normal pet name for him is "Nickie"; he calls Nora "Tiger." There are no two ways about it. Nick does have a roaming eye and he calms Nora with lines like "None are as beautiful as you."

Nora wears a size eight dress and is a member of the Junior Matrons' Breakfast Club and a charity called the Junior Guild. Nora enjoys her adventures as an amateur sleuth and believes her intuition is better than Nick's experience when it comes to solving crimes. She also never thinks in emergencies—"I have hunches." Asta often accompanies Nora and Nick calls the dog their child because of the way Nora babies him. Even though the dog is a male, Nora gave him a girl's name based on her Uncle Harry's theory that a sissy name will make a man out of a boy. When Asta needs to go for a walk he most often brings his leash to Nick. Nick enjoys reading the New York *Chronicle*; hates to have his sleep disturbed and drives a convertible with the license plate NICK 1.

845. Nick Barkley, *The Big Valley*, ABC, 1965–1969. Played by Peter Breck.

The Barkley Ranch in the San Joaquin Valley in Stockton, California (1870s) has a reputation for three things for its workers: good food, clean beds, fair treatment. Nicholas Barkley, the second born son of Victoria and Tom Barkley, is the ranch foreman and the man who sees to it that those standards are met. Nick, as he is called, was a young man (22) when his father was killed for standing up to railroad officials who wanted his land. In the six years that have passed since then (when the series begins) Nick has become tough—eager to use his fists or guns when necessary. Nick is proud of the Barkley name. It is a name that stands for justice and a name the people of the valley can look up to in times of trouble.

Nick has three brothers (Jarrod, Heath and Eugene) and a sister (Audra). He received his first saddle when he was six years old (he wrote "Nick, age 6—keep off" on it). Ten years later he fell down an open mine shaft and was almost killed. Nick fell in love for the first time when he was 18 with a girl named Jeannie Price (he met her in a town called Willow Springs). Jeannie's father ran the grocery store but Nick was too restless to settle down and left her, hoping to return for her one day. In 1877 he found that Jeannie (born in 1850) had died of typhoid fever in 1870.

Nick is an expert on horses (he rides a cutting horse named Coco; later Big Duke) and is responsible for buying horses for the ranch (and breaking wild ones). Audra loves to ride horses. Nick, however, doesn't like her to ride half-broken stock (he thinks it is much too dangerous for her; she thinks she can ride a horse "and break 'em with the best of them"). Nick enjoys a drink at The Empire Saloon in nearby Stockton (the saloon is also called The Golden Eagle and The Wagon Wheel).

Nick was the only Barkley child to marry — to grant a dying woman's wish (Julia Jenkins was the unwed mother of a young boy [Tommy]. She had a shady background and wanted her son to have a fresh start with a good last name).

See also: Audra Barkley, Heath Barkley, Jarrod Barkley, Victoria Barkley.

846. Nick Biancavilla, *Strong Medicine*, Lifetime, 2000–2004. Played by Brennan Elliott.

Nick Biancavilla is a young doctor with a great fear: his colleagues will discover he watches *The Golden Girls* reruns on TV. Nick would love to have a Rolex watch (but can't afford it) and play pro hockey. He feels his greatest achievement was graduating from medical school. He has put his knowledge of medicine to work as a staff doctor in the emergency room of the Rittenhouse Women's Health Clinic in Philadelphia. Nick is brash and impulsive and puts himself on the front lines, performing the procedures he feels are necessary — sometimes without time for the proper diagnosis.

Nick was born in Philadelphia and believes because of his Italian-American heritage, his father may have had ties to organized crime. He has four older sisters and has learned a lot about women from them. He feels he knows more about women than men twice his age. Nick is always eager to learn. He keeps abreast of all the latest medical advances and hopes to one day become head of an emergency hospital.

See also: Andy Campbell, Dana Stowe, Kayla Thornton, Lana Hawkins, Luisa Delgado, Peter Riggs.

847. Nick Boyle, *Poltergeist: The Legacy*, SHO, 1996–1998; Sci Fi, 1999. Played by Martin Cummings.

Nicholas Boyle is a member of the San Francisco Legacy House, an organization that investigates matters associated with the supernatural. Nick, as he is called, is 38 years old. His official title is researcher but his research often leads him outside the four walls of a library to physically battle demons.

Nick is an adventurer and spent time as a Navy S.E.A.L. His father was a colleague of Derek Rayne, the head of the San Francisco Legacy House and it was through this acquaintance that Nick became a part of the Legacy (hoping to find excitement). Nick has become an expert on the unnatural and frequently suspects that what appears to be a paranormal event may actually be the work of human beings. Nick has no patience. When he finds that something is wrong he likes to react immediately, usually going head first into dangerous situations. Experience has taught him that the forces of darkness can be dangerous and his keen sense of intelligence sometimes curbs his tendency to act first and think later. He drives a Mustang with the license plate LP 326C7.

See also: Alex Moreau, Derek Rayne, Kristen Adams, Rachel Corrigan.

848. Nick Marshall, *Dark Justice,* CBS, 1991–1993. Played by Ramy Zada, Bruce Abbott.

Nicholas Marshall is a Supreme Court Judge (city not specified). He is also a man who has stopped believing in the system and has formed the Night Watchmen, a group of vigilantes who bring justice to those who are guilty but beat the system (the group was originally called the Secret Vigilante Force).

Nick, as he is called, began his career as a police officer. He was married and had a daughter. As part of his job, Nick was forced to kill a mobster or be killed. Nick's wife and daughter were killed in revenge. Nick tried to fight back the only way he could—through the justice system.

As a cop he lost cases through loopholes. When he became a district attorney he lost cases to corrupt lawyers. As a judge he finds his hands tied by a strict interpretation of the law. Though bitter he still believes in the law but the only way to accomplish his goal was to become a vigilante and go beyond the law to deal justice.

Nick first reviews a case "to see how the scuzz got off" then determines what action should be taken to bring the criminal back to justice ("I can't balance the sides all the time, not even half the time. I do what I can and hope I get a break once in a while"). Nick rides a motorcycle with "850 Commando" printed on the side and the license plate IHD 469. "Justice may be blind," Nick says, "but it can see in the dark."

849. Nick O'Malley, *Special Unit 2,* UPN, 2001–2002. Played by Michael Landers.

Nicholas O'Malley is a police officer with Special Unit 2, a secret branch of the Chicago Police Department, who believes in the supernatural—everything from werewolves to trolls to vampires. He is not crazy. His first partner, Judy, was killed by a vicious Link (everything that is not man or beast) that "ripped her into 600 inch-size pieces." He joined Special Unit 2 to find and destroy these unearthly Links (the police department lingo for them).

Nick, as he is called, was born in Chicago and is considered a psychopath for his Rambo-like pursuit of Links. He is rude and obnoxious and often plunges head first into situations without thinking first (when he gets in too deep he often says, "Maybe I should have had a plan first"). Nick's Special Unit 2 I.D. number is 00PG-5905-332. He treats all Links the same—"Kill 'em" (he is also an expert on coming up with unique ways to destroy them. Unfortunately, none are feasible, as each Link is different). Nick becomes uptight if a Link gets the best of him. He seeks revenge "but only to protect the public," he says. Nick finds relaxation at strip clubs; his car license plate reads MIJ 528.

See also: Kate Benson.

850. Nick Russo, *Blossom,* NBC, 1991–1995. Played by Ted Wass.

Nicholas Russo is a musician who provided backup for such performers as Chuck Barry, Anita Baker and B.B. King. He won Cleo Awards for his music in television commercials and has played on sound tracks for such movies as *Dirty Dancing, Fame* and *Ghost.*

Nick, as he is called, is the father of three children (Blossom, Anthony and Joey) and is divorced from Madelyn (who left the family after 20 years of marriage to pursue her dream of becoming a singer in Europe). Nick was born in Southern California and now lives at 465 Hampton Drive. He grew up appreciating music and has geared his whole life to entertaining people. He is a graduate of Julliard and in high school was a member of a band called Neon Wilderness. Nick can play all types of music and entertains at various clubs. He is also struggling to raise three children as a single father. Blossom is his only daughter and very good; Joey is a bit dense and can find trouble simply by tying his shoelaces; Anthony has been the most troublesome (a drug addict who is trying to get his life back together). Nick is very strict with Anthony but a bit more lenient when disciplining Blossom and Joey. Blossom and Joey have not followed in Anthony's footsteps and Nick feels tough love is the only way to prevent Anthony from reverting to his old ways. Nick found romance in 1994 and married a widow named Carol on October 24, 1994.

See also: Anthony Russo, Blossom Russo, Six LeMeure.

851. Nick Slaughter, *Sweating Bullets,* CBS, 1991–1993. Played by Rob Stewart.

Nicholas Slaughter is a former operative for the D.E.A. (Drug Enforcement Agency) turned private detective. He is based on Key Mariah, a small coastal town in Florida and runs Nick Slaughter — Private Investigations from an office at 45 Lafayette Street. Nick, as he is called, charges $250 a day and uses tactics he learned with the D.E.A. to help him solve crimes.

Nick was born in Florida and is a graduate of Lakeside High School. He joined the Miami Police Department after graduating and five years later was recruited by the D.E.A. for his impressive arrest record. He quit the D.E.A., he says, for two reasons: "They ran out of bad guys"; "I got tired of seeing them railroad innocent people so some prosecutor could have an impressive record."

Nick doesn't pay taxes and owes the IRS a great deal of money. Sylvie, his secretary, doesn't trust him with sharp weapons or with beautiful women (he has a roving eye and can't make a commitment. He hates the "R" word — relationship). Nick falls to pieces when he meets a woman and things don't work out. His Jeep license plate reads BZN N57 (later NIR 548 and PZE 181).

See also: Sylvie Gerard.

852. Nick Stokes, *C.S.I.: Crime Scene Investigation,* CBS, 2000 (current). Played by George Eades.

Nick Stokes is a field operative with the Crime Scene Investigation Unit of the Metropolitan Las Vegas Police Department. He was born in Dallas, Texas, on August 18, 1971, and has one sister and five brothers. His father was a D.A. before becoming a judge. His mother worked as a public defender. Nick has a Bachelor of Science degree in criminal justice from Rice University. His specialty is hair and fiber analysis (he was also said to have attended Texas A&M University). Nick previously worked with the Dallas Police Department before being transferred to its crime lab, C.S.I. Level One. Gil Grissom then recruited him for his C.S.I. unit in Las Vegas. Nick likes being around people but is easily frustrated when a case upsets him — "Sometimes I hate this job." He

watches the Discovery Channel, which he claims is beneficial to his work.

See also: Catherine Willows, Gil Grissom, Sara Sidle, Warrick Brown.

853. Nicole Bradford, *My Two Dads,* NBC, 1987–1990. Played by Staci Keanan.

Nicole Bradford is the daughter of the late Marcie Bradford and is being raised by her two fathers — Joey Harris (Greg Evigan) and Michael Taylor (Paul Reiser). Joey and Michael are actually Nicole's guardians (she calls them "My Two Dads"). Michael and Joey both dated Marcie. When Marcie passed away, the actual biological father could not be determined and a judge (Margaret Wilbur) gave the responsibility of raising Nicole to both men.

Nicole and her two dads live at 627 North Brewster Street (Apartment B) in Manhattan. She is a very pretty 12-year-old girl when the series begins. Joey was initially an artist, then director for *Financial Update* magazine, artist again and finally teacher at New York University. Michael was originally a financial advisor at the Taft-Kelcher Agency then marketing manager for *Financial Update* magazine.

Nicole is the typical young lady. She is a student at Kennedy Junior High School. She has a teddy bear (Mr. Beebels) and likes boys but is not yet eager to date. She is experimenting with makeup and soon becomes a worry to Joey and Michael. Shortly after turning 13 Nicole also wanted to become a woman. She found an interest in boys and wanted to date (although her fathers restricted her dating to weekends only and only to movies). Nicole felt she was smart and pretty but had not yet developed and became jealous of girls who had. She felt breasts were the key for attention and tried padding her bra and wearing tight blouses. When that didn't work she spent $29.95 on the "Bust-O-Matic" breast developer only to discover that pretending to be someone you are not was more trouble than it was worth (it was also the toughest talk her fathers had to face in dealing with Nicole's approaching womanhood). Nicole is a good kid and very obedient although she does occasionally rebel against something when she feels she is right and her fathers are wrong. Michael feels his job as a father is to focus on Nicole's needs and wants. Joey feels it is his job to decide how to punish Nicole when she does something wrong.

854. Nikita, *La Femme Nikita,* USA, 1997–2001. Played by Peta Wilson.

Nikita, codename Josephine, is a beautiful but

deadly Level Two operative for Section One, a ruthless agency that will get any job done no matter what the cost in terms of life or equipment.

Nikita is the daughter of Roberta Wirth and Philip Jones. She was born in an undisclosed locale and attended Monroe High School. She does not know her father and her mother is an alcoholic. Life became intolerable as Nikita grew. Her mother's drinking caused constant fighting and eventually her home when Roberta's boyfriend (who didn't like Nikita) kicked Nikita out of the house. Nikita took to living on the streets. One night a police officer was stabbed to death. Nikita was in the wrong place at the wrong time. The killer saw Nikita, pushed her up against a wall and placed the murder weapon in her hand — just in time for arriving police to see Nikita holding the knife. Nikita was quickly tried, found guilty and sentenced to life in prison.

Section One framed Nikita. To convince the world that Nikita was dead, it revealed that she committed suicide in prison and is buried in Row 8, plot 30. Section One required the services of a girl with beauty who could also kill. Nikita is released from prison on the condition that she work for Section One (her other choice: execution).

Nikita does what is necessary to survive. She has blonde hair, is highly intelligent and not as ruthless as the agency she works for. Her greatest weakness is her compassion and sympathy for innocent people. She relies on her fierce instincts (and gorgeous features) to achieve the covert and extremely dangerous objectives of Section One (she knows that if she lets her conscience get in the way she will be eliminated). Nikita is highly trained and dedicated to fighting global terrorism by any means necessary — legal or otherwise. Nikita often violates protocol by acting on her own intuition (when she feels a mission is not going as planned). Nikita does not want to be treated differently ("It's not fair to the others") and will risk her life to safeguard the U.S.

Nikita is a martial arts expert. She is capable of handling any weapon and is proficient with explosives. She has been trained to kill and will not do so unless she has to (when she does kill it is because she feels the victim deserved it). Nikita collects sunglasses (she is never seen without a pair) and often carries a bag (such as a backpack or over-the-shoulder) that contains her gun and cell phone. She also sleeps with a gun under her pillow. Nikita does what she does because "If I don't play by the rules I die."

855. Nikki Franco, *V.I.P.*, Syn., 1998–2002. Played by Natalie Raitano.

Nicolette Franco is a member of V.I.P. (Vallery Irons Protection), a high profile Los Angeles protection agency that charges $25,000 a day plus expenses. Nikki, as she is called, was born in Los Angeles and is a member of the Franco crime family. Nikki, however, grew up on the straight and narrow and says, "I have nothing to do with the crime end of it" (her grandfather, Don Franco, is a Los Angeles mafia boss). Although Nikki is not a mobster, she is a very violent (and beautiful) woman.

Nikki believes bullets and guns are the only way to deal with the enemy. She has been influenced by Clint Eastwood's *Dirty Harry* movies and sees herself as a female version of that character (only more forceful and deadly). She carries a pair of 357 Magnums with her at all times; a grenade launcher is her favorite weapon (she carries one as "emergency equipment" in the back of her yellow Ford Mustang, plate VIP NIK; later it's a Dodge). Nikki is also an expert on bombs and explosives and has an "electronic sniffer" (a bomb detector shaped like a dog) she calls Rex. "When I get depressed I like to blow something up," says Nikki (who is also seen discharging alarming amounts of ammunition on a firing range when she gets upset). Nikki is a Catholic and a graduate of St. Theresa's High School for Girls. She likes high-speed racing and drove the XJ-219, an experimental electric car. Vallery Irons, her boss, calls her "Queen of Explosives" and "Car Crazy."

See also: Kay Simmons, Quick Williams, Tasha Dexter, Vallery Irons.

856. Nikki Merrick, *All About Us*, NBC, 2001–2002. Played by Marieh Delfino.

Nicole Merrick is a 16-year-old beauty who attends Belmont High School in Chicago. She is a sophomore and best friends with Alecia, Sierra and Christina. Nikki, as she is called, lives at 299 Linden Drive on the Gold Coast; 555-0134 is her cell phone number.

Nikki is self-centered and believes the key to friendship is total selfishness. She is also the most confident of her friends and has a positive attitude about everything — no matter how bleak things look (like facing a test she did not study for). Nikki is not a morning person and hates to be awakened early on non-school days. She enjoys cappuccino and has no sense of commitment. The more devious something is, the better Nikki likes it.

Nikki is the most fashionable of her girlfriends. She is into makeup and clothes and always feels she has to look her best. Nikki and her girlfriends are members of the Martha Stewart Cooking Club (they gather each Sunday at Alecia's home to test new recipes) and when a problem arises they hold ECS (Emergency Chat Session) to resolve matters. Nikki enjoys hanging out with her friends at a teen club called the Loft.

See also: Alecia Alcott, Christina Castelli, Sierra Jennings.

857. Nikki Page, *Over My Dead Body*, CBS, 1990–1991. Played by Jessica Lundy.

Nicole Page, called Nikki, was born in San Francisco, California. As a child she became addicted to the crime dramas on television and as she grew older she became fascinated with crime stories written by Maxwell Beckett, a former Scotland Yard Inspector turned author. Nikki set her sights on becoming an investigative reporter.

Nikki is a graduate of Union Bay High School and State College (where she majored in journalism). She acquired a first job as a journalist-trainee for the San Francisco *Union* (her actual job is an entry level position writing the obituary column; she does so under the name Miss Black). Nikki is pretty, brash and street smart. She aspires to bigger and better things — like helping her hero, Maxwell Beckett, solve crimes. (When Nikki witnesses a murder but no one believes her, she devises a plan to get Maxwell's help. She prints his obituary in the paper. The prank almost gets Nikki fired, but it unites her with Maxwell and together they solve a case of murder. Nikki now assists Maxwell and hopes to get the experience she needs to become a crime reporter). Nikki lives in Apartment 307 at 5045 Hode Street and rides a motorcycle. She is impulsive and too quick to involve herself in situations without thinking first (which causes friction between her and Maxwell as Maxwell prefers the calm, slow and thought out approach).

See also: Maxwell Beckett.

858. Nikki White, *Nikki*, WB, 2000–2002. Played by Nikki Cox.

Nikki White is the wife of Dwight White, a Las Vegas wrestler who performs under the name "The Cry Baby." Nikki was born as Nicole Carmichael in Paramus, New Jersey, on June 9, 1978. She attended St. Mark's Grammar School, then Paramus High School. She studied jazz, tap and ballet for 16 years. Nikki is very well endowed and claims, "I had to give up ballet lessons because my breasts were too big." Her dream is to use her expertise as a dancer to become a Las Vegas show-girl.

Before marrying and moving to Las Vegas, Nikki held the following jobs: counter girl at Burger World and 50 Flavors of Ice Cream; sales-girl at Murray's Pets; waitress at the Brick Oven.

In Las Vegas, Nikki and Dwight live at 262 Linden Drive, Apartment 26 (also seen as 25); 555-0816 is their phone number. Nikki first worked as a chorus girl (a calf dancer) at the Golden Calf Hotel and Casino. When the casino experienced a financial setback and Nikki was laid off, she found two temporary jobs: teaching children to dance at the Frances Lang School of Dance; weather girl on KAAC-TV's *Five O'clock News* program. When the Golden Calf closed (purchased by the U.S. Meat Corporation), Nikki found work as "The Meat Girl" (hands out meat samples) at the Rivera Hotel. This was followed by the role of Orchida (a super hero who was part girl, part flower) at the Comics Fair at the Las Vegas Convention Center. When this failed, she became a CWF Wrestling League Cheerleader (the girl who dances between matches). She also wrestled as "The Cheerleader of Doom." When the wrestling league disbanded Nikki became a salesgirl at American Auto Parts.

Nikki buys her lingerie at Victoria's Secret. She is sometimes afraid to audition for bigger stage roles "because in my mind I am a star. If the show fails, I'll just be a woman dancing at the Golden Calf." Nikki's stunning good looks were also her biggest disappointment (she was hired by Succulent Records as a singer. She was fired when she objected to them using her body with another girl's voice). No matter what happens, Nikki has a positive outlook on life. She also believes she has a super power — matchmaking — "I know when two people are meant for each other."

See also: Dwight White.

859. Niles Crane, *Frasier*, NBC, 1993–2004. Played by David Hyde Pierce.

Niles Crane is the younger brother of Frasier Crane and the son of Martin Crane, a retired police detective (his mother, Hester, is deceased). Niles was born in Seattle, Washington, and like Frasier, is a private practice psychiatrist. Niles lived on Wallace Lane as a child and attended the Bryce Academy. He acquired his degree from Oxford University and married the neurotic, well dressed, very thin, very beautiful but never seen Maris (whom he later divorced).

Niles lives at the luxurious Montana Hotel in Seattle. He has a pet parrot (Baby) and as children he and Frasier wrote as series of detective yarns called "The Crane Boys Mystery Stories." Niles has an I.Q. of 156 and spends $250 for a haircut ("I have problem follicles"). He is allergic to parchment ("My ear itches, I sneeze and I have a tough time at the library"). Niles has a fear of figures in authority and phobias about insects and what he calls "Chair Clusters" (chairs being placed too close to one another). He eats at Stefano's Restaurant and enjoys coffee with Frasier at the Café Nervosa. He and Frasier also attempted to run their own eatery called The Happy Brothers Restaurant. Niles' license plate reads SHRINK.

The episode of September 24, 2002, finds Niles marrying Daphne Moon (Jane Leeves), his father's live-in home car specialist. Daphne was born in Manchester, England, and as a child was the star of a British TV series called *Mind Your Knickers* (about a 12 year-old-girl in a private boarding school; Daphne played Emma). During his divorce from Maris, Niles was forced to temporarily abandon his apartment and moved into Apartment 8 of the Shangri La Apartments (at 52 Elm Street).

See also: Frasier Crane, Martin Crane.

860. Nina Van Horn, *Just Shoot Me*, NBC, 1997–2003. Played by Wendie Malick.

Nina Van Horn is a world-famous model turned fashion editor for *Blush*, a Manhattan-based magazine. Nina has appeared on the covers of such magazines as *Vogue*, *Blush*, *Redbook* and *Mademoiselle* and was the spokeswoman for Noxzema Skin Cream. She played a Fembot on the TV series *The Bionic Woman*; was a celebrity guest on *Jeopardy*; gave makeup advice on *Wake Up, New York*; and appeared on *Cops* ("but you can't see me; they pushed my face into the grass"). Nina wears sexy clothes "Because that's all I own" and auditioned for a TV commercial called Simple Time Stuffing (she was rejected for not being motherly enough).

Nina was a top model in the 1970s and '80s, but her past is a dark secret that she tries to hide from the public. Before changing her name to Nina Van Horn, she was known as Claire Noodleman. She is unaware of who her parents are and is hoping to one day find them. Nina was abandoned as an infant and placed in a feed troth of a farm family named Noodleman in Colby, Kansas. She came with a note attached: "Allergic to bananas" and was given the first name of Claire by the Noodleman's (who named her after their cat, who had run away). Claire grew up on the farm and developed a special skill: the ability to milk two cows at once with her feet. But Claire also had a special look. At the age of 12 she appeared on the cover of Blumgarten's Seed Catalogue. Her pose impressed a talent agent who changed her name to Nina Van Horn (after a porn star who lived in his building) and launched her career. In

1969 Nina became a sensation with her bikini poster "Jungle Beach." She next made a feature film, *Foxy Trouble* and its sequel, *Cop Full of Trouble*. She played regional theater in *A Doll's House* and in 1977 she was host of the TV series *A.M. Milwaukee*.

A later remembrance by Nina changes her background somewhat. Claire was abandoned and did grow up on a farm but made it on her own. She had an affair when she was 15 and gave birth a year later to a girl (Chloe) that she gave up for adoption. Claire yearned for the fast life and left home to pursue a modeling career in New York City. She changed her name to Nina Van Horn and wound up in Boston modeling hats; it was here that a talent agent discovered her. She was now allergic to peanut butter ("My lips swell up") and had a different farm talent: she was called "The Horse Calmer Downer" (she could calm horses during storms). Additional credits mentioned for Nina at this time were the 1974 Model of the Year Award and the host of the E-Channel's *American Awards Pre-Show*.

When Nina's career took a beating in the late 1970s she survived on whatever jobs she could find. She was working as a mermaid at a boat show when Jack Gallo, the publisher of *Blush*, discovered her. As a young girl Nina loved to try on her party dress and pretend to be a model. She bases her entire life on her looks and fears growing old and losing them.

See also: Dennis Finch, Jack Gallo, Maya Gallo.

861. 99, *Get Smart*, NBC, 1965–1969; CBS, 1969–1970. Played by Barbara Feldon.

She is known only as 99 (or Agent 99). She is also a spy. She is young, beautiful and intelligent and works with Agent 86 (Maxwell Smart) on dangerous missions for CONTROL, a secret organization that battles the evils of KAOS.

Ninety-Nine has a mysterious and mostly unknown past. She was born in Twin Falls, Idaho (an apparently rural community because 99 calls herself "a country girl"). It is believed her father was a spy (his cover was a salesman and its is possibly 99's exposure in her early years to espionage that whet her appetite to become a spy).

Ninety-Nine's stunning good looks helped her break into the modeling field but for unknown reasons she quit to join the CONTROL Spy School (based on dialogue it appears she joined two weeks after Max graduated and became a spy). Ninety-Nine is not only a top-notch spy but is capable of speaking several languages. She can play the harp and violin and dance. Her abilities have earned her the Lamont Cranston Award for Shadowing (the award is based on the old radio series *The Shadow*. The Shadow, alias Lamont Cranston, had the power to cloud men's minds so they could not see him).

Ninety-Nine and Max eventually marry and have twins (and like 99, have no names). They were voted Spy Couple of the Year in 1968. Ninety-Nine used a number of aliases throughout the series. Many sources state that 99's real name is Susan Hilton. She mentions this in the episode "99 Loses Control." However, the last scene (which was cut by some stations when first syndicated) clearly states it is an alias when 99 says to Max: "Max, Susan isn't my real name." Even when Max meets 99's mother, he calls her "99's mother" and "Mrs. 99." Her catch phrase (when Max fumbles) is "Oh Max."

In the TV movie update, *Get Smart Again* (ABC, February 26, 1989), 99 has turned author and is writing her memories in a book called *Out of CONTROL*. In the series update, *Get Smart* (Fox 1995), 99 is a congresswoman and still uses her agent's number ("I don't like to be called Mrs. Smart, that makes me feel like 100. Call me 99").

See also: The Chief, Maxwell Smart.

Nora Charles *see* **Nick and Nora Charles**

862. Nora Wilde, *The Naked Truth*, ABC, 1995–1996; NBC, 1996–1997. Played by Tea Leoni.

Nora Wilde is 27 years old, divorced, and working as a photographer for *The Comet*, a trashy tabloid that prints only celebrity scandals. Nora was born in Washington, D.C., on October 10, 1968. She enjoyed writing short stories as a child and excelled in school when it came to term papers and book reports. Nora is a graduate of Sarah Lawrence College (she was the editor of the school newspaper and created a sensation by writing about campus lesbians; she later learned her roommate, Janice, was a lesbian). Nora worked for the Washington *Post* and was a Pulitzer Prize nominee. She sponsors a South American child named Manuel ("I bought him from Sally Struthers." This refers to the 1990s TV ads in which Sally represented the Catholic Children's Charity).

Nora is a beautiful and sexy woman whose marriage (to Leland) was the biggest mistake of her life. Leland tried to prevent Nora from working (he wanted her all to himself). When Nora divorced him to get her freedom, he got back at her by using his wealth and influence to close all desirable jobs to her (why she wound up at *The Comet*). Nora is hoping to someday get back into the mainstream and cover traditional news. But

at the present time is unable and forces herself to dig up celebrity dirt (her first assignment: to get a picture of a pregnant Anna Nicole Smith. Her most embarrassing assignment: posing as a stripper for an expose on well-endowed girls — are they real or falsies? All went well until Nora stuffed her bra with M&M's ["The plain ones"], bent over and the candies spilled out).

When the series switched networks the paper became *The Inquisitor*. Nora first worked as an advice columnist, then as a reporter — something she feels is one step closer to achieving her goal. Nora has one fault that she will admit to — she has a difficult time lying (she laughs when she attempts to do so).

863. Norm Henderson, *The Norm Show*, ABC, 1999–2001. Played by Norm MacDonald.

Norman Henderson was a once famous hockey player called "The Agony of Defeat" by the press. He was born in Manhattan and is a graduate of James Monroe High School. Somewhere along the line, Norm, as he is called, found a liking for poker and gambling. That fondness has cost him a great deal: he was kicked out of hockey for gambling and tax evasion.

Norm received his press name when he was with the Oilers and was knocked into the goalie net during a championship game. Although Norm was said to be on the All Stars Team (jersey 18) he was also said to be "a bad hockey player compared to the professionals." As a result of his arrest for gambling, Norm was sentenced to five years of community service with the New York City Department of Social Services as a counselor.

Norm lives at 228 West 20th Street, Apartment 6E. He has a dog named Weiner Dog (as a kid he had a dog named Scooter) and works a second job as a driver with the Supreme Modeling Agency to pay his rent and gambling debts. Norm hides the spare key to his apartment (also seen as 4E) in the fake rock in the hallway. He enjoys Burt Reynolds movies and country and western music. He enjoys a beer at his favorite pub, The Bar.

864. Norm Peterson, *Cheers*, NBC, 1982–1993. Played by George Wendt.

Hilary Peterson, called Norm, is a regular at Cheers, the Boston-based bar run by Sam Malone. Norm is a person who truly enjoys eating and drinking beer. He was born in Boston and is married to the never-seen Vera. Norm loves Vera and puts up with all her nagging but he is loyal to the bar first — "Vera is somewhere down the line." But he also says, "I joke about her but she's all I got. I don't know what I'd do without her."

Norm first worked as an accountant for H.W. and Associates. He was then a "Corporate Killer" (fires people) for Talbot International Accounting. He held one additional job as an accountant (Masters, Holly and Dickson) before beginning his own home decorating business (first called AAAA Painting then K&P Painting). Norm was called "Moonglow" in high school. He enjoys meals at the Hungry Heifer Restaurant and Ho-Ho's are his favorite snack.

See also: Cliff Claven, Diane Chambers, Ernie Pantusso, Frasier Crane, Rebecca Howe, Sam Malone, Woody Boyd.

865. Number 6, *The Prisoner*, CBS, 1968. Played by Patrick McGoohan.

"I am not a number. I am a free man." These are the words constantly spoken by a former intelligence agent of the British government who was kidnapped after resigning his post and imprisoned in a resort village in an unknown locale from which there is no escape (the agent is assumed to be John Drake from the series *Secret Agent*, but this is never said on *The Prisoner*).

The agent is stripped of his dignity and called by his new designation of Number 6. Number 6 is free to roam the Village and it appears to be populated by other ex-agents. The mysterious, never-seen Number 1 rules the Village (his or her second in command, Number 2, is seen as the actual ruler of the Village). Number 6 is constantly interrogated in an attempt to learn the reason for his resignation (could the information he possess prove a threat to the British government?). Number 6 has a strong sense of justice and is not about to divulge any information — "You won't get it," he continually says. He also asks his captors who they are, who is Number 1 and "whose side are you on?" "That would be telling" is the common response he receives.

Number 6 is determined to keep his sanity despite the endless interrogation sessions he faces. He has a razor sharp mind and one goal — to bring down the Village from within. Number 6 is always seen wearing the black suit he was supplied with by his captors. He tore off the Number 6 I.D. badge in the first episode and never wore it again (refusing to cave into their new designation for him).

The agent lived at Number 1 Buckingham Place in London. He drove a Lotus Seven Series II car and it is assumed that *The Prisoner* is a continuation from the last episode of *Secret Agent* (wherein John Drake was assigned to capture a missing sci-entist. When John confronted the scientist and learned that he was wanted for a deadly mind transference device he developed, John let him escape. John felt betrayed and resigned as a result). It could also be assumed that if the Village leaders cooperated with Number 6 (telling them who they were) he may have cooperated with them. Number 6 was a man with remarkable training and a strong sense of loyalty who could not be broken — no matter how many times he was interrogated (he did manage to escape in the last episode by destroying the Village from within).

866. Oliver and Lisa Douglas, *Green Acres*, CBS, 1965–1971. Played by Eddie Albert, Eva Gabor.

Oliver Wendell Douglas and his glamorous so-cialite wife Lisa are a city couple who moved from a luxurious penthouse apartment at 255 Park Avenue in New York City to the rural town of Hooterville to become farmers in a run down shack on a 160-acres of near worthless land (the Haney Farm) Oliver calls Green Acres.

Oliver is a successful Manhattan attorney with a life-long dream "to buy a farm, move away from the city, plow my own fields, get my hands dirty, sweat and strain to make things grow. To join with other farmers, the backbone of the American economy." Oliver believes that because he was born on a farm (in Saratoga Springs, New York) his roots are in farming (his parents thought differently and groomed him to be a lawyer. They even named him after Associate Justice Oliver Wendell Holmes. Although Oliver insisted on becoming a farmer he graduated from Harvard and found his first job as a lawyer with the firm of Fenton, Harmon, Dillon and Clay in New York City. A rather vague dialogue in another episode changes this and explains that Oliver's parents were on vacation in upstate New York when Oliver's father had to stay to hear the results for one more horse race at Saratoga. Oliver's mother, Eunice, went into labor and Oliver was born on a nearby farm. They stayed for two days before returning to Manhattan. Oliver insists in this recollection that he was born on a farm and had to become a farmer).

Oliver grew up in New York City. During World War II Oliver joined the air force and became a fighter pilot (he mentioned being a lieutenant). His biggest regret was having to bomb farmlands. On one such bombing mission over Hungry, Oliver's plane engine failed and Oliver was forced to parachute to safety. He landed in a tree and was found by a beautiful woman named

Lisa, a sergeant in the Hungarian Underground (Lisa's job was "to blow up tanks." She would wear sexy clothes, distract the Germans and allow her comrades to destroy tanks).

Lisa is the daughter of a wealthy family and lives in a mansion in Budapest. She fell in love with Oliver the instant she saw him and told him they were going to be married — "You fell from the sky and I found you" and according to a legend "we must marry." Another episode drastically changes Oliver and Lisa's meeting. Oliver was on a cruise ship (the S.S. *Titanic* — "not the one you think"). He was a member of the ship's band (played guitar) as a way of paying for his passage to New York (where he was to join a corporate law firm). One evening he met Lisa, the wealthy daughter of the ship's owner. They spoke, fell in love and married. They set up housekeeping in New York and after becoming a successful lawyer lived on East 62nd Street, East 54th, East 37th, Sutton Place, Central Park South and finally Park Avenue (which gave Olive the best sunlight to grow his patio crops).

Oliver does his farming in a suit (he has 12 suits and each has a purpose — planting, plowing, harvesting crops, etc.). He purchased the farm from an ad in *Farm Gazette* magazine and is a member of the Hooterville Chamber of Commerce. Oliver had his own practice in New York and grew vegetables in his desk drawer. He collects and writes folk songs and makes little or no money as a farmer.

Lisa adapted to "farm livin'" after initially only agree to try it for six months. She calls the town "Hootersville" and dresses much too elegantly to be a farmer's wife. Lisa can't cook (she tries to prepare meals but nothing ever comes out right; even her "hotscakes," made with Hal's Hotcake Flour, are anything but light). She enrolled in Hooterville High School to take classes in home economics (called here domestic science class) but it didn't really work. She and Oliver have yet to master the electric problem (each appliance is numbered and no more than a seven can be used at one time to avoid blowing a fuse)

When Oliver becomes excited about farming he tends to make what the citizens of Hooterville call "his farmer's speech" (and only Lisa hears a patriotic fife playing in the background). Lisa has a milk cow named Eleanor and a group of chickens she calls "the girls" (she originally had only one named Alice). Eleanor gives just the right amount of milk Lisa requires. She merely places a glass under Eleanor and says, "One cup please." The girls also oblige Lisa with the exact amount of eggs Lisa requires to make Oliver's breakfast.

Lisa and Oliver shop for goods at Drucker's General Store.

See also: Fred and Doris Ziffel.

867. Oliver Beene, *Oliver Beene*, Fox, 2003–2004. Played by Grant Rosenmeyer.

Oliver Beene is the 11-year-old son of Jerry and Charlotte Beene and lives in Rego Park Queen in Apartment 10M of the Central Apartment Building on 27th Street. The series is set in the early 1960s and Oliver has an older brother named Ted. Jerry (Grant Shaud) is a dentist and Charlotte (Wendy Makkena) is a homemaker who appeared on TV in 1939 at the New York World's Fair ("The cameraman was told to find a pretty girl and he chose me").

Oliver and Ted (Andrew Lawrence) are students at P.S. 206 (originally said to be P.S. 304). Oliver is a young boy whose curiosity often gets the best of him (always landing him in trouble). He has a dog named Scruffles and enjoys the TV show *Romparama* (hosted by Ringmaster Bob). Oliver is also a bit paranoid, as he believes everybody listens to his conversations. Oliver was in a band called Oliver and the Otters and had a job delivering newspapers for the *Tribune* (at $6 a week). He reads *Atomic Man* comics and enjoys helping his mother bake cookies (he also feels that his mother wanted a girl because he attends beauty shop appointments with her — something he has been doing since he was an infant).

Fourteen-year-old Ted believes he is a ladies' man "but he is an idiot" and always fails to impress them by the dumb things he says. His greatest weakness is chocolate éclairs. Jerry's dream is to get a parking spot in front of the building. He is also an amateur inventor. Charlotte insists two inventions will hurt someone: the pop-up phone and the turbo veggie dicer. Charlotte is president of the building's Tenant Association and idolizes John F. Kennedy (she has a picture of him displayed with the family photos on the piano). Her social life, she says, "consists of the laundry room and the elevator."

Olivia Walton *see* **John and Olivia Walton**

868. Opie Taylor, *The Andy Griffith Show*, CBS, 1960–1968. Played by Ronny Howard.

Opie Taylor is the young son of Andy Taylor, the sheriff of Mayberry, a small, relatively peaceful town in North Carolina. Opie's mother died when he was very young and he and Andy are cared for their Aunt Bee. They live at 322 Maple Street (also given as 14 Maple Street).

Opie takes piano lessons (but is later seen playing the guitar and in a band called Freedom). He is captain (and a quarterback) on the Mayberry School football team. Opie has several pets: Oscar (lizard), Gulliver (dog), and Dinkie (parakeet). He enjoys fishing with his father at Meyer's Lake (where they are seen heading in the opening theme) and when it is time for dinner, Opie empties the dirt from his pants cuffs and washes his hands. When guests stay over for the night they stay in Opie's room (Opie enjoys sleeping on the ironing board between two chairs—"It's adventurous sleeping," he says).

Andy is good father and Opie is a very good son. He is very respectful and always (well almost always) does what he is told. He calls his father "Pa."

See also: Andy Taylor, Barney Fife, Bee Taylor.

869. Oscar Madison, *The Odd Couple*, ABC, 1970–1975. Played by Jack Klugman.

Oscar Trevor Madison is an irresponsible slob who now lives with Felix Unger, an excessively neat perfectionist. They share Apartment 1102 at 1049 Park Avenue and Central Park West at 74th Street in New York City.

Oscar is a sportswriter for the New York *Herald*. He first mentions he was born at Our Lady of Angels Hospital in Philadelphia (he later mentions being born in Chicago). He attended the Langley Tippy-Toe Dancing School and is a graduate of James K. Polk High School. He served a hitch in the army where he was a perfect example of what not to do—"In any other army in the world he would have been shot on sight." The IRS claims Oscar has the worst tax returns they have ever seen ("Winos who throw their returns through the windows have neater returns").

Culturally, Oscar is a hopeless case. His life is centered on sports and he has little regard for his health. He smokes cigars puts ketchup on everything and his normal nourishment is a can of beer. He eats at places like Edible Eddie's, April Fools Taco, and Heidi's Nautical Nosh. Lasagna and French fries is his favorite dinner; Boston cream pie is his favorite dessert.

Oscar first worked as a copywriter for *Playboy* magazine, then as a sportswriter for the *New York Times* before acquiring his current position. He was also the host of a radio program called *The Oscar Madison Sports Talk Show* (later called *Oscar Madison's Greatest Moment in Sports*). His favorite song is "Reckless" and his one serious vice is gambling. Oscar acquired his current apartment in 1962 after his wife, Blanche, divorced him due to excessive arguing. It is first mentioned that Oscar met Felix when they were jurors for the trial of

Leo Garvey (a man accused of driving his roommate crazy); Oscar later mentions he met Felix when they were children in Chicago.

See also: Felix Unger.

870. Oswald Harvey, *The Drew Carey Show*, ABC, 1995–2004. Played by Diedrich Bader.

Oswald Harvey is a man of few talents. He drinks beer, hangs out with his friends and drinks beer. He was born in Ohio and attended Rhodes High School (where he met his lifelong friends Drew Carey, Lewis Kiniski and Kate O'Brien). Oswald, Lewis and Drew were in a band called the Horn Dogs and together they invented a beer-coffee mix called Buzz Beer ("The working man's beer") that they sell at their favorite hangout, the Warsaw Tavern.

Oswald is a bit naïve and easily taken advantage of. He lives with Lewis above the Warsaw Tavern and they spent $8,000 to produce a C.D. called "The Lewis and Oswald Experience." Oswald was originally a rodeo clown. He quit to become a driver for Global Deliveries. He next became a male nurse then worked with Drew at an internet company (Never Ending Store Dot Com). He is unemployed for a time after getting fired but eventually buys the Warsaw Tavern (with a $50,000 settlement he got after his shoe lace became entangled in an escalator and he lost part of his pinky toe).

See also: Drew Carey, Kate O'Brien, Lewis Kiniski, Mimi Bobeck.

871. Otis Drexell, *Drexell's Class*, Fox, 1991–1992. Played by Dabney Coleman.

Otis Drexell pays his ex-wife, Mona, $900 a month in alimony (although he is behind in payments). He owes the IRS $153,000 in back taxes. Otis is a maverick corporate executive who told his bosses to "shove it" and was branded "the crookedest man in town." On the plus side, he and Mona produced two very pretty daughters, Melissa and Brenda.

Otis has custody of his daughters (although he really doesn't want it). They live in a rather untidy apartment at 603 Essex Drive in Cedar Bluffs in Cleveland, Ohio. There is a picture of the *Titanic* sinking on the living room wall and Otis's dinner plates come from White Castle ("Do you know how many hamburger dinners I had to eat to make a complete service for eight?"). His pride and joy is his autographed 1947 baseball.

Otis is obnoxious, cantankerous and believes smoking is the answer to a long life. He is also the fifth grade teacher at the Grantwood Avenue Elementary School. Isaac Grantwood, the man who invented the manure spreader for farmers, founded the school. The school's principal, Francine Itkin, says, "Otis is a drifter who failed in business and somehow crawled out of a sewer grate into my school to preach his amoral poison to 20 impressionable children."

Otis is a terrible teacher. He ignores school rules, is tardy and discourteous to fellow staff members. He also enjoys pinching the student teachers ("but only the female ones") and a ten-dollar bill attached to a test or homework assignment guarantees an A grade. Otis feels that because has lived a life of hard knocks his students should really learn what life is all about — not some "mumbo jumbo they read in books." He allows his students to get away with a lot but is a bit more responsible when it comes to his daughters, especially 16-year-old Melissa (A.J. Langer), who believes she is sexy and desirable (Otis believes she is a magnet for perverts). Brenda (Brittany Murphy) is 14 years old and more of a homebody and does the lions share of the work (keeping house). In college Otis had the nickname "Skippy."

872. Paige and Valerie Whitney, *Odd Man Out,* ABC, 1999. Played by Natalia Cigliuti, Marina Malota.

Paige and Valerie Whitney are the beautiful teenage daughters of Julia Whitney (Markie Post), a gorgeous, smart, and sexy widow who runs the Whitney Catering Service in South Beach, Florida. Julia was born in Connecticut and attended the University of Miami; her late husband was named Bill.

Paige is 16 years old and a sophomore at South Beach High School. She tells her friends she is an only child and yearns to be a model. Paige believes being beautiful is her goal in life and she needs to let the rest of the world see just how beautiful she is. A mirror is her best friend and she has a figure that will allow her to look good in any outfit (she especially likes to "borrow" her mother's sexy outfits but often finds, that because of her 34B bust line, she cannot fill out a blouse like her mother, who wears a 38C bra).

Julia is well aware of Paige's goal but would like her to wait until she graduates from college before becoming a model. Paige can't promise. She reads all the fashion magazines and did manage to acquire a modeling job on her own — as a foot model for a local shoe company. When Paige becomes depressed "I go to the mall to buy things I don't need with the money I don't have."

Paige and 13-year-old Valerie use Maybelline cosmetics. While Valerie does not express a desire to become a model she enjoys shopping at the mall with Paige and trying on Wonder Bras (she is not as developed as her girlfriends and is quite jealous of them). When Valerie needs to call a family member she screams out their name. Valerie believes the bathroom is essential for "lip gloss emergencies" and is unhappy over her mother's rule that she cannot watch TV during the day. When she gets upset Valerie goes to her room, slams the door and says, "I'm never coming out again." Like Paige, Valerie is very weight conscious (she picks the fat out of the morning breakfast sausage, as an example, to make sure she retains her slim figure). She is enrolled in South Bay Junior High.

873. Paige Matthews, *Charmed,* WB, 2001 (current). Played by Rose McGowan.

Paige Matthews is the half-sister of Prue, Piper and Phoebe Halliwell, witches who are known as the Power of Three. Paige is not only as beautiful a witch as her sisters, but she is also part White Lighter (a guardian angel of witches). Paige's mother is a witch (Patty Halliwell); her father is Sam, a White Lighter. Patty had an affair with after she divorced Victor (the father of Prue, Piper and Phoebe). Paige, the youngest of the sisters, was born at a time when it was forbidden for a witch and her White Lighter to be romantic. Patty and Sam kept their affair a secret because Patty feared her daughter would be denied her ability to become a good witch. Prue, Piper and Phoebe were toddlers at the time and thought "Mommy was just getting fat." Patty desperately wanted to keep the baby but she couldn't. She took her to a church and gave her to a nun (Sister Agnes). Patty told her "Let the name begin with a *P*" and orbed out (vanished in a sprinkling of white light). The nun, who believed she had a heavenly visit, named the baby Paige and found her a good home knowing that one day she would fulfill a preordained destiny.

Paige was raised by the Matthews family and was first seen by viewers working at the South Bay Social Services Center in San Francisco. She became a part of Piper and Phoebe's lives after Prue is killed by a demon and Phoebe has a vision of a girl being attacked by the same demon. Through their White Lighter, Leo, Phoebe and Piper learn that Paige is their half-sister and rescue her from and kill the demon that killed Prue. Paige learns that she is a witch and the Power of Three is reborn.

Paige has Prue's power to move objects by concentrating but can also do it by "orbing the object" (making it vanish from one place to reappear in another). As a child Paige had a plush clown she called Slappy. She is a graduate of Berkeley College and possesses a degree in social services. In order to fight demons full time, Paige gives up her apartment and moves into the house shared by her sisters at 1329 Prescott Street in San Francisco (also given as 7511 and 1829 Prescott). Paige also quits her full time job to work at Temp Jobs (originally called The Ritz, Teukolsky and Reuben Agency). She quits this a year later when she becomes head of the Magic School (which trains young witches and warlocks).

See also: Leo Wyatt, Phoebe Halliwell, Piper Halliwell, Prue Halliwell.

874. Paige Thatcher, *Life Goes On*, ABC, 1989–1993. Played by Monique Lanier, Tracey Needham.

Paige Thatcher is the daughter of Drew Thatcher and his first wife, Katherine Henning. Paige lives with her father, her stepmother, Libby, and her half sister (Becca) and brother (Corky) at 305 Woodridge Road in Glen Brook, Illinois.

Paige is called "Button" by Drew. She loves to paint and has two rabbits (Matilda and Sammy). Paige first worked as a receptionist at the Matthews Animal Hospital. The original Paige (Monique Lanier) left home at the end of the first season. When Paige (Tracey Needham) returned in November of 1990, she moved back home but seemed to lack direction. She worked at several temporary jobs then enrolled at Glen Oak Community College (studying acting). She next worked at the family diner (The Glen Brook Grill) then as a "cross worker" (doing what is necessary) at Stollmark Industries. Her final series job is co-owner of the Darlin Construction Company (which she began with a friend named Artie).

See also: Becca Thatcher, Corky Thatcher, Libby and Drew Thatcher.

875. Paladin, *Have Gun—Will Travel*, CBS, 1957–1963. Played by Richard Boone.

The Hotel Carlton in San Francisco (1870s) is the headquarters of a man known only as Paladin, a man who hires his guns and experience to people in trouble. His calling card reads "Have Gun—Will Travel. Wire Paladin, San Francisco."

Paladin is a connoisseur of the arts. He has box seats at the opera house, enjoys fine food (he even has his own recipes) and has an eye for the ladies. He smokes expensive cigars (he carries a spare in his boot), collects chessmen and is lucky at gambling. He also has a rule: never go anyplace without his gun. Paladin, a right-handed gunman,

carries a Colt .45 revolver ("The balance is excellent; the trigger responds to the pressure of one ounce. It was hand crafted to my specifications"). He rarely draws it — "But when I do I am to use it." He also carries a small derringer under his gun belt.

Paladin's work clothes are a black outfit with a chess knight — the Paladin — embossed in white on his black holster. He is a graduate of West Point and his experiences with the Union Army have given him knowledge of war tactics that he uses to help people. He has a talent with a gun, a devotion to duty and relaxes in luxury at the hotel, genuinely enjoying life between assignments. He reads newspapers from various states and sometimes sends his calling card to people he thinks may need his help. His fee is $1,000.

Little is known about Paladin; not even his real name. His legend began when he lost a large sum of money to a wealthy land baron in a poker game. To repay the debt the man agreed to kill an outlaw (Smoke) who had been plaguing the land baron. In a duel to the death the man kills Smoke. The man then adopts Smoke's black outfit and the symbol of the Paladin as his own. He calls himself Paladin and begins a policy of hiring out his guns for good, to those who are unable to protect themselves.

876. Pamela Barnes, *Dallas*, CBS, 1978–1991. Played by Victoria Principal.

Pamela Barnes, the eventual wife of Bobby Ewing, brother of Ewing Oil Company executive J.R. Ewing, was born in Corpus Christi, Texas. She is the daughter of William "Digger" Barnes and his wife Rebecca Blake Barnes. She has an older brother named Cliff. Rebecca died when Pamela was very young. Maggie, Digger's sister, took over the responsibility of raising Cliff and Pamela.

Pamela was a good student in school (she was a member of the cheerleading team and at the age of 15 performed at the Sun Bowl football game in El Paso). After graduating from high school Pamela found work as a salesgirl at a clothing boutique called The Store. It was shortly after that she met Ray Krebs, foreman of the Southfork Ranch in Braddock, Texas (home of the Ewing family) and was invited to a barbeque at the ranch. She met Bobby Ewing and the two fell in love. They married and became the Romeo and Juliet of Dallas (the Ewing and Barnes families are bitter enemies. Digger believes Jock, J.R.'s father, cheated him out of the oil business when they were partners many years ago). Pamela and Bobby eloped and married in New Orleans (the ten minute service was performed by a Southern Baptist minister). Their return to the Southfork Ranch caused much friction (she was a Barnes and not only considered an outcast but a spy for her father in his attempt to get his fair share of the Ewing fortune. Bobby disbelieved this and rigorously defended her). When Pamela became pregnant most of the hatreds were forgiven — except those of Jr. and Sue Ellen (J.R's wife), who still resented her. Pamela's happiness was short lived when she lost her baby after a fall in the barn. After recovering Pamela returned to work at The Store and eventually became a lawyer. Although Pamela had no desire to hurt anyone, she could never win the love — or even the acceptance of J.R. (whose goal seemed to get her out of the Ewing family).

See also: Bobby Ewing, J.R. Ewing, Lucy Ewing, Sue Ewing Ewing.

Pamela North *see* **Jerry and Pamela North**

877. Paris Geller, *Gilmore Girls,* WB, 2000 (current). Played by Liza Weil.

Paris Eustace Geller is a pretty teenage girl with one single ambition: to attend Harvard University. She is the classic overachiever and all her time and energy is devoted to accomplishing her goal. Paris attends the prestigious Chilton School in Connecticut (which has one of the highest reputations for excellence in the country). "Paris studies, thinks about studying and studies more," says her friend Rory Gilmore. Paris does so "because ten generations of Gellers went to Harvard." Paris has no social life. She is 16 years old (when the series begins) and is editor of the school newspaper, *The Franklin.* Paris does volunteer work for Rebuilding Together (building homes for charity), trains seeing eye dogs, manned a suicide hotline, volunteered in a trauma center, worked with dolphins, worked as a camp counselor, taught sign language, and organized a senior citizens center. Paris has been accumulating extra curricular activities since the fourth grade. She feels a prestigious college requires this. She scored a 750 in math and a 730 in verbal on her PSAT test. She is also student body president at Chilton. Paris is also a straight A student but with all her achievements, she was also not Harvard material. The rejection literally devastated Paris and sent her on a downward spiral that only a true friend like Rory could help her overcome (Paris's wealthy parents are never seen and pay little attention to her). While she could not have her dream, Paris accepted her invitation to Yale University and shared Suite 5 with Rory at Durfee Hall.

Paris was born in Connecticut. As a child she had a dog named Skippy. At Chilton Paris was capable of speaking 178 words per minute as a member of the debate team. She enjoys decaf coffee with soymilk and while still a straight A student, is not as focused on schoolwork the way she was at Chilton.

See also: Lorelai Gilmore, Richard and Emily Gilmore, Rory Gilmore.

878. Parker Lewis, *Parker Lewis Can't Lose,* Fox, 1990–1991. Played by Corin Nemec.

Parker Lewis is a sophomore at Santo Domingo High School in Santo Domingo, California. He is the son of Martin and Judy Lewis and has a 13-year-old sister named Shelly. Parker is an enterprising student who simply cannot lose; no matter what happens to him he always comes out on top. He is the "cool" kid and has an ingenious plan for every situation. He resists authority and lives by his own rules. He dreams of attending college and is a master of self-promotion. Parker records people (on both audio and video tape) for "blackmail purposes." The earliest he is at school is 7:52 A.M.

Parker is Dr. Retro on the school's radio station, WFLM (89.8 FM). His parents own Mondo Video, a movie rental store, and are a bit dense. Asking them for advice "is like looking for gasoline with a match — you're lucky to get out alive." Parker is a schemer who operates from his headquarters at school — an abandoned room above the boys' gym. He wears a Swatch Watch (model 150M) and enjoys meals at the Atlas Diner.

See also: Shelly Lewis.

879. Patricia Jones, *Decoy,* Syn., 1957–1958. Played by Beverly Garland.

Patricia Jones, nicknamed Casey, is a police woman with the 16th Precinct of the N.Y.P.D. Patricia is often called Casey Jones because of her addiction to sports, especially baseball (she was named after Casey, the character in the poem "Casey at the Bat"). She was born on July 3, 1936, and is the daughter of Vincent and Nicole Jones. Casey's father and grandfather were law enforcers and Casey was groomed to follow in their footsteps. She attended Mid Manhattan High School and is a graduate of City College. She enrolled in the police academy in 1953 and graduated with top honors. Although Casey is a uniformed officer (or supposed to be) she rarely wears her uniform and investigates crimes in her street clothes.

Casey is attractive and alluring and is somewhat of a loner. She is totally dedicated to her job and never uses her beauty to accomplish a goal.

She carries a gun and will use it if she has to. Casey is television's first police woman and she is not treated like a delicate object of admiration. She puts in long hours, works dangerous cases, gets shot at and does take beatings from thugs — seeing her with a bruise or disheveled clothing and hair is not unusual.

Casey lives at 110 Hope Street and Murray Hill 3–4643 is her phone number. She wears badge number 300 and earns $75 a week. Hoods call her "A Dame Copper."

880. Patrick Murphy, *Murphy's Law*, ABC, 1988–1989. Played by George Segal.

Daedalus Patrick Murphy never uses his first name (he is known more by his last name). Murphy is a recovering alcoholic who works as an investigator for the First Fidelity Casualty Insurance Company in San Francisco (he originally worked for Triax Insurance). He lives in a loft at 3116 Hillsdale with Kimiko Fannuchi, a beautiful Eurasian model.

Murphy was born in San Francisco and had a difficult childhood. His father walked out on him and his mother when he was ten years old (his last words to Murphy were "Go to hell, kid"). Murphy's mother raised him as best she could (he would call the breakfast his mother made out of leftovers "dangerous eggs"). Murphy was an average student in school but learned most of what he knows from the streets.

Murphy is now divorced (from Marissa; she called him "Paddy"). They lived on Baker Street and had a daughter (Kathleen). The marriage ended when Murphy took up drinking. Murphy is not one for taking his time. When he gets an assignment he jumps head first into a situation without thinking about the consequences. It is usually Kimiko, who is fascinated with Murphy, who assists him and keeps him on the straight and narrow (and also from getting killed). Murphy drives a sedan with the license plate SPM 162.

See also: Kimiko Fannuchi.

881. Patrick Owen, *I'm with Her*, ABC, 2003–2004. Played by David Sutcliffe.

Patrick Owen teaches English literature at Carter High School in San Francisco. He is also the boyfriend of Alex Young, a popular movie star (he and Alex met when her dog bit him and they found an instant attraction to each other). Patrick attended Harvard Law School but dropped out after two years feeling it was not the right career choice for him. He returned to his hometown of Connecticut and enrolled in State University to acquire a degree in teaching ("I love teaching kids

and I drive a '91 Jeep and make substantially less than Alex"). Patrick lives in Apartment 208 in West Hollywood and his classes are held in Room 127. In his youth Patrick won his eighth grade spelling bee and during summer school breaks he earns extra money by tutoring children.

See also: Alex Young.

882. Patty and Cathy Lane, *The Patty Duke Show*, ABC, 1963–1966. Played by Patty Duke.

Patricia Lane, called Patty, and Catherine Margaret Rollin Lane, nicknamed Cathy, are identical cousins who live together at 8 Remsen Drive in the Brooklyn Heights section of Brooklyn, New York. Patty was born in Brooklyn and is the daughter of Martin and Natalie Lane. Cathy was born in Glasgow, Scotland, and is the daughter of Kenneth Lane, a widower and Martin's look-a-like brother. Martin is the managing editor of the New York *Chronicle*; Kenneth is one of its foreign correspondents. Because Kenneth's assignments constantly uproot Cathy, Kenneth arranged for her to live with Martin and his family to enable her to complete her high school education. Patty also has a younger brother named Ross.

Cathy and Patty attend Brooklyn Heights High School. Cathy was previously enrolled in Mrs. Tuttles of Mountain Briar, a private school in Scotland (where she was the debate champion). Her father calls her "Kit Kat" and she has a built-in lie detector: she gets the hiccups when she lies (or tries to). At Brooklyn Heights High, Cathy is a member of the literary club while Patty is editor of the school newspaper, *The Bugle*. The Shake Shop (later called Leslie's Ice Cream Parlor) is their after school hangout.

Patty is the typical American teenage girl. She (and Cathy) were born in December of 1947 (they are 16 when the series begins; their birth signs are Sagittarius). Patty wears a size five dress (as does Cathy) and she is carefree and unpredictable. Patty has a knack for getting into trouble and finds pleasure in the little things in life. Cathy is sedate, enjoys reading poetry and is a straight A student (Patty is the average C student). Cathy is not as popular with boys as Patty and feels her European upbringing has hindered her in this respect (Cathy does date but does not have a steady boyfriend. Patty dates classmate Richard Harrison [Eddie Applegate]).

Patty attempted to make money as a waitress at a coffee house (The Pink Percolator) where she worked under the name "Pittsburgh Patty." She next tried to write a book called *I Was a Teenage Teenager* (a story about "love, war, poverty, death and cooking recipes." One hundred copies were published by the vanity press Frye Publishing). Patty and Cathy's joint efforts to make money were the Worldwide Dress Company (selling Catnip dresses designed by Cathy for $9.95), Mother Patty's Preserves (a jam based on a recipe Cathy found in a book by Charles III), and The Doctor's Baby Sitting Service (which folded when Patty had too many kids and no sitters).

Patty calls her father "Poppo" and has a dog named Tiger. Patty Duke also played a third-look-a-like cousin named Betsy Lane, a beautiful blonde bombshell who was born and raised in Atlanta, Georgia.

In the 1999 CBS TV movie update, *The Patty Duke Show—Still Rockin' in Brooklyn Heights*, Patty is divorced from Richard after 27 years of marriage; she is now the principal of Brooklyn Heights High School. Cathy is a widow and now lives in Scotland (with her 14-year-old son, Liam). Ross is a musician; Martin and Natalie have retired to Florida.

Paul Buchman *see* **Jamie and Paul Buchman**

883. Paul Hennessey, *Eight Simple Rules for Dating My Teenage Daughter*, ABC, 2002–2003. Played by John Ritter.

Paul Hennessey is a sports columnist for the *Detroit Post*. He is married to Cate and is the father of Bridget, Kerry and Rory. Paul and Cate have been married for 20 years and live on Oakdale Street in Michigan. As a kid Paul would sing songs to make the thunder stop during storms. He played the French horn in high school and was "yell captain" (cheerleader)—"I led cheers," he says. He was also on the school's basketball team and had originally planned on becoming a lawyer but followed his heart's desire to become a sports writer. He then attended Ohio State University (mentioned as Michigan State in another episode). Paul covered the Detroit Tigers before becoming a columnist but also mentions having a first job in a cannery (exactly what the job entailed is never mentioned. Every time Paul attempts to tell the story, Cate interrupts him with "Not the cannery story").

Paul is an over protective father, especially about his two beautiful daughters, Bridget and Kerry (they believe he is old fashioned). He is very particular about who dates his daughters and scrutinizes every date. He has also established "Eight Simple Rules:" *1.* Use your hands on my daughter and you'll lose them later. *2.* You make her cry, I make you cry. *3.* Safe sex is a myth. Anything you try will be hazardous to your health. *4.* Bring her home late, there's no next

date. *5.* Only deliverymen honk. Dates ring the doorbell. *6.* No complaining while waiting for her. If you're bored change my oil. *7.* If your pants hang off your hip, I'll gladly secure them with my staple gun. *8.* Dates must be in crowded public places. You want romance? Read a book. Paul is also worried about piercings and pays Vinnie, manager of the Navel Station, $20 a month to call him if Bridget or Kerry come in looking for a navel ring.

Paul's favorite movie is *Brigadoon* and would like nothing more than to watch a football game when Michigan is playing without interruptions from the family and their problems. Paul only calls family meetings when he thinks there is something important to say. He also makes the family observe two traditions: the yearly vacation "at the cabin by the lake" and the annual Halloween campout in the backyard tree house (where Paul dresses as "Man with axe in head").

It is the morning of November 4, 2003. Cate and the children are about to have breakfast when Cate receives a phone call telling her that Paul, shopping for milk, collapsed in Aisle 3 of the supermarket and died of a heart attack (reflecting the real life passing of John Ritter on September 11, 2003). The years listed for the series reflect John Ritter's run. The several episodes that followed were a loving tribute to John and the character he portrayed. He is mentioned and thought of by the family often. Paul's favorite bar, the City Room, paid tribute by introducing "The Paul Hennessey Sandwich."

See also: Bridget Hennessey, Cate Hennessey, Kerry Hennessey, Rory Hennessey.

884. Paul Lassiter, *Spin City*, ABC, 1996–2002. Played by Richard Kind.

Paul Thomas Lassiter is Press Secretary to Randall Winston, the Mayor of New York City. He is abrasive, steals office supplies and never shows up for work on time (he has, for example, taken 10,000 pens and sold them as City Hall souvenirs). He is also cheap, a moocher, cons and takes advantage of people. The fact that people do not know Paul is his greatest asset.

Paul's collects antique dolls and Denny's Restaurant menus. He was recording secretary of the audio/video club in college and drives a car with the license plate QAG 286. He gets up at 4 A.M. to do yoga and eats Rice-A-Roni out of the box (he also enjoys meatball sandwiches for lunch). To make sure nobody takes his morning donut at work, Paul puts his name on the bottom of one. Paul appears to be absent minded and is known as a slacker (he revises old memos, takes naps in the janitor's closet, places a cardboard cut out of himself at his desk and leaves early). He was spokesman for the New York State Department of Education and was married to a woman named Claudia (who left him to become a nun). Although Paul is not Jewish, he had a bar mitzvah (he faked being Jewish) and keeps his money "safe" in a no interest checking account (he also spends his mornings scouring the City Hall parking lot looking for loose change). Paul was a contestant on the TV game shows *Blind Date* and *Who Wants to be a Millionaire?* (where he won $1 million and invested it in a politically themed restaurant called Wonk).

See also: Caitlin Moore, Charlie Crawford, Michael Flaherty, Randall Winston, Stewart Bondek.

885. Pavel Chekov, *Star Trek*, NBC, 1966–1969. Played by Walter Koenig.

Pavel Andreievich Chekov was born in Russia in the year 2245. He attended Starfleet Academy (2263–67) and became an ensign. His first assignment was as a navigator under James T. Kirk, captain of the U.S.S. *Enterprise NCC-1701*. Pavel is an only child and he is proud of his Russian heritage (claiming often that Russia was responsible for implementing many of the innovations used by Starfleet).

See also: James T. Kirk, Leonard McCoy, Mr. Spock, Montgomery Scott, Uhura.

886. Peggy Bundy, *Married ... With Children*, Fox, 1987–1997. Played by Katey Sagal.

Peggy Bundy is the wife of Al Bundy, a shoe salesman who believes he has a pathetic life. They are the parents of Kelly and Bud and reside at 9674 (also seen as 9764) Jeopardy Lane in Chicago.

Peggy Wanker and Al Bundy were students at James K. Polk High School. They met at Johnny B. Goods (fast food hamburgers) fell in love and married after graduation. Twenty years later Al is still married "to my red-haired plaque."

Peggy was born in Wanker County, a community in Wisconsin that was founded by her ancestors (it is also mentioned as being in Milwaukee). Peggy knows a divorce will make Al happy but she won't give it to him. Peggy is a terrible wife and mother. She never shops for food, rarely cooks or cleans and spends her days on the sofa watching TV (especially *The Oprah Winfrey Show*) and eating bon bons. Although Peggy hates to work ("That's why I got married") she took a job at Muldin's Department Store to earn the money for a VCR. She also took an interior decorating class

at the Cook County School of Design (she turned Al's one place of refuge — the bathroom — into "a frilly pink nightmare." Al considered his "cold, white and soothing restroom" his "oasis from pantyhose and women").

Peggy is a 36C and wears the Perfect Figure Model 327 Bra. She has a stuffed parrot (Winky) and gives Al a tie on their anniversary (he gives her shoes). Peggy holds the record at Jim's Bowl-a-Rama for bowling a perfect 300 game. In an attempt to make money, Al groomed Peggy and Kelly as singers he called "Juggs — A New Mother and Daughter Duo" (like with everything else he does, it failed). Peggy drew a cartoon strip about Al for *Modern Gal* magazine called "Mr. Empty Pockets." Peggy and Al's bank checks read "Mrs. Peggy Bundy and the Nameless Shoe Salesman." When Kelly and Bud were young, they thought Al was the dim-witted handyman. To make up for this, Peggy instituted "Make Believe Daddy Day" on Friday afternoons. Peggy's overly romantic advances frighten Al the most. While never seen, Peggy's father was "Pa Wanker" and her mother was the grossly overweight "Ma Wanker" (who has to be transported from place to place by flatbed truck. Al once saw her in the nude and was so horrified by the sight that he went temporarily blind).

See also: Al Bundy, Bud Bundy, Kelly Bundy, Marcy Rhoades.

Penny Robinson *see* **John Robinson**

887. Pepper Anderson, *Police Woman*, NBC, 1974–1978. Played by Angie Dickinson.

Suzanne Anderson, nicknamed Pepper, is a police woman with the Criminal Conspiracy Division of the Los Angeles Police Department. She works with Joe Stiles and Pete Royster and her superior is Sergeant Bill Crowley.

Pepper, whose first name was also said to be Lee Ann, was born in California. She has a sister named Cheryl, who is autistic and attends the Austin School for Learning Disabilities. No mention is made of their parents and it appears as if Pepper is caring for Cheryl (she pays for her education and is the only relative ever seen with Cheryl). Little is revealed about Pepper's past. She was a good student in school but did not set her sights on becoming a law enforcer. Pepper was a very beautiful child and it appears her mother groomed her to become a model. Pepper attended modeling classes and broke into the field after graduating from U.C.L.A. Her picture appeared in the various glamour magazines but the life of a high fashion model bored her. For reasons that are not really explained, Pepper chose to join the L.A. Police Academy and become a cop. She graduated top in her class but was apparently not a rookie. She was assigned to the L.A.P.D.'s Vice Squad, where she worked for several years before her promotion to sergeant and the Criminal Conspiracy Division.

Pepper's beauty seems to attract seedy characters and she often acts as bait while working on cases. She wears a 38C bra and lives in an apartment on Melrose (the word "Pepper" can be seen on her bedroom wall. She chose the name Pepper "because I like it"). Pepper takes chances and often risks her life to bring criminals to justice. She gets shot, punched and often finds her clothes getting ripped — "It comes with the territory." Pepper drives a sedan with the license plate 635 CIN.

888. Perry Mason, *Perry Mason*, CBS, 1957–1966. Played by Raymond Burr.

This entry also contains information on Della Street (Barbara Hale), Perry's secretary.

Perry Mason is a brilliant criminal attorney working out of Los Angeles. He has an office (Suite 904) in the Brent Building and Madison 5-1190 is his office phone number.

Perry's retainer fees ranged from $1,000 to $5,000. He worked by the books and fought for clients with the odds stacked up against them. Perry used whatever legal tactics he could to win a case for his client but always within the bounds of the law. Plea bargaining was not in Perry's vocabulary; it is something he would never do as he felt risking the life of a client was better than ruining it with a suspicious way out or a reduced sentence.

Perry was not without compassion. If a client could not afford his services and Perry honestly believed the person was innocent, he would offer his services at a reduced rate (even without charge at times). While Perry did have an investigator (Paul Drake) he would often investigate his own cases and put his life at risk. While Perry was competent as a detective, it was in the courtroom where his abilities became evident. He was shrewd and never let it be known that at times he did not have sufficient evidence to defend a client (he always waited for that vital, last minute piece of evidence he needed to free a client). Perry delivered his statements with such eloquence that he could mesmerize jurors. He was also infamous for doing the unordinary — bringing in last minute witnesses that would ultimately clear his client. Perry was not one for home-cooked meals. He ate regularly at McQuade's Bar and Grill or at Clay's Grille.

Perry was tough, persistent and an unrelenting force for good when it came to his clients. Della Street his pretty, ever efficient secretary (and assistant) was the only woman who could tame his roughness. Della had as much or even more compassion than Perry and gave of herself to help her friends (or clients she felt were deeply in trouble). Della often helped Perry by donning various disguises but relying on her female intuition was her best means of helping Perry investigate a case. Della was always elegantly dressed and loved to wear perfume (she is somewhat of an expert on it). Hollywood 2-1799 is her phone number.

In a series of TV movies that appeared in the 1980s, Perry and Della reunited to once again defend clients. In the interim, Perry had become a judge; Della had become a secretary to Arthur Gordon of Arthur Gordon Industries. When Della is framed and arrested for Arthur's murder, she calls on her old friend Perry for help. Perry, eager to get away from what he considers a boring job, accepts the case. He clears Della, resigns from the Appeals Court ("Let's say I just got tired of writing opinions") and reestablishes his law practice with Della again by his side.

889. Pete and Gladys Porter, *Pete and Gladys*, CBS, 1960–1962. Played by Harry Morgan, Cara Williams.

The Porters, commonly called Pete and Gladys, are a happily married, somewhat quarrelsome couple who live at 36 Bleecker Street in Westwood, California (Granite 5-5055 is their phone number).

Pete and Gladys met in 1942 and eloped nine years later. They first lived at 726 Elm Street in Westwood on a block lined with Palm trees. Pete is an insurance salesman for the Springer, Slocum and Klever Insurance Company in Los Angeles (it was here that Pete first met Gladys Hooper, the firm's scatterbrained secretary). Although they have no children, Gladys retired from the work force to become a housewife.

Gladys looks up to Pete as a war hero ("He single handedly captured a Japanese patrol," she says). In reality Pete made up the story to impress Gladys (he did serve with the military during World War II, but as a clerk in a PX). Pete is an easy-going man who feels exasperation from all the harebrained situations Gladys involves him with. He always accepts her faults because he loves her. This attitude is a bit different from the Peter Porter character Harry Morgan portrayed on *December Bride* (CBS, 1954–1959, from which *Pete and Gladys* is a spinoff). Gladys was never seen but was always talked about. Pete claimed, "She was a tyrant and total boss. I'm not henpecked, I'm buzzard pecked." He also said, "I wear the pants in my family even though Gladys makes them, I still wear them."

Gladys, when seen, always appears as a very beautiful woman. However, in her unseen days, Pete says, "Gladys is a very attractive woman, but not in the morning with the mud pack on her face and those blinkers on her eyes. She looks like Citation [a famous 1950s racehorse] on a muddy track."

"A padlock, chains and a straight jacket are the symbols of my marriage," said Pete. He also mentioned on several occasions that they had a daughter named Linda (this unseen character was not carried over to the *Pete and Gladys* series).

Gladys is in no way like Pete said. She is not a tyrant; in fact she is afraid to anger Pete by her dumb antics (as he always yells at her). While she does sew she is only seen making her own dresses. Gladys is a total scatterbrain—"When strange things are looking to happen, somebody gives them Gladys's address" (says Pete because mishap appears to follow Gladys wherever she goes—and it is usually Pete who has to bail her out).

Gladys is the Entertainment Chairman of the Junior Matron's League of the Children's Hospital and a member of the Westwood Bowling League. Love keeps Pete and Gladys together—no matter how mad Pete gets at Gladys she knows he will forgive her.

890. Pete Kelly, *Pete Kelly's Blues*, NBC, 1959. Played by William Reynolds.

Pete Kelly is a cornet player and leader of The Big Seven, a jazz band that plays nightly at Lupo's, a brownstone turned funeral parlor turned speakeasy at 17 Cherry Street in Kansas City, Missouri. The series is set in 1927.

"Lupo's is a standard speakeasy," says Pete. "The booze is cut but the prices aren't. The beer is good and the whiskey is aged—if you get there later in the day." The band plays from 10:00 P.M. to 4:00 A.M. with a pizza break at midnight.

Pete was born in Chicago. He became fascinated with the cornet as a kid and set his goal to become a musician. Two versions are given regarding this. In the first, Pete mentions that a musician named Gus Trudeaux taught him how to play the cornet. They became friends but when Gus became involved with the mob Pete left Chicago and played with various bands and in various cities until he found his way to Kansas City and formed The Big Seven. Pete later says he was a struggling musician when he befriended Gus at a union meeting. The second version finds Pete already a cornet player and friends with a

piano player named Augie. He and Augie played the various clubs before they both drifted to Kansas City. Each apparently went their separate ways with Pete forming his own band.

Pete lives in a small room on Grand Avenue near Washington Square (he lived at 18th and Holstead in Chicago). Pete wants to do only one thing—play the cornet and enjoy doing it. That was not meant to be, as trouble seems to find him no matter where he goes. While not a cop or private detective, Pete helps the people he finds in trouble, often getting a beating and risking his life to do so.

Peter Brady *see* **Greg Brady**

891. Peter Farrell, *I Married Dora*, ABC, 1987–1988. Played by Daniel Hugh Kelly.

This entry also contains information on Dora Calderon (Elizabeth Pena), Peter's live-in housekeeper.

Peter Farrell is an architect with the firm of Hughes, Whitney and Lennox in Los Angeles. He is the father of Kate and Will and is raising them with the help of Dora Calderon, a young woman from El Salvador, who works as his housekeeper (Peter's wife left him for a younger man and no responsibilities). The Farrell's live at 46 LaPaloma Drive; 555-3636 is their phone number.

Peter was born in California and as a kid was called "Bunny" by his mother (after his favorite bedtime story "The Runaway Rabbit"). His mother's homemade cookies would change Peter "from a pouty puppy to a happy hippo." In high school Peter was a letterman (running back for his football team and he set a record for the most touchdowns in one game).

Peter has two very different children. Kate is 13 years old, very beautiful but somewhat dense; Will is younger and very smart. Peter feels he is obligated to spend more time dealing with Kate then Will due to the fact that Kate believes her best assets are her gorgeous hair and her love of Beastie Boys music. Peter mentioned that he attended Woodstock in 1969. Although Peter and Dora were never affectionate, Peter married her in 1988 when her Visa was about to expire to keep her in the U.S.

Dora was born in El Salvador and was a cheerleader in high school. She realizes that Peter's marriage to her is only one of convenience and that she is not really married to him. Dora allows Peter to date other women and asks only "to bring them home to meet your wife and children."

Dora is an expert housekeeper and a wonderful substitute mother to Kate and Will. Kate especially likes Dora because she was once 13 years old and knows how to help her with her problems (she doesn't think her father can help her "because he was never a 13-year-old girl"). Although Dora calls Peter "Mr. Peter," she does secretly love him (had the series continued, their eventual real marriage would have taken place).

See also: Kate Farrell.

892. Peter Gunn, *Peter Gunn*, NBC, 1958–1960; ABC, 1960–1961. Played by Craig Stevens.

Peter Gunn is a debonair, tough and handsome private detective operating out of Los Angeles. He resides at 351 Ellis Park Road and KR2-7056 is his phone number (JL1-7211 is his mobile car phone number). His company is known as Gunn Investigations and Peter Gunn's Private Detective Agency (which he established on July 5, 1957). Peter Gunn is actually the first private detective created for television. Prior detectives like Richard Diamond, Mike Hammer, Ellery Queen and Martin Kane, were all based on characters appearing in books, on radio or on the silver screen.

Peter was also a bit more sophisticated than his predecessors (although he inherited a flare for violence via fists and gunplay). He is always well dressed and more reserved and polished. His speech is more respectable and he frequents a classy hangout (Mother's, later called Edie's, a waterfront nightclub). However, Peter had a number of snitches and was seen frequenting such dives as the Green Café, Nate's Hot Dogs and a beatnik coffeehouse called Cookie's to acquire information.

Peter kept company with Edie Hart (Lola Albright), the glamorous and sophisticated singer at Mother's (later it's owner). She lived at the Bartell Hotel, Apartment 15 at 1709 Ver Banna Street; KL6-0699 was her phone number.

893. Peter Riggs, *Strong Medicine*, Lifetime, 2000 (current). Played by Josh Coxx.

Vegetarian Peter Riggs is a registered nurse (at the Rittenhouse Women's Health Clinic in Philadelphia) who occasionally sneaks a Philly Cheese steak. He first worked for the Peace Corps as a volunteer and idolizes the Dalai Lama. He is also a massage therapist, herbalist, midwife, acupuncturist, psychologist — and anything else that may be required for him to do his job and help women in need. Peter loves yoga, his motorcycle and his garden. He believes in alternate medicine and the new age holistic medicines. Peter has learned his jack-of-all-trades reputation from his travels with the Peace Corps (visiting and helping doctors in many third world countries). Peter feels his var-

ied medical knowledge has made him "every woman's everyman."

See also: Andy Campbell, Dana Stowe, Kayla Thornton, Lana Hawkins, Luisa Delgado, Nick Biancavilla.

894. Philip Banks, *The Fresh Prince of Bel Air*, NBC, 1990–1996. Played by James Avery.

Philip Zeke Banks is a wealthy lawyer who lives with his wife (Vivian) and children (Hilary, Carlton and Ashley) in a luxurious mansion in Bel Air, California ("two houses from Ronald and Nancy Reagan. We share the same pool man"). Also living with them is Will Smith, the son of Vivian's sister.

Philip was born on January 30. He is the son of Joe and Hattie Banks and grew up on a farm in Yamacrow, Nebraska. He had a pet pig (Melvin) and won the Young Farmer's of America Pig Passing Contest four years in a row. He was also the first black president of the Young Farmer's of America. Despite his achievement, Philip wanted to do more — he wanted to help people. He chose the legal profession and graduated from both Princeton University and Harvard Law School. He joined the law firm of Furth and Meyer, became a senior partner then a judge. He won the Urban Spirit Award for his community work and almost tarnished his good reputation when an investment turned sour and he became the "slum lord" of the Chalet Towers, an apartment building with sub standard living conditions. He was also part owner of a record shop (The Sound Explosion) and is an expert pool player (his pool stick is named Lucille).

See also: Ashley Banks, Carlton Banks, Hilary Banks, Will Smith.

895. Phlox, *Star Trek: Enterprise*, UPN, 2001–2005. Played by John Billingsley.

Phlox is a Denobulan and Chief Medical Officer under Jonathan Archer, Captain of the Star Ship U.S.S. *Enterprise NX-01*. Phlox was born on the planet Denobula and studied intergalactic medicine; he was personally asked by Captain Archer to become a part of his crew. Phlox has three wives on his home planet (who in turn have three husbands) and requires only six hours of sleep a year. He enjoys collecting animal and insect species from the various planets he visits and his office is in Sickbay on E-Deck.

See also: Charles Tucker, Hoshi Sato, Jonathan Archer, T'Pol, Travis Mayweather.

896. Phoebe Buffay, *Friends*, NBC, 1994–2004. Played by Lisa Kudrow.

Phoebe Buffay, called Pheebs, was born in New York City on February 16. She had a difficult childhood and was raised by a grandmother after her mother, a drug dealer, killed herself (by placing her head in an oven) and her father was sent to prison. Phoebe grew up on the streets and by the age of 14 had taken up a career mugging people. She turned her life around when she realized what she was doing was wrong. (Future friend Ross Geller, a teenager at the time, was one of the people Phoebe mugged). It is later revealed that Phoebe's real birth mother was Phoebe Abbott.

Phoebe lives at 5 Morton Street, Apartment 14, in Manhattan. She is a vegetarian and can speak fluent French. She worked as a waitress at a Dairy Queen before finding her career goal as masseuse. Phoebe first worked at Helping Hands, Inc. She next became partners with friend Monica Geller in a catering business that failed. Phoebe turned the catering van into a taxi and began Relax-a-Taxi (a cab with a massage table in the back; 2X85 was the cab I.D. number). Before finding a steady job at the Lavender Days Spa (in 2003) Phoebe worked as a telemarketer selling toner for Empire Office Supplies.

Phoebe has written 14 unpublished novels ("I've been the only one whose read them and they have been well received") and enjoys writing and singing folk songs (her most famous is "Smelly Cat"). Phoebe hangs out with her friends (Monica, Rachel, Joey, Chandler and Ross) at a coffee shop called Central Perk and won't eat turkey because "turkeys are beautiful and intelligent."

Phoebe has a pet mouse (Suzy) and a rat (Bob) that visit her apartment on occasion. She claims to make the best oatmeal raisin cookies in the world (but only makes them on occasion "because it wouldn't be fair to the other cookies"). Phoebe is somewhat of a psychic (by coincidence things happen and Phoebe believes it is due to her mystic powers). She pretended to be a vice cop with the 57th Precinct ("Who worked undercover as a whore") when she found a police badge on the street and has a dim-witted twin sister named Ursula (also played by Lisa Kudrow). Phoebe's other grandmother raised Ursula. Ursula works as a waitress at Riff's Bar in Manhattan and it was Ursula who starred in an X-rated film called *Buffay the Vampire Slayer* (using her sister's name). Phoebe keeps a little black book of all the men she has dated and when she doesn't remember something that she has to tell someone she uses the word "flimby." She also has a three dimensional picture of a woman (a doll glued against a city background) coming out of the frame she created and calls Gladys.

Phoebe dated all types of men but found her true love in Mike Hannigan, whom she married on February 12, 2004. The last episode has no conclusion for Phoebe (it is assumed she and Mike will live happily ever after).

See also: Chandler Bing, Joey Tribbiani, Monica Geller, Rachel Greene, Ross Geller.

897. Phoebe Figalilly, *Nanny and the Professor*, ABC, 1970–1971. Played by Juliet Mills.

Phoebe Figalilly is a very pretty young woman. She works as the nanny to Professor Harold Everett and cares for his three children, Hal, Prudence and Butch. Nanny, as Phoebe is called, resides with the family at 10327 Oak Street in Los Angeles and drives a 1930 Model A car she calls Arabella (named after her favorite aunt). Very little is known about Phoebe. She is British, wise, very feminine and has a natural instinct for childcare. She also has an uncanny ability to talk to and understand animals. Phoebe appears to be in her twenties; her exact age, however, seems to be much older (she has a passport with her birth date listed as April 18, 1864, making her 106 in 1970 when the series begins). Phoebe is also very secretive. She rarely discusses her past and has an air of mystery about her. She can make things happen as if by magic. She has psychic abilities and can spread love and joy wherever she goes. Is she a witch? A magician? An angel? Viewers were never told.

Professor Everett (Richard Long) teaches mathematics at Clinton College. He is a widower and was struggling to raise Hal Jr. (David Doremus), Prudence (Kim Richards) and Bentley, called Butch (Trent Lehman) on his own until Nanny magically appeared and offered her services. Of all the animals the children have, Nanny has a special affinity with Waldo, a sheepdog. She can also communicate with Jerome and Geraldine (baby goats), Mike and Myrtle (Guinea pigs) and Sebastian (a rooster).

Phoebe is very caring and very protective of the Everett children. She never uses her powers to help unless a lesson can be learned by her intrusion on fate. She uses magic to help a child overcome a fear or learn by discovering. She never raises her voice, never scolds and never has a harsh word for anyone. Nanny extracts revenge in fun ways — by making those who cross her see the error of their ways. She is "soft and sweet, wise and wonderful," as the theme says.

898. Phoebe Halliwell, *Charmed*, WB, 1998 (current). Played by Alyssa Milano.

Phoebe Halliwell is a Charmed One, a powerful witch who protects innocents threatened by evil. She is the daughter of Patty and Victor Halliwell and lives with her sisters, Prue and Piper in the house in which she was born in 1978. The house, located at 1329 Prescott in San Francisco (also given as 7511 and 1829 Prescott) is mystical. It was built on a spiritual nexus and pentagram as a battleground between good and evil. Phoebe's birth in the house makes her most connected to it and is more susceptible to evil than her sisters. Like her sisters, Phoebe inherited powers, although hers are passive (she can see the future). Each of the sisters inherited their powers from their ancestor, Melissa Warren, a 17th century witch who was burned at the stake. Before she died she willed her spirit to carry her abilities (the Power of Three) over time until it culminated in three sisters (Phoebe, Prue and Piper) who would become powerful good witches (Phoebe, Piper and Prue battle evil as the Power of Three). Phoebe later acquires the power to sense what others feel and is aided by *The Book of Shadows*, a mysterious journal that contains spells to banish demons.

Phoebe is the youngest of the sisters. She played at Kenwood Park, spent summers at Camp Skylark and is a graduate of Baker High School (where she was voted "Most Likely to Serve Time" as a result of a shoplifting incident). As a child Phoebe had an imaginary fairy she called Lily and was the first sister to experience evil when she saw "The Woogie Man," a force that thrives in the dark, in the basement of her home.

Phoebe is unemployed when the series begins. She was enrolled at the College of the Humanities and took whatever temporary jobs she could find. She lived previously in New York and worked as a hostess at the Rainbow Room and later the Chelsea Bar (she relocated to San Francisco when she and her sisters inherited the mystic house). Phoebe later found a steady job as an advice columnist ("Ask Phoebe") for a newspaper called *The Bay Mirror*. Phoebe occasionally hosts the call-in radio program, *Hotline*. Phoebe called Prue "Honey," "Sweetie" and "Darling." She wears a 36D bra and drives a car with the license plate 3B58 348. Her life changed dramatically when she married Cole Turner, the assistant D. A. Unknown to Phoebe at first, Cole was actually Beltizar, a powerful demon and member of the Brotherhood, who sought to kill the Charmed Ones by getting close to Phoebe. He was eventually exposed and banished by Phoebe, Piper and their half-sister, Paige (Prue had been killed by a demon prior to the banishing).

See also: Leo Wyatt, Paige Matthews, Piper Halliwell, Prue Halliwell.

899. Piper Halliwell, *Charmed,* WB, 1998 (current). Played by Holly Marie Combs.

Piper Halliwell, the daughter of Patty and Victor Halliwell, is a Charmed One, a good witch who helps people threatened by evil. Piper has two sisters (Prue and Phoebe) and a half-sister (Paige) and lives at 1329 Prescott (also given as 7511 and 1829 Prescott) in San Francisco.

Piper is 26 years old and has the abilities to freeze time and project fireballs from her hands. Her powers were one of three that were possessed by her ancestor, Melissa Warren, a 17th century witch who could also see the future and move objects with her mind. When Melinda was discovered to be a witch she was burned at the stake. Before she died she willed her spirit to carry her abilities (the Power of Three) from century to century until it culminated in three sisters (Piper, Prue and Phoebe) who would become powerful good witches (the Charmed Ones who use the Power of Three to battle evil).

Piper is a graduate of Baker High School. She played at Kenwood Park, attended Camp Skylark during the summer and had an imaginary fairy she and her sisters called Lily. She is helped in her fight against evil by the mysterious *Book of Shadows*, which contains spells to banish demons.

Piper most resembles her mother (who was killed by a warlock in 1978). Piper was originally a chef at the Restaurante (later changed to Quake, a trendy bar-restaurant). She quit to open her own eatery and nightclub, P-3 (named after her, Phoebe and Prue). Piper wears a 34B bra and has type A-B negative blood. She drives a car with the license plate 26A3 123. Piper is afraid of spiders and when she becomes nervous she babbles and waters the flowers she has all around the house.

Piper and her sisters are watched over by Leo Wyatt, a White Lighter (a guardian angel for witches). They fell in love, eventually married and became the parents of a mystical baby they named Wyatt.

See also: Leo Wyatt, Paige Matthews, Phoebe Halliwell, Prue Halliwell.

900. The Professor, *Gilligan's Island,* CBS, 1964–1967. Played by Russell Johnson.

Roy Hinkley, better known as the Professor, is one of seven castaways stranded on an uncharted island in the South Pacific (about 300 miles Southeast of Hawaii). The charter ship S.S. *Minnow* was caught in a tropical storm at sea and beached, stranding its skipper, Jonas Grumby, his first mate, Gilligan, and passengers Roy, Ginger Grant, Mary Ann Summers, and Thurston and Lovey Howell.

Roy was born in Cleveland, Ohio, and taught high school science. He is 35 years old and possesses degrees in biology, botany, and chemistry. He also has a master's degree in psychology and can speak the languages of various Hawaiian and African tribes. His extensive knowledge has earned him the nickname "The Professor."

In Cleveland Roy was a noted Boy Scout leader and had been the youngest Eagle Scout in the city. He was a chess champion and wrote a book called *Rust, the Real Menace.* He was in Hawaii doing research for his next book (*Fun with Ferns*) when he decided to relax and take a three-hour cruise. He discovered five different mutations of ragweed on his first week on the island.

Roy's extensive knowledge of various subjects made life on the island tolerable (as an example, he made a polo pony out of bamboo for Mr. Howell and a coconut battery charger for their radio. Yet with all his wisdom, Roy couldn't repair the *Minnow* or figure out how to make a raft from bamboo that would stay afloat). Roy keeps a diary of his experiences on the island and halibut with kumquat sauce is his favorite meal. He is the only one of the castaways to live alone in his own hut (Gilligan and Skipper share a hut as do Ginger and Mary Ann and the Howells).

See also: Gilligan, Ginger Grant, Mary Ann Summers, The Skipper, Thurston and Lovey Howell.

901. Prue Halliwell, *Charmed,* WB, 1998–2001. Played by Shannen Doherty.

Prudence Halliwell, called Prue, is a Charmed One, a powerful witch who protects people threatened by the supernatural. Prue is 28 years old and was born in San Francisco. She is the daughter of Patty and Victor Halliwell and currently lives at 1329 Prescott Street (also given as 7511 and 1829 Prescott). Prue has the power of astro projection (be in two places at once) and the ability to move objects with her mind. She inherited her powers from her ancestor, Melissa Warren, a 17th century witch who was burned at the stake (she possessed the abilities to see the future, move objects and freeze time). Before she died Melissa willed her spirit to carry her abilities (the Power of Three) across time until it culminated in three sisters (Prue and her sisters, Piper and Phoebe), making them powerful good witches.

Prue attended Camp Skylark during the summer, played at Kenwood Park and graduated from Baker High School and San Francisco State College. She and her sisters are aided by the mysterious *Book of Shadows,* which contains spells to banish demons. As children the sisters had an imaginary fairy they called Lily.

Prue originally worked as a curator at the American Museum of Natural History but quit when her partner took credit for an exhibit she designed. She next worked as an appraiser for the Buckland Auction House (she resigned when she identified a Monet painting as a fake but her superiors chose to ignore her and sell it as an original). With an interest in photography, Prue found work as a photographer at *4-One-5,* a trendy magazine. Prue wears a size 36C bra, drives a car with the plate 2WAC 231 and channels her powers through her eyes. Because Prue likes to wear low cut blouses, Piper calls her "an Einstein with cleavage."

After playing Prue for three years Shannen Doherty wanted to leave the series. At the end of the third season, the sisters battled a fierce demon called Shacks. During the confrontation Prue is killed. The sisters are no longer the Power of Three. Rather than replace Shannen, a fourth half-sister, Paige, was introduced to restore the Power of Three.

See also: Leo Wyatt, Paige Matthews, Phoebe Halliwell, Piper Halliwell.

902. Punky Brewster, *Punky Brewster,* NBC, 1984–1986; Syn., 1986–1988. Played by Soleil Moon Frye.

Penelope Brewster, nicknamed Punky, was born in Chicago in 1977. Her father abandoned her and her mother (Susan) six years later. Shortly after Punky turned seven, Susan found she could no longer care for Punky and abandoned her and her dog, Brandon, at a shopping mall. Punky believes "my mother just forgot about me" and begins to wander. She finds her way to 2520 Michigan Avenue and takes refuge in an empty apartment (2D) of an apartment house managed by Henry Warnimont, a 60-year-old gruff photographer. Henry finds Punky and eventually becomes her adoptive father when a search is made and no relations to Punky can be found.

Punky (and Brandon) now live with Henry in Apartment 2A. Punky originally slept on the couch in the living room. When Henry realized Punky needed her own space, he let her turn his den into her bedroom — "I'm not nobody anymore," exclaimed Punky, "I'm Punky Brewster!" Her bed is an old-fashioned flower cart with a mattress attached. Her window has the sun painted on it; the moon and stars are painted on the window shade. The room is painted in so many colors that Henry says, "It could blind a smurf."

Punky is a very charming girl and cares deeply for people. Despite the bad things that have happened to her, Punky tries to spread joy and happiness wherever she goes. Punky loves to wear miniskirts and believes everything will be all right no matter how bad things look—"That's Punky Power," she says. Orange is Punky's favorite color. She eats Sugar Beasties cereal for breakfast and has a tree house in the backyard. WATB is her favorite radio station (she says, "Rock and roll is the answer to everything"). She also won a trip to Disneyland by entering radio station WHXY's old time radio contest (she wrote the play "Gruesome Ghost Stories—The Mystery of Horror House").

Punky is a student at a school called Fenster Hall (at her unnamed prior school, she was teased as "Gunky Brewster"). Punky starred in the school's production of *The Saddest Raindrop* (Punky as a sad raindrop who finds happiness when a winter wind turns her into a beautiful snowflake). Punky attended Camp Kookalooki and as a young girl pretended to be Rapunzel and ran down the street with bathroom tissue hanging from her head.

Punky's fondest memory of Christmas was the warm feeling she got when her mother made cranberry pudding. On her first Christmas without her mother, Punky wished for Santa to reunite her with her mother. Henry made every attempt to grant that wish but was unable. Santa, however, did leave Punky something—her mother's musical jewelry box. And the gift Punky made for her mother (earrings) was gone. Was it a miracle? Punky thinks so "because all you have to do is believe."

See also: Margaux Kramer.

903. Purdy, *The New Avengers,* CBS, 1978–1979. Played by Joanna Lumley.

A beautiful woman, known only as Purdy, appears to be a high fashion model but is actually an Avenger, a Ministry agent who avenges crimes committed against the British government. She works with Mike Gambit and John Steed is her superior.

Her father named Purdy after the most respected and expensive shotgun in the world. She was born in India but had an international education (her father was a Brigadier in the British army and was constantly on the move). Purdy attended such schools as Roedean and La Sorbonne and was also a student of dance (she later became a professional ballerina). Her life changed after her father's death (shot by the enemy as a spy after joining the Secret Service). Purdy became a Ministry agent to even up the score.

Purdy is well versed in the martial arts, especially the French technique of Panach (fighting with the feet). She is also an expert at firearms and is capable of driving any car (she has a TR7 sports car). Purdy lives in a basement flat in London that is decorated in the Art Deco style. She is very meticulous when on a case and studies every aspect of a situation before proceeding. She feels careful planning lessens the risk factor.

See also: John Steed, Mike Gambit.

904. Quick Williams, *V.I.P.*, Syn., 1998–2002. Played by Shaun Baker.

Quick Williams is a bodyguard who works for V.I.P. (Vallery Irons Protection), a high profile protection service that charges $25,000 a day plus expenses.

Quick is a former boxer who uses the skills he learned in the ring to defend his clients. He first said he was called "The Iron Bull"; later he says, "The Boxer with the Mighty Quick Hands." He was forced to quit the ring when he refused to take a dive and was framed on drug charges.

Quick lives at 3420 Alto Cello Drive in Los Angeles; 323-555-7704 is his phone number. Astronaut Dex Dexter was Quick's hero as a kid ("I even had a toy action figure of him"). Quick took tap dancing lessons as a kid and served a hitch in the army after high school (stationed at Fort Irving but sentenced to a psychiatric ward for running naked across the base). Quick is quick with his fists and skilled in the martial arts. Although he works with four beautiful women (Vallery, Kay, Tasha and Nikki) Quick does not always take the beatings—Tasha and Nikki get equal rough treatment (Vallery and are Kay too feminine for the rough end of the business).

See also: Kay Simmons, Nikki Franco, Tasha Dexter, Vallery Irons.

905. Rachel Burke, *Profiler*, NBC, 1999–2000. Played by Jamie Luner.

Rachel Burke is an agent with the Violent Crimes Task Force (V.C.T.F.) unit of the FBI, a special agency that attempts to solve the baffling and bizarre crimes of any police department in the nation.

Rachel was born in Arlington, Virginia, and raised by a loving family. As she grew she began having visions (seeing people). When she was ten years old her best friend disappeared. The friend, a girl, was being raised by a nanny and was the daughter of parents who wished they never had a child. The girl knew this and felt her life was empty. Rachel envisioned the girl's death but was too late to help. The girl was found dead at the bottom of a well. The news devastated Rachel but Rachel believed her vision was a gift — to see what others could not and, although quite young, made a promise to help people with her abilities in later life.

Rachel graduated from the University of Virginia with a degree in psychology. She became an instructor for special agents at the Virginia FBI Training Center. Two years later she became a field agent "because I was sick of seeing criminals beat the system. They should be behind bars." Rachel's highly developed intuition allows her to think in pictures and visualize the frame of mind of both the killer and the victim. Such a person is called a Profiler and Rachel first worked with the Seattle Bureau then the Houston Bureau of the FBI before joining Bailey Monroe's V.C.T.F. unit in Atlanta, Georgia.

Rachel is not a psychic. She is a forensic psychologist. She has the unique ability to feel for the victims of crime and understand the criminal mind. Rachel can see into the criminal mind and explain the unexplained. She need not be present at a crime scene to receive images — "I could be brushing my teeth or grinding coffee when they come." Rachel has an 88 percent accuracy rate — "But it's that other 12 percent that bothers me." She devotes extra time to certain cases — "I can't sleep when I'm working on a tough case." Rachel lived previously in Arlington. She now lives in an apartment on Melrose; 555-0192 is her phone number.

See also: Bailey Monroe, Samantha Waters.

906. Rachel Corrigan, *Poltergeist: The Legacy*, SHO, 1996–1998; Sci Fi, 1999. Played by Helen Slater.

Rachel Corrigan is a member of the San Francisco Legacy House, an organization that battles the evils of the supernatural. Rachel works as the Legacy's psychological specialist. She is the mother of a ten-year-old daughter (Kathleen) and lives at Legacy House. Rachel is a firm believer in science and brings her medical expertise, skepticism and open mind to the mysteries she finds during case investigations. Rachel will use what science has to offer to try to expose unexplainable happenings as hoaxes (often she cannot and constantly places herself in dangerous situations).

Rachel is very dedicated to Kathleen (Alexandra Purvis). Kat, as she is called, shows promise of extraordinary psychic abilities. Rachel fears for Kat's safety. Kat is just developing her powers and Rachel would like to keep her away from the work of the Legacy but Kat's second sight often draws her into the events that haunt the Legacy and she

becomes a pawn in the fight for good against evil.

See also: Alex Moreau, Derek Rayne, Kristen Adams, Nick Boyle.

907. Rachel Greene, *Friends*, NBC, 1994–2004. Played by Jennifer Aniston.

Rachel Karen Greene is one of a group of six close friends who live in New York City. Rachel was born on Long Island and is a graduate of Lincoln High School. She is concerned about her appearance and cares about what other people think of her. When she was a young girl, Rachel experienced her first tragedy. While playing her hair became entangled in the chains of a swing. She cried for days after when her mother cut her hair to free her and made one side shorter than the other. As one of the most beautiful girls in high school, Rachel suffered a second trauma when a rumor was started that called her "The hermaphrodite cheerleader from Long Island." As a kid Rachel had a plush pink pony she called Cotton.

Rachel has a flair for fashion but first worked as a waitress at a Manhattan coffee shop called Central Perk. She quit for a job at Fortunato Fashions. This led to her becoming a Junior Miss (assistant buyer) then Personal Shopper (helps people shop) at Bloomingdale's. She next worked as a fashion consultant for Ralph Lauren (where she received a 45 percent discount on clothes). She is later a merchandising head. When Rachel is fired from Ralph Lauren for not being a team player (she sought a better job at Gucci), she is hired by Louis Viton Fashions.

Rachel buys 30 fashion magazines a month and has a secret closet in her apartment that hides all the junk she has collected over the years. She attempted to write a novel called *A Woman Undone* and claims that her favorite movie is *Dangerous Liaisons* but it is actually the silly comedy *Weekend at Bernie's*.

Rachel is friends with Monica, Phoebe, Joey, Ross and Chandler. She had a one-night stand with Ross (both were drunk) and became pregnant by him. On May 16, 2002, Rachel gave birth a daughter she and Ross name Emma (although she had contemplated Isabelle or Delilah). Emma was born at St. Vincent's Hospital and won first prize in the baby pageant "The Grand Supreme Little Darling Contest."

Rachel wears a size 32C bra (but says, "I'd get more attention if I were a 36D") and loves to show ample cleavage. Rachel is always elegantly dressed and fears people finding out that she is not as perfect as she appears (as a teenager she had plastic surgery to fix her nose; she felt it was not right for her face). The last episode finds Rachel giving up a job in Paris to stay in New York with Ross to raise Emma.

See also: Chandler Bing, Joey Tribbiani, Monica Geller, Phoebe Buffay, Ross Geller.

908. Rachel Gunn, *Rachel Gunn, R.N.*, Fox, 1992. Played by Christine Ebersole.

Rachel Gunn is a middle-aged nurse at Little Innocents Hospital. She oversees the Fourth Floor Nurse's Station and is called "The Iron Nightingale" by staff members.

Rachel lives at 668 Oak Street. She is pretty, brassy and cheap (she names her money and is obsessed with it). She also has one problem with being a nurse—"I can't stand the sight of blood. I faint." Rather than spend money on a vacation she sits in her backyard with her feet in a plastic pool and pretends to be in Fiji. Rachel keeps the lights off on Halloween so the UNICEF kids won't know she is home. She hates doctors for all the attention they get "and all the nonsense nurses get."

"Banana cream pie is my favorite dessert but I also like coconut and strawberry cream pies—except for coconut and strawberries." Rachel first worked as a Sherbet Girl at the Dip Queen Ice Cream Parlor. She had a dog named Tuffy as a child and her specialty is doing voices from *The Wizard of Oz* (her favorite movie, however, appears to be *Death Wish* with Charles Bronson as she has seen it 83 times).

909. Radar O'Reilly, *M*A*S*H*, CBS, 1972–1980. Played by Gary Burghoff.

Corporal Walter Eugene O'Reilly is the company clerk for the 4077 M*A*S*H (Mobile Army Surgical Hospital) unit in Korea during the war. He was born in Iowa and has the nickname "Radar" for his ability to perceive what others think. Radar writes the announcements heard over the P.A. system and drinks only Grape Nehi. Radar's serial number is 3911880 and he has mailed a jeep home piece by piece. He has a pet mouse (Daisy), rabbits (Bingo and Fluffy) and guinea pigs (Bongo, Babette, Mannie, Moe and Jack).

Radar manages to do the impossible: acquire needed items without the hassle of red tape (usually through bartering). As a kid Radar had an imaginary friend named Shirley and mentioned that his hobby is peeking through the hole in the nurses shower tent. He attempted to earn extra money by selling wing tip shoes by the Style Right Shoe Company of Iowa for $8.98 a pair.

Radar received a hardship discharge when his Uncle Ed died and he became the family's sole support. He left behind his most cherished pos-

session, his teddy bar (which he placed on the bed of his best friend, Captain Hawkeye Pierce). In a follow-up letter it was learned that Walter O'Reilly, gentleman farmer, had taken an evening job with the local grocery store to pay the bills. In an unsold pilot called *W*A*L*T*E*R* (CBS, July 17, 1984) it is learned that Radar gave up the family farm and moved to St. Louis to become a police officer.

See also: Benjamin Franklin Pierce, B.J. Hunnicutt, Charles Winchester, III, Frank Burns, Henry Blake, Margaret Houlihan, Sherman Potter, Trapper John McIntire.

910. Rafael Caine, *The Immortal*, Syn., 2000–2001. Played by Lorenzo Lamas.

Rafael Caine is a man who lives for only one purpose: to destroy demons. Rafael was born in 1620 and is the son of a wealthy father and mother who worked as importers. Rafael, called Rafe, became a part of the business when he became of age. In 1638 Rafe began an ocean voyage to Japan to acquire silk and spices for his father. En route the ship on which Rafe was traveling encountered a fierce storm at sea. The ship was destroyed but Rafe managed to swim to shore. After wandering for three days Rafe met a man named Yashiro. Yashiro welcomed Rafe into his home. For reasons that are not explained (why he did not attempt to return home) Rafe remained and eventually married Yashiro's daughter, Mikko. They built a home near a small stream and were blessed with a child. One day in 1643, demons killed Mikko and stole Rafe's daughter. An enraged Rafe forged a sword of revenge and swore an oath: "I'll hunt them forever and never rest until they're dead. With this sword I seek and oath of vengeance. The evil ones will know my name and fear it. I will send them back to hell with this blade and never stop until it is done." Rafe raises his sword to the heavens. Thunder sounds and he is encircled in a sphere of light. Rafe becomes the Chosen One and battled demons for centuries. He comes to our attention in the year 2000.

Rafe doesn't eat or drink. He can smell demons when they are near and has a plan for everything ("I make it up as I go along"). Rafe doesn't make mistakes when it comes to demons—"I make decisions." Rafe can be killed and if it should happen "the world would be plunged into darkness." In addition to his sword, Rafe carries two large knives, a small knife and a small rapid-fire gun. Rafe also carries with him a small wooden box that contains his most treasured item—a doll his daughter played with. Demons call Rafe "The Vengeful One."

911. Raina Washington, *The Division*, Lifetime, 2002–2004. Played by Taraji Henson.

Raina Washington is an inspector with the San Francisco Police Department. She is 35 years old and enjoys being a cop. She has set her goals on quickly moving up the departmental ranks.

Raina has good instincts, is disciplined and shows a great deal of compassion. As a child Raina had dreams of becoming a professional athlete (track and field). She actually made the Olympics but she felt pursuing that goal held few opportunities. For reasons that are not really explained, Raina chose police work (possibly because it would allow her to test her limits).

Raina's athletic training is also her greatest asset as a police officer. She graduated with top honors from the San Francisco Police Academy and while vivacious, she pushes herself beyond her limits — "I need to prove my abilities as an inspector. I know I'm good."

See also: Candace DeLorenzo, Jinny Exstead, Kate McCafferty, Magda Ramirez, Stacy Newland.

912. Ralph Furley, *Three's Company*, ABC, 1979–1984. Played by Don Knotts.

Playboy, ladies' man and all around swinger are the qualities Ralph Furley believes he possesses. Yet he also says "I failed at everything I tried and amounted to nothing. I'm the laughing stock of my family." No matter what he believes, Ralph is a gentle, kind and sweet man who puts his feelings aside to help others.

Ralph works as a landlord for his rich brother Bart, the new owner of the Ropers Apartment House in San Diego (the residence of Jack Tripper, Chrissy Snow and Janet Wood). Ralph had a pet cat named Patches as a kid and during World War II he worked in a deli and was engaged to a girl named Helga (who left him to run away with a salami salesman). Ralph wanted to serve his country but was classified 4F.

Ralph is a man in his late fifties but dresses in outlandish, bright colored mod clothes. He believes he has "a powerhouse body" and calls himself "The King of Romance" and the "The Prince of Passion." He also claims he has valuable antiques in his apartment (101; tenant Chrissy Snow says, "They're priceless all right, they're worth nothing"). Ralph confessed that he always felt inferior to Bart "because my parents told me so." Tenant Jack Tripper calls him" R.F." and he enjoys a beer at the Regal Beagle Pub.

See also: Chrissy Snow, Cindy Snow, Jack Tripper, Janet Wood, Stanley and Helen Roper, Terri Alden.

913. Ralph Kramden, *The Honeymooners*, CBS, 1955–1956. Played by Jackie Gleason.

Ralph Kramden is a bus driver for the Manhattan-based Gotham Bus Company. He is married to Alice and lives in a rather shabby apartment at 728 Chauncey Street in Bensonhurst, Brooklyn, New York (the address is also given as 328 and 358 Chauncey Street).

Ralph was born in Brooklyn and attended P.S. 73 grammar school. At the age of 14 he worked as a newspaper delivery boy. He had high hopes of playing the cornet in a band but his parents couldn't afford to give him music lessons (he later mentions that he hung out in pool halls and became an expert on popular music in his youth). It is first said that Ralph noticed Alice in a diner when she yelled to the waiter, "Hey Mac, a hot frank and a small orange drink." Next it is a snowy winter day when Ralph, assigned by the WPA to shovel snow, met Alice Gibson, who was handing out snow shovels. Finally, Ralph mentions he met Alice in a restaurant called Angie's when they both ordered spaghetti and meatballs.

Ralph drives bus number 247 (later 2969) along Madison Avenue. Over the course of his 14 years with the company (at 225 River Street) Ralph has been robbed six times (five times the crooks got nothing; the sixth time they got $45). His salary started at $42.50 a week and was later mentioned as being $60 then $62 a week. His astrological sign is Taurus and he owns two suits (one black, one blue). He has type A blood and is thought of as cheap. Ralph likes to be right about everything and he has a tendency to yell a lot. "Homina, homina, homina" is what Ralph says when he doesn't know what to say; and "I've got a big mouth" is what he says when he realizes he said something he shouldn't have.

Ralph is a member of the Raccoon Lodge (also called the International Order of the Friendly Sons of Raccoons and the International Loyal Order of Friendly Raccoons). Ralph is the treasurer; Alice is a member of the Ladies' Auxiliary of the lodge. Ralph also enjoys playing pool and bowling with his best friend, Ed Norton. Ralph dreams of making it big. He ventured into a number of money-making schemes that all failed: low cal pizza, a uranium mine in Asbury Park, glow-in-the-dark wallpaper, Kran-Mars Delicious Mystery Appetizer (an appetizer Ralph unknowingly made from dog food), and the Handy Housewife Helper (a combination peeler, can opener and apple corer) that he and Ed tried to sell in a TV commercial called "Chef of the Future." Ralph also started the Ralph Kramden Corporation and appeared as a contestant on the TV quiz show *The $99,000 Answer* (he lost when he couldn't name the composer of the song "Swanee River"). He also did a commercial for Chewsy Chews candy bars on *The Chewsy Chews Musical Hour* on TV.

See also: Alice Kramden, Ed Norton.

914. Randall Winston, *Spin City,* ABC, 1996–2002. Played by Barry Bostwick.

Randall Winston is a Manhattan Borough President (for six years) who was elected to the office of the Mayor of New York City. Randall is a man of wealth and to him eight hours is like three workdays. Randall's grandfather made the family fortune by bootlegging whiskey during the 1920s. It was Randall's father's money that put him through college. Although Randall is oblivious to other people's suffering, he feels that his most redeeming quality "is my trustfulness" (he also has a bad habit of using the nonsense word "further-the-less" as a real word). If Randall is attending an important meeting and it is time for his massage, he opts to leave for his massage. Randall knows how to play a crowd after a speech. However, if he sees a pretty girl staring at him he falls to pieces.

Randall was born in Fairfield, Connecticut, and grew up with a very demanding mother who overshadowed everything he did. She dictated his whole life and showed him no love. In college (Yale) Randall was interested in film making and made a movie the Yale *Daily News* called "an incoherent mess." Randall receives a death threat in the mail every Tuesday and keeps a large sum of cash in a fake bank in his office that he calls Don Quixote. He collects driftwood sculptors and enjoys watching *All My Children* and *Wheel of Fortune* (he succeeds in guessing the puzzle before the letters are revealed). Randall has his own action figure (the Mayor Winston Action Figure) and enjoys meals with his co-workers at the Landmark Tavern (he hates street vendor food — "It repulses me").

Randall was married to Helen, who received a million dollar divorce settlement. He had a brief romance with Judge Claire Simmons (Farrah Fawcett), whom he called "Claire Bear." Blue is Randall's favorite color and he has a polo pony named Little Miss Muffy. The Keebler Room is his favorite cigar bar. Randall reads the great books — on tape and in high school was on the football team. *The Sound of Music* and *West Side Story* were the two plays Randall performed in after college when he attempted to become an actor. He also hosts a weekly radio show he calls *The Mayor Winston Weekly Radio Show* and drives a 1966 Mustang. Randall also has a rather strange dream: being on a yacht and being fed strawberries by a young Angie Dickinson.

See also: Caitlin Moore, Charlie Crawford, Michael Flaherty, Paul Lassiter, Stewart Bondek.

915. Randi Wallace, *She-Wolf of London,* Syn., 1990–1991. Played by Kate Hodge.

Randi Wallace is a young woman marked by a pentagram — the sign of the wolf. When the full moon appears a dramatic change occurs: Randi becomes a hideous werewolf. Randi, however, was not always cursed. She was born and grew up in Los Angeles. She is the daughter of a middle class family and enjoyed horror movies; her favorite TV show was *Beyond the Beyond* (a space series about a ship called *Voyager*); she has seen each episode 100 times. At one point in her life Randi became a vegetarian and acquired a keen interest in myths and mythology. After graduating from high school Randi applied to the University of England to acquire her master's degree in the occult. Randi plans on writing her thesis on disproving the supernatural.

One night Randi finds the supernatural really exists. She was attacked and bitten by a werewolf while exploring the moors. Thirty days later, on the first full moon of the month, the beautiful coed becomes a vicious animal, seeking only to kill. Daylight returns Randi to her normal self and finding clothes becomes her top priority (the transformation rips the clothes from her body).

Randi has recollections of her transformations. Her high degree of morality prevents her from being a vicious killer. She now has a craving for meat and is still dangerous in her transformed state. Legend states that the curse can be lifted if the werewolf who caused the affliction is killed or if the victim is shot with a silver bullet by the one who loves her. The man who loves Randi is Ian Matheson, her professor and the only person she can trust.

Randi and Ian (Neil Dickson) live at Matheson Bed and Breakfast (which is run by Ian's parents). Ian is seeking an alternate cure for Randi and protects her on nights of a full moon by locking her in a cell. In England Randi's name means "Erotically Charged."

The series ended before Randi could be cured.

916. Randolph Agarn, *F Troop,* ABC, 1965–1967. Played by Larry Storch.

Randolph Agarn is a corporal stationed at Fort Courage in Kansas in 1866. He insists he has no middle name and is vice president of O'Rourke Enterprises, the illegal business run by Sergeant

Morgan O'Rourke out of the barracks and supply hut of the fort (Morgan is the founder and president).

Randolph is a nine-year veteran and is assigned the menial tasks for O'Rourke Enterprises (the business deals in anything that can make money and Randolph oversees the factory operations — the reservation of the friendly Hekawi Indians. Morgan has made the tribe so dependent on income from sales that Chief Wild Eagle and his people have forgotten the hard times they once lead).

Randolph is a kind and gentle man who finds it difficult to lie and scheme. He is always aware of what he is doing and just can't bring himself to take advantage of others. He treats everybody with respect but is so money hungry that he always complicates matters when he devises ideas that never work.

Randolph tends to get carried away by things (for example, by the beat of the tom toms at the Hekawi Festival of the Succotash and yelling "Kill the paleface"). He also has an array of strange cousins — from El Diablo to Lucky Pierre to Dimitri Agaronoff — who show up at the fort just in time to complicate a deal for O'Rourke Enterprises. Randolph has a horse named Barney and is always being told, "Agarn, I don't know why everybody says you're so dumb." It always dawns on him a few minutes later and he responds with "Who says I'm dumb?" Randolph also faints when he hears mention of large sums of money.

See also: Morgan O'Rourke, Wilton Parmenter, Wrangler Jane.

917. Raven Baxter, *That's So Raven*, Disney, 2003 (current). Played by Raven Symone.

Raven Baxter is the 16-year-old daughter of Victor and Tanya Baxter. Victor is a chef and Tanya a substitute teacher. She lives at 419 Miranda Place in San Francisco and has a ten-year-old brother named Corey.

Raven is not a typical teenager. While very pretty and always in style, she possesses psychic powers that enable her to see future events (usually those involving friends and family). Raven calls herself "a future seer" and cannot control what she sees (she can try to prevent something from happening but that is as far as she can go). According to the Sleevemore Center for Psychiatric Research, Raven registered a four on the Sleevemore Psychic Reader (indicating that her powers have not yet fully developed).

Raven is a sophomore at Bayside High School. She wears jersey 7 as a member of the volleyball team, the Barracudas, and is a sports writer for the school newspaper, *The Barracudian*. If Raven tries to lie her right eye twitches. Teachers consider her a showoff as she always raises her hand to answer questions. She used her abilities to make money as Tallulah on a telephone service called Psychic Sidekicks.

918. Raymond Barone, *Everybody Loves Raymond*, CBS, 1996–2005. Played by Ray Romano.

Raymond Albert Barone is a sportswriter for *Newsday*, a local New York newspaper based on Long Island. Raymond lives in Lynbrook, New York, at 320 Fowler Street (although 135 can be seen on the front door) with his wife Debra and children Ally, Jeffrey and Michael.

Raymond is the son of Frank and Marie Barone. He was born on Long Island in 1959 and is a graduate of Hillcrest High School (class of 1977; he had a C.B. radio at the time with the handle "Straight Shooter") and St. John's University (class of 1981). As a kid he had a teddy bear named Hector Von Fuzzy, a bird (Tweedy), a dog (Shamsky), and a cat (Whiskers). Raymond also took piano lessons from his mother (a piano teacher; his father worked for Polk Accounting). Ray, as he is sometimes called, became a sports fan at an early age and his hero, ball player Mickey Mantle, made him want to become a sportswriter. In later dialogue Ray claims that his brother, Robert's inability to throw a spiral ball started him on the road to critiquing.

Ray is an Italian Catholic but doesn't attend mass on Sunday "because of work. The football game is on at the same time." Ray's dream is to get published in *Sports Illustrated* magazine. Prior to his current job, Ray worked as a bed installer for Claude's Futons. He wears a size 11 shoe, eats Alpha Bits cereal for breakfast and enjoys Twix candy bars. Ray believes all he has is golf (which he plays at the Brookside Country Club) and reading *Golf Digest* magazine. Ray won the 1996 Sportswriter of the Year Award and the Association of Sportswriters Award in 2002 (which won him a promotion to head of sports features at *Newsday*). Ray appeared on the TV show *Sports Call* (talking about steroids in sports) and considers the biggest mistake in his life was to erase his and Debra's wedding video to tape a football game. His favorite hangout is Nemo's Pizzeria.

See also: Ally Barone, Debra Barone, Frank and Marie Barone, Robert Barone.

919. Reba Hart, *Reba*, WB, 2001 (current). Played by Reba McEntire.

This entry also contains information on Brock and Barbara Jean Hart (Christopher Rich, Melissa

Peterson), Cheyenne and Van Montgomery (Jo-Anna Garcia, Steve Howey), and Kyra and Jake Hart (Scarlett Pomers, Mitch Holleman).

Reba McKinney was born in McCallister, Oklahoma, on March 28 ("The year is not important," she says). Reba graduated from the University of Oklahoma with a degree in teaching but longed to become a professional singer. Her teaching career took her to Texas, where she began moonlighting as a singer in a local bar. There she met Brock Hart, a dental student working as a bartender. It was 1976 and they fell in love and married shortly after. They lived in a small apartment until Brock graduated and began his practice. They purchased a Colonial-style home at 4280 Oak Street and had three children: Cheyenne, Kyra and Jake.

When the series begins Reba and Brock are divorced. The children are living with Reba; Brock has married Barbara Jean Booker, the woman (his dental assistant) he had an affair with while still married to Reba. Also living with Reba is Van Montgomery, the teenager who impregnated 17-year-old Cheyenne (Van's wealthy parents, Stan and Sue, disowned him when they learned what happened). Although they were reckless, Cheyenne and Van do love each other and set up housekeeping in Cheyenne's bedroom. They later marry and have a daughter they name Elizabeth.

Reba appears to be living off the child support and alimony Brock pays (Brock does complain that the payments are draining him and that Barbara Jean is a spendthrift). To make ends meet, Reba first worked as a substitute teacher at Westchester High School then as Brock's receptionist. It bothers Reba that nobody puts milk on the shopping list and she has a hard time putting up with Van and Cheyenne, especially when they show affection in front of Kyra and Jake. Reba has a lot to say but no one will listen to her (so she often talks to herself).

Brock and Barbara Jean eventually move next door to Reba at 4282 Oak Street. Barbara Jean works as Brock's dental assistant and is a bit naïve. Reba is a bit hostile toward Barbara Jean for stealing her husband but Barbara Jean feels she and Reba can put that behind them and is now struggling to become her friend (Reba says, " Barbara Jean laughs like a horse and doesn't have the sense God gave paste"). Barbara Jean is a full-figured woman. In the second grade she experienced a sudden growth spurt and was called "Blondezella" by the other kids. She wanted to be a meter maid "but they wouldn't let me carry a gun." She had a pet cat (Clap Clap Kitty Cat) and is famous for her tuna casserole ("Three kinds of tuna and two kinds of potato chips"). Barbara Jean is very religious. She oversees her church's "Bowling for Jesus" fund and shops at the Joy for Jesus Gift Shop. She reads to the blind on Tuesday evenings and volunteers at the Church Service Camp, teaching blind high school children to cook.

Barbara Jean collects Beanie Babies (she has 450 of them and celebrates each new arrival with cake and ice cream). She also has 14 plush animals that have to be arranged in a specific order (however, Binky and Lulu cannot be next to each other "because they have a history." The history is not revealed). Barbara Jean is proud of the fact that she can stuff seven eggs in her mouth. Her favorite singer is Sting and hates TV host Bob Barker (who said she wasn't perky enough to be a contestant on *The Price Is Right*). Brock calls Barbara Jean "Sassy Shorts" and "Mrs. Boopy Woo Woo" (she calls him "Mr. Whoopie Boo Boo"). Brock is 45 years old (in 2003), three years older than Reba (making her previously undisclosed birth year 1961). He enjoys playing golf (he uses Naked Lady Golf Tees) and gave up his practice in 2004 to play professional golf. He and Barbara Jean also have a child together (Henry).

Cheyenne is Reba's oldest child, a very beautiful and sexy blonde who attended Westchester High School (where she met Van). Before becoming pregnant at 17, she was co-captain of the Wildcats football cheerleading team, the Pepettes. Cheyenne rallies at sporting events, stands up for herself and attends all school functions. After a year's absence from school Cheyenne begins taking classes at Houston University. She drops out when she decides to become a dentist (she scored a B plus on her test for hygienist and is now attending dental school). As a child Cheyenne took up ballet, piano and karate but gave up on them ("I'm flaky and I don't stick with things"). At summer camp, Cheyenne took a self-defense course and was called "Most Lethal and Most Peppy." Cheyenne has her hair done at Salon Verona and shops at Donna's Outlet.

Van was a quarterback for the Westchester High Wildcats football team (jersey 24). He won a football scholarship to college and attended Houston University for a short time (where he also worked as the grounds keeper). He quit to become a hopeful linebacker with the Thunderbears, an area football team (jersey 88). Van exercises on an elaborate machine called the ExerCist and held a job as Sauce and Cheese Captain at Fat Tony's Pizza Parlor. Van wears a size 12-shoe. He calls Reba "Mrs. H" and his red Mustang sports car "Rhonda."

Kyra is Reba's middle child, a sassy 12-year-old

girl. Her middle name is Eleanor and she is a straight A student at Oak Elementary, then Westchester High School. She is an expert chess player, reads *Teen* magazine and earns money babysitting. Kyra is an Honor Roll student and played first clarinet (then tuba) in the school band. Pot roast and macaroni and cheese are her favorite meals. She is a very independent girl and often defies Reba's authority.

Jake attends Oak Elementary School. He is seven years old and a Cub Scout. He takes jazz and tap classes and has a pet turtle named Speedy. He can't eat fast food because it upsets his stomach and likes chunky peanut butter and banana sandwiches.

920. Rebecca Howe, *Cheers,* NBC, 1987–1993. Played by Kirstie Alley.

Rebecca Howe was the manager of Cheers, a Boston-based bar, in 1987 (she was appointed by The Lillian corporation to manage the bar when its owner, Sam Malone, sold it). Her stay was short-lived. She was fired when she was falsely accused of letting her boyfriend (Roger Colcord) use her secret computer code ("Sweet Baby") to access corporate information. The corporation sold it back to Sam for 85 cents. Before Sam hired Rebecca as his bar manager (at $6 an hour), Rebecca worked as the Miracle Buff Girl at the Auto Show (Miracle Buff is a wax preservative).

Rebecca was born in San Diego. Her father is a naval captain and her mother a concert cellist. Rebecca was overweight as a teenager and found it difficult to live up to her parent's high expectations. Although she is slim and beautiful now, she hides her insecurities beneath her polished exterior. Rebecca is a graduate of the University of Connecticut (where she acquired a degree in business) and enjoys watching *Spenser: For Hire* on TV (Robert Urich, its star, is her favorite actor).

Rebecca is attractive and always fashionably dressed. She has a tendency to whine and is very easily exasperated. She has a bad habit of smoking and at one time carelessly tossed a lit cigarette into a trash can and damaged Cheers when the building caught fire (the bar regulars had to frequent the Cheers competition, Mr. Pubbs). In 1991 Rebecca and Sam became partners in Cheers when Rebecca invested $25,000 to expand the bar (adding a pool room and additional bathrooms).

See also: Carla LeBec, Cliff Claven, Diane Chambers, Ernie Pantusso, Norm Peterson, Sam Malone, Woody Boyd.

921. Reese Harden, *Movie Stars,* WB, 1999–2000. Played by Harry Hamlin.

Reese Harden is a popular movie star who has been dubbed "America's Leading Action Star." He is married to actress Jacey Wyatt ("America's Favorite Leading Lady") and they are the parents of Lori, Apache and Moonglow.

Reese is known as "Reese Harden, Action Star" and has made such films as *Clash of the Titans* (actually starring Harry Hamlin), *Lethal Impact, Fierce Impact* and *Sudden Vengeance.* He is represented by the CAA Agency and has been voted "The World's Sexiest Man" by *Appeal Weekly* magazine. Reese is also a People's Choice Award winner and "Makes those movies with the word *Lethal* in the title that gross three billion dollars."

Reese has his own Kimbro Toys action figure (Reese Harden, Navy Seal) and his picture adorns boxes of Flutie Flakes cereal (although he snacks on Honey Heroes cereal). Reese first met Jacey on the set of the film *Cyber Death 2000* (she played "The annoying mime who got vaporized"). Reese refuses to make a screen test (he feels he is a superstar and need not bother with such trivial matters). The one exception he has made is for the role of Batman (which has stiff competition). As a kid Reese had a pet turtle named Skippy.

See also: Jacey Wyatt, Lori Harden, Todd Harden.

922. Regina Grier, *The Steve Harvey Show,* WB, 1996–2002. Played by Wendy Raquel Robinson.

Regina Grier is the principal of Booker T. Washington High School in Chicago. She was born in Chicago and attended Booker T (as the school is called) before becoming a teacher then its principal. She holds the school title "The Undefeated Scrabble Champion of Booker T High."

Regina is very attractive and can have any man she desires. She is, however, very demanding and is seeking a man who can accept her as his superior. She also believes she has stunning looks and a dancer's legs "and that will get me any man I want." Regina is slim but loves to eat (she has a mini-fridge in her nightstand and enjoys Lucky Charms cereal for breakfast). Regina lives in Apartment 204 (address not given) and drives a Miata. *Essence* magazine chose her as their "I'm Every Woman Power Professional." She starts each day off with tea and a raspberry scone and offers office visitors a Chunky candy square. Regina became romantically involved with Steve Hightower, the music teacher she called "Hightower" (he fondly calls her "Piggy." Steve and Regina attended high school together and she was overweight).

Regina loves amusement parks, especially the roller coaster and had a pet pig named Bentley.

Chunky Monkey is her favorite flavor of ice cream and she also teaches dance classes with her Regina Grier Dance Ensemble of Chicago.

See also: Cedric Robinson, Lovita Jenkins, Steve Hightower.

923. Regine Hunter, *Living Single,* Fox, 1993–1997. Played by Kim Fields.

Regine Hunter's real first name is Regina—"but that is not classy enough for me." She is well endowed and honestly believes "my double d's got me into M.I.T." (where she also claims "My breasts made me Homecoming Queen").

Regine was born in Brooklyn, New York, and now resides in the Prospect Heights section (her apartment is seen as A, 1A and 3A). Regine was a beautiful child and has used her beauty to get what she wants. She is extremely feminine and a fanatic about her clothes (she works as a buyer for The Boutique in Manhattan). Regine can't bear to be without a man by her side (if too much time passes she feels she is losing her looks). Her attire consists of sexy but fashionable clothes and she shows ample cleavage to attract men. She is self-centered, self-absorbed and wants kids—"these genes are too good to waste." Her friends call her "loud and busty." Regine is on a mission to marry a man "who knows that fine wine doesn't come with a twist off cap." She believes that she is irresistible to men and that "sometimes life is not fair to me. That's why bras come in different sizes." Regine lives by a code she calls "The Three C's of Men:" "Catch, control and conquer." Regine has to be a standout wherever she goes. If she is in a room and a man does not look at her "then he must be gay." Being without a man for long periods (two or three days) causes Regine to panic and she goes on a chocolate eating binge.

See also: Synclaire James.

924. Remington Steele, *Remington Steele,* NBC, 1982–1986. Played by Pierce Brosnan.

Remington Steele is a man who does not really exist. The name was created by Laura Holt to stimulate business for her company, Remington Steele Investigations ("All was going well until he walked into my life" and assumed the persona of Remington Steele. "Who are you?" "Where do you come from?" are two questions Laura asks but are never answered).

"The mysterious Remington Steele" is just that—mysterious. He was born in Ireland on September 6, 1952, and was apparently an orphan. He grew up on the streets and was taught the art of crime by a master con artist (Daniel Chalmers). The man, now officially known as Remington Steele, was 12 years earlier (1970) making the rounds as a professional boxer called "The Kilkearney Kid." When his boxing career ended, he took up professional thievery to survive. It was during one such incident (an attempt to steal jewels being guarded by Laura) that the man assumes Remington's identity to avoid capture by the police. Rather than turn him in, Laura allows him to become her partner, Remington Steele.

Remington lives at 1594 Rossmore Street, Apartment 5A in Los Angeles (address also given as 5594 Rossmore). He has two cars: a 1936 Auburn (plate R. STEELE) and a blue Mercedes (plate IDR 0373). Remington is a fan of old movies and associates their plots with real life (he also solves cases based on their plots). He claims old movies are therapeutic in value and relax him (posters of *Casablanca, Hotel Imperial, Notorious* and *The Thin Man* can be seen on his apartment walls). Humphrey Bogart is his favorite actor and he has passports based on characters played by Bogart: Michael O'Leary (Ireland), Paul Fabre (France), John Morrill (England) and Richard Blaine (Australia). *The Honeymooners* is his favorite TV show.

Remington was voted one of the five most eligible bachelors by *Upbeat* magazine. He is also writing a book (*Remington Steele's Ten Most Famous Cases*) and squanders money on cases to wine and dine women. Remington Steele Investigations is located in Suite 1157 at 606 West Beverly Boulevard in Los Angeles.

See also: Laura Holt.

925. Ren Stevens, *Even Stevens,* Disney, 2000–2003. Played by Christy Carlson Romano.

Ren Stevens is a pretty 15-year-old girl who lives in Sacramento, California. She is the daughter of Eileen and Steven Stevens and has a brother named Louis. Ren is obsessed with being perfect in everything she does. She is a role model to other students at school and her only flaw may be that she files her nails when she is nervous. When Ren sets her mind on something she does it in style (for example, her first slumber party was by special invitation only—"Ren's Young Women's All Night Forum").

Ren first attended Lawrence Grammar School then Lawrence Jr. High School. She is her own best friend. Ren is the Administrative Assistant to the principal (a job she created) and head of the Yearbook Committee. She has been Student of the Month for 18 straight months and won "Student of the Semester Award" three semesters in a row. Ren is editor of the school newspaper, *The Wombat Reporter* and her picture hangs on the school's "Wombat Hall of Fame" wall (She has also been awarded the associated prize for being a top notch student — a $5 gift certificate for a Harry's Honey Ham). Ren reports the news on "The Wombat Report" for the school's closed circuit TV Station (Wombat TV) and hates it if anybody comes up with a better idea than her for a news story. Ren is a very pretty girl but doesn't use her looks to achieve a goal. Her brains are her ticket to success.

926. Reuben Gregory, *Amen*, NBC, 1986–1991. Played by Clifton Davis.

This entry also contains information on Thelma Frye (Anna Maria Horsford), the daughter of the church's deacon, Ernest Frye. Reverend Reuben Gregory is a young minister at the First Community Church of Philadelphia. Reuben has a B.A. from Morehouse College, a master's degree in religious education from Yale Divinity School, and a doctorate in Christian Studies from Union Theological Seminary. He was born in Cleveland and was raised by Christian parents. Reuben began his duties in Cleveland as the host of *Sunrise Semester* on a local station there.

Reuben has progressive ideas and is trying to implement them in a church that is behind the times. He has added music to the masses, gives stirring sermons and encourages people to join in and help the church serve the community. He holds a "Pastor's Pow Wow" to discuss church matters with his parishioners. In 1991 he began duties as a teacher (of theology) at Baxter Women's College.

Thelma Frye took an instant liking to Reuben. Although he tried to avoid her romantic advances they eventually married (1990). Thelma is a graduate of West Holmes High School (where she was called "The Undateable"). She was a member of the track team and won the 100-yard dash. Her favorite subjects were science, English and home economics. Before acquiring her real estate license and working for the firm of Underwood and Baines, Thelma hosted *Thelma's Kitchen*, a TV cooking show for Bake Rite Flour. Thelma calls Reuben "Sweet Potato."

See also: Ernest Frye.

927. Rhapsody Angel, *Captain Scarlet and the Mysterons*, Syn., 1967. Voiced by Liz Morgan.

Rhapsody Angel is a pilot for Spectrum, a futuristic organization that protects the Earth from alien invaders. Rhapsody was born in Chelsea, England, and is the daughter of aristocratic parents. She attended London University and attained degrees in law and sociology. After graduating she joined the Federal Agents Bureau and soon became a top operative. Her crime-solving skills eventually earned her a promotion to commander. Rhapsody quit the bureau to become chief security officer for an airline. This gave her the knowledge to start her own airline company. As Rhapsody's abilities grew so did her reputation. It was at this time that Spectrum asked her to become a pilot. Rhapsody enjoys chess and is quite an expert. The program is a puppet series filmed in Supermarionation.

See also: Captain Magenta, Captain Ochre, Captain Scarlet, Destiny Angel, Harmony Angel, Melody Angel, Symphony Angel.

928. Rhoda Miller, *My Living Doll*, CBS, 1964–1965. Played by Julie Newmar.

Rhoda Miller is made of low modulus polyethylene plastics, miniature computers "and assorted components." She is "the ultimate in feminine composition" but she is also a robot built by Dr. Carl Miller for a U.S. space project designed to send robots into space. Until she is ready, she has been placed in the care of Dr. Bob McDonald, a psychologist, to shape her personality.

Rhoda appears as a very beautiful woman. She is actually Air Force Model AF 709. She stands five feet, ten inches tall and measures 37-26-36. Rhoda has four "birthmarks" on her back that each act as an emergency control button. Her main "off switch" is located in her right elbow. Her eyes produce a source of power obtained from light (covering her eyes causes a system relaxation). Rhoda has microscopic sensors that keep her body temperature at a constant 98.6 degrees (so she feels human to the touch). Her memory bank contains 50 million items of information and her computer brain can compute any piece of programmed information in one second. Before he named her Rhoda Miller, Carl called his creation "Living Doll," "It," "709" or "The Robot." He sees her as just that, not a gorgeous woman.

Rhoda resides with Dr. MacDonald (Bob Cummings) at his home at 5600 Wiltshire Boulevard. Rhoda is not jerky in her movements or speech unless she has a system malfunction. To allow Rhoda to experience human contact (and acquire human abilities), she works as Bob's secretary (she types 240 words a minute with no mistakes and no coffee breaks).

929. Rhoda Morganstern, *Rhoda*, CBS, 1974–1978. Played by Valerie Harper.

Rhoda Jo Beth Morganstern is the daughter of Ida and Martin Morganstern. She was born in the Bronx, New York, in December of 1941 and lived near Fordham Road at 3517 Grand Concourse. In the third grade at P.S. 7 Rhoda won a science fair prize with a model of the human brain. As a teenager she attended Roosevelt High School and worked as an usherette at Lowe's State Theater. She was also a member of a street gang called the Sharkettes. When Rhoda was unable to find a job following graduation she moved to Minneapolis, Minnesota, where she acquired a job as a window dresser at Hempell's Department Store. She lives in an apartment at 119 North Weatherly and is best friends with her downstairs neighbor, Mary Richards. Rhoda is Jewish, has a gold fish named Goldfish and was fined $40 at the Minneapolis Zoo for feeding yogurt to a buffalo. Rhoda has a weight problem and tries to eat healthy but is often tempted by sweets ("I should just apply it to my hips").

In September of 1974 the role of Rhoda ended on *The Mary Tyler Moore Show* and Valerie Harper began her own series as *Rhoda*. Rhoda returns to New York for a two-week vacation that changes to a permanent stay when she meets and falls in love with Joe Gerard (David Groh), the owner of the New York Wrecking Company. They marry shortly after and set up housekeeping in Apartment 9B at 332 West 46th Street in Manhattan. It is at this time that Rhoda begins her own decorating business, Windows By Rhoda. In 1976, as Rhoda and Joe grow apart, they decide to divorce. Rhoda, now on her own once again, moves to a new apartment in the same building (6G; also seen as 4G) and acquires a job as the Doyle Costume Company.

The ABC TV movie update, *Mary and Rhoda* (February 7, 2000) updates the Rhoda character. She is now a professional photographer and the mother of Meredith, a medical student at Barnard College. Rhoda married for a second time (but divorced her husband, Jean Paul Russo, for cheating on her). Rhoda has resumed her maiden name and returned to New York to begin her photography career.

See also: Lou Grant, Mary Richards, Ted Baxter.

930. Ricardo Tubbs, *Miami Vice*, NBC, 1984–1989. Played by Philip Michael Thomas.

Ricardo Tubbs is an undercover detective with the Vice Squad of the Miami Metro Dade County Police Department (also called the Miami, Florida, Police Department). He is a partner with Sonny Crockett and the two use their own brand of justice to solve crimes.

Ricardo was born in the Bronx, New York, and was a detective with the Armed Robbery Division of the N.Y.P.D., Bronx Division. Another episode claims he was a narcotics detective with the N.Y.P.D. (tracking the killer of his brother by a drug dealer brought him to Florida and to Sonny, who was seeking the same man. At the conclusion of the case Ricardo was offered a chance to work with Sonny and he accepted).

Ricardo assumes the name of Ricardo Cooper to protect his identity. He is called Rico by Sonny and claims that his name stands for "tough, unique, bad, bold and sassy." Ricardo is single and lives in an apartment on Linden Avenue. He is much more careful than Sonny. He is also not as aggressive and prefers to take a less gung ho approach when it comes to questioning or chasing suspects. Ricardo will use his gun only when necessary. Despite his restraints he often finds himself in trouble with his superiors for following Sonny's unorthodox approaches on cases (he figures they are partners and somebody has to cover Sonny's back). Ricardo has an account at the Security Central Bank of Florida.

See also: Sonny Crockett.

931. Richard and Emily Gilmore, *Gilmore Girls*, WB, 2000 (current). Played by Edward Herrmann, Kelly Bishop.

Richard Gilmore and his wife Emily are the parents of Lorelai Gilmore and the grandparents of her daughter Rory. They are wealthy and live in Hartford, Connecticut. Richard is a graduate of Yale University and was first executive vice president of the Gerhman and Driscoll Insurance Company before retiring to begin his own insurance company, The Gilmore Group (in 2002). Richard gets up every morning at 5:30 A.M. and has half a grapefruit with his breakfast. He is a member of the Cigar Club (sits in an enclosed room twice a week with other cigar smokers) and Chuck Berry is his favorite singer.

Emily is a socialite who lives for charity functions. She is a member of the D.A.R. (Daughters of the American Revolution), the Edward R. Wardus Rare Manuscript Foundation, the Philharmonic Club, the Historical Society and the Hospital Committee. She is president of the Horticultural Society and co-chairman of the Starlight Foundation. Emily is also a perfectionist and, as Richard says, "can't hold onto a maid" (she is always replacing them when she finds the slightest fault).

See also: Lorelai Gilmore, Paris Geller, Rory Gilmore.

932. Richard Barrett, *The Champions*, NBC/Syn., 1968. Played by William Gaunt.

Richard Barrett is an agent for Nemesis, an international organization based in Geneva, Switzerland, that tackles dangerous matters. Richard was born in Salisbury, Wiltshire, England, in 1938. He and his partners, Sharron Macready and Craig Stirling, possess unique powers that were granted to them by the inhabitants of a lost city in the Himalayan Mountains.

During an assignment to recover deadly bacteria specimens in Tibet, the plane on which the agents are using is hit by enemy gunfire and crash lands in the mountains. The apparently lifeless agents are found by a mysterious old man and brought to his world "where their physical and mental capacities are enhanced and their sight, senses and hearing raised to their highest futuristic stage of mental and physical growth." In return for saving their lives and endowing them with powers, the agents are asked only to use their abilities to help keep the world safe (and of course to keep the secret of the lost city).

Richard is the unofficial head of the group (it is his plans that Craig and Sharron follow). He lives at 101 Barrington Place and is an expert in the martial arts. Nothing phases Richard and he will risk his life to accomplish a mission. He is a snappy dresser and believes that clothes make the man (he is most often seen in a brown suit). He is also a gourmet and enjoys eating at the finest restaurants.
See also: Craig Stirling, Sharron Macready.

933. Richard Diamond, *Richard Diamond, Private Detective,* CBS, 1957–1959; NBC, 1959–1960. Played by David Janssen.

Richard Diamond is a handsome New York–based private detective. He is a former officer with the 5th Precinct of the N.Y.P.D. and now operates from an office (306) in mid–Manhattan. Richard charges $100 a day plus expenses. He has an eye for the ladies and if a beautiful girl is in trouble and can't afford his rates, he lowers his fee to $50 a day. Richard lives at the Savoy Hotel, reads the New York *Chronicle* and doesn't come to the office on Tuesdays. He claims that a private eye is only as good as his snitches (he pays them as much as $10 for information).

Richard is tough and uses violence (fists and guns) when necessary to bring a case to a successful conclusion. He drives a convertible and ZM1 2173 and ZM1-2713 were given as his car phone calling numbers. He dines at the Lunch Counter and often uses an alias when going undercover "because some people are allergic to my profession." Last season episodes are set in Los Angeles where Richard has an office (117) in an unidentified building. He is still rugged and handsome but is less of a ladies' man as he now has a steady girlfriend, Karen Wells (Barbara Bain).
See also: Sam.

934. Richard Karinsky, *Caroline in the City,* NBC, 1995–1999. Played by Malcolm Gets.

Richard Karinsky is an artist who feels he is suffering for his art. He appears to always be depressed and is having a difficult time being accepted as a true artist. He works as the colorist for Caroline Duffy, the creator of a daily comic strip called "Caroline in the City."

Richard was born in New York City and lives at 424 East 6th Street. He showed interest in being an artist from his early childhood. When he drew an object it looked like what it was supposed to be. He excelled in art in high school and college but has yet to find recognition. He took the job with Caroline "because I won't be able to make money for my art until after I'm dead."

Richard's work reflects courage and originality but he is boring and has no sense of humor ("I'm working on my people skills," he says). Richard is very high strung and when he gets upset he stands in the corner of Caroline's kitchen and sulks. Richard always looks like a tortured artist. He doesn't come to work before ten in the morning, doesn't work on weekends and requires at least 90 minutes for lunch. Richard had his first public showing at the Arabia Gallery on Spring Street and was commissioned to paint a mural on the Reisman Building.
See also: Annie Spadaro, Caroline Duffy.

935. Richard Kimble, *The Fugitive,* ABC, 1963–1967; CBS, 2000–2001. Played by David Janssen (ABC), Tim Daly (CBS).

ABC Profile: Richard Kimble is the son of John and Elizabeth Kimble. He was born in Stafford, Indiana, on March 27, 1927. With ambitions of becoming a doctor, he attended Cornell University, began his internship in New York and completed training at Fairgreen County Hospital in Indiana. He became a resident doctor at Chicago's Memorial Hospital and specialized in pediatrics and obstetrics. He returned to open his own practice in Stafford and married Helen Waverly shortly after. Richard and Helen lived a happy life until Helen became pregnant and a stillbirth of their first child resulted. Helen was now unable to have children and she and Richard argued constantly over the prospect of adoption (Helen refused, feeling it would be living with a lie).

Richard Kimble stands six feet tall and weighs 175 pounds. He hair is listed as salt and pepper (although he dyes it black). He is also a fugitive, wanted for murder and interstate flight. Indiana court case 33972 found Richard Kimble guilty of the murder of his wife. His defense, that he returned home one night to find Helen dead and he saw a mysterious one-armed man leaving the scene of the crime, was dismissed when no evidence of such a man could be found. Richard was then arrested, booked (KB 7601863) and fingerprinted (classification: 19M 9400013 L24001). Richard received the death penalty and was assigned to Lt. Philip Gerard (Barry Morse). En route to State Prison, the train on which they are riding derailed allowing Richard to escape — to search for Fred Johnson, the mysterious one-armed man — and avoid capture by Gerard, who has vowed to apprehend his escaped prisoner.

CBS Profile: The revised version follows the same concept but changes the facts. At the conclusion of the trial, the State of Indiana vs. Dr. Richard Kimble, Richard was found guilty of murdering his wife (Helen). He was sentenced to death by lethal injection at the Joliet State Prison. "I didn't kill my wife," insisted Richard, who claims he returned home one night to find Helen lying on the floor in a pool of blood. Richard also encountered the intruder, a one-armed man who escaped when Richard chose to help Helen rather than chase the man (later discovered to be Fred Johnson). That night Richard and Helen discussed children and buying a new house. On his way home from the hospital, Richard stopped to buy her flowers. "If I didn't stop she might still be alive," he says.

Richard's police file number was 760813. Lt. Philip Gerard (Mykelti Williamson) was assigned to transport Kimble to Joliet in a police van (number 598). En route the van surves to avoid hitting a car and overturns. Richard escapes but is relentlessly pursued by Gerard, who is determined to recapture him.

Although both versions feature Richard receiving help from the various people he meets, the revised version features Richard using a website (*www.drrichardkimble.com*) that asks people for help and money for his defense (the police believe Richard killed Helen for her money — $20 million).

The ABC version ended with Richard being cleared when a witness to the crime came forward to reveal that it was Fred Johnson who killed Helen. The CBS version ended in an unresolved cliffhanger with Richard finding Johnson (but not being able to get a confession out of him) and Gerard closing in on both of them.

936. Richard Langley, *The Lone Gunmen*, Fox, 2001. Played by Dean Haglund.

Richard Langley, John Byers and Melvin Frohike are the Lone Gunmen, publishers of a newsletter called *The Lone Gunman* that attempts to expose criminals on all levels of society. The paper is based in Tacoma Park, Maryland, and is singular in title because it is the only publication that tells the stories no one else will.

Richard was born on a farm in Saltville, Nebraska. He has the nickname Ringo (after Beatle Ringo Starr) for his obsession with hard rock music (he is always seen wearing a hard rock T-shirt). Richard has long blond hair, black-rimmed glasses and looks like he stepped out of a *Wayne's World* movie (he resembles Garth).

Richard has extraordinary computer skills and feels he has the ability to become "a dot com gazillionaire." He sold illegal cable boxes before joining John and Melvin. Richard is also paranoid. He tapes all phone calls and can break into any computer system in the world. He serves as the team's communications expert.

See also: John Byers, Melvin Frohike.

937. Richie Cunningham, *Happy Days*, ABC, 1974–1980. Played by Ron Howard.

Richard Cunningham is the son of Howard and Marion Cunningham and lives with them and his sister, Joanie, at 618 Bridge Street in Milwaukee, Wisconsin (1950s).

Richie, as he is called, was born in Milwaukee. He weighs 175 pounds and is five feet, nine inches tall. He had the nickname "Freckles" at the age of nine and was said to resemble TV's Howdy Doody. His mother has a full page of Richie as a baby in the family photo album showing him attempting to eat his first bowl of oatmeal. In grammar school Richie received a medal for reading comprehension.

Richie first attended Jefferson High School then the University of Wisconsin. At Jefferson Richie wore jersey 17 as a member of the basketball team, was a member of the French Club, a reporter for the school newspaper, *The Bugle*, and his ROTC 3rd Squadron leader. He had aspirations to become a lawyer then a journalist. Blueberry pancakes and freshly squeezed orange juice is his favorite breakfast; meatloaf is his favorite dinner. Richie's first car was a 1952 Ford he called "The Love Bandit" (plate F 7193). He worked as a disc jockey at radio station WOW (where he earned $25 a week). He later worked as a cub reporter for the Milwaukee *Journal*.

Richie and his friends, Warren "Potsie" Weber (Anson Williams) and Ralph Malph (Donny

Most) formed a company called "Cheap Work" ("any job for money"). They also formed The Happy Days Band (later called The Velvet Clouds). They attended the same schools and in college were members of the Alpha Tau Omega fraternity (also called Pi Kappa Nu fraternity). Their favorite hangout is Arnold's Drive-In (fast food). Richie was written out of the series when he joined the army and was transferred to Greenland. He had married his girlfriend, Lori Beth Allen (Lynda Goodfriend) and they became the parents of son they named Richie, Jr.; Richie's trademark became the song "Blueberry Hill" (he would frequently sing the first line — "I found my thrill on Blueberry Hill").

See also: Fonzie, Howard and Marion Cunningham, Joanie Cunningham.

938. Rick Blaine, *Casablanca,* ABC, 1955–1956. Played by Charles McGraw.

Richard Blaine, called Rick by the few friends who know him, owns Rick's Café Americain, a saloon and casino in Casablanca (in French Morocco). Rick was born in New York City in 1914 and has a mostly unknown past. In 1935 he ran guns in Ethiopia and in 1937 fought with the Fascists in Spain. Although not a soldier during World War II, he fought with the resistance to thwart German plans. He opened a café in Paris after the war and later retreated to Casablanca. His piano player, Sam (Clarence Muse) has been with him from the start.

Rick stands for right against wrong. Few things impress Rick. When asked why he came to Casablanca he says, "to escape indiscretion in America" (although he also says, "I did it for my health — the waters." Casablanca is in the desert, however; and those indiscretions are not mentioned). Rick likes to run his business his way. He never drinks with customers and at times appears to be his best customer (he says he drinks to ease his nerves). His outward appearance appears to be one of indifference ("I stick my neck out for nobody") but inside he is sentimental and a soft heart — especially when it comes to women. Rick insists that he will not sell his bar at any price and claims "The world is not my problem. I run a saloon" (where he also lives one flight up). Rick has an interest in chess, never makes plans too ahead of time and dislikes disturbances in his bar.

939. Rick Hunter, *Hunter,* NBC, 1984–1991; 2003. Played by Fred Dryer.

Richard Hunter, called Rick, is a detective sergeant with Division 122 of the L.A.P.D. He was born on February 3, 1941, in Los Angeles and 991-

02-2042 is his Social Security number. He first lived at 5405 Ocean Front Drive in Los Angeles then at 1229 Riverside Drive in San Diego (when he became a lieutenant with the Robbery-Homicide Division of the San Diego Police Department in 2003). His telephone number is 619-555-0142 and his police I.D. number is 179.

Rick is the son of a mobster but rejected a life of crime to help people by becoming a cop. He is tough and honest and not afraid to use his gun. When he approaches an uncooperative suspect he warns him — "The worst part of your day is not when I show up but when I come back."

Rick was originally teamed with Dee Dee McCall (Stepfanie Kramer) then Joann Molinski (Darlanne Fluegel) and Christine Novak (Lauren Lane). His L.A. car codes were 1-William-56, 1-William-156 and L-56. In San Diego his car code is 930-Sam. The L.A. Division is also called Central Division, the Parker Division and Metro Division.

See also: Dee Dee McCall.

Ricky Ricardo *see* **Lucy and Ricky Ricardo**

940. Ricky Stratton, *Silver Spoons,* NBC, 1982–1986; Syn., 1986–1988. Played by Ricky Schroder.

Richard Stratton, called Ricky, is the son of Edward Stratton, III, the head of the Eddie Toys Division of Stratton Industries, and his ex-wife, Evelyn. Ricky, who calls himself "The Rickster" (also his computer password), lives at 123 Mockingbird Lane in Shallow Springs on Long Island.

Ricky first attended the Burton Military Academy. He next attended Fuller Jr. High School and finally Buck Minster Fuller High School. Ricky is the editor of the school newspaper, the Fuller *Flash* and uses the same pen his father did when he was in high school. Ricky was also a Muskrat with the Beaver Scouts.

Ricky has a pet frog (Oscar) that he raised from a tadpole. Leave it to Burgers and the Bun on the Run are his hangouts. He worked after school as a waiter at Chicken on a String. He and his father eat out once a week at Rick's Café. When Ricky became older he joined his father's company. He created a board game called "Rock Express" (about getting over obstacles to get to a rock concert). The game didn't sell.

See also: Edward Stratton, Kate Summers.

941. Ricky Wilder, *Camp Wilder,* ABC, 1992–1993. Played by Mary Page Keller.

Ricky Wilder is a young woman who lives at 1115 Fairlawn Drive in Santa Monica, California. She is divorced (from Dean) and the mother of a young daughter (Sophie). Ricky's parents were killed in a car accident and she also cares for her 16-year-old brother (Brody) and 13-year-old sister (Melissa).

Ricky was born in Santa Monica in 1964. As a child she wanted to be a ballerina "but I didn't study, couldn't dance and I was pudgy." In high school Ricky was insecure about her body and refused to take a shower with the other girls after gym until she was the last one. Ricky majored in oceanography in college and dreamed of working with explorer Jacques Costeau aboard his ship, the *Calypso*. But she met Dean, married and moved to Albuquerque, New Mexico, to begin a new life. Shortly after giving birth to Sophie Ricky realized Dean didn't love her. She divorced him and moved back to California.

Ricky also had dreams about becoming a maternity nurse. The urge became strong by the age of 12 and she decided to follow through. She became an emergency room nurse at Santa Monica General Hospital after graduation but soon had her doubts about the job ("Nursing is not what I dreamed it would be so I quit"). She used her college degree to become an education specialist at Sea Land (leading tours and teaching marine biology).

Ricky was not the best student at Santa Monica High. As a result she has a recurring nightmare "about being back in high school, dressed only in my bra and panties and taking a test, then realizing I haven't been to class all year." Ricky is a good mother to Sophie (who has a pet penguin named Rusty) and has opened her home to Brody and Melissa's friends (who has nicknamed their oasis from school "Camp Wilder").

942. Rico Amonte, *10–8: Officers on Duty*, ABC, 2003–2004. Played by Danny Nucci.

Rico Amonte is a rookie deputy with the Los Angeles Sheriff's Department (10-8 is code for sheriffs and deputies who are patrolling the streets). Rico was born in Flatbush, Brooklyn, New York, and grew up in a tough neighborhood. He earned money by participating in "Boxcar Fights" (fighting in abandoned railroad boxcars). Rico was headed for a life of trouble when his brother, an L.A.P.D. detective, changed his life by bringing him to California to become a police officer. Rico is now 28 years old and lives at 46873 Ocean Walk Drive in Venice.

Rico rides with his training partner, Sergeant John Henry Barnes. He believes "bad guys make good cops and good cops make bad guys." Rico cares about people and tries to help them — even when they do not want help. Rico carries a spare gun in his belt and his personal car license plate reads 4CPL 289. He rides in car 789 (plate 186 3592) and 21-Adam is his mobile code. Fontana's Bar is his favorite hangout.

943. Riley Veatch, *M.Y.O.B.*, NBC, 2000. Played by Katharine Towne.

Riley Veatch is a teenage girl who is aware that she is a character on a TV show and comments on and off camera about the situations that arise. She describes her program as "It's the whole fish-out-of-water odd couple, unrequited love combo you get most every night on every channel. So you don't want to watch? That's okay. *Law and Order* is bound to be on somewhere."

Riley is tough, the product of her all too human experiences. She was born in Akron, Ohio, but abandoned by Pearl Brown, her wacky, cult-prone birth mother. Riley was adopted soon after but also lost this mother ("She went crazy in a post office and tried to shoot up the place"). Riley developed acute personal survival instincts, a fierce independence, a distaste for pretense, and an extraordinary ability to sense the needs and desires of others.

At the age of 16 Riley traveled to California to find her only known relative, her mother's sister, Opal Brown (Lauren Graham). Riley is now living with Opal and attends Gossett High School (where Opal is the principal). Riley and Opal are hoping to find Pearl, who is rumored to be with some cult in Finland.

Riley has the ability to manipulate people and get them to do what she wants them to do. Opal is her direct opposite. She lacks Riley's self-confidence and skepticism about people and their motives. Opal has a clear-headed sense of responsibility and a fundamental optimism about life. They are both intelligent but neither can handle loneliness. As a kid Opal had a dog named Mr. Waggs. Even though there is a button on the microwave for popcorn, Opal has a knack for burning it.

944. Rita, *Thieves*, ABC, 2001. Played by Melissa George.

Rita (no last name) is an expert thief who works for the U.S. government — she steals items the government believes were stolen from them.

Rita was born in Australia on May 12, 1976. Rita's father, a pit boss, raised her and she learned her craft (stealing) from the streets. Rita prides herself on her skills and is also a blackjack dealer, computer whiz and weapons expert. She loves to fire a gun ("It gives me a rush") and has several bogus drivers licenses (Michelle Michael, Karen

Paldoni and Sheila Francis; 1150 Lamaria Street, Chicago, Illinois, is listed as her address). Her car license plate reads ADM 396 (later 756 AQU).

Rita is a very beautiful woman who uses her sexuality to help her achieve her goals. She is a vegetarian, takes herbal drugs and gets cranky after drinking coffee. She is meticulous and does things by a set of rules she has established for herself (to ensure that she never gets caught). When Rita dresses in pink it usually means she has a trick up her sleeve. Rita keeps her personal life just that—personal. She is sometimes impatient and likes to take the quickest way out to accomplish a goal (this usually means the use of plastic explosives). Rita is totally professional in everything she does and when she was operating on her own she never stole anything that her victim's couldn't afford to lose.

See also: Johnny Marucci.

945. Rita Lance, *Silk Stalkings*, CBS, 1991–1993; USA, 1993–1995. Played by Mitzi Kapture.

Rita Lee Lance, a stunning girl with a natural flair for investigation, is a sergeant with the Crimes of Passion Unit of the Palm Springs, Florida, Police Department. She and her partner, Chris Lorenzo, investigate high society murders called "Silk Stalkings."

Rita's real last name is Fontana. She was born in Florida in 1965. Her mother died in childbirth and her father, a wealthy businessman, killed himself several years later when he lost millions through bad investments. Rita was adopted and raised by her foster parents, Tom and Sue Lance; she took their last name because it meant so much to her. As a kid Rita enjoyed Mother Goose stories and was fascinated by "Suzy Pratt" detective books. She also enjoyed riding her Victory Flyer tricycle.

Rita, a graduate of Palm Beach High School and Florida State College, now lives at 400 East Palm Drive; 555-4793 is her phone number. Rita likes to pretend she is someone else to acquire information. She also suffers from an embolism in her brain that is located in an area that is difficult to reach and an operation could prove fatal. The swelling of the blood vessel is minor and with medication she can live a normal life. Rita has refused to have the operation, which could kill or paralyze her. "I'll take my chances," she says. "My philosophy is you aren't sick unless you admit you are." Chris is the only other person who knows; she hasn't told her captain, fearing she could be put on medical leave.

Rita loves golf (she and Chris call each other "Sam" after their hero, golfing great "Slammin'"

Sammy Snead). Rita worked with the Vice Squad when she first joined the force. In 1995 she was promoted to lieutenant and given the title Chief of Detectives. Her car code was 1-X-Ray 8.

See also: Chris Lorenzo.

946. Rita Nash, *Whoopi*, NBC, 2003–2004. Played by Elizabeth Regen.

Rita Nash is blonde, beautiful and white but speaks and acts like a stereotyped black "sista" to impress Mavis Rae, the owner of the LaMont Hotel in New York City, and the sister of her boyfriend, Courtney.

Rita was born in Manhattan and realized at an early age she was beautiful. She used her looks to manipulate boys but learned that beauty isn't the answer to everything when she lost the title of "Prom Queen of Lexington High" to a boy; she also attended P.S. 96 grammar school. Courtney doesn't seem to mind Rita's look, but Mavis does and feels Rita is embarrassing. Rita calls Mavis "Mae Rae." Rita works as a technician at the M.R.I. Imaging Center and has a pet ferret named Buddy ("He's not my pet, he's my animal companion"). Rita watches the African-American programs on the UPN network for research and her telephone answering machine message says, "Yo, this is Ree Ree. Holler back. Peace, peace." Rita calls her breasts "The Twins" and Courtney "Boo" and "Boo Boo" (all of which angers Mavis even more).

See also: Courtney Rae, Mavis Rae.

947. Ritchie Petrie, *The Dick Van Dyke Show*, CBS, 1961–1966. Played by Larry Matthews.

Richard Petrie, called Ritchie, is the son of Rob and Laura Petrie, a happily married couple who live at 148 Bonnie Meadow Road in New Rochelle, New York. Ritchie attends New Rochelle Elementary School and has the middle name of Rosebud (Robert Oscar Sam Edward Benjamin Ulysses David; one letter for each name various family members wanted for Rob and Laura's newborn baby).

Ritchie's favorite TV program is *The Uncle Spunky Show* and had two pet ducks (Stanley and Oliver). He greets his father when he comes home from work with lines like "What do you have for me?" (Rob gives him anything—from a paper clip to a rubber band and he is happy). Laura wanted to name Ritchie Robert or Roberta; Rob (Laura or Lawrence); Sally Rogers, Rob's co-worker (Valentino—"I was saving it for a parakeet but you can have it"); Buddy, Rob's co-worker (Exit—"if the kid is an actor his name will be in every theater in the country"); and Mel Cooley, Rob's boss, the producer of *The Alan Brady Show* (Allen, Alan or Allan — all after the show's star; Rob is head writer on the show).

In the series update, *The Dick Van Dyke Show Revisited* (CBS, May 11, 2004), Ritchie is married and now living in his parent's home in New Rochelle (Rob and Laura have relocated to Manhattan).

See also: Alan Brady, Buddy Sorrell, Laura Petrie, Rob Petrie, Sally Rogers.

948. River Tam, *Firefly*, Fox, 2002. Played by Summer Glau.

River Tam is a member of the *Serenity*, a futuristic Firefly class space ship that transverses the galaxy seeking jobs. River is a psychic and a former member of the Academy, a government school that performed unethical experiments on the brain. River was kept at the Academy against her will and is now a fugitive. She escaped with the help of her brother (Simon) and is now sought by the Academy for the potential she has. River found refuge on the *Serenity* after its captain, Malcolm Reynolds, rescued her.

Simon (Sean Mather), who serves as the doctor on the *Serenity*, and River are the children of wealthy parents, Gabriel and Regan Tam. River's psychic abilities are not fully developed. She can read most minds and sometimes annoys people by telling them what is on her mind. River's dress is quite conservative, if not unattractive, compared to ship mate Inara (who dresses provocatively).

See also: Inara Serra, Malcolm Reynolds.

949. Rob Petrie, *The Dick Van Dyke Show*, CBS, 1961–1966. Played by Dick Van Dyke.

Robert Simpson Petrie, called Rob, is the head writer of *The Alan Brady Show*, a mythical variety series. He is married to Laura and is the father of Ritchie. He lives at 148 Bonnie Meadow Road in New Rochelle, New York, in a home that cost him $27,990 (the house number was also given as 485).

Rob was born in Danville, Ohio, and attended Danville High School (where he played the lead in a production of *Romeo and Juliet* opposite his then girlfriend, Janie Layton. He was also called "Rapid Robert, the Devil of Danville High School." Not so much for his reputation with girls but for his fastball as a pitcher). Rob is next said to have joined the army, where as a sergeant, he was stationed at the Camp Crowder Army base in Joplin, Missouri (he is with Company A in some flashbacks; Company E in others). It was at this time that he met his future wife, Laura Meeker,

a beautiful dancer with the U.S.O. (United Serviceman's Organization).

Rob and Laura married while Rob was still in the service and first lived at the camp housing development. It was at this time that he wrote a song about nothing called "Bupkis." After his discharge, Rob and Laura moved to Ohio where Rob worked as a radio disc jockey at station WOFF (where he broke the stay awake record for broadcasting without sleep for 100 hours). He next found work in New York City as the head writer for Alan Brady when he impressed Alan with his comical wit.

Rob has freckles on his back that when connected form an outline of the Liberty Bell. He is allergic to chicken feathers and cats and enjoys cold spaghetti and meatballs for breakfast. His favorite dinner is franks and beans with sauerkraut. Rob wears a size 10D shoe and his wallet has a photo of actress Paula Marshall in it (it came with the wallet and he never removed it).

In the series update, *The Dick Van Dyke Show Revisited* (CBS, May 11, 2004), Rob and Laura have moved to Manhattan. Rob is retired (he hasn't written for Alan Brady since the show was cancelled almost 40 years ago) and Laura now runs a dance studio from their apartment.

See also: Alan Brady, Buddy Sorrell, Laura Petrie, Ritchie Petrie, Sally Rogers.

Robbie Sinclair *see* **Charlene Sinclair**

950. Robert Barone, *Everybody Loves Raymond*, CBS, 1996–2005. Played by Brad Garrett.

Robert Charles Barone is the younger brother of sportswriter Raymond Barone. He is a sergeant (then lieutenant) with the N.Y.P.D. and lives in Lynbrook, New York. He is the son of Frank and Marie Barone and is jealous of Raymond because of all the attention he gets. He also believes everything good happens to Raymond while everything bad happens to him. Robert is afraid of commitment and has trouble with relationships. He is currently married to Amy Louise MacDougall, a sweet girl with an offbeat family. His first wife, Joanna, was a stripper who left him for a man he arrested.

Robert became a police officer in 1967 but found an interest in law enforcement at the age of 11. Robert was the tallest boy in his class (he now stands six feet, eight and one half inches tall). One rainy day Raymond stole Robert's rubber boots and Robert had to walk to school without them. His shoes became rain soaked and he was teased and called "Sasquash." From that moment he vowed to fight crime.

Robert attended Hillcrest High School and St. John's University. He played drums as a kid but had to give them up because of nosebleeds. He took opera lessons for a year but suffered his most embarrassing moment as an infant. His mother wanted a daughter but his father didn't want any more children. To compensate, Marie dressed Robert in a pink dress and pretended he was a little girl. In grammar school Robert wrote the column "The View from Up Here" for the school newspaper. Deep down Robert always wanted to be a dancer (although Frank wanted him to get a job at Carvel so he could get free Fudgie the Whale cakes). As a kid he (and Raymond) had a dog named Shamsky (named after ball player Art Shamsky).

Although Robert puts onions on everything, he most enjoys spare ribs and key lime pie. He has his hair cut at the Hair Barn and he is afraid to eat out because he fears busboys. He separates his Good and Plenty candy into good and plenty (the pink ones are the good; the white ones the plenty because there are more of them). When Robert broke up an illegal rodeo, Nestor, the Happy Bull, gored him in the behind.

Robert won an accommodation at the police department for perfect attendance three years in a row (1994–96). His police car code is Two-Three Sergeant and when he taught traffic school he did so with the help of a dummy called Traffic Cop Timmy. To make extra money Robert sold Castle Door Alarm Systems.

Robert first lived with his parents, then in his own apartment (F). When he married Amy (Monica Horan) he and Amy moved into a new apartment (6). Amy was born in Connecticut and lived with her parents (Hank and Patricia) and her off-the-wall brother (Peter). Amy worked with Debra, Raymond's wife, at a P.R. firm in Manhattan. Although Debra quit when she had her first child (Ally), she and Amy remained friends. It was through Debra that Amy and Robert met.

See also: Ally Barone, Debra Barone, Frank and Marie Barone, Raymond Barone.

951. Robert McCall, *The Equalizer*, CBS, 1985–1989. Played by Edward Woodward.

Robert McCall is a man who believes in an eye for an eye. He is a former operative for a government organization called the Company (also referred to as the Agency). He now helps people facing insurmountable odds.

Robert lives on West 74th Street in New York City (555-4200; later 555-5247 is his phone number). Robert does not charge a fee for his services and he can be reached through a newspaper personal ad column ("Got a problem? Odds Against You? Call The Equalizer. 212-555-

4200"). He drives a 1985 Jaguar (plate 5809 AUG). He feels that after 25 years as an espionage agent, helping people is his way of repaying a debt he owes to humanity.

Robert was born on November 16, 1933, in England. Her served a hitch in the British Army and joined the Company in 1960. It was at this time that he met a woman named Manon Brevard. They had an affair and Manon became pregnant (she gave birth to a daughter named Yvette in 1963). Robert, however, was unaware that he was a father. He met Manon on an assignment and was unaware of Manon's pregnancy when he left. He later married a woman named Kay (they divorced due to his constant dedication to his work). They are the parents of Scott. A younger daughter, Kathy, died 18 months after her birth in 1973 due to a heart problem.

Robert is a vigilante but he is not as ruthless as he was when employed by the Company. He does incorporate tactics he learned over the years but he will try to avoid a violent confrontation if possible. He will only use a gun if he has no other choice.

952. Roberta Young, *Snoops*, ABC, 1999. Played by Paula Jai Parker.

Roberta Young is a beautiful 31-year-old woman who works as a private detective for Glenn Hall, Inc., a Los Angeles–based high tech private investigation agency.

Roberta is very sexy and believes cleavage is a necessary part of the job, especially when she is assigned to go undercover. She has no problem breaking the law and is skilled at picking locks and opening safes. Roberta was born in Los Angeles and is the daughter of wealthy parents. While she was given the best education money could buy and could have pursued any career goal, she chose the life of an investigator for the excitement it offers. Roberta is careless; she acts before she thinks and places her life in jeopardy by taking unnecessary chances. She is reluctant to use a gun (even the stun gun Glenn assigns to each operative) and loves her tube of lipstick — it doubles as a miniature video camera. Roberta is single, looking for a man (but not in a rush to get married). She lives in Apartment K at 73 Donal Road. If the occasion arises, whether at home or in the office, Roberta loves to show off her sexy figure in lingerie.

See also: Glenn Hall, Dana Platt.

953. Robin Kennedy, *Heart of the City*, ABC, 1986–1987. Played by Christina Applegate.

Robin Kennedy is the 16-year-old daughter of

Wes Kennedy, a Los Angeles police detective. Robin is sweet, innocent and the image of the pretty girl next door. That was just months ago before the death of her mother, Susan. Robin holds her father responsible for her mother's death (Susan rushed to the scene of a police shooting, fearing Wes was hurt, and was killed in a crossfire). Robin is now bitter and resentful and has changed her sweet image to one of questionable taste. She shortened her blonde hair, applied heavier makeup and dresses in clothes that make her look like a high priced call girl ("I may look like a tramp, but boys are not getting near me — no way, no chance. I dress to please myself, not some boy").

Robin was born in Los Angeles and lives at 5503 Pacific Way (house number 4607 is seen in the pilot). She attended the Palmer Street Grammar School and is currently a student at West Hollywood High School. She is a B student (despite her drastic change, she has maintained her grades) and is a talented dancer (she takes dancing lessons and appeared as Beauty in a "Beauty and the Beast" rock video for a singer named Radical Conrad). Robin claims "dance is a celebration to make people feel good." Although she is very attractive, Robin says, "I don't think I'm as beautiful as other people see me."

See also: Wes Kennedy.

The Robot (*Lost in Space*) see Dr. Zachary Smith

954. Robot Head 790, *Lexx,* Sci Fi, 2000–2002. Voiced by Jeffrey Hirschfield.

Robot Head 790 is a member of the crew of the *Lexx,* a space ship that is exploring the futuristic world of the Dark Universe. He was actually a robotic drone and was half machine and half organic (organs donated by unwilling humans). He was designated 790 and served in the army of His Divine Shadow, the evil leader of His Divine Order, the governing force in the now extinct Light Universe. Robot 790 controlled the computer that transformed women into love slaves. During the process to transform a cluster lizard into a beautiful woman, a confrontation begins. The lizard is transformed into a woman named Zev Bellringer but the cluster lizard part of her eats the robot's body and places its robotic head in the transformation machine (where it is programmed for love). The blue metallic head is placed on a motorized running board and only has eyes for Zev (790 has animated eyes and a superimposed human mouth). He travels with Kai, Stanley H. Tweedle and Zev on the *Lexx.* According to Zev, "790 is a confused junk head."

Robot Head 790 was first in love with the beautiful Zev and wished to be united with her (he called her "My Love Muffin"). A freak accident, however, smashed 790 into number of pieces. Kai, the undead assassin, rebuilt him and 790 found a new love — Kai. Robot Head 790 calls Kai "My Dead Guy," "My Dead Man" and "My Black Man of Death" (for the black clothes he wears). He would like nothing more than to lose Zev and Stanley so he and Kai can be alone on the *Lexx.* Kai is dead and has feeling for no one. But 790 believes Kai has eyes for Zev and is jealous, fearing Kai will leave him for Zev (790 constantly laments about wanting "My handsome dead man" and realizes Zev is a beautiful woman — "Deep down I am a woman too. I can feel the femininity, the softness, the need to love"). But being only a head 790 can do nothing but professes his love for "My gorgeous dead guy."

See also: Kai, Stanley H. Tweedle, Zev Bellringer.

955. Roc and Eleanor Emerson, *Roc,* Fox, 1991–1994. Played by Charles S. Dubin, Ella Joyce.

Roc Emerson is a man with a dream: to buy a semi-detached house. He is the son of Andrew and Loretta Emerson and lives at 864 Essex Street in Baltimore with his wife Eleanor, widowed father, and brother Joey.

Roc is a garbage man with District 36 of the Department of Sanitation. He currently lives in an attached house and saves every penny he can for his dream house. Roc's newspapers are from the previous day ("I read yesterday's news today") and he furnishes his home with some pretty nice items that he finds on his route. When Roc has to buy something he will only buy it on sale. Roc has to empty 175,214 garbage cans to make $2,000. Eleanor believes he is too frugal and wishes he weren't so cheap (she is trying to get him to do the impossible — buy an item at list price). Eleanor is a nurse at Harbor Hospital (Wing C) and shares Roc's dream (although she is not as cheap or stingy as Roc). *L.A. Law* is Eleanor's favorite TV show and she suffers from a recurring nightmare about being molested as a child by an adult care giver (Roc, like Eleanor, have virtually unknown pasts. Eleanor was often cared for by babysitters while her parents worked; Roc was like all kids — always in trouble even though his father, a railroad porter, tried to provide a decent life for him and Joey). Roc mentioned that he served a hitch in the army after dropping out of high school. In 1993 Eleanor and Roc become the parents of a boy they name Marcus. Roc enjoys coffee on breaks at work at the Depot Café (originally called the Landfill) and for a drink he frequents Charlene's Bar.

956. Roger Collins, *Dark Shadows*, ABC, 1966–1971. Played by Louis Edmonds.

Roger Collins is the brother of Elizabeth Collins Stoddard (Joan Bennett), the matriarch of the Collins family, wealthy shipbuilders in Collinsport, Maine. Roger is divorced from Laura (Diana Millay), and is the son of David (David Henesy).

Roger is tall and very distinguished. He oversees the Collins family holdings (the Collins Cannery) and is totally dedicated to money. While he has considerable power when it comes to business matters, he cannot override Elizabeth's decisions.

Roger resides in the Great Estate in Collinwood. He appears to be aware of the unearthly happenings that occur on the estate but sort of turns his head and pretends they are never really happening. He feels most comfortable standing near the fireplace with a glass of brandy in his hand. Roger is stubborn and rarely takes backtalk from anyone. He does not seem to fear anyone or any situation but resents Elizabeth for taking control of the family and the business—something he desperately wants to call his own.

Laura is another story. Roger and Laura have been divorced for five years when the series begins. She is possibly the only person Roger fears. Her whereabouts is not exactly known but he fears her because she is a Phoenix, a mythical creature that is born again in fire and rises from the ashes to claim the lives of her children. Laura loves David (now nine years old) but lost custody of him because she could not fight the powerful Collins family lawyers. Roger fears she will soon come for David and he is helpless to stop her (this became a recurring story line and Laura did return but failed to reclaim David).

See also: Angelique, Barnabas Collins, Victoria Winters, Willie Loomis.

957. Roland B. Hutton, Jr., *Good Morning, World*, CBS, 1967–1968. Played by Billy DeWolfe.

Roland B. Hutton, Jr., is a wealthy Los Angeles radio station owner. He was born in New York City and became interested in show business at an early age. He hoped to become a legend in his own time and broke into show business when he was a teenager. He performed on the New York vaudeville stage as Billy Jones in 1932. It was at this same time that he met Margaret MacBride, a wealthy society woman, and fell in love. Her family disapproved of actors, so Roland gave up show business to marry money.

Roland is now a widower. He lives in a luxurious home in Beverly Hills (address not given) and can't stand for anything to be broken in the house (which was featured in *Home and Terrace* magazine, pages 9–16). There is so much crystal in the house that Roland lives in the fear of sonic booms. Roland has a bust of himself in the master bedroom and many house rules that guests must follow (for example, number 4: No shoes on white carpets; number 1: No strangers allowed; number 7: No yelling).

Roland is a perfectionist and likes his employees to be as perfect as possible. He is easily exasperated and tends to yell to release tension. His worst employee is Larry Clark, half of the team of Lewis and Clark, early morning disc jockeys. Larry has little respect for Roland and purposely plays songs that annoy him (for example, "Pipati Papa" by Billy and the Bing Bongs. Larry has had to replace the record several times because Roland keeps breaking it).

See also: Dave and Linda Lewis.

958. Rory Gilmore, *Gilmore Girls*, WB, 2000 (current). Played by Alexis Bledel.

Lorelai Leigh Gilmore, called Rory, is the daughter of Lorelai Gilmore, the manager of the Independence Inn in Stars Hollow, Connecticut (she is later the owner of the Dragonfly Inn). Lorelai named her daughter after herself "because I was in the hospital whacked out on demurral and figured that if boys could be named after their father, girls should be named after her mother"). Rory was born on a snowy winters morning in Hartford, Connecticut in 1984. She is 16 years old when the series begins and is the brightness in all the darkness in Lorelai's life (Lorelai considers Rory "low maintenance like a Honda"). Rory and Lorelai are not only mother and daughter but they are best friends. Rory even inherited her mother's addiction to coffee.

When Rory was a child she had a dream of marrying Prince Charming ("Not the Snow White one, the Sleeping Beauty one"). Also at this time, when she learned the tree in the front of her house was a Weeping Willow, she spent hours trying to cheer it up. Rory had a plush chicken (Colonel Clucker) and the nickname "Droopy Draws" (which Lorelai called her after her loose-fitting pants fell to the floor). Rory played a broccoli in her kindergarten play, "A Salute to Vegetables" and learned the seven continents from her Hug-a-World Globe. Rory wears a size six coat (but Lorelai buys her a size eight "in case she grows"). She had a pet hamster named Skippy (whom Lorelai says was vicious—"He laughed at me after he bit me").

Rory likes the color blue, blueberry muffins, sunflowers and Twinkies snack cakes. She loves to read (a trait she inherited from her grandfather) and has a collection of books. She is a brilliant student and dreams of attending Harvard University to study journalism and become a reporter. She has a bulletin board of Harvard related material she calls "The Obsession Board" and a collection of Spice Girls memorabilia. Rory stands five feet, seven inches tall and works at the Independence Inn after school and on special occasions. She carries a book with her everywhere she goes ("It's a habit"). She was voted "Ice Cream Queen" at the Stars Hollow Ice Cream Shoppe and played Anita ("Portrait of a Young Girl Named Anita") is the 2003 Stars Hollow Festival of Living Pictures Festival.

Rory attended Stars Hollow Grammar School then Stars Hollow High School before transferring to Chilton Prep, a prestigious private school 14 miles from her home in Hartford. At Chilton, which was established in 1803, Rory has a 4.0 grade average and writes for the school newspaper, *The Franklin*. She is later senior class vice president and became valedictorian of her graduating class (she scored 740 in verbal and 760 in math on her PSAT test). Rory likes to get her homework done before Saturday night so she can devote time on Sunday to extra credit reports. At this time Lorelai joined the Booster Club to become an active part of Rory's school life.

Rory likes to eat Redi Whip whipped cream from the can and hates the baby pictures of her in the den (Lorelai threatens to show them to guests if Rory refuses to obey her). Rory's first taste for Harvard came at the age of four when Lorelai gave her a Harvard T-shirt (it was too big so Rory used it as a blanket). Rory was accepted to a number of colleges — including Harvard, but chose to attend Yale, which is closer to home and her life with Lorelai and the people of Stars Hollow (Yale is in Hartford, 30 miles from Rory's home). At Yale Rory resides in Durfee Hall (Suite 5). When she finds it difficult to study (too much noise) she finds serenity at her study tree on the campus grounds. Rory is majoring in journalism (now wanting to become a foreign correspondent) and writes for the school newspaper, *The Yale Daily News*.

Rory made her debut in society (to please her grandmother, Emily) at the Daughters of the American Revolution Debutante Ball. At Stars Hollow High School Rory was a member of the German Club; it disbanded when two of its three members quit after seeing the movie *Schindler's List*. Rory's only D grade in school occurred at Chilton (she was a late transfer and a bit behind.

She scored the grade for a report on Shakespeare). Rory delights in receiving gifts of rare first edition books from her grandfather (Richard). At Chilton, when Rory was on the debate team, she spoke 135 words per minute.

See also: Lorelai Gilmore, Paris Geller, Richard and Emily Gilmore.

959. Rory Hennessey, *Eight Simple Rules for Dating My Teenage Daughter*, ABC, 2002–2005. Played by Martin Spanjers.

Rory Joseph Hennessey is the 13-year-old son of sportswriter Paul Hennessey and his wife Cate, a nurse. He lives on Oakdale Street in Michigan with his 16-year-old sister Bridget and 14-year-old sister Kerry. Rory is mischievous and scheming. He loves to eavesdrop on his sisters and tattle on them. He knows how to get out of doing things because he tells his parents what they want to hear. Kerry feels Rory gets all the attention "because he's the boy." Rory attends Liberty Middle School (later Liberty High School) and is a member of the flag football team. He has his own web cast called "Web Master X" (where he wears a gorilla mask and reports on school activities). Rory lives to get his sisters in trouble. He has a tire under his bed ("it's part of my first car") and had a nasty ventriloquist's dummy he called Sheevie.

Rory enjoys going to the pet shop on feeding day to see the snakes being fed mice and started a car washing business wherein he charged $10 a car (he called himself "The Car Wash King").

See also: Bridget Hennessey, Cate Hennessey, Kerry Hennessey, Paul Hennessey.

960. Rose Nylund, *The Golden Girls*, NBC, 1985–1992. Played by Betty White.

Rose Nylund is one of four women over 50 who share a home at 6151 Richmond Street in Miami Beach, Florida. Her housemates are Blanche Devereaux, Dorothy Zbornak and Dorothy's mother, Sophia Petrillo.

Rose, the most naïve of the women, was born in the strange little farming town of St. Olaf, Minnesota, "The Broken Hip Capital of the Midwest" ("We revere our old people and put them on pedestals but they fall off and break bones"). Rose's natural father was Brother Martin, a monk. Her mother was Ingrid, a cook in the monastery. They had an affair but it ended when Ingrid discovered she was pregnant. She quit her job and later died giving birth to Rose. The baby was placed in a basket with hickory-smoked cheese, beefsteaks and crackers and left on the doorstep of the Lindstrom family (who raised Rose; in another episode Rose mentions it was the Gierkeckibiken family). Rose was raised as a Lutheran and heard rumors that her father was a clown in the Ringling Brothers and Barnum & Bailey Circus.

Rose attended St. Olaf's Grammar School, St. Olaf High School, Rockport Community College (where she was a member of the farmer's sorority, the Alpha Yams) and finally St. Paul's Business School. Rose had the following pets: Larry (mouse), Rusty and Jake (dogs), Scruffy (cat) and Lester (a pig who could predict Oscar Award winners by wagging his tail). Rose was struck by lightning ("But only once") and "put these hands into a chicken for a breech birth." People say Rose looks like Wilma Flintstone and Rose is known to do outrageous things (like eating raw cookie dough and running through the sprinklers without a bathing cap). Her mother called her "Twinkle Toes" and she has a teddy bear named Fernando (later called Mr. Longfellow).

Rose's favorite number is 12. She wrote the St. Olaf High School fight song ("Onward St. Olaf") and lost the "Little Miss Olaf Beauty Pageant" 22 years in a row (her talent was rat smelling). Her biggest disappointment was losing the title "Miss Butter Queen of St. Olaf" (her parents groomed her for 16 years. When the big day came she was a finalist but lost when her churn jammed).

Rose married Charlie Nylund, the owner of a tile grouting business, at St. Olaf's Shepherd Church (the St. Olaf wedding march is "The Cuckoo Song," which became famous when movie comedians Stan Laurel and Oliver Hardy used it as their theme song). When Charlie died Rose moved to Florida with her pet cat, Mr. Peepers.

Rose listens to all-talk radio WXBC and works as the production assistant at WSF-TV, Channel 8, for the consumer affairs program, *The Enrique Ross Show*. She is later associate producer of *Wake Up, Miami* (her first job was waitress at the Fountain Rock Coffee Shop, then a counselor at an unnamed grief center). Rose is also a Sunshine Girls Cadet leader and claims she always tells the truth ("I lied only once to get out of class to see a movie. I'm sorry I did because it must have been the day they taught everything — which explains why I am so dense").

See also: Blanche Devereaux, Dorothy Zbornak, Sophia Petrillo.

Roseanne Conner *see* **Dan and Roseanne Conner**

961. Rosie O'Neill, *The Trials of Rosie O'Neill*, CBS, 1990–1992. Played by Sharon Gless.

Fiona Rose O'Neill, called Rosie, is 43 years old and divorced from Patrick (who ran off with a younger woman named Bridget). She is the daughter of Bill and Charlotte O'Neill and was born in Waco, Texas. Rosie attended Brownie camp when she was in the fourth grade and is a graduate of Waco High School (where she liked history, gym and lunch. "I hated algebra"). She was sophomore class president, captain of the swimming and diving teams and, as she called herself "a porker." Rosie believed she had acting abilities and landed the lead role in the school production of *Carousel* (the school paper review read: "Rosie O'Neill in a triple threat on stage. She can't act, can't sing and can't dance"). Rosie graduated fifth in her class at Wellesley College (where she acquired her law degree). She worked for several lawyers over the course of 16 years before joining Patrick in their own practice in Beverly Hills. After the divorce Rosie left the law firm and took a job with the Central Felonies Division of the Los Angeles County Public Defender's Office. In Beverly Hills Rosie would help her rich clients gets richer. She now feels she can do something she always wanted to do — help people who actually need her.

Rosie lost her Beverly Hills home to Patrick in the divorce settlement. She now lives in Santa Monica (house number 418; 555-2363 is her phone number) and drives a Mercedes. Rosie is an idealist and says, "My real first name is Fiona but it sounds too soft and dreamy, like a fairy tale princess. I think my mother must have been expecting something else." Rosie wears a perfume called Temptation and her co-workers say that when she wears red "it washes her out."

Rosie has doubts about her figure and would like to improve things. Her remarks were quite unexpected for the time: "I'm thinking of having my tits done. I may not want them any bigger they're a nice size already. I just thought maybe I'll have them fluffed up a bit." Rosie is now dedicated to seeking justice for her clients. She will do what it takes (even bend the law) to come to a satisfactory conclusion. Rosie's best friend since the second grade has been Victoria Lindman, a now famous Broadway star. Tyne Daly played the role (reuniting her with Sharon, her former co-star on *Cagney and Lacey*).

962. Ross Geller, *Friends*, NBC, 1994–2004. Played by David Schwimmer.

Ross Geller was born on Long Island in New York on October 8. He is the son of Jack and Judy Geller and has a younger sister (Monica). Ross is considered a medical marvel because doctors had diagnosed Judy with an inability to conceive. As children he and Monica would compete against each other for "The Geller Award" (a troll doll nailed to a piece of wood). Ross attended Lincoln High School (where he wore a jacket that said "Geology Rocks" and had an affair with Anita Altman, the 50-year-old school librarian). He is intensely interested in science and as a teenager had an idea for a comic book called "Science Boy" (who had a superhuman thirst for knowledge). Ross was also fascinated by dinosaurs and majored in anthropology in college. He also played drums and keyboard and composed "wordless sound poems" (music with sound effects; each song ended with an explosion).

Ross now lives in Manhattan's West Village. He is a paleontologist with the Museum of Natural History (also called the Museum of Prehistoric History). He is afraid of spiders and is fascinated with aviator Amelia Earhart (he is determined to find out what happened to her). Ross had a pet monkey (Marcel) and his beeper number is 555-JIMBO.

Ross hangs out with Monica and friends Joey, Rachel, Chandler and Phoebe at a coffee shop called Central Perk. Ross is divorced. He was married to Carol but lost her to her lesbian lover (Susan). He has a son (Ben) by Carol and after an affair with Rachel became the father of her daughter, Emma. Ross later teaches paleontology at New York University and hates ice cream.

See also: Chandler Bing, Joey Tribbiani, Monica Geller, Phoebe Buffay, Rachel Greene.

963. Roxie King, *Sabrina, the Teenage Witch*, WB, 2000–2003. Played by Soleil Moon Frye.

This entry also contains information on Morgan Cavanaugh (Elisa Donovan), Roxie's friend and roommate. Roxie and Morgan are students at Adams College in Westbridge, Mass. They are friends with Sabrina Spellman (the teenage witch) and live with her at 133 Collins Road.

Roxie. Roxie is a very beautiful girl who never jokes, never giggles and is very concerned about helping people and saving the environment. Roxie is a sociology major and works at the college radio station (WAC, 98.9 FM). Sabrina and Roxie were co-hosts of the call-in show *Chick Chat*; Roxie later hosts her own program, *The Roxie King Show*. Roxie is embarrassed by the fact that she has a tattoo on her behind that reads "I Love Hanson" (in high school Roxie had a crush on the music group).

Morgan. Morgan is pretty but dense and self-absorbed (she believes, for example, that a musical B-flat is a bra size). She has a shallow exterior (and, according to Roxie, "A shallow interior") and is majoring in fashion design. Morgan does

have a flair for fashion and feels she is known for her fashion sense and great hair. She knows women are hard for men to understand "because we're a mystery." Morgan started a clothing line called Morgan Ware and claims that her only other talent is curling her eye lashes in a moving car. Although she feels she needs to find a man to pamper her, she did work for a time as a waitress at Hilda's Coffee House. Sabrina, Roxie and Morgan eat at Eve's Diner and were in the all-girl band Gal Palz.

See also: Sabrina Spellman.

Roy Bean *see* **Judge Roy Bean**

Rudy Huxtable *see* **Vanessa Huxtable**

964. Rupert Giles, *Buffy the Vampire Slayer*, WB, 1997–2001; UPN, 2001–2003. Played by Anthony Stewart Head.

Rupert Giles is a Watcher, a specially chosen individual who helps a slayer (like Buffy Summers) defeat whatever evil a Hellmouth dispenses (a Hellmouth is a mysterious portal that attracts evil).

Rupert's father and grandfather were Watchers, members of a secret society that is based in England. The society trains men and women to protect Chosen Ones (Slayers) through their knowledge of demons and proficiency with weapons. Rupert was born in England and is a graduate of Oxford University. He was working at the British Museum when he was chosen to protect Buffy Summers and guide her as she takes on the abilities of a Slayer. He now works as the librarian at Buffy's school (Sunnydale High) to cover his activities as a Watcher (the library also provides the perfect meeting place for Buffy and her assistants, Willow, Xander and Cordelia). Rupert later moved his base of operations to the Magic Box, a store at 1524 Maple Court that sold items dealing with the occult. Rupert can speak five languages and with the aid of the prophecies of ancient books and writings, he is able to defeat evil (his most important book is the *Codex*, a text of prophecies concerning the Slayer).

See also: Angel, Buffy Summers, Cordelia Chase, Dawn Summers, Willow Rosenberg, Xander Harris.

965. Ruthie Camden, *7th Heaven*, WB, 1996 (current). Played by Mackenzie Rosman.

Ruth Camden, called Ruthie, is the youngest daughter of Eric and Annie Camden, a Protestant minister and his wife, who live in Glen Oak, California. Ruthie was born in Glen Oak and has six siblings (Matt, Mary, Simon, Lucy and twins Sam and David). She is a pint sized snoop — "Everything that happens in this house is my business."

Ruthie is five years old when the series begins. She wanted to be an astronaut and live on the moon "because the Earth bores me." She attends the Eleanor Roosevelt School (a private institution that has its own stables; Ruthie has a horse named Ed). Ruthie shares a bedroom with Lucy and her side of the room reflects her fascination with Hello, Kitty dolls and posters ("Hello, Kitty is very important to me," she says). Ruthie has a security blanket (Blankey) and two favorite dolls (Amy and Zin Zin; Amy is lactose intolerant; Zin Zin is allergic to strawberries). Ruthie likes to ride bikes, write stories and drink orange soda; lasagna is her favorite dinner. She had an imaginary friend (Hooey) and *Xena: Warrior Princess* and the mythical *Snappy the Stegosaurus* are her favorite TV shows. Ruthie won her second grade art pageant with "A Camden Nose" (a totem pole of clay noses). When Ruthie feels guilty about something she becomes very unlady like and burps. Every Christmas Ruthie performs in the Glen Oak church's holiday pageant and always gets nervous — "I get dinosaurs in my stomach." Ruthie helps her mother care for the twins and held a job delivering newspapers for the *Gazette*. As a young girl Ruthie's favorite activity was getting her brother, Simon, into trouble. Ruthie later attends the Walter Reed School (where she is a straight A student) and earns money babysitting.

See also: Eric and Annie Camden, Lucy Camden, Mary Camden, Matt Camden.

966. Ryan Malloy, *Unhappily Ever After*, WB, 1995–1999. Played by Kevin Connolly.

This entry also contains information on Ryan's younger brother Ross (Justin Berfield). Ryan and Ross are the sons of Jack and Jennie Malloy. They have a voluptuous sister named Tiffany and according to Jack, Tiffany is the only reason why "The WB hasn't cancelled us long ago." The family resides at 30220 Oak Avenue in Van Nuys, California.

Ryan is rather naive and easily taken advantage of. He is an extremely poor student at Priddy High (although Howe High can be seen in the background). His average grade is F (which he believes stands for phenomenal). He is totally disorganized, easily confused and believes he is a loser when it comes to the opposite sex ("Girls find me completely repulsive"). He never has a date on Saturday nights and watches *Only the Lonely Late Night Theater* on TV.

Ryan works on occasion in the school's cafeteria. He tried to make extra money by selling sexy images of Tiffany over the Internet in a website called "Cyber Sex Tiffany" (which could be accessed at *www.tiffanymalloy.com*). Ryan appeared with Tiffany on the TV game show *Smart and Stupid Siblings* (where Ryan's ignorance actually won them the championship). Ryan also became a superhero of sorts (he thought he was) when he hid in a metal garbage can during a lightning storm and was struck by lightning.

Ross is totally neglected by the family. When Jennie abandoned the family Ross took over the role of mother (cooking, cleaning and being referred to as "Mom"). Tiffany calls Ross "a sad little man." He is constantly degraded and Jack does little or nothing for him (he feels ignoring him will toughen him up). Ross has a pet turtle (Skippy) and claims to know "the secret to attract chicks" (he washes his dirty bike with his shirt off). Although he takes abuse from the family, he has a fantasy — "To be hugged by my math teacher, 38 triple D Miss Bushnick."

See also: Jack Malloy, Jennie Malloy, Tiffany Malloy.

Sable *see* **Nicholas Flemming**

967. Sabrina Duncan, *Charlie's Angels*, ABC, 1976–1978. Played by Kate Jackson.

Sabrina Duncan is a graduate of the Los Angeles Police Academy. She was assigned to Division 28 but writing parking tickets is not exactly what she wanted. She wanted to be a street cop and fight crime. When the opportunity arose for her to find the life she wanted she quit the force and became an Angel — a detective for Charlie Townsend, the never-seen owner of Townsend Investigations in Los Angeles. Sabrina works with Jill Monroe and Kelly Garrett.

Sabrina, called "Bree" by Jill and Kelly is the thinker of the group, the one who usually comes up with the plans the Angels follow during a case. Sabrina is loyal and cares about people, but is sometimes too uptight. She promises to loosen up and become carefree because "I've got a guardian angel who keeps an eye on me."

Sabrina is an expert at fingerprint dusting and appreciates law officers who go by the book although she says, "So do I, but I use a different book" when she does things her way. Sabrina is prim and proper and always a lady, always stylishly dressed and most always receives the glamorous undercover assignments. She is also the only Angel who admits to having a fault — "We're the biggest chauvinists of them all. Who says the murderer can't be a woman?" Sabrina was also the only Angel who was married (to Bill Duncan) and divorced. Sabrina left at the end of the second season to marry for a second time (Charlie mentions that Sabrina is expecting a baby "and is quite thrilled about the whole thing"). Sabrina was replaced by Kris Monroe and was the only Angel never to be seen in a bikini or swimsuit.

See also: Charlie Townsend, Jill Monroe, Julie Rogers, Kelly Garrett, Kris Monroe, Tiffany Welles.

968. Sabrina Spellman, *Sabrina, the Teenage Witch*, ABC, 1996–2000; WB, 2000–2003. Played by Melissa Joan Hart.

Sabrina Spellman is a beautiful 16-year-old witch who is the daughter of a mortal mother (Diane Becker) and a warlock father (Edward Spellman). She lives at 133 Collins Road in Westbridge, Massachusetts, with her aunts Hilda and Zelda Spellman. Hilda and Zelda have been assigned by the Witch's Counsel to teach Sabrina the art of witchcraft (her mother is an archeologist on assignment in Peru; her father's duties in the Other Realm Foreign Service prevent him from caring for Sabrina).

Sabrina learns how to cast spells from the book *The Discovery of Magic*. She is forbidden to use her powers for profit, turn back time or conjure up pancakes (if a Spellman eats a pancake it becomes addictive). Levitation is the first power Sabrina learned and every 25 years she must have a magic tune-up. When she has to cook, she uses *The Magical Meals Cookbook*.

Sabrina is ticklish behind the ears, uses strawberry swirl lip-gloss and has the Other Realm (the home of witches) computer password "Sabrina is Hot." Each member of the Spellman family has an evil twin; Sabrina's is Katrina, an alluring blonde (also played by Melissa Joan Hart) who is as devious as Sabrina is good. Sabrina's catch phrase is "Woo Who" (which she says when something excites her).

Sabrina first attended Westbridge High School. She wrote for the school newspaper, *The Lantern*, and The Slicery (a pizza parlor) is her favorite hangout. Her first job was "The Lovely Assistant" to Magic Jolly at the World of Wonder. She then worked as a "pizza pie maker" at The Slicery, waitress as the Pork on a Fork, and through the Other Realm Employment Agency, a Sandman ("I put people in my neighborhood to sleep"). On her 18th birthday (a senior in high school) she became a waitress at The Coffee Shop (later called Hilda's Coffee House when her aunt becomes the owner).

With an interest in becoming a writer, Sabrina enrolled in Adams College as a journalist major. It was here that she befriended fellow students Roxie King and Morgan Cavanaugh and found a job as a writer for the school newspaper, *The Adams Advocate*, then as an apprentice on *The Boston Citizen*. Sabrina next became a writer for *Scorch*, a music industry magazine (2002) and a year later quit to become a free-lance writer (at which time the series ended). Her hangout at this time was Eve's Diner.

Sabrina's first love, Harvey Kinkel (Nate Richert) was actually her one true love. They dated in high school but drifted apart after graduation. He was the only mortal who knew Sabrina was a witch (accidentally caught her performing magic but promised and did keep her secret). She next fell for Josh (David Lissauer), a reporter on the *Citizen*. When he is transferred, Sabrina meets Aaron Jacobs (Dylan Neal), a band promoter who proposed marriage. Sabrina accepted but had doubts, especially when Harvey came back into her life. Sabrina's wedding day saw Sabrina realizing Harvey was her true love and returning to him. Aaron understood.

Sabrina produced a horror film for school called *The Blood of Mindy Adelman* and was co-host of *Chick Chat*, Roxie's call-in radio program on the college radio station (WAC, 98.9 FM). Sabrina wore jersey 35 as a member of the Marauders (her high school basketball team) and received her witch's license on her 17th birthday. She was also one of the Gal Palz, a band Sabrina formed with Roxie and Morgan for the TV show *National Superstars*.

See also: Amanda Wickham, Roxie King, Salem Saberhagen, Zelda Spellman.

969. Salem Saberhagen, *Sabrina, the Teenage Witch*, ABC, 1996–2000; WB, 2000–2003. Voiced by Nick Bakay.

Salem Saberhagen was once a powerful warlock who not only dreamed of taking over the world but he actually acted upon it. Salem was punished when his superiors, the Witch's Council, discovered his plan. He was sentenced to serve 100 years as a black American short hair cat.

Salem was turned into a cat in 1966 and is cared for by Hilda and Zelda Spellman, witch sisters who live at 133 Collins Road in Westbridge, Massachusetts, with their niece Sabrina. Hilda was a follower of Salem's preaching and in punishment she was sentenced to care for him.

"The sound of the can opener is the only thing that truly makes me feel alive," says Salem. His weakness is tassels and his favorite TV show is

V.I.P. starring Pamela Anderson. He craves squid and likes chocolate syrup in his bowl of milk (although he also takes Metamucil, a laxative, in his iced tea). At times yesterday's leftovers are today's lunch for Salem. When Salem is upset he eats "but when I'm happy I eat." The song "What's It All About, Alfie" makes Salem cry and his bedtime is 8:30 P.M. Salem attended the Other Realm High School and cast a spell that accidentially made the world forget a holiday called Bobeck. He was ostracized for eating a rat in public and uses Zelda's computer to get into chat rooms (where he pretends to be a woman). It pains Salem to be sincere and his one joy in life appears to be helping Sabrina, the teenage witch, solve her problems. Salem is also a coward and will run and hide at the first sign of trouble.

See also: Amanda Wickham, Sabrina Spellman, Zelda Spellman.

970. Sally Monroe, *Fly by Night,* CBS, 1991. Played by Shannon Tweed.

Sally Monroe is an enterprising young woman who owns Slick Air, a one-plane airline based at the Ellis Airport in Canada. Her flyer's read: "Slick Air. Non-stop daily service from Vancouver, Canada, and connecting you to the world. Private luxury charters. Highly trained security specialists. First in personal service. Call toll free—1-604-555-4567. Telex: 346-SLIC."

Sally, nicknamed Slick, was born in Alberta, Canada. She grew up as a normal child but dreamed about flying a plane one day. As Sally grew her dreamed seemed less likely to happen and she developed an interest in fashion and makeup. After graduating from high school Sally acquired a job at the Fancy Lady Beauty Salon. Sally seemed content. Then one day a Lear jet made an emergency landing just outside the shop's front window. Sally was green with envy as her childhood dreams began to resurface. She quit her job and with only $64 to her name applied for a position as a stewardess with Air Canada. It was not what she really wanted, but at least she was flying. Three years later an opportunity arose for Sally to buy a used cargo plane (a B-27 that transported zoo animals). Sally cons investors into helping her start Slick Air and hires an ex-Vietnam vet (Mack Sheppard) as her pilot.

Sally lives in a warehouse loft (number 283) at 1755 Vasser Road in Vancouver, British Columbia (she hides her spare key above the doorjamb). Sally earned her nickname of Slick by pulling off wild schemes that turned her failures into successes. Her car license plate reads SLICK-1 and 485 GKFT is her plane's I.D. number (the plane can handle 30 passengers). The Federal Trade Development Bank holds the mortgage on the plane and Sally's favorite hangout is the Bomber's Bar.

971. Sally Rogers, *The Dick Van Dyke Show,* CBS, 1961–1966. Played by Rose Marie.

Sally Rogers is one of three comedy writers who compose sketches for the mythical *Alan Brady Show* (Rob Petrie is the head writer; Buddy Sorrell a co-writer). Sally is a graduate of Herbert Hoover High School and worked as a writer for *The Milton Berle Show* before joining Alan's staff. Sally uses her quick wit and sense of humor to hide her loneliness. She is single and looking for (but never finding) Mr. Right. She has an on-and-off romance with her mother-dominated boyfriend Herman Glimshire (also called Woodrow Glimshire) and performs with Buddy as the variety act Gilbert and Solomon on weekends at Herbie's Hiawatha Lodge.

Sally wears a size 6½ shoe and accessorizes with a hair bow and a pearl necklace. Her pet cat, Mr. Henderson, is sometimes the only "person" she can talk to when she is sad. In the series update, *The Dick Van Dyke Show Revisited* (CBS, May 11, 2004), Sally is retired and living in Manhattan with her husband, Herman Glimshire.

See also: Alan Brady, Buddy Sorrell, Laura Petrie, Ritchie Petrie, Rob Petrie.

972. Sally Solomon, *Third Rock from the Sun,* NBC, 1996–2001. Played by Kristen Johnston.

On orders from the Big Giant Head, ruler of a world called the Home Planet, four aliens are dispatched over three billion galaxies to study life on Earth. They take up residence at 417 Pensdale Drive in Rutherford, Ohio. Here the Security Officer becomes Sally Solomon. Dick Solomon becomes her supervisor. The Transmitter becomes Harry and the Information Officer is Tommy (all posing as her brothers).

Sally is a beautiful woman who is actually a male on the Home Planet. One of the aliens had to become a woman to study human female behavior "and I lost," says Sally. While Sally possesses a degree in interstellar exploration, she has a difficult time being a woman ("I can't adjust to mood swings"). She calls her breasts "The Girls, Monique and Cindy." She also felt she had a great body and others should see it. She volunteered to pose nude for *Playboy* magazine's "Co-Ed's of the Midwest" issue "but I was rejected for being too old."

Sally is a lieutenant on her home world. She has a superior brain, the ability to digest glass but is untidy at home (leaves her clothes all over the house). Sally uses Lemon Pledge on her furniture and hates "chick flicks." She has a "pet" tomato plant (Jeremy) and started her own business (Sally's Actual Salon, a Real Business) as a tax dodge that was soon shut down. Sally also worked as a fact checker; the weather girl (Sally Storm) on WRTF-TV; and as a consultant at Bower and Stein, Inc., a human resources company.

Sally dated police officer Don Leslie Orville (Wayne Knight). He bowls on a team called the Three Amigos, takes sick days "to catch up on my soaps" and puts money into expired parking meters so he doesn't have to do the paperwork. The last episode finds Sally being transferred back to the Home Planet.

See also: Dick Solomon, Harry Solomon, Tommy Solomon.

973. Sam, *Richard Diamond, Private Detective*, CBS, 1957–1959. Played by Mary Tyler Moore, Roxanne Brooks.

Sam is a mysterious but beautiful girl who operates the Hi Fi Answering Service in New York City. Sam (real name Samantha) is never fully seen. She is the assistant to Richard Diamond, a rugged private detective. Richard has never seen Sam—"The only thing I know about her is what she tells me—and that ain't much." Samuel, as Richard sometimes calls her, has a deep, sexy voice. She is situated in a dimly lit room (presumably in Manhattan) near a switchboard that is designed to accentuate her shapely legs and well-developed chest. Sam's face is never clearly seen (always in a shadow). She wears tight blouses and sweaters and slit skirts or dresses raised just enough to show a bit of thigh. She wears the then famous "torpedo bra" (38B) and size ten stockings, medium length. When Roxanne Brooks took over the role, a bit more of Sam was seen. She still had the shapely legs, sexy voice and large bosom but several quick, better-lit scenes revealed she was a brunette, definitely gorgeous and wore a headset.

Sam answers Richard's office calls on the fourth ring. When she calls Richard she says, "It's me, Mr. D." Richard concludes his conversations with her with "As usual, Samuel, thank you." Richard also receives clients from Sam—"Richard, I have a friend who needs help—a female friend." Murray Hill 4-9099 was Sam's answering service number when Mary Tyler Moore played the role; OL4-1654 when Roxanne Brooks became Sam.

See also: Richard Diamond.

974. Sam Beckett, *Quantum Leap*, NBC, 1989–1993. Played by Scott Bakula.

Samuel Beckett is the son of John and Thelma Beckett. He was born on a farm in Elkridge, Indiana, on August 8, 1953, at 12:30 P.M. He became interested in science at an early age. At the age of nine, Sam, as he is called, saw a Tarzan movie and became fascinated by Tarzan swinging from vine to vine. He rigged his own homemade vine from the barn roof, attempted to swing and failed. As a result he became afraid of heights.

Sam is a graduate of Elkridge High School and M.I.T. (where he acquired a degree in quantum physics). Sam's writings won him a Noble Peace Prize and was called "The next Einstein." One of Sam's theories was the possibility of time travel. He received a government grant to work on a project called Quantum Leap (located in a secret lab 30 miles outside the town of Destiny County, New Mexico). Sam's progress is developing normally until the government threatens to cut off funding. To save the project, Sam steps into the unit's acceleration chamber and vanishes. He is sent in time and can travel (leap) only within 30 years of his own lifetime. A system malfunction traps Sam in time—where he is destined to remain until he can be retrieved. Sam now "bounces around in time" and assumes the identities of people he has never known to correct a mistake they made and set history straight. He receives help from Al Calavicci, a project observer who appears in a holographic image. Only Sam, some dogs, children and mentally unstable people can also see Al. Sam's computer (Ziggy) monitor's his adventures in time. Al carries a slightly defective Ziggy as his hand-held link to the computer when he appears to Sam.

The episode of November 10, 1992 ("Deliver Us from Evil, March 19, 1966"), relates the reason why Sam believes he has been sent back in time. In 1966 he encounters Alia, a futuristic time traveler and her hologram, Zoey. Alia takes orders from an artificial intelligence (Lafus) that controls her assignments. Alia, however, is evil and Sam's direct opposite. Her assignments are to destroy people's lives, not save them (as Sam does). But for Sam to kill (or she to kill him) would mean they would both destroy each other. Sam concludes that he is trapped in time to stop Alia by fixing what she creates (Alia believes she has to stop Sam from changing the fates she created).

In the last episode, "Mirror Image, August 8, 1953," Sam leaps into himself. He never returned home. Sam built Quantum Leap "to make the world a better place; to make right what was once wrong."

See also: Al Calavicci.

975. Sam Buckhart, *Law of the Plainsman*, NBC, 1959–1960. Played by Michael Ansara.

Sam Buckhart is a Harvard-educated Apache Indian who works as a U.S. Marshal in the territory of New Mexico during the 1880s.

Sam Buckhart is the name given to a young brave by a U.S. Army captain. Sam was born and raised on the Apache Indian reservation in New Mexico. He grew up as every Native American at the time, struggling to survive and hating the white man for their unfair treatment of them. When Sam was 14 years old Fate moved its giant hand. During a battle between the Apache and the cavalry, the brave encountered a wounded army captain. Instead of killing the captain the brave befriended him and summoned help. The captain and the brave (now named Sam Buckhart) soon became blood brothers. Two years later, after the captain is killed in an Indian ambush, Sam inherits a great deal of money — money that enables him to attend Harvard University (as once did the captain). Wishing to help his people, Sam decides to become a law enforcer upon graduation.

Sam's job is not an easy one. He is hated because he is an Indian doing a white man's job. He encounters numerous prejudices as he tries to perform his job. Sam is based in the town of Santa Fe, New Mexico, and he has a ward, Tess Logan (Gina Gillespie), a very pretty seven-year-old girl he rescued from a wagon train massacre. Sam shows no signs of prejudice. He sees no color line if he has to pursue a wanted Indian. He is fair and will not kill unless he has no other choice. Sam is fast with his gun but more apt with his fists. He has sworn to uphold the Constitution of the United States and he hopes to ease the tension between the white man and the Indian.

976. Sam Malone, *Cheers*, NBC, 1982–1993. Played by Ted Danson.

Samuel Malone, called Sam, is the owner of Cheers, a bar located at 112½ Beacon Street in Boston. He purchased the bar from Gus O'Malley in 1976. In 1987 when Sam became bored with the bar he sold it to the Lillian Corporation and with the money bought a ketch to sail around the world. The ketch sank shortly after and stranded him on an uncharted atoll he called "No Brains Atoll" (for selling the bar that he now missed). He eventually purchases back the bar (for 85 cents) when the corporation becomes involved in a scandal and wanted noting to do with Cheers.

Sam was born in Boston and wore jersey 16 as a relief pitcher for the Boston Red Sox. He was nicknamed "Mayday" and when his career began to falter he turned to drink. Alcoholism eventu-

ally cost him his reputation and his career in baseball. It was during this time that he found a bottle cap on the field that became his good luck charm. It was also at this time that he bought Cheers (although drinking when he purchased it, he did manage to clean up his act and now runs a respectable establishment).

Sam attended Boston Prep School and is a graduate of Boston University. He is gruff in his tone of voice but is actually a kind-hearted individual who will help any friend in need. Sam had an eye for the ladies but most of his romantic escapades revolved around Diane Chambers, his prim and proper bar maid (they had planned to marry but a wedding never occurred. See Diane Chambers for more information). Sam recalled that he first noticed the difference between men and women when he was in the sixth grade. He has been a womanizer ever since. He has a little black book and feels he has "the look" that attracts women.

Sam appeared on TV in commercials for Field's Beer and worked as a substitute sportscaster at Wrigley Field. He has a dream of opening a waterfront bar called Sam's Place. While he is generous with his money Sam is also eager to make a buck. He pooled resources and joined with bar patrons Norm Peterson and Cliff Claven to open the ill-fated Tan 'n' Wash (a tanning salon and coin-operated laundry).

See also: Carla LeBec, Cliff Claven, Diane Chambers, Ernie Pantusso, Norm Peterson, Rebecca Howe, Woody Boyd.

977. Samantha and Patti Russell, *My Sister Sam*, CBS, 1986–1988. Played by Pam Dawber (Samantha), Rebecca Schaeffer (Patti).

Samantha and Patricia Russell are sisters who share Apartment 5C at 1345 Benchley Street in San Francisco (555-6687 is their phone number).

Samantha, called Sam, and Patricia, nicknamed Patti, were born in Oregon (Sam on April 6, 1957; Patti on October 27, 1970). Sam's fascination for photography came at an early age when she received an instamatic camera for Christmas. She kept a photo journal of her activities and eventually turned that fascination into a career. Sam is a graduate of Bennett High School. She was a straight A student (with the exception of a C-minus in Spanish) and was a member of the photography club. After graduating from Oregon State University Sam moved to San Francisco to begin her own business (Russell Scouts Photography). Shortly after, her parents are killed in a car accident. Fourteen-year-old Patti is sent to live with her Uncle Bob and Aunt Elsie. Patti, however, yearned to live with Sam and two years later became her roommate and responsibility.

Patti, now 16, attends Millard Fillmore High School. She is bright and cheery but not as academically motivated as Sam. She has found an interest in fashion, makeup and boys and those take priority over schoolwork. Patti is very much like Sam in that she is also very caring. Patti and Sam respect each other and that is what makes their relationship work. Patti is enthusiastic about everything and her energy seems never ending (sometimes exhausting Sam, who can't keep up with her). She is a bit untidy and often thinks life is unfair when she is sick on a weekend rather than a school day. She likes movies but not old ones "because there's no reality."

Sam has high hopes of becoming a famous photographer. She has made it her goal to make the cover of a national magazine before she turns 30 (her biggest disappointment occurred when *Epicure* magazine rejected her "Table Settings" photo for its cover). She would also like to become an independent artist — "no deadlines and no clients telling you what to do." Sam is very organized (she alphabetizes her fruit juices and arranges her shoes so the toes point north). This upsets Patti who is just the opposite (she's not a slob, just untidy). Patti and Sam attempted an ill fated business venture to market decorated sweatshirts at the Serendipity Boutique.

978. Samantha Carter, *Stargate SG-1,* Sci Fi, 1997 (current). Played by Amanda Tapping.

Samantha Carter is a lieutenant colonel (later major) in the U.S. Air Force who works as the second-in-command (under Jack O'Neill) at Stargate Command in Colorado (see Jack O'Neill for details).

Samantha is the only woman on Jack's team. She is an expert astrophysicist and followed in her father's footsteps and joined the air force (her father, Jacob, was a general; her mother was killed in a car accident when Samantha was very young). While Samantha is a very sexy and beautiful woman, she has an almost non-existent social life as all her energies are devoted to the Stargate program. Samantha (and fellow team mate Daniel Jackson) was responsible for deciphering the Stargate address system when the first Stargate was found in Creek Mountain. She also created the computer that activates the Stargate and allows travel to other planets via its dimensional portal.

Samantha is overly brave (often puts her life on the line for others) and extremely loyal to her team. She is intelligent and apparently the Earth's leading authority on the Stargate. She also has an impressive combat record (especially her 100 hours of air missions during the Persian Gulf War in 1991) and devoted two years of her life (1994–96) at the Pentagon to make the Stargate program a reality.

See also: Daniel Jackson, Jack O'Neill, Teal'c.

979. Samantha Jones, *Sex and the City,* HBO, 1998–2004. Played by Kim Cattrall.

Samantha Jones is a beautiful woman who believes in being seductive and having a good time. She demands the best in whatever she does and whomever she chooses to date.

Samantha is a public relations consultant who dresses to draw attention to herself. She knows she has the look and strives to make a lasting impression. Her wardrobe is anything that can make her look sexy — from deeply plunging, cleavage revealing necklines, to provocative skirts and dresses. For that extra special look, Samantha wears fake nipples to impress people. However, it is at night when Samantha makes the bar scene, that she shines in dazzling outfits that turn not only the heads of men — but women also. Samantha is, in the simplest of terms, a sex kitten. She is very promiscuous and looks only to be pleased sexually (she experimented with making love to another woman but found she couldn't handle it when her lover wanted a commitment and more intimacy. Samantha knew she couldn't commit and left her). Samantha knows what she wants and radiates confidence in everything she does. She lives in a luxurious apartment (45) and enjoyed posing nude for a photographic session. Samantha enjoys a drink (a Cosmopolitan) with her close friends, Carrie, Miranda and Charlotte.

See also: Carrie Bradshaw, Charlotte York, Miranda Hobbes.

980. Samantha Kanisky, *Gimme a Break,* NBC, 1981–1987. Played by Lara Jill Miller.

Samantha Kanisky is the youngest daughter of Carl and Margaret Kanisky. Carl is the police chief of Glen Lawn, California; Margaret died when Samantha was a toddler. She lives at 2938 Maple Drive with her sisters Katie and Julie and their live-in housekeeper, Nell Harper.

Samantha is the youngest of the girls and the closest to Nell (she looks upon her as a substitute mother). Samantha attends Glen Lawn Elementary School and wears braces ("loud music makes my braces vibrate"). Samantha, called "Baby" by Nell, loves sports, especially hockey, and always accompanies her father to sporting events (the more violent and bloody the better). She also likes horror movies and always roots for the monsters.

Samantha enjoys helping Nell cook, clean the house and shop. She later attends Lincoln High School then, in 1986, moves to New Jersey with Nell to begin a new life when her father passes away. Samantha now attends Littlefield College and as a child had an imaginary friend named Debbie Jo.

See also: Julie Kanisky, Katie Kanisky, Nell Harper.

981. Samantha McPherson, *Popular,* WB, 1999–2001. Played by Carly Pope.

Samantha McPherson, known as Sam to her friends, is a sophomore at John F. Kennedy High School in Los Angeles. Sam was born in Los Angeles in 1983 and grew up in a middle class family. She previously attended Ocean Park Elementary School. Samantha has never been one of the popular girls at school. She believes she is pretty "but I will never be a *17* magazine girl because they don't airbrush in real life." Samantha is on the yearbook committee, *The Camelot,* at school and hopes to become a journalist (she is editor of the school newspaper, *The Zapruder Reporter*). Samantha eats Post Honey Combs cereal for breakfast and is known to snore. She has small breasts and wishes she were more amply endowed. Samantha listens to KRCQ radio and is a volunteer for the Teen Peer Hotline. Her hangout is a coffee shop called Roscoe's.

See also: Brooke McQueen, Mary Cherry.

982. Samantha Micelli, *Who's the Boss?,* ABC, 1984–1992. Played by Alyssa Milano.

Samantha Micelli, affectionately called Sam, is the daughter of Tony Micelli, a widower who works as the live-in housekeeper to Angela Bower, an ad company owner. They live at 3344 Oak Hills Drive in Fairfield, Connecticut.

Samantha was born in Brooklyn, New York, in 1972. She was attending P.S. 86 when her mother died and Tony applied as Angela's housekeeper to give Samantha a better life.

Samantha receives an allowance of $15 a week and now attends Fairfield Jr. High School. She is very pretty tomboy and loves sports (she wears a size 5½ hockey skate). Samantha calls French toast "Mr. Frenchie" and pasta, her favorite dinner, is "Mr. Linguini." Her tomboyish ways came to an end when she became 12 and wanted her first bra ("The one with the little pink bow. Tony thought pink bows were to "girly" and bought her a no bow Model 304 "My Training Bra"). Samantha was a member of the Bulldogs baseball team and her first job experience was as Angela's girl Friday at her agency. Samantha later worked as a waitress at the Yellow Submarine (fast food). Her first car was a yellow 1968 Oldsmobile (plate SAM'S CAR) with red reflectors on the sides, five rear brake lights and an old tire as a rear bumper. Sam called it "My yellow nightmare."

Samantha later attends Ridgemont College (1990). She chose to live on campus (two miles from her home) and in 1992 married Hank Tomopopolus, a would-be puppeteer. As a child Samantha had a teddy bear she called Freddy Fuzz Face.

See also: Angela Bower, Tony Micelli.

983. Samantha Stevens, *Bewitched,* ABC, 1964–1972. Played by Elizabeth Montgomery.

Samantha (last name unpronounceable according to her mother) is the daughter of Maurice and Endora. She is a "cauldron stirring, broom riding witch" and was a dream of a child. Although her parents had separated, Samantha adjusted to the fact that she was a child of divorce. She was raised primarily by Endora and was brought up to live the life of a witch, to blend into society, but to never forget her powers or her heritage. One day in 1964 Samantha met a mortal named Darrin Stevens (Dick York, Dick Sargent). It was a love at first sight for both of them and they married. They set up housekeeping in Westport, Connecticut (at 1164 Morning Glory Circle), and eventually became the parents of two children, witches Tabitha and Adam. More importantly, Samantha broke family tradition by marrying a mortal and brought disgrace upon her family (and also by agreeing not to use her powers to please her husband — something her parents can't comprehend).

Darrin works in Manhattan as an account executive at the advertising firm of McMann and Tate. His office phone number is 555-6059 and he drives a car with the license plate 4R6 558. Darrin's favorite hangout is Joe's Bar and Grill (also called Mulvaney's Bar). He is often the recipient of Endora's efforts to show Samantha what a fool she married by casting spells on him (for example, always having to tell the truth; speaking in rhyme; slowly shrinking). Maurice also enjoys transforming Darrin into things (for example, a donkey, a statue, an old pair of galoshes). "Duspin," "Dustin," "Dobbin" and "Duncan" are the names Maurice calls Darrin; for Endora it's "Derwood," "Dumbo" and "Dum Dum."

Samantha's marriage has also upset the Witch's Counsel, powerful women who rule witches. When they become upset they take away Samantha's powers and short-circuit her (so she can experience "a power failure"). Darrin calls Samantha "Sam." Samantha evokes her powers by wrinkling her nose (the musical effect that is heard is called "Samantha's Twitch"). Being an earthbound witch exposes Samantha to a number of unusual conditions (like rhyming words, voracious appetite, uncontrollable laughing and crying, and a buildup of unused magic called "Gravititus Inflamatious").

Ordinary doctors are unable to help Samantha. When she needs assistance she uses the atmospheric continuum to contact her family physician, Dr. Bombay (Bernard Fox). Although called a "witch doctor" by Darrin, he can usually cure Samantha's afflictions.

When Samantha has a craving for food only ringtail pheasant can satisfy her.

Elizabeth Montgomery (using the name Pandora Spocks) also played Serena, Samantha's mischievous cousin, a girl who calls herself "The goddess of love." Serena is a member of the Cosmos Club and is entertainment chairwoman of the Cosmos Cotillion. She enjoys demonstrating her unperfected karate and doesn't trust anyone over 3,000 years old. Serena wrote the song "Kisses in the Wind" and has a birthmark on her face that changes with each appearance (usually on the left side of her face near her lower eyelid. It takes the form of, among other things, an anchor, a question mark, a heart, and the letter *S* for Serena). Samantha and Darrin's last name is also spelled as Stephens in some sources.

See also: Endora.

984. Samantha Stepjak, *Someone Like Me,* NBC, 1994. Played by Nikki Cox.

Samantha Stepjak is the daughter of Steve and Jean Stepjak. She was born on August 6, 1978, and lives at 1402 Manton Drive in Parkwood, St. Louis, with her sister (Gaby) and brother (Evan).

Samantha is a sophomore at Parkwood High School. She has an advantage over every other girl at school—"I'm the most beautiful." Samantha realized at an early age she had super model potential and used her looks to get what she wanted. Samantha also began to develop early and made other girls envious by being the first one in her class to wear a bra. Samantha is now amply endowed and is admired by other girls for her breasts (as one adolescent girl said, "I hope to get breasts that great too").

Samantha loves to roller skate but her mother will not let her go to the local skating rink (Skateland) because "drug addicts hang out there" (her mother doesn't seem to mind the sexy clothes Samantha wears for a girl so young, or all the cleavage she shows). Samantha can have her choice of any boy at school but appears to date

what her father calls "losers" (boys who are barely passing and look to be suited for digging ditches). Then too, Samantha is not the brightest girl in school. Her looks and wardrobe come first; school is somewhere down the line. Each morning before school Samantha takes inventory — "Lipstick, eyeliner, scrungie, brush, Walkman." She always forgets one thing — her books.

Gaby, Samantha's younger sister, admires Samantha for only one thing — her beauty. Samantha feels that she has only one job to perform around the house — "To brighten Gaby's day." Although Gaby and Samantha love each other, Samantha feels that the only way she can get Gaby to do something for her is to bribe her with clothes (Gaby loves Samantha's wardrobe but doesn't have the figure yet to wear most of them).

See also: Gaby Stepjak.

985. Samantha Waters, *Profiler,* NBC, 1996–1999. Played by Ally Walker.

Samantha Waters is a forensic psychologist with a unique ability to feel for the victims of crime and understand the criminal mind. Police call such people Profilers.

Samantha is not a psychic. Her highly developed intuition allows her to think in pictures and visualize the frame of mind of both the killer and the victim. She looks beyond the obvious and rarely takes a guess ("I need more to go on. Without a crystal ball, there is not much more I can tell you"). Samantha works for Bailey Monroe, head of the V.C.T.F. (Violent Crimes Task Force), a special Atlanta-based unit of the FBI that attempts to solve the baffling crimes of any police department in the nation.

Samantha is a widow and lives with her daughter Chloe at 501 Almada (in a converted firehouse station). As a child Samantha and her mother enjoyed solving puzzles. It made Samantha feel alive. As she grew her interest in solving mysteries also grew. It is this enthusiasm that made Samantha choose law enforcement as her career goal. Her abilities were immediately put to use by the FBI. Samantha performed well but in 1993 it all came to a tragic end. Samantha was about to uncover the identity of a fiendish killer the FBI labeled Jack of All Trades. To distract Samantha, Jack killed her husband. A devastated Samantha resigned and moved to the country to live an anonymous life with Chloe. Jack too disappeared. He resurfaced in 1996 and so did Samantha when Bailey coaxed her out of retirement to find Jack (she does so three years later and resigns to be with Chloe).

Samantha can't sleep when she is working on a

tough case. She sometimes feels scared "but I'm not going to quit." She is also a workaholic and often runs herself down. Her hobby of photography seems to relax her — "It offers me an escape from the dark corners."

See also: Rachel Burke.

986. Sandra Clark, *227*, NBC, 1985–1989. Played by Jackee Harry.

Sandra Clark says that her favorite letter of the alphabet is *M* ("for money men and me"). She is beautiful and sexy and believes she is a threat to other men's wives ("They are jealous of my sexy walk, the way I act and the way I flaunt what I have").

Sandra was born in Washington, D.C., and lives in Apartment J of an apartment house identified only as 227 (its street number). Sandra is a graduate of Waverly High School and first came to 227 when she was a student at Georgetown University (where she had the nickname "Sparkles" for her bubbly personality).

Sandra flaunts what she has to get what she wants. She calls her stunning figure, especially her breasts (which she proudly displays in low cut necklines) "my equipment." When she feels sick she shops ("It makes me feel better") and she doesn't like to be yelled at ("Don't yell at me, I'm sensitive"). Sandra works as an agent for Winslow Travel. Her prior jobs were receptionist for an unnamed talent agency; receptionist for the Stumper and Nathan Construction Company; sales clerk at Benson's Department Store; door-to-door salesgirl for Luscious Lingerie; "The Tuna Lady" in TV commercials for tuna fish; and TV weather girl on Channel 87.

Sandra left 227 in 1989 and moved to New York for a job as a fashion designer at Midway Productions. When she discovered that Midway produced X-rated films, she turned the job down and found work as the assistant manager of the Sensations Health and Fitness Club.

987. Sandy Stockton, *Funny Face* (CBS, 1971), *The Sandy Duncan Show* (CBS, 1972). Played by Sandy Duncan.

Sandra Stockton, called Sandy, is a student teacher at UCLA. She was born in Illinois and as early as she could remember, she wanted to become a teacher (her teachers so impressed her that she wanted to become just like them). Sandy is a graduate of Illinois State University and relocated to Los Angeles to begin her career as a teacher. She lives in Apartment 2A of the Royal Weatherly Hotel at 130 North Weatherly Boulevard; 555-3444 is her phone number. To help pay her ex-penses, Sandy acquires a job as an actress for Maggie Prescott (Nita Talbot), a former model turned owner of the Prescott Advertising Agency on West Pico Street (555-3174 is its phone number). Sandy appeared in two TV commercials — "The Yummy Peanut Butter Girl" and spokes girl for "Jack E. Appleseed Used Cars in the Heart of the San Fernando Valley."

Sandy is very pretty and single. She is full of life and always on the go (she never seems to get tired). She enjoys the company of other people and she is extremely loyal to those she considers her friends. Sandy was brought up to be a caring person. She sometimes cares too much as she feels it is her duty to help people in trouble (she eventually solves the problem but complicates matters in the process).

When the series switched titles Sandy was still depicted as a pretty single girl who enjoys life. Her job, however, was changed. She was now a part-time secretary to Bert Quinn (Tom Bosley), head of the Quinn and Cohen Advertising Agency (at 5099 Lincoln Boulevard). Sandy was still a student teacher at UCLA but less time was devoted to this aspect of her life; her time at the agency (trying to solve problems) was the main focus of her life.

988. Sara Brennan, *Happy Family*, NBC, 2003–2004. Played by Melanie Paxson.

Sara Brennan is the daughter of Peter and Anne Brennan, a happily married couple who live in suburban Philadelphia. She is a graduate of Lincoln High School and Penn State University but rather than follow in her father's footsteps and become a dentist, she chose the life of a financier (she is currently vice president of Keystone Financial). As a kid Sara stole a marshmallow from an open bag at a supermarket. She felt so guilty that she got a job at the store and quit before they could pay her. A year later Sara spent the summer dressed as a donut — not because she worked in a donut store but "because I wanted to."

As a youngster Sara had a pet dog named Bootsy. She now has a pet parrot she calls Eric (who is Jewish; Sara is Catholic). Sara believes that she always does the right thing. She has no boyfriends, no social life and feels she will never find a man. She is very pretty but her parents believe Eric is to blame (Sara takes Eric on dates with her, babies him, and even has a painting of herself with Eric. The painting is based on a photograph of her and Eric on vacation). Sara chooses the films for movie night Thursday at her parent's home and is very negative about herself (if someone says, for example, "You have lovely skin," Sara responds with "Yea, when my exima isn't flaring up"). Despite her neurotic tendencies, Sara appears to be happy most of the time.

989. Sara Joy Pitts, *Madame's Place*, Syn., 1982–1983. Played by Judy Landers.

Sara Joy Pitts is young, beautiful and sexy. She is the daughter of Marmalina, the sister of Madame, the vibrant but rather unattractive host of *Madame's Place*, a late night TV talk show (Madame is a puppet manipulated and voiced by Wayland Flowers).

Sara Joy was born in Georgia but is no puppet. She is a flesh and blood girl who has been overly influenced by the success of her aunt and now wants to become an actress "like my Auntie Madame." Marmalina sent Sara Joy to Hollywood to live with Madame and learn how to become a star. Sara Joy measures 37-24-36 and is all body and no brains (Madame describes her as "a sex pot who doesn't realize she is a sex pot"). Madame appears to be in her sixties and didn't recall she had a niece. When Sara Joy first arrived she thought she was getting "a boob-o-gram" and said her name sounded like a limerick: "There once was a girl named Sara Joy Pitts who had big..."

Sara Joy is so sweet and so adorable that, as Madame says, "You can't help but love her no matter how many dumb things she does." Sara Joy loves to dress in very low cut and off the shoulder blouses as well as short shorts (or what the producers could get away with at the time without being censored). Although Sara Joy comes from a rural background, she seems to enjoy life in the big city and is fascinated by all the activity that surrounds her (the show is broadcast from Madame's home). Sara Joy's favorite TV show is *The Young and the Stupid* (which she watches with the sound off because "It's so sad it makes me cry"). Sara Joy never became an actress. She helped Madame around the house and remained a lure to attract viewers.

See also: Madame.

990. Sara Pezzini, *Witchblade*, TNT, 2001. Played by Yancy Butler.

Sara Pezzini is a homicide detective with the 11th Precinct of the N.Y.P.D. She wears badge 322 and drives a car with the license plate RFD 960. She also possesses the Witchblade, a mysterious, ancient bracelet that attaches itself to strong women. It is said to be "a branch ripped from the tree of knowledge to balance good and evil." The Witchblade has a mind of its own. When it attaches itself to Sara she gains extraordinary abilities to fight evil. It becomes a chameleon-like powerhouse: a bullet-deflecting bracelet, a bayonet-like knife, a Samurai sword, a suit of armor—whatever its preordained champion needs to protect herself as she battles "to cleanse the world and make it pure." A gift of the Witchblade is the power to slip back and forth in time. A refusal to wear the bracelet or fight its power could result in Sara's death.

Cleopatra, Joan of Arc and World War II spy Elizabeth Bronte were three of the women throughout time who were chosen to wield the Witchblade. Sara showed the same courage and concealed vulnerability and was thus chosen to wear the Witchblade. Sara is also a continuation of the lives of these great women. During the 1940s Elizabeth Bronte had a daughter who did not wield the Witchblade. This daughter had a child and from that child Sara was born. To ensure that Sara would eventually wield the Witchblade, unknown powers arranged for a man named Lazar to kidnap the infant Sara and give her to James Pezzini (an incorruptible police detective) to raise. When Sara acquires the Witchblade, it bonds with her and gives her a unique genetic makeup — something no other person has.

The Witchblade has many powers and only Sara can know them all. She can see things other people cannot (for example, what happened at a crime scene by looking at a photo or visiting the scene). She can acquire strength and pierce the veil of the senses to extract more from the universe than the normal person. Sara cannot fight the powers of the Witchblade. If she fails to use its power she will die. She also cannot rid herself of the Witchblade (it will return to her. If she tries to abandon it the bracelet will punish her by inflicting pain).

The Witchblade appears as a gold band with a red ruby. Sara cannot remove it from her wrist. Only women can wear it because they are closer to nature than men and the Witchblade finds them superior. Sara also has two marks on her chest that represent the light and dark powers of the Witchblade (Sara disbelieves this and says "I got them from shrapnel during a SWAT raid eleven months ago").

Sara believes she was born in New York City and is the daughter of James Pezzini. She lives in a Greenwich Village loft (416). She goes into a deep depression when something upsets her and relaxes by shooting pool. (Sara acquired the Witchblade during a shootout in a museum. A bullet shattered a glass Joan of Arc exhibit and the bracelet was set free to find Sara.)

991. Sara Sidle, *C.S.I.: Crime Scene Investigation*, CBS, 2000 (current). Played by Jorga Fox.

Sara Sidle, employee number 037-784, is a field operative with the Crime Scene Investigation unit of the Metropolitan Las Vegas Police Department. She was born in Tamalas Bay in San Francisco on September 16, 1971, and is the only daughter of former hippies who ran a bed and breakfast. Following in her parent's footsteps was not for Sara.

As a child Sara became interested in police work. She listened to police scanners at home and studied forensic magazines in her spare time. After graduating from high school Sara enrolled in Harvard University and acquired a Bachelor of Sciences degree. She next enrolled in graduate school and acquired a degree in theoretical physics. She next joined the San Francisco Police Department where she worked for five years in the coroner's office. She was transferred to its crime lad and was eventually recruited by Gil Grissom, head of the Las Vegas C.S.I. Sara is an expert on arson fires and her specialty is material and element analysis. She likes plants and maxes out on overtime each month. Gil believes she becomes too involved in cases, especially when a victim survives and Sara has vowed to find the culprit responsible for the assault. If an unknown substance is found, Sara delights in trying to figure out what it is.

See also: Catherine Willows, Gil Grissom, Nick Stokes, Warrick Brown.

992. Sarah and Ernie Henderson, *Harry and the Hendersons*, Syn., 1991–1993. Played by Carol Ann Plante, Zachary Bostrom.

Sarah and Ernie Henderson are the children of George and Nancy Henderson, a happily married couple who live at 410 Forest Drive in Seattle. Also living with them is Harry, a Sasquash who has befriended them.

Fifteen-year-old Sarah first attended Madison High School then Northern College of the Arts. She (and Ernie) were born in Seattle. Sarah is a member of Madison's track team and is a talented singer and dancer (she wrote the song "Somewhere Out There" for the Homecoming Dance). Sarah is not too happy living with a Big Foot in the house and fears her friends will find out and become the talk of the town (she hopes to write a book about Harry and her family one day — "But I'm going to use a pen name. I don't want anyone to think I'm nuts"). Sarah has the middle name of Nicole. She worked at Photo Quickie and has aspirations to become an actress (she starred in the Community Theater production of *Beauty and the Beast*). She has a special white lace bra she calls "My lucky bra" and she only wears it when she needs something special to happen. She has a pet hamster (Melissa) and played saxophone in the school orchestra.

Ernie is the closest to Harry ("Ernie" was the first word he spoke). Ernie attends Madison Jr. High School and was a member of the Padres Pee Wee league baseball team. Although Ernie dislikes girls, he became friendly with Darcy Farg (Courtney Peldon), a very pretty and very rich but spoiled girl who lived next door. Ernie is not as studious as Sarah and finds himself getting into more trouble with Harry than he does on his own or with Darcy.

See also: George and Nancy Henderson.

993. Sarah Powell, *Charles in Charge*, Syn., 1987–1990. Played by Josie Davis.

Sarah Powell is a very sweet and charming young girl. She is the daughter of Ellen and Robert Powell and lives at 10 Barrington Court in New Brunswick, New Jersey. She has an older sister (Jamie) and a younger brother (Adam) and is cared for by Charles, the live-in housekeeper (her mother is a real estate broker and her father is a naval commander stationed overseas).

Sarah is a student at Central High School. She keeps a daily diary of her activities and is hoping to one day become a writer. Sarah earns money as a teenage correspondent for the New Brunswick *Herald* and had her first story, "What It Is Like to be a Teenager," published in *Teen* magazine. She is very studious and a straight A student. Sarah is a member of the Shakespeare Club at school and first mentioned Elizabeth Barrett Browning was her favorite poet (later it's Emily Dickinson).

If Sarah had three wishes she would ask for "world peace, a cleaner environment and an end of world hunger." Sarah is tall and thin and not as shapely or fashion conscious as Jamie. She is sensitive and comfortable the way she is. She has a pet turtle (Ross) and a favorite doll (Rebecca).

See also: Buddy Lembeck, Charles, Jamie Powell, Lila Pembroke.

994. Sarah Rush, *Too Close for Comfort*, ABC, 1980–1983. Played by Lydia Cornell.

Sarah Rush is a girl who considers herself a perfect 10. She was born in San Francisco on June 9, 1970, and is the daughter of Henry and Muriel Rush. She lives with her older sister, Jackie, in the downstairs apartment of her parent's home on Buena Vista Street in San Francisco.

Sarah is a graduate of Union Bay High School and is currently attending State College. Sarah is a very beautiful blonde and wears a 36C bra. She feels her looks are not always a blessing because she sometimes attracts men she wants nothing to do with. Sarah works at whatever part-time jobs she can find to pay her half of the rent ($150). Her first job was as a "wench waitress" at the Fox and Hound Bar (she got the job because her figure fit the available costume). When this job became too much for her easily upset, overly concerned father to handle, she quit and became a teller at the Bay City Bank. Sarah also worked as the local weather girl for KTSF-TV's *Dawn in San Francisco* program.

Sarah is not easily motivated. She is a rather sloppy housekeeper and has more dates in one week than most girls have in a month. Sarah is a bit naïve, likes attention but doesn't dress in clothes that are too revealing. She sometimes gets too much attention and wishes she were less attractive just to get a good eight hours of sleep at night.

See also: Henry and Muriel Rush, Jackie Rush.

995. Sarah Stewart, *Raising Dad,* WB, 2001–2002. Played by Kat Dennings.

Sarah Stewart is the 15-year-old daughter of Matt Stewart, a high school creative writing teacher. She has a sister (Emily) and lives at 803 Linden Avenue in Massachusetts. Sarah attends Barrington High School and has a 10:00 P.M. curfew. She is a B student and a member of the drama club (where she directed "The Lemon Grove," a lost play by Anton Chekov).

Sarah first worked in the attendance office of Barrington High, then as a waitress at Pulp Fiction, a juice bar and bookstore on Center Street. Sarah believes her father is a control freak. She is very obedient and only seriously defied his wishes once by seeing an R-rated movie (*Love to Love*) with Emily at the Circle Theater.

See also: Emily Stewart, Matt Stewart.

996. Screech Powers, *Saved by the Bell,* NBC, 1989–2000. Played by Dustin Diamond.

Samuel Powers, nicknamed Screech, is a student at Bayside High School in Palisades, California. He was born on February 9, 1975, and is the only regular student who spanned the entire series run, including the Disney version, *Good Morning, Miss Bliss* (1988–1989).

Screech was first seen as a student at J.F.K. Junior High School in Indianapolis, Indiana (1988–89). Here he was depicted as a nerd. He had two pet mice (Spin and Marty) and was the glue monitor ("Believe me, it's not as glamorous as it sounds"). Screech is suddenly in Palisades and attending Bayside High when the series was retitled for NBC.

Screech lives at 88 Edgemont Road. He has a dog (Hound Dog), lizard (Oscar), spider (Ted), white rats (Spin and Marty), roach (Herbert), mouse (Arnold) and a homemade robot (Kevin). Screech wears a size 11-shoe and is a member of the photography, science, chess, insect and glee clubs at school. He hosts "Screech's Mystery Theater" on the school radio station (Tiger Radio) and won fifth runner-up in an ALF look-a-like contest. Screech named his first zit Murray and invented Zit-Off, a blemish cream that removed pimples but left a maroon after-effect. He also tried to market Screech's Secret Sauce (A spaghetti sauce that sold for $3 a jar. Its slogan: "The Sauce You Gotta Have, but the Secret, She's-a-mine"). He scored a 1200 on his SAT test. During the summer of 1991 Screech worked as a waiter at the Malibu Sands Beach Club. His after school hangout is the Max (fast food).

Screech next appeared in the first spinoff series, *Saved by the Bell: The College Years* (NBC, 1993–94). He is attending California State University and shares a room with former Bayside High pals Zack Morris and A.C. Slater. From 1994 until 2000 Screech becomes the assistant to Richard Belding, the principal of Bayside High. He also works with Richard as his assistant at the Palisades Hills Country Club (1994–95) and weekends with Richard in stores called The Sweet Tooth (1995–96), Yukon Yogurt (1996–97), and Gimmicks and Gadgets (1998–2000). Screech was also advisor for the school's newspaper, the *Bayside Breeze* and was host (with Richard) of "From the Principal's Office" on Tiger Radio (now KGAB, 98.6 FM).

See also: Jesse Spano, Kelly Kapowski, Lisa Turtle, Zack Morris.

997. Seven of Nine, *Star Trek: Voyager,* UPN, 1996–2001. Played by Jeri Ryan.

Seven of Nine is a member of the Starship U.S.S. *Voyager*. She has no rank or specific assignment, but her knowledge of foreign species and technology is critical to *Voyager*'s survival in space (they are lost in the Delta Quadrant and seeking a way back to Earth).

Seven of Nine is actually Annika Hansen, an Earth girl who was born in the Tendara Colony on star date 25479. She is the daughter of Erin and Magnus Hansen, exo-biologists who were studying an evil alien race called the Borg. The Hansens were on their ship, *The Raven*, when they were assimilated by the alien race. The Borg is a collective — a billion minds thinking as one. Annika was a young girl at the time and received the Borg designation Seven of Nine. After living as a Borg drone for 20 years, Annika was rescued by the crew of *Voyager* when she was disconnected from the Borg collective mind (the upper spinal column in her neutro-transceiver was neutralized). Although a deadly Borg when first released, she received extreme medical treatments to return her to her human form. Eighty-two percent of her Borg implants were safely removed; she requires the remaining bio implants to survive. Her human metabolism and immune system have also been restored through the Borg nanoprobes in her bloodstream (she has 3.6 million nanoprobes in her body. The misuse of one could spell disaster). While physically human in appearance, Seven of Nine does retain evidence of her Borg assimilation: an ocular implant over her left eye and assimilation tubes on her left arm.

Seven of Nine insists on absolute perfection. As a Borg she was responsible for destroying countless millions. She requires weekly maintenance checks with the Doctor and must rejuvenate in her alcove (which takes 30 megawatts of electricity to power). When she is bad (disobeying Captain Janeway), Seven of Nine is sent to Cargo Bay Two as punishment. As a child Annika was afraid of the dark and her father called her "Muffin."

See also: B'Elanna Torres, Chakotay, The Doctor, Harry Kim, Kathryn Janeway, Tuvok.

998. Shalimar Fox, *Mutant X*, Syn., 2001–2004. Played by Victoria Pratt.

Shalimar Fox is a beautiful woman who possesses extraordinary martial arts skills and the ability to move at an accelerated rate. She was created by Adam Kane at Genomex, a secret genetics laboratory and now works for Adam as an agent of Mutant X, a group of rouge, genetically engineered people who battle evil wherever they find it (see Adam Kane for information on Genomex).

Shalimar and fellow agents Emma and Brennan are Adam's "children" (as he calls them). Shalimar has been with Adam for ten years and was the first mutant he recruited (he found her in a sleazy hotel and helped her come to terms with who she is). Shalimar is incredibly strong and has enhanced hearing. Her eyes become cat-like when she becomes angry and she is also reckless and leaves herself wide open for attack. She is very territorial and protective of the people she loves — "I'm feral and when I sense anything that threatens my family I'll fight to the death." Shalimar often wonders if her life will ever be her own — "I can't help but wonder if my life was all planned

out for me before I was born or whether Genomex wrote it into my genes and I'm just acting what some scientist wanted to happen."

See also: Adam Kane, Brennan Mulray, Emma DeLauro, Lexa Pierce.

999. Shane Phillips, *She Spies*, Syn., 2002–2004. Played by Natashia Williams.

Shane Phillips is a member of She Spies, a government organization that battles crime and corruption. Shane was born in Los Angeles. She is African-American and from a rich family. She rebelled against her parents and made good by becoming a master thief. She was eventually caught and sent to Terminal Island Prison in San Pedro, California. She was later released to the government when they needed an agent with her skills.

Shane's father wanted a boy and raised her as though she were his son. Shane became "macho," as she says, and was taught things like boxing. She used what she was taught for all the wrong reasons — crime. "I wish I would have spent more time as a girl," she says. Shane is an expert in Brazilian jujitsu and is happy to kick, body punch or slam her way into a situation. She is tough in a fight and will use any means possible to defend herself. Shane is an expert on explosives, safe cracking and alarm systems. She reads *Spy* magazine and makes a wonderful peach cobbler.

Shane wasn't allowed to play with dolls as a kid — "I use to rip their heads off and it freaked out the neighbors." When she was six years old Shane dreamed of becoming a veterinarian. She was a member of the Indian Princesses scouts and was called "Little Pain on the Prairie." She spent most of her childhood at boarding schools because her mother was too busy with her career to care for her. Her least favorite assignment is body disposal.

See also: Cassie McBain, D.D. Cummings.

1000. Sharron Macready, *The Champions*, NBC/Syn., 1968. Played by Alexandra Bastedo.

Sharron Macready is an agent for Nemesis, an international organization based in Geneva, Switzerland, that tackles extremely dangerous matters. She works with agents Craig Stirling and Richard Barrett.

Sharron was born in England and resides at 36 Bristol Court. She was a former operative for the C.I.D. (Criminal Investigation Division) of New Scotland Yard whose outstanding series of arrests prompted Nemesis to draft her. Sharron is intelligent, very capable and resourceful. She, as well as Craig and Richard, possess extraordinary powers that they use to battle evil ("Their mental and physical capacities fused to computer efficiency; their sight, sense and hearing raised to their highest futuristic state of mental and physical strength"; see Richard Barrett for further information).

While seductive in any outfit, Sharron prefers not to use her sex appeal as part of her assignment. She also has training in medical procedures and can withstand physical and mental punishment. Sharron is a black belt in karate and able to outwit the enemy by quickly assessing a situation and acting upon it.

See also: Craig Stirling, Richard Barrett.

Shauni McClain *see* **The Girls of Baywatch**

1001. Sheena, *Sheena, Queen of the Jungle* (Syn., 1956–1957); *Sheena* (Syn., 2000–2002). Played by Irish McCalla (1956), Gena Lee Nolin (2000).

Sheena is a beautiful white jungle goddess who protects her adopted homeland, Africa, from evil.

Irish McCalla Profile: *Sheena, Queen of the Jungle.* Sheena, 28 years old when the series begins, was a young girl when the plane on which she was traveling crashed in the jungles of Kenya, East Africa. Her parents and the pilot were killed and the young girl was found by a native chief (Logi) who named her Sheena and raised her to respect good men and hate evil ones. Sheena is blonde and stands five feet, nine inches tall. She weighs 141 pounds and measures 39½-24½-38. Her wardrobe consists of a conservative leg-revealing leopard skin dress with a black belt (the symbol of a lion can be seen in the center of the belt). She also wears a metal band on each arm above her elbow that is embossed with the symbol of a lion. Sheena carries a spear and a knife (in back of her waist belt) and an ivory horn to summon animals for help.

Sheena is assisted by her chimpanzee Chim and is called "The White Jungle Goddess" by superstitious natives. She prefers to "move through the trees" (swing by vine from one to another) rather than walking through the jungle ("Faster my way," she says). Sheena, TV's first female superhero, risks her life to protect her jungle domain from the unscrupulous characters who invade it. Sheena will not kill and relies on her friend, Bob Rayburn (Christian Drake), to help her collar the bad guys (Bob was a big game hunter hired by the commissioner to ensure the safety of safaris; he was originally said to be a white trader).

Gena Lee Nolin Profile: *Sheena.* Cheryl Hamilton was five years old when a tragic event changed the course of her life. Cheryl's parents were scientists exploring a cave in Africa when they were killed in a rockslide. Cheryl was found wandering in the jungle shortly after by Kali (Margo Moorer), a member of the Kia tribe. Kali raised Cheryl as her own daughter and named her Shi-ena but Cheryl preferred Sheena.

Sheena is 25 years old when the series begins. She lives in the La Mista, a dangerous area in Maltoka, Africa, and protects her adopted homeland from evil with the ability to morph (change into animals). Kali's people possessed the power to morph. When civilization came to Africa, the Kia tribe, with the exception of Kali, chose to become animals. Kali passed the knowledge of morphing to Sheena. For Sheena to become an animal she must first feel the spirit of the animal inside her (what she calls "The Manta"). She then looks into the eyes of the animal and the transformation begins. Once she becomes an animal Sheena is prone to two dangers: retaining part of that animal if she remains in that form for too long; and injury (if Sheena is hurt in her animal form, she will retain that injury when she becomes human).

Sheena cannot talk to animals but can communicate with them. She is a friend with all animals except rogues (she is also unable to morph into a rogue because there is no focus). Sheena can follow animals and humans by their scents and will only kill a human if one threatens to kill her. Sheena was taught to fight by Kali and educates herself by reading.

Sheena lives in a cave in the LaMista, which is also home to a legendary creature called the Darak'na. It is said that when evildoers come to Africa, the Darak'na will strike. The Darak'na ("Shadow" in English) is actually Sheena using a power Kali taught her to battle evil when evil fights unfair. The Darak'na is a vicious cat-like creature with razor-sharp claws (and Sheena does kill as the Darak'na). Sheena becomes the creature by covering herself with mud. She then concentrates and the change occurs. Sheena retains her human thought processes but loses her top, exposing her mud-covered breasts (no explanation is given as to why the Darak'na is topless or how Sheena regains her top when she becomes her normal self). Sheena receives help from Matt Cutter (John Allen Nelson), a former CIA sniper who now runs Cutter Enterprises.

1002. Shelly Lewis, *Parker Lewis Can't Lose,* Fox, 1990–1992. Played by Maia Brewton.

Shelly Lewis is the daughter of Judy and Martin Lewis. She lives in Santo Domingo, California and has an older brother named Parker. Shelly is 13 years old and a freshman at Santo Domingo High School. She hates Parker for all the bad things he does and gets away with. Shelly is looking forward to the day she can get the goods on him and make her parents see that Parker is really as bad as she is.

Shelly's idol is Grace Musso, the stern, authoritarian principal of the school (Parker says Grace is more than a principal, "she is a psychopath with tenure" as she is also trying to bring down Parker). Shelly weighs 77 pounds and is Grace's "pretty, two-faced sugar plum freshman obedience trainee" (Parker calls her "Santo Domingo's hellcat" and is sure she is adopted. At home he calls her "Shelly Belly"). Shelly is feared by students (as she reports any insubordination directly to Grace) and is a member of the snobbish Vogues, an all-girl clique that is the terror of the school.

Shelly has an 11:00 P.M. curfew. If she helps Parker in any way a red warning light is flashed on the screen. Parker says "My sister is capable of many things: humiliating me in public, reading my diary, selling my baby pictures, but getting a date, that's another story." Shelly is so feared that boys just won't approach her. Parker decided to change that (to get her off his back) and tried to refine Shelly and bring out her natural beauty for her first date in what he called "Operation Pretty Woman — changing a 72 pound swamp monster into Julia Roberts." Shelly's favorite movie is *Fatal Attraction* (she has seen it 15 times) and has a collection of My Little Ponies ("The world's largest," according to Parker).

See also: Parker Lewis.

1003. Shelly Williams, *Eve*, UPN, 2003 (current). Played by Eve Jihan Jeffers.

This entry also contains information on Rita LeFleur (Ali Landry) and Janie Egan (Natalie Deselle-Reed), Shelly's friends and co-workers.

Shelly, Rita and Janie are partners in a dress making business called Diva Style in Miami Beach, Florida. Shelly is a single girl and lives in Apartment 1 over the store (located at 6950 South Beach Boulevard). She won the Miami Fashion Award and the Rodney Starr Award for her designs. Shelly sometimes becomes too emotional over her designs (especially wedding dresses) and cries when she has to give them up to a client. Shelly takes her frustrations out on the store mannequins and had to take out three loans to pay for her share of the business.

Shelly is a size 4. She believes her beauty is a burden — "No man is safe and I shouldn't be allowed to walk on the streets." She also believes she shouldn't have to pay for dates "because I'm an old fashioned girl." She has two special outfits: her intellectual white skirt and her "Shelly I can't live

without you gold pants." Shelly has to be perfect when she goes out on a date and claims to make delicious fudge brownies (after tasting them people secretly wish Shelly would stop making them). As a child Shelly had a dog named Chanel Number 5 and would play Electra Woman and Dyna Girl (a 1970s TV series) with her older sister Simone (Shelly was always Dyna Girl; Simone is now an investment banker). Shelly recalled a "delightful" incident when she was five years old: she ate a whole quart of strawberry ice cream and then went on an amusement park Ferris wheel. Before the ride could be shut down "everybody was covered in strawberry."

When clients see Shelly they say, "You should be a model not a designer." "I get that a lot," she says. Shelly claims she is an expert at getting rid of men without hurting their feelings ("I make them feel good about themselves"). Her favorite movie is *The Divine Secrets of the Ya Ya Sisterhood* (although she likes old movies like *Casablanca*). Shelly wears vanilla oil as a perfume and hates people who know what they will be doing in advance (she likes to take it day by day).

Shelly, Rita and Janie met in design school. Rita is a penniless ex-model who made $3.6 million and squandered it. She appeared on the cover of *Sports Illustrated* in a turquoise bikini and would not go out in public until "I was camera ready." She gave up college to model in Milan and developed an eating disorder as a model. She is afraid of housework, uses a different cup for everything she drinks and eats no carb ice cream. Rita holds the title of Miss New Orleans French Quarter (she was born in Baton Rouge, Louisiana). When Rita needs something, she uses her Scarlett O'Hara voice. Rita says she will never use her fabulous body for prostitution "but if I do I'd like to be like Julia Roberts in *Pretty Woman*."

Janie considers herself "the good wise woman's friend." She is the only one of the friends who is married (to Marty, who is in the Navy). She loves to gossip but says, "I do not gossip." She has a tendency to cry at anything that is sad and is usually the peacemaker when Shelly and Rita are at odds (which is often). Janie enjoys a foot-long hot dog, extra large popcorn, sugar babies and a diet coke at the movies. She, Shelly and Rita enjoy a drink at the Z Lounge.

1004. Sherman Potter, *M*A*S*H*, CBS, 1975–1983. Played by Harry Morgan.

Colonel Sherman Potter is a career army man. He was appointed to head the 4077 M*A*S*H (Mobile Army Surgical Hospital) unit in Korea during the war when its former commander,

Henry Blake, was killed when his transport plane was shot down by the enemy.

Sherman was born in Riverbend, Missouri (later he says Hannibal, Missouri) and is married to Mildred (who calls him "Puddin' Head"). Sherman began practicing medicine in 1932 and was a horse soldier during World War II. He is fond of horses (he has one on the base named Sophie) and finds relief from the insanity of war by painting (he paints sitting on a saddle and wearing a cowboy hat. Pictures of horses are on the wall behind his desk). Although he finds fellow officers Hawkeye Pierce and B.J. Hunnicutt's antics a violation of army rules, he puts up with them (even shares drinks with them). He considered his troops at the 4077 "The best group of people I ever worked with." In the spinoff series, *After M*A*S*H* (CBS, 1983–84), it is learned that Sherman retired from the army in 1953 and has returned to his hometown to become Chief of Staff at the General Pershing V.A. Hospital.

See also: Benjamin Franklin Pierce, B.J. Hunnicutt, Charles Winchester, III, Frank Burns, Henry Blake, Margaret Houlihan, Radar O'Reilly, Trapper John McIntire.

1005. Shirley Feeney, *Laverne and Shirley*, ABC, 1976–1982. Played by Cindy Williams.

Shirley Feeney lives with her best friend, Laverne DeFazio, in Apartment A at 730 Knapp Street in Milwaukee, Wisconsin (the series is set in the 1960s and the address is also given as 730 Hampton Street).

Shirley, an Irish Protestant, was born in Wisconsin. She is a graduate of Fillmore High School and served a hitch in the army (trained at Camp McCallister). She and Laverne played prostitutes in the army training film *This Can Happen to You* and she wrote of her experiences under the pen name S. Wilhelmina Feeney. Shirley works with Laverne in the beer bottle capping division of the Shotz Brewery (at $1.35 an hour). She has a plush cat (Boo Boo Kitty) and is famous for "My Shirley Feeney Scarf Dance." Shirley greets people with "Hi yoooo" and says "Bye yoooo" for goodbye. Shirley never orders chicken with extra barbeque sauce because "It's too messy and gets under my nails" and has a recurring dream wherein she marries her singing idol, Ringo Starr. She has nightmares about her kindergarten days when a bully named Candy Zarvorkes made her eat a box of Crayola Crayons.

Shirley is a bit naïve and highly concerned about her reputation. She tries to be prim and proper and lady like at all times but finds herself fighting and yelling to accomplish something.

Shirley later moves to California with Laverne to begin a new life. They acquire an apartment at 113½ Laurel Vista Drive and work as gift wrappers at Bardwell's Department Store. Shirley was written out of the series a year before it ended when she married Dr. Walter Meeney and began a new life with him as Shirley Feeney-Meeney.

See also: Laverne DeFazio, Lenny and Squiggy.

1006. Shirley Partridge, *The Partridge Family*, ABC, 1970–1974. Played by Shirley Jones.

This entry also contains information on Shirley's children: Keith (David Cassidy), Laurie (Susan Dey), and Danny (Danny Bonaduce). She has two other children, Tracy (Suzanne Crough) and Chris (Jeremy Gelbwaks, Brian Foster).

Shirley. Shirley is a widow. She and her children live at 698 Sycamore Road in San Pueblo, California (address also given as the 700 block on Vassario Road). Shirley is the daughter of Walter and Amanda Renfrew. She worked as a teller at the Bank of San Pueblo before becoming a part of the Partridge Family, a singing group formed by ten-year-old Danny (Shirley and Keith are the lead singers). Shirley is blessed with five good children and has only minor problems to deal with (basically Danny's misguided efforts to make money). When time permitted Shirley returned to school (San Pueblo Jr. College) to complete her courses in psychology (she married after beginning college but had to drop out when she became pregnant with Keith). When someone calls on the family at home, Shirley worries about how the house looks (while Keith worries about how his hair looks). Shirley is very sweet, very caring and performing with her children makes her feel like a child herself.

Keith. Keith is the eldest child (born in 1952). Laurie says "Most mothers have to worry about drugs and violence with their sons. But all your ding-a-ling son does is think about girls." Keith writes the songs his family sings, plays guitar and is lead vocalist. He first attended San Pueblo High School then San Pueblo Jr. College. He is a member of the school basketball team (jersey 15) and his favorite foods are meat loaf and steak and potatoes. Laurie believes Keith dates dumb girls "because they fall for all his corny pickup lines." Keith reads *Playpen* magazine ("for the short stories") and made an experimental film about his family called *16½*. Muldoon Point is his "make out spot."

Laurie. Laurie was born on December 10, 1954. She attends San Pueblo High School (where she was Homecoming Queen) and is later a student at San Pueblo Jr. College. Laurie believes in standing up for what she believes in. She is a teenage woman's libber and reads *Liberal Outlook* magazine. Laurie plays keyboard and sings backup. She sometimes objects to Keith's love song lyrics as she feels they are degrading to women. Laurie enjoys helping her mother with cooking and housework and never uses her beauty to manipulate boys. Laurie dates on occasion, is not overly fashion conscious (she dresses to please herself) and presents few problems for her mother.

Danny. Danny, like Keith and Laurie, was born in San Pueblo, California. He is ten years old and delights in devising schemes to accomplish something ("He usually comes up with six to eight schemes a week," says Shirley. Their agent, Reuben Kincaid, believes "he's a 40-year-old midget in a kid outfit"). Danny plays bass guitar and is very addicted to making money. Danny is a bit awkward around girls and hangs out at the Sweet Shoppe and the Taco Stand. He keeps his money in a "piggy bank" that resembles an Old West safe in his room. He has a stamp collection and his one share of AT&T preferred stock is his most cherished possession. Danny reads *U.S. Finance and Monetary Report* magazine and it was he who organized his family into a band.

1007. Sierra Jennings, *All About Us*, NBC, 2001–2002. Played by Crystal Grant.

Sierra Jennings is a sophomore at Belmont High School in Chicago. She is 16 years old and best friends with Christina, Alecia and Nikki. Sierra is a very pretty, fashionably dressed girl who has her feet planted firmly on the ground. She lives at 864 Montgomery Place and has a pet cat named Buster. Sierra and her girl friends hangout at a teen club called The Loft. She is a member of the Martha Stewart Cooking Club (she and the girls test new recipes on Sunday afternoons) and when a problem arises an ECS (Emergency Chat Session) is held to resolve a matter that exists among the friends.

Sierra is so feminine and elegant that she attracts more boys than she wants. She is looking for a boy who will treat her with respect, not a good time date. She is also an activist of sorts (limited to what she can do at her age) and will stand up and fight for what she believes in (usually school issues).

Sierra is very smart and a careful planner. Rushing into things is not the way she approaches life as she feels people who act before they think are asking for nothing but trouble. She is highly motivated and likes to get things done (Nikki believes Sierra accomplishes what she does because

she is a conniver. "I wish I was that conniving," she says).

See also: Alecia Alcott, Christina Castelli, Nikki Merrick.

1008. Simon Camden, *7th Heaven*, WB, 1996 (current). Played by David Gallagher.

Simon Camden is the third born child of Eric and Annie Camden, a Protestant minister and his wife, who live in Glen Oak, California. He has six siblings: Matt, Mary, Lucy, Ruthie and twins Sam and David.

Simon likes working with figures and numbers. He was so good that his parents allowed him to handle their finances. Simon was also good at saving money and was called "The Bank of Simon" by his family. He first attended Walter Reed Jr. High School, then Kennedy High School. He delivered papers for the *Gazette*, was a waiter at Pete's Pizza, and a janitor after school (at Kennedy High) with his girlfriend, Cecilia (Ashlee Simpson); her father owns a janitorial service. Simon was smart and basically a good kid but became shattered emotionally when he was involved in a fatal car accident that claimed the life of a young man. Although the accident was not Simon's fault, Simon could not ease his mind while living in Glen Oak and chose to attend college out of state (at which time David Gallagher left the series). He returns on occasion as a guest star.

See also: Eric and Annie Camden, Lucy Camden, Mary Camden, Matt Camden, Ruthie Camden.

1009. Simon Templar, *The Saint*, Syn., 1963–1966; NBC, 1967–1969. Played by Roger Moore.

Simon Templar is a wealthy adventurer who makes it his business to help people in trouble. He is considered criminal by the police (for constantly breaking the law) but is actually on their side and helps them solve baffling crimes (especially Claud Eustace Teal, Chief Inspector of Scotland Yard).

Simon is called "The Saint" but no explanation is given as to how or why (it could be that he helps people and is sort of their patron saint; or it could be that he breaks the law to accomplish things but also upholds it — he is both a devil and a saint). Simon's background is also a mystery. Nothing is known about his youth or even his early adult life. He is British, well educated, and apparently a man of independent means. He does not work and he accepts no fees for his services. He finds pleasure in helping people and delights in the adventures it affords him. Simon is very generous with his money. He carries Diner's Club and American Express credit cards, an international driver's license and passport wherever he goes. In London (where Simon lives) he drives a white Volvo 1800 with the license plate ST-1.

Simon is a master among thieves (another reason for his "wanted by the police" reputation). He appeals to women and the woman he meets, "the most glamorous in the world," appeal to him ("Luscious figures, provocative eyes and haunting voices"). Simon is "lean, tall and well able to look out after himself. His voice and manners are deceptively lazy."

Simon is "a roaring adventurer who loves a fight; a dashing daredevil, debonair, preposterously handsome; a pirate or philanthropist as the occasion demands. He lives for the pursuit of excitement, for the one triumphant moment that is his alone." Simon is fearless and risks his life to help complete strangers. He battles injustice more than crime. He often acts alone and is shot at and beaten up for his intrusion in matters that really do not concern him (it should be the police who help, not a loner who just happens to be in the wrong place at the wrong time).

1010. Simone Foster, *Head of the Class*, ABC, 1986–1991. Played by Khrystyne Haje.

Simone Foster is a student in the I.H.P. (Individual Honors Program) at Fillmore High School in New York City. She is the daughter of Maureen and Robert Foster and was born on May 14, 1970. She lives at 3406 Riverdale Drive and is considered the prettiest girl in the Honors Program. Simone is sweet, shy and very sensitive. She has been a straight A student all her life. Her specialty is English and her greatest gift is her romantic vision of life. Simone is not from a wealthy family (her father works in the book binding department of a publisher) and dresses in clothes that fit her budget. She honestly enjoys school and spends her spare time doing charity work. The mythical Robert T. Lasker is her favorite poet and she is a member of the school's chess club (where she loses her femininity and is called "Mister").

See also: Arvin Engen, Charlie Moore, Darlene Merriman, Dennis Blunden.

1011. Sister Bertrille, *The Flying Nun*, ABC, 1967–1970. Played by Sally Field.

Sister Bertrille is a nun with the order of the Sisters of San Tanco. She is assigned to the Convent San Tanco in San Juan, Puerto Rico, and has taken a vow of poverty. She lives in a convent and works with the poor people of the community. She most enjoys teaching the children (mothers consider the convent a day care center).

Sister Bertrille's real name is Elsie Ethrington. She was born in Santa Monica, California, and is the daughter of Russell and Mary Ethrington. Elsie attended Westside High School (where she was voted "The Most Far Out Girl of 1965") and was a member of a rock band called The Gorries. Elsie was a typical teenager and enjoyed movies, the beach and hanging out with her friends. In 1966 she became so impressed by her aunt's work as a missionary that she chose to devote her life to helping those less fortunate. After graduating from high school (1966) Elsie joined a nunnery. A year later she received her first assignment at the Convent San Tanco. Prior to her joining the nunnery Elsie worked as a counselor at Camp Laughing Water.

Elsie had never known poverty before. She now wants to do all she can to help the people of San Tanco. Shortly after her arrival on the island, Sister Bertrille (the name taken by Elsie when she became a nun) discovers she has the ability to fly. Her white cornets (headgear) have sides that resemble wings. Elsie weighs only 90 pounds and San Juan is an area affected by trade winds. A strong gale of wind enables her to soar above the ground. By manipulating her cornets she acquires some control over her flights but landings are difficult (she crashes into things).

Elsie cares deeply about people. She always has and always caused more problems than solutions when she tried to help somebody in trouble. She now feels with her gift of flight she can help those who really need help.

1012. Sister Steve, *Father Dowling Mysteries*, NBC, 1989; ABC, 1990–1991. Played by Tracy Nelson.

Stephanie Oskowski was born in Chicago in 1966. She was an unruly child and grew up on the streets. While she loved her parents she often disobeyed them. Her years at St. Michael's Grammar School were normal, but when she left a Catholic school for a public high school she fell in with a crowd who enjoyed hanging out on the streets rather than attending classes. She enjoyed playing stickball and learned some unique talents: how to pick locks and how to hot wire cars. It was at this time that Steve, as Stephanie was called, met Father Frank Dowling, the pastor of St. Michael's Church. He caught her stealing from F.W. Woolworth and made it his business to help her. He took her under his wing and straightened her out. Steve and Frank became friends. Steve became so impressed by Frank's work that she decided to become a nun. With the help of Father Dowling, Steve was accepted at the Holy Mother Convent.

She became a nun and took the name Sister Stephanie (although Frank calls her Sister Steve).

Steve believes she made the right decision about becoming a nun. She now works with Frank at St. Michael's (where she also teaches at St. Michael's Grammar School). Steve's middle name (taken at Confirmation) is Sivle — Elvis spelled backward (after her favorite singer, Elvis Presley). While Steve is caring and dedicated to God, she also finds pure pleasure in helping Frank do what he does best — solve crimes (both consider themselves amateur sleuths). Steve's street smarts and ability to think like a criminal make her and Frank (who thinks like Sherlock Holmes) the perfect crime fighting team. As a child Steve enjoyed going to the zoo to visit Diogenes, a monkey she befriended.

See also: Father Dowling.

1013. Six, *Tripping the Rift*, Sci Fi, 2004. Voiced by Gina Gershon.

Tripping the Rift is a computer generated adult science fiction series. This entry also contains information on Chode (Stephen Root), Darph Bobo (Terrence Scammell), Gus (Maurice LaMarche), Spaceship Bob (John Melendez), T'nuk (Gayle Garfinkle) and Whip (Rick Jones).

Six. Six of One (her full name and a parody of *Star Trek: Voyager*'s Seven of Nine) is an android that is also a beautiful, busty, long-legged sex machine. She was built for love "and can fake over 2,000 orgasms in over 600 languages."

Six, she is often called, operates as the science officer on the *Jupiter 42*, a futuristic smuggling ship. Although Six lives to make love she likes to do it in private offline. She becomes upset when people treat her like a slut ("I am a professional, not an addict") and would like nothing more than "being a droid that has rockin' sex" but her duties on the ship derail that ambition.

Six knows she is drop dead gorgeous — and not supposed to have a brain. She is supposed to be a pretty toy but she works with a group of less-intellectual beings and has thus taken on the responsibility of keeping the *Jupiter 42* in orbit.

Chode. Chode, a parody of Captain Kirk of *Star Trek* fame, is a three-eyed purple being (similar to a dog's chew toy) who captains the *Jupiter 42*. He is from a race that enslaves its people (they believe society makes the man, not the individual). Chode has a crush on Six and loves to drink, smoke pot and curse like a sailor. He hates paying bills and believes in slavery. He is not the best of captains and has a knack for getting himself into situations that require rescuing.

Darph Bobo. Darph is a spoof of the evil Darth Vader character in *Star Wars* films. He is a clown, a creation of the Dark Clowns, beings bent on dominating the galaxy. Darph was a student of Ben Dover, a great clown warrior who taught peace and harmony. Darph (who resembles an evil Bozo the Clown) dislikes Dover's teachings and chose a path of destruction (he was teased as a child and now feels he has the power to get even by taking his anger out on anyone who crosses him). Darph enjoys being evil and crushing people under his large clown shoes.

Gus. Gus could be considered a parody on *Star Wars* C-3P0. Gus is a robot who works as the *Jupiter 42*'s inept engineer. He is actually Captain Chode's robot slave (robots have no rights and must be servants). Over time Gus has developed his own ideals and is uncooperative and cynical (this goes against the robot code of being helpful and courteous). Is Gus gay? He gives that impression especially when he yearns to become "the funny one" on the futuristic TV show *Queer Eye for the Space Guy*. Gus is an excellent cook (quiche Lorraine is his specialty) and he enjoys frosting cupcakes, Judy Garland movies and loosening his metal parts with hot penetrating oil. He hates his master and always having to travel in the baggage compartment.

Spaceship Bob. Bob is the artificial intelligence that controls the *Jupiter 42*. He is afraid of the vast regions of space and suffers from panic attacks. He would like to jettison his entire crew of morons so he can be left alone, but he can't because he needs their help in running the ship. Bob is afraid to make a commitment and making a decision is very upsetting to him.

T'nuk. T'nuk could be considered a spoof of the beautiful alien women seen on *Star Trek*. She is just the opposite — hideous and not very bright (she has a triangle-shaped head with protruding eyes, sagging breasts and is grossly overweight. She has four feet and when standing resembles a mythical creature like a Hind). T'nuk is Chode's partner in their smuggling operations. She is always suspicious and always made the butt of jokes at parties. She doesn't appreciate men who do not appreciate her. T'nuk admires Six and dreams of becoming a sex slave.

Whip. Whip has only one ambition in life: have sex before his moronic crew gets him killed. He is lazy, drinks any brand of beer and holds the pointless job as foreman on the *Jupiter 42* (the job suits him because he is use to avoiding work and since there is no need for a foreman on a ship he does no work). Whip resembles a lizard with two arms and legs. He believes he is irresistible to women and also hates exercising and getting up before noon.

1014. Six LeMeure, *Blossom*, NBC, 1991–1995. Played by Jenna Von Oy.

Six Dorothy LeMeure is a 13-year-old girl who wonders about things — "I wonder what my husband will look like naked or if I'll laugh the first time I see him. I wonder what it will be like to have a mortgage, a baby and breasts." She also worries "that my father will go into my room and read the lyrics on my album covers if I stay away from home for too long."

Six is the cute, smart-mouthed girlfriend of Blossom Russo. She lives next door to Blossom (on Hampton Drive) and attends Tyler High School. Six is so named because her father had six beers the night he made love to his wife and a baby was conceived. Six (and Blossom) love to shop at the mall after school. They eat lunch together in the school cafeteria and each saves the other a seat when the other is going to be late. Six considers Blossom to be "a real decent person with moral values" (why her parents like her being friends with Blossom but six worries that Blossom's niceness is going to rub off on her). Six enjoys dancing "to get all sweaty and dizzy and see stars." She is on the school's debate team and she has a real knack for getting into mischief at school and winding up in detention ("If detention were frequent flyer miles I'd have enough miles for a free trip to Hawaii"). Six does volunteer work at the Beacon Light Mission. In the last episode Six was accepted to West Orlando State, Northridge and San Diego State College but had made no decision as to which one to attend.

See also: Anthony Russo, Blossom Russo, Joey Russo, Nick Russo.

1015. The Skipper, *Gilligan's Island*, CBS, 1964–1967. Played by Alan Hale, Jr.

Jonas Grumby, called the Skipper, is captain of the S.S. *Minnow*, a small charter boat based in Hawaii. Gilligan, his bumbling first mate, assists him. It was during a three-hour tour that his ship became engulfed by a tropical storm at sea and was beached on an uncharted island 300 miles southeast of Hawaii. Jonas, Gilligan and their passengers, Ginger Grant, Mary Ann Summers, the Professor, and Thurston and Lovey Howell, are now stranded and have made the island their home.

It was the Skipper's quick thinking that saved the lives of his crew and passengers. Jonas lost everything when the *Minnow* was destroyed but plans to use the insurance money to start over again. Jonas met Gilligan during a hitch in the Navy (Gilligan saved Jonas's life when he pushed him out of the way of a depth charge that had come loose on the ship they were aboard). Jonas saw action during World War II in the South Pacific and earned the rank of captain. He played football in high school and is an excellent poker player. His favorite steak sandwich is "a filet between two top sirloins." Jonas is superstitious and is concerned about voodoo curses (as he has witnessed a number of peculiar happenings in his dealings with native tribes). The Skipper calls Gilligan "Little Buddy" and hates it when Gilligan reminds him "I'm your crew."

See also: Gilligan, Ginger Grant, Mary Ann Summers, The Professor, Thurston and Lovey Howell.

1016. Sledge Hammer, *Sledge Hammer*, ABC, 1986–1987. Played by David Rasche.

Sledge Hammer is a man who loves violence. He is a cop who shoots first and asks questions later. His car license plate reads I LOVE VIOLENCE and Sledge Hammer is the name given to him by his parents. He is said to be "dirtier than Harry and meaner than Bronson" and "I make Rambo look like Pee Wee Herman."

Sledge enjoyed violent movies while growing up (television was too tame for his tastes). He had a toy gun as a companion and when he played cops and robbers he was always the cop who never brought a robber in alive. Sledge was a bully of sorts in school (he would protect the wimpy kids from the bullies by beating up "the bad guys"). He lived and breathed violence. After graduating from high school he joined the police academy and upon graduation acquired his best friend, Gun, a .44 Magnum (he talks to it and sometimes imagines it talks back to him).

Sledge lives at 5517 Stafford Street (Apartment 13) in an unspecified American city. He is a detective with an unnamed police precinct, wears badge number 6316 and carries a bazooka in the trunk of his car ("For taking out suspects," he says). Sledge is considered a menace by the department — not only to himself and innocent victims but also to other police officers. Sledge upholds the law but has a misguided interpretation of it. He considers jay walking, for example, a serious crime and fires warning shots at such people. He feels that the only way to capture a criminal is to be more dangerous than they are. He has been sited for police brutality (beating up suspects) and takes Gun wherever he goes — to bed, grocery shopping, to visit his mother. Sledge is trigger happy and believes "all cops are wusses except me. I never let my guard down." Sledge has been shot at many times and wounded many times. The flesh wounds don't faze him; but when a good sports jacket is ruined by a bullet hole he becomes angered. Sledge prefers the solitude of his apartment for target practice. He is not concerned about bullets piercing the walls or even being evicted. Sledge was married to a woman named Susan. They divorced after three years ("She fell for a geek — someone who works in the Peace Corps"). Despite all his apparent recklessness Sledge does have a good side — he donates to a charity called Toy Guns for Tots.

1017. Sock Miller, *The People's Choice*, CBS, 1955–1958. Played by Jackie Cooper.

Socrates Miller, called Sock, is the people's choice, voted 5th District Councilman of New City, California. Sock was born in California and raised by his Aunt Augusta (called Aunt Gus) after his parents were killed in a car accident when he was three years old. Sock was a marine sergeant and served in Korea during the war (he was the platoon's bayonet champion). He is a graduate of Cornell University (where he was in the Phi Delta Kappa fraternity) and works as an ornithologist for the government's Bureau of Fish and Wildlife. His job is to "follow the birds" (he files reports on migratory birds and their flights predict climatic conditions and aid farmers when planting crops). Since getting back from Korea, Sock has logged 80,000 miles following birds.

Sock lives with Aunt Gus and his dog (Cleo) in a trailer camp in New City Paradise Park. He is romantically involved with Amanda Peoples (Patricia Breslin), the mayor's daughter, and marries her in 1957. Shortly after, Sock applies for a position as a lawyer with Barker Amalgamated in New York City (now that he is married he hopes to settle down). Sock is hired — but as the sales manager for Barkerville, a housing development with 294 houses for sale "20 miles from nowhere." Houses sell for $15,995 and Sock and Amanda (called Mandy) live rent-free in model house 119. Mandy was born in New City and is a graduate of Valley High School. Sock calls her his "Ruby Throated Hummingbird." Mandy's father, Mayor John Peoples, calls Sock "Nature Boy."

1018. Sondra Huxtable, *The Cosby Show*, NBC, 1984–1992. Played by Sabrina LeBeauf.

Sondra Huxtable is the eldest child of Cliff and Clair Huxtable. She lives at 10 Stigwood Avenue in Brooklyn, New York, and has four siblings (Theo, Denise, Vanessa and Rudy). Sondra was born in Brooklyn at the Children's Hospital in 1953. She attended Central High School and is a graduate of Princeton University (it cost her parents $79,648.72 and she broke a long-standing

family tradition by not attending Hillman College in Georgia — her parent's alma mater). Sondra was a pre-law student at Princeton when she met (and married) Elvin Tibideaux (Geoffrey Owens), a pre-med student. They became the parents of twins (Winnie and Nelson) and put their careers on hold to open the Wilderness Store. They first lived in a small apartment (5B) in Brooklyn, then with Cliff and Clair and in1990 in New Jersey when they buy their first home. Elvin called Sondra "Muffin." When their business failed, Sondra became a full time housewife and mother while Elvin found work as Inspector 36 at Benrix Industries (he checked pill bottles for their safety seals). He was fired when an efficiency expert said they didn't require 36 inspectors. With Cliff's help Elvin enrolled in medical school and became a doctor in 1990. Sondra resumed her education and became a lawyer in 1991.

See also: Cliff and Clair Huxtable, Denise Huxtable, Theo Huxtable, Vanessa and Rudy Huxtable.

1019. Sonny Crockett, *Miami Vice*, NBC, 1984–1989. Played by Don Johnson.

James Crockett, nicknamed Sonny, is a detective with the Miami Metro Dade Police Department (also called the Miami, Florida, Police Department). He is partners with Ricardo Tubbs; divorced from Caroline and the father of Billy.

Sonny was born in Florida in 1949 and is a graduate of the University of Miami (where he played football as a member of the Gators; he wore jersey 88). Sonny appeared to have a promising career as a professional player until "I traded the whole thing in for two years in Nam" (in another episode he mentions his career ended when he injured his knee). He became a cop after the Korean War. He first taught in rookie school and was first assigned to the Robbery Division. Four years later he was transferred to the Vice Squad and finally to Metro Dade's Organized Crime Bureau. Because of the sensitive nature of his work, Sonny has been given the undercover identity of Sonny Burnett, an enterprising businessman.

Sonny lives away from the pressures of society on a boat he calls *The Saint Vidas Dance*. Sonny is a drug dealer this week, an outlaw the next. "I'm trying to get by on four hours of sleep a day. I go undercover for weeks at a time. It's disastrous on a marriage, hell on the nervous system."

Sonny gets high from the action he encounters but suffers from a gambling and drinking problem. He prefers to do things his way and has been suspended for misconduct. Once on a case he doesn't request backup and he won't submit progress reports (he fears leaks in his department could compromise his cases).

Sonny lives on the boat with Elvis, an alligator who was the former mascot of the Gators football team. Elvis was benched for taking a bite out of a player and now "works" as Sonny's watchdog and dope sniffer. Elvis shows his teeth when strangers appear and ticks — he ate a clock. Elvis is also high (he devoured a bag of LSD while searching a Key West bus depot for drugs). Sonny has an account at the Dade County Federal Bank and says of himself and Tubbs: "We're just tollbooths on a highway when it comes to bustin' drug runners."

See also: Ricardo Tubbs.

1020. Sonny Mann, *It's a Living*, ABC, 1980–1982; Syn., 1985–1989. Played by Paul Kreppel.

Sonny Mann is a one-man entertainment center who performs nightly at Above the Top, a 13th Floor Los Angeles Restaurant. Sonny was born in Reno, Nevada, and his real last name is Manischevitz (he changed it when he became a singer). Sonny calls himself "The Singing Sex Symbol" and dreams of becoming rich and famous (he puts on elaborate shows when record producers dine at the restaurant).

Sonny's idol is singer Jack Jones. Sonny also performs at Vinnie's Romper Room and the Playpen Lounge at Chuck's Game Room in Las Vegas. Sonny pictures himself as a ladies' man and wrote the book *Mann to Mann* (a guide for picking up girls). When no publisher would touch it, he had 750 copies printed for himself. Sonny has a Franklin Mint All Nation doll collection and *Rocky and His Friends* is his favorite TV show (he is a charter member of the Bullwinkle the Moose Fan Club). He had a dog named Buster as a kid.

See also: Amy Tompkins, Cassie Cranston, Dot Higgins, Ginger St. James, Jan Hoffmeyer, Lois Adams, Maggie McBirney.

1021. Sophia Petrillo, *The Golden Girls*, NBC, 1985–1992. Played by Estelle Getty.

Sophia Petrillo is the mother of Dorothy Zbornak and lives with her and housemates Blanche Devereaux and Rose Nylund at 6151 Richmond Street in Miami Beach, Florida. Sophia is a widow (her late husband was named Sal) and is a senior citizen who lived previously at the Shady Pines Retirement Home.

Sophia was born in Sicily, Italy. She and Sal immigrated to the U.S. and set up housekeeping on Canarsie Street in Brooklyn, New York (where her daughter, Dorothy, was born).

Sophia had a part-time job at the Pecos Pete Chow Wagon Diner, then at Meals on Wheels, and finally as activities director for the Cypress Grove Retirement Home. Sophia calls Dorothy "Big Foot" and "Pussycat" and became somewhat senile as the series progressed. She plays bingo at St. Dominick's Church and buys her shoes at Shim Shacks. Sophie and Dorothy are Catholic. In the spinoff series, *The Golden Palace* (CBS, 1992–1993), Sophia, Blanche and Rose pool their resources to open the Golden Palace, a 42-room Miami Hotel.

See also: Blanche Devereaux, Dorothy Zbornak, Rose Nylund.

1022. The Sorceress, *BeastMaster*, Syn., 1999–2002. Played by Monika Schnarre, Dylan Bierk.

The age of darkness, magic and nature produced many strange beings. Two are the Sorceress (Monika Schnarre) and the New Sorceress (Dylan Bierk). The Sorceress is a beautiful woman who has been studying and learning supernatural magic for untold ages. She is fascinated by her ability to combine the elements of nature and myth to create both natural and unnatural forces. She lives in a mountain cave and appears and disappears in a purple mist. She uses what she calls "My Third Eye" (a telescope she acquired from Baha the Slave Trader) that lets her see what others cannot through a human female eye. The Sorceress is controlled by the Ancient One, the magical ruler of the land, who is teaching her how to use her developing powers "to keep the world from sinking into darkness."

According to the Ancient One, a Sorceress "is not supposed to have a heart or fall in love" or interfere with human destiny without her teacher being present. When the Sorceress begins challenging her teacher and defying his wishes, the Ancient One becomes displeased with her and imprisons her in a crystal rock. He replaces her with a new protégé called the New Sorceress. The New Sorceress is unaware of who she really is or where she came from. She is eager to learn about the fascinating world in which she finds herself and is not fully aware of the extent of her powers. The New Sorceress enjoys meddling in human affairs and uses what powers she has to help good defeat evil.

See also: The Ancient One, Arina, Dar, Curupira, Iara, Tao.

1023. Spenser, *Spenser: For Hire*, ABC, 1985–1988. Played by Robert Urich.

Spenser (no first name) is a sophisticated Boston-based private detective. He was born in Laramie, Wyoming. His mother died in childbirth and his father and his mother's two brothers raised him. He rejected the family business (carpentry) and joined the army after graduating from high school. He served time in Korea during the war (where he learned how to box). He became a semi-professional boxer for a short time after his discharge. He next joined the Massachusetts Police Department and worked as a state trooper before becoming an investigator for the district attorney in Suffolk County. He quit when he found he had trouble accepting authority. Spenser turned his talents to becoming his own boss and making his own rules as a private detective.

Spenser lives at 357 Masave Street in Boston (he first lived in an apartment that was destroyed by a fire, then in an abandoned firehouse that was reactivated). He first drives a green (then gray) Mustang. Spenser has a sense of chivalry and decency toward all people. While he does help people solve their problems (and bring criminals to justice) he also enjoys the excitement and considers himself a thug for hire. Spenser is a gourmet cook and enjoys a beer with each meal. He keeps in shape by lifting weights and quotes poetry and lines from books. He is also sensitive and romantic but too quick to act and often finds himself in hot water for doing so.

1024. Spike, *Buffy the Vampire Slayer*, WB, 1997–2001; UPN, 2001–2003. Played by James Marsters.

The character of Spike also appeared on *Angel* (WB, 2003–2004). William the Bloody, called Spike, is a vampire who fluctuates between good and evil. When he is good he helps Buffy (then Angel) battle demons. When he is bad he becomes a vicious vampire who preys on the living. William the Bloody received his nickname for his habit of torturing people with railroad spikes. He was born in Prague and originally came to America for the Hellmouth that exists under Sunnydale High School in California. A Hellmouth is a mysterious portal that attracts evil and a Slayer (such as Buffy Summers) destroys whatever it dispenses. Spike hoped the Hellmouth would cure Drusilla (Juliet Landau), the woman he loves. Drusilla was young woman who enjoyed life—until she met Angel (as a vampire). Angel drove Drusilla insane by killing her family for fun. He then turned her into a vampire and let her roam free. Drusilla met William shortly after and in 1897 turned him into a creature of the undead. Drusilla is not only evil but she is insane. She eventually left Spike for other demons.

Spike is next captured by the Initiative, a government organization that hunts vampires and demons. Spike is called Hostile 17 and is rendered harmless to humans when a computer chip is placed in his brain (if he tries to harm anyone the chip produces extreme pain). It is at this time that Spike becomes "good" and helps Buffy battle demons "out of the evilness of my heart."

The last episode of *Buffy* (May 20, 2003), found Spike helping Buffy and Angel defeat an army of vampires seeking to take over the world. Buffy and Angel survived but it appeared Spike did not. When *Angel* began its new season in the fall of 2003, Spike was reincarnated, first as a spirit, then as an actual being when a magic amulet releases him from the spirit world. He has now become a savior and an important aid to Angel in stopping evil. Spike wears a black coat that he took from the body of a female slayer he killed in New York City.

See also: Angel, Buffy Summers, Fred Berkel.

1025. Stacey Colbert, *Ned and Stacey*, Fox, 1995–1996. Played by Debra Messing.

Stacey Colbert is a young woman who works as a newspaper columnist for the *Village Voice* in Manhattan. Stacey was born in Trenton, New Jersey, and is a graduate of Trenton High School and Brandice College (where she majored in journalism). She is now a gorgeous red head but in grammar school she was gawky, wore braces and was a head taller than other girls in her class. The one thing she wished for (but never got) were larger breasts (she is rather small compared to her older sister Amanda). Stacey's father called her "Cookie" and each year on his birthday she gave him slippers (and each year he would say "What, slippers again?"). When Stacey had a problem she and her father would talk things over at Hogan's Diner. A good day for Stacey can only happen "if I have a good hair day." She enjoys snacks at her sister's Manhattan coffee shop (Amanda's-A-Muffins).

Stacey is sweet, kind, gentle and very caring. She will do anything to help a friend if she is asked. She lives on Long Island but wishes she lived in Manhattan to be closer to work. When her friend Ned Dorsey (Thomas Hayden Church) learns that he needs to have a wife to get a promotion (at the Spencer Haywood Advertising Agency) he asks Stacey to pose as his wife; in return he will let her live rent-free in his Manhattan apartment. Stacey is now "married," and happy and trying to get along with a man who is her complete opposite (Ned is neat, loves to cook and maneuvers and manipulates his way through life—"I exploit people, that's what I do").

Stacks (*B.J. and the Bear*) *see* **B.J. McKay**

1026. Stacy Newland, *The Division*, Lifetime, 2004. Played by Amy Jo Johnson.

Stacy Newland is a services aide with the San Francisco Police Department. She is 24 years old and not exactly sure what she wants to do with her life ("I don't know which direction I should be heading in yet"). She is an overachiever but she often becomes bored with something once she achieves it (in high school, for example, Stacy became a cheerleader to be like her two sisters, star cheerleaders. She dropped out when she became bored with it).

Stacy is the youngest of three children and from an upper middle class family. She has lived in the shadow of two perfect sisters — girls who did everything to please their parents. Stacy tried to follow suit. She became engaged but called off the marriage to become different. She joined the San Francisco Police Academy and graduated top in her class. She not only became the black sheep of the family but she jumped into a situation without giving it much thought and now isn't sure if she is ready to patrol the streets (hence her services aide job). Stacy realizes her thrilling but less traditional life has upset her parents but she is determined not to cave in and give up her new career. She is determined to prove herself — to herself and her parents. Although Stacy considers herself to be an eager beaver she has a habit of irritating people with her desire to help people with their problems.

See also: Candace DeLorenzo, Jinny Exstead, Kate McCafferty, Magda Ramirez, Raina Washington.

1027. Stanley and Helen Roper, *Three's Company* (ABC, 1977–1978), *The Ropers* (ABC, 1979–1980). Played by Norman Fell, Audra Lindley.

Stanley and Helen Roper are a somewhat happily married couple who own the Roper Apartment Building in San Diego, California (the residence of Jack Tripper, Chrissy Snow and Janet Wood). Helen and Stanley later sell the building and move to the Royal Condominium Town House Complex in nearby Chevia Hills (they reside in a home at 46 Peacock Drive and 555-3099 is their phone number).

Helen was a U.S.O. (United Serviceman's Organization) entertainer during World War II (she met Stanley, a soldier, during a show). Helen is seeking only one thing from Stanley — romance. Stanley, however, is not interested in any kind of romantic encounters with Helen. Stanley likes women, especially young women, but can't let Helen know (he fears he will then have to make love to her). Stanley has a collection of girlie magazines hidden in the bathroom.

Helen accepts all of Stanley's nonsense and endless excuses why he won't be romantic because she loves him. Helen's main goal is to break down the barriers that prevent Stanley from becoming romantic. Stanley claims that if he saw Helen come to bed in the nude he'd be the first one to complain. If Helen were to write an autobiography she'd call it "Not Tonight" (as Stanley always says).

Stanley has a weird sense of humor and it seems it is always at the expense of someone else's misfortune (Helen says his sense of humor is a birth defect). Stanley enjoys peeping at the gorgeous blonde in Apartment 107 through his front window (or with binoculars) but simply cannot get interested in Helen. Helen complains that Stanley snores and is opposed to any weirdoes or hanky panky in the building. She also says that Stanley uses foul language when he gets angry and takes a nap every afternoon.

Stanley's favorite TV show is *Name That Tune* ("ever since he guessed the National Anthem in seven notes," says Helen). Hot Cocoa is Stanley's favorite bedtime drink and he enjoys the comic section of the Sunday paper ("Andy Capp" is his favorite strip). Stanley likes to enter contests. Helen has a dog (Muffin) and a parakeet (Stanley). Her mother calls Stanley Hubert. Helen is apparently Stanley's second love. He mentioned the only other girl he ever loved was Gloria Mealy.

See also: Chrissy Snow, Cindy Snow, Jack Tripper, Janet Wood, Ralph Furley, Terri Alden

1028. Stanley Beemish, *Mr. Terrific*, CBS, 1967. Played by Stephen Strimpell.

Stanley Beemish is, according to the opening theme narration, "a weak and droopy daffodil." He is also girl shy, accident-prone and a bit naïve. These are the qualities the U.S. government's Bureau of Special Projects requires to transform an ordinary man into a superhero.

Stanley is a high school graduate and co-owner of a gas station called Hal and Stanley's Service Station on Northeastern and Wyoming Streets in Washington, D.C. When a government scientist accidentally invents a source of power he calls "The Power Pill," it is found to make the strongest of men quite ill. But what will it do to a weak, sniveling coward? The government is determined to find out and their search leads them to the gas station and Stanley Beemish. Though reluctant at first, Stanley agrees to test the pill. Seconds after taking it, he is transformed into an heroic crime fighter he calls Mr. Terrific. Bureau Chief Burton J. Reed swears Stanley in and Stanley must now lead a double life — private citizen and the government's secret weapon against crime.

Stanley is not your run of the mill superhero. He wears a jacket with wing-like sleeves (which he flaps to fly), a pair of goggles and a scarf — all of which she stores in his locker at the gas station. In addition to flying, the pills endow Stanley with incredible strength and an immunity to harm. However, Stanley has difficulty flying and landings become difficult (he can't navigate). He also has difficulty finding assigned targets when airborne (his scarf constantly obstructs his vision).

The Purple Alert is sounded when Mr. Terrific is needed. The bitter tasting pills have to be candy coated for Stanley to take. He is given a box of three pills for each assignment. The initial pill endows him with the strength of 1,000 men and lasts one hour. The two booster pills last 10 minutes each (and naturally, wear off at crucial moments and Stanley has to solve cases as his normal, bumbling self).

1029. Stanley H. Tweedle, *Lexx*, Sci Fi, 2000– 2002. Played by Brian Downey.

Stanley H. Tweedle is captain of the *Lexx*, a space ship that is exploring a futuristic world called the Dark Universe. Stanley is also a coward. He prefers to talk his way out of a situation and refrains from using violence.

Stanley was a security guard for His Divine Shadow, the evil leader of His Divine Order, the force that governs the Light Universe. In reality, however, Stanley fought against His Divine Shadow as a member of the rebel group the Ostro-B Pair Legation. Stanley held the lowest rank possible (four) and worked as the Assistant Deputy Backup Courier for His Divine Shadow. During an assignment to deliver amino acid codes to the rebel group, His Divine Shadow's army attacked the rebels and all members of the legation were killed. The codes fell into enemy hands and 94 planets of His Divine Order were destroyed. Stanley became known as Arch Traitor Stanley Tweedle. He redeemed himself by joining forces with two former members of His Divine Shadow, Zev and Kai. Together they killed His Divine Shadow and escaped the destruction of the Light Universe in the *Lexx*. Stanley is able to control *Lexx* by the Light Hand Key he stole from His Divine Shadow.

Stanley is always seen wearing his red cap with his former rank, Level 4, on it. He is brave depending on the situation and has a three-stage philosophy: "When you're scared you're hungry.

When you're not hungry you're thinking about sex. When you're thinking about sex you're scared."

See Also: Kai, Robot Head 790, Zev Bellringer.

Stephanie Holden *see* **The Girls of Baywatch**

Stephanie Kaye *see* **The Girls of Degrassi**

1030. Stephanie Mills, *All in the Family*, CBS, 1978–1979. Played by Danielle Brisebois.

The character of Stephanie Mills also appeared on *Archie Bunker's Place* (CBS, 1979–1983). Stephanie Mills is a young girl who lives with Archie and Edith Bunker at 704 Hauser Street in Queens, New York. She is the daughter Edith's "no good cousin" Floyd Mills and has had an unsteady upbringing since her mother was killed in a car accident (Floyd took up drinking and has not been a good parent. Stephanie has had to fend for herself — cook, clean and care for her father). When Edith becomes concerned for Stephanie's welfare, she convinces Archie to let her live with them.

Stephanie is Jewish (Archie says he is a Christian; Edith is Episcopalian). She is a member of the Temple Beth Shalom and attends Ditmars High School. Stephanie was born on May 16, 1965, and is shy and insecure. Any change in Archie's life is a traumatic experience for him. But with Stephanie he had little to complain or worry about. She loved watching cartoons on TV, her stuffed animals and roller-skating. As she grew and lost interest in her tomboyish ways, she found an interest in boys, dating and makeup. "Now it's boys, boys, boys," says Archie. Archie is afraid to let Stephanie grow up because he fears, at age 13 she will ruin the best years of her life — "Your obsolescence" (he means, of course, adolescence). Archie feels Stephanie is not going to grow up around him and will let her have a boy who is a friend "but not a boyfriend."

Stephanie is a good student at school and enjoys doing homework. As Stephanie matured her wardrobe also changed from loose fitting clothes to slightly tighter, figure-revealing outfits (which, of course upset Archie, who cannot deal with female issues, like Stephanie's blossoming womanhood). Despite her rocky upbringing, Stephanie respects Edith and especially Archie, whom she believes is old-fashioned and needs to lighten up and get with the times (something Archie can not do because he was raised to fear everything he does not understand).

See also: Archie Bunker, Billie Bunker, Edith Bunker, Gloria and Mike Stivic.

1031. Stephanie Tanner, *Full House*, ABC, 1987–1995. Played by Jodie Sweetin.

Stephanie Judith Tanner is the middle daughter of Danny and Pamela Tanner and lives at 1882 Gerard Street in San Francisco, California, with her sisters D.J. and Michelle. Her mother is deceased.

Stephanie is sweet and adorable and always in a good mood. Even when she is sad she tries not to let it depress her. She is a student at Frasier Street Elementary School, then DiMaggio Jr. High School. Stephanie carries a "Jetsons" lunchbox to school and is a member of the Giants Little League baseball team (she wore jersey 8). She was a sensation as a pitcher and threw what Danny called "The Tanner Twister" ("a curve ball like no other girl").

Emily is Stephanie's favorite doll and Mr. Bear her favorite plush toy. Stephanie used the name Dawn for several weeks after the kids at school made fun of her name and called her "Step on Me." She earned the nickname "Sneeze Burger" when she sneezed during the taking of class pictures. Stephanie is a Capricorn and was a member of the Honeybees Scout Troop. She made a TV commercial for Oat Boats cereal and enjoys strawberry yogurt and pizza. Her catch phrase is "How rude."

See also: Danny Tanner, D.J. Tanner, Jesse Katsopolis, Joey Gladstone, Michelle Tanner.

1032. Stephanie Vanderkellen, *Newhart*, CBS, 1982–1990. Played by Julia Duffy.

Stephanie Vanderkellen is the spoiled daughter of a wealthy family who works as a maid at the Stratford Inn at 28 Westbrook Road in River City, Vermont. Stephanie was born in Vermont and is the daughter of Arthur and Mary Vanderkellen. She took the job to experience real life. She is very moody and looks down on people of lower social status. She likes to get things her way and pouts when she doesn't. Stephanie has to always be in fashion — even in her duties as a housekeeper at the inn. She wears only the latest fashions (which she buys at Peck's Department Store) and has a boyfriend (Michael Harris) who is not rich but struggles to provide the life to which Stephanie has become accustomed.

Michael (Peter Scolari) is an executive at WPIV-TV, Channel 8 (where Stephanie played twins Judy and Jody Bumpter in a sitcom called *Seein' Double*). When Michael is fired for insulting the boss's daughter, he first works as a salesman at Circus of Shoes, then as a produce clerk at Menke's Market and a mime. When it all came crashing down around him, he became a resident at the Pine Valley Psychiatric Hospital.

Michael is totally devoted to Stephanie. He calls her "Cupcake," "Gumdrop," and "Muffin" and constantly showers her with gifts. He has a special area of his apartment (9B) devoted to pictures of Stephanie that he calls "Cupcake Corner." To further please Stephanie with gifts, Michael has created "Cupcake Day," which comes between Valentine's Day and Easter. In 1989 Stephanie and Michael married. Stephanie became pregnant and gave birth to a girl she and Michael named Baby Stephanie.

Michael was born in Vermont and is the son of Ted and Lily Harris. He showed talent as a singer and dancer and as a child was the singing assistant on the TV show *Captain Cookie's Clubhouse*.

See also: Dick and Joanna Loudon, George Utley, Larry, Darryl and Darryl.

1033. Steve Austin, *The Six Million Dollar Man*, ABC, 1973–1978. Played by Lee Majors.

Steve Austin is a cybernetic organism, a cyborg — part human, part machine. Steve was born in Ojai, California, and lives on a ranch on Decatur Road (which he brought to find peace and quiet away from his hectic life as an astronaut). There is a highway sign that reads "The Home of American Astronaut Steve Austin" that one sees as they enter Ojai. Steve is a graduate of Ojai High School and dated Jaime Sommers, the girl who would become the Bionic Woman.

Steve was a colonel in the U.S. Air Force when he was chosen to test the M-3F5, an experimental plane. During the test flight, the plane experienced a blowout, crashed and exploded. Steve was seriously injured (legs broken beyond repair; a crushed right arm; a damaged left eye). With only one hope of saving him, Oscar Goldman, head of the O.S.I. (Office of Scientific Intelligence) arranges for Steve to have a bionic operation to replace his damaged limbs with atomic powered, artificial limbs. In a $6 million operation, Steve's eye is replaced with a Bionic Visual Cortex Terminal. His arm is replaced with an upper assembly Bionic Neuro Link Forearm and a Neuro Link Hand, Right. A Bionic Neuro Link, Bi-Pedal Assembly replaces his legs.

The synthetic parts endow Steve with superhuman abilities; abilities the government requires for special, super sensitive and highly dangerous missions. Steve can run as fast as 60 miles an hour. He has incredible strength and can see and pinpoint objects at incredible distances. He is able to leap to great heights. When at home (rarely) Steve drives a car with the license plate 299 KKL and enjoys a meal at the Capri (a pizza parlor). The

O.S.I was originally called the O.S.O. (Office of Strategic Operations).

See also: Jaime Sommers.

1034. Steve Douglas, *My Three Sons*, ABC, 1960–1965; CBS, 1965–1972. Played by Fred MacMurray.

Steve Douglas is a widower and the father of three sons (Mike, Robbie and Chip). He stands six feet, two inches tall and lives at 837 Mill Street in the town of Bryant Park. Steve works as an aeronautical engineer for Universal Research and Development. William Michael Francis Aloysius O'Casey, affectionately called "Bub" (William Frawley), Steve's father-in-law, cares for the family. Ernie Thompson, a young orphan later lives with them when Mike (Tim Considine) graduates from college and moves east to become a psychology professor. Bub first says his nickname came from Mike (who couldn't pronounce Grandpa) then from Chip (who couldn't say Bill).

Steve was born in 1913 in an unspecified Midwest locale. He is a graduate of Midwest University (class of 1935) and married Louise O'Casey, Bub's daughter, when he was 21 years old. Louise died 12 years later on the night before Chip's first birthday. Steve attended Beaver Dam High School (1927–31) and was a member of the school's baseball team; he also played the saxophone in the school band. Steve married Barbara Harper in 1969, two years after he was transferred to North Hollywood, California. Barbara (Beverly Garland) was a widowed schoolteacher with a young daughter named Dodie (Dawn Lyn).

Steve enjoys wearing a cardigan sweater and relaxing by smoking a pipe in his easy chair in the living room. He likes Italian food (at Luigi's Restaurant) and ice cream is his favorite dessert. He has a dog (Tramp) and Bryant Park 6100 (then Larson 0-6719) is his phone number. He drives a car with the license plate JXN 127.

Mike was the oldest of the children. He attended Bryant Park High School then State College. He married Sally Ann Morrison (Meredith MacRae) in 1963. Robbie (Don Grady) attended Webster Elementary School then Bryant Park High. He and Katie Miller (Tina Cole) marry and become the parents of triplets (Charley, Steve, Jr. and Robbie II). Chip, real name Richard (Stanley Livingston) attends Buchanan Elementary School, then Bryant Park High. He and Polly Williams (Ronne Troup) marry in 1970.

Bub was a member of Brotherhood of the Cavaliers and left the series in 1964 (returned to Ireland to help his Aunt Kate celebrate her 104th birthday). Bub's brother, Charlie O'Casey (William Demarest), a retired Merchant Marine then cared for the family (he was affectionately called Uncle Charlie).

1035. Steve Hightower, *The Steve Harvey Show*, WB, 1996–2002. Played by Steve Harvey.

Steve Hightower is the music teacher at Booker T. Washington High School in Chicago. He lives in Apartment 1412 (undisclosed address) and is single. He tries to use his past glory as a professional musician to attract women. Steve was born in Chicago and is a graduate of Booker T (as the school is called) but chose to follow a dream in the music business rather than attend college. Steve, a talented piano and sax player, formed a group called The High Tops. The group played funk music and achieved one gold record. Creative differences led to the group's breakup and Steve turned his talents to teaching what he loves.

Steve won a Grammy Award and was honored by the Funk Café in Detroit as "The King of Funk Music." At Booker T, Steve is famous for squashing the 1996 mysterious meat riot in the cafeteria. Steve is always hoping for another big break. He keeps active by performing with his friend, Cedric Robinson, in charity functions as The Soul Teachers. He also attempted to become a manager by forming an all-girl group he called Jailbait for his company, Steve Hightower Management.

Steve wears a size 12 shoe and likes his grilled cheese sandwiches "with the edges burned." He often pretends to be somebody he is not to meet women (for example, he joined the Sexually Addicted Group "to meet funky women"). Steve's classes are held in Room 104 and he became romantically involved with the school's principal, Regina Grier (whom he affectionately calls "Piggy"). They were in high school together and she was a bit overweight. Steve drives a Ford Taurus.

See also: Cedric Robinson, Lovita Jenkins, Regina Grier.

1036. Steve McGarrett, *Hawaii Five-0*, CBS, 1968–1980. Played by Jack Lord.

Steven McGarrett is the head of Five-0, a special investigative branch of the Hawaiian Police Department (it is housed in the Iolani Palace, the only palace on American soil).

Steve was born in San Francisco. He attended Union High School and is a graduate of the Annapolis Naval Academy. He is a Capricorn (born in the 1930s) and has a younger sister (Mary Ann). He served with Naval Intelligence as was stationed in Japan during the Korean War. He remained with the navy until 1961 (at which time he moved to Hawaii). While not made clear, he apparently became a detective with the Hawaiian P.D. At an unspecified time after this, Steve was appointed to head Five-0.

Steve mentions his middle name as being Aloysius; in another episode he has the middle initial of J. He lives a 404 Pikoi Street in Honolulu and has an account at the National Bank of Oahu. Steve has his hair cut every Tuesday and his car license plate reads 163 958. Steve is also a navy reservist and keeps in shape by jogging along the beach. Steve claims to be a health food nut but sneaks an occasional junk food treat when he gets the urge. He is an excellent cook (lasagna and chicken cacciatore are his favorite meals) and he only has a drink on special occasions. Steve plays tennis to relax and enjoys his hobby of collecting Asian art objects. He has never been married because he believes that he can't be a good cop and a husband at the same time.

Steve works with Danny Williams (James MacArthur), whom he calls Dan-O (the term "Book 'em Dan-O" became associated with the series). Their arch enemy is Wo Fat (Khigh Dhiegh), a master criminal who eluded capture until the last episode ("Woe to Wo Fat").

1037. Steve Urkel, *Family Matters*, ABC, 1989–1997; CBS, 1997–1998. Played by Jaleel White.

Steven Quincy Urkel, called Steve, is a nerd with an unrelenting crush on his next-door neighbor, Laura Winslow. Steve was born in Chicago and attends Vanderbilt High School. He is equipment manager of the golf club and basketball team and says, "I'm 98 percent brain, two percent brawn." Steve has a stay-away fund (relatives send him money so he will not visit) and after people see Steve they remark, "I thank God I never had children."

Steve is a stringer for the school newspaper, *The Muskrat Times* and created a robot in his own image he called the Urkelbot (which has artificial intelligence and can think on its own). He later made one in Laura's image he called the Laurabot). He won the *Amateur Weekly* magazine contest with his Transformation Machine (which changes him into Stefan Urquette, a sophisticated ladies' man). He also invented the XJ-3, The Jet Propelled Urkel Pack that enables him to propel himself into the air. Steve has a lab in the basement of his home and he accomplishes things through science.

Steve does the difficult *New York Times* crossword puzzle in ink and is a straight A student (with the exception of a C he got in home economics when he tried to make bread and the yeast

didn't rise). Steve is interested in insects (he attends the Entomology Exhibit each year) and has a pet Peruvian stick bug named Pablo (for which he paid $486.52). Steve plays the accordion and anchovy paste on a dog biscuit is his favorite snack. His catch phrase is "Did I do that?"

Steve idolizes Laura. If Laura talks to another boy Steve becomes ill ("It shatters my heart"). He eats his lunch on Laura placemats, has a photo of Laura on his desk and pictures of her on his locker door. He calls her "Laura my love" and must walk 20 feet behind her at school (as she wants nothing to do with him). Steve drives the ultra compact Isetta 300 (a car with two wheels in the back; one centered in the front). The license plate was originally P27 128 then URKMAN.

After a relentless but ultimately fruitless pursuit of Laura, Steve realized she would never be his. To his surprise, the gorgeous Myra Monkhouse (Michelle Thomas) became attracted to him (for his intelligence). However, in the last episode, Laura returned to Steve and they became engaged. Steve was then chosen by the ISP (International Space Program) to test his invention, the AGF 5000 (Artificial Gravity Field). During the flight, dubbed "Nerd Watch '98," Steve's lifeline becomes detached from the mother ship (*Explorer*) and Steve is last seen drifting into endless space.

See also: Carl Winslow, Laura Winslow.

1038. Steven and Elyse Keaton, *Family Ties*, NBC, 1982–1989. Played by Michael Gross, Meredith Baxter.

Steven Richard Keaton and Elyse Catherine O'Donnell were students at Berkeley College when they met in the 1960s. They were flower children and married shortly after attending Woodstock in 1969. They lived in a California commune when their first child, Alex, was born (they had contemplated naming him Moon Muffin). At Berkeley Steven wrote a play called "A Draft Card for Burning" (as a protest to the Vietnam War) and was president of the South Campus aluminum can recycling program. He majored in communication arts. Elise majored in architecture. After graduating, Steven and Elyse moved to Columbus, Ohio, to begin new lives: Steven as manager of public TV station WKS, Channel 3; Elyse as a free-lance architect. They first lived in a small apartment on Rosewood Avenue, then in their series house in Leland Heights. They became the parents of three additional children: Mallory, Jennifer and Andrew. Another episode relates that Elyse was 15 and Steven was 18 when they first met in Berkeley, California. She married Steven three years later after graduating from high school.

Elyse is a fan of folk music and has a dream of becoming a folk singer. She worked briefly for the firm of Norvacks, Jenkins and St. Claire and the Cavanaugh Building in Columbus was the first structure she designed. Elyse and Steven are very good parents. They listen before they punish and feel that talking face-to-face about a problem is the best way to deal with that problem. While both parents tell their children "You can speak to us about anything," it is more often Elyse who deals with the problems of Mallory and Jennifer becoming women.

See also: Alex P. Keaton, Jennifer Keaton, Mallory Keaton

1039. Stewart Bondek, *Spin City,* ABC, 1996–2002. Played by Alan Ruck.

Stewart Bondek works as an aide to Randall Winston, the Mayor of New York City. Stewart is a rather unsavory character who delights in belittling other people, especially women. He has unconventional sex with girls he picks up at the bus station, thinks he is a ladies' man and hits on all the girls he sees. Large breasted woman excite Stewart and he calls "well stacked" girls "sweater meat." He has a beauty pageant paperweight on his desk that he purchased at a sex shop called the Knocker Locker; his Internet name is "Boob Meister." Stewart stays up all night watching Internet porn and claims to be an activist — if there was a petition to close a strip club within ten blocks of a school, "I would be right there to see that the school is closed."

Playing practical jokes amuses Stewart. He makes prank phone calls to pass the time and reads the personal ads for laughs (he finds the most pathetic ones and calls them "to give them a ray of hope"). Stewart collects a paycheck for all this and doesn't appear to do anything else. He doesn't take messages, attend meetings or even offer to volunteer for anything. Believing he is God's gift to women and hitting on girls is apparently the qualifications he needs for the job.

See also: Caitlin Moore, Charlie Crawford, Michael Flaherty, Paul Lassiter, Randall Winston.

1040. Stewart Sullivan, *Department S,* Syn., 1971–1972. Played by Joel Fabiani.

Stewart Sullivan was born in New York City and worked with the FBI before joining Department S, the Paris, France-based branch of Interpol (the International Police Force) that solves complex crimes.

Stewart has a shrewd mind and athletic abilities. He works with Annabelle Hurst and Jason King and is the team leader (he reports to their superior, Sir Curtis Seretse). He believes in the direct approach (planning before proceeding on a case) and that Jason's mind is sometimes faster than a computer in deciphering information. He expects progress reports from Jason and Annabelle as cases unfold and is usually the one who coordinates travel plans when a case requires the team to be in different places at the same time. He is an expert on explosives and provides the muscle when needed. Stewart lives in an apartment on Madeleine Drive and his car license plate reads YYM 297.

Stripperella *see* **Erotica Jones**

1041. Sue Ellen Ewing, *Dallas,* CBS, 1978–1991. Played by Linda Gray.

Sue Ellen Shepherd was born in Dallas, Texas, in 1947. She is the daughter of a caring mother (Patricia Shepherd) and an alcoholic father (not named), who deserted the family (and later died) after the birth of Sue Ellen's sister, Kristen.

Sue Ellen was a straight A student in high school. She attended the University of Texas at Austin and became the reigning beauty on campus. She became a varsity cheerleader and through her mother's urging, became a contestant in the 1967 Miss America Pageant. It was here that she met and fell in love with one of the judges — J.R. Ewing, then vice president of the Ewing Oil Company in Braddock, Texas. Sue Ellen won the pageant title and J.R.'s heart. They dated and married in 1971. They became the parents of John Ross Ewing, III, in 1979. Both were unfaithful. They divorced in 1981, remarried in 1982 and divorced again in 1988.

Living with the unscrupulous J.R. drove Sue Ellen to drinking and she eventually became an alcoholic. Sue Ellen was the founder of the Home for Wayward Boys, President of the Daughters of the Alamo and head of the fund-raising committee for the unfortunate. Sue Ellen loved to cook, was a graceful hostess at social functions and even tried her hand at business when she started Valentine Lingerie in 1986.

See also: Bobby Ewing, J.R. Ewing, Lucy Ewing, Pamela Barnes.

1042. Sue Thomas, *Sue Thomas, F.B.Eye,* PAX, 2002–2005. Played by Deanne Bray.

Suzanne Thomas, called Sue, is a young woman who sees what she cannot hear. She is deaf and reads lips to understand the world around her. Sue was born in Ohio and was apparently healthy.

She enjoyed playing outdoors with her friends and appeared to be typically normal. One day while watching a "Sylvester and Tweety Pie" cartoon on TV, Sue began to experience a hearing loss. Before the cartoon ended she was totally deaf. This became obvious to her mother when Sue approached the TV and turned up the volume in an effort to hear it. Sue was taken to several doctors but each was unable to explain the reason for her sudden hearing loss. Despite her handicap, Sue's mother was determined to see that her daughter would lead a normal life. A special tutor was hired and Sue was taught how to speak and hear things by reading lips and eyes. Sue was educated in normal schools and survived from kindergarten through college graduation. Sue was made fun of (called "a retard" in early grammar school) but her strong will and determination to be normal helped her survive a challenging school career. "You can never let them see you're scared," Sue's mother would tell her. "They'll think you don't belong."

"Keep moving forward; God will let you now if you're on the right track" is a philosophy Sue's mother taught her and that she now lives by to help her in her daily life. An abused golden retriever named Levi becomes Sue's hearing aid dog (trained to let her know when somebody is trying to get her attention, when the phone rings, etc.). "Nobody wanted him," she says, "except me. I knew he would make a good hearing aid dog." While not babied because of her impairment, Sue feels she must take her place in the world. She applies for and receives a position with the FBI in Washington, D.C. ("Never in a million years did I think I'd be working for the FBI"). Her enthusiasm turns to disappointment when she finds her job is Fingerprinting (examining fingerprints, identifying them and routing them for filing). "It's a fancy name for where they put people with disabilities," she says.

Sue does not consider herself disabled. With a hope of convincing personnel that she is suited for something better, Sue approaches Jack Hudson, an FBI agent she mistakes for the personnel director. When Jack sees that she is deaf but can look around a room and see what people are saying, he hits upon an idea to use her skills in his surveillance unit. She is given her own badge and becomes part of the investigative team. "We're going to make it, Levi," she said, "as long as we stick together."

Sue first lived in a loft over the Rock, Rattle and Roll Bowling Alley then is an apartment at 11 Hayden Place. She has a special phone that allows her to speak and "hear" the other party on a message unit that displays words. Sue's official title is Special Investigative Assistant; NC 5V2 is the license plate of her FBI–issued car. Sue tries to be open and honest about everything. She plays music because she likes to feel the vibrations. When she can't decide between coffee and tea at the vending machine she chooses hot chocolate. Sue is an excellent cook and is famous for her meatloaf. Sue also did a TV PSA (Public Service Announcement) for the government urging people to get out and vote.

Summer Quinn *see* **The Girls of Baywatch**

Superman *see* **Clark Kent**

Susan Bradford *see* **Mary Bradford**

1043. Sundance, *Hotel De Paree,* CBS, 1959–1960. Played by Earl Holliman.

He is only known as Sundance. He is an ex-gunfighter who is now the law enforcement officer of Georgetown, Colorado, during the 1870s. He is also part owner of the town's elegant Hotel De Paree, "one of the West's most colorful gathering places."

Sundance, also known as "The Sundance Kid," has a very mysterious past. He was born in Tombstone, Arizona (possibly in 1847), and grew up in an era of ruthlessness and lawlessness. Sundance learned at an early age how to use a gun — sometimes the only way his father could protect their ranch from outlaws and Indians.

Sundance served with the Union Army during the Civil War and became a wanderer after the conflict. He had a strong sense of justice and would help people in trouble as he roamed from town to town. At times he had to use his gun to defend himself and he gained a reputation as a gunfighter. It was a reputation he didn't want and figured he could shed it by becoming a lawman. Now he only wears his gun (a Colt .45) when he needs to (otherwise he patrols the town without a gun).

Sundance figures he acquired his nickname by his trademark — a black Stetson with a hatband of ten small mirrors (when the sun shines on them they produce blinding flashes of light — "sort of like a sun dance"). Sundance has a dog he calls Useless and enjoys whittling. He is opposed to killing (if he has to use his guns he will shoot to wound) and believes a fair trial is the right path to take — not the hangman's noose by a lynch mob.

1044. Susan Ivanova, *Babylon 5,* TNT, 1993–1997. Played by Claudia Christian.

Susan Ivanova is a lieutenant commander on *Babylon 5*, a five-mile long space station built in the 23rd century and located in neutral space (its purpose is to maintain peace among the various alien races). Susan is an extremely loyal and loving person. She stands by the station's captain, John Sheridan, and obeys his every command.

Susan is also a very beautiful woman who, despite the 250,000 people who live on the ship, is somewhat of a loner. She inherited telepathic abilities but hers have not yet fully developed and Susan has to be careful not to succumb to the same fate as her mother (who committed suicide when her powers overwhelmed her).

Susan is a very strong willed and caring person. She has a good sense of humor and dislikes people who ask dumb questions. Susan left *Babylon 5* at the end of the fourth season to take command of the Army of Light.

See also: Delenn, Elizabeth Lochley, John Sheridan, Lyta Alexander.

1045. Susan Keane, *Suddenly Susan*, NBC, 1996–2000. Played by Brooke Shields.

Susan Keane writes the column "Suddenly Susan" for *The* Gate, a trendy San Francisco magazine. She is beautiful and sexy and living in an apartment she can't afford. She is still paying off student loans and needs a new oven ("A repairman died in the old oven while trying to fix it"). Susan has a bright outlook about everything and thinks she is adorable. She fears telling a lie "because bad things happen when I don't tell the truth." Although she has the look of a super model, Susan hates to have her picture taken "because I always look I'm just reentering Earth" (her friend Vickie says, "Susan is pretty in person but nasty on film").

Susan was born in San Francisco on May 29 and weighed 10 pounds, 4 ounces at birth (her mother was in labor for 23 hours). When she was 10 years old Susan went on a hunger strike when Sizzler discontinued the rib sandwich. In junior high school Susan says, "I was a pie-loving kid who was overweight." She attended Hillcrest High School (where she wrote for the school newspaper) and majored in journalism at State University. Susan now lives at 3135 Washington Street and 555-4858 is her phone number. Lemon peel chicken is her favorite dinner and tequila is her favorite drink. She has a dog (Duchess) that she keeps at her mother's home and enjoys reruns of *Charlie's Angels*. Susan ran for (but lost) a seat on the San Francisco Board of Supervisors (her slogan was "I'm Keen on Keane"). Susan feels her life is filled with misadventure and

uses that as the basis for her columns — "It's about life and what happens to me" (her articles "have to be 1800 words and funny"). She is also a member of the Vixens (jersey 31), an all-girl basketball team. Susan enjoys dinner at Chan's Restaurant and has a drink with her co-workers at Buckey's Tavern (later O'Malley's and McMurphy's Bar).

See also: Vickie Groener.

1046. Susan Mayer, *Desperate Housewives*, ABC, 2004 (current). Played by Teri Hatcher.

Susan Mayer is a divorcee with a teenage daughter (Julie) who lives at 4353 Wisteria Lane in a seemingly perfect city called Fairview. Susan is divorced from Carl (who left her for his young secretary). She is very beautiful and sexy and seeking a new man in her life. She and Julie (Andrea Bowen) are very close and share each other's joys and sorrows. For a 12-year-old girl Julie is very knowledgeable and looks out for her mother; she even offers her dating tips — tips that are perfectly logical but Susan appears to be misfortune prone when it comes to men. She is known for her streak of bad luck and just when romance appears to be blossoming, a dark cloud casts its shadow and Susan is alone again.

Susan works as a children's book illustrator ("I'm very popular with the under five set"). She is a caring mother, excellent housekeeper but can only cook macaroni (and rarely do it well). Susan and Julie live on "store bought" meals and when Susan entertains a male guest she prepares him a home cooked meal prepared by a local take out diner. Susan drives a car with the license plate ERQ 346 and is a member of the monthly Wisteria Lane Book Club (with her friends Gabrielle, Bree and Lynette). Susan enjoys taking long, relaxing mid day showers and on one occasion managed to lock herself out of her house totally naked. It was mentioned that Susan was born in Ohio.

See also: Bree Van De Kamp, Edie Britt, Gabrielle Solis, Lynette Scavo.

1047. Susie McNamara, *Private Secretary*, CBS, 1953–1957. Played by Ann Sothern.

Susan Camille McNamara is a private secretary to Peter Sands, the owner of International Artists, Inc., a theatrical agency located on the 22nd floor (Suite 2201) of a building at 10 East 56th Street in New York City.

Susie, as she is called, was born in Mumford, Indiana, in 1925. She is descended from Scottish ancestors and is a graduate of Mumford High School (Mumford is also mentioned as being in Iowa). There was little excitement for Susan in Mumford. She had her schoolwork, she listened to radio programs and enjoyed actress Ann Sothern (the star of *Maizy* feature films). A big Saturday night in Mumford for Susie "was to get all dressed up, go to city hall and watch them polish the cannon." Susie is a Libra and incurably romantic. Life changed dramatically for her when she enlisted in the navy and became a WAVE. She served for three years (1942–45) and after her enlistment ended found her job with Mr. Sands.

Susie lives in Apartment H of the Brockhurst Apartments on East 92nd Street. She can type 65 words a minute and take 125 words per minute by shorthand. She enjoys meals at the Penguin Club and is a very sweet and generous person. She feels obligated to help people (mostly clients) she sees are in trouble and, as with most sitcoms of the day, only makes matters worse. Despite the problems she causes trying to solve problems, Peter calls her "The most faithful and loyal secretary I ever had."

1048. Suzanne Sugarbaker, *Designing Women*, CBS, 1986–1991. Played by Delta Burke.

Suzanne and Julia Sugarbaker are sisters who run the Sugarbakers Design Firm (later Sugarbaker and Associates — Interior Design) at 1521 Sycamore Street in Atlanta, Georgia (404-555-8600; later 555-6787 is their phone number).

"Julia got the brains and Suzanne got the boobs" is how employee Mary Jo Shively describes the sisters. Suzanne is not as intellectual as Julia. She attended Chapel High School and Southern State College but isn't as enthused about art like Julia ("I'm sick of seeing small busted women with big butts"). Suzanne exercises with a baton to the tune of "St. Louis Blues." She is extremely feminine and flaunts her sexuality. She was crowned "Miss Georgia World of 1976" and her talent was baton twirling. Julia speaks proudly of the event: "She was the only woman in pageant history to sweep every category except congeniality... When she walked down the runway in her swimsuit, five contestants quit on the spot. She did not just twirl a baton, that baton was on fire. And when she threw that baton in the air, it flew higher, further and faster than any baton had flown before, hitting a transformer and showering the darkened arena with sparks. And when that baton came down, my sister caught it and 12,000 people jumped to their feet for 16½ minutes of uninterrupted, thundering ovation as flames illuminated her tear-stained face. And that is the night the lights went out in Georgia!"

Suzanne has a pet pig (Noel) and a never-seen, nasty maid named Consuela (she howls at the moon, makes necklaces out of chicken bones and

is "totally psychotic," says Julia). Suzanne is divorced (from Dash Goff, author of the book *Being Belled*). Her favorite TV show is *Sensational Breakthroughs* (a thirty-minute commercial for new products). Suzanne wears a size 6½ shoe and is very fashion conscious. She will show ample cleavage to get what she wants from men. Suzanne left the firm in 1991 when she moved to Japan to take advantage of its economy.

See also: Anthony Bouvier, Charlene Frazier, Julia Sugarbaker, Mary Jo Shively.

1049. Sydney and Michael Hughley, *The Hughleys*, ABC, 1998–1999; UPN, 1999–2002. Played by Ashley Monique Clark, Dee Jay Daniels.

Sydney and Michael Hughley are the children of Darryl and Yvonne Hughley. They were born in Los Angeles but now live in West Hills, California. Sydney is 10 years old and attends West Hills Elementary School. She has two dolls (Heather and Jasmine) and is six inches taller than most of the boys in her class. She is a Brownie and a member of the school's soccer team and called "Sugar" by Darryl. Becoming a teenager has not been easy for Sydney. While purchasing her first bra went well, her first period was a nightmare: Darryl "celebrated her womanhood" by throwing a party (and inviting all her friends). Sydney snores and even before she was born she was embarrassed: Darryl took a picture of Yvonne in mid contraction seconds before Sydney's birth and used that picture as their 1988 Christmas card. While Sydney is considered the good child, she did shock her parents by drinking beer, piercing her navel and dressing provocatively (a cleavage revealing top at age 13). "Sydney 2002" is her computer screen name.

While Sydney is enrolled in the accelerated class at school, Michael is having a difficult time due to his dyslexia. He is on the school's soccer team, the Scary Spiders. He is also mischievous and has V.I.P. seating in detention. He enjoys going to Jiffy Lube with Darryl and as a toddler was prone "to getting stuck in things" (like a chair, a bucket, the banister railing). He is afraid of heights and attempted to become a rap star called L'il Spooner.

See also: Darryl Hughley, Yvonne Hughley.

1050. Sydney Bristow, *Alias*, ABC, 2001 (current). Played by Jennifer Garner.

Sydney Bristow appears to be an ordinary girl. In reality she is a spy for the CIA. Sydney was born in Los Angeles and is the daughter of Jack and Irina Bristow, a couple who were also spies. Sydney, however, was not aware of this. She believed her father sold airplane parts for Jennings Aerospace and that her mother had died in an automobile accident (in reality, Irina faked her death to distance herself from Jack and protect Sydney. She was a Russian KGB spy who married Jack [a CIA agent] to infiltrate the CIA. She was responsible for killing 25 agents before disappearing and going into seclusion). While it appeared Sydney had a normal childhood, she was secretly a subject of "The Christmas Project," an experimental CIA program designed to subconsciously train and program children for intelligence work in later life.

Sydney was an A student in high school (her only D occurred in a home economics class) but her college career made her feel out of place and she was unsure of her future.

One fall afternoon on the Berkeley campus Sydney was approached by a man. "He said he might be interested in talking to me about a job. When I asked why me all he told me was that I fit a profile ... I needed the money ... and he offered me the job." The job was to become a spy. Sydney was trained and advanced quickly — "They said I was a natural." Her actual status as a student provides her with the perfect cover. She has a photographic memory, is an expert shot and skilled in the martial arts. She carries lock picks in the heels of her shoes, is proficient with explosives and a master of disguise. She is also shocked to learn that her superior is her father — who had to lie to her to protect her as a child — what she didn't know would save her life.

Sydney lives in an apartment at 425 Cochran Place in Los Angeles. She is extremely careful during assignments — "I have to be. If I get careless, it's over for me." Sydney's cover is also that of a banker for Credit Dauphine (Jack's cover is that of the Portfolio Manager). Sydney is a beautiful woman who risks her life during every assignment. She is not always prim and proper and uses her sexuality to accomplish a mission. She gets shot, tortured and beaten up. She gets bruises, cuts and is often seen with blood on her body and clothes. She is also careful about who she dates because one slip of the tongue and it could cost her boyfriend his life. Sydney is considered a rogue agent and rarely follows protocol. She does, however, want to serve her country as best she can.

1051. Sydney Fox, *Relic Hunter*, Syn., 1999–2002. Played by Tia Carrere.

Sydney Fox is a beautiful professor of ancient studies at Trinity College in California who also recovers lost treasures on behalf of the university museum. "Part of what I do is search for relics.

Every relic tells a human story and gives us an insight into our lives."

Sydney is the daughter of Randall Fox, a dam builder who believes in defying everything. Sydney's interest in relics began when she was a student at St. Theresa's Catholic School for Girls. Here Sydney befriended a teacher who hunted for relics as a side-line and learned "Relics don't belong to people or individuals. They belong to the world." Sydney next attended Franklin High School (where she was a cheerleader and played Maria in her senior play, *West Side Story*; no mention is made of her interest in relics at this time). At some period after this (not specified) Sydney again became interested in relics and majored in ancient civilizations at Trinity College. She is a Boston Red Sox baseball fan and does what she can to find relics and save them from unscrupulous characters.

Sydney can be either a temptress or an Amazon — whatever she has to get the job done. Her assignments take her to the far, desolate corners of the globe and the first thing Sydney does when she gets out of a scrape "is to go to a hotel, take a bath and have a glass of whatever they call wine." Although she is gorgeous, Sydney is not treated as such on assignments. She sweats, is beaten up, drugged, shot at and often finds herself in a fistfight with the enemy. She is no lady when she gets mad and is quite capable of taking care of herself. Sydney is an expert in the martial arts, an expert shot with a gun or the crossbow she likes to use and in her spare time teaches Tai Chi classes at the university.

1052. Sydney Guilford, *Civil Wars*, ABC, 1991–1993. Played by Mariel Hemingway.

Sydney Guilford is a beautiful matrimonial lawyer and a senior partner in the firm of Guilford, Levinson and Howell (located in Room 712 of an unidentified building in Manhattan).

Sydney was born in Minneapolis and lived at 213 Minnetaka Trail. She is a child of divorce and was brought up by her mother Harriet. She attended Madison High School (where she was a cheerleader) and received her degree in law from Harvard.

"If it weren't for the misery of others" Sydney would be out of a job. Sydney is divorced and is not ready for another relationship. She sometimes wishes she were not so attractive just to avoid a problem she has with men hitting on her (she suspects that sooner or later she is going to have the same problem with women). Although this really bothers Sydney, she has no solution for it. She doesn't like to leave the house without makeup and enjoys wearing stunning outfits. Sydney lives in an apartment on East 74th Street in Manhattan. She carries a gun for protection and orders mineral water before each meal (she is not a good cook and rarely eats at home). Although she doesn't want attention drawn to her, Sydney felt comfortable enough to pose nude for a photo layout in *New Yorker* magazine.

1053. Sydney Kells, *Sydney,* CBS, 1990. Played by Valerie Bertinelli.

Sydney Kells is a young woman who works as an investigator for the law firm of Fenton, Benton and Sloane in Century City, California. Sydney was born in Los Angeles on April 12, 1965. She has brown hair and brown eyes. She is five feet, five inches tall and weighs 110 pounds. Her right thumbprint appears on her private investigators license (number M-83456).

Sydney became addicted to crime shows on TV while growing up and set her sights on becoming a detective. She cried when Dick Sargent replaced Dick York on her favorite TV show *Bewitched.* Sydney is a graduate of Harrison High School and U.C.L.A. She is single and lives at 1144 Oliphant Street. She is a sloppy housekeeper, a terrible cook and lives with a cat named Calvin. A Hershey Bar with almonds on white bread is her favorite meal and chocolate milk is her favorite drink. The only nutritional meal she has is when she has dinner with her mother (Linda) on Thursday nights.

Because of her name people believe Sydney is "a fat, middle-aged bald man." When it comes to her work Sydney is a totally different person. She is focused, proficient and always brings a case to a successful conclusion. She often wishes she could run her life like her cases. Sydney hangs out at the Blue Collar Bar and was profiled by the L.A. *Times* in a story called "A Week in the Life of Sydney Kells."

1054. Sydney Kovack, *Partners in Crime,* NBC, 1984. Played by Loni Anderson.

Sydney Kovack is a beautiful blonde and partners with an equally beautiful brunette (Carole Stanwyck) in the San Francisco–based Caulfield Detective Agency. Sydney was the second wife of the late Raymond Caulfield; Carole was his first wife and they inherited his mansion and agency after his death.

Sydney is a stunning, street-wise girl who was born in San Francisco and grew up in the Mission District where she learned all the tricks of the con artist's trade — from picking locks to picking pockets. As a kid Sydney ran numbers for her fa-

ther (a bookie) and had a mean left hook (she sent three school bullies to the dentist). Sydney is now an aspiring musician (bass fiddle) and hopes to one-day play with the San Francisco Symphony Orchestra. Her biggest break came when she played in a band for a singer named Rochelle Robbins. Sydney has been studying the bass for 20 years and has played professionally for 15 years.

Sydney wears a size medium dress and measures 36-24-36. She lives at 921 Hayworth Street, Apartment C and drives a car with the license plate IPCE 467. Sydney can hot wire a car, carries lock picks with her at all times and only plays tennis because she feels she looks fabulous in a tennis outfit.

See also: Carole Stanwyck.

1055. Sylvie Girard, *Sweating Bullets,* CBS, 1991–1993. Played by Carolyn Dunn.

Sylvie Girard "is the brains of the outfit" for Nick Slaughter, a former DEA (Drug Enforcement Agency) operative turned private detective (Nick Slaughter — Private Investigator). The agency is based at 45 Lafayette Street in Key Mariah, a small coastal town in Florida.

Sylvie was born in Miami and is a graduate of Miami State University. She is the daughter of a brick laying company owner and was a beauty contestant in the 1985 Miss Brick and Mortar Pageant (as a favor to her father). Sylvie used her degree in business management to land a job as a consultant for a travel agency that catered to the rich and famous. She was fired when a yacht left in her care disappeared (she met Nick when she hired him to find the yacht).

Sylvie believes she and Nick work well as a team because the disorganized Nick needs all the help she can give him (she earns 25 percent of what he makes each month). Sylvie is not one for violence (if she can find an easy way out of a situation she will try to convince Nick to do it). She is an expert at manipulating and reading people. She can sweet talk men into almost anything and uses that talent to keep the agency afloat.

See also: Nick Slaughter.

1056. Symphony Angel, *Captain Scarlet and the Mysterons,* Syn., 1967. Voiced by Janna Hill.

Symphony Angel is a pilot for Spectrum, a futuristic organization that protects the Earth from alien invaders. Symphony was born in Cedar Rapids, Iowa, in 2034. She was a brilliant child and excelled in mathematics at school. She earned seven degrees in math and technology from college. Her abilities led her to become a spy for the Universal Secret Service. Symphony revolutionized the spy game with innovative techniques that are now used all over the world. During training as a pilot for special U.S.S. missions, Symphony fell in love with flying. She later joined a charter air company and proved her abilities as an extraordinary pilot. It was at this time that Spectrum asked her to become a part of their team. Symphony enjoys experimenting with fashion, makeup and creating new hairstyles for herself and the other Angels. The program is a puppet series filmed in Supermarionation.

See also: Captain Magenta, Captain Ochre, Captain Scarlet, Destiny Angel, Harmony Angel, Melody Angel, Rhapsody Angel.

1057. Synclaire James, *Living Single*, Fox, 1993–1997. Played by Kim Coles.

Synclaire James is the perky receptionist at *Flavor*, a contemporary monthly magazine aimed at African-American women ("It's called *Flavor* because we've got taste").

Synclaire was born in Missouri and is a graduate of Howard University. As a child she had a pet turtle (Fred) and a plush cat (Mr. Jammers). She now has a pet hamster (Robespierre) and lives in an apartment house in Prospect Heights, Brooklyn. Synclaire is a full figured woman but feels her head is too big for her body (she applied for a job at Chuckie Cheese but lost the position "because my head was too big for the rat head"). Prior to her job at *Flavor*, Synclaire worked as a cashier, telephone solicitor, babysitter, and order taker at Turkey Burger Hut.

Synclaire's desk is decorated with troll dolls "to spread joy and happiness in the office." She uses what she calls "an emotional filing system" (things that make her boss, Khadjah James, happy are in the front; "the things that make her weary are in the back; and the things that upset her are not within her reach"). Synclaire makes Christmas ornaments out of the plastic eggs in which Leggs panty hose come and feels sad at the end of the day "because I have to say goodbye to the makeup that got me through the day." When she feels blue Syncalire wears wind chime earrings.

1058. Tamera Campbell, *Sister, Sister*, ABC, 1994–1995; WB, 1995–1999. Played by Tamera Mowry.

This entry also contains information on Tia Landry (Tia Mowry), Tamera's identical twin sister. Tamera and Tia are the children of a black artist (Rachel Gavin) and a white globetrotting photojournalist (Matt Sullivan). The twins were born in Florida in 1980.

Rachel died in childbirth and Matt, on assign-ment at the time, was unable to claim the babies (who were given up for adoption when no relatives could be found). Tamera was adopted by Ray Campbell (Tim Reid); Tia by Lisa Landry (Jackee Harry). Fourteen years later Tia and Tamera meet by chance at Fashion Fantasy in a mall. Ray and Lisa realize the girls need to be together. Because Ray owns a house, it is agreed upon that Lisa will move in with him (at $350 a month for rent). Ray owns Campbell's Limousine Service (also called Ray's Limos); Lisa is a fashion designer and runs a cart business, Fashions by Lisa, at the Northland Mall.

Tamera and Tia share a bedroom in Ray's home at 243 Maple Drive in Detroit, Michigan. Tia is the neat sister. She alphabetizes her CDs, dusts the vacuum cleaner and folds her dirty laundry before placing it in the hamper. Tamera is the untidy sister. She rarely cleans her side of the room, plays loud music and leaves her clothes lying around.

Tia is also the smart sister. She was the only one in kindergarten who knew her ABCs backwards and sees college as a place to learn and work. Tamera got by in school and sees college as a place to have fun with learning somewhere down the line. The girls first attended Roosevelt High School. Here Tamera won the first "Golden Casey Award" (for singing in a talent contest when the school dedicated its gym to its most famous alumni, Casey Kasem). She is also the star pitcher for the school's basketball team, the Tigers. Tia is not as sports oriented as Tamera. Tia is an Honors Student and loves to paint and play the piano (Tamera loves to sing and is more of a flirt with boys). Tia scored a 1560 on her SAT test; Tamera a 1080. They both chose to attend Michigan State University (where they appeared in their freshman year talent show as the Singing Simones). The Cellar is their college eatery hangout.

Tia and Tamera first worked for Ray (washing cars) then at Rocket Burger (fast food). Tia next worked for Book 'Em Joe, a coffee and bookshop in the mall. Tamera became "Lady J," the host of a listener call-in program on WTSE (her college radio station). Tia and Tamera had a pet hamster (M.C. Hamster) and Tamera becomes easily upset if someone mentions Lulu (her dog, who ran away when she was a child). Tia has a plush animal (Mr. Froggy) and when she gets angry she applies polish to her toenails. Tia and Tamera appeared on the TV game show *Slime Party* but went their separate ways after college: Tia won an internship with the Women's National Basketball Association and Tamera appeared to be following in her father's footsteps and become a photojournalist.

1059. Tammy Tarleton, *Tammy,* ABC, 1965–1966. Played by Debbie Watson.

Tammy Tarleton was born on the *Ellen B,* a riverboat that is moored on the Louisiana Shore in Ducheau County on May 14, 1948. Tammy's parents died when she was very young (a cause or their names not mentioned) and she was raised by her grandfather, Mordecai (Denver Pyle).

Tammy grew up as a backwoods rural girl. She was taught the word of the Lord by her grandfather and how to fish, cook and fend for herself. Her family is poor but proud and Tammy delights in the little things that life has to offer. Tammy was taught the basics of life but her thirst for education led her to take classes at nearby Seminole College. She next attended an unnamed secretarial school where she showed an amazing ability to type 200 words per minute. She also excelled in shorthand and filing. Tammy acquired her first job as a secretary to John Brent, the owner of Brent Enterprises, at Brentwood Hall (a short distance from the *Ellen B*).

Tammy possesses enthusiasm and the ability to overcome adverse situations through her philosophy of love and understanding. She lived a sheltered life and is a bit naïve when it comes to certain matters. Her speech is also from a time long gone (called "river talk") and she enjoys the company of people. She has an undying willingness to help people but that is also her greatest downfall: people take advantage of her. Tammy cannot find what she calls "the bad in people." Her upbringing has taught her that good exists in everyone and that is what she looks for in everyone she meets. Tammy is an excellent cook and is known for her "river vittles" (for example, hog liver soup, poke week salad, stuffed catfish and mustard greens). Her companion is her pet goat, Nan.

1060. Tao, *BeastMaster,* Syn., 1999–2002. Played by Jackson Raine.

Tao, whose name means "The Way," is the traveling companion of Dar, the man who can communicate with animals (the BeastMaster). They met in an age of darkness and magic when Dar saved Tao from an attack from an evil tribe called Terron. Tao is from a land called Xinca (pronounced Chinka) that is located in the Middle of the World ("where the earth touches the sky"); his people are called Eirons (the green rock ring he wears on his finger is a symbol of his people). Tao was embarked on a mission by the Elders to spread the word of his people and bring followers to his village. His other duties were to map the world.

Tao is a natural sorcerer (makes potions from herbs and plants) and studies weapons "because you can learn a lot about a man by the way he fights." He feels that the future holds many promises for mankind (by studying Dar's eagle, Sharak, for example, Tao believes that man may one day fly). Tao's people were a society open to new thinking and new ideas. He believes in the natural process of things and provides commentary on his beliefs as he and Dar encounter the good and evils of a dark age.

See also: The Ancient One, Arina, Dar, Curupira, Iara, The Sorceress.

1061. Tara King, *The Avengers,* ABC, 1968–1969. Played by Linda Thorson.

Tara King is a beautiful and shapely Avenger, an agent of the Ministry who avenges crimes committed against the British government.

Tara works with John Steed, the Ministry's top agent, and is a replacement for Emma Peel (Steed's prior partner who returned to her husband, previously listed as missing, but found alive in the Amazonian jungle). Tara was born in England and is the daughter of a prosperous farmer. She had everything she wanted growing up and attended a prestigious finishing school where she acquired the sophistication of the young international set. Tara has survival skills, can ski and fly an airplane. She, however, does not have any particular fighting skills. She knows judo but will use whatever is handy as a weapon to protect herself. She lives at 9 Primrose Crescent and drives a red Lotus Europa MKI (plate PPW 999F). Tara is the most voluptuous of Steed's partners (she has a 39 inch bosom) and loves to outfit herself in tight sweaters and miniskirts. She loves music, auto racing and is the most affectionate of Steed's partners (they give each other an occasional hug or kiss). Steed (as John is most always called) and Tara met by accident. She was Recruit 69 and tackled Steed during a training exercise, thinking he was part of the exercise. Tara had come to admire Steed (hearing about his daring adventures) but never met him. It was Steed's superior, the wheel chair-bound Mother, who felt they would make the perfect crime fighting team.

See also: Catherine Gale, Emma Peel, John Steed.

1062. Tasha Dexter, *V.I.P.,* Syn., 1998–2002. Played by Molly Culver.

Tasha Dexter is a highly skilled specialist who works for V.I.P. (Vallery Irons Protection), a Los Angeles–based protective service that charges $25,000 a day plus expenses. Tasha works with

Nikki Franco, Kay Simmons and Quick Williams; her boss is Vallery Irons.

Tasha is the most ruthless of the V.I.P. girls. She has a short attention span "and I got an itchy trigger finger if the baddies take too long to answer my questions." She also says, "I do all the dangerous work and Val gets all the credit." Tasha also gets uptight around Vallery because "no matter what case we're on, Vallery needs protection" (Vallery is totally unqualified for the job and is actually just a figure head who involves herself in cases and complicates matters).

Tasha was a CIA double agent ("I was a spy for the Soviet Union before I switched sides") and can speak six languages. She is well versed in the martial arts, will "sleep with the enemy" to get information but gets really angry "if I did it for nothing and it didn't pay off in results." Tasha is a licensed helicopter pilot. She was a former KGB operative, a member of the Israeli Army and was an agent for M.I.-5 (Military Intelligence). She also spent one year in a KGB prison (exactly why a woman with so many talents and experience took a job as a body guard is not really made clear).

Tasha mentioned she was a fashion model before becoming a spy and has been married and divorced four times. Although Tasha is no longer a spy, she treats each assignment as if it were a military operation. She is quick to use violence and rarely asks questions first. VIP TSH is her blue Mustang license plate and 310-555-9816 is her phone number. Tasha is an average cook but claims she is famous for her veggie lasagna. *Born Free* is her favorite movie.

See also: Kay Simmons, Nikki Franco, Quick Williams, Vallery Irons.

1063. Tate, *Tate,* NBC, 1960. Played by David McLean.

Tate (no other name given) is a restless gunfighter who wanders from town to town siding with justice against criminal elements. Tate was born in Kansas City in the 1840s. He grew up in an era of lawlessness and had the nickname Curley (people now say "You're too ugly to be called that now"). He was a hard-nosed kid and constantly rebelled against authority. "I got some schoolin'," he says. When he was old enough he joined the Union Army. In May of 1863 during the Battle of Vicksburg, his arm was smashed ("I didn't run fast enough") and is now preserved in a black leather casing. The Civil War toughened him ("He's ugly as ever and twice as mean looking"). Despite his handicap, he is lightning fast on the draw "and can shoot five times without reloading."

Tate takes everything personally. The one thing you do not want to do is get him angry because he is quick to settle things by violence (gunplay). Tate appears to like the lifestyle he has chosen and he never stays in one place long enough to call it home. No matter where he goes he always finds someone in need of help. Once the help has been provided, Tate is off to wherever the trail leads him. As for the lady folk, Tate is not much of a romantic. He enjoys a woman's company but ever since the death of his one and only true love (a girl named Mary Ellen) he avoids situations that could lead to commitments.

1064. Tattoo, *Fantasy Island,* ABC, 1978–1984. Played by Herve Villechaize.

The four foot tall Tattoo assists Mr. Roarke, the mysterious owner of Fantasy Island, a tropical resort where dreams become a reality. Tattoo and Mr. Roarke have been close friends for many years. Tattoo helps Mr. Roarke, whom he calls "Boss," prepare guests for their fantasies and is most famous for ringing the tower bell and proclaiming "Da plane, da plane," as the seaplane carrying guests approaches the island. In addition to his romantic French accent, Tattoo is always elegantly dressed (most often in white like his mentor) and rides around the island in his red hybrid golf cart-station wagon. Tattoo, known by no other name, is a trusting individual with an eye for the ladies. He longs for a family but has never found the right woman. He is hoping to make a fortune with one of his endless ventures (for example, greeting cards, selling encyclopedias).

See also: Mr. Roarke.

1065. Teal'c, *Stargate SG-1,* Sci Fi, 1997 (current). Played by Christopher Judge.

Teal'c is an alien whose name means strength. He is a warrior and part of the Stargate SG-1 team (see Jack O'Neill for details).

Teal'c grew up in a society called Jaffa. He is actually a human who was used by his planet's enslavers, the Goa'uld, as an incubator for infant Goa'uld parasites. Unlike other Jaffa who joined with their Goa'uld, Teal'c did not join with his (although he carries the Goa'uld larva in his stomach). The male Jaffa were brought up as warriors to serve the Goa'uld. Teal'c had served the Goa'uld for many years (he is over 100 years old) and has acquired knowledge in many languages, races and technology.

Teal'c was married to Drey'auc (now deceased) and lived on the planet Chulak with their son Rya'c (now a Goa'uld warrior). Teal'c next became a First Prime and served the leader Apophis, a cruel dictator who forced Teal'c to perform many horrific deeds (killing innocent people and selecting candidates for Goa'uld implantation). His life changed when Jack O'Neill and his team (Samantha Carter and Daniel Jackson) were captured on Chulak. Teal'c believed the Goa'uld were not the all-powerful gods they professed to be and helped the Stargate team escape. He accepted Jack's invitation to join the team to give him the opportunity to fight the Goa'uld on whatever planet they may infest. The Goa'uld have branded Teal'c a traitor and a bounty has been placed on him.

Teal'c is strong and totally dedicated to Jack and his team. His knowledge of alien races proves invaluable to the team's survival on unexplored planets. He is often silent and his expressions are stronger than words. Although raised as a warrior, Teal'c will not kill unless he is forced to.

See also: Daniel Jackson, Jack O'Neill, Samantha Carter.

1066. Ted Baxter, *The Mary Tyler Moore Show*, CBS, 1970–1977. Played by Ted Knight.

Ted Baxter is a man who is in love with himself and who believes he has many talents. He is employed by WJM-TV, Channel 6 in Minneapolis, Minnesota, and is the sole anchor on the station's *Six O'clock News* program. Ted's background is limited to his constant rambling, "that it all began in a 6,000-watt radio station in Fresno, California." Ted's life-long hero has been CBS newsman Walter Cronkite and he hopes to become anchor of the network's evening newscast in New York City. Unfortunately Ted cannot see that he is incompetent. He has trouble pronouncing words and relies on the station's news writer, Murray Slaughter, to make him look intelligent (he especially likes to agree with what the President has to say and hopes he and Murray think alike).

Ted earns $31,000 a year. He pays a high school senior $5 a year to prepare his taxes and calls the station's control room "The technical place" (Murray calls Ted's cue cards "idiot cards"). Ted is a Republican and has a fake newspaper headline that reads "Ted Baxter Wins Three Emmys." He attempted his own business (The Ted Baxter Famous Broadcasting School) and hates to part with money (he cries when he has to). Ted also found work as a commercial spokesman as Farmer Ted for Ma and Pa's Country Sausage. *Snow White* is Ted's favorite movie and he has a dog named WJM. He dines at Antonio's Restaurant. Ted likes to read other people's mail and has made it a goal to be a part of everyone's business. He ends each broadcast with "Good Night and Good News."

Although Ted considers himself a confirmed bachelor, one woman managed to steal his heart — Georgette Franklin (Georgia Engel), a window dresser at Hempell's Department Store. They dated for a short time before marrying in 1974.

See also: Lou Grant, Rhoda Morganstern, Mary Richards.

1067. Tedde Cochran, *The Geena Davis Show*, ABC, 2000–2001. Played by Geena Davis.

Scantily clad pictures of Tedde Cochran appear in *Esquire* magazine in a layout called "Women We Love." Although Tedde was "Miss Congeniality" in a Junior Miss Pageant, she is a wholesome, down-to-earth girl. She was born in New York City and attended Columbia University (where she majored in public relations and advertising). She now runs a semi-successful PR agency called Tedde Cochran, Inc. in Manhattan.

Tedde attended Roosevelt High School and was each year voted class president. She likes to eat cereal from the box (her favorite is Fruity Pebbles) and pop tarts are her favorite fast food breakfast. Although Tedde believes she is independent, she longs for a family and a home in the suburbs.

1068. Templeton Peck, *The A-Team*, NBC, 1983–1987. Played by Dirk Benedict.

Templeton Peck, known as "Face" and "The Faceman," is a member of the A-Team, military fugitives who help people in trouble (see Hannibal Smith for further information).

Face (as he is most often called) was a lieutenant in Vietnam and served in the 5th Special Forces Group with B.A. Baracus, Hannibal Smith and H.M. Murdock. His Social Security number is 522-70-5044 and 61-5683-2 is his FBI file number. Face is a master con artist and the team's means of getting what they need without paying for it. He was orphaned at the age of five. He wandered into and was raised at the Guardian Angels Orphanage in Los Angeles. Face claims he learned most of his cons from his favorite TV show — *Dragnet*. He is an expert at bending the rules and has such a face that everybody believes what he is saying. His favorite scam is Miracle Films ("If it's a good picture, it's a Miracle") and has a script called "The Beast of the Yellow Night" ready for "production." Face lives in a beach house (that he scams) at 1347 Old Balboa Road and his license plate reads IHG 581.

See also: B.A. Baracus, Hannibal Smith, H.M. Murdock.

1069. Terri Alden, *Three's Company*, ABC, 1981–1984. Played by Priscilla Barnes.

Theresa Alden, called Terri, is a gorgeous blonde who becomes Janet Wood and Jack Tripper's new roommate when Cindy Snow leaves to attend college. Terri shares a bedroom with Janet in Apartment 201 of a Santa Monica building owned by Bart Furley but managed by is brother, Ralph Furley.

Terri was born in Indiana and had contemplated entering the medical profession ever since she knew about doctors and nurses (she also attempted to play the violin but was awful). She now works as a nurse at Wiltshire Memorial Hospital in Los Angeles. Terri is warm and caring but easily exasperated. She is independent and doesn't like to be told what to do or bossed around. She hates to be criticized and was the only one of the roommates to fall for Jack (when he bought a false moustache to impress girls). Terri is very persistent when she has her mind set on something and is a pain (as Jack calls her) until she gets someone to listen to what she has to say.

Terri reads *All Woman* magazine. After a day at the hospital dealing with transfusions, broken bones, knife wounds and other gory things, Terri likes to go to the local pub (the Regal Beagle) and relax with her favorite drink — a Bloody Mary. If Terri has to work the graveyard shift at the hospital, she has her favorite breakfast — pizza with anchovies.

Terri is constantly hit on by men and knows how to defend herself (she has a tendency to fall for men who are married or gay according to dialogue between Jack and Janet). Creamy garlic is Terri's favorite flavor of salad dressing. In the last episode, Terri leaves for a job opportunity in Hawaii.

See also: Chrissy Snow, Cindy Snow, Jack Tripper, Janet Wood, Ralph Furley, Stanley and Helen Roper.

Thalia Menninger *see* **Dobie Gillis**

1070. Thelma Evans, *Good Times*, CBS, 1974–1979. Played by BernNadette Stanis.

Thelma Evans is the daughter of James and Florida Evans. She was born on June 15, 1957, in Tuckahoe, New York, and now lives with her family at 963 North Gilbert (Apartment 17C of the Cabrini Housing Project) on the South Side of Chicago (address also given as 763).

Thelma is a very pretty girl who is fashionably dressed although her clothes are mostly home made or bargain basement garments that are reworked by her mother. The family is poor and the times are hard and Thelma helps as much as she can by doing chores around the house. Thelma

held various part time jobs and is not the smartest girl in school. She tries and that is what pleases her parents. Thelma has aspirations to become an actress and enrolled in classes at the Community Workshop (her high school is not named).

Thelma is a young girl in bad times in a bad area. She is responsible, caring and not a tease. She has respect for her developing figure and will not throw herself at any boy. Thelma is not argumentative and appears to make friends wherever she goes. She gets along with her younger brother (Michael) but is constantly at odds with her older brother J.J. (the two constantly insult each other). Thelma sees J.J. as a "Beanpole"; J.J. sees Thelma as having "a face whose mold could make gorilla cookies").

Thelma found true love and married Keith Anderson (Ben Powers), a former football player turned driver for the Windy City Cab Company. Despite her rough upbringing Thelma has matured into a fine, sensible young woman and is totally devoted to her family (even J.J.) and her husband.

See also: James and Florida Evans, J.J. Evans.

1071. Thelma Harper, *Mama's Family*, NBC, 1983–1984; Syn., 1986. Played by Vicki Lawrence.

Thelma Mae Harper is a cantankerous widow who lives at 1542 Ray Lane (also called Ray Way) in Raytown, U.S.A. Thelma Crowley was born and raised in Raytown. She attended Raytown Grammar School but drooped out of Raytown High School (she became frustrated by teachers who always called on her even though her hand wasn't raised). Thelma developed at an early age and in adult hood wore a 44D bra. During World War II Thelma was a hostess at the USO (United Serviceman's Organization) Raytown Canteen. She was jump rope champion of the second grade and as a teenager was called "Hot Pants" (a false loose reputation started by a boy who couldn't have his way with her).

Thelma was married to Carl Harper (who called her "Snooky Ookems"). They became the parents of Eunice, Ellen and Vinton. When Carl died Thelma became "a cranky old woman" everyone calls Mama. Mama wears a perfume called Obsession and has named her two porcelain lawn flamingos Milly and Willy. Her most treasured recipe is Million Dollar Fudge and she teaches ballet to retired people at the Senior Center (she also has a dance group she calls Mama's Girls). Mama made all her children take tap-dancing lessons; "There ain't a Harper who can't sing and dance," says Mama. Mama held a job as a receptionist for the Raytown Travel Agency and as a checker at Food Circus. She shops at Neidermeyer's Department Store. She is a member of the Raytown Community Church League and the founder of M.O.P. (Mothers Opposing Pornography). Mama cleans her oven with Easy-Off and believes she can force people to tell the truth with a stare she calls "The Look." She attempted to market Mother Harper's Miracle Tonic (a cold remedy with a touch of vanilla extract and 35 percent alcohol that intoxicated users). Mama's house was originally a brothel called Ma Beaudine's and was located at 10 Decatur Road. Mama also won first runner-up in the Lovely Be Lady Grandma U.S.A. Pageant. The town was founded by James Ray.

See also: Naomi Harper, Vinton Harper.

Thelma Frye *see* **Reuben Gregory**

1072. Theo Huxtable, *The Cosby Show*, NBC, 1984–1992. Played by Malcolm-Jamal Warner.

Theodore Aloysius Huxtable is the only son of Cliff and Clair Huxtable and lives at 10 Stigwood Avenue in Brooklyn, New York, with his four sisters (Sondra, Denise, Vanessa and Rudy). Theo, as he is called, was born in Brooklyn at Children's Hospital in 1968. Being the only male offspring does not give him any special privileges. He is treated (and punished) just as fairly as his sisters. Theo is a bit naïve and easily taken advantage of (especially by pretty girls. When Theo sees a girl he thinks he is in love with he tends to remain in the clouds for days).

Theo was called "Monster Man Huxtable" on the wrestling team at Central High School. While not a top-notch student his grades were good enough to earn him admission into New York University in Manhattan (Theo chose to live on campus in Apartment 10B in Greenwich Village). In 1991 he became a psychology major and acquired a job as a junior counselor at the Seton Hall Communications Center (he taught the Rosa Parks Group). The following year Theo graduated from N.Y.U. with a bachelor's degree and enrolled in the school's department of psychology grad program. It cost Cliff and Clair $100,000 for Theo's education.

See also: Cliff and Clair Huxtable, Denise Huxtable, Sondra Huxtable, Vanessa and Rudy Huxtable.

Theodore Cleaver *see* **Beaver Cleaver**

1073. Theo Kojak, *Kojak*, CBS, 1973–1978. Played by Telly Savalas.

Theo Kojak is a tough, no nonsense detective with the Manhattan South Precinct of the N.Y.P.D. He began his career as an officer with the 26th Precinct and his dedication to duty quickly led him up the department ranks (he is now a lieutenant).

Theo is a 24 hour, seven days a week cop. He works on hunches, which often pay off. Although he is a strict by-the-books police officer, he will bend the rules to draw a case to a successful conclusion. This is especially true if he takes a personal interest in a case. He becomes fixated and doesn't care what it takes to solve it — "I don't care about my badge; I don't care about my pension. But somebody's gonna take the fall for what they did."

Theo is very proud of his Greek heritage. He lives at 215 River Street in Lower Manhattan and smokes pencil-thin cigars. He is also famous for being the only cop on the force who loves lollipops — the round Tootsie Roll Pops. Theo is abrasive and has to be to deal with the gory cases he sometimes investigates. Because of the nature of cases he will not allow a female detective in the unit. Stella's is Theo's favorite eatery and his car license plate reads 394 AFL (later 383 JDZ). "Who loves ya, baby" is his favorite expression.

1074. Thomas Banacek, *Banacek*, NBC, 1972–1974. Played by George Peppard.

Thomas Banacek is a Boston-based free-lance insurance company investigator who recovers valuable lost or stolen objects for ten percent of their insured value. He has a 66 percent success rate and companies find it cheaper to hire him than to assign their own agents to a case.

Thomas was born on Scully Square in Boston. His father was born in Warsaw, Poland, and was a research scientist. He came to America and worked as a mathematician for an insurance company. After 20 years a computer replaced him. Because of this Thomas will not work a nine-to-five job for any insurance company — "I don't work for anybody. I work for myself."

Thomas's official business is restoring antiques (his one-man operation is called "T. Banacek Restorations"). *The Assurance Reports* is his official research material. The recovery and rewards section lists current and unsolved insurance company cases. If a case is more than 60 days old it becomes public domain and anyone can attempt to solve it (these are the cases he likes to take); he can't, however, tackle other cases unless he is hired to do so. When he is hired to solve a case he gets, in addition to ten percent, $100 a day plus expenses. And what does he do if he can't solve a case — "I get a little bit older." Thomas also has a saying for every occasion, usually that begins with "There's an old Polish proverb that goes..."

Thomas lives on Beacon Hill and enjoys an extravagant lifestyle. He has exquisite taste in food, wine and women. He is intrigued by the how of a case (how the crime was committed) and why it was impossible for the police or insurance company to solve.

1075. Thomas Magnum, *Magnum, P.I.*, CBS, 1980–1988. Played by Tom Selleck.

Thomas Sullivan Magnum hates to be called Tommy. He lives at Robin's Nest, the estate of pulp writer Robin Masters in return for providing its security. The estate is located on Concord Road (later Kalohoa Drive) on the North Shore of Hawaii.

Thomas was born in Tidewater, Virginia, in 1944. He was a fan of Roy Rogers movies and would pretend to be a hero and keep the neighborhood free of outlaws. He earned $12 a week plus a penny for each paper he sold as a delivery boy for the *Daily Sentinel*. For reasons that are not explained, Thomas chose a naval career and attended Annapolis. He served with the VM02 Unit in DaNang during the Vietnam War and was later assigned to Naval Intelligence. He resigned shortly after "when I woke up one morning and realized I was 33 and never 23." He turned his attention to investigating and became a private detective. He charges $200 a day plus expenses and will lower his rate by $25 if a client can't afford him. Thomas is writing a book called *How to Be a World Class Private Investigator*. He held a temporary job as the house detective at the Hawaiian Gardens Hotel but was angry because he couldn't carry a gun.

Thomas is a member of the King Kamehameha Club and drives a red Ferrari (plate ROBIN 1 but also seen as 5GE 478 and 308 TTS). *Stalag 17* is Thomas's favorite movie and he enjoys working the *New York Times* Sunday crossword puzzle. He exercises by swimming, playing volleyball and running. "Rosebud" is his computer password for the estate's computer system. Thomas narrates stories, talks to the camera, acts as a big brother toward women and hangs his head when he becomes frustrated. He can be reached by phone at 555-2131.

1076. Thurgood Stubbs, *The P.J.'s*, Fox, 1999–2000; WB, 2000. Voiced by Eddie Murphy.

Thurgood Stubbs is the "supa" (maintenance engineer) of the 13-story Hilton Jacobs Building in the Projects (the P.J.'s) of an unnamed crime-ridden city. Thurgood is 48 years old ("but looks 60") and is married to Muriel (Loretta Devine).

Thurgood is rude, obnoxious and overweight (he buys exercise videos but never watches them). He has an extremely poor diet (fried, fatty foods, take out and endless junk snacks). Thurgood was born and raised in the Projects. He grew up poor and lives a comfortable life and his home (a basement apartment) is furnished with treasures — the furniture other people discarded. In his youth Thurgood was a professional wrestler (the Conquering Conquistador) with the NWA (Negro Wrestling Association).

Wheel of Fortune is Thurgood's favorite TV show. He drinks an alcoholic beverage called Mule 40 (he tried to make his own wine and called it Baron von Thurgood's Spring Frolic). He believes he is the world's greatest gumbo chef, uses Old English 800 cologne, and makes chocolate milk by combining Choco Puffs cereal with milk in a blender. For Thurgood, rent day is as much fun as eviction day.

Thurgood has a pet rat named Whiskers. His hero is action film star Jackie Chan and Thurgood served as the technical advisor on a film being made in the Projects called *Hell Hole 2*. Thurgood started a band with his tenants called Thurgood and the Stub Tones and with his friend Smokey had a program on the Project's radio station (WHJS) called *Thurgood and Smokey's Laugh Riot* (Smokey is a homeless man who lives in a cardboard box and is always being picked up with the trash. He once worked as a rat trainer called Ratman Carruthers). Thurgood also purchased the abandoned movie theater on Al Sharpton Boulevard for one dollar from H.U.D. (Housing and Urban Development) and turned it into the Thurgood Stubbs Neighborhood Theater.

Muriel is totally devoted to Thurgood. She is always seen in a pink blouse with "Paris" on it. She keeps a daily record of her activities in her journal and is president of Women United to Save Our Projects. The series is a puppet animation project filmed in Fomation.

1077. Thurston and Lovey Howell, *Gilligan's Island*, CBS, 1964–1967. Played by Jim Backus, Natalie Schafer.

Thurston and Lovey Howell are a wealthy married couple (called "The Millionaire and His Wife" in the opening theme) who are stranded on an uncharted island 300 miles Southeast of Hawaii. The Howells and fellow passengers Ginger, Mary Ann and The Professor were on a three hour sight seeing tour when their ship, the S.S. *Minnow*, was caught in a tropical storm at sea and beached. Jonas Grumby, the ship's captain, and his first mate, Gilligan, have also made the island their home.

For a three hour tour the Howells packed a fabulous wardrobe and a considerable amount of cash (the reason is never explained). Thurston, called "The Wolf of Wall Street," is a multi-millionaire who heads Howell Industries (he later says he is retired and doesn't work — "Dear Dad left me everything"). Amalgamated is Thurston's favorite stock and he has a teddy bear (his security blanket) named Teddy. The New York Stock Exchange is his favorite club and the Social Register his favorite reading matter.

Thurston claims to have attended SMU (Super Millionaires University); later he says Harvard (where he met Lovey; they married in 1944). Thurston has been convicted six times on antitrust suits and is constantly being investigated by the IRS for tax evasion. Thurston is a shrewd businessman and an apparent terror on his employees but generous and caring about his fellow castaways. Thurston refuses (but sometimes has) to do manual labor. He shares a hut with Lovey and tries to spend his days relaxing, listening to the stock market reports on their salvaged radio, playing golf or riding Bruce, his bamboo practice polo pony.

Lovey's real name is Eunice Wentworth. She is also wealthy and inherited her riches from her family (the diamond broach she is seen wearing has been in her family since Columbus received it from Queen Isabella). Lovey holds the title "Queen of the Pitted Prune Parade" and is considered one of the world's most socially active women. She most misses the social season and yearns to return to the mainland. Lovey is known to associate with royalty but has adjusted to living with people well below her social scale. Like her husband, she despises having to work.

See also: Gilligan, Ginger Grant, Mary Ann Summers, The Professor, The Skipper.

Tia Landry *see* **Tamera Campbell**

1078. Tia Russell, *Uncle Buck*, CBS, 1990–1991. Played by Dah-ve Chodan.

Tia Russell is the 16-year-old daughter of Robert and Margaret Russell. Tia, her sister, Maizy, and brother, Miles are now cared for by their Uncle Buck, who became their guardian after their parents were killed in a car accident.

Maizy has a fake I.D. that says she is 21. She hates being 16 and wants to become a woman now, not tomorrow. She is fascinated by "older guys" (21) and is restricted from dating them. Tia

dresses too sexy for one so young and gets away with it (Buck complains "She dresses too damn sexy" but doesn't really stop her).

Tia first attended the Livingston Avenue Grammar School then Monroe High School. She receives an allowance of $10 a week and works as a salesgirl at the French Collection, a boutique in the mall. Tia was a Blue Bell as a child and since she was old enough to realize she was beautiful, she has dreamed of becoming a fashion model. She believes she has the skill right now: "I can walk and wear lip gloss at the same time." Tia is an average student at school and likes the attention she gets when the boys stare at her. At home she is an angel and rarely defies her uncle because she knows she can get away with anything. She drinks Minute Maid orange juice and roast chicken is her favorite meal.

See also: Buck Russell, Maizy Russell.

1079. The Tick, *The Tick*, Fox, 2001. Played by Patrick Warburton.

A man dressed only in an electric blue body suit with exaggerated muscles and twitching antennae, calls himself the Tick. He is a superhero but has no idea who he really is, where he came from or how he acquired his powers. The Tick has speed and strength but is not always in control of them. He is also unable to distinguish between living things and inanimate objects. He thus creates considerable havoc as he goes about dispensing justice.

The Tick has made a city called the City home ("City, City, I am the Tick and you have melted my heart. From this day forth I will spread my buttery justice over your every nook and cranny. Hear, oh hear me, my City, your toast will never go bare again").

The Tick began his life as a crime fighter at a bus station (where he established a base of operations on the rooftop to battle the menace of the coffee vending machine that was directly below him. Should the vending machine not dispense coffee once the money was inserted, the Tick would come to the rescue "and shake the vending menace." When he was told "You have freed us from the tyranny of the coffee machine" by the bus depot manager, the Tick felt his job was done and he moved on).

The Tick lives at 370 Pleasant Avenue in an apartment he shares with Arthur (David Burke), a dissatisfied bookkeeper for World Wide Fishladder and Sons, who assists the Tick as a superhero he calls the Moth. The Tick doesn't understand insults ("It doesn't comprehend"). He claims "I have to keep my head clear to deal with evil." The

Tick is also bulletproof and calls himself "The Mysterious Blue Avenger" and "The Big Blue Bug of Justice." The Tick enjoys meals at the Tick Tock Diner and he can be reached by phone at 555-0197.

See also: Captain Liberty.

1080. Tiffany Malloy, *Unhappily Ever After*, WB, 1995–1999. Played by Nikki Cox.

Tiffany Malloy is 16 years old and beautiful. She could be considered the only child of Jack and Jennie Malloy because Jack only cares about Tiffany (he calls his sons, Ryan and Ross "the accident" and "the mistake"). Tiffany wasn't planned on either but "if it wasn't for Tiffany, the WB would have cancelled us long ago," says Jack.

Tiffany was born on May 16, 1979, in Van Nuys, California. She lives with her family (and three dogs — Jasper, Emily and Annie) at 30220 Oak Avenue. Tiffany knows she is gorgeous and makes sure everyone else becomes aware of that fact. She is well endowed and wears low cut blouses, miniskirts and tight jeans. She is proud of the fact that she is voluptuous and has built her whole life around her physical beauty. She hopes to one day own a Corvette "because I look gorgeous and have to have a flashy car to put me in." To weigh herself makes her happy. But in 1995 it happened and Tiffany cried — "Oh help me, help me, I'm deformed" — when she saw that she got her first (and only) pimple.

Tiffany's motto is "I will never trade my purity except for financial security." She is a straight A student at Priddy High School (although Howe High can be seen in the background) then Northridge Junior College. Her worst day in school occurred when she got a B on a book report on *The Scarlet Letter* ("Now I have a B for bad"). At college Tiffany wrote for the school newspaper, *The North Ridgeon.* Tiffany is on the debate team and is a National Merit Scholar.

Tiffany collects money for the homeless ("so they can buy cheap wine") and is considered a real nice person. When that bothered her and she wanted to see what it would be like to be bad (or as Tiffany said, "Not so nice"), she changed her name to "Toughany," got a Popeye iron-on tattoo and stole a lipstick (Bad Girl Scarlet) from a department store. She became so overcome by guilt that she returned the lipstick and dropped the image.

Other than being beautiful Tiffany has little talent. In grade school she acted in *Swan Lake* ("but I drowned in the paper water"). She tried twirling a baton ("but I couldn't catch it") and she tried to play the accordion but never did (Tiffany looked at her breasts, then the camera and shook her head "no"). Tiffany joined the volleyball team (jersey 17) in high school because of the cute red uniform. To get money from her father Tiffany does "the pouty lips and Bambi eyes thing." When she needed money for a car she became a counter girl at the Granny Goodness Ice Cream Parlor. She was also the spokesgirl for Ultra Bank and a waitress at Cali-Burger Dreamin' (where the owner named a burger after Tiffany — "The Tiffalicious Tiffany Burger — the Most Beautiful Burger Named After the Most Beautiful Girl").

Tiffany has a fear of the closet in the kitchen (when she was young Ryan locked her in and she feared the closet monster would get her. She has been haunted by the incident ever since). In the last episode, Tiffany's dream comes true when she is accepted into Harvard.

See also: Jack Malloy, Jennie Malloy, Ryan Malloy.

1081. Tiffany Smith, *California Dreams*, NBC, 1992–1997. Played by Kelly Packard.

Tiffany Smith is a very pretty teenage girl who attends Pacific Coast High School in California. She is also a member of the California Dreams, a soft rock music group. Tiffany plays guitar and sings. She is the typical California beach girl and loves to surf. She also loves to wear bikinis and inevitably attracts the opposite sex but "I can't figure out why the boys stop swimming to watch me."

Tiffany was born in California on July 3, 1976, and is a child of divorce. She is close to her father (who raised her) and sees her mother only on special occasions. As a child Tiffany would pretend to live in a fairy tale forest and it was through her pretend friends that Tiffany gained respect for all of God's creatures. She is very fond of animals (although she has no pets) and is especially protective of the beach and its creatures (she protests the big companies who dump waste into the ocean). She also works with Save the Dolphins and lives partly by the surfer's code of fun in the sun. Tiffany hangs out at Sharkey's (the beach eatery; also where the band plays on occasion) and she drives a car with the license plate IM TIFFI. In her spare time Tiffany volunteers as a candy stripper at Cliffside Hospital.

See also: Jenny Garrison.

1082. Tiffany Welles, *Charlie's Angels*, ABC, 1979–1980. Played by Shelley Hack.

Tiffany Welles is an Angel. She appears to have just stepped out of the pages of the latest fashion magazine but is actually a private detective for Charlie Townsend, the never-seen owner of the

Los Angeles–based Townsend Investigations. Tiffany works with fellow detectives (called Angels by Charlie) Kelly Garrett and Kris Monroe.

Tiffany was born in Boston and is the daughter of a detective lieutenant with the Boston Police Department. Tiffany is a debutante and was a nurse's aide while in high school. She is a graduate of Whitney College in California (where she was a member of the Kappa Omega Sorority) and the Boston Police Academy. Tiffany graduated with top honors from the academy and acquired the job with Charlie through a connection — her father and Charlie are good friends.

At Whitney College Tiffany was a resident of Tracy Hall (her dorm room) and during one summer she worked with Hans Kemper, a famous ghost hunter. Tiffany learned she was a sensitive and could communicate with spirits. She had a brief period where she became involved with the occult and conducted séances.

Tiffany is always elegantly dressed and soft spoken (making her look more like a model than a detective). She is a crusader for women's rights and is called "Tiff" by Kris and Kelly. She also appears to be the most fragile and delicate of the Angels. Her stunning good looks and air of sophistication were also her greatest weapon as she could fool even the most brilliant criminals — who would never suspect she was one of Charlie's Angels.

See also: Charlie Townsend, Jill Monroe, Julie Rogers, Kelly Garrett, Kris Monroe, Sabrina Duncan.

1083. Tim Speedle, *C.S.I.: Miami,* CBS, 2002–2004. Played by Rory Cochrane.

Tim Speedle is a chief investigator for the Crime Scene Investigation Unit of the Miami Dade Police Department. Tim was born in Syracuse, New York, on June 24, 1973. He stands six feet tall and weighs 153 pounds. Tim is a graduate of Columbia University in New York and has a B.S. degree in biology. He is single and his specialty is trace and impressions evidence.

Tim's father was an entrepreneur and ran a chain of family restaurants; his mother was a volunteer with Social Services. He grew up around abandoned and neglected children and gained a sense of compassion to help people solve problems beyond their control. The library became Tim's hangout in high school. He read everything science had to offer and won the state science championships four years in a row. At Columbia University he devoted himself to the science of paralysis (as a result of a best friend being stricken with such a disease). A year later, while vacation-

ing in Florida, Tim accompanied his uncle, a police officer, to the Miami Crime Lab and became fascinated by what he saw. He studied and observed and knew what he had to do. He interned at the Miami Crime Lab for six months before he became a part of the unit. He calls his boss, Horatio Caine, "H" and believes in using his gut instinct. Rory Cochrane left the series in 2004 for other ventures. His character was killed (shot) during a case investigation.

See also: Alexx Woods, Calleigh Duquesne, Erik Delko, Horatio Caine.

1084. Tim Taylor, *Home Improvement,* ABC, 1991–1999. Played by Tim Allen.

Tim Taylor, called "The Tool Man" for his supposed knowledge of tools, is the host of *Tool Time,* a Detroit cable TV home improvement program that airs Saturday's on Channel 122 (also given as Channel 112; it is simulcast in Spanish on Channel 88). Tim is married to Jill and is the father of Randy, Mark and Brad. They live at 508 Glen View Road.

Tim worked as a salesman for Binford Tools (the show's sponsor) when the owner, John Binford, selected him to host the program. Tim appears to be a master of any project on TV but is a klutz at home when it comes to repairing things. He has blown up five toasters, a washing machine, and two blenders. His remedy, "It needs more power" rarely works (he has, for example, a blender that can puree a brick). The motto of Binford Tools is "If it doesn't say Binford on it, somebody else makes it."

Tim was born in Detroit and attended Adams High School and Michigan State College (where he met Jill). Tim became fascinated by tools at an early age. His hobby is restoring classic cars (he spent three years building a 1933 Blue Goose Roadster; he later worked on a 1946 Ford). He won "The Car Guy of the Year Award" for his devotion to automobiles and wrote the book *How to Maintain Your Bench Grinder.* He takes five sugars in his coffee and trout almandine is his favorite dinner. His oasis away from the wife and kids is his garage, where he maintains a workshop (Jill has her washer and dryer there). When Jill gets angry at Tim she slams the workshop door. The vibration knocks his Binford tools off their pegboard hooks. Tim can't resist the Sears Home Improvement Sale and was the youngest person to ever join the Triple A. "Monkey Town" is his favorite video game and his hangout is Harry's Hardware Store.

See also: Al Borland, Jill Taylor, Wilson Wilson, Jr.

1085. T.J. Henderson, *Smart Guy*, WB, 1998–1999. Played by Tahj Mowry.

T.J. Henderson is a 12-year-old genius who attends Piedmont High School in Washington, D.C. He was born on August 19, 1986, and has an older brother (Marcus) and sister (Yvette). His father, Floyd (a widower) runs the Henderson Construction Company ("Everything Under One Roof").

T.J. has an I.Q. of 180 and feels he is "a 12-year-old brain stick in the mud" as getting high school to like him is a serious problem. He is the youngest member of his freshman class and still considered a baby. He tries to fit in but has little success. T.J. is brilliant in every subject matter and would make a great teacher when he grows up, but he won't consider it—"It pays jack," he says.

T.J. lives at 11 Wyler Road. He receives an allowance of $10 a week and is allergic to shellfish. He is equipment manager of the school's basketball team, reads *Sister Girl* magazine and appeared in a Destiny's Child music video. The Dawgburger is his favorite after school hangout.

See also: Yvette Henderson.

Tobias Funke *see* **Michael Bluth**

1086. Todd Harden, *Movie Stars*, WB, 1999–2000. Played by Mark Benninghofen.

Todd Harden is the brother of Reese Harden, a famous feature film action star. Todd is also an actor but gets all the least desirable roles. His credits include: *Starship Troopers* ("The guy who gets crushed by a giant roach"), *Fargo* (the leg sticking out of the wood chipper), *Babe, Pig in the City* (voice of Nick the Ferret), *Titanic* (frozen corpse number three), *Outbreak* (E-boli victim number eight), *Lethal Weapon 4* (body bag victim), *The Sixth Sense* ("Corpse with gaping head wound"). Todd did Shakespeare in the Park (at the Santa Monica Dog Park) and played Santa Claus at the Northridge Mall.

Todd was born in California and now lives in an apartment that overlooks a homeless guy with a sock puppet named Eddie. Todd attended Julliard and the Actors School and went to Hollywood with great expectations for a role in *The Sting II*. His brother, Reese, tagged along "to race motorcycles and chase chicks." Reese got into an altercation with a producer, punched his lights out and got the job. Todd now feels Reese has taken all the glory but believes there is a star-making role out there for him—he just hasn't found it yet.

Todd starred in a Mentos TV commercial and frequents the Juice Bar (he later opens his own juice bar, "L.A.'s Hottest Spot, Squeeze This"). Todd also opened his own acting school—Todd Harden's Acting School for Actors. He wrote a one-man play called "Fillmore, the Forgotten President." Todd was also the host of the E-Channel special "Behind the Scenes of the Making of *Space Ark*, a Cinematic Journey" (which stars Reese). Todd also became a director—of school plays at Buchanan Prep (*Hansel and Gretel, Rumplestiltskin* and *Death of a Salesman*). The series ended before Todd got his big break.

See also: Jacey Wyatt, Lori Harden, Reese Harden.

1087. Tom Bradford, *Eight Is Enough*, ABC, 1977–1981. Played by Dick Van Patten.

This entry also contains information on Joan Bradford (Diana Hyland), Tom's first wife, and Abby Bradford (Betty Buckley), Tom's second wife.

Thomas Bradford and his wife Joan are the parents of eight children (Nancy, Tommy, Elizabeth, Nicholas, Susan, Joanie, Mary and David). They remember their children's names by the saying "Never Try Eating Nectarines Since Juice May Dispense" (each capital letter stands for a child's name). The family lives in a white house with maroon shutters at 1436 Oak Street in Sacramento, California. Tom, as he is called, works as a columnist for the Sacramento *Register*; Joan is a freelance photographer.

Tom Bradford and Joan Wells were married in 1950. At this time Tom was the editor of a small magazine that went bankrupt. Three months later he found a job with the *Register*. Joanie (as Tom called her) liked to read, enjoyed poetry and bought Christmas gifts for the children months in advance. Joanie "died" shortly after the series began when Diana lost her life to cancer in 1977. Tom wears a size 38 regular suit and disliked the sound Joanie made when she filed her fingernails. Tom and Joanie struggled to raise eight children basically on what Tom made as Joanie became a full time housewife and mother. Their sacrifices at the time were difficult but the family pulled together and developed a close relationship.

Two years after Joan's passing Tom married Sandra Sue Abbott. Abby, as she is called, loved children and took on the responsibility of helping Tom raise the children. Abby is a widow (her late husband, Frank, was a P.O.W. who died in Vietnam) and previously lived at 1412 Compton Place. She works as a counselor at Memorial High School. Her transition to mother was made most difficult by Joanie. Joanie was named after her mother and had her mother's eyes, smile and sensitivity. She mistakenly believed that Abby resented her because she looked so much like her mother. As a kid Abby had a horse named Blaze. She wrote her college thesis on "Modern Sex Roles."

Tom is an excellent cook (noted for his chili con Bradford). When he was a kid, his sister, Vivian called him "Tommy Bellybutton." Abby has a car, a British MG she calls Gwendolyn (plate YNH 872). Tom drives a sedan (plate CUI 842). In the NBC TV movie update, *Eight Is Enough: A Family Reunion* (October 18, 1987), Tom is now the managing editor of the *Register* and Abby owns her own restaurant, the Delta Supper Club.

See also: David Bradford (for information on David, Tommy and Nicholas Bradford), Mary Bradford (for information on Mary, Susan, Nancy and Elizabeth Bradford).

1088. Tom Brewster, *Sugarfoot*, ABC, 1957–1960. Played by Will Hutchins.

Thomas Brewster is a Sugarfoot, a western term for "a cowboy who is working his way up to be a tenderfoot." Tom, as he is called, was born in Oklahoma in the 1840s. Although raised in an era of violence and lawlessness Tom acquired an interest in the law from Henry Davis, a judge who inspired him into becoming a lawyer.

It is the West of the 1870s when the series begins and Tom is a law school correspondent (he receives lessons from Kansas City and learns law from his book *Blackstone's Commentary, Volume 9*, which he carries with him at all times). Right now Tom is a wanderer but plans to hang his shingle in a place that needs him and which he needs.

Tom is peaceful, laid-back, idealistic and romantic. He is looked upon as a gullible coward by rough neck cowboys but is skilled with his gun, his fists and a knife. Tom calls his guns "tools of the devil." He wears his father's gun and believes that "shootin; ain't always the answer." He drinks only root beer "with a twist of cherry" and carries a "Home, Sweet Home" plaque with him as he wanders from town to town "tryin' to earn a little livin' money." While Tom struggled to avoid trouble (he wanted only to study his law books) trouble was all that he found. He stopped only long enough to help people and his knowledge of the law and strong sense of justice helped him overcome difficult situations when defending clients.

1089. Tom Chang, *Black Sash*, WB, 2003. Played by Russell Wong.

Tom Chang was born in San Francisco and attended Marina Park High School. He has been

betrayed by the world and now fights back as a mysterious bounty hunter. After graduating from State College Tom entered the police academy and became an officer with the San Francisco P.D. He eventually worked his way up from rookie to an undercover narcotics detective. His first assignment was also his downfall. While attempting to trace the trail of heroin being smuggled into the U.S. from Hong Kong by a ruthless gang called the Triads, Tom was framed with ten kilos of heroin and sentenced to five years of hard time in Hong Kong. His family, his friends and his reputation were all gone when he was released. Tom returned to San Francisco and opened a school called simply Martial Arts — his cover for operations as a bounty hunter with one goal in mind — bring criminals to justice. Tom is bitter but careful in what he does. He is well versed in the martial arts and has waged a secret war on crime as a way of getting even for the wrong done to him.

1090. Tommy and Willie Barry, *Dave's World*, CBS, 1993–1997. Played by Zane Carney (Tommy), Andrew Ducote (Willie).

Thomas and William Barry are the children of Dave and Beth Barry, a happily married couple who live "West of Maple Street" in Dade County, Florida. Tommy and Willie, as they are called, attend the Collins Street Elementary School. They are obedient children and cause few problems for Dave (who tends to be lenient) and Beth (who is a bit more strict and believes in a firm hand). Willie is allergic to mushrooms and played a slice of bread in his school play "Nutrition Is Our Friend" (he also played a fungus in the play "Bacteria to the Future"). He also has a number of pets: Mr. Moto, Sloppy Joe and Bruiser (ants), Jiminy, Gory, Buster and Moon Unit (crickets), Donald (turtle), Mr. Fish (fish), Puffy (rabbit) and Jerry (gerbil). Willie starred in a TV commercial for Oliver Twistie Meats.

Tommy has a plush dinosaur named Rappie. He sometimes has a hard time sleeping at night because he fears "the slimy creature living under my bed." He played Ahab in his school's production of *Moby Dick* and he and Willie eat Fruit Rings cereal for breakfast.

See also: Beth Barry, Dave Barry, Kenny Beckett.

Tommy Bradford *see* **David Bradford**

1091. Tommy Solomon, *Third Rock from the Sun*, NBC, 1996–2001. Played by Joseph Gordon-Levitt.

Tommy Solomon is the Earth name for one of four aliens from the Home Planet who traveled across three billion galaxies to study life on Earth. Tommy is the Information Officer. The leader became Dick Solomon (Tommy's brother); Sally Solomon, Dick's sister, is the Security Officer; and Harry Solomon, Dick's younger brother, is the Transmitter (reports telepathically to their supreme leader, the Big Giant Head). Tommy's relationship varies by episodes. Sometimes he is Dick's brother; other times he is Dick's son. They live at 417 Pensdale Drive in Rutherford, Ohio.

Tommy is extremely intelligent and is actually the oldest of the aliens but was chosen to portray the youngest to study Earth's culture. He attends Rutherford High School, then Pendleton University, and is the editor of the school newspaper, the *Zephyr*. He is required to be a model student and was a member of a band called the Whiskey Kings (where he played the guitar). Tommy held a job at Fetzels Homemade Pretzels and briefly attended the Picnee County School for the Gifted when he was found to be an above average student. The last episode finds Tommy and his three comrades being transported back to the Home Planet.

See also: Dick Solomon, Harry Solomon, Sally Solomon.

1092. Toni Childs, *Girlfriends*, UPN, 2000 (current). Played by Jill Marie Jones.

Antoinette Marie Childs, called Toni, is a beautiful woman who dreams of marrying a millionaire. She is extremely sexy and loves to show ample cleavage in low cut blouses and dresses. She is, as her friend Maya says, "a golddigger who dates rich men for what monetary gifts they can give her." Toni is instantly attracted to rich men but backs down when things get too serious (she grew up in a poor family and doesn't want to be poor again).

Toni was born in Fresno, California, and is the daughter of Eugene and Verdetta Childs. She is a graduate of U.C.L.A. and now lives at the El Royale Apartments (Apartment 303) in Larchmont Village. Toni is a real estate broker and first worked for Colonoda Realty before starting her own business—Toni Childs Realty ("I Specialize in Class") in an office on Sunset Plaza.

Toni is self-centered and hates to be told she is not the youngest at a bar she attends. She sizes a man by the clothes he wears; if they are not expensive she will not give him a second look. She also believes that other women are jealous of her looks, style and sex appeal. Toni reads *Forbes* magazine and when she feels depressed, a nutty buddy ice cream cone raises her spirits. Toni, a Catholic, carries a L'il Jesus statue with her everywhere she goes and considers mini kashas her good luck food. She enjoys lunch with her girlfriends (Lynn, Maya and Joan) at a restaurant called Skia's.

See also: Joan Clayton, Lynn Searcy, Maya Wilkes.

Tonto *see* **John Reid**

1093. Tony Almeida, *24*, Fox, 2002 (current). Played Carlos Bernard.

Anthony Almeida is a former CIA agent who now works with Jack Bauer as a member of the U.S. government's Counter Terrorism Unit (CTU). He is married to Michelle Dessler (Reiko Aylesworth), an employee of the CTU (she uses her maiden name) and is an expert on hand-to-hand combat (he is also a certified instructor).

Tony, as he is called, has a Master's degree in computer science from Stanford University and a Bachelor's degree in engineering from San Diego State University. He was a first lieutenant with the Marines and acquired his experience at the Marine Scout Sniper School and Surveillance and Target Acquisition Platoon School. He performed his first CTU mission in 2000 (with Jack in Operation Proteus). He was then the special agent in charge of the Los Angeles Domestic Unit (where he also served as the Systems Validation Analyst). Tony is a bit impulsive and while he follows orders he sometimes finds his gut instinct is more reliable than what he has been told to do.

See also: David Palmer, Jack Bauer.

1094. Tony Baretta, *Baretta*, ABC, 1975–1978. Played by Robert Blake.

Anthony Baretta, nicknamed Tony, is an Italian American detective with the 53rd Precinct in an unidentified Eastern city that is presumed to be Newark, New Jersey. Tony wears badge number 609 and is a loner (his companion is Fred, a cockatoo who thinks he is a chicken).

Tony is single and lives in Apartment 2C of the King Edward Hotel. He is unorthodox and likes to do things his way. Tony often breaks all the rules to catch a criminal and feels that his best weapon against crime is his ability to go undercover as various characters. Tony's normal dress is a T-shirt and jeans with a cap tilted slightly over his forehead. He is often seen carrying an unlit cigarette in his hand or placed behind his ear. When he finally collars a suspect he says, "And that's the name of the tune."

Ross's Billiard Academy is Tony's favorite hangout. He drives a beat up 1966 blue Chevy 4-door Impala he calls "The Blue Ghost" (plate 532 BEN). While Tony had numerous girlfriends (whom he referred to as "My cousins") he never stayed with one long enough to contemplate marriage.

1095. Tony Canetti, *Hudson Street,* ABC, 1995. Played by Tony Danza.

Anthony Canetti, called Tony, is a homicide detective with Precinct Number 7 on Hudson Street in Hoboken, New Jersey. He is divorced from Lucy and the father of Mickey. Tony, the son of Victor and Anna Canetti, was born in Hoboken in 1950. He attended Hoboken High School and worked after school in his father's shoe store, Canetti's Discount Shoes. A botched robbery attempt cost Victor his life. The incident made Tony realize he had to do something about it and he decided to become a cop. He graduated from rookie school and started his career as a beat cop. He upheld the law and he made people feel safe. He made friends and acquired snitches ("Information engineers," as he calls them) he could trust. He proved his abilities and worked his way up to plainclothes detective.

Tony is single and lives near the precinct on Hudson Street. He is very conservative and treasures his Italian heritage. Tony is careful when it comes to his investigations and likes to take things step by step. Previous experience has taught him that rushing causes mistakes and loopholes for criminals to be set free. Tony enjoys meals at a diner called the Pool Hall and he has a love-hate relationship with Melanie Clifford (Lori Loughlin), a young woman who dreams of becoming a reporter for the *New York Times.* She now works as a police reporter in the pressroom of Precinct 7 and worked previously as the obituary editor for the *Hoboken Record.* Melanie was born in New Jersey, is single and lives at 11 Wilson Street.

1096. Tony Micelli, *Who's the Boss?,* ABC, 1984–1992. Played by Tony Danza.

Arthur Morton Micelli, called Tony, is the live-in housekeeper to Angela Bower, an ad agency owner who lives at 3344 Oak Hill Drive in Fairfield County, Connecticut. Tony, a widower, took the job to get away from the congestion of the big city and provide a better life for his daughter, Samantha.

Tony was born in Brooklyn, New York on April 23, 1952. He is a Catholic and attended P.S. 86 grammar school (although he later says he was an altar boy at the Blessed Sacrament Church which would mean he would have to attend Blessed Sacrament Elementary School). He next attended Pitkin High School (where he was a member of a band called the Dream Tones). Tony joined the navy after graduation and after his enlistment ended became a second baseman for the St. Louis Cardinals. Two years later his career ended when he injured his arm. He returned to Brooklyn and acquired a job as a fish truck driver. At some point (not specified) he was married and Samantha was born. Tony's wife died when Samantha was a young girl. It was at this time that Tony applied for the position as housekeeper.

Tony does his grocery shopping at Food Town. He is a very tidy housekeeper and an excellent cook. He plays golf at the Ridgemont Golf Club and is a member of a bowling league called Dr. Whittier's Drill Team. He is the manager of a softball team called Tony's Tigers and posed as "Mr. November" for a calendar. When Samantha began college Tony decided to complete his education and enrolled in night classes in business at Ridgemont College. He later changed his major to education and soon became a substitute teacher at the Nelson Academy for Boys (where he taught English, science and history). He also taught history and was the baseball coach at Wells College in Iowa. Tony became a legend at Ridgemont College when he "liberated the monkeys from the bio lab." Tony first drives a 1967 Chevy van (plate 780 AGN) then a Jeep Cherokee (plate PH 3925) and finally a sedan (plate 518 68Q).

See also: Angela Bower, Samantha Micelli.

1097. Tony Scali, *The Commish,* ABC, 1991–1995. Played by Michael Chiklis.

Anthony Scali, called Tony, is the Police Commissioner of Eastbridge, a suburban New York Community. Tony is married to Rachel (Theresa Saldana) and the father of David and Sarah. They live at 1209 Beach Street.

Tony was born in Brooklyn, New York, and attended St. Mary's High School. He became interested in law enforcement by watching crime shows on TV and obtained a law degree from Fordham University in the Bronx but chose to become a cop rather than practice law.

Tony was previously with the N.Y.P.D. in Manhattan. His outstanding arrest record came to the attention of the Eastbridge Mayor who hired him as their commissioner. Tony is affectionately called "The Commish" by those her works with. Tony is hard on criminals but a softie at heart. He keeps abreast of the current changes in the law by reading whatever material comes his way. He studies the reactions to questions he asks of suspects and always says, "Gotya" when he apprehends a criminal.

Tony is Catholic. Rachel, a teacher at Eastbridge Grammar School, is Jewish. They are raising David in the Jewish faith and Sarah as a Catholic. Tony drives a car with the plate HCM 1971; LLQ 118 is Rachel's license plate number.

1098. Tony Soprano, *The Sopranos*, HBO, 1999 (current). Played by James Gandolfini.

Anthony Soprano is the acting boss for the DiMeo family, a powerful criminal organization in New Jersey. Tony, as he is called, was born in New Jersey in 1959. He grew up in both Newark and West Orange and now lives at 633 Stag Trail Road in North Caldwell, New Jersey.

Tony's father, Johnny Boy Soprano, was a ruthless wise guy for the DiMeo family (he died of lung cancer when Tony was a teenager). His mother, Livia, was emotionally abused by Johnny and was never able to show affection (she died some 20 years later from a stroke). Tony's grandfather, Corrado Soprano, and his wife, Mari Angela D'Agostino, arrived in New York from Ariano, Italy, in 1911. Corrado became a stonemason and the father of Corrado Soprano, Jr. (later to become known as Uncle Junior), Giovanni (better known as Johnny Boy, eventually to become Tony's father), and Ercoli (known as Eckley) who was born with a mental disorder and spent his life in an institution. Junior and Johnny Boy were troublesome from the beginning. They dropped out of high school and wanted no part of their father's life. Instead they aligned themselves to the DiMeo crime family and set the path for future generations of Sopranos.

It was in the 1930s that the Soprano family became active in the crime world (basically Essex County). Johnny Boy established himself in the gambling end of the business. Sometime later Domenico "Dom" DiMeo, the last surviving head of the family, was arrested on a number of felony charges and given several life sentences. When Jackie Aprile, the man Dom chose to run the family, died, Johnny Boy was elevated to boss at the same time Tony began to make a name for himself in the underworld (and eventually becoming the acting boss).

Tony's childhood was anything but normal. As early as he can remember violence was a part of his life. He recalled seeing his father nearly beat to death a bookie for being late with a numbers payment and his father chopping off a dead beat's finger with a meat cleaver. With events such as these coupled with abuse he suffered at home (constantly hit by his father when he disobeyed),

Tony had no choice but to follow in his father's footsteps.

Tony's high school life was basically normal and it was at this time that he met his future wife, Carmela DeAngelis, a girl with faint ties to the mob (her cousin was a mobster). They married after high school and became the parents of Meadow and Anthony Jr. Although Tony does not abuse his children, he is unfaithful and strains his relationship with Carmela. Tony is street smart and has the ability to exonerate himself of criminal charges — a situation that frustrates the FBI, who are eager to put Tony behind bars.

See also: Carmela Soprano, Janice Soprano, Meadow Soprano.

1099. Tootie Ramsey, *The Facts of Life*, NBC, 1979–1988. Played by Kim Fields.

Dorothy Ramsey, called Tootie, is a student at the Eastland School for Girls in Peekskill, New York. She is the daughter of Jason and Diane Ramsey and is a darling girl with a bad habit of eavesdropping. She is the youngest of the series regulars (Blair, Jo, and Natalie) and lived on roller skates her first year at Eastland. She is best friends (and roommate) with Natalie and enjoys meddling in other student's affairs. Tootie has a cat (Jeffrey), two pet rabbits (Romeo and Juliet) and hopes to become an actress (she was the first black girl at Eastland to play Juliet in *Romeo and Juliet*). Tootie is the most ambitious of the girls and enjoys playing checkers with Natalie. Tootie worked at Edna's Edibles, a gourmet food store, and at Over Our heads, a novelty store. She later attended nearby Langley College and in the last episode had been accepted to study acting at London's Royal Academy of Dramatic Arts.

The ABC TV movie, *The Facts of Life Reunion* (November 18, 2001), finds Tootie as the host of daily TV talk show called *Wake Up, Los Angeles*. She is also said to be married and have a daughter named Tisha.

See also: Blair Warner, Edna Garrett, Jo Polniaszek, Natalie Greene.

1100. Topanga Lawrence, *Boy Meets World*, ABC, 1993–2000. Played by Danielle Fishel.

Topanga Lawrence is a girl who cares about other people and will go out of her way to help them. She was born at St. Vincent's Hospital in Philadelphia and lives at 703 North Turtle Dove Drive. She is 11 years old when the series begins and attends John Adams Jr. High School. She first attended Jefferson Elementary School, where she met her on-and-off boyfriend, Cory Matthews. Her after school hangouts at this time were Chubbys (a diner) and Peg Leg Pete's Diner. Topanga next attended John Adams High School (where she was anchor girl for the school's TV program, "The News Now"), then Pennbrook University (where she lived on campus at the McKay Dorm; her hangout was a diner called Captain Randy's). She became engaged to Cory in 1998 (he proposed to her over dinner at Barellie's Restaurant) and married him on November 5, 1999.

See also: Cory Matthews.

1101. T'Pol, *Star Trek: Enterprise*, UPN, 2001–2005. Played by Jolene Blalock.

T'Pol is a beautiful Vulcan and serves as the Science Officer under Jonathan Archer on the U.S.S. Star Ship *Enterprise NX-01*. Prior to joining *Enterprise* T'Pol served as the Deputy Science Officer on the Vulcan ship *Seleya*. One year later, in 2149, she became part of the Vulcan Consulate on Earth (Vulcans and Earthlings had formed a friendship in the mid–21st century). T'Pol was next assigned as an observer on *Enterprise*, when it began its first mission in 2151. She remained as its science officer until 2153 when she resigned her commission with the Vulcan High Command to accompany Jonathan Archer on a mission to destroy an alien (Xindi) weapon that is being built to destroy Earth.

Vulcans are a highly developed race and look down upon humans as an inferior race. They also find working closely with humans unpleasant because of an order they emit. T'Pol finds her experiences with humans gratifying and has a nasal numbing implant to allow her to work closely with them. T'Pol has shown a strong ability to adapt to her human environment—something that is rare in Vulcans. Whether tall tales or factual, T'Pol believes that in the Earth year 1957 her ancestors paved the way for Vulcan-human relationships. At this time a Vulcan ship crash-landed in Carbon Creek, a small mining town in Pennsylvania. To blend in, the Vulcans posed as humans, thus initiating first contact long before the first documented events of 2063.

T'Pol, like Mr. Spock (see entry) of the series *Star Trek*, has the ability to mind meld. She has great admiration for V'Lar, a legendary Vulcan ambassador, and her great-grandmother, TiMir (who was part of that 1957 crash landing). T'Pol's behavior can be considered radical when compared to other Vulcans. She is fiercely independent and defies tradition. This was best displayed when T'Pol, betrothed as a child to a Vulcan named Koss, refused to marry him in order to continue her work with Captain Archer.

See also: Hoshi Sato, Jonathan Archer, Phlox, Travis Mayweather.

1102. Tracee Banks, *Malibu, Ca.*, Syn., 1998–2000. Played by Priscilla Lee Taylor.

Tracee Banks is a beautiful, busty blonde who believes she is the most gorgeous girl "in Malibu Beach and California and the whole U.S. of A. except for alien chicks who may appear on *Star Trek*."

Tracee was born in Malibu Beach on June 9, 1980. She lives at 147 Ocean Drive and yearns to become an actress. She believes she has what it takes—"I'm a glamorous, head-turning knockout." Tracee loves to hang out at the beach and wears bikinis to show off her stunning figure. She is also a bit naïve and easily fooled and says, "I may be an airhead, but I'm one hot babe."

Tracee began her acting career with a gust shot on the TV series *Baywatch*. She next played the Dancing Doritos Chip in a TV commercial ("I was the only chip who got dipped in the salsa") and acquired the role of Dr. Sheila Lowenstein, a brain surgeon, on the TV series *Malibu Hospital*. Her favorite color is pink (her wardrobe, lingerie and even bed sheets are pink). If her acting career fails, Tracee claims she will "fall back on the doctor thing—marry one, not be one."

Tracee holds the title "Miss Shock Absorber of 1998." She appeared on the cover of *Soap Opera Today* magazine and starred as Juliet in an avant-garde production of Romeo and Juliet called "Rome-Yo and L'il Juliet." Tracee also did a PSA (Public Service Announcement) for "Stay in School" and drives a pink Cadillac (with pink tires, pink seat covers and a pink steering wheel) she calls Barbie. She wears a size six shoe and as a kid had a dog named Bo Bo.

See also: Murray Updike.

1103. Tracy Callahan, *Lenny*, CBS, 1990–1991. Played by Alexis Caldwell.

Tracy Callahan is the 10-year-old daughter of Lenny and Shelly Callahan and lives at 11 Cherry Wood Lane in Boston with her sister Kelly.

Tracy was born on May 16, 1980, in Boston and receives an allowance of two dollars a week. She has a doll (Wendy) and a pet hamster (Fuzzball). Tracy is very bright and very knowledgeable for one so young (she watches a lot of TV, especially the Medical Channel, and is an expert on all types of diseases). Tracy attends St. Theodore's Elementary School and hides her money in a box under her bed.

Tracy is addicted to peanut butter and eats Nutri Grain cereal for breakfast. She is a member of the Indian Braves Scout Troop and belongs to the Muttinhead Tribe (her name is Little Fawn). Her father believes that for a ten-year-old girl, Tracy is somewhat unusual. He did ask her, "When you look out into space at night do you get homesick?" Tracy is a talented dancer and performed her first recital as a daffodil in "The Flower Dance."

See also: Kelly Callahan, Lenny and Shelly Callahan.

1104. Tracy Doyle, *Eye to Eye*, ABC, 1985. Played by Stephanie Faracy.

If you dial 213-555-8751 you may hear "Hi, this is Tracy. I'm not in right now. Wait a second I think I hear myself coming up the elevator. No, it wasn't me, better leave a message." Tracy Doyle is a pretty, unassuming young woman who works as a private detective. She is a partner with Oscar Poole (Charles Durning) in a company called Doyle and Pool—Private Investigations (at 112 Beverly Court in Los Angeles).

Tracy was born in California in 1960 and is the daughter of Howard and Patricia Doyle. Her father walked out on her and her mother when she was five years old. Howard, however, was not all bad. He established the agency with Oscar and always sent his wife money. In 1985 Howard attempted to reestablish ties with Tracy but was killed while investigating a case before he could do so. When Tracy learned what had happened, she convinced Oscar to let her help him find Howard's killer. Tracy finds the case exciting and after apprehending the culprit, teams with Oscar.

Tracy lives in a loft over a factory at 120 Waverly Boulevard. She is also a Jill of all trades. She sells real estate and star maps, does interior decorating, caters parties, and is a Smoke Enders counselor "and the personal manager of a singer." Tracy has a dog named Pal and is called "Doll" and "Pussycat" by Oscar. Tracy is over eager when it comes to investigating crimes and becomes rather careless. She likes to get things done fast and doesn't think before she acts (Oscar usually takes a beating because of this). Tracy accomplishes most things by accident and it is often her dumb luck that enables her and Oscar to solve a crime. Tracy and Oscar enjoy meals at Tail of the Pup.

1105. Trance Gemini, *Andromeda*, Syn., 2000–2005. Played by Laura Bertram.

Trance Gemini is a member of the *Andromeda Ascendant*, a futuristic battle ship piloted by Captain Dylan Hunt. Trance appears as a beautiful alien girl with red hair; her actual form is a golden glowing ball of energy. She was born in a futuristic time to transverse all universes in a force from one side to the other. She is the Avatar of the Sun—"A star. All things come from the same thing—all from me. Humans are elements of the Sun. As I make you I am able to destroy you. As I destroy you I am able to create. I am all gravity and we exist in all universes between them. What destroys you in this universe will deliver you to the next."

Trance does not fear the darkness or the light—"It's about balance. They cannot exist without each other." She is skilled as a doctor (she claims baking a pie is harder than performing brain surgery) and is an expert meteorologist (can tell you anything you may want to know about the weather). Trance loves chocolate and plants (hydroponics is her specialty) and tends to give them Earth names (like Walter). While Trance can do many things she is incapable of piloting *Andromeda* (when she does she short circuits the slipstream drive, which powers the ship. It requires full confidence to operate and Trance cannot obtain this under pressure). Trance is also a marvelous cook (if not inventive) and can prepare meals from dirt and spores.

See also: Andromeda, Beka Valentine, Dylan Hunt.

1106. Trapper John McIntire, *M*A*S*H*, CBS, 1972–1995. Played by Wayne Rogers.

John McIntire, nicknamed Trapper John, is a doctor assigned to the 4077th M*A*S*H (Mobile Army Surgical Hospital) unit in Korea during the war. He is a captain and tent mate of Hawkeye Pierce (who calls him "Champion of the oppressed and molester of registered nurses"). Trapper misses his family most—his wife, Louise, and their children, Kathy and Becky. Trapper weighs 175 pounds and fought in the Army's Inner Camp Boxing Tournament as "Kid Doctor" (he was a boxing champion in college also).

Trapper enjoys smoking cigars, poker and playing practical jokes. When the locals need medical help, Trapper is the one they turn to. He reads *Field and Stream* and *Popular Mechanics* magazines. Trapper played a Harpo Marx–like surgeon in the army film *Yankee Doodle Doctor* and was transferred stateside when Wayne Rogers left the series. Captain B.J. Hunnicutt replaced him.

See also: Benjamin Franklin Pierce, B.J. Hunnicutt, Charles Winchester, III, Frank Burns, Henry Blake, Margaret Houlihan, Radar O'Reilly, Sherman Potter.

1107. Travis Mayweather, *Star Trek: Enterprise*, UPN, 2001–2005. Played by Anthony Montgomery.

Ensign Travis Mayweather is a Helmsman under Jonathan Archer, Captain of the Star Ship U.S.S. *Enterprise NX-01*. Travis's parents operated the E.C.S. (Earth Cargo Ship) *Horizon* that carried a fuel called dilithium between the Draylax and Vega Colonies. Travis was born aboard the vessel in the year 2126. He was raised aboard the ship and grew up with a fascination for space and travel. He became well versed in navigation and learned to do many different jobs at the same time (his mother, Rianna, for example, doubled as the ship's medical officer and chief engineer). As Travis grew older he felt life on the *Horizon* was not for him. He joined Starfleet and created a bit of tension when he told his father he would not be following in his footsteps. It was his father, however, who brought Travis to the attention of Captain Archer (when Travis's father learned that Jonathan was seeking candidates for *Enterprise* he sent him a one sentence recommendation: "I've never seen a more natural stick and rudder man in my life") and Travis was immediately recruited.

See also: Charles Tucker, Hoshi Sato, Jonathan Archer, Phlox, T'Pol.

1108. Trek Sanders, *Team Knight Rider*, Syn., 1997–1998. Played by Nick Wechsler.

Kevin Sanders, nicknamed Trek for his fascination with *Star Trek*, is a scientific genius and a member of TKR (Team Knight Rider) an agency of the Foundation for Law and Government that tackles highly dangerous cases.

Trek, as he is called, has an I.Q. of 200. He graduated from M.I.T. at the age of 12 and immediately went to work for a Washington Think Tank. He soon tired of this and put his genius to work developing new technology and selling it on the open market. He became a millionaire by the time he was 20. The following year he was broke. Making money soon became a game with him: invent something, make a fortune, lose it, and invent something else. TKR intrigued him and he offered them his services.

Trek is a computer whiz but not the most ambitious member of the team. He appears to absorb knowledge in all fields and can take nothing and come up with a solution to the team's problem. Trek rides a highly sophisticated and talking motorcycle named Plato (who is also Trek's best friend). Plato is an expert on pop culture and entertainment trivia. He often speaks in a code of movie and TV program quotes that is only understood by Trek.

See also: Duke DePalma, Erica West, Jenny Andrews, Kyle Stewart.

1109. Troy Tempest, *Stingray*, Syn., 1965. Voiced by Don Mason.

Troy Tempest is a member of the World Aquanaut Security Patrol and captain of *Stingray*, a futuristic submarine that patrols the ocean floor.

Troy was born in New York City in the year 2038. He was not the best student in school (constantly inattentive) but his fascination for tropical fish and swimming led him to enroll in the World Naval Academy in San Diego. He graduated with honors and become a part of the World Navy's Submarine Service. His experiences here led to a transfer to the World Aquanaut Security Patrol and eventually the captain of *Stingray*.

Troy believed that life under the sea existed — and proved it in 2064 when he made contact with the people of Pacifica (most notably the beautiful Marina). Troy loves sailing and is a man who carefully plots every move he makes. He never rushes into a situation and is very protective of the various life forms he encounters (he is not one for violence or shooting first and asking questions later). *Stingray* is a Gerry Anderson puppet series filmed in Supermarionation.

See also: Atlanta Shore, Marina.

1110. Tru Davies, *Tru Calling*, Fox, 2003–2005. Played by Eliza Dushku.

Tru Davies is a young woman who can go back in time 24 hours to relive the events of the day to change destinies. She believes it is a curse not a calling — "A calling gives you something you're destined to do, something that gives your life meaning. What I do is more like a curse."

Tru is the daughter of Richard and Elise Davies. She was born in Manhattan and has an older sister (Meredith) and younger brother (Harrison). Life changed for Tru in 1991 when she was 10 years old. One night, while alone with her mother, an intruder entered the Davies home. Elise knew something was going to happen and hid Tru in her bedroom closet. Though Tru could not see what was happening, she heard the intruder shoot her mother dead. The killer was never found and the shooting has haunted Tru all her life (unknown to Tru, her father hired a hit man to kill Elise so he could marry another woman). At the funeral Tru believed she heard her mother say "I'm okay." Tru wished she could go back in time and change that fatal day but nothing happened.

Tru graduated from Grover Cleveland High School in 1999. With an interest in medicine, Tru enrolled at New York University (where she was a track star) and later became an intern at a local hospital. In 2003, at age 22, Tru acquired a night job at the City Morgue (330 West 7th Street) in Manhattan. Her duties required her to work in the crypt where victims of untimely deaths are stored and to assist on autopsies. On her first night, Tru is stunned to hear a female voice calling her name. She traces the voice to a recent victim who tells her "Help Me." Instantly, Tru is transported back in time 24 hours to relive the events of the day to alter the destinies of those who died too soon.

Tru calls her experiences "rewinding" or "the day has rewound." She suspected but didn't know at first, that her mother was able to so the same thing. Her mother, however, couldn't save herself. Tru is caring and will listen to people. She believes that is the reason why she was chosen to do what she does. She has no idea, however, when she was chosen or how it is possible to relive a day (her memories of what happened on the day she is reliving is the key to her saving people's lives). Tru lives at 1723 Oakland Street, Apartment 3, in Manhattan. She drives a car with the license plate RTM 356 and enjoys meals at the Standard Diner. Tru says, "I have 24 hours to relive the past to change the future."

See also: Jack Harper.

1111. Tuvok, *Star Trek: Voyager*, UPN, 1995–2001. Played by Tim Russ.

Tuvok, Security Chief of the Starfleet space ship U.S.S. *Voyager*, was born on the planet Vulcan in the year 2264. He followed in his parent's footsteps and joined Starfleet Academy in 2289. He graduated at the age of 29 in 2293 and was assigned to the U.S.S. *Excelsior*. He married T'Pel in 2304 and became the father of Sek and Asil. In 2298 Tuvok resigned from Starfleet service to raise his children and explore his people's regime of non-emotion. He then became a Starfleet teacher and cadet trainer. In 2343 he was assigned to the U.S.S. *Wyoming*. He later served with Kathryn Janeway aboard the U.S.S. *Billings* and in 2371 joined Captain Janeway as her Security Chief on *Voyager*. Three years later he was promoted to Lieutenant Commander.

Tuvok is a skilled botanist and has a fondness for growing orchids. He practices keetharn meditation and is a master at the Vulcan game Kai-ton. Right before his assignment on the *Wyoming*, Tuvok taught archery at the Vulcan Institute for Defensive Arts (he has a keen interest in the study of violence).

See also: B'Elanna Torres, Chakotay, The Doc-

tor, Harry Kim, Kathryn Janeway, Neelix, Seven of Nine.

1112. Tyger Hayes, *Bare Essence*, NBC, 1983. Played by Genie Francis.

Patricia Louise Hayes works as an executive at the Kellerco Perfume Company in New York City (the company is responsible for creating a perfume called Bare Essence). Tyger, as Patricia is called, is a girl of many talents: "I can drive a truck, an 18-wheeler, keep books — accurate too. Talk to teamsters and get them to do what I want. Play poker and win. Work all night and the next day too — I'm a horse, I never get sick. I cook, simple food but good; and I can out talk and out run any sheriff in three Southern states." And Tyger also plays football — "I always play quarterback."

Tyger is the daughter of Jack and Roberta Hayes. She was born in Los Angeles on November 3, 1961. Her parents divorced when she was six years old (Tyger cried so hard she had the hiccups for two days. When she went back to school she told everyone that her mother died). Her father was a low budget Hollywood horror filmmaker and raised Tyger alone. When Tyger graduated from high school, she enrolled at UCLA. She attended classes for four years but never graduated. The reason: assisting her father on such films as *Halloween Sorority Massacre, Flight Inferno, The Wolfman of Tucson* and *Scream Blood, Mama*. In 1982 her father died of a heart attack. At the funeral Tyger was reunited with her mother, now a wealthy society woman known as Lady Bobbi Rowan. Bobbi's invitation for Tyger to come and live with her in New York (on Gramercy Park) leads her to recall something her mother once said — "Women dress for other women but I know the smell good for men" and to her joining Kellerco to become a business tycoon.

1113. Uhura, *Star Trek*, NBC, 1966–1969. Played by Nichelle Nichols.

Uhura, a lieutenant and communications officer aboard the Star Ship U.S.S. *Enterprise* was born in the United States of Africa in the year 2239. Uhura is a beautiful African-American, and one of the earliest role models for black girls on television. Uhura speaks fluent Swahili and her name translates to mean Freedom. She has a lovely singing voice and can play the Vulcan harp. Uhura is a graduate of Starfleet Academy and in the year 2266 became the Communications Officer under James T. Kirk, captain of the *Enterprise*. Her childhood remains a mystery and it is only known that her mother's name was M'Umbha. Uhura and Captain Kirk are famous or initiating television's first interracial kiss.

See also: Hikaru Sulu, James T. Kirk, Leonard McCoy, Mr. Spock, Montgomery Scott, Pavel Chekov.

1114. Uncle Fester, *The Addmas Family*, ABC, 1964–1966. Played by Jackie Coogan.

Uncle Fester, as this character is called, is somehow related to the eccentric Addams family of Cemetery Ridge, but to what member is not made clear. He is said to be the brother of Gomez (making him Fester Addams) and the uncle of Gomez's wife, Morticia (making him Fester Frump). No matter what, he lives with Gomez and Morticia and their children, Wednesday and Pugsley, at 000 Cemetery Lane.

Fester thrives on electricity and needs to be charged when he runs low (indicated by a feeling of depression). He relieves headaches by placing his head in a vise and tightening it until the headache "pops out." He sleeps on a bed of nails and relaxes with various torture devises in the playroom (actually the dungeon). Fester's right ear produces D.C. (direct current); the left ear is A.C. (alternating current). He can operate appliances simply by plugging it into the needed ear.

Fester claims to know all about women "because I had a mother" and once worked as an advice-to-the-lovelorn columnist but quit when everybody started suing him. He prides himself on his knowledge of explosives (he plays with dynamite caps) and claims to be psychic (he tries but always fails to read minds in a Japanese-made crystal ball). He is also mechanically inclined but has never succeeded in inventing anything of use. Fester likes thunderstorms, lightning, rain, fog, cloudy days and moon bathing. He enjoys exploring caves and the tunnels beneath the house. He hates strangers coming to the house (he threatens them with Genevieve, his Revolutionary War rifle; his philosophy is "Shoot 'em in the back"). He has a hangman's noose collection and in his grammar school's production of George Washington, Fester played the cherry tree. Halloween is his favorite holiday.

See also: Gomez Addams, Morticia Addams, Wednesday and Pugsley Addams.

1115. Uncle Martin, *My Favorite Martian*, CBS, 1963–1966. Played by Ray Walston.

Exagitious 12½ was born on the planet Mars. He is a professor of anthropology whose specialty is the planet Earth. On an exploratory mission to Earth, the Martian's silver spacecraft is cruising along at 9,000 miles an hour when it has a near miss with the U.S. Air Force's test of an X-15 plane. The incident damages the spacecraft and Exagitious crash lands near the desert in California. Tim O'Hara (Bill Bixby), a reporter for the Los Angeles *Sun*, witnessed the incident. Tim befriends the stranded Martian and takes him to his home at 21 Elm Street in a building owned by Lorelei Brown (Pamela Britton), a pretty but scatterbrained widow. To protect Exagitious, Tim introduces him as Uncle Martin, a relative who has come to live with his nephew, Tim. Uncle Martin and Tim later retrieve the spacecraft and hide it in Lorelei's garage. Uncle Martin now needs to find rare minerals (presently unknown on Earth) to repair his craft and return home.

Uncle Martin looks like an ordinary human male but is quite old and has some peculiarities. He is 450 years old based on the Martian calendar of 300 weeks to the year and 8672 days to the week. Uncle Martin has visited Earth many times and has known and advised many famous people (like William Shakespeare, Thomas Jefferson and Rembrandt). "Earth is a nice place to visit," he says, "but I wouldn't want to live here." Uncle Martin has a normal body temperature of 131 degrees and his blood pressure reading is a normal 218.

Uncle Martin is puzzled by earthly emotions and thinks humans lack intelligence (Martians use all of their brain, not a portion of it). Uncle Martin needs an accurate barometer so he can monitor storms. Thunderstorms are his worst fear on Earth because if he is struck by lightning and not properly grounded by the antennae in the back of his head, he gets a condition called "Popsy" (uncontrollable appearing and disappearing). Uncle Martin is prone to short circuits, has the ability to project his dreams, can read minds (unless there is a conscious effort to shut him out), speak to and understand animals, levitate (with his right index figure), and appear and disappear by raising his antennae. Uncle Martin weighs more on Earth because of gravity and claims to be the greatest living authority on the history of Earth.

1116. Valerie Tyler, *What I Like About You*, WB, 2002 (current). Played by Jennie Garth.

Valerie Tyler is a beautiful single woman who lives in Apartment 34C on Bleecker Street in Manhattan with her 16-year-old sister, Holly Tyler. Valerie is an account executive (later managing director) of the Harper and Diggs Public Relations Firm. She was born on April 21, 1974, and is a graduate of Styvesant High School (where she was a cheerleader and called "Pickles" because "I liked pickles") and Columbia University. Valerie first worked as the assistant manager of the Hobby Hutch and carries a toothbrush and paste with her at all times so she can brush after every meal. Valerie prides herself on never being late for work and eats a Mounds bar when something bothers her. Her favorite donut is a chocolate-chocolate with chocolate sprinkles and she "accidentially" appeared in an X-rated film (in college Valerie played a bar tender in a low budget student film that was shelved when the director ran out of money. Years later he reworked the film by adding sex scenes and Valerie became known as "The Butt Tender").

Valerie has a collection of stuffed animals that are arranged by groups because she once had a dream they came to life to play. As a child Valerie had a teddy bear she called Biddy Bear. When she outgrew it she gave it to Holly (who named him Lorenzo).

Valerie alphabetizes her soups, loves playing Scrabble (but hates losing) and chooses Meryl Streep films for her and Holly's weekly movie night. The second season finds Valerie beginning her own PR firm, Valco, and moving with Holly into loft 3D on Spring Street. Valerie calls her breasts "The Girls" and is always fashionably dressed. She also likes to be perfect — "That's who I am, that's what I do." Michael Bolton is her favorite singer.

See also: Holly Tyler, Lauren (no last name).

1117. Vallery Irons, *V.I.P.,* Syn., 1998–2002. Played by Pamela Anderson.

Vallery Irons Protection (V.I.P.) is a Los Angeles–based service owned by Vallery Irons, a beautiful young woman with no special skills, little business experience and no knowledge of computers, but who is an expert on fashion and makeup. The agency charges $25,000 a day plus expenses.

Vallery was born in Vancouver, B.C., Canada, on July 1, 1973. She is five feet, six inches tall and weighs 120 pounds. She has green eyes, blonde hair and a mole on her left shoulder. Her bra size varies by episodes: 38D, 36DD and 34D (she buys her lingerie at Sheer Elegance). Vallery loves to wear very low cut, cleavage revealing blouses, very tight jeans and see-through blouses that reveal her sexy bras. She doesn't appear to have any shame as she flaunts what she has for all to see.

Vallery was first said to live at 10867 Whittier Boulevard, then 299 Ocean Avenue and finally 209 Ocean Avenue. Her phone number is 310-555-1836 and 904-38-2832 is her Social Security

number. The Commerce Bank of Beverly Hills lists Vallery as the Chief Executive Officer of V.I.P. (located at 9100 Sunset Boulevard, Beverly Hills, 90210-0176); 310-555-9276 is the agency's phone number and 904-382812 is her Federal I.D. number. V.I.P. was also said to be located on the ninth floor at 3500 Hollywood Boulevard and 310-555-1847 and 555-1-VIP (later 555-0199) were its phone numbers. Vallery's employees are Nikki Franco, Kay Simmons, Quick Williams and Tasha Dexter.

Vallery is called "The Bodyguard to the Stars." Her knowledge of criminal activity comes from watching reruns of *Law and Order.* She also enjoys watching the interview program *Donny and Marie* (the real series with Donny and Marie Osmond) and enjoys going to the 7–11 "to see what the latest Slurpee flavor is." She hyperventilates when she gets scared and did a TV commercial for Oliver King's Rare Treasures. Vallery's purpose at V.I.P. is "to pull in the rich and famous." While called "The best in the business" (thanks to the efforts of her employees who do all the dirty work while Vallery takes all the bows), Vallery "is better at fashion and makeup than she is at protecting." Her haphazard crime fighting skills (accomplishes everything by accident) have led criminals to believe that her incompetence is her secret weapon.

Vallery has a wardrobe of 8,762 outfits and loves short skirts and high heels. The lingerie company, Cleo's Passion, introduced a line of sexy lingerie and active wear called "The Vallery Irons Undercover Collection — Undergarments to Cover You." Vallery has the ability to have a good time in any situation. She has several strong convictions: "I don't eat meat, I don't cheat at Yahtzee and I don't date men who kill other people." She reads *Vogue* and *Open Toe* magazines and frequents a bar called Foam. She has a robot dog (Bowser) and a red Viper (then Jaguar) with the license plate VIP VAL. Although Vallery drives quite recklessly (and never gets a ticket) she hates car chases — "You gotta watch out for speed bumps and baby squirrels."

Vallery is the daughter of Carol and Jed Irons. Jed was a CIA agent who abandoned his family to protect them when a mission went wrong and he was framed for killing agents. Vallery believed her father was a house painter; her mother works for STX Consolidated, a computer company in Canada. As a child Vallery had an invisible friend named Dirk. She attended Eastern Vancouver High School (class of 1990). She was an *A* student, a gymnast and captain of the girls volleyball team. She is currently taking classes in hypnotism at

U.C.L.A. Vallery's computer password at V.I.P. is "Val Gal." Vallery also has to deal with a girl she calls "The Evil Me," an ex–undercover cop named Joan Archer (Pamela Anderson in a dual role) who was drummed out of the police department and uses Vallery's identity to commit crimes.

See also: Kay Simmons, Nikki Franco, Quick Williams, Tasha Dexter.

1118. Van Ray, *Fastlane*, Fox, 2002–2003. Played by Peter Facinelli.

Van Ray is an L.A.P.D. detective who uses an abbreviated version of his real first name (Donovan). He currently works under Billie Chambers, the head of the Candy Store, a police warehouse that stores (and uses) seized weapons and cars.

Van was born in Los Angeles and is the son of Raymond Ray, an expert counterfeiter known as "Ray Ray" (who is serving time in prison). Van possesses a great deal of knowledge about counterfeiting and it sometimes helps him in his undercover work (he uses the alias Van Strummer). Van has a weakness for beautiful women and "becomes dumb around them," says his partner, Deaquon Hayes. Van trusts people and sometimes gets emotionally involved in his assignments. He hates the fact that he has to lie to people to get the job done and often takes unnecessary chances. He is always out to even up the score. Van enjoys racing cars and being frisked by a gorgeous girl when he goes undercover. His beeper code is "Van To Go" and EHO 537 is his car license plate number.

See also: Billie Chambers, Deaquon Hayes.

1119. Vanessa and Rudy Huxtable, *The Cosby Show*, NBC, 1984–1992. Played by Tempestt Bledsoe, Keshia Knight Pulliam.

Vanessa and Rudy are the youngest children of Cliff and Claire Huxtable, a professional couple who live at 10 Stigwood Avenue in Brooklyn, New York. They have two older sisters (Sondra and Denise) and a brother (Theo).

Vanessa. Vanessa is the fourth-born child and first attended Central High School, then Lincoln University in Philadelphia. Vanessa is a young lady who is anxious to grow up (her mother fears she is going to miss the best years of her life if she doesn't slow down). She started a rock group called The Lipsticks. When Vanessa appeared in her costume (a miniskirt and a stuffed bra worn over a leotard) Clair quickly put an end to the group when she felt it was too suggestive.

Vanessa likes to wear makeup (Clair believes too much) and buys her cosmetics at Nathan's Department Store. She has a 10 P.M. curfew and

Clare feels that Vanessa constantly lies about where she goes "so she can neck in the woods."

Rudy. Rudy is the youngest of the children. She has a teddy bear named Bobo and a goldfish she calls Lamont (Cliff originally had a rule about pets of any kind because he felt his kids were not responsible enough to care for them). Vanilla is Rudy's favorite flavor of ice cream. When she joined the Pee Wee League football team (jersey 32) and proved to be a sensation, Cliff nicknamed her "The Gray Ghost." Rudy likes to throw video parties for her friends (beginning when she was nine years old) and her bedtime is 9:30 P.M. because when Cliff was nine years old his bedtime was 9:30. Cliff looks upon Rudy as his little girl and doesn't want her growing up; Rudy says, "It's a new age Dad, get with it."

See also: Cliff and Claire Huxtable, Denise Huxtable, Sondra Huxtable, Theo Huxtable.

1120. Velvet Brown, *National Velvet*, NBC, 1960–1962. Played by Lori Martin.

This entry also contains information on Edwina (Carole Wells) and Donald Brown (Joey Scott), Velvet's older sister and younger brother.

Velvet. Velvet Brown is a 12-year-old girl with a powerful dream: to win the Grand National Steeplechase. Velvet is the daughter of Herbert and Martha Brown, the owners of the Brown Dairy Farm in a Mid-western community called the Valley (on the outskirts of Birch City). Velvet was born on May 16, 1948. She is a student at Valley Elementary School and won her chestnut horse in a raffle at the state fair. A week later, while training the horse, she remarks, "I just decided something. You hold your head so high and you look so proud. I'm going to call you King." Mi Taylor (James McCallion), the ranch hand who is helping Velvet train the horse, remarks, "That's not much of a racing name. There has to be something ahead of it, like Regal King." Velvet thinks for a moment and says, "How about Blaze King?" "That's not bad at all," says Mi, and it becomes the chestnut's official name.

Velvet is a member of the Pioneers Club (children who go exploring). She is a good student at school and spends her spare moments training for her dream. Velvet won her first steeplechase race at the state fair and next won her first loving cup when she entered the Junior Hurdles at the Valley Hunt Club. Velvet's most difficult task in training King was breaking him to saddle. Once this was achieved Velvet was forbidden by her parents to ride King bare back.

Velvet is a very obedient girl and does what is asked of her without complaining. She has chores to perform in the house and on the farm and is quite wise for one so young. She also appears to have an affinity for animals and enjoys working with Mi, a former steeplechase rider in England (he was born in Ireland and his career ended when he was thrown from a horse during a race. The fall injured Mi's leg and he now walks with a limp). Velvet and Mi enjoys playing checkers together. Velvet is a sensitive girl and always seeks to help anyone she believes is in trouble. She is very pretty but not as feminine as her older sister (who loves to wear makeup and dresses). She attributes this to her work with King and the chores she performs on the farm. Velvet is also not too interested in boys (a godsend for her parents) as all her energies are devoted to fulfilling a dream.

Edwina. Edwina is a beautiful 16-year-old girl and a sophomore at Valley High School. Winna, as she is called, was born on August 12, 1944, and is very sweet and very feminine (she almost always wears a dress — not only at school but around the farm). She is a member of the Teen Club and has a 9 P.M. curfew. She is not permitted to date on school nights (the local make out spot is Honeymoon Lane). While Edwina loves King, she prefers her canaries (which she breeds). She never calls any by a name and reads a magazine called *The Canary Breeders Journal*. She also has "My lucky doll" (name not given) that she has had for ten years and comforts her when she is sad.

Donald. Donald is the baby of the family. He is six years old and is a realistic and typical little boy. He is mischievous and curious and gets hurt (for example, falling down the stairs). He loves all animals and adopts anything he believes is a stray. Donald has a bug collection (which he keeps in a jar with a string around his neck), fibs, blames his sisters for something he did, and is often confused by words he doesn't understand (he calls them "big words"). Donald attends Valley Elementary School and is the mascot for the Pioneers Club. Blueberry pie is his favorite dessert.

1121. Venus Flytrap, *WKRP in Cincinnati*, CBS, 1978–1982. Played by Tim Reid.

Venus Flytrap is the night disc jockey at WKRP, a 5,000-watt radio station (1590 AM) in Cincinnati, Ohio. Venus is really Gordon Simms and uses the alias Venus Flytrap to avoid capture by the military. Gordon was a private in the army and served ten months and 29 days before he realized he made a big mistake by enlisting. He couldn't stand it any longer and went AWOL (Absent Without Leave). He is now wanted as a military fugitive but feels somewhat safe being a nondescript disc jockey at a low rated insignificant radio station.

Venus plays a mix of rock and romantic music. He is a ladies' man and to set the mood for his programs, he usually burns scented candles in the broadcast booth. He also romances his lady friends while spinning records (the station is behind the times and doesn't use tapes) and has a glass or two of wine during each show.

Venus tries to remain inconspicuous in all situations that involve his duties away from the safety of the WKRP studios (suite 1412 of the nine story Flem Building). He fears any attention being brought to him and rarely voices his objections to station policy. While he does fear getting caught, he never associates a woman as being with the military (he believes its a military guy out to get him).

See also: Arthur Carlson, Bailey Quarters, Dr. Johnny Fever, Jennifer Marlowe, Les Nessman.

1122. Vera Gorman, *Alice*, CBS, 1976–1985. Played by Beth Howland.

Vera Gorman is the insecure waitress who works for Mel Sharples, the owner of Mel's Diner at 1030 Bush Highway in Phoenix, Arizona.

Vera was born in Los Angeles, California. She was a good child and excelled at school. She took tap dancing lessons at Miss Dana's Academy of Tippy Tappy Toe Dancing (dancer Donald O'Connor is Vera's hero). Vera's life changed when she was a student at Berkeley. It was the late sixties and she was content (she enjoyed painting peace signs on rocks). One day, while walking on campus, she encountered a group of protestors. She was pushed and shoved and her handbag, filled with peace rocks, hit a policeman in the head. Vera was arrested and the incident so upset her that she quit school and moved to Boston to live with her Aunt Agatha. It is not explained how Vera came to be in Phoenix or how she acquired the waitress job.

Vera is now shy, nervous and a bit clumsy (Mel calls her "Dingie"). She lives at the Sun Rise Apartments and has a pet cat (Mel), two hamsters (Mitzi and Harold) and a guppy (Sidney). Her piggybank is named Irving. Vera is pretty but has few dates (she feels she has no sex appeal). She has the ability to count money by hearing it and plays the cello (Mel put her tap dancing abilities to the test when he staged "Mel's Diner Presents the Vera Gorman Tap Dancing Marathon." Vera broke the tap dancing record of 26 hours and 54 minutes by dancing for 27 straight hours).

Daffy Duck is Vera's favorite cartoon. She has seen the movie *The African Queen* 14 times and has a poster from the film *Watcher on the Rhine* on her living room wall. *One Day After Another* is her favorite TV soap opera. Vera believes everything she sees on TV is real (for example, when Mary Richards of *The Mary Tyler Moore Show* was fired in the last episode, Vera cried for her). When Vera finds herself in a situation that requires her to be in a high place, she tells her brain that she is on the ground floor "so I don't get scared." Vera refuses to serve Mel's Boston clam chowder "because the clams came from Seattle" and gets upset when she opens a jar of baby gherkins (she believes farmers sneak into the fields at night to snatch the baby cucumbers from their mothers). Yum Nutties is Vera's favorite candy and she doesn't go to drive-in movies "because I don't have a car. I'd look foolish standing there with the sound box around my neck." Vera also worked for a short time at Herb's 24-Hour Gas Station.

See also: Alice Hyatt, Flo Castleberry, Jolene Hunnicutt, Mel Sharples.

1123. Vern Albright, *My Little Margie*, CBS, 1952–1953; NBC, 1953–1955. Played by Charles Farrell.

Vernon Albright is an investment counselor for the Manhattan firm of Honeywell and Todd. He is also the father of Margie Albright, a very beautiful 21-year-old girl who delights in meddling in his business affairs.

Vern, as he is called, was born on December 10, 1902, in Boston. He is a graduate of Boston University (where he starred in several school plays). He served as a captain in the army during World War II and he relaxes (or tries to) by playing golf. Vern enjoys watching "old Charlie Farrell movies on TV" ("I wouldn't miss them for anything," he says, referring to the films he made in his real-life career as an actor).

Vern has a bad habit of "staying out all night and exhausting himself." Margie worries because he is not a young man. Vern does it "because it's fun" and believes age has noting to do with it. "I have the constitution of a 17-year-old boy" (Margie wishes he'd give it back). Although Vern raised Margie by himself after his wife's death (in childbirth), Margie feels "I've raised him from my childhood. He's nearly 50 now and you'd think he'd settle down, wouldn't you? Today he looks better in shorts on a tennis court than fellows 25. Girls wink at him and what's worse, he winks back at them." She wants "a nice old comfortable father" and she tries to look after him — "but he just won't settle down."

Vern and Margie live at the Carlton Arms Hotel (Apartment 10A); Carlton 3-8966 is their phone number. Vern has his shoes polished at Joe's Shoe Stand and eats Boomies, "The Atomic Energy Cereal" for breakfast (Margie collects the box tops for the Junior League Toy Drive). Vern is dating his neighbor Roberta Townsend (Hillary Brooke) and was the co-host with Margie of a TV show called *Captain Stratosphere* on WBCA-TV. They were billed as "The Father and Daughter Space Team" but the show was only seen once (in the episode "Margie's Millionth Member") and never mentioned again.

See also: Freddie Wilson, Margie Albright.

1124. Veronica Chase, *Veronica's Closet*, NBC, 1997–2000. Played by Kirstie Alley.

Veronica's Closet is a chain of lingerie stores (and mail order catalogue) owned by Veronica Chase, a former model turned multi-millionaire "by simply selling bras and panties."

Veronica was born in Kansas City, Kansas, and attended the Royal Oaks Elementary School. She had a mostly normal childhood but did begin to develop early and had her first bra when she was in the sixth grade. Although teased by the boys, Veronica paid no attention to it. By the time Veronica was a sophomore at Kansas City High School, she was a 38C and not only the envy of all the girls, but much sought after by the boys. Still, Veronica thought nothing much of it and relished in all the attention she was getting. Following graduation, a not highly motivated Veronica found work as a waitress at Dairy Queen. It was here that a photographer saw what Veronica didn't — a great figure that should be shared with the world. He talked her into modeling a macramé swimsuit and her career took off. She modeled not only swimwear but lingerie as well and was said to be extremely sexy. Apparently Frederick's of Hollywood or Victoria's Secret did not exist in Veronica's world because finding sexy lingerie was a problem. She had an idea to start a manufacturing company that would fill that gap. It eventually grew into a worldwide enterprise with Veronica designing most of the lingerie herself.

Veronica's Closet is based in New York City with offices at 609 7th Avenue. Veronica appeared on the covers of numerous magazines, including *Harper's Bazaar*, *U.S.*, *Time*, *Life*, *Glamour* and of course, the covers of her own catalogues. She is called "The Queen of Romance" and the Sherman Toy Company produced a role model doll for girls based on Veronica (less busty and heavier than a Barbie doll). While described as having a fabulous figure, Veronica apparently never posed nude or did a *Playboy* or *Penthouse* layout. She lives at 703

Park Avenue and has a dog named Buddy. She was called "Princess" by her father and becomes easily exasperated when the slightest thing goes wrong at work. She lives in the lap of luxury but only a hot bubble bath seems to relax her.

1125. Veronica Layton, *The Lost World,* Syn., 1998–2002. Played by Jennifer O'Dell.

Veronica Layton is a beautiful young woman who is called "The Child of the Plateau." The Plateau is a lost world of unknown civilizations and prehistoric creatures that has survived the ages. Veronica was born on the Plateau and cannot leave it; she is its future protector. Veronica has a symbol of rule called the Eye of Heaven (a pendant given to her by her mother, Abigail). It is activated by concentrating and glows in a golden light that protects Veronica from harm. However, there are two contradicting stories regarding Veronica and her parents. In the first version, Veronica states that her botanist parents, Abigail and Thomas Layton are missing — "They went out for samples and never came back." She has been living on the plateau for 11 years and believes they are still alive. Thomas and Abigail met in a world outside of the Plateau. How Thomas knew of the Plateau or how to get to it is not explained (refraction of light appears to conceal its presence). He knew the Plateau held many secrets and he wanted to uncover them. Abigail was just as eager and they set up a life on the Plateau. Veronica was born there but does not know her purpose or how to escape.

A later version claims that Thomas Layton was a botanist who somehow found the Plateau and there met a woman named Abigail. While they never formally married, they bonded to each other. Veronica was born on the Plateau (like her mother and her grandmother, who were protectors of the Plateau and cannot leave). In this version Thomas is apparently killed trying to protect Abigail and a 10-year-old Veronica from a hostile invader. Veronica was hiding in the dense jungle and does not know the fate of her parents. She believes her mother is in a land called Avalon (where the protectors of the Plateau live) but is not able to find it.

Veronica has survived eleven years alone on the Plateau. She lives in a tree house built by her father and has opened her home to George Challenger, Marguerite Krux, John Roxton and Ned Malone, four explorers (the Challenger Expedition) who have come to the Plateau to uncover its secrets but who are now stranded and unable to unravel the mystery that offers escape.

Veronica is a very brave woman who risks her life to protect her newfound friends. She will face a dinosaur with only her knife as a weapon and will fight to the death to protect her home from hostile tribes. Veronica is actually the only hope the Challenger Expedition has of getting off the plateau. Her search to find her mother could also lead them to uncovering the unknown path to the outside world.

See also: George Challenger, Finn, John Roxton, Marguerite Krux, Ned Malone.

1126. Veronica Mars, *Veronica Mars,* UPN, 2004 (current). Played by Kristen Bell.

Veronica Mars is the daughter of Keith and Lee Ann Mars. She was born in Neptune, California, in 1987, and lives with her father in Apartment 10 of the Sunset Cliffs Apartments. Keith and Lee Ann are now separated. Neptune is seen as being located in Balboa County.

Veronica claims "Neptune is a town without a middle class. There are two types of people in Neptune — millionaires and the people who work for millionaires. I fall into the second group." Veronica is a junior at Neptune High School and works for her father, a private detective (owner of Mars Investigations; 555-0137 is its phone number). Veronica is a secretary, but tails philanderers, cheating spouses and investigates false injury claims.

Veronica is not a big fan of high school ("My grades are okay"). She attends because she has to and joined the Pep Squad for the P.E. credits. Two years earlier Veronica was a victim of date rape and has become very vengeful — if you cross her she will find a way to get even ("I believe in the old school — and eye for an eye"). Veronica is a computer whiz and enjoys working as a photographer for the school newspaper, *The Navigator* ("Every girl's gotta have a hobby. Photography is mine").

Veronica can pick locks with a hairpin and goes undercover when she has to — as a dumb blonde or brunette. When she can't pick a lock she uses bolt cutters. While very pretty Veronica is gutsy and will take nothing from anyone. Veronica lies, steals evidence and cheats to accomplish a goal. Trouble seems to follow her around and she will help people for reasons that are sometimes known only to her.

Veronica will not crash a party. She did it once and was given a drugged drink. She has no memory of the party and recalls only "that I woke up in my bra and panties." She is now very careful with whom she associates and where she goes. Veronica claims that the most disturbing part of her job is finding information that could prove harmful to a client. "Should I tell them or is it better if they do not know the results?"

Veronica has a dog (Buddy), drives a car (plate 6BL A504) and she can be reached by phone at 555-0196. The *South Park* movie is her favorite film. She uses the web site *www.preyingeye.com* for research. Waffles and ice cream is her favorite dessert and she most enjoys Italian food. When Veronica bakes a cake "They tend to lean a little to the left."

1127. Vic Nardozzo, *The Michael Richards Show*, NBC, 2000. Played by Michael Richards.

Victor Nardozzo, better known as Vic, was born in Los Angeles. He had an almost normal upbringing until he became hooked on television cop shows and set his goal on becoming a private eye when he grew up. Vic attended the Lakeside Grammar School, U.S. Grant High School and the U.S.A. Detective School. He set himself up in business but found little work. After becoming the technical consultant on the detective series *The Eliminator*, Vic found steady employment at the McKay Detective Agency in Los Angeles.

Vic considers his ability to penetrate any situation his greatest ability ("Just ask the judges at the Mr. Universe Contest," he says). Beside his chameleon-like abilities, Vic feels he is a master of disguises (Mr. Rollin is his favorite alias) and he is proud of the fact that he never has to use a gun.

Vic carries Lady Be Brave pepper spray in his inside jacket pocket, eats at Poquito Mas, "The Original Baja Taco Stand," and shops at Frugal Simpleton ("Where Simple People Shop"). Vic's license plate reads 2ZRZ 458.

1128. Vicki Lawson, *Small Wonder*, Syn., 1985–1989. Played by Tiffany Brissette.

Vicki Lawson is the robotic daughter of Ted and Joanie Lawson, a married couple who live at 16 Maple Drive in Los Angeles. Ted, a robotics engineer for United Robotronics, created Vicki as part of a secret experiment to help handicapped children. Vicki is extremely realistic and looks exactly like a very pretty 10-year-old girl. She is in the experimental stage and needs to learn how to become human before she can be marketed.

Voice Imput Child Identicate, Vicki for short, is made of a highly advanced, flexible plastic, metal, transistors, wires and microchips. The Waffer Scale Integration System gives Vicki life. Vicki generates FM radio waves and has built-in micro generators with a 440-volt capability (which provides electricity. She can for example power appliances and jump-start a car). Her control box is located in her back and its logic code is ML 5500. Vicki has a built-in tape recorder

(she can be used like an answering machine) and the command "Stop" turns her off from whatever she is doing. Once Vicki does something (for example, smiling, climbing a ladder) she is programmed to do it. She can imitate any voice and has one problem that Ted can't solve — she takes things literally (for example, when someone told her to "go soak you head," she did and blew three transistors). "It's not in my memory bank" is Vicki's response when someone says something she doesn't understand. The LES (Logic and Emotional Stimulator) is the emotional program for Vicki.

Vicki sleeps standing up in "Vicki's Closet." She has an electrical outlet under each arm and she possesses incredible strength. Her brown eyes are solar cells and provide power. Joanie dresses Vicki in a cute white and red dress and she is sophisticated enough to blend in with real children and attend school (Washington Elementary, then Grant Jr. High). Ted hopes her exposure to real children will mature her enough to do what she was built to do. Ted redesigned Vicki on occasion (to account for Tiffany's growth spurts) and originally failed when he first tried creating Vicki. Vicki's prototype is Vanessa (also played by Tiffany Brissette), an evil girl who opposed everything good. The series ended before Vicki matured enough to market.

1129. Vickie Groener, *Suddenly Susan*, NBC, 1996–2000. Played by Kathy Griffin.

Victoria Groener is a woman who enjoys other people's misery. She also feels she is a man magnet but confesses, "I'm a tramp at heart." Vickie, as she is called, works as the food critic for *The Gate*, a trendy San Francisco magazine. Vickie also writes about the hip scene and calls herself "The Empress of Hip."

Vickie was born in San Francisco and is a graduate of Hillcrest High School. She was nasty as a child and she is just as nasty as an adult. She dresses in what she calls "trashy clothes" at the office in the hope that she will be sexually harassed. Vickie loves to show cleavage (although she often wishes "I had more to show") and wore a padded bra when she took a second job as hostess at Juggs, a bar that features big breasted girls.

Vickie claims she is mean because she is not as gorgeous as her co-worker Susan Keane ("I'm not as beautiful as Susan, but I'm cute and spunky"). She also feels she will never have a positive outlook on life because girls like Susan get all the breaks while she has to struggle for what she wants. Vickie enjoys taking yoga classes and *Felicity* is her favorite TV series. She has a fake handicap parking permit and when she gets depressed over losing a man "I need pizza, booze and male strippers to get me over it." Sweet and sour shrimp is her favorite meal and she is a member of the Vixens (jersey 1), an all-girl basketball team.

See also: Susan Keane.

1130. Victor Bergman, *Space: 1999*, Syn., 1975–1977. Played by Barry Morse.

Professor Victor Bergman is the guiding force behind Moonbase Alpha, a project established on the moon as an early warning system to repel alien invaders. A radioactive chain reaction blasted the moon out of orbit in 1999 and it now wanders seeking a new planet to affix itself. Victor was visiting Moonbase for study when the explosion occurred and he is now marooned with 300 others.

Victor was born in London, England, on June 27, 1940. He has a degree in technology from Oxford University and is the oldest member of Moonbase. He is also the wisest (he constantly figures out ways to deal with the aliens they encounter). Victor is bright but has a mechanical heart that makes him slow to react to emotional situations (as a child he suffered from an illness that required a heart replacement). Victor believes in old world theories and customs and while he accepts the new technology, he appears happiest when he can recall something from his past to achieve a goal. Victor was responsible for most of Moonbase Alpha's planning and construction. He has also made many contributions to the World Space Mission (where his knowledge has enabled missions to Mars and Venus).

See also: Alan Carter, Helena Russell, John Koenig, Maya.

1131. Victoria Barkley, *The Big Valley*, ABC, 1965–1969. Played by Barbara Stanwyck.

Victoria Barkley is the matriarch of the Barkley Ranch, a 30,000-acre spread in the San Joaquin Valley in Stockton, California, during the 1870s. Victoria is a middle-aged woman and the mother of four children: Jarrod, Nick, Audra and Eugene. Heath, her husband's illegitimate son, also lives with her.

It was the mid–1830s when Victoria and her late husband, Thomas, left Ohio to find a new life in California. A hazardous trek over many months brought them to the San Joaquin Valley where they settled and established their ranch. Over time the Barkleys became a powerful family with a name that stood for right against wrong; a name the people of the Valley could look to for wisdom and leadership in troubled times. Victoria lost

Thomas when he was killed fighting railroad officials seeking his land.

Victoria is a strong-willed woman who does not take a back seat while others run her ranch. She involves herself in the ranch operations and is not always depicted as a woman of leisure, elegantly dressed and entertaining guests. Victoria does become a part of the violence and lawlessness of the Old West. She has been kidnapped, has killed (to save Audra's life), has been drugged, shot at, stranded in the desert and beaten and through it all remains a lady. Victoria rides a horse named Misty Girl and enjoys her meals most when the whole family is present at the dinner table (at which times matters of the ranch are usually discussed).

See also: Audra Barkley, Heath Barkley, Jarrod Barkley, Nick Barkley.

1132. Victoria Winters, *Dark Shadows*, 1966–1968. Played by Alexandra Moltke.

Victoria Winters is a beautiful young woman searching for clues to her unknown past. She has visions of living in another time and another place and believes that Collinsport, a fishing village in Maine, holds the key to unlocking the mystery.

Victoria was orphaned at a young age (abandoned by her parents) and raised in a foundling home. She helped the nuns who ran the orphanage and learned well to care for those younger than her. Victoria was never adopted. She grew up in the orphanage and it was through the home that she was hired to care for David Collins, the young son of Roger Collins (the brother of Elizabeth Collins Stoddard, the matriarch of the Collins family). When Victoria received the employment offer she felt it was more than a coincidence but an opportunity to learn the truth about her parentage — a quest that never succeeded. It is when Victoria becomes David's governess that the mysteries that surround the various family members are also linked to Victoria. Her efforts to uncover the truth involve her in the world of the supernatural. Victoria is sweet but unworldly and she has very little power to affect her own destiny.

Victoria sums up her goal from her opening speech in the first episode: "My name is Victoria Winters. My journey is beginning. A journey that I hope will open the doors of life to me and link my past with my future. A journey that will bring me to a strange and dark place, to the edge of the sea high atop Widow's Hill and a house called Collinwood. A world I've never known with people I've never met. People who tonight are still only shadows in my mind but who will soon fill the days and nights of my tomorrows."

Victoria has long brown hair and brown eyes. She is tall and slender and somewhat of a loner. She is very caring of David and protects him at all costs. Victoria appears to be well educated and she is smart — not just school smart but keen enough to stray from dangerous situations that surround her everyday. Betty Durkin and Carolyn Groves later took over the role of Victoria Winters

See also: Angelique, Barnabas Collins, Roger Collins, Willie Loomis.

1133. Vincent, *Beauty and the Beast,* CBS, 1987–1990. Played by Ron Pearlman.

Vincent, the "beast" of the title, is a mysterious individual who lives beneath the streets of Manhattan in "The Tunnel World," a long forgotten subterranean world beneath New York's subways. Vincent is tall and very strong. He appears vicious but is gentle and kind. His face is described as "a mask of a cat's face with long hair." He was touched by the writings of an author named Bridget O'Donnell whose books "helped me through the dark times and made me think."

Vincent knows only one man as his father, Dr. Jacob Wells (Roy Dotrice), a research scientist called Father, who leads the people of the Tunnels. Jacob worked for the Chittenden Research Institute. He was black listed in 1952 by the House of Un-American Activities for questioning Atomic Energy Commission activities. Unable to face life as he knew it, Jacob retreated to the underworld and established himself as Father. A short time later Father found an abandoned, misfit infant in front of St. Vincent's Hospital. The baby was named after the hospital and raised by Father. Father was never able to find the baby's birth parents. Vincent has no positive answers regarding his birth ("I have ideas but I'll never know. I was born and I survived"). Vincent is now Father's right hand man and helps him guide the community of misfit people who live in the Tunnels.

The underworld people have contacts above the ground called Helpers and only one stranger knows of their existence — Catherine Chandler, an investigative reporter for the D.A. whose life was saved by Father. Vincent now works with Catherine and helps her gather the evidence she needs to bring criminals to justice. He can sense when Catherine is in danger and comes to her rescue. Vincent is unable to show his face in public fearing what might happen. He finds that on Halloween he can walk the streets above his world and be like everyone else.

See also: Catherine Chandler.

1134. Vinnie Barbarino, *Welcome Back, Kotter,* ABC, 1975–1979. Played by John Travolta.

Vincent Barbarino is a teenage tough guy who likes to be called Vinnie. He is a Sweathog, a student in special education classes at James Buchanan High School in Bensonhurst, Brooklyn, New York.

Vinnie is the leader of the Sweathogs — "Room 11 is my place [where classes are held] and these [the Sweathogs] are my people." When it comes to homework "Barbarino don't do reports for no one." Vinnie once opened a book and studied for 15 minutes "but nothin' happened." He hasn't read a book since. Vinnie manages to get away with doing assignments because his teacher, Gabe Kotter, once a Sweathog himself, knows that forcing him will only make him resent school even more (Vinnie believes he is getting away with it because he tells Mr. Kotter "It will hurt my sainted mother if she hears bad things about me"; he also claims bad news causes his mother to throw her rosary beads at him).

Vinnie is a ladies' man and calls himself "The Sweathog Heartthrob" because he can ask out any girl he wants ("I have a stupefying talent with female girls of the opposite sex"). Vinnie is famous for a dance called "The Barbarino" ("Barb-bar-bar-Barbarino"). When asked a question Vinnie responds with "What?" When the question is repeated he says, "Where?" Vinnie ran for student body president with the slogan "Vote for Vinnie and Nobody Gets Hurt." He had a "law and order" platform: Vinnie made the laws and fellow Sweathog Juan Epstein, his Secretary of Fear and campaign manager, kept the order. Vinnie received 47 votes and lost. Vinnie is famous for the term "Up Your Nose with a Rubber Hose" (which is Sweathog slang for farewell or goodbye). He later worked as an orderly at the local hospital and he would like to become an actor (like his idol Marlon Brando) "and be discovered in a drug store."

See also: Arnold Horshack, Freddie Washington, Gabe and Julie Kotter, Juan Epstein.

1135. Vinnie Verducci, *Vinnie and Bobby,* Fox, 1992. Played by Matt LeBlanc.

Vincent Verducci, called Vinnie, is a former boxer who now works for the Rand Construction Company in Chicago. Vinnie was born in Chicago on March 3, 1971. He is a graduate of James K. Polk High School and became a lightweight boxer after graduation (the best he could do with the poor grades he had). When this failed (more losses than wins) he found a job at the Rolling Hills Country Club. His good looks got him the job by the owner (Alexandra Stone) who needed someone to dazzle the female members and keep them from bothering her. When Vinnie tired of this he became a construction worker.

Vinnie first lived at 116 East Hampton, Apartment 3A, then at 623 Cypress Avenue, Apartment 3B (which he shares with fellow construction worker Bobby Grazzo). Vinnie is a bit dense and tends to believe what people tell him. He is "hoping to become smarter" and is attending classes at Dick Butkus Community College (the only school that would accept his D average from Polk High). Vinnie is hoping to become a businessman with his name on the door.

Vinnie believes he is a ladies' man and attracts women by flexing his muscles (he calls them "Thunder and Lightning"). He has an American Express credit card (with a $500 limit) and a motorcycle he calls Ruby. Vinnie frequents a restaurant called Martino's and picks up girls (or tries to) at Smoke's, a pool hall and bar. Macadamia nut ice cream his favorite dessert and as a kid he had a pet cat named Mr. Fluffy.

See also: Mona Mullins (the girl with a crush on Vinnie).

1136. Vinton Harper, *Mama's Family,* NBC, 1983–1984; Syn., 1986. Played by Ken Berry.

Vinton Harper is the only son of Thelma and Carl Harper. He lives with his mother (called Mama) and wife (Naomi) in Mama's house at 1542 Ray Lane in Raytown, U.S.A. Vinton was born in Raytown on April 23. He weighed eight pounds, two ounces and was 22 inches long. He is a graduate of Raytown High School and now works as a locksmith for Kwick Keys. He is proud of his *TV Guide* collection (which dates back to 1958) and is a member of the Mystic Order of the Cobra Club. His favorite hangout is the Bigger Jigger Bar.

Vint, as he is also called, took tap dancing lessons as a kid and was teased at school for carrying a Binky Bunny lunchbox (made by Mama). He had a pet rabbit named Fluffy and believes that the secret to bowling is "the thumb hold." When Vinton won a talent contest at the Bigger Jigger by imitating dancer Fred Astaire, success went to his head and he attempted to break into show business as Vinnie Vegas. Vinton has an insurance policy with Mutual of Raytown and he eats Dino Puffs cereal for breakfast (not for the high fiber count but for the surprise dinosaur that comes in the box).

See also: Naomi Harper, Thelma Harper.

1137. Wally Cleaver, *Leave It to Beaver,* CBS, 1957–1958; ABC, 1958–1963.

Wallace Cleaver, called Wally, is the eldest son of Ward and June Cleaver. He lives with his brother Beaver at 211 Pine Street, then 211 Lakewood Avenue, in Mayfield (the original house address is also given as 211 Pine Avenue).

Wally attended the Grant Avenue Elementary School, Mayfield High School and State College. In high school Wally was a three-letter man and 53.2 seconds was his best time on the swim team. He was also captain of the varsity football team and history was his worst subject. He first mentions he wants to be an engineer then a tree surgeon and finally an electrical engineer to work on missiles. His high school homeroom was 211 and 10-30-11 was his locker combination. He wears Arabian Knights aftershave lotion and held the following jobs: soda jerk at Gibson's Soda Fountain; candy and ice cream vendor weekends at Friends Lake; and loading dock worker at the Mayfield Dairy. He drove a rundown green convertible with the license plate JHJ 355. He is a friend with the trouble-making Eddie Haskell and the slightly overweight Lumpy Rutherford. Julie Foster (Cheryl Holdridge) was his on-and-off girlfriend.

In the CBS TV movie update, *Still the Beaver* (March 19, 1983), Wally has become a lawyer and is married to Mary Ellen (Janice Kent). The updated series, *The New Leave It to Beaver* (TBS, 1986–1989) finds Wally living next door to his mother (at 213 Pine Street) and now the father of Kelly (Kaleena Kiff).

See also: Beaver Cleaver, Eddie Haskell, June Cleaver, Lumpy Rutherford, Ward Cleaver.

1138. Wally Porter, *Love and War,* CBS, 1992–1994. Played by Susan Dey.

Wallis Porter is a beautiful 35-year-old business woman who owns the Blue Shamrock, a quaint 1940s-like bar in Manhattan. Wally, as she is called, lives at 1016 East 74th Street (Apartment C) and is struggling to run the bar and get her life back together after her divorce from a two-bit actor named Kip Zakaris.

Wally is anything but the man people believe she is when they hear her name. She was born in Connecticut on August 6, 1957, and is the daughter of Lillian and Marshall Porter. Lillian was a world-famous chef and groomed Wally to follow in her footsteps. Wally could cook gourmet meals by the age of ten. After graduating from Yale, Wally enrolled in the Cordon Bleu School in Paris and mastered the art of cooking. She can debone a chicken in 20 seconds. She can serve 12 dinners in 21 minutes and once received a letter from chef Julia Child telling her that her *coq au vin* was the best she ever tasted.

Wally's talents led the way for her to open her own eatery, the trendy Chez Wally Restaurant on 72nd Street in New York City. The business quickly became a success and Wally's reputation grew as that of a master chef. Her downfall came when she met Kip after seeing him in an off-Broadway production of *West Side Story* (where he played "Jet Number 2"). They fell in love and married but after 5½ years Wally was unable to stand Kip any longer (he became very conceited) and they divorced. When Kip got her restaurant in the divorce settlement, Wally walked out of the courtroom and wandered into the Blue Shamrock. She ordered one too many double vodkas and bought the bar for $70,000 from its owner.

Wally is Episcopalian. She was named "The Most Promising Chef in New York" and has a hard time serving lobster ("I name them and get attached to them"). Despite her cooking abilities and knowledge of business, Wally soon found life closing in around her. She needed to "find myself" and left suddenly for Paris (she gave ownership of the Shamrock to its bartender, Abe Hancock). It was at this time that Abe hired chef Dana Palladino to replace Wally.

See also: Dana Palladino, Jack Stein.

1139. Walter Nebecher, *Automan*, ABC, 1983–1984. Played by Desi Arnaz, Jr.

This entry also contains information on Automan (Chuck Wagner), "The world's first automated man."

Walter Nebecher is head of the computer department of the Parker Division of the Los Angeles Police Department. He was born in the city and now lives at 3611 Alameda, Apartment 2. Walter grew up admiring police and private detectives on TV and hoped to devote his life to battling the criminal elements. What he wound up with, however, was an inside desk job (in an office he calls "The Cage").

Walter has an advanced knowledge of computers and electronics. He begins experimenting with holographic images in an attempt to create a game in which he can be the conquering hero. He invents an image he calls Automan and programs it with all the knowledge of sleuthing from Sherlock Holmes to James Bond. Walter now hopes to use Automan as part of his computer to help solve crimes. However, an accidental increase of power produces the unexpected: Automan jumps from the computer to the real world and becomes a life-size image that is able to operate apart from the computer that created him.

Automan is a force for good and is accompanied by Cursor, a glowing hexagon that can create anything Automan needs (like the AutoCar, which can make 90 degree right angle turns). Walter has programmed Automan to be honest and to sound and feel human. A glitch, however, had gotten into the program and Automan is afraid of the dark.

Automan learns by observing people ("I do what they do — only better. On a scale of one to ten think of me as an eleven"). Automan lives with Walter. He needs to be recharged often ("If I'm away from my computer for too long I have a power failure and can't function"). When Automan needs to become human he asks Cursor to make him acceptable based on the situations he encounters. Since Automan is an electronic display he is prone to interference from above-the-ground power lines. Walter uses the word "Crime Fighter" to bring Automan from the computer to the real world. Since Automan physically assists Walter on cases, he first introduced Automan as, "This is my assistant, Auto" (Automan later adopted the alias of Agent Man of the FBI). When Automan introduces himself to people he calls himself Auto J. Man. Automan enjoys TV and his favorite series is *Abilene*. Veronica Everly is his favorite actress (he has seen her film, *Queen of the Nile*, 100 times).

1140. Walter Tatum, *Moon Over Miami*, NBC, 1993. Played by Bill Campbell.

Walter Tatum is the owner of Walter Tatum, Inc. (also called the Walter Tatum Detective Agency) in South Beach (at 668 Strand) in Miami Beach, Florida.

Walter was born in Florida and raised by his grandparents, Nate and Adelaide Tatum, since he was two years old (his parents were killed in a plane crash). Although his grandfather was a famous musician (played sax) with the Benny Goodman Band Walter was fascinated by police and detective shows on TV. But rather than become a cop he thought he could better protect people if he were a lawyer.

Walter studied and apprenticed. One summer while working for the Legal Aid Society, Walter's life changed. He saw a private detective help an old lady get her water turned back on. The detective did more for the woman than a whole team of lawyers. Walter quit law and became an apprentice to the detective (Gavin Mills) who had influenced him. When he felt the time was right Walter opened his own agency.

Walter charges $200 a day plus expenses and can be reached by phone at 555-3666. His car license plate reads WCU 72N. What Walter saw on TV and what he learned from Gavin don't exactly mix now that he has his own agency. He has one employee, Gwen Cross, who is supposed to be his secretary and receptionist but feels more comfortable helping him solve crimes. A romantic relationship appeared to be developing between Gwen and Walter but the series ended before anything was established. Walter likes to take his time on a case and study the clues. Gwen is impulsive and likes to rush in and get the job done. The two bicker, the two get into trouble and they often solve crimes by pure luck.

See also: Gwen Cross.

1141. Ward Cleaver, *Leave It to Beaver,* CBS, 1957–1958; ABC, 1958–1963. Played by Hugh Beaumont.

Ward Cleaver, the husband of June and the father of Wally and Beaver, was born in 1918. He has four siblings (two brothers and two sisters) and was born in Shaker Heights, Ohio, and raised on a farm. At some point thereafter (possibly as a teenager) he moved to Mayfield (the series setting) and lived on Shannon Avenue. He now lives with his family at 211 Pine Street, then at 211 Lakewood Avenue. In another episode, it is mentioned that Ward was born and raised in Mayfield.

As a child Ward washed windows to earn money and was interested in playing baseball (he carried a heavy unabridged dictionary to school to strengthen his pitching arm). He fished for eels (with liver as bait) near "the old drain pipe" and shot rats at the local dump. Ward read *Weird Tales* magazine and had seen the 1931 movie *Dracula* with Bela Lugosi four times. At one point he was a member of the 4H Club and won first prize for his hog at a state fair. Ward was a second string halfback on his high school football team and also a member of the shot put team. In college he was on the school's basketball team but was said to be both a philosophy and engineering major. He served as an engineer with the Seabees during World War II. He now works as a businessman in an unnamed profession in a modern office building with the street number 9034; Fred Rutherford is his boss. He drives a car with the license plate WJG 865 (later KHG 865). Ward reads the *Mayfield Press,* still enjoys fishing (at Crystal Lake) and takes his coffee with cream and no sugar.

See also: Beaver Cleaver, Eddie Haskell, June Cleaver, Lumpy Rutherford, Wally Cleaver.

1142. Warwick Brown, *C.S.I.: Crime Scene Investigation,* CBS, 2000 (current). Played by Gary Dourdan.

Warrick Brown is a field operative for the Crime Scene Investigation Unit of the Metropol-

itan Las Vegas Police Department. Warrick was born in Las Vegas on October 10, 1970. His father abandoned him and his mother when he was still an infant. Warrick's mother died when he was seven and his grandmother raised him. He had a normal high school education but had to work to put himself through college. His jobs included taxi driver, bell captain at the Sahara Hotel and Casino, selling helicopter rides over the Grand Canyon and grave digger. Warrick graduated from the University of Las Vegas with a Bachelor of Science degree in chemistry and immediately went to work for the Las Vegas P.D. He was soon recruited by Gil Grissom to become a member of his C.S.I. unit. His specialty is audio and video analysis. Warrick is a stickler for gathering evidence and brilliant at piecing together fragments of objects to make them whole or identifiable. He can visually detect evidence others may have overlooked but suffers from a gambling problem that he has yet to get fully under control.

See also: Catherine Willows, Gil Grissom, Nick Stokes, Sara Sidle.

Wayloo Marie Holmes *see* **Laurette Barber**

1143. Webster Long, *Webster,* ABC, 1983–1987; Syn., 1987–1988. Played by Emmanuel Lewis.

Webster Long is a seven-year-old African-American who is being raised by his godfather, George Papadopolis, and his wife Katherine.

Webster was born in Chicago in 1976 and is the son of Travis and Gert Long. Travis was a former pro quarterback and called Webster "Little Quarterback." When Travis and Gert were killed in a car accident Webster was sent to live with George when there was no one else to care for him. He lives in Apartment 14B at 534 Steiner Boulevard in Chicago.

Webster attends Clemens Elementary School (where he plays triangle in the school band). He calls George "George" and Katherine "Mam" (it sounds like "Mom" to him). He has two pet frogs (Fred and Peggy), a snake (Dr. Plotsman) and a homemade robot (Mr. Spielberg). Webster keeps his "menstoes' (mementoes) in an old cigar box and eats Sweeties and Farina Pops cereal for breakfast. His favorite number is 3. Webster was a member of the Boy Braves Scout Troop (where he earned a merit badge for helping the Great Walnutto, a 1940s radio magician, make a comeback). He enjoys feeding pigeons in the park (Charlie is his favorite) and his favorite TV show is the mythical game show *Don't Jump.*

See also: George and Katherine Papadopolis.

1144. Wednesday and Pugsley Addams, *The Addams Family*, ABC, 1964–1966. Played by Lisa Loring, Ken Weatherwax.

Wednesday and Pugsley Addams are the children of Gomez and Morticia Addams, an eccentric couple who live at 000 Cemetery Lane in the town of Cemetery Ridge. They attend the Sherwood Elementary School. Wednesday is the older child and loves all that is morbid. She likes to play autopsy and has a headless doll named Marie Antoinette. She also has a pet spider (Homer) and enjoys dressing in black like her mother. Wednesday is most happy when it thunderstorms or the weather is gloomy. Bright, sunshine and clear days make her feel sad.

Pugsley is an overweight boy who enjoys helping his father blow up his Lionel O-gauge electric trains. He has a pet octopus (Aristotle) and a jaguar named Fang. He plays with dynamite caps and can control an explosion. Pugsley is an inventor of sorts (he created, for example, a ray gun and an anti gravity machine). He is a happy and curious boy who finds pleasure in things his family finds disturbing (for example, the Boy Scouts, sports). He eats licorice sticks while reading his comic books and enjoys playing in the torture room of the house.

See also: Gomez Addams, Morticia Addams.

1145. Wendy Lubbock, *Just the Ten of Us*, ABC, 1988–1990. Played by Brooke Theiss.

Seventeen-year-old Wendy Lubbock is a junior at Saint Augustine's, a Catholic high school in Eureka, California. She has seven siblings and is the daughter of Graham and Elizabeth Lubbock. Wendy was born on Long Island in New York on May 17, 1971.

Wendy is the sexiest and most beautiful of the Lubbock girls (her sisters are Marie, Connie, Cindy and Sherry). She is boy crazy and totally self-absorbed. She wears a size five dress, a 34B bra, a 7½ shoe and the lipstick shades Dawn at His Place and Midnight Passion. Wendy enjoys shopping at the Eureka Mall and has the ability to take a precious moment of one of her sisters and drag it into the gutter. She doesn't understand "big words" ("They confuse me") and says, "Attitude gets me men. I think I'm beautiful. I fool people. I'm not as perfect as you think I am. I've got fat ankles" (which she calls "my shame"). Wendy also claims that girls like her are a tease: "I show a little cleavage, some thigh and even a glimpse of my bikini line to get attention." (Marie, who is hoping to become a nun believes Wendy is "wicked and evil" for saying such things). Wendy, Connie, Cindy and Marie formed a singing group called The Lubbock Babes (they played regularly at Danny's Pizza Parlor).

See also: Cindy Lubbock, Connie Lubbock, Graham and Elizabeth Lubbock.

1146. Wes Kennedy, *Heart of the City*, ABC, 1986–1987. Played by Robert Desiderio.

Wesley Kennedy is a detective with the Los Angeles Police Department. He is the father of Robin and Kevin and his late wife was named Susan (killed in a crossfire at the site of a police shooting). Wes, as he is called, lives at 5503 Pacific Way and drives a car with the license plate ICYD 198.

Wes was born in Los Angeles and attended West Hollywood High School. He has a photographic memory and could have become anything he wanted; he chose to become a cop. He graduated with top honors from the Los Angeles Police Academy and was assigned duty as a street cop. Before long he had an impressive record of arrests and convictions. He was then chosen to head a S.W.A.T. (Special Weapons and Tactics) team. As a commander of S.W.A.T., Wes solved 24 percent of his caseload, which is more than ten percent higher than the rate of other cops in the precinct. He resigned after Susan was killed but remained with the precinct; he is now a plainclothes detective with the Homicide and Robbery Division.

Wes remained a cop "to get the animals off the streets. It's what I do; it's what has to be done." Wes was an impatient cop — get the job done first, ask questions later (he was often reprimanded for "too many shootings"). He is now more relaxed and much more careful now that he has the sole responsibility of raising Robin and Kevin. The series begins 18 months after Susan's death. Wes has found a new love, Kathy Priester (Kay Lenz), a waitress at a diner called Trio's Grill. He is very protective of her and has made it a policy of not involving her in any police matters.

See also: Robin Kennedy.

1147. Wesley Owens, *Mr. Belvedere*, ABC, 1985–1990. Played by Brice Beckham.

Wesley Owens is the youngest member of the Owens family. He lives with his parents, George and Marsha, and his siblings (Heather and Kevin) at 200 Spring Valley Road in Beaver Falls, Pittsburgh. Lynn Belvedere, a British butler, cares for them.

Wesley was born in Beaver Falls and is the most mischievous of the children. He attended Conklin Elementary School, Allegheny Junior High and finally Beaver Falls Junior High. He is a member of the Colts, a Little League baseball team, and the Junior Pioneers (Group 12). He has a pet dog

(Spot), a snake (Captain Nemo) and a hamster (Inky). His favorite sandwiches are tuna fish and marshmallow spread and bologna and marshmallow spread on raisin bread. To make some extra spending money, Wesley sold Heather's lingerie, claiming it belonged to Madonna. Wesley is called "Wesman" by George and delights in playing practical jokes. Wesley was also on the school's football team (jersey 31) and attended Camp Chippewa. He also made a home movie about Mr. Belvedere called "The Housekeeper from Hell."

See also: George and Marsha Owens, Heather Owens, Kevin Owens.

1148. Whitley Gilbert, *A Different World*, NBC, 1987–1993. Played by Jasmine Guy.

Whitley Gilbert is a student at Hillman College in Georgia. She is rich, beautiful and spoiled and her passion is art and shopping. Whitley was born in Richmond, Virginia, on February 14, 1967. Her grandparents donated the money for the school's Gilbert Hall (built in 1925) and her parents donated the money for the Dorothy Dwight Hall, the dorm room in which she now lives (in Room 20S).

Whitley is always fashionably dressed (she considers herself "The Ebony Fashion Queen"). She is proud of the fact that her beauty allows her to steal men from other girls. She despises anyone touching or wearing her clothes and will only use a bar of soap once then discard it. She will not eat cheese or allow anyone to eat cheese in her presence. Whitley locks her phone and sleeps with a tape recording of either the sounds of the sea and seagulls or of crickets chirping in the forest.

Whitley has taken dance lessons since she was a little girl (jazz, ballet and tap). She was also crowned "Miss Magnolia" as a child. She is an art major at Hillman and later became an art buyer "with my own office" at E.H. Wright Investments.

See also: Dwayne Wayne (the student Whitley marries).

1149. Wilbur Post, *Mister Ed*, Syn., 1960–1961; CBS, 1961–1966. Played by Alan Young.

Wilbur Post is an independent architect who has an office in the barn of his horse Mister Ed, a talkative animal who has chosen only to speak to Wilbur because he "is the only human he liked well enough to talk to."

Wilbur is married to Carol Carlyle, a former dancer, and they live at 17230 Valley Spring Lane in Los Angeles (the address is also given as 17290 Valley Spring Lane, 1720 Valley Road, 17340 Valley Boulevard and 17230 Valley Stream Road).

Wilbur was born in Connecticut but was relocated to Los Angeles shortly after when his parents moved to California. He loved animals as child and is a graduate of Mulholland High School (where his best subject was algebra) and U.C.L.A. (where he studied architecture). He joined the Air Force after college (he made 50 parachute jumps and Donald Duck was his squad room mascot. He claims to have gotten the courage to jump from his time as a child when he would walk along the tops of fences). Wilbur's office phone number is Poplar 9-1769 and he drives a Studebaker with the license plate FIM 921 (in certain scenes it reads IJM 921). Wilbur is a Taurus (born in May) and he is a member of the Lawndale Men's Club. Ed's antics cause Wilbur to become the fall guy. He appears unstable to most people and is looked upon as a fool by others as he tries to hide the fact that he has a talking (and mischievous) horse. Carol doesn't know what to believe half the time but Wilbur's explanations to why he acted a certain way often satisfy her. Last season episodes find Wilbur and Ed solving crimes for the Secret Intelligence Agency.

See also: Carol Post, Mister Ed.

Will Robinson *see* **John Robinson**

1150. Will Smith, *The Fresh Prince of Bel Air*, NBC, 1990–1996. Played by Will Smith.

Will Smith is a young man who was given a better chance to succeed in life when his mother, Viola, saw he was hanging out with the wrong crowd and sent him to live with his uncle, Philip Banks, his wife, Vivian, and their children, Hilary, Carlton and Ashley, in fashionable Bel Air, California.

Will was born in West Philadelphia on July 3, 1973. He attended West Philly High School and carried his books in a pizza box so no one would know he was attempting to learn something. In California Will first attended the Bel Air Academy then the University of Los Angeles. He plays ball at the L.A. Recreational Center and held the following jobs: car salesman at Mulholland Motors; waiter at the Brawny Deep (where he dressed as a pirate); waiter at the Peacock Stop, the college hangout; waiter at Chesler's Touchdown, the off-campus sports bar; assistant talent coordinator (books guests) for the TV talk show *Hilary* (which stars his cousin Hilary).

Will first lived in the family mansion then in the pool house out back. He danced on the TV show *Soul Train* and attempted to write a book called *Celebrity Houses at Night*. He also tried to impress girls as a member of the Bel Air Poetry Club by pretending to be a famous poet named Raphael De La Ghetto. During the summer of 1994 Will returned home to visit his mother and took a job as a cook-waiter at Duke's House of Cheese Steaks.

See also: Ashley Banks, Carlton Banks, Hilary Banks, Philip Banks.

1151. Will Truman, *Will and Grace*, NBC, 1998 (current). Played by Eric McCormick.

William Truman is a gay lawyer with a private practice in Manhattan (he later works as a corporate lawyer for the firm of Doucette and Stein). Will, as he is called, was born in New York City and is the son of George and Marilyn Truman. As a child he had a dog named Daisy and an Easy Bake Oven (which he says accounts for the fact that in his adult life he is a great cook).

Will is a best friend with Grace Adler, a beautiful straight woman he met at New York University (Grace discovered Will was gay "when he put his hand on my boob and said is that a cashmere sweater?"). In a later episode, Grace says she learned Will was gay when he told her at Christmas time. In college Will hoped to become a playwright and wrote a play called "Bye, Bye Sexual," which told of him coming out of the closet. When his professor told him it was bad he switched his major to law.

Will lives at 155 Riverdale Drive, Apartment 9C. He embroiders his own kitchen aprons (from McCall patterns) and had one entered in the Statewide Needlepoint Competition. He is a huge Barry Manilow fan ("I'm a fanilow") and in college was in an improv group with Grace called The Zaniacs.

Will's most treasured item is Squatsy, a garden gnome he bought for his parents when he was a child. He enjoys coffee with Grace at Kitty's Coffee Shop and they dine at a Mexican restaurant called Pablo's Cantina. Will frequents such gay bars as The Tight End, Adam's Bar and Crisco Disco. When he needs to blow off steam, he goes to the sweater department of Burgdorf's Department Store.

See also: Grace Adler, Jack McFarland, Karen Walker.

1152. William Riker, *Star Trek: The Next Generation*, Syn., 1987–1994. Played by Jonathan Frakes.

William Thomas Ryker is a captain under Jean-Luc Picard, commander of the Galaxy Class Star Ship U.S.S. *Enterprise NCC-1701-E*. William is the son of Kyle and Betty Riker and was born in Valdez, Alaska, on August 19, 2335. He is a graduate of Star Fleet Academy (2353–57) and is married to Deanna Troi.

William is well versed in legal issues. His first assignment was an ensign aboard the U.S.S. *Pegasus* in 2358. He became a lieutenant in 2361 and a year later was assigned to the Star Ship U.S.S. *Potemkin*. Six weeks later, when he rescued the ship's away team on Nervalla IV, he was promoted to lieutenant commander and transferred to the U.S.S. *Hood*. In 2364 he was assigned to *Enterprise*.

See also: Beverly Crusher, Data, Deanna Troi, Geordi La Forge, Jean-Luc Picard, Natasha Yar.

1153. Willie Loomis, *Dark Shadows*, ABC, 1966–1971. Played by John Karlen.

Willie Loomis is the caretaker for the powerful Collins family at Collinsport in Maine. He is somewhat unkempt, thin and stands five feet, seven inches tall. Willie was born on a farm in the Mid-West and was the youngest of three brothers. He was considered small and weak and was constantly teased by his brothers. When a fire destroyed the family farm Willie became a drifter and earned his meager living as a thief. He eventually found his way to Maine where he was hired to care for the gardens of the Collinwood estate.

Willie is a coward at heart and very predictable. He rarely thinks before he acts and when he drinks too much (at the Blue Whale Bar) he tends to brag about what he has done. He is easily manipulated and loyal when he has to be (usually when his life is on the line). Willie has a fascination for jewelry and it was this obsession that led him to break into a crypt at Eagle Hill Cemetery and release a 19th century vampire (Barnabas Collins) on the modern-day world (see Barnabas Collins for details).

Willie has a bad reputation for lying and cheating and is looked down upon by almost everyone on the great estate and in town. He is also a sneak and learns much of what he knows by eavesdropping. He can be described simply as immature and is only responsible when someone takes charge of him.

See also: Angelique, Barnabas Collins, Roger Collins, Victoria Winters.

1154. Willis Jackson, *Diff'rent Strokes*, NBC, 1978–1985; ABC, 1985–1986. Played by Todd Bridges.

Willis Jackson and his brother Arnold are the black adopted children of Phillip Drummond, a multi-millionaire who lives at 679 Park Avenue (Penthouse A; sometimes seen as B) in Manhattan. Phillip is a widower and has a young daughter named Kimberly.

Willis was born in Harlem and was the son of Lucy Jackson. He and Arnold lived at 259 East 135th Street (Apartment 12) and Lucy earned a living as Phillip's housekeeper. When Lucy passed away, Phillip kept a promise he made to her to look after her sons (he later adopts them).

Willis is the older brother and the one who looks out for Arnold (even though Arnold feels he can take care of himself). Willis had a doll named Wendy Wetems as a kid but quickly outgrew that, fearing to get teased (or worse) if word got around the neighborhood. He attended Roosevelt Jr. High School, Garfield High School then an unnamed college. While Willis was a very good kid, he did experience what it was like to go on the wild side when he joined a gang called the Tarantulas. He quickly gave it up when he realized the gang was up to no good. He formed a band called The Afro Desiacs and held a job at Kruger's Garage. Willis is a bit conceited and thinks he is a ladies' man. He likes looking into the mirror and "tries to act like Superfly with the girls but I come off like Big Bird." He dated Charlene DuPres (Janet Jackson) and "Say what?" is his favorite expression.

See also: Arnold Jackson, Edna Garrett, Kimberly Drummond.

1155. Willow Rosenberg, *Buffy the Vampire Slayer*, WB, 1997–2001; UPN, 2001–2003. Played by Alyson Hannigan.

Willow Rosenberg is a 16-year-old computer genius who attends Sunnydale High School in Sunnydale, California. She is pretty, shy and sensitive. She is a straight A student and has the powers of an apprentice witch. Willow is friends with Buffy Summers (the vampire slayer) and helps her Watcher, Rupert Giles, battle demons (mostly with her research at first, then with her powers as a witch as she matured).

Willow gets headaches and nosebleeds when she uses a transformation spell. She was first in love with her childhood friend, Xander Harris, but realized they could never be more than just friends. Three years later, when Willow begins classes at the University of Sunnydale, she reveals that she is a lesbian. She bonds with Tara (Amber Benson), a lesbian who is also a witch (they share Room 217 at Stevenson Hall and combine their powers to help Buffy defeat evil). Although she accepts the term "witch," Willow calls herself by the proper designation, "a powerful she witch." Willow went from good to evil and back to good over the course of the series and tried to always use her powers for good. When she became evil (possessed by forces or calling on powers to sophisticated for her to comprehend) no one was safe and she would kill any human who crossed her.

See also: Buffy Summers, Dawn Summers, Rupert Giles, Xander Harris.

1156. Wilson Wilson, Jr., *Home Improvement*, ABC, 1991–1999. Played by Earl Hindman.

Wilson Wilson, Jr., lives at 510 Glenview Road in Detroit, Michigan, and is the neighbor of Tim Taylor, the host of TV's *Tool Time*, and his wife Jill.

Wilson is the son of Wilson Wilson, Sr., a famous scientist. Wilson's face is never fully seen (it is always obstructed by something, usually the picket fence that divides his and Tim's property. Wilson only appears to give Tim or Jill advice on something that is troubling them).

Wilson was born in Michigan. He attended the Greenville School for Boys (where he played Juliet in *Romeo and Juliet*) and attended Oxford University in England for one semester. He was a pilot during World War II, worked as a park ranger, and writes the column, "Rock Beat" (about rocks) for the Wichita *Star*. Wilson is a scholar. He has had dinner with Albert Einstein, knows world leaders, and can talk brilliantly on any subject. He is interested in insect mating, hangs ancient Crete bells in his backyard to attract friendly spirits, and is a trained midwife. He sculpts shrines out of yak butter and his idea of a romantic dinner is haggis (sheep's liver wrapped dumpling style). Wilson celebrates unusual holidays (like the end of the Punic Wars), raises spiders, sings to his plants, and plays the Alpine Horn (used for herding sheep) in the Alpine Horn and Yodel Festival.

Wilson is a widower. He met his late wife Kathryn in Ecuador and they married in 1969. He has a mynah bird (Mozart) and a scarecrow he calls Oliver. Wilson greets Tim with "Hi-dee-ho, neighbor" and Jill with "Hi-ho, neighborette."

See also: Al Borland, Jill Taylor, Tim Taylor.

1157. Wilton Parmenter, *F Troop*, ABC, 1965–1967. Played by Ken Berry.

Wilton Parmenter is a captain, called "The Scourge of the West," who commands a misfit platoon of soldiers at Fort Courage, the U.S. Army's cavalry outpost in Kansas (1866).

Wilton was born in Philadelphia in June of 1842. He is from a very proud military family and grew up hearing of the exploits of such relatives as Colonel Jupiter Parmenter and General Thor X.

Parmenter. Naturally, Wilton was groomed to follow in their footsteps. In 1865 Wilton joined the Union Army and became a private in charge of officers laundry with the Quartermasters Corps. Wilton is nothing like his relatives. He is timid, weak, easily fooled and terribly accident-prone. For reasons that are known only to higher authorities, Fate stepped in. One day while performing his chores, an excess of pollen caused Wilton to sneeze and blurt out what sounded like "Charge!" Troopers on standby were prompted into action that foiled a Confederate plan and brought victory to the Union (the battle supposedly ended the Civil War). Wilton was promoted to captain and assigned the command of F Troop. His sneeze also earned him a reputation that is feared by the various Indian tribes (who fear reprisal if they do not keep the peace).

Wilton accomplishes his achievements by accident. He believes the "ferocious" Hewaki Indians are kept in line by his reputation (unknown to him, the Hewakis are a friendly tribe and pretend to live in fear of him). Wilton is not the monster his reputation makes him out to be. He is kind and gentle and hopes to make his troops the best fighting unit in the cavalry. His main problem, however, is not his troops or the Indians, but avoiding the matrimonial plans of Wrangler Jane, the girl who fell in love with Wilton at first sight and has now made it her goal to marry him.

See also: Morgan O'Rourke, Randolph Agarn, Wrangler Jane.

1158. Winnie Cooper, *The Wonder Years*, ABC, 1988–1993. Played by Danica McKellar.

Gwendolyn Cooper was born in Any Town, U.S.A., on July 16, 1956. She is very pretty, very sweet and is depicted as the 1960s girl next door. She is best friends with Kevin Arnold and became very close as they grew from childhood to adulthood. They shared their first kiss while sitting on a rock in Harper's Woods.

Winnie, as she is called, attended Hillcrest Grammar School and Robert F. Kennedy Jr. High School. She had to leave Kennedy Jr. High in the spring of 1970 when her family moved to a new home four miles away. She completed her education at Lincoln Jr. High. She then enrolled at McKinley High School. Although her relationship with Kevin became rocky over the years, Kevin says that "I'm a part of Winnie and Winnie is a part of me. For as long as I live I will never let her go."

At Kennedy Jr. High Winnie was a member of the cheerleading team for the Wildcats and starred in a production of *Our Town* (Kevin worked the spotlight). Winnie was a young girl Kevin had a hard time figuring out. He had a "Star Trek" dream one night in which he was Captain Kirk and Winnie was a beautiful alien with long hair and a short skirt ("Hey, it's my fantasy. I figured I might as well do things right"). But even as Captain Kirk, Kevin was still mystified by Winnie.

Kevin always found Winnie to be a friend, a person he could share his deepest thoughts with. She listened and she cared. Winnie worked as a lifeguard at the Cascades Resort and Tennis Club during the summer of 1973 (and Kevin was right here with her, working as a busboy). It appeared that Winnie and Kevin were meant to be with each other forever. In the last episode Winnie and Kevin make a promise to never let their friendship end. Kevin's words during the final seconds of the show tell us what happened after they graduated from high school: "Winnie left the next summer [1974] to study art history in Paris. Still, we never forgot our promise. We wrote to each other once a week for eight years. I was there [the airport] to meet her when she came home — with my wife and my first son... Things never turn out exactly as you planned. Growing up happens in a heartbeat... The memories of childhood stay with you for the long haul ... and the thing is, after all these years, I still look back in wonder."

See also: Jack and Norma Arnold, Kevin Arnold.

1159. Winnie Goodwin, *Free Spirit*, ABC, 1989–1990. Played by Corinne Bohrer.

Winnie Goodwin works as the live-in housekeeper to a divorced attorney (Thomas Harper) and his children (Jessica, Robin and Gene). Winnie appears as a beautiful blonde. She is very kind and very gentle but is actually a good witch. She resides with the family at 33 Essex Drive in Connecticut.

Winnie is a member of an organization of witches that helps needy earthlings through a public service duty program. Winnie was born in Salem, Massachusetts, on June 9, 1665. She is the daughter of Melissa and Ethan Goodwin, a witch and a warlock who had to struggle to keep their true identities a secret (fearing to be burned at the stake if it were discovered they were witches). Winnie was taught everything she needed to know by her mother: how to use her powers, how to control them, and how not to be exposed. Winnie grew up as normal a girl as possible but was frustrated by the fact that she had to hide who she really was. Even as time passed and the mystique surrounding witches began to fade,

Winnie had to be careful about letting people know who she really is.

Winnie worked as a housekeeper to witches for many years before her turn of duty came up for public service. Winnie appeared at the Harper household as a result of the children's wish that they had someone to take care of them. Winnie feels comfortable revealing her true nature to children because children do not hold the same misconceptions about witches as adults. Winnie can use magic to solve family problems but she prefers not to (she feels talking and disciplining is the better course of action). Winnie tries to be helpful and a good influence but she is a bit of a klutz and sometimes complicates situations when she feels a slight touch of magic is needed. Some people would say Winnie is a slightly "dizzy blonde" as she tends to become nervous and anxious when something doesn't go exactly as she planned. While Winnie enjoys holidays like Christmas and Easter, she fears Halloween "because it strains my powers."

Wonder Woman *see* **Diana Prince**

1160. Wood Newton, *Evening Shade*, CBS, 1990–1994. Played by Burt Reynolds.

Woodrow Newton is the physical education teacher and coach of the Mules (a losing football team) at Evening Shade High School in the small town of Evening Shade, Arkansas. Wood, as he is called, is married to Ava and is the father of Molly, Will and Taylor. They have a dog named Brownie and live at 2102 Willow Lane.

Wood was born in Evening Shade and played football for Evening Shade High School (he was called "Thumper" and wore jersey 37). After graduating from the University of Arkansas he became a quarterback for the Pittsburgh Steelers (he was called "Clutch" and wore jersey 22). Wood was Honorable Mention, All-American one year and All-American the next. He was the Southwest Conference Most Valuable Player, runner-up for the Heisman Trophy and NFL rookie quarterback. Wood single-handedly won the Eastern Division playoff game, completing six passes with a minute and 53 seconds left on the clock; and with ten seconds left and no time outs, he scored the winning touchdown with a broken collarbone. Although he had a fantastic football career, Wood holds the record for the most fumbles and most yardage lost.

Wood's favorite song is "Blueberry Hill" (selection B-5 on the jukebox at Blue's Barbecue Villa, the local diner). His good luck charm is a towel he dyed black when he was with the Steelers.

Wood recalled his first sexual experience was with Big Ruthie Ralston at the Purple Dawn Whorehouse in Hot Springs, Arkansas. Wood also had a small role (as Colonel Rodney Stone) in the TV miniseries *The Blue and the Gray II*.

See also: Ava Newton, Merleen and Harlan Eldridge, Molly and Taylor Newton.

1161. Woody Banner, *Hey Landlord!*, NBC, 1966–1967. Played by Will Hutchins.

Woodrow Banner, called Woody, is the owner of an old brownstone at 14th Street in Manhattan. He inherited the building from his late uncle and has converted it into a ten-room apartment house. Woody is called "The Boy Landlord" by some of the tenants.

Woody was born on a farm in Ohio. He is the son of Lloyd and Marcy Banner and has a sister named Bonnie (played by Sally Field). Woody was a Boy Scout (a member of the Skunk Troop) and attended Fillmore High School in Toledo. He was first on the school's football team (quit when the tackling dummy broke and he substituted for it) then on the swim team. Woody next attended Ohio State University and had contemplated becoming a writer. He moved to New York to pursue that goal after graduation but became a bit sidetracked when he became a landlord. He shares his cluttered, messy apartment with his college friend (Chuck Hookstratten) and is more interested in pursuing girls than becoming a writer.

See also: Chuck Hookstratten.

1162. Woody Boyd, *Cheers*, NBC, 1985–1992. Played by Woody Harrelson.

Huckleberry Tiberius Boyd, called Woody, is the assistant bartender at Cheers, a Boston bar owned by Sam Malone.

Woody was born in Hanover, Indiana, and yearned to be a bartender. He wrote to all the bars in the big cities. One was Cheers. Ernie Pantusso, Sam's assistant, was the only person who wrote back to him. They became pen pals. When Woody came to Boston to look up Ernie, he learned that he recently died. Sam felt that Ernie would have wanted Woody to have the bartending job and gave it to him.

Woody is a graduate of Hanover High School and invented a game called "Hide Bob's Pants." He enjoys duck hunting (he uses an empty Good & Plenty candy box as a duck caller), fishing and sports. He had a dog named Truman and Small Pox was the first childhood disease he had. Woody is a friendly person with a backwoods aura that makes him very likeable. Although Woody had set his sights on becoming a bartender, he later felt he could become an actor and pursued that goal (he did a TV commercial for a vegetable drink called Veggie Boy that combined broccoli, cauliflower and kale juice).

Woody mentioned having a girlfriend named Beth Curtis in Hannibal but he married Kelly Gaines (Jackie Swanson), the very rich and very spoiled daughter of the Boston Gaines (Elliott and Roxanne). Kelly has a collection of over 1,000 Barbie dolls and Woody wrote her a song called "The Kelly Song." The last episode finds Woody running for and becoming third district councilman with the Boston City Council.

See also: Carla LeBec, Cliff Claven, Diane Chambers, Ernie Pantusso, Norm Peterson, Rebecca Howe, Sam Malone.

1163. Wrangler Jane, *F Troop*, ABC, 1965–1967. Played by Melody Patterson.

Jane Angelica Thrift, better known as Wrangler Jane, is a very beautiful and independent young woman who lives in Fort Courage, a U.S. Army cavalry outpost in Kansas (1866).

Jane was born in Kansas on November 11, 1846, and is what then could be considered a cowgirl. Her background is a mystery (she never mentions her parents or her upbringing). Jane prefers her male look (dresses like a cowboy in buckskins) even though she measures 36-24-34. She has long blonde hair and a seductive walk. When she has to (and that's not often), Jane wears a size 10 dress to show her beau, Captain Wilton Parmenter, that she is all-woman (she becomes extremely jealous if she sees Wilton with another girl).

Jane is a sharpshooter (can outdraw any man), bust broncos, trick ride (perform stunt tricks like any rodeo rider) and has a unique affinity with animals (she can tame wild horses).

Jane earns a living as the owner of Wrangler Jane's (the post office, general merchandise and hay and feed store). Jane wears a holster (gun on a the right side of her hips) and lives in a lovely home right outside of town. She is also a great cook and housekeeper (but she only lets this side of her life be known to the reluctant to marry Wilton Parmenter). Jane rides a horse named Pecos and is a talented singer (she performed the songs "Lemon Tree" and "Mr. Tambourine Man" with a rock band 100 years ahead of its time called The Termites).

See also: Morgan O'Rourke, Randolph Agarn, Wilton Parmenter.

1164. Xander Harris, *Buffy the Vampire Slayer*, WB, 1997–2001; UPN, 2001–2003. Played by Nicholas Brendon.

Alexander Harris, called Xander, is a sophomore at Sunnydale High School in Sunnydale, California. He is friends with Willow Rosenberg and Buffy Summers and helps them battle the evils of Hellmouth, a mysterious portal that dispenses evil. Xander is an only child and comes from a family of blue-collar workers. He is sensitive and hides those feelings with a jovial outlook on life. He first worked as a kitchen helper at a nightclub called Fabulous Ladies. When he chose not to attend college, he turned his skills as a carpenter into his profession.

Xander's choice of a girlfriend was rather unique. He chose Anya (Emma Caulfield), an 1100-year-old former demon trying to adjust to a mortal life. Anya's real name is Audi. When she matured she developed the powers of a vengeance demon to protect wronged women and punish evil men. She became known as Anyanka. Anya, as she is called, can teleport herself from one place to another. She was stripped of her powers when she began using them for evil. She now helps Buffy (the vampire slayer) Willow (a powerful witch) and Buffy's Watcher, Rupert Giles, battle demons.

See also: Buffy Summers, Dawn Summers, Rupert Giles, Willow Rosenberg.

1165. Xena, *Xena: Warrior Princess*, Syn., 1995–2001. Played by Lucy Lawless.

Xena was once a ruthless warrior in the age of mythology who changed her ways to become a champion of those threatened by evil. Xena did not exist in ancient Greek or Roman mythology, but her essence is based on the gods and warriors of the time.

Xena was born in the ancient Greek village of Amphipolis and cared for by her mother, Cyrene. She has two brothers, Lyceus and Toris. Her father is unknown to his children and deserted the family when Xena was very young. Xena worked with her mother in the family-owned tavern and had a relatively normal life until she became 17. At this time, the warlord Cortese threatened Amphipolis and Xena organized a group of reluctant-to-fight villagers into a small army. Xena's army managed to defeat Cortese but many villagers were killed, including Xena's brother Lyceus. Now hated and feeling guilty for the misery she caused, Xena left her home to build an army to defend Amphipolis against future attacks.

Xena's good intentions turned to evil when she became corrupted by power and fought for the thrill of battle. She soon earned a reputation as a ruthless warrior princess. It is not until she meets Hercules that Xena is made to see her evil ways and vows to redeem herself by helping others.

Xena is proficient in the art of swordplay. Her weapon of choice is the deadly Chakram (a flat, round piece of iron with razor sharp blades that when thrown act as a boomerang). Those who oppose Xena also have to fear "The Pinch," a deadly technique she uses to stop the flow of blood to the brain (when she pinches a nerve on the back of the neck). Despite her evil ways, Xena would never kill women or children. She travels with a young woman named Gabrielle.

See also: Callisto, Gabrielle.

1166. Yancy Derringer, *Yancy Derringer,* CBS, 1958–1959. Played by Jock Mahoney.

Marchancy Derringer, called Yancy, is a man who loves the city of New Orleans and the South. He is also a man who will act when something happens; a man who will fight for right against wrong any way he can and not get caught by the law for doing it. Yancy is, as he calls himself, "a rogue, scoundrel, gentleman, gambler and fool" as he works undercover to help city administrator John Colton uphold the peace.

Yancy was born in New Orleans on the Waverly Plantation in 1842. He left in 1860 and joined the Confederacy. He was shot during the Battle of Cold Harbor and spent one year in a Yankee prison. When he got out (possibly in 1865) he went out West to strike it rich but didn't. He then returned to New Orleans (1868) to begin a new life.

Yancy comes from a well-to-do family. In addition to operating the plantation, he owns a riverboat (the *Sultana*) and a silver mine near Virginia City, Nevada. Yancy carries a derringer (several): in his hat, up his sleeve, in his belt and in his boot. He is always neatly dressed in white (he buys his "fancy duds" at Devereaux's Gentlemen's Apparel) and has a dog named Old Dixie. Yancy is not one who looks for a fight. If he can avoid a situation he will. He is assisted by Pahoo-Ta-Wah ("Wolf Who Stands in Water"), a non-speaking Pawnee Indian who saved Yancy's life and went against his faith (for helping a white man). Pahoo is now responsible for Yancy's life and carries a shotgun with him at all times (it is not made clear when Pahoo saved Yancy's life; it probably happened when he was out West looking for gold).

Yancy is a ladies' man, a gourmet and quite well educated (exactly where he found the time for an education is not stated. It can only be assumed his early years on the plantation were spent in deep study). Yancy enjoys meals at the Sazarack Restaurant.

1167. Yvette Henderson, *Smart Guy,* WB, 1998–2000. Played by Essence Atkins.

Yvette Henderson is the sister of a genius. Her brother, T.J., has an I.Q. of 180 and at the age of 12 is a freshman in high school — the same school that is attended by Yvette.

Yvette was born on May 26, 1981, in Washington, D.C. She lives at 11 Wyler Road with her father Floyd (a widower) and two brothers, T.J. and Marcus.

Yvette is a junior at Piedmont High School (where she is a writer for the newspaper, *The Piedmont Times,* and a member of the student council). Yvette is smart but not as smart as T.J. (Marcus is not as smart as either one). She is very attractive but feels her one serious shortcoming is "my small bust line." While Yvette felt larger breasts would mean attention she never really pursued it beyond the thinking stage (like wearing a padded bra).

Yvette is very studious and believes that a good education is the only way to make it in life. She works as a salesgirl at Stylo Wear, a clothing store in the mall. Yvette's dream is to attend Princeton. Her big disappointment came in the last episode when she was not accepted to Princeton. Had the series been renewed Yvette would have become a freshman at Georgetown University.

See also: T.J. Henderson.

1168. Yvonne Hughley, *The Hughleys,* ABC, 1998–1999; UPN, 1999–2002. Played by Elise Neal.

Yvonne Hughley is the wife of Darryl L. Hughley, the owner of the Hughley Vending Machine Company in West Hills, California. She lives at 317 Crestview and is the mother of two children (Sydney and Michael).

Yvonne is the daughter of James and Paulette Williams and grew up in Tucson, Arizona. She met Darryl, then an employee of the Perrymore Vending Machine Company, when she was a student at the University of Southern California (majoring in business administration). Although they were from different sides of the track (Darryl was a high school dropout) they fell in love and married in 1987. They first lived in a room above a beauty salon owned by Darryl's aunt. It was at this time that Yvonne convinced Darryl to follow his dream and begin his own company. When Yvonne became pregnant with their daughter (Sydney) they moved to an apartment in Los Angeles. Eight years later they relocated to the suburbs to give their children a better life.

Darryl romanced Yvonne, whom he calls Vonnie, with poetry "borrowed from Barry Manilow songs." Yvonne put her career on hold to raise their children. In later years she worked as Darryl's receptionist, fund raising director at West Hills Hospital and finally as a marketing executive at the Staples Sports Center in Los Angeles. Yvonne enjoys helping people and the community. She is a member of the West Hills School District P.T.A., the Car Pooling Mothers and the Neighborhood Safety Committee. She drives a Minivan and *Catcher in the Rye* is her favorite book. She is an excellent cook and her only fault appears to be an addiction to gambling (which she appears to have under control — except when she goes to Las Vegas and becomes addicted to the slot machine).

See also: Darryl Hughley, Sydney and Michael Hughley.

1169. Zack Morris, *Saved by the Bell*, NBC, 1989–1993. Played by Mark-Paul Gosselaar.

Zachary Morris, called Zack, is a student at Bayside High School in Palisades, California. Zack is actually part of the original series, *Good Morning, Miss Bliss* (Disney, 1988–1989) wherein he was an eighth grader at J.F.K. Junior High School in Indianapolis, Indiana. Here Zack was the schemer and always trying to impress girls. At Bayside, Zack is exactly the same — only older, more of a schemer and more interested in girls, especially fellow student Kelly Kapowski.

Zack is a natural born con artist and his antics often land him in detention. He was the disc jockey "Wolfman Zack" on the Bayside radio station Tiger Radio and "Nitro Man" on a teen hot line he started. In an attempt to make money he devised "The Girls of Bayside High Swimsuit Calendar" (wherein students Kelly, Lisa and Jesse posed in bikinis). He next formed Kelly, Lisa and Jesse into Hot Sundae, a band that he later joined and renamed The Zack Attack (Zack played guitar). In his senior year the band became known as The Five Aces. He and his friends hang out at The Max, the after school eatery.

Although the school's principal, Richard Belding, called Zack his "Zack Ache" Zack managed to graduate and attended California State University (as depicted the 1993–94 NBC spinoff series, *Saved by the Bell: The College Years*). Kelly also attended the school and Zack proposed to her in the last episode. They married in the NBC TV movie, *Saved by the Bell: Wedding in Las Vegas* (October 7, 1994). Zack worked as a waiter at the Malibu Beach Sands Club during the summer of 1991. He was originally accepted into Yale University in the last episode of *Saved by the Bell* but

wound up at California State University for the spinoff series. Here he was a finance major and lived in dorm room 218B and was a member of the Sigma Alpha Fraternity.

See also: Jesse Spano, Kelly Kapowski, Lisa Turtle, Screech Powers.

1170. Zeb and Esther Walton, *The Waltons*, CBS, 1972–1981. Played by Will Geer (to 1979), Ellen Corby.

Zebulon Walton and his wife Esther are the patriarchs of the Walton Family. Zeb, as he is called, and Ellen are the parents of John Walton (who is married to Olivia) and the grandparents to their children John-Boy, Mary Ellen, Jason, Erin, Ben, Elizabeth and Jim-Bob. They live together as a family in Jefferson County, Virginia. The series is set beginning in 1931.

Zeb and Esther have been married to each other for over 50 years. Zeb has a gruff exterior but is kind and gentle at heart. He works with John in the family timber mill and is always eager to give advice to anyone who asks for it (which he usually does through a story). Zeb's bones tell him the weather: "They feel one way for good weather, another way for bad weather." He enjoys fishing, singing at church on Sundays and a sip (or more) of "Papa's Recipe," liquor made by the two elderly Baldwin sisters (Miss Emily and Miss Mamie). Zeb calls Olivia "Livie" and "Daughter." He passed away in 1979.

Esther was a very strong and independent woman who loved her family dearly. She enjoyed helping Olivia care for the children as well as cooking and cleaning the house. She too had a gruff look about her but was gentle and full of motherly advice for any of the children who needed someone to talk to. Esther was also very religious and enjoyed Sunday mass with the family. Ellen Corby suffered a stroke in 1977. She returned to the series in March of 1978 and it was explained that Esther had suffered a stroke and been hospitalized. As a result, Esther (as Ellen) were victims of aphasia (speech difficulty). Although partially crippled, Esther was still a strong force in keeping the family together in trying times.

See also: John and Olivia Walton, John-Boy Walton (for information on John-Boy, Jason, Ben and Jim-Bob), Mary Ellen Walton (for information on Mary Ellen, Erin and Elizabeth).

1171. Zelda and Hilda Spellman, *Sabrina, the Teenage Witch*, ABC, 1996–2000; WB, 2000–2002. Played by Beth Broderick (Zelda), Caroline Rhea (Hilda).

Zelda and Hilda Spellman are single sisters and witches who live at 133 Collins Road in Westbridge, Massachusetts. They are the guardians of Sabrina, a witch who is also their niece, and Salem Saberhagen, a warlock who was turned into a cat for trying to take over the world.

Zelda is the older sister (she only says she is "500 plus years old"). She is extremely bright and has a four digit I.Q. She attended the Other Realm University (the Other Realm is where witches live) and has a degree in quantum physics. She was also credited with discovering 17 moons and has three degrees in intergalactic studies. She applies this knowledge as a teacher at Adams College. In addition to science, Zelda is also interested in psychiatry, slug reproduction and art (she was an intern for Leonardo da Vinci and a model for Goya; nude postcards of her sold at the art museum). "Chem Kitten" is Zelda's on-line computer name and she drinks only bottled water. As a child Zelda had an interest in bees. Zelda is also quite attractive and will date only intellectuals (when she breaks up with a man she cooks; her favorite meal to prepare is honey calf marrow).

Hildegarde, called Hilda, has the middle name Antoinette. She first mentions she is 620 years old but in the episode of January 19, 2001, she turns 650. Hilda attended the Other Realm High School then Clown University (she hates it when people refer to it as clown school). In her youth Hilda worked as a blacksmith, donkey walker, fisherman and with Zelda, a Wild West singing duo called the Spellman Sisters. Every 25 years Hilda and Zelda require a magic tune-up and every 200 years they report for Scare Duty (teaching pre-teen witches how to scare people).

Hilda is a talented musician (plays violin) and first went into business for herself by buying a clock shop she called Hickory Dickory Clock (where she and Zelda helped lost travelers in time through the Lost in Time Clock). When the business failed Hilda purchased a coffee shop near the campus of Adams College she called Hilda's Coffee House.

Hilda is fond of Devil's Food Cake with deviled ham and her and Zelda's favorite holiday is Halloween (they decorate the house and sing Halloween carols). Hilda and Zelda are not fond of Thanksgiving because the Puritans who started it were not fond of witches.

Hilda and Zelda were written out at the end of the 2002 season to allow stories to focus on Sabrina and her friends Roxie and Morgan. Hilda had married while Zelda left to pursue new life goals. *See also:* Amanda Wickham, Roxie King, Sabrina Spellman, Salem Saberhagen.

Zelda Gilroy *see* **Dobie Gillis**

1172. Zev Bellringer, *Lexx*, Sci Fi, 2000–2002. Played by Eva Haberman, Xenia Seeberg.

Zev Bellringer is 4,000 years old and was born on B3-K, a planet in a futuristic world called the Light Universe. She is a beautiful female with a body designed for sex. Zev, however, was not always gorgeous. She was born part human and part cluster lizard. She was unattractive, tough and hardened by life. She grew up in a box and at an early age was given up by her parents. She was placed in an electronic holocare home as a candidate for a wife bank. Zev had been deprived of love and human contact as a child and she proved to be unfit as a wife. When she failed to perform wifely duties with her first mate, she was charged with crimes of humiliation and sentenced to love slave transformation. The operation not only humanized her lizard-like skin but also reshaped her body with a Marilyn Monroe–like figure and a somewhat uncontrollable urge for sex. But Zev also retained her tough, independent quality as well as her "lizard scream" (called "lizard growls" in closed captioning dialogue), which she does when she gets upset—"It's the cluster lizard in me, my more aggressive side." Another side effect of the operation was the infusion of her lizard blood with human blood—it makes her crave raw meat ("I'm half human and half cluster lizard—a very nasty thing. It eats human flesh but prefers the brain").

Zev was a slave for His Divine Shadow, the evil leader of His Divine Order (ruler of the Light Universe). She became a part of the space ship *Lexx* when she helped fugitives Kai and Stanley kill His Divine Shadow and destroy the Light Universe. She now journeys with Kai and Stanley as they explore the mysterious worlds of the Dark Universe.

Zev describes he cluster lizard side as "a hot tempered and nasty little animal. It's a predator without feelings." Zev, when played by Eva Haberman, had white hair and a more conservative dress than Xenia Seeberg as Zev (who was blonde and wore a sexy outfit she called her "cluster skin"—tan bikini-like top with a tan miniskirt and black boots). Earth alcohol has a strange effect on Zev—she becomes intoxicated and playful. When someone tells her "You're so beautiful," Zev replies with "I wasn't always you know." *See also:* Kai, Robot Head 790, Stanley H. Tweedle.

1173. Zoe Bean, *Zoe, Duncan, Jack and Jane*, WB, 1999–2000. Played by Selma Blair.

Zoe Bean is a 16-year-old girl who attends Fielding High School in New York City. She is a close friend with Jane Cooper, her brother Jack, and Duncan Milch. They go to school together and hang out at a coffee shop called Café and Pastries in Greenwich Village.

Zoe was born in Manhattan on November 1, 1983, and lives with her single mother, Iris (Mary Page Keller) in Chelsea (Apartment 16). She has a dog named Wally and is sometimes mistaken for actress Alyssa Milano (rather than disappoint people, Zoe signs autographs in Alyssa's name). Zoe considers herself "a very sexy young thing" and has "womanly wily womanly ways." Zoe is very pretty and attracted to the types of boys she would like to avoid. When she breaks up with a boy Zoe wears a purple dress Jane calls "the available skirt."

Zoe feels that her head is too big for her body and that her breasts are too small but "I can't do anything about it" and learns to accept who she is. She is also very protective of her mother and screens all her dates because she feels her mother dates freaks and can do better. Iris asks only one thing of Zoe when a date calls: "Be nice, Zoe" (Zoe also hates her mother to show cleavage to attract men. Yet when Zoe and Jane prepare for a date, they wear push-up bras "for cleavage purposes only").

Second season episodes are titled *Zoe...* and set three years later. Zoe is now in college and majoring in psychology. She shares an apartment with Jane (who is studying photography). Zoe's mother is said to be in Arizona. She pays Zoe's rent and tuition but Zoe has to pay for everything else. Zoe works as a hostess (later manager) of Chang Hi, a Chinese restaurant in Manhattan. She eats Life cereal for breakfast and enjoys Breyer's fat free ice cream as a dessert.

See also: Jane Cooper.

Zorro *see* **Don Diego de la Vega**

Zotoh Zhaan *see* **John Crichton**

Appendix A
Characters by Series

The A-Team: B.A. Baracus, Hannibal Smith, H.M. Murdock, Templeton Peck.

According to Jim: Cheryl, Jim.

The Addams Family: Gomez Addams, Morticia Addams, Uncle Fester, Wednesday and Pugsley Addams.

Adventures in Paradise: Adam Troy.

The Adventures of Brisco County, Jr.: Brisco County, Jr.

The Adventures of Superman: Clark Kent, Lois Lane.

Alias: Sidney Bristow.

Alice: Alice Hyatt, Flo Castleberry, Jolene Hunnicutt, Mel Sharples, Vera Gorman.

ALF: ALF.

Aliens in the Family: Cookie Brody (also for information on Bobut).

All About the Andersons: Anthony Anderson.

All About Us: Alecia Alcott, Christina Castelli, Nikki Merrick, Sierra Jennings.

All in the Family: Archie Bunker, Edith Bunker, Gloria and Mike Stivic.

All of Us: Neesee James

Ally McBeal: Ally McBeal, Elaine Vassal, John Cage, Ling Woo.

Amen: Ernest Frye, Reuben Gregory (also contains information on Thelma Frye).

Andromeda: Andromeda, Beka Valentine, Dylan Hunt, Trance Gemini.

The Andy Griffith Show: Andy Taylor, Barney Fife, Bee Taylor, Gomer Pyle, Goober Pyle, Opie Taylor.

Angel: Angel, Cordelia Chase, Fred Berkel.

Ann Jillian: Ann McNeal (also contains information on Lucy McNeal), Melissa Santos.

Anne of Green Gables: Anne Shirley.

Annette: Annette McCleod.

Archie Bunker's Place: Archie Bunker, Billie Bunker, Stephanie Mills.

Arrested Development: Michael Bluth (also for information on Buster Bluth, Gob Bluth, Lindsay Funke, Tobias Funke).

Automan: Walter Nebecher (also for information on Automan).

The Avengers: Catherine Gale, Emma Peel, John Steed, Tara King.

Babylon 5: Delenn, Elizabeth Lochley, John Sheridan, Lyta Alexander, Susan Ivanova.

Bachelor Father: Bentley Gregg (also for information on Kelly Gregg).

Banacek: Thomas Banacek.

Bare Essence: Tyger Hayes.

Baretta: Tony Baretta.

Barnaby Jones: Barnaby Jones.

Batman: Barbara Gordon, Bruce Wayne, Dick Grayson.

Baywatch: Mitch Buchannon (see also *The Girls of Baywatch* for information on April Giminski, Carolyn Holden, C.J. Parker, Donna Marco, Jesse Owens, Jill Riley, Neely Capshaw, Shauni McClain, Stephanie Holden, Summer Quinn).

BeastMaster: The Ancient One, Arina, Curupira, Dar, Iara, The Sorceress, Tao.

Beauty and the Beast: Catherine Chandler, Vincent,

Becker: John Becker.

The Bernie Mac Show: Bernie Mac (also contains information on Wanda Mac).

Bette: Bette (also contains information on Rose, Bette's daughter).

The Beverly Hillbillies: Elly Mae Clampett, Granny, Jed Clampett, Jethro Bodine.

Beverly Hills, 90210: Brenda and Brandon Walsh (also contains information on Andrea Zuckerman, Donna Martin, Kelly Taylor).

Bewitched: Endora (also contains information on Maurice), Samantha Stevens (also for information on Darrin Stevens).

The Bickersons: John and Blanche Bickerson.

Big Eddie: Eddie and Ginger Smith

The Big Valley: Audra Barkley, Heath Barkley, Jarrod Barkley, Nick Barkley, Victoria Barkley.

The Bionic Woman: Jaime Sommers.

Birds of Prey: Barbara Gordon, Dinah Lance, Helena Kyle.

B.J. and the Bear: B.J. McKay (also for information on Callie Everett, Cindy Grant, Stacks).

Black Sash: Tom Chang.

Black Scorpion: Darcy Walker.

Blossom: Anthony Russo, Blossom Russo, Joey Russo, Nick Russo, Six LeMeure.

Bob: Bob McKay (also contains information on Kaye and Trish McKay).

The Bob Newhart Show: Bob and Emily Hartley.

Bob Patterson: Bob Patterson.

Bonanza: Adam Cartwright, Ben Cartwright, Hoss Cartwright, Little Joe Cartwright.

Boy Meets World: Cory Matthews, Topanga Lawrence.

The Brady Bunch: Alice Nelson, Carol and Mike Brady, Greg Brady (also for information on Peter and Bobby Brady), Marcia Brady (also for information on Jan and Cindy Brady).

Branded: Jason McCord.

Bronco: Bronco Layne.

Buffy the Vampire Slayer: Angel, Buffy Summers, Cordelia Chase, Dawn Summers, Rupert Giles, Spike, Willow Rosenberg, Xander Harris.

Byrds of Paradise: Franny Byrd.

Café Americain: Holly Aldridge.

Cagney and Lacey: Chris Cagney, Mary Beth Lacey.

Camp Wilder: Ricky Wilder.

Can't Hurry Love: Annie O'Donnell.

Captain Nice: Carter Nash.

Captain Scarlet and the Mysterons: Captain Magenta, Captain Ochre, Captain Scarlet, Destiny Angel, Harmony Angel, Rhapsody Angel, Symphony Angel.

Car 54, Where Are You?: Francis Muldoon, Gunther Toody.

Caroline in the City: Annie Spadaro, Caroline Duffy, Richard Karinsky.

Casablanca: Rick Blaine.

The Champions: Craig Stirling, Richard Barrett, Sharron Macready.

Charles in Charge: Buddy Lembeck, Charles, Jamie Powell, Lila Pembroke, Sarah Powell.

Charlie's Angels: Charlie Townsend, Jill Monroe, Julie Rogers, Kelly Garrett, Kris Monroe, Sabrina Duncan, Tiffany Welles.

Charmed: Leo Wyatt, Paige Matthews, Phoebe Halliwell, Piper Halliwell, Prue Halliwell.

Cheers: Carla LeBec, Cliff Claven, Diane Chambers, Ernie Pantusso, Frasier Crane (also for information on Lilith), Norm Peterson, Rebecca Howe, Sam Malone, Woody Boyd.

Cheyenne: Cheyenne Bodie.

China Beach: Colleen McMurphy, K.C., Laurette Barber (also for information on Cherry White, Lila Garreau and Waylou Marie Holmes).

Christy: Christy Huddleston.

Civil Wars: Sydney Guilford.

Clarissa Explains It All: Clarissa Darling, Ferguson Darling.

Cleopatra 2525: Cleopatra (also for information on Hel and Sarge).

Clueless: Amber Mariens, Cher Horowitz, Dee Davenport.

Coach: Christine Armstrong, Hayden Fox, Luther Van Dam.

Cold Case: Lily Rush.

Columbo: Columbo.

The Commish: Tony Scali.

Cosby: Hilton Lucas (also contains information on Ruth and Erica Lucas).

The Cosby Show: Cliff and Clair Huxtable, Denise Huxtable, Sondra Huxtable, Theo Huxtable, Vanessa and Rudy Huxtable.

The Critic: Jay Sherman.

Crossing Jordan: Garrett Macy, Jordan Cavanaugh.

C.S.I.: Crime Scene Investigation: Catherine Willows, Gil Grissom, Nick Stokes, Sara Sidle, Warrick Brown.

C.S.I.: Miami: Alexx Woods, Calleigh Duquesne, Eric Delko, Horatio Caine, Tim Speedle.

Cybill: Cybill Sheridan.

DAG: Jerome Daggett.

Dallas: Bobby Ewing, J.R. Ewing, Lucy Ewing, Pamela Barnes, Sue Ellen Ewing.

Darcy's Wild Life: Darcy Fields.

Dark Angel: Max Guevara.

Dark Justice: Nick Marshall.

Dark Shadows: Angelique, Barnabas Collins, Roger Collins, Victoria Winters, Willie Loomis.

A Date with Judy: Judy Foster.

Dave's World: Beth Barry, Dave Barry, Kenny Beckett, Tommy and Willie Barry.

Davis Rules: Dwight Davis.

Dear John: John Lacey, Kate McCarron, Kirk Morris, Louise Mercer, Mary Beth Sutton.

Decoy: Patricia Jones.

Delta: Delta Bishop.

Department S: Annabelle Hurst, Jason Kin, Stewart Sullivan.

Designing Women: Anthony Bouvier, Charlene Frazier, Julia Sugarbaker, Mary Jo Shively, Suzanne Sugarbaker.

Desperate Housewives: Bree Van De Kamp, Edie Britt, Gabrielle Solis, Lynette Scavo, Susan Mayer.

Destry: Harrison Destry.

Dharma and Greg: Abby O'Neill, Dharma Montgomery, Edward and Kitty Montgomery, Greg Montgomery, Larry Finkelstein.

Diagnosis Murder: Mark Sloan.

The Dick Van Dyke Show: Alan Brady, Buddy Sorrell, Laura Petrie, Ritchie Petrie, Rob Petrie, Sally Rogers.

Diff'rent Strokes: Arnold Jackson, Edna Garrett, Kimberly Drummond, Willis Jackson.

A Different World: Dwayne Wayne, Whitley Gilbert.

Dinosaurs: Charlene Sinclair (also for information on Robbie and Baby Sinclair), Earl and Fran Sinclair.

The District: Jack Mannion.

Dobie Gillis: Chatsworth Osborne, Jr., Dobie Gillis (also for information on Thalia Menninger and Zelda Gilroy), Maynard G. Krebs.

Doc: Clint Cassidy.

Dr. Quinn, Medicine Woman: Byron Sully, Michaela Quinn.

Dr. Vegas: Billy Grant.

Doctor Who: Doctor Who.

Dog and Cat: J.Z. Kane.

Doogie Howser, M.D.: Doogie Howser.

Double Trouble: Allison and Kate Foster.

Down Home: Kate McCrorey.

Dragnet: Joe Friday.

The Drew Carey Show: Drew Carey, Kate O'Brien, Lewis Kiniski, Mimi Bobeck, Oswald Harvey.

Drexell's Class: Otis Drexell.

Duffy's Tavern: Archie.

The Dukes of Hazzard: Boss Hogg, Daisy Duke (also for information on Bo, Luke and Uncle Jesse Duke).

Early Edition: Gary Hobson.

Easy Street: L.K. McGuire.

The Eddie Capra Mysteries: Eddie Capra.

Eight Is Enough: David Bradford (also for information on Tommy and Nicholas Bradford), Mary Bradford (also for information on Joanie, Nancy and Elizabeth Bradford), Tom Bradford (also for information on Joan and Abby Bradford).

8 Simple Rules for Dating My Teenage Daughter: Bridget Hennessey, Cate Hennessey, Kerry Hennessey, Paul Hennessey, Rory Hennessey.

18 Wheels of Justice: Katherine Spencer.

Electra Woman and Dyna Girl: Electra Woman and Dyna Girl.

Ellen: Ellen Morgan.

The Ellen Show: Ellen Richmond.

Empty Nest: Barbara Weston, Carol Weston, Emily Weston, Harry Weston.

The Equalizer: Robert McCall.

Eve: Shelley Williams (also for information on Janie Egan, Rita LeFleur)

Even Stevens: Ren Stevens.

Evening Shade: Ava Newton, Merleen and Harlan Eldridge, Molly and Taylor Newton, Wood Newton.

Everybody Loves Raymond: Ally Barone, Debra Barone, Frank and Marie Barone, Raymond Barone, Robert Barone.

Eye to Eye: Tracy Doyle.

F Troop: Morgan O'Rourke, Randolph Agarn, Wilton Parmenter, Wrangler Jane.

The Facts of Life: Blair Warner, Edna Garrett, Jo Polniaszek, Natalie Greene, Tootie Ramsey.

The Fall Guy: Colt Seavers.

Family Affair: Bill Davis, Buffy and Jody Davis, Cissy Davis.

Family Matters: Carl Winslow (also for information on Harriette Winslow), Laura Winslow (also for information on Eddie Winslow), Steve Urkel.

Family Ties: Alex P. Keaton, Jennifer Keaton, Mallory Keaton, Steven and Elyse Keaton.

Fantasy Island: Mr. Roarke, Tattoo.

Farscape: John Crichton (also for information on Aeryn Sun, Chiana, Ka D'Argo, Zoyoh Zhann).

Fastlane: Billie Chambers, Deaquon Hayes, Van Ray.

Father Dowling Mysteries: Father Dowling, Sister Steve.

La Femme Nikita: Nikita.

Ferris Bueller: Jeannie Bueller.

The Fighting Fitzgeralds: Fitz Fitzgerald.

Firefly: Inara Serra, Malcolm Reynolds, River Tam.

The Flash: Barry Allen.

The Flintstones: Barney and Betty Rubble, Fred and Wilma Flintstone.

Fly by Night: Sally Monroe.

Flying Blind: Alicia Smith, Neil Barash.

The Flying Nun: Sister Bertrille.

Forever Knight: Nicholas Knight.

Frasier: Frasier Crane, Martin Crane, Niles Crane.

Free Spirit: Winnie Goodwin.

The Fresh Prince of Bel Air: Ashley Banks, Carlton Banks, Hilary Banks, Philip Banks, Will Smith.

Friends: Chandler Bing, Joey Tribbiani, Monica Geller, Phoebe Buffay, Rachel Greene, Ross Geller.

The Fugitive: Richard Kimble (David Janssen, 1963; Tim Daly, 2000).

Full House: Danny Tanner, D.J. Tanner, Jesse Katsopolis, Joey Gladstone, Michelle Tanner, Stephanie Tanner.

Funny Face: Sandy Stockton.

Gabriel's Fire: Gabriel Bird.

The Gallery of Madame Liu Tsong: Liu Tsong.

The Geena Davis Show: Tedde Cochran.

The George Lopez Show: Carmen Lopez, George and Angie Lopez.

Get a Life: Chris Peterson.

Get Christie Love: Christie Love.

Get Smart: The Chief, Maxwell Smart, 99.

The Ghost and Mrs. Muir: Carolyn Muir, Daniel Gregg.

Gidget: Gidget Lawrence.

Gilligan's Island: Gilligan, Ginger Grant, Mary Ann Summers, The Professor, The Skipper, Thurston and Lovey Howell.

Gilmore Girls: Lorelai Gilmore, Paris Geller, Richard and Emily Gilmore, Rory Gilmore.

Gimme a Break: Julie Kanisky, Katie Kanisky, Nell Harper, Samantha Kanisky.

The Girl from U.N.C.L.E.: April Dancer, Mark Slate.

Girlfriends: Joan Clayton, Lynn Searcy, Maya Wilkes, Toni Childs.

Going Places: Alex Burton.

The Golden Girls: Blanche Devereaux, Dorothy Zbornak, Rose Nylund, Sophia Petrillo.

Gomer Pyle, U.S.M.C.: Gomer Pyle.

Good Morning World: Dave and Linda Lewis, Roland B. Hutton, Jr.

Good Sports: Bobby Tannen, Gayle Roberts.

Good Times: James and Florida Evans, J.J. Evans, Thelma Evans.

Grace Under Fire: Grace Kelly, Libby Kelly.

The Great Defender: Frankie Colletti, Lou Frischetti.

Green Acres: Fred and Doris Ziffel (also contains information on Arnold Ziffel), Oliver and Lisa Douglas.

Grosse Pointe: Courtney Scott, Hunter Fallow, Marcy Sternfeld.

Grounded for Life: Claudia and Sean Finnerty, Lily Finnerty.

Growing Pains: Carol Seaver, Jason and Maggie Seaver, Mike Seaver.

Gunsmoke: Matt Dillon (also for information on Doc Adams, Festus Haggen, Kitty Russell).

Hack: Mike Olshansky.

Half and Half: Dee Dee Thorne, Mona Thorne.

Happy Days: Fonzie, Howard and Marion Cunningham, Joanie Cunningham, Richie Cunningham.

Happy Family: Sara Brennan.

Harry and the Hendersons: George and Nancy Henderson, Sarah and Ernie Henderson.

Harry O: Harry Orwell.

Hart to Hart: Jonathan and Jennifer Hart.

Have Gun — Will Travel: Paladin.

Hawaii Five-O: Steve McGarrett.

Hazel: George and Dorothy Baxter, Hazel Burke.

Head of the Class: Arvid Engen, Charlie Moore, Darlene Merriman, Dennis Blunden, Simone Foster.

Heart of the City: Robin Kennedy, Wes Kennedy.

Hearts Afire: Dee Dee Star, Georgie Lahti.

Herman's Head: Herman Brooks.

Hey Landlord!: Chuck Hookstratten, Woody Banner.

High Society: Ellie Walker.

Highway to Heaven: Jonathan Smith (also contains information on Mark Gordon).

Highlander: Duncan MacLeod.

Highlander: The Raven: Amanda.

Home Improvement: Al Borland, Jill Taylor, Tim Taylor, Wilson Wilson, Jr.

Honey West: Honey West.

The Honeymooners: Alice Kramden, Ed Norton, Ralph Kramden.

Hope and Faith: Faith Fairfield, Hope Shanoski.

Hotel De Paree: Sundance.

House: Gregory House.

How to Marry a Millionaire: Greta Hanson, Gwen Kirby, Loco Jones, Mike McCall.

Howdy Doody: Howdy Doody (also contains information on Buffalo Bob Smith).

Hudson Street: Tony Canetti.

The Hughleys: Darryl Hughley, Sydney and Michael Hughley, Yvonne Hughley.

Hunter: Dee Dee McCall, Rick Hunter.

I Dream of Jeannie: Anthony Nelson, Jeannie.

I Love Lucy: Fred and Ethel Mertz, Lucy and Ricky Ricardo.

I Married Dora: Kate Farrell, Peter Farrell (also for information on Dora Calderon).

I Spy: Alexander Scott, Kelly Robinson.

I'm with Her: Alex Young (also contains information on Sherry), Patrick Owen.

The Immortal (1970): Ben Richards.

The Immortal (2000): Rafael Caine.

Isis: Andrea Thomas.

It's a Living: Amy Tompkins, Cassie Cranston, Dot Higgins, Ginger St. James, Jan Hoffmeyer, Lois Adams, Sonny Mann.

Jack of All Trades: Emilia Rothschild, Jack Stiles.

The Jackie Thomas Show: Jackie Thomas.

The Jeffersons: George and Louise Jefferson.

Jennifer Slept Here: Jennifer Farrell.

Jenny: Jenny McMillan.

Jessie: Jessie Hayden.

Joan of Arcadia: Helen and William Girardi, Joan Girardi.

Joey: Gina Tribbiani, Joey Tribbiani.

Johnny Midnight: Johnny Midnight

Johnny Ringo: Johnny Ringo.

Johnny Staccato: Johnny Staccato.

Judge Roy Bean: Judge Roy Bean.

Just Cause: Alexandra DeMonico, Hamilton Whitney III.

Just Shoot Me: Dennis Finch, Jack Gallo, Maya Gallo, Nina Van Horn.

Just the Ten of Us: Cindy Lubbock, Connie Lubbock, Graham and Elizabeth Lubbock, Marie Lubbock, Wendy Lubbock.

Karen Sisco: Karen Sisco.

Kate and Allie: Allie Lowell, Kate McArdle.

Katie Joplin: Katie Joplin.

The King of Queens: Arthur Spooner, Carrie Heffernan, Doug Heffernan.

Knight Rider: KITT, Michael Knight.

Kojak: Theo Kojak.

Kolchak: The Night Stalker: Carl Kolchak.

Kristen: Kristen Yancey.

Kung Fu: Kwai Chang Caine.

Lady Blue: Katy Mahoney.

Laverne and Shirley: Laverne DeFazio, Lenny and Squiggy, Shirley Feeney.

The Law and Harry McGraw: Harry McGraw.

Law of the Plainsman: Sam Buckhart.

Lawman: Dan Troop.

LAX: Harley Random.

Leave It to Beaver: Beaver Cleaver, Eddie Haskell, June Cleaver, Lumpy Rutherford, Wally Cleaver, Ward Cleaver.

Leg Work: Claire McCarron.

Lenny: Kelly Callahan, Lenny and Shelly Callahan, Tracy Callahan.

Lexx: Kai, Robot Head 790, Stanley H. Tweedle, Zev Bellringer.

Life Goes On: Becca Thatcher, Corky Thatcher, Libby and Drew Thatcher, Paige Thatcher.

The Life of Riley: Chester and Peg Riley.

Life with Luigi: Luigi Basco.

Little Men: Jo Bhaer (also for information on Bess Lawrence, Nan Harding).

Living Dolls: Caroline Weldon, Charlie Briscoe, Emily Franklin, Martha Lambert.

Living Single: Regine Hunter, Synclaire James.

Lizzie McGuire: Lizzie McGuire, Matt McGuire.

The Lone Gunmen: John Byers, Melvin Frohike, Richard Langley.

The Lone Ranger: John Reid (also contains information on Tonto).

Longstreet: Michael Longstreet.

Lost in Space: Dr. Zachary Smith (also for information on The Robot), John Robinson (also for information on Maureen, Judy, Penny and Will Robinson).

The Lost World: Finn, George Challenger, John Roxton, Marguerite Krux, Ned Malone, Veronica Layton.

Love and War: Dana Palladino, Jack Stein, Wally Porter.

Love That Bob: Bob Collins.

MacGyver: MacGyver.

Mad About You: Jamie and Paul Buchman.

Madame's Place: Madame, Sara Joy Pitts.

Maggie Winters: Maggie Winters.

Magnum, P.I.: Jonathan Higgins, Thomas Magnum.

Major Dad: Elizabeth Cooper (also for information on Robin and Casey Cooper), John and Polly MacGillis.

Malibu, Ca.: Murray Updike, Tracee Banks.

Malcolm in the Middle: Lois and Hal Wilkerson (also for information on Malcolm, Francis, Reese and Dewey Wilkerson).

Mama's Family: Naomi Harper, Thelma Harper, Vinton Harper.

The Man from Atlantis: Mark Harris.

The Man from U.N.C.L.E.: Illya Kuryakin, Napoleon Solo.

Mann and Machine: Eve Madison.

Mannix: Joe Mannix.

M.A.N.T.I.S.: Miles Hawkins.

Margie: Margie Clayton.

Married People: Cindy and Allen Campbell, Elizabeth and Russell Meyers.

Married ... With Children: Al Bundy, Bud Bundy, Kelly Bundy, Marcy Rhoades (also for information on Jefferson D'Arcy, Steve Rhoades), Peg Bundy.

Martin: Martin Payne (also contains information on Gina Waters).

Mary Hartman, Mary Hartman: Mary Hartman.

The Mary Tyler Moore Show: Lou Grant, Mary Richards, Rhoda Morganstern, Ted Baxter.

M*A*S*H: Benjamin Franklin Pierce, B.J. Hunnicutt, Charles Winchester III, Frank Burns, Henry Blake, Margaret Houlihan, Maxwell Klinger, Radar O'Reilly, Sherman Potter, Trapper John McIntire.

The Master: John McCallister.

Matlock: Ben Matlock.

Matt Houston: Matt Houston.

Maverick: Bart and Bret Maverick.

Maybe It's Me: Molly Stage.

Maybe This Time: Julia Wallace (also for information on Gracie Wallace).

Meet Corliss Archer: Corliss Archer.

Miami Vice: Ricardo Tubbs, Sonny Crockett.

The Michael Richards Show: Vic Nardozzo.

Michael Shayne: Michael Shayne.

The Millionaire: John Beresford Tipton.

Miss Match: Katie Fox.

Mr. and Mrs. North: Jerry and Pamela North.

Mr. Belvedere: George and Marsha Owens, Heather Owens, Kevin Owens, Wesley Owens.

Mister Ed: Carol Post, Mister Ed, Wilbur Post

Mr. Terrific: Stanley Beemish.

Moesha: Moesha Mitchell.

Molloy: Courtney Martin, Molloy Martin.

Monk: Adrian Monk (also contains information on Sharona Fleming).

Moon Over Miami: Gwen Cross, Walter Tatum.

Moonlighting: David Addison, Maddie Hayes.

Mork and Mindy: Mindy McConnell, Mork.

Movie Stars: Jacey Wyatt, Lori Harden, Reese Harden, Todd Harden.

Mrs. Columbo: Kate Columbo.

The Mullets: Dwayne and Denny Mullet (also for information on Mandy Mullet).

The Munsters: Eddie Munster, Grandpa, Herman Munster, Lily Munster, Marilyn Munster.

Murder, She Wrote: Jessica Fletcher.

Murphy Brown: Corky Sherwood, Frank Fontana, Jim Dial, Miles Silverberg, Murphy Brown.

Murphy's Law: Kimiko Fannuchi, Patrick Murphy.

Mutant X: Adam Kane, Brennan Mulwray, Emma DeLauro, Lexa Pierce, Shalimar Fox.

My Favorite Martian: Uncle Martin.

My Friend Irma: Irma Peterson.

My Life and Times: Ben Miller.

My Little Margie: Freddie Wilson, Margie Albright, Vern Albright.

My Living Doll: Rhoda Miller,

My Three Sons: Steve Douglas (also contains information on Mike, Robbie and Chip Douglas).

My Two Dads: Nicole Bradford (also contains information on Joey Harris and Michael Taylor).

My Wife and Kids: Michael and Jay Kyle (also for information on Claire, Michael, Jr., and Cady Kyle).

M.Y.O.B.: Riley Veatch (also contains information on Opal Brown).

The Nancy Drew Mysteries: Nancy Drew.

The Nanny: C.C. Babcock, Fran Fine, Gracie Sheffield, Maggie Sheffield, Maxwell Sheffield.

Nanny and the Professor: Phoebe Figalilly.

Nash Bridges: Caitlin Cross, Cassidy Bridges, Joe Dominiquez, Nash Bridges.

National Velvet: Velvet Brown (also for information on Edwina and Donald Brown).

Ned and Stacey: Stacey Colbert (also contains information on Ned Dorsey).

Nero Wolfe: Nero Wolfe.

The New Avengers: Mike Gambit, Purdy.

Newhart: Dick and Joanna Louden, George Utley, Larry, Darryl and Darryl, Stephanie Vanderkellen.

Night Court: Bull Shannon, Christine Sullivan, Dan Fielding, Harry T. Stone, Mac Robinson.

Nikki: Dwight White, Nikki White.

Norm: Norm Henderson.

Northern Exposure: Joel Fleischman (also for information on Maggie O'Connell).

Nurses: Casey McAfee.

The Odd Couple: Felix Unger, Oscar Madison.

Odd Man Out: Paige and Valerie Whitney.

Oliver Beene: Oliver Beene.

Once a Hero: Brad Steele.

One Day at a Time: Ann Romano, Barbara Cooper, Dwayne Schneider, Julie Cooper.

The 100 Lives of Black Jack Savage: Barry Tarberry, Black Jack Savage.

One on One: Breanna Barnes, Duane O'Dell Knox, Flex Washington.

Our House: Gus Witherspoon, Jessie Witherspoon (also for information on Kris, David and Molly Witherspoon).

Our Miss Brooks: Connie Brooks.

Out of This World: Donna Garland (also contains information on Troy of Anterias), Evie Garland, Kyle Applegate.

Over My Dead Body: Maxwell Beckett, Nikki Page.

Paper Moon: Addie Loggins (also contains information on Moses Pray).

Parker Lewis Can't Loose: Grace Musso, Parker Lewis, Shelly Lewis.

Partners in Crime: Carole Stanwyck, Sydney Kovack.

The Partridge Family: Shirley Partridge (also for information on Keith, Laurie and Danny Partridge).

Party of Five: Bailey Salinger, Charlie Salinger, Claudia Salinger, Julia Salinger.

The Patty Duke Show: Patty and Cathy Lane.

The People's Choice: Sock Miller.

Perfect Strangers: Balki Bartokomous, Larry Appleton.

Perry Mason: Perry Mason (also for information on Della Street).

The Persuaders: Brett Sinclair, Danny Wilde.

Pete and Gladys: Pete and Gladys Porter.

Pete Kelly's Blues: Pete Kelly.

Peter Gunn: Peter Gunn.

Phenom: Angela Doolan.

The Pitts: Liz and Bob Pitts.

The P.J.'s: Thurgood Stubbs.

Please Don't Eat the Daisies: Joan and Jim Nash.

Police Woman: Pepper Anderson.

Poltergeist: The Legacy: Alex Moreau, Derek Rayne, Kristen Adams, Nick Boyle, Rachel Corrigan (also contains information on Kat Corrigan).

Popular: Brooke McQueen, Mary Cherry, Samantha McPherson.

Princesses: Georgy De La Rue.

The Prisoner: Number 6.

Private Secretary: Susie McNamara.

Profiler: Rachel Burke, Samantha Waters.

Punky Brewster: Marguax Kramer, Punky Brewster.

Quantum Leap: Al Calavicci, Sam Beckett.

The Queen of Swords: Dona Alvarado.

Quintuplets: Bob and Carol Chase (also for information on Paige, Penny, Parker, Pierce and Patton Chase).

Rachel Gunn, R.N.: Rachel Gunn.

Raising Dad: Emily Stewart, Matt Stewart, Sarah Stewart.

The Real McCoys: Amos McCoy, Hassie McCoy (also contains information on Little Luke McCoy), Luke and Kate McCoy.

Reba: Reba Hart (also contains information on Brock, Barbara Jean, Cheyenne, Kyra, Jake and Van).

The Rebel: Johnny Yuma.

Relic Hunter: Sydney Fox.

Remington Steele: Laura Holt, Remington Steele.

The Reporter: Danny Taylor.

Richard Diamond, Private Detective: Richard Diamond, Sam.

RoboCop: Alex Murphy.

Roc: Roc and Eleanor Emerson.

The Rockford Files: Jim Rockford.

Roseanne: Becky Conner, Dan and Roseanne Conner, Darlene Conner, Jackie Harris.

Run of the House: Kurt Franklin (also for information on Brooke, Chris and Sally Franklin).

Sable: Nicholas Flemming.

Sabrina, the Teenage Witch: Amanda Wickham, Roxie King (also contains information on Morgan Cavanaugh), Sabrina Spellman, Salem Saberhagen, Zelda and Hilda Spellman.

The Saint: Simon Templar.

Sanford and Son: Fred Sanford, Lamont Sanford.

Saved by the Bell: Jesse Spano, Kelly Kapowski, Lisa Turtle, Screech Powers, Zack Morris.

Scarecrow and Mrs. King: Amanda King, Lee Stetson.

Sea Hunt: Mike Nelson.

Secret Agent: John Drake.

The Secret World of Alex Mack: Alex Mack, Annie Mack.

Seinfeld: Cosmo Kramer, Elaine Benes, George Costanza, Jerry Seinfeld.

The Sentinel: Jim Ellison.

7th Heaven: Eric and Annie Camden, Lucy Camden, Mary Camden, Matt Camden, Ruthie Camden, Simon Camden.

Sex and the City: Carrie Bradshaw, Charlotte York, Miranda Hobbes, Samantha Jones.

She Spies: Cassie McBain, D.D. Cummings, Shane Phillips.

She-Wolf of London: Randi Wallace.

Sheena: Sheena (Irish McCalla, 1956; Gena Lee Nolin, 2000).

Silk Stalkings: Chris Lorenzo, Rita Lee Lance.

Silver Spoons: Edward Stratton III, Kate Summers, Ricky Stratton.

The Simpson: Bart Simpson, Homer Simpson, Lisa Simpson, Marge Simpson.

Sister, Sister: Tamera Campbell (also contains information on Tia Landry).

Sisters: Georgie Reed (also for information on Alex, Teddy and Frankie Reed).

Sledge Hammer: Sledge Hammer.

Small Wonder: Vicki Lawson.

Smart Guy: T.J. Henderson, Yvette Henderson.

Snoops: Dana Platt, Glenn Hall, Roberta Young.

Someone Like Me: Gaby Stepjak, Samantha Stepjak.

The Sopranos: Carmela Soprano, Janice Soprano, Meadow Soprano, Tony Soprano.

Space: 1999: Alan Carter, Helena Russell, John Koenig, Maya, Victor Bergman.

Special Unit 2: Kate Benson, Nick O'Malley.

Spin City: Caitlin Moore, Charlie Crawford, Michael Flaherty, Paul Lassiter, Randall Winston, Stewart Bondek.

Star Trek: Hikaru Sulu, James T. Kirk, Leonard McCoy, Mr. Spock, Montgomery Scott, Pavel Chekov, Uhura.

Star Trek: Deep Space Nine: Benjamin Sisko, Ezri Dax, Jadzia Dax, Kira Nerys.

Star Trek: Enterprise: Charles Tucker, Hoshi Sato, Jonathan Archer, Phlox, T'Pol, Travis Mayweather.

Star Trek: The Next Generation: Beverly Crusher, Data, Deanna Troi, Geordi La Forge, Jean-Luc Picard, Natasha Yar, William Riker.

Star Trek: Voyager: B'Elanna Torres, Chakotay, The Doctor, Harry Kim, Kathryn Janeway, Seven of Nine, Tuvok.

Stargate SG-1: Daniel Jackson, Jack O'Neill, Samantha Carter, Teal'c.

Starsky and Hutch: Dave Starsky, Ken Hutchinson.

Step by Step: Alicia Lambert, Carol and Frank Lambert, Dana Foster, J.T. Lambert, Karen Foster.

The Steve Harvey Show: Cedric Robinson, Lovita Jenkins, Regina Grier, Steve Hightower.

Still Standing: Bill Miller, Brian Miller, Judy Miller, Lauren Miller.

Stingray: Alantha Shore, Marina, Troy Tempest.

Strange Luck: Chance Harper.

Stripperella: Erotica Jones.

Strong Medicine: Andy Campbell, Dana Stowe, Kayla Thornton, Lana Hawkins, Nick Biancavilla.

Suddenly Susan: Susan Keane, Vickie Groener.

Sue Thomas, F.B.Eye: Sue Thomas.

Sugarfoot: Tom Brewster.

Supercar: Mike Mercury.

Suzanne Pleshette is Maggie Briggs: Maggie Briggs.

Sweating Bullets: Nick Slaughter, Sylvie Girard.

Sweet Valley High: Elizabeth and Jessica Wakefield.

Sydney: Sydney Kells.

Tammy: Tammy Tarleton.

Tate: Tate (no other name).

Taxi: Alex Reiger, Elaine Nardo, Jim Ignatowski, Latka Gravas, Louie DePalma.

Team Knight Rider: Duke DePalma, Erica West, Jenny Andrews, Kyle Stewart, Trek Sanders.

10–8: Officers on Duty: Rico Amonte.

That Girl: Ann Marie, Donald Hollinger.

That's Life: Lydia DeLucca.

That's So Raven: Raven Baxter.

Thicker Than Water: Ernie Paine, Jonas Paine, Nellie Paine.

Thieves: Johnny Marucci, Rita.

The Thin Man: Nick and Nora Charles.

Third Rock from the Sun: Dick Solomon (also contains information on Mary Albright), Harry Solomon, Sally Solomon, Tommy Solomon.

This Is Alice: Alice Holliday.

Three Sisters: Annie, Bess and Nora Bernstein.

Three's Company: Chrissy Snow, Cindy Snow, Jack Tripper, Janet Wood, Ralph Furley, Stanley and Helen Roper, Terri Alden.

The Tick: Captain Liberty, The Tick.

Time Traxx: Darien Lambert.

Titus: Christopher Titus (also contains information on Ken Titus).

Too Close for Comfort: Henry and Muriel Rush, Jackie Rush, Sarah Rush.

The Torkelsons: Dorothy Jane Torkelson, Millicent Torkelson.

Touched by an Angel: Monica (no other name).

Tracker: Cole (no other name)

The Trials of Rosie O'Neill: Rosie O'Neill.

Tripping the Rift: Six (also for information on Chode, Darph Bobo, Gus, Space Ship Bob, T'nuk, Whip).

Tru Calling: Jack Harper, Tru Davies.

24: David Palmer, Jack Bauer, Tony Almeida.

Two of a Kind: Mary Kate and Ashley Burke.

2000 Malibu Road: Jade O'Keefe, Lindsay Wallace (also contains information on Joy Wallace).

227: Sandra Clark.

Uncle Buck: Buck Russell, Maizy Russell, Tia Russell.

Undercover: Dylan Del'Amico, Kate Del'Amico.

Unhappily Ever After: Jack Malloy, Jennie Malloy, Ryan Malloy (also contains information on Ross Malloy), Tiffany Malloy.

Vegas: Dan Tanna.

Veronica Mars: Veronica Mars.

Veronica's Closet: Veronica Chase.

Vinnie and Bobby: Mona Mullins, Vinnie Verducci.

V.I.P.: Kay Simmons, Nikki Franco, Quick Williams, Tasha Dexter, Vallery Irons.

Voyage to the Bottom of the Sea: Harrison Nelson, Lee Crane.

Walker, Texas Ranger: Alexandra Cahill, Cordell Walker, Jimmy Trevette.

The Waltons: John and Olivia Walton, John-Boy Walton (also for information on Jason, Ben and Jim-Bob Walton), Mary Ellen Walton (also for information on Erin and Elizabeth Walton).

Wanted: Dead or Alive: Josh Randall.

Watching Ellie: Ellie Riggs.

We Got It Made: Mickey MacKenzie.

Webster: George and Katherine Papadopolis, Webster Long.

Welcome Back, Kotter: Arnold Horshack, Freddie Washington, Gabe and Julie Kotter, Juan Epstein, Vinnie Barbarino.

The Westerner: Dave Blassingame.

What About Joan: Joan Gallagher.

What I Like About You: Holly Tyler, Valerie Tyler.

Who's the Boss?: Angela Bower, Samantha Micelli, Tony Micelli.

Whoopi: Courtney Rae, Mavis Rae, Rita Nash.

The Wild Wild West: Artemus Gordon, James T. West

Will and Grace: Grace Adler, Jack McFarland, Karen Walker, Will Truman.

Witchblade: Sara Pezzini.

WKRP in Cincinnati: Arthur Carlson, Bailey Quarters, Dr. Johnny Fever, Herb Tarlek, Jennifer Marlowe, Les Nessman, Venus Flytrap.

Wonder Woman: Diana Prince.

The Wonder Years: Jack and Norma Arnold, Kevin Arnold, Winnie Cooper.

Wonderfalls: Jaye Tyler.

The X-Files: Dana Scully, Fox Mulder.

Xena: Warrior Princess: Gabrielle, Xena.

Yancy Derringer: Yancy Derringer.

Yes Dear: Christine and Jimmy Hughes, Kim and Greg Warner.

Zoe, Duncan, Jack and Jane: Jane Cooper, Zoe Bean.

Zorro: Don Diego de la Vega.

Appendix B

Characters by Last Name

Addams, Gomez **see** Gomez Addams
Addams, Morticia **see** Morticia Addams
Addams, Wednesday **see** Wednesday Addams
Addison, David **see** David Addison
Adler, Grace **see** Grace Adler
Agarn, Randolph **see** Randolph Agarn
Albright, Margie **see** Margie Albright
Albright, Vern **see** Vern Albright
Alcott, Alecia **see** Alecia Alcott
Alden, Terri **see** Terri Alden
Alexander, Lyta **see** Lyta Alexander
Alvarado, Dona **see** Dona Alvarardo
Amonte, Rico **see** Rico Amonte
Anderson, Anthony **see** Anthony Anderson
Anderson, Pepper **see** Pepper Anderson
Appleton, Larry **see** Larry Appleton
Archer, Corliss **see** Corliss Archer
Archer, Jonathan **see** Jonathan Archer
Armstrong, Christine **see** Christine Armstrong
Arnold, Jack **see** Jack and Norma Arnold
Arnold, Kevin **see** Kevin Arnold
Austin, Steve **see** Steve Austin

Babcock, C.C. **see** C.C. Babcock
Baker, Jon **see** Jon Baker
Banacek, Thomas **see** Thomas Banacek
Banks, Ashley **see** Ashley Banks
Banks, Carlton **see** Carlton Banks
Banks, Hilary **see** Hilary Banks
Banks, Philip **see** Philip Banks
Banks, Tracee **see** Tracee Banks
Baracus, B.A. **see** B.A. Baracus
Barbarino, Vinnie **see** Vinnie Barbarino
Baretta, Tony **see** Tony Baretta
Barkley, Audra **see** Audra Barkley
Barkley, Heath **see** Heath Barkley
Barkley, Jarrod **see** Jarrod Barkley
Barkley, Nick **see** Nick Barkley
Barkley, Victoria **see** Victoria Barkley
Barnes, Breanna **see** Breanna Barnes
Barnes, Pamela **see** Pamela Barnes
Barone, Ally **see** Ally Barone
Barone, Debra **see** Debra Barone
Barone, Frank **see** Frank and Marie Barone
Barone, Raymond, **see** Raymond Barone
Barone, Robert **see** Robert Barone
Barry, Beth **see** Beth Barry
Barry, Dave **see** Dave Barry

Bartokomous, Balki **see** Balki Bartokomous
Basco, Luigi **see** Luigi Basco
Bauer, Jack **see** Jack Bauer
Baxter, George **see** George and Dorothy Baxter
Baxter, Raven **see** Raven Baxter
Baxter, Ted **see** Ted Baxter
Bean, Zoe **see** Zoe Bean
Becker, John **see** John Becker
Beckett, Maxwell **see** Maxwell Beckett
Beckett, Sam **see** Sam Beckett
Beemish, Stanley **see** Stanley Beemish
Beene, Oliver **see** Oliver Beene
Bellringer, Zev **see** Zev Bellringer
Belvedere, Lynn **see** Lynn Belvedere
Benes, Elaine **see** Elaine Benes
Benson, Kate **see** Kate Benson
Bergman, Victor **see** Victor Bergman
Bing, Chandler **see** Chandler Bing
Bird, Gabriel **see** Gabriel Bird
Bishop, Delta **see** Delta Bishop
Blaine, Rick **see** Rick Blaine
Blake, Henry **see** Henry Blake
Blunden, Dennis **see** Dennis Blunden
Bluth, Michael **see** Michael Bluth
Bobeck, Mimi **see** Mimi Bobeck
Bodie, Cheyenne **see** Cheyenne Bodie
Bodine, Jethro **see** Jethro Bodine
Borland, Al **see** Al Borland
Bosley, John **see** John Bosley
Bouvier, Anthony **see** Anthony Bouvier
Boyd, Woody **see** Woody Boyd
Bradford, David **see** David Bradford
Bradford, Mary **see** Mary Bradford
Bradford, Tom **see** Tom Bradford
Bradshaw, Carrie **see** Carrie Bradshaw
Brady, Alan **see** Alan Brady
Brady, Carol **see** Carol and Mike Brady
Brady, Greg **see** Greg Brady
Brady, Marcia **see** Marcia Brady
Brewster, Punky **see** Punky Brewster
Brewster, Tom **see** Tom Brewster
Bridges, Cassidy **see** Cassidy Bridges
Bridges, Nash **see** Nash Bridges
Briggs, Maggie **see** Maggie Briggs
Briscoe, Charlie **see** Charlie Briscoe
Bristow, Sydney **see** Charlie Bristow
Britt, Edie **see** Edie Britt
Brody, Cookie **see** Cookie Brody

Brody, Melanie **see** *The Girls of Degrassi*
Brooks, Connie **see** Connie Brooks
Brown, Velvet **see** Velvet Brown
Brown, Warwick **see** Warwick Brown
Buchannon, Mitch **see** Mitch Buchannon
Buchman, Jamie **see** Jamie and Paul Buchman
Buckhart, Sam **see** Sam Buckhart
Buffay, Phoebe **see** Phoebe Buffay
Bundy, Al **see** Al Bundy
Bundy, Bud **see** Bud Bundy
Bundy, Kelly **see** Kelly Bundy
Bundy, Peggy **see** Peggy Bundy
Bunker, Archie **see** Archie Bunker
Bunker, Billie **see** Billie Bunker
Bunker, Edith **see** Edith Bunker
Burke, Hazel **see** Hazel Burke
Burke, Rachel **see** Rachel Burke
Burns, Frank **see** Frank Burns
Burton, Alex **see** Alex Burton

Cage, John **see** John Cage
Cagney, Chris **see** Chris Cagney
Cahill, Alexandra **see** Alexandra Cahill
Caine, Horatio **see** Horatio Caine
Caine, Kwai Chang **see** Kwai Chang Caine
Caine, Rafael **see** Rafael Caine
Calavicci, Al **see** Al Calavicci
Calderon, Dora **see** Peter Farrell
Camden, Eric **see** Eric and Annie Camden
Camden, Lucy **see** Lucy Camden
Camden, Mary **see** Mary Camden
Camden, Matt **see** Matt Camden
Camden, Ruthie **see** Ruthie Camden
Camden, Simon **see** Simon Camden
Campbell, Andy **see** Andy Campbell
Capshaw, Neely **see** *The Girls of Baywatch*
Carlson, Arthur **see** Arthur Carlson
Carter, Alan **see** Alan Carter
Carter, Samantha **see** Samantha Carter
Cartwright, Adam **see** Adam Cartwright
Cartwright, Ben **see** Ben Cartwright
Cartwright, Hoss **see** Hoss Cartwright
Cartwright, Little Joe **see** Little Joe Cartwright
Cassidy, Clint **see** Clint Cassidy
Castleberry, Florence Jean **see** Florence Jean Castleberry
Castelli, Christina **see** Christina Castelli
Cavanaugh, Jordan **see** Jordan Cavanaugh
Chambers, Billie **see** Billie Chambers
Challenger, George **see** George Challenger
Chambers, Diane **see** Diane Chambers
Chandler, Catherine **see** Catherine Chandler
Charles, Nick **see** Nick and Nora Charles
Chase, Bob **see** Bob and Carol Chase
Chase, Cordelia **see** Cordelia Chase
Chase, Veronica **see** Veronica Chase
Chekov, Pavel **see** Pavel Chekov
Cherry, Mary **see** Mary Cherry
Childs, Toni **see** Toni Childs
Clampett, Elly Mae **see** Elly Mae Clampett
Clampett, Jed **see** Jed Clampett
Clark, Sandra **see** Sandra Clark
Claven, Cliff **see** Cliff Claven
Clayton, Joan **see** Joan Clayton
Clayton, Margie **see** Margie Clayton

Cleaver, Beaver **see** Beaver Cleaver
Cleaver, June **see** June Cleaver
Cleaver, Wally **see** Wally Cleaver
Cleaver, Ward **see** Ward Cleaver
Cochran, Teddie **see** Teddie Cochran
Colletti, Frankie **see** Frankie Colletti
Collins, Barnabas **see** Barnabas Collins
Collins, Bob **see** Bob Collins
Collins, Roger **see** Roger Collins
Columbo, Kate **see** Kate Columbo
Conner, Becky **see** Becky Conner
Conner, Dan **see** Dan and Roseanne Conner
Conner, Darlene **see** Darlene Conner
Cooper, Barbara **see** Barbara Cooper
Cooper, Julie **see** Julie Cooper
Cooper, Winnie **see** Winnie Cooper
Corrigan, Rachel **see** Rachel Corrigan
Costanza, George **see** George Costanza
Crane, Frasier **see** Frasier Crane
Crane, Martin **see** Martin Crane
Crane, Niles **see** Niles Crane
Cranston, Cassie **see** Cassie Cranston
Crawford, Charlie **see** Charlie Crawford
Crockett, Sonny **see** Sonny Crockett
Cross, Caitlin **see** Caitlin Cross
Crusher, Beverly **see** Beverly Crusher
Cummings, D.D. **see** D.D. Cummings
Cunningham, Howard **see** Howard and Marion Cunningham
Cunningham, Joanie **see** Joanie Cunningham
Cunningham, Richie **see** Richie Cunningham

Daggett, Jerome **see** Jerome Daggett
Dancer, April **see** April Dancer
D'Arcy, Jefferson **see** Marcy Rhoades
Darling, Clarissa **see** Clarissa Darling
Darling, Ferguson **see** Ferguson Darling
Davenport, Dee **see** Dee Davenport
Davies, Tru **see** Tru Davies
Davis, Bill **see** Bill Davis
Davis, Buffy **see** Buffy and Jody Davis
Davis, Cissy **see** Cissy Davis
Davis, Dwight **see** Dwight Davis
Dax, Ezri **see** Ezri Dax
Dax, Jadzia **see** Jadzia Dax
DeFazio, Laverne **see** Laverne DeFazio
Del'Amico, Dylan **see** Dylan Del'Amico
Del'Amico, Kate **see** Kate Del'Amico
DeLa Rue, Georgy **see** Georgy DeLa Rue
DeLauro, Emma **see** Emma DeLauro
Delgado, Luisa **see** Luisa Delgado
Delko, Eric **see** Eric Delko
DeLorenzo, Candace **see** Candace DeLorenzo
DeLucca, Lydia **see** Lydia DeLucca
DeMonaco, Alexandra **see** Alexandra DeMonaco
DePalma, Duke **see** Duke DePalma
DePalma, Louie **see** Louie DePalma
Derringer, Yancy **see** Yancy Derringer
Destry, Harrison **see** Harrison Destry
Devereaux, Blanche **see** Blanche Devereaux
Dexter, Tasha **see** Tasha Dexter
Dial, Jim **see** Jim Dial
Diamond, Richard **see** Richard Diamond
Dillon, Matt **see** Matt Dillon

Performer Index

References are to entry numbers